55th Annual Meeting of the Association for Computational Linguistics (ACL 2017)

Short Papers

Vancouver, Canada
30 July – 4 August 2017

ISBN: 978-1-5108-4568-8

ACL 2017

The 55th Annual Meeting of the Association for Computational Linguistics

Proceedings of the Conference, Vol. 2 (Short Papers)

July 30 - August 4, 2017
Vancouver, Canada

Preface: General Chair

Welcome to ACL 2017 in Vancouver, Canada! This is the 55th annual meeting of the Association for Computational Linguistics. A tremendous amount of knowledge has been presented at more than half a century's worth of our conferences. Hopefully, some of it is still relevant now that deep learning has solved language. We are anticipating one of the largest ACL conferences ever. We had a record number of papers submitted to the conference, and a record number of industry partners joining us as sponsors of the conference. We are on track to be one of the best attended ACL conferences to date. I hope that this year's conference is intellectually stimulating and that you take home many new ideas and techniques that will help extend your own research.

Each year, the ACL conference is organized by a dedicated team of volunteers. Please thank this year's organizers for their service to the community when you see them at the conference. Without these people, this conference would not happen: Regina Barzilay and Min-Yen Kan (Program Co-Chairs), Priscilla Rasmussen and Anoop Sarkar (Local Organizing Committee), Wei Xu and Jonathan Berant (Workshop Chairs), Maja Popović and Jordan Boyd-Graber (Tutorial Chairs), Wei Lu, Sameer Singh and Margaret Mitchell (Publication Chairs), Heng Ji and Mohit Bansal (Demonstration Chairs), Spandana Gella, Allyson Ettinger, and Matthieu Labeau (Student Research Workshop Organizers), Cecilia Ovesdotter Alm, Mark Dredze, and Marine Carpuat (Faculty Advisors to the Student Research Workshop), Charley Chan (Publicity Chair), Christian Federmann (Conference Handbook Chair), Maryam Siahbani (Student Volunteer Coordinator), and Nitin Madnani (Webmaster and Appmaster).

The organizers have been working for more than a year to put together the conference. Far more than a year in advance, the ACL 2017 Coordinating Committee helped to select the venue and to pick the General Chair and the Program Co-Chairs. This consisted of members from NAACL and ACL executive boards. Representing NAACL we had Hal Daumé III, Michael White, Joel Tetreault, and Emily Bender. Representing ACL we had Pushpak Bhattacharyya, Dragomir Radev, Graeme Hirst, Yejin Choi, and Priscilla Rasmussen. I would like to extend a personal thanks to Graeme and Priscilla who often serve as the ACL's institutional memory, and who have helped fill in many details along the way.

I would like to extend a special thanks to our Program Co-Chairs, Regina Barzilay and Min-Yen Kan. They documented their work creating the program by running a blog. They used their blog as a platform for engaging the ACL community in many of the decision making processes including soliciting suggestions for the conference's area chairs and invited speakers. They hosted discussions with Marti Hearst and Joakim Nivre about the value of publishing pre-prints of submitted paper on arXiv and how they relate to double blind reviewing. They even invited several prominent members of our community to provide last-minute writing advice. If you weren't following the blog in the lead-up to the conference, I highly recommend taking a look through it now. You can find it linked from the ACL 2017 web page.

This year's program looks like it will be excellent! We owe a huge thank you to Regina Barzilay and Min-Yen Kan. They selected this year's papers from 1,318 submissions with the help of 44 area chairs and more than 1,200 reviewers. Thanks to Regina, Min, the area chairs, the reviewers and the authors. Beyond the papers, we have talks by luminaries in the field of NLP, including ACL President Joakim Nivre, invited speakers Mirella Lapata and Noah Smith, and the recipient of this year's Lifetime Achievement Award. We also have an excellent set of workshops and tutorials. On the tutorial day, there will also be a special workshop on Women and Underrepresented Minorities in Natural Language Processing. Thank you to our workshop organizers and tutorial presenters.

This year's conference features two outreach activities that I would like to highlight. First, on Sunday, July 30, 2017, there will be a workshop on Women and Underrepresented Minorities in Natural Language Processing organized by Libby Barak, Isabelle Augenstein, Chloé Braud, He He, and Margaret Mitchell. The goals of the workshop are to increase awareness of the work women and underrepresented groups do, support women and underrepresented groups in continuing to pursue their research, and motivate long-term resources for underrepresented groups within ACL. Second, for the first time ever, ACL is offering subsidized on-site childcare at the conference hotel. The goal of this is to allow ACL participants with children to more readily be able to attend the conference. Since childcare duties often fall disproportionately on women, our hope is that by having professional childcare on-site that we will allow more women to participate, and therefore to help promote their careers. My hope is that the childcare will be continued in future conferences.

I would like to thank our many sponsors for their generous contributions. Our platinum sponsors are Alibaba, Amazon, Apple, Baidu, Bloomberg, Facebook, Google, Samsung and Tencent. Our gold sponsors are eBay, Elsevier, IBM Research, KPMG, Maluuba, Microsoft, Naver Line, NEC, Recruit Institute of Technology, and SAP. Our silver sponsors are Adobe, Bosch, CVTE, Duolingo, Huawei, Nuance, Oracle, and Sogou. Our bronze sponsors are Grammarly, Toutiao, and Yandex. Our supporters include Newsela and four professional master's degree programs from Brandeis, Columbia, NYU and the University of Washington. We would like to acknowledge the generous support of the National Science Foundation which has awarded a $15,000 grant to the ACL Student Research Workshop. Finally, NVIDIA donated several Titan X GPU cards for us to raffle off during the conference.

Lastly, I would like to thank everyone else who helped to make this conference a success. Thank you to our area chairs, our army of reviewers, our workshop organizers, our tutorial presenters, our invited speakers, and our authors. Best regards to all of you.

Welcome to ACL 2017!

Chris Callison-Burch
General Chair

This page intentionally left blank.

Preface: Program Committee Co-Chairs

Welcome to the 55th Annual Meeting of the Association for Computational Linguistics! This year, ACL received 751 long paper submissions and 567 short paper submissions[1]. Of the long papers, 195 were accepted for presentation at ACL — 117 as oral presentations and 78 as poster presentations (25% acceptance rate). 107 short papers were accepted — 34 as oral and 73 as poster presentations (acceptance rate of 18%). In addition, ACL will also feature 21 presentations of papers accepted in the *Transactions of the Association for Computational Linguistics* (TACL). Including the student research workshop and software demonstrations, the ACL program swells to a massive total of 367 paper presentations on the scientific program, representing the largest ACL program to date.

ACL 2017 will have two distinguished invited speakers: Noah A. Smith (Associate Professor of Computer Science and Engineering at the University of Washington) and Mirella Lapata (Professor in the School of Informatics at the University of Edinburgh). Both are well-renowned for their contributions to the field of computational linguistics and are excellent orators. We are honored that they have accepted our invitation to address the membership at this exciting juncture in our field's history, addressing key issues in representation learning and multimodal machine translation.

To manage the tremendous growth of our field, we introduced some changes to the conference. With the rotation of the annual meeting to the Americas, we anticipated a heavy load of submissions and early on we decided to have both the long and short paper deadlines merged to reduce reviewing load and to force authors to take a stand on their submissions' format. The joint deadline allowed us to only load our reviewers once, and also enabled us to have an extended period for more lengthy dialogue among authors, reviewers and area chairs.

In addition, oral presentations were shortened to fourteen (twelve) minutes for long (short) papers, plus time for questions. While this places a greater demand on speakers to be concise, we believe it is worth the effort, allowing far more work to be presented orally. We also took advantage of the many halls available and expanded the number of parallel talks to five during most of the conference sessions.

In keeping with changes introduced in the ACL community from last year, we continued the practice of recognizing outstanding papers at ACL. The 22 outstanding papers (15 long, 7 short, 1.6% of submissions) represent a broad spectrum of exciting contributions and have been specially placed on the final day of the main conference where the program is focused into two parallel sessions of these outstanding contributions. From these, a best paper and a best short paper those will be announced in the awards session on Wednesday afternoon.

Chris has already mentioned our introduction of the chairs' blog[2], where we strove to make the selection process of the internal workings of the scientific committee more transparent. We have publicly documented our calls for area chairs, reviewers and accepted papers selection process. Via the blog, we communicated several innovations in the conference organization workflow, of which we would call attention to two key ones here.

In the review process, we pioneered the use of the Toronto Paper Matching System, a topic model based approach to the assignment of reviewers to papers. We hope this decision will spur other program chairs to adopt the system, as increased coverage will better the reviewer/submission matching process, ultimately leading to a higher quality program.

For posterity, we also introduced the usage of hyperlinks in the bibliography reference sections of papers,

---

[1] These numbers exclude papers that were not reviewed due to formatting, anonymity, or double submission violations or that were withdrawn prior to review, which was unfortunately a substantial number.

[2] https://chairs-blog.acl2017.org/

and have worked with the ACL Anthology to ensure that digital object identifiers (DOIs) appear in the footer of each paper. These steps will help broaden the long-term impact of the work that our community has on the scientific world at large.

There are many individuals we wish to thank for their contributions to ACL 2017, some multiple times:

- The 61 area chairs who volunteered for our extra duty. They recruited reviewers, led discussions on each paper, replied to authors' direct comments to them and carefully assessed each submission. Their input was instrumental in guiding the final decisions on papers and selecting the outstanding papers.

- Our full program committee of BUG hard-working individuals who reviewed the conference's 1,318 submissions (including secondary reviewers).

- TACL editors-in-chief Mark Johnson, Lillian Lee, and Kristina Toutanova, for coordinating with us on TACL presentations at ACL.

- Noah Smith and Katrin Erk, program co-chairs of ACL 2016 and Ani Nenkova and Owen Rambow, program co-chairs of NAACL 2016, who we consulted several times on short order for help and advice.

- Wei Lu and Sameer Singh, our well-organized publication chairs, with direction and oversight from publication chair mentor Meg Mitchell. Also, Christian Federmann who helped with the local handbook.

- The responsive team at Softconf led by Rich Gerber, who worked quickly to resolve problems and who strove to integrate the use of the Toronto Paper Matching System (TPMS) for our use.

- Priscilla Rasmussen and Anoop Sarkar and the local organization team, especially webmaster Nitin Madnani.

- Christopher Calliston-Burch, our general chair, who kept us coordinated with the rest of the ACL 2017 team and helped us free our time to concentrate on the key duty of organizing the scientific program.

- Key-Sun Choi, Jing Jiang, Graham Neubig, Emily Pitler, and Bonnie Webber who carefully reviewed papers under consideration for best paper recognition.

- Our senior correspondents for the blog, who contributed guest posts and advice for writing and reviewing: Waleed Ammar, Yoav Artzi, Tim Baldwin, Marco Baroni, Claire Cardie, Xavier Carreras, Hal Daumé, Kevin Duh, Chris Dyer, Marti Hearst, Mirella Lapata, Emily M. Bender, Aurélien Max, Kathy McKeown, Ray Mooney, Ani Nenkova, Joakim Nivre, Philip Resnik, and Joel Tetreault. Without them, the participation of the community through the productive comments, and without you the readership, our blog for disseminating information about the decision processes would not have been possible and a success.

We hope that you enjoy ACL 2017 in Vancouver!

ACL 2017 program co-chairs
Regina Barzilay, Massachusetts Institute of Technology
Min-Yen Kan, National University of Singapore

Organizing Committee

General Chair:

Chris Callison-Burch, University of Pennsylvania

Program Co-Chairs:

Regina Barzilay, Massachusetts Institute of Technology
Min-Yen Kan, National University of Singapore

Local Organizing Committee:

Priscilla Rasmussen, ACL
Anoop Sarkar, Simon Fraser University

Workshop Chairs:

Wei Xu, Ohio State University
Jonathan Berant, Tel Aviv University

Tutorial Chairs:

Maja Popović, Humboldt-Universität zu Berlin
Jordan Boyd-Graber, University of Colorado, Boulder

Publication Chairs:

Wei Lu, Singapore University of Technology and Design
Sameer Singh, University of California, Irvine
Margaret Mitchell, Google (Advisory)

Demonstration Chairs:

Heng Ji, Rensselaer Polytechnic Institute
Mohit Bansal, University of North Carolina, Chapel Hill

Student Research Workshop Organizers:

Spandana Gella, University of Edinburgh
Allyson Ettinger, University of Maryland, College Park
Matthieu Labeau, Laboratoire d'Informatique pour la Mécanique et les Sciences de l'Ingénieur (LIMSI)

Faculty Advisors to the Student Research Workshop:

Cecilia Ovesdotter Alm, Rochester Institute of Technology
Mark Dredze, Johns Hopkins University
Marine Carpuat, University of Maryland, College Park

Publicity Chair:

Charley Chan, Bloomberg

Conference Handbook Chair:

Christian Federmann, Microsoft

Student Volunteer Coordinator:

Maryam Siahbani, University of the Fraser Valley

Webmaster and Appmaster:

Nitin Madnani, Educational Testing Service

Program Committee

Program Committee Co-Chairs

Regina Barzilay, Massachusetts Institute of Technology
Min-Yen Kan, National University of Singapore

Area Chairs

Mausam (Information Extraction and NLP Applications Area)
Omri Abend (Multilingual Area)
Eugene Agichtein (Information Extraction and NLP Applications Area)
Ron Artstein (Dialogue and Interactive Systems Area)
Alexandra Balahur (Sentiment Analysis and Opinion Mining Area)
Mohit Bansal (Vision, Robotics and Grounding Area)
Chia-Hui Chang (Information Extraction and NLP Applications Area)
Grzegorz Chrupała (Machine Learning Area)
Mona Diab (Multilingual Area)
Jason Eisner (Phonology, Morphology and Word Segmentation Area)
Manaal Faruqui (Semantics Area)
Raquel Fernandez (Dialogue and Interactive Systems Area)
Karën Fort (Multidisciplinary Area)
Amir Globerson (Machine Learning Area)
Hannaneh Hajishirzi (Semantics Area)
Chiori Hori (Speech Area)
Tommi Jaakkola (Machine Learning Area)
Yangfeng Ji (Discourse and Pragmatics Area)
Jing Jiang (Information Extraction and NLP Applications Area)
Sarvnaz Karimi (Information Extraction and NLP Applications Area)
Anna Korhonen (Semantics Area)
Zornitsa Kozareva (Information Extraction and NLP Applications Area)
Lun-Wei Ku (Sentiment Analysis and Opinion Mining Area)
Nate Kushman (Vision, Robotics and Grounding Area)
Chia-ying Lee (Speech Area)
Oliver Lemon (Dialogue and Interactive Systems Area)
Roger Levy (Cognitive Modeling and Psycholinguistics Area)
Sujian Li (Discourse and Pragmatics Area)
Wenjie Li (Summarization and Generation Area)
Kang Liu (Information Extraction and NLP Applications Area)
Tie-Yan Liu (Information Extraction and NLP Applications Area)
Yang Liu (Machine Translation Area)
Zhiyuan Liu (Social Media Area)
Minh-Thang Luong (Machine Translation Area)
Saif M Mohammad (Sentiment Analysis and Opinion Mining Area)
Alexander M Rush (Summarization and Generation Area)
Haitao Mi (Machine Translation Area)
Alessandro Moschitti (Information Extraction and NLP Applications Area)
Smaranda Muresan (Information Extraction and NLP Applications Area)
Preslav Nakov (Semantics Area)
Graham Neubig (Machine Translation Area)

Aurélie Névéol (Biomedical Area)
Shimei Pan (Social Media Area)
Michael Piotrowski (Multidisciplinary Area)
Emily Pitler (Tagging, Chunking, Syntax and Parsing Area)
Barbara Plank (Tagging, Chunking, Syntax and Parsing Area)
Sujith Ravi (Machine Learning Area)
Verena Rieser (Summarization and Generation Area)
Sophie Rosset (Resources and Evaluation Area)
Mehroosh Sadrzadeh (Semantics Area)
Hinrich Schütze (Phonology, Morphology and Word Segmentation Area)
Anders Søgaard (Cognitive Modeling and Psycholinguistics Area)
Karin Verspoor (Biomedical Area)
Aline Villavicencio (Semantics Area)
Svitlana Volkova (Social Media Area)
Bonnie Webber (Discourse and Pragmatics Area)
Deyi Xiong (Machine Translation Area)
William Yang Wang (Machine Learning Area)
Wajdi Zaghouani (Resources and Evaluation Area)
Yue Zhang (Tagging, Chunking, Syntax and Parsing Area)
Hai Zhao (Tagging, Chunking, Syntax and Parsing Area)

Primary Reviewers

Reviewers who are acknowledged by the program committee for providing one or more outstanding reviews are marked with "*".

Balamurali A R, Mourad Abbas, Omri Abend, Amjad Abu-Jbara, Gilles Adda, Heike Adel, Stergos Afantenos, Apoorv Agarwal, Eneko Agirre, Željko Agić, Alan Akbik, Ahmet Aker, Mohammed Alam, Hanan Aldarmaki, Enrique Alfonseca, Afra Alishahi, Laura Alonso Alemany, David Alvarez-Melis, Maxime Amblard, Maryam Aminian, Silvio Amir, Waleed Ammar, Daniel Andrade, Jacob Andreas*, Nicholas Andrews*, Ion Androutsopoulos, Galia Angelova, Jean-Yves Antoine*, Emilia Apostolova, Jun Araki, Yuki Arase, Lora Aroyo, Philip Arthur, Yoav Artzi*, Masayuki Asahara, Giuseppe Attardi, AiTi Aw, Ahmed Hassan Awadallah, Wilker Aziz

Collin Baker, Alexandra Balahur, Niranjan Balasubramanian, Timothy Baldwin, Tyler Baldwin, Miguel Ballesteros, David Bamman, Rafael E. Banchs, Carmen Banea, Ritwik Banerjee, Srinivas Bangalore, Libby Barak, Alistair Baron, Marco Baroni, Alberto Barrón-Cedeño, Roberto Basili, David Batista, Daniel Bauer, Timo Baumann, Daniel Beck, Srikanta Bedathur, Beata Beigman Klebanov, Kedar Bellare, Charley Beller, Islam Beltagy, Anja Belz, Yassine Benajiba, Fabrício Benevenuto, Luciana Benotti*, Jonathan Berant, Taylor Berg-Kirkpatrick, Sabine Bergler*, Robert Berwick, Laurent Besacier, Steven Bethard, Archna Bhatia, Chris Biemann, Joachim Bingel, Or Biran, Alexandra Birch, Arianna Bisazza, Yonatan Bisk, Prakhar Biyani, Johannes Bjerva, Anders Björkelund, Philippe Blache, Frédéric Blain, Eduardo Blanco, Nate Blaylock, Bernd Bohnet, Gemma Boleda, Danushka Bollegala, Claire Bonial, Francesca Bonin, Kalina Bontcheva, Benjamin Börschinger, Johan Bos, Elizabeth Boschee, Florian Boudin, Fethi Bougares, Samuel Bowman, Johan Boye, Kristy Boyer, Cem Bozsahin, David Bracewell, S.R.K. Branavan, Pavel Braslavski, Adrian Brasoveanu, Ted Briscoe, Chris Brockett, Julian Brooke, Elia Bruni, William Bryce, Marco Büchler, Christian Buck, Paul Buitelaar, Harry Bunt, Manuel Burghardt, David Burkett, Hendrik Buschmeier, Miriam Butt

José G. C. de Souza, Deng Cai, Jose Camacho-Collados, Berkant Barla Cambazoglu, Erik Cambria, Burcu Can, Marie Candito, Hailong Cao, Kris Cao*, Yuan Cao, Ziqiang Cao, Cornelia Caragea, Jesus Cardeńosa, Giuseppe Carenini, Marine Carpuat, Xavier Carreras, John Carroll, Paula Carvalho, Francisco Casacuberta, Helena Caseli, Tommaso Caselli*, Taylor Cassidy, Vittorio Castelli, Giuseppe Castellucci, Asli Celikyilmaz*, Daniel Cer, Özlem Çetinoğlu, Mauro Cettolo, Arun Chaganty, Joyce Chai, Soumen Chakrabarti, Gaël de Chalendar, Yllias Chali, Nathanael Chambers, Jane Chandlee, Muthu Kumar Chandrasekaran, Angel Chang*, Baobao Chang, Kai-Wei Chang, Ming-Wei Chang, Snigdha Chaturvedi, Wanxiang Che, Ciprian Chelba, Bin Chen, Boxing Chen, Chen Chen, Hsin-Hsi Chen, John Chen, Kehai Chen, Kuang-hua Chen, Qingcai Chen, Tao Chen, Wenliang Chen, Xinchi Chen, Yubo Chen, Yun-Nung Chen, Zhiyuan Chen, Jianpeng Cheng, Colin Cherry, Sean Chester, Jackie Chi Kit Cheung*, David Chiang, Jen-Tzung Chien, Hai Leong Chieu, Laura Chiticariu, Eunsol Choi, Kostadin Cholakov, Shamil Chollampatt, Jan Chorowski, Christos Christodoulopoulos, Tagyoung Chung, Kenneth Church, Mark Cieliebak*, Philipp Cimiano, Alina Maria Ciobanu*, Alexander Clark*, Jonathan Clark, Stephen Clark, Ann Clifton, Maximin Coavoux, Kevin Cohen, Nigel Collier, Michael Collins, Sandra Collovini, Miriam Connor, John Conroy*, Matthieu Constant, Danish Contractor, Mark Core, Ryan Cotterell, Benoit Crabbé, Danilo Croce*, Fabien Cromieres, Montse Cuadros, Heriberto Cuayahuitl, Silviu-Petru Cucerzan, Aron Culotta*

Luis Fernando D'Haro, Giovanni Da San Martino, Walter Daelemans, Daniel Dahlmeier, Amitava Das, Dipanjan Das, Rajarshi Das, Pradeep Dasigi, Johannes Daxenberger, Munmun De Choudhury, Eric De La Clergerie, Thierry Declerck, Luciano Del Corro, Louise Deléger, Felice Dell'Orletta, Claudio Delli Bovi, Li Deng, Lingjia Deng, Pascal Denis, Michael Denkowski, Tejaswini Deoskar, Leon Derczynski, Nina Dethlefs, Ann Devitt, Jacob Devlin, Lipika Dey, Barbara Di Eugenio, Giuseppe Di Fabbrizio, Gaël Dias, Fernando Diaz, Georgiana Dinu, Liviu P. Dinu, Stefanie Dipper, Dmitriy Dligach, Simon Dobnik, Ellen Dodge, Jesse Dodge, Daxiang Dong, Li Dong, Doug Downey, Gabriel Doyle, A. Seza Doğruöz, Eduard Dragut, Mark Dras*, Markus Dreyer, Lan Du, Nan Duan, Xiangyu Duan, Kevin Duh*, Long Duong, Emmanuel Dupoux, Nadir Durrani, Greg Durrett, Ondřej Dušek*, Marc Dymetman

Judith Eckle-Kohler, Steffen Eger*, Markus Egg, Koji Eguchi, Patrick Ehlen, Maud Ehrmann*, Vladimir Eidelman, Andreas Eisele, Jacob Eisenstein*, Heba Elfardy, Michael Elhadad*, Desmond Elliott*, Micha Elsner, Nikos Engonopoulos, Messina Enza, Katrin Erk, Arash Eshghi, Miquel Esplà-Gomis

James Fan, Federico Fancellu, Licheng Fang, Benamara Farah, Stefano Faralli, Richárd Farkas, Afsaneh Fazly, Geli Fei, Anna Feldman, Minwei Feng, Yansong Feng, Olivier Ferret, Oliver Ferschke, Simone Filice, Denis Filimonov, Katja Filippova*, Andrew Finch, Nicolas Fiorini, Orhan Firat*, Radu Florian, Evandro Fonseca, Markus Forsberg, Eric Fosler-Lussier, George Foster, James Foulds*, Marc Franco-Salvador, Alexander Fraser, Dayne Freitag, Lea Frermann, Annemarie Friedrich, Piotr W. Fuglewicz, Akinori Fujino, Fumiyo Fukumoto, Robert Futrelle

Robert Gaizauskas, Olivier Galibert*, Irina Galinskaya, Michel Galley*, Michael Gamon, Kuzman Ganchev, Siva Reddy Gangireddy, Jianfeng Gao, Claire Gardent*, Matt Gardner, Guillermo Garrido, Justin Garten, Milica Gasic, Eric Gaussier, Tao Ge, Georgi Georgiev, Kallirroi Georgila, Pablo Gervás*, George Giannakopoulos, C Lee Giles, Kevin Gimpel*, Maite Giménez*, Roxana Girju, Adrià de Gispert, Dimitra Gkatzia*, Goran Glavaš, Amir Globerson, Yoav Goldberg, Dan Goldwasser, Carlos Gómez-Rodríguez*, Graciela Gonzalez, Edgar Gonzàlez Pellicer, Kyle Gorman, Matthew R. Gormley, Isao Goto, Cyril Goutte, Amit Goyal, Kartik Goyal, Pawan Goyal, Joao Graca, Yvette Graham, Roger Granada, Stephan Greene, Jiatao Gu, Bruno Guillaume, Liane Guillou, Curry Guinn, Hongyu Guo, James Gung, Jiang Guo, Weiwei Guo, Yufan Guo, Yuhong Guo, Abhijeet Gupta, Rahul Gupta, Yoan Gutiérrez, Francisco Guzmán,

Thanh-Le Ha, Christian Hadiwinoto, Gholamreza Haffari, Matthias Hagen, Udo Hahn, Jörg Hakenberg, Dilek Hakkani-Tur, Keith Hall, William L. Hamilton, Michael Hammond, Xianpei Han, Sanda Harabagiu, Christian Hardmeier, Kazi Saidul Hasan, Sadid A. Hasan, Saša Hasan, Eva Hasler, Hany Hassan, Helen Hastie, Claudia Hauff, He He*, Hua He, Luheng He, Shizhu He, Xiaodong He, Yulan He, Peter Heeman, Carmen Heger, Serge Heiden, Georg Heigold, Michael Heilman, James Henderson, Matthew Henderson, Aron Henriksson, Aurélie Herbelot*, Ulf Hermjakob, Daniel Hershcovich, Jack Hessel, Kristina Hettne, Felix Hieber, Ryuichiro Higashinaka, Erhard Hinrichs, Tsutomu Hirao, Keikichi Hirose, Julian Hitschler, Cong Duy Vu Hoang, Julia Hockenmaier, Kai Hong*, Yu Hong, Ales Horak, Andrea Horbach, Takaaki Hori, Yufang Hou, Julian Hough, Dirk Hovy*, Eduard Hovy, Chun-Nan Hsu, Baotian Hu, Yuening Hu, Yuheng Hu, Hen-Hsen Huang, Hongzhao Huang, Liang Huang, Lifu Huang, Minlie Huang, Ruihong Huang, Songfang Huang, Xuanjing Huang, Yi-Ting Huang, Luwen Huangfu, Mans Hulden, Tim Hunter, Seung-won Hwang

Ignacio Iacobacci, Nancy Ide, Marco Idiart, Gonzalo Iglesias, Ryu Iida, Kenji Imamura, Diana Inkpen, Naoya Inoue, Hitoshi Isahara, Mohit Iyyer

Tommi Jaakkola, Cassandra L. Jacobs, Guillaume Jacquet, Evan Jaffe, Jagadeesh Jagarlamudi, Siddharth Jain, Aren Jansen, Sujay Kumar Jauhar, Laura Jehl, Minwoo Jeong, Yacine Jernite, Rahul Jha, Donghong Ji, Guoliang Ji, Sittichai Jiampojamarn, Hui Jiang, Antonio Jimeno Yepes, Salud María Jiménez-Zafra, Richard Johansson, Kyle Johnson, Melvin Johnson Premkumar, Kristiina Jokinen, Arne Jonsson, Aditya Joshi, Mahesh Joshi, Shafiq Joty, Dan Jurafsky*, David Jurgens

Besim Kabashi, Ákos Kádár, Sylvain Kahane*, Juliette Kahn, Herman Kamper, Jaap Kamps, Hiroshi Kanayama, Hung-Yu Kao, Justine Kao, Mladen Karan, Dimitri Kartsaklis, Arzoo Katiyar, David Kauchak, Daisuke Kawahara, Anna Kazantseva, Hideto Kazawa, Andrew Kehler, Simon Keizer, Frank Keller, Casey Kennington, Mitesh M. Khapra, Douwe Kiela, Halil Kilicoglu*, Jin-Dong Kim, Jooyeon Kim, Seokhwan Kim, Suin Kim, Yoon Kim, Young-Bum Kim, Irwin King, Brian Kingsbury, Svetlana Kiritchenko, Dietrich Klakow, Alexandre Klementiev, Sigrid Klerke, Roman Klinger, Julien Kloetzer, Simon Kocbek, Arne Köhn*, Daniël de Kok, Prasanth Kolachina, Varada Kolhatkar, Mamoru Komachi, Kazunori Komatani, Rik Koncel-Kedziorski, Fang Kong, Lingpeng Kong, Ioannis Konstas*, Selcuk Kopru, Valia Kordoni, Yannis Korkontzelos, Bhushan Kotnis, Alexander Kotov, Mikhail Kozhevnikov, Martin Krallinger, Julia Kreutzer*, Jayant Krishnamurthy*, Kriste Krstovski, Canasai Kruengkrai, Germán Kruszewski, Mark Kröll, Lun-Wei Ku*, Marco Kuhlmann, Jonas Kuhn, Roland Kuhn, Shankar Kumar, Jonathan K. Kummerfeld, Sadao Kurohashi, Polina Kuznetsova, Tom Kwiatkowski,

Igor Labutov, Wai Lam, Patrik Lambert, Man Lan, Ian Lane, Ni Lao, Mirella Lapata, Shalom Lappin, Romain Laroche, Kornel Laskowski, Jey Han Lau, Alon Lavie, Angeliki Lazaridou, Phong Le*, Joseph Le Roux, Robert Leaman, Kenton Lee, Lung-Hao Lee, Moontae Lee, Sungjin Lee, Yoong Keok Lee, Young-Suk Lee, Els Lefever, Tao Lei, Jochen L. Leidner, Alessandro Lenci, Yves Lepage*, Johannes Leveling, Tomer Levinboim, Gina-Anne Levow*, Omer Levy*, Roger Levy, Dave Lewis, Mike Lewis, Binyang Li, Chen Li, Cheng-Te Li, Chenliang Li, Fangtao Li, Haizhou Li, Hang Li, Jiwei Li, Junhui Li, Junyi Jessy Li, Lishuang Li, Peifeng Li, Peng Li, Qi Li, Qing Li, Shaohua Li, Sheng Li, Shoushan Li, Xiaoli Li, Yanran Li, Yunyao Li, Zhenghua Li, Maria Liakata*, Kexin Liao*, Xiangwen Liao, Chin-Yew Lin, Chu-Cheng Lin, Chuan-Jie Lin, Shou-de Lin, Victoria Lin, Ziheng Lin, Wang Ling, Xiao Ling, Tal Linzen, Christina Lioma, Pierre Lison, Marina Litvak, Bing Liu, Fei Liu, Hongfang Liu, Jiangming Liu, Lemao Liu, Qian Liu, Qun Liu, Tie-Yan Liu, Ting Liu, Xiaobing Liu, Yang Liu, Nikola Ljubešić, Chi-kiu Lo, Henning Lobin, Varvara Logacheva, Lucelene Lopes, Adam Lopez, Oier Lopez de Lacalle, Aurelio Lopez-Lopez, Annie Louis, Bin Lu, Yi Luan, Andy Luecking, Michal Lukasik, Xiaoqiang Luo, Anh Tuan Luu

Ji Ma, Qingsong Ma, Shuming Ma, Xuezhe Ma, Wolfgang Macherey, Nitin Madnani, Saad Mahamood, Cerstin Mahlow, Wolfgang Maier, Prodromos Malakasiotis, Andreas Maletti, Shervin Malmasi, Titus von der Malsburg, Suresh Manandhar, Gideon Mann, Diego Marcheggiani, Daniel Marcu, David Mareček, Matthew Marge, Benjamin Marie, Katja Markert, Marie-Catherine de Marneffe, Erwin Marsi, Patricio Martinez-Barco, André F. T. Martins*, Sebastian Martschat, Héctor Martínez Alonso, Eugenio Martínez-Cámara*, Fernando Martínez-Santiago, Yann Mathet, Shigeki Matsubara, Yuichiroh Matsubayashi, Yuji Matsumoto, Takuya Matsuzaki, Austin Matthews, Jonathan May, David McClosky, Tara McIntosh, Kathy McKeown, Michael McTear, Yashar Mehdad, Sameep Mehta, Hongyuan Mei*, Yelena Mejova, Oren Melamud, Fandong Meng, Adam Meyers, Yishu Miao, Rada Mihalcea, Todor Mihaylov, Timothy Miller, Tristan Miller*, David Mimno, Bonan Min, Zhao-Yan Ming, Shachar Mirkin, Seyed Abolghasem Mirroshandel, Abhijit Mishra, Prasenjit Mitra, Makoto Miwa, Daichi Mochihashi, Ashutosh Modi, Marie-Francine Moens, Samaneh Moghaddam, Abdelrahman Mohamed, Behrang Mohit, Mitra Mohtarami, Karo Moilanen, Luis Gerardo Mojica de la Vega, Manuel Montes, Andres Montoyo, Taesun Moon, Michael Moortgat, Roser Morante, Hajime Morita, Lili Mou, Dana Movshovitz-Attias, Arjun Mukherjee, Philippe Muller, Yugo Murawaki, Brian Murphy, Gabriel Murray*, Reinhard Muskens, Sung-Hyon Myaeng

Masaaki Nagata, Ajay Nagesh, Vinita Nahar, Iftekhar Naim, Tetsuji Nakagawa, Mikio Nakano, Yukiko Nakano, Ndapandula Nakashole, Ramesh Nallapati, Courtney Napoles, Jason Naradowsky, Karthik Narasimhan*, Shashi Narayan, Alexis Nasr, Vivi Nastase, Borja Navarro, Roberto Navigli, Adeline Nazarenko*, Mark-Jan Nederhof, Arvind Neelakantan, Sapna Negi, Matteo Negri, Aida Nematzadeh, Guenter Neumann, Mariana Neves, Denis Newman-Griffis, Dominick Ng, Hwee Tou Ng, Jun-Ping Ng, Vincent Ng, Dong Nguyen*, Thien Huu Nguyen, Truc-Vien T. Nguyen, Viet-An Nguyen, Garrett Nicolai, Massimo Nicosia, Vlad Niculae*, Jian-Yun Nie, Jan Niehues, Luis Nieto Piña*, Ivelina Nikolova, Malvina Nissim*, Joakim Nivre*, Hiroshi Noji, Gertjan van Noord, Joel Nothman

Brendan O'Connor, Timothy O'Donnell, Yusuke Oda, Stephan Oepen, Kemal Oflazer*, Alice Oh*, Jong-Hoon Oh, Tomoko Ohta, Kiyonori Ohtake, Hidekazu Oiwa, Naoaki Okazaki, Manabu Okumura, Hiroshi G. Okuno, Constantin Orasan, Vicente Ordonez, Petya Osenova, Mari Ostendorf*, Myle Ott, Katja Ovchinnikova, Cecilia Ovesdotter Alm

Muntsa Padró, Valeria de Paiva, Alexis Palmer, Martha Palmer, Alessio Palmero Aprosio, Sinno Jialin Pan*, Xiaoman Pan, Denis Paperno, Ankur Parikh, Cecile Paris, Seong-Bae Park, Tommaso Pasini, Marco Passarotti*, Peyman Passban, Panupong Pasupat, Siddharth Patwardhan, Michael J. Paul*, Adam Pauls, Ellie Pavlick*, Adam Pease, Pavel Pecina, Ted Pedersen, Nanyun Peng, Xiaochang Peng, Gerald Penn, Marco Pennacchiotti, Bryan Perozzi, Casper Petersen, Slav Petrov, Eva Pettersson, Anselmo Peñas, Hieu Pham, Nghia The Pham, Lawrence Phillips, Davide Picca, Karl Pichotta, Olivier Pietquin, Mohammad Taher Pilehvar, Yuval Pinter, Paul Piwek, Thierry Poibeau, Tamara Polajnar, Heather Pon-Barry, Simone Paolo Ponzetto, Andrei Popescu-Belis, Maja Popović, Fred Popowich, François Portet*, Matt Post*, Christopher Potts, Vinodkumar Prabhakaran, Daniel Preoţiuc-Pietro, Emily Prud'hommeaux*, Laurent Prévot, Jay Pujara, Matthew Purver, James Pustejovsky

Juan Antonio Pérez-Ortiz, Ashequl Qadir, Peng Qi, Longhua Qian, Xian Qian, Lu Qin, Long Qiu, Xipeng Qiu, Lizhen Qu, Ariadna Quattoni, Chris Quirk* Alexandre Rademaker, Will Radford, Alessandro Raganato, Afshin Rahimi*, Altaf Rahman, Maya Ramanath, Rohan Ramanath, A Ramanathan, Arti Ramesh, Gabriela Ramirez-de-la-Rosa, Carlos Ramisch, Anita Ramm, Vivek Kumar Rangarajan Sridhar, Ari Rappoport, Mohammad Sadegh Rasooli, Pushpendre Rastogi, Antoine Raux, Sravana Reddy, Ines Rehbein*, Georg Rehm, Roi Reichart, Ehud Reiter, Zhaochun Ren, Corentin Ribeyre, Matthew Richardson, Martin Riedl, Jason Riesa, German Rigau, Ellen Riloff*, Laura Rimell*, Alan Ritter, Brian Roark*, Molly Roberts, Tim Rocktäschel, Oleg Rokhlenko, Salvatore Romeo, Andrew Rosenberg, Sara Rosenthal*, Paolo Rosso, Benjamin Roth, Michael Roth, Sascha Rothe, Masoud Rouhizadeh, Mickael Rouvier, Alla Rozovskaya, Josef Ruppenhofer, Delia Rusu, Attapol Rutherford

Mrinmaya Sachan, Kugatsu Sadamitsu, Fatiha Sadat, Mehrnoosh Sadrzadeh, Markus Saers, Kenji Sagae, Horacio Saggion, Saurav Sahay, Magnus Sahlgren, Patrick Saint-dizier, Hassan Sajjad, Sakriani Sakti, Mohammad Salameh, Bahar Salehi, Avneesh Saluja, Rajhans Samdani, Mark Sammons, Germán Sanchis-Trilles, Ryohei Sasano, Agata Savary*, Asad Sayeed, Carolina Scarton, Tatjana Scheffler, Christian Scheible, David Schlangen, Natalie Schluter, Allen Schmaltz*, Helmut Schmid, Alexandra Schofield, William Schuler, Sebastian Schuster, Lane Schwartz, Roy Schwartz*, Christof Schöch, Diarmuid Ó Séaghdha, Djamé Seddah, Abigail See, Nina Seemann, Satoshi Sekine, Mark Seligman, Minjoon Seo, Burr Settles, Lei Sha, Kashif Shah, Rebecca Sharp, Shiqi Shen, Shuming Shi, Hiroyuki Shindo, Koichi Shinoda, Chaitanya Shivade, Eyal Shnarch*, Milad Shokouhi, Ekaterina Shutova, Advaith Siddharthan, Avirup Sil, Carina Silberer, Yanchuan Sim, Patrick Simianer, Kiril Simov, Kairit Sirts, Amy Siu, Gabriel Skantze, Kevin Small, Noah A. Smith, Pavel Smrz, Richard Socher, Artem Sokolov, Thamar Solorio, Swapna Somasundaran, Hyun-Je Song, Min Song, Sa-kwang Song, Yang Song, Yangqiu Song, Radu Soricut, Aitor Soroa, Matthias Sperber, Caroline Sporleder, Vivek Srikumar, Somayajulu Sripada, Shashank Srivastava, Edward Stabler, Jan Šnajder*, Sanja Štajner, Gabriel Stanovsky*, Manfred Stede, Mark Steedman, Josef Steinberger, Amanda Stent, Mark Stevenson, Brandon Stewart, Matthew Stone, Svetlana Stoyanchev, Veselin Stoyanov, Carlo Strapparava, Karl Stratos, Kristina Striegnitz*, Emma Strubell, Tomek Strzalkowski, Sara Stymne, Maik Stührenberg, Jinsong Su, Keh-Yih Su, Yu Su, L V Subramaniam, Katsuhito Sudoh, Ang Sun, Huan Sun, Le Sun, Weiwei Sun, Xu Sun, Simon Suster, Hisami Suzuki, Jun Suzuki, Yoshimi Suzuki, Swabha Swayamdipta, Stan Szpakowicz, Idan Szpektor, Felipe Sánchez-Martínez, Pascale Sébillot, Anders Søgaard

Prasad Tadepalli, Kaveh Taghipour, Hiroya Takamura, David Talbot, Partha Talukdar, Aleš Tamchyna, Akihiro Tamura, Chenhao Tan*, Liling Tan, Niket Tandon, Duyu Tang, Jiliang Tang, Christoph Teichmann, Serra Sinem Tekiroglu, Irina Temnikova, Joel Tetreault, Kapil Thadani*, Sam Thomson, Jörg Tiedemann, Ivan Titov, Katrin Tomanek, Gaurav Singh Tomar, Marc Tomlinson, Sara Tonelli, Antonio Toral, Kentaro Torisawa, Ke M. Tran, Isabel Trancoso, Ming-Feng Tsai, Richard Tzong-Han Tsai, Reut Tsarfaty*, Oren Tsur, Yoshimasa Tsuruoka, Yulia Tsvetkov, Cunchao Tu, Zhaopeng Tu, Gokhan Tur, Marco Turchi, Ferhan Ture, Oscar Täckström

Raghavendra Udupa, Stefan Ultes, Lyle Ungar, Shyam Upadhyay, L. Alfonso Urena Lopez, Olga Uryupina

Alessandro Valitutti*, Benjamin Van Durme*, Tim Van de Cruys, Lucy Vanderwende*, Vasudeva Varma, Paola Velardi, Sumithra Velupillai, Sriram Venkatapathy, Yannick Versley, Tim Vieira, David Vilar, Martín Villalba*, Veronika Vincze, Sami Virpioja*, Andreas Vlachos, Rob Voigt, Ngoc Thang Vu, Ivan Vulić, Yogarshi Vyas, V.G.Vinod Vydiswaran, Ekaterina Vylomova

Houfeng Wang, Henning Wachsmuth, Joachim Wagner, Matthew Walter*, Stephen Wan, Xiaojun Wan, Baoxun Wang, Chang Wang, Chong Wang, Dingquan Wang, Hongning Wang, Lu Wang, Mingxuan Wang, Pidong Wang, Rui Wang, Shaojun Wang, Tong Wang, Yu-Chun Wang, Wei Wang, Wenya Wang, William Yang Wang, Xiaolin Wang, Xiaolong Wang, Yiou Wang, Zhiguo Wang, Zhongqing Wang*, Leo Wanner, Nigel Ward, Shinji Watanabe, Taro Watanabe, Aleksander Wawer, Bonnie Webber, Ingmar Weber, Julie Weeds, Furu Wei, Zhongyu Wei, Gerhard Weikum, David Weir, Michael White, Antoine Widlöcher, Michael Wiegand*, Jason D Williams*, Shuly Wintner, Sam Wiseman, Michael Witbrock, Silke Witt-Ehsani, Travis Wolfe, Kam-Fai Wong, Jian Wu, Yuanbin Wu, Joern Wuebker

Aris Xanthos, Rui Xia, Yunqing Xia, Bing Xiang, Min Xiao, Tong Xiao, Xinyan Xiao, Boyi Xie, Pengtao Xie, Shasha Xie, Chenyan Xiong, Feiyu Xu, Hua Xu, Ruifeng Xu, Wei Xu, Wenduan Xu, Huichao Xue, Nianwen Xue

Yadollah Yaghoobzadeh, Ichiro Yamada, Bishan Yang, Cheng Yang, Diyi Yang, Grace Hui Yang, Min Yang, Yaqin Yang, Yi Yang, Roman Yangarber, Mark Yatskar, Meliha Yetisgen, Wen-tau Yih, Pengcheng Yin, Wenpeng Yin, Anssi Yli-Jyrä, Dani Yogatama, Naoki Yoshinaga, Bei Yu, Dian Yu, Dianhai Yu, Kai Yu, Liang-Chih Yu, Mo Yu, Zhou Yu, François Yvon

Marcos Zampieri, Menno van Zaanen, Fabio Massimo Zanzotto, Amir Zeldes*, Daojian Zeng, Xiaodong Zeng, Kalliopi Zervanou*, Luke Zettlemoyer, Deniz Zeyrek, Feifei Zhai, Congle Zhang, Dongdong Zhang, Guchun Zhang, Jiajun Zhang, Jian Zhang, Jianwen Zhang, Lei Zhang, Meishan Zhang, Min Zhang, Qi Zhang, Renxian Zhang, Sicong Zhang, Wei Zhang*, Zhisong Zhang, Bing Zhao, Dongyan Zhao, Jun Zhao, Shiqi Zhao, Tiejun Zhao, Wayne Xin Zhao, Alisa Zhila, Guodong Zhou, Xinjie Zhou, Muhua Zhu, Xiaodan Zhu, Xiaoning Zhu, Ayah Zirikly, Chengqing Zong, Bowei Zou

Secondary Reviewers

Naveed Afzal, Yamen Ajjour

Jeremy Barnes, Joost Bastings, Joachim Bingel, Luana Bulat

Iacer Calixto, Lea Canales, Kai Chen, Tongfei Chen, Hao Cheng, Jianpeng Cheng, Yiming Cui

Marco Damonte, Saman Daneshvar, Tobias Domhan, Daxiang Dong, Li Dong

Mohamed Eldesouki

Stefano Faralli, Bin Fu

Srinivasa P. Gadde, Qiaozi Gao, Luca Gilardi, Sujatha Das Gollapalli, J. Manuel Gomez, Stig-Arne Grönroos, Lin Gui

Casper Hansen, Lihong He, Martin Horn

Oana Inel

Gongye Jin

Roman Kern, Vaibhav Kesarwani, Joo-Kyung Kim, Seongchan Kim, Christine Köhn, Santosh Kosgi

Ronja Laarmann-Quante, Egoitz Laparra, Anais Lefeuvre-Halftermeyer, Guanlin Li, Jing Li, Minglei Li, Xiang Li, Xiaolong Li, Chen Liang, Ming Liao, Sijia Liu, Pranay Lohia

Chunpeng Ma, Shuming Ma, Tengfei Ma, Ana Marasovic

Toan Nguyen, Eric Nichols, Sergiu Nisioi

Gözde Özbal

Alexis Palmer, Suraj Pandey, Nikolaos Pappas, José M. Perea-Ortega, Marten Postma

Longhua Qian

Masoud Rouhizadeh Abeed Sarker, Andrew Schneider, Roxane Segers, Pararth Shah, Samiulla Shaikh, Xing Shi, Tomohide Shibata, Samiulla Shiekh, Miikka Silfverberg

Bo Wang*, Boli Wang, Jianxiang Wang, Jingjing Wang, Rui Wang, Shuai Wang, Shuting Wang, Tsung-Hsien Wen, John Wieting

Nan Yang, Yi Yang, Mark Yatskar, Yichun Yin

Sheng Zhang, Kai Zhao, Imed Zitouni

Outstanding Papers

With twin upward trends in the interest in computational linguistics and natural language processing and the size of our annual meeting, ACL has begun the practice of recognizing outstanding papers that represent a select cross-section of the entire field, as nominated by reviewers and vetted by the area chairs and program co-chairs. These papers have been centrally located in the program, on the last day of our meeting, in a more focused two parallel tracks format.

This year, we have nominated 15 long papers and 7 short papers, representing 1.8% of all submissions and approximately 5% of the accepted ACL program. Congratulations, authors!

(in alphabetical order by first author surname)

Long Papers

- Jan Buys and Phil Blunsom. *Robust Incremental Neural Semantic Graph Parsing.*
- Xinchi Chen, Zhan Shi, Xipeng Qiu and Xuanjing Huang. *Adversarial Multi-Criteria Learning for Chinese Word Segmentation.*
- Ryan Cotterell and Jason Eisner. *Probabilistic Typology: Deep Generative Models of Vowel Inventories.*
- Yanzhuo Ding, Yang Liu, Huanbo Luan and Maosong Sun. *Visualizing and Understanding Neural Machine Translation.*
- Milan Gritta, Mohammad Taher Pilehvar, Nut Limsopatham and Nigel Collier. *Vancouver Welcomes You! Minimalist Location Metonymy Resolution.*
- Daniel Hershcovich, Omri Abend and Ari Rappoport. *A Transition-Based Directed Acyclic Graph Parser for UCCA.*
- Shuhei Kurita, Daisuke Kawahara and Sadao Kurohashi. *Neural Joint Model for Transition-based Chinese Syntactic Analysis.*
- Ryan Lowe, Michael Noseworthy, Iulian Vlad Serban, Nicolas Angelard-Gontier, Yoshua Bengio and Joelle Pineau. *Towards an Automatic Turing Test: Learning to Evaluate Dialogue Responses.*
- Yasuhide Miura, Motoki Taniguchi, Tomoki Taniguchi and Tomoko Ohkuma. *Unifying Text, Metadata, and User Network Representations with a Neural Network for Geolocation Prediction.*
- Ramakanth Pasunuru and Mohit Bansal. *Multi-Task Video Captioning with Visual and Entailment Generation.*
- Maxim Rabinovich, Mitchell Stern and Dan Klein. *Abstract Syntax Networks for Code Generation and Semantic Parsing.*
- Ines Rehbein and Josef Ruppenhofer. *Detecting annotation noise in automatically labelled data.*
- Jiwei Tan, Xiaojun Wan and Jianguo Xiao. *Abstractive Document Summarization with a Graph-Based Attentional Neural Model.*
- Mingbin Xu, Hui Jiang and Sedtawut Watcharawittayakul. *A Local Detection Approach for Named Entity Recognition and Mention Detection.*
- Suncong Zheng, Feng Wang, Hongyun Bao, Yuexing Hao, Peng Zhou and Bo Xu. *Joint Extraction of Entities and Relations Based on a Novel Tagging Scheme.*

Short Papers

- Xinyu Hua and Lu Wang. *Understanding and Detecting Diverse Supporting Arguments on Controversial Issues.*
- Jindřich Libovický and Jindřich Helcl. *Attention Strategies for Multi-Source Sequence-to-Sequence Learning.*
- Bogdan Ludusan, Reiko Mazuka, Mathieu Bernard, Alejandrina Cristia and Emmanuel Dupoux. *The Role of Prosody and Speech Register in Word Segmentation: A Computational Modelling Perspective.*
- Afshin Rahimi, Trevor Cohn and Timothy Baldwin. *A Neural Model for User Geolocation and Lexical Dialectology.*
- Keisuke Sakaguchi, Matt Post and Benjamin Van Durme. *Error-repair Dependency Parsing for Ungrammatical Texts.*
- Alane Suhr, Mike Lewis, James Yeh and Yoav Artzi. *A Corpus of Compositional Language for Visual Reasoning.*
- Yizhong Wang, Sujian Li and Houfeng Wang. *A Two-stage Parsing Method for Text-level Discourse Analysis.*

Table of Contents

Conference Program

Monday, July 31st

11:46–11:58   Session 1A: Information Extraction 1 (NN)

11:46–11:58   *Classifying Temporal Relations by Bidirectional LSTM over Dependency Paths*
Fei Cheng and Yusuke Miyao

11:46–11:58   Session 1B: Semantics 1

11:46–11:58   *AMR-to-text Generation with Synchronous Node Replacement Grammar*
Linfeng Song, Xiaochang Peng, Yue Zhang, Zhiguo Wang and Daniel Gildea

11:46–11:58   Session 1C: Discourse 1

11:46–11:58   *Lexical Features in Coreference Resolution: To be Used With Caution*
Nafise Sadat Moosavi and Michael Strube

11:46–11:58   Session 1D: Machine Translation 1

11:46–11:58   *Alternative Objective Functions for Training MT Evaluation Metrics*
Miloš Stanojević and Khalil Sima'an

13:30–15:02   Session 5A: Multidisciplinary 1

13:30–13:48   *Exploring Neural Text Simplification Models*
Sergiu Nisioi, Sanja Štajner, Simone Paolo Ponzetto and Liviu P. Dinu

14:40–15:02   *On the Challenges of Translating NLP Research into Commercial Products*
Daniel Dahlmeier

14:27–15:02   Session 5B: Language and Resources 1

14:27–14:39   *Sentence Alignment Methods for Improving Text Simplification Systems*
Sanja Štajner, Marc Franco-Salvador, Simone Paolo Ponzetto, Paolo Rosso and Heiner Stuckenschmidt

14:40–15:02   *Understanding Task Design Trade-offs in Crowdsourced Paraphrase Collection*
Youxuan Jiang, Jonathan K. Kummerfeld and Walter S. Lasecki

14:27–15:02   Session 5C: Syntax 2 (NN)

14:27–14:39   *Arc-swift: A Novel Transition System for Dependency Parsing*
Peng Qi and Christopher D. Manning

14:40–15:02   *A Generative Parser with a Discriminative Recognition Algorithm*
Jianpeng Cheng, Adam Lopez and Mirella Lapata

Tuesday, August 1st (continued)

16:22–17:00   Session 6D: Machine Learning 2

16:22–16:40   *Information-Theory Interpretation of the Skip-Gram Negative-Sampling Objective Function*
Oren Melamud and Jacob Goldberger

16:41–17:00   *Implicitly-Defined Neural Networks for Sequence Labeling*
Michaeel Kazi and Brian Thompson

Wednesday, August 2nd

11:37–12:25   Session 7A: Outstanding Papers 1

11:37–11:49   *The Role of Prosody and Speech Register in Word Segmentation: A Computational Modelling Perspective*
Bogdan Ludusan, Reiko Mazuka, Mathieu Bernard, Alejandrina Cristia and Emmanuel Dupoux

11:50–12:12   *A Two-Stage Parsing Method for Text-Level Discourse Analysis*
Yizhong Wang, Sujian Li and Houfeng Wang

12:13–12:25   *Error-repair Dependency Parsing for Ungrammatical Texts*
Keisuke Sakaguchi, Matt Post and Benjamin Van Durme

11:18–12:25   Session 7B: Outstanding Papers 2

11:18–11:36   *Attention Strategies for Multi-Source Sequence-to-Sequence Learning*
Jindřich Libovický and Jindřich Helcl

11:37–11:49   *Understanding and Detecting Diverse Supporting Arguments on Controversial Issues*
Xinyu Hua and Lu Wang

11:50–12:12   *A Neural Model for User Geolocation and Lexical Dialectology*
Afshin Rahimi, Trevor Cohn and Timothy Baldwin

12:13–12:25   *A Corpus of Natural Language for Visual Reasoning*
Alane Suhr, Mike Lewis, James Yeh and Yoav Artzi

Monday, July 31st

18:00–21:30   Session P1: Poster Session 1

Neural Architecture for Temporal Relation Extraction: A Bi-LSTM Approach for Detecting Narrative Containers
Julien Tourille, Olivier Ferret, Aurelie Neveol and Xavier Tannier

How to Make Context More Useful? An Empirical Study on Context-Aware Neural Conversational Models
Zhiliang Tian, Rui Yan, Lili Mou, Yiping Song, Yansong Feng and Dongyan Zhao

Cross-lingual and cross-domain discourse segmentation of entire documents
Chloé Braud, Ophélie Lacroix and Anders Søgaard

Detecting Good Arguments in a Non-Topic-Specific Way: An Oxymoron?
Beata Beigman Klebanov, Binod Gyawali and Yi Song

Argumentation Quality Assessment: Theory vs. Practice
Henning Wachsmuth, Nona Naderi, Ivan Habernal, Yufang Hou, Graeme Hirst, Iryna Gurevych and Benno Stein

A Recurrent Neural Model with Attention for the Recognition of Chinese Implicit Discourse Relations
Samuel Rönnqvist, Niko Schenk and Christian Chiarcos

Discourse Annotation of Non-native Spontaneous Spoken Responses Using the Rhetorical Structure Theory Framework
Xinhao Wang, James Bruno, Hillary Molloy, Keelan Evanini and Klaus Zechner

Improving Implicit Discourse Relation Recognition with Discourse-specific Word Embeddings
Changxing Wu, Xiaodong Shi, Yidong Chen, Jinsong Su and Boli Wang

Oracle Summaries of Compressive Summarization
Tsutomu Hirao, Masaaki Nishino and Masaaki Nagata

Japanese Sentence Compression with a Large Training Dataset
Shun Hasegawa, Yuta Kikuchi, Hiroya Takamura and Manabu Okumura

19:00–22:00 Session P2: Poster Session 2

AliMe Chat: A Sequence to Sequence and Rerank based Chatbot Engine
Minghui Qiu, Feng-Lin Li, Siyu Wang, Xing Gao, Yan Chen, Weipeng Zhao, Haiqing Chen, Jun Huang and Wei Chu

A Conditional Variational Framework for Dialog Generation
Xiaoyu Shen, Hui Su, Yanran Li, Wenjie Li, Shuzi Niu, Yang Zhao, Akiko Aizawa and Guoping Long

Question Answering through Transfer Learning from Large Fine-grained Supervision Data
Sewon Min, Minjoon Seo and Hannaneh Hajishirzi

Self-Crowdsourcing Training for Relation Extraction
Azad Abad, Moin Nabi and Alessandro Moschitti

A Generative Attentional Neural Network Model for Dialogue Act Classification
Quan Hung Tran, Gholamreza Haffari and Ingrid Zukerman

Salience Rank: Efficient Keyphrase Extraction with Topic Modeling
Nedelina Teneva and Weiwei Cheng

List-only Entity Linking
Ying Lin, Chin-Yew Lin and Heng Ji

Improving Native Language Identification by Using Spelling Errors
Lingzhen Chen, Carlo Strapparava and Vivi Nastase

Disfluency Detection using a Noisy Channel Model and a Deep Neural Language Model
Paria Jamshid Lou and Mark Johnson

On the Equivalence of Holographic and Complex Embeddings for Link Prediction
Katsuhiko Hayashi and Masashi Shimbo

Classifying Temporal Relations by Bidirectional LSTM over Dependency Paths

Fei Cheng and **Yusuke Miyao**
Research Center for Financial Smart Data
National Institute of Informatics
2-1-2 Hitotsubashi, Chiyoda-ku, Tokyo, Japan
{fei-cheng, yusuke}@nii.ac.jp

Abstract

Temporal relation classification is becoming an active research field. Lots of methods have been proposed, while most of them focus on extracting features from external resources. Less attention has been paid to a significant advance in a closely related task: relation extraction. In this work, we borrow a state-of-the-art method in relation extraction by adopting bidirectional long short-term memory (Bi-LSTM) along dependency paths (DP). We make a "common root" assumption to extend DP representations of cross-sentence links. In the final comparison to two state-of-the-art systems on TimeBank-Dense, our model achieves comparable performance, without using external knowledge and manually annotated attributes of entities (class, tense, polarity, etc.).

1 Introduction

Recently, the need for extracting temporal information from text is motivated rapidly by many NLP tasks such as: question answering (QA), information extraction (IE), etc. Along with the TimeBank[1] (Pustejovsky et al., 2003) and other temporal information annotated corpora, a series of temporal evaluation challenges (TempEval-1,2,3) (Verhagen et al., 2009, 2010; UzZaman et al., 2012) are attracting growing research efforts.

Temporal relation classification is a task to identify the pairs of temporal entities (events or temporal expressions) that have a temporal link and classify the temporal relations between them. For instance, we show an event-event (E-E) link with 'DURING' type in *(i)*, an event-time (E-T) link with 'INCLUDES' type in *(ii)* and an event-DCT (document creation time, E-D) with 'BEFORE' type in *(iii)*.

(i) *There was no **hint** of trouble in the last **conversation** between controllers and TWA pilot Steven Snyder.*

(ii) *In Washington **today**, the Federal Aviation Administration **released** air traffic control tapes.*

(iii) *The U.S. Navy **has** 27 ships in the maritime barricade of Iraq.*

Marcu and Echihabi (2002) propose an approach considering word-based pairs as useful features. The following researchers (Laokulrat et al., 2013; Chambers et al., 2014; Mani et al., 2006; D'Souza and Ng, 2013) focus on extracting lexical, syntactic or semantic information from various external knowledge bases such as: WordNet (Miller, 1995) and VerbOcean (Chklovski and Pantel, 2004). However, these feature based methods rely on hand-crafted efforts and external resources. In addition, these works require the features of entity attributes (class, tense, polarity, etc.), which are manually annotated to achieve high performance. Consequently, they are hard to obtain in practical application scenarios.

In relation extraction, there is an explosion of the works done with the dependency path (DP) based methods, which employ various models along dependency paths (Bunescu and Mooney, 2005; Plank and Moschitti, 2013). In recent years, the DP-based neural networks (Socher et al., 2011; Xu et al., 2015a,b) show state-of-the-art performance, with less requirements on explicit features. Intuitively, the DP-based approaches have the potential to classify temporal relations.

Both relation extraction and temporal relation classification require the identification of relation-

---

[1] https://catalog.ldc.upenn.edu/LDC2006T08

1

Proceedings of the 55th Annual Meeting of the Association for Computational Linguistics (Short Papers), pages 1–6
Vancouver, Canada, July 30 - August 4, 2017. ©2017 Association for Computational Linguistics
https://doi.org/10.18653/v1/P17-2001

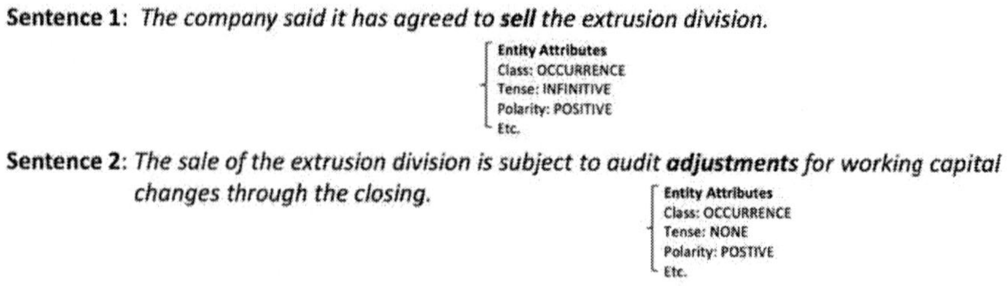

Figure 1: An example of the sentences with entity attributes annotated in TimeBank.

ship between entities in texts. However, temporal relation classification is more challenging, since it includes three different type of entities: 'event', 'time expression' and DCT. Cross-sentence links also add additional complexity into the task. Due to the outstanding performance of DP-based neural networks revealed in relation extraction, we borrow this state-of-the-art approach to temporal relation classification.

In Section 2 of this paper, we review related work and introduce TimeBank-Dense. We discuss the cross-sentence link problem and the architectures of our E-E, E-T and E-D classifiers in Section 3. In Section 4, the experiments are performed on TimeBank-Dense and we compare our model to the baseline and two state-of-the-art systems. The final conclusion is made in Section 5.

2 Background

2.1 Related Work

Current state-of-the-art temporal relation classifiers exploit a variety of features. Laokulrat et al. (2013); Chambers et al. (2014) extract lexical and morphological features derived from WordNet synsets. Mani et al. (2006); D'Souza and Ng (2013) incorporate semantic relations between verbs from VerbOcean as features. In addition, most of the systems include the entity attributes (Figure 1) specified in TimeML [2] as basic features, which actually need heavy human annotations.

In this work, we push this work into a more practical level by using only word, part-of-speech (POS), dependency parsing information, without incorporating entity attributes, as well as any other external resources.

In relation extraction, Bunescu and Mooney (2005) propose an observation that a relation can be captured by the shortest dependency path

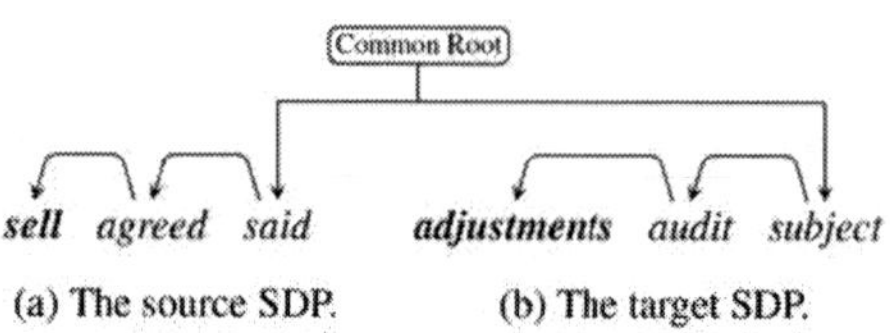

Figure 2: An example of the DP representation of a cross-sentence link between the two sentences in Figure 1.

(SDP) between the two entities in the entire dependency graph. Plank and Moschitti (2013) extract syntactic and semantic information in a tree kernel. Following this line, researchers (Socher et al., 2011; Xu et al., 2015a,b) achieve state-of-the-art performance by building various neural networks over dependency path.

Our system is similar to the work by Xu et al. (2015b). They perform LSTM with max pooling separately on each feature channel along dependency path. In contrast, our system adopts bidirectional LSTM on the concatenation of feature embeddings.

2.2 TimeBank-Dense

In the original TimeBank, temporal links have been created on those pairs with semantic connections, which led to a sparse annotation style. Cassidy et al. (2014) [3] propose a mechanism to force annotators to create complete graphs over the entities in neighboring sentences. Compared to 6,418 links in 183 TimeBank documents, TimeBank-Dense achieves greater density with 12,715 links in 36 documents.

We follow a similar experiment setting to the other two systems (Mirza and Tonelli, 2016; Chambers et al., 2014) with the same 9 documents

---

[2]http://timeml.org/

[3]https://www.usna.edu/Users/cs/nchamber/caevo

as test data and the others as training data (15% of training data is split as validation data for early stopping).

3 The Proposed Method

3.1 Cross-sentence Dependency Paths

Intuitively, the dependency path based idea can be introduced into the temporal relation classification task. However, around 64% E-E, E-T links in TimeBank-Dense are with the ends in two neighboring sentences, called cross-sentence links.

A crucial obstacle is how to represent the dependency path of a cross-sentence link. In this work, we make a naive assumption that two neighboring sentences share a "common root". Therefore, a cross-sentence dependency path can be represented as two shortest dependency path branches from the ends to the "common root", as shown in Figure 2.

Stanford CoreNLP[4] is used to parsing syntactic structures of sentences in this work.

3.2 Temporal Relation Classifiers

Long short-term memory (LSTM) (Hochreiter and Schmidhuber, 1997) is a natural choice for processing sequential dependency paths. As the reversed order also takes useful information, a backward representation can be achieved by feeding LSTM with the same input in reverse. We adopt the concatenation of the forward and backward LSTMs outputs, referred to as bidirectional LSTM (Graves and Schmidhuber, 2005).

Figure 3a shows the neural network architecture of our E-E, E-T classifier. Given an E-E or E-T temporal link, our system first generates two SDP branches: 1) the source entity to common root, 2) the target entity to common root. For each word along a SDP branch, concatenation of word, POS and dependency relation (DEP) embeddings (word-level) is fed into Bi-LSTM. The forward and backward outputs of both source and target branches are all concatenated, and fed into a fully connected hidden units layer. The final Softmax layer generates multi-class predictions. Since an E-D link contains single event SDP branch, our system applies a similar architecture, but with single branch Bi-LSTM with outputs fed into the penultimate hidden layer, as shown in Figure 3b.

In this work, we use word2vec[5] (Mikolov et al.,

<hr>

[4] http://stanfordnlp.github.io/CoreNLP/
[5] https://code.google.com/archive/p/word2vec/

LINK type	E-D	E-E	E-T
AFTER	.493	.477	.350
BEFORE	.552	.380	.311
SIMULTANEOUS	-	-	-
INCLUDES	.305	.185	.254
IS_INCLUDED	.513	.296	.204
VAGUE	.482	.656	.616
Overall	.491	.544	.480

Table 1: The best sentence-level 5-fold CV performance (Micro-average Overall F1-score).

2013a,b) to train 200-dimensions word embeddings on English Gigaword 4th edition with skip-gram model and other default settings. For either of POS or DEP, we adopt the 50-dimensions lookup table initialized randomly.

4 Experiments

4.1 Hyper-parameters and Cross-validation

The grid search exploring a full hyper-parameter space takes time for three classifiers (E-E, E-T and E-D). Empirically, we set each single LSTM output with the same dimensions (equal to 300) as the concatenation of word, POS, DEP embeddings. The hidden layer is set as 200-dimensions.

Our system adopts dependency paths as input, which means that the entities in the same sentences contain highly covered word sequence input. Simple cross-validation (CV) on links can not reflect the generalization ability of our model correctly. We use a grouped 5-fold CV based on the source entity ids (document id + sentence id) of links. This schema can reduce bias separately in either the source SDP or the target SDP. Although document level CV can avoid this issue, it's not feasible for TimeBank-Dense because it contains only 27 training documents.

Early stopping is used to save the best model based on the validation data. In each run of the 5-fold cross-validation, we split 80% of 'original training' as 'tentative training' and 20% as 'tentative test'. 85% of 'tentative training' is used to learning and 15% is used for validation. We also adopt early stopping in the final system on the validation data (15% of 'original training'). The patience is set as 10.

Dropout (Srivastava et al., 2014) recently is proved to be an useful approach to prevent neural networks from over-fitting. We adopt dropout

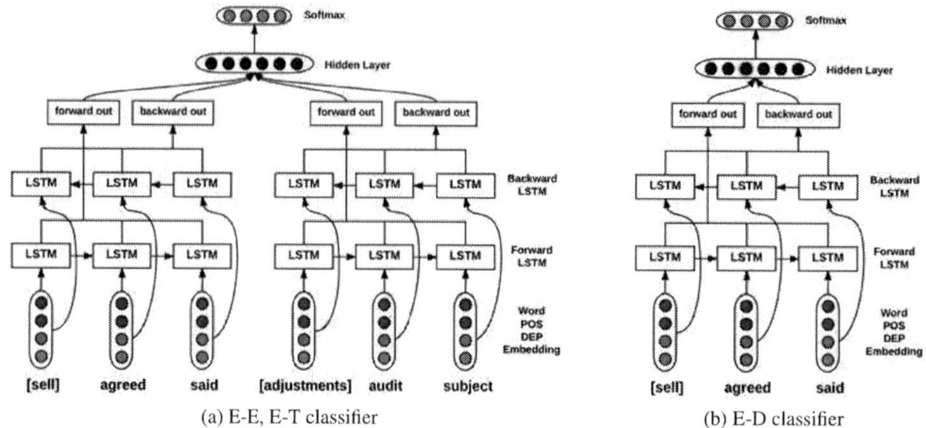

(a) E-E, E-T classifier   (b) E-D classifier

Figure 3: The DP-based Bi-LSTM temporal relation classifier.

	Our	Mirza	Our	Mirza
LINK type	**E-D**	**E-D**	**E-E**	**E-E**
AFTER	**.582**	.466	**.440**	.430
BEFORE	.634	**.671**	.460	**.471**
SIMULTA.	-	-	-	-
INCLUDES	.056	**.250**	.025	**.049**
IS_INCLUD.	.595	**.600**	.170	**.250**
VAGUE	**.526**	.502	**.624**	.613
Overall	**.546**	.534	**.529**	.519

Table 2: The detailed comparison of E-E and E-T against relation types to Mirza and Tonelli (2016) (Micro-average Overall F1-score) on test data.

Systems	E-D	E-E	E-T	Overall
Baseline	.471	.502	.437	.486
Proposed	.546	**.529**	.471	**.520**
Mirza	.534	.519	.468	.512
CAEVO	**.553**	.494	**.494**	.502

Table 3: The final comparison of E-E, E-T and E-D to the baseline and two state-of-the-art systems on test data.

separately after the following layers: embeddings, LSTM, and hidden layer to investigate the impact of dropout on performance. Table 1 shows the best CV results recorded in tuning dropout. The hyperparameter setting with the best CV performance is adopted in the final system.

4.2 Overall Performance

Recently, Mirza and Tonelli (2016) report state-of-the-art performance on TimeBank-Dense. They show the new attempt to mine the value of low-dimensions word embeddings by concatenating them with sparse traditional features. Their traditional features include entity attributes, temporal signals, semantic information of WordNet, etc., which means it's a hard setting for challenging their performance. In Table 2 and 3, 'Mirza' denotes their system.

Table 2 shows the detailed comparison to their work. Our system achieves higher performance on 'AFTER', 'VAGUE', while lower on 'BEFORE', 'INCLUDES' (5% of all data) and 'IS_INCLUDED' (4% of all data). It is likely that their rich traditional features help the classifiers to capture more minority-class links. On the whole, our system reaches better 'Overall' on both E-E and E-D. As their E-T classifier does not include word embeddings, the E-T results are not listed.

The final comparison is shown in Table 3. An one-layer fully connected hidden units baseline (200-dimensions) with word, POS embeddings as input (without any dependency information) is provided. The significant out-performance of our proposed model over the baseline indicates the effectiveness of the dependency path information and our Bi-LSTM in classifying temporal links. As a hybrid system, 'CAEVO' (Chambers et al., 2014) includes hand-crafted rules for their E-T and E-D classifiers. For instance, the temporal prepositions *in*, *on*, *over*, *during*, and *within* indicate 'IN_INCLUDED' relations. Their system is superior in E-T and E-D. 'Miza' takes the pure feature-based methods and performs slightly better in E-E and overall, compared to 'CAEVO'. Our system shows the highest scores in E-E and overall among the four systems. In general, our system achieves comparable performance to two state-of-the-art systems, without using any hand-crafted features, rules, or external resources.

5 Conclusion

We borrow the idea of the dependency path based neural networks into temporal relation classification. A "common root" assumption adapts our model to cross-sentence links. Our model adopts bidirectional LSTM for capturing both forward and backward orders information. We observe the significant benefit of the DP-based Bi-LSTM model by comparing it to the baseline. Our model achieves comparable performance to two state-of-the-art systems without using any explicit features (class, tense, polarity, etc.) or external resources, which indicates that our model can capture such information automatically.

6 Acknowledgments

We thank the anonymous reviewers for the insightful comments.

References

Razvan Bunescu and Raymond Mooney. 2005. A shortest path dependency kernel for relation extraction. In *Proceedings of Human Language Technology Conference and Conference on Empirical Methods in Natural Language Processing.* Association for Computational Linguistics, Vancouver, British Columbia, Canada, pages 724–731. http://www.aclweb.org/anthology/H/H05/H05-1091.

Taylor Cassidy, Bill McDowell, Nathanael Chambers, and Steven Bethard. 2014. An annotation framework for dense event ordering. In *Proceedings of the 52nd Annual Meeting of the Association for Computational Linguistics (Volume 2: Short Papers).* Association for Computational Linguistics, Baltimore, Maryland, pages 501–506. http://www.aclweb.org/anthology/P14-2082.

Nathanael Chambers, Taylor Cassidy, Bill McDowell, and Steven Bethard. 2014. Dense event ordering with a multi-pass architecture. *Transactions of the Association for Computational Linguistics* 2:273–284. http://aclweb.org/anthology/Q/Q14/Q14-1022.pdf.

Timothy Chklovski and Patrick Pantel. 2004. Verbocean: Mining the web for fine-grained semantic verb relations. In Dekang Lin and Dekai Wu, editors, *Proceedings of EMNLP 2004.* Association for Computational Linguistics, Barcelona, Spain, pages 33–40. https://www.aclweb.org/anthology/W/W04/W04-3205.pdf.

Jennifer D'Souza and Vincent Ng. 2013. Classifying temporal relations with rich linguistic knowledge. In *Proceedings of the 2013 Conference of the North American Chapter of the Association for Computational Linguistics: Human Language Technologies.* Association for Computational Linguistics, Atlanta, Georgia, pages 918–927. http://www.aclweb.org/anthology/N13-1112.

Alex Graves and Jürgen Schmidhuber. 2005. Framewise phoneme classification with bidirectional lstm and other neural network architectures. *Neural Networks* 18(5):602–610. https://doi.org/10.1016/j.neunet.2005.06.042.

Sepp Hochreiter and Jürgen Schmidhuber. 1997. Long short-term memory. *Neural computation* 9(8):1735–1780. https://doi.org/10.1162/neco.1997.9.8.1735.

Natsuda Laokulrat, Makoto Miwa, Yoshimasa Tsuruoka, and Takashi Chikayama. 2013. Uttime: Temporal relation classification using deep syntactic features. In *Second Joint Conference on Lexical and Computational Semantics (* SEM).* volume 2, pages 88–92. http://aclweb.org/anthology/S/S13/S13-2015.pdf.

Inderjeet Mani, Marc Verhagen, Ben Wellner, Chong Min Lee, and James Pustejovsky. 2006. Machine learning of temporal relations. In *Proceedings of the 21st International Conference on Computational Linguistics and 44th Annual Meeting of the Association for Computational Linguistics.* Association for Computational Linguistics, Sydney, Australia, pages 753–760. https://doi.org/10.3115/1220175.1220270.

Daniel Marcu and Abdessamad Echihabi. 2002. An unsupervised approach to recognizing discourse relations. In *Proceedings of 40th Annual Meeting of the Association for Computational Linguistics.* Association for Computational Linguistics, Philadelphia, Pennsylvania, USA, pages 368–375. https://doi.org/10.3115/1073083.1073145.

Tomas Mikolov, Kai Chen, Greg Corrado, and Jeffrey Dean. 2013a. Efficient estimation of word representations in vector space. *arXiv preprint arXiv:1301.3781* http://arxiv.org/pdf/1301.3781v3.pdf.

Tomas Mikolov, Ilya Sutskever, Kai Chen, Greg S Corrado, and Jeff Dean. 2013b. Distributed representations of words and phrases and their compositionality. In *Advances in neural information processing systems.* pages 3111–3119. https://arxiv.org/pdf/1310.4546.pdf.

George A Miller. 1995. Wordnet: a lexical database for english. *Communications of the ACM* 38(11):39–41. https://doi.org/10.1145/219717.219748.

Paramita Mirza and Sara Tonelli. 2016. On the contribution of word embeddings to temporal relation classification. In *Proceedings of COLING 2016, the 26th International Conference on Computational Linguistics: Technical Papers*. The COLING 2016 Organizing Committee, Osaka, Japan, pages 2818–2828. http://aclweb.org/anthology/C16-1265.

Barbara Plank and Alessandro Moschitti. 2013. Embedding semantic similarity in tree kernels for domain adaptation of relation extraction. In *Proceedings of the 51st Annual Meeting of the Association for Computational Linguistics (Volume 1: Long Papers)*. Association for Computational Linguistics, Sofia, Bulgaria, pages 1498–1507. http://www.aclweb.org/anthology/P13-1147.

James Pustejovsky, Patrick Hanks, Roser Sauri, Andrew See, Robert Gaizauskas, Andrea Setzer, Dragomir Radev, Beth Sundheim, David Day, Lisa Ferro, et al. 2003. The timebank corpus. In *Corpus linguistics*. volume 2003, page 40. https://catalog.ldc.upenn.edu/LDC2006T08.

Richard Socher, Jeffrey Pennington, Eric H. Huang, Andrew Y. Ng, and Christopher D. Manning. 2011. Semi-supervised recursive autoencoders for predicting sentiment distributions. In *Proceedings of the 2011 Conference on Empirical Methods in Natural Language Processing*. Association for Computational Linguistics, Edinburgh, Scotland, UK., pages 151–161. http://www.aclweb.org/anthology/D11-1014.

Nitish Srivastava, Geoffrey E Hinton, Alex Krizhevsky, Ilya Sutskever, and Ruslan Salakhutdinov. 2014. Dropout: a simple way to prevent neural networks from overfitting. *Journal of Machine Learning Research* 15(1):1929–1958. http://jmlr.org/papers/v15/srivastava14a.html.

Naushad UzZaman, Hector Llorens, James Allen, Leon Derczynski, Marc Verhagen, and James Pustejovsky. 2012. Tempeval-3: Evaluating events, time expressions, and temporal relations. *arXiv preprint arXiv:1206.5333* http://aclweb.org/anthology/S/S13/S13-2001.pdf.

Marc Verhagen, Robert Gaizauskas, Frank Schilder, Mark Hepple, Jessica Moszkowicz, and James Pustejovsky. 2009. The tempeval challenge: identifying temporal relations in text. *Language Resources and Evaluation* 43(2):161–179. https://doi.org/10.1007/s10579-009-9086-z.

Marc Verhagen, Roser Sauri, Tommaso Caselli, and James Pustejovsky. 2010. Semeval-2010 task 13: Tempeval-2. In *Proceedings of the 5th international workshop on semantic evaluation*. Association for Computational Linguistics, pages 57–62. http://www.aclweb.org/anthology/S10-1010.

Kun Xu, Yansong Feng, Songfang Huang, and Dongyan Zhao. 2015a. Semantic relation classification via convolutional neural networks with simple negative sampling. In *Proceedings of the 2015 Conference on Empirical Methods in Natural Language Processing*. Association for Computational Linguistics, Lisbon, Portugal, pages 536–540. http://aclweb.org/anthology/D15-1062.

Yan Xu, Lili Mou, Ge Li, Yunchuan Chen, Hao Peng, and Zhi Jin. 2015b. Classifying relations via long short term memory networks along shortest dependency paths. In *Proceedings of the 2015 Conference on Empirical Methods in Natural Language Processing*. Association for Computational Linguistics, Lisbon, Portugal, pages 1785–1794. http://aclweb.org/anthology/D15-1206.

AMR-to-text Generation with Synchronous Node Replacement Grammar

Linfeng Song, Xiaochang Peng, Yue Zhang, Zhiguo Wang and **Daniel Gildea**
Department of Computer Science, University of Rochester, Rochester, NY 14627
IBM T.J. Watson Research Center, Yorktown Heights, NY 10598
Singapore University of Technology and Design

Abstract

This paper addresses the task of AMR-to-text generation by leveraging synchronous node replacement grammar. During training, graph-to-string rules are learned using a heuristic extraction algorithm. At test time, a graph transducer is applied to collapse input AMRs and generate output sentences. Evaluated on a standard benchmark, our method gives the state-of-the-art result.

1 Introduction

Abstract Meaning Representation (AMR) (Banarescu et al., 2013) is a semantic formalism encoding the meaning of a sentence as a rooted, directed graph. AMR uses a graph to represent meaning, where nodes (such as "boy", "want-01") represent concepts, and edges (such as "ARG0", "ARG1") represent relations between concepts. Encoding many semantic phenomena into a graph structure, AMR is useful for NLP tasks such as machine translation (Jones et al., 2012; Tamchyna et al., 2015), question answering (Mitra and Baral, 2015), summarization (Takase et al., 2016) and event detection (Li et al., 2015).

AMR-to-text generation is challenging as function words and syntactic structures are abstracted away, making an AMR graph correspond to multiple realizations. Despite much literature so far on text-to-AMR parsing (Flanigan et al., 2014; Wang et al., 2015; Peng et al., 2015; Vanderwende et al., 2015; Pust et al., 2015; Artzi et al., 2015; Groschwitz et al., 2015; Goodman et al., 2016; Zhou et al., 2016; Peng et al., 2017), there has been little work on AMR-to-text generation (Flanigan et al., 2016; Song et al., 2016; Pourdamghani et al., 2016).

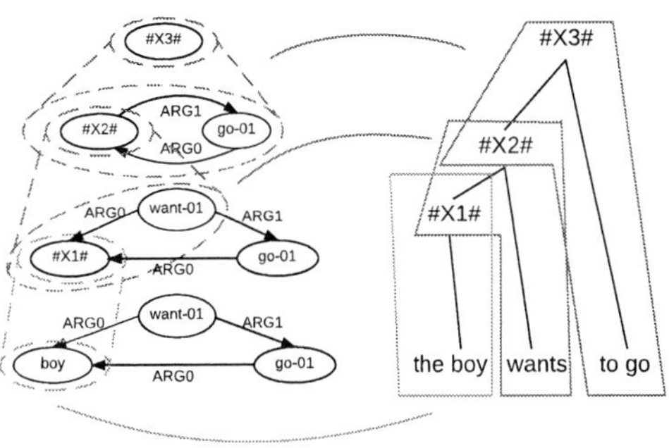

Figure 1: Graph-to-string derivation.

Flanigan et al. (2016) transform a given AMR graph into a spanning tree, before translating it to a sentence using a tree-to-string transducer. Their method leverages existing machine translation techniques, capturing hierarchical correspondences between the spanning tree and the surface string. However, it suffers from error propagation since the output is constrained given a spanning tree due to the projective correspondence between them. Information loss in the graph-to-tree transformation step cannot be recovered. Song et al. (2016) directly generate sentences using graphfragment-to-string rules. They cast the task of finding a sequence of disjoint rules to transduce an AMR graph into a sentence as a traveling salesman problem, using local features and a language model to rank candidate sentences. However, their method does not learn hierarchical structural correspondences between AMR graphs and strings.

We propose to leverage the advantages of hierarchical rules without suffering from graph-to-tree errors by directly learning graph-to-string rules. As shown in Figure 1, we learn a synchronous node replacement grammar (NRG) from a corpus of aligned AMR and sentence pairs. At test time, we apply a graph transducer to collapse input

7

Proceedings of the 55th Annual Meeting of the Association for Computational Linguistics (Short Papers), pages 7–13
Vancouver, Canada, July 30 - August 4, 2017. ©2017 Association for Computational Linguistics
https://doi.org/10.18653/v1/P17-2002

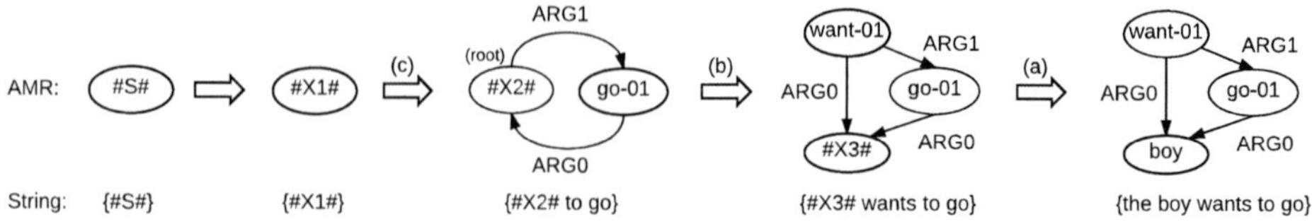

Figure 2: Example deduction procedure

ID.	F	E
(a)	(b / boy)	the boy
(b)	(w / want-01 :ARG0 (X / #X#))	#X# wants

(c)	(X / #X#
	    :ARG1 (g / go-01
	      :ARG0 X))
		#X# to go

(d)	(w / want-01 :ARG0 (b / boy))	the boy wants

Table 1: Example rule set

AMR graphs and generate output strings according to the learned grammar. Our system makes use of a log-linear model with real-valued features, tuned using MERT (Och, 2003), and beam search decoding. It gives a BLEU score of 25.62 on LDC2015E86, which is the state-of-the-art on this dataset.

2 Synchronous Node Replacement Grammar

2.1 Grammar Definition

A synchronous node replacement grammar (NRG) is a rewriting formalism: $G = \langle N, \Sigma, \Delta, P, S \rangle$, where N is a finite set of nonterminals, Σ and Δ are finite sets of terminal symbols for the source and target sides, respectively. $S \in N$ is the start symbol, and P is a finite set of productions. Each instance of P takes the form $X_i \to (\langle F, E \rangle, \sim)$, where $X_i \in N$ is a nonterminal node, F is a rooted, connected AMR fragment with edge labels over Σ and node labels over $N \cup \Sigma$, E is a corresponding target string over $N \cup \Delta$ and $\sim$ denotes the alignment of nonterminal symbols between F and E. A classic NRG (Engelfriet and Rozenberg, 1997, Chapter 1) also defines C, which is an embedding mechanism defining how F is connected to the rest of the graph when replacing X_i with F on the graph. Here we omit defining C and allow arbitrary connections.[1] Following Chiang

Data: training corpus C
Result: rule instances R

```
1  R ← [];
2  for (Sent, AMR, ∼) in C do
3      R_cur ← FRAGMENTEXTRACT(Sent, AMR, ∼);
4      for r_i in R_cur do
5          R.APPEND(r_i) ;
6          for r_j in R_cur/{r_i} do
7              if r_i.CONTAINS(r_j) then
8                  r_ij ← r_i.COLLAPSE(r_j);
9                  R.APPEND(r_ij) ;
10             end
11         end
12     end
13 end
```

Algorithm 1: Rule extraction

(2005), we use only one nonterminal X in addition to S, and use subscripts to distinguish different non-terminal instances.

Figure 2 shows an example derivation process for the sentence "the boy wants to go" given the rule set in Table 1. Given the start symbol S, which is first replaced with X_1, rule (c) is applied to generate "X_2 to go" and its AMR counterpart. Then rule (b) is used to generate "X_3 wants" and its AMR counterpart from X_2. Finally, rule (a) is used to generate "the boy" and its AMR counterpart from X_3. Our graph-to-string rules are inspired by synchronous grammars for machine translation (Wu, 1997; Yamada and Knight, 2002; Gildea, 2003; Chiang, 2005; Huang et al., 2006; Liu et al., 2006; Shen et al., 2008; Xie et al., 2011; Meng et al., 2013).

2.2 Induced Rules

There are three types of rules in our system, namely *induced rules*, *concept rules* and *graph glue rules*. Here we first introduce induced rules, which are obtained by a two-step procedure on a training corpus. Shown in Algorithm 1, the first step is to extract a set of initial rules from training $\langle$sentence, AMR, $\sim \rangle$[2] pairs (Line 2) using the phrase-to-graph-fragment extraction algorithm of Peng et al. (2015) (Line 3). Here an *initial rule*

---

[1] This may over generate, but does not affect our case, as in our bottom-up decoding procedure (section 3) when F is replaced with X_i, nodes previously connected to F are reconnected to X_i

[2] $\sim$ denotes alignment between words and AMR labels.

contains only terminal symbols in both F and E. As a next step, we match between pairs of initial rules r_i and r_j, and generate r_{ij} by collapsing r_i with r_j, if r_i contains r_j (Line 6-8). Here r_i contains r_j, if $r_j.F$ is a subgraph of $r_i.F$ and $r_j.E$ is a sub-phrase of $r_i.E$. When collapsing r_i with r_j, we replace the corresponding subgraph in $r_i.F$ with a new non-terminal node, and the sub-phrase in $r_i.E$ with the same non-terminal. For example, we obtain rule (b) by collapsing (d) with (a) in Table 1. All initial and generated rules are stored in a rule list R (Lines 5 and 9), which will be further normalized to obtain the final induced rule set.

2.3 Concept Rules and Glue Rules

In addition to induced rules, we adopt concept rules (Song et al., 2016) and graph glue rules to ensure existence of derivations. For a concept rule, F is a single node in the input AMR graph, and E is a morphological string of the node concept. A concept rule is used in case no induced rule can cover the node. We refer to the verbalization list[3] and AMR guidelines[4] for creating more complex concept rules. For example, one concept rule created from the verbalization list is "(k / keep-01 :ARG1 (p / peace)) ||| peacekeeping".

Inspired by Chiang (2005), we define graph glue rules to concatenate non-terminal nodes connected with an edge, when no induced rules can be applied. Three glue rules are defined for each type of edge label. Taking the edge label "ARG0" as an example, we create the following glue rules:

ID.	F	E
r_1	(X1 / #X1# :ARG0 (X2 / #X2#))	#X1# #X2#
r_2	(X1 / #X1# :ARG0 (X2 / #X2#))	#X2# #X1#
r_3	(X1 / #X1# :ARG0 X1)	#X1#

where for both r_1 and r_2, F contains two non-terminal nodes with a directed edge connecting them, and E is the concatenation the two non-terminals in either the monotonic or the inverse order. For r_3, F contains one non-terminal node with a self-pointing edge, and E is the non-terminal. With concept rules and glue rules in our final rule set, it is easily guaranteed that there are legal derivations for any input AMR graph.

3 Model

We adopt a log-linear model for scoring search hypotheses. Given an input AMR graph, we find the highest scored derivation t^* from all possible derivations t:

$$t^* = \underset{t}{\arg\max} \exp \sum_i w_i f_i(g, t), \qquad (1)$$

where g denotes the input AMR, $f_i(\cdot, \cdot)$ and w_i represent a feature and the corresponding weight, respectively. The feature set that we adopt includes phrase-to-graph and graph-to-phrase translation probabilities and their corresponding lexicalized translation probabilities (section 3.1), language model score, word count, rule count, reordering model score (section 3.2) and moving distance (section 3.3). The language model score, word count and phrase count features are adopted from SMT (Koehn et al., 2003; Chiang, 2005).

We perform bottom-up search to transduce input AMRs to surface strings. Each hypothesis contains the current AMR graph, translations of collapsed subgraphs, the feature vector and the current model score. Beam search is adopted, where hypotheses with the same number of collapsed edges and nodes are put into the same beam.

3.1 Translation Probabilities

Production rules serve as a basis for scoring hypotheses. We associate each synchronous NRG rule $n \rightarrow (\langle F, E \rangle, \sim)$ with a set of probabilities. First, phrase-to-fragment translation probabilities are defined based on maximum likelihood estimation (MLE), as shown in Equation 2, where $c_{\langle F,E \rangle}$ is the fractional count of $\langle F, E \rangle$.

$$p(F|E) = \frac{c_{\langle F,E \rangle}}{\sum_{F'} c_{\langle F',E \rangle}} \qquad (2)$$

In addition, lexicalized translation probabilities are defined as:

$$p_w(F|E) = \prod_{l \in F} \sum_{w \in E} p(l|w) \qquad (3)$$

Here l is a label (including both edge labels such as "ARG0" and concept labels such as "want-01") in the AMR fragment F, and w is a word in the phrase E. Equation 3 can be regarded as a "soft" version of the lexicalized translation probabilities adopted by SMT, which picks the alignment yielding the maximum lexicalized probability for each translation rule. In addition to $p(F|E)$ and $p_w(F|E)$, we use features in the reverse direction, namely $p(E|F)$ and $p_w(E|F)$, the definitions of which are omitted as they are consistent with

---

[3]http://amr.isi.edu/download/lists/verbalization-list-v1.06.txt
[4]https://github.com/amrisi/amr-guidelines

Equations 2 and 3, respectively. The probabilities associated with concept rules and glue rules are manually set to 0.0001.

3.2 Reordering Model

Although the word order is defined for induced rules, it is not the case for glue rules. We learn a reordering model that helps to decide whether the translations of the nodes should be monotonic or inverse given the directed connecting edge label. The probabilistic model using smoothed counts is defined as:

$$p(M|h,l,t) =$$
$$\frac{1.0 + \sum_h \sum_t c(h,l,t,M)}{2.0 + \sum_{o \in \{M,I\}} \sum_h \sum_t c(h,l,t,o)} \quad (4)$$

$c(h,l,t,M)$ is the count of monotonic translations of head h and tail t, connected by edge l.

3.3 Moving Distance

The moving distance feature captures the distances between the subgraph roots of two consecutive rule matches in the decoding process, which controls a bias towards collapsing nearby subgraphs consecutively.

4 Experiments

4.1 Setup

We use LDC2015E86 as our experimental dataset, which contains 16833 training, 1368 dev and 1371 test instances. Each instance contains a sentence, an AMR graph and the alignment generated by a heuristic aligner. Rules are extracted from the training data, and model parameters are tuned on the dev set. For tuning and testing, we filter out sentences with more than 30 words, resulting in 1103 dev instances and 1055 test instances. We train a 4-gram language model (LM) on gigaword (LDC2011T07), and use BLEU (Papineni et al., 2002) as the evaluation metric. MERT is used (Och, 2003) to tune model parameters on k-best outputs on the devset, where k is set 50.

We investigate the effectiveness of rules and features by ablation tests: "NoInducedRule" does not adopt induced rules, "NoConceptRule" does not adopt concept rules, "NoMovingDistance" does not adopt the moving distance feature, and "NoReorderModel" disables the reordering model. Given an AMR graph, if *NoConceptRule* cannot produce a legal derivation, we concatenate

System	Dev	Test
TSP-gen	21.12	22.44
JAMR-gen	23.00	23.00
All	**25.24**	**25.62**
NoInducedRule	16.75	17.43
NoConceptRule	23.99	24.86
NoMovingDistance	23.48	24.06
NoReorderModel	25.09	25.43

Table 2: Main results.

existing translation fragments into a final translation, and if a subgraph can not be translated, the empty string is used as the output. We also compare our method with previous works, in particular JAMR-gen (Flanigan et al., 2016) and TSP-gen (Song et al., 2016), on the same dataset.

4.2 Main results

The results are shown in Table 2. First, *All* outperforms all baselines. *NoInducedRule* leads to the greatest performance drop compared with *All*, demonstrating that induced rules play a very important role in our system. On the other hand, *NoConceptRule* does not lead to much performance drop. This observation is consistent with the observation of Song et al. (2016) for their TSP-based system. *NoMovingDistance* leads to a significant performance drop, empirically verifying the fact that the translations of nearby subgraphs are also close. Finally, *NoReorderingModel* does not affect the performance significantly, which can be because the most important reordering patterns are already covered by the hierarchical induced rules. Compared with *TSP-gen* and *JAMR-gen*, our final model *All* improves the BLEU from 22.44 and 23.00 to 25.62, showing the advantage of our model. To our knowledge, this is the best result reported so far on the task.

4.3 Grammar analysis

We have shown the effectiveness of our synchronous node replacement grammar (SNRG) on the AMR-to-text generation task. Here we further analyze our grammar as it is relatively less studied than the hyperedge replacement grammar (HRG) (Drewes et al., 1997).

Statistics on the whole rule set

We first categorize our rule set by the number of terminals and nonterminals in the AMR fragment F, and show the percentages of each type in Figure 3. Each rule contains at most 1 nonterminal, as we collapse each initial rule only once. First

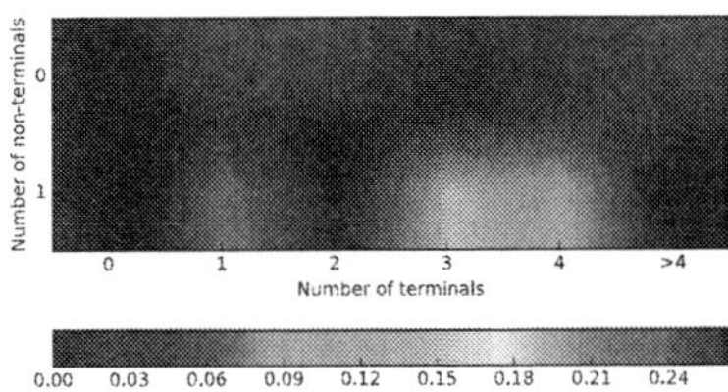

Figure 3: Statistics on the right-hand side.

	Glue	Nonterminal	Terminal
1-best	30.0%	30.1%	39.9%

Table 3: Rules used for decoding.

of all, the percentage of rules containing nonterminals are much more than those without nonterminals, as we collapse each pair of initial rules (in Algorithm 1) and the results can be quadratic the number of initial rules. In addition, most rules are small containing 1 to 3 terminals, meaning that they represent small pieces of meaning and are easier to matched on a new AMR graph. Finally, there are a few large rules, which represent complex meaning.

Statistics on the rules used for decoding

In addition, we collect the rules that our well-tuned system used for generating the 1-best output on the testset, and categorize them into 3 types: (1) glue rules, (2) nonterminal rules, which are not glue rules but contain nonterminals on the right-hand side and (3) terminal rules, whose right-hand side only contain terminals. Over the rules used on the 1-best result, more than 30% are non-terminal rules, showing that the induced rules play an important role. On the other hand, 30% are glue rules. The reason is that the data sparsity for graph grammars is more severe than string-based grammars (such as CFG), as the graph structures are more complex than strings. Finally, terminal rules take the largest percentage, while most are *induced rules*, but not *concept rules*.

Rule examples

Finally, we show some rules in Table 4, where F and E are the right-hand-side AMR fragment and phrase, respectively. For the first rule, the root of F is a verb ("give-01") whose subject is a nonterminal and object is a AMR fragment "(p / person :ARG0-of (u / use-01))", which means "user". So it is easy to see that the corresponding phrase E conveys the same meaning. For the second rule, "(s3 / stay-01 :accompanier (i / i))" means "stay

F:	(g / give-01 :ARG0 (X1 / #X1#) :ARG2 (p / person :ARG0-of (u / use-01)))
E:	#X1# has given users an
F:	(X1 / #X1# :ARG2 (s3 / stay-01 :ARG1 X1 :accompanier (i / i)))
E:	#X1# staying with me

Table 4: Example rules.

```
(u / understand-01
  :ARG0 (y / you)
  :ARG1 (t2 / thing
    :ARG1-of (f2 / feel-01
      :ARG0 (p2 / person
        :example (p / person :wiki -
          :name (t / name :op1 "TMT")
          :location (c / city :wiki "Fairfax,_Virginia"
            :name (f / name :op1 "Fairfax")))))
  :time (n / now))
```

Trans: now, you have to understand that people feel about such as tmt fairfax

Ref: now you understand how people like tmt in fairfax feel .

Table 5: Generation example.

with me", which is also covered by its phrase.

4.4 Generation example

Finally, we show an example in Table 5, where the top is the input AMR graph, and the bottom is the generation result. Generally, most of the meaning of the input AMR are correctly translated, such as ":example", which means "such as", and "thing", which is an abstract concept and should not be translated, while there are a few errors, such as "that" in the result should be "what", and there should be an "in" between "tmt" and "fairfax".

5 Conclusion

We showed that synchronous node replacement grammar is useful for AMR-to-text generation by developing a system that learns a synchronous NRG in the training time, and applies a graph transducer to collapse input AMR graphs and generate output strings according to the learned grammar at test time. Our method performs better than the previous systems, empirically proving the advantages of our graph-to-string rules.

Acknowledgement

This work was funded by a Google Faculty Research Award. Yue Zhang is funded by NSFC61572245 and T2MOE201301 from Singapore Ministry of Education.

References

Yoav Artzi, Kenton Lee, and Luke Zettlemoyer. 2015. Broad-coverage CCG semantic parsing with AMR. In *Conference on Empirical Methods in Natural Language Processing (EMNLP-15)*. pages 1699–1710.

Laura Banarescu, Claire Bonial, Shu Cai, Madalina Georgescu, Kira Griffitt, Ulf Hermjakob, Kevin Knight, Philipp Koehn, Martha Palmer, and Nathan Schneider. 2013. Abstract meaning representation for sembanking. In *Proceedings of the 7th Linguistic Annotation Workshop and Interoperability with Discourse*. pages 178–186.

David Chiang. 2005. A hierarchical phrase-based model for statistical machine translation. In *Proceedings of the 43rd Annual Meeting of the Association for Computational Linguistics (ACL-05)*. Ann Arbor, Michigan, pages 263–270.

Frank Drewes, Hans-Jörg Kreowski, and Annegret Habel. 1997. Hyperedge replacement, graph grammars. *Handbook of Graph Grammars* 1:95–162.

J. Engelfriet and G. Rozenberg. 1997. Node replacement graph grammars. In Grzegorz Rozenberg, editor, *Handbook of Graph Grammars and Computing by Graph Transformation*, World Scientific Publishing Co., Inc., River Edge, NJ, USA, pages 1–94.

Jeffrey Flanigan, Chris Dyer, Noah A. Smith, and Jaime Carbonell. 2016. Generation from abstract meaning representation using tree transducers. In *Proceedings of the 2016 Meeting of the North American chapter of the Association for Computational Linguistics (NAACL-16)*. pages 731–739.

Jeffrey Flanigan, Sam Thomson, Jaime Carbonell, Chris Dyer, and Noah A. Smith. 2014. A discriminative graph-based parser for the abstract meaning representation. In *Proceedings of the 52nd Annual Meeting of the Association for Computational Linguistics (ACL-14)*. pages 1426–1436.

Daniel Gildea. 2003. Loosely tree-based alignment for machine translation. In *Proceedings of the 41th Annual Conference of the Association for Computational Linguistics (ACL-03)*. Sapporo, Japan, pages 80–87.

James Goodman, Andreas Vlachos, and Jason Naradowsky. 2016. Noise reduction and targeted exploration in imitation learning for abstract meaning representation parsing. In *Proceedings of the 54th Annual Meeting of the Association for Computational Linguistics (ACL-16)*. Berlin, Germany, pages 1–11.

Jonas Groschwitz, Alexander Koller, and Christoph Teichmann. 2015. Graph parsing with s-graph grammars. In *Proceedings of the 53rd Annual Meeting of the Association for Computational Linguistics (ACL-15)*. Beijing, China, pages 1481–1490.

Liang Huang, Kevin Knight, and Aravind Joshi. 2006. Statistical syntax-directed translation with extended domain of locality. In *Proceedings of Association for Machine Translation in the Americas (AMTA-2006)*. pages 66–73.

Bevan Jones, Jacob Andreas, Daniel Bauer, Karl Moritz Hermann, and Kevin Knight. 2012. Semantics-based machine translation with hyperedge replacement grammars. In *Proceedings of the International Conference on Computational Linguistics (COLING-12)*. pages 1359–1376.

Philipp Koehn, Franz Josef Och, and Daniel Marcu. 2003. Statistical phrase-based translation. In *Proceedings of the 2003 Meeting of the North American chapter of the Association for Computational Linguistics (NAACL-03)*. pages 48–54.

Xiang Li, Thien Huu Nguyen, Kai Cao, and Ralph Grishman. 2015. Improving event detection with abstract meaning representation. In *Proceedings of the First Workshop on Computing News Storylines*. Beijing, China, pages 11–15.

Yang Liu, Qun Liu, and Shouxun Lin. 2006. Tree-to-string alignment template for statistical machine translation. In *Proceedings of the 44th Annual Meeting of the Association for Computational Linguistics (ACL-06)*. Sydney, Australia, pages 609–616.

Fandong Meng, Jun Xie, Linfeng Song, Yajuan Lü, and Qun Liu. 2013. Translation with source constituency and dependency trees. In *Conference on Empirical Methods in Natural Language Processing (EMNLP-13)*. Seattle, Washington, USA, pages 1066–1076.

Arindam Mitra and Chitta Baral. 2015. Addressing a question answering challenge by combining statistical methods with inductive rule learning and reasoning. In *Proceedings of the National Conference on Artificial Intelligence (AAAI-16)*.

Franz Josef Och. 2003. Minimum error rate training in statistical machine translation. In *Proceedings of the 41st Annual Meeting of the Association for Computational Linguistics (ACL-03)*. Sapporo, Japan, pages 160–167.

Kishore Papineni, Salim Roukos, Todd Ward, and Wei-Jing Zhu. 2002. BLEU: a method for automatic evaluation of machine translation. In *Proceedings of the 40th Annual Meeting of the Association for Computational Linguistics (ACL-02)*. pages 311–318.

Xiaochang Peng, Linfeng Song, and Daniel Gildea. 2015. A synchronous hyperedge replacement grammar based approach for AMR parsing. In *Proceedings of the Nineteenth Conference on Computational Natural Language Learning (CoNLL-15)*. pages 731–739.

Xiaochang Peng, Chuan Wang, Daniel Gildea, and Nianwen Xue. 2017. Addressing the data sparsity issue in neural amr parsing. In *Proceedings of the*

15th Conference of the European Chapter of the Association for Computational Linguistics (EACL-17). Valencia, Spain, pages 366–375.

Nima Pourdamghani, Kevin Knight, and Ulf Hermjakob. 2016. Generating English from abstract meaning representations. In *International Conference on Natural Language Generation (INLG-16)*. Edinburgh, UK, pages 21–25.

Michael Pust, Ulf Hermjakob, Kevin Knight, Daniel Marcu, and Jonathan May. 2015. Parsing English into abstract meaning representation using syntax-based machine translation. In *Conference on Empirical Methods in Natural Language Processing (EMNLP-15)*. pages 1143–1154.

Libin Shen, Jinxi Xu, and Ralph Weischedel. 2008. A new string-to-dependency machine translation algorithm with a target dependency language model. In *Proceedings of the 46th Annual Meeting of the Association for Computational Linguistics (ACL-08)*. Columbus, Ohio, pages 577–585.

Linfeng Song, Yue Zhang, Xiaochang Peng, Zhiguo Wang, and Daniel Gildea. 2016. AMR-to-text generation as a traveling salesman problem. In *Conference on Empirical Methods in Natural Language Processing (EMNLP-16)*. Austin, Texas, pages 2084–2089.

Sho Takase, Jun Suzuki, Naoaki Okazaki, Tsutomu Hirao, and Masaaki Nagata. 2016. Neural headline generation on abstract meaning representation. In *Conference on Empirical Methods in Natural Language Processing (EMNLP-16)*. Austin, Texas, pages 1054–1059.

Aleš Tamchyna, Chris Quirk, and Michel Galley. 2015. A discriminative model for semantics-to-string translation. In *Proceedings of the 1st Workshop on Semantics-Driven Statistical Machine Translation (S2MT 2015)*. Beijing, China, pages 30–36.

Lucy Vanderwende, Arul Menezes, and Chris Quirk. 2015. An AMR parser for English, French, German, Spanish and Japanese and a new AMR-annotated corpus. In *Proceedings of the 2015 Meeting of the North American chapter of the Association for Computational Linguistics (NAACL-15)*. pages 26–30.

Chuan Wang, Nianwen Xue, and Sameer Pradhan. 2015. A transition-based algorithm for AMR parsing. In *Proceedings of the 2015 Meeting of the North American chapter of the Association for Computational Linguistics (NAACL-15)*. pages 366–375.

Dekai Wu. 1997. Stochastic inversion transduction grammars and bilingual parsing of parallel corpora. *Computational linguistics* 23(3):377–403.

Jun Xie, Haitao Mi, and Qun Liu. 2011. A novel dependency-to-string model for statistical machine translation. In *Conference on Empirical Methods in Natural Language Processing (EMNLP-11)*. Edinburgh, Scotland, UK., pages 216–226.

Kenji Yamada and Kevin Knight. 2002. A decoder for syntax-based statistical MT. In *Proceedings of the 40th Annual Meeting of the Association for Computational Linguistics (ACL-02)*. Philadelphia, Pennsylvania, USA, pages 303–310.

Junsheng Zhou, Feiyu Xu, Hans Uszkoreit, Weiguang QU, Ran Li, and Yanhui Gu. 2016. AMR parsing with an incremental joint model. In *Conference on Empirical Methods in Natural Language Processing (EMNLP-16)*. Austin, Texas, pages 680–689.

Lexical Features in Coreference Resolution: To be Used With Caution

Nafise Sadat Moosavi and **Michael Strube**
Heidelberg Institute for Theoretical Studies gGmbH
Schloss-Wolfsbrunnenweg 35
69118 Heidelberg, Germany
{nafise.moosavi|michael.strube}@h-its.org

Abstract

Lexical features are a major source of information in state-of-the-art coreference resolvers. Lexical features implicitly model some of the linguistic phenomena at a fine granularity level. They are especially useful for representing the context of mentions. In this paper we investigate a drawback of using many lexical features in state-of-the-art coreference resolvers. We show that if coreference resolvers mainly rely on lexical features, they can hardly generalize to unseen domains. Furthermore, we show that the current coreference resolution evaluation is clearly flawed by only evaluating on a specific split of a specific dataset in which there is a notable overlap between the training, development and test sets.

1 Introduction

Similar to many other tasks, lexical features are a major source of information in current coreference resolvers. Coreference resolution is a set partitioning problem in which each resulting partition refers to an entity. As shown by Durrett and Klein (2013), lexical features implicitly model some linguistic phenomena, which were previously modeled by heuristic features, but at a finer level of granularity. However, we question whether the knowledge that is mainly captured by lexical features can be generalized to other domains.

The introduction of the CoNLL dataset enabled a significant boost in the performance of coreference resolvers, i.e. about 10 percent difference between the CoNLL score of the currently best coreference resolver, deep-coref by Clark and Manning (2016b), and the winner of the CoNLL 2011 shared task, the Stanford rule-based system

by Lee et al. (2013). However, this substantial improvement does not seem to be visible in downstream tasks. Worse, the difference between state-of-the-art coreference resolvers and the rule-based system drops significantly when they are applied on a new dataset, even with consistent definitions of mentions and coreference relations (Ghaddar and Langlais, 2016a).

In this paper, we show that if we mainly rely on lexical features, as it is the case in state-of-the-art coreference resolvers, overfitting become more sever. Overfitting to the training dataset is a problem that cannot be completely avoided. However, there is a notable overlap between the CoNLL training, development and test sets that encourages overfitting. Therefore, the current coreference evaluation scheme is flawed by only evaluating on this overlapped validation set. To ensure meaningful improvements in coreference resolution, we believe an out-of-domain evaluation is a must in the coreference literature.

2 Lexical Features

The large difference in performance between coreference resolvers that use lexical features and ones which do not, implies the importance of lexical features. Durrett and Klein (2013) show that lexical features implicitly capture some phenomena, e.g. definiteness and syntactic roles, which were previously modeled by heuristic features. Durrett and Klein (2013) use exact surface forms as lexical features. However, when word embeddings are used instead of surface forms, the use of lexical features is even more beneficial. Word embeddings are an efficient way of capturing semantic relatedness. Especially, they provide an efficient way for describing the context of mentions.

Durrett and Klein (2013) show that the addition of some heuristic features like gender, num-

Proceedings of the 55th Annual Meeting of the Association for Computational Linguistics (Short Papers), pages 14–19
Vancouver, Canada, July 30 - August 4, 2017. ©2017 Association for Computational Linguistics
https://doi.org/10.18653/v1/P17-2003

	MUC			B^3			$CEAF_e$			CoNLL	LEA		
	R	P	F_1	R	P	F_1	R	P	F_1	Avg. F_1	R	P	F_1
CoNLL test set													
rule-based	64.29	65.19	64.74	49.18	56.79	52.71	52.45	46.58	49.34	55.60	43.72	51.53	47.30
berkeley	67.56	74.09	70.67	53.93	63.50	58.33	53.29	56.22	54.72	61.24	49.66	59.17	54.00
cort	67.83	78.35	72.71	54.34	68.42	60.57	53.10	61.10	56.82	63.37	50.40	64.46	56.57
deep-coref [conll]	70.55	79.13	74.59	58.17	69.01	63.13	54.20	63.44	58.45	65.39	54.55	65.35	59.46
deep-coref [lea]	70.43	79.57	74.72	58.08	69.26	63.18	54.43	64.17	58.90	65.60	54.55	65.68	59.60
WikiCoref													
rule-based	60.42	61.56	60.99	43.34	53.53	47.90	50.89	42.70	46.44	51.77	38.79	48.92	43.27
berkeley	68.52	55.96	61.61	59.08	39.72	47.51	48.06	40.44	43.92	51.01	-	-	-
cort	70.39	53.63	60.88	60.81	37.58	46.45	47.88	38.18	42.48	49.94	-	-	-
deep-coref [conll]	58.59	66.63	62.35	44.40	54.87	49.08	42.47	51.47	46.54	52.65	40.36	50.73	44.95
deep-coref [lea]	57.48	70.55	63.35	42.12	60.13	49.54	41.40	53.08	46.52	53.14	38.22	55.98	45.43
deep-coref⁻	55.07	71.81	62.33	38.05	61.82	47.11	38.46	50.31	43.60	51.01	34.11	57.15	42.72

Table 1: Comparison of the results on the CoNLL test set and WikiCoref.

ber, person and animacy agreements and syntactic roles on top of their lexical features does not result in a significant improvement.

deep-coref, the state-of-the-art coreference resolver, follows the same approach. Clark and Manning (2016b) capture the required information for resolving coreference relations by using a large number of lexical features and a small set of non-lexical features including string match, distance, mention type, speaker and genre features. The main difference is that Clark and Manning (2016b) use word embeddings instead of the exact surface forms that are used by Durrett and Klein (2013).

Based on the error analysis by cort (Martschat and Strube, 2014), in comparison to systems that do not use word embeddings, deep-coref has fewer recall and precision errors especially for pronouns. For example, deep-coref correctly recognizes around 83 percent of non-anaphoric "it" in the CoNLL development set. This could be a direct result of a better context representation by word embeddings.

3 Out-of-Domain Evaluation

Aside from the evident success of lexical features, it is debatable how well the knowledge that is mainly captured by the lexical information of the training data can be generalized to other domains. As reported by Ghaddar and Langlais (2016b), state-of-the-art coreference resolvers trained on the CoNLL dataset perform poorly, i.e. worse than the rule-based system (Lee et al., 2013), on the new dataset, WikiCoref (Ghaddar and Langlais, 2016b), even though WikiCoref is annotated with the same annotation guidelines as the CoNLL dataset. The results of some of recent coreference resolvers on this dataset are listed in Table 1.

The results are reported using *MUC* (Vilain

et al., 1995), B^3 (Bagga and Baldwin, 1998), $CEAF_e$ (Luo, 2005), the average F_1 score of these three metrics, i.e. CoNLL score, and *LEA* (Moosavi and Strube, 2016).

berkeley is the mention-ranking model of Durrett and Klein (2013) with the FINAL feature set including the head, first, last, preceding and following words of a mention, the ancestry, length, gender and number of a mention, distance of two mentions, whether the anaphor and antecedent are nested, same speaker and a small set of string match features.

cort is the mention-ranking model of Martschat and Strube (2015). *cort* uses the following set of features: the head, first, last, preceding and following words of a mention, the ancestry, length, gender, number, type, semantic class, dependency relation and dependency governor of a mention, the named entity type of the head word, distance of two mentions, same speaker, whether the anaphor and antecedent are nested, and a set of string match features. *berkeley* and *cort* scores in Table 1 are taken from Ghaddar and Langlais (2016a).

deep-coref is the mention-ranking model of Clark and Manning (2016b). *deep-coref* incorporates a large set of embeddings, i.e. embeddings of the head, first, last, two previous/following words, and the dependency governor of a mention in addition to the averaged embeddings of the five previous/following words, all words of the mention, sentence words, and document words. *deep-coref* also incorporates type, length, and position of a mention, whether the mention is nested in any other mention, distance of two mentions, speaker features and a small set of string match features.

For *deep-coref [conll]* the averaged CoNLL score is used to select the best trained model on the development set. *deep-coref [lea]* uses the *LEA*

			genre			
bc	bn	mz	nw	pt	tc	wb
			train+dev			
43%	50%	51%	45%	77%	38%	39%
			train			
41%	49%	39%	44%	76%	37%	38%

Table 2: Ratio of non-pronominal coreferent mentions in the test set that are seen as coreferent in the training data.

metric (Moosavi and Strube, 2016) for choosing the best model. It is worth noting that the results of *deep-coref*'s ranking model may be slightly different at various experiments. However, the performance of *deep-coref [lea]* is always higher than that of *deep-coref [conll]*.

We add WikiCoref's words to *deep-coref*'s dictionary for both *deep-coref [conll]* and *deep-coref [lea]*. *deep-coref⁻* reports the performance of *deep-coref [lea]* in which WikiCoref's words are not incorporated into the dictionary. Therefore, for *deep-coref⁻*, WikiCoref's words that do not exist in CoNLL will be initialized randomly instead of using pre-trained *word2vec* word embeddings. The performance gain of *deep-coref [lea]* in comparison to *deep-coref⁻* indicates the benefit of using pre-trained word embeddings and word embeddings in general. Henceforth, we refer to *deep-coref [lea]* as *deep-coref*.

4 Why do Improvements Fade Away?

In this section, we investigate how much lexical features contribute to the fact that current improvements in coreference resolution do not properly apply to a new domain.

Table 2 shows the ratio of non-pronominal coreferent mentions in the CoNLL test set that also appear as coreferent mentions in the training data. These high ratios indicate a high degree of overlap between the mentions of the CoNLL datasets.

The highest overlap between the training and test sets exists in genre *pt* (Bible). The *tc* (telephone conversation) genre has the lowest overlap for non-pronominal mentions. However, this genre includes a large number of pronouns. We choose *wb* (weblog) and *pt* for our analysis as two genres with low and high degree of overlap.

Table 3 shows the results of the examined coreference resolvers when the test set only includes one genre, i.e. *pt* or *wb*, in two different settings: (1) the training set includes all genres (in-domain evaluation), and (2) the corresponding genre of the test set is excluded from the training and development sets (out-of-domain evaluation).

berkeley-final is the coreference resolver of Durrett and Klein (2013) with the FINAL feature set explained in Section 3. *berkeley-surface* is the same coreference resolver with only surface features, i.e. ancestry, gender, number, same speaker and nested features are excluded from the FINAL feature set.

cort−lexical is a version of *cort* in which no lexical feature is used, i.e. the head, first, last, governor, preceding and following words of a mention are excluded.

For in-domain evaluations we train *deep-coref*'s ranking model for 100 iterations, i.e. the setting used by Clark and Manning (2016a). However, based on the performance on the development set, we only train the model for 50 iterations in out-of-domain evaluations.

The results of the *pt* genre show that when there is a high overlap between the training and test datasets, the performance of all learning-based classifiers significantly improves. *deep-coref* has the largest gain from including *pt* in the training data that is more than 13% based on the *LEA* score. *cort* uses both lexical and a relatively large number of non-lexical features while *berkeley-surface* is a pure lexicalized system. However, the difference between the *berkeley-surface*'s performances when *pt* is included or excluded from the training data is lower than that of *cort*. *berkeley* uses feature-value pruning so lexical features that occur fewer than 20 times are pruned from the training data. Maybe, this is the reason that *berkeley*'s performance difference is less than other lexicalized systems in highly overlapping datasets.

For a less overlapping genre, i.e. *wb*, the performance gain of including the genre in the training data is significantly lower for all lexicalized systems. Interestingly, the performance of *berkeley-final*, *cort* and *cort−lexical* increases for the *wb* genre when this genre is excluded from the training set. *deep-coref*, which uses a complex deep neural network and mainly lexical features, has the highest gain from the redundancy in the training and test datasets. As we use more complex neural networks, there is more capacity for brute-force memorization of the training dataset.

It is also worth noting that the performance gains and drops in out-of-domain evaluations are

	CoNLL	LEA			CoNLL	LEA		
	Avg. F_1	R	P	F_1	Avg. F_1	R	P	F_1
				pt				
		in-domain				out-of-domain		
rule-based	-	-	-	-	65.01	50.58	65.02	56.90
berkeley-surface	69.15	58.57	65.24	61.73	63.01	46.56	62.13	53.23
berkeley-final	70.71	60.48	67.29	63.70	64.24	47.10	65.77	54.89
cort	72.56	61.82	70.70	65.96	64.60	46.85	67.69	55.37
cort−lexical	69.48	54.26	70.33	61.26	64.32	45.63	68.51	54.77
deep-coref	75.61	68.48	73.70	71.00	66.06	52.44	63.84	57.58
				wb				
		in-domain				out-of-domain		
rule-based	-	-	-	-	53.80	45.19	44.98	45.08
berkeley-surface	56.37	45.72	47.20	46.45	55.14	45.94	44.59	45.26
berkeley-final	56.08	44.20	50.45	47.12	57.31	50.33	46.17	48.16
cort	59.29	50.37	51.56	50.96	58.87	51.47	50.96	51.21
cort−lexical	56.83	51.00	47.34	49.10	57.10	51.50	47.83	49.60
deep-coref	61.46	48.04	60.99	53.75	57.17	50.29	47.27	48.74

Table 3: In-domain and out-of-domain evaluations for a high and a low overlapped genres.

Antecedent		Anaphor		
		Proper	Nominal	Pronominal
Proper	seen	80%	85%	77%
	all	3221	261	1200
Nominal	seen	75%	93%	95%
	all	69	1673	1315
Pronominal	seen	58%	99%	100%
	all	85	74	4737

Table 4: Ratio of links created by deep-coref for which the head-pair is seen in the training data.

		Anaphor		
		Proper	Nominal	Pronominal
Antecedent		Correct decisions		
Proper	seen	82%	85%	78%
	all	2603	150	921
Nominal	seen	76%	94%	96%
	all	42	1058	890
Pronominal	seen	63%	98%	100%
	all	49	44	3998
		Incorrect decisions		
Proper	seen	73%	85%	76%
	all	618	111	279
Nominal	sen	74%	92%	94%
	all	27	615	425
Pronominal	seen	50%	100%	100%
	all	36	30	739

Table 5: Ratio of links created by deep-coref for which the head-pair is seen in the training data.

not entirely because of lexical features, as the performance of *cort−lexical* also drops significantly in *pt* out-of-domain evaluation. The classifier may also memorize other properties of the seen mentions in the training data. However, in comparison to features like gender and number agreement or syntactic roles, lexical features have the highest potential for overfitting.

We further analyze the output of *deep-coref* on the development set. The *all* rows in Table 4 show the number of pairwise links that are created by *deep-coref* on the development set for different mention types. The *seen* rows show the ratio of each category of links for which the (antecedent head, anaphor head) pair is seen in the training set. All ratios are surprisingly high. The most worrisome cases are those in which both mentions are either a proper name or a common noun.

Table 5 further divides the links of Table 4 based on whether they are correct coreferent links. The results of Table 5 show that most of the incorrect links are also made between the mentions that are both seen in the training data.

The high ratios indicate that (1) there is a high overlap between the mention pairs of the training and development sets, and (2) even though that *deep-coref* uses generalized word embeddings instead of exact surface forms, it is strongly biased towards the seen mentions.

We analyze the links that are created by Stanford's rule-based system and compute the ratio of the links that exist in the training set. All corresponding ratios are lower than those of *deep-coref* in Table 5. However, the ratios are surprisingly high for a system that does not use the training data. This analysis emphasizes the overlap in the CoNLL datasets. Because of this high overlap, it is not easy to assess the generalizability of a coreference resolver to unseen mentions on the CoNLL dataset given its official split.

We also compute the ratios of Table 5 for the missing links that are associated with the recall er-

| | | Anaphor | | |
Antecedent		Proper	Nominal	Pronominal
Proper	seen	63%	51%	75%
	all	818	418	278
Nominal	seen	44%	73%	90%
	all	168	892	538
Pronominal	seen	82%	90%	100%
	all	49	59	444

Table 6: Ratio of deep-coref's recall errors for which the head-pair exists in the training data.

rors of *deep-coref*. We compute the recall errors by cort error analysis tool (Martschat and Strube, 2014). Table 6 shows the corresponding ratios for recall errors. The lower ratios of Table 6 in comparison to those of Table 4 emphasize the bias of *deep-coref* towards the seen mentions.

For example, the *deep-coref* links include 31 cases in which both mentions are either proper names or common nouns and the head of one of the mentions is "country". For all these links, "country" is linked to a mention that is seen in the training data. Therefore, this raises the question how the classifier would perform on a text about countries not mentioned in the training data.

Memorizing the pairs in which one of them is a common noun could help the classifier to capture world knowledge to some extent. From the seen pairs like (Haiti, his country), and (Guangzhou, the city) the classifier could learn that "Haiti" is a country and "Guangzhou" is a city. However, it is questionable how useful word knowledge is if it is mainly based on the training data.

The coreference relation of two nominal noun phrases with no head match can be very hard to resolve. The resolution of such pairs has been referred to as capturing semantic similarity (Clark and Manning, 2016b). *deep-coref* links 49 such pairs on the development set. Among all these links, only 5 pairs are unseen on the training set and all of them are incorrect links.

The effect of lexical features is also analyzed by Levy et al. (2015) for tasks like hypernymy and entailment. They show that state-of-the-art classifiers memorize words from the training data. The classifiers benefit from this lexical memorization when there are common words between the training and test sets.

5 Discussion

We show the extensive use of lexical features biases coreference resolvers towards seen mentions. This bias holds us back from developing more robust and generalizable coreference resolvers. After all, while coreference resolution is an important step for text understanding, it is not an end-task. Coreference resolvers are going to be used in tasks and domains for which coreference annotated corpora may not be available. Therefore, generalizability should be brought into attention in developing coreference resolvers.

Moreover, we show that there is a significant overlap between the training and validation sets in the CoNLL dataset. The *LEA* metric (Moosavi and Strube, 2016) is introduced as an attempt to make coreference evaluations more reliable. However, in order to ensure valid developments on coreference resolution, it is not enough to have reliable evaluation metrics. The validation set on which the evaluations are performed also needs to be reliable. A dataset is reliable for evaluations if a considerable improvement on this dataset indicates a better solution for the coreference problem instead of a better exploitation of the dataset itself.

This paper is not intended to argue against the use of lexical features. Especially, when word embeddings are used as lexical features. The incorporation of word embeddings is an efficient way for capturing semantic relatedness. Maybe we should use them more for describing the context and less for describing the mentions themselves. Pruning rare lexical features plus incorporating more generalizable features could also help to prevent overfitting.

To ensure more meaningful improvements, we ask to incorporate out-of-domain evaluations in the current coreference evaluation scheme. Out-of-domain evaluations could be performed by using either the existing genres of the CoNLL dataset or by using other existing coreference annotated datasets like WikiCoref, MUC or ACE.

Acknowledgments

The authors would like to thank Kevin Clark for answering all of our questions regarding deep-coref. We would also like to thank the three anonymous reviewers for their thoughtful comments. This work has been funded by the Klaus Tschira Foundation, Heidelberg, Germany. The first author has been supported by a Heidelberg Institute for Theoretical Studies PhD. scholarship.

References

Amit Bagga and Breck Baldwin. 1998. Algorithms for scoring coreference chains. In *Proceedings of the 1st International Conference on Language Resources and Evaluation*, Granada, Spain, 28–30 May 1998. pages 563–566.

Kevin Clark and Christopher D. Manning. 2016a. Deep reinforcement learning for mention-ranking coreference models. In *Proceedings of the 2016 Conference on Empirical Methods in Natural Language Processing*, Austin, Tex., 1–5 November 2016. pages 2256–2262. https://www.aclweb.org/anthology/D16-1245.pdf.

Kevin Clark and Christopher D. Manning. 2016b. Improving coreference resolution by learning entity-level distributed representations. In *Proceedings of the 54th Annual Meeting of the Association for Computational Linguistics (Volume 1: Long Papers)*, Berlin, Germany, 7–12 August 2016. http://www.aclweb.org/anthology/P16-1061.pdf.

Greg Durrett and Dan Klein. 2013. Easy victories and uphill battles in coreference resolution. In *Proceedings of the 2013 Conference on Empirical Methods in Natural Language Processing*, Seattle, Wash., 18–21 October 2013. pages 1971–1982. http://www.aclweb.org/anthology/D13-1203.pdf.

Abbas Ghaddar and Philippe Langlais. 2016a. Coreference in Wikipedia: Main concept resolution. In *Proceedings of the 20th Conference on Computational Natural Language Learning*, Berlin, Germany, 11–12 August 2016. pages 229–238. https://www.aclweb.org/anthology/K16-1023.pdf.

Abbas Ghaddar and Philippe Langlais. 2016b. WikiCoref: An English coreference-annotated corpus of Wikipedia articles. In *Proceedings of the 10th International Conference on Language Resources and Evaluation*, Portorož, Slovenia, 23–28 May 2016. http://www.lrec-conf.org/proceedings/lrec2016/pdf/192_Paper.pdf.

Heeyoung Lee, Angel Chang, Yves Peirsman, Nathanael Chambers, Mihai Surdeanu, and Dan Jurafsky. 2013. Deterministic coreference resolution based on entity-centric, precision-ranked rules. *Computational Linguistics* 39(4):885–916. https://www.aclweb.org/anthology/J13-4004.pdf.

Omer Levy, Steffen Remus, Chris Biemann, and Ido Dagan. 2015. Do supervised distributional methods really learn lexical inference relations? In *Proceedings of the 2015 Conference of the North American Chapter of the Association for Computational Linguistics: Human Language Technologies*, Denver, Col., 31 May – 5 June 2015. pages 970–976. http://www.aclweb.org/anthology/N15-1098.

Xiaoqiang Luo. 2005. On coreference resolution performance metrics. In *Proceedings of the Human Language Technology Conference and the 2005 Conference on Empirical Methods in Natural Language Processing*, Vancouver, B.C., Canada, 6–8 October 2005. pages 25–32.

Sebastian Martschat and Michael Strube. 2014. Recall error analysis for coreference resolution. In *Proceedings of the 2014 Conference on Empirical Methods in Natural Language Processing*, Doha, Qatar, 25–29 October 2014. pages 2070–2081. http://www.aclweb.org/anthology/D14-1221.pdf.

Sebastian Martschat and Michael Strube. 2015. Latent structures for coreference resolution. *Transactions of the Association for Computational Linguistics* 3:405–418. http://www.aclweb.org/anthology/Q15-1029.pdf.

Nafise Sadat Moosavi and Michael Strube. 2016. Which coreference evaluation metric do you trust? A proposal for a link-based entity aware metric. In *Proceedings of the 54th Annual Meeting of the Association for Computational Linguistics (Volume 1: Long Papers)*, Berlin, Germany, 7–12 August 2016. pages 632–642. http://www.aclweb.org/anthology/P16-1060.pdf.

Sameer Pradhan, Xiaoqiang Luo, Marta Recasens, Eduard Hovy, Vincent Ng, and Michael Strube. 2014. Scoring coreference partitions of predicted mentions: A reference implementation. In *Proceedings of the 52nd Annual Meeting of the Association for Computational Linguistics (Volume 2: Short Papers)*, Baltimore, Md., 22–27 June 2014. pages 30–35. http://www.aclweb.org/anthology/P14-2006.pdf.

Marc Vilain, John Burger, John Aberdeen, Dennis Connolly, and Lynette Hirschman. 1995. A model-theoretic coreference scoring scheme. In *Proceedings of the 6th Message Understanding Conference (MUC-6)*. Morgan Kaufmann, San Mateo, Cal., pages 45–52.

Alternative Objective Functions
for Training MT Evaluation Metrics

Miloš Stanojević
ILLC
University of Amsterdam
m.stanojevic@uva.nl

Khalil Sima'an
ILLC
University of Amsterdam
k.simaan@uva.nl

Abstract

MT evaluation metrics are tested for correlation with human judgments either at the sentence- or the corpus-level. *Trained* metrics ignore corpus-level judgments and are trained for high sentence-level correlation only. We show that training only for one objective (sentence or corpus level), can not only harm the performance on the other objective, but it can also be suboptimal for the objective being optimized. To this end we present a metric trained for corpus-level and show empirical comparison against a metric trained for sentence-level exemplifying how their performance may vary per language pair, type and level of judgment. Subsequently we propose a model trained to optimize *both objectives* simultaneously and show that it is far more stable than–and *on average* outperforms–both models on both objectives.

1   Introduction

Ever since BLEU (Papineni et al., 2002) many proposals for an improved automatic evaluation metric for Machine Translation (MT) have been made. Some proposals use additional information for extracting quality indicators, like paraphrasing (Denkowski and Lavie, 2011), syntactic trees (Liu and Gildea, 2005; Stanojević and Sima'an, 2015) or shallow semantics (Rios et al., 2011; Lo et al., 2012) etc. Whereas others use different matching strategies, like n-grams (Papineni et al., 2002), treelets (Liu and Gildea, 2005) and skip-bigrams (Lin and Och, 2004). Most metrics use several indicators of translation quality which are often combined in a linear model whose weights are estimated on a training set of human judgments.

Because the most widely available type of human judgments are relative ranking (RR) judgments, the main machine learning method used for training the metrics were based on the learning-to-rank framework (Li, 2011). While the effectiveness of this framework for training evaluation metrics has been confirmed many times, e.g., (Ye et al., 2007; Duh, 2008; Stanojević and Sima'an, 2014; Ma et al., 2016), so far there is no prior work exploring alternative objective functions for training learning-to-rank models. Without exception, all existing learning-to-rank models are trained to rank sentences while completely ignoring the corpora judgments, likely because human judgments come in the form of sentence rankings.

It might seem that sentence and corpus level tasks are very similar but that is not the case. Empirically it has been shown that many metrics that perform well on the sentence level do not perform well on the corpus level and vice versa. By training to rank sentences the model does not necessarily learn to give scores that are well scaled, but only to give higher scores to better translations. Training for the corpus level score would force the metric to give well scaled scores on the sentence level.

Human judgments of sentences can be aggregated in different ways to hypothesize human judgments of full corpora. However, this fact has not been used so far to train learning-to-rank models that are good for ranking different corpora.

This work fills-in this gap by exploring the merits of different objective functions that take corpus level judgments into consideration. We first create a learning-to-rank model for ranking corpora and compare it to the standard learning-to-rank model that is trained for ranking sentences. This comparison shows that performance of these two objectives can vary radically depending on the chosen meta-evaluation method. To tackle this prob-

20

Proceedings of the 55th Annual Meeting of the Association for Computational Linguistics (Short Papers), pages 20–25
Vancouver, Canada, July 30 - August 4, 2017. ©2017 Association for Computational Linguistics
https://doi.org/10.18653/v1/P17-2004

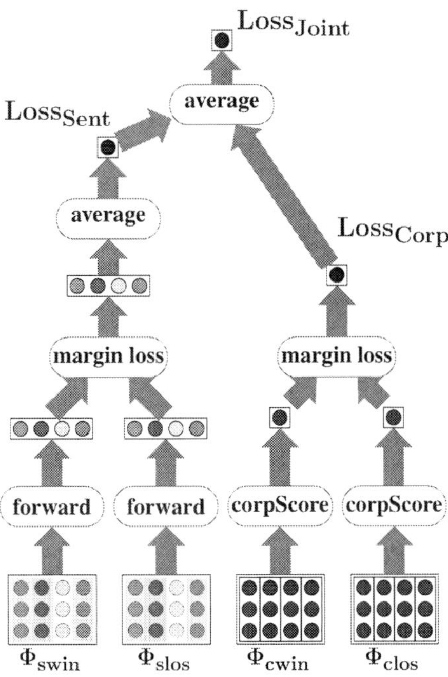

Figure 1: Computation Graph

lem we contribute a new objective function, inspired by multi-task learning, in which we train for both objectives simultaneously. This multi-objective model behaves a lot more stable over all methods of meta-evaluation and achieves a higher correlation than both single objective models.

2 Models

All the models that we define have one basic function in common, we call it a $forward(\cdot)$ function, that maps the features of any sentence to a single real number. That function can be any differentiable function including multi-layer neural networks as in (Ma et al., 2016), but here we will stick with the standard linear model:

$$forward(\phi) = \phi^T \mathbf{w} + b$$

Here ϕ is a vector with feature values of a sentence, $\mathbf{w}$ is a weight vector and b is a bias term. Usually in training we would like to process a mini-batch of feature vectors $\mathbf{\Phi}$, where $\mathbf{\Phi}$ is a matrix in which each column is a feature vector of individual sentence in the mini-batch or in the corpus. By using broadcasting we can rewrite the previous definition of the $forward(\cdot)$ function as:

$$forward(\mathbf{\Phi}) = \mathbf{\Phi}^T \mathbf{w} + b$$

Now we can define the score of a sentence as a sigmoid function applied over the output of the $forward(\cdot)$ function because we want to get a score between 0 and 1:

$$sentScore(\phi) = \sigma(forward(\phi))$$

As the corpus level score we will use just the average of sentence level scores:

$$corpScore(\mathbf{\Phi}) = \frac{1}{m} \sum sentScore(\mathbf{\Phi})$$

where m is the number of sentences in the corpus.

Next we present several objective functions that are illustrated by the computation graph in Figure 1.

2.1 Training for Sentence Level Accuracy

Here we use the training objective very similar to BEER (Stanojević and Sima'an, 2014) which is a learning-to-rank framework that finds a separating hyper-plane between "good" and "bad" translations. Unlike BEER, we use a max-margin objective instead of logistic regression.

For each mini-batch we randomly select m human relative ranking pairwise judgments and after extracting features for all the sentences taking part in these judgments we put features in two matrices Φ_{swin} and Φ_{slos}. These matrices are structured in such a way that for judgment i the column i in Φ_{swin} contains the features of the "good" translation in the judgment and the column i in Φ_{slos} the features of the "bad" translation.

We would like to maximize the average margin that would separate sentence level scores of pairs of translations in each judgment. Because the squashing sigmoid function does not influence the ranking we can directly optimize on the unsquashed forward pass and require that the margin between "good" and "bad" translation is at least 1:

$$\Delta_{sent} = forward(\Phi_{swin}) - forward(\Phi_{slos})$$

$$Loss_{Sent} = \frac{1}{m} \sum max(0, 1 - \Delta_{sent})$$

2.2 Training for Corpus Level Accuracy

At the corpus level we would like to do a similar thing as on the sentence level: maximize the distance between the scores of "good" and "bad" corpora. In this case we have additional information that is not present on the sentence level: we know not only which corpus is (according to humans) better, but also by *how much* it is better. For that we can use one of the heuristics such as the Expected Wins (Koehn, 2012). We can use this information to guide the learning model by how much it should separate the scores of two corpora.

For doing this we use an approach similar to Max-Margin Markov Networks (Taskar et al., 2003) where for each training instance we dynamically scale the margin that should be enforced. We want the margin between the scores Δ_{corp} to be at least as big as the margin between the human scores Δ_{human} assigned to these systems. In one mini-batch we will use only a randomly chosen pair of corpora with feature matrices Φ_{cwin} and Φ_{clos} for which we have a human comparison. The corpus level loss function is given by:

$$\Delta_{corp} = corpScore(\Phi_{cwin}) - corpScore(\Phi_{clos})$$
$$Loss_{Corp} = max(0, \Delta_{human} - \Delta_{corp})$$

2.3 Training Jointly for Sentence and Corpus Level Accuracy

In this model we optimize both objectives jointly in the style of multi-task learning (Caruana, 1997). Here we employ the simplest approach of just tasking the interpolation of the previously introduced loss functions.

$$Loss_{Joint} = \alpha \cdot Loss_{Sent} + (1 - \alpha) \cdot Loss_{Corp}$$

The interpolation is controlled by the hyperparameter α which could in principle be tuned for good performance, but here we just fix it to 0.5 to give both objectives equal importance.

2.4 Feature Functions

The feature functions that are used are reimplementation of many (but not all) feature functions of BEER. Because the point of this paper is about the exploration of different objective functions we did not try to experiment with more complex feature functions based on paraphrasing, function words or permutation trees.

We use just simple precision, recall and 3 types of F-score (with β parameters 1, 2 and 0.5) over different "pieces" of translation:

- character n-grams of orders 1,2,3,4 and 5

- word n-grams of orders 1,2,3 and 4

- skip-bigrams of maximum skip 2 and ∞ (similar to ROUGE-S2 and ROUGE-S* (Lin and Och, 2004))

One final feature deals with length-disbalance. If the length of the system and reference translation are a and b respectively then this feature is computed as $\frac{max(a,b) - min(a,b)}{min(a,b)}$. It is computed both for word and character length.

3 Experiments

Experiments are conducted on WMT13 (Macháček and Bojar, 2013), WMT14 (Machacek and Bojar, 2014) and WMT16 (Bojar et al., 2016) datasets which were used as training, validation and testing datasets respectively.

All of the models are implemented using TensorFlow[1] and trained with L2 regularization $\lambda = 0.001$ and ADAM optimizer with learning rate 0.001. The mini-batch size for sentence level judgments is 2000 and for the corpus level is one comparison. Each model is trained for 200 epochs out of which the one performing best on the validation set for the objective function being optimized is used during the test time.

We show the results for the relative ranking (RR) judgments correlation in Table 1. For all language pairs that are of the form *en-X* we show it under the column X and for all the language pairs that have English on the target side we present their average under the column *en*.

RR corpus vs. sentence objective The corpusobjective is better than the sentence-objective for both corpus and sentence level RR judgments on 5 out of 7 languages and also on average correlation.

RR joint vs. single-objectives Training for the joint objective improves even more on both levels of RR correlation and outperforms both singleobjective models on average and on 4 out of 7 languages.

Making confident conclusions from these results is difficult because, to the best of our knowledge, there is no principled way of measuring statistical significance on the RR judgments. That is why we also tested on direct assessment (DA) judgments available from WMT16. On DA we can measure statistical significance on the sentence level using Williams test (Graham et al., 2015) and on the corpus level using combination of hybrid-supersampling and Williams test (Graham and Liu, 2016). The results of correlation with human judgment are for sentence and corpus level are shown in Table 2.

---

[1] https://www.tensorflow.org/

Objective	en	cs	de	fi	ro	ru	tr	Average
sent	**0.963**	0.977	0.737	0.938	0.922	0.905	0.937	0.912
corpus	0.944	0.982	**0.765**	0.940	0.917	**0.907**	**0.954**	0.916
joint	**0.963**	**0.983**	0.748	**0.951**	**0.933**	0.905	0.946	**0.918**

(a) Corpus level

Objective	en	cs	de	fi	ro	ru	tr	Average
sent	0.347	0.405	0.345	0.304	0.293	0.382	0.304	0.340
corpus	0.337	**0.414**	0.349	**0.307**	0.292	0.385	**0.325**	0.344
joint	**0.350**	0.410	**0.356**	0.296	**0.299**	**0.396**	0.312	**0.346**

(b) Sentence level

Table 1: Relative Ranking (RR) Correlation. The corpus level correlation is measured with Pearson r and sentence level with Kendall τ

Objective	en-ru	cs-en	de-en	fi-en	ro-en	ru-en	tr-en	Average
sent	**0.9113**$_J^C$	0.9839^C	0.8483^C	**0.9556**$_J^C$	0.8348^C	0.8888^C	**0.9706**$_J^C$	0.9133
corpus	0.9086	0.9790	0.8032	0.9121	0.7933	0.8857	0.9011	0.8833
joint	0.9111^C	**0.9844**$_S^C$	**0.8488**$_S^C$	0.9545^C	**0.8399**$_S^C$	**0.8935**$_S^C$	0.9647^C	**0.9138**

(a) Corpus level

Objective	en-ru	cs-en	de-en	fi-en	ro-en	ru-en	tr-en	Average
sent	0.6655^C	0.6478^C	0.4930^C	0.4608^C	0.5066^C	0.5535^C	0.5800^C	0.5582
corpus	0.5632	0.5676	0.3913	0.3644	0.3771	0.4306	0.4579	0.4503
joint	0.6668^C	**0.6631**$_C^S$	**0.5019**$_C^S$	0.4608^C	**0.5276**$_C^S$	0.5564^C	0.5830^C	**0.5657**

(b) Sentence level

Table 2: Direct Assessment (DA) Pearson r Correlation. Super- and sub-scripts S, C and J signify that the model outperforms with statistical significance ($p < 0.05$) the model trained for sentence, corpus or joint objective respectively. Bold marks that the system has outperformed both other models significantly.

DA corpus vs. other objectives On DA judgments the results for corpus level objective are completely different than on the RR judgments. On DA judgments the corpus-objective model is significantly outperformed on both levels and on all languages by both of the other objectives.

This shows that gambling on one objective function (being that sentence or corpus level objective) could give unpredictable results. This is precisely the motivation for creating the joint model with multi-objective training.

DA joint vs. single objectives By choosing to jointly optimize both objectives we get a much more stable model that performs well both on DA and RR judgments and on both levels of judgment. On the DA sentence level, the joint model was *not* outperformed by any other model and on 3 out of 7 language pairs it significantly outperforms both alternative objectives. On the corpus level results are a bit mixed, but still joint objective outperforms both other models on 4 out of 7 language pairs and also it gives higher correlation on average.

4   Conclusion

In this work we found that altering the objective function for training MT metrics can have radical effects on performance. Also the effects of the objective functions can sometimes be unexpected: the sentence objective might not be good for sentence level correlation (in case of RR judgments) and the corpus objective might not be good for corpus level correlation (in case of DA judgments). The difference among objectives is better explained by different types of human judgments: the corpus objective is better for RR while sentence objective is better for DA judgments.

Finally, the best results are achieved by training for both objectives at the same time. This gives an evaluation metric that is far more stable in its performance over all methods of meta-evaluation.

Acknowledgments

This work is supported by NWO VICI grant nr. 277-89-002, DatAptor project STW grant nr. 12271 and QT21 project H2020 nr. 645452.

References

Ondřej Bojar, Yvette Graham, Amir Kamran, and Miloš Stanojević. 2016. Results of the wmt16 metrics shared task. In *Proceedings of the First Conference on Machine Translation*. Association for Computational Linguistics, Berlin, Germany, pages 199–231. http://www.aclweb.org/anthology/W/W16/W16-2302.

Rich Caruana. 1997. Multitask learning. *Machine Learning* 28(1):41–75. https://doi.org/10.1023/A:1007379606734.

Michael Denkowski and Alon Lavie. 2011. Meteor 1.3: Automatic Metric for Reliable Optimization and Evaluation of Machine Translation Systems. In *Proceedings of the EMNLP 2011 Workshop on Statistical Machine Translation*.

Kevin Duh. 2008. Ranking vs. Regression in Machine Translation Evaluation. In *Proceedings of the Third Workshop on Statistical Machine Translation*. Association for Computational Linguistics, Stroudsburg, PA, USA, StatMT '08, pages 191–194. http://dl.acm.org/citation.cfm?id=1626394.1626425.

Yvette Graham and Qun Liu. 2016. Achieving accurate conclusions in evaluation of automatic machine translation metrics. In *Proceedings of the 15th Annual Conference of the North American Chapter of the Association for Computational Linguistics: Human Language Technologies*. Association for Computational Linguistics, San Diego, CA.

Yvette Graham, Nitika Mathur, and Timothy Baldwin. 2015. Accurate evaluation of segment-level machine translation metrics. In *Proceedings of the 2015 Conference of the North American Chapter of the Association for Computational Linguistics Human Language Technologies*. Denver, Colorado.

Philipp Koehn. 2012. Simulating human judgment in machine translation evaluation campaigns. In *Proceedings of International Workshop on Spoken Language Translation*. http://www.mt-archive.info/IWSLT-2012-Koehn.pdf.

Hang Li. 2011. *Learning to Rank for Information Retrieval and Natural Language Processing*. Synthesis Lectures on Human Language Technologies. Morgan & Claypool Publishers.

Chin-Yew Lin and Franz Josef Och. 2004. Automatic Evaluation of Machine Translation Quality Using Longest Common Subsequence and Skip-bigram Statistics. In *Proceedings of the 42Nd Annual Meeting on Association for Computational Linguistics*. Association for Computational Linguistics, Stroudsburg, PA, USA, ACL '04. https://doi.org/10.3115/1218955.1219032.

Ding Liu and Daniel Gildea. 2005. Syntactic features for evaluation of machine translation. In *Proceedings of the ACL Workshop on Intrinsic and Extrinsic Evaluation Measures for Machine Translation and/or Summarization*. Association for Computational Linguistics, Ann Arbor, Michigan, pages 25–32. http://www.aclweb.org/anthology/W/W05/W05-0904.

Chi-kiu Lo, Anand Karthik Tumuluru, and Dekai Wu. 2012. Fully automatic semantic mt evaluation. In *Proceedings of the Seventh Workshop on Statistical Machine Translation*. Association for Computational Linguistics, Stroudsburg, PA, USA, WMT '12, pages 243–252. http://dl.acm.org/citation.cfm?id=2393015.2393048.

Qingsong Ma, Fandong Meng, Daqi Zheng, Mingxuan Wang, Yvette Graham, Wenbin Jiang, and Qun Liu. 2016. Maxsd: A neural machine translation evaluation metric optimized by maximizing similarity distance. In Chin-Yew Lin, Nianwen Xue, Dongyan Zhao, Xuanjing Huang, and Yansong Feng, editors, *Natural Language Understanding and Intelligent Applications: 5th CCF Conference on Natural Language Processing and Chinese Computing and 24th International Conference on Computer Processing of Oriental Languages*. Springer International Publishing, Kunming, China, pages 153–161.

Matous Machacek and Ondrej Bojar. 2014. Results of the wmt14 metrics shared task. In *Proceedings of the Ninth Workshop on Statistical Machine Translation*. Association for Computational Linguistics, Baltimore, Maryland, USA, pages 293–301. http://www.aclweb.org/anthology/W/W14/W14-3336.

Matouš Macháček and Ondřej Bojar. 2013. Results of the WMT13 metrics shared task. In *Proceedings of the Eighth Workshop on Statistical Machine Translation*. Association for Computational Linguistics, Sofia, Bulgaria, pages 45–51. http://www.aclweb.org/anthology/W13-2202.

Kishore Papineni, Salim Roukos, Todd Ward, and Wei-Jing Zhu. 2002. BLEU: A Method for Automatic Evaluation of Machine Translation. In *Proceedings of the 40th Annual Meeting on Association for Computational Linguistics*. Association for Computational Linguistics, Stroudsburg, PA, USA, ACL '02, pages 311–318. https://doi.org/10.3115/1073083.1073135.

Miguel Rios, Wilker Aziz, and Lucia Specia. 2011. Tine: A metric to assess mt adequacy. In *Proceedings of the Sixth Workshop on Statistical Machine Translation*. Association for Computational Linguistics, Edinburgh, Scotland, pages 116–122. http://www.aclweb.org/anthology/W11-2112.

Miloš Stanojević and Khalil Sima'an. 2014. Fitting Sentence Level Translation Evaluation with Many Dense Features. In *Proceedings of the 2014 Conference on Empirical Methods in Natural Language Processing (EMNLP)*. Association for Computational Linguistics, Doha, Qatar, pages 202–206. http://www.aclweb.org/anthology/D14-1025.

Miloš Stanojević and Khalil Sima'an. 2015. BEER 1.1: ILLC UvA submission to metrics and tuning task. In *Proceedings of the Tenth Workshop on Statistical Machine Translation*. Association for Computational Linguistics, Lisbon, Portugal, pages 396–401. http://aclweb.org/anthology/W15-3050.

Ben Taskar, Carlos Guestrin, and Daphne Koller. 2003. Max-Margin Markov Networks. In *NIPS 2014 - Advances in Neural Information Processing Systems 27*.

Yang Ye, Ming Zhou, and Chin-Yew Lin. 2007. Sentence Level Machine Translation Evaluation As a Ranking Problem: One Step Aside from BLEU. In *Proceedings of the Second Workshop on Statistical Machine Translation*. Association for Computational Linguistics, Stroudsburg, PA, USA, StatMT '07, pages 240–247. http://dl.acm.org/citation.cfm?id=1626355.1626391.

A Principled Framework for Evaluating Summarizers: Comparing Models of Summary Quality against Human Judgments

Maxime Peyrard and **Judith Eckle-Kohler**

Research Training Group AIPHES and UKP Lab
Computer Science Department, Technische Universität Darmstadt
`www.aiphes.tu-darmstadt.de`, `www.ukp.tu-darmstadt.de`

Abstract

We present a new framework for evaluating extractive summarizers, which is based on a principled representation as optimization problem. We prove that every extractive summarizer can be decomposed into an objective function and an optimization technique. We perform a comparative analysis and evaluation of several objective functions embedded in well-known summarizers regarding their correlation with human judgments. Our comparison of these correlations across two datasets yields surprising insights into the role and performance of objective functions in the different summarizers.

1 Introduction

The task of extractive summarization (ES) can naturally be cast as a discrete optimization problem where the text source is considered as a set of sentences and the summary is created by selecting an optimal subset of the sentences under a length constraint (McDonald, 2007; Lin and Bilmes, 2011).

In this work, we go one step further and mathematically prove that ES is equivalent to the problem of choosing (i) an objective function θ for scoring system summaries, and (ii) an optimizer O. We use (θ, O) to denote the resulting *decomposition* of any extractive summarizer. Our proposed decomposition enables a principled analysis and evaluation of existing summarizers, and addresses a major issue in the current evaluation of ES.

This issue concerns the traditional "intrinsic" evaluation comparing system summaries against human reference summaries. This kind of evaluation is actually an end-to-end evaluation of summarization systems which is performed *after θ has been optimized by O*. This is highly problematic from an evaluation point of view, because first, θ is typically not optimized exactly, and second, there might be side-effects caused by the particular optimization technique O, e.g., a sentence extracted to maximize θ might be suitable because of other properties not included in θ. Moreover, the commonly used evaluation metric ROUGE yields a noisy surrogate evaluation (despite its good correlation with human judgments) compared to the much more meaningful evaluation based on human judgments. As a result, the current end-to-end evaluation does not provide any insights into the *task of automatic summarization*.

The (θ, O) decomposition we propose addresses this issue: it enables a well-defined and principled evaluation of extractive summarizers on the level of their components θ and O. In this work, we focus on the analysis and evaluation of θ, because θ is a model of the quality indicators of a summary, and thus crucial in order to understand the properties of "good" summaries. Specifically, we compare θ functions of different summarizers by measuring the correlation of their θ functions with human judgments.

Our goal is to provide an evaluation framework which the research community could build upon in future research to identify the best possible θ and use it in optimization-based systems. We believe that the identification of such a θ is the central question of summarization, because this optimal θ would represent an optimal definition of summary quality both from an algorithmic point of view and from the human perspective.

In summary, our contribution is twofold: (i) We present a novel and principled evaluation framework for ES which allows evaluating the objective function and the optimization technique separately and independently. (ii) We compare well-known summarization systems regarding their implicit choices of θ by measuring the correlation

Proceedings of the 55th Annual Meeting of the Association for Computational Linguistics (Short Papers), pages 26–31
Vancouver, Canada, July 30 - August 4, 2017. ©2017 Association for Computational Linguistics
https://doi.org/10.18653/v1/P17-2005

of their θ functions with human judgments on two datasets from the Text Analysis Conference (TAC). Our comparative evaluation yields surprising results and shows that extractive summarization is not solved yet.

The code used in our experiments, including a general evaluation tool is available at `github.com/UKPLab/acl2017-theta_evaluation_summarization`.

2 Evaluation Framework

2.1 (θ, O) decomposition

Let $D = \{s_i\}$ be a document collection considered as a set of sentences. A summary S is then a subset of D, or we can say that S is an element of $\mathcal{P}(D)$, the power set of D.

Objective function We define an objective function to be a function that takes a summary of the document collection D and outputs a score:

$$\theta \; : \; \begin{array}{ccc} \mathcal{P}(D) & \to & \mathbb{R} \\ S & \mapsto & \theta_D(S) \end{array} \tag{1}$$

Optimizer Then the task of ES is to select the set of sentences S^* with maximal $\theta(S^*)$ under a length constraint:

$$S^* = \underset{S}{\operatorname{argmax}} \, \theta(S)$$
$$len(S) = \sum_{s \in S} len(s) \leq c \tag{2}$$

We use O to denote the technique which solves this optimization problem. O is an operator which takes an objective function θ from the set of all objective functions Θ and a document collection D from the set of all document collections $\mathcal{D}$, and outputs a summary S^*:

$$O \; : \; \begin{array}{ccc} \Theta \times \mathcal{D} & \to & S \\ (\theta, D) & \mapsto & S^* \end{array} \tag{3}$$

Decomposition Theorem Now we show that the problem of ES is equivalent to the problem of choosing a decomposition (θ, O).

We formalize an extractive summarizer σ as a set function which takes a document collection $D \in \mathcal{D}$ and outputs a summary $S_{D,\sigma} \in \mathcal{P}(D)$. With this formalism, it is clear that every (θ, O) tuple forms a summarizer because $O(\theta, \cdot)$ produces a summary from a document collection.

But the other direction is also true: for every extractive summarizer there exists at least one tuple (θ, O) which perfectly describes the summarizer:

Theorem 1 $\forall \sigma, \exists(\theta, O)$ *such that:*
$$\forall D \in \mathcal{D}, \sigma(D) = O(\theta, D)$$

This theorem is quite intuitive, especially since it is common to use a similar decomposition in optimization-based summarization systems. In the next section we illustrate the theorem by way of several examples, and provide a rigorous proof of the existence in the supplemental material.

2.2 Examples of θ

We analyze a range of different summarizers regarding their (mostly implicit) θ.

ICSI (Gillick and Favre, 2009) is a global linear optimization that extracts a summary by solving a maximum coverage problem considering the most frequent bigrams in the source documents. ICSI has been among the best systems in a classical ROUGE evaluation (Hong et al., 2014). For ICSI, the identification of θ is trivial because it was formulated as an optimization task. If c_i is the i-th bigram selected in the summary and w_i its weight computed from D, then:

$$\theta_{ICSI}(S) = \sum_{c_i \in S} c_i * w_i \tag{4}$$

LexRank (Erkan and Radev, 2004) is a well-known graph-based approach. A similarity graph $G(V, E)$ is constructed where V is the set of sentences and an edge e_{ij} is drawn between sentences v_i and v_j if and only if the cosine similarity between them is above a given threshold. Sentences are scored according to their PageRank score in G. We observe that $\theta_{LexRank}$ is given by:

$$\theta_{LexRank}(S) = \sum_{s \in S} PR_G(s) \tag{5}$$

where PR is the PageRank score of sentence s.

KL-Greedy (Haghighi and Vanderwende, 2009) minimizes the Kullback Leibler (KL) divergence between the word distributions in the summary and D (i.e $\theta_{KL} = -KL$). Recently, Peyrard and Eckle-Kohler (2016) optimized KL and Jensen Shannon (JS) divergence with a genetic algorithm. In this work, we use KL and JS for both unigram and bigram distributions.

LSA (Steinberger and Jezek, 2004) is an approach involving a dimensionality reduction of the term-document matrix via Singular Value Decomposition (SVD). The sentences extracted should cover the most important latent topics:

$$\theta_{LSA} = \sum_{t \in S} \lambda_t \tag{6}$$

where t is a latent topic identified by SVD on the term-document matrix and λ_t the associated singular value.

Edmundson (Edmundson, 1969) is an older heuristic method which scores sentences according to cue-phrases, overlap with title, term frequency and sentence position. $\theta_{Edmundson}$ is simply a weighted sum of these heuristics.

TF⋆IDF (Luhn, 1958) scores sentences with the TF*IDF of their terms. The best sentences are then greedily extracted. We use both the unigram and bigram versions in our experiments.

3 Experiments

Now we compare the summarizers analyzed above by measuring the correlation of their θ functions with human judgments.

Datasets We use two multi-document summarization datasets from the Text Analysis Conference (TAC) shared task: TAC-2008 and TAC-2009.[1] TAC-2008 and TAC-2009 contain 48 and 44 topics, respectively. Each topic consists of 10 news articles to be summarized in a maximum of 100 words. We use only the so-called initial summaries (A summaries), but not the update part.

For each topic, there are 4 human reference summaries along with a manually created Pyramid set. In both editions, all system summaries and the 4 reference summaries were manually evaluated by NIST assessors for readability, content selection (with Pyramid) and overall responsiveness. At the time of the shared tasks, 57 systems were submitted to TAC-2008 and 55 to TAC-2009. For our experiments, we use the Pyramid and the responsiveness annotations.

System Comparison For each θ, we compute the scores of all system and all manual summaries for any given topic. These scores are compared with the human scores. We include the manual summaries in our computation because this yields a more diverse set of summaries with a wider range of scores. Since an ideal summarizer would create summaries as well as humans, an ideal θ would also be able to correctly score human summaries with high scores.

For comparison, we also report the correlation between pyramid and responsiveness.

Correlations are measured with 3 metrics: Pearson's r, Spearman's ρ and Normalized Discounted Cumulative Gain (Ndcg). Pearson's r is a value correlation metric which depicts linear relationships between the scores produced by θ and the human judgments. Spearman's ρ is a rank correlation metric which compares the ordering of systems induced by θ and the ordering of systems induced by human judgments. Ndcg is a metric that compares ranked lists and puts more emphasis on the top elements by logarithmic decay weighting. Intuitively, it captures how well θ can recognize the best summaries. The optimization scenario benefits from high Ndcg scores because only summaries with high θ scores are extracted.

Previous work on correlation analysis averaged scores over topics for each system and then computed the correlation between averaged scores (Louis and Nenkova, 2013; Nenkova et al., 2007). An alternative and more natural option which we use here is to compute the correlation for each topic and average these correlations over topics (CORRELATION-AVERAGE). Since we want to estimate how well θ functions measure the quality of summaries, we find the summary level averaging more meaningful.

Analysis The results of our correlation analysis are presented in Table 1.

In our (θ, O) formulation, the end-to-end approach maps a set of documents to exactly one summary selected by the system. We call the (classical and well known) evaluation of this single summary end-to-end evaluation because it measures the end product of the system. This is in contrast to our proposed evaluation of the assumption made by individual summarizers shown in Table 1. A system summary was extracted by a given system because it was high scoring using its θ, but we ask the question whether optimizing this θ made sense in the first place.

We first observe that scores are relatively low. Summarization is not a solved problem and the systems we investigated can not identify correctly what makes a good summary. This is in contrast to the picture in the classical end-to-end evaluation with ROUGE where state-of-the-art systems score relatively high. Some Ndcg scores are higher (for TAC-2008) which explains why these systems can extract relatively good summaries in the end-to-end evaluation. In this classical evaluation, only the single best summary is evaluated, which means that a system does not need to be able to rank all

---

[1] http://tac.nist.gov/2009/Summarization/, http://tac.nist.gov/2008/Summarization/

| | TAC-2008 | | | | | | TAC-2009 | | | | | |
| | responsiveness | | | Pyramid | | | responsiveness | | | Pyramid | | |
θ	r	ρ	Ndcg	r	ρ	Ndcg	r	ρ	Ndcg	r	ρ	Ndcg
TF*IDF-1	.1777	.2257	.5031	.1850	.2386	.3575	.1996	.2282	.3826	.2514	.2890	.2280
TF*IDF-2	.0489	.1548	.5952	.0507	.1833	.4811	.0061	.1736	.4984	.1073	.2383	.3844
ICSI	.1069	.1885	.6153	.1147	.2294	.5228	.1050	.1821	.5707	.1379	.2466	.5016
JS-1	**.2504**	**.2762**	.4411	**.2798**	**.3205**	.2804	.2021	.2282	.3896	.2616	.3042	.2272
JS-2	.0383	.1698	.5873	.0410	.2038	.4804	.0284	.1475	.5646	.0021	.2084	.4734
LexRank	.1995	.1821	.6618	.2498	.2168	.5935	.2831	.2585	.6028	**.3714**	.3421	.5764
LSA	.0437	.1137	**.6772**	.1144	.1131	**.5997**	**.2965**	.2127	**.6641**	.3677	.2935	**.6467**
Edmunds.	.2223	.2686	.6372	.2665	.3164	.5521	.2598	**.2604**	.5852	.3647	**.3720**	.5594
KL-1	.1796	.2249	.4899	.2016	.2690	.3439	.1827	.2275	.4047	.2423	.2981	.2466
KL-2	.0023	.1661	.6165	.0023	.1928	.5135	.0437	.1435	.6171	.0211	.2060	.5462
Pyramid	.7031	.6606	.8528	—	—	—	.7174	.6414	.8520	—	—	—

Table 1: Correlation of θ functions with human judgments across various systems.

possible summaries correctly.

We see that systems with high end-to-end ROUGE scores (according to Hong et al. (2014)) do not necessarily have a good model of summary quality. Indeed, the best performing θ functions are not part of the systems performing best with ROUGE. For example, ICSI is the best system according to ROUGE, but it is not clear that it has the best model of summary quality. In TAC-2009, LexRank, LSA and the heuristic Edmundson have better correlations with human judgments. The difference with end-to-end evaluation might stem from the fact that ICSI solves the optimization problem exactly, while LexRank and Edmundson use greedy optimizers. There might also be some side-effects from which ICSI profits: extracting sentences to improve θ might lead to accidentally selecting suitable sentences, because θ can merely correlate well with properties of good summaries, while not modeling these properties itself.

It is worth noting that systems perform differently on TAC2009 and TAC2008. There are several differences between TAC2008 and TAC2009 like redundancy level or guidelines for annotations; for example, responsiveness is scored out of 5 in 2008 and out of 10 in 2009. The LSA summarizer ranks among the best systems in TAC2009 with pearson's r but is closer to the worst systems in TAC2008. While this is difficult to explain we hypothesize that the model of summary quality from LSA is sensitive to the slight variations and therefore not robust. In general, any system which claims to have a better θ than previous works should indeed report results on several datasets to ensure robustness and generality.

Interestingly, we observe that the correlation between Pyramid and responsiveness is better than in any system, but still not particularly high. Responsiveness is an overall annotation while Pyramid is a manual measure of content only. These results confirm the intuition that humans take into account much more aspects when evaluating summaries.

4 Related Work and Discussion

While correlation analyses on human judgment data have been performed in the context of validating automatic summary evaluation metrics (Louis and Nenkova, 2013; Nenkova et al., 2007; Lin, 2004), there is no prior work which uses these data for a principled comparison of summarizers.

Much previous work focused on efficient optimizers O, such as ILP, which impose constraints on the θ function. Linear (Gillick and Favre, 2009) and submodular (Lin and Bilmes, 2011) θ functions are widespread in the summarization community because they can be optimized efficiently and effectively via ILP (Schrijver, 1986) and the greedy algorithm for submodularity (Fujishige, 2005). A greedy approach is often used when θ does not have convenient properties that can be leveraged by a classical optimizer (Haghighi and Vanderwende, 2009).

Such interdependencies of O and θ limit the expressiveness of θ. However, realistic θ functions are unlikely to be linear or submodular, and in the well-studied field of optimization there exist a range of different techniques developed to tackle difficult combinatorial problems (Schrijver, 2003; Blum and Roli, 2003).

A recent example of such a technique adapted to extractive summarization are meta-heuristics used to optimize non-linear, non-submodular objective functions (Peyrard and Eckle-Kohler, 2016).

Other methods like Markov Chain Monte Carlo (Metropolis et al., 1953) or Monte-Carlo Tree Search (Suttner and Ertel, 1991; Silver et al., 2016) could also be adapted to summarization and thus become realistic choices for O. General purpose optimization techniques are especially appealing, because they offer a decoupling of θ and O and allow investigating complex θ functions without making any assumption on their mathematical properties. In particular, this supports future work on identifying an "optimal" θ as a model of relevant quality aspects of a summary.

5 Conclusion

We presented a novel evaluation framework for ES which is based on the proof that ES is equivalent to the problem of choosing an objective function θ and an optimizer O. This principled and well-defined framework allows evaluating θ and O of any extractive summarizer – separately and independently. We believe that our framework can serve as a basis for future work on identifying an "optimal" θ function, which would provide an answer to the central question of what are the properties of a "good" summary.

Acknowledgments

This work has been supported by the German Research Foundation (DFG) as part of the Research Training Group "Adaptive Preparation of Information from Heterogeneous Sources" (AIPHES) under grant No. GRK 1994/1, and via the German-Israeli Project Cooperation (DIP, grant No. GU 798/17-1).

References

Christian Blum and Andrea Roli. 2003. Metaheuristics in Combinatorial Optimization: Overview and Conceptual Comparison. *ACM Computing Surveys* 35(3):268–308.

H. P. Edmundson. 1969. New Methods in Automatic Extracting. *Journal of the Association for Computing Machinery* 16(2):264–285.

Günes Erkan and Dragomir R. Radev. 2004. LexRank: Graph-based Lexical Centrality As Salience in Text Summarization. *Journal of Artificial Intelligence Research* pages 457–479.

Satoru Fujishige. 2005. *Submodular functions and optimization*. Annals of discrete mathematics. Elsevier, Amsterdam, Boston, Paris.

Dan Gillick and Benoit Favre. 2009. A Scalable Global Model for Summarization. In *Proceedings of the Workshop on Integer Linear Programming for Natural Language Processing*. Association for Computational Linguistics, Boulder, Colorado, pages 10–18.

Aria Haghighi and Lucy Vanderwende. 2009. Exploring Content Models for Multi-document Summarization. In *Proceedings of Human Language Technologies: The 2009 Annual Conference of the North American Chapter of the Association for Computational Linguistics*. Association for Computational Linguistics, Boulder, Colorado, pages 362–370.

Kai Hong, John Conroy, benoit Favre, Alex Kulesza, Hui Lin, and Ani Nenkova. 2014. A Repository of State of the Art and Competitive Baseline Summaries for Generic News Summarization. In *Proceedings of the Ninth International Conference on Language Resources and Evaluation (LREC'14)*. European Language Resources Association (ELRA), Reykjavik, Iceland, pages 1608–1616.

Chin-Yew Lin. 2004. ROUGE: A Package for Automatic Evaluation of Summaries. In *Text Summarization Branches Out: Proceedings of the ACL-04 Workshop*. Association for Computational Linguistics, Barcelona, Spain, pages 74–81.

Hui Lin and Jeff A. Bilmes. 2011. A Class of Submodular Functions for Document Summarization. In *Proceedings of the 49th Annual Meeting of the Association for Computational Linguistics: Human Language Technologies*. Association for Computational Linguistics, Portland, Oregon, USA, pages 510–520.

Annie Louis and Ani Nenkova. 2013. Automatically Assessing Machine Summary Content Without a Gold Standard. *Computational Linguistics* 39(2):267–300.

Hans Peter Luhn. 1958. The Automatic Creation of Literature Abstracts. *IBM Journal of Research Development* 2:159–165.

Ryan McDonald. 2007. A Study of Global Inference Algorithms in Multi-document Summarization. In *Proceedings of the 29th European Conference on IR Research*. Springer-Verlag, Rome, Italy, pages 557–564.

Nicholas Metropolis, Arianna Rosenbluth, Marshall Rosenbluth, Augusta Teller, and Edward Teller. 1953. Equation of State Calculations by Fast Computing Machines. *Journal of Chemical Physics* 21:1087 – 1092.

Ani Nenkova, Rebecca Passonneau, and Kathleen McKeown. 2007. The Pyramid Method: Incorporating Human Content Selection Variation in Summarization Evaluation. *ACM Transactions on Speech and Language Processing (TSLP)* 4(2).

Maxime Peyrard and Judith Eckle-Kohler. 2016. A General Optimization Framework for Multi-Document Summarization Using Genetic Algorithms and Swarm Intelligence. In *Proceedings of the 26th International Conference on Computational Linguistics (COLING 2016)*. The COLING 2016 Organizing Committee, Osaka, Japan, pages 247–257.

Alexander Schrijver. 1986. *Theory of Linear and Integer Programming*. John Wiley & Sons, Inc., New York, NY, USA.

Alexander Schrijver. 2003. *Combinatorial Optimization - Polyhedra and Efficiency*. Springer, New York.

David Silver, Aja Huang, Chris J. Maddison, Arthur Guez, Laurent Sifre, George van den Driessche, Julian Schrittwieser, Ioannis Antonoglou, Veda Panneershelvam, Marc Lanctot, Sander Dieleman, Dominik Grewe, John Nham, Nal Kalchbrenner, Ilya Sutskever, Timothy Lillicrap, Madeleine Leach, Koray Kavukcuoglu, Thore Graepel, and Demis Hassabis. 2016. Mastering the game of Go with deep neural networks and tree search. *Nature* 529(7587):484–489.

Josef Steinberger and Karel Jezek. 2004. Using latent semantic analysis in text summarization and summary evaluation. In *Proceedings of the 7th International Conference on Information Systems Implementation and Modelling (ISIM '04)*. Rožnov pod Radhoštěm, Czech Republic, pages 93–100.

Christian Suttner and Wolfgang Ertel. 1991. Using Back-Propagation Networks for Guiding the Search of a Theorem Prover. *International Journal of Neural Networks Research & Applications* 2(1):3–16.

Vector space models for evaluating semantic fluency in autism

Emily Prud'hommeaux[†], Jan van Santen[°], Douglas Gliner[†]
[†]Rochester Institute of Technology, [°]Oregon Health & Science University
{emilypx,dgg5503}@rit.edu, vansantj@ohsu.edu

Abstract

A common test administered during neurological examination is the semantic fluency test, in which the patient must list as many examples of a given semantic category as possible under timed conditions. Poor performance is associated with neurological conditions characterized by impairments in executive function, such as dementia, schizophrenia, and autism spectrum disorder (ASD). Methods for analyzing semantic fluency responses at the level of detail necessary to uncover these differences have typically relied on subjective manual annotation. In this paper, we explore automated approaches for scoring semantic fluency responses that leverage ontological resources and distributional semantic models to characterize the semantic fluency responses produced by young children with and without ASD. Using these methods, we find significant differences in the semantic fluency responses of children with ASD, demonstrating the utility of using objective methods for clinical language analysis.

1 Introduction

Semantic fluency tasks, in which patients undergoing neuropsychological evaluation must list as many items as possible in a particular semantic category in a fixed, brief period of time, are widely used by clinicians to evaluate language, development, and cognition. Performance on such tasks is usually measured in terms of the raw number of appropriate items produced. A more detailed analysis of these lists, however, can reveal patterns associated with a variety of neurological conditions, including autism, dementia, and schizophrenia.

Semantic fluency responses hold particular promise for shedding light on the language of children with autism spectrum disorder (ASD). ASD has been associated with atypical semantics and pragmatic expression since the condition was was first identified over 70 years ago (Kanner, 1943). One linguistic feature of ASD, referenced in many of the diagnostic instruments for the disorder, is the use of words that are meaningful but unexpected (Lord et al., 2002; Rutter et al., 2003), a phenomenon that could play an important role in the production of semantically related words.

In this paper, we present NLP-informed approaches for automatically approximating the subjective manual methods described in the psychology literature for analyzing semantic fluency responses. Applying these methods to data collected from young children with and without ASD, we find that none of the standard manual measures of semantic fluency are able to distinguish children with ASD from those without. Several computationally derived measures, however, are significantly different between diagnostic groups. These results indicate that computationally derived measures of semantic fluency tap into subtle differences that would be difficult to detect using standard manual metrics, lending support for the clinical utility of computational linguistic analysis.

2 Background

The semantic fluency task is a subtype of a more general word-generation task commonly referred to as verbal fluency. In such tasks, a participant must verbally produce a list of words belonging to some category (e.g., animals) within a predetermined amount of time, usually 60 seconds. Performance on verbal fluency tasks has been correlated with executive function, and differences in verbal fluency scores have been noted in a variety of neurological conditions including dementia

32

Proceedings of the 55th Annual Meeting of the Association for Computational Linguistics (Short Papers), pages 32–37
Vancouver, Canada, July 30 - August 4, 2017. ©2017 Association for Computational Linguistics
https://doi.org/10.18653/v1/P17-2006

(Henry et al., 2004), schizophrenia (Frith et al., 1995), and autism (Turner, 1999; Geurts et al., 2004; Spek et al., 2009; Begeer et al., 2014).

The rate at which speakers generate words in a semantic fluency response has been observed to vary throughout the timed period, typically with several related words being produced in close succession followed by a pause before a new burst of related words (Bousfield et al., 1954). Troyer et al. (1997) proposed two cognitive processes underlying this pattern: clustering and switching. Clustering refers to the tendency of speakers to list words in clusters according to their membership in a particular subcategory of the larger semantic category (e.g., *pets* for the larger category of *animals*). Switching is the decision made by the speaker to abandon a subcategory when it has been exhausted and to list items in a new subcategory.

Autism is associated with deficits in executive function, and thus we should expect to see consistent patterns demonstrating deficits in semantic fluency performance in the ASD population. Several studies have found overall weaker performance, in terms of raw item count, in individuals with ASD (Turner, 1999; Geurts et al., 2004; Spek et al., 2009); other more recent studies, however, have not been able to replicate this finding (Lopez et al., 2005; Inokuchi and Kamio, 2013; Begeer et al., 2014). Similarly conflicting results have been reported when evaluating the semantic relatedness of adjacent words, with some finding smaller clusters in ASD (Turner, 1999), some finding larger clusters (Begeer et al., 2014), and still others finding no differences (Spek et al., 2009).

One likely source of these discrepancies is the subjectivity inherent in the cluster assignment task. Troyer et al. (1997) provide examples of common clusters and their member animals, but they note the difficulty in assigning items to subcategories, explaining that their proposed subcategories were not generated using any existing taxonomy but instead grew organically out of the patterns observed in the data. An additional complication is that a word's subcategory membership is dependent on its context. The word *camel*, for instance, could be assigned to any number of categories (e.g., *desert animal, zoo animal*), depending on the nearby words. This is particularly problematic when analyzing the responses of children, whose semantic categories might not align with those of an adult annotator.

In response to these challenges, some recent work has focused on modeling the cluster-switch behavior using computational linguistic methods, in particular, using latent semantic analysis to calculate the semantic similarity between adjacent words. Mean scores over these similarity values can capture a individual's tendency to use a naming strategy relying on similarity (Nicodemus et al., 2014; Rosenstein et al., 2015). Other work has focused on setting thresholds over these similarity values in order to delineate the boundaries between clusters or chains of related words (Rosenstein et al., 2015; Pakhomov and Hemmy, 2014). None of these studies, however, has compared the output of the automated methods to manual annotations in order to determine their accuracy. Furthermore, the thresholds used for cluster boundary identification in these studies were set by "rule of thumb" rather than empirically or probabilistically.

To our knowledge, this is the first attempt to use distributional semantic models to analyze semantic fluency responses in children with autism spectrum disorder. More importantly, it is the first study that uses machine learning to validate the utility of these models for replicating and, perhaps improving upon, human annotation methods of semantic fluency responses.

3 Data

The participants in this study were 22 children with typical development (TD) and 22 high-functioning children with ASD, ranging in age from 4 to 9 years. ASD was diagnosed via clinical consensus according to the Diagnostic and Statistical Manual of Mental Disorders, 4th Edition (DSM-IV-TR) criteria for Autistic Disorder (American Psychiatric Association, 2000) and the established thresholds on two commonly used diagnostic instruments: the Autism Diagnostic Observation Schedule (ADOS) (Lord et al., 2002) and the Social Communication Questionnaire (SCQ) (Rutter et al., 2003). None of the participants analyzed here met the criteria for language impairment, and the two groups were selected so that there were no statistically significant differences (via two-tailed t-test) between the groups in chronological age, verbal IQ, and full scale IQ. In addition to the experimental corpus, we had access to a development set of 55 semantic fluency responses that were discarded after the groups were matched on these three criteria.

During administration of the task, the clinician asked the child to name as many animals as he could as quickly as possible. The children's responses were timed and recorded. The audio was then transcribed by a speech-language pathologist, and the transcripts were reviewed to remove extraneous dialogue and to standardize spelling. Two manual annotations were performed: (1) semantic clusters (Troyer et al., 1997), in which a cluster consists of two or more animals belonging to same subcategory (*giraffe, elephant, lion*); and (2) semantic chains (Pakhomov and Hemmy, 2014), in which each animal shares something in common at least with the immediately preceding animal (*elephant, lion, cat*). Inter-annotator agreement for labeling cluster boundaries according to the Troyer criteria was low (Cohen's $\kappa < 0.4$); we therefore limit our discussion to semantic chains, whose boundaries were labeled with more substantial agreement ($\kappa = 0.71$).

4   Features

4.1   Manually derived measures

Performance on a verbal fluency task is normally evaluated by counting the number of unique items produced in the designated time period. Credit is given both to a general category such as *fish* and to examples of that category, such as *salmon*; however, a morphological or descriptive variation of another item (e.g., *doggy* for *dog*) is considered a repetition and does not contribute to the total. We report this count, along with the number of semantic chains and mean length of semantic chain.

4.2   Semantic similarity measures

There are a number of ways to measure the semantic similarity between two words, some relying on manually curated knowledge bases and other derived distributionally from large text corpora. A high mean similarity between adjacent word pairs in a list of words might suggest that the list contains a small number of large clusters of strongly related words (a cluster-and-switch strategy) or a sequence of items each of which is closely related to the previous item but not necessarily to the items before that (a chaining strategy). In either case, the participant is tapping into semantic subcategories when producing his response. A lower mean similarity should indicate that a participant has produced a large number of small clusters or has selected items from the larger category seemingly at random.

One possible way to capture relatedness is by using a manually curated lexical ontology that implicitly encodes the similarity between pairs of words, such as WordNet (Fellbaum, 1998). Various algorithms have been proposed for assigning similarities scores for two synsets in WordNet by traversing the hierarchical trees connecting those synsets. Here we calculate the mean path similarity for each adjacent word pair in a participant's generated wordlist. Words not appearing in WordNet were manually replaced with equivalent synsets (e.g., *puppy dog* was replaced with *puppy*). When multiple synsets were associated with a given item, we used the first synset whose hypernym included the synset for *animal* or *imaginary being* (e.g., *pegasus*).

One disadvantage inherent in the WordNet ontology of animal names is that it is derived from the biological taxonomy of the animal kingdom; that is, the degree to which two animals are semantically related within WordNet is determined primarily by their biological similarity and not by semantic features (e.g., region of origin, usual habitat) that a non-zoologist might use to organize animals names. In order to model multiple dimensions of similarity, we turn to the use of vector space models. We explore two vector-space representations: latent semantic analysis (LSA) (Landauer et al., 1998) and continuous space neural word embeddings (Bengio et al., 2003). Using the gensim Python library (Řehůřek and Sojka, 2010), we built an LSA model and a word2vec model, both with 400 dimensions but otherwise using default parameters settings, on the full text of Wikipedia downloaded in November, 2016. For each model, we take the mean of the set of cosine similarities between each adjacent pair of items in a participant's response. We also calculate the mean similarity over 100 random permutations of a participant's wordlist to capture "global coherence", as proposed by Nicodemus et al. (2014).

4.3   Measures of identifying semantic chains

Previous work in using word embeddings to model clustering relied on a simple cosine similarity threshold, determined heuristically (set arbitrarily 0.9 in Rosenstein et al. (2015), and at the 75th percentile in Pakhomov and Hemmy (2014)), in which a cluster boundary is inserted between any two adjacent words whose similarity did not exceed that threshold. We instead propose to empirically determine the optimal value of such a thresh-

Feature	TD	ASD	t
Raw count	12.0	10.2	1.043
Manual chain count	6.14	4.86	1.603
Manual chain length	2.0	2.13	-0.572
WordNet path similarity	0.169	0.1697	0.1721
LSA cosine similarity	0.365	0.308	1.636
LSA coherence	0.311	0.248	1.934*
w2v cosine similarity	0.427	0.392	1.710*
w2v coherence	0.409	0.375	1.530
LSA chain count	4.09	4.31	-0.316
LSA chain length	3.38	1.87	2.310*
w2v chain count	4.14	4.41	-0.3800
w2v chain length	3.07	1.91	1.9265*
SVM chain count	4.09	4.86	-1.0894
SVM chain length	3.66	2.19	2.4164*

Table 1: Mean values by diagnostic group for semantic fluency metrics ($*p < 0.05$, one-tailed).

old. First, while leaving one subject out, we iteratively sweep through a range of possible values for the threshold to determine the value that maximizes the accuracy of semantic chain boundary identification for the rest of the participants. We then apply that threshold to the left-out subject.

In addition to thresholding over individual similarity metrics, we also use three similarity metrics (WordNet path similarity, LSA cosine similarity, and word2vec cosine similarity) as features within a support vector machine to classify any pair of adjacent words as either containing a semantic chain boundary or as belonging to the same semantic chain. Using all two-word sequences found in the children's responses and the manual indications of the locations of cluster boundaries, we perform leave-one-out cross validation to predict whether the second word in each word pair represents the start of a new chain or a continuation of the previous chain.

Although the methods all achieved reasonable boundary identification accuracy, with AUC ranging from 0.65 to 0.8, we note that the goal of determining cluster boundaries in this way is not to replicate human cluster boundary insertion, which we know to be subjective and difficult to perform reliably. Rather, we are attempting to develop an objective way to insert boundaries that does not rely on an annotator's ability to infer another individual's semantic organization of the world.

5 Results

Table 1 shows the mean value for each group and the t-statistic for each of the features. In contrast to some previous work (Turner, 1999; Geurts et al., 2004; Spek et al., 2009), we find no between-group differences in raw item count. These re-

sults, however, support other work that did not find such differences when comparing groups matched on verbal ability, as our groups are (Lopez et al., 2005; Inokuchi and Kamio, 2013).

Mean cosine similarity derived using the word2vec model is significantly different between the two groups, with the TD group showing a higher mean similarity between adjacent items. We also see that the global coherence measure, derived by taking the mean similarity over 100 random orderings of each list, is significantly higher in the TD group when derived using LSA.

Although there are no between-group differences in the manually derived measures of chain count and chain length, we find differences in chain length when derived using both thresholding over similarity measures and machine learning. In all three cases, children with typical development have longer semantic chains than children with ASD, suggesting that TD children employ the semantic chaining strategy that is reportedly preferred by neurotypical adults. In short, there are differences in the semantic fluency responses of young children with ASD, and these differences would be difficult to reliably detect without appealing to computational techniques.

Figure 1 shows two semantic fluency responses, one produced by a child with ASD and one by a child with TD, with plots indicating the cosine similarities between adjacent words derived from both the LSA and word2vec models. Semantic chain boundaries proposed by the SVM are indicated with vertical dashed lines. Note that LSA and word2vec similarity values are only somewhat correlated, underscoring the potential utility of combining the two scores for chain boundary identification. As expected given the results in Table 1, the child with ASD has generally lower cosine similarity scores and many more chain boundaries than the typically developing child.

6 Discussion and future work

One problem with applying the chaining and clustering paradigms to children is that the semantic features linking animals for a child might be very different those of adults. Well over half of the children in this study included the sequence *cat, bear* or *bear, cat*, despite the lack of clear relation between the two words from an adult's perspective. We found, however, that our automated methods usually grouped these two words together, recognizing some similarity that adults seem to miss. At

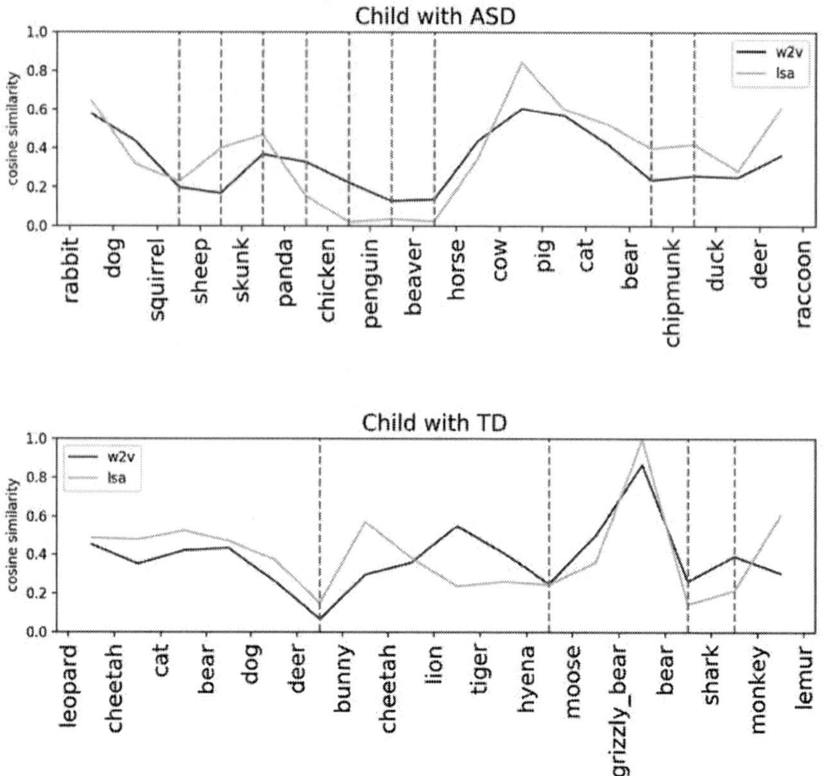

Figure 1: Plots of successive word-pair cosine similarity values derived using LSA and word2vec models for a child with ASD (upper panel) and a child with TD (lower panel). Vertical dashed lines indicate semantic chain boundaries proposed by the SVM.

the same time, relying on large corpora of adult-focused texts may introduce problems: the lowest similarity values found in our data set involved the word *turkey*, suggesting a preponderance in the data of the country rather than the bird. More sensitive text normalization methods could likely resolve this problem, but we also plan to build LSA and neural word embedding models using child language data (e.g., the CHILDES corpus (MacWhinney, 2000)) and child-oriented texts in the public domain.

Future work will focus on improving our methods for identifying semantic chains while accounting for different methods of semantic organization by combining information gained from the rich but out-of-domain data scenarios described here with in-domain experimental data. In addition to incorporating more child-oriented training data, we plan to use graph-based models to capture the ways in which speakers proceed through the semantic space (Abbott et al., 2015).

As the contradictory results in the literature indicate, the precise nature of the linguistic deficits associated with ASD is somewhat unclear. Many of the most widely reported linguistic deficits fail to obtain when participants are carefully matched, particularly on verbal IQ. The atypical language features that do persist under strict matching are usually semantic or pragmatic and, hence, more difficult to detect using easily scored standard language assessment instruments. Methods leveraging large corpora that reflect neurotypical language use may prove to be one of the more useful tools for identifying atypical language in ASD.

Acknowledgments

This work was supported in part by NIH grants R01DC013996, R01DC012033, and R01DC007129. Any opinions, findings, conclusions or recommendations expressed in this publication are those of the authors and do not necessarily reflect the views of the NIH.

References

Joshua T Abbott, Joseph L Austerweil, and Thomas L Griffiths. 2015. Random walks on semantic networks can resemble optimal foraging. *Psychological Review* 122(3):558–569.

American Psychiatric Association. 2000. *DSM-IV-TR: Diagnostic and Statistical Manual of Mental Disorders*. American Psychiatric Publishing, Washington, DC.

Sander Begeer, Marlies Wierda, Anke M Scheeren, Jan-Pieter Teunisse, Hans M Koot, and Hilde M Geurts. 2014. Verbal fluency in children with autism spectrum disorders: Clustering and switching strategies. *Autism* 18(8):1014–1018.

Yoshua Bengio, Réjean Ducharme, Pascal Vincent, and Christian Jauvin. 2003. A neural probabilistic language model. *Journal of machine learning research* 3:1137–1155.

Weston Ashmore Bousfield, CHW Sedgewick, and BH Cohen. 1954. Certain temporal characteristics of the recall of verbal associates. *The American Journal of Psychology* 67(1):111–118.

Christian Fellbaum. 1998. *WordNet: An Electronic Lexical Database*. MIT Press, Cambridge, MA.

CD Frith, KJ Friston, S Herold, D Silbersweig, P Fletcher, C Cahill, RJ Dolan, RS Frackowiak, and PF Liddle. 1995. Regional brain activity in chronic schizophrenic patients during the performance of a verbal fluency task. *The British Journal of Psychiatry* 167(3):343–349.

Hilde M Geurts, Sylvie Verté, Jaap Oosterlaan, Herbert Roeyers, and Joseph A Sergeant. 2004. How specific are executive functioning deficits in attention deficit hyperactivity disorder and autism? *Journal of child psychology and psychiatry* 45(4):836–854.

Julie D Henry, John R Crawford, and Louise H Phillips. 2004. Verbal fluency performance in dementia of the Alzheimer's type: A meta-analysis. *Neuropsychologia* 42(9):1212–1222.

Eiko Inokuchi and Yoko Kamio. 2013. Qualitative analyses of verbal fluency in adolescents and young adults with high-functioning autism spectrum disorder. *Research in Autism Spectrum Disorders* 7:1403–1410.

Leo Kanner. 1943. Autistic disturbances of affective content. *Nervous Child* 2:217–250.

Thomas K Landauer, Peter W Foltz, and Darrell Laham. 1998. An introduction to latent semantic analysis. *Discourse processes* 25(2-3):259–284.

Brian Lopez, Alan Lincoln, Sally Ozonoff, and Zona Lai. 2005. Examining the relationship between executive functions and restricted, repetitive symptoms of autistic disorder. *Journal of Autism and Developmental Disorders* 35(4).

Catherine Lord, Michael Rutter, Pamela DiLavore, and Susan Risi. 2002. *Autism Diagnostic Observation Schedule (ADOS)*. Western Psychological Services, Los Angeles.

Brian MacWhinney. 2000. *The CHILDES project: The database*, volume 2. Psychology Press.

Kristin K Nicodemus, Brita Elvevåg, Peter W Foltz, Mark Rosenstein, Catherine Diaz-Asper, and Daniel R Weinberger. 2014. Category fluency, latent semantic analysis and schizophrenia: a candidate gene approach. *Cortex* 55:182–191.

Serguei V.S. Pakhomov and Laura S. Hemmy. 2014. A computational linguistic measure of clustering behavior on semantic verbal fluency task predicts risk of future dementia in the nun study. *Cortex* 55:97–106.

Radim Řehůřek and Petr Sojka. 2010. Software Framework for Topic Modelling with Large Corpora. In *Proceedings of the LREC 2010 Workshop on New Challenges for NLP Frameworks*. pages 45–50.

Mark Rosenstein, Peter W. Foltz, Anja Vaskinn, and Brita Elvevg. 2015. Practical issues in developing semantic frameworks for the analysis of verbal fluency data: A norwegian data case study. In *Proceedings of the 2nd Workshop on Computational Linguistics and Clinical Psychology*. pages 124–133.

Michael Rutter, Anthony Bailey, and Catherine Lord. 2003. *Social Communication Questionnaire (SCQ)*. Western Psychological Services, Los Angeles.

Annelies Spek, Tjeerd Schatorjé, Evert Scholte, and Ina van Berckelaer-Onnes. 2009. Verbal fluency in adults with high functioning autism or asperger syndrome. *Neuropsychologia* 47(3):652–656.

Angela K Troyer, Morris Moscovitch, and Gordon Winocur. 1997. Clustering and switching as two components of verbal fluency: evidence from younger and older healthy adults. *Neuropsychology* 11(1):138–146.

Michelle A Turner. 1999. Generating novel ideas: Fluency performance in high-functioning and learning disabled individuals with autism. *Journal of Child Psychology and Psychiatry* 40(2):189–201.

Neural Architectures for Multilingual Semantic Parsing

Raymond Hendy Susanto and **Wei Lu**
Singapore University of Technology and Design
{raymond_susanto, luwei}@sutd.edu.sg

Abstract

In this paper, we address semantic parsing in a multilingual context. We train one multilingual model that is capable of parsing natural language sentences from multiple different languages into their corresponding formal semantic representations. We extend an existing sequence-to-tree model to a multi-task learning framework which shares the decoder for generating semantic representations. We report evaluation results on the multilingual GeoQuery corpus and introduce a new multilingual version of the ATIS corpus.

1 Introduction

In this work, we address *multilingual* semantic parsing – the task of mapping natural language sentences coming from multiple different languages into their corresponding formal semantic representations. We consider two multilingual scenarios: 1) the *single-source* setting, where the input consists of a single sentence in a single language, and 2) the *multi-source* setting, where the input consists of parallel sentences in multiple languages. Previous work handled the former by means of monolingual models (Wong and Mooney, 2006; Lu et al., 2008; Jones et al., 2012), while the latter has only been explored by Jie and Lu (2014) who ensembled many monolingual models together. Unfortunately, training a model for each language separately ignores the shared information among the source languages, which may be potentially beneficial for typologically related languages. Practically, it is also inconvenient to train, tune, and configure a new model for each language, which can be a laborious process.

In this work, we propose a parsing architecture that accepts as input sentences in several languages. We extend an existing sequence-to-tree model (Dong and Lapata, 2016) to a multi-task learning framework, motivated by its success in other fields, e.g., neural machine translation (MT) (Dong et al., 2015; Firat et al., 2016). Our model consists of *multiple encoders*, one for each language, and *one decoder* that is shared across source languages for generating semantic representations. In this way, the proposed model potentially benefits from having a generic decoder that works well across languages. Intuitively, the model encourages each source language encoder to find a common structured representation for the decoder. We further modify the attention mechanism (Bahdanau et al., 2015) to integrate multi-source information, such that it can learn where to focus during parsing; i.e., which input positions in which languages.

Our contributions are as follows:

- We investigate semantic parsing in two multilingual scenarios that are relatively unexplored in past research,

- We present novel extensions to the sequence-to-tree architecture that integrates multilingual information for semantic parsing, and

- We release a new ATIS semantic dataset annotated in two new languages.

2 Related Work

In this section, we summarize semantic parsing approaches from previous works. Wong and Mooney (2006) created WASP, a semantic parser based on statistical machine translation. Lu et al. (2008) proposed generative hybrid tree structures, which were augmented with a discriminative re-ranker. CCG-based semantic parsing systems have been developed, such as ZC07 (Zettlemoyer and Collins, 2007) and UBL (Kwiatkowski et al.,

Proceedings of the 55th Annual Meeting of the Association for Computational Linguistics (Short Papers), pages 38–44
Vancouver, Canada, July 30 - August 4, 2017. ©2017 Association for Computational Linguistics
https://doi.org/10.18653/v1/P17-2007

2010). Researchers have proposed sequence-to-sequence parsing models (Jia and Liang, 2016; Dong and Lapata, 2016; Kočiský et al., 2016). Recently, Susanto and Lu (2017) extended the hybrid tree with neural features.

Recent progress in multilingual NLP has moved towards building a unified model that can work across different languages, such as in multilingual dependency parsing (Ammar et al., 2016), multilingual MT (Firat et al., 2016), and multilingual word embedding (Guo et al., 2016). Nonetheless, multilingual approaches for semantic parsing are relatively unexplored, which motivates this work. Jones et al. (2012) evaluated an individually-trained tree transducer on a multilingual semantic dataset. Jie and Lu (2014) ensembled monolingual hybrid tree models on the same dataset.

3 Model

In this section, we describe our approach to multilingual semantic parsing, which extends the sequence-to-tree model by Dong and Lapata (2016). Unlike the mainstream approach that trains one monolingual parser per source language, our approach integrates N *encoders*, one for each language, into a single model. This model encodes a sentence from the n-th language $X = x_1, x_2, ..., x_{|X|}$ as a vector and then uses a shared *decoder* to decode the encoded vector into its corresponding logical form $Y = y_1, y_2, ..., y_{|Y|}$. We consider two types of input: 1) a single sentence in one of N languages in the *single-source* setting and 2) parallel sentences in N languages in the *multi-source* setting. We elaborate on each setting in Section 3.1 and 3.2, respectively.

The encoder is implemented as a unidirectional RNN with long short-term memory (LSTM) units (Hochreiter and Schmidhuber, 1997), which takes a sequence of natural language tokens as input. Similar to previous multi-task frameworks, e.g., in neural MT (Firat et al., 2016; Zoph and Knight, 2016), we create one encoder per source language, i.e., $\{\Psi^n_{\text{enc}}\}^N_{n=1}$. For the n-th language, it updates the hidden vector at time step t by:

$$\mathbf{h}^n_t = \Psi^n_{\text{enc}}(\mathbf{h}^n_{t-1}, \mathbf{E}^n_x[x_t]) \qquad (1)$$

where Ψ^n_{enc} is the LSTM function and $\mathbf{E}^n_x \in \mathbb{R}^{|V| \times d}$ is an embedding matrix containing row vectors of the source tokens in the n-th language. Each encoder may be configured differently, such

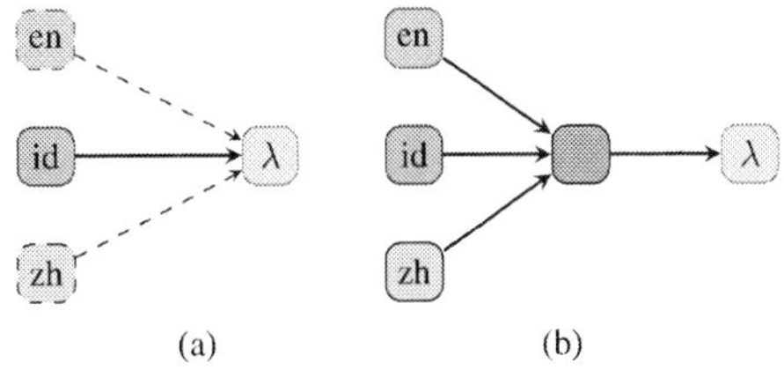

Figure 1: Illustration of the model with three language encoders and a shared logical form decoder (in λ-calculus). Two scenarios are considered: (a) *single-source* and (b) *multi-source* with a combiner module (in grey color).

as by the number of hidden units and the embedding dimension for the source symbol.

In the basic sequence-to-sequence model, the decoder generates each target token in a linear fashion. However, in semantic parsing, such a model ignores the hierarchical structure of logical forms. In order to alleviate this issue, Dong and Lapata (2016) proposed a decoder that generates logical forms in a top-down manner, where they define a "non-terminal" token <n> to indicate subtrees. At each depth in the tree, logical forms are generated sequentially until the end-of-sequence token is output.

Unlike in the single language setting, here we define a single, shared decoder Ψ_{dec} as opposed to one decoder per source language. We augment the parent non-terminal's information $\mathbf{p}$ when computing the decoder state $\mathbf{z}_t$, as follows:

$$\mathbf{z}_t = \Psi_{\text{dec}}(\mathbf{z}_{t-1}, \mathbf{E}_y[\tilde{y}_{t-1}], \mathbf{p}) \qquad (2)$$

where Ψ_{dec} is the LSTM function and $\tilde{y}_{t-1}$ is the previous target symbol.

The attention mechanism (Bahdanau et al., 2015; Luong et al., 2015) computes a time-dependent context vector $\mathbf{c}_t$ (as defined later in Section 3.1 and 3.2), which is subsequently used for computing the probability distribution over the next symbol, as follows:

$$\tilde{\mathbf{z}}_t = \tanh(\mathbf{U}\mathbf{z}_t + \mathbf{V}\mathbf{c}_t) \qquad (3)$$

$$p(y_t|y_{<t}, X) \propto \exp(\mathbf{W}\tilde{\mathbf{z}}_t) \qquad (4)$$

where $\mathbf{U}$, $\mathbf{V}$, and $\mathbf{W}$ are weight matrices. Finally, the model is trained to maximize the following conditional log-likelihood:

$$\mathcal{L}(\theta) = \sum_{(X,Y)\in\mathcal{D}} \sum_{t=1}^{|Y|} \log p(y_t|y_{<t}, X) \qquad (5)$$

where (X, Y) refers to a ground-truth sentence-semantics pair in the training data $\mathcal{D}$.

We use the same formulation above for the encoders and the decoder in both multilingual settings. Each setting differs in terms of: 1) the decoder state initialization, 2) the computation of the context vector $\mathbf{c}_t$, and 3) the training procedure, which are described in the following sections.

3.1 Single-Source Setting

In this setting, the input is a source sentence coming from the n-th language. Figure 1 (a) depicts a scenario where the model is parsing Indonesian input, with English and Chinese being non-active.

The last state of the n-th encoder is used to initialize the first state of the decoder. We may need to first project the encoder vector into a suitable dimension for the decoder, i.e., $\mathbf{z}_0 = \phi_{\text{dec}}^n(\mathbf{h}_{|X|}^n)$, where ϕ_{dec}^n can be an affine transformation. Similarly, we may do so before computing the attention scores, i.e., $\tilde{\mathbf{h}}_k^n = \phi_{\text{att}}^n(\mathbf{h}_k^n)$. Then, we compute the context vector $\mathbf{c}_t^n$ as a weighted sum of the hidden vectors in the n-th encoder:

$$\alpha_{k,t}^n = \frac{\exp(\tilde{\mathbf{h}}_k^n \cdot \mathbf{z}_t)}{\sum_{k'=1}^{|X|} \exp(\tilde{\mathbf{h}}_{k'}^n \cdot \mathbf{z}_t)} \tag{6}$$

$$\mathbf{c}_t^n = \sum_{k=1}^{|X|} \alpha_{k,t}^n \tilde{\mathbf{h}}_k^n \tag{7}$$

We set $\mathbf{c}_t = \mathbf{c}_t^n$ for computing Equation 3. We propose two variants of the model under this setting. In the first version, we define separate weight matrices for each language, i.e., $\{\mathbf{U}^n, \mathbf{V}^n, \mathbf{W}^n\}_{n=1}^N$. In the second version, the three weight matrices are shared across languages, essentially reducing the number of parameters by a factor of N.

The training data consists of the union of sentence-semantics pairs in N languages, where the source sentences are not necessarily parallel. We implement a scheduling mechanism that cycles through all languages during training, one language at a time. Specifically, model parameters are updated after one batch from one language before moving to the next one. Similar to Firat et al. (2016), this mechanism prevents excessive updates from a specific language.

3.2 Multi-Source Setting

In this setting, the input are semantically equivalent sentences in N languages. Figure 1 (b) depicts a scenario where the model is parsing English, Indonesian, and Chinese *simultaneously*. It includes a *combiner* module (denoted by the grey box), which we will explain next.

The decoder state at the first time step is initialized by first combining the N final states from each encoder, i.e., $\mathbf{z}_0 = \phi_{\text{init}}(\mathbf{h}_{|X|}^1, \cdots, \mathbf{h}_{|X|}^N)$, where we implement ϕ_{init} by max-pooling.

We propose two ways of computing $\mathbf{c}_t$ that integrates source-side information from multiple encoders. First, we consider **word-level combination**, where we combine N encoder states at every time step, as follows:

$$\alpha_{k,t}^n = \frac{\exp(\tilde{\mathbf{h}}_k^n \cdot \mathbf{z}_t)}{\sum_{n'=1}^N \sum_{k'=1}^{|X|} \exp(\tilde{\mathbf{h}}_{k'}^{n'} \cdot \mathbf{z}_t)} \tag{8}$$

$$\mathbf{c}_t = \sum_{n=1}^N \sum_{k=1}^{|X|} \alpha_{k,t}^n \tilde{\mathbf{h}}_k^n \tag{9}$$

Alternatively, in **sentence-level combination**, we first compute the context vector for each language in the same way as Equation 6 and 7. Then, we perform a simple concatenation of N context vectors: $\mathbf{c}_t = [\mathbf{c}_t^1; \cdots ; \mathbf{c}_t^N]$.

Unlike the single-source setting, the training data consists of N-way parallel sentence-semantics pairs. That is, each training instance consists of N semantically equivalent sentences and their corresponding logical form.

4 Experiments and Results

4.1 Datasets and Settings

We conduct our experiments on two multilingual benchmark datasets, which we describe below. Both datasets use a meaning representation based on lambda calculus.

The GeoQuery (**GEO**) dataset is a standard benchmark evaluation for semantic parsing. The multilingual version consists of 880 instances of natural language queries related to US geography facts in four languages (English, German, Greek, and Thai) (Jones et al., 2012). We use the standard split which consists of 600 training examples and 280 test examples.

The **ATIS** dataset contains natural language queries to a flight database. The data is split into 4,434 instances for training, 491 for development, and 448 for evaluation, same as Zettlemoyer and Collins (2007). The original version only includes English. In this work, we annotate the corpus in Indonesian and Chinese. The Chinese corpus was annotated (with segmentations) by hiring professional translation service. The Indonesian corpus was annotated by a native Indonesian speaker.

We use the same pre-processing as Dong and Lapata (2016), where entities and numbers are replaced with their type names and unique IDs.[1] English words are stemmed using NLTK (Bird et al., 2009). Each query is paired with its corresponding semantic representation in lambda calculus (Zettlemoyer and Collins, 2005).

In all experiments, following Dong and Lapata (2016), we use a one-layer LSTM with 200-dimensional cells and embeddings. We use a mini-batch size of 20 with RMSProp updates (Tieleman and Hinton, 2012) for a fixed number of epochs, with gradient clipping at 5. Parameters are uniformly initialized at [-0.08,0.08] and regularized using dropout (Srivastava et al., 2014). Input sequences are reversed. See Appendix A for detailed experimental settings.

For each model configuration, all experiments are repeated 3 times with different random seed values, in order to make sure that our findings are reliable. We found empirically that the random seed may affect SEQ2TREE performance. This is especially important due to the relatively small dataset. As previously done in multi-task sequence-to-sequence learning (Luong et al., 2016), we report the average performance for the baseline and our model. The evaluation metric is defined in terms of exact match accuracy with the ground-truth logical forms. See Appendix B for the accuracy of individual runs.

4.2 Results

Table 1 compares the performance of the monolingual sequence-to-tree model (Dong and Lapata, 2016), SINGLE, and our multilingual model, MULTI, with separate and shared output parameters under the single-source setting as described in Section 3.1. On average, both variants of the multilingual model outperform the monolingual model by up to 1.34% average accuracy on GEO. Parameter sharing is shown to be helpful, in particular for GEO. We observe that the average performance increase on ATIS mainly comes from Chinese and Indonesian. We also learn that although including English is often helpful for the other languages, it may affect its individual performance.

Table 2 shows the average performance on

---

[1] See Section 3.6 of (Dong and Lapata, 2016).

	SINGLE	MULTI	
		separate	shared
GEO			
en	84.40	85.00	**85.48**
de	70.24	71.19	**72.86**
el	74.40	75.12	**75.60**
th	72.86	72.26	**73.33**
avg.	75.48	75.89	**76.82**
ATIS			
en	**81.85**	81.40	81.77
id	74.85	74.03	**75.45**
zh	73.66	**75.89**	73.96
avg.	76.79	**77.11**	77.06

Table 1: Single-source parsing results in terms of average accuracy % over 3 runs. Best results are in **bold**.

	RANKING	MULTI	
		word	sentence
GEO			
en+de+el	83.21	85.48	**86.43**
en+de+th	82.02	**86.19**	85.48
en+el+th	82.62	**85.60**	85.24
de+el+th	**79.64**	72.14	76.43
en+de+el+th	82.50	85.48	**86.79**
ATIS			
en+id	82.81	**83.93**	83.78
en+zh	82.81	**82.96**	**82.96**
id+zh	**78.50**	76.79	77.75
en+id+zh	83.11	82.22	**83.85**

Table 2: Multi-source parsing results in terms of average accuracy % over 3 runs. Best results are in **bold**.

multi-source parsing by combining 3 to 4 languages for GEO and 2 to 3 languages for ATIS. For RANKING, we combine the predictions from each language by selecting the one with the highest probability. Indeed, we observe that system combination at the *model* level is able to give better performance on average (up to 4.29% on GEO) than doing so at the *output* level. Combining at the word level and sentence level shows comparable performance on both datasets. It can be seen that the benefit is more apparent when we include English in the system combination.

Regarding comparison to previous monolingual works, we want to highlight that there exist two different versions of the GeoQuery dataset annotated with completely different semantic representations: semantic tree and lambda calculus. As noted in Section 5 of Lu (2014), results obtained from these two versions are not comparable. We use lambda calculus same as Dong and Lapata (2016). Under the multilingual setting, the closest work is Jie and Lu (2014). Nonetheless, they used the semantic tree version of GeoQuery. They eval-

Model	Input	Output
SINGLE (en)	list the airlines with flights to or from ci0	lambda $0 e (and (airline $0) (exists $1 (and (flight $1) (or (from $1 ci0) (to $1 ci0)) (airline $1 $0))))
SINGLE (id)	daftarkan maskapai dengan penerbangan ke atau dari ci0	lambda $0 e (and (airline $0) (exists $1 (and (flight $1) (from $1 ci0) (airline $1 $0))))
SINGLE (zh)	请列出 有 航班 起降 ci0 的 航空 公司	lambda $0 e (and (airline $0) (services $0 ci0))
MULTI	(en+id+zh)	lambda $0 e (exists $1 (and (flight $1) (or (from $1 ci0) (to $1 ci0)) (= (airline:e $1) $0)))
GOLD	(en+id+zh)	lambda $0 e (exists $1 (and (flight $1) (or (from $1 ci0) (to $1 ci0)) (= (airline:e $1) $0)))

Table 3: Example output from monolingual and multilingual models trained on ATIS.

Model	Number of parameters	
	GEO	ATIS
SINGLE/RANKING	3.7×10^6	3.1×10^6
MULTI (single)		
- separate	2.3×10^6	2.1×10^6
- shared	2.0×10^6	1.9×10^6
MULTI (multi)		
- word	2.0×10^6	1.9×10^6
- sentence	2.1×10^6	1.9×10^6

Table 4: Model size

uated extrinsically on a database query task while we use exact match accuracy, so their work is not directly comparable to ours.

5 Analysis

In this section, we report a qualitative analysis of our multilingual model. Table 3 shows example output from the monolingual model, SINGLE, trained on the three languages in ATIS and the multilingual model, MULTI, with sentence-level combination. This example demonstrates a scenario when the multilingual model successfully parses the three input sentences into the correct logical form, whereas the individual models are unable to do so.

Figure 2 shows the alignments produced by MULTI (sentence) when parsing ATIS in the multi-source setting. Each cell in the alignment matrix corresponds to $\alpha_{k,t}^n$ which is computed by Equation 6. Semantically related words are strongly aligned, such as the alignments between *ground* (en), *darat* (id), 地面 (zh) and *ground_transport*. This shows that such correspondences can be jointly learned by our multilingual model.

In Table 4, we summarize the number of parameters in the baseline and our multilingual model. The number of parameters in SINGLE and RANKING is equal to the sum of the number of parameters in their monolingual components. It can be seen that the size of our multilingual model is about 50-60% smaller than that of the baseline.

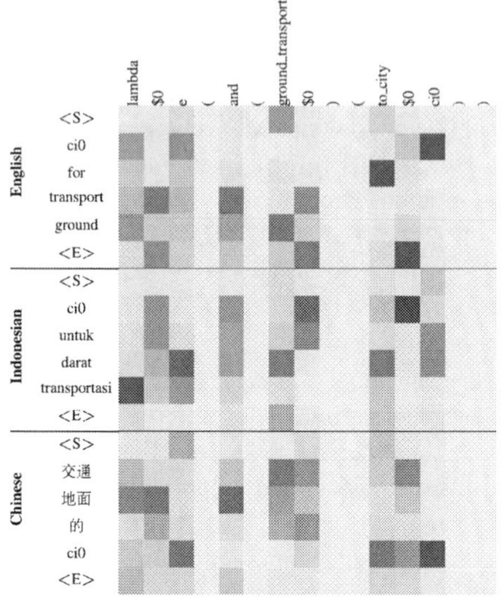

Figure 2: Attention score matrices computed by MULTI when parsing English, Indonesian, and Chinese inputs from ATIS. Darker color represents higher attention score.

6 Conclusion

We have presented a multilingual semantic parser that extends the sequence-to-tree model to a multi-task learning framework. Through experiments, we show that our multilingual model performs better on average than 1) monolingual models in the single-source setting and 2) ensemble ranking in the multi-source setting. We hope that this work will stimulate further research in multilingual semantic parsing. Our code and data is available at http://statnlp.org/research/sp/.

Acknowledgments

We would like to thank Christopher Bryant, Li Dong, and the anonymous reviewers for helpful comments and feedback. This work is supported by MOE Tier 1 grant SUTDT12015008, and is partially supported by project 61472191 under the National Natural Science Foundation of China.

References

Waleed Ammar, George Mulcaire, Miguel Ballesteros, Chris Dyer, and Noah Smith. 2016. Many languages, one parser. *Transactions of the Association for Computational Linguistics* 4:431–444.

Dzmitry Bahdanau, Kyunghyun Cho, and Yoshua Bengio. 2015. Neural machine translation by jointly learning to align and translate. In *Proceedings of ICLR*.

Steven Bird, Ewan Klein, and Edward Loper. 2009. *Natural language processing with Python: analyzing text with the natural language toolkit.* " O'Reilly Media, Inc.".

Daxiang Dong, Hua Wu, Wei He, Dianhai Yu, and Haifeng Wang. 2015. Multi-task learning for multiple language translation. In *Proceedings of ACL*. https://doi.org/10.3115/v1/P15-1166.

Li Dong and Mirella Lapata. 2016. Language to logical form with neural attention. In *Proceedings of ACL*. https://doi.org/10.18653/v1/P16-1004.

Orhan Firat, Kyunghyun Cho, and Yoshua Bengio. 2016. Multi-way, multilingual neural machine translation with a shared attention mechanism. In *Proceedings of NAACL*. https://doi.org/10.18653/v1/N16-1101.

Jiang Guo, Wanxiang Che, David Yarowsky, Haifeng Wang, and Ting Liu. 2016. A representation learning framework for multi-source transfer parsing. In *Proceedings of AAAI*.

Sepp Hochreiter and Jürgen Schmidhuber. 1997. Long short-term memory. *Neural computation* 9(8):1735–1780.

Robin Jia and Percy Liang. 2016. Data recombination for neural semantic parsing. In *Proceedings of ACL*. https://doi.org/10.18653/v1/P16-1002.

Zhanming Jie and Wei Lu. 2014. Multilingual semantic parsing: Parsing multiple languages into semantic representations. In *Proceedings of COLING*. http://aclweb.org/anthology/C14-1122.

Bevan Keeley Jones, Mark Johnson, and Sharon Goldwater. 2012. Semantic parsing with bayesian tree transducers. In *Proceedings of ACL*. http://aclweb.org/anthology/P12-1051.

Tomáš Kočiský, Gábor Melis, Edward Grefenstette, Chris Dyer, Wang Ling, Phil Blunsom, and Karl Moritz Hermann. 2016. Semantic parsing with semi-supervised sequential autoencoders. In *Proceedings of EMNLP*. https://doi.org/10.18653/v1/D16-1116.

Tom Kwiatkowski, Luke Zettlemoyer, Sharon Goldwater, and Mark Steedman. 2010. Inducing probabilistic ccg grammars from logical form with higher-order unification. In *Proceedings of EMNLP*. http://aclweb.org/anthology/D10-1119.

Wei Lu. 2014. Semantic parsing with relaxed hybrid trees. In *Proceedings of EMNLP*. http://aclweb.org/anthology/D14-1137.

Wei Lu, Hwee Tou Ng, Wee Sun Lee, and Luke S Zettlemoyer. 2008. A generative model for parsing natural language to meaning representations. In *Proceedings of EMNLP*. http://aclweb.org/anthology/D08-1082.

Minh-Thang Luong, Quoc V Le, Ilya Sutskever, Oriol Vinyals, and Lukasz Kaiser. 2016. Multi-task sequence to sequence learning. In *Proceedings of ICLR*.

Minh-Thang Luong, Hieu Pham, and Christopher D Manning. 2015. Effective approaches to attention-based neural machine translation. In *Proceedings of EMNLP*. https://doi.org/10.18653/v1/D15-1166.

Nitish Srivastava, Geoffrey E Hinton, Alex Krizhevsky, Ilya Sutskever, and Ruslan Salakhutdinov. 2014. Dropout: a simple way to prevent neural networks from overfitting. *Journal of Machine Learning Research* 15(1):1929–1958.

Raymond Hendy Susanto and Wei Lu. 2017. Semantic parsing with neural hybrid trees. In *Proceedings of AAAI*.

Tijmen Tieleman and Geoffrey Hinton. 2012. Lecture 6.5-rmsprop: Divide the gradient by a running average of its recent magnitude. *COURSERA: Neural networks for machine learning* 4(2).

Yuk Wah Wong and Raymond J Mooney. 2006. Learning for semantic parsing with statistical machine translation. In *Proceedings of NAACL*. http://aclweb.org/anthology/N06-1056.

Luke S Zettlemoyer and Michael Collins. 2005. Learning to map sentences to logical form: Structured classification with probabilistic categorial grammars. In *Proceedings of UAI*.

Luke S Zettlemoyer and Michael Collins. 2007. Online learning of relaxed ccg grammars for parsing to logical form. In *Proceedings of EMNLP-CoNLL*. http://aclweb.org/anthology/D07-1071.

Barret Zoph and Kevin Knight. 2016. Multi-source neural translation. In *Proceedings of NAACL*. https://doi.org/10.18653/v1/N16-1004.

A Hyperparameters

Table 5 lists the number of training epochs and the dropout probability used in the LSTM cell and the hidden layers before the softmax classifiers, which were chosen based on preliminary experiments on a held-out dataset. We use a training schedule where we switch to the next language after training one mini-batch for GEO and 500 for ATIS. For

	SINGLE			MULTI					
					separate			shared	
	1	2	3	1	2	3	1	2	3
GEO									
en	**87.14**	83.57	82.50	85.71	83.93	85.36	85.36	83.93	**87.14**
de	70.00	70.36	70.36	71.79	71.79	70.00	73.57	**73.93**	71.07
el	76.43	72.50	74.29	**77.14**	72.14	76.07	76.43	74.64	75.71
th	72.50	73.57	72.50	72.14	72.14	72.50	72.50	71.07	**76.43**
ATIS									
en	**84.60**	79.24	81.70	82.14	81.03	81.03	82.59	80.36	82.37
id	75.67	74.55	74.33	75.67	72.54	73.88	**76.56**	75.45	74.33
zh	74.33	73.66	72.99	74.11	76.12	**77.46**	75.67	72.54	73.66

Table 6: Single-source parsing results showing the accuracy of the 3 runs. Best results are in **bold**.

	RANKING			MULTI					
					word			sentence	
	1	2	3	1	2	3	1	2	3
GEO									
en+de+el	85.00	82.50	82.14	87.14	84.64	84.64	**87.50**	85.36	86.43
en+de+th	84.29	81.07	80.71	**87.86**	85.00	85.71	85.71	86.43	84.29
en+el+th	84.29	82.14	81.43	**87.50**	84.29	85.00	84.64	85.71	85.36
de+el+th	**80.00**	79.29	79.64	71.07	72.86	72.50	77.86	74.64	76.79
en+de+el+th	83.93	81.79	81.79	85.71	86.07	84.64	**87.50**	86.79	86.07
ATIS									
en+id	83.48	82.14	82.81	83.48	83.48	84.82	85.27	80.58	**85.49**
en+zh	84.60	80.80	83.04	83.26	82.14	83.48	**85.49**	80.13	83.26
id+zh	79.24	78.57	77.68	77.46	78.35	74.55	**80.58**	78.13	74.55
en+id+zh	84.15	81.92	83.26	82.14	81.25	83.26	**85.49**	81.03	85.04

Table 7: Multi-source parsing results showing the accuracy of the 3 runs. Best results are in **bold**.

all multilingual models, we initialize the encoders using the encoder weights learned by the monolingual models. For the multi-source setting, we also initialize the decoder using the first language in the list of the combined languages.

B Additional Experimental Results

In Table 6 and 7, we report the accuracy of the 3 runs for each model and dataset. In both settings, we observe that the best accuracy on both datasets is often achieved by MULTI. This is the same conclusion that we reached when averaging the results over all runs.

	#epochs	dropout (LSTM)	dropout (output layer)
GEO			
SINGLE	90	0.1	0.4
MULTI (single)	340	0.1	0.4
MULTI (multi)	150	0.1	0.4
ATIS			
SINGLE	130	0.3	0.3
MULTI (single)	390	0.3	0.3
MULTI (multi)	250	0.3	0.3

Table 5: Hyperparameter values

Incorporating Uncertainty into Deep Learning for Spoken Language Assessment

Andrey Malinin, Anton Ragni, Kate M. Knill, Mark J. F. Gales
University of Cambridge, Department of Engineering
Trumpington St, Cambridge CB2 1PZ, UK
{am969, ar527, kate.knill, mjfg}@eng.cam.ac.uk

Abstract

There is a growing demand for automatic assessment of spoken English proficiency. These systems need to handle large variations in input data owing to the wide range of candidate skill levels and L1s, and errors from ASR. Some candidates will be a poor match to the training data set, undermining the validity of the predicted grade. For high stakes tests it is essential for such systems not only to grade well, but also to provide a measure of their uncertainty in their predictions, enabling rejection to human graders. Previous work examined Gaussian Process (GP) graders which, though successful, do not scale well with large data sets. Deep Neural Networks (DNN) may also be used to provide uncertainty using Monte-Carlo Dropout (MCD). This paper proposes a novel method to yield uncertainty and compares it to GPs and DNNs with MCD. The proposed approach *explicitly* teaches a DNN to have low uncertainty on training data and high uncertainty on generated artificial data. On experiments conducted on data from the Business Language Testing Service (BULATS), the proposed approach is found to outperform GPs and DNNs with MCD in uncertainty-based rejection whilst achieving comparable grading performance.

1 Introduction

Systems for automatic assessment of spontaneous spoken language proficiency (Fig. 1) are becoming increasingly important to meet the demand for English second language learning. Such systems are able to provide throughput and consistency which are unachievable with human examiners. This is a challenging task. There is a large vari-

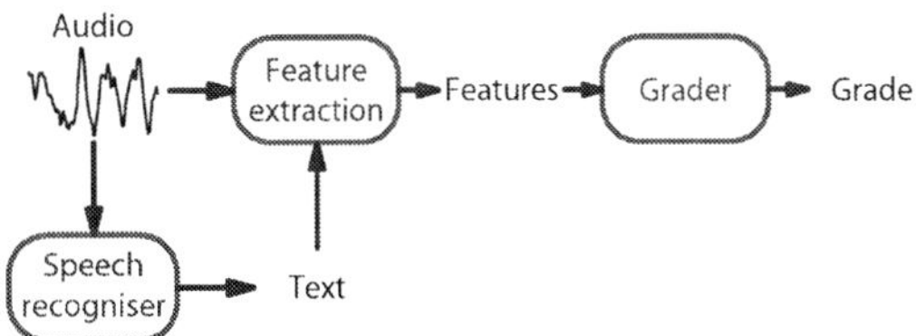

Figure 1: Automatic Assessment System

ation in the quality of spoken English across all proficiency levels. In addition, candidates of the same skill level will have different accents, voices, mispronunciations, and sentence construction errors. All of which are heavily influenced by the candidate's L1 language and compounded by ASR errors. It is therefore impossible in practice to observe all these variants in training. At test time, the predicted grade's validity will decrease the more the candidate is mismatched to the data used to train the system. For deployment of these systems to high-stakes tests the performance on all candidates needs to be consistent and highly correlated with human graders. To achieve this it is important that these systems can detect outlier speakers who need to be examined by, for example, human graders.

Previously, separate models were used to filter out "non-scorable" candidates (Yoon and Xie, 2014; Zechner et al., 2009; Higgins et al., 2011; Xie et al., 2012). However, such models reject candidates based on whether they can be scored at all, rather than an automatic grader's uncertainty [1] in its predictions. It was shown by van Dalen et al. (2015) that Gaussian Process (GP) graders give

---

[1] Uncertainty is used in the sense of the inverse of confidence to be consistent with Gal and Ghahramani (2016) and van Dalen et al. (2015).

Proceedings of the 55th Annual Meeting of the Association for Computational Linguistics (Short Papers), pages 45–50
Vancouver, Canada, July 30 - August 4, 2017. ©2017 Association for Computational Linguistics
https://doi.org/10.18653/v1/P17-2008

state-of-the-art performance for automatic assessment and yield meaningful uncertainty estimates for rejection of candidates. There are, however, computational constraints on training set sizes for GPs. In contrast, Deep Neural Networks (DNNs) are able to scale to large data sets, but lack a native measure of uncertainty. However, Gal and Ghahramani (2016) have shown that Monte-Carlo Dropout (MCD) can be used to derive an uncertainty estimate for a DNN.

Alternatively, a Deep Density Network (DDN), which is a Mixture Density Network (Bishop, 1994) with only one mixture component, may be used to yield a mean and variance corresponding to the predicted grade and the uncertainty in the prediction. Similar to GP and DNNs with MCD, a standard DDN provides an *implicit* modelling of uncertainty in its prediction. This implicit model may not be optimal for the task at hand. Hence, a novel approach to *explicitly* model uncertainty is proposed in which the DDN is trained in a multi-task fashion to model a low variance real data distribution and a high variance artificial data distribution which represents candidates with unseen characteristics.

2 Prediction Uncertainty

The principled method for dealing with uncertainty in statistical modelling is the Bayesian approach, where a conditional posterior distribution over grades, g, given inputs, x, and training data $\mathcal{D} = \{\hat{g}, \hat{x}\}$ is computed by marginalizing over all models:

$$p(g|x, \mathcal{D}) = \int p(g|x, \mathcal{M})p(\mathcal{M}|\mathcal{D})\mathrm{d}\mathcal{M} \quad (1)$$

where $p(\mathcal{M}|\mathcal{D})$ is a prior over a model given the data. Given the posterior, the predictive mean and the variance (uncertainty) can be computed using:

$$\mu_g(x) = \int p(g|x, \mathcal{D})g\mathrm{d}g \quad (2)$$

$$\sigma_g^2(x) = \int p(g|x, \mathcal{D})g^2\mathrm{d}g - \mu_g^2(x) \quad (3)$$

2.1 Gaussian Processes

Eq. 2, 3 can be analytically solved for a class of models called Gaussian Processes (GP) (Rasmussen and Williams, 2006), a powerful nonparametric model for regression. The GP induces a conditional posterior in the form of a normal distribution over grades g given an input x and training data $\mathcal{D}$:

$$p(g|x; \mathcal{D}) = \mathcal{N}(g; \mu_g(x|\mathcal{D}), \sigma_g^2(x|\mathcal{D})) \quad (4)$$

With mean function $\mu_g(x|\mathcal{D})$ and variance function $\sigma_g^2(x|\mathcal{D})$, which is a function of the similarity of an input x to the training data inputs $\hat{x}$, where the similarity metric is defined by a covariance function $k(.,.)$. The nature of GP variance means that the model is uncertain in predictions for inputs far away from the training data, given appropriate choice of $k(.,.)$. Unfortunately, without sparsification approaches, the computational and memory requirements of GPs become prohibitively expensive for large data sets. Furthermore, GPs are known to scale poorly to higher dimensional features (Rasmussen and Williams, 2006).

2.2 Monte-Carlo Dropout

Alternatively, a grader can be constructed using Deep Neural Networks (DNNs) which have a very flexible architecture and scale well to large data sets. DNNs, however, lack a native measure of uncertainty. Uncertainty estimates for DNNs can be computed using a Monte-Carlo ensemble approximation to Eq. 2, 3:

$$\hat{\mu}_g(x) = \frac{1}{N}\sum_{i=1}^{N} f(x; \mathcal{M}^{(i)}) \quad (5)$$

$$\hat{\sigma}_g^2(x) = \frac{1}{N}\sum_{i=1}^{N} \left(f(x; \mathcal{M}^{(i)})\right)^2 - \hat{\mu}_g^2(x) \quad (6)$$

where there are N DNN models in the ensemble, $\mathcal{M}^{(i)}$ is a DNN with a particular architecture and parameters sampled from $p(\mathcal{M}|\mathcal{D})$ using Monte Carlo Dropout (MCD) (Srivastava et al., 2014), and $f(x; \mathcal{M}^{(i)})$ are the DNN predictions. Recent work by Gal and Ghahramani (2016) showed that MCD is equivalent to approximate variational inference in GPs, and can be used to yield meaningful uncertainty estimates for DNNs. Furthermore, Gal and Ghahramani (2016) show that different choices of DNN activation functions correspond to different GP covariance functions. MCD uncertainty assumes that for inputs further from the training data, different subnets will produce increasingly differing outputs, leading to larger variances. Unfortunately, it is difficult to know beforehand which activation functions accomplish this in practice.

3 Deep Density Networks

Instead of relying on a Monte Carlo approximation to Eq. 1, a DNN can be modified to produce a prediction of both a mean and a variance:

$$\mu_g(\boldsymbol{x}) = f_\mu(\boldsymbol{x}; \mathcal{M}) \qquad (7)$$

$$\sigma_g^2(\boldsymbol{x}) = f_{\sigma^2}(\boldsymbol{x}; \mathcal{M}) \qquad (8)$$

parametrising a normal distribution over grades conditioned on the input, similar to a GP. This architecture is a Deep Density Network (DDN), which is a Mixture Density Network (MDN) (Bishop, 1994) with only one mixture component. DDNs are trained by maximizing the likelihood of the training data. The variance of the DDN represents the natural spread of grades at a given input. This is an *implicit* measure of uncertainty, like GP and MCD variance, because it is learned automatically as part of the model. However, this doesn't enforce higher variance further away from training points in DDNs. It is possible to *explic-*

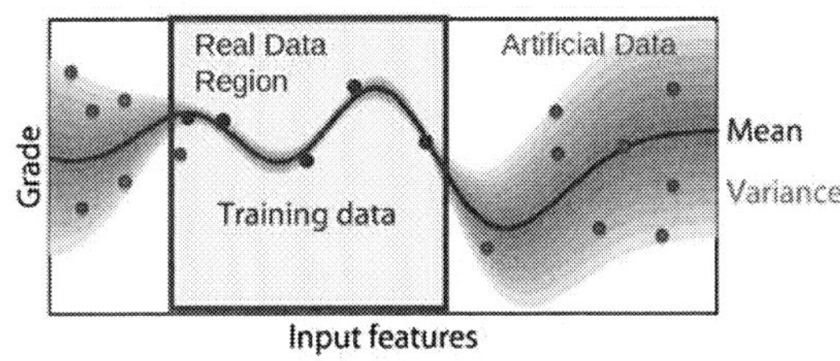

Figure 2: Desired variance characteristic

itly teach a DDN to predict a high or low variance for inputs which are unlike or similar to the training data, respectively (Fig. 2). This requires a novel training procedure. Two normal distributions are constructed: a low-variance real (training) data distribution p_D and a high-variance artificial data distribution p_N, which models data outside the real training data region. The DDN needs to model both distributions in a multi-task (MT) fashion. The loss function for training the DDN with explicitly specified uncertainty is the expectation over the training data of the KL divergence between the distribution it parametrizes and both the real and artificial data distributions:

$$\mathcal{L} = \mathrm{E}_{\hat{\mathbf{x}}}[\mathrm{KL}(p_D||p(g|\hat{\boldsymbol{x}}; \mathcal{M})] + \\ \alpha \cdot \mathrm{E}_{\tilde{\mathbf{x}}}[\mathrm{KL}(p_N||p(g|\tilde{\boldsymbol{x}}; \mathcal{M})] \qquad (9)$$

where α is the multi-task weight.

The DDN with explicit uncertainty is trained in a two stage fashion. First, a standard DDN $\mathcal{M}_0$ is trained, then a DDN $\mathcal{M}$ is instantiated using the parameters of $\mathcal{M}_0$ and trained in a multi-task fashion. The real data distribution p_D is defined by $\mathcal{M}_0$ (Eq. 7, 8). The artificial data distribution p_N is constructed by generating artificial inputs $\tilde{\boldsymbol{x}}$ and the associated mean and variance targets $\mu(\tilde{\boldsymbol{x}}), \sigma^2(\tilde{\boldsymbol{x}})$:

$$p_N = \mathcal{N}(g; f_\mu(\tilde{\boldsymbol{x}}; \mathcal{M}_0), \sigma^2(\tilde{\boldsymbol{x}})) \qquad (10)$$

The predictions of $\mathcal{M}_0$ are used as the targets for $\mu(\tilde{\boldsymbol{x}})$. The target variance $\sigma^2(\tilde{\boldsymbol{x}})$ should depend on the similarity of $\tilde{\boldsymbol{x}}$ to the training data. Here, this variance is modelled by the squared normalized Euclidean distance from the mean of $\hat{\boldsymbol{x}}$, with a diagonal covariance matrix, scaled by a hyperparameter λ. The artificial inputs $\tilde{\boldsymbol{x}}$ need to be different to, but related to the real data $\hat{\boldsymbol{x}}$. Ideally, they should represent candidates with unseen characteristics, such as L1, accent and proficiency. A simple approach to generating $\tilde{\boldsymbol{x}}$ is to use a Factor Analysis (FA) (Murphy, 2012) model trained on $\hat{\boldsymbol{x}}$. The generative model of FA is:

$$\tilde{\boldsymbol{x}} \sim \mathcal{N}(\boldsymbol{W}\boldsymbol{z} + \boldsymbol{\mu}, \gamma\boldsymbol{\Psi}), \, \boldsymbol{z} \sim \mathcal{N}(\boldsymbol{0}, \gamma\boldsymbol{I}) \qquad (11)$$

where $\boldsymbol{W}$ is the loading matrix, $\boldsymbol{\Psi}$ the diagonal residual noise variance, $\boldsymbol{\mu}$ the mean, all derived from $\hat{\boldsymbol{x}}$, and γ is used to control the distance of the generated data from the real training data region. During training the artificial inputs are sampled from the FA model.

4 Experimental Results

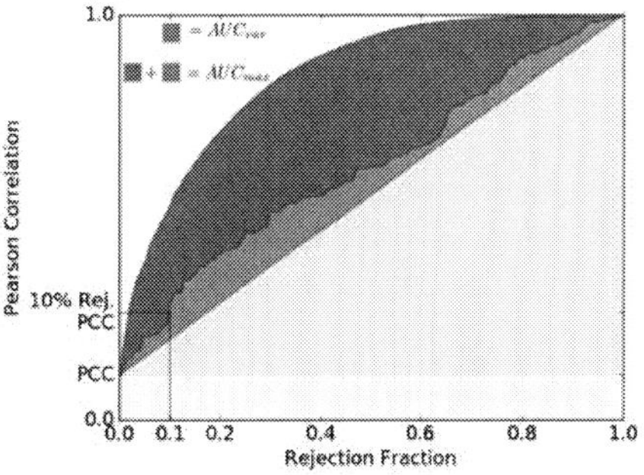

Figure 3: An example Rejection Plot

$$\mathrm{AUC_{RR}} = \frac{\mathrm{AUC_{var}}}{\mathrm{AUC_{max}}} \qquad (12)$$

As previously stated, the operating scenario is to use a model's estimate of the uncertainty in

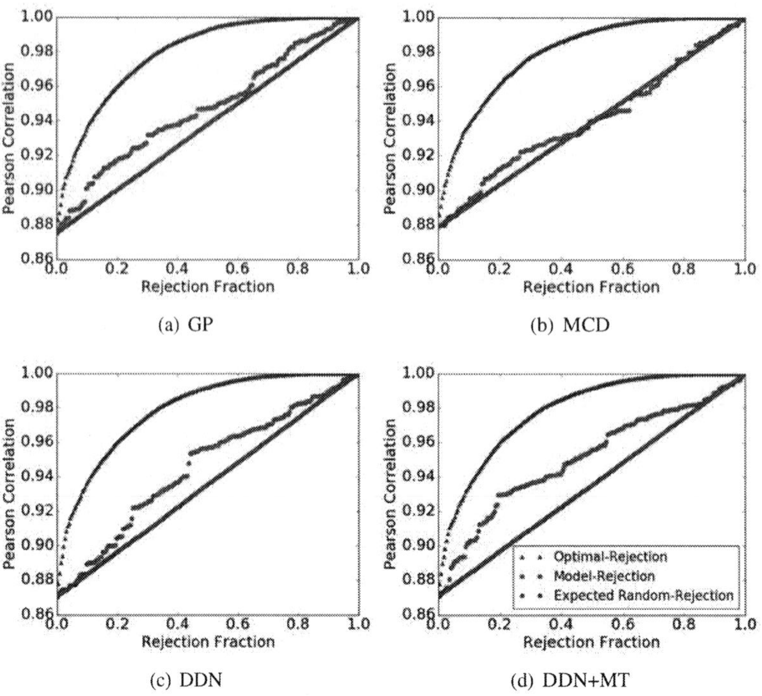

Figure 4: Rejection Plots for models

its prediction to reject candidates to be assessed by human graders for high-stakes tests, maximizing the increase in performance while rejecting the least number of candidates. The rejection process is illustrated using a rejection plot (Fig. 3). As the rejection fraction is increased, model predictions are replaced with human scores in some particular order, increasing overall correlation with human graders. Fig. 3 has 3 curves representing different orderings: expected random rejection, optimal rejection and model rejection. The expected random performance curve is a straight line from the base predictive performance to 1.0, representing rejection in a random order. The optimal rejection curve is constructed by rejecting predictions in order of decreasing mean square error relative to human graders. A rejection curve derived from a model should sit between the random and optimal curves. In this work, model rejection is in order of decreasing predicted variance.

The following metrics are used to assess and compare models: Pearson Correlation Coefficient (PCC) with human graders, the standard performance metric in assessment (Zechner et al., 2009; Higgins et al., 2011); 10% rejection PCC, which illustrates the predictive performance at a partic-

ular operating point, i.e. rejecting 10% of candidates; and Area under a model's rejection curve (AUC) (Fig 3). However, AUC is influenced by the base PCC of a model, making it difficult to compare the rejection performance. Thus, a metric independent of predictive performance is needed. The proposed metric, AUC_{RR} (Eq. 12), is the ratio of the areas under the actual (AUC_{var}) and optimal (AUC_{max}) rejection curves relative to the random rejection curve. Ratios of 1.0 and 0.0 correspond to perfect and random rejection, respectively.

All experiments were done using 33-dimensional pronunciation, fluency and acoustic features derived from audio and ASR transcriptions of responses to questions from the BULATS exam (Chambers and Ingham, 2011). The ASR system has a WER of 32% on a development set. The training and test sets have 4300 and 224 candidates, respectively. Each candidate provided a response to 21 questions, and the features used are aggregated over all 21 questions into a single feature vector. The test data was graded by expert graders at Cambridge English. These experts have inter-grader PCCs in the range 0.95-0.97. Candidates are equally distributed across CEFR grade levels (Europe, 2001).

The input features where whitened by subtracting the mean and dividing by the standard deviation for each dimension computed on all training speakers. The Adam optimizer (Kingma and Ba, 2015), dropout (Srivastava et al., 2014) regularization with a dropout keep probability of 0.6 and an exponentially decaying learning rate are used with decay factor of 0.86 per epoch, batch size 50. All networks have 2 hidden layers with 180 rectified linear units (ReLU) in each layer. DNN and DDN models were implemented in Tensorflow (Abadi et al., 2015). Models were initialized using the Xavier Initializer (Glorot and Bengio, 2010). A validation set of 100 candidates was selected from the training data to tune the model and hyper-parameters. GPs were run using Scikit-Learn (Pedregosa et al., 2011) using a squared exponential covariance function.

Grader	PCC	10% Rej. PCC	AUC	AUC_{RR}
GP	0.876	0.897	0.942	0.233
MCD	0.879	0.892	0.937	0.040
MCD_{tanh}	0.865	0.886	0.938	0.226
DDN	0.871	0.887	0.941	0.230
+MT	0.871	0.902	0.947	0.364

Table 1: Grading and rejection performance

The Gaussian Process grader, GP, is a competitive baseline (Tab. 1). GP variance clearly yields uncertainty which is useful for rejection. A DNN with ReLU activation, MCD, achieves grading performance similar to the GP. However, MCD fails to yield an informative uncertainty for rejection, with performance barely above random. If the tanh activation function, MCD_{tanh}, is used instead, then a DNN is able to provide a meaningful measure of uncertainty using MCD, at the cost of grading performance. It is likely that ReLU activations correspond to a GP covariance function which is not suited for rejection on this data.

The standard DDN has comparable grading performance to the GP and DNNs. AUC_{RR} of the DDN is on par with the GP, but the 10% rejection PCC is lower, indicating that the DDN is not as effective at rejecting the worst outlier candidates. The approach proposed in this work, a DDN trained in a multi-task fashion (DDN+MT), achieves significantly higher rejection performance, resulting in the best AUC_{RR} and 10% rejection PCC, showing its better capability to detect outlier candidates. Note, AUC reflects similar trends to AUC_{RR}, but not

as clearly, which is demonstrated by Fig. 4. The model was found to be insensitive to the choice of hyper-parameters α and γ, but λ needed to be set to produce target noise variances $\sigma^2(\tilde{x})$ larger than data variances $\sigma^2(\hat{x})$.

5 Conclusions and Future Work

A novel method for explicitly training DDNs to yield uncertainty estimates is proposed. A DDN is a density estimator which is trained to model two distributions in a multi-task fashion (1) the low variance (uncertainty) true data distribution and (2) a generated high variance artificial data distribution. The model is trained by minimizing the KL divergence between the DDN and the true data distribution (1) and between the DDN and the artificial data distribution (2). The DDN should assign its prediction of low or high variance (uncertainty) if the input is similar or dissimilar to the true data respectively. The artificial data distribution is given by a factor analysis model trained on the real data. During training the artificial data is sampled from this distribution.

This method outperforms GPs and Monte-Carlo Dropout in uncertainty based rejection for automatic assessment. However, the effect of the nature of artificial data on rejection performance should be further investigated and other data generation methods, such as Variational Auto-Encoders (Kingma and Welling, 2014), and metrics to assess similarity between artificial and real training data should be examined. The proposed approach must also be assessed on other tasks and datasets.

Acknowledgments

This research was funded under the ALTA Institute, University of Cambridge as well as the Engineering and Physical Sciences Research Council. Thanks to Cambridge English, University of Cambridge, for support and access to the BULATS data.

References

Martín Abadi, Ashish Agarwal, Paul Barham, Eugene Brevdo, Zhifeng Chen, Craig Citro, Greg S. Corrado, Andy Davis, Jeffrey Dean, Matthieu Devin, Sanjay Ghemawat, Ian Goodfellow, Andrew Harp, Geoffrey Irving, Michael Isard, Yangqing Jia, Rafal Jozefowicz, Lukasz Kaiser, Manjunath Kudlur, Josh Levenberg, Dan Mané, Rajat Monga, Sherry Moore, Derek Murray, Chris Olah, Mike Schuster, Jonathon Shlens, Benoit Steiner, Ilya Sutskever, Kunal Talwar, Paul Tucker, Vincent Vanhoucke, Vijay Vasudevan, Fernanda Viégas, Oriol Vinyals, Pete Warden, Martin Wattenberg, Martin Wicke, Yuan Yu, and Xiaoqiang Zheng. 2015. TensorFlow: Large-scale machine learning on heterogeneous systems. Software available from tensorflow.org. http://tensorflow.org/.

C. M. Bishop. 1994. Mixture density networks. *Technical Report NCRG 4288, Neural Computing Research Group, Department of Computer Science, Aston University* .

Lucy Chambers and Kate Ingham. 2011. The BULATS online speaking test. *Research Notes* 43:21–25.

Council of Europe. 2001. *Common European framework of reference for languages: Learning, teaching, assessment*. Cambridge, U.K: Press Syndicate of the University of Cambridge.

Yarin Gal and Zoubin Ghahramani. 2016. Dropout as a Bayesian Approximation: Representing Model Uncertainty in Deep Learning. In *Proceedings of the 33rd International Conference on Machine Learning (ICML-16)*.

Xavier Glorot and Yoshua Bengio. 2010. Understanding the difficulty of training deep feedforward neural networks. In *Aistats*. volume 9, pages 249–256.

Derrick Higgins, Xiaoming Xi, Klaus Zechner, and David Williamson. 2011. A three-stage approach to the automated scoring of spontaneous spoken responses. *Computer Speech and Language* 25(2):282–306.

Diederik P. Kingma and Jimmy Ba. 2015. Adam: A Method for Stochastic Optimization. In *Proceedings of the 3rd International Conference on Learning Representations (ICLR)*.

Diederik P. Kingma and Max Welling. 2014. Auto-encoding variational bayes. In *Proceedings of the 2nd International Conference on Learning Representations (ICLR)*.

Kevin P. Murphy. 2012. *Machine Learning*. The MIT Press.

F. Pedregosa, G. Varoquaux, A. Gramfort, V. Michel, B. Thirion, O. Grisel, M. Blondel, P. Prettenhofer, R. Weiss, V. Dubourg, J. Vanderplas, A. Passos, D. Cournapeau, M. Brucher, M. Perrot, and E. Duchesnay. 2011. Scikit-learn: Machine learning in Python. *Journal of Machine Learning Research* 12:2825–2830.

Carl Edward Rasmussen and Christopher K. I. Williams. 2006. *Gaussian Processes for Machine Learning*. MIT Press.

Nitish Srivastava, Geoffrey E Hinton, Alex Krizhevsky, Ilya Sutskever, and Ruslan Salakhutdinov. 2014. Dropout: a simple way to prevent neural networks from overfitting. *Journal of Machine Learning Research* 15(1):1929–1958.

Rogier C. van Dalen, Kate M. Knill, and Mark J. F. Gales. 2015. Automatically Grading Learners' English Using a Gaussian Process. In *Proceedings of the ISCA Workshop on Speech and Language Technology for Education (SLaTE)*.

Shasha Xie, Keelan Evanini, and Klaus Zechner. 2012. Exploring Content Features for Automated Speech Scoring. In *Proceedings of the 2012 Conference of the North American Chapter of the Association for Computational Linguistics: Human Language Technologies (NAACL-HLT)*.

Su-Youn Yoon and Shasha Xie. 2014. Similarity-Based Non-Scorable Response Detection for Automated Speech Scoring. In *Proceedings of the Ninth Workshop on Innovative Use of NLP for Building Educational Applications*.

Klaus Zechner, Derrick Higgins, Xiaoming Xi, and David M. Williamson. 2009. Automatic scoring of non-native spontaneous speech in tests of spoken english. *Speech Communication* 51(10):883–895. Spoken Language Technology for Education Spoken Language.

Incorporating Dialectal Variability
for Socially Equitable Language Identification

David Jurgens
Stanford University

Yulia Tsvetkov
Stanford University

Dan Jurafsky
Stanford University

{jurgens,tsvetkov,jurafsky}@stanford.edu

Abstract

Language identification (LID) is a critical first step for processing multilingual text. Yet most LID systems are not designed to handle the linguistic diversity of global platforms like Twitter, where local dialects and rampant code-switching lead language classifiers to systematically miss minority dialect speakers and multilingual speakers. We propose a new dataset and a character-based sequence-to-sequence model for LID designed to support dialectal and multilingual language varieties. Our model achieves state-of-the-art performance on multiple LID benchmarks. Furthermore, in a case study using Twitter for health tracking, our method substantially increases the availability of texts written by underrepresented populations, enabling the development of "socially inclusive" NLP tools.

1 Introduction

Language identification (LID) is an essential first step for NLP on multilingual text. In global settings like Twitter, this text is written by authors from diverse linguistic backgrounds, who may communicate with regional dialects (Gonçalves and Sánchez, 2014) or even include parallel translations in the same message to address different audiences (Ling et al., 2013, 2016). Such dialectal variation is frequent in all languages and even macro-dialects such as American and British English are composed of local dialects that vary across city and socioeconomic development level (Labov, 1964; Orton et al., 1998). Yet current systems for broad-coverage LID—trained on dozens of languages—have largely leveraged European-centric corpora and not taken into account demo-

1. @username R u a wizard or wat gan sef: in d mornin - u tweet, afternoon - u tweet, nyt gan u dey tweet. beta get ur IT placement wiv twitter
2. Be the lord lantern jaysus me heart after that match!!!
3. Aku hanya mengagumimu dari jauh sekarang . RDK ({}) * last tweet about you -_- , maybe

Figure 1: Challenges for socially-equitable LID in Twitter include dialectal text, shown from Nigeria (#1) and Ireland (#2), and multilingual text (Indonesian and English) in #3.

graphic and dialectal variation. As a result, these systems systematically misclassify texts from populations with millions of speakers whose local speech differs from the majority dialects (Hovy and Spruit, 2016; Blodgett et al., 2016).

Multiple systems have been proposed for broad-coverage LID at the global level (McCandless, 2010; Lui and Baldwin, 2012; Brown, 2014; Jaech et al., 2016). However, only a handful of techniques have addressed the challenge of *linguistic variability* of global data, such as the dialectal variability and multilingual text seen in Figure 1. These techniques have typically focused only on limited aspects of variability, e.g., individual dialects like African American Vernacular English (Blodgett et al., 2016), online speech (Nguyen and Doğruöz, 2013), similar languages (Bergsma et al., 2012; Zampieri et al., 2014a), or word-level code switching (Solorio et al., 2014; Rijhwani et al., 2017).

In this work, our goal is to devise a *socially equitable* LID, that will enable a massively multilingual, broad-coverage identification of populations speaking underrepresented dialects, multilingual messages, and other linguistic varieties. We first construct a large-scale dataset of Twitter posts across the world (§2). Then, we introduce an LID system, EQUILID, that produces per-token language assignments and obtains state-of-the-art performance on four LID tasks (§3), outperforming broad-coverage LID benchmarks by

51

Proceedings of the 55th Annual Meeting of the Association for Computational Linguistics (Short Papers), pages 51–57
Vancouver, Canada, July 30 - August 4, 2017. ©2017 Association for Computational Linguistics
https://doi.org/10.18653/v1/P17-2009

up to 300%. Finally, we present a case study on using Twitter for health monitoring and show that (1) current widely-used systems suffer from lower recall rates for texts from developing countries, and (2) our system substantially reduces this disparity and enables socially-equitable LID.

2 Curating Socially-Representative Text

Despite known linguistic variation in languages, current broad-coverage LID systems are trained primarily on European-centric sources (e.g., Lui and Baldwin, 2014), often due to data availability. Further, even when training incorporates seemingly-global texts from Wikipedia, their authors are still primarily from highly-developed countries (Graham et al., 2014). This latent bias can significantly affect downstream applications (as we later show in §4), since language ID is often assumed to be a solved problem (McNamee, 2005) and most studies employ off-the-shelf LID systems without considering how they were trained.

We aim to create a socially-representative corpus for LID that captures the variation within a language, such as orthography, dialect, formality, topic, and spelling. Motivated by the recent language survey of Twitter (Trampus, 2016), we next describe how we construct this corpus for 70 languages along three dimensions: geography, social and topical diversity, and multilinguality.

Geographic Diversity We create a large-scale dataset of geographically-diverse text by bootstrapping with a *people-centric* approach (Bamman, 2015) that treats location and languages-spoken as demographic attributes to be inferred for authors. By inferring both for Twitter users and then collecting documents from monolingual users, we ensure that we capture regional variation in a language, rather than focusing on a particular aspect of linguistic variety.

Individuals' locations are inferred using the method of Compton et al. (2014) as implemented by Jurgens et al. (2015). The method first identifies the individuals who have reliable ground truth locations from geotagged tweets and then infers the locations of other individuals as the geographic center of their friends' locations, iteratively applying this inference method to the whole social network. The method is accurate to within tens of kilometers on urban and rural users (Johnson et al., 2017), which is sufficient for the city-level analysis we use here. We use a network of 2.3B edges

from reciprocal mentions to locate 132M users.

To identify monolingual users, we classify multiple tweets by the same individual and consider an author monolingual if they had at least 20 tweets and 95% were labeled with one language ℓ. All tweets by that author are then treated as being ℓ. We use this relabeling process to automatically identify misclassified tweets, which when aggregated geographically, can potentially capture regional dialects and topics.[1] We construct separate sets of monolinguals using langid.py and CLD2 as classifiers to mitigate the biases of each.

Social and Topical Diversity Authors modulate their writing style for different social registers (Eisenstein, 2015; Tatman, 2015). Therefore, we include corpora from different levels of formality across a wide range of topics. Texts were gathered for all of the 70 languages from (1) Wikipedia articles and their more informal Talk pages, (2) Bible and Quran translations (3) JRC-Acquis (Steinberger et al., 2006), a collection of European legislation, (4) the UN Declaration of Human Rights, (5) the Watchtower online magazines, (6) the 2014 and 2015 iterations of the Distinguishing Similar Languages shared task (Zampieri et al., 2014b, 2015), and (7) the Twitter70 dataset (Trampus, 2016). We also include single-language corpora drawn from slang websites (e.g., Urban Dictionary) and the African American Vernacular English data from Blodgett et al. (2016). For all sources, we extract instances sequentially by aggregating sentences up to 140 characters.

Multilingual Diversity Authors are known to generate multilingual texts on Twitter (Ling et al., 2013, 2014), with Rijhwani et al. (2017) estimating that 3.5% of tweets are code-switched. To capture the potential diversity in multilingual documents, we perform data augmentation to synthetically construct multilingual documents of tweet length by (1) sampling texts for two languages from arbitrary sources, (2) with 50% chance for each, truncating a text at the first occurrence of phrasal punctuation, and (3) concatenating the two texts together and adding it to the dataset (if $\leq$ 140 characters). We create only sentence-level or phrase-level code-switching rather than word-level switches to avoid classifier ambiguity for loan words, which is known to be a significant challenge (Çetinoğlu et al., 2016).

---

[1] A manual analysis of 500 tweets confirmed that nearly all cases (98.6%) where the classifier's label differed from the author's inferred language were misclassifications.

Corpus Summary The geographically-diverse corpus was constructed from two Twitter datasets: 1.3B tweets drawn from a 10% sample of all tweets from March 2014 and 14.2M tweets drawn from 1% sample of all geotagged tweets from November 2016. Ultimately, we collected 97.8M tweets from 1.5M users across 197 countries and in 53 languages. After identifying monolingual authors in the dataset, 9.4% of the instances (9.1M) were labeled by CLD2 or langid.py with a different language than that spoken by its author; since nearly all are misclassifications, we view these posts as valuable data to correct systematic bias.

A total of 258M instances were collected for the topically and socially-diverse corpora. Multilingual instances were created by sampling text from all language pairs; a total of 3.2M synthetic instances were created. Full details are reported in Supplementary Material.

3 Equitable LID Classifier

We introduce EQUILID, and evaluate it on monolingual and multilingual tweet-length text.

Model Character-based neural network architectures are particularly suitable for LID, as they facilitate modeling nuanced orthographic and phonological properties of languages (Jaech et al., 2016; Samih et al., 2016), e.g., capturing regular morpheme occurrences within the words of a language. Further, character-based methods significantly reduce the model complexity compared to word-based methods; the latter require separate neural representations for each word form and therefore are prohibitive in multilingual environments that easily contain tens of millions of unique words. We use an encoder–decoder architecture (Cho et al., 2014; Sutskever et al., 2014) with an attention mechanism (Bahdanau et al., 2015). The encoder and the decoder are 3-layer recurrent neural networks with 512 gated recurrent units (Chung et al., 2014). The model is trained to tokenize character sequence input based on white space and output a sequence with each token's language, with extra token types for punctuation, hashtags, and user mentions.

Setup The data from our socially-representative corpus (§2) was split into training, development, and test sets (80%/10%/10%, respectively), separately partitioning the data from each source (e.g., Wikipedia). Due to different sizes, we imposed a maximum of 50K instances per source and language to reduce training bias. A total 52.3M instances were used for the final datasets. Multilingual instances were generated from texts within their respective split to prevent test-train leakage. For the Twitter70 dataset, we use identical training, development, and test splits as Jaech et al. (2016). The same trained model is used for all evaluations. All parameter optimization was performed on the development set using adadelta (Zeiler, 2012) with mini-batches of size 64 to train the models. The model was trained for 2.7M steps, which is roughly three epochs.

Comparison Systems We compare against two broad-coverage LID systems, langid.py (Lui and Baldwin, 2012) and CLD2 (McCandless, 2010), both of which have been widely used for Twitter within in the NLP community. CLD2 is trained on web page text, while langid.py was trained on newswire, JRC-Acquis, web pages, and Wikipedia. As neither was designed for Twitter, we preprocess text to remove user mentions, hashtags, and URLs for a more fair comparison. For multilingual documents, we substitute langid.py (Lui and Baldwin, 2012) with its extension, Polyglot, described in Lui et al. (2014) and designed for that particular task.

We also include the results reported in Jaech et al. (2016), who trained separate models for two benchmarks used here. Their architecture uses a convolutional network to transform each input word into a vector using its characters and then feed the word vectors to an LSTM encoder that decodes to per-word soft-max distributions over languages. These word-language distributions are averaged to identify the most-probable language for the input text. In contrast, our architecture uses only character-based representations and produces per-token language assignments.

Benchmarks We test the monolingual setting with three datasets: (1) the test portion of the geographically-diverse corpus from §2, which covers 53 languages (2) the test portion of the Twitter70 dataset, which covers 70 languages and (3) the TweetLID shared task (Zubiaga et al., 2016), which covers 6 languages. The TweetLID data includes Galician, which is not one of the 70 languages we include due to its relative infrequency. Therefore, we report results only on the non-Galician portions of the data. Multilingual LID is tested using the test data portion of the

| | Geo.-Diverse Tweets | | Tweet 70 | | TweetLID† | Multilingual Tweets | |
System	Macro-F1	Micro-F1	Macro-F1	Micro-F1	Macro-F1	Macro-F1	Micro-F1
langid.py°	0.234	0.960	0.378	0.769	0.580	0.302	0.240
CLD2	0.217	0.930	0.497	0.741	0.544	0.360	0.629
Jaech et al. (2016)‡			0.912		0.787		
EQUILID	**0.598**	**0.982**	**0.920**	**0.905**	**0.796**	**0.886**	**0.853**

Table 1: Results on the four benchmarks. ‡ results reported in Jaech et al. (2016) are separate models optimized for each benchmark † excludes Galician. ° For multilingual tweets, we use the extension to langid.py described in Lui et al. (2014).

synthetically-constructed multilingual data from 70 languages. Models are evaluated using macro-averaged and micro-averaged F1. Macro-averaged F1 denotes the average F1 for each language, independent of how many instances were seen for that language. Micro-averaged F1 denotes the F1 measured from all instances and is sensitive to the skew in the distribution of languages in the dataset. **Results** EQUILID attains state-of-the-art performance over the other broad-coverage LID systems on all benchmarks. We attribute this increase to more representative training data; indeed, Jaech et al. (2016) reported langid.py obtains a substantially higher F1 of 0.879 when retrained only on Twitter70 data, underscoring the fact that broad-coverage systems are typically not trained on data as linguistically diverse as seen in social media. Despite being trained for general-purpose, EQUILID also outperformed the benchmark-optimized models of Jaech et al. (2016).

In the multilingual setting, EQUILID substantially outperforms both Polyglot and CLD2, with over a 300% increase in Macro-F1 over the former. Further, because our model can also identify the spans in each language, we view its performance as an important step towards an all-languages solution for detecting sentence and phrase-level switching between languages. Indeed, in the Twitter70 dataset, EQUILID found roughly 5% of the test data are unmarked instances of code-switching, one of which is the third example in Figure 1.

Error Analysis To identify main sources of classification errors, we manually analyzed the outputs of EQUILID on the test set of Twitter70. The dataset contains 9,572 test instances, 90.5% of which were classified correctly by our system; we discuss below sources of errors in the remaining 909 misclassified instances.

Classification of closely related languages with overlapping vocabularies written in a same script is the biggest source of errors (374 misclassified instances, 41.1% of all errors). Slavic languages

are the most challenging, with 177 Bosnian and 65 Slovenian tweets classified as Croatian. This is unsurprising, considering that even for a human annotator this task is challenging (or impossible). For example, a misclassified Bosnian tweet *Sočni čokoladni biskvit recept* ("juicy chocolate biscuit recipe") would be the same in Croatian. Indo-Iranian languages contribute 39 errors, with Bengali, Marathi, Nepali, Punjabi, and Urdu tweets classified as Hindi. Among Germanic languages, Danish, Norwegian, and Swedish are frequently confused, contributing 22 errors.

Another major source of errors is due to transliteration and code switching with English: 328 messages in Hindi, Urdu, Tagalog, Telugu, and Punjabi were classified as English, contributing 36.1% of errors. A Hindi-labeled tweet *dost tha or rahega ... dont wory ... but dherya rakhe* ("he was and will remain a friend ... don't worry ... but have faith") is a characteristic example, misclassified by our system as English. Reducing these types of errors is currently difficult due to the lack of transliterated examples for these languages.

4 Case Study: Health Monitoring

We conclude with a real-world case study on using Twitter posts as a real-time source of information for tracking health and well-being trends (Paul and Dredze, 2011; Achrekar et al., 2011; Aramaki et al., 2011). This information is especially critical for regions where local authorities may not have sufficient resources to identify trends otherwise. Commonly, trend-tracking approaches first apply language identification to select language-specific content, and then apply sophisticated NLP techniques to identify content related to their target phenomena, e.g., distinguishing a flu comment from a hangover-related one. This setting is where socially-inclusive LID systems can make real, practical impact: LID systems that effectively classify languages of underrepresented dialects can substantially increase the recall of data for trend-tracking approaches, and thus help reveal dangerous trends in infectious diseases in the areas that need it most.

Language varieties are associated, among other factors, with social class (Labov, 1964; Ash, 2002) and ethnic identity (Rose, 2006; Mendoza-Denton, 1997; Dubois and Horvath, 1998). As a case study, we evaluate the efficacy of LID systems in identifying English tweets containing health lexicons, across regions with varying Human Development Index (HDI).[2] We compare EQUILID against langid.py and CLD2.

Setup A list of health-related terms was compiled from lexicons for influenza (Lamb et al., 2013); psychological well-being (Smith et al., 2016; Preoţiuc-Pietro et al., 2015); and temporal orientation lexica correlated with age, gender and personality traits (Park et al., 2016). We incorporate the 100 highest-weighted alphanumeric terms from each lexicon, for a total of 385 unique terms.

To analyze the possible effect of regional language, we selected 25 countries with English-speaking populations and constructed 62 bounding boxes for major cities therein for study (listed in Supplementary Material). Using the Gnip API, a total of 984K tweets were collected during January 2016 which used at least one term and were authored within one of the bounding boxes. As these tweets are required to contain domain-specific terms, the vast majority are English.[3] We therefore measure each system's performance according to what percent of these tweets they classify as English, which estimates their Recall.

Results To understand how Human Development Index relates to LID performance, we train a Logit Regression to predict whether a tweet with one of the target terms will be recognized as English according to the HDI of the tweet's origin country. Figure 2 reveals increasing disparity in LID accuracy for developing countries by the two baseline models. In contrast, EQUILID outperforms both systems at all levels of HDI and provides 30% more observations for countries with the lowest development levels. This performance improvement is increasingly critical in the global environment as more English text is generated from populous developing countries such as Nigeria (HDI

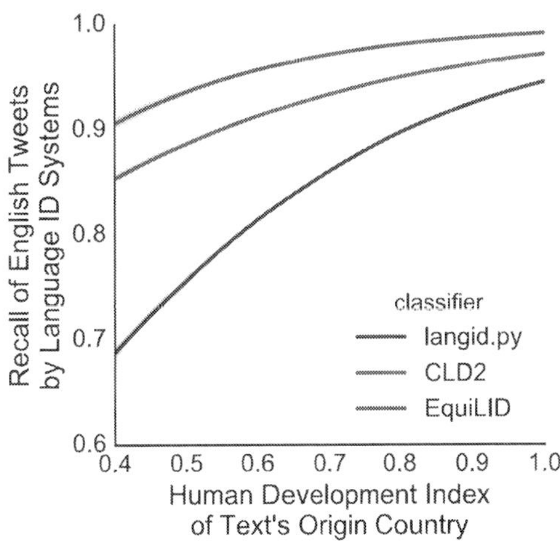

Figure 2: Estimated recall of tweets with health-related terms according to a logit regression on the Human Development Index of the tweet's origin country; bands show 95% confidence interval.

0.527) and India (HDI 0.624), which have tens of millions of anglophones each. EQUILID provides a 23.9% and 17.4% improvement in recall of English tweets for each country, respectively. This study corroborates our hypothesis that socially-equitable training corpora are an essential first step towards socially-equitable NLP.

5 Conclusion

Globally-spoken languages often vary in how they are spoken according to regional dialects, topics, or sociolinguistic factors. However, most LID systems are not designed and trained for this linguistic diversity, which has downstream consequences for what types of text are considered a part of the language. In this work, we introduce a socially-equitable LID system, EQUILID, built by (1) creating a dataset representative of the types of diversity within languages and (2) explicitly modeling multilingual and codes-switched communication for arbitrary language pairs. We demonstrate that EQUILID significantly outperforms current broad-coverage LID systems and, in a real-world case study on tracking health-related content, show that EQUILID substantially reduces the LID performance disparity between developing and developed countries. Our work continues a recent emphasis on NLP for social good by ensuring NLP tools fully represent all people. The EQUILID system is publicly available at `https://github.com/davidjurgens/equilid` and data is available upon request.

---

[2]HDI is a composite of life expectancy, education, and income per capita indicators, used to rank countries into tiers of human development.

[3]A manual analysis of a random sample of 1000 tweets showed that 99.4% were in English.

Acknowledgments

We thank the anonymous reviewers, the Stanford Data Science Initiative, and Twitter and Gnip for providing access to part of data used in this study. This work was supported by the National Science Foundation through awards IIS-1514268, IIS-1159679, and IIS-1526745.

References

Harshavardhan Achrekar, Avinash Gandhe, Ross Lazarus, Ssu-Hsin Yu, and Benyuan Liu. 2011. Predicting flu trends using Twitter data. In *Proc. IEEE Computer Communications Workshops*. pages 702–707.

Eiji Aramaki, Sachiko Maskawa, and Mizuki Morita. 2011. Twitter catches the flu: detecting influenza epidemics using Twitter. In *Proc. EMNLP*. pages 1568–1576.

Sharon Ash. 2002. Social class. *The handbook of language variation and change* 24:402.

Dzmitry Bahdanau, Kyunghyun Cho, and Yoshua Bengio. 2015. Neural machine translation by jointly learning to align and translate. In *Proc. ICLR*.

David Bamman. 2015. *People-Centric Natural Language Processing*. Ph.D. thesis, Carnegie Mellon University.

Shane Bergsma, Paul McNamee, Mossaab Bagdouri, Clayton Fink, and Theresa Wilson. 2012. Language identification for creating language-specific Twitter collections. In *Proc. of the Second Workshop on Language in Social Media*. pages 65–74.

Su Lin Blodgett, Lisa Green, and Brendan O'Connor. 2016. Demographic dialectal variation in social media: A case study of African-American English. In *Proc. EMNLP*.

Ralf D Brown. 2014. Non-linear mapping for improved identification of 1300+ languages. In *Proc. EMNLP*. pages 627–632.

Özlem Çetinoğlu, Sarah Schulz, and Ngoc Thang Vu. 2016. Challenges of computational processing of code-switching. In *Proc. of the Second Workshop on Computational Approaches to Code Switching*.

Kyunghyun Cho, Bart van Merrienboer, Caglar Gulcehre, Dzmitry Bahdanau, Fethi Bougares, Holger Schwenk, and Yoshua Bengio. 2014. Learning phrase representations using RNN encoder–decoder for statistical machine translation. In *Proc. EMNLP*.

Junyoung Chung, Caglar Gulcehre, KyungHyun Cho, and Yoshua Bengio. 2014. Empirical evaluation of gated recurrent neural networks on sequence modeling. In *Proc. NIPS Deep Learning workshop*.

Ryan Compton, David Jurgens, and David Allen. 2014. Geotagging one hundred million twitter accounts with total variation minimization. In *Big Data (Big Data), 2014 IEEE International Conference on*. IEEE, pages 393–401.

Sylvie Dubois and Barbara M Horvath. 1998. From accent to marker in Cajun English: A study of dialect formation in progress. *English World-Wide* 19(2):161–188.

Jacob Eisenstein. 2015. Systematic patterning in phonologically-motivated orthographic variation. *Journal of Sociolinguistics* 19(2):161–188.

Bruno Gonçalves and David Sánchez. 2014. Crowdsourcing dialect characterization through Twitter. *PloS one* 9(11):e112074.

Mark Graham, Bernie Hogan, Ralph K Straumann, and Ahmed Medhat. 2014. Uneven geographies of user-generated information: patterns of increasing informational poverty. *Annals of the Association of American Geographers* 104(4):746–764.

Dirk Hovy and Shannon L Spruit. 2016. The social impact of natural language processing. In *Proc. ACL*. pages 591–598.

Aaron Jaech, George Mulcaire, Shobhit Hathi, Mari Ostendorf, and Noah A Smith. 2016. Hierarchical character-word models for language identification. In *Proc. of the 2nd Workshop on Computational Approaches to Code Switching*.

I. Johnson, C. McMahon, J. Schning, and B. Hecht. 2017. The effect of population and "structural" biases on social media-based algorithms – a case study in geolocation inference across the urban-rural spectrum. In *Proc. CHI*.

David Jurgens, Tyler Finnethy, James McCorriston, Yi Tian Xu, and Derek Ruths. 2015. Geolocation prediction in twitter using social networks: A critical analysis and review of current practice. In *Proc. ICWSM*.

William Labov. 1964. *The social stratification of English in New York City*. Ph.D. thesis, Columbia university.

Alex Lamb, Michael J Paul, and Mark Dredze. 2013. Separating fact from fear: Tracking flu infections on Twitter. In *Proc. HLT-NAACL*. pages 789–795.

Wang Ling, Luis Marujo, Chris Dyer, Alan Black, and Isabel Trancoso. 2014. Crowdsourcing high-quality parallel data extraction from Twitter. In *Proc. WMT*.

Wang Ling, Luís Marujo, Chris Dyer, Alan W Black, and Isabel Trancoso. 2016. Mining parallel corpora from Sina Weibo and Twitter. *Computational Linguistics* .

Wang Ling, Guang Xiang, Chris Dyer, Alan W Black, and Isabel Trancoso. 2013. Microblogs as parallel corpora. In *Proc. ACL*. pages 176–186.

Marco Lui and Timothy Baldwin. 2012. langid.py: An off-the-shelf language identification tool. In *Proc. ACL (system demonstrations)*. pages 25–30.

Marco Lui and Timothy Baldwin. 2014. Accurate language identification of Twitter messages. In *Proc. of the 5th Workshop on Language Analysis for Social Media*. pages 17–25.

Marco Lui, Jey Han Lau, and Timothy Baldwin. 2014. Automatic detection and language identification of multilingual documents. *TACL* 2:27–40.

Michael McCandless. 2010. Accuracy and performance of Google's compact language detector. Blog post.

Paul McNamee. 2005. Language identification: a solved problem suitable for undergraduate instruction. *Journal of Computing Sciences in Colleges* 20(3):94–101.

Norma Catalina Mendoza-Denton. 1997. *Chicana/Mexicana identity and linguistic variation: An ethnographic and sociolinguistic study of gang affiliation in an urban high school*. Ph.D. thesis, Stanford University.

Dong-Phuong Nguyen and A Seza Doğruöz. 2013. Word level language identification in online multilingual communication. In *Proc. EMNLP*. pages 857–862.

Harold Orton, Stewart Sanderson, and John Widdowson. 1998. *The linguistic atlas of England*. Psychology Press.

Gregory Park, H Andrew Schwartz, Maarten Sap, Margaret L Kern, Evan Weingarten, Johannes C Eichstaedt, Jonah Berger, David J Stillwell, Michal Kosinski, Lyle H Ungar, et al. 2016. Living in the past, present, and future: Measuring temporal orientation with language. *Journal of personality* .

Michael J Paul and Mark Dredze. 2011. You are what you tweet: Analyzing Twitter for public health. In *Proc. ICWSM* .

Daniel Preoţiuc-Pietro, Svitlana Volkova, Vasileios Lampos, Yoram Bachrach, and Nikolaos Aletras. 2015. Studying user income through language, behaviour and affect in social media. *PloS one* 10(9):e0138717.

Shruti Rijhwani, Royal Sequiera, Monojit Choudhury, Kalika Bali, and Chandra Sekhar Maddila. 2017. Estimating code-switching on twitter with a novel generalized word-level language detection technique. In *Proc. ACL*.

Mary Aleene Rose. 2006. *Language, place and identity in later life*. Stanford University.

Younes Samih, Suraj Maharjan, Mohammed Attia, Laura Kallmeyer, and Thamar Solorio. 2016. Multilingual code-switching identification via LSTM recurrent neural networks. In *Proc. of the 2nd Workshop on Computational Approaches to Code Switching*.

Laura K. Smith, Salvatore Giorgi, Rishi Solanki, Johannes C. Eichstaedt, H. Andrew Schwartz, Muhammad Abdul-Mageed, Anneke Buffone, and Lyle H. Ungar. 2016. Does 'well-being' translate on Twitter? In *Proc. EMNLP*.

Thamar Solorio, Elizabeth Blair, Suraj Maharjan, Steven Bethard, Mona Diab, Mahmoud Gohneim, Abdelati Hawwari, Fahad AlGhamdi, Julia Hirschberg, Alison Chang, and Pascale Fung. 2014. Overview for the first shared task on language identification in code-switched data. In *Proc. of the First Workshop on Computational Approaches to Code Switching*. pages 62–72.

Ralf Steinberger, Bruno Pouliquen, Anna Widiger, Camelia Ignat, Tomaz Erjavec, Dan Tufis, and Dániel Varga. 2006. The jrc-acquis: A multilingual aligned parallel corpus with 20+ languages. *arXiv preprint cs/0609058* .

Ilya Sutskever, Oriol Vinyals, and Quoc VV Le. 2014. Sequence to sequence learning with neural networks. In *Proc. NIPS*.

Rachael Tatman. 2015. # go awn: Sociophonetic variation in variant spellings on twitter. *Working Papers of the Linguistics Circle* 25(2):97–108.

Mitja Trampus. 2016. Evaluating language identification performance. Blog post. Https://blog.twitter.com/2015/evaluating-language-identification-performance.

Marcos Zampieri, Liling Tan, Nikola Ljubešic, and Jörg Tiedemann. 2014a. A report on the DSL shared task 2014. In *Proc. of the First Workshop on Applying NLP Tools to Similar Languages, Varieties and Dialects*. pages 58–67.

Marcos Zampieri, Liling Tan, Nikola Ljubešic, and Jörg Tiedemann. 2014b. A report on the dsl shared task 2014. In *Proc. of the First Workshop on Applying NLP Tools to Similar Languages, Varieties and Dialects*. pages 58–67.

Marcos Zampieri, Liling Tan, Nikola Ljubešic, Jörg Tiedemann, and Preslav Nakov. 2015. Overview of the DSL shared task 2015. In *Proc. of the Joint Workshop on Language Technology for Closely Related Languages, Varieties and Dialects*. pages 1–9.

Matthew D Zeiler. 2012. Adadelta: an adaptive learning rate method. *arXiv preprint arXiv:1212.5701* .

Arkaitz Zubiaga, Inaki San Vicente, Pablo Gamallo, José Ramom Pichel, Inaki Alegria, Nora Aranberri, Aitzol Ezeiza, and Víctor Fresno. 2016. TweetLID: a benchmark for tweet language identification. *Language Resources and Evaluation* 50(4):729–766.

Evaluating Compound Splitters Extrinsically with Textual Entailment

Glorianna Jagfeld   **Patrick Ziering**
Institute for Natural Language Processing
University of Stuttgart
{jagfelga,zierinpk}
@ims.uni-stuttgart.de

Lonneke van der Plas
Institute of Linguistics
University of Malta, Malta
Lonneke.vanderPlas
@um.edu.mt

Abstract

Traditionally, compound splitters are evaluated intrinsically on gold-standard data or extrinsically on the task of statistical machine translation. We explore a novel way for the extrinsic evaluation of compound splitters, namely recognizing textual entailment. Compound splitting has great potential for this novel task that is both transparent and well-defined. Moreover, we show that it addresses certain aspects that are either ignored in intrinsic evaluations or compensated for by task-internal mechanisms in statistical machine translation. We show significant improvements using different compound splitting methods on a German textual entailment dataset.

1 Introduction

Closed compounding, i.e., the formation of a one-word unit composing several lexemes, is a common linguistic phenomenon in several languages such as German, Dutch, Greek, and Finnish. The goal of compound splitting is to obtain the constituents of a compound to increase its semantic transparency. For example, for the German compound *Apfelsaft* 'apple$_1$ juice$_2$' the desired output of a compound splitter is *Apfel$_1$ Saft$_2$*.

Intrinsic evaluation of compound splitting measures the correctness of the determined split point (Riedl and Biemann, 2016) and the resulting lemmas by means of precision, recall, F_1-score and accuracy (e.g., Koehn and Knight (2003)). In *extrinsic evaluation* setups, compound splitting is applied to the input data of an external natural language processing (NLP) task that benefits from split compounds. As closed compounding introduces semantic opaqueness and vastly increases the vocabulary size of a language, many NLP tasks

benefit from compound splitters. Still, previous work that evaluates compound splitting with extrinsic evaluation methods mostly focuses on statistical machine translation (SMT) (e.g., Nießen and Ney (2000), Koehn and Knight (2003)). Some other external tasks such as information retrieval (Kraaij and Pohlmann, 1998) or speech recognition (Larson et al., 2000) have been shown to benefit from prior compound splitting, yet these works have not compared the extrinsic performance of different compound splitting methods.

Interestingly, the performance found in intrinsic evaluations does not automatically propagate to performance in downstream evaluations as shown in (Fritzinger and Fraser, 2010) for SMT, where oversplit compounds are simply learned as phrases (Dyer, 2009; Weller et al., 2014). Oversplitting is an example of a feature that might not be measured in intrinsic evaluations, because some available gold standards contain positive examples only (Ziering and van der Plas, 2016). It is highly relevant to increase the number of extrinsic tasks for the evaluation of compound splitting to be able to evaluate features that intrinsic evaluations and known extrinsic evaluations ignore.

In this paper we investigate the suitability of Recognizing Textual Entailment (RTE) for the task of compound splitting, inspired by the fact that previous work in RTE underlined the potential benefits of compound splitting for this task (Zeller, 2016). Textual Entailment (TE) is a directional relationship between an entailing text fragment T and an entailed hypothesis, H, saying that the meaning of T entails (or implies) the meaning of H. This relation holds if 'typically, a human, reading T, would infer that H is most likely true' (Dagan et al., 2006). The following is an example of an entailing T-H pair:

T: Yoko Ono unveiled a bronze statue of her late husband, John Lennon.
H: Yoko Ono is John Lennon's widow.

58

Proceedings of the 55th Annual Meeting of the Association for Computational Linguistics (Short Papers), pages 58–63
Vancouver, Canada, July 30 - August 4, 2017. ©2017 Association for Computational Linguistics
https://doi.org/10.18653/v1/P17-2010

We opted for exploring the use of RTE as an extrinsic evaluation for compound splitting for three main reasons: first, in contrast to SMT systems, most RTE systems are less complex. In fact, we deliberately chose an RTE system that reaches good performance with a method that is transparent, i.e., a method that allows for exploring the effect of compounding.[1] It is not our goal to reach state-of-the-art performance for the RTE task. We aim to find a suitable alternative extrinsic evaluation for compound splitting. Second, human agreement on the binary RTE decisions is very high, e.g., on the dataset used in our experiments, an average agreement rate of 87.8% with a κ level of 0.75 was reported (Giampiccolo et al., 2007). Third, the potential benefits for RTE are large. According to Zeller (2016, p. 182) the number of T/H pairs in their phenomenon-specific RTE dataset would rise by about 16 percentage points by compound splitting. In the dataset we use in our experiments, about three-quarters of the T-H pairs contain at least one closed compound.

2 Relevance of Compound Splitting for RTE

The approach to RTE taken in this paper follows the *Lexical Overlap Hypothesis* (LOH), which states that the higher the number of lexical matches between T and H, the more likely the T-H pair is entailing rather than non-entailing (Zeller, 2016). In other words, H is more likely to be entailed by T if most of its lexical content also occurs in T. While this hypothesis is a simplification of the TE problem, it has been shown to perform reasonably well for some datasets (Noh et al., 2015). We argue that the brittleness of the chosen LOH-based RTE system may actually be a strength in terms of evaluation, since it will penalize oversplitting more severely than, e.g., an RNN-based RTE system or a phrase-based MT method that can recover from systematic oversplitting by chunking the splits.

Under the LOH, the problem caused by the opacity of closed compounds becomes evident. As shown in the example below, missing information on the constituents of closed compounds hinders the matching of words from T in H1. Conversely, compound splitting also helps to detect non-entailing T-H pairs. By compound splitting, we increase the number of uncovered tokens in H2, which makes a non-entailment decision more likely[2].

T: Kinder lieben Frucht**säfte**$_1$ aus **Äpfeln**$_2$ '*Children love fruit juices*$_1$ *made of apples*$_2$'

H1: Peters Sohn liebt **Apfel**$_3$**saft**$_4$ 'Peter's son loves **apple**$_3$ **juice**$_4$'

H2: Peters Sohn liebt **Apfel**$_5$**kuchen**$_6$**stücke**$_7$ 'Peter's son loves **pieces**$_7$ of **apple**$_5$ **pie**$_6$'

3 Materials and Methods

In this section we explain the splitters and the RTE framework used in our experiments.

3.1 Inspected Compound Splitters

Our proposed extrinsic evaluation approach for compound splitting is language-independent as we do not use any language-specific parameters. However, in the present work we test it on the most prominent closed-compounding language, German (Ziering and van der Plas, 2014). We inspect the impact of three different types of automatic compound splitting[3] methods that follow a generate-and-rank principle, where the candidate splits are ranked according to the geometric mean of the constituents' frequencies in a given training corpus (Koehn and Knight, 2003).

FF2010 The compound splitter by Fritzinger and Fraser (2010) relies on the output of the German morphological analyzer SMOR (Schmid et al., 2004) to generate several plausible compound splits (e.g., due to word sense ambiguity).

WH2012 As an alternative method, we use the statistical approach presented in Weller and Heid (2012) for German compound splitting. Instead of using the knowledge-rich SMOR, it includes an extensive list of hand-crafted transformation rules that allows to map constituents to corpus lemmas (e.g., by truncating linking morphemes) to generate all possible splits with up to four constituents per compound. Moreover, misleading lemmas are removed from the training corpus using hand-crafted filters.

---

[1] We did not opt for neural RTE systems (Bowman et al., 2015), albeit state-of-the-art, in this first study because of the opacity of the models and the inclusion of phrase-level information, which will make interpretation of the effect harder.

[2] Note that we need to apply lemmatization prior to determining the lexical matches between T and H.

[3] The compound splitters are designed to split compounds with any content word as head, i.e., noun compounds (*Hunde|hütte* 'doghouse'), verb compounds (*eis|laufen* 'to ice-skate') and adjective compounds (*hunde|müde* 'dog-tired') and disregard constructions with a functional modifier (as in the particle verb *auf|stehen* 'to stand up').

System	Acc	Entailment			Non-entailment		
		P	**R**	**F$_1$**	**P**	**R**	**F$_1$**
INIT	64.13	62.50	74.57	68.00	66.67	53.20	59.18
manual splitting $\star$	67.88	65.08	80.20	71.85	72.64	54.99	62.59
ZvdP2016	66.63	64.55	77.02	70.23	69.87	55.75	62.02
FF2010 $\star$	**67.38**	**65.48**	76.53	**70.58**	**70.19**	**57.80**	**63.39**
WH2012	66.00	63.73	**77.75**	70.04	69.77	53.71	60.69

Table 1: Results on RTE performance without (INIT) and with prior compound splitting. $\star$: significant difference of the performance in comparison to INIT

ZvdP2016 Finally, the method using least language-specific knowledge was proposed by Ziering and van der Plas (2016). Instead of using a morphological analyzer or manually compiling a hand-crafted list of rules, they recursively generate all possible binary splits by learning constituent transformations from regular inflection derived from a monolingual lemmatized corpus, e.g., the s-suffix in the case of a genitive marker is often used as linking morpheme. The recursion stops if a non-splitting (atomic) analysis is ranked highest.

Additionally, to provide an upper bound, we manually split development and test data.

3.2 RTE Framework

We conduct our RTE experiments using the open-source Excitement Open Platform (EOP) (Padó et al., 2015; Magnini et al., 2014), which provides comprehensive implementations of algorithms and lexical resources for textual inference. We use the alignment-based algorithm P1EDA (Noh et al., 2015) in all our experiments as it has been shown to be simple and transparent while yielding relatively good results. P1EDA is based on the LOH for RTE explained in Section 2. The algorithm works in three steps: First, it extracts all possible alignments between sequences of identical lemmas in T and H. Then, it extracts various features[4] from the alignments. Finally, these features are given as input to a multinomial logistic regression classifier which is trained on annotated data. For the sake of simplicity, for now we only use one basic aligner which aligns (sequences of) words in T and H that consist of identical lemmas. We will investigate the impact of prior compound splitting given additional lexical resources (such as a derivational morphology lex-

icon (Zeller et al., 2013)) in future work. We use TreeTagger (Schmid, 1995) as integrated in EOP to provide tokenization, lemmatization and Part-of-Speech tagging as linguistic preprocessing.

We train and evaluate all models on the German translation of the RTE-3 dataset (Dagan et al., 2006; Magnini et al., 2014). The training and test dataset contain 800 T-H pairs each. In both sets, entailing and non-entailing T-H pairs are equally distributed (chance baseline of 50% accuracy).

We apply a compound splitter on the RTE training and test dataset *before* we input the data to the EOP pipeline. We replace all compounds by their constituents, separated by white-space. Thus, they are subsequently treated as individual words by EOP and the lexical aligner can benefit from the increased transparency of the compounds.

4 Results and Discussion

Table 1 shows accuracy, precision, recall and F$_1$-score for the entailment and non-entailment class on the RTE-3 dataset. As reflected in the results, reducing the opacity of compounds via the application of a compound splitter improves the subsequent RTE performance. This holds for all compound splitters that we used in our experiments. It is also noticeable that the different compound splitters yield different results in the downstream task, with FF2010 being the most beneficial and significantly[5] outperforming the initial RTE setup without prior compound splitting (INIT) by up to four percentage points in accuracy and F$_1$-score.

As expected, manual splitting performs best overall. The performance difference with FF2010 is however not statistically significant. This is not surprising because FF2010 reaches an accuracy of around 90% in intrinsic evaluations (Ziering and van der Plas, 2016) and the small underperfor-

---

[4] We use a similar feature set as Noh et al. (2015), namely the ratio of aligned vs. unaligned words in H with respect to all words, content words, and named entities.

[5] McNemar test (McNemar, 1947), $p < 0.05$

mance is leveled out by the small size of the test set. Moreover, manual inspections revealed that FF2010 has a higher recall than manual splitting in the non-entailment class due to its undersplitting which results in less lexical overlap between T and H, pointing to the non-entailment class.

When we compare these results from the extrinsic evaluation with intrinsic evaluation results (in terms of splitting accuracy) reported in Ziering and van der Plas (2016), we see the same performance ordering with respect to the three compound splitters, while the current extrinsic evaluation on RTE differentiates between the best system (FF2010) and the two others in that only the former reached statistically significant improvements over the INIT baseline.

To analyze the possible causes of difference in performance between the systems and to see the benefits of using RTE for compound splitting evaluation we performed a manual error analysis. First, we examined all entailment classifications that were correct using FF2010 and incorrect when using the INIT baseline. Using FF2010, the classifier was able to correctly classify an additional 36 entailing and 25 non-entailing T-H pairs. As expected, most of the hypotheses in these pairs contained correctly split compounds where the RTE system could benefit from the increased transparency. Conversely, we also examined the 28 T-H pairs that the classifier missed to identify as entailing while they were correct in INIT. Most of the examples were cases in which there was almost no lexical overlap between T and H even with compound splitting.

Furthermore, we compared the correct entailment classifications of FF2010 with the other two splitters. For ZvdP2016, most errors can be attributed to oversplitting. Precisely, 25 out of its 37 (67.5%) misclassifications compared to FF2010 can be attributed to this problem. For example, ZvdP2016 oversplit the name *Landowska* into *Line Dow Ska*[6] that appeared in both T and H in an non-entailing pair, which artificially increased the coverage ratio of words in H and therefore pointed to the incorrect entailment classification. For WH2012, oversplitting is also a major contributor of RTE errors, however it appeares not as predominant as for ZvdP2016. 10 out of its 29 (34.5%) misclassifications compared to FF2010

____

[6]Misleading knowledge about verbal inflection automatically derived from a lemmatized corpus is responsible for the oversplitting by ZvdP2016.

can be attributed to oversplitting, while 4 (13.8%) missclassifications are due to undersplitting. For example, in an entailing T-H pair WH2012 correctly split *Amazonas-Regenwald* 'Amazon rainforest' in H into *Amazonas Regen Wald*, however it oversplit *Amazonas* in T into *Amazon As* 'Amazon ace' and thus, *Amazonas* in H remained unaligned. To the contrary, FF2010 did not split *Amazonas* in T, which lead to a higher token coverage ratio in H. Again, in the H *Die EU senkt die Fangquoten* 'The EU lowers the fishing quota' of another entailing T-H pair, WH2010 correctly split $Fang_1 quoten_2$ 'fishing quota' in H into $fangen_1 Quote_2$ but failed to split *EU-Quote* in T, failing to cover both *EU* and *Quote* in H.

Our closer inspections also showed that compound splitting does not always suffice to reveal a lexical match between T and H as shown in the following example:

T: Ben **fährt**$_1$ einen **Mercedes**$_2$ *'Ben drives$_1$ a Mercedes$_2$'*

H: Ben ist **Auto**$_3$**fahrer**$_4$ 'Ben is a **car**$_3$ **driver**$_4$'

Given a correct splitting of *Autofahrer* to *Auto Fahrer*, a derivational morphology resource (Zeller et al., 2013) would be required to discover the relationship between *fahren* and *Fahrer* and a synonym database to find that *Mercedes* is a hyponym of *Auto*. This does not weaken the claim that RTE is useful for evaluating compound splitters. It just shows that deeper, semantic compound analysis could improve RTE further.

Besides, the error analysis shed some light on the treatment of compound heads and modifiers. It seems advisable to weight the compound head and modifiers differently when computing the ratio of aligned tokens in H. As illustrated by the following example, coverage of the head should be more important for the entailment decision than of the modifiers. Given a correct split of $Kinder_1 buch_2$ into $Kind_1 Buch_2$, H1 and H2 have the same token coverage ratio while only H1 is entailed by T.

T: Yuki kauft ein **Kinder**$_1$**buch**$_2$ *'Yuki buys a children's$_1$ book$_2$'*

H1: Yuki kauft ein **Buch** 'Yuki buys a **book**'

H2: Yuki ist ein **Kind** 'Yuki is a **child**'

It should be noted that the transparency gain using compound splitting is limited to closed compounds that are compositional with respect to at least one constituent. Splitting compounds in

H that are fairly non-compositional with respect to all constituents (e.g., *Maulwurf* 'mole' (lit. 'mouth throw')) is counterproductive. However, since most compounds (in particular ad-hoc productions) are compositional, this is only a side issue. In fact, we did not observe any cases of non-compositional compounds in the course of our error analysis.

In summary, compound splitting is a complex task that comprises many subtasks. The multiple evaluation methods available, both intrinsic and extrinsic, vary in their suitability to evaluate them. One of these subtasks concerns the ability of compound splitters to determine whether to split or not, which is an integral part of compound analysis. While aspects such as oversplitting were not consistently evaluated in previous intrinsic evaluations, or compensated for by task-internal mechanisms in SMT, RTE proved more strict in this respect. Moreover, the transparency of the models made it possible to better estimate the impact of splitting. Despite the small size of the dataset, we were able to show significant differences, partly due to the clear definition of this binary classification task.

On a side note, to the best of our knowledge, the result we obtained using the FF2010 compound splitter is the best result on the German RTE-3 dataset that has been reported using EOP. Notably, we obtain an accuracy which is almost three percentage points higher than the results of Noh et al. (2015), although they include further (language-specific) linguistic knowledge.

5 Conclusion

Inspired by the potential benefits of compound splitting from the RTE literature and supported by the transparency of the models and the clear definition of this binary classification task, we set out to explore whether RTE is a suitable method to extrinsically evaluate the performance of compound splitting. We compared several compound splitters on a German textual entailment dataset and found that compound splitting is helpful for RTE across the board. More importantly, we found that certain aspects of compound splitters, neglected in previous evaluations, such as oversplitting, had a large impact on this task and nicely differentiated the systems tested. We conclude that RTE represents a suitable alternative to SMT for the extrinsic evaluation of compound splitters.

In future work, we would like to investigate the interaction between additional lexical resources (such as GermaNet (Hamp and Feldweg, 1997; Henrich and Hinrichs, 2010) or DErivBase (Zeller et al., 2013)) and compound splitting, and the impact on the RTE performance.

Acknowledgments

We thank Sebastian Padó and Britta Zeller for their inspiring ideas about using compound splitting for improving RTE, and for their support in using the RTE framework. We are also grateful to the anonymous reviewers for their helpful feedback. This research was funded by the German Research Foundation (Collaborative Research Centre 732, Project D11).

References

Samuel R Bowman, Gabor Angeli, Christopher Potts, and Christopher D Manning. 2015. A large annotated corpus for learning natural language inference. In *Proceedings of the Conference on Empirical Methods in Natural Language Processing*.

Ido Dagan, Oren Glickman, and Bernardo Magnini. 2006. The PASCAL Recognising Textual Entailment Challenge. In *Proceedings of the First International Conference on Machine Learning Challenges: Evaluating Predictive Uncertainty Visual Object Classification, and Recognizing Textual Entailment*. Springer-Verlag, Berlin, Heidelberg, MLCW'05.

Chris Dyer. 2009. Using a Maximum Entropy Model to Build Segmentation Lattices for MT. In *Proceedings of NAACL-HLT 2009*. NAACL '09.

Fabienne Fritzinger and Alexander Fraser. 2010. How to Avoid Burning Ducks: Combining Linguistic Analysis and Corpus Statistics for German Compound Processing. In *Proceedings of the ACL 2010 Joint 5th Workshop on Statistical Machine Translation and Metrics MATR*.

Danilo Giampiccolo, Bernardo Magnini, Ido Dagan, and Bill Dolan. 2007. The Third PASCAL Recognizing Textual Entailment Challenge. In *Proceedings of the ACL-PASCAL Workshop on Textual Entailment and Paraphrasing*. Stroudsburg, PA, USA, RTE '07.

Birgit Hamp and Helmut Feldweg. 1997. GermaNet - a Lexical-Semantic Net for German. In *Proceedings of ACL workshop Automatic Information Extraction and Building of Lexical Semantic Resources for NLP Applications*.

Verena Henrich and Erhard Hinrichs. 2010. GernEdiT - The GermaNet Editing Tool. In Nicoletta Calzolari (Conference Chair), Khalid Choukri, Bente

Maegaard, Joseph Mariani, Jan Odijk, Stelios Piperidis, Mike Rosner, and Daniel Tapias, editors, *Proceedings of the Seventh International Conference on Language Resources and Evaluation (LREC'10)*. European Language Resources Association (ELRA), Valletta, Malta.

Philipp Koehn and Kevin Knight. 2003. Empirical Methods for Compound Splitting. In *EACL*.

Wessel Kraaij and Renée Pohlmann. 1998. Comparing the Effect of Syntactic vs. Statistical Phrase Index Strategies for Dutch. In *Proceedings ECDL'98*.

Martha Larson, Daniel Willett, Joachim Köhler, and Gerhard Rigoll. 2000. Compound splitting and lexical unit recombination for improved performance of a speech recognition system for German parliamentary speeches. In *Sixth International Conference on Spoken Language Processing, ICSLP / INTERSPEECH*.

Bernardo Magnini, Roberto Zanoli, Ido Dagan, Kathrin Eichler, Günter Neumann, Tae-Gil Noh, Sebastian Pado, Asher Stern, and Omer Levy. 2014. The Excitement Open Platform for Textual Inferences. In *Proceedings of the ACL 2014 System Demonstrations*.

Quinn McNemar. 1947. Note on the sampling error of the difference between correlated proportions or percentages. *Psychometrika* 12(2).

Sonja Nießen and Hermann Ney. 2000. Improving SMT quality with morpho-syntactic analysis. In *COLING 2000*.

Tae-Gil Noh, Sebastian Padó, Vered Shwartz, Ido Dagan, Vivi Nastase, Kathrin Eichler, Lili Kotlerman, and Meni Adler. 2015. Multi-Level Alignments As An Extensible Representation Basis for Textual Entailment Algorithms. In *Proceedings of the Fourth Joint Conference on Lexical and Computational Semantics, *SEM 2015*. Denver, Colorado, USA.

Sebastian Padó, Tae-Gil Noh, Asher Stern, Rui Wang, and Roberto Zanoli. 2015. Design and Realization of a Modular Architecture for Textual Entailment. *Natural Language Engineering* 21(2).

Martin Riedl and Chris Biemann. 2016. Unsupervised Compound Splitting With Distributional Semantics Rivals Supervised Methods. In *NAACL-HTL 2016*.

Helmut Schmid. 1995. Improvements In Part-of-Speech Tagging With an Application To German. In *In Proceedings of the ACL SIGDAT-Workshop*.

Helmut Schmid, Arne Fitschen, and Ulrich Heid. 2004. SMOR: A German Computational Morphology Covering Derivation, Composition, and Inflection. In *LREC 2004*.

Marion Weller, Fabienne Cap, Stefan Müller, Sabine Schulte im Walde, and Alexander Fraser. 2014. Distinguishing Degrees of Compositionality in Compound Splitting for Statistical Machine Translation. In *ComAComA 2014*.

Marion Weller and Ulrich Heid. 2012. Analyzing and Aligning German compound nouns. In *LREC 2012*.

Britta Dorothee Zeller. 2016. *Induction, Semantic Validation and Evaluation of a Derivational Morphology Lexicon for German*. Ph.D. thesis, Heidelberg, Germany.

Britta Dorothee Zeller, Jan Snajder, and Sebastian Padó. 2013. DErivBase: Inducing and Evaluating a Derivational Morphology Resource for German. In *ACL (1)*. The Association for Computer Linguistics.

Patrick Ziering and Lonneke van der Plas. 2014. What good are 'Nominalkomposita' for 'noun compounds': Multilingual Extraction and Structure Analysis of Nominal Compositions using Linguistic Restrictors. In *Proceedings of COLING 2014, the 25th International Conference on Computational Linguistics: Technical Papers*.

Patrick Ziering and Lonneke van der Plas. 2016. Towards Unsupervised and Language-independent Compound Splitting using Inflectional Morphological Transformations. In *Proceedings of NAACL-HLT 2016*.

An Analysis of Action Recognition Datasets for Language and Vision Tasks

Spandana Gella and **Frank Keller**
Institute for Language, Cognition and Computation
School of Informatics, University of Edinburgh
10 Crichton Street, Edinburgh EH8 9AB
S.Gella@sms.ed.ac.uk, keller@inf.ed.ac.uk

Abstract

A large amount of recent research has focused on tasks that combine language and vision, resulting in a proliferation of datasets and methods. One such task is action recognition, whose applications include image annotation, scene understanding and image retrieval. In this survey, we categorize the existing approaches based on how they conceptualize this problem and provide a detailed review of existing datasets, highlighting their diversity as well as advantages and disadvantages. We focus on recently developed datasets which link visual information with linguistic resources and provide a fine-grained syntactic and semantic analysis of actions in images.

1 Introduction

Action recognition is the task of identifying the action being depicted in a video or still image. The task is useful for a range of applications such as generating descriptions, image/video retrieval, surveillance, and human–computer interaction. It has been widely studied in computer vision, often on videos (Nagel, 1994; Forsyth et al., 2005), where motion and temporal information provide cues for recognizing actions (Taylor et al., 2010). However, many actions are recognizable from still images, see the examples in Figure 1. Due to the absence of motion cues and temporal features (Ikizler et al., 2008) action recognition from stills is more challenging. Most of the existing work can be categorized into four tasks: (a) action classification (AC); (b) determining human–object interaction (HOI); (c) visual verb sense disambiguation (VSD); and (d) visual semantic role labeling (VSRL). In Figure 2 we illustrate each of these

Figure 1: Examples of actions in still images

tasks and show how they are related to each other.

Until recently, action recognition was studied as action classification on small-scale datasets with a limited number of predefined actions labels (Ikizler et al., 2008; Gupta et al., 2009; Yao and Fei-Fei, 2010; Everingham et al., 2010; Yao et al., 2011). Often the labels in action classification tasks are verb phrases or a combination of verb and object such as *playing baseball*, *riding horse*. These datasets have helped in building models and understanding which aspects of an image are important for classifying actions, but most methods are not scalable to larger numbers of actions (Ramanathan et al., 2015). Action classification models are trained on images annotated with mutually exclusive labels, i.e., the assumption is that only a single label is relevant for a given image. This ignores the fact that actions such as *holding bicycle* and *riding bicycle* can co-occur in the same image. To address these issues and also to understand the range of possible interactions between humans and objects, the human–object interaction (HOI) detection task has been proposed, in which all possible interactions between a human and a given object have to be identified (Le et al., 2014; Chao et al., 2015; Lu et al., 2016).

However, both action classification and HOI detection do not consider the ambiguity that arises when verbs are used as labels, e.g., the verb *play* has multiple meanings in different contexts. On the other hand, action labels consisting of verb-object pairs can miss important generalizations:

Proceedings of the 55th Annual Meeting of the Association for Computational Linguistics (Short Papers), pages 64–71
Vancouver, Canada, July 30 - August 4, 2017. ©2017 Association for Computational Linguistics
https://doi.org/10.18653/v1/P17-2011

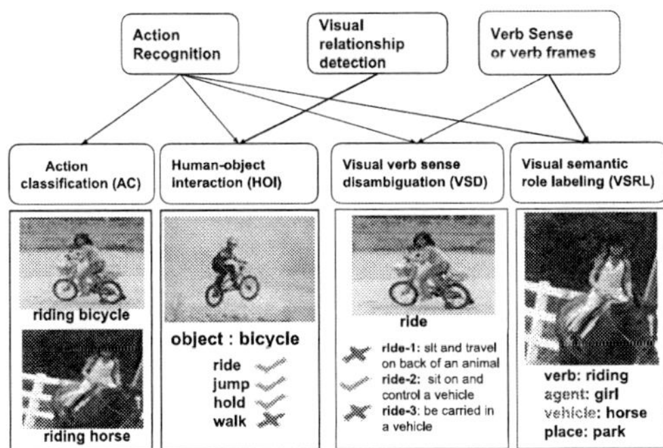

Figure 2: Categorization of action recognition tasks in images

riding horse and *riding elephant* both instantiate the same verb semantics, i.e., *riding animal.* Thirdly, existing action labels miss generalizations across verbs, e.g., the fact that *fixing bike* and *repairing bike* are semantically equivalent, in spite of the use of different verbs. These observations have led authors to argue that actions should be analyzed at the level of verb senses. Gella et al. (2016) propose the new task of visual verb sense disambiguation (VSD), in which a verb–image pair is annotated with a verb sense taken from an existing lexical database (OntoNotes in this case). While VSD handles distinction between different verb senses, it does not identify or localize the objects that participate in the action denoted by the verb. Recent work (Gupta and Malik, 2015; Yatskar et al., 2016) has filled this gap by proposing the task of visual semantic role labeling (VSRL), in which images are labeled with verb frames, and the objects that fill the semantic roles of the frame are identified in the image.

In this paper, we provide a unified view of action recognition tasks, pointing out their strengths and weaknesses. We survey existing literature and provide insights into existing datasets and models for action recognition tasks.

2 Datasets for Action Recognition

We give an overview of commonly used datasets for action recognition tasks in Table 1 and group them according to subtask. We observe that the number of verbs covered in these datasets is often smaller than the number of action labels reported (see Table 1, columns #V and #L) and in many cases the action label involves object reference. A few of the first action recognition datasets such as the Ikizler and Willow datasets (Ikizler et al.,

2008; Delaitre et al., 2010) had action labels such as *throwing* and *running*; they were taken from the sports domain and exhibited diversity in camera view point, background and resolution. Then datasets were created to capture variation in human poses in the sports domain for actions such as *tennis serve* and *cricket bowling*; typically features based on poses and body parts were used to build models (Gupta et al., 2009). Further datasets were created based on the intuition that object information helps in modeling action recognition (Li and Fei-Fei, 2007; Ikizler-Cinbis and Sclaroff, 2010), which resulted in the use of action labels such as *riding horse* or *riding bike* (Everingham et al., 2010; Yao et al., 2011). Not only were most of these datasets domain specific, but the labels were also manually selected and mutually exclusive, i.e., two actions cannot co-occur in the same image. Also, most of these datasets do not localize objects or identify their semantic roles.

2.1 Identifying Visual Verbs and Verb Senses

The limitations with early datasets (small scale, domain specificity, and the use of ad-hoc labels that combine verb and object) have been recently addressed in a number of broad-coverage datasets that offer linguistically motivated labels. Often these datasets use existing linguistic resources such as VerbNet (Schuler, 2005), OntoNotes (Hovy et al., 2006) and FrameNet (Baker et al., 1998) to classify verbs and their senses. This allows for a more general, semantically motivated treatment of verbs and verb phrases, and also takes into account that not all verbs are depictable. For example, abstract verbs such as *presuming* and *acquiring* are not depictable at all, while other verbs have both depictable and non-depictable senses: *play* is non-depictable in *playing with emotions*, but depictable in *playing instrument* and *playing sport*. The process of identifying depictable verbs or verb senses is used by Ronchi and Perona (2015), Gella et al. (2016) and Yatskar et al. (2016) to identify visual verbs, visual verb senses, and the semantic roles of the participating objects respectively. In all the cases the process of identifying visual verbs or senses is carried out by human annotators via crowd-sourcing platforms. Visualness labels for 935 OntoNotes verb senses corresponding to 154 verbs is provided by Gella et al. (2016), while Yatskar et al. (2016) provides visualness labels for 9683 FrameNet verbs.

Dataset	Task	#L	#V	Obj	Imgs	Sen	Des	Cln	ML	Resource	Example Labels
Ikizler (Ikizler et al., 2008)	AC	6	6	0	467	N	N	Y	N	—	running, walking
Sports Dataset (Gupta et al., 2009)	AC	6	6	4	300	N	N	Y	N	—	tennis serve, cricket bowling
Willow (Delaitre et al., 2010)	AC	7	6	5	986	N	N	Y	Y	—	riding bike, photographing
PPMI (Yao and Fei-Fei, 2010)	AC	24	2	12	4.8k	N	N	Y	N	—	play guitar, hold violin
Stanford 40 Actions (Yao et al., 2011)	AC	40	33	31	9.5k	N	N	Y	N	—	cut vegetables, ride horse
PASCAL 2012 (Everingham et al., 2015)	AC	11	9	6	4.5k	N	N	Y	Y	—	riding bike, riding horse
89 Actions (Le et al., 2013)	AC	89	36	19	2k	N	N	Y	N	—	ride bike, fix bike
MPII Human Pose (Andriluka et al., 2014)	AC	410	–	66	40.5k	N	N	Y	N	—	riding car, hair styling
TUHOI (Le et al., 2014)	HOI	2974	–	189	10.8k	N	N	Y	Y	—	sit on chair, play with dog
COCO-a (Ronchi and Perona, 2015)	HOI	–	140	80	10k	N	Y	Y	Y	VerbNet	walk bike, hold bike
Google Images (Ramanathan et al., 2015)	AC	2880	–	–	102k	N	N	N	N	—	riding horse, riding camel
HICO (Chao et al., 2015)	HOI	600	111	80	47k	Y	N	Y	Y	WordNet	ride#v#1 bike; hold#v#2 bike
VCOCO-SRL (Gupta and Malik, 2015)	VSRL	–	26	48	10k	N	Y	Y	Y	—	verb: hit; instr: bat; obj: ball
imSitu (Yatskar et al., 2016)	VSRL	–	504	11k	126k	Y	N	Y	N	FrameNet WordNet	verb: ride; agent: girl#n#2 vehicle: bike#n#1; place: road#n#2
VerSe (Gella et al., 2016)	VSD	163	90	–	3.5k	Y	Y	Y	N	OntoNotes	ride.v.01, play.v.02
Visual Genome (Krishna et al., 2016)	VRD	42.3k	–	33.8k	108k	N	N	Y	Y	—	man playing frisbee

Table 1: Comparison of various existing action recognition datasets. #L denotes number of action labels in the dataset; #V denotes number of verbs covered in the dataset; Obj indicates number of objects annotated; Sen indicates whether sense ambiguity is explicitly handled; Des indicates whether image descriptions are included; Cln indicates whether dataset is manually verified; ML indicates the possibility of multiple labels per image; Resource indicates linguistic resource used to label actions.

2.2 Datasets Beyond Action Classification

Over the last few years tasks that combine language and vision such as image description and visual question answering have gained much attention. This has led to the creation of new, large datasets such as MSCOCO (Chen et al., 2015) and the VQA dataset (Antol et al., 2015). Although these datasets are not created for action recognition, a number of attempts have been made to use the verbs present in image descriptions to annotate actions. The COCO-a, VerSe and VCOCO-SRL datasets all use the MSCOCO image descriptions to annotate fine-grained aspects of interaction and semantic roles.

HICO: The HICO dataset has 47.8k images annotated with 600 categories of human-object interactions with 111 verbs applying to 80 object categories of MSCOCO. It is annotated to include diverse interactions for objects and has an average of 6.5 distinct interactions per object category. Unlike other HOI datasets such as TUHOI which label interactions as verbs and ignore senses, the HOI categories of HICO are based on WordNet (Miller, 1995) verb senses. The HICO dataset also has multiple annotations per object and it incorporates the information that certain interactions such as *riding a bike* and *holding a bike* often co-occur. However, it fails to include annotations to distinguish between multiple senses of a verb.

Visual Genome: The dataset created by Krishna et al. (2016) has dense annotations of objects, attributes, and relationships between objects. The Visual Genome dataset contains 105k images with 40k unique relationships between objects. Unlike other HOI datasets such as HICO, visual genome relationships also include prepositions, comparative and prepositional phrases such as *near* and *taller than*, making the visual relationship task more generic than action recognition. Krishna et al. (2016) combine all the annotations of objects, relationships, and attributes into directed graphs known as scene graphs.

COCO-a: Ronchi and Perona (2015) present Visual VerbNet (VVN), a list of 140 common visual verbs manually mined from English VerbNet (Schuler, 2005). The coverage of visual verbs in this dataset is not complete, as many visual verbs such as *dive*, *perform* and *shoot* are not included. This also highlights a bias in this dataset as the authors relied on occurrence in MSCOCO as a verification step to consider a verb as visual. They annotated 10k images containing human subjects with one of the 140 visual verbs, for 80 MSCOCO objects. This dataset has better coverage of human-object interactions than the HICO dataset despite of missing many visual verbs.

VerSe: Gella et al. (2016) created a dataset of 3.5k images sampled from the MSCOCO and TUHOI datasets and annotated it with 90 verbs and their OntoNotes senses to distinguish different verb senses using visual context. This is the first dataset that aims to annotate all visual senses of a verb. However, the total number of images annotated and number of images for some senses is relatively small, which makes it difficult to use this dataset to train models. The authors further divided their 90 verbs into motion and non-motion verbs according to Levin (1993) verb classes and analyzed visual ambiguity in the task of visual sense disambiguation.

VCOCO-SRL: Gupta and Malik (2015) annotated a dataset of 16k person instances in 10k images with 26 verbs and associated objects in the scene with the semantic roles for each action. The main aim of the dataset is to build models for visual semantic role labeling in images. This task involves identifying the actions depicted in an image, along with the people and objects that instantiate the semantic roles of the actions. In the VCOCO-SRL dataset, each person instance is annotated with a mean of 2.8 actions simultaneously.

imSitu: Yatskar et al. (2016) annotated a large dataset of 125k images with 504 verbs, 1.7k semantic roles and 11k objects. They used FrameNet verbs, frames and associated objects or scenes with roles to develop the dataset. They annotate every image with a single verb and the semantic roles of the objects present in the image. VCOCO-SRL the is dataset most similar to imSitu, however VCOCO-SRL includes localization information of agents and all objects and provides multiple action annotations per image. On the other hand, imSitu is the dataset that covers highest number of verbs, while also omitting many commonly studied polysemous verbs such as *play*.

2.3 Diversity in Datasets

With the exception of a few datasets such as COCO-a, VerSe, imSitu all action recognition datasets have manually picked labels or focus on covering actions in specific domains such as sports. Alternatively, many datasets only cover actions relevant to specific object categories such as musical instruments, animals and vehicles. In the real world, people interact with many more objects and perform actions relevant to a wide range of domains such as personal care, household activities, or socializing. This limits the diversity and coverage of existing action recognition datasets. Recently proposed datasets partly handle this issue by using generic linguistic resources to extend the vocabulary of verbs in action labels. The diversity issue has also been high-

lighted and addressed in recent video action recognition datasets (Caba Heilbron et al., 2015; Sigurdsson et al., 2016), which include generic household activities. An analysis of various image description and question answering datasets by Ferraro et al. (2015) shows the bias in the distribution of word categories. Image description datasets have a higher distribution of nouns compared to other word categories, indicating that the descriptions are object specific, limiting their usefulness for action-based tasks.

3 Relevant Language and Vision Tasks

Template based description generation systems for both videos and images rely on identifying subject–verb–object triples and use language modeling to generate or rank descriptions (Yang et al., 2011; Thomason et al., 2014; Bernardi et al., 2016). Understanding actions also plays an important role in question answering, especially when the question is pertaining to an action depicted in the image. There are some specifically curated question answering datasets which target human activities or relationships between a pair of objects (Yu et al., 2015). Mallya and Lazebnik (2016) have shown that systems trained on action recognition datasets could be used to improve the accuracy of visual question answering systems that handle questions related to human activity and human–object relationships. Action recognition datasets could be used to learn actions that are visually similar such as *interacting with panda* and *feeding a panda* or *tickling a baby* and *calming a baby*, which cannot be learned from text alone (Ramanathan et al., 2015). Visual semantic role labeling is a crucial step for grounding actions in the physical world (Yang et al., 2016).

4 Action Recognition Models

Most of the models proposed for action classification and human–object interaction tasks rely on identifying higher-level visual cues present in the image, including human bodies or body parts (Ikizler et al., 2008; Gupta et al., 2009; Yao et al., 2011; Andriluka et al., 2014), objects (Gupta et al., 2009), and scenes (Li and Fei-Fei, 2007). Higher-level visual cues are obtained through low-level features extracted from the image such as Scale Invariant Feature Transforms (SIFT), Histogram of Oriented Gradients (HOG), and Spatial Envelopes (Gist) features (Lowe, 1999; Dalal and Triggs,

2005). These are useful in identifying key points, detecting humans, and scene or background information in images, respectively. In addition to identifying humans and objects, the relative position or angle between a human and an object is useful in learning human–object interactions (Le et al., 2014). Most of the existing approaches rely on learning supervised classifiers over low-level features to predict action labels.

More recent approaches are based on end-to-end convolutional neural network architectures which learn visual cues such as objects and image features for action recognition (Chao et al., 2015; Zhou et al., 2016; Mallya and Lazebnik, 2016). While most of the action classification models rely solely on visual information, models proposed for human–object interaction or visual relationship detection sometimes combine human and object identification (using visual features) with linguistic knowledge (Le et al., 2014; Krishna et al., 2016; Lu et al., 2016). Other work on identifying actions, especially methods that focus on relationships that are infrequent or unseen, utilize word vectors learned on large text corpora as an additional source of information (Lu et al., 2016). Similarly, Gella et al. (2016) show that embeddings generated from textual data associated with images (object labels, image descriptions) is useful for visual verb sense disambiguation, and is complementary to visual information.

5　Discussion

Linguistic resources such as WordNet, OntoNotes, and FrameNet play a key role in textual sense disambiguation and semantic role labeling. The visual action disambiguation and visual semantic role labeling tasks are extensions of their textual counterparts, where context is provided as an image instead of as text. Linguistic resources therefore have to play a key role if we are to make rapid progress in these language and vision tasks. However, as we have shown in this paper, only a few of the existing datasets for action recognition and related tasks are based on linguistic resources (Chao et al., 2015; Gella et al., 2016; Yatskar et al., 2016). This is despite the fact that the WordNet noun hierarchy (for example) has played an important role in recent progress in object recognition, by virtue of underlying the ImageNet database, the de-facto standard for this task (Russakovsky et al., 2015). The success of ImageNet for objects has

in turn helped NLP tasks such as bilingual lexicon induction (Vulić et al., 2016). In our view, language and vision datasets that are based on the WordNet, OntoNotes, or FrameNet verb sense inventories can play a similar role for tasks such as action recognition or visual semantic role labeling, and ultimately be useful also for more distantly related tasks such as language grounding.

Another argument for linking language and vision datasets with linguistic resources is that this enables us to deploy the datasets in a multilingual setting. For example a polysemous verb such as *ride* in English has multiple translations in German and Spanish, depending on the context and the objects involved. Riding a horse is translated as *reiten* in German and *cabalgar* in Spanish, whereas riding a bicycle is translated as *fahren* in German and *pedalear* in Spanish. In contrast, some polysemous verb (e.g., English *play*) are always translated as the same verb, independent of sense (*spielen* in German). Such sense mappings are discoverable from multilingual lexical resources (e.g., BabelNet, Navigli and Ponzetto 2010), which makes it possible to construct language and vision models that are applicable to multiple languages. This opportunity is lost if language and vision dataset are constructed in isolation, instead of using existing linguistic resources.

6　Conclusions

In this paper, we have shown the evolution of action recognition datasets and tasks from simple ad-hoc labels to the fine-grained annotation of verb semantics. It is encouraging to see the recent increase in datasets that deal with sense ambiguity and annotate semantic roles, while using standard linguistic resources. One major remaining issue with existing datasets is their limited coverage, and the skewed distribution of verbs or verb senses. Another challenge is the inconsistency in annotation schemes and task definitions across datasets. For example Chao et al. (2015) used WordNet senses as interaction labels, while Gella et al. (2016) used the more coarse-grained OntoNotes senses. Yatskar et al. (2016) used FrameNet frames for semantic role annotation, while Gupta and Malik (2015) used manually curated roles. If we are to develop robust, domain independent models, then we need to standardize annotation schemes and use the same linguistic resources across datasets.

References

Mykhaylo Andriluka, Leonid Pishchulin, Peter Gehler, and Bernt Schiele. 2014. 2d human pose estimation: New benchmark and state of the art analysis. In *Proceedings of the IEEE Conference on Computer Vision and Pattern Recognition*. pages 3686–3693.

Stanislaw Antol, Aishwarya Agrawal, Jiasen Lu, Margaret Mitchell, Dhruv Batra, C. Lawrence Zitnick, and Devi Parikh. 2015. VQA: visual question answering. In *2015 IEEE International Conference on Computer Vision, ICCV 2015, Santiago, Chile, December 7-13, 2015*. pages 2425–2433.

Collin F Baker, Charles J Fillmore, and John B Lowe. 1998. The berkeley framenet project. In *Proceedings of the 36th Annual Meeting of the Association for Computational Linguistics and 17th International Conference on Computational Linguistics-Volume 1*. Association for Computational Linguistics, pages 86–90.

Raffaella Bernardi, Ruket Cakici, Desmond Elliott, Aykut Erdem, Erkut Erdem, Nazli Ikizler-Cinbis, Frank Keller, Adrian Muscat, and Barbara Plank. 2016. Automatic description generation from images: A survey of models, datasets, and evaluation measures. *Journal of Artifical Intelligence Research* 55:409–442.

Fabian Caba Heilbron, Victor Escorcia, Bernard Ghanem, and Juan Carlos Niebles. 2015. Activitynet: A large-scale video benchmark for human activity understanding. In *Proceedings of the IEEE Conference on Computer Vision and Pattern Recognition*. pages 961–970.

Yu-Wei Chao, Zhan Wang, Yugeng He, Jiaxuan Wang, and Jia Deng. 2015. HICO: A benchmark for recognizing human-object interactions in images. In *2015 IEEE International Conference on Computer Vision, ICCV 2015, Santiago, Chile, December 7-13, 2015*. pages 1017–1025.

Xinlei Chen, Hao Fang, Tsung-Yi Lin, Ramakrishna Vedantam, Saurabh Gupta, Piotr Dollár, and C. Lawrence Zitnick. 2015. Microsoft COCO captions: Data collection and evaluation server. *CoRR* abs/1504.00325.

Navneet Dalal and Bill Triggs. 2005. Histograms of oriented gradients for human detection. In *Computer Vision and Pattern Recognition, 2005. CVPR 2005. IEEE Computer Society Conference on*. IEEE, volume 1, pages 886–893.

Vincent Delaitre, Ivan Laptev, and Josef Sivic. 2010. Recognizing human actions in still images: a study of bag-of-features and part-based representations. In *BMVC 2010-21st British Machine Vision Conference*.

Mark Everingham, S. M. Ali Eslami, Luc Van Gool, Christopher K. I. Williams, John M. Winn, and Andrew Zisserman. 2015. The Pascal visual object classes challenge: A retrospective. *International Journal of Computer Vision* 111(1):98–136.

Mark Everingham, Luc J. Van Gool, Christopher K. I. Williams, John M. Winn, and Andrew Zisserman. 2010. The Pascal visual object classes (VOC) challenge. *International Journal of Computer Vision* 88(2):303–338.

Francis Ferraro, Nasrin Mostafazadeh, Ting-Hao (Kenneth) Huang, Lucy Vanderwende, Jacob Devlin, Michel Galley, and Margaret Mitchell. 2015. A survey of current datasets for vision and language research. In *Proceedings of the 2015 Conference on Empirical Methods in Natural Language Processing, EMNLP 2015, Lisbon, Portugal, September 17-21, 2015*. pages 207–213.

David A. Forsyth, Okan Arikan, Leslie Ikemoto, James F. O'Brien, and Deva Ramanan. 2005. Computational studies of human motion: Part 1, tracking and motion synthesis. *Foundations and Trends in Computer Graphics and Vision* 1(2/3).

Spandana Gella, Mirella Lapata, and Frank Keller. 2016. Unsupervised visual sense disambiguation for verbs using multimodal embeddings. In *Proceedings of the 2016 Conference on North American Chapter of the Association for Computational Linguistics: Human Language Technologies, San Diego California, USA, June 12-17, 2016*. pages 182–192.

Abhinav Gupta, Aniruddha Kembhavi, and Larry S. Davis. 2009. Observing human-object interactions: Using spatial and functional compatibility for recognition. *IEEE Transactions on Pattern Analysis and Machine Intelligence* 31(10):1775–1789.

Saurabh Gupta and Jitendra Malik. 2015. Visual semantic role labeling. *CoRR* abs/1505.04474.

Eduard H. Hovy, Mitchell P. Marcus, Martha Palmer, Lance A. Ramshaw, and Ralph M. Weischedel. 2006. Ontonotes: The 90% solution. In *Human Language Technology Conference of the North American Chapter of the Association of Computational Linguistics, Proceedings, June 4-9, 2006, New York, New York, USA*. pages 57–60.

Nazli Ikizler, Ramazan Gokberk Cinbis, Selen Pehlivan, and Pinar Duygulu. 2008. Recognizing actions from still images. In *19th International Conference on Pattern Recognition (ICPR 2008), December 8-11, 2008, Tampa, Florida, USA*. pages 1–4.

Nazli Ikizler-Cinbis and Stan Sclaroff. 2010. Object, scene and actions: Combining multiple features for human action recognition. In *European conference on computer vision*. Springer, pages 494–507.

Ranjay Krishna, Yuke Zhu, Oliver Groth, Justin Johnson, Kenji Hata, Joshua Kravitz, Stephanie Chen, Yannis Kalantidis, Li-Jia Li, David A Shamma, et al. 2016. Visual genome: Connecting language and vision using crowdsourced dense image annotations. *arXiv preprint arXiv:1602.07332* .

Dieu Thu Le, Raffaella Bernardi, and Jasper Uijlings. 2013. Exploiting language models to recognize unseen actions. In *Proceedings of the 3rd ACM conference on International conference on multimedia retrieval*. ACM, pages 231–238.

Dieu-Thu Le, Jasper Uijlings, and Raffaella Bernardi. 2014. *Proceedings of the Third Workshop on Vision and Language*, Dublin City University and the Association for Computational Linguistics, chapter TUHOI: Trento Universal Human Object Interaction Dataset, pages 17–24.

Beth Levin. 1993. *English verb classes and alternations: A preliminary investigation.* University of Chicago Press.

Li-Jia Li and Li Fei-Fei. 2007. What, where and who? classifying events by scene and object recognition. In *Computer Vision, 2007. ICCV 2007. IEEE 11th International Conference on*. IEEE, pages 1–8.

David G Lowe. 1999. Object recognition from local scale-invariant features. In *Computer vision, 1999. The proceedings of the seventh IEEE international conference on*. Ieee, volume 2, pages 1150–1157.

Cewu Lu, Ranjay Krishna, Michael Bernstein, and Li Fei-Fei. 2016. Visual relationship detection with language priors. In *European Conference on Computer Vision*. Springer, pages 852–869.

Arun Mallya and Svetlana Lazebnik. 2016. Learning models for actions and person-object interactions with transfer to question answering. In *European Conference on Computer Vision*. Springer, pages 414–428.

George A Miller. 1995. Wordnet: a lexical database for english. *Communications of the ACM* 38(11):39–41.

Hans-Hellmut Nagel. 1994. A vision of "vision and language" comprises action: An example from road traffic. *Artif. Intell. Rev.* 8(2-3):189–214.

Roberto Navigli and Simone Paolo Ponzetto. 2010. Babelnet: Building a very large multilingual semantic network. In *ACL 2010, Proceedings of the 48th Annual Meeting of the Association for Computational Linguistics, July 11-16, 2010, Uppsala, Sweden*. pages 216–225.

Vignesh Ramanathan, Congcong Li, Jia Deng, Wei Han, Zhen Li, Kunlong Gu, Yang Song, Samy Bengio, Chuck Rossenberg, and Li Fei-Fei. 2015. Learning semantic relationships for better action retrieval in images. In *Proceedings of the IEEE Conference on Computer Vision and Pattern Recognition*. pages 1100–1109.

Matteo Ruggero Ronchi and Pietro Perona. 2015. Describing common human visual actions in images. In *Proceedings of the British Machine Vision Conference (BMVC 2015)*. BMVA Press, pages 52.1–52.12.

Olga Russakovsky, Jia Deng, Hao Su, Jonathan Krause, Sanjeev Satheesh, Sean Ma, Zhiheng Huang, Andrej Karpathy, Aditya Khosla, Michael S. Bernstein, Alexander C. Berg, and Fei-Fei Li. 2015. Imagenet large scale visual recognition challenge. *International Journal of Computer Vision* 115(3):211–252.

Karin Kipper Schuler. 2005. *VerbNet: A broad-coverage, comprehensive verb lexicon.* Ph.D. thesis, University of Pennsylvania.

Gunnar A Sigurdsson, Gül Varol, Xiaolong Wang, Ali Farhadi, Ivan Laptev, and Abhinav Gupta. 2016. Hollywood in homes: Crowdsourcing data collection for activity understanding. In *European Conference on Computer Vision*. Springer, pages 510–526.

Graham W Taylor, Rob Fergus, Yann LeCun, and Christoph Bregler. 2010. Convolutional learning of spatio-temporal features. In *European conference on computer vision*. Springer, pages 140–153.

Jesse Thomason, Subhashini Venugopalan, Sergio Guadarrama, Kate Saenko, and Raymond J. Mooney. 2014. Integrating language and vision to generate natural language descriptions of videos in the wild. In *COLING 2014, 25th International Conference on Computational Linguistics,Proceedings of the Conference: Technical Papers, August 23-29, 2014, Dublin, Ireland*. pages 1218–1227.

Ivan Vulić, Douwe Kiela, Stephen Clark, and Marie-Francine Moens. 2016. Multi-modal representations for improved bilingual lexicon learning. In *Proceedings of the 54th Annual Meeting of the Association for Computational Linguistics*. ACL, pages 188–194.

Shaohua Yang, Qiaozi Gao, Changsong Liu, Caiming Xiong, Song-Chun Zhu, and Joyce Y. Chai. 2016. Grounded semantic role labeling. In *NAACL HLT 2016, The 2016 Conference of the North American Chapter of the Association for Computational Linguistics: Human Language Technologies, San Diego California, USA, June 12-17, 2016*. pages 149–159.

Yezhou Yang, Ching Lik Teo, Hal Daumé III, and Yiannis Aloimonos. 2011. Corpus-guided sentence generation of natural images. In *Proceedings of the Conference on Empirical Methods in Natural Language Processing*. Association for Computational Linguistics, pages 444–454.

Bangpeng Yao and Li Fei-Fei. 2010. Grouplet: A structured image representation for recognizing human and object interactions. In *Computer Vision and Pattern Recognition (CVPR), 2010 IEEE Conference on*. IEEE, pages 9–16.

Bangpeng Yao, Xiaoye Jiang, Aditya Khosla, Andy Lai Lin, Leonidas Guibas, and Li Fei-Fei. 2011. Human action recognition by learning bases of action attributes and parts. In *Computer Vision (ICCV), 2011 IEEE International Conference on*. IEEE, pages 1331–1338.

Mark Yatskar, Luke Zettlemoyer, and Ali Farhadi. 2016. Situation recognition: Visual semantic role labeling for image understanding. In *2016 IEEE Conference on Computer Vision and Pattern Recognition, CVPR 2016, Las Vegas, NV, USA, June 26-July 1, 2016*.

Licheng Yu, Eunbyung Park, Alexander C. Berg, and Tamara L. Berg. 2015. Visual madlibs: Fill in the blank description generation and question answering. In *2015 IEEE International Conference on Computer Vision, ICCV 2015, Santiago, Chile, December 7-13, 2015*. pages 2461–2469.

Bolei Zhou, Aditya Khosla, Agata Lapedriza, Aude Oliva, and Antonio Torralba. 2016. Learning deep features for discriminative localization. In *Proceedings of the IEEE Conference on Computer Vision and Pattern Recognition*. pages 2921–2929.

Learning to Parse and Translate Improves Neural Machine Translation

Akiko Eriguchi[†], **Yoshimasa Tsuruoka**[†], and **Kyunghyun Cho**[‡]

[†]The University of Tokyo, 7-3-1 Hongo, Bunkyo-ku, Tokyo, Japan
`{eriguchi, tsuruoka}@logos.t.u-tokyo.ac.jp`
[‡]New York University, New York, NY 10012, USA
`kyunghyun.cho@nyu.edu`

Abstract

There has been relatively little attention to incorporating linguistic prior to neural machine translation. Much of the previous work was further constrained to considering linguistic prior on the source side. In this paper, we propose a hybrid model, called NMT+RNNG, that learns to parse and translate by combining the recurrent neural network grammar into the attention-based neural machine translation. Our approach encourages the neural machine translation model to incorporate linguistic prior during training, and lets it translate on its own afterward. Extensive experiments with four language pairs show the effectiveness of the proposed NMT+RNNG.

1 Introduction

Neural Machine Translation (NMT) has enjoyed impressive success without relying on much, if any, prior linguistic knowledge. Some of the most recent studies have for instance demonstrated that NMT systems work comparably to other systems even when the source and target sentences are given simply as flat sequences of characters (Lee et al., 2016; Chung et al., 2016) or statistically, not linguistically, motivated subword units (Sennrich et al., 2016; Wu et al., 2016). Shi et al. (2016) recently made an observation that the encoder of NMT captures syntactic properties of a source sentence automatically, indirectly suggesting that explicit linguistic prior may not be necessary.

On the other hand, there have only been a couple of recent studies showing the potential benefit of explicitly encoding the linguistic prior into NMT. Sennrich and Haddow (2016) for instance proposed to augment each source word with its corresponding part-of-speech tag, lemmatized form and dependency label. Eriguchi et al. (2016) instead replaced the sequential encoder with a tree-based encoder which computes the representation of the source sentence following its parse tree. Stahlberg et al. (2016) let the lattice from a hierarchical phrase-based system guide the decoding process of neural machine translation, which results in two separate models rather than a single end-to-end one. Despite the promising improvements, these explicit approaches are limited in that the trained translation model strictly requires the availability of external tools during inference time. More recently, researchers have proposed methods to incorporate target-side syntax into NMT models. Alvarez-Melis and Jaakkola (2017) have proposed a doubly-recurrent neural network that can generate a tree-structured sentence, but its effectiveness in a full scale NMT task is yet to be shown. Aharoni and Goldberg (2017) introduced a method to serialize a parsed tree and to train the serialized parsed sentences.

We propose to *implicitly* incorporate linguistic prior based on the idea of multi-task learning (Caruana, 1998; Collobert et al., 2011). More specifically, we design a hybrid decoder for NMT, called NMT+RNNG[1], that combines a usual conditional language model and a recently proposed recurrent neural network grammars (RNNGs, Dyer et al., 2016). This is done by plugging in the conventional language model decoder in the place of the buffer in RNNG, while sharing a subset of parameters, such as word vectors, between the language model and RNNG. We train this hybrid model to maximize both the log-probability of a target sentence and the log-probability of a parse action sequence. We use an external parser (Andor et al., 2016) to generate target parse actions, but unlike the previous explicit approaches, we do not need it during test time.

---

[1]Our code is available at `https://github.com/tempra28/nmtrnng`.

Proceedings of the 55th Annual Meeting of the Association for Computational Linguistics (Short Papers), pages 72–78
Vancouver, Canada, July 30 - August 4, 2017. ©2017 Association for Computational Linguistics
https://doi.org/10.18653/v1/P17-2012

We evaluate the proposed NMT+RNNG on four language pairs ({JP, Cs, De, Ru}-En). We observe significant improvements in terms of BLEU scores on three out of four language pairs and RIBES scores on all the language pairs.

2 Neural Machine Translation

Neural machine translation is a recently proposed framework for building a machine translation system based purely on neural networks. It is often built as an attention-based encoder-decoder network (Cho et al., 2015) with two recurrent networks—encoder and decoder—and an attention model. The encoder, which is often implemented as a bidirectional recurrent network with long short-term memory units (LSTM, Hochreiter and Schmidhuber, 1997) or gated recurrent units (GRU, Cho et al., 2014), first reads a source sentence represented as a sequence of words $x = (x_1, x_2, \ldots, x_N)$. The encoder returns a sequence of hidden states $h = (h_1, h_2, \ldots, h_N)$. Each hidden state h_i is a concatenation of those from the forward and backward recurrent network: $h_i = \left[\overrightarrow{h}_i; \overleftarrow{h}_i\right]$, where

$$\overrightarrow{h}_i = \overrightarrow{f}_{\text{enc}}(\overrightarrow{h}_{i-1}, V_x(x_i)),$$
$$\overleftarrow{h}_i = \overleftarrow{f}_{\text{enc}}(\overleftarrow{h}_{i+1}, V_x(x_i)).$$

$V_x(x_i)$ refers to the word vector of the i-th source word.

The decoder is implemented as a conditional recurrent language model which models the target sentence, or translation, as

$$\log p(\boldsymbol{y}|\boldsymbol{x}) = \sum_j \log p(y_j|\boldsymbol{y}_{<j}, \boldsymbol{x}),$$

where $\boldsymbol{y} = (y_1, \ldots, y_M)$. Each of the conditional probabilities in the r.h.s is computed by

$$p(y_j = y|\boldsymbol{y}_{<j}, \boldsymbol{x}) = softmax(W_y^\top \tilde{s}_j), \quad (1)$$
$$\tilde{s}_j = \tanh(\boldsymbol{W}_c[s_j; c_j]), \quad (2)$$
$$s_j = f_{\text{dec}}(s_{j-1}, [V_y(y_{j-1}); \tilde{s}_{j-1}]), \quad (3)$$

where f_{dec} is a recurrent activation function, such as LSTM or GRU, and W_y is the output word vector of the word y.

c_j is a time-dependent context vector that is computed by the attention model using the sequence h of hidden states from the encoder. The attention model first compares the current hidden state s_j against each of the hidden states and assigns a scalar score: $\beta_{i,j} = \exp(h_i^\top \boldsymbol{W}_d s_j)$ (Luong et al., 2015). These scores are then normalized across the hidden states to sum to 1, that is $\alpha_{i,j} = \frac{\beta_{i,j}}{\sum_i \beta_{i,j}}$. The time-dependent context vector is then a weighted-sum of the hidden states with these attention weights: $c_j = \sum_i \alpha_{i,j} h_i$.

3 Recurrent Neural Network Grammars

A recurrent neural network grammar (RNNG, Dyer et al., 2016) is a probabilistic syntax-based language model. Unlike a usual recurrent language model (see, e.g., Mikolov et al., 2010), an RNNG simultaneously models both tokens and their tree-based composition. This is done by having a (output) buffer, stack and action history, each of which is implemented as a stack LSTM (sLSTM, Dyer et al., 2015). At each time step, the action sLSTM predicts the next action based on the (current) hidden states of the buffer, stack and action sLSTM. That is,

$$p(a_t = a|\boldsymbol{a}_{<t}) \propto e^{W_a^\top f_{\text{action}}(h_t^{\text{buffer}}, h_t^{\text{stack}}, h_t^{\text{action}})}, \quad (4)$$

where W_a is the vector of the action a. If the selected action is *shift*, the word at the beginning of the buffer is moved to the stack. When the *reduce* action is selected, the top-two words in the stack are reduced to build a partial tree. Additionally, the action may be one of many possible non-terminal symbols, in which case the predicted non-terminal symbol is pushed to the stack.

The hidden states of the buffer, stack and action sLSTM are correspondingly updated by

$$h_t^{\text{buffer}} = \text{StackLSTM}(h_{\text{top}}^{\text{buffer}}, V_y(y_{t-1})), \quad (5)$$
$$h_t^{\text{stack}} = \text{StackLSTM}(h_{\text{top}}^{\text{stack}}, r_t),$$
$$h_t^{\text{action}} = \text{StackLSTM}(h_{\text{top}}^{\text{action}}, V_a(a_{t-1})),$$

where V_y and V_a are functions returning the target word and action vectors. The input vector r_t of the stack sLSTM is computed recursively by

$$r_t = \tanh(\boldsymbol{W}_r[r^d; r^p; V_a(a_t)]),$$

where r^d and r^p are the corresponding vectors of the parent and dependent phrases, respectively (Dyer et al., 2015). This process is iterated until a complete parse tree is built. Note that the original paper of RNNG (Dyer et al., 2016) uses constituency trees, but we employ dependency trees in this paper. Both types of trees are represented as a sequence of the three types of actions in a transition-based parsing model.

When the complete sentence is provided, the buffer simply summarizes the shifted words. When the RNNG is used as a generator, the buffer further generates the next word when the selected action is shift. The latter can be done by replacing the buffer with a recurrent language model, which is the idea on which our proposal is based.

4 Learning to Parse and Translate

4.1 NMT+RNNG

Our main proposal in this paper is to hybridize the decoder of the neural machine translation and the RNNG. We continue from the earlier observation that we can replace the buffer of RNNG to a recurrent language model that simultaneously summarizes the shifted words as well as generates future words. We replace the RNNG's buffer with the neural translation model's decoder in two steps.

Construction First, we replace the hidden state of the buffer h^{buffer} (in Eq. (5)) with the hidden state of the decoder of the attention-based neural machine translation from Eq. (3). As is clear from those two equations, both the buffer sLSTM and the translation decoder take as input the previous hidden state ($h^{\text{buffer}}_{\text{top}}$ and s_{j-1}, respectively) and the previously decoded word (or the previously shifted word in the case of the RNNG's buffer), and returns its summary state. The only difference is that the translation decoder additionally considers the state $\tilde{s}_{j-1}$. Once the buffer of the RNNG is replaced with the NMT decoder in our proposed model, the NMT decoder is also under control of the actions provided by the RNNG.[2] Second, we let the next word prediction of the translation decoder as a generator of RNNG. In other words, the generator of RNNG will output a word, when asked by the shift action, according to the conditional distribution defined by the translation decoder in Eq. (1). Once the buffer sLSTM is replaced with the neural translation decoder, the action sLSTM naturally takes as input the translation decoder's hidden state when computing the action conditional distribution in Eq. (4). We call this hybrid model *NMT+RNNG*.

---

[2]The j-th hidden state in Eq. (3) is calculated only when the action (*shift*) is predicted by the RNNG. This is why our proposed model can handle the sequences of words and actions which have different lengths.

Learning and Inference After this integration, our hybrid NMT+RNNG models the conditional distribution over all possible pairs of translation and its parse given a source sentence, i.e., $p(\boldsymbol{y}, \boldsymbol{a}|\boldsymbol{x})$. Assuming the availability of parse annotation in the target-side of a parallel corpus, we train the whole model jointly to maximize $\mathbb{E}_{(\boldsymbol{x},\boldsymbol{y},\boldsymbol{a})\sim\text{data}}\left[\log p(\boldsymbol{y}, \boldsymbol{a}|\boldsymbol{x})\right]$. In doing so, we notice that there are two separate paths through which the neural translation decoder receives error signal. First, the decoder is updated in order to maximize the conditional probability of the correct next word, which has already existed in the original neural machine translation. Second, the decoder is updated also to maximize the conditional probability of the correct parsing action, which is a novel learning signal introduced by the proposed hybridization. Furthermore, the second learning signal affects the encoder as well, encouraging the whole neural translation model to be aware of the syntactic structure of the target language. Later in the experiments, we show that this additional learning signal is useful for translation, even though we discard the RNNG (the stack and action sLSTMs) in the inference time.

4.2 Knowledge Distillation for Parsing

A major challenge in training the proposed hybrid model is that there is not a parallel corpus augmented with gold-standard target-side parse, and vice versa. In other words, we must either parse the target-side sentences of an existing parallel corpus or translate sentences with existing gold-standard parses. As the target task of the proposed model is translation, we start with a parallel corpus and annotate the target-side sentences. It is however costly to manually annotate any corpus of reasonable size (Table 6 in Alonso et al., 2016).

We instead resort to noisy, but automated annotation using an existing parser. This approach of automated annotation can be considered along the line of recently proposed techniques of knowledge distillation (Hinton et al., 2015) and distant supervision (Mintz et al., 2009). In knowledge distillation, a teacher network is trained purely on a training set with ground-truth annotations, and the annotations predicted by this teacher are used to train a student network, which is similar to our approach where the external parser could be thought of as a teacher and the proposed hybrid network's RNNG as a student. On the other hand, what we

	Train.	Dev.	Test	Voc. (*src, tgt, act*)
Cs-En	134,453	2,656	2,999	(33,867, 27,347, 82)
De-En	166,313	2,169	2,999	(33,820, 30,684, 80)
Ru-En	131,492	2,818	2,998	(32,442, 27,979, 82)
Jp-En	100,000	1,790	1,812	(23,509, 28,591, 80)

Table 1: Statistics of parallel corpora.

propose here is a special case of distant supervision in that the external parser provides noisy annotations to otherwise an unlabeled training set.

Specifically, we use SyntaxNet, released by Andor et al. (2016), on a target sentence.[3] We convert a parse tree into a sequence of one of three transition actions (SHIFT, REDUCE-L, REDUCE-R). We label each REDUCE action with a corresponding dependency label and treat it as a more fine-grained action.

5 Experiments

5.1 Language Pairs and Corpora

We compare the proposed NMT+RNNG against the baseline model on four different language pairs–Jp-En, Cs-En, De-En and Ru-En. The basic statistics of the training data are presented in Table 1. We mapped all the low-frequency words to the unique symbol "UNK" and inserted a special symbol "EOS" at the end of both source and target sentences.

Ja   We use the ASPEC corpus ("train1.txt") from the WAT'16 Jp-En translation task. We tokenize each Japanese sentence with *KyTea* (Neubig et al., 2011) and preprocess according to the recommendations from WAT'16 (WAT, 2016). We use the first 100K sentence pairs of length shorter than 50 for training. The vocabulary is constructed with all the unique tokens that appear at least twice in the training corpus. We use "dev.txt" and "test.txt" provided by WAT'16 respectively as development and test sets.

Cs, De and Ru   We use News Commentary v8. We removed noisy metacharacters and used the tokenizer from Moses (Koehn et al., 2007) to build a vocabulary of each language using unique tokens that appear at least 6, 6 and 5 times respectively for Cs, Ru and De. The target-side (English) vocabulary was constructed with all the unique tokens

appearing more than three times in each corpus. We also excluded the sentence pairs which include empty lines in either a source sentence or a target sentence. We only use sentence pairs of length 50 or less for training. We use "newstest2015" and "newstest2016" as development and test sets respectively.

5.2 Models, Learning and Inference

In all our experiments, each recurrent network has a single layer of LSTM units of 256 dimensions, and the word vectors and the action vectors are of 256 and 128 dimensions, respectively. To reduce computational overhead, we use BlackOut (Ji et al., 2015) with 2000 negative samples and $\alpha = 0.4$. When employing BlackOut, we shared the negative samples of each target word in a sentence in training time (Hashimoto and Tsuruoka, 2017), which is similar to the previous work (Zoph et al., 2016). For the proposed NMT+RNNG, we share the target word vectors between the decoder (buffer) and the stack sLSTM.

Each weight is initialized from the uniform distribution $[-0.1, 0.1]$. The bias vectors and the weights of the softmax and BlackOut are initialized to be zero. The forget gate biases of LSTMs and Stack-LSTMs are initialized to 1 as recommended in Józefowicz et al. (2015). We use stochastic gradient descent with minibatches of 128 examples. The learning rate starts from 1.0, and is halved each time the perplexity on the development set increases. We clip the norm of the gradient (Pascanu et al., 2012) with the threshold set to 3.0 (2.0 for the baseline models on Ru-En and Cs-En to avoid NaN and Inf). When the perplexity of development data increased in training time, we halved the learning rate of stochastic gradient descent and reloaded the previous model. The RNNG's stack computes the vector of a dependency parse tree which consists of the generated target words by the buffer. Since the complete parse tree has a "ROOT" node, the special token of the end of a sentence ("EOS") is considered as the ROOT. We use beam search in the inference time, with the beam width selected based on the development set performance.

It took about 15 minutes per epoch and about 20 minutes respectively for the baseline and the proposed model to train a full JP-EN parallel corpus in our implementation.[4]

---

[3]When the target sentence is parsed as data preprocessing, we use all the vocabularies in a corpus and do not cut off any words. We use the plain SyntaxNet and do not train it furthermore.

[4]We run all the experiments on multi-core CPUs (10

|| De-En	Ru-En	Cs-En	Jp-En
BLEU				
NMT	16.61	12.03	11.22	17.88
NMT+RNNG	16.41	**12.46**[†]	**12.06**[†]	**18.84**[†]
RIBES				
NMT	73.75	69.56	69.59	71.27
NMT+RNNG	**75.03**[†]	**71.04**[†]	**70.39**[†]	**72.25**[†]

Table 2: BLEU and RIBES scores by the baseline and proposed models on the test set. We use the bootstrap resampling method from Koehn (2004) to compute the statistical significance. We use † to mark those significant cases with $p < 0.005$.

Jp-En (Dev)	BLEU
NMT+RNNG	18.60
w/o Buffer	18.02
w/o Action	17.94
w/o Stack	17.58
NMT	17.75

Table 3: Effect of each component in RNNG.

5.3 Results and Analysis

In Table 2, we report the translation qualities of the tested models on all the four language pairs. We report both BLEU (Papineni et al., 2002) and RIBES (Isozaki et al., 2010). Except for De-En, measured in BLEU, we observe the statistically significant improvement by the proposed NMT+RNNG over the baseline model. It is worthwhile to note that these significant improvements have been achieved *without* any additional parameters nor computational overhead in the inference time.

Ablation Since each component in RNNG may be omitted, we ablate each component in the proposed NMT+RNNG to verify their necessity.[5] As shown in Table 3, we see that the best performance could only be achieved when all the three components were present. Removing the stack had the most adverse effect, which was found to be the case for parsing as well by Kuncoro et al. (2017).

Generated Sentences with Parsed Actions
The decoder part of our proposed model consists of two components: the NMT decoder to gener-

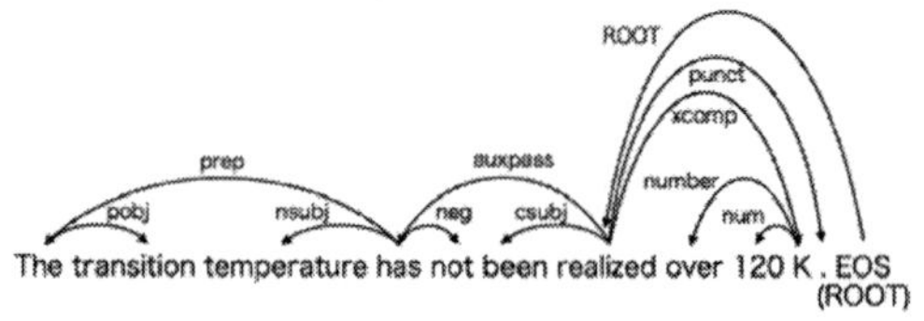

Figure 1: An example of translation and its dependency relations obtained by our proposed model.

ate a translated sentence and the RNNG decoder to predict its parsing actions. The proposed model can therefore output a dependency structure along with a translated sentence. Figure 1 shows an example of JP-EN translation in the development dataset and its dependency parse tree obtained by the proposed model. The special symbol ("EOS") is treated as the root node ("ROOT") of the parsed tree. The translated sentence was generated by using beam search, which is the same setting of NMT+RNNG shown in Table 3. The parsing actions were obtained by greedy search. The resulting dependency structure is mostly correct but contains a few errors; for example, dependency relation between "The" and " transition" should not be "pobj".

6 Conclusion

We propose a hybrid model, to which we refer as NMT+RNNG, that combines the decoder of an attention-based neural translation model with the RNNG. This model learns to parse and translate simultaneously, and training it encourages both the encoder and decoder to better incorporate linguistic priors. Our experiments confirmed its effectiveness on four language pairs ({JP, Cs, De, Ru}-En). The RNNG can in principle be trained without ground-truth parses, and this would eliminate the need of external parsers completely. We leave the investigation into this possibility for future research.

Acknowledgments

We thank Yuchen Qiao and Kenjiro Taura for their help to speed up the implementations of training and also Kazuma Hashimoto for his valuable comments and discussions. This work was supported by JST CREST Grant Number JPMJCR1513 and JSPS KAKENHI Grant Number 15J12597 and

---

threads on Intel(R) Xeon(R) CPU E5-2680 v2 @2.80GHz)

[5] Since the buffer is the decoder, it is not possible to completely remove it. Instead we simply remove the dependency of the action distribution on it.

16H01715. KC thanks support by eBay, Facebook, Google and NVIDIA.

References

Roee Aharoni and Yoav Goldberg. 2017. Towards string-to-tree neural machine translation. In *Proceedings of the 55th Annual Meeting of the Association for Computational Linguistics*. to appear.

Héctor Martínez Alonso, Djamé Seddah, and Benoît Sagot. 2016. From noisy questions to minecraft texts: Annotation challenges in extreme syntax scenario. In *Proceedings of the 2nd Workshop on Noisy User-generated Text (WNUT)*. pages 13–23.

David Alvarez-Melis and Tommi S. Jaakkola. 2017. Tree-structured decoding with doubly-recurrent neural networks. In *Proceedings of International Conference on Learning Representations 2017*.

Daniel Andor, Chris Alberti, David Weiss, Aliaksei Severyn, Alessandro Presta, Kuzman Ganchev, Slav Petrov, and Michael Collins. 2016. Globally normalized transition-based neural networks. In *Proceedings of the 54th Annual Meeting of the Association for Computational Linguistics*. pages 2442–2452.

Rich Caruana. 1998. Multitask learning. In *Learning to learn*, Springer, pages 95–133.

Kyunghyun Cho, Aaron Courville, and Yoshua Bengio. 2015. Describing multimedia content using attention-based encoder-decoder networks. *IEEE Transactions on Multimedia* 17(11):1875–1886.

Kyunghyun Cho, Bart van Merrienboer, Caglar Gulcehre, Dzmitry Bahdanau, Fethi Bougares, Holger Schwenk, and Yoshua Bengio. 2014. Learning phrase representations using rnn encoder–decoder for statistical machine translation. In *Proceedings of the 2014 Conference on Empirical Methods in Natural Language Processing*. pages 1724–1734.

Junyoung Chung, Kyunghyun Cho, and Yoshua Bengio. 2016. A character-level decoder without explicit segmentation for neural machine translation. In *Proceedings of the 54th Annual Meeting of the Association for Computational Linguistics*. Association for Computational Linguistics, pages 1693–1703.

Ronan Collobert, Jason Weston, Léon Bottou, Michael Karlen, Koray Kavukcuoglu, and Pavel Kuksa. 2011. Natural language processing (almost) from scratch. *Journal of Machine Learning Research* 12:2493–2537.

Chris Dyer, Miguel Ballesteros, Wang Ling, Austin Matthews, and A. Noah Smith. 2015. Transition-based dependency parsing with stack long short-term memory. In *Proceedings of the 53rd Annual Meeting of the Association for Computational Linguistics and the 7th International Joint Conference on Natural Language Processing*. pages 334–343.

Chris Dyer, Adhiguna Kuncoro, Miguel Ballesteros, and A. Noah Smith. 2016. Recurrent neural network grammars. In *Proceedings of the 2016 Conference of the North American Chapter of the Association for Computational Linguistics: Human Language Technologies*. pages 199–209.

Akiko Eriguchi, Kazuma Hashimoto, and Yoshimasa Tsuruoka. 2016. Tree-to-sequence attentional neural machine translation. In *Proceedings of the 54th Annual Meeting of the Association for Computational Linguistics*. pages 823–833.

Kazuma Hashimoto and Yoshimasa Tsuruoka. 2017. Neural Machine Translation with Source-Side Latent Graph Parsing. *arXiv preprint arXiv:1702.02265* .

Geoffrey Hinton, Oriol Vinyals, and Jeff Dean. 2015. Distilling the knowledge in a neural network. *arXiv preprint arXiv:1503.02531* .

Sepp Hochreiter and Jürgen Schmidhuber. 1997. Long short-term memory. *Neural Comput.* 9(8):1735–1780.

Hideki Isozaki, Tsutomu Hirao, Kevin Duh, Katsuhito Sudoh, and Hajime Tsukada. 2010. Automatic evaluation of translation quality for distant language pairs. In *Proceedings of the 2010 Conference on Empirical Methods in Natural Language Processing*. pages 944–952.

Shihao Ji, S. V. N. Vishwanathan, Nadathur Satish, Michael J. Anderson, and Pradeep Dubey. 2015. Blackout: Speeding up recurrent neural network language models with very large vocabularies. *Proceedings of International Conference on Learning Representations 2015* .

Rafal Józefowicz, Wojciech Zaremba, and Ilya Sutskever. 2015. An empirical exploration of recurrent network architectures. In *Proceedings of the 32nd International Conference on Machine Learning*. pages 2342–2350.

Philipp Koehn. 2004. Statistical significance tests for machine translation evaluation. In *Proceedings of the 2004 Conference on Empirical Methods in Natural Language Processing*. pages 388–395.

Philipp Koehn, Hieu Hoang, Alexandra Birch, Chris Callison-Burch, Marcello Federico, Nicola Bertoldi, Brooke Cowan, Wade Shen, Christine Moran, Richard Zens, Chris Dyer, Ondrej Bojar, Alexandra Constantin, and Evan Herbst. 2007. Moses: Open source toolkit for statistical machine translation. In *Proceedings of the 45th Annual Meeting of the Association for Computational Linguistics Companion Volume Proceedings of the Demo and Poster Sessions*. pages 177–180.

Adhiguna Kuncoro, Miguel Ballesteros, Lingpeng Kong, Chris Dyer, Graham Neubig, and Noah A. Smith. 2017. What do recurrent neural network grammars learn about syntax? In *Proceedings of the 15th Conference of the European Chapter of the Association for Computational Linguistics: Volume 1, Long Papers.* pages 1249–1258.

Jason Lee, Kyunghyun Cho, and Thomas Hofmann. 2016. Fully character-level neural machine translation without explicit segmentation. *arXiv preprint arXiv:1610.03017* .

Thang Luong, Hieu Pham, and Christopher D. Manning. 2015. Effective approaches to attention-based neural machine translation. In *Proceedings of the 2015 Conference on Empirical Methods in Natural Language Processing.* pages 1412–1421.

Tomáš Mikolov, Martin Karafiát, Lukáš Burget, Jan Černocký, and Sanjeev Khudanpur. 2010. Recurrent neural network based language model. In *Proceedings of the 11th Annual Conference of the International Speech Communication Association (INTERSPEECH 2010).* International Speech Communication Association, pages 1045–1048.

Mike Mintz, Steven Bills, Rion Snow, and Dan Jurafsky. 2009. Distant supervision for relation extraction without labeled data. In *Proceedings of the Joint Conference of the 47th Annual Meeting of the ACL and the 4th International Joint Conference on Natural Language Processing of the AFNLP.* pages 1003–1011.

Graham Neubig, Yosuke Nakata, and Shinsuke Mori. 2011. Pointwise prediction for robust, adaptable japanese morphological analysis. In *Proceedings of the 49th Annual Meeting of the Association for Computational Linguistics: Human Language Technologies.* pages 529–533.

Kishore Papineni, Salim Roukos, Todd Ward, and Wei-Jing Zhu. 2002. Bleu: A method for automatic evaluation of machine translation. In *Proceedings of the 40th Annual Meeting on Association for Computational Linguistics.* pages 311–318.

Razvan Pascanu, Tomas Mikolov, and Yoshua Bengio. 2012. Understanding the exploding gradient problem. *arXiv preprint arXiv:1211.5063* abs/1211.5063.

Rico Sennrich and Barry Haddow. 2016. Linguistic input features improve neural machine translation. In *Proceedings of the First Conference on Machine Translation.* pages 83–91.

Rico Sennrich, Barry Haddow, and Alexandra Birch. 2016. Neural machine translation of rare words with subword units. In *Proceedings of the 54th Annual Meeting of the Association for Computational Linguistics.* pages 1715–1725.

Xing Shi, Inkit Padhi, and Kevin Knight. 2016. Does string-based neural mt learn source syntax? In *Proceedings of the 2016 Conference on Empirical Methods in Natural Language Processing.* pages 1526–1534.

Felix Stahlberg, Eva Hasler, Aurelien Waite, and Bill Byrne. 2016. Syntactically guided neural machine translation. In *Proceedings of the 54th Annual Meeting of the Association for Computational Linguistics.* pages 299–305.

WAT. 2016. `http://lotus.kuee.kyoto-u.ac.jp/WAT/baseline/dataPreparationJE.html`.

Yonghui Wu, Mike Schuster, Zhifeng Chen, Quoc V. Le, Mohammad Norouzi, Wolfgang Macherey, Maxim Krikun, Yuan Cao, Qin Gao, Klaus Macherey, Jeff Klingner, Apurva Shah, Melvin Johnson, Xiaobing Liu, Lukasz Kaiser, Stephan Gouws, Yoshikiyo Kato, Taku Kudo, Hideto Kazawa, Keith Stevens, George Kurian, Nishant Patil, Wei Wang, Cliff Young, Jason Smith, Jason Riesa, Alex Rudnick, Oriol Vinyals, Greg Corrado, Macduff Hughes, and Jeffrey Dean. 2016. Google's neural machine translation system: Bridging the gap between human and machine translation. *arXiv preprint arXiv:1609.08144* .

Barret Zoph, Ashish Vaswani, Jonathan May, and Kevin Knight. 2016. Simple, Fast Noise-Contrastive Estimation for Large RNN Vocabularies. In *Proceedings of the 2016 Conference of the North American Chapter of the Association for Computational Linguistics: Human Language Technologies.* pages 1217–1222.

On the Distribution of Lexical Features at Multiple Levels of Analysis

Fatemeh Almodaresi[†]   **Lyle Ungar**[§]   **Vivek Kulkarni**[†]   **Mohsen Zakeri**[†]
Salvatore Giorgi[§]   **H. Andrew Schwartz**[†]

[†]Stony Brook University   [§]University of Pennsylvania

`{falmodaresit,has}@cs.stonybrook.edu`

Abstract

Natural language processing has increasingly moved from modeling documents and words toward studying the people behind the language. This move to working with data at the user or community level has presented the field with different characteristics of linguistic data. In this paper, we empirically characterize various lexical distributions at different levels of analysis, showing that, while most features are decidedly sparse and non-normal at the message-level (as with traditional NLP), they follow the central limit theorem to become much more Log-normal or even Normal at the user- and county-levels. Finally, we demonstrate that modeling lexical features for the correct level of analysis leads to marked improvements in common social scientific prediction tasks.

1 Introduction

NLP for studying people has grown rapidly as more than one-third of the human population use social media actively.[1] While traditional NLP tasks (e.g. POS tagging, parsing, sentiment analysis) mostly work at the word, sentence, or document level, the increased focus on social scientific applications has shifted attention to new levels of analysis (e.g. user-level and community-level) (Koppel et al., 2009; Sarawgi et al., 2011; Schwartz et al., 2013a; Coppersmith et al., 2014; Flekova et al., 2016).

Figure 1 shows the distribution of two unigrams, 'the' and 'love' at three levels of analysis. While both words have zero counts in most messages, 'the' starts to look Normal across

users, and both words are approximately Normal at the county level. Methods performing optimally at the document level may suffer at the user or community level due to this shift in the distribution of lexical features.[2]

In this paper, we ask a fundamental statistical question: *How does the shift in unit-of-analysis from document-level to user-or-community level shift lexical distributions in social media?*[3] The central limit theorem suggests that count data is better approximated by a *Normal* distribution as one increases the number of events, or as one aggregates more features (e.g. combining words using LDA topics or hand-built word sets). However, we do not know how far towards a Normal these new levels of analysis bring us.

Related work. The question we ask harks back to work from pioneers in corpus-based computational linguistics, including Shannon (1948) who suggested that probabilistic distributions of ngrams could be used to solve a range of communications problems, and Mosteller and Wallace (1963) who found that a negative binomial distribution seemed to model unigram usage by authors of the Federalist Papers. Numerous works have since continued the tradition of examining the distribution of lexical features. For example, McCallum et al. (1998) compares the results of probabilistic models based on multivariate Bernoulli with those based on multinomial distributions for document classification. Jansche

---

[1]Social Insights; Global social media research summary 2017

[2]While the distribution of word frequencies (i.e. a *Zipfian* distribution) is often discussed in NLP, it is important to note that we are focused on the distribution of single features (e.g. words) over documents, users, or communities.

[3]While other sources of corpora can also be aggregated to the user- or community-level (e.g. newswire, books), we believe the question of distributions is particularly important in social media because it often contains very short posts and a growing body of work in NLP for social science focuses on social media.

Proceedings of the 55th Annual Meeting of the Association for Computational Linguistics (Short Papers), pages 79–84
Vancouver, Canada, July 30 - August 4, 2017. ©2017 Association for Computational Linguistics
https://doi.org/10.18653/v1/P17-2013

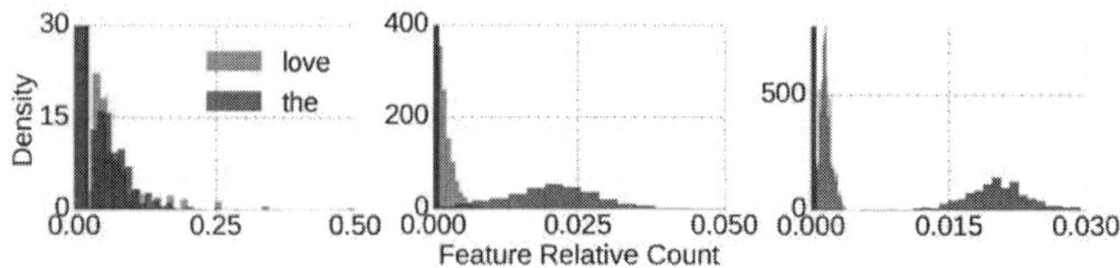

Figure 1: Histograms for unigrams "the" (a very frequent feature) and "love" (less frequent) at different levels of analysis: message, user, and community (from left to right). The bars at zero are cut-off at the message and user levels to increase readability of the remaining distribution.

(2003) extended this line of work, observing lexical count data often display an extra probability mass concentrated at zero and suggesting Zero-Inflated negative binomial distributions can capture this phenomenon better and are easier to implement than alternatives such as overdispersed binomial models. While these works are numerous, none, to the best of our knowledge, have focused on distributions across social media or at multiple levels of analysis.

Contributions. Our study is perhaps unconventional in modern computational linguistics due to the elementary nature of our contributions, focusing on understanding the empirical distributions of lexical features in Twitter. First, we use zero-inflated kernel density estimated plots to show how distributions of different language features (words, LDA topics, and hand-curated word sets) vary with level of analysis (message, user, and county). Second, we quantify which distributions best describe the different feature types and analysis levels of social media. Finally, we show the utility of such information, finding that using the appropriate model for each feature type improves Naive Bayes classification results across three common social scientific tasks: sarcasm detection at the message-level, gender identification at the user-level, and political ideology classification at the community-level.

2 Methods

Examining data at three different levels of analysis and across three different lexical feature types (unigrams, data-driven topics, and manual lexica), we seek to (1) visually characterize distributions, (2) empirically test which distributions best fit the data, and (3) evaluate classification models utilizing multiple distributions at each level. Unigrams underlie all data where as each level of analysis

and feature type represent a different degree of aggregation and covariance structure.

Data preparation. We start with a set of about two million Twitter posts and supplemental information about the users: their ID, county, and gender. The data was based on that of Volkova et al. (2013), who provide tweet ids and gender, and mapped to counties using the method of Schwartz et al. (2013a). We limit our data to users who have used at least 1000 words and counties that have at least 30 users and a total word count of 5000. Applying these constraints, the final set of data consists of 1,639,750 tweets (representing the message-level) from 5,226 users in 420 different counties (representing the community-level).

We consider three lexical features that are commonly used in NLP for social science: *1-grams* (the top 10,000 most common unigrams found with happierFunTokenizing social media tokenizer), 2000 LDA *topics* downloaded from Schwartz et al. (2013b)), and *lexica* (64 categories from the linguistic inquiry and word count dictionary (Pennebaker et al., 2007)). Note that the features progress from most sparse (1grams) to least sparse (lexica).

Distributions. Figure 2 shows the empirical distributions of different lexical features at different levels of analysis. 500 features were sampled from the top 20,000 unigrams [4], 2000 social media LDA topics (Schwartz et al., 2013a), and all 64 categories from the LIWC lexica (Pennebaker et al., 2007). To encode the variables continuously we used relative frequencies for unigrams and lexica (count of word or category divided by count of all words), and probability of topics, calculated from the posterior probabilities from the LDA models. Each line in the kernel density plot

---

[4] In social media analyses, the top 20,000 features are often used (Schwartz and Ungar, 2015)

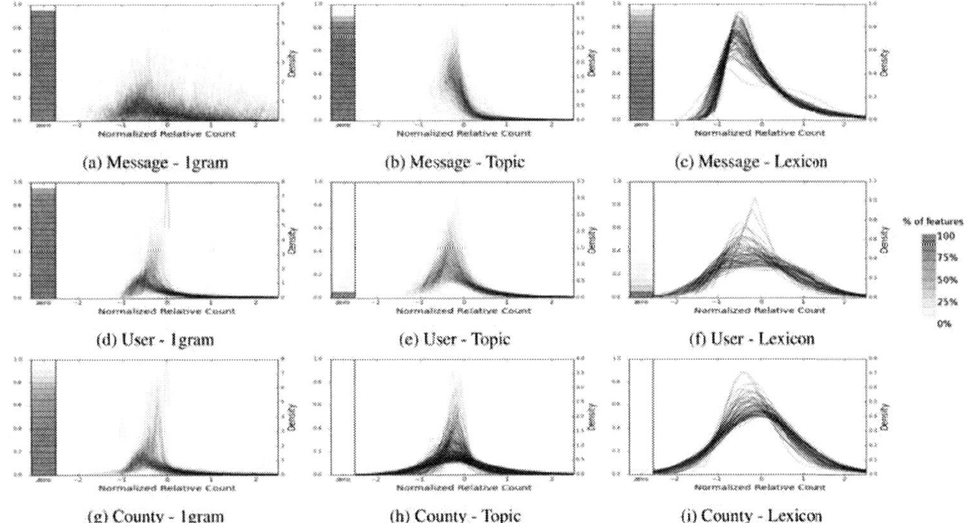

Figure 2: Kernel Density Estimate (KDE) plots showing the distribution of 500 random features at different levels of analysis. Each row represents a specific level of analysis (county, user, message) and each column represents a specific type of feature (Lexicon, Topic, Unigram). The bar on the left of each plot represents the percentage of observations that are zero for each feature where the shading represents the percent of features reaching the given threshold. As the bar gets darker it means more features out of 500 are zero in that percentage of individuals. The right portion of each plot is based on standardized relative frequencies of the variables (mean centered and divided by the standard deviation).

is semi-transparent such that an aggregate trend across multiple features will emerge darkest. As we move along a row ranging specific features (unigrams) to generic features (lexicon), the empirical distribution gradually changes from resembling a "power law" (or binomial distribution with low number of trials and probability of success) to something more "Normal". Similar shifts are also observed as we move across levels of modeling.

We investigate whether the best-fitting distributions vary across the three levels of analysis and three types of lexical features. We consider the following candidate distributions to see how well they fit each of these empirical distributions:

- *Continuous Distributions*: (a) Power-law, (b), Log-normal and (c) Normal

- *Discrete Distributions*: (a) Bernoulli, (b) Multinomial, (c) Poisson, and (d) Zero Inflated Poisson

Since most of the distributions outlined above are standard distributions, we only briefly describe the zero-inflated variants which handle excess zero counts. Zero-inflated models explicitly model the idea that a distribution does not fully capture the mass at 0 in real world data. They assume that the data is generated from two components. The first

component is governed by a Bernoulli distribution that generates excess zeros, while the second component generates counts, some of which also could be zero (Jansche, 2003).

3 Evaluation

We evaluate the distributions we considered by first characterizing the goodness of fit at different levels of analyses and then by their predictive performance on social media prediction tasks, both of which we describe below.

3.1 Goodness of fit

Following the central limit theorem, we seek to determine across the range levels of analysis and feature types, whether the distribution can be approximated by a Normal. Focusing just on the non-zero portions of data encoded as relative frequencies, we quantify the fit of each candidate distribution to the data.

We estimate the parameters for each distribution using MLE on a training data set (i.e. 80% of data). Then, we evaluate their likelihoods of a held-out test dataset, given the estimated parameters. Since we are trying to approximate the discrete distribution with a continuous model, all data were converted to relative frequencies. Finally, the distribution under which the test data is most likely

Dist	Message			User			County		
	1gram	Topic	Lex.	1gram	Topic	Lex.	1gram	Topic	Lex.
Power Law	**71**	10	0	4	0	0	7	0	0
Log-Normal	25	**89**	**100**	**96**	**97**	**64**	**92**	**86**	44
Normal	4	1	0	0	3	36	1	14	**56**

Table 1: Percentage of best-fitted distributions in each level of message, user, and county for different types of features such as "Lexicons", "Topics", and "1grams". Note that the best-fitting distribution for each feature type is a function of the level of analysis.

is chosen as the 'best fit' distribution. We repeat this 100 times and pick the most likely distribution over all these 100 independent runs.

Results. Table 1 shows the percentage of features in each level that were best fit from an underlying distribution of Normal, Log-Normal, or Power Law. We see empirically that there is a trend toward Normal approximation moving from message to county level, as well as 1grams to lexica. In fact, a majority of lexica at the county-level were best approximated by a Normal distribution.

3.2 Predictive Power

In the previous section, we showed that the distribution of lexical features depends on the scale of analysis considered (for example, the message level or the user level). Here, we demonstrate that predictive models which use these lexical features as co-variates can leverage this information to boost predictive performance. We consider three predictive tasks using a generative predictive model. The primary purpose of this evaluation is not to characterize the best distribution at a level or task, but to demonstrate that the choice of distribution assumed when modeling features significantly affects the predictive performance.

Predictive Tasks : We consider the following common predictive tasks and also outline details of the datasets considered:

1. **Sarcasm Detection (Message level)**: This task consists of determining whether tweets contain a sarcastic expression (Bamman and Smith, 2015). The dataset consists of 16,833 messages with an average of 12 words per message.

2. **Gender Identification (User level)**: This task involves determining the gender of the author utilizing a previously described Twitter dataset (Volkova et al., 2013). This dataset consists of 5,044 users each of which have at least a 1,000 tokens as is standard in user-level analyses (Schwartz et al., 2013b).

3. **Ideology Classification (Community level)**: We utilized county voting records from 2012 along with a dataset of tweets mapped to counties. This data consists of 2,175 counties with atleast 10,000 unigrams as is common in community level analyses (Eichstaedt et al., 2015).

We consider a Naive Bayes classifier (a generative model) which enables one to directly incorporate the inferred feature distribution at a particular level of analysis, the results of which we discuss in Table 2. Variable encoding for the classifiers varied from binary encoding of present or not (Bernoulli), to counts (Poisson, Zero-inflated Poisson), multivariate counts (Multinomial), and continuous relative frequencies (Normal). All distributions have closed form MLE solutions except for Zero-Inflated Poisson, in which case we used LBFGS optimization to fit both of its parameters (Head and Zerner, 1985).

Results. We report macro F1-score for each of the underlying distributions in Table 2. For each of the tasks, we used 80% of the data for training and evaluate on the held-out 20%. We observe a similar pattern as that observed in the goodness of fit setting, with a shift in the best performing distribution from Bernoulli (which simply models if a feature exists or not) toward something more Gaussian (Poisson or Normal) as we move along from message-level to county-level analysis and from unigrams to lexica. Specifically note that at higher levels of analysis (at user and county levels) as the distribution of features becomes closer to Normal, modeling features as Bernoulli is clearly sub-optimal where as at the message level modeling unigrams as a Bernoulli is superior. These observations underscore the main insight that the distribution family used to model features can be con-

Feature Distribution	Message (Sarcasm)			User (Gender)			County (Political Ideology)		
	1gram	Topic	Lex.	1gram	Topic	Lex.	1gram	Topic	Lex.
most frequent class	.33	.33	.33	.31	.31	.31	.42	.42	.42
Bernoulli	**.71**	.62	.61	**.68**	.52	.48	.66	.42	.42
Multinomial	.70	.63	.63	.66	.54	.64	.60	.74	.71
Poisson	.70	.59	**.64**	.51	.47	.49	.73	.60	**.73**
ZeroInflated-Poisson	.34	**.64**	.63	.50	.47	.49	**.75**	.74	**.73**
Normal	.57	.47	.54	.51	**.59**	**.65**	.56	**.78**	.70

Table 2: F1-Score of Naive Bayes classifiers using various distributions and levels of analysis across tasks of sarcasm detection, gender identification, and political ideology classification. Observe that predictive power is once again a function of the distribution family used to model feature distribution and depends on level of analysis.

sidered a function of level of analysis and feature-type considered and has a significant bearing on predictive performance.

4 Conclusion

While computational linguistics has a long history of studying the distributions of lexical features, social media and social scientific studies have brought about a need to understand how these change at multiple levels of analyses. Here, we explored empirical distributions of different types of linguistic features (unigrams, topics, lexica) in three different levels of analysis in Twitter data (message, user, and community). To show which distribution can better describe features of different levels, we approached the problem in three different ways: (1) visualization of empirical distributions, (2) goodness-of-fit comparisons, and (3) for predictive tasks.

We showed that the best-fit distribution depends on feature-type (i.e. unigram versus lexica) and the level of analysis (i.e. message-, user-, or community-level). Following the central limit theorem, all user-level features were predominantly Log-normal, while a power law best fit unigrams at the message level and a Normal distribution best approximated lexica at the community level. Finally, we demonstrated that predictive performance can also vary considerably by the level of analysis and feature-type, following a similar trend from Bernoulli distributions at the message-level to Poisson or Normal at the community-level. Our results underscore the significance of the level of analysis for the ever-growing focus in NLP on social scientific problems which seek to not only better model words and documents but also the people and communities generating them.

Acknowledgements

This work was supported in part by the Templeton Religion Trust, Grant TRT-0048.

References

David Bamman and Noah A Smith. 2015. Contextualized sarcasm detection on twitter. In *Proceedings to the International Conference on Web-blogs and Social Media*. pages 574–577.

Glen Coppersmith, Mark Dredze, and Craig Harman. 2014. Quantifying mental health signals in twitter. In *Proceedings of the ACL workshop on Computational Linguistics and Clinical Psychology*.

Johannes C Eichstaedt, H Andrew Schwartz, Margaret L Kern, Gregory Park, Darwin R Labarthe, Raina M Merchant, Sneha Jha, Megha Agrawal, Lukasz A Dziurzynski, Maarten Sap, et al. 2015. Psychological language on twitter predicts county-level heart disease mortality. *Psychological Science* 1:11.

Lucie Flekova, Jordan Carpenter, Salvatore Giorgi, Lyle Ungar, and Daniel Preoctiuc-Pietro. 2016. Analyzing Biases in Human Perception of User Age and Gender from Text. In *Proceedings of the 54th annual meeting of the Association for Computational Linguistics*. ACL.

John D Head and Michael C Zerner. 1985. A broyden-fletchergoldfarbshanno optimization procedure for molecular geometries. *Chemical physics letters* 122(3):264–270.

Martin Jansche. 2003. Parametric models of linguistic count data. In *Proceedings of the 41st Annual Meeting on Association for Computational Linguistics-Volume 1*. Association for Computational Linguistics, pages 288–295.

Moshe Koppel, Jonathan Schler, and Shlomo Argamon. 2009. Computational methods in authorship attribution. *Journal of the American Society for information Science and Technology* 60(1):9–26.

Andrew McCallum, Kamal Nigam, et al. 1998. A comparison of event models for naive bayes text classification. In *AAAI-98 workshop on learning for text categorization*. Citeseer, volume 752, pages 41–48.

Frederick Mosteller and David L Wallace. 1963. Inference in an authorship problem: A comparative study of discrimination methods applied to the authorship of the disputed federalist papers. *Journal of the American Statistical Association* 58(302):275–309.

James W Pennebaker, Roger J Booth, and Martha E Francis. 2007. Liwc2007: Linguistic inquiry and word count. *Austin, Texas: LIWC.net* .

Ruchita Sarawgi, Kailash Gajulapalli, and Yejin Choi. 2011. Gender attribution: tracing stylometric evidence beyond topic and genre. In *Proceedings of the Fifteenth Conference on Computational Natural Language Learning*. Association for Computational Linguistics, pages 78–86.

H Andrew Schwartz, Johannes C Eichstaedt, Margaret L Kern, Lukasz Dziurzynski, Richard E Lucas, Megha Agrawal, Gregory J Park, Shrinidhi K Lakshmikanth, Sneha Jha, Martin EP Seligman, et al. 2013a. Characterizing geographic variation in wellbeing using tweets. In *Proceedings of the 7th International AAAI Conference on Web and Social Media*. ICWSM.

H Andrew Schwartz, Johannes C Eichstaedt, Margaret L Kern, Lukasz Dziurzynski, Stephanie M Ramones, Megha Agrawal, Achal Shah, Michal Kosinski, David Stillwell, Martin EP Seligman, et al. 2013b. Personality, gender, and age in the language of social media: The open-vocabulary approach. *PloS one* 8(9):e73791.

H Andrew Schwartz and Lyle H Ungar. 2015. Data-driven content analysis of social media a systematic overview of automated methods. *The ANNALS of the American Academy of Political and Social Science* 659(1):78–94.

Claude E Shannon. 1948. A mathematical theory of communication, bell system technical journal 27: 379-423 and 623–656. *Mathematical Reviews (MathSciNet): MR10, 133e* .

Svitlana Volkova, Theresa Wilson, and David Yarowsky. 2013. Exploring demographic language variations to improve multilingual sentiment analysis in social media. In *Proceedings of the Conference on Empirical Methods in Natural Language Processing*. EMNLP, pages 1815–1827.

Exploring Neural Text Simplification Models

Sergiu Nisioi[1,3,*]   Sanja Štajner[2,*]   Simone Paolo Ponzetto[2]   Liviu P. Dinu[1]

[1]Human Language Technologies Research Center, University of Bucharest, Romania
[2]Data and Web Science Group, University of Mannheim, Germany
[3]Oracle Corporation, Romania
{sergiu.nisioi,ldinu}@fmi.unibuc.ro
{sanja,simone}@informatik.uni-mannheim.de

Abstract

We present the first attempt at using sequence to sequence neural networks to model text simplification (TS). Unlike the previously proposed automated TS systems, our neural text simplification (NTS) systems are able to simultaneously perform lexical simplification and content reduction. An extensive human evaluation of the output has shown that NTS systems achieve almost perfect grammaticality and meaning preservation of output sentences and higher level of simplification than the state-of-the-art automated TS systems.

1 Introduction

Neural sequence to sequence models have been successfully used in many applications (Graves, 2012), from speech and signal processing to text processing or dialogue systems (Serban et al., 2015). Neural machine translation (Cho et al., 2014; Bahdanau et al., 2014) is a particular type of sequence to sequence model that recently attracted a lot of attention from industry (Wu et al., 2016) and academia, especially due to the capability to obtain state-of-the-art results for various translation tasks (Bojar et al., 2016). Unlike classical statistical machine translation (SMT) systems (Koehn, 2010), neural networks are being trained end-to-end, without the need to have external decoders, language models or phrase tables. The architectures are relatively simpler and more flexible, making possible the use of character models (Luong and Manning, 2016) or even training multilingual systems in one go (Firat et al., 2016).

Automated text simplification (ATS) systems are meant to transform original texts into differ-

ent (simpler) variants which would be understood by wider audiences and more successfully processed by various NLP tools. In the last several years, great attention has been given to addressing ATS as a monolingual machine translation problem translating from 'original' to 'simple' sentences. So far, attempts were made at standard phrase-based SMT (PBSMT) models (Specia, 2010; Štajner et al., 2015), PBSMT models with added phrasal deletion rules (Coster and Kauchak, 2011) or reranking of the n-best outputs according to their dissimilarity to the output (Wubben et al., 2012), tree-based translation models (Zhu et al., 2010; Paetzold and Specia, 2013), and syntax-based MT with specially designed tuning function (Xu et al., 2016). Recently, lexical simplification (LS) was addressed by unsupervised approaches leveraging word-embeddings, with reported good success (Glavaš and Štajner, 2015; Paetzold and Specia, 2016).

To the best of our knowledge, our work is the first to address the applicability of neural sequence to sequence models for ATS. We make use of the recent advances in neural machine translation (NMT) and adapt the existing architectures for our specific task. We also perform an extensive human evaluation to directly compare our systems with the current state-of-the-art (supervised) MT-based and unsupervised lexical simplification systems.

2 Neural Text Simplification (NTS)

We use the OpenNMT framework (Klein et al., 2017) to train and build our architecture with two LSTM layers (Hochreiter and Schmidhuber, 1997), hidden states of size 500 and 500 hidden units, and a 0.3 dropout probability (Srivastava et al., 2014). The vocabulary size is set to 50,000 and we train the model for 15 epochs with plain SGD optimizer, and after epoch 8 we halve the

---

*Both authors have contributed equally to this work

Proceedings of the 55th Annual Meeting of the Association for Computational Linguistics (Short Papers), pages 85–91
Vancouver, Canada, July 30 - August 4, 2017. ©2017 Association for Computational Linguistics
https://doi.org/10.18653/v1/P17-2014

learning rate. At the end of each epoch we save the current state of the model and predict the perplexity values of the models on the development set. We employ early-stopping and select the model resulted from the epoch with the best perplexity to avoid over-fitting. The parameters are initialized over uniform distribution with support [-0.1, 0.1]. Additionally, for the decoder we employ global attention in combination with input feeding as described by Luong et al. (2015). The architecture[1] is depicted in Figure 1, with the input feeding approach represented only for the last hidden state of the decoder.

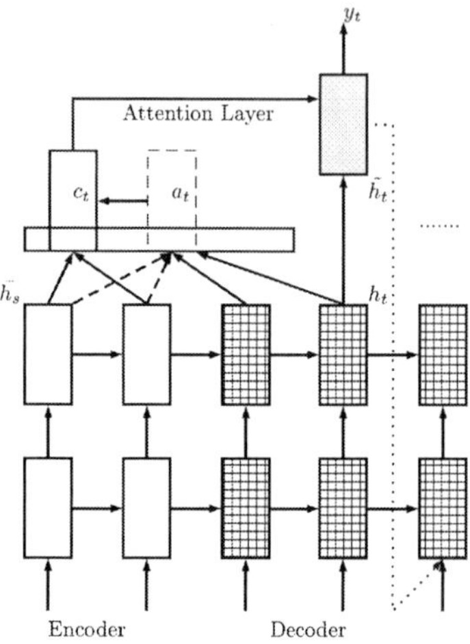

Figure 1: Architecture of the neural simplification model with global attention and input feeding.

For the attention layer, we compute a context vector c_t by using the information provided from the hidden states of the source sentence and by computing a weighted average with the alignment weights a_t. The new hidden state is obtained using a concatenation of the previous hidden state and the context vector:

$$\tilde{h}_t = \tanh W[c_t; h_t]$$

The global alignment weights a_t are being computed with a softmax function over the general scoring method for attention:

$$a_t(s) = \frac{\exp h_t^T W_{as} \bar{h}_s}{\sum_{s'} \exp h_t^T W_{as'} \bar{h}_{s'}}$$

Input feeding is a process that sends the previous hidden state obtained using the alignment

method, to the input at the next step, presumably making the model keep track of anterior alignment decisions. Luong et al. (2015) showed this approach can increase the evaluation scores for neural machine translation, while in our case, for monolingual data, we believe it can be helpful to create better alignments. Our approach does not involve the use of character-based models (Sennrich et al., 2015; Luong and Manning, 2016) to handle out of vocabulary words and entities. Instead, we make use of alignment probabilities between the predictions and the original sentences to retrieve the original words.

2.1 Word2vec Embeddings

Furthermore, we are interested to explore whether large scale pre-trained embeddings can improve text simplification models. Kauchak (2013) indicates that combining normal data with simplified data can increase the performance of ATS systems. Therefore, we construct a secondary model (NTS-w2v) using a combination of pre-trained word2vec from Google News corpus (Mikolov et al., 2013a) of size 300 and locally trained embeddings of size 200. To ensure good representations of low-frequency words, we use word2vec (Řehůřek and Sojka, 2010; Mikolov et al., 2013b) to train skip-gram with hierarchical softmax and we set a window of 10 words.

Following Garten et al. (2015) who showed that simple concatenation can improve the word representations, we construct two different sets of embeddings for the encoder and for the decoder. The former are constructed using the word2vec trained on the original English texts combined with Google News and the later (decoder) embeddings are built from word2vec trained on the simplified version of the training data combined with Google News. To merge the local and global embeddings, we concatenate the representations for each word in the vocabulary, thus obtaining a new representation of size 500. If a word is missing in the global embeddings, we replace it with a sample from a Gaussian distribution with mean 0 and standard deviation of 0.9. The remaining parameters are left unchanged from the previous model description.

2.2 Prediction Ranking

To ensure the best predictions and the best simplified sentences at each step, we use beam search to sample multiple outputs from the two systems

[1]The architecture configurations, data, and the pretrained models are released in `https://github.com/senisioi/NeuralTextSimplification`

described previously (NTS and NTS-w2v). Beam search works by generating the first k hypotheses at each step ordered by the log-likelihood of the target sentence given the input sentence. By default, we use a beam size of 5 and take the first hypothesis, but we also observe that higher beam size and lower-ranked hypotheses can generate good simplification results. Therefore, we generate the first two candidate hypotheses for each beam size from 5 to 12. We then attempt to find the best beam size and hypothesis based on two metrics: the traditional MT-evaluation metric, BLEU (Papineni et al., 2002; Bird et al., 2009) with NIST smoothing (Bird et al., 2009), and SARI (Xu et al., 2016), a recent text-simplification metric.

2.3 Dataset

To train our models, we use the publicly available dataset provided by Hwang et al. (2015) based on manual and automatic alignments between standard English Wikipedia and Simple English Wikipedia (EW–SEW). We discard the uncategorized matches, and use only *good matches* and *partial matches* which were above the 0.45 threshold (Hwang et al., 2015), totaling to 280K aligned sentences (around 150K full matches and 130K partial matches). It is one of the largest freely available resources for text simplification, and unlike the previously used EW–SEW corpus[2] (Kauchak, 2013), which only contains *full matches* (167K pairs), the newer dataset also contains *partial matches*. Therefore, it is not only larger, but it also allows for learning sentence shortening (dropping irrelevant parts) transformations (see Table 3, Appendix A).

	original	simplified
locations	158,394	127,349
persons	161,808	127,742
organizations	130,679	101,239
misc	95,168	71,138
vocabulary	187,137	144,132
tokens	7,400,499	5,634,834

Table 1: The number of tokens and entities in the corpus.

We use the Stanford NER system (Finkel et al., 2005) to get an approximate number of locations, persons, organizations and miscellaneous entities in the corpus. A brief analysis of the vocabulary is rendered in Table 1.

The dataset we use contains an abundant amount of named entities and consequently a large amount of low frequency words, but the majority of entities are not part of the model's 50,000 words vocabulary due to their small frequency. These words are replaced with 'UNK' symbols during training. At prediction time, we replace the unknown words with the highest probability score from the attention layer. We believe it is important to ensure that the models learn good word representations, either during the model training or through word2vec, in order to accurately create alignments between source and target sentences.

Given that in TS there is not only one best simplification, and that the quality of simplifications in Simple English Wikipedia has been disputed before (Amancio and Specia, 2014; Xu et al., 2015), for tuning and testing we use the dataset previously released by Xu et al. (2016), which contains 2000 sentences for tuning and 359 for testing, each with eight simplification variants obtained by eight Amazon Mechanical Turkers.[3] The tune subset is also used as reference corpus in combination with BLEU and SARI to select the best beam size and hypothesis for prediction reranking.

3 Evaluation

For the first 70 original sentences of the Xu *et al.*'s (2016) test set[4] we perform three types of human evaluation to assess the output of our best systems and three ATS systems of different architectures: (1) the PBSMT system with reranking of n-best outputs (Wubben et al., 2012), which represent the best PBSMT approach to ATS, trained and tuned over the same datasets as our systems; (2) the state-of-the-art SBMT system (Xu et al., 2016) with modified tuning function (using SARI) and using PPDB paraphrase database (Ganitkevitch et al., 2013);[5] and (3) one of the state-of-the-art unsupervised lexical simplification (LS) systems that leverages word-embeddings (Glavaš and

---

[3] None of the 359 test sentences was present in the datasets we used for training and tuning.

[4] https://github.com/cocoxu/
simplification/

[5] For the first two systems, we use publicly available output at: https://github.com/
cocoxu/simplification/tree/master/data/
systemoutputs

---

[2] http://www.cs.pomona.edu/~dkauchak/
simplification/

Štajner, 2015).[6]

We evaluate the output of all systems using three types of human evaluation.

Correctness and Number of Changes. First, we count the total number of changes made by each system (*Total*), counting the change of a whole phrase (e.g. *"become defunct"* → *"was dissolved"*) as one change. Those changes that preserve the original meaning and grammaticality of the sentence (assessed by two native English speakers) and, at the same time, make the sentence easier to understand (assessed by two non-native fluent English speakers) are marked as *Correct*. In the case of content reduction, we instructed the annotators to count the deletion of each array of consecutive words as one change and consider the meaning unchanged if the main information of the sentence was retained and unchanged. The sentences for which the two annotators did not agree were given to a third annotator to obtain the majority vote.

Grammaticality and Meaning Preservation. Second, three native English speakers rate the grammaticality (G) and meaning preservation (M) of each (whole) sentence with at least one change on a 1–5 Likert scale (1 – very bad; 5 – very good). The obtained inter-annotator agreement (quadratic Cohens kappa) was 0.78 for G and 0.63 for M.

Simplicity of sentences. Third, the three non-native fluent English speakers were shown original (reference) sentences and target (output) sentences, one pair at the time, and asked whether the target sentence is: +2 – much simpler; +1 – somewhat simpler; 0 – equally difficult; -1 – somewhat more difficult; -2 – much more difficult, than the reference sentence. The obtained inter-annotator agreement (quadratic Cohens kappa) was 0.66.

While the correctness of changes takes into account the influence of each individual change on grammaticality, meaning and simplicity of a sentence, the *Scores (G and M)* and *Rank (S)* take into account the mutual influence of all changes within a sentence.

4   Results and Discussion

The results of the human evaluation (Table 2) revealed that all NTS models achieve higher percentage of correct changes and more simplified output than any of the state-of-the-art ATS systems with different architectures (PBSMT-R, SBMT, and LightLS). We also notice that the best models according to BLEU are obtained with hypothesis 1 and the maximum beam size for both models, while the SARI re-ranker prefers hypothesis 2 and beam size 5 for the first NTS and the maximum beam size for the custom word embeddings model.

The NTS with custom word2vec embeddings ranked with the text simplification specific metric (SARI) obtained the highest total number of changes among the neural systems, one of the highest percentage of correct changes, the second highest simplicity score, and solid grammaticality and meaning preservation scores. An example of the output of different systems is presented in Table 4 (Appendix A).

The use of different metrics for ranking the NTS predictions optimizes the output towards different evaluation objectives: SARI leads to the highest number of total changes, BLEU to the highest percentage of correct changes, and the default beam scores to the best grammaticality (G) and meaning preservation (M). In addition, custom composed global and local word embeddings in combination with SARI metric improve the default translation system, given the joint scores for each evaluation criterion.

Here is important to note that for ATS systems, the precision of the system (correctness of changes, grammaticality, meaning preservation, and simplicity of the output) is more important than the recall (the total number of changes made). The low recall would just leave the sentences similar to their originals thus not improving much the understanding or reading speed of the target users, or not improving much the NLP systems in which they are used as a pre-processing step. A low precision, on the other hand, would make texts even more difficult to read and understand, and would worsen the performances of the NLP systems in which ATS is used as a pre-processing step.

5   Conclusions

We presented a first attempt at modelling sentence simplification with a neural sequence to sequence model. Our extensive human evaluation showed that our NTS systems, if the output is ranked with the right metric, can significantly[7] outperform the best phrase-based and syntax-based MT approaches, and unsupervised lexical ATS approach,

---

[6]For the LightLS system (Glavaš and Štajner, 2015) we use the output of the original system provided by the authors.

[7]Wilcoxon's signed rank test, $p < 0.001$.

Approach	Changes		Scores		Rank	SARI	BLEU
	Total	Correct	G	M	S		
NTS default (beam 5, hypothesis 1)	36	72.2%	**4.92**	**4.31**	+0.46	30.65	84.51
NTS SARI (beam 5, hypothesis 2)	72	51.6%	4.19	3.62	+0.38	37.25	80.69
NTS BLEU (beam 12, hypothesis 1)	44	73.7%	4.77	4.15	**+0.92**	30.77	84.70
NTS-w2v default (beam 5, hypothesis 1)	31	54.8%	4.79	4.17	+0.21	31.11	**87.50**
NTS-w2v SARI (beam 12, hypothesis 2)	110	68.1%	4.53	3.83	**+0.63**	36.10	79.38
NTS-w2v BLEU (beam 12, hypothesis 1)	61	**76.9%**	4.67	4.00	+0.40	30.67	85.03
PBSMT-R (Wubben et al., 2012)	**171**	41.0%	3.10	2.71	−0.55	34.07	67.79
SBMT (SARI+PPDB) (Xu et al., 2016)	143	34.3%	4.28	3.57	+0.03	**38.59**	73.62
LightLS (Unsupervised) (Glavaš and Štajner, 2015)	132	26.6%	4.47	2.67	−0.01	34.96	83.54

Table 2: Human evaluation results (the highest scores by each evaluation criterion are shown in bold).

by grammaticality, meaning preservation and simplicity of the output sentences, the percentage of correct transformations, while at the same time achieving more than 1.5 changes per sentence, on average. Furthermore, we discovered that NTS systems are capable of correctly performing significant content reduction, thus being the only TS models proposed so far which can jointly perform lexical simplification and content reduction.

Acknowledgments

This work has been partially supported by a grant of the Romanian National Authority for Scientific Research and Innovation, CNCS/CCCDI UEFIS-CDI, project number PN-III-P2-2.1-53BG/2016, within PNCDI III, and by the SFB 884 on the Political Economy of Reforms at the University of Mannheim (project C4), funded by the German Research Foundation (DFG).

References

Marcelo Adriano Amancio and Lucia Specia. 2014. An Analysis of Crowdsourced Text Simplifications . In *Proceedings of the 3rd Workshop on Predicting and Improving Text Readability for Target Reader Populations (PITR)*. pages 123–130.

Dzmitry Bahdanau, Kyunghyun Cho, and Yoshua Bengio. 2014. Neural machine translation by jointly learning to align and translate. *CoRR* abs/1409.0473. http://arxiv.org/abs/1409.0473.

Steven Bird, Ewan Klein, and Edward Loper. 2009. *Natural language processing with Python: analyzing text with the natural language toolkit.* " O'Reilly Media, Inc.".

Ondřej Bojar, Rajen Chatterjee, Christian Federmann, Yvette Graham, Barry Haddow, Matthias Huck, Antonio Jimeno Yepes, Philipp Koehn, Varvara Logacheva, Christof Monz, Matteo Negri, Aurelie Neveol, Mariana Neves, Martin Popel, Matt Post, Raphael Rubino, Carolina Scarton, Lucia Specia, Marco Turchi, Karin Verspoor, and Marcos Zampieri. 2016. Findings of the 2016 conference on machine translation. In *Proceedings of the First Conference on Machine Translation.* Association for Computational Linguistics, pages 131–198.

Kyunghyun Cho, Bart van Merrienboer, Çaglar Gülçehre, Dzmitry Bahdanau, Fethi Bougares, Holger Schwenk, and Yoshua Bengio. 2014. Learning phrase representations using RNN encoder-decoder for statistical machine translation. In *Proceedings of the 2014 Conference on Empirical Methods in Natural Language Processing.* pages 1724–1734.

William Coster and David Kauchak. 2011. Simple English Wikipedia: a new text simplification task. In *Proceedings of ACL&HLT.* pages 665–669.

Jenny Rose Finkel, Trond Grenager, and Christopher Manning. 2005. Incorporating non-local information into information extraction systems by gibbs sampling. In *Proceedings of the 43rd annual meeting on association for computational linguistics.* Association for Computational Linguistics, pages 363–370.

Orhan Firat, KyungHyun Cho, and Yoshua Bengio. 2016. Multi-way, multilingual neural machine translation with a shared attention mechanism. *CoRR* abs/1601.01073.

Juri Ganitkevitch, Benjamin Van Durme, and Chris Callison-Burch. 2013. PPDB: The Paraphrase Database. In *Proceedings of NAACL-HLT.* pages 758–764.

Justin Garten, Kenji Sagae, Volkan Ustun, and Morteza Dehghani. 2015. Combining distributed vector representations for words. In *Proceedings of NAACL-HLT.* pages 95–101.

Goran Glavaš and Sanja Štajner. 2015. Simplifying Lexical Simplification: Do We Need Simplified Corpora? In *Proceedings of the ACL&IJCNLP 2015 (Volume 2: Short Papers).* pages 63–68.

Alex Graves. 2012. *Supervised sequence labelling with recurrent neural networks*, volume 385. Springer.

Sepp Hochreiter and Jürgen Schmidhuber. 1997. Long short-term memory. *Neural Computation* 9(8):1735–1780.

William Hwang, Hannaneh Hajishirzi, Mari Ostendorf, and Wei Wu. 2015. Aligning Sentences from Standard Wikipedia to Simple Wikipedia. In *Proceedings of NAACL&HLT*. pages 211–217.

David Kauchak. 2013. Improving text simplification language modeling using unsimplified text data. In *Proceedings of the 51st Annual Meeting of the Association for Computational Linguistics (Volume 1: Long Papers)*. ACL, pages 1537–1546.

G. Klein, Y. Kim, Y. Deng, J. Senellart, and A. M. Rush. 2017. OpenNMT: Open-Source Toolkit for Neural Machine Translation. *ArXiv e-prints* .

Philipp Koehn. 2010. Statistical machine translation.

Minh-Thang Luong and Christopher D Manning. 2016. Achieving open vocabulary neural machine translation with hybrid word-character models. *arXiv preprint arXiv:1604.00788* .

Thang Luong, Hieu Pham, and Christopher D. Manning. 2015. Effective approaches to attention-based neural machine translation. In *EMNLP*. The Association for Computational Linguistics, pages 1412–1421.

Tomas Mikolov, Kai Chen, Greg Corrado, and Jeffrey Dean. 2013a. Efficient estimation of word representations in vector space. In *Proceedings of Workshop at International Conference on Learning Representations*.

Tomas Mikolov, Ilya Sutskever, Kai Chen, Greg S Corrado, and Jeff Dean. 2013b. Distributed representations of words and phrases and their compositionality. In *Advances in neural information processing systems*. pages 3111–3119.

Gustavo Henrique Paetzold and Lucia Specia. 2013. Text simplification as tree transduction. In *Proceedings of the 9th Brazilian Symposium in Information and Human Language Technology*. pages 116–125.

Gustavo Henrique Paetzold and Lucia Specia. 2016. Unsupervised lexical simplification for non-native speakers. In *Proceedings of the 30th AAAI*.

Kishore Papineni, Salim Roukos, Todd Ward, and Wei-Jing Zhu. 2002. BLEU: a method for automatic evaluation of machine translation. In *Proceedings of ACL*.

Radim Řehůřek and Petr Sojka. 2010. Software Framework for Topic Modelling with Large Corpora. In *Proceedings of the LREC 2010 Workshop on New Challenges for NLP Frameworks*. ELRA, Valletta, Malta, pages 45–50.

Rico Sennrich, Barry Haddow, and Alexandra Birch. 2015. Neural machine translation of rare words with subword units. *arXiv preprint arXiv:1508.07909* .

Iulian V Serban, Alessandro Sordoni, Yoshua Bengio, Aaron Courville, and Joelle Pineau. 2015. Building end-to-end dialogue systems using generative hierarchical neural network models. *arXiv preprint arXiv:1507.04808* .

Lucia Specia. 2010. Translating from complex to simplified sentences. In *Proceedings of the 9th international conference on Computational Processing of the Portuguese Language (PROPOR)*. Springer Berlin Heidelberg, volume 6001 of *Lecture Notes in Computer Science*, pages 30–39.

Nitish Srivastava, Geoffrey E Hinton, Alex Krizhevsky, Ilya Sutskever, and Ruslan Salakhutdinov. 2014. Dropout: a simple way to prevent neural networks from overfitting. *Journal of Machine Learning Research* 15(1):1929–1958.

Sanja Štajner, Hannah Bechara, and Horacio Saggion. 2015. A Deeper Exploration of the Standard PB-SMT Approach to Text Simplification and its Evaluation. In *Proceedings of ACL&IJCNLP (Volume 2: Short Papers)*. pages 823–828.

Yonghui Wu, Mike Schuster, Zhifeng Chen, Quoc V Le, Mohammad Norouzi, Wolfgang Macherey, Maxim Krikun, Yuan Cao, Qin Gao, Klaus Macherey, et al. 2016. Google's neural machine translation system: Bridging the gap between human and machine translation. *arXiv preprint arXiv:1609.08144* .

Sander Wubben, Antal van den Bosch, and Emiel Krahmer. 2012. Sentence simplification by monolingual machine translation. In *Proceedings of the 50th Annual Meeting of the Association for Computational Linguistics (ACL): Long Papers - Volume 1*. Association for Computational Linguistics, pages 1015–1024.

Wei Xu, Chris Callison-Burch, and Courtney Napoles. 2015. Problems in Current Text Simplification Research: New Data Can Help. *Transactions of the Association for Computational Linguistics (TACL)* 3:283–297.

Wei Xu, Courtney Napoles, Ellie Pavlick, Quanze Chen, and Chris Callison-Burch. 2016. Optimizing statistical machine translation for text simplification. *Transactions of the Association for Computational Linguistics* 4:401–415.

Z. Zhu, D. Berndard, and I. Gurevych. 2010. A Monolingual Tree-based Translation Model for Sentence Simplification. In *Proceedings of the 23rd International Conference on Computational Linguistics (Coling 2010)*. pages 1353–1361.

A Appendix - Data Sample and System Output

Match	Transformation	Sentence pair
Full	syntactic simplification; reordering of sentence constituents	"During the 13th century, gingerbread was brought to Sweden by German immigrants." and "German immigrants brought it to Sweden during the 13th century."
Full	lexical paraphrasing	"During the 13th century, gingerbread was brought to Sweden by German immigrants." and "German immigrants brought it to Sweden during the 13th century."
Partial	strong paraphrasing	"Gingerbread foods vary, ranging from a soft, moist loaf cake to something close to a ginger biscuit." and "Gingerbread is a word which describes different sweet food products from soft cakes to a ginger biscuit."
Partial	adding explanations	"Humidity is the amount of water vapor in the air." and "Humidity (adjective: humid) refers to water vapor in the air, but not to liquid droplets in fog, clouds, or rain."
Partial	sentence compression; dropping irrelevant information	"Falaj irrigation is an ancient system dating back thousands of years and is used widely in Oman, the UAE, China, Iran and other countries." and "The ancient falaj system of irrigation is still in use in some areas."

Table 3: Examples of full and partial matches from the EW–SEW dataset (Hwang et al., 2015).

System	Output
NTS-w2v default	Perry Saturn (with terri) defeated Eddie Guerrero (with chyna) to win the WWF European Championship (8:10); Saturn pinned Guerrero after a diving elbow drop.
NTS-w2v SARI	Perry Saturn **pinned Guerrero to win the WWF European Championship.**
NTS-w2v BLEU	Perry Saturn pinned Guerrero after a diving **drop** drop.
NTS default	**He** (with terri) defeated Eddie Guerrero (with chyna) to win the WWF European Championship (8:10); Saturn pinned Guerrero after a diving elbow drop.
NTS BLEU/SARI	**He** defeated Eddie Guerrero (with Chyna) to win the WWF European Championship (8:10); Saturn pinned Guerrero after a diving elbow drop.
LightLS (Glavaš and Štajner, 2015)	Perry Saturn (with terri) defeated Eddie Guerrero (with chyna) to win the WWF European Championship (8:10); Saturn pinned Guerrero after a **swimming shoulder fall**.
SBMT (Xu et al., 2016)	Perry Saturn (with terri) **beat** Eddie Guerrero (with chyna) to win the WWF European **League** (8:10); Saturn pinned Guerrero after a diving elbow drop.
PBSMT-R (Wubben et al., 2012)	Perry Saturn with terri **and** Eddie Guerrero , chyna , to win the European Championship **then-wwf** 8:10); **he** pinned Guerrero after a diving elbow drop.
Original	Perry Saturn (with terri) defeated Eddie Guerrero (with chyna) to win the WWF European Championship (8:10); Saturn pinned Guerrero after a diving elbow drop.

Table 4: Output examples, differences to the original sentence are shown in bold.

On the Challenges of Translating NLP Research into Commercial Products

Daniel Dahlmeier
SAP Innovation Center Singapore
`d.dahlmeier@sap.com`

Abstract

This paper highlights challenges in industrial research related to translating research in natural language processing into commercial products. While the interest in natural language processing from industry is significant, the transfer of research to commercial products is non-trivial and its challenges are often unknown to or underestimated by many researchers. I discuss current obstacles and provide suggestions for increasing the chances for translating research to commercial success based on my experience in industrial research.

1 Introduction

Natural language processing (NLP) has made significant progress over the last two decades, in particular due to the success of data-driven machine learning methods. Recently, deep learning has led to another wave of remarkable improvements in NLP and other areas of machine learning and artificial intelligence (AI). Not surprisingly, many industry players are investing heavily in machine learning and AI to create new products and services (MIT Technology Review, 2016).

However, translating research into a successful product has its own challenges. Traditionally, technology transfer is often assumed to happen in a linear transition from pure research to applied research to commercialization (Stokes, 1997). The model assumes that the discoveries from researchers will naturally be picked up by engineers and industry players who will use it to build new products. In reality, the transfer from research to commercial products is considerably more complex and far from guaranteed. In fact, many research projects fail to successfully transfer their discoveries to commercial products.

In this position paper, I highlight some of the reasons why it is so difficult to translate NLP research into successful products. This paper does not contain any new algorithms, experiments, or results. Instead, it seeks to share my experience working at the intersection of academic research and industry with the aim to stimulate a discussion how technology transfer of NLP research can be improved. I want to emphasize upfront that the paper is not arguing that all NLP researchers should focus their efforts on building commercial products nor does every new product require a research breakthrough to be successful. The paper's aim is rather to discuss how we can improve *use-inspired basic research* that satisfies both the desire for fundamental understanding and considerations of use, sometimes referred to as *Pasteur's quadrant* (Stokes, 1997).

The contributions of this paper are twofold. First, I highlight common obstacles in the path of transferring research into commercial products. Second, I offer suggestions for increasing the chances of success based on my experience at SAP, the world's largest enterprise software company.

2 Challenges to Innovation

This section highlights challenges in NLP research that make it difficult to translate the results into impactful innovation.

2.1 Lack of Value Focus

The first step to creating a successful product is understanding your customers. That is why many methodologies for creating new products or business models start with a *user persona* and how to create value for the user (Ries, 2011; Osterwalder et al., 2014). Similarly, to conduct research with practical impact, it is worthwhile to consider what potential applications the research could enable

Proceedings of the 55th Annual Meeting of the Association for Computational Linguistics (Short Papers), pages 92–96
Vancouver, Canada, July 30 - August 4, 2017. ©2017 Association for Computational Linguistics
https://doi.org/10.18653/v1/P17-2015

and what the *value proposition* for a potential user might be. The value proposition is closely linked to the user persona and the tasks that she tries to solve in her daily life (Christensen and Raynor, 2013). Thus, choosing the right research task is important when aiming for impactful research. It is instructive that NLP tasks which solve practical problems, like machine translation or sentiment analysis, have seen significant adoption in commercial applications. But many applications that are requested by industry are still beyond the capabilities of current NLP research, for example chatbots that can respond to arbitrary user questions.

It is also important for researchers to understand that the priorities in industry are different from priorities in academic research. In academic research, the priorities are to create contributions to the body of knowledge in the field, e.g., defining a new task, a novel, elegant model, or a new state-of-the-art benchmark result. In industry the priorities are creating innovative products that delight users and create new revenue streams. To have the best of both worlds, researchers should occasionally take a step back and consider what value proposition their work has for people outside the NLP community.

2.2 Lack of Reproducibility

Reproducible research is one of the pillars of the scientific method and thus important to good research work in general. But the ability to reproduce a model is also a prerequisite to incorporating it into a product. As NLP models often depend on a complex set of parameters and pre-processing steps which cannot always be explained in all detail in a paper, it is often hard to reproduce other's results. The author himself has his own experience trying to (unsuccessfully) reproduce published results. As problems to reproduce research are seldom reported (but see (Bikel, 2004) for an exception), it is also hard for researchers to find information on how to improve their implementation when they struggle to re-produce published results.

2.3 Lack of (Domain) Data

Data is the fuel that powers machine learning and most of NLP research. While the "big data" revolution has given us access to large quantities of text data from some domains, for many industry problems there is no or very limited data available to conduct research on. For example, in my group we have been working on text classi-

fication for customer service tickets. While there are many datasets available for text classification, these are primarily from newswire or online reviews. For customer service, there is no public dataset to compare to. Due to the confidential nature of the data and data privacy concerns, companies who have such data cannot easily release it for research purposes. Some companies host shared tasks or data science competitions in which they make data available, for example on Kaggle[1], but access to data remains one of the biggest obstacles for researcher who want to work on industry problems.

Even when there is data available from public sources, e.g., from the web, using the data for commercial purposes can be tricky from a legal standpoint. Crawling data from web (or using corpora created by others in this manner) might be acceptable for research purposes, but when building a commercial product the exact license, copyright, etc. of every data source needs to be checked. The same holds for publicly available NLP models derived from such data.

For everyone who believes that working in industry solves all data problem, I note here that working with real data sets has its own challenges. Real data sets are often small, noisy, scrambled, or otherwise incomplete, making it hard to achieve good results. To effectively use the data, researchers also have to understand the data schema and the business process behind the data. This can be challenging without and in-depth domain knowledge.

2.4 Overemphasis on Test Scores

The empirical evaluation of statistical methods on common benchmarks has without a doubt revolutionized NLP (Johnson, 2009). However, sometimes the score on the test set is taken as the *only* factor that determines the success of a piece of research. For practical applications, the test score on a benchmark dataset is only one criteria among many when it comes to choosing an algorithm for practical use. Other factors include the time and costs required to implement the method, the computational resources required, speed and performance, the ease of integration, support for multi-lingual input, the ability to adapt and customize the method, the ability to incorporate prior knowledge, and the ability to interpret and explain

---

[1] https://www.kaggle.com

the model. For example, in our text categorization work, we encountered the requirement to accommodate changes in the the output classes, i.e., adding, merging, splitting, and removing classes, without re-training the model from scratch. These factors are currently underrepresented in NLP research.

2.5 Difficulty of Adoption

No matter how good an NLP model is, it cannot have practical impact if it is never implemented. But in any application, the NLP model will only be one component in a larger software system. How easily the NLP component can work together with the remaining components is important for the ease of adoption of the method into productive applications. Unlike rule-based methods, statistical NLP models often require expensive collection and labeling of data, data pre-processing, model (re-)training, parameter tuning, and monitoring of the model to avoid model staleness. This makes it harder to adopt statistical models in practical applications (Chiticariu et al., 2013).

2.6 Timelines

The time horizon within which stakeholders expect results is generally shorter in industry projects. While research grants typically run for three to five years, industry research is under pressure to deliver tangible outcomes in less than two years. For projects with actual customers and proof of concepts, timelines are usually not longer than a few months. This results in the following chicken and egg problem: it is difficult to produce groundbreaking research within a short time frame but long investments into research are hard to justify if the value the research will ultimately produce is not clear. That is why academic research is generally better equipped to focus on fundamental research questions. Fundamental research does not exclude practical usage but incremental research that fine-tunes every aspect of the implementation of an NLP model is often better done in industry labs.

3 Bridging the Gap

In this section, I offer some suggestions about how the disconnect between NLP research and commercial products can be reduced.

3.1 A "Recipe" for Qualifying a Research Problem

The following approach describes the criteria that we typically apply in our team when we evaluate new machine learning use cases, including NLP use cases.

First, we make sure we understand the "job to be done": what is the business problem, who is the potential user and what problem are we trying to solve? Once we have understood the task, a first question to ask is whether the task actually requires NLP. Is the data volume so high that automation is needed? Would it be easier or cheaper to solve the task manually? Can the task be solved via simple rules? Typically, tasks with high data volume and complex or ambiguous rules are good candidates for NLP.

To ensure that the use cases we work on have practical relevance, we include stakeholders from the lines of business and industry units in the company in any new project right from the beginning and gather feedback from actual customers.

Once we believe that NLP is required, we try to formulate the problem as a machine learning task. The simple template *given X, predict Y* together with the question *what are the inputs and what are the outputs?* helps significantly to get from a vague idea to a concrete task formulation. At this stage, we can often already map the problem to a standard NLP task, e.g., text classification, sequence tagging, or sequence-to-sequence learning.

Next, we establish whether data is available. If real data is not available easily, can we work with publicly available proxy data? For example for learning to classify customer service tickets, we can start with text classification on public datasets. If it is unlikely that data will be available in the foreseeable future, we do not proceed with a use case.

Next, we make a best guess whether the problem can be solved with the current state of the art in NLP. Is there an intuitive regularity in the data which we believe a statistical model could pick up? Can we represent the input via meaningful features? Do we have a way to measure the success of the method with a well-defined metric?

Finally, we determine the right approach to execute the use case. If it is a hard problem which needs at least a few more years of research before it becomes useful, we would most likely decide on a research project. We fund external research projects at top universities around the world, where we provide the research problem and the data and let others try to crack the tough problems. We also sponsor Ph.D. students who are working at SAP during their studies.

If we think that the use case has a strong business case and the technology is mature enough, we will move it to building a proof of concept, and ultimately a commercial product. While this "recipe" for qualifying an NLP use case is simple and common sense, we have found it helpful in prioritizing use cases.

Researchers in academia might not have access to a business unit to provide feedback on research ideas but many funding bodies are trying to encourage increased collaborations between industry and academia. The European Union, for example, has specifically funded an initiative, LT-innovate[2] to encourage commercial exploitation of NLP research.

3.2 Engineering Approach to NLP

I believe that a more rigorous application of (software) engineering principles and tools can greatly increase the odds of having practical impact with NLP research.

To address the problem of reproducibility, I suggest the following. First, the community should be more stringent about reproducibility. In some research communities, for example databases, the criteria for reproducible research are a lot stricter. If the results are not reproducible, the results are generally not considered valid. However, the large number of parameters and implementation details in NLP systems makes it hard to exactly reproduce published results based on the paper alone. Therefore, we should encourage the dissemination of results through software tools that make code reproducible. To reproduce the results in a paper, we essentially need the code, the data, and the parameters of the experimental run that produced the results of the experiment. Fortunately, the open source community has created great tools that make this possible. First, social code repository platforms, such as GitHub[3], make it easy to share code and data. In fact, the ease of sharing and contributing to code has arguably accelerated the progress in machine learning significantly. Second, interactive computational environments,

such as Jupyter notebooks[4], that tie together data, code, and documentation, allow for reproducible results that can easily be shared and published. Finally, software containers, such as Docker[5], allow light-weight virtualization that pulls in all software dependencies and allow the same code to run in a reliable and reproducible manner. If a Jupyter notebook or Dockerfile is published with the paper, it should be easier for other researchers to reproduce results and integrate them into larger systems. Projects like CodaLab[6] try to build online platforms for reproducible research with similar goals.

On the problem of data availability, there is already a considerable amount of work in the area of building NLP models in low-resource environments (see for example (Duong et al., 2014; Garrette and Baldridge, 2013; Wang et al., 2015)) which deals with limited data availability. Techniques like domain adaptation, semi-supervised learning and transfer learning (Pan and Yang, 2010) are extremely relevant to address the problem of data availability for industry applications. Finally, recent work on learning models from private data (Papernot et al., 2016) and federated learning across many devices (McMahan et al., 2016) appear to be promising directions for practical NLP engineering research.

3.3 Industry Papers

I believe that there is an opportunity to increase the exchange between industry and the research community by establishing an industry paper submission format, potentially with its own industry track at NLP conferences. Such a track could offer a venue to discuss practical challenges in building large-scale NLP systems and deploying NLP models in production settings, such as scalability, trade-offs between accuracy and computational costs, robustness, data quality, etc. This would help to counter-balance the overemphasis on test scores in pure research papers and aid the adoption of research in industry applications. Industry tracks are common in other communities and have strong participation from industry players there.

---

4 Related Work

Wagstaff (2012) argues for making machine learning research more relevant. He laments a hyper-focus on UCI benchmark datasets and abstract metrics. Spector *et al.* (2012) present Google's hybrid approach to research, which tries to avoid separation between research and engineering. Recently, several groups at Google have published papers on practical challenges in deploying machine learning in production (Sculley et al., 2014; McMahan et al., 2013; Breck et al., 2016). Belz (2009) discusses the practical applications of NLP research. Mani (2011) gives suggestions for improving the review process. None of the works provides a detailed discussion on the difficulties in bringing NLP research to commercial products – the main contribution of this paper.

5 Conclusion

I have highlighted difficulties that exist for researchers who try to bring NLP research into commercially products and offered suggestions for improving the odds of commercial success. I hope that my experience can stimulate creative thought and a healthy discussion in the NLP community.

References

Anja Belz. 2009. That's nice... what can you do with it? *Computational Linguistics* 35(1).

Daniel Bikel. 2004. Intricacies of Collins' parsing model. *Computational Linguistics* 30(4).

Eric Breck, Shanqing Cai, Eric Nielsen, Michael Salib, and D. Sculley. 2016. Whats your ML test score? A rubric for ML production systems. In *Proceedings of Reliable Machine Learning in the Wild - NIPS 2016 Workshop (2016)*.

Laura Chiticariu, Yunyao Li, and Frederick R. Reiss. 2013. Rule-based information extraction is dead! long live rule-based information extraction systems! In *Proceedings of EMNLP*.

Clayton M. Christensen and Michael E. Raynor. 2013. *The Innovator's Solution: Creating and Sustaining Successful Srowth*. Harvard Business Review Press.

Long Duong, Trevor Cohn, Karin Verspoor, Steven Bird, and Paul Cook. 2014. What can we get from 1000 tokens? A case study of multilingual POS tagging for resource-poor languages. In *Proceedings of EMNLP*.

Dan Garrette and Jason Baldridge. 2013. Learning a part-of-speech tagger from two hours of annotation. In *Proceedings of HLT-NAACL*.

Mark Johnson. 2009. How the statistical revolution changes (computational) linguistics. In *Proceedings of the EACL 2009 Workshop on the Interaction between Linguistics and Computational Linguistics*.

Inderjeet Mani. 2011. Improving our reviewing processes. *Computational Linguistics* 37(1).

H. Brendan McMahan, Gary Holt, D. Sculley, Michael Young, Dietmar Ebner, Julian Grady, Lan Nie, Todd Phillips, Eugene Davydov, Daniel Golovin, Sharat Chikkerur, Dan Liu, Martin Wattenberg, Arnar Mar Hrafnkelsson, Tom Boulos, and Jeremy Kubica. 2013. Ad click prediction: a view from the trenches. In *Proceedings of ACM SIGKDD*.

H. Brendan McMahan, Eider Moore, Daniel Ramage, Seth Hampson, and Blaise Agera y Arcas. 2016. Communication-efficient learning of deep networks from decentralized data. In *Proceedings of AISTATS*.

MIT Technology Review. 2016. AI Takes Off. https://www.technologyreview.com/business-report/ai-takes-off/. Online; accessed 22 April 2017.

Alexander Osterwalder, Yves Pigneur, Gregory Bernarda, and Alan Smith. 2014. *Value proposition design: How to create products and services customers want*. John Wiley & Sons.

Sinno Jialin Pan and Qiang Yang. 2010. A survey on transfer learning. *IEEE Transactions on knowledge and data engineering* 22(10).

Nicolas Papernot, Martín Abadi, Úlfar Erlingsson, Ian Goodfellow, and Kunal Talwar. 2016. Semi-supervised knowledge transfer for deep learning from private training data.

Eric Ries. 2011. *The lean startup: How today's entrepreneurs use continuous innovation to create radically successful businesses*. Crown Business.

D. Sculley, Gary Holt, Daniel Golovin, Eugene Davydov, Todd Phillips, Dietmar Ebner, Vinay Chaudhary, and Michael Young. 2014. Machine learning: The high interest credit card of technical debt. In *Proceedings of SE4ML: Software Engineering for Machine Learning (NIPS 2014 Workshop)*.

Alfred Spector, Peter Norvig, and Slav Petrov. 2012. Google's hybrid approach to research. *Communications of the ACM* 55(7).

Donald E. Stokes. 1997. *Pasteur's quadrant: Basic Science and Technological Innovation*. Brookings Institution Press.

Kiri Wagstaff. 2012. Machine learning that matters. In *Proceedings of ICML*.

Yushi Wang, Jonathan Berant, and Percy Liang. 2015. Building a semantic parser overnight. In *Proceedings of ACL*.

Sentence Alignment Methods for Improving Text Simplification Systems

Sanja Štajner[1], Marc Franco-Salvador[2,3],
Simone Paolo Ponzetto[1], Paolo Rosso[3], Heiner Stuckenschmidt[1]

[1] DWS Research Group, University of Mannheim, Germany
[2] Symanto Research, Nuremberg, Germany
[3] PRHLT Research Center, Universitat Politècnica de València, Spain
{sanja,simone,heiner}@informatik.uni-mannheim.de
marc.franco@symanto.net, prosso@prhlt.upv.es

Abstract

We provide several methods for sentence-alignment of texts with different complexity levels. Using the best of them, we sentence-align the Newsela corpora, thus providing large training materials for automatic text simplification (ATS) systems. We show that using this dataset, even the standard phrase-based statistical machine translation models for ATS can outperform the state-of-the-art ATS systems.

1 Introduction

Automated text simplification (ATS) tries to automatically transform (syntactically, lexically and/or semantically) complex sentences into their simpler variants without significantly altering the original meaning. It has attracted much attention recently as it could make texts more accessible to wider audiences (Aluísio and Gasperin, 2010; Saggion et al., 2015), and used as a pre-processing step, improve performances of various NLP tasks and systems (Vickrey and Koller, 2008; Evans, 2011; Štajner and Popović, 2016).

However, the state-of-the-art ATS systems still do not reach satisfying performances and require some human post-editing (Štajner and Popović, 2016). While the best supervised approaches generally lead to grammatical output with preserved original meaning, they are overcautious, making almost no changes to the input sentences (Specia, 2010; Štajner et al., 2015), probably due to the limited size or bad quality of parallel TS corpora used for training. The largest existing sentence-aligned TS dataset for English is the English Wikipedia – Simple English Wikipedia

(EW–SEW) dataset, which contains 160-280,000 sentence pairs, depending on whether we want to model only traditional sentence rewritings or also to model content reduction and stronger paraphrasing (Hwang et al., 2015). For Spanish, the largest existing parallel TS corpus contains only 1,000 sentence pairs thus impeding the use of fully supervised approaches. The best unsupervised lexical simplification (LS) systems for English which leverage word-embeddings (Glavaš and Štajner, 2015; Paetzold and Specia, 2016) seem to perform more lexical substitutions but at the cost of having less grammatical output and more often changed meaning. However, there have been no direct comparisons of supervised and unsupervised state-of-the-art approaches so far.

The Newsela corpora[1] offers over 2,000 original news articles in English and around 250 in Spanish, manually simplified to 3–4 different complexity levels following strict guidelines (Xu et al., 2015). Although it was suggested that it has better quality than the EW–SEW corpus (Xu et al., 2015), Newsela has not yet been used for training end-to-end ATS systems, due to the lack of its sentence (and paragraph) alignments. Such alignments, between various text complexity levels, would offer large training datasets for modelling different levels of simplification, i.e. 'mild' simplifications (using the alignments from the neighbouring levels) and 'heavy' simplifications (using the alignments of level pairs: 0–3, 0–4, 1–4).

Contributions. We: (1) provide several methods for paragraph- and sentence alignment of parallel texts, and for assessing similarity level between pairs of text snippets, as freely avail-

---

[1]Freely available: https://newsela.com/data/

Proceedings of the 55th Annual Meeting of the Association for Computational Linguistics (Short Papers), pages 97–102
Vancouver, Canada, July 30 - August 4, 2017. ©2017 Association for Computational Linguistics
https://doi.org/10.18653/v1/P17-2016

able software;[2] (2) compare the performances of lexically- and semantically-based alignment methods across various text complexity levels; (3) test the hypothesis that the original order of information is preserved during manual simplification (Bott and Saggion, 2011) by offering customized MST-LIS alignment strategy (Section 3.1); and (4) show that the new sentence-alignments lead to the state-of-the-art ATS systems even in a basic phrase-based statistical machine translation (PB-SMT) approach to text simplifications.

2 Related Work

The current state-of-the-art systems for automatic sentence-alignment of original and manually simplified texts are the GSWN method (Hwang et al., 2015) used for sentence-alignment of original and simple English Wikipedia, and the HMM-based method (Bott and Saggion, 2011) used for sentence-alignment of the Spanish Simplext corpus (Saggion et al., 2015).

The HMM-based method can be applied to any language as it does not require any language-specific resources. It is based on two hypotheses: (H1) that the original order of information is preserved, and (H2) that every 'simple' sentence has at least one corresponding 'original' sentence (it can have more than one in the case of 'n-1' or 'n-m' alignments).

As Simple Wikipedia does not represent direct simplification of the 'original' Wikipedia articles ('simple' articles were written independently of the 'original' ones), GSWN method does not assume H1 or H2. The main limitations of this method are that it only allows for '1-1' sentence alignments – which is very restricting for TS as it does not allow for sentence splitting ('1-n'), and summarisation and compression ('n-1' and 'n-m') alignments – and it is language-dependent as it requires English Wiktionary.

Unlike the GSWN method, all the methods we apply are language-independent, resource-light and allow for '1-n', 'n-1', and 'n-m' alignments. Similar to the HMM-method, our methods assume the hypothesis H2. We provide them in both variants, using the hypothesis H1 and without it (Section 3.1).

3 Approach

Having a set of 'simple' text snippets S and a set of 'complex' text snippets C, we offer two strategies (Section 3.1) to obtain the alignments (s_i, c_j), where $s_i \in S$, $c_j \in C$. Each alignment strategy, in turn, can use one of the three methods (Section 3.2) to calculate similarity scores between text snippets (either paragraphs or sentences).

3.1 Alignment strategies

Most Similar Text (MST): Given one of the similarity methods (Section 3.2), MST compares similarity scores of all possible pairs (s_i, c_j), and aligns each $s_i \in S$ with the closest one in C.

MST with Longest Increasing Sequence (MST-LIS): MST-LIS uses the hypothesis H1. It first uses the MST strategy, and then postprocess the output by extracting – from all obtained alignments – only those alignments $l_i \in L$, which contain the longest increasing sequence of offsets j_k in C. In order to allow for '1–n' alignments (i.e. sentence splitting), we allow for repeated offsets of C ('complex' text snippets) in L. The 'simple' text snippets not contained in L are included in the set U of unaligned snippets. Finally, we align each $u_m \in U$ by restricting the search space in C to those offsets of 'complex' text snippets that correspond to the previous and the next aligned 'simple' snippets. For instance, if $L = \{(s_1, c_4), (s_3, c_7)\}$ and $U = \{s_2\}$, then the search space for the alignments of s_2 is reduced to $\{c_4...c_7\}$. We denote this strategy with an '*' in the results (Table 2), e.g. C3G*.

3.2 Similarity Methods

C3G: We employ the Character N-Gram (CNG) (Mcnamee and Mayfield, 2004) similarity model (for $n = 3$) with log TF-IDF weighting (Salton and McGill, 1986) and compare vectors using the cosine similarity.

WAVG: We use the continuous skip-gram model (Mikolov et al., 2013b) of the TensorFlow toolkit[3] to process the whole English Wikipedia and generate continuous representations of its words.[4] For each text snippet, we average its word vectors to obtain a single representation of its content as this setting has shown good results

---

[2]https://github.com/neosyon/
SimpTextAlign

[3]https://www.tensorflow.org/
[4]We use 300-dimensional vectors, context windows of size 10, and 20 negative words for each sample, in all our continuous word-based models.

Match	Transformation	Original	Simple
Full	syntactic simplification; reordering of sentence constituents	During the 13th century, gingerbread was brought to Sweden by German immigrants.	German immigrants brought it to Sweden during the 13th century.
Full	lexical paraphrasing	During the 13th century, gingerbread was brought to Sweden by German immigrants.	German immigrants brought it to Sweden during the 13th century.
Partial	strong paraphrasing	Gingerbread foods vary, ranging from a soft, moist loaf cake to something close to a ginger biscuit.	Gingerbread is a word which describes different sweet food products from soft cakes to a ginger biscuit.
Partial	adding explanations	Humidity is the amount of water vapor in the air.	Humidity (adjective: humid) refers to water vapor in the air, but not to liquid droplets in fog, clouds, or rain.
Partial	sentence compression	Falaj irrigation is an ancient system dating back thousands of years and is used widely in Oman, the UAE, China, Iran and other countries.	The ancient falaj system of irrigation is still in use in some areas.

Table 1: Examples of full and partial matches from the EW–SEW dataset (Hwang et al., 2015).

in other NLP tasks (e.g. for selecting out-of-the-list words (Mikolov et al., 2013a)). Finally, the similarity between text snippets is estimated using the cosine similarity.

CWASA: We employ the Continuous Word Alignment-based Similarity Analysis (CWASA) model (Franco-Salvador et al., 2016), which finds the optimal word alignment by computing cosine similarity between continuous representations of all words (instead of averaging word vectors as in the case of WAVG). It was originally proposed for plagiarism detection with excellent results, especially for longer text snippets.

4   Manual Evaluation

To compare the performances of different alignment methods, we randomly selected 10 original texts (Level 0) and their corresponding simpler versions at Levels 1, 3 and 4. Instead of creating a 'gold standard' and then automatically evaluating the performances, we asked two annotators to rate each pair of automatically aligned paragraphs and sentences – by each of the possible six alignment methods and the HMM-based method (Bott and Saggion, 2011) – for three pairs of text complexity levels (0–1, 0–4, and 3–4) on a 0–2 scale, where: **0** – no semantic overlap in the content; **1** – partial semantic overlap (*partial matches*); **2** – same semantic content (*good matches*). This resulted in a total of 1526 paragraph- and 1086 sentence-alignments for the 0–1 pairs, and 1218 paragraph- and 1266 sentence-alignments for the 0–4 and 3–4 pairs. In the context of TS, both good- and partial matches

are important. While full semantic overlap models full paraphrases ('1-1' alignments), partial overlap models sentence splitting ("1-n" alignments), deleting irrelevant sentence parts, adding explanations, or summarizing ('n-m' alignments). Several examples of full and partial matches from the EW–SEW dataset (Hwang et al., 2015) are given in Table 1.

We expect that the automatic-alignment task is the easiest between the 0–1 text complexity levels, and much more difficult between the 0-4 levels (Level 4 is obtained after four stages of simplification and thus contains stronger paraphrases and less lexical overlap with Level 0 than Level 1 has). We also explore whether the task is equally difficult whenever we align two neighbouring levels, or the difficulty of the task depends on the level complexity (0–1 vs. 3–4). The obtained inter-annotator agreement, weighted Cohen's κ (on 400 double-annotated instances) was between 0.71 and 0.74 depending on the task and levels.

The results of the manual analysis (Table 2) showed that: (1) all applied methods significantly ($p < 0.001$) outperformed the HMM method on both paragraph- and sentence-alignment tasks;[5] (2) the methods which do not assume hypothesis H1 (C3G, CWASA, and WAVG) led to (not significantly) higher percentage of correct alignments than their counterparts which do assume

---

[5]Although some of our methods share the same percentage of good+partial matches with the HMM method on the paragraph-alignment 0–1 task, there is still significant difference in the obtained scores (in some cases, our methods led to good matches whereas the HMM only led to partial matches).

Method	Sentence			Paragraph		
	0–1	0–4	3–4	0–1	0–4	3–4
C3G	98.3	56.1	81.1	**98.6**	**86.8**	**95.2**
C3G*	96.7	54.7	78.8	95.4	77.0	92.3
CWASA	98.3	45.3	79.7	98.2	83.3	94.1
CWASA*	96.1	42.1	76.4	95.4	74.1	90.5
WAVG	97.8	56.1	79.7	96.8	75.9	91.7
WAVG*	96.1	50.0	79.7	96.8	69.5	89.3
C3G-2s	**98.5**	**57.8**	**83.5**	/	/	/
HMM	86.2	25.2	65.6	96.8	41.2	65.5

Table 2: Percentage of good+partial sentence- and paragraph-alignments on the English Newsela corpus. All results are significantly better ($p < 0.001$, Wilcoxon's signed rank test) than those obtained by the HMM method (Bott and Saggion, 2011). The best scores are in bold.

H1 (C3G*, CWASA*, WAVG*); (3) the difference in the performances of the lexical approach (C3G) and semantic approaches (CWASA and WAVG) was significant only in the 0–4 sentence-alignment task, where CWASA performed significantly worse ($p < 0.001$) than the other two methods, and in the 0–4 paragraph-alignment task, where WAVG performed significantly worse than C3G; (4) the 2-step C3G alignment-method (*C3G-2s*), which first aligns paragraphs using the best paragraph-alignment method (C3G) and then within each paragraph align sentences with the best sentence-alignment method (C3G), led to more good+partial alignments than the 'direct' sentence-alignment C3G method.

5 Extrinsic Evaluation

Finally, we test our new English Newsela (C3G-2s) sentence-alignments (both for the neighbouring levels – *neighb.* and for all levels – *all*) and Newsela sentence-alignments for neighboring levels obtained with HMM-method[6] (Bott and Saggion, 2011) in the ATS task using standard PBSMT models[7] in the Moses toolkit (Koehn et al., 2007). We vary the training dataset and the corpus used to build language models (LMs), while keeping always the same 2,000 sentence pairs for tuning (Xu et al., 2016) and the first 70 sentence

pairs of their test set[8] for our human evaluation. Using that particular test set allow us to compare our (PBSMT) systems with the output of the state-of-the-art syntax-based MT (SBMT) system for TS (Xu et al., 2016) which is not freely available. We compare: (1) the performance of the standard PBSMT model which uses only the already available EW–SEW dataset (Hwang et al., 2015) with the performances of the same PBSMT models but this time using the combination of the EW–SEW dataset and our newly-created Newsela datasets; (2) the latter PBSMT models (which use both EW–SEW and new Newsela datasets) against the state-of-the-art supervised ATS system (Xu et al., 2016), and one of the recently proposed unsupervised lexical simplification systems, the LightLS system (Glavaš and Štajner, 2015).[9]

We perform three types of human evaluation on the outputs of all systems. First, we count the total number of changes made by each system (*Total*), counting the change of a whole phrase (e.g. *"become defunct"* → *"was dissolved"*) as one change. We mark as *Correct* those changes that preserve the original meaning and grammaticality of the sentence (assessed by two native English speakers) and, at the same time, make the sentence easier to understand (assessed by two non-native fluent English speakers).[10] Second, three native English speakers rate the grammaticality (*G*) and meaning preservation (*M*) of each sentence with at least one change on a 1–5 Likert scale (1 – very bad; 5 – very good). Third, the three non-native fluent English speakers were shown original (reference) sentences and target (output) sentences (one pair at the time) and asked whether the target sentence is: +2 – much simpler; +1 – somewhat simpler; 0 – equally difficult; -1 – somewhat more difficult; -2 – much more difficult, than the reference sentence. While the correctness of changes takes into account the influence of each individual change on grammaticality, meaning and simplicity of a sentence, the *Scores (G and M)* and *Rank (S)* take into account the mutual influence of all changes within a sentence.

Adding our sentence-aligned Newsela corpus

---

[6]Given that the performance of the HMM-method was poor for non-neighboring levels (Table 2).

[7]GIZA++ implementation of the IBM word alignment model 4 (Och and Ney, 2003), refinement and phrase-extraction heuristics (Koehn et al., 2003), the minimum error rate training (Och, 2003) for tuning, and 5-gram LMs with Kneser-Ney smoothing trained with SRILM (Stolcke, 2002).

[8]Both freely available from: `https://github.com/cocoxu/simplification/`

[9]We use the output of the original SBMT (Xu et al., 2016) and LightLS (Glavaš and Štajner, 2015) systems, obtained from the authors.

[10]Those cases in which the two annotators did not agree are additionally evaluated by a third annotator to obtain majority.

Approach	Training		LM		Changes		Scores		Rank
	Dataset	Size (sent)	Corpus	Size (sent)	Total	Correct	G	M	S
PBSMT	Wiki(Good+Partial)	284,499	Wiki	391,572	76	27 (35.5%)	4.09	3.31	0.26
PBSMT	Newsela(neighb. C3G-2s)+Wiki	593,947	Newsela+Wiki	766,446	81	38 (46.9%)	4.40	**3.84**	**0.30**
PBSMT	Newsela(all C3G-2s)+Wiki	764,572	Newsela+Wiki	766,446	87	42 (**48.3%**)	4.25	3.73	**0.30**
PBSMT	Newsela(neighb.-HMM)+Wiki	584,106	Newsela+Wiki	766,446	75	33 (44.0%)	4.20	3.65	0.20
s.o.t.a.	supervised SBMT (PPDB+SARI) (Xu et al., 2016)				**143**	49 (34.3%)	4.28	3.57	0.03
	unsupervised (LightLS) (Glavaš and Štajner, 2015)				132	35 (26.6%)	**4.47**	2.67	-0.01

Table 3: Extrinsic evaluation (PBSMT-based automatic text simplification systems vs. state of the art).

System	Output
Original	He advocates applying a user-centered design process in product development cycles and also works towards popularizing interaction design as a mainstream discipline.
PBSMT (Newsela neighb. C3G-2s + Wiki)	He **advocates a** user-centered design process in product development cycles and also works **for** popularizing interaction design as a mainstream discipline.
PBSMT (Newsela all C3G-2s + Wiki)	He **supports a** user-centered design process in product development cycles and also works **for** popularizing interaction design as a mainstream discipline.
PBSMT (Newsela HMM neighb. + Wiki)	He **advocates a** user-centered design process in product development cycles and also works towards popularizing interaction design as a mainstream discipline.
PBSMT (Wiki)	He advocates applying a user-centered design process in product development cycles and also works towards popularizing interaction design as a mainstream discipline.
SBMT (Xu et al., 2016)	He advocates **using** a user-centered design process in product development cycles and also works **for** popularizing *trade* design as a *whole field*.
LightLS	He *argues allowing* a user-centered design process in product development cycles and also works towards popularizing interaction design as a mainstream discipline.

Table 4: Outputs of different ATS systems (the correct changes/simplifications are shown in bold and the incorrect ones in italics).

(either *neighb. C3G-2l* or *all C3G-2l*) to the currently best sentence-aligned Wiki corpus (Hwang et al., 2015) in a standard PBSMT setup significantly[11] improves grammaticality (*G*) and meaning preservation (*M*), and increases the percentage of correct changes (Table 3). It also significantly outperforms the state-of-the-art ATS systems by simplicity rankings (*S*), meaning preservation (*M*), and number of correct changes (*Correct*), while achieving almost equally good grammaticality (*G*).

The level of simplification applied in the training dataset (*Newsela neighb. C3G-2s* vs. *Newsela all C3G-2s*) significantly influences G and M scores.

The use of the HMM-method for aligning Newsela (instead of ours) lead to significantly worse simplifications by all five criteria.

An example of the outputs of different ATS systems is presented in Table 4.

6 Conclusions

We provided several methods for paragraph- and sentence-alignment from parallel TS corpora, made the software publicly available, and showed that the use of the new sentence-aligned (freely available) Newsela dataset leads to state-of-the-art ATS systems even in a basic PBSMT setup. We also showed that lexically-based C3G method is superior to semantically-based methods (CWASA and WAVG) in aligning paraphraphs and sentences with 'heavy' simplifications (0–4 alignments), and that 2-step sentence alignment (aligning first paragraphs and then sentences within the paragraphs) lead to more correct alignments than the 'direct' sentence alignment.

---

[11]Wilcoxon's signed rank test, $p < 0.001$.

Acknowledgments

This work has been partially supported by the SFB 884 on the Political Economy of Reforms at the University of Mannheim (project C4), funded by the German Research Foundation (DFG), and also by the SomEMBED TIN2015-71147-C2-1-P MINECO research project.

References

Sandra Maria Aluísio and Caroline Gasperin. 2010. Fostering Digital Inclusion and Accessibility: The PorSimples project for Simplification of Portuguese Texts. In *Proceedings of YIWCALA Workshop at NAACL-HLT 2010*. pages 46–53.

Stefan Bott and Horacio Saggion. 2011. An Unsupervised Alignment Algorithm for Text Simplification Corpus Construction. In *Proceedings of the Workshop on Monolingual Text-To-Text Generation*. ACL, pages 20–26.

Richard J. Evans. 2011. Comparing methods for the syntactic simplification of sentences in information extraction. *Literary and Linguistic Computing* 26(4):371–388.

Marc Franco-Salvador, Parth Gupta, Paolo Rosso, and Rafael E. Banchs. 2016. Cross-language plagiarism detection over continuous-space- and knowledge graph-based representations of language. *Knowledge-Based Systems* 111:87 – 99.

Goran Glavaš and Sanja Štajner. 2015. Simplifying Lexical Simplification: Do We Need Simplified Corpora? In *Proceedings of the ACL&IJCNLP 2015 (Volume 2: Short Papers)*. pages 63–68.

William Hwang, Hannaneh Hajishirzi, Mari Ostendorf, and Wei Wu. 2015. Aligning Sentences from Standard Wikipedia to Simple Wikipedia. In *Proceedings of NAACL&HLT*. pages 211–217.

Philipp Koehn, Hieu Hoang, Alexandra Birch, Chris Callison-Burch, Marcello Federico, Nicola Bertoldi, Brooke Cowan, Wade Shen, Christine Moran, Richard Zens, Chris Dyer, Ondrej Bojar, Alexandra Constantin, and Evan Herbst. 2007. Moses: Open source toolkit for statistical machine translation. In *Proceedings of the ACL*. pages 177–180.

Philipp Koehn, Franz Josef Och, and Daniel Marcu. 2003. Statistical phrase-based translation. In *Proceedings of the NAACL&HLT, Vol. 1*. pages 48–54.

Paul Mcnamee and James Mayfield. 2004. Character n-gram tokenization for European language text retrieval. *Information Retrieval* 7(1):73–97.

Tomas Mikolov, Kai Chen, Greg Corrado, and Jeffrey Dean. 2013a. Efficient estimation of word representations in vector space. In *Proceedings of Workshop at International Conference on Learning Representations*.

Tomas Mikolov, Ilya Sutskever, Kai Chen, Greg S Corrado, and Jeff Dean. 2013b. Distributed representations of words and phrases and their compositionality. In *Advances in Neural Information Processing Systems 26*. pages 3111–3119.

Franz Och. 2003. Minimum Error Rate Training in Statistical Machine Translation. In *Proceedings of the ACL*. pages 160–167.

Franz Josef Och and Hermann Ney. 2003. A systematic comparison of various statistical alignment models. *Computational Linguistics* 29(1):19–51.

Gustavo Henrique Paetzold and Lucia Specia. 2016. Unsupervised lexical simplification for non-native speakers. In *Proceedings of the 30th AAAI*.

Horacio Saggion, Sanja Štajner, Stefan Bott, Simon Mille, Luz Rello, and Biljana Drndarevic. 2015. Making It Simplext: Implementation and Evaluation of a Text Simplification System for Spanish. *ACM Transactions on Accessible Computing* 6(4):14:1–14:36.

Gerard Salton and Michael J. McGill. 1986. *Introduction to Modern Information Retrieval*. McGraw-Hill, Inc.

Lucia Specia. 2010. Translating from complex to simplified sentences. In *Proceedings of the 9th PROPOR*. Springer Berlin Heidelberg, volume 6001 of *Lecture Notes in Computer Science*, pages 30–39.

Andreas Stolcke. 2002. SRILM - an Extensible Language Modeling Toolkit. In *Proceedings of the International Conference on Spoken Language Processing (ICSLP)*. pages 901–904.

David Vickrey and Daphne Koller. 2008. Sentence simplification for semantic role labeling. In *Proceedings of ACL&HLT*. volume 344–352.

Sanja Štajner, Hannah Bechara, and Horacio Saggion. 2015. A Deeper Exploration of the Standard PB-SMT Approach to Text Simplification and its Evaluation. In *Proceedings of ACL&IJCNLP (Volume 2: Short Papers)*. pages 823–828.

Sanja Štajner and Maja Popović. 2016. Can Text Simplification Help Machine Translation? *Baltic Journal of Modern Computing* 4(2):230–242.

Wei Xu, Chris Callison-Burch, and Courtney Napoles. 2015. Problems in Current Text Simplification Research: New Data Can Help. *Transactions of the Association for Computational Linguistics (TACL)* 3:283–297.

Wei Xu, Courtney Napoles, Ellie Pavlick, Quanze Chen, and Chris Callison-Burch. 2016. Optimizing statistical machine translation for text simplification. *Transactions of the Association for Computational Linguistics* 4:401–415.

Understanding Task Design Trade-offs in Crowdsourced Paraphrase Collection

Youxuan Jiang, Jonathan K. Kummerfeld and **Walter S. Lasecki**
Computer Science & Engineering
University of Michigan, Ann Arbor
{lyjiang,jkummerf,wlasecki}@umich.edu

Abstract

Linguistically diverse datasets are critical for training and evaluating robust machine learning systems, but data collection is a costly process that often requires experts. Crowdsourcing the process of paraphrase generation is an effective means of expanding natural language datasets, but there has been limited analysis of the trade-offs that arise when designing tasks. In this paper, we present the first systematic study of the key factors in crowdsourcing paraphrase collection. We consider variations in instructions, incentives, data domains, and workflows. We manually analyzed paraphrases for correctness, grammaticality, and linguistic diversity. Our observations provide new insight into the trade-offs between accuracy and diversity in crowd responses that arise as a result of task design, providing guidance for future paraphrase generation procedures.

1 Introduction

Paraphrases are useful for a range of tasks, including machine translation evaluation (Kauchak and Barzilay, 2006), semantic parsing (Wang et al., 2015), and question answering (Fader et al., 2013). Crowdsourcing has been widely used as a scalable and cost-effective means of generating paraphrases (Negri et al., 2012; Wang et al., 2012; Tschirsich and Hintz, 2013), but there has been limited analysis of the factors influencing diversity and correctness of the paraphrases workers write.

In this paper, we perform a systematic investigation of design decisions for crowdsourcing paraphrases, including the first exploration of worker incentives for paraphrasing. For worker incentives, we either provide a bonus payment when a paraphrase is novel (encouraging diversity) or

when it matches a paraphrase from another worker (encouraging agreement/correctness). We also varied the type of example paraphrases shown to workers, the number of paraphrases requested from each worker per sentence, the subject domain of the data, whether to show answers to questions, and whether the prompt sentence is the same for multiple workers or varies, with alternative prompts drawn from the output of other workers.

Effective paraphrasing has two desired properties: correctness and diversity. To measure correctness, we hand-labeled all paraphrases with semantic equivalence and grammaticality scores. For diversity, we measure the fraction of paraphrases that are distinct, as well as Paraphrase In N-gram Changes (PINC), a measure of n-gram variation. We have released all 2,600 paraphrases along with accuracy annotations. Our analysis shows that the most important factor is how workers are primed for a task, with the choice of examples and the prompt sentence affecting diversity and correctness significantly.

2 Related Work

Previous work on crowdsourced paraphrase generation fits into two categories: work on modifying the creation process or workflow, and studying the effect of prompting or priming on crowd worker output. Beyond crowdsourced generation, other work has explored using experts or automated systems to generate paraphrases.

2.1 Workflows for Crowd-Paraphrasing

The most common approach to crowdsourcing paraphrase generation is to provide a sentence as a prompt and request a single paraphrase from a worker. One frequent addition is to ask a different set of workers to evaluate whether a generated paraphrase is correct (Buzek et al., 2010; Burrows et al., 2013). Negri et al. (2012) also explored an alternate workflow in which each worker writes

Proceedings of the 55th Annual Meeting of the Association for Computational Linguistics (Short Papers), pages 103–109
Vancouver, Canada, July 30 - August 4, 2017. ©2017 Association for Computational Linguistics
https://doi.org/10.18653/v1/P17-2017

two paraphrases, which are then given to other workers as the prompt sentence, forming a binary tree of paraphrases. They found that paraphrases deeper in the tree were more diverse, but understanding how correctness and grammaticality vary across such a tree still remains an open question. Near real-time crowdsourcing (Bigham et al., 2010) allowed Lasecki et al. (2013a) to elicit variations on entire conversations by providing a setting and goal to pairs of crowd workers. Continuous real-time crowdsourcing (Lasecki et al., 2011) allows Chorus Lasecki et al. (2013b) users to hold conversations with groups of crowd workers as if the crowd was a single individual, allowing for the collection of example conversations in more realistic settings. The only prior work regarding incentives we are aware of is by Chklovski (2005), who collected paraphrases in a game where the goal was to match an existing paraphrase, with extra points awarded for doing so with fewer hints. The disadvantage of this approach was that 29% of the collected paraphrases were duplicates. In our experiments, duplication ranged from 1% to 13% in each condition.

2.2 The Effects of Priming

When crowd workers perform a task, they are *primed* (influenced) by the examples, instructions, and context that they see. This priming can result in systematic variations in the resulting paraphrases. Mitchell et al. (2014) showed that providing context, in the form of previous utterances from a dialogue, only provides benefits once four or more are included. Kumaran et al. (2014) provided drawings as prompts, obtaining diverse paraphrases, but without exact semantic equivalence. When each sentence expresses a small set of slot-filler predicates, Wang et al. (2012) found that providing the list of predicates led to slightly faster paraphrasing than giving either a complete sentence or a short sentence for each predicate. We further expand on this work by exploring how the type of examples shown affects paraphrasing.

2.3 Expert and Automated Generation

Finally, there are two general lines of research on paraphrasing not focused on using crowds. The first of these is the automatic collection of paraphrases from parallel data sources, such as translations of the same text or captions for the same image (Ganitkevitch et al., 2013; Chen and Dolan, 2011; Bouamor et al., 2012; Pavlick et al.,

Paraphrase/Reword Sentences

For each sentence below, please write 2 new sentence that express the same meaning in different ways (paraphrase/reword).

For example: 'Which 400 level courses don't have labs?' could be rewritten as:

- Of all the 400 level courses, which ones do not include labs?
- What are the 400 level courses without lab sessions?

BONUS: You will receive 5 cents bonus for each sentence you write that matches one written by another worker on the task.

Figure 1: Baseline task instructions.

2015). These resources are extremely large, but usually (1) do not provide the strong semantic equivalence we are interested in, and (2) focus on phrases rather than complete sentences. The second line of work explores the creation of lattices that compactly encode hundreds of thousands of paraphrases (Dreyer and Marcu, 2012; Bojar et al., 2013). Unfortunately, these lattices are typically expensive to produce, taking experts one to three hours per sentence.

3 Experimental Design

We conducted a series of experiments to investigate factors in crowdsourced paraphrase creation. To do so in a controlled manner, we studied a single variation per condition.

3.1 Definition of Valid Paraphrases

This project was motivated by the need for strongly equivalent paraphrases in semantic parsing datasets. We consider two sentences paraphrases if they would have equivalent interpretations when represented as a structured query, i.e., "a pair of units of text deemed to be interchangeable" (Dras, 1999). For example:

Prompt: *Which upper-level classes are four credits?*
Are there any four credit upper-level classes?

We considered the above two questions as paraphrases since they are both requests for a list of classes, explicit and implicit, respectively, although the second one is a polar question and the first one is not. However:

Prompt:*Which is easier out of EECS 378 and EECS 280?*
Is EECS 378 easier than EECS 280?

We did not consider the above two questions as paraphrases since the first one is requesting one of two class options and the second one is requesting a yes or no answer.

3.2 Baseline

We used Amazon Mechanical Turk, presenting workers with the instructions and examples in Figure 1. Workers were shown prompt sentences one at a time, and asked to provide two paraphrases for each. To avoid confusion or training effects between different conditions, we only allowed workers to participate once across all conditions. The initial instructions shown to workers were the same across all conditions (variations were only seen after a worker accepted the task).

Workers were paid 5 cents per paraphrase they wrote plus, once all workers were done, a 5 cent bonus for paraphrases that matched another worker's paraphrase in the same condition. While we do not actually want duplicate paraphrases, this incentive may encourage workers to more closely follow the instructions, producing grammatical and correct sentences. We chose this payment rate to give around minimum wage, estimating time based on prior work.

3.3 Conditions

Examples We provided workers with an example prompt sentence and two paraphrases, as shown in Figure 1. We showed either: no examples (No Examples), two examples with lexical changes only (Lexical Examples), one example with lexical changes and one with syntactic changes (Mixed Examples), or two examples that each contained both lexical and syntactic changes (Baseline). The variations between these conditions may prime workers differently, leading them to generate different paraphrases.

Incentive The 5 cent bonus payment per paraphrase was either not included (No Bonus), awarded for each sentence that was a duplicate at the end of the task (Baseline), or awarded for each sentence that did not match any other worker's paraphrase (Novelty Bonus). Bonuses that depend on other workers' actions may encourage either creativity or conformity. We did not vary the base level of payment because prior work has found that workers work quality is not increased by increased financial incentives due to an anchoring effect relative to the base rate we define (Mason and Watts, 2010).

Workflow We considered three variations to workflow. First, for each sentence, we either asked workers to provide two paraphrases (Baseline), or one (One Paraphrase). Asking for multiple paraphrases reduces duplication (since workers will not repeat themselves), but may result in lower diversity. Second, since our baseline prompt sentences are questions, we ran a condition with answers shown to workers (Answers). Third, we started all conditions with the same set of prompt sentences, but once workers had produced paraphrases, we had the option to either prompt future workers with the original prompt, or to use paraphrase from another worker. Treating sentences as points and the act of paraphrasing as creating an edge, the space can be characterized as a graph. We prompted workers with either the original sentences only (Baseline), or formed a chain structured graph by randomly choosing a sentence that was (1) not a duplicate, and (2) furthest from the original sentence (Chain). These changes could impact paraphrasing because the prompt sentence is a form of priming.

Data domains We ran with five data sources: questions about university courses (Baseline), messages from dialogues between two students in a simulated academic advising session (ADVISING), questions about US geography (GEOQUERY Tang and Mooney, 2001), text from the Wall Street Journal section of the Penn Treebank (WSJ Marcus et al., 1993), and discussions on the Ubuntu IRC channel (UBUNTU). We randomly selected 20 sentences as prompts from each data source with the lengths representative of the sentence length distribution in that source.

3.4 Metrics

Semantic Equivalence For a paraphrase to be valid, its meaning must match the original sentence. To assess this match, two of the authors—one native speaker and one non-native but fluent speaker—rated every sentence independently, then discussed every case of disagreement to determine a consensus judgement. Prior to the consensus-finding step, the inter-annotator agreement kappa scores were .50 for correctness (moderate agreement), and .36 for grammaticality (fair agreement) (Altman, 1990). For the results in Table 1, we used a χ^2 test to measure significance, since this is a binary classification process.

Grammaticality We also judged whether the sentences were grammatical, again with two annotators rating every sentence and resolving disagreements. Again, since this was a binary classification, we used a χ^2 test for significance.

Time The time it takes to write paraphrases is important for estimating time-to-completion, and ensuring workers receive fair payment. We measured the time between when a worker submitted one pair of paraphrases and the next. The first paraphrase was excluded since it would skew the data by including the time spent reading the instructions and understanding the task. We report the median time to avoid skewing due to outliers, e.g. a value of five minutes when a worker probably took a break. We apply Mood's Median test for statistical significance.

Diversity We use two metrics for diversity, measured over correct sentences only. First, a simple measurement of exact duplication: the number of distinct paraphrases divided by the total number of paraphrases, as a percentage (Distinct). Second, a measure of n-gram diversity (PINC Chen and Dolan, 2011)[1]. In both cases, a higher score means greater diversity. For PINC, we used a t-test for statistical significance, and for Distinct we used a permutation test.

4   Results

We collected 2600 paraphrases: 10 paraphrases per sentence, for 20 sentences, for each of the 13 conditions. The cost, including initial testing, was \$196.30, of which \$20.30 was for bonus payments. Table 1 shows the results for all metrics.

4.1   Discussion: Task Variation

Qualitatively, we observed a wide variety of lexical and syntactic changes, as shown by these example prompts and paraphrases (one low PINC and one high PINC in each case):

Prompt: *How long has EECS 280 been offered for?*
How long has EECS 280 been offered?
EECS 280 has been in the course listings how many years?

Prompt: *Can I take 280 on Mondays and Wednesdays?*
On Mondays and Wednesdays, can I take 280?
Is 280 available as a Monday/Wednesday class?

There was relatively little variation in grammaticality or time across the conditions. The times

---

[1] We also considered BLEU (Papineni et al., 2002), which measures n-gram overlap and is used as a proxy for correctness in MT. As expected, it strongly correlated with PINC.

	Accuracy (%)		Time	Diversity	
Condition	Corr	Gram	(s)	Distinct	PINC
Baseline	74	97	36	99	68
Lexical Examples	**90**†	98	**27**	**93**	**55**†
Mixed Examples	**89**†	96	36	**87**†	**58**†
No Examples	84	96	30	95	63
Novelty Bonus	72	96	30	99	69
No Bonus	78	94	28	99	66
One Paraphrase	82	**89**	38	96	65
Chain	68	94	**25**	98	**74**
Answers	80	94	**29**	96	65
ADVISING	78	94	31	97	70
GEOQUERY	77	**85**†	**25**†	**94**	**63**
WSJ	68	**90**	**61**†	**94**†	**38**†
UBUNTU	**56**†	92	44	97	67

Table 1: Variation across conditions for a range of metrics (defined in § 3.4). Bold indicates a statistically significant difference compared to the baseline at the 0.05 level, and a † indicates significance at the 0.01 level, both after applying the Holm-Bonferroni method across each row (Holm, 1979).

we observed are consistent with prior work: e.g. Wang et al. (2015) report ∼28 sec/paraphrase.

Priming had a major impact, with the shift to lexical examples leading to a significant improvement in correctness, but much lower diversity. The surprising increase in correctness when providing no examples has a p-value of 0.07 and probably reflects random variation in the pool of workers. Meanwhile, changing the incentives by providing either a bonus for novelty, or no bonus at all, did not substantially impact any of the metrics.

Changing the number of paraphrases written by each worker did not significantly impact diversity (we worried that collecting more than one may lead to a decrease). We further confirmed this by calculating PINC between the two paraphrases provided by each user, which produced scores similar to comparing with the prompt. However, the One Paraphrase condition did have lower grammaticality, emphasizing the value of evaluating and filtering out workers who write ungrammatical paraphrases.

Changing the source of the prompt sentence to create a chain of paraphrases led to a significant increase in diversity. This fits our intuition that the prompt is a form of priming. However, correctness decreases along the chain, suggesting the need to check paraphrases against the original sentence during the overall process, possibly using other workers as described in § 2.1. Meanwhile, showing the answer to the question being paraphrased did not significantly affect correctness or diversity, and in 2.5% of cases workers incorrectly used the answer as part of their paraphrase.

We also analyzed the distribution of incorrect or ungrammatical paraphrases by worker. 7% of workers accounted for 25% of incorrect paraphrases, while the best 30% of workers made no mistakes at all. Similarly, 8% of workers wrote 50% of the ungrammatical paraphrases, while 70% of workers wrote only grammatical paraphrases. Many crowdsourcing tasks address these issues by showing workers some gold standard instances, to evaluate workers' performance during annotation. Unfortunately, in paraphrasing there is no single correct answer, though other workers could be used to check outputs.

Finally, we checked the distribution of incorrect paraphrases per prompt sentence. Two prompts accounted for 22% of incorrect paraphrases:

Prompt:*Which is easier out of EECS 378 and EECS 280?*
Is EECS 378 easier than EECS 280?

Prompt: *Is Professor Stout the only person who teaches Algorithms?*
Are there professors other than Stout who teach Algorithms?

These paraphrases are not semantically equivalent to the original question, but they would elicit equivalent information, which explains why workers provided them. Providing negative examples may help guide workers to avoid such mistakes.

4.2 Discussion: Domains

The bottom section of Table 1 shows measurements using the baseline setup, but with variations in the source domain of data. The only significant change in correctness is on UBUNTU, which is probably due to the extensive use of jargon in the dataset, for example:

Prompt: *ok, what does journalctl show*
That journalistic show is about what?

For grammaticality, GEOQUERY is particularly low; common mistakes included confusion between singular/plural and has/have. WSJ is the domain with the greatest variations. It has considerably longer sentences on average, which explains the greater time taken. This could also explain the lower distinctness and PINC score, because workers would often retain large parts of the sentence, sometimes re-arranged, but otherwise unchanged.

5 Conclusion

While previous work has used crowdsourcing to generate paraphrases, we perform the first systematic study of factors influencing the process. We find that the most substantial variations are caused by priming effects: using simpler examples leads to lower diversity, but more frequent semantic equivalence. Meanwhile, prompting workers with paraphrases collected from other workers (rather than re-using the original prompt) increases diversity. Our findings provide clear guidance for future paraphrase generation, supporting the creation of larger, more diverse future datasets.

6 Acknowledgements

We would like to thank the members of the UMich/IBM Sapphire project, as well as all of our study participants and the anonymous reviewers for their helpful suggestions on this work.

This material is based in part upon work supported by IBM under contract 4915012629 . Any opinions, findings, conclusions or recommendations expressed above are those of the authors and do not necessarily reflect the views of IBM.

References

Douglas G Altman. 1990. *Practical statistics for medical research.* CRC press. https://www.crcpress.com/Practical-Statistics-for-Medical-Research/Altman/p/book/9780412276309.

Jeffrey P Bigham, Chandrika Jayant, Hanjie Ji, Greg Little, Andrew Miller, Robert C Miller, Robin Miller, Aubrey Tatarowicz, Brandyn White, Samual White, et al. 2010. Vizwiz: nearly real-time answers to visual questions. In *Proc. of the 23nd annual ACM symposium on User interface software and technology.* ACM, pages 333–342. http://dl.acm.org/citation.cfm?id=1866029.1866080.

Ondřej Bojar, Matouš Macháček, Aleš Tamchyna, and Daniel Zeman. 2013. *Scratching the surface of possible translations,* Springer Berlin Heidelberg, Berlin, Heidelberg, pages 465–474. http://dx.doi.org/10.1007/978-3-642-40585-3_59.

Houda Bouamor, Aurlien Max, Gabriel Illouz, and Anne Vilnat. 2012. A contrastive review of paraphrase acquisition techniques. In *Proc. of the Eight International Conference on Language Resources and Evaluation (LREC'12).* http://www.lrec-conf.org/proceedings/lrec2012/pdf/555_paper.pdf.

Steven Burrows, Martin Potthast, and Benno Stein. 2013. Paraphrase acquisition via crowdsourcing and machine learning. *ACM Transactions on Intelligent Systems and Technology* 4(3):43:1–43:21. http://doi.acm.org/10.1145/2483669.2483676.

Olivia Buzek, Philip Resnik, and Ben Bederson. 2010. Error driven paraphrase annotation using mechanical turk. In *Proc. of the NAACL HLT 2010 Workshop on Creating Speech and Language Data with Amazon's Mechanical Turk.* http://www.aclweb.org/anthology/W10-0735.

David Chen and William Dolan. 2011. Collecting highly parallel data for paraphrase evaluation. In *Proc. of the 49th Annual Meeting of the Association for Computational Linguistics: Human Language Technologies.* http://www.aclweb.org/anthology/P11-1020.

Timothy Chklovski. 2005. Collecting paraphrase corpora from volunteer contributors. In *Proc. of the 3rd International Conference on Knowledge Capture.* http://doi.acm.org/10.1145/1088622.1088644.

Mark Dras. 1999. *Tree adjoining grammar and the reluctant paraphrasing of text.* Ph.D. thesis, Macquarie University NSW 2109 Australia. http://web.science.mq.edu.au/ madras/papers/thesis.pdf.

Markus Dreyer and Daniel Marcu. 2012. HyTER: Meaning-equivalent semantics for translation evaluation. In *Proc. of the 2012 Conference of the North American Chapter of the Association for Computational Linguistics: Human Language Technologies.* http://www.aclweb.org/anthology/N12-1017.

Anthony Fader, Luke Zettlemoyer, and Oren Etzioni. 2013. Paraphrase-driven learning for open question answering. In *Proc. of the 51st Annual Meeting of the Association for Computational Linguistics (Volume 1: Long Papers).* http://www.aclweb.org/anthology/P/P13/P13-1158.pdf.

Juri Ganitkevitch, Benjamin Van Durme, and Chris Callison-Burch. 2013. PPDB: The paraphrase database. In *Proc. of the 2013 Conference of the North American Chapter of the Association for Computational Linguistics: Human Language Technologies.* http://aclweb.org/anthology/N/N13/N13-1092.pdf.

Sture Holm. 1979. A simple sequentially rejective multiple test procedure. *Scandinavian Journal of Statistics* 6(2):65–70. http://www.jstor.org/stable/4615733.

David Kauchak and Regina Barzilay. 2006. Paraphrasing for automatic evaluation. In *Proc. of the Human Language Technology Conference of the NAACL, Main Conference.* http://www.aclweb.org/anthology/N/N06/N06-1058.pdf.

A Kumaran, Melissa Densmore, and Shaishav Kumar. 2014. Online gaming for crowdsourcing phrase-equivalents. In *Proc. of COLING 2014, the 25th International Conference on Computational Linguistics: Technical Papers.* http://www.aclweb.org/anthology/C14-1117.

Walter S. Lasecki, Ece Kamar, and Dan Bohus. 2013a. Conversations in the crowd: Collecting data for task-oriented dialog learning. In *Scaling Speech, Language Understanding and Dialogue through Crowdsourcing Workshop at the First AAAI Conference on Human Computation and Crowdsourcing.* http://www.aaai.org/ocs/index.php/HCOMP/HCOMP13/paper/view/7637.

Walter S Lasecki, Kyle I Murray, Samuel White, Robert C Miller, and Jeffrey P Bigham. 2011. Realtime crowd control of existing interfaces. In *Proc. of the 24th annual ACM symposium on User interface software and technology.* ACM, pages 23–32. http://dl.acm.org/citation.cfm?id=2047200.

Walter S Lasecki, Rachel Wesley, Jeffrey Nichols, Anand Kulkarni, James F Allen, and Jeffrey P Bigham. 2013b. Chorus: a crowd-powered conversational assistant. In *Proc. of the 26th annual ACM symposium on User interface software and technology.* ACM, pages 151–162. http://dl.acm.org/citation.cfm?id=2502057.

Mitchell P. Marcus, Beatrice Santorini, and Mary Ann Marcinkiewicz. 1993. Building a large annotated corpus of English: The Penn Treebank. *Computational Linguistics* 19(2):313–330. http://aclweb.org/anthology/J93-2004.

Winter Mason and Duncan J Watts. 2010. Financial incentives and the performance of crowds. *ACM SigKDD Explorations Newsletter* 11(2):100–108. http://dl.acm.org/citation.cfm?id=1600175.

Margaret Mitchell, Dan Bohus, and Ece Kamar. 2014. Crowdsourcing language generation templates for dialogue systems. In *Proc. of the INLG and SIGDIAL 2014 Joint Session.* http://www.aclweb.org/anthology/W14-5003.

Matteo Negri, Yashar Mehdad, Alessandro Marchetti, Danilo Giampiccolo, and Luisa Bentivogli. 2012. Chinese whispers: Cooperative paraphrase acquisition. In *Proc. of the Eighth International Conference on Language Resources and Evaluation (LREC'12).* http://www.lrec-conf.org/proceedings/lrec2012/pdf/772_Paper.pdf.

Kishore Papineni, Salim Roukos, Todd Ward, and Wei-Jing Zhu. 2002. BLEU: a method for automatic evaluation of machine translation. In *Proc. of the 40th Annual Meeting of the Association for Computational Linguistics.* http://www.aclweb.org/anthology/P/P02/P02-1040.pdf.

Ellie Pavlick, Pushpendre Rastogi, Juri Ganitkevich, and Chris Callison-Burch Ben Van Durme. 2015. PPDB 2.0: Better paraphrase ranking, fine-grained entailment relations, word embeddings, and style classification. In *Proc. of the 53rd Annual Meeting of the Association for Computational Linguistics (ACL 2015)*. http://aclweb.org/anthology/P/P15/P15-2070.pdf.

Lappoon R. Tang and Raymond J. Mooney. 2001. Using multiple clause constructors in inductive logic programming for semantic parsing. In *Proc. of the 12th European Conference on Machine Learning*. https://link.springer.com/chapter/10.1007/3-540-44795-4$_4$0.

Martin Tschirsich and Gerold Hintz. 2013. Leveraging crowdsourcing for paraphrase recognition. In *Proc. of the 7th Linguistic Annotation Workshop and Interoperability with Discourse*. http://www.aclweb.org/anthology/W13-2325.

W. Y. Wang, D. Bohus, E. Kamar, and E. Horvitz. 2012. Crowdsourcing the acquisition of natural language corpora: Methods and observations. In *2012 IEEE Spoken Language Technology Workshop (SLT)*. http://ieeexplore.ieee.org/document/6424200/.

Yushi Wang, Jonathan Berant, and Percy Liang. 2015. Building a semantic parser overnight. In *Proc. of the 53rd Annual Meeting of the Association for Computational Linguistics and the 7th International Joint Conference on Natural Language Processing (Volume 1: Long Papers)*. http://www.aclweb.org/anthology/P15-1129.

Arc-swift: A Novel Transition System for Dependency Parsing

Peng Qi   **Christopher D. Manning**
Computer Science Department
Stanford University
{pengqi, manning}@cs.stanford.edu

Abstract

Transition-based dependency parsers often need sequences of local shift and reduce operations to produce certain attachments. Correct individual decisions hence require global information about the sentence context and mistakes cause error propagation. This paper proposes a novel transition system, *arc-swift*, that enables direct attachments between tokens farther apart with a single transition. This allows the parser to leverage lexical information more directly in transition decisions. Hence, *arc-swift* can achieve significantly better performance with a very small beam size. Our parsers reduce error by 3.7–7.6% relative to those using existing transition systems on the Penn Treebank dependency parsing task and English Universal Dependencies.

1 Introduction

Dependency parsing is a longstanding natural language processing task, with its outputs crucial to various downstream tasks including relation extraction (Schmitz et al., 2012; Angeli et al., 2015), language modeling (Gubbins and Vlachos, 2013), and natural logic inference (Bowman et al., 2016).

Attractive for their linear time complexity and amenability to conventional classification methods, *transition-based* dependency parsers have sparked much research interest recently. A transition-based parser makes sequential predictions of transitions between states under the restrictions of a *transition system* (Nivre, 2003). Transition-based parsers have been shown to excel at parsing shorter-range dependency structures, as well as languages where non-projective parses are less pervasive (McDonald and Nivre, 2007).

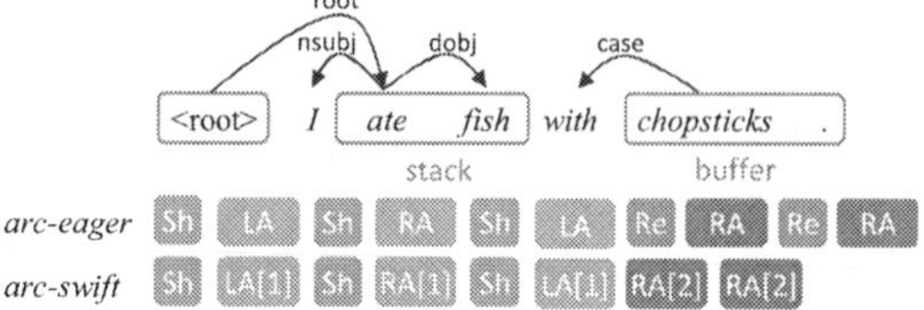

Figure 1: An example of the state of a transition-based dependency parser, and the transition sequences used by *arc-eager* and *arc-swift* to induce the correct parse. The state shown is generated by the first six transitions of both systems.

However, the transition systems employed in state-of-the-art dependency parsers usually define very local transitions. At each step, only one or two words are affected, with very local attachments made. As a result, distant attachments require long and not immediately obvious transition sequences (e.g., *ate→chopsticks* in Figure 1, which requires two transitions). This is further aggravated by the usually local lexical information leveraged to make transition predictions (Chen and Manning, 2014; Andor et al., 2016).

In this paper, we introduce a novel transition system, *arc-swift*, which defines non-local transitions that directly induce attachments of distance up to n (n = the number of tokens in the sentence). Such an approach is connected to *graph-based* dependency parsing, in that it leverages pairwise scores between tokens in making parsing decisions (McDonald et al., 2005).

We make two main contributions in this paper. Firstly, we introduce a novel transition system for dependency parsing, which alleviates the difficulty of distant attachments in previous systems by allowing direct attachments anywhere in the stack. Secondly, we compare parsers by the number of mistakes they make in common linguistic con-

Proceedings of the 55th Annual Meeting of the Association for Computational Linguistics (Short Papers), pages 110–117
Vancouver, Canada, July 30 - August 4, 2017. ©2017 Association for Computational Linguistics
https://doi.org/10.18653/v1/P17-2018

arc-standard		*arc-hybrid*	
Shift	$(\sigma, i|\beta, A) \Rightarrow (\sigma|i, \beta, A)$	**Shift**	$(\sigma, i|\beta, A) \Rightarrow (\sigma|i, \beta, A)$
LArc	$(\sigma|i|j, \beta, A) \Rightarrow (\sigma|j, \beta, A \cup \{(j \to i)\})$	**LArc**	$(\sigma|i, j|\beta, A) \Rightarrow (\sigma, j|\beta, A \cup \{(j \to i)\})$
RArc	$(\sigma|i|j, \beta, A) \Rightarrow (\sigma|i, \beta, A \cup \{(i \to j)\})$	**RArc**	$(\sigma|i|j, \beta, A) \Rightarrow (\sigma|i, \beta, A \cup \{(i \to j)\})$

arc-eager		*arc-swift*	
Shift	$(\sigma, i|\beta, A) \Rightarrow (\sigma|i, \beta, A)$	**Shift**	$(\sigma, i|\beta, A) \Rightarrow (\sigma|i, \beta, A)$
LArc	$(\sigma|i, j|\beta, A) \Rightarrow (\sigma, j|\beta, A \cup \{(j \to i)\})$	**LArc**[k]	$(\sigma|i_k|\ldots|i_1, j|\beta, A)$ $\Rightarrow (\sigma, j|\beta, A \cup \{(j \to i_k)\})$
RArc	$(\sigma|i, j|\beta, A) \Rightarrow (\sigma|i|j, \beta, A \cup \{(i \to j)\})$	**RArc**[k]	$(\sigma|i_k|\ldots|i_1, j|\beta, A)$ $\Rightarrow (\sigma|i_k|j, \beta, A \cup \{(i_k \to j)\})$
Reduce	$(\sigma|i, \beta, A) \Rightarrow (\sigma, \beta, A)$		

Figure 2: Transitions defined by different transition systems.

structions. We show that *arc-swift* parsers reduce errors in attaching prepositional phrases and conjunctions compared to parsers using existing transition systems.

2 Transition-based Dependency Parsing

Transition-based dependency parsing is performed by predicting transitions between states (see Figure 1 for an example). Parser states are usually written as $(\sigma|i, j|\beta, A)$, where $\sigma|i$ denotes the *stack* with token i on the top, $j|\beta$ denotes the *buffer* with token j at its leftmost, and A the set of dependency arcs. Given a state, the goal of a dependency parser is to predict a *transition* to a new state that would lead to the correct parse. A *transition system* defines a set of transitions that are sound and complete for parsers, that is, every transition sequence would derive a well-formed parse tree, and every possible parse tree can also be derived from some transition sequence.[1]

Arc-standard (Nivre, 2004) is one of the first transition systems proposed for dependency parsing. It defines three transitions: shift, left arc (LArc), and right arc (RArc) (see Figure 2 for definitions, same for the following transition systems), where all arc-inducing transitions operate on the stack. This system builds the parse bottom-up, i.e., a constituent is only attached to its head after it has received all of its dependents. A potential drawback is that during parsing, it is difficult to predict if a constituent has consumed all of its right dependents. *Arc-eager* (Nivre, 2003) remedies this drawback by defining arc-inducing transitions that operate between the stack and the buffer. As a result, a constituent no longer needs to be complete

before it can be attached to its head to the left, as a right arc doesn't prevent the attached dependent from taking further dependents of its own.[2] Kuhlmann et al. (2011) propose a hybrid system derived from a tabular parsing scheme, which they have shown both *arc-standard* and *arc-eager* can be derived from. *Arc-hybrid* combines LArc from *arc-eager* and RArc from *arc-standard* to build dependencies bottom-up.

3 Non-local Transitions with *arc-swift*

The traditional transition systems discussed in Section 2 only allow very local transitions affecting one or two words, which makes long-distance dependencies difficult to predict. To illustrate the limitation of local transitions, consider parsing the following sentences:

> *I ate fish with ketchup.*
> *I ate fish with chopsticks.*

The two sentences have almost identical structures, with the notable difference that the prepositional phrase is complementing the direct object in the first case, and the main verb in the second.

For *arc-standard* and *arc-hybrid*, the parser would have to decide between Shift and RArc when the parser state is as shown in Figure 3a, where $\star$ stands for either "*ketchup*" or "*chopsticks*".[3] Similarly, an *arc-eager* parser would deal with the state shown in Figure 3b. Making the correct transition requires information about context words "*ate*" and "*fish*", as well as "$\star$".

---

[1] We only focus on projective parses for the scope of this paper.

[2] A side-effect of *arc-eager* is that there is sometimes *spurious ambiguity* between Shift and Reduce transitions. For the example in Figure 1, the first Reduce can be inserted before the third Shift without changing the correctness of the resulting parse, i.e., both are feasible at that time.

[3] For this example, we assume that the sentence is being parsed into Universal Dependencies.

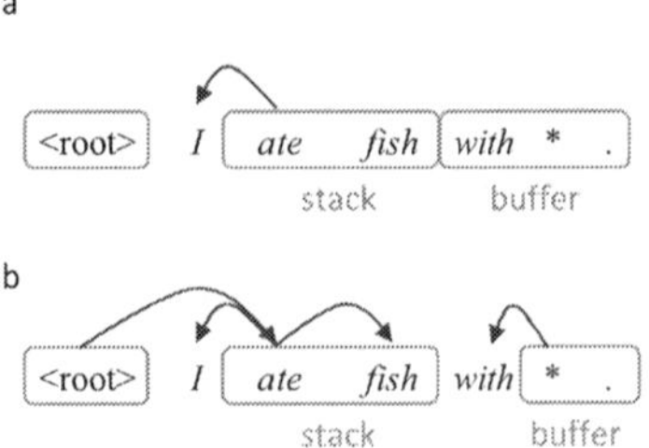

Figure 3: Parser states that present difficult transition decisions in traditional systems. In these states, parsers would need to incorporate context about "ate", "fish", and "⋆" to make the correct local transition.

Parsers employing traditional transition systems would usually incorporate more features about the context in the transition decision, or employ beam search during parsing (Chen and Manning, 2014; Andor et al., 2016).

In contrast, inspired by graph-based parsers, we propose *arc-swift*, which defines non-local transitions as shown in Figure 2. This allows direct comparison of different attachment points, and provides a direct solution to parsing the two example sentences. When the *arc-swift* parser encounters a state identical to Figure 3b, it could directly compare transitions RArc[1] and RArc[2] instead of evaluating between local transitions. This results in a direct attachment much like that in a graph-based parser, informed by lexical information about affinity of the pairs of words.

Arc-swift also bears much resemblance to *arc-eager*. In fact, an LArc[k] transition can be viewed as $k - 1$ Reduce operations followed by one LArc in *arc-eager*, and similarly for RArc[k]. Reduce is no longer needed in *arc-swift* as it becomes part of LArc[k] and RArc[k], removing the ambiguity in derived transitions in *arc-eager*. *arc-swift* is also equivalent to *arc-eager* in terms of soundness and completeness.[4] A caveat is that the worst-case time complexity of *arc-swift* is $O(n^2)$ instead of $O(n)$, which existing transition-based parsers enjoy. However, in practice the runtime is nearly linear, thanks to the usually small number of reducible tokens in the stack.

4 Experiments

4.1 Data and Model

We use the Wall Street Journal portion of Penn Treebank with standard parsing splits (PTB-SD), along with Universal Dependencies v1.3 (Nivre et al., 2016) (EN-UD). PTB-SD is converted to Stanford Dependencies (De Marneffe and Manning, 2008) with CoreNLP 3.3.0 (Manning et al., 2014) following previous work. We report labelled and unlabelled attachment scores (LAS/UAS), removing punctuation from all evaluations.

Our model is very similar to that of (Kiperwasser and Goldberg, 2016), where features are extracted from tokens with bidirectional LSTMs, and concatenated for classification. For the three traditional transition systems, features of the top 3 tokens on the stack and the leftmost token in the buffer are concatenated as classifier input. For *arc-swift*, features of the head and dependent tokens for each arc-inducing transition are concatenated to compute scores for classification, and features of the leftmost buffer token is used for Shift. For other details we defer to Appendix A. The full specification of the model can also be found in our released code online at `https://github.com/qipeng/arc-swift`.

4.2 Results

We use static oracles for all transition systems, and for *arc-eager* we implement oracles that always Shift/Reduce when ambiguity is present (*arc-eager-S/R*). We evaluate our parsers with greedy parsing (i.e., beam size 1). The results are shown in Table 1.[5] Note that K&G 2016 is trained with a dynamic oracle (Goldberg and Nivre, 2012), Andor 2016 with a CRF-like loss, and both Andor 2016 and Weiss 2015 employed beam search (with sizes 32 and 8, respectively).

For each pair of the systems we implemented, we studied the statistical significance of their difference by performing a paired test with 10,000 bootstrap samples on PTB-SD. The resulting p-values are analyzed with a 10-group Bonferroni-Holm test, with results shown in Table 2. We note

---

[4]This is easy to show because in *arc-eager*, all Reduce transitions can be viewed as preparing for a later LArc or RArc transition. We also note that similar to *arc-eager* transitions, *arc-swift* transitions must also satisfy certain pre-conditions. Specifically, an RArc[k] transition requires that the top $k - 1$ elements in the stack are already attached; LArc[k] additionally requires that the k-th element is unattached, resulting in no more than one feasible LArc candidate for any parser state.

[5]In the interest of space, we abbreviate all transition systems (TS) as follows in tables: *asw* for *arc-swift*, *asd* for *arc-standard*, *aeS/R* for *arc-eager-S/R*, and *ah* for *arc-hybrid*.

Model	TS	PTB-SD		EN-UD	
		UAS	LAS	UAS	LAS
This work	*asd*	94.0	91.7	85.6	81.5
This work	*aeS*	94.0	91.8	85.4	81.4
This work	*aeR*	93.8	91.7	85.2	81.2
This work	*ah*	93.9	91.7	85.4	81.3
This work	*asw*	94.3	92.2	**86.1**	**82.2**
Andor 2016	*asd*	**94.6**	**92.8**	84.8*	80.4*
K&G 2016	*ah*	93.9	91.9		
Weiss 2015	*asd*	94.0	92.1		
C&M 2014	*asd*	91.8	89.6		

Table 1: Performance of parsers using different transition systems on the Penn Treebank dataset. *: Obtained from their published results online.[6]

	aeS	*asd*	*ah*	*aeR*
asw	***/***	***/***	***/***	***/***
aeS		-/-	-/-	*/-
asd			-/-	*/-
ah				-/-

Table 2: Significance test for transition systems. Each grid shows adjusted test result for UAS and LAS, respectively, showing whether the system on the row is significantly better than that on the column. "***" stands for $p < 0.001$, "**" $p < 0.01$, "*" $p < 0.05$, and "-" $p \geq 0.05$.

that with almost the same implementation, *arc-swift* parsers significantly outperform those using traditional transition systems. We also analyzed the performance of parsers on attachments of different distances. As shown in Figure 4, *arc-swift* is equally accurate as existing systems for short dependencies, but is more robust for longer ones.

While *arc-swift* introduces direct long-distance transitions, it also shortens the overall sequence necessary to induce the same parse. A parser could potentially benefit from both factors: direct attachments could make an easier classification task, and shorter sequences limit the effect of error propagation. However, since the two effects are correlated in a transition system, precise attribution of the gain is out of the scope of this paper.

Computational efficiency. We study the computational efficiency of the *arc-swift* parser by

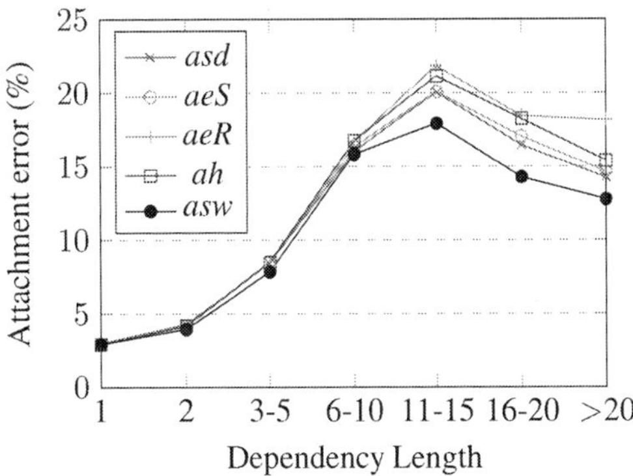

Figure 4: Parser attachment errors on PTB-SD binned by the length of the gold dependency.

comparing it to an *arc-eager* parser. On the PTB-SD development set, the average transition sequence length per sentence of *arc-swift* is 77.5% of that of *arc-eager*. At each step of parsing, *arc-swift* needs to evaluate only about 1.24 times the number of transition candidates as *arc-eager*, which results in very similar runtime. In contrast, beam search with beam size 2 for *arc-eager* requires evaluating 4 times the number of transition candidates compared to greedy parsing, which results in a UAS 0.14% worse and LAS 0.22% worse for *arc-eager* compared to greedily decoded *arc-swift*.

4.3 Linguistic Analysis

We automatically extracted all labelled attachment errors by error type (incorrect attachment or relation), and categorized a few top parser errors by hand into linguistic constructions. Results on PTB-SD are shown in Table 3.[7] We note that the *arc-swift* parser improves accuracy on prepositional phrase (PP) and conjunction attachments, while it remains comparable to other parsers on other common errors. Analysis on EN-UD shows a similar trend. As shown in the table, there are still many parser errors unaccounted for in our analysis. We leave this to future work.

[6]https://github.com/tensorflow/models/blob/master/syntaxnet/g3doc/universal.md

[7]We notice that for some examples the parsers predicted a *ccomp* (complement clause) attachment to verbs "says" and "said", where the CoreNLP output simply labelled the relation as *dep* (unspecified). For other examples the relation between the prepositions in "out of" is labelled as *prep* (preposition) instead of *pcomp* (prepositional complement). We suspect this is due to the converter's inability to handle certain corner cases, but further study is warranted.

	asw	*aeS*	*asd*
PP attachment	545	569	571
Noun/Adjective confusion	221	230	221
Conjunction attachment	156	170	164
Adverbial attachment	123	122	143
Total Errors	3884	4100	4106

Table 3: Common parser errors on PTB-SD. The top 4 common errors are categorized and shown in this table. Errors not shown are in a long-tail distribution and warrant analyses in future work.

5 Related Work

Previous work has also explored augmenting transition systems to facilitate longer-range attachments. Attardi (2006) extended the *arc-standard* system for non-projective parsing, with arc-inducing transitions that are very similar to those in *arc-swift*. A notable difference is that their transitions retain tokens between the head and dependent. Fernández-González and Gómez-Rodríguez (2012) augmented the *arc-eager* system with transitions that operate on the buffer, which shorten the transition sequence by reducing the number of Shift transitions needed. However, limited by the sparse feature-based classifiers used, both of these parsers just mentioned only allow direct attachments of distance up to 3 and 2, respectively. More recently, Sartorio et al. (2013) extended *arc-standard* with transitions that directly attach to left and right "spines" of the top two nodes in the stack. While this work shares very similar motivations as *arc-swift*, it requires additional data structures to keep track of the left and right spines of nodes. This transition system also introduces *spurious ambiguity* where multiple transition sequences could lead to the same correct parse, which necessitates easy-first training to achieve a more noticeable improvement over *arc-standard*. In contrast, *arc-swift* can be easily implemented given the parser state alone, and does not give rise to spurious ambiguity.

For a comprehensive study of transition systems for dependency parsing, we refer the reader to (Bohnet et al., 2016), which proposed a generalized framework that could derive all of the traditional transition systems we described by configuring the size of the active token set and the maximum arc length, among other control parameters. However, this framework does not cover *arc-swift* in its original form, as the authors limit each of their transitions to reduce at most one token from the active token set (the buffer). On the other hand, the framework presented in (Gómez-Rodríguez and Nivre, 2013) does not explicitly make this constraint, and therefore generalizes to *arc-swift*. However, we note that *arc-swift* still falls out of the scope of existing discussions in that work, by introducing multiple Reduces in a single transition.

6 Conclusion

In this paper, we introduced *arc-swift*, a novel transition system for dependency parsing. We also performed linguistic analyses on parser outputs and showed *arc-swift* parsers reduce errors in conjunction and adverbial attachments compared to parsers using traditional transition systems.

Acknowledgments

We thank Timothy Dozat, Arun Chaganty, Danqi Chen, and the anonymous reviewers for helpful discussions. Stanford University gratefully acknowledges the support of the Defense Advanced Research Projects Agency (DARPA) Deep Exploration and Filtering of Text (DEFT) Program under Air Force Research Laboratory (AFRL) contract No. FA8750-13-2-0040. Any opinions, findings, and conclusion or recommendations expressed in this material are those of the authors and do not necessarily reflect the view of the DARPA, AFRL, or the US government.

References

Daniel Andor, Chris Alberti, David Weiss, Aliaksei Severyn, Alessandro Presta, Kuzman Ganchev, Slav Petrov, and Michael Collins. 2016. Globally normalized transition-based neural networks. In *Proceedings of the 54th Annual Meeting of the Association for Computational Linguistics*. https://www.aclweb.org/anthology/P16-1231.

Gabor Angeli, Melvin Johnson Premkumar, and Christopher D Manning. 2015. Leveraging linguistic structure for open domain information extraction. In *Proceedings of the 53rd Annual Meeting of the Association for Computational Linguistics (ACL 2015)*. http://www.aclweb.org/anthology/P15-1034.

Giuseppe Attardi. 2006. Experiments with a multilanguage non-projective dependency parser. In *Proceedings of the Tenth Conference on Computational Natural Language Learning*. Association for Computational Linguistics, pages 166–170. http://www.aclweb.org/anthology/W06-2922.

Bernd Bohnet, Ryan McDonald, Emily Pitler, and Ji Ma. 2016. Generalized transition-based dependency parsing via control parameters. In *Proceedings of the 54th Annual Meeting of the Association for Computational Linguistics*. volume 1, pages 150–160. https://www.aclweb.org/anthology/P16-1015.

Samuel R Bowman, Jon Gauthier, Abhinav Rastogi, Raghav Gupta, Christopher D Manning, and Christopher Potts. 2016. A fast unified model for parsing and sentence understanding. In *Proceedings of the 54th Annual Meeting of the Association for Computational Linguistics (ACL 2016)*. http://www.aclweb.org/anthology/P16-1139.

Danqi Chen and Christopher D Manning. 2014. A fast and accurate dependency parser using neural networks. In *EMNLP*. pages 740–750. http://www.aclweb.org/anthology/D14-1082.

Marie-Catherine De Marneffe and Christopher D Manning. 2008. The Stanford typed dependencies representation. In *COLING 2008: Proceedings of the Workshop on Cross-framework and Cross-domain Parser Evaluation*. pages 1–8. http://www.aclweb.org/anthology/W08-1301.

Daniel Fernández-González and Carlos Gómez-Rodríguez. 2012. Improving transition-based dependency parsing with buffer transitions. In *Proceedings of the 2012 Joint Conference on Empirical Methods in Natural Language Processing and Computational Natural Language Learning*. pages 308–319. http://www.aclweb.org/anthology/D12-1029.

Yoav Goldberg and Joakim Nivre. 2012. A dynamic oracle for arc-eager dependency parsing. In *COLING*. pages 959–976. http://www.aclweb.org/anthology/C12-1059.

Carlos Gómez-Rodríguez and Joakim Nivre. 2013. Divisible transition systems and multiplanar dependency parsing. *Computational Linguistics* 39(4):799–845.

Joseph Gubbins and Andreas Vlachos. 2013. Dependency language models for sentence completion. In *EMNLP*. volume 13, pages 1405–1410. http://www.aclweb.org/anthology/D13-1143.

Sepp Hochreiter and Jürgen Schmidhuber. 1997. Long short-term memory. *Neural computation* 9(8):1735–1780.

Diederik Kingma and Jimmy Ba. 2014. Adam: A method for stochastic optimization. *arXiv preprint arXiv:1412.6980* .

Eliyahu Kiperwasser and Yoav Goldberg. 2016. Simple and accurate dependency parsing using bidirectional lstm feature representations. *Transactions of the Association for Computational Linguistics (TACL)* https://aclweb.org/anthology/Q16-1023.

Marco Kuhlmann, Carlos Gómez-Rodríguez, and Giorgio Satta. 2011. Dynamic programming algorithms for transition-based dependency parsers. In *Proceedings of the 49th Annual Meeting of the Association for Computational Linguistics: Human Language Technologies*. pages 673–682. http://www.aclweb.org/anthology/P11-1068.

Christopher D. Manning, Mihai Surdeanu, John Bauer, Jenny Finkel, Steven J. Bethard, and David McClosky. 2014. The Stanford CoreNLP natural language processing toolkit. In *Association for Computational Linguistics (ACL) System Demonstrations*. pages 55–60. http://www.aclweb.org/anthology/P/P14/P14-5010.

Ryan McDonald, Fernando Pereira, Kiril Ribarov, and Jan Hajič. 2005. Non-projective dependency parsing using spanning tree algorithms. In *Proceedings of the conference on Human Language Technology and Empirical Methods in Natural Language Processing*. pages 523–530. http://www.aclweb.org/anthology/H05-1066.

Ryan T McDonald and Joakim Nivre. 2007. Characterizing the errors of data-driven dependency parsing models. In *EMNLP-CoNLL*. pages 122–131. http://www.aclweb.org/anthology/D07-1013.

Joakim Nivre. 2003. An efficient algorithm for projective dependency parsing. In *Proceedings of the 8th International Workshop on Parsing Technologies*. pages 149–160. http://stp.lingfil.uu.se/ nivre/docs/iwpt03.pdf.

Joakim Nivre. 2004. Incrementality in deterministic dependency parsing. In *Proceedings of the Workshop on Incremental Parsing: Bringing Engineering and Cognition Together*. pages 50–57. https://www.aclweb.org/anthology/W04-0308.

Joakim Nivre, Marie-Catherine de Marneffe, Filip Ginter, Yoav Goldberg, Jan Hajic, Christopher D Manning, Ryan McDonald, Slav Petrov, Sampo Pyysalo, Natalia Silveira, et al. 2016. Universal dependencies v1: A multilingual treebank collection. In *Proceedings of the 10th International Conference on Language Resources and Evaluation (LREC 2016)*. pages 1659–1666.

Jeffrey Pennington, Richard Socher, and Christopher D. Manning. 2014. Glove: Global vectors for word representation. In *Empirical Methods in Natural Language Processing (EMNLP)*. pages 1532–1543. http://www.aclweb.org/anthology/D14-1162.

Francesco Sartorio, Giorgio Satta, and Joakim Nivre. 2013. A transition-based dependency parser using a dynamic parsing strategy. In *Association for Computational Linguistics*. pages 135–144. http://www.aclweb.org/anthology/P13-1014.

Michael Schmitz, Robert Bart, Stephen Soderland, Oren Etzioni, et al. 2012. Open language learning for information extraction. In *Proceedings* of the 2012 Joint Conference on Empirical Methods in Natural Language Processing and Computational Natural Language Learning. pages 523–534. https://www.aclweb.org/anthology/D12-1048.

David Weiss, Chris Alberti, Michael Collins, and Slav Petrov. 2015. Structured training for neural network transition-based parsing. In *Proceedings of the 53rd Annual Meeting of the Association for Computational Linguistics (ACL 2015)*. http://www.aclweb.org/anthology/P15-1032.

A Model and Training Details

Our model setup is similar to that of (Kiperwasser and Goldberg, 2016) (See Figure 5). We employ two blocks of bidirectional long short-term memory (BiLSTM) networks (Hochreiter and Schmidhuber, 1997) that share very similar structures, one for part-of-speech (POS) tagging, the other for parsing. Both BiLSTMs have 400 hidden units in each direction, and the output of both are concatenated and fed into a dense layer of rectified linear units (ReLU) before 32-dimensional representations are derived as classification features. As the input to the tagger BiLSTM, we represent words with 100-dimensional word embeddings, initialized with GloVe vectors (Pennington et al., 2014).[8] The output distribution of the tagger classifier is used to compute a weighted sum of 32-dimensional POS embeddings, which is then concatenated with the output of the tagger BiLSTM (800-dimensional per token) as the input to the parser BiLSTM. For the parser BiLSTM, we use two separate sets of dense layers to derive a "head" and a "dependent" representation for each token. These representations are later merged according to the parser state to make transition predictions.

For traditional transition systems, we follow (Kiperwasser and Goldberg, 2016) by featurizing the top 3 tokens on the stack and the leftmost token in the buffer. To derive features for each token, we take its head representation v_{head} and dependent representation v_{dep}, and perform the following biaffine combination

$$
\begin{aligned}
v_{\text{feat},i} &= [f(v_{\text{head}}, v_{\text{dep}})]_i \\
&= \text{ReLU}\big(v_{\text{head}}^\top W_i v_{\text{dep}} + b_i^\top v_{\text{head}} \\
&\quad + c_i^\top v_{\text{dep}} + d_i\big)
\end{aligned}
\tag{1}
$$

where $W_i \in \mathbb{R}^{32\times32}$, $b_i, c_i \in \mathbb{R}^{32}$, and d_i is a scalar for $i = 1, \ldots, 32$. The resulting 32-dimensional features are concatenated as the input

---

[8] We also kept the vectors of the top 400k words trained on Wikipedia and English Gigaword for a broader coverage of unseen words.

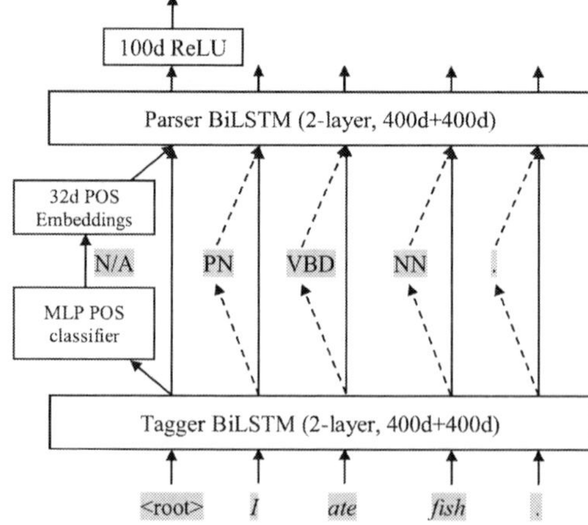

Figure 5: Illustration of the model.

to a fixed-dimensional softmax classifier for transition decisions.

For *arc-swift*, we featurize for each arc-inducing transition with the same composition function in Equation (1) with v_{head} of the head token and v_{dep} of the dependent token of the arc to be induced. For Shift, we simply combine v_{head} and v_{dep} of the leftmost token in the buffer with the biaffine combination, and obtain its score by computing the inner-product of the feature and a vector. At each step, the scores of all feasible transitions are normalized to a probability distribution by a softmax function.

In all of our experiments, the parsers are trained to maximize the log likelihood of the desired transition sequence, along with the tagger being trained to maximize the log likelihood of the correct POS tag for each token.

To train the parsers, we use the ADAM optimizer (Kingma and Ba, 2014), with $\beta_2 = 0.9$, an initial learning rate of 0.001, and minibatches of size 32 sentences. Parsers are trained for 10 passes through the dataset on PTB-SD. We also find that annealing the learning rate by a factor of 0.5 for every pass after the 5th helped improve performance. For EN-UD, we train for 30 passes, and anneal the learning rate for every 3 passes after the 15th due to the smaller size of the dataset. For all of the biaffine combination layers and dense layers, we dropout their units with a small probability of 5%. Also during training time, we randomly replace 10% of the input words by an artificial $\langle$UNK$\rangle$ token, which is then used to replace all unseen words in the development and test sets. Finally, we repeat each experiment with 3 independent random initializations, and use the average result for reporting and statistical significance tests.

The code for the full specification of our models and aforementioned training details are available at `https://github.com/qipeng/arc-swift`.

A Generative Parser with a Discriminative Recognition Algorithm

Jianpeng Cheng   **Adam Lopez** and **Mirella Lapata**
School of Informatics, University of Edinburgh
`jianpeng.cheng@ed.ac.uk, {alopez,mlap}@inf.ed.ac.uk`

Abstract

Generative models defining joint distributions over parse trees and sentences are useful for parsing and language modeling, but impose restrictions on the scope of features and are often outperformed by discriminative models. We propose a framework for parsing and language modeling which marries a generative model with a discriminative recognition model in an encoder-decoder setting. We provide interpretations of the framework based on expectation maximization and variational inference, and show that it enables parsing and language modeling within a single implementation. On the English Penn Treebank, our framework obtains competitive performance on constituency parsing while matching the state-of-the-art single-model language modeling score.[1]

1   Introduction

Generative models defining joint distributions over parse trees and sentences are good theoretical models for interpreting natural language data, and appealing tools for tasks such as parsing, grammar induction and language modeling (Collins, 1999; Henderson, 2003; Titov and Henderson, 2007; Petrov and Klein, 2007; Dyer et al., 2016). However, they often impose strong independence assumptions which restrict the use of arbitrary features for effective disambiguation. Moreover, generative parsers are typically trained by maximizing the joint probability of the parse tree and the sentence—an objective that only indirectly relates to the goal of parsing. At test time, these models require a relatively expensive recognition algo-

rithm (Collins, 1999; Titov and Henderson, 2007) to recover the parse tree, but the parsing performance consistently lags behind their discriminative competitors (Nivre et al., 2007; Huang, 2008; Goldberg and Elhadad, 2010), which are directly trained to maximize the conditional probability of the parse tree given the sentence, where linear-time decoding algorithms exist (e.g., for transition-based parsers).

In this work, we propose a parsing and language modeling framework that marries a generative model with a discriminative recognition algorithm in order to have the best of both worlds. The idea of combining these two types of models is not new. For example, Collins and Koo (2005) propose to use a generative model to generate candidate constituency trees and a discriminative model to rank them. Sangati et al. (2009) follow the opposite direction and employ a generative model to re-rank the dependency trees produced by a discriminative parser. However, previous work combines the two types of models in a goal-oriented, pipeline fashion, which lacks model interpretations and focuses solely on parsing.

In comparison, our framework unifies generative and discriminative parsers with a single objective, which connects to expectation maximization and variational inference in grammar induction settings. In a nutshell, we treat parse trees as latent factors generating natural language sentences and parsing as a posterior inference task. We showcase the framework using Recurrent Neural Network Grammars (RNNGs; Dyer et al. 2016), a recently proposed probabilistic model of phrase-structure trees based on neural transition systems. Different from this work which introduces separately trained discriminative and generative models, we integrate the two in an auto-encoder which fits our training objective. We show how the framework enables grammar induction, parsing and language

---

[1] Our code is available at `https://github.com/cheng6076/virnng.git`.

Proceedings of the 55th Annual Meeting of the Association for Computational Linguistics (Short Papers), pages 118–124
Vancouver, Canada, July 30 - August 4, 2017. ©2017 Association for Computational Linguistics
https://doi.org/10.18653/v1/P17-2019

modeling within a single implementation. On the English Penn Treebank, we achieve competitive performance on constituency parsing and state-of-the-art single-model language modeling score.

2 Preliminaries

In this section we briefly describe Recurrent Neural Network Grammars (RNNGs; Dyer et al. 2016), a top-down transition-based algorithm for parsing and generation. There are two versions of RNNG, one discriminative, the other generative. We follow the original paper in presenting the discriminative variant first.

The discriminative RNNG follows a shift-reduce parser that converts a sequence of words into a parse tree. As in standard shift-reduce parsers, the RNNG uses a buffer to store unprocessed terminal symbols and a stack to store partially completed syntactic constituents. At each timestep, one of the following three operations[2] is performed:

- NT(X) introduces an open non-terminal X onto the top of the stack, represented as an open parenthesis followed by X, e.g., (NP.

- SHIFT fetches the terminal in the front of the buffer and pushes it onto the top of the stack.

- REDUCE completes a subtree by repeatedly popping the stack until an open non-terminal is encountered. The non-terminal is popped as well, after which a composite term representing the entire subtree is pushed back onto the top of the stack, e.g., (NP *the cat*).

The above transition system can be adapted with minor modifications to an algorithm that generates trees and sentences. In generator transitions, there is no input buffer of unprocessed words but there is an output buffer for storing words that have been generated. To reflect the change, the previous SHIFT operation is modified into a GEN operation defined as follows:

- GEN generates a terminal symbol and add it to the stack and the output buffer.

---

[2]To be precise, the total number of operations under our description is |X|+2 since the NT operation varies with the non-terminal choice X.

3 Methodology

Our framework unifies generative and discriminative parsers within a single training objective. For illustration, we adopt the two RNNG variants introduced above with our customized features. Our starting point is the generative model (§ 3.1), which allows us to make explicit claims about the generative process of natural language sentences. Since this model alone lacks a bottom-up recognition mechanism, we introduce a discriminative recognition model (§ 3.2) and connect it with the generative model in an encoder-decoder setting. To offer a clear interpretation of the training objective (§ 3.3), we first consider the parse tree as latent and the sentence as observed. We then discuss extensions that account for labeled parse trees. Finally, we present various inference techniques for parsing and language modeling within the framework (§ 3.4).

3.1 Decoder (Generative Model)

The decoder is a generative RNNG that models the joint probability $p(x, y)$ of a latent parse tree y and an observed sentence x. Since the parse tree is defined by a sequence of transition actions a, we write $p(x, y)$ as $p(x, a)$.[3] The joint distribution $p(x, a)$ is factorized into a sequence of transition probabilities and terminal probabilities (when actions are GEN), which are parametrized by a transitional state embedding $\mathbf{u}$:

$$
\begin{aligned}
p(x, a) &= p(a)p(x|a) \\
&= \prod_{t=1}^{|a|} p(a_t|\mathbf{u}_t)p(x_t|\mathbf{u}_t)^{\mathbb{I}(a_t=\text{GEN})} \quad (1)
\end{aligned}
$$

where $\mathbb{I}$ is an indicator function and $\mathbf{u}_t$ represents the state embedding at time step t. Specifically, the conditional probability of the next action is:

$$
p(a_t|\mathbf{u}_t) = \prod_{t=1}^{|a|} \frac{\exp(\mathbf{a}_t\mathbf{u}_t^{\mathrm{T}} + b_a)}{\sum_{a' \in \mathcal{A}} \exp(\mathbf{a}'\mathbf{u}_t^{\mathrm{T}} + b_{a'})} \quad (2)
$$

where $\mathbf{a}_t$ represents the action embedding at time step t, $\mathcal{A}$ the action space and b_a the bias. Similarly, the next word probability (when GEN is invoked) is computed as:

$$
p(w_t|\mathbf{u}_t) = \prod_{t=1}^{|a|} \frac{\exp(\mathbf{w}_t\mathbf{u}_t^{\mathrm{T}} + b_w)}{\sum_{w' \in \mathcal{W}} \exp(\mathbf{w}'\mathbf{u}_t^{\mathrm{T}} + b_{w'})} \quad (3)
$$

---

[3]We assume that the action probability does not take the actual terminal choice into account.

where $\mathcal{W}$ denotes all words in the vocabulary.

To satisfy the independence assumptions imposed by the generative model, $\mathbf{u}_t$ uses only a restricted set of features defined over the output buffer and the stack — we consider $p(a)$ as a context insensitive prior distribution. Specifically, we use the following features: 1) the stack embedding $\mathbf{d}_t$ which encodes the stack of the decoder and is obtained with a stack-LSTM (Dyer et al., 2015, 2016); 2) the output buffer embedding $\mathbf{o}_t$; we use a standard LSTM to compose the output buffer and $\mathbf{o}_t$ is represented as the most recent state of the LSTM; and 3) the parent non-terminal embedding $\mathbf{n}_t$ which is accessible in the generative model because the RNNG employs a depth-first generation order. Finally, $\mathbf{u}_t$ is computed as:

$$\mathbf{u}_t = \mathbf{W}_2 \tanh(\mathbf{W}_1[\mathbf{d}_t, \mathbf{o}_t, \mathbf{n}_t] + b_d) \quad (4)$$

where $\mathbf{W}$s are weight parameters and b_d the bias.

3.2 Encoder (Recognition Model)

The encoder is a discriminative RNNG that computes the conditional probability $q(a|x)$ of the transition action sequence a given an observed sentence x. This conditional probability is factorized over time steps as:

$$q(a|x) = \prod_{t=1}^{|a|} q(a_t|\mathbf{v}_t) \quad (5)$$

where $\mathbf{v}_t$ is the transitional state embedding of the encoder at time step t.

The next action is predicted similarly to Equation (2), but conditioned on $\mathbf{v}_t$. Thanks to the discriminative property, $\mathbf{v}_t$ has access to any contextual features defined over the entire sentence and the stack — $q(a|x)$ acts as a context sensitive posterior approximation. Our features[4] are: 1) the stack embedding $\mathbf{e}_t$ obtained with a stack-LSTM that encodes the stack of the encoder; 2) the input buffer embedding $\mathbf{i}_t$; we use a bidirectional LSTM to compose the input buffer and represent each word as a concatenation of forward and backward LSTM states; $\mathbf{i}_t$ is the representation of the word on top of the buffer; 3) to incorporate more global features and a more sophisticated look-ahead mechanism for the buffer, we also use an adaptive buffer embedding $\bar{\mathbf{i}}_t$; the latter is computed by having the stack embedding $\mathbf{e}_t$ attend to

all remaining embeddings on the buffer with the attention function in Vinyals et al. (2015); and 4) the parent non-terminal embedding $\mathbf{n}_t$. Finally, $\mathbf{v}_t$ is computed as follows:

$$\mathbf{v}_t = \mathbf{W}_4 \tanh(\mathbf{W}_3[\mathbf{e}_t, \mathbf{i}_t, \bar{\mathbf{i}}_t, \mathbf{n}_t] + b_e) \quad (6)$$

where $\mathbf{W}$s are weight parameters and b_e the bias.

3.3 Training

Consider an auto-encoder whose encoder infers the latent parse tree and the decoder generates the observed sentence from the parse tree.[5] The maximum likelihood estimate of the decoder parameters is determined by the log marginal likelihood of the sentence:

$$\log p(x) = \log \sum_a p(x, a) \quad (7)$$

We follow expectation-maximization and variational inference techniques to construct an evidence lower bound of the above quantity (by Jensen's Inequality), denoted as follows:

$$\log p(x) \geq \mathbb{E}_{q(a|x)} \log \frac{p(x, a)}{q(a|x)} = \mathcal{L}_x \quad (8)$$

where $p(x, a) = p(x|a)p(a)$ comes from the decoder or the generative model, and $q(a|x)$ comes from the encoder or the recognition model. The objective function[6] in Equation (8), denoted by $\mathcal{L}_x$, is unsupervised and suited to a grammar induction task. This objective can be optimized with the methods shown in Miao and Blunsom (2016).

Next, consider the case when the parse tree is observed. We can directly maximize the log likelihood of the parse tree for the encoder output $\log q(a|x)$ and the decoder output $\log p(a)$:

$$\mathcal{L}_a = \log q(a|x) + \log p(a) \quad (9)$$

This supervised objective leverages extra information of labeled parse trees to regularize the distribution $q(a|x)$ and $p(a)$, and the final objective is:

$$\mathcal{L} = \mathcal{L}_x + \mathcal{L}_a \quad (10)$$

where $\mathcal{L}_x$ and $\mathcal{L}_a$ can be balanced with the task focus (e.g, language modeling or parsing).

---

[4]Compared to Dyer et al. (2016), the new features we introduce are 3) and 4), which we found empirically useful.

[5]Here, GEN and SHIFT refer to the same action with different definitions for encoding and decoding.

[6]See § 4 and Appendix A for comparison between this objective and the importance sampler of Dyer et al. (2016).

Learned word embedding dimensions	40
Pretrained word embedding dimensions	50
POS tag embedding dimensions	20
Encoder LSTM dimensions	128
Decoder LSTM dimensions	256
LSTM layer	2
Encoder dropout	0.2
Decoder dropout	0.3

Table 1: Hyperparameters.

Discrimina- tive parsers	Socher et al. (2013)	90.4
	Zhu et al. (2013)	90.4
	Dyer et al. (2016)	91.7
	Cross and Huang (2016)	89.9
	Vinyals et al. (2015)	92.8
Generative parsers	Petrov and Klein (2007)	90.1
	Shindo et al. (2012)	92.4
	Dyer et al. (2016)	93.3
This work	$\mathrm{argmax}_a\, q(a\|x)$	89.3
	$\mathrm{argmax}_a\, p(a, x)$	90.1

Table 2: Parsing results (F1) on the PTB test set.

3.4 Inference

We consider two inference tasks, namely parsing and language modeling.

Parsing In parsing, we are interested in the parse tree that maximizes the posterior $p(a|x)$ (or the joint $p(a, x)$). However, the decoder alone does not have a bottom-up recognition mechanism for computing the posterior. Thanks to the encoder, we can compute an approximated posterior $q(a|x)$ in linear time and select the parse tree that maximizes this approximation. An alternative is to generate candidate trees by sampling from $q(a|x)$, re-rank them with respect to the joint $p(x, a)$ (which is proportional to the true posterior), and select the sample that maximizes the true posterior.

Language Modeling In language modeling, our goal is to compute the marginal probability $p(x) = \sum_a p(x, a)$, which is typically intractable. To approximate this quantity, we can use Equation (8) to compute a lower bound of the log likelihood $\log p(x)$ and then exponentiate it to get a pessimistic approximation of $p(x)$.[7]

Another way of computing $p(x)$ (without lower bounding) would be to use the variational approximation $q(a|x)$ as the proposal distribution as in the importance sampler of Dyer et al. (2016). However, this is beyond the scope of this work and we leave detailed discussions to Appendix A.

4 Related Work

Our framework is related to a class of variational autoencoders (Kingma and Welling, 2014), which use neural networks for posterior approximation in variational inference. This technique has been previously used for topic modeling (Miao et al.,

---

[7]As a reminder, the language modeling objective is $\exp(NLL/T)$, where NLL denotes the total negative log likelihood of the test data and T the token counts.

2016) and sentence compression (Miao and Blunsom, 2016). Another interpretation of the proposed framework is from the perspective of guided policy search in reinforcement learning (Bachman and Precup, 2015), where a generative parser is trained to imitate the trace of a discriminative parser. Further connections can be drawn with the importance-sampling based inference of Dyer et al. (2016). There, a generative RNNG and a discriminative RNNG are trained separately; during language modeling, the output of the discriminative model serves as the proposal distribution of an importance sampler $p(x) = \mathbb{E}_{q(a|x)} \frac{p(x,a)}{q(a|x)}$. Compared to their work, we unify the generative and discriminative RNNGs in a single framework, and adopt a joint training objective.

5 Experiments

We performed experiments on the English Penn Treebank dataset; we used sections 2–21 for training, 24 for validation, and 23 for testing. Following Dyer et al. (2015), we represent each word in three ways: as a learned vector, a pretrained vector, and a POS tag vector. The encoder word embedding is the concatenation of all three vectors while the decoder uses only the first two since we do not consider POS tags in generation. Table 1 presents details on the hyper-parameters we used. To find the MAP parse tree $\mathrm{argmax}_a\, p(a, x)$ (where $p(a, x)$ is used rank the output of $q(a|x)$) and to compute the language modeling perplexity with the evidence lower bound (where $a \sim q(a|x)$), we collect 100 samples from $q(a|x)$, same as Dyer et al. (2016).

Experimental results for constituency parsing and language modeling are shown in Tables 2 and 3, respectively. As can be seen, the single framework we propose obtains competitive pars-

KN-5	255.2
LSTM	113.4
Dyer et al. (2016)	102.4
This work: $a \sim q(a\|x)$	99.8

Table 3: Language modeling results (perplexity).

ing performance. Comparing the two inference methods for parsing, ranking approximated MAP trees from $q(a|x)$ with respect to $p(a, x)$ yields a small improvement, as in Dyer et al. (2016). It is worth noting that our parsing performance lags behind Dyer et al. (2016). We believe this is due to implementation disparities, such as the modeling of the reduce operation. While Dyer et al. (2016) use an LSTM as the syntactic composition function of each subtree, we adopt a rather simple composition function based on embedding averaging for memory concern.

On language modeling, our framework achieves lower perplexity compared to Dyer et al. (2016) and baseline models. This gain possibly comes from the joint optimization of both the generative and discriminative components towards a language modeling objective. However, we acknowledge a subtle difference between Dyer et al. (2016) and our approach compared to baseline language models: while the latter incrementally estimate the next word probability, our approach (and Dyer et al. 2016) directly assigns probability to the entire sentence. Overall, the advantage of our framework compared to Dyer et al. (2016) is that it opens an avenue to unsupervised training.

6 Conclusions

We proposed a framework that integrates a generative parser with a discriminative recognition model and showed how it can be instantiated with RNNGs. We demonstrated that a unified framework, which relates to expectation maximization and variational inference, enables effective parsing and language modeling algorithms. Evaluation on the English Penn Treebank, revealed that our framework obtains competitive performance on constituency parsing and state-of-the-art results on single-model language modeling. In the future, we would like to perform grammar induction based on Equation (8), with gradient descent and posterior regularization techniques (Ganchev et al., 2010).

Acknowledgments We thank three anonymous reviewers and members of the ILCC for valuable feedback, and Muhua Zhu and James Cross for help with data preparation. The support of the European Research Council under award number 681760 "Translating Multiple Modalities into Text" is gratefully acknowledged.

References

Philip Bachman and Doina Precup. 2015. Data generation as sequential decision making. In *Advances in Neural Information Processing Systems*, MIT Press, pages 3249–3257.

Michael Collins. 1999. *Head-Driven Statistical Models for Natural Language Parsing*. Ph.D. thesis, University of Pennsylvania, Pennsylvania, Philadelphia.

Michael Collins and Terry Koo. 2005. Discriminative reranking for natural language parsing. *Computational Linguistics* 31(1):25–70.

James Cross and Liang Huang. 2016. Incremental parsing with minimal features using bi-directional lstm. In *Proceedings of the 54th Annual Meeting of the Association for Computational Linguistics (Volume 2: Short Papers)*. Berlin, Germany, pages 32–37.

Chris Dyer, Miguel Ballesteros, Wang Ling, Austin Matthews, and Noah A. Smith. 2015. Transition-based dependency parsing with stack long short-term memory. In *Proceedings of the 53rd Annual Meeting of the Association for Computational Linguistics and the 7th International Joint Conference on Natural Language Processing (Volume 1: Long Papers)*. Beijing, China, pages 334–343.

Chris Dyer, Adhiguna Kuncoro, Miguel Ballesteros, and Noah A. Smith. 2016. Recurrent neural network grammars. In *Proceedings of the 2016 Conference of the North American Chapter of the Association for Computational Linguistics: Human Language Technologies*. San Diego, California, pages 199–209.

Kuzman Ganchev, Jennifer Gillenwater, Ben Taskar, et al. 2010. Posterior regularization for structured latent variable models. *Journal of Machine Learning Research* 11(Jul):2001–2049.

Zoubin Ghahramani and Matthew J. Beal. 2000. Variational inference for Bayesian mixtures of factor analysers. In *Advances in Neural Information Processing Systems*, MIT Press, pages 449–455.

Yoav Goldberg and Michael Elhadad. 2010. An efficient algorithm for easy-first non-directional dependency parsing. In *Human Language Technologies: The 2010 Annual Conference of the North American Chapter of the Association for Computational Linguistics*. Los Angeles, California, pages 742–750.

James Henderson. 2003. Inducing history representations for broad coverage statistical parsing. In *Proceedings of the 2003 Human Language Technology Conference of the North American Chapter of the Association for Computational Linguistics*. Edmonton, Canada, pages 24–31.

Liang Huang. 2008. Forest reranking: Discriminative parsing with non-local features. In *Proceedings of ACL-08: HLT*. Columbus, Ohio, pages 586–594.

Diederik P Kingma, Shakir Mohamed, Danilo Jimenez Rezende, and Max Welling. 2014. Semi-supervised learning with deep generative models. In *Advances in Neural Information Processing Systems*, MIT Press, pages 3581–3589.

Diederik P Kingma and Max Welling. 2014. Auto-encoding variational Bayes. In *Proceedings of the International Conference on Learning Representations*. Banff, Canada.

Yishu Miao and Phil Blunsom. 2016. Language as a latent variable: Discrete generative models for sentence compression. In *Proceedings of the 2016 Conference on Empirical Methods in Natural Language Processing*. Austin, Texas, pages 319–328.

Yishu Miao, Lei Yu, and Phil Blunsom. 2016. Neural variational inference for text processing. In *Proceedings of The 33rd International Conference on Machine Learning*. New York, New York, USA, pages 1727–1736.

Andriy Mnih and Karol Gregor. 2014. Neural variational inference and learning in belief networks. In *Proceedings of the 31st International Conference on Machine Learning*. Beijing, China, pages 1791–1799.

Joakim Nivre, Johan Hall, Jens Nilsson, Atanas Chanev, Gülsen Eryigit, Sandra Kübler, Svetoslav Marinov, and Erwin Marsi. 2007. Maltparser: A language-independent system for data-driven dependency parsing. *Natural Language Engineering* 13(2):95–135.

Jeffrey Pennington, Richard Socher, and Christopher Manning. 2014. Glove: Global vectors for word representation. In *Proceedings of the 2014 Conference on Empirical Methods in Natural Language Processing (EMNLP)*. Doha, Qatar, pages 1532–1543.

Slav Petrov and Dan Klein. 2007. Improved inference for unlexicalized parsing. In *Human Language Technologies 2007: The Conference of the North American Chapter of the Association for Computational Linguistics; Proceedings of the Main Conference*. Rochester, New York, pages 404–411.

Reuven Y Rubinstein and Dirk P Kroese. 2008. *Simulation and the Monte Carlo method*. John Wiley & Sons.

Federico Sangati, Willem Zuidema, and Rens Bod. 2009. A generative re-ranking model for dependency parsing. In *Proceedings of the 11th International Conference on Parsing Technologies (IWPT'09)*. Paris, France, pages 238–241.

Hiroyuki Shindo, Yusuke Miyao, Akinori Fujino, and Masaaki Nagata. 2012. Bayesian symbol-refined tree substitution grammars for syntactic parsing. In *Proceedings of the 50th Annual Meeting of the Association for Computational Linguistics: Long Papers-Volume 1*. Jeju Island, Korea, pages 440–448.

Richard Socher, John Bauer, Christopher D. Manning, and Ng Andrew Y. 2013. Parsing with compositional vector grammars. In *Proceedings of the 51st Annual Meeting of the Association for Computational Linguistics (Volume 1: Long Papers)*. Sofia, Bulgaria, pages 455–465.

Ivan Titov and James Henderson. 2007. Constituent parsing with incremental sigmoid belief networks. In *Proceedings of the 45th Annual Meeting of the Association of Computational Linguistics*. Prague, Czech Republic, pages 632–639.

Oriol Vinyals, Łukasz Kaiser, Terry Koo, Slav Petrov, Ilya Sutskever, and Geoffrey Hinton. 2015. Grammar as a foreign language. In *Advances in Neural Information Processing Systems*, MIT Press, pages 2773–2781.

Muhua Zhu, Yue Zhang, Wenliang Chen, Min Zhang, and Jingbo Zhu. 2013. Fast and accurate shift-reduce constituent parsing. In *Proceedings of the 51st Annual Meeting of the Association for Computational Linguistics (Volume 1: Long Papers)*. Sofia, Bulgaria, pages 434–443.

A Comparison to Importance Sampling (Dyer et al., 2016)

In this appendix we highlight the connections between importance sampling and variational inference, thereby comparing our method with Dyer et al. (2016).

Consider a simple directed graphical model with discrete latent variables a (e.g., a is the transition action sequence) and observed variables x (e.g., x is the sentence). The model evidence, or the marginal likelihood $p(x) = \sum_a p(x, a)$ is often intractable to compute. Importance sampling transforms the above quantity into an expectation over a distribution $q(a)$, which is known and easy to sample from:

$$p(x) = \sum_a p(x, a) \frac{q(a)}{q(a)} = \mathbb{E}_{q(a)} w(x, a) \quad (11)$$

where $q(a)$ is the proposal distribution and $w(x, a) = \frac{p(x,a)}{q(a)}$ the importance weight.

The proposal distribution can potentially depend on the observations x, i.e., $q(a) \triangleq q(a|x)$.

A challenge with importance sampling lies in choosing a proposal distribution which leads to low variance. As shown in Rubinstein and Kroese (2008), the optimal choice of the proposal distribution is in fact the true posterior $p(a|x)$, in which case the importance weight $\frac{p(a,x)}{p(a|x)} = p(x)$ is constant with respect to a. In Dyer et al. (2016), the proposal distribution depends on x, i.e., $q(a) \triangleq q(a|x)$, and is computed with a separately-trained, discriminative model. This proposal choice is close to optimal, since in a fully supervised setting a is also observed and the discriminative model can be trained to approximate the true posterior well. We hypothesize that the performance of their importance sampler is dependent on this specific proposal distribution. Besides, their training strategy does not generalize to an unsupervised setting.

In comparison, variational inference approach approximates the log marginal likelihood $\log p(x)$ with the evidence lower bound. It is a natural choice when one aims to optimize Equation (11) directly:

$$
\begin{aligned}
\log p(x) &= \log \sum_a p(x, a) \frac{q(a)}{q(a)} \\
&\geq \mathbb{E}_{q(a)} \log \frac{p(x, a)}{q(a)}
\end{aligned}
\tag{12}
$$

where $q(a)$ is the variational approximation of the true posterior. Again, the variational approximation can potentially depend on the observation x (i.e., $q(a) \triangleq q(a|x)$) and can be computed with a discriminative model. Equation (12) is a well-defined, unsupervised training objective which allows us to jointly optimize generative (i.e., $p(x, a)$) and discriminative (i.e., $q(a|x)$) models. To further support the observed variable a, we augment this objective with supervised terms shown in Equation (10), following Kingma et al. (2014) and Miao and Blunsom (2016).

Equation (12) can be also used to approximate the marginal likelihood $p(x)$ (e.g., in language modeling) with its lower bound. An alternative choice without lower bounding is to use the variational approximation $q(a|x)$ as the proposal distribution in importance sampling (Equation (11)). Ghahramani and Beal (2000) show that this proposal distribution leads to improved results of importance samplers. However, a potential drawback of importance sampling-based approach is that it is prone to numerical underflow. In practice, we observed similar language modeling performance for both methods.

Hybrid Neural Network Alignment and Lexicon Model in Direct HMM for Statistical Machine Translation

Weiyue Wang, Tamer Alkhouli, Derui Zhu, Hermann Ney

Human Language Technology and Pattern Recognition, Computer Science Department
RWTH Aachen University, 52056 Aachen, Germany
`<surname>@i6.informatik.rwth-aachen.de`

Abstract

Recently, the neural machine translation systems showed their promising performance and surpassed the phrase-based systems for most translation tasks. Retreating into conventional concepts machine translation while utilizing effective neural models is vital for comprehending the leap accomplished by neural machine translation over phrase-based methods. This work proposes a direct hidden Markov model (HMM) with neural network-based lexicon and alignment models, which are trained jointly using the Baum-Welch algorithm. The direct HMM is applied to rerank the n-best list created by a state-of-the-art phrase-based translation system and it provides improvements by up to 1.0% BLEU scores on two different translation tasks.

1 Introduction

The hidden Markov model (HMM) was first introduced to statistical machine translation for addressing the word alignment problem (Vogel et al., 1996). Then the HMM-based approach was widely used along with the IBM models (Brown et al., 1993) for aligning the source and target words. In the conventional approach, the Bayes' theorem is used and the HMM is applied to the inverse translation model

$$\Pr(e_1^I | f_1^J) = \Pr(e_1^I) \cdot \Pr(f_1^J | e_1^I)$$
$$= \sum_{a_1^J} \Pr(f_1^J, a_1^J | e_1^I) \qquad (1)$$

In this case, as a part of a noisy channel model, the marginalisation becomes intractable for every e.

This work proposes a novel concept focusing on direct HMM for $\Pr(e_1^I | f_1^J)$, in which the alignment direction is from target to source positions. This specific property allows us to introduce dependencies into the translation model that take the full source sentence into account. This aspect will be important for the future decoder to be developed. The lexicon and alignment probabilities in the HMM are modeled using feed-forward neural networks (FFNN) and they are trained jointly. The trained HMM is then applied for reranking the n-best lists created by a state-of-the-art open source phrase-based translation system. The experiments are conducted on the IWSLT 2016 German→English and BOLT Chinese→English translation tasks. The FFNN-based hybrid HMM provides improvements by up to 1.0% BLEU scores.

2 Related Work

In order to discuss related work, we will consider the following two key concepts that are essential for the work to be presented:

- **Neural lexicon and alignment models**

  The idea of using neural networks for lexicon modeling is not new (Schwenk, 2012; Sundermeyer et al., 2014; Devlin et al., 2014). Apart from differences in the neural network architecture, the important difference to this work is that those approaches did not include the concepts of HMM models and end-to-end training. In addition to neural lexicon modeling, (Alkhouli et al., 2016) also applied a neural network for alignment modeling like this work, but their training procedure was based on the maximum approximation and on predefined GIZA++ (Och and Ney, 2003) alignments.

125

Proceedings of the 55th Annual Meeting of the Association for Computational Linguistics (Short Papers), pages 125–131
Vancouver, Canada, July 30 - August 4, 2017. ©2017 Association for Computational Linguistics
https://doi.org/10.18653/v1/P17-2020

There were other studies that focused on feature-rich alignment models (Blunsom and Cohn, 2006; Berg-Kirkpatrick et al., 2010; Dyer et al., 2011), but those studies did not use a neural network to automatically learn features (as we do in this work). (Yang et al., 2013) used neural network-based lexicon and alignment models inside the HMM alignment model, but they model alignments using a simple distortion model that has no dependence on lexical context. Their goal was to improve the alignment quality in the context of a phrase-based translation system. However, apart from (Dyer et al., 2011), no results on translation were reported.

The idea of using neural networks is the basis of the state-of-the-art attention-based approach to machine translation (Bahdanau et al., 2015; Luong et al., 2015). However, that approach is not based on the principle of an explicit and separate lexicon model.

- **End-to-end training**

The HMM in combination with the neural translation model lends itself to what is usually called end-to-end training. The training criterion is the logarithm of the target sentence posterior probability. This criterion results in a specific training algorithm that can be interpreted as a combination of forward-backward algorithm (as in EM style training of HHMs) and backpropagation. To the best of our knowledge, this end-to-end training has not been considered before for machine translation. In the context of signal processing and recognition, the connectionist temporal classification (CTC) approach (Graves et al., 2006) leads to a similar training procedure. (Tran et al., 2016) studied neural networks for unsupervised training for a part-of-speech tagging task. In their approach, the training criterion for this problem results in a combination of EM framework and backpropagation, which has a certain similarity to the training algorithm for translation as presented in this work.

3 Definition of neural network-based HMM

Similar to hidden alignments $a_j = j \to i$ between the source string $f_1^J = f_1...f_j...f_J$ and the target

string $e_1^I = e_1...e_i...e_I$ in the conventional HMM, we define the alignments in direct HMM as $b_i = i \to j$. Then the model can be defined as:

$$\Pr(e_1^I|f_1^J) = \sum_{b_1^I} \Pr(e_1^I, b_1^I|f_1^J) \tag{2}$$

$$\Pr(e_1^I, b_1^I|f_1^J)$$
$$= \prod_{i=1}^{I} p(e_i, b_i|b_1^{i-1}, e_1^{i-1}, f_1^J)$$
$$= \prod_{i=1}^{I} \underbrace{p(e_i|b_1^i, e_1^{i-1}, f_1^J)}_{\text{lexicon model}} \cdot \underbrace{p(b_i|b_1^{i-1}, e_1^{i-1}, f_1^J)}_{\text{alignment model}} \tag{3}$$

Our feed-forward alignment model has the same architecture (Figure 1) as the one proposed in (Alkhouli et al., 2016). Thus the alignment probability can be modeled by:

$$p(b_i|b_1^{i-1}, e_1^{i-1}, f_1^J) = p(\Delta_i|f_{b_{i-1}-\gamma_m}^{b_{i-1}+\gamma_m}, e_{i-n}^{i-1}) \tag{4}$$

where $\gamma_m = \frac{m-1}{2}$ and m indicates the window size. $\Delta_i = b_i - b_{i-1}$ denotes the jump from the predecessor position to the current position. Thus, the jump over the source is estimated based on a m-words source context window and n predecessor target words.

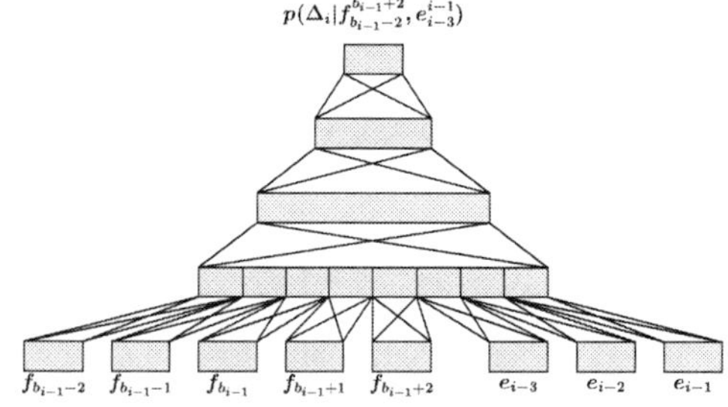

Figure 1: A feed-forward alignment neural network with 3 target history words, 5-gram source window, a projection layer, 2 non-linear hidden layers and a small output layer to predict jumps.

For the lexicon model, we assume a similar dependence as in the alignment model with a shift, namely on the source words within a window centred on the aligned source word and n predecessor target words. To overcome the high costs of the softmax function for large vocabularies, we adopt the class-factored output layer consisting of a class layer and a word layer (Goodman, 2001; Morin and Bengio, 2005). The model in this case is defined as

$$p(e_i|b_1^i, e_1^{i-1}, f_1^J)$$
$$= p(e_i|f_{b_i-\gamma_m}^{b_i+\gamma_m}, e_{i-n}^{i-1})$$
$$= p(e_i|c(e_i), f_{b_i-\gamma_m}^{b_i+\gamma_m}, e_{i-n}^{i-1}) \cdot p(c(e_i)|f_{b_i-\gamma_m}^{b_i+\gamma_m}, e_{i-n}^{i-1}) \tag{5}$$

where c denotes a word mapping that assigns each target word to a single class, where the number of classes is chosen to be much smaller than the vocabulary size. The lexicon model architecture is shown in Figure 2.

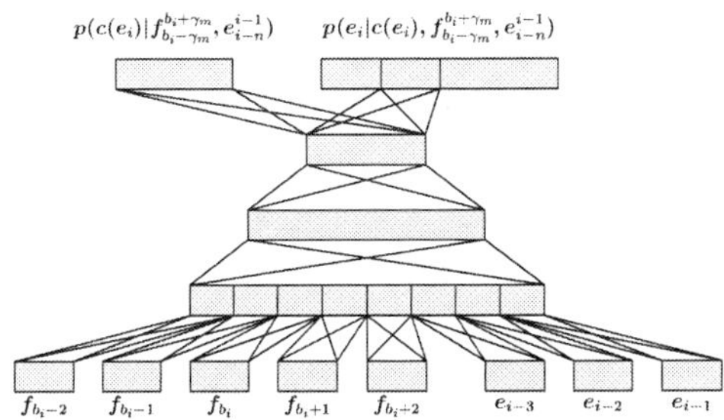

Figure 2: A feed-forward lexicon neural network with the same structure as the alignment model, except a class-factored output layer.

4 Training

The training data of the direct HMM are the source and target sequences, without any alignment information. In the training of direct HMM including neural network-based models, the weights have to be updated along with the posterior probabilities calculated by the Baum-Welch algorithm. Similar to the training procedure used in (Berg-Kirkpatrick et al., 2010), we apply the EM algorithm and define the auxiliary function as

$$Q(\theta; \hat{\theta})$$
$$= \sum_{b_1^I} p(b_1^I|f_1^J, e_1^I, \theta) \log p(e_1^I, b_1^I|f_1^J, \hat{\theta})$$
$$= \sum_{b_1^I} p(b_1^I|f_1^J, e_1^I, \theta) \sum_{i=1}^{I} [\log p(e_i|f_{b_i-\gamma_m}^{b_i+\gamma_m}, e_{i-n}^{i-1}, \hat{\alpha})$$
$$+ \log p(\Delta_i|f_{b_{i-1}-\gamma_m}^{b_{i-1}+\gamma_m}, e_{i-n}^{i-1}, \hat{\beta})]$$
$$= \sum_i \sum_j p_i(j|e_1^I, f_1^J, \theta) \log p(e_i|f_{j-\gamma_m}^{j+\gamma_m}, e_{i-n}^{i-1}, \hat{\alpha})$$
$$+ \sum_i \sum_{j'} \sum_j p_i(j', j|e_1^I, f_1^J, \theta) \log p(\Delta_i|f_{j'-\gamma_m}^{j'+\gamma_m}, e_{i-n}^{i-1}, \hat{\beta}) \tag{6}$$

where $\hat{\theta} = \{\hat{\alpha}, \hat{\beta}\}$, $j' = b_{i-1}$ and

$$p_i(j|e_1^I, f_1^J, \theta) = \sum_{b_1^I:b_i=j} p(b_1^I|e_1^I, f_1^J, \theta) \tag{7}$$

Then the parameters can be separated for lexicon model and alignment model:

$$Q(\theta; \hat{\theta}) = Q_{\text{lex}}(\theta; \hat{\alpha}) + Q_{\text{align}}(\theta; \hat{\beta}) \tag{8}$$

where

$$\frac{\partial Q_{\text{lex}}(\theta, \hat{\alpha})}{\partial \hat{\alpha}} = \sum_i \sum_j \overbrace{p_i(j|e_1^I, f_1^J, \theta)}^{\text{forward-backward algorithm}}$$
$$\cdot \underbrace{\frac{\partial}{\partial \hat{\alpha}} \log p(e_i|f_{j-\gamma_m}^{j+\gamma_m}, e_{i-n}^{i-1}, \hat{\alpha})}_{\text{backpropagation}} \tag{9}$$

$$\frac{\partial Q_{\text{align}}(\theta, \hat{\beta})}{\partial \hat{\beta}} = \sum_i \sum_{j'} \sum_j \overbrace{p_i(j', j|e_1^I, f_1^J, \theta)}^{\text{forward-backward algorithm}}$$
$$\cdot \underbrace{\frac{\partial}{\partial \hat{\beta}} \log p(\Delta_i|f_{j'-\gamma_m}^{j'+\gamma_m}, e_{i-n}^{i-1}, \hat{\beta})}_{\text{backpropagation}} \tag{10}$$

From Equations (9) and (10) we can observe that the marginalisation of hidden alignments ($\sum_j p_i(j|e_1^I, f_1^J, \theta)$) is the only difference compared to the derivative of neural network training based on word-aligned data. In this approach we iterate over all source positions and the word alignment toolkit such as GIZA++ is not required. Furthermore, the word-aligned data generated e.g. by GIZA++ might contain unaligned and multiply aligned words, which make the data difficult to use for training neural networks. Thus the heuristic-based approaches (Sundermeyer et al., 2014; Devlin et al., 2014) have to be used in order to guarantee the one-on-one alignments, which may negatively influence the quality of the alignments. By contrast, the neural network-based HMM is not constrained by these heuristics. In addition, even though the training process of the direct HMM takes more time than the neural network training on the word-aligned data, we should note that generating the word-aligned data using GIZA++ is also a time-consuming process.

In general, our training procedure can be summarized as follows:

1. One iteration IBM-1 model training to create lexicon table for initializing the forward-backward table.

2. In the first epoch, for each sentence pair calculate and save the entire table of posterior probabilities $p_i(b|e_1^I, f_1^J)$ (also $p_i(b', b|e_1^I, f_1^J)$ for alignment model) using forward-backward algorithm based on the results of IBM-1 model.

3. Training neural network lexicon and alignment models based on the posterior probabilities.

4. From the second epoch onwards:

   (a) For each sentence pair, calculating the posterior probabilities based on the lexicon and alignment probabilities estimated by neural network models.

   (b) Updating weights of neural networks based on the posterior probabilities.

   (c) Repeating step 4 until the perplexity converges.

In this work the IBM-1 initialization is required. We tried to train neural network models from scratch, but the perplexity converges towards a bad local minimum and gets stuck in it. We also attempted other heuristics for initialization, such as assigning probability 0.9 to diagonal alignments and spreading the left 0.1 evenly among other source positions. The resulted perplexity is much higher compared to initializing using IBM-1.

5 Experimental Results

The experiments are conducted on the IWSLT 2016 German→English and BOLT Chinese→English translation tasks, which consist of $20M$ and $4M$ parallel sentence pairs respectively. The feed-forward neural network alignment and lexicon models are jointly trained on the subset of about $200K$ sentence pairs. As an initial research of this topic, our new model is only applied for reranking n-best lists created by a phrase-based decoder. The maximum size of the n-best lists is 500. The translation quality is evaluated by case-insensitive BLEU (Papineni et al., 2002) and TER (Snover et al., 2006) metrics using MultEval (Clark et al., 2011). The scaling factors are tuned with MERT (Och, 2003) with BLEU as optimization criterion on the development sets. For the translation experiments, the averaged scores are presented on the development set from three optimization runs.

Our direct HMM consists of a feed-forward neural network lexicon model with following configuration:

- Five one-hot input vectors for source words and three for target words

- Projection layer size 100 for each word

- Two non-linear hidden layers with 1000 and 500 nodes respectively

- A class-factored output layer with 1000 singleton classes dedicated to the most frequent words, and 1000 classes shared among the rest of the words.

and a feed-forward neural network alignment model with the same configuration as the lexicon model, except a small output layer with 201 nodes, which reflects that the aligned position can jump within the scope from -100 to 100 (Alkhouli et al., 2016).

We conducted experiments on the source and target window size of both network models. Larger source and target windows could not provide significant improvements on BLEU scores, at least for rescoring experiments.

The model is applied for reranking the n-best lists created by the Jane toolkit (Vilar et al., 2010; Wuebker et al., 2012) with a log-linear framework containing phrasal and lexical smoothing models for both directions, word and phrase penalties, a distance-based reordering model, enhanced low frequency features (Chen et al., 2011), a hierarchical reordering model (Galley and Manning, 2008), a word class language mode (Wuebker et al., 2013) and an n-gram language model. The word alignments used for the training of phrase-tables are generated by GIZA++, which performs the alignment training sequentially for IBM-1, HMM and IBM-4. More details about our phrase-based baseline system can be found in (Peter et al., 2015).

The experimental results are demonstrated in Table 1. The rescoring experiments are conducted by adding HMM probability as feature and tuned with MERT. The applied attention-based neural network is a neural machine translation system similar to (Bahdanau et al., 2015). The decoder and encoder word embeddings are of size 620, the encoder uses a bidirectional layer with 1000 LSTMs (Hochreiter and Schmidhuber, 1997) to encode the source side. A layer with 1000 LSTMs

Table 1: Experimental results of rescoring using neural network-based direct HMM. The model with *sum* denotes the system proposed in this work, while the model with *Viterbi* denotes the model with the same neural network structure, which was trained based on the word-aligned data (alignments generated by GIZA++) (Alkhouli et al., 2016). Improvements by systems marked by $*$ have a 95% statistical significance from the *NN-based direct HMM (Viterbi)* system, whereas † denotes the 95% statistical significant improvements with respect to the *attention-based system* in rescoring. [1] was used in reranking the n-best lists, while [2] denotes the stand-alone attention-based decoder.

| | IWSLT | | | | BOLT | | | |
| | TEDX.tst.2014 | | MSLT.dev2016 | | DEV12 | | P1R6 | |
	BLEU[%]	TER[%]	BLEU[%]	TER[%]	BLEU[%]	TER[%]	BLEU[%]	TER[%]
Phrase-based translation system	25.9	55.7	39.7	39.8	17.9	68.3	17.1	67.4
+ NN-based direct HMM (Viterbi)	26.6	54.9	40.2	39.3	18.5	67.6	17.8	66.8
+ NN-based direct HMM (sum)	26.9	**54.7**	**40.6***	**38.9***†	18.9*	67.3*†	18.3*	66.4
+ attention-based system [1]	26.8	55.0	40.4	39.3	18.9*	67.6	18.0	66.4*
Stand-alone attention-based system [2]	**27.0**	54.8	40.4	39.2	**19.6***†	**67.0***†	**18.5***†	**66.1***

is used by the decoder. The data is converted into subword units using byte pair encoding with 20000 operations (Sennrich et al., 2016). During training a batch size of 50 is used. More details about our neural machine translation system can be found in (Peter et al., 2016).

With n-best rescoring, all neural network-based systems achieve significant improvements over the phrase-based system. The neural network-based HMMs provide promising performance, even with simple feed-forward neural networks. The direct HMM trained by the EM procedure with marginalizing the hidden alignments outperformed the same model trained on the word-aligned data. For the rescoring tasks, it provides comparable performance with the attention-based network. The neural network-based HMM also helps the phrase-based system achieve comparable results with the stand-alone attention-based system on the German→English task.

6 Conclusion and Future Work

This work aims to close the gap between the conventional word alignment models and the novel neural machine translation. The proposed direct HMM consists of neural network-based alignment and lexicon models, both models are trained jointly and without any alignment information. With the simple feed-forward neural network models, the HMM model already provides promising results and significantly improves the strong phrase-based translation system.

As future work, we are searching for alternatives to initialize the training instead of using IBM-1. We will investigate recurrent model structures, such as the LSTM representation for source and target word embeddings (Luong et al., 2015). In addition to the network structure, we will implement a stand-alone decoder based on this novel model. The first step would be to apply maximum approximation for the search problem as elucidated in (Yu et al., 2017). Then we plan to investigate heuristics for marginalizing the hidden alignment during search.

Acknowledgments

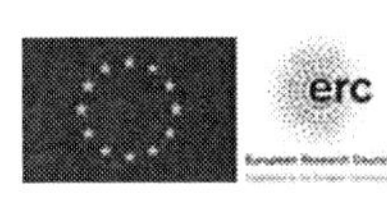

The work reported in this paper results from two projects, SEQCLAS and QT21. SEQCLAS has received funding from the European Research Council (ERC) under the European Union's Horizon 2020 research and innovation programme under grant agreement n° 694537. QT21 has received funding from the European Union's Horizon 2020 research and innovation programme under grant agreement n° 645452. The work reflects only the authors' views and neither the European Commission nor the European Research Council Executive Agency are responsible for any use that may be made of the information it contains.

Tamer Alkhouli was partly funded by the 2016 Google PhD Fellowship for North America, Europe and the Middle East.

The authors would like to thank Jan-Thorsten Peter for providing the attention-based neural network models.

References

Tamer Alkhouli, Gabriel Bretschner, Jan-Thorsten Peter, Mohammed Hethnawi, Andreas Guta, and Hermann Ney. 2016. Alignment-Based Neural Machine Translation. In *Proceedings of the ACL 2016 First Conference on Machine Translation (WMT 2016)*. Berlin, Germany, pages 54–65.

Dzmitry Bahdanau, Kyunghyun Cho, and Yoshua Bengio. 2015. Neural Machine Translation by Jointly Learning to Align and Translate. In *Proceedings of the 3rd International Conference on Learning Representations*. San Diego, CA, USA.

Taylor Berg-Kirkpatrick, Alexandre Bouchard-Côté, John DeNero, and Dan Klein. 2010. Painless Unsupervised Learning with Features. In *Proceedings of the 2010 Annual Conference of the North American Chapter of the ACL*. Los Angeles, CA, USA, pages 582–590.

Phil Blunsom and Trevor Cohn. 2006. Discriminative Word Alignment with Conditional Random Fields. In *Proceedings of the 21st International Conference on Computational Linguistics and 44th Annual Meeting of the ACL*. Sydney, Australia, pages 65–72.

Peter F. Brown, Vincent J. Della Pietra, Stephen A. Della Pietra, and Robert L. Mercer. 1993. The Mathematics of Statistical Machine Translation: Parameter Estimation. *Computational Linguistics* 19(2):263–311.

Boxing Chen, Roland Kuhn, George Foster, and Howard Johnson. 2011. Unpacking and Transforming Feature Functions: New Ways to Smooth Phrase Tables. In *Proceedings of MT Summit XIII*. Xiamen, China, pages 269–275.

Jonathan H. Clark, Chris Dyer, Alon Lavie, and Noah A. Smith. 2011. Better Hypothesis Testing for Statistical Machine Translation: Controlling for Optimizer Instability. In *Proceedings of the 49th Annual Meeting of the Association for Computational Linguistics*. Portland, OR, USA, pages 176–181.

Jacob Devlin, Rabih Zbib, Zhongqiang Huang, Thomas Lamar, Richard Schwartz, and John Makhoul. 2014. Fast and robust neural network joint models for statistical machine translation. In *Proceedings of the 52nd Annual Meeting of the Association for Computational Linguistics*. Baltimore, MD, USA, pages 1370–1380.

Chris Dyer, Jonathan Clark, Alon Lavie, and Noah A. Smith. 2011. Unsupervised Word Alignment with Arbitrary Features. In *Proceedings of the 49th Annual Meeting of the Association for Computational Linguistics*. Portland, OR, USA, pages 409–419.

Michel Galley and Christopher D. Manning. 2008. A simple and effective hierarchical phrase reordering model. In *Proceedings of the 2008 Conference on Empirical Methods in Natural Language Processing*. Honolulu, HI, USA, pages 848–856.

Joshua Goodman. 2001. Classes for fast maximum entropy training. In *Proceedings of the IEEE International Conference on Acoustics, Speech, and Signal Processing*. Salt Lake City, UT, USA, pages 561–564.

Alex Graves, Santiago Fernández, Faustino Gomez, and Jürgen Schmidhuber. 2006. Connectionist Temporal Classification: Labelling Unsegmented Sequence Data with Recurrent Neural Networks. In *Proceedings of the 23rd International Conference on Machine Learning*. Pittsburgh, PA, USA, pages 369–376.

Sepp Hochreiter and Jürgen Schmidhuber. 1997. Long Short-Term Memory. *Neural Computation* 9(8):1735–1780.

Minh-Thang Luong, Hieu Pham, and Christopher D. Manning. 2015. Effective approaches to attention-based neural machine translation. In *Conference on Empirical Methods in Natural Language Processing*. Lisbon, Portugal, pages 1412–1421.

Frederic Morin and Yoshua Bengio. 2005. Hierarchical probabilistic neural network language model. In *Proceedings of the international workshop on artificial intelligence and statistics*. Barbados, pages 246–252.

Franz Josef Och. 2003. Minimum Error Rate Training in Statistical Machine Translation. In *Proceedings of the 41st Annual Meeting on Association for Computational Linguistics*. Sapporo, Japan, pages 160–167.

Franz Josef Och and Hermann Ney. 2003. A Systematic Comparison of Various Statistical Alignment Models. *Computational Linguistics* 29:19–51.

Kishore Papineni, Salim Roukos, Todd Ward, and Wei-Jing Zhu. 2002. BLEU: A Method for Automatic Evaluation of Machine Translation. In *Proceedings of the 40th Annual Meeting on Association for Computational Linguistics*. Philadelphia, PA, USA, pages 311–318.

Jan-Thorsten Peter, Andreas Guta, Nick Rossenbach, Miguel Graça, and Hermann Ney. 2016. The RWTH Aachen Machine Translation System for IWSLT 2016. In *International Workshop on Spoken Language Translation*. Seattle, WA, USA.

Jan-Thorsten Peter, Farzad Toutounchi, Joern Wuebker, and Hermann Ney. 2015. The RWTH Aachen German-English Machine Translation System for WMT 2015. In *EMNLP 2015 Tenth Workshop on Statistical Machine Translation*. Lisbon, Portugal, pages 158–163.

Holger Schwenk. 2012. Continuous Space Translation Models for Phrase-Based Statistical Machine Translation. In *Proceedings of the 24th International Conference on Computational Linguistics*. Mumbai, India, pages 1071–1080.

Rico Sennrich, Barry Haddow, and Alexandra Birch. 2016. Neural Machine Translation of Rare Words with Subword Units. In *Proceedings of the 54th Annual Meeting of the Association for Computational Linguistics*. Berlin, Germany, pages 1715–1725.

Matthew Snover, Bonnie Dorr, Richard Schwartz, Linnea Micciulla, and John Makhoul. 2006. A study of translation edit rate with targeted human annotation. In *Proceedings of the Conference of the Association for Machine Translation in the Americas*. Cambridge, MA, USA, pages 223–231.

Martin Sundermeyer, Tamer Alkhouli, Joern Wuebker, and Hermann Ney. 2014. Translation Modeling with Bidirectional Recurrent Neural Networks. In *Conference on Empirical Methods in Natural Language Processing*. Doha, Qatar, pages 14–25.

Ke Tran, Yonatan Bisk, Ashish Vaswani, Daniel Marcu, and Kevin Knight. 2016. Unsupervised Neural Hidden Markov Models. In *Proceedings of the Workshop on Structured Prediction for NLP*. Austin, TX, USA, pages 63–71.

David Vilar, Daniel Stein, Matthias Huck, and Hermann Ney. 2010. Jane: Open Source Hierarchical Translation, Extended with Reordering and Lexicon Models. In *ACL 2010 Joint Fifth Workshop on Statistical Machine Translation and Metrics MATR*. Uppsala, Sweden, pages 262–270.

Stephan Vogel, Hermann Ney, and Christoph Tillmann. 1996. HMM-based Word Alignment in Statistical Translation. In *Proceedings of the 16th Conference on Computational Linguistics - Volume 2*. Copenhagen, Denmark, COLING '96, pages 836–841.

Joern Wuebker, Matthias Huck, Stephan Peitz, Malte Nuhn, Markus Freitag, Jan-Thorsten Peter, Saab Mansour, and Hermann Ney. 2012. Jane 2: Open Source Phrase-based and Hierarchical Statistical Machine Translation. In *International Conference on Computational Linguistics*. Mumbai, India, pages 483–491.

Joern Wuebker, Stephan Peitz, Felix Rietig, and Hermann Ney. 2013. Improving Statistical Machine Translation with Word Class Models. In *Proceedings of the 2013 Conference on Empirical Methods in Natural Language Processing*. Seattle, WA, USA, pages 1377–1381.

Nan Yang, Shujie Liu, Mu Li, Ming Zhou, and Nenghai Yu. 2013. Word Alignment Modeling with Context Dependent Deep Neural Network. In *Proceedings of the 51st Annual Meeting of the Association for Computational Linguistics*. Sofia, Bulgaria, pages 166–175.

Lei Yu, Phil Blunsom, Chris Dyer, Edward Grefenstette, and Tomáš Kočiský. 2017. The Neural Noisy Channel. In *Proceedings of the 5th International Conference on Learning Representations*. Toulon, France.

Towards String-to-Tree Neural Machine Translation

Roee Aharoni & Yoav Goldberg
Computer Science Department
Bar-Ilan University
Ramat-Gan, Israel
{roee.aharoni,yoav.goldberg}@gmail.com

Abstract

We present a simple method to incorporate syntactic information about the target language in a neural machine translation system by translating into linearized, lexicalized constituency trees. Experiments on the WMT16 German-English news translation task shown improved BLEU scores when compared to a syntax-agnostic NMT baseline trained on the same dataset. An analysis of the translations from the syntax-aware system shows that it performs more reordering during translation in comparison to the baseline. A small-scale human evaluation also showed an advantage to the syntax-aware system.

1 Introduction and Model

Neural Machine Translation (NMT) (Kalchbrenner and Blunsom, 2013; Sutskever et al., 2014; Bahdanau et al., 2014) has recently became the state-of-the-art approach to machine translation (Bojar et al., 2016), while being much simpler than the previously dominant phrase-based statistical machine translation (SMT) approaches (Koehn, 2010). NMT models usually do not make explicit use of syntactic information about the languages at hand. However, a large body of work was dedicated to syntax-based SMT (Williams et al., 2016). One prominent approach to syntax-based SMT is string-to-tree (S2T) translation (Yamada and Knight, 2001, 2002), in which a source-language string is translated into a target-language tree. S2T approaches to SMT help to ensure the resulting translations have valid syntactic structure, while also mediating flexible reordering between the source and target languages. The main formalism driving current S2T SMT systems is GHKM rules (Galley et al., 2004, 2006), which are

synchronous transduction grammar (STSG) fragments, extracted from word-aligned sentence pairs with syntactic trees on one side. The GHKM translation rules allow flexible reordering on all levels of the parse-tree.

We suggest that NMT can also benefit from the incorporation of syntactic knowledge, and propose a simple method of performing string-to-tree neural machine translation. Our method is inspired by recent works in syntactic parsing, which model trees as sequences (Vinyals et al., 2015; Choe and Charniak, 2016). Namely, we translate a source sentence into a linearized, lexicalized constituency tree, as demonstrated in Figure 2. Figure 1 shows a translation from our neural S2T model compared to one from a vanilla NMT model for the same source sentence, as well as the attention-induced word alignments of the two models.

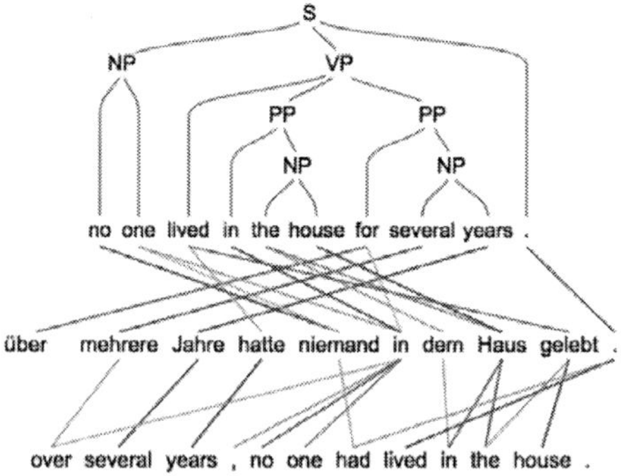

Figure 1: Top - a lexicalized tree translation predicted by the bpe2tree model. Bottom - a translation for the same sentence from the bpe2bpe model. The blue lines are drawn according to the attention weights predicted by each model.

Note that the linearized trees we predict are different in their structure from those in Vinyals et al. (2015) as instead of having part of speech tags as terminals, they contain the words of the translated sentence. We intentionally omit the POS informa-

Proceedings of the 55th Annual Meeting of the Association for Computational Linguistics (Short Papers), pages 132–140
Vancouver, Canada, July 30 - August 4, 2017. ©2017 Association for Computational Linguistics
https://doi.org/10.18653/v1/P17-2021

| **Jane hatte eine Katze .** $\rightarrow$ $(_{ROOT}$ $(_S$ $(_{NP}$ **Jane** $)_{NP}$ $(_{VP}$ **had** $(_{NP}$ **a cat** $)_{NP}$ $)_{VP}$ **.** $)_S$ $)_{ROOT}$ |

Figure 2: An example of a translation from a string to a linearized, lexicalized constituency tree.

tion as including it would result in significantly longer sequences. The S2T model is trained on parallel corpora in which the target sentences are automatically parsed. Since this modeling keeps the form of a sequence-to-sequence learning task, we can employ the conventional attention-based sequence to sequence paradigm (Bahdanau et al., 2014) as-is, while enriching the output with syntactic information.

Related Work Some recent works did propose to incorporate syntactic or other linguistic knowledge into NMT systems, although mainly on the source side: Eriguchi et al. (2016a,b) replace the encoder in an attention-based model with a Tree-LSTM (Tai et al., 2015) over a constituency parse tree; Bastings et al. (2017) encoded sentences using graph-convolutional networks over dependency trees; Sennrich and Haddow (2016) proposed a factored NMT approach, where each source word embedding is concatenated to embeddings of linguistic features of the word; Luong et al. (2015) incorporated syntactic knowledge via multi-task sequence to sequence learning: their system included a single encoder with multiple decoders, one of which attempts to predict the parse-tree of the source sentence; Stahlberg et al. (2016) proposed a hybrid approach in which translations are scored by combining scores from an NMT system with scores from a Hiero (Chiang, 2005, 2007) system. Shi et al. (2016) explored the syntactic knowledge encoded by an NMT encoder, showing the encoded vector can be used to predict syntactic information like constituency trees, voice and tense with high accuracy.

In parallel and highly related to our work, Eriguchi et al. (2017) proposed to model the target syntax in NMT in the form of dependency trees by using an RNNG-based decoder (Dyer et al., 2016), while Nadejde et al. (2017) incorporated target syntax by predicting CCG tags serialized into the target translation. Our work differs from those by modeling syntax using constituency trees, as was previously common in the "traditional" syntax-based machine translation literature.

2 Experiments & Results

Experimental Setup We first experiment in a resource-rich setting by using the German-English

portion of the WMT16 news translation task (Bojar et al., 2016), with 4.5 million sentence pairs. We then experiment in a low-resource scenario using the German, Russian and Czech to English training data from the News Commentary v8 corpus, following Eriguchi et al. (2017). In all cases we parse the English sentences into constituency trees using the BLLIP parser (Charniak and Johnson, 2005).[1] To enable an open vocabulary translation we used sub-word units obtained via BPE (Sennrich et al., 2016b) on both source and target.[2]

In each experiment we train two models. A **baseline** model (bpe2bpe), trained to translate from the source language sentences to English sentences without any syntactic annotation, and a **string-to-linearized-tree** model (bpe2tree), trained to translate into English linearized constituency trees as shown in Figure 2. Words are segmented into sub-word units using the BPE model we learn on the raw parallel data. We use the NEMATUS (Sennrich et al., 2017)[3] implementation of an attention-based NMT model.[4] We trained the models until there was no improvement on the development set in 10 consecutive checkpoints. Note that the only difference between the baseline and the bpe2tree model is the syntactic information, as they have a nearly-identical amount of model parameters (the only additional parameters to the syntax-aware system are the embeddings for the brackets of the trees).

For all models we report results of the best performing single model on the dev-set (newstest2013+newstest2014 in the resource rich setting, newstest2015 in the rest, as measured by BLEU) when translating newstest2015 and newstest2016, similarly to Sennrich et al. (2016a); Eriguchi et al. (2017). To evaluate the string-totree translations we derive the surface form by removing the symbols that stand for non-terminals in the tree, followed by merging the sub-words. We also report the results of an ensemble of the last 5 checkpoints saved during each model training. We compute BLEU scores using the

---

[1] https://github.com/BLLIP/bllip-parser
[2] https://github.com/rsennrich/subword-nmt
[3] https://github.com/rsennrich/nematus
[4] Further technical details of the setup and training are available in the supplementary material.

133

`mteval-v13a.pl` script from the Moses toolkit (Koehn et al., 2007).

system	newstest2015	newstest2016
bpe2bpe	27.33	31.19
bpe2tree	27.36	32.13
bpe2bpe ens.	28.62	32.38
bpe2tree ens.	28.7	33.24

Table 1: BLEU results for the WMT16 experiment

Results As shown in Table 1, for the resource-rich setting, the single models (bpe2bpe, bpe2tree) perform similarly in terms of BLEU on newstest2015. On newstest2016 we witness an advantage to the bpe2tree model. A similar trend is found when evaluating the model ensembles: while they improve results for both models, we again see an advantage to the bpe2tree model on newstest2016. Table 2 shows the results in the low-resource setting, where the bpe2tree model is consistently better than the bpe2bpe baseline. We find this interesting as the syntax-aware system performs a much harder task (predicting trees on top of the translations, thus handling much longer output sequences) while having a nearly-identical amount of model parameters. In order to better understand where or how the syntactic information improves translation quality, we perform a closer analysis of the WMT16 experiment.

3 Analysis

The Resulting Trees Our model produced valid trees for 5970 out of 6003 sentences in the development set. While we did not perform an in-depth error-analysis, the trees seem to follow the syntax of English, and most choices seem reasonable.

Quantifying Reordering English and German differ in word order, requiring a significant amount of reordering to generate a fluent translation. A major benefit of S2T models in SMT is facilitating reordering. Does this also hold for our neural S2T model? We compare the amount of reordering in the bpe2bpe and bpe2tree models using a distortion score based on the alignments derived from the attention weights of the corresponding systems. We first convert the attention weights to hard alignments by taking for each target word the source word with highest attention weight. For an n-word target sentence t and source sentence s let $a(i)$ be the position of the source word aligned to the target word in position i. We define:

	system	newstest2015	newstest2016
DE-EN	bpe2bpe	13.81	14.16
	bpe2tree	14.55	16.13
	bpe2bpe ens.	14.42	15.07
	bpe2tree ens.	15.69	17.21
RU-EN	bpe2bpe	12.58	11.37
	bpe2tree	12.92	11.94
	bpe2bpe ens.	13.36	11.91
	bpe2tree ens.	13.66	12.89
CS-EN	bpe2bpe	10.85	11.23
	bpe2tree	11.54	11.65
	bpe2bpe ens.	11.46	11.77
	bpe2tree ens.	12.43	12.68

Table 2: BLEU results for the low-resource experiments (News Commentary v8)

$$d(s, t) = \frac{1}{n} \sum_{i=2}^{n} |a(i) - a(i - 1)|$$

For example, for the translations in Figure 1, the above score for the bpe2tree model is 2.73, while the score for the bpe2bpe model is 1.27 as the bpe2tree model did more reordering. Note that for the bpe2tree model we compute the score only on tokens which correspond to terminals (words or sub-words) in the tree. We compute this score for each source-target pair on newstest2015 for each model. Figure 3 shows a histogram of the binned score counts. The bpe2tree model has more translations with distortion scores in bins 1-onward and significantly less translations in the least-reordering bin (0) when compared to the bpe2bpe model, indicating that the syntactic information encouraged the model to perform more reordering.[5] Figure 4 tracks the distortion scores throughout the learning process, plotting the average dev-set scores for the model checkpoints saved every 30k updates. Interestingly, both models obey to the following trend: open with a relatively high distortion score, followed by a steep decrease, and from there ascend gradually. The bpe2tree model usually has a higher distortion score during training, as we would expect after our previous findings from Figure 3.

Tying Reordering and Syntax The bpe2tree model generates translations with their constituency tree and their attention-derived alignments. We can use this information to extract GHKM rules (Galley et al., 2004).[6] We derive

---

[5] We also note that in bins 4-6 the bpe2bpe model had slightly more translations, but this was not consistent among different runs, unlike the gaps in bins 0-3 which were consistent and contain most of the translations.

[6] `github.com/joshua-decoder/galley-ghkm`

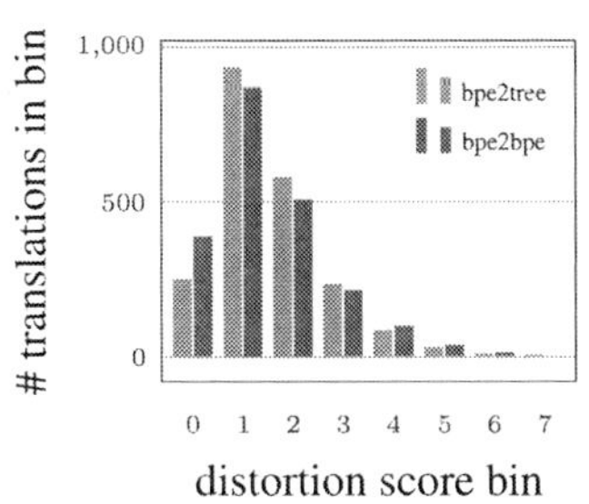

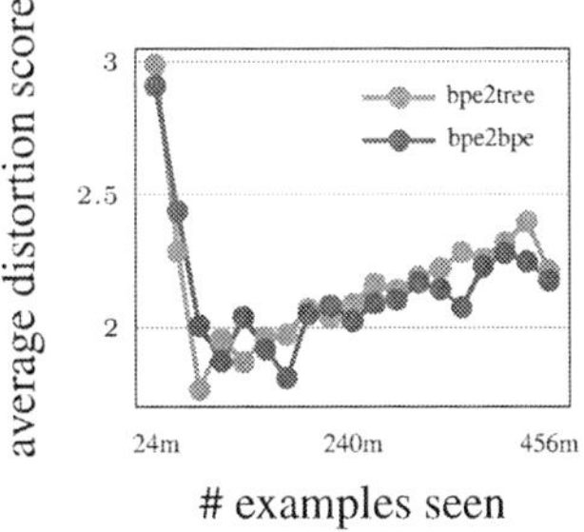

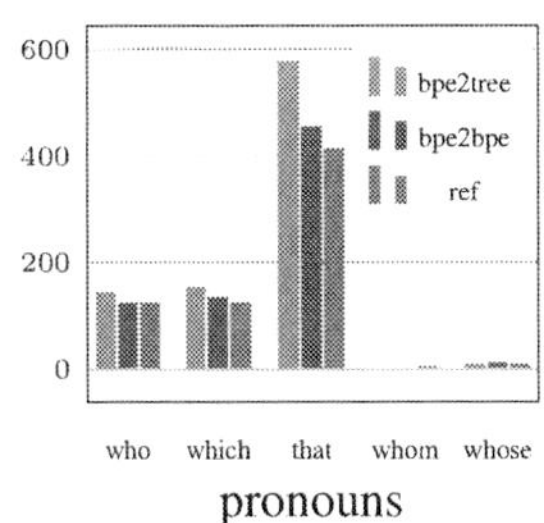

Figure 3: newstest2015 DE-EN translations binned by distortion amount

Figure 4: Average distortion score on the dev-set during different training stages

Figure 5: Amount of English relative pronouns in newstest2015 translations

LHS	Top-5 RHS, sorted according to count.
VP(x0:TER x1:NP)	(244) x0 x1 (157) **x1 x0** (80) x0 x1 ",/." (56) **x1 x0 ",/."** (17) x0 "eine" x1
VP(x0:TER PP(x1:TER x2:NP))	(90) **x1 x2 x0** (65) x0 x1 x2 (31) **x1 x2 x0 ",/."** (13) x0 x1 x2 ",/." (7) **x1 "der" x2 x0**
VP(x0:TER x1:PP)	(113) **x1 x0** (82) x0 x1 (38) **x1 x0 ",/."** (18) x0 x1 ",/." (5) ",/." x0 x1
S(x0:NP VP(x1:TER x2:NP))	(69) x0 x1 x2 (51) **x0 x2 x1** (35) x0 x1 x2 ",/." (20) **x0 x2 x1 ",/."** (6) "die" x0 x1 x2
VP(x0:TER x1:NP x2:PP)	(52) x0 x1 x2 (38) **x1 x2 x0** (20) **x1 x2 x0 ",/."** (11) x0 x1 x2 ",/." (9) **x2 x1 x0**
VP(x0:TER x1:NP PP(x2:TER x3:NP))	(40) x0 x1 x2 x3 (32) **x1 x2 x3 x0** (18) **x1 x2 x3 x0 ",/."** (8) x0 x1 x2 x3 ",/." (5) **x2 x3 x1 x0**
VP(x0:TER NP(x1:NP x2:PP))	(61) x0 x1 x2 (38) **x1 x2 x0** (19) x0 x1 x2 ",/." (8) x0 "eine" x1 x2 (8) **x1 x2 x0 ",/."**
NP(x0:NP PP(x1:TER x2:NP))	(728) x0 x1 x2 (110) "die" x0 x1 x2 (107) x0 x1 x2 ",/." (56) x0 x1 "der" x2 (54) "der" x0 x1 x2
S(VP(x0:TER x1:NP))	(41) **x1 x0** (26) x0 x1 (14) **x1 x0 ",/."** (7) **"die" x1 x0** (5) x0 x1 ",/."
VP(x0:TER x1:VP)	(73) x0 x1 (38) **x1 x0** (25) x0 x1 ",/." (15) **x1 x0 ",/."** (9) ",/." x0 x1

Table 3: Top dev-set GHKM Rules with reordering. Numbers: rule counts. Bolded: reordering rules.

src	Dutzende türkischer Polizisten wegen "Verschwörung" gegen die Regierung <u>festgenommen</u>	
ref	Tens of Turkish Policemen Arrested over 'Plotting' against Gov't	
2tree	dozens of Turkish police <u>arrested</u> for "conspiracy" against the government.	
2bpe	dozens of turkish policemen on "conspiracy" against the government <u>arrested</u>	
src	Die Menschen in London <u>weinten</u>, als ich unsere Geschichte erzhlte.	Er ging einen Monat nicht zu Arbeit.
ref	People in London were crying when I told our story.	He ended up spending a month off work.
2tree	the people of london <u>wept</u> as I told our story.	he <u>did</u> not go to work a month.
2bpe	the people of London, <u>when</u> I told our story.	he went <u>one</u> month to work.
src	Achenbach <u>habe</u> für 121 Millionen Euro Wertgegenstände für Albrecht angekauft.	
ref	Achenbach purchased valuables for Albrecht for 121 million euros.	
2tree	Achenbach <u>has</u> bought valuables for Albrecht for 121 million euros.	
2bpe	Achenbach have purchased <u>value of</u> 121 million Euros for Albrecht.	
src	Apollo <u>investierte</u> 2008 1 Milliarde $ in Norwegian Cruise.	Könntest du mal mit dem "ich liebe dich" <u>aufhören</u>?
ref	Apollo made a $1 billion investment in Norwegian Cruise in 2008.	Could you stop with the "I love you"?
2tree	Apollo <u>invested</u> EUR $1 billion in Norwegian Cruise in 2008.	Could you stop saying "I love you<u>?</u>
2bpe	Apollo invested <u>2008</u> $1 billion in Norwegian Cruise.	Can you say with the "I love you" <u>stop</u>?
src	Gerade in dieser schweren Phase hat er gezeigt, dass er für uns ein sehr wichtiger Spieler ist", <u>konstatierte</u> Barisic.	
ref	Especially during these difficult times, he showed that he is a very important player for us", Barisic stated.	
2tree	Especially at this difficult time he has shown that he is a very important player for us," <u>said</u> Barisic.	
2bpe	It is precisely during this difficult period that he <u>has shown us to be</u> a very important player, "Barisic said.	
src	Hopfen und Malz <u>-</u> auch in China eine beliebte Kombination.	"Ich weiß jetzt, dass ich das kann <u>-</u> prima!"
ref	Hops and malt - a popular combination even in China.	"I now know that I can do it - brilliant!"
2tree	Hops and malt <u>-</u> a popular combination in China.	"I now know that I can do that!
2bpe	Hops and malt - <u>even</u> in China, a popular combination.	I know now that I can that - prima!"
src	Die Ukraine hatte gewarnt, Russland könnte auch die Gasversorgung für Europa <u>unterbrechen</u>.	
ref	Ukraine warned that Russia could also suspend the gas supply to Europe.	
2tree	Ukraine had warned that Russia could also <u>stop</u> the supply of gas to Europe.	
2bpe	Ukraine had been warned, and Russia could <u>also cut</u> gas supplies to Europe.	
src	Bis dahin <u>gab</u> es in Kollbach im Schulverband Petershausen-Kollbach drei Klassen und in Petershausen fünf.	
ref	Until then, the school district association of Petershausen-Kollbach had three classes in Kollbach and five in Petershausen.	
2tree	until then, in Kollbach there <u>were</u> three classes and five classes in Petershausen.	
2bpe	until then <u>there</u> were three classes and in Petershausen five at the school board in Petershausen-Kollbach.	

Table 4: Translation examples from newstest2015. The underlines correspond to the source word attended by the first opening bracket (these are consistently the main verbs or structural markers) and the target words this source word was most strongly aligned to. See the supplementary material for an attention weight matrix example when predicting a tree (Figure 6) and additional output examples.

hard alignments for that purpose by treating every source/target token-pair with attention score above 0.5 as an alignment. Extracting rules from the dev-set predictions resulted in 233,657 rules, where 22,914 of them (9.8%) included reordering, i.e. contained variables ordered differently in the source and the target. We grouped the rules by their LHS (corresponding to a target syntactic structure), and sorted them by the total number of RHS (corresponding to a source sequential structure) with reordering. Table 3 shows the top 10 extracted LHS, together with the top-5 RHS, for each rule. The most common rule, $\text{VP}(x_0\text{:TER } x_1\text{:NP}) \rightarrow x_1\ x_0$, found in 184 sentences in the dev set (8.4%), is indicating that the sequence $x_1\ x_0$ in German was reordered to form a verb phrase in English, in which x_0 is a terminal and x_1 is a noun phrase. The extracted GHKM rules reveal very sensible German-English reordering patterns.

Relative Constructions Browsing the produced trees hints at a tendency of the syntax-aware model to favor using relative-clause structures and subordination over other syntactic constructions (i.e., "several cameras *that* are all priced..." vs. "several cameras, all priced..."). To quantify this, we count the English relative pronouns (who, which, that[7], whom, whose) found in the newstest2015 translations of each model and in the reference translations, as shown in Figure 5. The bpe2tree model produces more relative constructions compared to the bpe2bpe model, and both models produce more such constructions than found in the reference.

Main Verbs While not discussed until this point, the generated opening and closing brackets also have attention weights, providing another opportunity to to peak into the model's behavior. Figure 6 in the supplementary material presents an example of a complete attention matrix, including the syntactic brackets. While making full sense of the attention patterns of the syntactic elements remains a challenge, one clear trend is that opening the very first bracket of the sentence *consistently attends to the main verb or to structural markers* (i.e. question marks, hyphens) in the source sentence, suggesting a planning-ahead behavior of the decoder. The underlines in Table 4 correspond to the source word attended by the first opening bracket, and the target word this source word was

---

[7]"that" also functions as a determiner. We do not distinguish the two cases.

most strongly aligned to. In general, we find the alignments from the syntax-based system more sensible (i.e. in Figure 1 – the bpe2bpe alignments are off-by-1).

Qualitative Analysis and Human Evaluations
The bpe2tree translations read better than their bpe2bpe counterparts, both syntactically and semantically, and we highlight some examples which demonstrate this. Table 4 lists some representative examples, highlighting improvements that correspond to syntactic phenomena involving reordering or global structure. We also performed a small-scale human-evaluation using mechanical turk on the first 500 sentences in the dev-set. Further details are available in the supplementary material. The results are summarized in the following table:

2bpe weakly better	100
2bpe strongly better	54
2tree weakly better	122
2tree strongly better	64
both good	26
both bad	3
disagree	131

As can be seen, in 186 cases (37.2%) the human evaluators preferred the bpe2tree translations, vs. 154 cases (30.8%) for bpe2bpe, with the rest of the cases (30%) being neutral.

4   Conclusions and Future Work

We present a simple string-to-tree neural translation model, and show it produces results which are better than those of a neural string-to-string model. While this work shows syntactic information about the target side can be beneficial for NMT, this paper only scratches the surface with what can be done on the subject. First, better models can be proposed to alleviate the long sequence problem in the linearized approach or allow a more natural tree decoding scheme (Alvarez-Melis and Jaakkola, 2017). Comparing our approach to other syntax aware NMT models like Eriguchi et al. (2017) and Nadejde et al. (2017) may also be of interest. A Contrastive evaluation (Sennrich, 2016) of a syntax-aware system vs. a syntax-agnostic system may also shed light on the benefits of incorporating syntax into NMT.

Acknowledgments

This work was supported by the Intel Collaborative Research Institute for Computational Intelligence (ICRI-CI), and The Israeli Science Foundation (grant number 1555/15).

References

David Alvarez-Melis and Tommi S. Jaakkola. 2017. Tree-structured decoding with doubly recurrent neural networks. *International Conference on Learning Representations (ICLR)* .

Dzmitry Bahdanau, Kyunghyun Cho, and Yoshua Bengio. 2014. Neural machine translation by jointly learning to align and translate. *arXiv preprint arXiv:1409.0473* .

Joost Bastings, Ivan Titov, Wilker Aziz, Diego Marcheggiani, and Khalil Simaan. 2017. Graph convolutional encoders for syntax-aware neural machine translation. *arXiv preprint arXiv:1704.04675* .

Ondřej Bojar, Rajen Chatterjee, Christian Federmann, Yvette Graham, Barry Haddow, Matthias Huck, Antonio Jimeno Yepes, Philipp Koehn, Varvara Logacheva, Christof Monz, Matteo Negri, Aurelie Neveol, Mariana Neves, Martin Popel, Matt Post, Raphael Rubino, Carolina Scarton, Lucia Specia, Marco Turchi, Karin Verspoor, and Marcos Zampieri. 2016. Findings of the 2016 conference on machine translation. In *Proceedings of the First Conference on Machine Translation*. Association for Computational Linguistics, Berlin, Germany, pages 131–198.

Eugene Charniak and Mark Johnson. 2005. Coarse-to-fine n-best parsing and maxent discriminative reranking. In *Proceedings of the 43rd Annual Meeting on Association for Computational Linguistics*. Association for Computational Linguistics, pages 173–180.

David Chiang. 2005. A hierarchical phrase-based model for statistical machine translation. In *Proceedings of the 43rd Annual Meeting on Association for Computational Linguistics*. Association for Computational Linguistics, pages 263–270.

David Chiang. 2007. Hierarchical phrase-based translation. *computational linguistics* 33(2):201–228.

Do Kook Choe and Eugene Charniak. 2016. Parsing as language modeling. In *Proceedings of the 2016 Conference on Empirical Methods in Natural Language Processing*. Association for Computational Linguistics, Austin, Texas, pages 2331–2336. https://aclweb.org/anthology/D16-1257.

Chris Dyer, Adhiguna Kuncoro, Miguel Ballesteros, and Noah A. Smith. 2016. Recurrent neural network grammars. In *Proceedings of the 2016 Conference of the North American Chapter of the Association for Computational Linguistics: Human Language Technologies*. Association for Computational Linguistics, San Diego, California, pages 199–209. http://www.aclweb.org/anthology/N16-1024.

Akiko Eriguchi, Kazuma Hashimoto, and Yoshimasa Tsuruoka. 2016a. Character-based decoding in tree-to-sequence attention-based neural machine translation. In *Proceedings of the 3rd Workshop on Asian Translation (WAT2016)*. pages 175–183.

Akiko Eriguchi, Kazuma Hashimoto, and Yoshimasa Tsuruoka. 2016b. Tree-to-sequence attentional neural machine translation. In *Proceedings of the 54th Annual Meeting of the Association for Computational Linguistics (Volume 1: Long Papers)*. Association for Computational Linguistics, Berlin, Germany, pages 823–833. http://www.aclweb.org/anthology/P16-1078.

Akiko Eriguchi, Yoshimasa Tsuruoka, and Kyunghyun Cho. 2017. Learning to parse and translate improves neural machine translation. *arXiv preprint arXiv:1702.03525* http://arxiv.org/abs/1702.03525.

Michel Galley, Jonathan Graehl, Kevin Knight, Daniel Marcu, Steve DeNeefe, Wei Wang, and Ignacio Thayer. 2006. Scalable inference and training of context-rich syntactic translation models. In *Proceedings of the 21st International Conference on Computational Linguistics and the 44th annual meeting of the Association for Computational Linguistics*. Association for Computational Linguistics, pages 961–968.

Michel Galley, Mark Hopkins, Kevin Knight, and Daniel Marcu. 2004. What's in a translation rule? In Daniel Marcu Susan Dumais and Salim Roukos, editors, *HLT-NAACL 2004: Main Proceedings*. Association for Computational Linguistics, Boston, Massachusetts, USA, pages 273–280.

Nal Kalchbrenner and Phil Blunsom. 2013. Recurrent continuous translation models. In *Proceedings of the 2013 Conference on Empirical Methods in Natural Language Processing*. Association for Computational Linguistics, Seattle, Washington, USA, pages 1700–1709. http://www.aclweb.org/anthology/D13-1176.

Philipp Koehn. 2010. *Statistical Machine Translation*. Cambridge University Press, New York, NY, USA, 1st edition.

Philipp Koehn, Hieu Hoang, Alexandra Birch, Chris Callison-Burch, Marcello Federico, Nicola Bertoldi, Brooke Cowan, Wade Shen, Christine Moran, Richard Zens, et al. 2007. Moses: Open source toolkit for statistical machine translation. In *Proceedings of the 45th annual meeting of the ACL on interactive poster and demonstration sessions*. Association for Computational Linguistics, pages 177–180.

Minh-Thang Luong, Quoc V Le, Ilya Sutskever, Oriol Vinyals, and Lukasz Kaiser. 2015. Multi-task sequence to sequence learning. *arXiv preprint arXiv:1511.06114* .

Maria Nadejde, Siva Reddy, Rico Sennrich, Tomasz Dwojak, Marcin Junczys-Dowmunt, Philipp Koehn, and Alexandra Birch. 2017. Syntax-aware neural machine translation using CCG. *arXiv preprint arXiv:1702.01147* .

Rico Sennrich. 2016. How grammatical is character-level neural machine translation? assessing mt quality with contrastive translation pairs. *arXiv preprint arXiv:1612.04629* .

Rico Sennrich, Orhan Firat, Kyunghyun Cho, Alexandra Birch, Barry Haddow, Julian Hitschler, Marcin Junczys-Dowmunt, Samuel L"aubli, Antonio Valerio Miceli Barone, Jozef Mokry, and Maria Nadejde. 2017. Nematus: a Toolkit for Neural Machine Translation. In *Proceedings of the Demonstrations at the 15th Conference of the European Chapter of the Association for Computational Linguistics*. Valencia, Spain.

Rico Sennrich and Barry Haddow. 2016. Linguistic input features improve neural machine translation. In *Proceedings of the First Conference on Machine Translation*. Association for Computational Linguistics, Berlin, Germany, pages 83–91. http://www.aclweb.org/anthology/W16-2209.

Rico Sennrich, Barry Haddow, and Alexandra Birch. 2016a. Edinburgh neural machine translation systems for wmt 16. In *Proceedings of the First Conference on Machine Translation*. Association for Computational Linguistics, Berlin, Germany, pages 371–376. http://www.aclweb.org/anthology/W16-2323.

Rico Sennrich, Barry Haddow, and Alexandra Birch. 2016b. Neural machine translation of rare words with subword units. In *Proceedings of the 54th Annual Meeting of the Association for Computational Linguistics (Volume 1: Long Papers)*. Association for Computational Linguistics, Berlin, Germany, pages 1715–1725. http://www.aclweb.org/anthology/P16-1162.

Xing Shi, Inkit Padhi, and Kevin Knight. 2016. Does string-based neural mt learn source syntax? In *Proceedings of the 2016 Conference on Empirical Methods in Natural Language Processing*. Association for Computational Linguistics, Austin, Texas, pages 1526–1534. https://aclweb.org/anthology/D16-1159.

Felix Stahlberg, Eva Hasler, Aurelien Waite, and Bill Byrne. 2016. Syntactically guided neural machine translation. In *Proceedings of the 54th Annual Meeting of the Association for Computational Linguistics (Volume 2: Short Papers)*. Association for Computational Linguistics, Berlin, Germany, pages 299–305. http://anthology.aclweb.org/P16-2049.

Ilya Sutskever, Oriol Vinyals, and Quoc V. Le. 2014. Sequence to sequence learning with neural networks. *arXiv preprint arXiv:1409.3215* .

Kai Sheng Tai, Richard Socher, and Christopher D. Manning. 2015. Improved semantic representations from tree-structured long short-term memory networks. In *Proceedings of the 53rd Annual Meeting of the Association for Computational Linguistics and the 7th International Joint Conference on Natural Language Processing (Volume 1: Long Papers)*. Association for Computational Linguistics, Beijing, China, pages 1556–1566. http://www.aclweb.org/anthology/P15-1150.

Oriol Vinyals, Łukasz Kaiser, Terry Koo, Slav Petrov, Ilya Sutskever, and Geoffrey Hinton. 2015. Grammar as a foreign language. In *Advances in Neural Information Processing Systems*. pages 2773–2781.

P. Williams, M. Gertz, and M. Post. 2016. *Syntax-Based Statistical Machine Translation*. Morgan & Claypool publishing.

Kenji Yamada and Kevin Knight. 2001. A syntax-based statistical translation model. In *Proceedings of the 39th Annual Meeting on Association for Computational Linguistics*. Association for Computational Linguistics, pages 523–530.

Kenji Yamada and Kevin Knight. 2002. A decoder for syntax-based statistical mt. In *Proceedings of the 40th Annual Meeting on Association for Computational Linguistics*. Association for Computational Linguistics, pages 303–310.

Matthew D Zeiler. 2012. Adadelta: an adaptive learning rate method. *arXiv preprint arXiv:1212.5701* .

A Supplementary Material

Data The English side of the corpus was tokenized (into Penn treebank format) and truecased using the scripts provided in Moses (Koehn et al., 2007). We ran the BPE process on a concatenation of the source and target corpus, with 89500 BPE operations in the WMT experiment and with 45k operations in the other experiments. This resulted in an input vocabulary of 84924 tokens and an output vocabulary of 78499 tokens in the WMT16 experiment. The linearized constituency trees are obtained by simply replacing the POS tags in the parse trees with the corresponding word or subwords. The output vocabulary in the bpe2tree models includes the target subwords and the tree symbols which correspond to an opening or closing of a specific phrase type.

Hyperparameters The word embedding size was set to 500/256 and the encoder and decoder sizes were set to 1024/256 (WMT16/other experiments). For optimization we used Adadelta (Zeiler, 2012) with minibatch size of 40. For decoding we used beam search with a beam size of 12. We trained the bpe2tree WMT16 model on sequences with a maximum length of 150 tokens (the average length for a linearized tree in the training set was about 50 tokens). It was trained for two weeks on a single Nvidia TitanX GPU. The bpe2bpe WMT16 model was trained on sequences with a maximum length of 50 tokens, and with minibatch size of 80. It was trained for one week on a single Nvidia TitanX GPU. Only in the low-resource experiments we applied dropout as described in Sennrich et al. (2016a) for Romanian-English.

Human Evaluation We performed human-evaluation on the Mechnical Turk platform. Each sentence was evaluated using two annotators. For each sentence, we presented the annotators with the English reference sentence, followed by the outputs of the two systems. The German source was not shown, and the two system's outputs were shown in random order. The annotators were instructed to answer "Which of the two sentences, in your view, is a better portrayal of the the reference sentence." They were then given 6 options: "sent 1 is better", "sent 2 is better", "sent 1 is a little better", "sent 2 is a little better", "both sentences are equally good", "both sentences are equally bad". We then ignore differences between "better" and "a little better". We count as "strongly better" the cases where both annotators indicated the same sentence as better, as "weakly better" the cases were one annotator chose a sentence and the other indicated they are both good/bad. Other cases are treated as either "both good" / "both bad" or as disagreements.

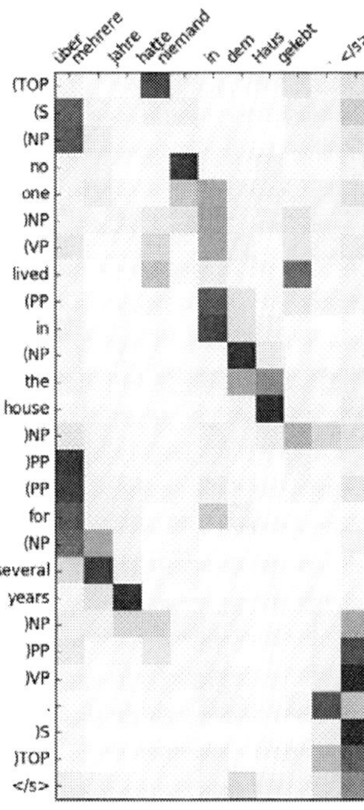

Figure 6: The attention weights for the string-to-tree translation in Figure 1

Additional Output Examples from both models, in the format of Figure 1. Notice the improved translation and alignment quality in the tree-based translations, as well as the overall high structural quality of the resulting trees. The few syntactic mistakes in these examples are attachment errors of SBAR and PP phrases, which will also challenge dedicated parsers.

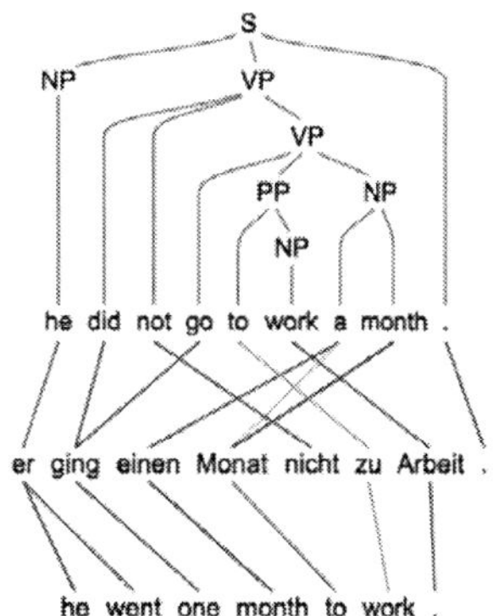

139

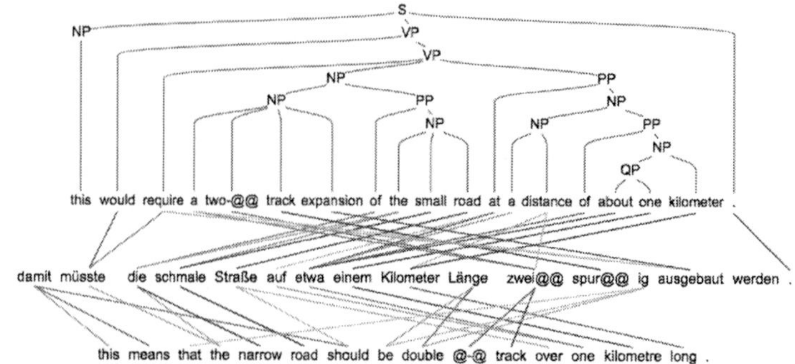

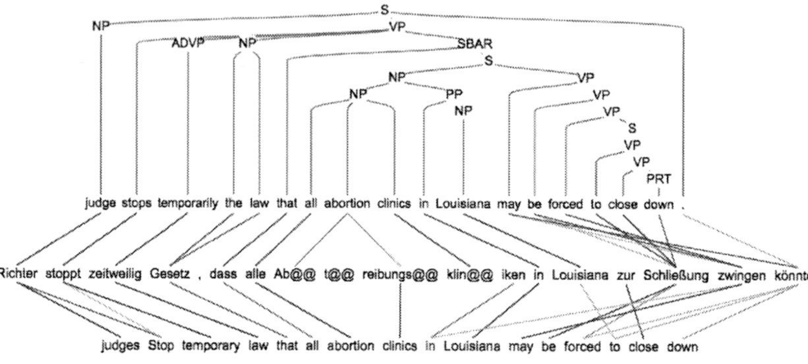

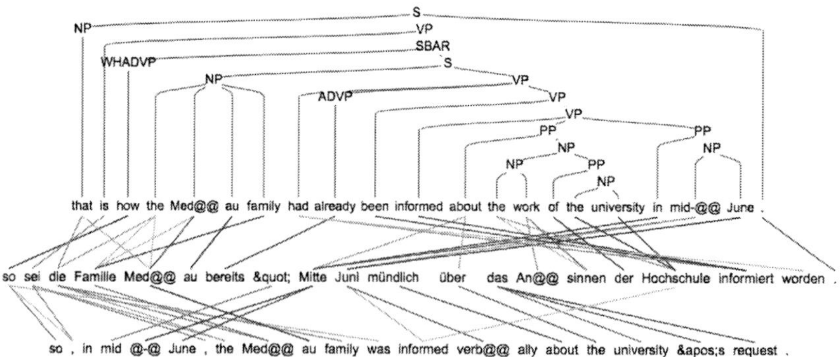

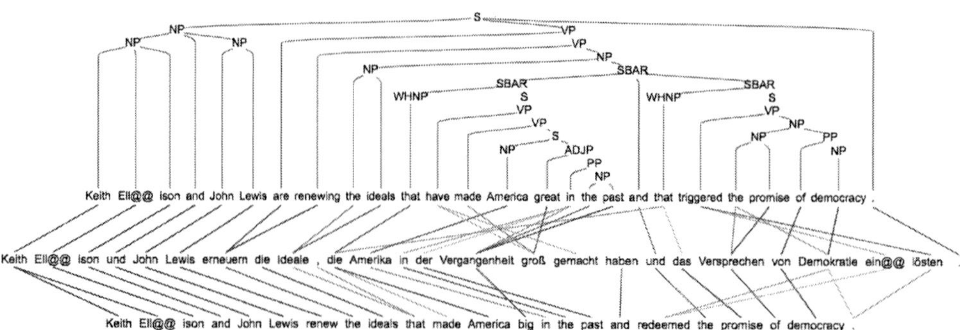

Learning Lexico-Functional Patterns for First-Person Affect

Lena Reed, Jiaqi Wu, Shereen Oraby
Pranav Anand and Marilyn Walker
University of California Santa Cruz
{lireed,jwu64,soraby,panand,mawalker}@ucsc.edu

Abstract

Informal first-person narratives are a unique resource for computational models of everyday events and people's affective reactions to them. People blogging about their day tend not to explicitly say *I am happy*. Instead they describe situations from which other humans can readily infer their affective reactions. However current sentiment dictionaries are missing much of the information needed to make similar inferences. We build on recent work that models affect in terms of lexical predicate functions and affect on the predicate's arguments. We present a method to learn proxies for these functions from first-person narratives. We construct a novel fine-grained test set, and show that the patterns we learn improve our ability to predict first-person affective reactions to everyday events, from a Stanford sentiment baseline of .67F to .75F.

1 Introduction

Across social media, thousands of posts daily take the form of informal FIRST-PERSON NARRATIVES. These narratives provide a rich resource for computational modeling of how people feel about the events they report on. Being able to reliably predict the affect a person may feel towards events they encounter has a range of potential applications, including monitoring mood and mental health (Isaacs et al., 2013) and getting conversational assistants to respond appropriately (Bowden et al., 2017). Moreover, as these narratives are told from the perspective of a protagonist, this research could be used to understand other types of protagonist-framed narratives, like those in fiction.

We are interested in the opinions that a protagonist has, not the author per se. This is sometimes referred to as internal sentiment or self reflective sentiment. While in many situations that is overlaid with the author's opinions, in first-personal narratives, because the author is the protagonist, the two perspectives align. Here, we use the term *affect* to reference this protagonist-centered notion of opinion.

A central obstacle to reliable affect prediction is that that people tend not to *explicitly* flag their affective state, by saying *I am happy*. Large-scale sentiment dictionaries focus on compiling lexical items that bear a consistent affect all on their own (Wilson et al., 2005). But people tend to describe situations, such as *My friend bought me flowers*, or *I got a parking ticket*, from which other humans can readily infer their *implicit* affective reactions.

One approach to this problem aims to directly learn units larger than a lexical item that reliably bear some marker of polarity or emotion (Vu et al., 2014; Li et al., 2014; Ding and Riloff, 2016; Goyal et al., 2010; Russo et al., 2015; Kiritchenko et al., 2014; Reckman et al., 2013).

X	Y	E_{hve}	E_{lck}	Example
+	+	+	-	*I have a new kitten.*
+	-	-	+	*I got a parking ticket.*
-	+	-	+	*My rival got a prize.*
-	-	+	-	*My rival got a reprimand.*
X have/lack Y				

Table 1: Functions for verbs of possession.

Another approach aims to model the speaker's affect to an event compositionally, e.g. Anand and Reschke (2010) (A&R) proposed that the affect a lexical predicate communicates should be modeled as an n-ary function, taking as inputs the affect that the speaker bears towards each partici-

Proceedings of the 55th Annual Meeting of the Association for Computational Linguistics (Short Papers), pages 141–147
Vancouver, Canada, July 30 - August 4, 2017. ©2017 Association for Computational Linguistics
https://doi.org/10.18653/v1/P17-2022

pant. Table 1 contains A&R's functions for verbs of possession: a state in which *X has Y* or *X lacks Y* does not convey a clear affect unless we know what the speaker thinks of both X and Y. If the speaker has positive affect toward both X and Y (Row 1), then we infer that her attitude toward the event is positive, but if either is negative, then we infer that the speaker is negative toward the event. Similarly, Rashkin et al. (2016) represent the typical affect communicated by particular predicates via connotation frames. Here we are finding the internal sentiment of the speaker, or, as Rashkin et al. refer to it, the "mental state" of the speaker.

Inspired by A&R's framework, our work learns lexico-functional patterns (patterns involving lexical items or pairs of lexical items in specific grammatical relations that we show to capture functor-argument relations in A&R's sense), about the effects of combining particular arguments with particular verbs (event types) from first-person narratives. Our novel observation is that learning these compositional functions is greatly simplified in the case of first-person affect. People bear positive affect to themselves, so sentences with first-person elements, e.g. *I/we/me*, reduce the problem for an approach like A&R's to learning the polarity that results from composing the verb with *only one* of its arguments, i.e. only Rows 1, 2 in Table 1 need to be learned for first person subjects. First-person narratives are full of such sentences. See Table 2. We show that the learned patterns are often consonant with A&R's predictions, but are richer, including e.g. many private state descriptions (Wiebe et al., 2004; Wiebe, 1990).

Positive Sentences
We had a marvelous visit and drank coffee and ate home-made chocolate chip cookies.
Now, I could swim both froggy and free style swimming!!

Negative Sentences
But last week, he said that he doesn't know if he has the same feelings for me anymore.
I didn't want to lose him.

Table 2: Sentences from the training data

In addition, we demonstrate that these lexico-functional patterns improve the performance of several off-the-shelf sentiment analyzers. We show that Stanford sentiment (Socher et al., 2013) has a best performance of 0.67 macro F on our test set. We then supplement it with our learned patterns and demonstrate significant improvements. Our final ensemble achieves 0.75 F on the test set.

We discuss related work in more detail in Sec. 5.

2 Bootstrapping a First-Person Sentiment Corpus

We start with a set of first-person narratives (weblogs) drawn from the Spinn3r corpus, that cover a wide range of topics (Burton et al., 2009; Gordon and Swanson, 2009). To reduce noise, we restrict the blogs to those from well-known blogging sites (Ding and Riloff, 2016), and select 15,466 stories whose length ranges from 225 to 375 words.

Pattern Template	Class	Example Instantiations
<subj> ActVP	neg	<I> **cry** at the thought of it and I'm crying now.
<subj> ActInfVP	pos	<I> **got to swim** from the boat to a little sandbar.
<subj> AuxVP Dobj	neg	Yesterday <**it**> **was** my 1st **molar**, today it's my 2nd molar.
ActVP <dobj>	pos	As I bake often, I have **used** <**several different kinds of recipes**>.
PassInfVP <dobj>	pos	When we arrived at the Embarcadero, we were **surprised** to find < **a music festival taking place**>...
Subj AuxVP <dobj>	neg	Our **relationship was** <**non existant**> for over a year after that.
NP Prep <np>	neg	he hurt me countless times but I still forgave him and i still tried to prove to him that I did **care for** <**him**>.
ActVP Prep <np>	neg	I didn't think anything of it until I thought about when he **cheated on** <**me**>.
InfVP Prep <np>	pos	...my friend from college who was so generous **to offer** his place to <**us**>...

Table 3: AutoSlog-TS Templates and Example Instantiations

We hand-annotate a set of 477 positive and 440 negative stories, and use these to bootstrap a larger set of 1,420 negative and 2,288 positive stories. To bootstrap, we apply AutoSlog-TS, a weakly supervised pattern learner that only requires training sets os stories labeled broadly as POSITIVE or NEGATIVE (Riloff, 1996; Riloff and Wiebe, 2003). AutoSlog uses a set of syntactic templates to define different types of linguistic expressions. The left-hand side of Table 3 lists examples of AutoSlog patterns and the right-hand side illustrates a specific lexical-syntactic pattern that corresponds to each general pattern template, as instantiated in first-person stories.[1] When bootstrapping a larger positive and negative story corpus, we use the whole story, not just the first person sentences.

The left-hand-side of Table 3 shows that the learned patterns can involve syntactic arguments

---

[1] The examples are shown as general expressions for readability, but the actual patterns must match the syntactic constraints associated with the pattern template.

of the verbal predicate, which means that these patterns are proxies for one column of verbal function tables like those in Table 1. However, they can also include verb-particle constructions, such as *cheated on*, or verb-head-of-preposition constructions. In each case though, because these patterns are localized to a verb and only one element, they allow us to learn highly specific patterns that could be incorporated into a dictionary such as +-Effect (Choi and Wiebe, 2014). AutoSlog simultaneously harvests both (syntactically constrained) MWE patterns and more compositionally regular verb-argument groups at the same time.

AutoSlog-TS computes statistics on the strength of association of each pattern with each class, i.e. $P(\text{POSITIVE} \mid p)$ and $P(\text{NEGATIVE} \mid p)$, along with the pattern's overall frequency. We define three parameters for each class: θ_f, the frequency with which a pattern occurs, θ_p, the probability with which a pattern is associated with the given class and θ_n, the number of patterns that must occur in the text for it to be labeled. These parameters are tuned on the dev set (Riloff, 1996; Oraby et al., 2015; Riloff and Wiebe, 2003).

To bootstrap a larger corpus, we want settings that have lower recall but very high precision. We select $\theta_p = 0.7$, $\theta_f = 10$ and $\theta_n = 3$ for the positive class and $\theta_p = 0.85$, $\theta_f = 10$ and $\theta_n = 4$ for the negative class for bootstrapping.

3 Experimental Setup

Our experimental setup involves first creating a corpus of training and test **sentences**, then applying AutoSlog-TS a second time to learn linguistic patterns. We then set up methods for cascading classifiers to explore whether ensemble classifiers improve our results.

Training Set: From the bootstrapped set of stories, we create a corpus of sentences. A critical simplifying assumption of our method is that a multi-sentence story can be labelled as a whole as positive or negative, and that each of its sentences **inherit** this polarity. This means we can learn the polarity of events in such narratives from their (noisy) inherited polarity without labelling individual sentences. Our training set consists of 46,255 positive and 25,069 negative sentences.

Test Set: We create the test set by selecting 4k random first-person sentences. First-person sentences either contain an explicit first person marker, i.e. *we* and *my* or start with either a progressive verb or pleonastic *it*. To collect gold labels, we designed a qualifier and a HIT for Mechanical Turk, and put

these out for annotation by 5 Turkers, who label each instance as positive, negative, or neutral. To ensure the high quality of the test set, we select sentences that were labelled consistently positive or negative by 4 or 5 Turkers. We collected 1,266 positive and 1,440 negative sentences.

Dev Set: We created the dev set using the same method as the test set, having Turkers annotate 2k random first-person sentences. We collected 498 positive and 754 negative sentences. The 4k test and dev sentences available for download at https://nlds.soe.ucsc.edu/first-person-sentiment.

AutoSlog First-Person Sentence Classifier. In order to learn new affect functions, we develop a second **sentence-level** classifier using AutoSlog-TS. We run AutoSlog over the training corpus, using the dev set to tune the parameters θ_f, θ_p and θ_n (**?**), in order to maximize macro F-score. Our best parameters on the dev set for positive is $\theta_f=18$, $\theta_p=0.85$ and $\theta_n=1$ and for negative is $\theta_f=1$, $\theta_p=0.5$ and $\theta_n=1$. We specify that if the sentence is in both classes we rename it as neutral. We will refer to this classifier as the AutoSlog classifier.

Baseline First-Person Sentence Classifiers. Our goal is to see whether the knowledge we learn using AutoSlog-TS complements existing sentiment classifiers. We thus experiment with a number of baseline classifiers: the default SVM classifier from Weka with unigram features (Hall et al., 2005), a version of the NRC-Canada sentiment classifier (Mohammad et al., 2013), provided to us by Qadir and Riloff (2014), and the Stanford Sentiment classifier (Socher et al., 2013).

Retrained Stanford. The Stanford Sentiment classifier is a based on Recursive Neural Networks, and trained on a compositional Sentiment Treebank, which includes fine-grained sentiment labels for 215,154 phrases from 11,855 sentences from movie reviews. It can accurately predict some compositional semantic effects and handle negation. However since it was trained on movie reviews, it is likely to be missing labelled data for some common phrases in our blogs. Thus we also retrained it (RETRAINED STANFORD) on high precision phrases from AutoSlog extracted from our training data of positive and negative blogs. This provides 67,710 additional phrases, including 58,972 positive phrases and 8,738 negative phrases. The retrained model includes **both** the labels from the original Sentiment Treebank and the AutoSlog high precision phrases.

4 Results and Analysis

We present our experimental results and analyze the results in terms of the lexico-functional linguistic patterns we learn.

Baseline Classifiers. Rows 1-3 of Table 4 show the results for the three baselines, in terms of F-score for each class and the macro F. Stanford outperforms both NRC and SVM, but misses many cases of positive sentiment.

AutoSlog Classifier. Row 4 of Table 4 shows the results for the AutoSlog classifier. Although AutoSlog itself does not perform highly, the patterns that it learns represent a different type of knowledge than what is contained in many sentiment analysis tools. We therefore hypothesized that a cascading classifier, which supplements one of the baseline sentiment classifiers with the lexico-functional patterns that AutoSlog learns might yield higher performance.

Retrained Stanford. Row 5 of Table 4 shows the results for RETRAINED STANFORD. The F-scores for RETRAINED STANFORD are almost identical to the standard Stanford classifier. This may be because our data is a small percentage of the entire number of phrases used in training Stanford. Although RETRAINED STANFORD prioritizes our phrases, it would not make sense to remove the original training data.

Cascading Classifiers. We implement cascading classifiers to test our hypothesis. The cascade classifier has primary and secondary classifiers, and we invoke the secondary classifiers only if the primary assigns a prediction of *neutral* to a test instance, which reflects the lack of sentiment-bearing lexical items. We also have a cascade classifier with a tertiary classifier, which is invoked in the same fashion as the secondary classifier after the primary and secondary classifiers have been run. The cascading classifiers are named in the order the classifier is employed, primary, secondary or primary, secondary, tertiary. For our cascading classifiers, we combine our baseline classifiers (NRC and Stanford), with our AutoSlog classifier. We do not use SVM as a primary classifier since it has no neutral label. The results for the cascading experiments are in Rows 6-9 of Table 4.

Cascading NRC and AutoSlog provides the best performance, improving both the positive and negative classes, for a macro F of 0.71. This shows that the learned implicit polarity information from AutoSlog improves NRC's performance.

Since our best two-classifier cascade comes

from combining NRC and AutoSlog, we also test a cascade that adds Stanford or SVM. We achieve our best macro F of 0.75 for the combination with SVM.

	Classifier	Pos F1	Neg F1	Macro F
1	SVM	0.66	0.60	0.64
2	NRC	0.58	0.69	0.64
3	Stanford	0.54	0.73	0.67
4	AutoSlog (ASlog)	0.11	0.68	0.53
5	Retrained Stanford	0.53	0.73	0.67
6	NRC, ASlog	0.60	0.78	0.71
7	Stanford, ASlog	0.55	0.76	0.70
8	NRC, ASlog, Stanford	0.64	**0.79**	0.74
9	NRC, ASlog, SVM	**0.70**	0.78	**0.75**

Table 4: Test Set Results

Analysis and Discussion. Here we discuss how the patterns we learned from AutoSlog can supplement the knowledge encoded in current sentiment classifiers, and in newly evolving sentiment resources (Goyal et al., 2010; Choi and Wiebe, 2014; Balahur et al., 2012; Ruppenhofer and Brandes, 2015).

POS PATTERNS	Basic Entailment
HAVE_FUN	property
HAVE_PARTY	possession
HEADED_FOR	location
NEG PATTERNS	**Basic Entailment**
HAVE_CANCER	property
LOST	possession
NOT_COME_HOME	location
NOT_GOING_KILL	existence

Table 5: Highly predictable AutoSlog extracted case frames and functional description

Tables 5 and 6 illustrate several learned lexico-functional patterns for positive events used in the AutoSlog classifier. The patterns shown in Table 5 are predicted by A&R's framework, some functions of which can be seen in Table 1. For example, we find a range of basic state descriptions (have_party, have_cancer) whose basic entailment category is either *possessive* or *property* state. Since E_{have} is positive for a first-person subject only if the object is positive, and negative if the object is negative, we predict that *parties* are good to possess and that *cancer* is a bad property to have. In this way, we can recruit the existing function for *have* to induce new positive or negative things to "possess." In line with A&R's claims, many events are identified with their final results: *headed for* results in being at a desired location, while *not coming home* results in something failing to be at a desired location. We find it a welcome result that our semi-supervised methods yield patterns that correspond to the A&R classes, thus validating our suspicion that first-person sentences furnish a simplifying test ground for discovering functional patterns in the wild.

However, many patterns are not covered by A&R's general classes, see Table 6. Looking first at verbs, one major correlation is between positive classes and public events and negative classes and private states. Verbs extracted from the positive class tend to be eventive and agentive describing more dynamic activities and interactions, such as `played`, `swim`, `enjoyed`, and `danced`. Even many positive *have* uses are light verbs describing an activity such as *have lunch*.

Description	POS PATTERNS
activities	HAVE_DINNER, HAVE_WEDDING
success	GOT_SEE, WENT_WELL
planning	HEADED_FOR, SET_UP
free time	HAVE_TIME, TIME_WITH
social bonding	PICTURE_OF, OLD_FRIENDS
Description	NEG PATTERNS
activities	HAVE_X-RAY, GET_EXAM
knowledge	REALIZE, NOT_KNOW_WHAT
unmet desire	WANTS, NEED_MONEY
social bonding	NOT_TRUST

Table 6: Highly predictable AutoSlog case frames outside A&R's functional system

Verbs from the negative class are strikingly different. They are very often stative, where the author is the experiencer (cognitive subject) of that private state. While this state vs. event distinction is not one existing computational models of sentiment or affect discuss explicitly, it replicates a finding that consistently emerges in clinical psychology, one that is explicitly argued for in cognitive-behavioral accounts of the mood that particular activities evoke (Lewinsohn et al., 1985; MacPhillamy and Lewinsohn, 1982; Russo et al., 2015). In addition, Table 6 reveals several novel result state categories. The success, planning, and unmet desire frames are all ultimately about goal-fulfillment (or lack thereof). While the success and unmet desire cases could be understood as having or lacking something, the planning cases indicate steps achieved toward a desired end-state. Previous work on learning affect from eventuality descriptions has largely focused on actions. Our results indicate that private state descriptions are another rich source of evidence.

5 Related Work

Previous work learns phrasal markers of implicit polarity via bootstrapping from large-scale text sources, e.g. Vu et al. (2014)

learn emotion-specific event types by extracting `emotion,event` pairs on Twitter. Li et al. (2014) uses Twitter to bootstrap 'major life events' and typical replies to those events.

Ding and Riloff (2016) extract subj-verb-obj triples from blog posts. They then apply label propagation to spread polarity from sentences to events. However, the triples they learn do not focus on first-person experiencers. They also filter private states out of the verbs used to learn their triples, whereas we have found that verbs relating to private states such as *need, want* and *realize* are important indicators of first-person affect.

Balahur et al. (2012) use the narratives produced by the ISEAR questionnaire (Scherer et al., 1986) for first-person examples of particular emotions and extract sequences of subject-verb-object triples, which they annotate for basic emotions.

Recent work has built on this idea, and developed methods to automatically expand Anand & Reschke's verb classes to create completely new lexical resources (Balahur et al., 2012; Choi and Wiebe, 2014; Deng et al., 2013; Deng and Wiebe, 2014; Ruppenhofer and Brandes, 2015). Choi & Wiebe's work comes closest to ours in trying to induce (not annotate) lexical functions, but we attempt to infer these from stories directly, whereas they use a structured lexical resource.

6 Conclusion

We show that we can learn lexico-functional linguistic patterns that reliably predict first-person affect. We constructed a dataset of positive and negative first-person experiencer sentences and used them to learn such patterns. We then showed that the performance of current sentiment classifiers can be enhanced by augmenting them with these patterns. By adding our AutoSlog classifier's results to existing classifiers we were able to improve from a baseline 0.67 to 0.75 Macro F with a cascading classifier of NRC, AutoSlog and SVM. In addition, we analyze the linguistic functions that indicate positivity and negativity for the first person experiencer, and show that they are very different. In first-person descriptions, positivity is often signaled by active participations in events, while negativity involves private states. In future work, we plan to explore the integration of these observations into sentiment resources such as the +-Effect lexicon (Choi and Wiebe, 2014). We plan to apply these high precision first-person lexical patterns beyond blog data and with other person-marking.

References

Pranav Anand and Kevin Reschke. 2010. Verb classes as evaluativity functor classes. *Proceedings of Verb* pages 98–103.

Alexandra Balahur, Jesus M. Hermida, and Andres Montoyo. 2012. Building and exploiting emotinet, a knowledge base for emotion detection based on the appraisal theory model. *IEEE Trans. Affect. Comput.* 3(1):88–101.

Kevin Bowden, Shereen Oraby, Amita Misra, Jiaqu Wu, Stephanie Lukin, and Marilyn Walker. 2017. Data-driven dialogue systems for social agents. In *International Workshop on Spoken Dialogue Systems*.

Kevin Burton, Akshay Java, and Ian Soboroff. 2009. The icwsm 2009 spinn3r dataset. In *Proceedings of the Annual Conference on Weblogs and Social Media (ICWSM)*.

Yoonjung Choi and Janyce Wiebe. 2014. +/-effectwordnet: Sense-level lexicon acquisition for opinion inference. In *EMNLP*.

Lingjia Deng, Yoonjung Choi, and Janyce Wiebe. 2013. Benefactive/malefactive event and writer attitude annotation. In *ACL*. pages 120–125.

Lingjia Deng and Janyce Wiebe. 2014. Sentiment propagation via implicature constraints. In *EACL*. pages 377–385.

Haibo Ding and Ellen Riloff. 2016. Acquiring knowledge of affective events from blogs using label propagation. In *AAAI*.

Andrew Gordon and Reid Swanson. 2009. Identifying personal stories in millions of weblog entries. In *Third International Conference on Weblogs and Social Media, Data Challenge Workshop, San Jose, CA*.

Amit Goyal, Ellen Riloff, and Hal Daumé III. 2010. Automatically producing plot unit representations for narrative text. In *Proceedings of the 2010 Conference on Empirical Methods in Natural Language Processing*. pages 77–86.

M. Hall, F. Eibe, G. Holms, B. Pfahringer, P. Reutemann, and I. Witten. 2005. The weka data mining software: An update. *SIGKDD Explorations* 11(1).

Ellen Isaacs, Artie Konrad, Alan Walendowski, Thomas Lennig, Victoria Hollis, and Steve Whittaker. 2013. Echoes from the past: how technology mediated reflection improves well-being. In *Proceedings of the SIGCHI Conference on Human Factors in Computing Systems*. ACM, pages 1071–1080.

Svetlana Kiritchenko, Xiaodan Zhu, and Saif M. Mohammad. 2014. Sentiment analysis of short informal texts. *J. Artif. Int. Res.* 50(1):723–762.

Peter M Lewinsohn, Robin M Mermelstein, Carolyn Alexander, and Douglas J MacPhillamy. 1985. The unpleasant events schedule: A scale for the measurement of aversive events. *Journal of Clinical Psychology* 41(4):483–498.

Jiwei Li, Xun Wang, and Eduard Hovy. 2014. What a nasty day: Exploring mood-weather relationship from twitter. In *Proceedings of the 23rd ACM International Conference on Conference on Information and Knowledge Management*. ACM, New York, NY, USA, CIKM '14, pages 1309–1318. https://doi.org/10.1145/2661829.2662090.

Douglas J MacPhillamy and Peter M Lewinsohn. 1982. The pleasant events schedule: Studies on reliability, validity, and scale intercorrelation. *Journal of Consulting and Clinical Psychology* 50(3):363.

Saif M. Mohammad, Svetlana Kiritchenko, and Xiaodan Zhu. 2013. Nrc-canada: Building the state-of-the-art in sentiment analysis of tweets. In *Proceedings of the seventh international workshop on Semantic Evaluation Exercises (SemEval-2013)*. Atlanta, Georgia, USA.

Shereen Oraby, Lena Reed, Ryan Compton, Ellen Riloff, Marilyn Walker, and Steve Whittaker. 2015. And thats a fact: Distinguishing factual and emotional argumentation in online dialogue. In *Proceedings of the 2nd Workshop on Argumentation Mining*. pages 116–126.

Ashequl Qadir and Ellen Riloff. 2014. Learning emotion indicators from tweets: Hashtags, hashtag patterns, and phrases. In *Proceedings of the Conference on Empirical Methods in Natural Language Processing (EMNLP), Association for Computational Linguistics*. pages 1203–1209.

Hannah Rashkin, Sameer Singh, and Yejin Choi. 2016. Connotation frames: A data-driven investigation. In *Proceedings of the 54th Annual Meeting of the Association for Computational Linguistics (Volume 1: Long Papers)*. Association for Computational Linguistics, Berlin, Germany, pages 311–321. http://www.aclweb.org/anthology/P16-1030.

Hilke Reckman, Cheyanne Baird, Jean Crawford, Richard Crowell, Linnea Micciulla, Saratendu Sethi, and Fruzsina Veress. 2013. teragram: Rule-based detection of sentiment phrases using sas sentiment analysis. In *SemEval@NAACL-HLT*.

E. Riloff and J. Wiebe. 2003. Learning extraction patterns for subjective expressions. In *Proceedings of the 2003 conference on Empirical methods in natural language processing-Volume 10*. Association for Computational Linguistics, pages 105–112.

Ellen Riloff. 1996. Automatically generating extraction patterns from untagged text. In *Proceedings of the Thirteenth National Conference on Artificial Intelligence - Volume 2*. pages 1044–1049.

Josef Ruppenhofer and Jasper Brandes. 2015. Extending effect annotation with lexical decomposition. In *6th Workshop on Computational Approaches to Subjectivity, Sentiment and Social Media Analysis Wass 2015*. page 67.

Irene Russo, Tommaso Caselli, and Carlo Strapparava. 2015. Semeval-2015 task 9: Clipeval implicit polarity of events. In *Proceedings of the 9th International Workshop on Semantic Evaluation, SemEval*.

Klaus R. Scherer, Harald G. Wallbott, and Angela B. Summerfield. 1986. Experiencing emotion : a cross-cultural study. Cambridge University Press.

Richard Socher, Alex Perelygin, Jean Y. Wu, Jason Chuang, Christopher D. Manning, Andrew Y. Ng, and Christopher Potts. 2013. Recursive deep models for semantic compositionality over a sentiment treebank. *Conference on Empirical Methods in Natural Language Processing (EMNLP) 2013*.

Hoa Trong Vu, Graham Neubig, Sakriani Sakti, Tomoki Toda, and Satoshi Nakamura. 2014. Acquiring a dictionary of emotion-provoking events. *EACL 2014* page 128.

J. Wiebe, T. Wilson, R. Bruce, M. Bell, and M. Martin. 2004. Learning subjective language. *Computational linguistics* 30(3):277–308.

Janyce M Wiebe. 1990. Identifying subjective characters in narrative. In *Proceedings of the 13th conference on Computational linguistics-Volume 2*. Association for Computational Linguistics, pages 401–406.

T. Wilson, P. Hoffmann, S. Somasundaran, J. Kessler, J. Wiebe, Y. Choi, C. Cardie, E. Riloff, and S. Patwardhan. 2005. Opinionfinder: A system for subjectivity analysis. In *Proceedings of HLT/EMNLP on Interactive Demonstrations*. Association for Computational Linguistics, pages 34–35.

Lifelong Learning CRF for Supervised Aspect Extraction

Lei Shu, Hu Xu, Bing Liu

Department of Computer Science, University of Illinois at Chicago, USA

{lshu3, hxu48, liub}@uic.edu

Abstract

This paper makes a focused contribution to supervised aspect extraction. It shows that if the system has performed aspect extraction from many past domains and retained their results as knowledge, Conditional Random Fields (CRF) can leverage this knowledge in a lifelong learning manner to extract in a new domain markedly better than the traditional CRF without using this prior knowledge. The key innovation is that even after CRF training, the model can still improve its extraction with experiences in its applications.

1 Introduction

Aspect extraction is a key task of opinion mining (Liu, 2012). It extracts opinion targets from opinion text. For example, from the sentence *"The screen is great"*, it aims to extract "screen", which is a product feature, also called an *aspect*.

Aspect extraction is commonly done using a supervised or an unsupervised approach. The unsupervised approach includes methods such as frequent pattern mining (Hu and Liu, 2004; Popescu and Etzioni, 2005; Zhu et al., 2009), syntactic rules-based extraction (Zhuang et al., 2006; Wang and Wang, 2008; Wu et al., 2009; Zhang et al., 2010; Qiu et al., 2011; Poria et al., 2014), topic modeling (Mei et al., 2007; Titov and McDonald, 2008; Li et al., 2010; Brody and Elhadad, 2010; Wang et al., 2010; Moghaddam and Ester, 2011; Mukherjee and Liu, 2012; Lin and He, 2009; Zhao et al., 2010; Jo and Oh, 2011; Fang and Huang, 2012; Wang et al., 2016), word alignment (Liu et al., 2013), label propagation (Zhou et al., 2013; Shu et al., 2016), and others (Zhao et al., 2015).

This paper focuses on the supervised approach (Jakob and Gurevych, 2010; Choi and Cardie,

2010; Mitchell et al., 2013) using Conditional Random Fields (CRF) (Lafferty et al., 2001). It shows that the results of CRF can be significantly improved by leveraging some prior knowledge automatically mined from the extraction results of previous domains, including domains without labeled data. The improvement is possible because although every product (domain) is different, there is a fair amount of aspects sharing across domains (Chen and Liu, 2014). For example, every review domain has the aspect *price* and reviews of many products have the aspect *battery life* or *screen*. Those shared aspects may not appear in the training data but appear in unlabeled data and the test data. We can exploit such sharing to help CRF perform much better.

Due to leveraging the knowledge gained from the past to help the new domain extraction, we are using the idea of *lifelong machine learning* (LML) (Chen and Liu, 2016; Thrun, 1998; Silver et al., 2013), which is a continuous learning paradigm that retains the knowledge learned in the past and uses it to help future learning and problem solving with possible adaptations.

The setting of the proposed approach L-CRF (*Lifelong CRF*) is as follows: A CRF model M has been trained with a labeled training review dataset. At a particular point in time, M has extracted aspects from data in n previous domains $D_1, \dots, D_n$ (which are unlabeled) and the extracted sets of aspects are $A_1, \dots, A_n$. Now, the system is faced with a new domain data D_{n+1}. M can leverage some *reliable prior knowledge* in $A_1, \dots, A_n$ to make a better extraction from D_{n+1} than without leveraging this prior knowledge.

The key innovation of L-CRF is that even after supervised training, the model can still improve its extraction in testing or its applications with experiences. Note that L-CRF is different from semi-supervised learning (Zhu, 2005) as the n previous

Proceedings of the 55th Annual Meeting of the Association for Computational Linguistics (Short Papers), pages 148–154
Vancouver, Canada, July 30 - August 4, 2017. ©2017 Association for Computational Linguistics
https://doi.org/10.18653/v1/P17-2023

(unlabeled) domain data used in extraction are not used or not available during model training.

There are prior LML works for aspect extraction (Chen et al., 2014; Liu et al., 2016), but they were all unsupervised methods. Supervised LML methods exist (Chen et al., 2015; Ruvolo and Eaton, 2013), but they are for classification rather than for sequence learning or labeling like CRF. A semi-supervised LML method is used in NELL (Mitchell et al., 2015), but it is heuristic pattern-based. It doesn't use sequence learning and is not for aspect extraction. LML is related to transfer learning and multi-task learning (Pan and Yang, 2010), but they are also quite different (see (Chen and Liu, 2016) for details).

To the best of our knowledge, this is the first paper that uses LML to help a supervised extraction method to markedly improve its results.

2 Conditional Random Fields

CRF learns from an observation sequence $\mathbf{x}$ to estimate a label sequence $\mathbf{y}$: $p(\mathbf{y}|\mathbf{x}; \boldsymbol{\theta})$, where $\boldsymbol{\theta}$ is a set of weights. Let l be the l-th position in the sequence. The core parts of CRF are a set of feature functions $\mathcal{F} = \{f_h(y_l, y_{l-1}, \mathbf{x}_l)\}_{h=1}^{H}$ and their corresponding weights $\boldsymbol{\theta} = \{\theta_h\}_{h=1}^{H}$.

Feature Functions: We use two types of feature functions (FF). One is *Label-Label (LL)* FF:

$$f_{ij}^{LL}(y_l, y_{l-1}) = \mathbb{1}\{y_l = i\}\mathbb{1}\{y_{l-1} = j\}, \forall i, j \in \mathcal{Y}, \quad (1)$$

where $\mathcal{Y}$ is the set of labels, and $\mathbb{1}\{\cdot\}$ an indicator function. The other is *Label-Word (LW)* FF:

$$f_{iv}^{LW}(y_l, \mathbf{x}_l) = \mathbb{1}\{y_l = i\}\mathbb{1}\{x_l = v\}, \forall i \in \mathcal{Y}, \forall v \in \mathcal{V}, \quad (2)$$

where $\mathcal{V}$ is the vocabulary. This FF returns 1 when the l-th word is v and the l-th label is v's specific label i; otherwise 0. $\mathbf{x}_l$ is the current word, and is represented as a multi-dimensional vector. Each dimension in the vector is a feature of $\mathbf{x}_l$.

Following the previous work in (Jakob and Gurevych, 2010), we use the feature set {W, -1W, +1W, P, -1P, +1P, G}, where W is the word and P is its POS-tag, -1W is the previous word, -1P is its POS-tag, +1W is the next word, +1P is its POS-tag, and G is the generalized dependency feature.

Under the Label-Word FF type, we have two sub-types of FF: *Label-dimension* FF and *Label-G* FF. Label-dimension FF is for the first 6 features, and Label-G is for the G feature.

The *Label-dimension (Ld)* FF is defined as

$$f_{iv^d}^{Ld}(y_l, \mathbf{x}_l) = \mathbb{1}\{y_l = i\}\mathbb{1}\{x_l^d = v^d\}, \forall i \in \mathcal{Y}, \forall v^d \in \mathcal{V}^d, \quad (3)$$

where $\mathcal{V}^d$ is the set of observed values in feature $d \in \{W, -1W, +1W, P, -1P, +1P\}$ and we call $\mathcal{V}^d$ feature d's feature values. Eq. (3) is a FF that returns 1 when $\mathbf{x}_l$'s feature d equals to the feature value v^d and the variable y_l (lth label) equals to the label value i; otherwise 0.

We describe G and its feature function next, which also holds the key to the proposed L-CRF.

3 General Dependency Feature (G)

Feature G uses generalized dependency relations. What is interesting about this feature is that it enables L-CRF to use past knowledge in its sequence prediction at the test time in order to perform much better. This will become clear shortly. This feature takes a *dependency pattern* as its value, which is generalized from dependency relations.

The general dependency feature (G) of the variable $\mathbf{x}_l$ takes a set of feature values $\mathcal{V}^G$. Each feature value v^G is a dependency pattern. The *Label-G (LG)* FF is defined as:

$$f_{iv^G}^{LG}(y_l, \mathbf{x}_l) = \mathbb{1}\{y_l = i\}\mathbb{1}\{\mathbf{x}_l^G = v^G\}, \forall i \in \mathcal{Y}, \forall v^G \in \mathcal{V}^G. \quad (4)$$

Such a FF returns 1 when the dependency feature of the variable $\mathbf{x}_l$ equals to a dependency pattern v^G and the variable y_l equals to the label value i.

3.1 Dependency Relation

Dependency relations have been shown useful in many sentiment analysis applications (Johansson and Moschitti, 2010; Jakob and Gurevych, 2010). A dependency relation [1] is a quintuple-tuple: *(type, gov, govpos, dep, deppos)*, where *type* is the type of the dependency relation, *gov* is the *governor word*, *govpos* is the POS tag of the governor word, *dep* is the *dependent word*, and *deppos* is the POS tag of the dependent word. The l-th word can either be the governor word or the dependent word in a dependency relation.

3.2 Dependency Pattern

We generalize dependency relations into *dependency patterns* using the following steps:

1. For each dependency relation, replace the current word (governor word or dependent word) and its POS tag with a wildcard since we already have the word (W) and the POS tag (P) features.

---

[1] We obtain dependency relations using Stanford CoreNLP: http://stanfordnlp.github.io/CoreNLP/.

Index	Word	Dependency Relations
1	The	{(det, battery, 2, NN , The, 1, DT) }
2	battery	{(nsubj, great, 7, JJ , battery, 2, NN), (det, battery, 2, NN , The, 1, DT), (nmod, battery, 2, NN, camera, 5, NN) }
3	of	{(case, camera, 5, NN, of, 3, IN) }
4	this	{(det, camera, 5, NN, this, 4, DT) }
5	camera	{(case, camera, 5, NN, of, 3, IN), (det, camera, 5, NN, this, 4, DT), (nmod, battery, 2, NN, camera, 5, NN) }
6	is	{(cop, great, 7, JJ , is, 6, VBZ) }
7	great	{(root, ROOT, 0, VBZ, great, 7, JJ), (nsubj, great, 7, JJ , battery, 2, NN), (cop, great, 7, JJ , is, 6, VBZ) }

Table 1: Dependency relations parsed from "The battery of this camera is great"

2. Replace the context word (the word other than the l-th word) in each dependency relation with a knowledge label to form a more general dependency pattern. Let the set of aspects annotated in the training data be K^t. If the context word in the dependency relation appears in K^t, we replace it with a knowledge label 'A' (aspect); otherwise 'O' (other).

For example, we work on the sentence "The battery of this camera is great." The dependency relations are given in Table 1. Assume the current word is "battery," and "camera" is annotated as an aspect. The original dependency relation between "camera" and "battery" produced by a parser is (nmod, battery, NN, camera, NN). Note that we do not use the word positions in the relations in Table 1. Since the current word's information (the word itself and its POS-tag) in the dependency relation is redundant, we replace it with a wild-card. The relation becomes (nmod, *, camera, NN). Secondly, since "camera" is in K^t, we replace "camera" with a general label 'A'. The final dependency pattern becomes (nmod,*, A, NN).

We now explain why dependency patterns can enable a CRF model to leverage the past knowledge. The key is the knowledge label 'A' above, which indicates a likely aspect. Recall that our problem setting is that when we need to extract from the new domain D_{n+1} using a trained CRF model M, we have already extracted from many previous domains $D_1, \ldots, D_n$ and retained their extracted sets of aspects $A_1, \ldots, A_n$. Then, we can mine reliable aspects from $A_1, \ldots, A_n$ and add them in K^t, which enables many knowledge labels in the dependency patterns of the new data A_{n+1} due to sharing of aspects across domains. This enriches the dependency pattern features, which consequently allows more aspects to be extracted from the new domain D_{n+1}.

4 The Proposed L-CRF Algorithm

We now present the L-CRF algorithm. As the dependency patterns for the general dependency fea-

Algorithm 1 Lifelong Extraction of L-CRF

1: $K_p \leftarrow \emptyset$
2: **loop**
3:     $F \leftarrow$ FeatureGeneration(D_{n+1}, K)
4:     $A_{n+1} \leftarrow$ Apply-CRF-Model(M, F)
5:     $S \leftarrow S \cup \{A_{n+1}\}$
6:     $K_{n+1} \leftarrow$ Frequent-Aspects-Mining(S, λ)
7:     **if** $K_p = K_{n+1}$ **then**
8:         **break**
9:     **else**
10:         $K \leftarrow K^t \cup K_{n+1}$
11:         $K_p \leftarrow K_{n+1}$
12:         $S \leftarrow S - \{A_{n+1}\}$
13:     **end if**
14: **end loop**

ture do not use any actual words and they can also use the prior knowledge, they are quite powerful for cross-domain extraction (the test domain is not used in training).

Let K be a set of *reliable aspects* mined from the aspects extracted in past domain datasets using the CRF model M. Note that we assume that M has already been trained using some labeled training data D^t. Initially, K is K^t (the set of all annotated aspects in the training data D^t). The more domains M has worked on, the more aspects it extracts, and the larger the set K gets. When faced with a new domain D_{n+1}, K allows the general dependency feature to generate more dependency patterns related to aspects due to more knowledge labels 'A' as we explained in the previous section. Consequently, CRF has more informed features to produce better extraction results.

L-CRF works in two phases: *training phase* and *lifelong extraction phase*. The training phase trains a CRF model M using the training data D^t, which is the same as normal CRF training, and will not be discussed further. In the lifelong extraction phase, M is used to extract aspects from coming domains (M does not change and the domain data are unlabeled). All the results from the domains are retained in past aspect store S. At

Domain	# Sent.	# Asp.	# non-asp. words
Computer	536	1173	7675
Camera	609	1640	9849
Router	509	1239	7264
Phone	497	980	7478
Speaker	510	1299	7546
DVD Player	506	928	7552
Mp3 Player	505	1180	7607

Table 2: Annotation details of the datasets

a particular time, it is assumed M has been applied to n past domains, and is now faced with the $n + 1$ domain. L-CRF uses M and reliable aspects (denoted K_{n+1}) mined from S and K^t ($K = K^t \cup K_{n+1}$) to extract from D_{n+1}. Note that aspects K_t from the training data are considered always reliable as they are manually labeled, thus a subset of K. We cannot use all extracted aspects from past domains as reliable aspects due to many extraction errors. But those aspects that appear in multiple past domains are more likely to be correct. Thus K contains those frequent aspects in S. The lifelong extraction phase is in Algorithm 1.

Lifelong Extraction Phase: Algorithm 1 performs extraction on D_{n+1} iteratively.

1. It generates features (F) on the data D_{n+1} (line 3), and applies the CRF model M on F to produce a set of aspects A_{n+1} (line 4).

2. A_{n+1} is added to S, the past aspect store. From S, we mine a set of frequent aspects K_{n+1}. The frequency threshold is λ.

3. If K_{n+1} is the same as K_p from the previous iteration, the algorithm exits as no new aspects can be found. We use an iterative process because each extraction gives new results, which may increase the size of K, the reliable past aspects or past knowledge. The increased K may produce more dependency patterns, which can enable more extractions.

4. Else: some additional reliable aspects are found. M may extract additional aspects in the next iteration. Lines 10 and 11 update the two sets for the next iteration.

5 Experiments

We now evaluate the proposed L-CRF method and compare with baselines.

5.1 Evaluation Datasets

We use two types of data for our experiments. The first type consists of seven (7) annotated benchmark review datasets from 7 domains (types of products). Since they are annotated, they are used in training and testing. The first 4 datasets are from (Hu and Liu, 2004), which actually has 5 datasets from 4 domains. Since we are mainly interested in results at the domain level, we did not use one of the domain-repeated datasets. The last 3 datasets of three domains (products) are from (Liu et al., 2016). These datasets are used to make up our CRF training data D^t and test data D_{n+1}. The annotation details are given in Table 2.

The second type has 50 unlabeled review datasets from 50 domains or types of products (Chen and Liu, 2014). Each dataset has 1000 reviews. They are used as the past domain data, i.e., $D_1, \ldots, D_n$ ($n = 50$). Since they are not labeled, they cannot be used for training or testing.

5.2 Baseline Methods

We compare L-CRF with CRF. We will not compare with unsupervised methods, which have been shown improvable by lifelong learning (Chen et al., 2014; Liu et al., 2016). The frequency threshold λ in Algorithm 1 used in our experiment to judge which extracted aspects are considered reliable is empirically set to 2.

CRF: We use the linear chain CRF from [2]. Note that CRF uses all features including dependency features as the proposed L-CRF but does not employ the 50 domains unlabeled data used for lifelong learning

CRF+R: It treats the reliable aspect set K as a dictionary. It adds those reliable aspects in K that are not extracted by CRF but are in the test data to the final results. We want to see whether incorporating K into the CRF extraction through dependency patterns in L-CRF is actually needed.

We do not compare with domain adaptation or transfer learning because domain adaption basically uses the source domain labeled data to help learning in the target domain with few or no labeled data. Our 50 domains used in lifelong learning have no labels. So they cannot help in transfer learning. Although in transfer learning, the target domain usually has a large quantity of unlabeled data, but the 50 domains are not used as the target domains in our experiments.

---

[2] https://github.com/huangzhengsjtu/pcrf/

Training	Testing	Cross-Domain								
		CRF			CRF+R			L-CRF		
		$\mathcal{P}$	$\mathcal{R}$	$\mathcal{F}_1$	$\mathcal{P}$	$\mathcal{R}$	$\mathcal{F}_1$	$\mathcal{P}$	$\mathcal{R}$	$\mathcal{F}_1$
−Computer	Computer	86.6	51.4	64.5	23.2	90.4	37.0	82.2	62.7	71.1
−Camera	Camera	84.3	48.3	61.4	21.8	86.8	34.9	81.9	60.6	69.6
−Router	Router	86.3	48.3	61.9	24.8	92.6	39.2	82.8	60.8	70.1
−Phone	Phone	72.5	50.6	59.6	20.8	81.2	33.1	70.1	59.5	64.4
−Speaker	Speaker	87.3	60.6	71.6	22.4	91.2	35.9	84.5	71.5	77.4
−DVDplayer	DVDplayer	72.7	63.2	67.6	16.4	90.7	27.7	69.7	71.5	70.6
−Mp3player	Mp3player	87.5	49.4	63.2	20.6	91.9	33.7	84.1	60.7	70.5
Average		82.5	53.1	64.3	21.4	89.3	34.5	79.3	63.9	70.5
		In-Domain								
−Computer	−Computer	84.0	71.4	77.2	23.2	93.9	37.3	81.6	75.8	78.6
−Camera	−Camera	83.7	70.3	76.4	20.8	93.7	34.1	80.7	75.4	77.9
−Router	−Router	85.3	71.8	78.0	22.8	93.9	36.8	82.6	76.2	79.3
−Phone	−Phone	85.0	71.1	77.5	25.1	93.7	39.6	82.9	74.7	78.6
−Speaker	−Speaker	83.8	70.3	76.5	20.1	94.3	33.2	80.1	75.8	77.9
−DVDplayer	−DVDplayer	85.0	72.2	78.1	20.9	94.2	34.3	81.6	76.7	79.1
−Mp3player	−Mp3player	83.2	72.6	77.5	20.4	94.5	33.5	79.8	77.7	78.7
Average		84.3	71.4	77.3	21.9	94.0	35.5	81.3	76.0	78.6

Table 3: Aspect extraction results in precision, recall and F_1 score: Cross-Domain and In-Domain ($-$X means all except domain X)

5.3 Experiment Setting

To compare the systems using the same training and test data, for each dataset we use 200 sentences for training and 200 sentences for testing to avoid bias towards any dataset or domain because we will combine multiple domain datasets for CRF training. We conducted both cross-domain and in-domain tests. Our problem setting is cross-domain. In-domain is used for completeness. In both cases, we assume that extraction has been done for the 50 domains.

Cross-domain experiments: We combine 6 labeled domain datasets for training (1200 sentences) and test on the 7th domain (not used in training). This gives us 7 *cross-domain* results. This set of tests is particularly interesting as it is desirable to have the trained model used in cross-domain situations to save manual labeling effort.

In-domain experiments: We train and test on the same 6 domains (1200 sentences for training and 1200 sentences for testing). This also gives us 7 *in-domain* results.

Evaluating Measures: We use the popular precision $\mathcal{P}$, recall $\mathcal{R}$, and $\mathcal{F}_1$-score.

5.4 Results and Analysis

All the experiment results are given in Table 3.

Cross-domain: Each $-$X in column 1 means that domain X is not used in training. X in column 2 means that domain X is used in testing. We can see that L-CRF is markedly better than CRF and CRF+R in $\mathcal{F}_1$. CRF+R is very poor due to poor precisions, which shows treating the reliable aspects set K as a dictionary isn't a good idea.

In-domain: $-$X in training and test columns means that the other 6 domains are used in both training and testing (thus in-domain). We again see that L-CRF is consistently better than CRF and CRF+R in $\mathcal{F}_1$. The amount of gain is smaller. This is expected because most aspects appeared in training probably also appear in the test data as they are reviews from the same 6 products.

6 Conclusion

This paper proposed a lifelong learning method to enable CRF to leverage the knowledge gained from extraction results of previous domains (unlabeled) to improve its extraction. Experimental results showed the effectiveness of L-CRF. The current approach does not change the CRF model itself. In our future work, we plan to modify CRF so that it can consider previous extraction results as well as the knowledge in previous CRF models.

Acknowledgments

This work was supported in part by grants from National Science Foundation (NSF) under grant no. IIS-1407927 and IIS-1650900.

References

Samuel Brody and Noemie Elhadad. 2010. An unsupervised aspect-sentiment model for online reviews. In *NAACL '10*. pages 804–812.

Zhiyuan Chen and Bing Liu. 2014. Topic modeling using topics from many domains, lifelong learning and big data. In *ICML '14*. pages 703–711.

Zhiyuan Chen and Bing Liu. 2016. *Lifelong Machine Learning*. Morgan & Claypool Publishers.

Zhiyuan Chen, Nianzu Ma, and Bing Liu. 2015. Lifelong learning for sentiment classification. *Volume 2: Short Papers* page 750.

Zhiyuan Chen, Arjun Mukherjee, and Bing Liu. 2014. Aspect extraction with automated prior knowledge learning. In *ACL '14*. pages 347–358.

Yejin Choi and Claire Cardie. 2010. Hierarchical sequential learning for extracting opinions and their attributes. In *ACL '10*. pages 269–274.

Lei Fang and Minlie Huang. 2012. Fine granular aspect analysis using latent structural models. In *ACL '12*. pages 333–337.

Minqing Hu and Bing Liu. 2004. Mining and summarizing customer reviews. In *KDD '04*. pages 168–177.

Niklas Jakob and Iryna Gurevych. 2010. Extracting opinion targets in a single- and cross-domain setting with conditional random fields. In *EMNLP '10*. pages 1035–1045.

Yohan Jo and Alice H. Oh. 2011. Aspect and sentiment unification model for online review analysis. In *WSDM '11*. pages 815–824.

Richard Johansson and Alessandro Moschitti. 2010. Syntactic and semantic structure for opinion expression detection. In *Proceedings of the Fourteenth Conference on Computational Natural Language Learning*. pages 67–76.

John Lafferty, Andrew McCallum, and Fernando CN Pereira. 2001. Conditional random fields: Probabilistic models for segmenting and labeling sequence data. In *ICML '01*. pages 282–289.

Fangtao Li, Minlie Huang, and Xiaoyan Zhu. 2010. Sentiment analysis with global topics and local dependency. In *AAAI '10*. pages 1371–1376.

Chenghua Lin and Yulan He. 2009. Joint sentiment/topic model for sentiment analysis. In *CIKM '09*. pages 375–384.

Bing Liu. 2012. *Sentiment Analysis and Opinion Mining*. Morgan & Claypool Publishers.

Kang Liu, Liheng Xu, Yang Liu, and Jun Zhao. 2013. Opinion target extraction using partially-supervised word alignment model. In *IJCAI '13*. pages 2134–2140.

Qian Liu, Bing Liu, Yuanlin Zhang, Doo Soon Kim, and Zhiqiang Gao. 2016. Improving opinion aspect extraction using semantic similarity and aspect associations. In *Thirtieth AAAI Conference on Artificial Intelligence*.

Qiaozhu Mei, Xu Ling, Matthew Wondra, Hang Su, and ChengXiang Zhai. 2007. Topic sentiment mixture: Modeling facets and opinions in weblogs. In *WWW '07*. pages 171–180.

Margaret Mitchell, Jacqui Aguilar, Theresa Wilson, and Benjamin Van Durme. 2013. Open domain targeted sentiment. In *ACL '13*. pages 1643–1654.

T Mitchell, W Cohen, E Hruschka, P Talukdar, J Betteridge, A Carlson, B Dalvi, M Gardner, B Kisiel, J Krishnamurthy, N Lao, K Mazaitis, T Mohamed, N Nakashole, E Platanios, A Ritter, M Samadi, B Settles, R Wang, D Wijaya, A Gupta, X Chen, A Saparov, M Greaves, and J Welling. 2015. Never-ending learning. In *AAAI'2015*.

Samaneh Moghaddam and Martin Ester. 2011. ILDA: interdependent lda model for learning latent aspects and their ratings from online product reviews. In *SIGIR '11*. pages 665–674.

Arjun Mukherjee and Bing Liu. 2012. Aspect extraction through semi-supervised modeling. In *ACL '12*. volume 1, pages 339–348.

Sinno Jialin Pan and Qiang Yang. 2010. A survey on transfer learning. *IEEE Transactions on knowledge and data engineering* 22(10):1345–1359.

Ana-Maria Popescu and Oren Etzioni. 2005. Extracting product features and opinions from reviews. In *HLT-EMNLP '05*. pages 339–346.

Soujanya Poria, Erik Cambria, Lun-Wei Ku, Chen Gui, and Alexander Gelbukh. 2014. A rule-based approach to aspect extraction from product reviews. In *Proceedings of the second workshop on natural language processing for social media (SocialNLP)*. pages 28–37.

Guang Qiu, Bing Liu, Jiajun Bu, and Chun Chen. 2011. Opinion word expansion and target extraction through double propagation. *Computational Linguistics* 37(1):9–27.

Paul Ruvolo and Eric Eaton. 2013. Ella: An efficient lifelong learning algorithm. *ICML (1)* 28:507–515.

Lei Shu, Bing Liu, Hu Xu, and Annice Kim. 2016. Lifelong-rl: Lifelong relaxation labeling for separating entities and aspects in opinion targets. In *Proceedings of the Conference on Empirical Methods in Natural Language Processing (EMNLP)*.

Daniel L Silver, Qiang Yang, and Lianghao Li. 2013. Lifelong machine learning systems: Beyond learning algorithms. In *AAAI Spring Symposium: Lifelong Machine Learning*. Citeseer, pages 49–55.

Sebastian Thrun. 1998. Lifelong learning algorithms. In *Learning to learn*, Springer, pages 181–209.

Ivan Titov and Ryan McDonald. 2008. A joint model of text and aspect ratings for sentiment summarization. In *ACL '08: HLT*. pages 308–316.

Bo Wang and Houfeng Wang. 2008. Bootstrapping both product features and opinion words from chinese customer reviews with cross-inducing. In *IJC-NLP '08*. pages 289–295.

Hongning Wang, Yue Lu, and Chengxiang Zhai. 2010. Latent aspect rating analysis on review text data: A rating regression approach. In *KDD '10*. pages 783–792.

Shuai Wang, Zhiyuan Chen, and Bing Liu. 2016. Mining aspect-specic opinion using a holistic lifelong topic model. In *WWW '16*.

Yuanbin Wu, Qi Zhang, Xuanjing Huang, and Lide Wu. 2009. Phrase dependency parsing for opinion mining. In *EMNLP '09*. pages 1533–1541.

Lei Zhang, Bing Liu, Suk Hwan Lim, and Eamonn O'Brien-Strain. 2010. Extracting and ranking product features in opinion documents. In *COLING '10: Posters*. pages 1462–1470.

Wayne Xin Zhao, Jing Jiang, Hongfei Yan, and Xiaoming Li. 2010. Jointly modeling aspects and opinions with a maxent-lda hybrid. In *EMNLP '10*. pages 56–65.

Yanyan Zhao, Bing Qin, and Ting Liu. 2015. Creating a fine-grained corpus for chinese sentiment analysis. *IEEE Intelligent Systems* 30(1):36–43.

Xinjie Zhou, Xiaojun Wan, and Jianguo Xiao. 2013. Collective opinion target extraction in Chinese microblogs. In *EMNLP '13*. pages 1840–1850.

Jingbo Zhu, Huizhen Wang, Benjamin K. Tsou, and Muhua Zhu. 2009. Multi-aspect opinion polling from textual reviews. In *CIKM '09*. pages 1799–1802.

Xiaojin Zhu. 2005. Semi-supervised learning literature survey .

Li Zhuang, Feng Jing, and Xiao-Yan Zhu. 2006. Movie review mining and summarization. In *CIKM '06*. pages 43–50.

Exploiting Domain Knowledge via Grouped Weight Sharing with Application to Text Categorization

Ye Zhang[1]   Matthew Lease[2]   Byron C. Wallace[3]

[1]Department of Computer Science, University of Texas at Austin
[2]School of Information, University of Texas at Austin
[3]College of Computer & Information Science, Northeastern University
yezhang@utexas.edu, ml@utexas.edu, byron@ccs.neu.edu

Abstract

A fundamental advantage of neural models for NLP is their ability to learn representations from scratch. However, in practice this often means ignoring existing external linguistic resources, e.g., WordNet or domain specific ontologies such as the Unified Medical Language System (UMLS). We propose a general, novel method for exploiting such resources via *weight sharing*. Prior work on weight sharing in neural networks has considered it largely as a means of model compression. In contrast, we treat weight sharing as a flexible mechanism for incorporating prior knowledge into neural models. We show that this approach consistently yields improved performance on classification tasks compared to baseline strategies that do not exploit weight sharing.

1 Introduction

Neural models are powerful in part due to their ability to learn good representations of raw textual inputs, mitigating the need for extensive task-specific feature engineering (Collobert et al., 2011). However, a downside of learning from scratch is failing to capitalize on prior linguistic or semantic knowledge, often encoded in existing resources such as ontologies. Such prior knowledge can be particularly valuable when estimating highly flexible models. In this work, we address how to exploit known relationships between words when training neural models for NLP tasks.

We propose exploiting the *feature-hashing* trick, originally proposed as a means of neural network compression (Chen et al., 2015). Here we instead view the partial parameter sharing induced by feature hashing as a flexible mechanism for tying together network node weights that we believe

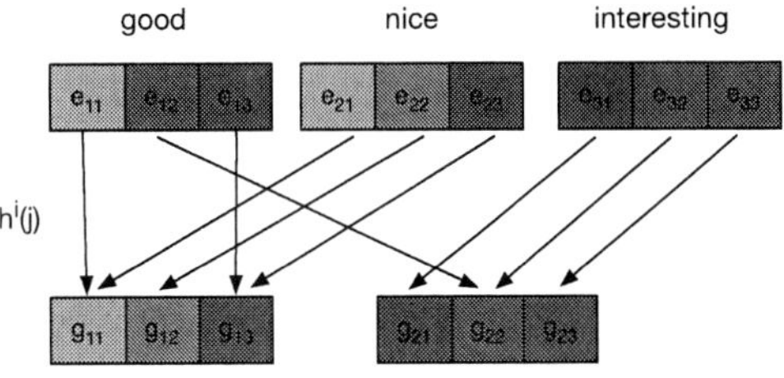

Figure 1: An example of grouped partial weight sharing. Here there are two groups. We stochastically select embedding weights to be shared between words belonging to the same group(s).

to be similar *a priori*. In effect, this acts as a regularizer that constrains the model to learn weights that agree with the domain knowledge codified in external resources like ontologies.

More specifically, as external resources we use Brown clusters (Brown et al., 1992), WordNet (Miller, 1995) and the Unified Medical Language System (UMLS) (Bodenreider, 2004). From these we derive groups of words with similar meaning. We then use feature hashing to share a subset of weights between the embeddings of words that belong to the same semantic group(s). This forces the model to respect prior domain knowledge, insofar as words similar under a given ontology are compelled to have similar embeddings.

Our contribution is a novel, simple and flexible method for injecting domain knowledge into neural models via stochastic weight sharing. Results on seven diverse classification tasks (three sentiment and four biomedical) show that our method consistently improves performance over (1) baselines that fail to capitalize on domain knowledge, and (2) an approach that uses *retrofitting* (Faruqui et al., 2014) as a preprocessing step to encode domain knowledge prior to training.

Proceedings of the 55th Annual Meeting of the Association for Computational Linguistics (Short Papers), pages 155–160
Vancouver, Canada, July 30 - August 4, 2017. ©2017 Association for Computational Linguistics
https://doi.org/10.18653/v1/P17-2024

2 Grouped Weight Sharing

We incorporate similarity relations codified in existing resources (here derived from Brown clusters, SentiWordNet and the UMLS) as prior knowledge in a Convolutional Neural Network (CNN).[1] To achieve this we construct a shared embedding matrix such that words known *a priori* to be similar are constrained to share some fraction of embedding weights.

Concretely, suppose we have N groups of words derived from an external resource. Note that one could derive such groups in several ways; e.g., using the synsets in SentiWordNet. We denote groups by $\{g_1, g_2, ..., g_N\}$. Each group is associated with an embedding $\mathbf{g}_{g_i}$, which we initialize by averaging the pre-trained embeddings of each word in the group.

To exploit both grouped and independent word weights, we adopt a two-channel CNN model (Zhang et al., 2016b). The embedding matrix of the first channel is initialized with pre-trained word vectors. We denote this input by $\mathbf{E}^p \in \mathbb{R}^{V \times d}$ (V is the vocabulary size and d the dimension of the word embeddings). The second channel input matrix is initialized with our proposed weight-sharing embedding $\mathbf{E}^s \in \mathbb{R}^{V \times d}$. $\mathbf{E}^s$ is initialized by drawing from both $\mathbf{E}^p$ and the external resource following the process we describe below.

Given an input text sequence of length l, we construct sequence embedding representations $\mathbf{W}^p \in \mathbb{R}^{l \times d}$ and $\mathbf{W}^s \in \mathbb{R}^{l \times d}$ using the corresponding embedding matrices. We then apply independent sets of linear convolution filters on these two matrices. Each filter will generate a feature map vector $\mathbf{v} \in \mathbb{R}^{l-h+1}$ (h is the filter height). We perform 1-max pooling over each $\mathbf{v}$, extracting one scalar per feature map. Finally, we concatenate scalars from all of the feature maps (from both channels) into a feature vector which is fed to a softmax function to predict the label (Figure 2).

We initialize $\mathbf{E}^s$ as follows. Each row $\mathbf{e}_i \in \mathbb{R}^d$ of $\mathbf{E}_s$ is the embedding of word i. Words may belong to one or more groups. A mapping function $G(i)$ retrieves the groups that word i belongs to, i.e., $G(i)$ returns a subset of $\{g_1, g_2, ..., g_N\}$, which we denote by $\{g_1^{(i)}, g_2^{(i)} ... g_K^{(i)}\}$, where K is the number of groups that contain word i. To initialize $\mathbf{E}^s$, for each dimension j of each word embedding $\mathbf{e}_i$, we use a hash function h^i to map

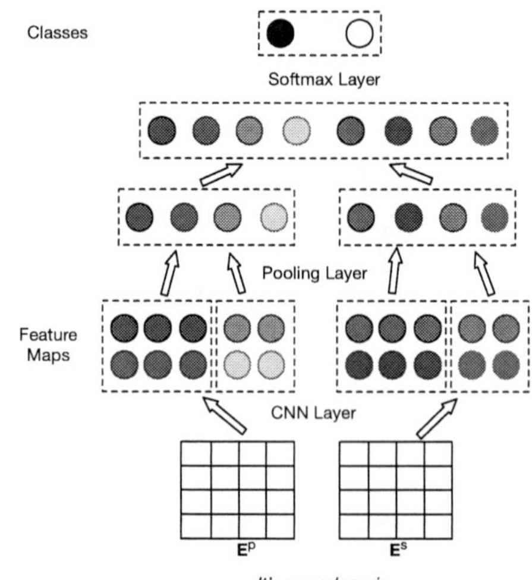

Figure 2: Proposed two-channel model. The first channel input is a standard pre-trained embedding matrix. The second channel receives a partially shared embedding matrix constructed using external linguistic resources.

(hash) the index j to one of the K group IDs: $h^i : \mathbb{N} \to \{g_1^{(i)}, g_2^{(i)} ... g_K^{(i)}\}$. Following (Weinberger et al., 2009; Shi et al., 2009), we use a second hash function b to remove bias induced by hashing. This is a signing function, i.e., it maps (i, j) tuples to $\{+1, -1\}$ [2]. We then set $\mathbf{e}_{i,j}$ to the product of $\mathbf{g}_{h^i(j),j}$ and $b(i, j)$. h and b are both approximately uniform hash functions. **Algorithm** 1 provides the full initialization procedure.

Algorithm 1 Initialization of $\mathbf{E}^s$

1: **for** i in $\{1, \ldots, V\}$ **do**
2:     $\{g_1^{(i)}, g_2^{(i)}, \ldots, g_K^{(i)}\} := G(i)$.
3:     **for** $j \in \{1, \ldots, d\}$ **do**
4:         $\mathbf{e}_{i,j} := \mathbf{g}_{h^i(j),j} \cdot b(i, j)$
5:     **end for**
6: **end for**

For illustration, consider Figure 1. Here g_1 contains three words: *good*, *nice* and *amazing*, while g_2 has two words: *good* and *interesting*. The group embeddings $\mathbf{g}_{g_1}$, $\mathbf{g}_{g_2}$ are initialized as averages over the pre-trained embeddings of the words they comprise. Here, embedding parameters $\mathbf{e}_{1,1}$ and $\mathbf{e}_{2,1}$ are both mapped to $\mathbf{g}_{g_1,1}$, and thus share this value. Similarly, $\mathbf{e}_{1,3}$ and $\mathbf{e}_{2,3}$ will share value at $\mathbf{g}_{g_1,3}$. We have elided the second hash function b from this figure for simplicity.

---

[1] The idea of sharing weights to reflect known similarity is general and could be applied with other neural architectures.

[2] Empirically, we found that using this signing function does not affect performance.

During training, we update $\mathbf{E}^p$ as usual using back-propagation (Rumelhart et al., 1986). We update $\mathbf{E}^s$ and group embeddings $\mathbf{g}$ in a manner similar to Chen et al. (2015). In the forward propagation before each training step (mini-batch), we derive the value of $\mathbf{e}_{i,j}$ from $\mathbf{g}$:

$$\mathbf{e}_{i,j} \coloneqq \mathbf{g}_{h^i(j),j} * b(i,j) \qquad (1)$$

We use this newly updated $\mathbf{e}_{i,j}$ to perform forward propagation in the CNN.

During backward propagation, we first compute the gradient of $\mathbf{E}^s$, and then we use this to derive the gradient w.r.t $\mathbf{g}s$. To do this, for each dimension j in $\mathbf{g}_{g_k}$, we aggregate the gradients w.r.t $\mathbf{E}^s$ whose elements are mapped to this dimension:

$$\nabla \mathbf{g}_{g_k,j} \coloneqq \sum_{(i,j)} \nabla \mathbf{E}^s_{i,j} \cdot \delta_{h^i(j)=g_k} \cdot b(i,j) \qquad (2)$$

where $\delta_{h^i(j)=g_k} = 1$ when $h^i(j) = g_k$, and 0 otherwise. Each training step involves executing Equations 1 and 2. Once the shared gradient is calculated, gradient descent proceeds as usual. We update all parameters aside from the shared weights in the standard way.

The number of parameters in our approach scales linearly with the number of channels. But the gradients can actually be back-propagated in a distributed way for each channel, since the convolutional and embedding layers are independent across these. Thus training time scales approximately linearly with the number of parameters in one channel (if the gradient is back-propagated in a distributed way).

3 Experimental Setup

3.1 Datasets

We use three sentiment datasets: a movie review (**MR**) dataset (Pang and Lee, 2005)[3]; a customer review (**CR**) dataset (Hu and Liu, 2004)[4]; and an opinion dataset (**MPQA**) (Wiebe et al., 2005)[5].

We also use four biomedical datasets, which concern *systematic reviews*. The task here is to classify published articles describing clinical trials as *relevant* or *not* to a well-specified clinical question. Articles deemed relevant are included in the corresponding review, which is a synthesis of all pertinent evidence (Wallace et al., 2010). We use data from reviews that concerned: clopidogrel (CL) for cardiovascular conditions (Dahabreh et al., 2013); biomarkers for assessing iron deficiency in anemia (AN) experienced by patients with kidney disease (Chung et al., 2012); statins (ST) (Cohen et al., 2006); and proton beam (PB) therapy (Terasawa et al., 2009).

3.2 Implementation Details and Baselines

We use SentiWordNet (Baccianella et al., 2010)[6] for the sentiment tasks. SentiWordNet assigns to each synset of wordnet three sentiment scores: positivity, negativity and objectivity, constrained to sum to 1. We keep only the synsets with positivity or negativity scores greater than 0, i.e., we remove synsets deemed objective. The synsets in SentiWordNet constitute our groups. We also use the Brown clustering algorithm[7] on the three sentiment datasets. We generate 1000 clusters and treat each as a group.

For the biomedical datasets, we use the Medical Subject Headings (MeSH) terms[8] attached to each abstract to classify them. Each MeSH term has a tree number indicating the path from the root in the UMLS. For example, 'Alagille Syndrome' has tree number 'C06.552.150.125'; periods denote tree splits, numbers are nodes. We induce groups comprising MeSH terms that share the same first three parent nodes, e.g., all terms with 'C06.552.150' as their tree number prefix constitute one group.

We compare our approach to several baselines. All use pre-trained embeddings to initialize $\mathbf{E}^p$, but we explore several approaches to exploiting $\mathbf{E}^s$: (1) randomly initialize $\mathbf{E}^s$; (2) initialize $\mathbf{E}^s$ to reflect the group embedding $\mathbf{g}$, but do not share weights during the training process, i.e., do not constrain their weights to be equal when we perform back-propagation; (3) use linguistic resources to *retro-fit* (Faruqui et al., 2014) the pre-trained embeddings, and use these to initialize $\mathbf{E}^s$. For *retro-fitting*, we first construct a graph derived from SentiWordNet. Then we run belief-propagation on the graph to encourage linked words to have similar vectors. This is a preprocessing step only; we do not impose weight sharing constraints during training.

---

[3]www.cs.cornell.edu/people/pabo/movie-review-data/
[4]www.cs.uic.edu/~liub/FBS/sentiment-analysis.html
[5]mpqa.cs.pitt.edu/corpora/mpqa_corpus/
[6]sentiwordnet.isti.cnr.it
[7]github.com/percyliang/brown-cluster
[8]www.nlm.nih.gov/bsd/disted/meshtutorial/

	total #instances	vocabulary size	#positive instances	#negative instances
MR	10662	18765	5331	5331
CR	3773	5340	2406	1367
MPQA	10604	6246	3311	7293
AN	5653	5554	653	5000
CL	8288	3684	768	7520
ST	3464	2965	173	3291
PB	4749	3086	243	4506

Table 1: Corpora statistics.

For the sentiment datasets we use three filter heights (3,4,5) for each of the two CNN channels. For the biomedical datasets, we use only one filter height (1), because the inputs are unstructured MeSH terms.[9] In both cases we use 100 filters of each unique height. For the sentiment datasets, we use Google word2vec (Mikolov et al., 2013)[10] to initialize E^p. For the biomedical datasets, we use word2vec trained on biomedical texts (Moen and Ananiadou, 2013)[11] to initialize E^p. For parameter estimation, we use Adadelta (Zeiler, 2012). Because the biomedical datasets are imbalanced, we use downsampling (Zhang et al., 2016a; Zhang and Wallace, 2015) to effectively train on balanced subsets of the data.

We developed our approach using the MR sentiment dataset, tuning our approach to constructing groups from the available resources – experiments on other sentiment datasets were run after we finalized the model and hyperparameters. Similarly, we used the anemia (AN) review as a development set for the biomedical tasks, especially w.r.t. constructing groups from MeSH terms using UMLS.

4 Results

We replicate each experiment five times (each is a 10-fold cross validation), and report the mean (min, max) across these replications. Results on the sentiment and biomedical corpora in are presented in Tables 2 and 3, respectively.[12] These exploit different external resources to induce the word groupings that in turn inform weight sharing. We report AUC for the biomedical datasets because these are highly imbalanced (see Table 1).

Our method improves performance compared to all relevant baselines (including an approach that also exploits external knowledge via retrofitting) in six of seven cases. Informing weight *initialization* using external resources improves performance independently, but additional gains are realized by also enforcing sharing during training.

We note that our aim here is not necessarily to achieve state-of-art results on any given dataset, but rather to evaluate the proposed method for incorporating external linguistic resources into neural models via weight sharing. We have therefore compared to baselines that enable us to assess this.

5 Related Work

Neural Models for NLP. Recently there has been enormous interest in neural models for NLP generally (Collobert et al., 2011; Goldberg, 2016). Most relevant to this work, simple CNN based models (which we have built on here) have proven extremely effective for text categorization (Kim, 2014; Zhang and Wallace, 2015).

Exploiting Linguistic Resources. A potential drawback to learning from scratch in end-to-end neural models is a failure to capitalize on existing knowledge sources. There have been efforts to exploit such resources specifically to induce better word vectors (Yu and Dredze, 2014; Faruqui et al., 2014; Yu et al., 2016; Xu et al., 2014). But these models do not attempt to exploit external resources jointly during training for a particular downstream task (which uses word embeddings as inputs), as we do here.

Past work on sparse linear models has shown the potential of exploiting linguistic knowledge in statistical NLP models. For example, Yogatama and Smith (2014) used external resources to inform structured, grouped regularization of log-linear text classification models, yielding improvements over standard regularization approaches. Elsewhere, Doshi-Velez et al. (2015) proposed a variant of LDA that exploits *a priori* known tree-

---

[9] For this work we are ignoring title and abstract texts.

[10] `code.google.com/archive/p/word2vec/`

[11] `bio.nlplab.org/`

[12] Sentiment task results are not directly comparable to prior work due to different preprocessing steps.

Method	MR	CR	MPQA
p only	81.02 (80.84,81.24)	84.34 (84.21,84.53)	89.41 (89.22,89.58)
p + r	81.25 (81.19,81.32)	84.33 (84.24,84.38)	89.63 (89.58,89.71)
p + retro	81.35 (81.23,81.51)	84.16 (84.09,84.28)	89.61 (89.48,89.77)
p + S (no sharing)	81.39 (81.32,81.43)	84.13 (84.06,84.21)	89.71 (89.67,89.75)
p + B (no sharing)	81.50 (81.29,81.63)	84.60 (84.53,84.66)	89.57 (89.52,89.61)
p + S (sharing)	81.69 (81.60,81.78)	84.34 (84.24,84.43)	89.84 (89.74,90.13)
p + B (sharing)	**81.83 (81.80,81.87)**	**84.68 (84.64,84.72)**	**89.97 (89.74,90.13)**

Table 2: Accuracy mean (min, max) on sentiment datasets. 'p': channel initialized with the pre-trained embeddings E^p. 'r': channel randomly initialized. 'retro': initialized with retofitted embeddings. 'S/B (no sharing)': channel initialized with E^s (using SentiWordNet or Brown clusters), but weights are not shared during training. 'S/B (sharing)': proposed weight-sharing method.

Method	AN	CL	ST	PB
p only	86.63 (86.57,86.67)	88.73 (88.51,89.00)	67.15 (66.00, 67.91)	90.11 (89.46, 91.03)
p + r	85.67 (85.46,85.95)	88.87 (88.56,89.03)	67.72 (67.65,67.86)	90.12 (89.87,90.47)
p + retro	86.46 (86.32,86.65)	89.27 (88.89,90.01)	**67.78 (67.56,68.00)**	90.07 (89.92,90.20)
p + U	86.60 (86.32,87.01)	88.93 (88.67,89.13)	67.78 (67.71,67.85)	90.23 (89.84,90.47)
p + U(s)	**87.15 (87.00,87.29)**	**89.29 (89.09,89.51)**	67.73 (67.58,67.88)	**90.99 (90.46,91.59)**

Table 3: AUC mean (min, max) on the biomedical datasets. Abbreviations are as in Table 2, except here the external resource is the UMLS MeSH ontology ('U'). 'U(s)' is the proposed weight sharing method utilizing ULMS.

structured relations between tokens (e.g., derived from the UMLS) in topic modeling.

Weight-sharing in NNs. Recent work has considered stochastically sharing weights in neural models. Notably, Chen et al. (2015). proposed randomly sharing weights in neural networks. Elsewhere, Han et al. (2015) proposed quantized weight sharing as an intermediate step in their deep compression model. In these works, the primary motivation was *model compression*, whereas here we view the hashing trick as a mechanism to encode domain knowledge.

6 Conclusion

We have proposed a novel method for incorporating prior semantic knowledge into neural models via stochastic weight sharing. We have showed it generally improves text classification performance vs. model variants which do not exploit external resources and vs. an approach based on retrofitting prior to training. In future work, we will investigate generalizing our approach beyond classification, and to inform weight sharing using other varieties and sources of linguistic knowledge.

Acknowledgements. This work was made possible by NPRP grant NPRP 7-1313-1-245 from the Qatar National Research Fund (a member of Qatar Foundation). The statements made herein are solely the responsibility of the authors.

References

Stefano Baccianella, Andrea Esuli, and Fabrizio Sebastiani. 2010. Sentiwordnet 3.0: An enhanced lexical resource for sentiment analysis and opinion mining. In *LREC*. volume 10, pages 2200–2204.

Olivier Bodenreider. 2004. The unified medical language system (umls): integrating biomedical terminology. *Nucleic acids research* 32(suppl 1):D267–D270.

Peter F Brown, Peter V Desouza, Robert L Mercer, Vincent J Della Pietra, and Jenifer C Lai. 1992. Class-based n-gram models of natural language. *Computational linguistics* 18(4):467–479.

Wenlin Chen, James T Wilson, Stephen Tyree, Kilian Q Weinberger, and Yixin Chen. 2015. Compressing neural networks with the hashing trick. In *ICML*. pages 2285–2294.

Mei Chung, Denish Moorthy, Nira Hadar, Priyanka Salvi, Ramon C Iovin, and Joseph Lau. 2012. *Biomarkers for Assessing and Managing Iron Deficiency Anemia in Late-Stage Chronic Kidney Disease*. AHRQ Comparative Effectiveness Reviews. Agency for Healthcare Research and Quality (US), Rockville (MD).

Aaron M Cohen, William R Hersh, K Peterson, and Po-Yin Yen. 2006. Reducing workload in systematic review preparation using automated citation classification. *Journal of the American Medical Informatics Association* 13(2):206–219.

Ronan Collobert, Jason Weston, Léon Bottou, Michael Karlen, Koray Kavukcuoglu, and Pavel Kuksa. 2011. Natural language processing (almost) from scratch. *Journal of Machine Learning Research* 12(Aug):2493–2537.

Issa J Dahabreh, Denish Moorthy, Jenny L Lamont, Minghua L Chen, David M Kent, and Joseph Lau. 2013. Testing of cyp2c19 variants and platelet reactivity for guiding antiplatelet treatment .

Finale Doshi-Velez, Byron C Wallace, and Ryan Adams. 2015. Graph-sparse lda: A topic model with structured sparsity. In *AAAI Conference on Artificial Intelligence*. pages 2575–2581.

Manaal Faruqui, Jesse Dodge, Sujay K Jauhar, Chris Dyer, Eduard Hovy, and Noah A Smith. 2014. Retrofitting word vectors to semantic lexicons. *arXiv preprint arXiv:1411.4166* .

Yoav Goldberg. 2016. A primer on neural network models for natural language processing. *Journal of Artificial Intelligence Research* 57:345–420.

Song Han, Huizi Mao, and William J Dally. 2015. Deep compression: Compressing deep neural networks with pruning, trained quantization and huffman coding. *arXiv preprint arXiv:1510.00149* .

Minqing Hu and Bing Liu. 2004. Mining and summarizing customer reviews. In *Proceedings of the 10th ACM SIGKDD international conference on Knowledge discovery and data mining*. pages 168–177.

Yoon Kim. 2014. Convolutional neural networks for sentence classification. *arXiv preprint arXiv:1408.5882* .

Tomas Mikolov, Kai Chen, Greg Corrado, and Jeffrey Dean. 2013. Efficient estimation of word representations in vector space. *arXiv preprint arXiv:1301.3781* .

George A Miller. 1995. Wordnet: a lexical database for english. *Communications of the ACM* 38(11):39–41.

SPFGH Moen and Tapio Salakoski2 Sophia Ananiadou. 2013. Distributional semantics resources for biomedical text processing.

Bo Pang and Lillian Lee. 2005. Seeing stars: Exploiting class relationships for sentiment categorization with respect to rating scales. In *Proc. of the ACL*.

D.E. Rumelhart, G.E. Hintont, and R.J. Williams. 1986. Learning representations by back-propagating errors. *Nature* 323(6088):533–536.

Qinfeng Shi, James Petterson, Gideon Dror, John Langford, Alex Smola, and SVN Vishwanathan. 2009. Hash kernels for structured data. *Journal of Machine Learning Research* 10(Nov):2615–2637.

T. Terasawa, T. Dvorak, S. Ip, G. Raman, J. Lau, and T. A. Trikalinos. 2009. Charged Particle Radiation Therapy for Cancer: A Systematic Review. *Ann. Intern. Med.* .

Byron C Wallace, Thomas A Trikalinos, Joseph Lau, Carla Brodley, and Christopher H Schmid. 2010. Semi-automated screening of biomedical citations for systematic reviews. *BMC bioinformatics* 11(1):55.

Kilian Weinberger, Anirban Dasgupta, John Langford, Alex Smola, and Josh Attenberg. 2009. Feature hashing for large scale multitask learning. In *Proceedings of the 26th Annual International Conference on Machine Learning*. pages 1113–1120.

Janyce Wiebe, Theresa Wilson, and Claire Cardie. 2005. Annotating expressions of opinions and emotions in language. *Language resources and evaluation* 39(2):165–210.

Chang Xu, Yalong Bai, Jiang Bian, Bin Gao, Gang Wang, Xiaoguang Liu, and Tie-Yan Liu. 2014. Rc-net: A general framework for incorporating knowledge into word representations. In *Proceedings of the 23rd ACM International Conference on Conference on Information and Knowledge Management*. ACM, pages 1219–1228.

Dani Yogatama and Noah A Smith. 2014. Linguistic structured sparsity in text categorization. In *Meeting of the Association for Computational Linguistics*. pages 786–796.

Mo Yu and Mark Dredze. 2014. Improving lexical embeddings with semantic knowledge. In *ACL*. pages 545–550.

Zhiguo Yu, Trevor Cohen, Elmer V Bernstam, and Byron C Wallace. 2016. Retrofitting word vectors of mesh terms to improve semantic similarity measures. *Intl. Workshop on Health Text Mining and Information Analysis at EMNLP* pages 43–51.

Matthew D. Zeiler. 2012. Adadelta: An adaptive learning rate method.

Ye Zhang, Iain Marshall, and Byron C Wallace. 2016a. Rationale-augmented convolutional neural networks for text classification. *arXiv preprint arXiv:1605.04469* .

Ye Zhang, Stephen Roller, and Byron C Wallace. 2016b. MGNC-CNN: A simple approach to exploiting multiple word embeddings for sentence classification pages 1522–1527.

Ye Zhang and Byron C Wallace. 2015. A sensitivity analysis of (and practitioners' guide to) convolutional neural networks for sentence classification. *arXiv preprint arXiv:1510.03820* .

Improving Neural Parsing by
Disentangling Model Combination and Reranking Effects

Daniel Fried[*] **Mitchell Stern**[*] **Dan Klein**

Computer Science Division
University of California, Berkeley
{dfried,mitchell,klein}@cs.berkeley.edu

Abstract

Recent work has proposed several generative neural models for constituency parsing that achieve state-of-the-art results. Since direct search in these generative models is difficult, they have primarily been used to rescore candidate outputs from base parsers in which decoding is more straightforward. We first present an algorithm for direct search in these generative models. We then demonstrate that the rescoring results are at least partly due to implicit model combination rather than reranking effects. Finally, we show that explicit model combination can improve performance even further, resulting in new state-of-the-art numbers on the PTB of 94.25 F1 when training only on gold data and 94.66 F1 when using external data.

1 Introduction

Recent work on neural constituency parsing (Dyer et al., 2016; Choe and Charniak, 2016) has found multiple cases where generative *scoring models* for which inference is complex outperform *base models* for which inference is simpler. Let A be a parser that we want to parse with (here one of the generative models), and let B be a base parser that we use to propose candidate parses which are then scored by the less-tractable parser A. We denote this cross-scoring setup by B → A. The papers above repeatedly saw that the cross-scoring setup B → A under which their generative models were applied outperformed the standard single-parser setup B → B. We term this a *cross-scoring gain*.

This paper asks two questions. First, *why* do recent discriminative-to-generative cross-scoring se-

tups B → A outperform their base parsers B? Perhaps generative models A are simply superior to the base models B and direct generative parsing (A → A) would be better still if it were feasible. If so, we would characterize the cross-scoring gain from B → B to B → A as a *reranking gain*. However, it's also possible that the hybrid system B → A shows gains merely from subtle model combination effects. If so, scoring candidates using some combined score A + B would be even better, which we would characterize as a *model combination gain*. It might even be the case that B is a better parser overall (i.e. B → B outperforms A → A).

Of course, many real hybrids will exhibit both reranking and model combination gains. In this paper, we present experiments to isolate the degree to which each gain occurs for each of two state-of-the-art generative neural parsing models: the Recurrent Neural Network Grammar generative parser (RG) of Dyer et al. (2016), and the LSTM language modeling generative parser (LM) of Choe and Charniak (2016).

In particular, we present and use a beam-based search procedure with an augmented state space that can search directly in the generative models, allowing us to explore A → A for these generative parsers A independent of any base parsers. Our findings suggest the presence of model combination effects in both generative parsers: when parses found by searching directly in the generative parser are added to a list of candidates from a strong base parser (the RNNG discriminative parser, RD (Dyer et al., 2016)), performance decreases when compared to using just candidates from the base parser, i.e., B ∪ A → A has lower evaluation performance than B → A (Section 3.1).

This result suggests that both generative models benefit from fortuitous search errors in the rescoring setting – there are trees with higher probability

---

[*]Equal contribution.

Proceedings of the 55th Annual Meeting of the Association for Computational Linguistics (Short Papers), pages 161–166
Vancouver, Canada, July 30 - August 4, 2017. ©2017 Association for Computational Linguistics
https://doi.org/10.18653/v1/P17-2025

under the generative model than any tree proposed by the base parser, but which would decrease evaluation performance if selected. Because of this, we hypothesize that model combination effects between the base and generative models are partially responsible for the high performance of the generative reranking systems, rather than the generative model being generally superior.

Here we consider our second question: if cross-scoring gains are at least partly due to implicit model combination, can we gain even more by combining the models explicitly? We find that this is indeed the case: simply taking a weighted average of the scores of both models when selecting a parse from the base parser's candidate list improves over using only the score of the generative model, in many cases substantially (Section 3.2). Using this technique, in combination with ensembling, we obtain new state-of-the-art results on the Penn Treebank: 94.25 F1 when training only on gold parse trees and 94.66 F1 when using external silver data.

2 Decoding in generative neural models

All of the parsers we investigate in this work (the discriminative parser RD, and the two generative parsers RG and LM, see Section 1) produce parse trees in a depth-first, left-to-right traversal, using the same basic *actions*: NT(X), which opens a new constituent with the non-terminal symbol X; SHIFT / GEN(w), which adds a word; and RE-DUCE, which closes the current constituent. We refer to Dyer et al. (2016) for a complete description of these actions, and the constraints on them necessary to ensure valid parse trees.[1]

The primary difference between the actions in the discriminative and generative models is that, whereas the discriminative model uses a SHIFT action which is fixed to produce the next word in the sentence, the generative models use GEN(w) to define a distribution over all possible words w in the lexicon. This stems from the generative model's definition of a joint probability $p(x, y)$ over all possible sentences x and parses y. To use a generative model as a parser, we are interested in finding the maximum probability parse for a given sentence. This is made more complicated by not

having an explicit representation for $p(y|x)$, as we do in the discriminative setting. However, we can start by applying similar approximate search procedures as are used for the discriminative parser, constraining the set of actions such that it is only possible to produce the observed sentence: i.e. only allow a GEN(w) action when w is the next terminal in the sentence, and prohibit GEN actions if all terminals have been produced.

2.1 Action-synchronous beam search

Past work on discriminative neural constituency parsers has shown the effectiveness of beam search with a small beam (Vinyals et al., 2015) or even greedy search, as in the case of RD (Dyer et al., 2016). The standard beam search procedure, which we refer to as *action-synchronous*, maintains a beam of K partially-completed parses that all have the same number of actions taken. At each stage, a pool of successors is constructed by extending each candidate in the beam with each of its possible next actions. The K highest-probability successors are chosen as the next beam.

Unfortunately, we find that action-synchronous beam search breaks down for both generative models we explore in this work, failing to find parses that are high scoring under the model. This stems from the probabilities of the actions NT(X) for all labels X almost always being greater than the probability of GEN(w) for the particular word w which must be produced next in a given sentence. Qualitatively, the search procedure prefers to open constituents repeatedly up until the maximum number allowed by the model. While these long chains of non-terminals will usually have lower probability than the correct sequence at the point where they finally generate the next word, they often have higher probability up until the word is generated, and so they tend to push the correct sequence off the beam before this point is reached. This search failure produces very low evaluation performance: with a beam of size $K = 100$, action-synchronous beam search achieves 29.1 F1 for RG and 27.4 F1 for LM on the development set.

2.2 Word-synchronous beam search

To deal with this issue, we force partial parse candidates to compete with each other on a word-by-word level, rather than solely on the level of individual actions. The *word-synchronous* beam search we apply is very similar to approximate

---

[1] The action space for LM differs from RG in two ways: 1) LM has separate reduce actions REDUCE(X) for each non-terminal X, and 2) LM allows any action to have non-zero probability at all times, even those that may be structurally invalid.

model	Word-synchronous beam size, K_w					
	10	20	40	60	80	100
RG	74.1	80.1	85.3	87.5	88.7	89.6
LM	83.7	88.6	90.9	91.6	92.0	92.2

Table 1: F1 on the development set for word-synchronous beam search when searching in the RNNG generative (RG) and LSTM generative (LM) models. K_a is set to $10 \times K_w$.

decoding procedures developed for other generative models (Henderson, 2003; Titov and Henderson, 2010; Buys and Blunsom, 2015) and can be viewed as a simplified version of the procedure used in the generative top-down parsers of Roark (2001) and Charniak (2010).

In word-synchronous search, we augment the beam state space, identifying beams by tuples $(|W|, |A_w|)$, where $|W|$ is the number of words that have been produced so far in the sentence, and $|A_w|$ is the number of structural actions that have been taken since the last word was produced. Intuitively, we want candidates with the same $|W| = w$ to compete against each other. For a beam of partial parses in the state $(|W| = w, |A_w| = a)$, we generate a beam of successors by taking all of the next possible actions for each partial parse in the beam. If the action is NT(X) or REDUCE, we place the resulting partial parse in the beam for state $(|W| = w, |A_w| = a + 1)$; otherwise, if the action is GEN, we place it in a list for $(|W| = w + 1, |A_w| = 0)$. After all partial parses in the beam have been processed, we check to see if there are a sufficient number of partial parses that have produced the next word: if the beam $(|W| = w + 1, |A_w| = 0)$ contains at least K_w partial parses (the *word beam size*), we prune it to this size and continue search using this beam. Otherwise, we continue building candidates for this word by pruning the beam $(|W| = w, |A_w| = a + 1)$ to size K_a (the *action beam size*), and continuing search from there.

In practice, we found it to be most effective to use a value for K_w that is a fraction of the value for K_a. In all the experiments we present here, we fix $K_a = 10 \times K_w$, with K_w ranging from 10 to 100. Table 1 shows F1 for decoding in both generative models on the development set, using the top-scoring parse found for a sentence when searching with the given beam size. RG has comparatively larger gains in performance between the larger beam sizes, while still underperforming LM, suggesting that more search is necessary in this model.

3 Experiments

Using the above decoding procedures, we attempt to separate reranking effects from model combination effects through a set of reranking experiments. Our base experiments are performed on the Penn Treebank (Marcus et al., 1993), using sections 2-21 for training, section 22 for development, and section 23 for testing. For the LSTM generative model (LM), we use the pre-trained model released by Choe and Charniak (2016). We train RNNG discriminative (RD) and generative (RG) models, following Dyer et al. (2016) by using the same hyperparameter settings, and using pre-trained word embeddings from Ling et al. (2015) for the discriminative model. The automatically-predicted part-of-speech tags we use as input for RD are the same as those used by Cross and Huang (2016).

In each experiment, we obtain a set of candidate parses for each sentence by performing beam search in one or more parsers. We use action-synchronous beam search (Section 2.1) with beam size $K = 100$ for RD and word-synchronous beam (Section 2.2) with $K_w = 100$ and $K_a = 1000$ for the generative models RG and LM.

In the case that we are using only the scores from a single generative model to rescore candidates taken from the discriminative parser, this setup is close to the reranking procedures originally proposed for these generative models. For RG, the original work also used RD to produce candidates, but drew samples from it, whereas we use a beam search to approximate its k-best list. The LM generative model was originally used to rerank a 50-best list taken from the Charniak parser (Charniak, 2000). In comparison, we found higher performance for the LM model when using a candidate list from the RD parser: 93.66 F1 versus 92.79 F1 on the development data. This may be attributable to having a stronger set of candidates: with beam size 100, RD has an oracle F1 of 98.2, compared to 95.9 for the 50-best list from the Charniak parser.

3.1 Augmenting the candidate set

We first experiment with combining the candidate lists from multiple models, which allows us to look for potential model errors and model combination effects. Consider the standard reranking setup B → A, where we search in B to get a set of candidate parses for each sentence, and

| | Scoring models | | |
Candidates	RD	RG	RD + RG
RD	92.22	93.45	93.87
RG	90.24	89.55	90.53
RD ∪ RG	92.22	92.78	93.92

| | Scoring models | | |
Candidates	RD	LM	RD + LM
RD	92.22	93.66	93.99
LM	92.57	92.20	93.07
RD ∪ LM	92.24	93.47	94.15

Table 2: Development F1 scores on section 22 of the PTB when using various models to produce candidates and to score them. ∪ denotes taking the union of candidates from each of two models; + denotes using a weighted average of the models' log-probabilities.

choose the top scoring candidate from these under A. We extend this by also searching directly in A to find high-scoring candidates for each sentence, and combining them with the candidate list proposed by B by taking the union, A ∪ B. We then choose the highest scoring candidate from this list under A. If A generally prefers parses outside of the candidate list from B, but these decrease evaluation performance (i.e., if B ∪ A → A is worse than B → A), this suggests a model combination effect is occurring: A makes errors which are hidden by having a limited candidate list from B.

This does seem to be the case for both generative models, as shown in Table 2, which presents F1 scores on the development set when varying the models used to produce the candidates and to score them. Each row is a different candidate set, where the third row in each table presents results for the augmented candidate sets; each column is a different scoring model, where the third column is the *score combination* setting described below. Going from RD → RG to the augmented candidate setting RD ∪ RG → RG decreases performance from 93.45 F1 to 92.78 F1 on the development set. This difference is statistically significant at the $p < 0.05$ level under a paired bootstrap test. We see a smaller, but still significant, effect in the case of LM: RD → LM achieves 93.66, compared to 93.47 for RD ∪ LM → LM.

We can also consider the performance of RG → RG and LM → LM (where we do not use candidates from RD at all, but return the highest-scoring parse from searching directly in one of the generative models) as an indicator of reranking effects: absolute performance is higher for LM (92.20 F1) than for RG (89.55). Taken together,

these results suggest that model combination contributes to the success of both models, but to a larger extent for RG. A reranking effect may be a larger contributor to the success of LM, as this model achieves stronger performance on its own for the described search setting.

3.2 Score combination

If the cross-scoring setup exhibits an implicit model combination effect, where strong performance results from searching in one model and scoring with the other, we might expect substantial further improvements in performance by explicitly combining the scores of both models. To do so, we score each parse by taking a weighted sum of the log-probabilities assigned by both models (Hayashi et al., 2013), using an interpolation parameter which we tune to maximize F1 on the development set.

These results are given in columns RD + RG and RD + LM in Table 2. We find that combining the scores of both models improves on using the score of either model alone, regardless of the source of candidates. These improvements are statistically significant in all cases. Score combination also more than compensates for the decrease in performance we saw previously when adding in candidates from the generative model: RD ∪ RG → RD + RG improves upon both RD → RG and RD ∪ RG → RG, and the same effect holds for LM.

3.3 Strengthening model combination

Given the success of model combination between the base model and a single generative model, we also investigate the hypothesis that the generative models are complementary. The Model Combination block of Table 3 shows full results on the test set for these experiments, in the PTB column. The same trends we observed on the development data, on which the interpolation parameters were tuned, hold here: score combination improves results for all models (row 3 vs. row 2; row 6 vs. row 5), with candidate augmentation from the generative models giving a further increase (rows 4 and 7).[2] Combining candidates and scores from all three models (row 9), we obtain 93.94 F1.

---

[2]These increases, from adding score combination and candidate augmentation, are all significant with $p < 0.05$ in the PTB setting. In the +S data setting, all are significant except for the difference between row 5 and row 6.

Model	PTB	+S
Liu and Zhang (2017)	91.7	–
Dyer et al. (2016)-discriminative	91.7	–
Dyer et al. (2016)-generative	93.3	–
Choe and Charniak (2016)	92.6	93.8
Model Combination		
1) RD → RD	91.51	91.73
2) RD → RG	92.73	93.29
3) RD → RD + RG	93.27	93.64
4) RD ∪ RG → RD + RG	93.45	93.75
5) RD → LM	93.31	94.18
6) RD → RD + LM	93.71	94.27
7) RD ∪ LM → RD + LM	93.89	94.63
8) RD → RD + RG + LM	93.63	94.33
9) RD ∪ RG ∪ LM → RD + RG + LM	**93.94**	**94.66**
Ensembling		
10) RD (8) → RD (8)	92.72	92.53
11) RD (8) → RD (8) + RG (8)	94.09	94.22
12) RD (8) → RD (8) + LM	93.97	94.56
13) RD (8) → RD (8) + RG (8) + LM	**94.25**	**94.62**

Table 3: Test F1 scores on section 23 of the PTB, by tree-bank training data conditions: either using only the training sections of the PTB, or using additional silver data (+S).

Semi-supervised silver data Choe and Charniak (2016) found a substantial increase in performance by training on external data in addition to trees from the Penn Treebank. This *silver dataset* was obtained by parsing the entire New York Times section of the fifth Gigaword corpus using a product of eight Berkeley parsers (Petrov, 2010) and ZPar (Zhu et al., 2013), then retaining 24 million sentences on which both parsers agreed. For our experiments we train RD and RG using the same silver dataset.[3] The +S column in Table 3 shows these results, where we observe gains over the PTB models in nearly every case. As in the PTB training data setting, using all models for candidates and score combinations is best, achieving 94.66 F1 (row 9).

Ensembling Finally, we compare to another commonly used model combination method: ensembling multiple instances of the same model type trained from different random initializations. We train ensembles of 8 copies each of RD and RG in both the PTB and silver data settings, combining scores from models within an ensemble by

averaging the models' distributions for each action (in beam search as well as rescoring). These results are shown in the bottom section, Ensembling, of Table 3.

Performance when using only the ensembled RD models (row 10) is lower than rescoring a single RD model with score combinations of single models, either RD + RG (row 3) or RD + LM (row 6). In the PTB setting, ensembling with score combination achieves the best overall result of 94.25 (row 13). In the silver training data setting, while this does improve on the analogous unensembled result (row 8), it is not better than the combination of single models when candidates from the generative models are also included (row 9).

4 Discussion

Searching directly in the generative models yields results that are partly surprising, as it reveals the presence of parses which the generative models prefer, but which lead to lower performance than the candidates proposed by the base model. However, the results are also unsurprising in the sense that explicitly combining scores allows the reranking setup to achieve better performance than implicit combination, which uses only the scores of a single model. Additionally, we see support for the hypothesis that the generative models can achieve good results on their own, with the LSTM generative model showing particularly strong and self-contained performance.

While this search procedure allows us to explore these generative models, disentangling reranking and model combination effects, the increase in performance from augmenting the candidate lists with the results of the search may not be worth the required computational cost in a practical parser. However, we do obtain a gain over state-of-the-art results using simple model score combination on only the base candidates, which can be implemented with minimal cost over the basic reranking setup. This provides a concrete improvement for these particular generative reranking procedures for parsing. More generally, it supports the idea that hybrid systems, which rely on one model to produce a set of candidates and another to determine which candidates are good, should explore combining their scores and candidates when possible.

---

[3]When training with silver data, we use a 1-to-1 ratio of silver data updates per gold data updates, which we found to give significantly faster convergence times on development set perplexity for RD and RG compared to the 10-to-1 ratio used by Choe and Charniak (2016) for LM.

Acknowledgments

We would like to thank Adhiguna Kuncoro and Do Kook Choe for their help providing data and answering questions about their work, as well as Jacob Andreas, John DeNero, and the anonymous reviewers for their suggestions. DF is supported by an NDSEG fellowship. MS is supported by an NSF Graduate Research Fellowship.

References

Jan Buys and Phil Blunsom. 2015. Generative incremental dependency parsing with neural networks. In *Proceedings of the Annual Meeting of the Association for Computational Linguistics*.

Eugene Charniak. 2000. A maximum-entropy-inspired parser. In *Proceedings of the Annual Meeting of the North American Chapter of the Association for Computational Linguistics*.

Eugene Charniak. 2010. Top-down nearly-context-sensitive parsing. In *Proceedings of the Conference on Empirical Methods in Natural Language Processing*.

Do Kook Choe and Eugene Charniak. 2016. Parsing as language modeling. In *Proceedings of the Conference on Empirical Methods in Natural Language Processing*.

James Cross and Liang Huang. 2016. Span-based constituency parsing with a structure-label system and provably optimal dynamic oracles. In *Proceedings of the Conference on Empirical Methods in Natural Language Processing*.

Chris Dyer, Adhiguna Kuncoro, Miguel Ballesteros, and Noah A Smith. 2016. Recurrent neural network grammars. In *Proceedings of the Annual Meeting of the North American Chapter of the Association for Computational Linguistics*.

Katsuhiko Hayashi, Shuhei Kondo, and Yuji Matsumoto. 2013. Efficient stacked dependency parsing by forest reranking. *Transactions of the Association for Computational Linguistics* 1:139–150.

James Henderson. 2003. Inducing history representations for broad coverage statistical parsing. In *Proceedings of the Human Language Technology Conference of the North American Chapter of the Association for Computational Linguistics*.

Wang Ling, Chris Dyer, Alan Black, and Isabel Trancoso. 2015. Two/too simple adaptations of word2vec for syntax problems. In *Proceedings of the Human Language Technology Conference of the North American Chapter of the Association for Computational Linguistics*.

Jiangming Liu and Yue Zhang. 2017. Shift-reduce constituent parsing with neural lookahead features. *Transactions of the Association for Computational Linguistics* 5:45–58.

Mitchell P Marcus, Mary Ann Marcinkiewicz, and Beatrice Santorini. 1993. Building a large annotated corpus of English: The Penn treebank. *Computational Linguistics* 19(2):313–330.

Slav Petrov. 2010. Products of random latent variable grammars. In *Proceedings of the Human Language Technology Conference of the North American Chapter of the Association for Computational Linguistics*.

Brian Roark. 2001. Probabilistic top-down parsing and language modeling. *Computational Linguistics* 27(2):249–276.

Ivan Titov and James Henderson. 2010. A latent variable model for generative dependency parsing. In *Trends in Parsing Technology*, Springer, pages 35–55.

Oriol Vinyals, Łukasz Kaiser, Terry Koo, Slav Petrov, Ilya Sutskever, and Geoffrey Hinton. 2015. Grammar as a foreign language. In *Advances in Neural Information Processing Systems*. pages 2773–2781.

Muhua Zhu, Yue Zhang, Wenliang Chen, Min Zhang, and Jingbo Zhu. 2013. Fast and accurate shift-reduce constituent parsing. In *Proceedings of the Annual Meeting of the Association for Computational Linguistics*.

Information-Theory Interpretation of the
Skip-Gram Negative-Sampling Objective Function

Oren Melamud
IBM Research
Yorktown Heights, NY, USA
`oren.melamud@ibm.com`

Jacob Goldberger
Faculty of Engineering
Bar-Ilan University, Israel
`jacob.goldberger@biu.ac.il`

Abstract

In this paper, we define a measure of dependency between two random variables, based on the Jensen-Shannon (JS) divergence between their joint distribution and the product of their marginal distributions. Then, we show that *word2vec*'s skip-gram with negative sampling embedding algorithm finds the optimal low-dimensional approximation of this JS dependency measure between the words and their contexts. The gap between the optimal score and the low-dimensional approximation is demonstrated on a standard text corpus.

1 Introduction

Continuous word representations, derived from unlabeled text, have proven useful in many NLP tasks. Such word representations (or embeddings) associate a low-dimensional, real-valued vector with each word, typically induced via neural language models or matrix factorization.

Substantial benefit arises when embeddings can be efficiently trained on large volumes of data. Hence the recent considerable interest in the continuous bag-of-words (CBOW) and skip-gram with negative sampling (SGNS) models, described in (Mikolov et al., 2013), as implemented in the open-source toolkit *word2vec*. These models are based on a relatively simple log-linear method and avoid hidden layers typical to neural networks. Consequently, they can be trained to produce high-quality word embeddings on large corpora like the entirety of English Wikipedia in several hours, compared to days or even weeks in the case of other continuous models. Recent studies obtained state-of-the-art results by using skip-gram embeddings on a variety of natural language processing tasks, such as named entity extraction (Passos et al., 2014)

and dependency parsing (Bansal et al., 2014). In recent years, there were several attempts to mathematically interpret word embedding models (Arora et al., 2016; Pennington et al., 2014; Stratos et al., 2015). Our study pursues this established line of work, attempting to explain the objective function of the SGNS word embedding algorithm.

In the SGNS model, the energy function takes the form of a dot product between the vectors of an observed word and an observed context. The objective function is a binary logistic regression classifier that treats a word and its observed context as a positive example, and a word and a randomly sampled context as a negative example. Levy and Goldberg (2014) offered a motivation for this function by showing that it obtains its global maximum value at the word-context pointwise mutual information (PMI) matrix. In this study, we take their analysis one step further and provide an information-theoretical interpretation of the SGNS objective function. In Section 2, we define a new measure of mutual information between random variables based the Jensen-Shennon divergence (Lin, 1991) instead of the KL divergence. In Section 3, we show that the value of the SGNS objective computed at the PMI matrix is this information measure. We then derive an explicit expression for the information loss caused by the low-dimensional embedding learned by the SGNS algorithm. Finally, in Section 4, we illustrate this by computing the information loss caused by actual SGNS embeddings learned on a standard text corpus.

2 A Dependency Measure based on Jensen-Shannon

In this section, we define a dependency measure between two random variables, which is based on the Jensen-Shannon divergence. Later, in Section 3, we show how it relates to the SGNS objective function.

Proceedings of the 55th Annual Meeting of the Association for Computational Linguistics (Short Papers), pages 167–171
Vancouver, Canada, July 30 - August 4, 2017. ©2017 Association for Computational Linguistics
https://doi.org/10.18653/v1/P17-2026

There are several standard methods of measuring the distance between two discrete probability distributions, defined on a given finite set $\mathcal{A}$. The Kullback-Leibler (KL) divergence of a distribution p from a distribution q is defined as follows: $KL(p\|q) = \sum_{i \in \mathcal{A}} p_i \log \frac{p_i}{q_i}$. The mutual information between two jointly distributed random variables X and Y is defined as the KL divergence of the joint distribution $p(x, y)$ from the product $p(x)p(y)$ of the marginal distributions of X and Y, i.e. $I(X; Y) = KL(p(x, y)\|p(x)p(y))$.

The Jensen-Shannon (JS) divergence (Lin, 1991) between distributions p and q is:

$$JS_\alpha(p, q) = \alpha KL(p\|r) + (1-\alpha)KL(q\|r) \quad (1)$$

$$= H(r) - \alpha H(p) - (1-\alpha)H(q)$$

such that $0 < \alpha < 1$, $r = \alpha p + (1 - \alpha)q$ and H is the entropy function (i.e. $H(p) = -\sum_i p_i \log p_i$). Unlike KL divergence, JS divergence is bounded from above and $0 \leq JS_\alpha(p, q) \leq 1$.

We next propose a new measure for mutual-information using the JS-divergence between $p(x, y)$ and $p(x)p(y)$ instead of the KL-divergence. We define the Jensen-Shannon Mutual information (JSMI) as follows:

$$JSMI_\alpha(X, Y) = JS_\alpha(p(x, y), p(x)p(y)). \quad (2)$$

It can be easily verified that X and Y are independent if and only if $JSMI_\alpha(X, Y) = 0$.

We next derive an alternative definition of the JSMI dependency measure. Assume we choose between the two distributions, $p(x, y)$ and the product of marginal distributions $p(x)p(y)$, according to a binary random variable Z, such that $p(Z = 1) = \alpha$. We first sample a binary value for Z and next, we sample a r.v. W as follows:

$$p(W = (x, y)|Z) = \begin{cases} p(x)p(y) & \text{if} \quad Z = 0 \\ p(x, y) & \text{if} \quad Z = 1. \end{cases} \quad (3)$$

The divergence measure $JSMI_\alpha(X, Y)$ can be alternatively defined in terms of mutual information between W and Z. The mutual-information between W and Z is:

$$I(W; Z) = H(W) - \sum_{i=0,1} p(Z = i)H(W|Z = i)$$

$$= H(\alpha p(x, y) + (1-\alpha)p(x)p(y))$$

$$-\alpha H(p(x, y)) - (1-\alpha)H(p(x)p(y)).$$

Eq. (1) thus implies that:

$$JSMI_\alpha(X, Y) = I(W; Z). \quad (4)$$

Applying Bayes rule we obtain:

$$p(Z = 1|W = (x, y)) \quad (5)$$

$$= \frac{\alpha p(x, y)}{\alpha p(x, y) + (1-\alpha)p(x)p(y)}$$

$$= \frac{1}{1 + \exp(-\log(\frac{\alpha p(x,y)}{(1-\alpha)p(x)p(y)}))} = \sigma(\text{pmi}_{x,y})$$

such that $\sigma(u) = \frac{1}{1+\exp(-u)}$ is the sigmoid function and

$$\text{pmi}_{x,y} = \log \frac{p(x, y)}{p(x)p(y)} + \log \frac{\alpha}{1-\alpha} \quad (6)$$

is a shifted version of the PMI function. Equations (4) and (5) imply that:

$$JSMI_\alpha(X, Y) = H(Z) - H(Z|W) \quad (7)$$

$$= h(\alpha) + \alpha \sum_{x,y} p(x, y) \log \sigma(\text{pmi}_{x,y})$$

$$+ (1-\alpha) \sum_{x,y} p(x)p(y) \log \sigma(-\text{pmi}_{x,y})$$

such that $h(\alpha) = -\alpha \log(\alpha) - (1-\alpha)\log(1-\alpha)$ is the binary entropy function.

3 The Skip-Gram Embedding Algorithm

The SGNS embedding algorithm (Mikolov et al., 2013) represents each word x and each context y as d-dimensional vectors $\vec{x}$ and $\vec{y}$, with the purpose that words that are "similar" to each other will have similar vector representations. We can represent a given d-dimensional embedding by a matrix m, such that $m(x, y) = \vec{x} \cdot \vec{y}$. The rank of the embedding matrix m is (at most) d.

Let $p(x, y)$ be the normalized number of co-occurrences of word x and context-word y in a given corpus and let $p(x)$ and $p(y)$ be the corresponding unigram distributions. Consider a binary classifier that treats a word and its observed context as a positive example, and a word and a randomly sampled context as a negative example. The classification is made based on the embedding in such a way that the probability that (x, y) is a positive example is $\sigma(\vec{x} \cdot \vec{y})$. The objective function ideally maximized by the SGNS word embedding algorithm is the expectation of the log-likelihood function of the embedding:

$$S(m) = h(\frac{1}{k+1}) + \frac{1}{k+1} \sum_{x,y} p(x,y) \log \sigma(\vec{x} \cdot \vec{y})$$

$$+ \frac{k}{k+1} \sum_{x,y} p(x)p(y) \log \sigma(-\vec{x} \cdot \vec{y}). \tag{8}$$

Note that the term $h(\frac{1}{k+1})$, which does not appear in the original SGNS objective function (Mikolov et al., 2013), is a constant number that was added here to simplify the following presentation.

The sparsity of $p(x,y)$ (which is obtained as normalized counts from a given learning corpus) makes it feasible to compute the second term of (8). The number of summed-over elements in the third term of (8), however, is quadratic in the size of the vocabulary, making it hard to compute. Therefore, in practice, we can approximate the expectation by sampling of 'negative' examples. The actual SGNS score, then, is:

$$S(m) \approx h(\frac{1}{k+1}) + \frac{1}{k+1} \cdot \frac{1}{n} \sum_{t=1}^{n} (\log \sigma(\vec{x}_t \cdot \vec{y}_t)$$

$$+ \sum_{i=1}^{k} \log \sigma(-\vec{x}_t \cdot \vec{y}_{ti})). \tag{9}$$

such that t goes over all the word-context pairs in a given corpus. The negative examples y_{ti} are created for each pair (x_t, y_t) by drawing k random contexts from the context-word distribution $p(y)$.

As pointed out in (Levy et al., 2015), k has two distinct functions in the SGNS objective function. First, it is used to better estimate the distribution of negative examples. Second, it is used as a weight on the probability of observing a positive example versus a negative example; a higher k means that negative examples are more probable.

We can compute the SGNS score function $S(m)$ for every real-valued matrix $m = (m_{x,y})$. Levy and Goldberg (2014) showed that the function achieves its global maximal value when for each word-pair (x,y) the inner product of the embedding vectors $\vec{x} \cdot \vec{y}$ is equal to pmi(x,y). In other words they showed that $S(m) \leq S(\text{pmi})$ for every matrix m. We next show that the value of the function $S(m)$ at its maximum point, the PMI matrix, has a concrete interpretation, namely it is exactly the Jensen-Shannon Mutual Information (JSMI) between words and their contexts.

Theorem 1: The value of the SGNS score with k negative samples (8) at the PMI matrix satisfies:

$$S(\text{pmi}) = \text{JSMI}_\alpha(X, Y)$$

such that $\alpha = \frac{1}{k+1}$.

Proof: It can be easily verified that by substituting $\alpha = \frac{1}{k+1}$ in the definition of JSMI (Eq. (7)), we exactly obtain the SGNS score (8) at the PMI matrix. $\square$

Levy and Goldberg (2014) showed that SGNS's objective achieves its maximal value at the PMI matrix. However, this result reveals nothing about the more interesting lower dimensional case, where the PMI matrix factorization is forced to compress the joint distribution and thereby learn a meaningful embedding. We next derive an explicit description of the approximation criterion that quantifies the gap between $S(m)$ and $S(\text{pmi})$.

Given the word co-occurrences joint distribution $p(x,y)$, we obtained in Eq. (5) a conditional distribution on the alphabet of (Z, W) as follows:

$$p(Z=1|W=(x,y)) = \sigma(\text{pmi}_{x,y}).$$

In a similar way, given any matrix m, we can define a conditional distribution p_m on the alphabet of (Z, W) as follows:

$$p_m(Z=1|W=(x,y)) = \sigma(m_{x,y}).$$

Note that in the special case where m is the PMI matrix, $p_{\text{pmi}}(z|w)$ coincides with the original $p(z|w)$ that was defined in Eq. (5).

Theorem 2: The difference between the SGNS score at the PMI matrix and the SGNS score at a given matrix m can be written as:

$$S(\text{pmi}) - S(m) = \text{KL}(p_{\text{pmi}}(Z|W)\|p_m(Z|W)) \tag{10}$$

Proof:

$$S(\text{pmi}) - S(m) = \sum_{x,y} (\alpha p(x,y) \log \frac{\sigma(\text{pmi}_{x,y})}{\sigma(m_{x,y})}$$

$$+ (1-\alpha)p(x)p(y) \log \frac{\sigma(-\text{pmi}_{x,y})}{\sigma(-m_{x,y})})$$

$$= \sum_{x,y} (\alpha p(x,y) \log \frac{p_{\text{pmi}}(Z=1|x,y)}{p_m(Z=1|x,y)}$$

$$+ (1-\alpha)p(x)p(y) \log \frac{p_{\text{pmi}}(Z=0|x,y)}{p_m(Z=0|x,y)})$$

$$= \sum_{w,z} p(W=w, Z=z) \log \frac{p_{\text{pmi}}(Z=z|W=w)}{p_m(Z=z|W=w)}$$

$$= \text{KL}(p_{\text{pmi}}(Z|W)||p_m(Z|W)). \square$$

The KL divergence between two distributions is always non-negative and is zero only if the two distributions are the same. Therefore, we red-erive the results of (Levy and Goldberg, 2014) that $S(\text{pmi}) = \max_m S(m)$. Theorem 2 can be viewed as an instance of the well-known connection between maximizing log-likelihood and minimizing KL divergence between the estimated and the true data-generating distribution. In this case, the true distribution is the pmi-based classifier $p_{\text{pmi}}(Z|W)$.

Combining theorems 1 and 2 we obtain that $S(m) \leq \text{JSMI}_\alpha(X, Y)$ for every low-dimensional embedding matrix. The difference $\text{JSMI}_\alpha(X, Y) - S(m)$ is the information loss caused by the low-dimensional embedding. We can view it as a Jensen-Shannon variant of the information bottleneck principle (Tishby et al., 1999; Globerson et al., 2007) that is defined in terms of the KL divergence. The optimal d-dimensional embedding, is the best d-dimensional approximation of the JSMI dependency measure in the sense that it minimizes the information loss. The JSMI is the upper bound that any embedding can obtain. To illustrate that, in the next section we compute the JSMI between words and their contexts based on a standard text corpus and show the information gap between the JSMI and the actual SGNS score as a function of the embedding dimension d.

From Theorem 2 we can also derive an explicit information-theoretic interpretation of the score function $S(m)$ (7) as the difference between two KL-divergence terms:

$$S(m) = S(\text{pmi}) - (S(\text{pmi}) - S(m)) =$$

$$I(Z; W) - (S(\text{pmi}) - S(m)) =$$

$$\text{KL}(p(Z|W)||p(Z)) - \text{KL}(p(Z|W)||p_m(Z|W))$$

The word embedding problem can be also viewed as a factorization of the PMI matrix. Previous works suggested other criteria for matrix factorization such as least-squares (Eckart and Young, 1936) and KL-divergence between the original matrix and the low-rank matrix approximation (Lee and Seung, 2000). We have shown that the SGNS algorithm factorizes the PMI matrix based on the JSMI-based criterion stated in Eq. (10).

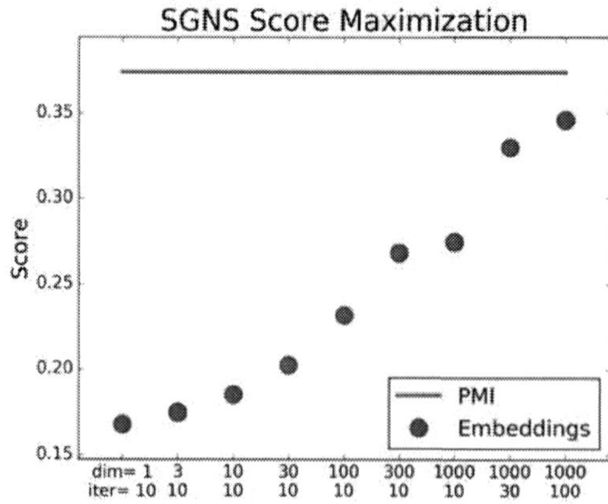

Figure 1: SGNS objective function score of trained embeddings models, compared to the optimal PMI-based score. *dim* and *iter* denote the dimensionality and training iterations used for each model.

4 Experiments

In this section we use *word2vec* to train real skip-gram with negative sampling (SGNS) embedding models. By measuring the value of their objective function and comparing it against the optimal one using exact PMI values, we demonstrate how a well-trained model minimizes the difference in Eq. (10). We note that this is an intrinsic measure that does not necessarily reflect the usefulness of the learned embeddings for other tasks.

We used the Penn Tree Bank (PTB), a popular small-scale corpus, for our experiments. A version of this dataset is available from Tomas Mikolov.[1] It consists of 929K training words with a 10K word vocabulary, which we used to train our models. To learn the SGNS word embeddings, we used word2vec's default parameter values: window-size = 5, min-count = 5, and number of negative samples $k = 5$. We varied the dimensionality of the embeddings and the number of training iterations performed. Once the models were trained, we measured their score (9) on the training corpus.

Based on the same learning corpus, we computed $S(\text{pmi}) = \text{JSMI}_\alpha(X, Y)$ for $\alpha = \frac{1}{k+1} = 1/6$. Note that $p(x, y) = 0$ implies that $\text{pmi}_{x,y} = -\infty$ and therefore $\log \sigma(-\text{pmi}_{x,y}) = 0$. Hence, as in the second term, to compute the third term of $S(m)$ (8) for the case of $m = \text{pmi}$, we can sum only

---

[1] http://www.fit.vutbr.cz/~imikolov/rnnlm/simple-examples.tgz

over the positive pairs (x, y) that actually appear in the corpus.[2] In other words, for the special case $m = $ pmi, it is feasible to compute the exact score (8) and not just its approximation (9) that is based on negative sampling. Figure 1 illustrates the optimal PMI-based score, compared with the scores obtained by different models with varied embedding dimensionality and number of training iterations. As can be seen, the embeddings score gets close to the optimal value using higher dimensionality and more training iterations, but doesn't surpass it.

5 Conclusion

In this study, we developed a new correlation measure between random variables, denoted JSMI. This measure is based on the JS divergence and differs from the standard mutual information measure that is based on the KL divergence. We showed that the optimization of skip-gram embeddings with negative sampling finds the best low-dimensional approximation of the JSMI measure. Thus, we provided an information theory framework that hopefully contributes to a better understanding of this embedding algorithm. Furthermore, although we focused here on the case of word-context joint distributions, the connection we haven shown between the PMI matrix and the JSMI function is valid for every joint distribution of two random variables.

Acknowledgments

This work is supported by the Intel Collaborative Research Institute for Computational Intelligence (ICRI-CI).

References

Sanjeev Arora, Yuanzhi Li, Yingyu Liang, Tengyu Ma, and Andrej Risteski. 2016. A latent variable model approach to pmi-based word embeddings. *Transactions of the Association for Computational Linguistics* 4:385–399.

Mohit Bansal, Kevin Gimpel, and Karen Livescu. 2014. Tailoring continuous word representations for dependency parsing. In *Association for Computational Linguistics (ACL)*.

Carl Eckart and Gale Young. 1936. The approximation of one matrix by another of lower rank. *Psychometrika* 1:211–218.

Amir Globerson, Gal Chechik, Fernando Pereira, and Naftaly Tishby. 2007. Euclidean embedding of co-occurrence data. *Journal of Machine Learning Research* 8:2265–2295.

Daniel D. Lee and H. Sebastian Seung. 2000. Algorithms for nonnegative matrix factorization. In *Advances in Neural Information Processing Systems*.

Omer Levy and Yoav Goldberg. 2014. Neural word embedding as implicit matrix factorization. In *Advances in Neural Information Processing Systems*.

Omer Levy, Yoav Goldberg, and Ido Dagan. 2015. Improving distributional similarity with lessons learned from word embeddings. *Trans. of the Association for Computational Linguistics* 3:211–225.

Jianhua Lin. 1991. Divergence measures based on the shannon entropy. *IEEE Transactions on Information Theory* 37(1):145–151.

Tomas Mikolov, Ilya Sutskever, Kai Chen, Greg Corrado, and Jeffrey Dean. 2013. Distributed representations of words and phrases and their compositionality. In *Advances in Neural Information Processing Systems*.

Alexandre Passos, Vineet Kumar, and Andrew McCallum. 2014. Lexicon infused phrase embeddings for named entity resolution. In *Conference on Natural Language Learning (CoNLL)*.

Jeffrey Pennington, Richard Socher, and Christopher D Manning. 2014. Glove: Global vectors for word representation. In *EMNLP*. volume 14, pages 1532–1543.

Karl Stratos, Michael Collins, and Daniel J Hsu. 2015. Model-based word embeddings from decompositions of count matrices. In *ACL (1)*. pages 1282–1291.

Naftaly Tishby, Fernando C. Pereira, and William Bialek. 1999. The information bottleneck method. In *Allerton Conf. on Communication, Control, and Computing*.

---

[2] We used the exact same positive co-occurrence pairs sampled by word2vec during the training of the SGNS embeddings to compute $S(\text{pmi})$.

Implicitly-Defined Neural Networks for Sequence Labeling *

Michaeel Kazi, Brian Thompson
MIT Lincoln Laboratory
244 Wood St, Lexington, MA, 02420, USA
{first.last}@ll.mit.edu

Abstract

In this work, we propose a novel, implicitly-defined neural network architecture and describe a method to compute its components. The proposed architecture forgoes the causality assumption used to formulate recurrent neural networks and instead couples the hidden states of the network, allowing improvement on problems with complex, long-distance dependencies. Initial experiments demonstrate the new architecture outperforms both the Stanford Parser and baseline bidirectional networks on the Penn Treebank Part-of-Speech tagging task and a baseline bidirectional network on an additional artificial random biased walk task.

1 Introduction

Feedforward neural networks were designed to approximate and interpolate functions. Recurrent Neural Networks (RNNs) were developed to predict sequences. RNNs can be 'unwrapped' and thought of as very deep feedforward networks, with weights shared between each layer. Computation proceeds one step at a time, like the trajectory of an ordinary differential equation when solving an initial value problem. The path of an initial value problem depends only on the current state and the current value of the forcing function. In a RNN, the analogy is the current hidden state and the current input sequence. However, in certain applications in natural language processing, especially those with long-distance dependencies or where grammar matters, sequence predic-

tion may be better thought of as a boundary value problem. Changing the value of the forcing function (analogously, of an input sequence element) at any point in the sequence will affect the values everywhere else. The bidirectional recurrent network (Schuster and Paliwal, 1997) attempts to addresses this problem by creating a network with two recurrent hidden states – one that progresses in the forward direction and one that progresses in the reverse. This allows information to flow in both directions, but each state can only consider information from one direction. In practice many algorithms require more than two passes through the data to determine an answer. We provide a novel mechanism that is able to process information in both directions, with the motivation being a program which iterates over itself until convergence.

1.1 Related Work

Bidirectional, long-distance dependencies in sequences have been an issue as long as there have been NLP tasks, and there are many approaches to dealing with them.

Hidden Markov models (HMMs) (Rabiner, 1989) have been used extensively for sequence-based tasks, but they rely on the Markov assumption – that a hidden variable changes its state based only on its current state and observables. In finding maximum likelihood state sequences, the Forward-Backward algorithm can take into account the entire set of observables, but the underlying model is still local.

In recent years, popularity of the Long Short-Term Memory (LSTM) (Hochreiter and Schmidhuber, 1997) and variants such as the Gated Recurrent Unit (GRU) (Cho et al., 2014) has soared, as they enable RNNs to process long sequences without the problem of vanishing or exploding gradients (Pascanu et al., 2013). However, these models

*This work is sponsored by the Air Force Research Laboratory under Air Force contract FA-8721-05-C-0002. Opinions, interpretations, conclusions and recommendations are those of the authors and are not necessarily endorsed by the United States Government.

172

Proceedings of the 55th Annual Meeting of the Association for Computational Linguistics (Short Papers), pages 172–177
Vancouver, Canada, July 30 - August 4, 2017. ©2017 Association for Computational Linguistics
https://doi.org/10.18653/v1/P17-2027

only allow for information/gradient information to flow in the forward direction.

The Bidirectional LSTM (b-LSTM) (Graves and Schmidhuber, 2005), a natural extension of (Schuster and Paliwal, 1997), incorporates past and future hidden states via two separate recurrent networks, allowing information/gradients to flow in both directions of a sequence. This is a very loose coupling, however.

In contrast to these methods, our work goes a step further, fully coupling the entire sequences of hidden states of an RNN. Our work is similar to (Finkel et al., 2005), which augments a CRF with long-distance constraints. However, our work differs in that we extend an RNN and uses Netwon-Krylov (Knoll and Keyes, 2004) instead of Gibbs Sampling.

2 The Implicit Neural Network (INN)

2.1 Traditional Recurrent Neural Networks

A typical recurrent neural network has a (possibly transformed) input sequence $[\xi_1, \xi_2, \ldots, \xi_n]$ and initial state h_s and iteratively produces future states:

$$
\begin{aligned}
h_1 &= f(\xi_1, h_s) \\
h_2 &= f(\xi_2, h_1) \\
&\ldots \\
h_n &= f(\xi_n, h_{n-1})
\end{aligned}
$$

The LSTM, GRU, and related variants follow this formula, with different choices for the state transition function. Computation proceeds linearly, with each next state depending only on inputs and previously computed hidden states.

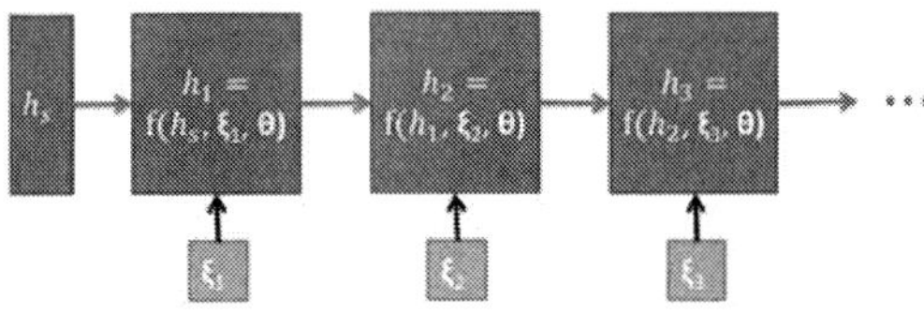

Figure 1: Traditional RNN structure.

2.2 Proposed Architecture

In this work, we relax this assumption by allowing $h_t = f(\xi_t, h_{t-1}, h_{t+1})^1$. This leads to an implicit set of equations for the entire sequence of hidden states, which can be thought of as a single tensor

---

[1] A wider stencil can also be used, e.g. $f(h_{t-2}, h_{t-1}, \ldots)$.

H:

$$
H = [h_1, h_2, \ldots, h_n]
$$

This yields a system of nonlinear equations. This setup has the potential to arrive at nonlocal, whole sequence-dependent results. We also hope such a system is more 'stable', in the sense that the predicted sequence may drift less from the true meaning, since errors will not compound with each time step in the same way.

There are many potential ways to architect a neural network – in fact, this flexibility is one of deep learning's best features – but we restrict our discussion to the structure depicted in Figure 2. In this setup, we have the following variables:

$$
\begin{array}{c|c}
\text{data} & X \\
\text{labels} & Y \\
\text{parameters} & \theta
\end{array}
$$

and functions:

$$
\begin{array}{l|l}
\text{input layer transformation} & \xi = g(\theta, X) \\
\textbf{implicit hidden layer def.} & H = F(\theta, \xi, H) \\
\text{loss function} & L = \ell(\theta, H, Y)
\end{array}
$$

Our implicit definition function, F, is made up of local state transitions and forms a system of nonlinear equations that require solving, denoting n as the length of the input sequence and h_s, h_e as boundary states:

$$
\begin{aligned}
h_1 &= f(h_s, h_2, \xi_1) \\
&\ldots \\
h_i &= f(h_{i-1}, h_{i+1}, \xi_i) \\
&\ldots \\
h_n &= f(h_{n-1}, h_e, \xi_n)
\end{aligned}
$$

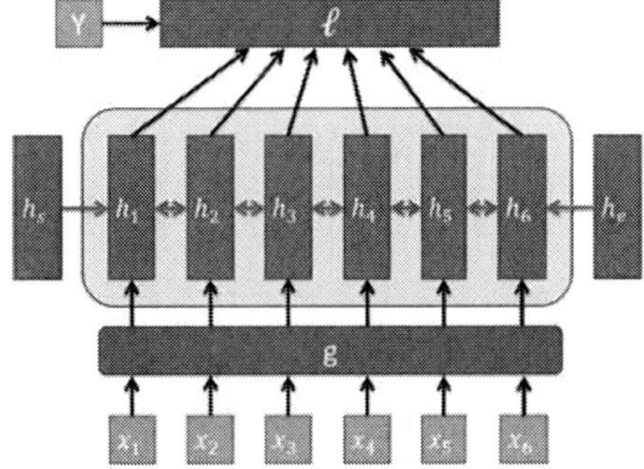

Figure 2: Proposed INN Architecture

2.3 Computing the forward pass

To evaluate the network, we must solve the equation $H = F(H)$. We computed this via an approximate Newton solve, where we successively refine an approximation H_n of H:

$$H_{n+1} = H_n - (I - \nabla_H F)^{-1}(H_n - F(H_n))$$

Let k be the dimension of a single hidden state. $(I - \nabla_H F)$ is a sparse matrix, since $\nabla_H F$ is zero except for k pairs of $n \times n$ block matrices, corresponding to the influence of the left and right neighbors of each state.

Because of this sparsity, we can apply Krylov subspace methods (Knoll and Keyes, 2004), specifically the BiCG-STAB method (Van der Vorst, 1992), since the system is non-symmetric. This has the added advantage of only relying on matrix-vector multiplies of the gradient of F.

2.4 Gradients

In order to train the model, we perform stochastic gradient descent. We take the gradient of the loss function:

$$\nabla_\theta L = \nabla_\theta \ell + \nabla_H \ell \nabla_\theta H$$

The gradient of the hidden units with respect to the parameters can found via the implicit definition:

$$\begin{aligned}
\nabla_\theta H &= \nabla_\theta F + \nabla_H F \nabla_\theta H + \nabla_\xi F \nabla_\theta \xi \\
&= (I - \nabla_H F)^{-1}(\nabla_\theta F + \nabla_\xi F \nabla_\theta \xi)
\end{aligned}$$

where the factorization follows from the noting that

$$(I - \nabla_H F)\nabla_\theta H = \nabla_\theta F + \nabla_\xi F \nabla_\theta \xi.$$

The entire gradient is thus:

$$\begin{aligned}
\nabla_\theta L =& \nabla_H \ell (I - \nabla_H F)^{-1}(\nabla_\theta F + \nabla_\xi F \nabla_\theta \xi) \\
& + \nabla_\theta \ell
\end{aligned}$$

$$(1)$$

Once again, the inverse of $I - \nabla_H F$ appears, and we can compute it via Krylov subspace methods. It is worth mentioning the technique of computing parameter updates by implicit differentiation and conjugate gradients have been applied before, in the context of energy minimization models in image labeling and denoising (Domke, 2012).

2.5 Transition Functions

Recall the original GRU equations (Cho et al., 2014), with slight notational modifications:

final h	$h_t = (1 - z_t)\hat{h}_t + z_t \tilde{h}_t$
candidate h	$\tilde{h}_t = \tanh(W x_t + U(r_t \hat{h}_t) + \tilde{b})$
update weight	$z_t = \sigma(W_z x_t + U_z \hat{h}_t + b_z)$
reset gate	$r_t = \sigma(W_r x_t + U_r \hat{h}_t + b_r)$

We make the following substitution for $\hat{h}_t$ (which was set to h_{t-1} in the original GRU definition):

state comb.	$\hat{h}_t = s h_{t-1} + (1 - s)h_{t+1}$
switch	$s = \frac{s_p}{s_p + s_n}$
prev. switch	$s_p = \sigma(W_p x_t + U_p h_{t-1} + b_p)$
next switch	$s_n = \sigma(W_n x_t + U_n h_{t+1} + b_n)$

$$(2)$$

This modification makes the architecture both implicit and bidirectional, since $\hat{h}_t$ is a linear combination of previous and future hidden states. The switch variable s is determined by a competition between two sigmoidal units s_p and s_n, representing the contributions of the previous and next hidden states, respectively.

2.6 Implementation Details

We implemented the implicit GRU structure using Theano (Bergstra et al., 2011). The product $\nabla_H F v$ for various v, required for the BiCG-STAB method, was computed via the `Rop` operator. In computing $\nabla_\theta L$ (Equation 1), we noted it is more efficient to compute $\nabla_H \ell (I - \nabla_H F)^{-1}$ first, and thus used the `Lop` operator.

All experiments used a batch size of 20. To batch solve the linear equations, we simply solved a single, very large block diagonal system of equations: each sequence in the batch was a single block matrix, and we input the encompassing matrix into our Theano BiCG solver. (In practice the block diagonal system is represented as a 3-tensor, but it is equivalent.) In this setup, each step does receive separate update directions, but one global step length. h_S and h_e were fixed at zero, but could be trained as parameters.

In solving multiple simultaneous systems of equations, we noted some elements converged significantly faster than others. For this reason, we found it helpful to run Newton's method from two separate initializations for each element in our batch, one selected randomly and the other set to a "one-step" approximation: Hidden states of a traditional GRU were computed in both forward (h_i^f) and reverse (h_i^b) directions, and h_i was initialized to $f(h_{i-1}^f, h_{i+1}^b, \xi_i)$. If either of the two candidates converged, we took its value and stopped computing the other. We also limited both the number Newton iterations and BiCG-STAB iterations per Newton iteration to 40.

3 Experiments

3.1 Biased random walks

We developed an artificial task with bidirectional sequence-level dependencies to explore the performance of our model. Our task was to find the point at which a random walk, in the spirit of the Wiener Process (Durrett, 2010), changes from a zero to nonzero mean. We trained a network to predict when the walk is no longer unbiased. We generated algorithmic data for this problem, the specifics of which are as follows: First, we chose an integer interval length N uniformly in the range 1 to 40. Then, we chose a (continuous) time $t' \in [0, N)$, and a direction $v \in \mathcal{R}^d$. We produced the input sequence $x_i \in \mathcal{R}^d$, setting $x_0 = 0$ and iteratively computing $x_{i+1} = x_i + \mathcal{N}(0, 1)$. After time t, a bias term of $b \cdot v$ was added at each time step $(b \cdot v \cdot (t' - t))$ for the first time step greater than t'. b is a global scalar parameter. The network was fed in these elements, and asked to predict $y = 0$ for times $t \le t'$ and $y = 1$ for times $t > t'$.

For each architecture, ξ was simply the unmodified input vectors, zero-padded to the embedding dimension size. The output was a simple binary logistic regression. We produced 50,000 random training examples, 2500 random validation examples, and 5000 random test examples. The implicit algorithm used a hidden dimension of 200, and the b-LSTM had an embedding dimension ranging from 100 to 1000. b-LSTM dimension of 300 was the point where the total number of parameters were roughly equal.

The results are shown in Table 1. The b-LSTM scores reported are the maximum over sweeps from 100 to 1500 hidden dimension size. The INN outperforms the best b-LSTM in the more challenging cases where the bias size b is small.

3.2 Part-of-speech tagging

We next applied our model to a real-world problem. Part-of-speech tagging fits naturally in the sequence labeling framework, and has the advantage of a standard dataset that we can use to compare our network with other techniques. To train a part-of-speech tagger, we simply let L be a softmax layer transforming each hidden unit output into a part of speech tag. Our input encoding ξ, is a concatenation of three sets of features, adapted from (Huang et al., 2015): first, word vectors for 39,000 case-insensitive vocabulary words; second, six additional 'word vector' components indicating the presence of the top-2000 most common prefixes and suffixes of words, for affix lengths 2 to 4; and finally, eight other binary features to indicate the presence of numbers, symbols, punctuation, and more rich case data.

We trained the Part of Speech (POS) tagger on the Penn Treebank Wall Street Journal corpus (Marcus et al., 1993), blocks 0-18, validated on 19-21, and tested on 22-24, per convention. Training was done using stochastic gradient descent, with an initial learning rate of 0.5. The learning rate was halved if validation perplexity increased. Word vectors were of dimension 320, prefix and suffix vectors were of dimension 20. Hidden unit size was equal to feature input size, so in this case, 448.

As shown in Table 2, the INN outperformed baseline GRU, bidirectional GRU, LSTM, and b-LSTM networks, all with 628-dimensional hidden layers (1256 for the bidirectional architectures), The INN also outperforms the Stanford Part-of-Speech tagger (Toutanova et al., 2003) (model `wsj-0-18-bidirectional-distsim.tagger` from 10-31-2016). Note that performance gains past approximately 97% are difficult due to errors/inconsistencies in the dataset, ambiguity, and complex linguistic constructions including dependencies across sentence boundaries (Manning, 2011).

b	INN Error	b-LSTM Error
2.0	0.0226	**0.0210**
1.0	**0.0518**	0.0589
0.75	**0.0782**	0.0879
0.5	**0.119**	0.132
0.25	**0.189**	0.205

Table 1: Biased walk classification performance.

Architecture	WSJ Accuracy
GRU	96.43
LSTM	96.47
Bidirectional GRU	97.28
b-LSTM	97.25
INN	**97.37**
Stanford POS Tagger	97.33

Table 2: Tagging performance relative to recurrent architectures and Stanford POS Tagger.

4 Time Complexity

The implicit experiments in this paper took approximately 3-5 days to run on a single Tesla K40, while the explicit experiments took approximately 1-3 hours. Running time of the solver is approximately $n_n \times n_b \times t_b$ where n_n is the number of Newton iterations, n_b is the number of BiCG-STAB iterations, and t_b is the time for a single BiCG-STAB iteration. t_b is proportional to the number of non-zero entries in the matrix (Van der Vorst, 1992), in our case $n(2k^2 + 1)$. Newton's method has second order convergence (Isaacson and Keller, 1994), and while the specific bound depends on the norm of $(I - \nabla_H F)^{-1}$ and the norm of its derivatives, convergence is well-behaved. For n_b, however, we are not aware of a bound. For symmetric matrices, the Conjugate Gradient method is known to take $O(\sqrt{\kappa})$ iterations (Shewchuk et al., 1994), where κ is the condition number of the matrix. However, our matrix is nonsymmetric, and we expect κ to vary from problem to problem. Because of this, we empirically estimated the correlation between sequence length and total time to compute a batch of 20 hidden layer states.

For the random walk experiment with $b = 0.5$, we found the the average run time for a given sequence length to be approximately $0.17n^{1.8}$, with $r^2 = 0.994$. Note that the exponent would have been larger had we not truncated the number of BiCG-STAB iterations to 40, as the inner iteration frequently hit this limit for larger n. However, the average number of Newton iterations did not go above 10, indicating that exiting early from the BiCG-STAB loop did not prevent the Newton solver from converging. Run times for the other random walk experiments were very similar, indicating run time does not depend on b; However, for the POS task runtime was $0.29n^{1.3}$, with $r^2 = 0.910$.

5 Conclusion and Future Work

We have introduced a novel, implicitly defined neural network architecture based on the GRU and shown that it outperforms a b-LSTM on an artificial random walk task and slightly outperforms both the Stanford Parser and a baseline bidirectional network on the Penn Treebank Part-of-Speech tagging task.

In future work, we intend to consider implicit variations of other architectures, such as the LSTM, as well as additional, more challenging, and/or data-rich applications. We also plan to explore ways to speed up the computation of $(I - \nabla_H F)^{-1}$. Potential speedups include approximating the hidden state values by reducing the number of Newton and/or BiCG-STAB iterations, using cached previous solutions as initial values, and modifying the gradient update strategy to keep the batch full at every Newton iteration.

6 Acknowledgements

This work would not be possible without the support and funding of the Air Force Research Laboratory. We also acknowledge Nick Malyska, Elizabeth Salesky, and Jonathan Taylor at MIT Lincoln Lab for interesting technical discussions related to this work.

References

James Bergstra, Frédéric Bastien, Olivier Breuleux, Pascal Lamblin, Razvan Pascanu, Olivier Delalleau, Guillaume Desjardins, David Warde-Farley, Ian Goodfellow, Arnaud Bergeron, et al. 2011. Theano: Deep learning on gpus with python. In *NIPS 2011, BigLearning Workshop, Granada, Spain.*

Kyunghyun Cho, Bart van Merriënboer, Dzmitry Bahdanau, and Yoshua Bengio. 2014. On the properties of neural machine translation: Encoder–decoder approaches. *Syntax, Semantics and Structure in Statistical Translation* page 103.

Justin Domke. 2012. Generic methods for optimization-based modeling. In *AISTATS.* volume 22, pages 318–326.

Richard Durrett. 2010. *Probability : theory and examples.* Cambridge University Press, Cambridge New York.

Jenny Rose Finkel, Trond Grenager, and Christopher Manning. 2005. Incorporating non-local information into information extraction systems by gibbs sampling. In *Proceedings of the 43rd Annual Meeting on Association for Computational Linguistics.* Association for Computational Linguistics, pages 363–370.

Alex Graves and Jürgen Schmidhuber. 2005. Framewise phoneme classification with bidirectional lstm and other neural network architectures. *Neural Networks* 18(5):602–610.

Sepp Hochreiter and Jürgen Schmidhuber. 1997. Long short-term memory. *Neural computation* 9(8):1735–1780.

Zhiheng Huang, Wei Xu, and Kai Yu. 2015. Bidirectional lstm-crf models for sequence tagging. *arXiv preprint arXiv:1508.01991* .

Eugene Isaacson and Herbert Bishop Keller. 1994. *Analysis of numerical methods.* Courier Corporation, New York.

Dana A Knoll and David E Keyes. 2004. Jacobian-free newton–krylov methods: a survey of approaches and applications. *Journal of Computational Physics* 193(2):357–397.

Christopher D Manning. 2011. Part-of-speech tagging from 97% to 100%: is it time for some linguistics? In *International Conference on Intelligent Text Processing and Computational Linguistics.* Springer, pages 171–189.

Mitchell P Marcus, Mary Ann Marcinkiewicz, and Beatrice Santorini. 1993. Building a large annotated corpus of english: The penn treebank. *Computational linguistics* 19(2):313–330.

Razvan Pascanu, Tomas Mikolov, and Yoshua Bengio. 2013. On the difficulty of training recurrent neural networks. *ICML (3)* 28:1310–1318.

Lawrence R Rabiner. 1989. A tutorial on hidden markov models and selected applications in speech recognition. *Proceedings of the IEEE* 77(2):257–286.

Mike Schuster and Kuldip K Paliwal. 1997. Bidirectional recurrent neural networks. *Signal Processing, IEEE Transactions on* 45(11):2673–2681.

Jonathan Richard Shewchuk et al. 1994. An introduction to the conjugate gradient method without the agonizing pain.

Kristina Toutanova, Dan Klein, Christopher D Manning, and Yoram Singer. 2003. Feature-rich part-of-speech tagging with a cyclic dependency network. In *Proceedings of the 2003 Conference of the North American Chapter of the Association for Computational Linguistics on Human Language Technology-Volume 1.* Association for Computational Linguistics, pages 173–180.

Henk A Van der Vorst. 1992. Bi-cgstab: A fast and smoothly converging variant of bi-cg for the solution of nonsymmetric linear systems. *SIAM Journal on scientific and Statistical Computing* 13(2):631–644.

The Role of Prosody and Speech Register in Word Segmentation: A Computational Modelling Perspective

Bogdan Ludusan
LSCP
EHESS/ENS/PSL/CNRS
29 rue d'Ulm, 75005 Paris, France
bogdan.ludusan@ens.fr

Reiko Mazuka
Language Development Lab
RIKEN Brain Science Institute
2-1 Hirosawa, Wako, 351-0198, Japan
mazuka@brain.riken.jp

Mathieu Bernard
Alejandrina Cristia
Emmanuel Dupoux
LSCP - EHESS/ENS/PSL/CNRS
29 rue d'Ulm, 75005 Paris, France
{mmathieubernardd, alecristia,
emmanuel.dupoux}@gmail.com

Abstract

This study explores the role of speech register and prosody for the task of word segmentation. Since these two factors are thought to play an important role in early language acquisition, we aim to quantify their contribution for this task. We study a Japanese corpus containing both infant- and adult-directed speech and we apply four different word segmentation models, with and without knowledge of prosodic boundaries. The results showed that the difference between registers is smaller than previously reported and that prosodic boundary information helps more adult- than infant-directed speech.

1 Introduction

Infants start learning their native language even before birth and, already during their first year of life, they succeed in acquiring linguistic structure at several levels, including phonetic and lexical knowledge. One extraordinary aspect of the learning process is infants' ability to segment continuous speech into words, while having little or no knowledge of the sounds of their native language.

Several hypotheses have been proposed in the experimental literature to explain how they achieve this feat. Among the main classes of cues put forward, prosodic cues (e.g. stress, prosodic boundaries) have been shown to be particularly useful in early-stage word segmentation (Christophe et al., 2003; Curtin et al., 2005; Seidl and Johnson, 2006). Previous work suggests that

these cues may be emphasized in the speech register often used when addressing infants (infant-directed speech; IDS). This register is characterized by shorter utterances, repeated words and exaggerated prosody (see (Cristia, 2013) for a review). It has been shown that IDS can facilitate segmentation performance in infants (Thiessen et al., 2005), when compared to the register that parents use when talking to adults (adult-directed speech; ADS).

The process of word segmentation has received considerable attention also from the computational linguistics community, where various computational models have been proposed (e.g. (Brent and Cartwright, 1996; Goldwater et al., 2009)). Yet, despite the role that prosodic cues play in early word segmentation, only lexical stress has been addressed in detail, in the computational modelling literature (e.g. (Börschinger and Johnson, 2014; Doyle and Levy, 2013; Lignos, 2011)). As for prosodic boundary information, it was investigated in only one previous study (Ludusan et al., 2015). That study found that that an Adaptor Grammar model (Johnson et al., 2007) performed better on both English and Japanese corpora when prosodic boundary information was added to its grammar. These previous studies investigated the effect of prosodic cues while keeping register constant, investigating either IDS (e.g. (Börschinger and Johnson, 2014)) or ADS (Ludusan et al., 2015). Other work focuses on register only. For instance, (Fourtassi et al., 2013) used the Adaptor Grammar framework to examine English and Japanese corpora of infant- and adult-directed speech, concluding that IDS was easier to segment

Proceedings of the 55th Annual Meeting of the Association for Computational Linguistics (Short Papers), pages 178–183
Vancouver, Canada, July 30 - August 4, 2017. ©2017 Association for Computational Linguistics
https://doi.org/10.18653/v1/P17-2028

than ADS. However, the corpora were not parallel or necessarily directly comparable, as, the ADS in Japanese was transcribed from academic presentation speeches, whereas the IDS came from spontaneous conversational speech.

We aim to put together these two lines of research, by conducting the first computational study of word segmentation that takes into account both variables: speech register and prosodic boundary information. This investigation extends the previously mentioned studies, by allowing us to observe not only the effect of each individual variable, but also any interaction between the two. More importantly, it is performed in a more controlled manner as it makes use of a large corpus of spontaneous verbal interactions, containing both IDS and ADS uttered by the same speakers. Furthermore, we do not limit ourselves to a specific model, but test several, different, unsupervised segmentation models in order to increase the generalizability of the findings.

2 Methods

Several unsupervised segmentation algorithms were employed. We selected 2 sub-lexical and 2 lexical models, all of which are made freely available through the CDSwordSeg package[1].

The first model performs transition-probability-based segmentation (TP) employing the *relative algorithm* of Saksida et al. (2016). It takes in input transcribed utterances, segmented at the syllable level and computes the forward transitional probabilities between every pair of syllables in the corpus. The transition probability between two syllables X and Y is defined as the frequency of the pair (X,Y) divided by the frequency of the syllable X. Once probabilities are computed, word boundaries are posited using local minima of the probability function. As this algorithm only attempts to posit boundaries based on phonological information it is called a 'sub-lexical' model.

Diphone-based segmentation (DiBS) is another sub-lexical model, which uses diphones instead of syllables pairs (Daland and Pierrehumbert, 2011). The input is represented as a sequence of phonemes and the model tries to place boundaries based on the identity of each consecutive sequence of two phonemes. The goal is accomplished by computing the probability of a word boundary falling within such a sequence, with the

---

[1]https://github.com/alecristia/CDSwordSeg

probability being rewritten using Bayes' rule. The information needed for the computation of the word boundary probability is estimated on a small subset of the corpus, using the gold word boundaries. Thereafter, a boundary is placed between every diphone whose probability is above a predetermined threshold.

Monaghan and Christiansen (2010)'s PUDDLE is a lexical model which utilizes previously seen utterances to extract lexical and phonotactic information knowledge later used to "chunk" sequences. In a nutshell, it is an incremental algorithm that initially memorizes whole utterances into its long-term lexical storage, from which possible word-final and word-initial diphones are extracted. The model continues to consider each utterance as a lexical unit, unless sub-sequences of the given utterance have already been stored in the word list. In that case, it cuts the utterance based on the words which it already knows and considers the newly segmented chunks as word candidates. In order for the word candidates to be added to the lexical list, they have to respect two rules: 1) the final diphones of the left chunk and the beginning diphones of the right chunk must be on the list of permissible final diphones; and 2) both chunks have to contain at least one vowel. Once a candidate is added to the lexical list, its beginning and final diphones are included into the list of permissible diphones.

The last model was a unigram implementation of Adaptor Grammar (AG) (Johnson et al., 2007). AG is a hierarchical Bayesian model based on an extension of probabilistic context free grammars. It alternates between using the previously learned grammar to parse an utterance into a hierarchical tree structure made up of words and phonemes, and updating the grammar by learning probabilities associated to rules and entire tree fragments, called adapted non-terminals. The unigram model is the simplest grammar, considering utterances as being composed of words, which are represented as a sequence of phonemes.

3 Materials

The RIKEN corpus (Mazuka et al., 2006) contains recordings of 22 Japanese mothers interacting with their 18 to 24-month old infants, while playing with toys or reading a book. The same mothers were then recorded while talking to an experimenter. Out of the total 14.5 hours of recordings, about 11 hours represent infant-directed speech, while the rest adult-directed speech.

The corpus was annotated at both segmental and prosodic levels. We made use in this study of the prosodic boundary annotation, labelled using the X-JToBI standard (Maekawa et al., 2002). X-JToBI defines prosodic breaks based on the degree of their perceived disjuncture, ranging from level 0 (the weakest) to level 3 (the strongest). We use here level 2 and level 3 prosodic breaks, which in the Japanese prosodic organization (Venditti, 2005) correspond, respectively, to accentual phrases and intonational phrases. Accentual phrases are sequences of words that carry at most one pitch accent; for instance, a noun with a postposition will typically only have one accent. Intonational phrases are made up of sequences of accentual phrases, and constitute the domain where pitch range is defined such that, for instance, the onset of an intonational phrase will be marked by a reset the pitch level.

An additional dataset, part of the Corpus of Spontaneous Japanese (CSJ) (Maekawa, 2003), was considered as control. It contains academic speech and was previously used to investigate either the effect of speech register (Fourtassi et al., 2013) or that of prosodic boundaries (Ludusan et al., 2015) on unsupervised word segmentation. The same levels of annotations are available as for the RIKEN corpus. Statistics about the number of utterances and word token and types, for all three corpora, can be found in Table 1.

4 Experimental settings

The transitional probabilities used by TP were computed on the entire input dataset, while the estimation of the probabilities needed by DiBS was performed on the first 200 utterances of the corpus. PUDDLE, being an incremental algorithm, was evaluated using a five-fold cross-validation. For AG, the process was repeated five times for each register and prosodic boundary condition, and the average across the five runs was reported.

Dataset	#utts	#tokens	#types
CSJ	20,052	216,932	7,340
ADS	3,582	22,844	2,022
IDS	14,570	51,315	2,850

Table 1: Statistics regarding the utterances and words contained in the investigated corpora.

Each run had 2000 iterations and Minimum Bayes Risk (Johnson and Goldwater, 2009) decoding was used for the evaluation.

Each algorithm was run on the ADS, IDS and CSJ datasets for each of the 3 cases considered: no prosody (*base*), level 3 prosodic breaks (*brk3*) and level 2 and level 3 prosodic breaks (*brk23*). For the base case, the system had in input a file containing on each line an utterance, defined as being an intonational phrase or a filler phrase followed by a pause longer than 200 ms. In the brk3 and brk23 cases, each prosodic phrase was considered as a standalone utterance, and thus was written on a separate line. During the evaluation of the brk3 and brk23 cases, the original utterances were rebuilt by concatenating all the prosodic phrases contained in them, after which they were compared against the reference.

Additionally, we checked whether the size difference between the ADS and IDS datasets might have an effect on the results obtained. For this, we created two additional, balanced, subsets of the IDS data. The first one contained an equal number of words from each speaker as in their ADS data, while the second one an equal number of utterances, for each speaker, as in their ADS production. As there was no significant difference between the results with the two balanced subsets and the entire IDS corpus, we will present here only the latter results.

5 Results and discussion

The segmentation evaluation was performed against the gold word segmentation, provided with the corpus. A classical metric, the token F-score, was used as evaluation measure. It is defined as the harmonic average between the token precision (how many word tokens, out of the total number of segmented words, were correct) and token recall (how many word tokens, out of the total number of words in the reference data, were found).

Next, we illustrate the obtained token F-score for the three corpora (IDS, ADS and CSJ) in Figure 1, for the three cases (base, brk3 and brk23) and for the four algorithms investigated (TP, DiBS, PUDDLE and AG). We observe that the largest differences are between algorithms. It appears that models employing sub-lexical information fare worse than the ones working at the lexical level. DiBS gives the lowest performance (.132 token F-score for CSJ base), followed by TP, PUDDLE

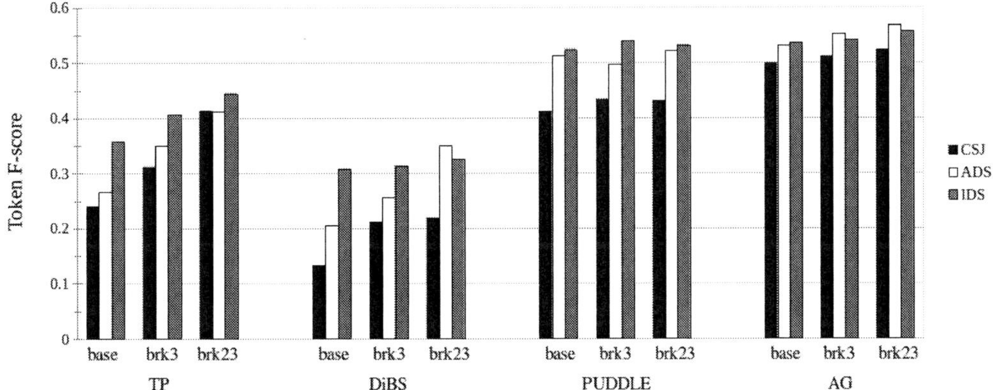

Figure 1: Segmentation results obtained using four algorithms: TP, DiBS, PUDDLE and AG on the IDS, ADS and CSJ datasets, when no prosodic information was provided (base), when utterances where additionally broken at boundaries of type 3 (brk3), and when utterances where additionally broken at boundaries of type 2 and 3 (brk23).

and AG giving the best performance (.567 token F-score for ADS brk23). The goal of the present study, however, is not to pit algorithms against each other, but rather to sample from plausible segmentation strategies that infants could potentially use so as to provide more representative and generalizable results.

Register effects found in the comparison between IDS and CSJ with the AG model replicate previous work (Fourtassi et al., 2013). We considerably extend knowledge by additionally including a casual ADS sample matched to the IDS, and investigating 3 additional algorithms. This allows us to conclude that differences between IDS and ADS are considerably smaller than previous work could have suggested. This is expected in view of previous reports that using un-matched materials leads to an overestimation of the differences between IDS and ADS (Batchelder, 2002). Interestingly, we also found that the size and direction of this difference was dependent on the algorithm used. An important advantage can be observed in the IDS-ADS comparison for the sub-lexical algorithms (maximally 9% for TP and 10.3% for DiBS), which decreases for PUDDLE and AG (maximally 1-1.1%), and can sometimes reverse when prosodic information is taken into account (DiBS brk23, AG brk3 and brk23).

Turning to prosodic boundaries, breaking utterances using internal prosodic breaks seems to help to a different degree the two classes of segmentation models and the three corpora, in ways that re-

semble a crossed interaction. The performance of sub-lexical models improves more with the use of prosodic information than that of lexical models, and this for all corpora. By and large, performance is boosted by additional prosodic breaks more for CSJ and ADS than IDS. This boost is, however, rather variable for PUDDLE, with apparent declines when, for instance, type 3 breaks are added for ADS. These results only partially replicate those reported in (Ludusan et al., 2015). Overall, the improvement brought by prosodic boundaries is smaller. TP brk23 brings an absolute improvement of 17.3% over TP base, for CSJ, but the improvement brought for AG (3.6%) is modest compared to what was previously reported (12.3%).[2]

Overall, we observe that some of our conclusions are dependent on the actual corpus being used. For this reason, we further analysed several measures which could play a role in the segmentation process. The first one, the average number of words per utterance was highest for CSJ, followed by ADS and the lowest for IDS. This would be expected taken into account the characteristics of IDS (Cristia, 2013). It is important to note that the smallest difference with respect to utterance length

---

[2]These differences might stem from the model used (we used here a unigram model, while a colloc3-syll model was previously used) or from the way in which the prosodic information was integrated (at the input level, in the current study, compared to at the grammar level, before). Indeed, a model that makes explicit in its grammar the prosodic boundaries and, thus, learns word boundaries jointly with prosodic boundaries could be more powerful. These aspects will have to be investigated in a future study.

Set	cond	phn	typ	wrd	ambig
CSJ	base			10.82	.02918
	brk3	3.498	.584	5.25	.01996
	brk23			2.75	.01195
ADS	base			6.38	.02981
	brk3	3.089	.579	3.57	.02217
	brk23			2.53	.01746
IDS	base			3.52	.03099
	brk3	3.402	.522	2.48	.02681
	brk23			2.06	.02425

Table 2: Detailed statistics on the three corpora used: average number of phonemes per word token (phn), average number of types per tokens (typ), average number of words per utterance (wrd), and segmentation ambiguity (ambig).

between the base and brk23 was obtained for IDS, the same register that seems to take advantage the least by the information on prosodic boundaries.

Besides the length of the utterance, the length of the words plays an important role in the segmentation task. Longer words would increase the possibility of having substrings which are words on their own, thus decreasing the segmentation performance. As expected, CSJ has the highest average word length, but IDS was found to have a very similar word length, followed by ADS. The unexpected value obtained for IDS might be due to the high number of long onomatopoeia present in the corpus. Thus, any IDS advantage due to having shorter utterances might be reversed by having longer words. We computed also the average number of types per token, which can give information about the distribution of the words in the corpora. In order not to have a measure biased by the size of the corpus, we computed it as a moving average over a window of 100 words. It shows a slightly higher vocabulary diversity for CSJ and ADS, than IDS, suggesting a more difficult segmentation.

The segmental ambiguity score (Fourtassi et al., 2013) measures the number of different parses of a sentence given the gold lexicon, by computing the average entropy in parses, taken into account the probability of each parse. Fourtassi and colleagues argue that this measure captures the intrinsic difficulty of the segmentation problem and predicts segmentation scores across languages (but see Phillips and Pearl (2014)). Here, we found that segmentation ambiguity decreases with the use of prosodic information (by preventing segmentations that would straddle a prosodic break). In contrast, there is not much difference between registers; if anything, IDS is more ambiguous than the two adult corpora; we speculate that this may be due to the presence of many onomatopoeia in IDS (over 8% of the total word tokens) some of which contain a lot of reduplications, which would increase segmentation ambiguity. This may explain why, when prosody equates sentence lengths, the advantage of IDS over ADS becomes small or even reverts to a detrimental effect.

6 Conclusions

We examined the performance of 4 different word segmentation algorithms on two matched corpora of spontaneous ADS and IDS, and a control corpus of more formal ADS, all of them with and without prosodic breaks. We found that, overall, sub-lexical algorithms perform less well than lexical algorithms, that IDS was overall slightly easier or equal to informal ADS, itself easier than formal ADS. In addition, across all algorithms and registers, we observed that prosody helped word segmentation. However, the impact of prosody was unequal and showed an interaction with register: It helped more ADS than IDS to the point that, with prosody taken into account, spontaneous ADS and IDS yield somewhat similar scores.

This has impact for theories of language acquisition, since IDS has been assumed to provide infants with 'hyperspeech', i.e. a simplified kind of input that facilitates language acquisition. If our observations are true, as far as word segmentation goes, it is not the case that IDS is massively easier to segment than ADS, at least at the stage when infants have acquired the ability to use prosodic breaks to constrain word segmentation. Of course, our observations would need to be confirmed and replicated with other languages and recording procedures. To conclude, our study illustrates the interest of testing theories of language acquisition using quantitative tools.

Acknowledgments

BL, MB and ED's research was funded by the European Research Council (ERC-2011-AdG-295810 BOOTPHON), and AC by the Agence Nationale pour la Recherche (ANR-14-CE30-0003 MechELex). It was also supported by the Canon Foundation in Europe and the Agence Nationale pour la Recherche (ANR-10-LABX-0087 IEC, ANR-10-IDEX-0001-02 PSL*).

References

Eleanor Olds Batchelder. 2002. Bootstrapping the lexicon: A computational model of infant speech segmentation. *Cognition* 83(2):167–206.

Benjamin Börschinger and Mark Johnson. 2014. Exploring the role of stress in bayesian word segmentation using adaptor grammars. *Transactions of the Association for Computational Linguistics* 2:93–104.

Michael R Brent and Timothy A Cartwright. 1996. Distributional regularity and phonotactic constraints are useful for segmentation. *Cognition* 61(1):93–125.

Anne Christophe, Ariel Gout, Sharon Peperkamp, and James Morgan. 2003. Discovering words in the continuous speech stream: the role of prosody. *Journal of phonetics* 31(3):585–598.

Alejandrina Cristia. 2013. Input to language: The phonetics and perception of infant-directed speech. *Language and Linguistics Compass* 7(3):157–170.

Suzanne Curtin, Toben H Mintz, and Morten H Christiansen. 2005. Stress changes the representational landscape: Evidence from word segmentation. *Cognition* 96(3):233–262.

Robert Daland and Janet B Pierrehumbert. 2011. Learning diphone-based segmentation. *Cognitive science* 35(1):119–155.

Gabriel Doyle and Roger Levy. 2013. Combining multiple information types in bayesian word segmentation. In *Proceedings of NAACL-HLT*. pages 117–126.

Abdellah Fourtassi, Benjamin Börschinger, Mark Johnson, and Emmanuel Dupoux. 2013. Whyisenglishsoeasytosegment. In *Proceedings of the Fourth Annual Workshop on Cognitive Modeling and Computational Linguistics*. pages 1–10.

Sharon Goldwater, Thomas L Griffiths, and Mark Johnson. 2009. A bayesian framework for word segmentation: Exploring the effects of context. *Cognition* 112(1):21–54.

Mark Johnson and Sharon Goldwater. 2009. Improving nonparameteric bayesian inference: experiments on unsupervised word segmentation with adaptor grammars. In *Proceedings of NAACL-HLT*. pages 317–325.

Mark Johnson, Thomas Griffiths, and Sharon Goldwater. 2007. Adaptor grammars: A framework for specifying compositional nonparametric bayesian models. *Advances in neural information processing systems* 19:641.

Constantine Lignos. 2011. Modeling infant word segmentation. In *Proceedings of the Fifteenth Conference on Computational Natural Language Learning*. pages 29–38.

Bogdan Ludusan, Gabriel Synnaeve, and Emmanuel Dupoux. 2015. Prosodic boundary information helps unsupervised word segmentation. In *Proceedings of NAACL-HLT*. pages 953–963.

K. Maekawa. 2003. Corpus of Spontaneous Japanese: Its design and evaluation. In *ISCA & IEEE Workshop on Spontaneous Speech Processing and Recognition*.

Kikuo Maekawa, Hideaki Kikuchi, Yosuke Igarashi, and Jennifer Venditti. 2002. X-JToBI: an extended J-ToBI for spontaneous speech. In *Proceedings of INTERSPEECH*. pages 1545–1548.

Reiko Mazuka, Yosuke Igarashi, and Ken'ya Nishikawa. 2006. Input for learning Japanese: RIKEN Japanese mother-infant conversation corpus (COE Workshop session 2). *IEICE Technical Report* 106(165):11–15.

Padraic Monaghan and Morten H Christiansen. 2010. Words in puddles of sound: modelling psycholinguistic effects in speech segmentation. *Journal of child language* 37(03):545–564.

Lawrence Phillips and Lisa Pearl. 2014. Bayesian inference as a viable cross-linguistic word segmentation strategy: It's all about what's useful. In *Proceedings of CogSci*. pages 2775–2780.

Amanda Saksida, Alan Langus, and Marina Nespor. 2016. Co-occurrence statistics as a language-dependent cue for speech segmentation. *Developmental science* .

Amanda Seidl and Elizabeth K Johnson. 2006. Infant word segmentation revisited: Edge alignment facilitates target extraction. *Developmental science* 9(6):565–573.

Erik D Thiessen, Emily A Hill, and Jenny R Saffran. 2005. Infant-directed speech facilitates word segmentation. *Infancy* 7(1):53–71.

Jennifer Venditti. 2005. The J-ToBI model of Japanese intonation. In Sun-Ah Jun, editor, *Prosodic typology: The phonology of intonation and phrasing*, Oxford University Press, Oxford, pages 172–200.

A Two-Stage Parsing Method for Text-Level Discourse Analysis

Yizhong Wang   **Sujian Li**   **Houfeng Wang**

Key Laboratory of Computational Linguistics, Peking University, MOE, China

{yizhong, lisujian, wanghf}@pku.edu.cn

Abstract

Previous work introduced transition-based algorithms to form a unified architecture of parsing rhetorical structures (including span, nuclearity and relation), but did not achieve satisfactory performance. In this paper, we propose that transition-based model is more appropriate for parsing the naked discourse tree (i.e., identifying span and nuclearity) due to data sparsity. At the same time, we argue that relation labeling can benefit from naked tree structure and should be treated elaborately with consideration of three kinds of relations including within-sentence, across-sentence and across-paragraph relations. Thus, we design a pipelined two-stage parsing method for generating an RST tree from text. Experimental results show that our method achieves state-of-the-art performance, especially on span and nuclearity identification.

1 Introduction

A typical document is usually organized in a coherent way that each text unit is relevant to its context and plays a role in the entire semantics. Text-level discourse analysis tries to identify such discourse structure of a document and its success can benefit many downstream tasks, such as sentiment analysis (Polanyi and van den Berg, 2011) and document summarization (Louis et al., 2010).

One most influential text-level discourse parsing theory is Rhetorical Structure Theory (RST) (Mann and Thompson, 1988), under which a text is parsed to a hierarchical discourse tree. The leaf nodes of this tree correspond to Elementary Discourse Units (EDUs, usually clauses) and then leaf nodes are recursively connected by rhetorical rela-

tions to form larger text spans until the final tree is built. RST also depicts which part is more important in a relation by tagging *Nucleus* or *Satellite*. Generally, each relation at least includes a *Nucleus* and there are three nuclearity types: *Nucleus-Satellite (NS)*, *Satellite-Nucleus (SN)* and *Nucleus-Nucleus (NN)*. Therefore, the performance of RST discourse parsing can be evaluated from three aspects: span, nuclearity and relation.

To parse discourse trees, transition-based parsing model, which gains significant success in dependency parsing (Yamada and Matsumoto, 2003; Nivre et al., 2006) , was introduced to discourse analysis. Marcu (1999) first employed a transition system to derive a discourse parse tree. In such a system, action labels are designed by combining shift-reduce action with nuclearity and relation labels, so that one classifier can determine span, nuclearity and relation simultaneously via judging actions. More recent studies followed this research line and enhanced the performance by either tuning the models (Sagae, 2009) or using more effective features (Ji and Eisenstein, 2014; Heilman and Sagae, 2015). Though these transition-based models show advantages in the unified processing of span, nuclearity and relation, they report weaker performance than other methods, like CYK-like algorithms (Li et al., 2014, 2016) or greedy bottom-up algorithms that merge adjacent spans (Hernault et al., 2010; Feng and Hirst, 2014).

In such cases, we analyze that the labelled data can not sufficiently support the classifier to distinguish among the information-rich actions (e.g., Reduce-NS-Contrast) , since there exist very few labelled text-level discourse corpus available for training. The limited training data will cause unbalanced actions and lead to the problems of data sparsity and overfitting. Thus, we propose to use the transition-based model to parse a naked dis-

Proceedings of the 55th Annual Meeting of the Association for Computational Linguistics (Short Papers), pages 184–188
Vancouver, Canada, July 30 - August 4, 2017. ©2017 Association for Computational Linguistics
https://doi.org/10.18653/v1/P17-2029

course tree (i.e., identifying span and nuclearity) in the first stage. The benefits are three-fold. First, we can still use the transition based model which is a good tree construction tool. Second, much fewer actions need to be identified in the tree construction process. Third, we could separately label relations, which needs careful consideration.

In the second stage, relation labels for each span are determined independently. Prior studies (Joty et al., 2013; Feng and Hirst, 2014) have found that rhetorical relations distribute differently intra-sententially vs. multi-sententially. They discriminate the two levels by training two models with different feature sets. We take a further step and argue that relations between paragraphs are usually more loosely connected than those between sentences within the same paragraph. Therefore we train three separate classifiers for labeling relations at three levels: within-sentence, across-sentence and across-paragraph. Different features are used for each classifier and the naked tree structure generated in the first stage is also leveraged as features. Experiments on the RST-DT corpus demonstrate the effectiveness of our pipelined two-stage discourse parsing model.

2 Our Method

Our discourse parsing process is composed of two stages: tree structure construction and relation labeling. In this work, we follow the convention to use the gold standard EDU segmentations and focus on building a tree with nuclearity and relation labels assigned for each inner node.

2.1 Tree Structure Construction

In a typical transition-based system for discourse parsing, the parsing process is modeled as a sequence of *shift* and *reduce* actions, which are applied to a stack and a queue. The stack is initialized to be empty and the queue contains all EDUs in the document. At each step, the parser performs either *shift* or *reduce*. *Shift* pushes the first EDU in the queue to the top of the stack, while *reduce* pops and merges the top elements in the stack to get a new subtree, which is then pushed back to the top of the stack. A parse tree can be finally constructed until the queue is empty and the stack only contains the complete tree. Only one classifier is learned to judge the actions at each step.

To derive a discourse tree in a unified framework, prior systems design multiple reduce actions

with consideration of both nuclearity and relation types. With 3 nuclearity types and 18 relation types, the number of reduce actions exceeds 40, leading to the data sparsity problem.

In our parsing model, a transition-based system is responsible for building the naked tree without relation labels. We only design four types of actions, including: Shift, Reduce-NN, Reduce-NS, Reduce-SN. We identify span and nuclearity simultaneously in the transition-based tree construction, since nuclearity is actually closely related to the tree structure, just as the left-arc and right-arc action in dependency parsing. The number of the four actions on the training set of RST-DT corpus is shown in Table 1. Though the four actions still have an unbalanced distribution, the relatively large number of occurrences assures that the classifier in our system can be trained more sufficiently.

Shift	Reduce-NN	Reduce-NS	Reduce-SN
19443	4329	11702	3065

Table 1: Statistics of the Four Actions

2.2 Relation Labeling

The most challenging subtask of discourse parsing is relation labeling. In a binarized RST discourse tree, a relation label can be determined for each internal node, describing the relation between its left and right subtrees[1].

We conduct relation labeling after the naked tree structure has been constructed. On one hand, the naked tree structure can provide more information to support relation classification, verified in (Feng and Hirst, 2014). For example, some relations tend to appear around the tree root while other relaitons would like to keep away from the root. On the other hand, we can elaborately distinguish relations at different levels, including within-sentence, across-sentence, across-paragraph. We add across-paragraph level because some relations, like textual-organization and topic-change are observed to mainly occur between paragraphs.

Therefore, we adopt three classifiers for labeling relations at different levels. We first traverse the naked tree in post order and ignore leaf nodes, since we only need to judge relations for internal nodes. Next, for each internal node, we determine

---

[1]Relation label is actually assigned to the satellite subtree and a "Span" label is assigned to the nucleus substree.

whether its left and right subtrees are in different
paragraphs, or the same paragraph, or the same
sentence. For each level, we predict a relation label using the corresponding classifier.

2.3 Training

We use SVM classifiers for the four classification
tasks (one action classifier and three relation classifiers). We take the linear kernel for fast training
and use squared hinge loss with L_1 penalty on the
error term. The penalty coefficient C is set to 1.

The four classifiers are learned with offline
training. Training instances for the action classifier are generated by converting gold parse trees
into a sequence of actions. Then we extract features for each action before it is performed. Training instances for relation classifiers are prepared
by traversing the gold parse trees and extracting
features for the relation of each internal node.

3 Features

This section details the features used in our model,
which are a key to the four classifiers in discourse
parsing.

For the action classifier, features are extracted
from the top 2 elements S_1, S_2 in the stack and the
first EDU Q_1 in the queue. We design the feature
sets for the action classifier as follows:

- **Status features:** the previous action; number of
  elements in the stack and queue.

- **Position features:** whether S_1, S_2 or S_1, Q_1
  are in the same sentence or paragraph; whether
  they are start or end of a sentence, paragraph or
  document; distance from S_1, S_2, Q_1 to the start
  and end of document.

- **Structural features:** nuclearity type (NN, NS
  or SN) of S_1, S_2; number of EDUs and sentences in S_1, S_2; length comparison of S_1, S_2
  with respect to EDUs and sentences.

- **Dependency features:** whether dependency relations exist between S_1, S_2 or between S_1, Q_1;
  the dependency direction and relation type.

- **N-gram features:** the first and the last n words
  and their POS tags in the text of S_1, S_2, Q_1,
  where $n \in \{1, 2\}$.

- **Nucleus features:** the dependency heads of
  the nucleus EDUs[2] for S_1, S_2, Q_1 and their
  POS tags; brown clusters (Brown et al., 1992;

Turian et al., 2010) of all the words in the nucleus EDUs of S_1, S_2, Q_1.

Next, we list all the features used for the three
relation classifiers. Given an internal node P in the
naked tree, we aim to predict the relation between
its left child C_{left} and right child C_{right}. Dependency features, N-gram features and nucleus features discussed above are also needed, the only
difference is that these features are applied to the
left and right children. Other features include:

- **Refined Structural features:** nuclearity type
  of node P; distance from P, C_{left}, C_{right} to
  the start and end of the document / paragraph /
  sentence with respect to paragraphs / sentences
  / EDUs; number of paragraphs / sentences /
  EDUs in C_{left} and C_{right}; length comparison
  of C_{left} and C_{right} with respect to paragraphs /
  sentences / EDUs.

- **Tree features:** depth and height of the node P
  in the tree; nuclearity type of P and P's grand-
  parent node, if they exist. This feature type benefits from our stagewise parsing method.

Relation labeling classifiers at different levels
pick somewhat different features from all the features. N-gram and structural features work for the
three classifiers. Dependency features are only
used for within-sentence classifier. Nucleus features and tree features are only used for across-
sentence and across-paragraph classifiers.

4 Experiments

We evaluate our parser on RST Discourse Treebank (RST-DT) (Carlson et al., 2003) and thor-
oughly analyze different components of our
method. Results show our parsing model achieves
state-of-the-art performance on the text-level discourse parsing task.

4.1 Setup

RST-DT annotates 385 documents (347 for
training and 38 for testing) from the Wall
Street Journal using Rhetorical Structure Theory (Mann and Thompson, 1988). Convention-
ally, we use 18 coarse-grained relations and bi-
narize non-binary relations with right-branching
(Sagae and Lavie, 2005). For preprocessing, we
use the Stanford CoreNLP toolkit (Manning et al.,
2014) to lemmatize words, get POS tags, segment
sentences and syntactically parse them.

To directly compare with other discourse parsing systems, we employ the same evaluation met-

---

[2]Nucleus EDU is defined by recursively selecting the Nucleus in the binary tree until an EDU (leaf node) is reached.

rics, i.e. the precision, recall and F-score [3] with respect to span (S), nuclearity (N) and relation (R), as defined by Marcu (2000).

4.2 Results and Analysis

We compare our system against other state-of-the-art discourse parsers, shown in Table 2. Among them, Joty et al. (2013), Li et al. (2014) and Li et al. (2016) all employ CKY-like algorithms to search global optimal parsing result. Ji and Eisenstein (2014) and Heilman and Sagae (2015) use transition-based parsing systems with improvements on the feature representation. Feng and Hirst (2014) adopts a greedy approach that merges two adjacent spans at each step and two CRFs are used to predict the structure and the relation separately.

From Table 2, we can see that our method outperforms all the others with respect to span and nuclearity, and exceeds most systems on relation labeling. Especially, our method significantly outperforms other transition-based models (Ji and Eisenstein, 2014; Heilman and Sagae, 2015) on building the naked tree structure (span and nuclearity). This is mainly due to the proper design of actions in our transition-based system. The reason that Ji and Eisenstein (2014) achieve a high score of relation labeling may be that their latent representations are more advantageous in capturing semantics, which will inspire us to refine our features in future work.

Model	S	N	R
Joty et al. (2013)	82.7	68.4	55.7
Li et al. (2014)	84.0	70.8	58.6
Ji and Eisenstein (2014)	82.1	71.1	**61.6**
Feng and Hirst (2014)	85.7	71.0	58.2
Heilman and Sagae (2015)	83.5	69.3	57.4
Li et al. (2016)	85.8	71.1	58.9
Ours	**86.0**	**72.4**	59.7
Human [4]	88.7	77.7	65.8

Table 2: Performance comparison with state-of-the-art parsers.

To further explore the influence of different components in our model, we implement three simplified versions (i.e., *Simp*-1/2/3), as is shown in Table 3. **Stage** means whether two-stage strat-

egy is adopted, **Level** denotes whether three kinds of relations (i.e., within-sentence, across-sentence, and across-paragraph) are differently classified, and **Tree** represents whether relation labeling uses tree features generated in the first stage.

The simplest model *Simp*-1 is almost the same as (Heilman and Sagae, 2015) except that we employ more features. That *Simp*-1 has a high performance also means that transition-based method has potentials for constructing discourse trees. *Simp*-2 adopts the two-stage strategy, but uses only one classifier to classify all the relations. We can observe that the pipelined two stages bring a significant improvement with respect to all the aspects, compared to *Simp*-1. The difference between *Simp*-3 and Ours is that *Simp*-3 does not exploit the tree structure features generated in the first stage. We can see that the three-level relation classification and tree features together bring an improvement of about 1 percent on relation labeling. Compared with prior work, this slight improvement is also valuable and more efficacious features need to be explored.

Model	Stage	Level	Tree	S	N	R
Simp-1	No	No	No	84.4	70.7	57.7
Simp-2	Yes	No	No	86.0	72.4	58.6
Simp-3	Yes	Yes	No	86.0	72.4	59.4
Ours	Yes	Yes	Yes	86.0	72.4	59.7

Table 3: Comparison with simplified versions.

Though the three-level relation labeling does not achieve prominent improvement, we get some interesting results via analyzing the performance on each relation. The *Attribution* and *Same-Unit* relations are the top 2 relations that we successfully classify with F-score as 0.87 and 0.83 respectively and over 90 percent of these two relations occur within sentences. This means that within-sentence relations are relatively easy to cope with. We also compare our final model with *Simp*-1 and results show that the Textual-Organization and Topic-Comment relaitons gain an increase by 20% and 8% respectively. Most of the Textual-Organization and Topic-Comment relations are loosely across paragraphs and their numbers (i.e., 148 and 130 instances in training data) are also relatively small. We can see that our method can improve on predicting infrequent relations and partly solve the data sparsity problem. At the same time, we infer that relations indeed belong to different levels and deserve fine treatment.

---

[3] Precision, recall and F-score are the same when manual segmentation is used.

[4] The human agreement on the annotations of RST corpus

5 Conclusion

In this paper, we design a novel two-stage method for text-level discourse analysis. The first stage adopts the transition-based algorithm to construct naked trees with consideration of span and nuclearity. The second stage categorizes relations into three levels and uses three classifiers for relation labeling. This pipelined design can mitigate the data sparsity problem in tree construction, and provide a new view of elaborately treating relations. Comprehensive experiments show the effectiveness of our proposed method.

Acknowledgments

We thank the anonymous reviewers for their insightful comments on this paper. This work was partially supported by National Natural Science Foundation of China (61572049 and 61333018). The correspondence author of this paper is Sujian Li.

References

Peter F Brown, Peter V Desouza, Robert L Mercer, Vincent J Della Pietra, and Jenifer C Lai. 1992. Class-based n-gram models of natural language. *Computational linguistics* 18(4):467–479.

Lynn Carlson, Daniel Marcu, and Mary Ellen Okurowski. 2003. Building a discourse-tagged corpus in the framework of rhetorical structure theory. In *Current and new directions in discourse and dialogue*, Springer, pages 85–112.

Vanessa Wei Feng and Graeme Hirst. 2014. A linear-time bottom-up discourse parser with constraints and post-editing. In *ACL*. pages 511–521.

Michael Heilman and Kenji Sagae. 2015. Fast rhetorical structure theory discourse parsing. *arXiv preprint arXiv:1505.02425*.

Hugo Hernault, Helmut Prendinger, David A DuVerle, Mitsuru Ishizuka, and Tim Paek. 2010. Hilda: a discourse parser using support vector machine classification. *Dialogue and Discourse* 1(3):1–33.

Yangfeng Ji and Jacob Eisenstein. 2014. Representation learning for text-level discourse parsing. In *ACL*. pages 13–24.

Shafiq R Joty, Giuseppe Carenini, Raymond T Ng, and Yashar Mehdad. 2013. Combining intra-and multi-sentential rhetorical parsing for document-level discourse analysis. In *ACL (1)*. pages 486–496.

Jiwei Li, Rumeng Li, and Eduard H Hovy. 2014. Recursive deep models for discourse parsing. In *EMNLP*. pages 2061–2069.

Qi Li, Tianshi Li, and Baobao Chang. 2016. Discourse parsing with attention-based hierarchical neural networks pages 362–371.

Annie Louis, Aravind Joshi, and Ani Nenkova. 2010. Discourse indicators for content selection in summarization. In *Proceedings of the 11th Annual Meeting of the Special Interest Group on Discourse and Dialogue*. Association for Computational Linguistics, pages 147–156.

William C Mann and Sandra A Thompson. 1988. Rhetorical structure theory: Toward a functional theory of text organization. *Text-Interdisciplinary Journal for the Study of Discourse* 8(3):243–281.

Christopher D. Manning, Mihai Surdeanu, John Bauer, Jenny Finkel, Steven J. Bethard, and David McClosky. 2014. The stanford corenlp natural language processing toolkit. In *Association for Computational Linguistics (ACL) System Demonstrations*. pages 55–60.

Daniel Marcu. 1999. A decision-based approach to rhetorical parsing. In *Proceedings of the 37th annual meeting of the Association for Computational Linguistics on Computational Linguistics*. Association for Computational Linguistics, pages 365–372.

Daniel Marcu. 2000. *The theory and practice of discourse parsing and summarization*. MIT press.

Joakim Nivre, Johan Hall, Jens Nilsson, Gülşen Eryiit, and Svetoslav Marinov. 2006. Labeled pseudo-projective dependency parsing with support vector machines. In *Proceedings of the Tenth Conference on Computational Natural Language Learning*. Association for Computational Linguistics, pages 221–225.

Livia Polanyi and Martin van den Berg. 2011. Discourse structure and sentiment. In *Data Mining Workshops (ICDMW), 2011 IEEE 11th International Conference on*. IEEE, pages 97–102.

Kenji Sagae. 2009. Analysis of discourse structure with syntactic dependencies and data-driven shift-reduce parsing. In *Proceedings of the 11th International Conference on Parsing Technologies*. Association for Computational Linguistics, pages 81–84.

Kenji Sagae and Alon Lavie. 2005. A classifier-based parser with linear run-time complexity. In *Proceedings of the Ninth International Workshop on Parsing Technology*. Association for Computational Linguistics, pages 125–132.

Joseph Turian, Lev Ratinov, and Yoshua Bengio. 2010. Word representations: a simple and general method for semi-supervised learning. In *ACL*. Association for Computational Linguistics, pages 384–394.

Hiroyasu Yamada and Yuji Matsumoto. 2003. Statistical dependency analysis with support vector machines. In *Proceedings of IWPT*. volume 3, pages 195–206.

Error-repair Dependency Parsing for Ungrammatical Texts

Keisuke Sakaguchi[†] and **Matt Post**[‡] and **Benjamin Van Durme**[††]
[†]Center for Language and Speech Processing, Johns Hopkins University
[‡]Human Language Technology Center of Excellence, Johns Hopkins University
{keisuke,post,vandurme}@cs.jhu.edu

Abstract

We propose a new dependency parsing scheme which jointly parses a sentence and repairs grammatical errors by extending the non-directional transition-based formalism of Goldberg and Elhadad (2010) with three additional actions: SUBSTITUTE, DELETE, INSERT. Because these actions may cause an infinite loop in derivation, we also introduce simple constraints that ensure the parser termination. We evaluate our model with respect to dependency accuracy and grammaticality improvements for ungrammatical sentences, demonstrating the robustness and applicability of our scheme.

1 Introduction

Robustness has always been a desirable property for natural language parsers: humans generate a variety of noisy outputs, such as ungrammatical webpages, speech disfluencies, and the text in language learner's essays. Such *non-canonical* text contains grammatical errors such as substitutions, insertions, and deletions. For example, a non-native speaker of English might write *"*I look in forward hear from you"*, where *in* is inserted, *to* is deleted, and *hearing* is substituted incorrectly.

We propose a novel dependency parsing scheme that jointly parses and repairs ungrammatical sentences with these sorts of errors. The parser is based on the *non-directional easy-first* (EF) parser introduced by Goldberg and Elhadad (2010) (GE herein), which iteratively adds the most probable arc until the parse tree is completed. These actions are called ATTACHLEFT and ATTACHRIGHT depending on the direction of the arc. We extend the EF parsing scheme to be robust for ungrammatical inputs by correcting grammatical er-

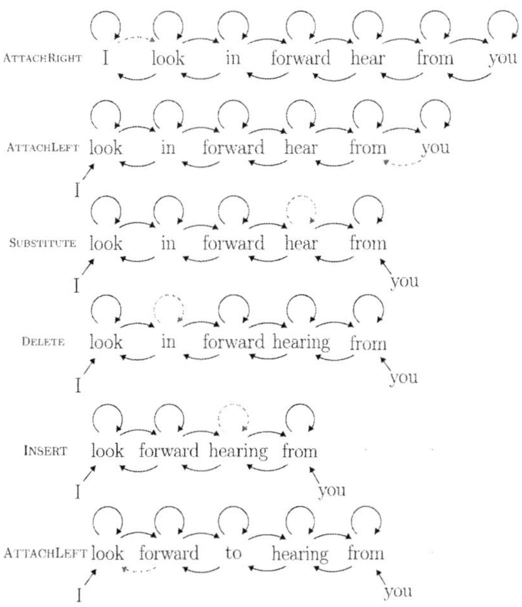

Figure 1: Illustrative example of partial derivation under error-repair easy-first non-directional dependency parsing. Solid arrows represent ATTACHRIGHT and ATTACHLEFT in Goldberg and Elhadad (2010). Dotted arcs correspond to actions for each step. Following the notation by GE: arcs are directed from a child to its parent.

rors with three new actions: SUBSTITUTE, INSERT, and DELETE. These new actions do not add an arc between tokens but instead they edit a single token. As a result, the parser is able to jointly parse and correct grammatical errors in the input sentence. We call this new scheme *Error-Repair Non-Directional Easy-First parsing* (EREF). Since the new actions may greatly increase the search space (e.g., infinite substitutions), we also introduce simple constraints to avoid such issues.

We first describe the technical details of EREF (§2) and then evaluate our EREF parser with respect to dependency accuracy (robustness) and grammaticality improvements (§3). Finally, we

Proceedings of the 55th Annual Meeting of the Association for Computational Linguistics (Short Papers), pages 189–195
Vancouver, Canada, July 30 - August 4, 2017. ©2017 Association for Computational Linguistics
https://doi.org/10.18653/v1/P17-2030

position this effort at the intersection of noisy text parsing and grammatical error correction (§4).

2 Model

Non-directional Easy-first Parsing   Let us begin with a brief review of a non-directional easy-first (EF) parsing scheme proposed by GE, which is the foundation of our proposed scheme described in the following sections.

The EF parser has a list of partial structures p_1, ..., p_k (called *pending*) initialized with sentence tokens w_1, ..., w_n, and it keeps updating *pending* through derivations. Unlike left-to-right (e.g., shift-reduce) parsing algorithms (Yamada and Matsumoto, 2003; Nivre, 2004), EF iteratively selects the best pair of adjoining tokens and chooses the direction of attachment: ATTACHLEFT or ATTACHRIGHT. Once the action is committed, the corresponding dependency arc is added and the child token is removed from *pending*. The first two derivations in Figure 1 depict ATTACHRIGHT and ATTACHLEFT. Pseudocode is shown in Algorithm 1 (lines 1, 3-12).

The parser is trained using the structured perceptron (Collins, 2002) to choose actions to take given a set of features expanded from templates. The cost of actions is computed at every step by checking the *validity*: whether a new arc is included in the gold parse and whether the child already has all its children. See GE for further description of feature templates and structured perceptron training. Since it is possible that there are multiple *valid* sequence of actions and it is important to examine a large search space, the parser is allowed to explore (possibly incorrect) actions with a certain probability, termed *learning with exploration* by Goldberg and Nivre (2013).

Error-repair variant of EF   Error-repair non-directional easy-first parsing scheme (EREF) is a variant of EF. We add three new actions: SUBSTITUTE, DELETE, INSERT as $Acts_{ER}$. We do not deal with a swapping action (Nivre, 2009) to deal with word reordering errors, since the errors are even less frequent than other error types (Leacock et al., 2014). SUBSTITUTE replaces a token to a grammatically more probable token, DELETE removes an unnecessary token, and INSERT inserts a new token at a designated index. These actions are shown in Figure 1 and Algorithm 1 (lines 13-25). Because the length of *pending* decreases as an attachment occurs, the parser

---

Algorithm 1: Error-repair non-directional parsing

Input: ungrammatical sentence$= w_1 \ldots w_n$
Output: a set of dependency arcs (*Arcs*),
        repaired sentence ($\hat{w}_1 \ldots \hat{w}_m$)

```
1  Acts = { ATTACHLEFT, ATTACHRIGHT }
2  Acts_ER = { DELETE, INSERT, SUBSTITUTE }
3  Arcs = { }
4  pending = p_1...p_n ← w_1...w_n
5  repaired = ŵ_1...ŵ_n ← w_1...w_n
6  while len (pending) > 1 do
7      best ←   argmax     score (act (i))
                act∈Acts∪Acts_ER
8      s.t. 1 ≤ i ≤ len(pending) ∩ isLegal(act, pending)
9      if best ∈ Acts then
10         (parent, child) ← edgeFor(best)
11         Arcs.add((parent, child))
12         pending.remove(child)
13     else if best = SUBSTITUTE then
14         c = bestCandidate(best, repaired)
15         pending.replace(p_i, c)
16         repaired.replace(ŵ_{p_i.idx}, c)
17     else if best = DELETE then
18         pending.remove(p_i)
19         repaired.remove(ŵ_{p_i.idx})
20         Arcs.updateIndex()
21     else if best = INSERT then
22         c = bestCandidate(best, repaired)
23         pending.insert(i, c)
24         repaired.insert(p_i.idx, c)
25         Arcs.updateIndex()
26 end
27 return Arcs, repaired
```

---

also keeps the token indices in *repaired* (line 5), which holds all tokens in a sentence throughout the parsing process. Furthermore, the parser updates token indices in *pending* and *repaired* when INSERT or DELETE occurs. Technically, when a token at i is deleted/inserted, the parser decrements/increments the indices that are $k >= i$ (before executing the action) in *pending*, *repaired*, and parents and children in a (partial) dependency tree (*Arcs*).

To find the best candidate for SUBSTITUTE and INSERT efficiently, we restrict candidates to the same part-of-speech or pre-defined candidate list. We select the best candidate by comparing each n-gram language model score with the same surrounding context.

Similar to EF, while training the parser, the cost

Algorithm 2: Check validity during training

1 **Function** *isValid(act, repaired, Gold)*
2   d_{before} = *editDistance(repaired, Gold)*
3   *repaired*$^+$ = *repaired*.apply(*act*)
4   d_{after} = *editDistance(repaired*$^+$*, Gold)*
5   **if** $d_{\text{before}} > d_{\text{after}}$ **then return** *true*;
6   **else return** *false*;
7 **end**

for *Acts*$_{\text{ER}}$ is based on *validity*. The *validity* of the new actions is computed by taking the edit distance (d) between the *Gold* tokens ($w_1^* \dots w_r^*$) and the sentence state that the parser stores in *repaired* ($\hat{w}_1 \dots \hat{w}_m$). When the edit distance after taking an action (d_{after}) is smaller than before (d_{before}), we regard the action as *valid* (Algorithm 2).

One serious concern of EREF is that the new actions may cause an infinite loop during parsing (e.g., infinite SUBSTITUTE, or an alternative DELETE and INSERT sequence.). To avoid this, we introduce two constraints: (1) *edit flag* and (2) *edit limit*. *Edit flag* is assigned for each token as a property, and a parser is not allowed to execute *Acts*$_{\text{ER}}$ on a token if its flag is on. The flag is turned on when a parser executes *Acts*$_{\text{ER}}$ on a token whose flag is off. In INSERT action, the flag of the inserted token is activated, while the subsequent token (which gave rise to the INSERT) is not. *Edit limit* is set to be the number of tokens in a sentence, and the parser is not allowed to perform *Acts*$_{\text{ER}}$ when the total number of execution of *Acts*$_{\text{ER}}$ exceeds the limit. These two constraints prevent the parser from falling into an infinite loop as well as parsing in the same order of time complexity as GE. We also add the following constraints to avoid unreasonable derivations: (i) a word with a dependent cannot be deleted and (ii) any child words cannot be substituted. All the constraints are implemented in the *isLegal*() function in Algorithm 1 (line 8). We note that these constraints not only prevent undesirable derivations but also leads to an efficiency in exploring the search space during training.

3   Experiment

Data and Evaluation   We evaluate EREF with respect to dependency parsing accuracy (Exp1) and grammaticality improvement (Exp2).[1]

---

[1] Code for the experiments is available at `http://github.com/keisks/error-repair-parsing`

In the first experiment, as in GE, we train and evaluate our parser on the English dataset from the Penn Treebank (Marcus et al., 1993) with the Penn2Malt conversion program (Sections 2-21 for training, 22 for tuning, and 23 for test). We use the PTB for the dependency experiment, since there are no ungrammatical text corpora that has dependency annotation on the *corrected* texts by human.

We choose the following most frequent error types that are used in CoNLL 2013 shared task (Ng et al., 2013):

1. Determiner (substitution, deletion, insertion)
2. Preposition (substitution, deletion, insertion)
3. Noun number (singular vs. plural)
4. Verb form (tense and aspect)
5. Subject verb agreement

Regarding the candidate sets for INSERT and SUBSTITUTE actions, following Rozovskaya and Roth (2014), we focus on the most common candidates for each error type, setting the determiner candidates to be {*a, an, the,* ϕ (as deletion)}, preposition candidates to be {*on, about, from, for, of, to, at, in, with, by,* ϕ}, and verb forms to be {VB(P|Z|G|D|N)}. We build a 5-gram language model on English Gigaword with the KenLM Toolkit (Heafield, 2011) for EREF to select the best candidate.

We manually inject grammatical errors into PTB with certain error-rates similarly to the Gen-ERRate toolkit by Foster and Andersen (2009), which is designed to create synthetic errors into sentences to improve grammatical error detection.

We train and tune EREF models with different token-level error injection rates from 5% (E05) to 20% (E20), because language learner corpora have generally around 5% to 15% of token level errors depending on learners' proficiency (Leacock et al., 2014). Since the error injection is stochastic, we train each model with 10 runs and take an average of parser performance on the test set.

As a baseline, we use the original parser as described by GE, which is equivalent to EREF with training on an error-free corpus (E00). Since the EF baseline does not allow error correction during parsing, we pre-process the test data with a grammatical error correction system similar to Rozovskaya and Roth (2014), where a combination of classifiers for each error type corrects grammatical errors.

For evaluation, we jointly parse and correct grammatical errors in the test set with different

(%)	Baseline	E05	E10	E15	E20
0	**91.43**	91.12	90.87	90.61	90.29
5	89.99	**90.00**	89.87	89.72	89.48
10	87.84	87.99	88.07	**88.14**	88.04
15	85.64	86.18	86.54	86.75	**86.82**
20	84.12	84.78	85.28	85.50	**85.76**
∇	-0.37	-0.32	-0.28	-0.26	**-0.23**

Table 1: Unlabeled dependency accuracy results with the 5x5 models and test sets. ∇ shows the slope of deterioration in parser performance.

	E05	E10	E15	E20
# edited sents (out of 5,124)	175	391	583	861
grammaticality (source)	2.92	2.95	2.95	2.89
grammaticality (this work)	2.96	2.99	**3.27**	**2.98**

Table 2: Grammaticality scores by 1-4 scale regression model (Heilman et al., 2014). The first row shows the number of sentences that are made (at least one) change. Bold numbers show statistically significant improvements.

Successful cases
I 'm looking forward to [-see-] {+seeing+} you next summer
I 've never [-approve-] {+approved+} his deal
There is not {+a+} possibility to travel

Failure cases
I 've [-assisted-] {+assisting+} your new musical show
I am writing to complain [-about-] {+with+} somethings
I hope you liked {+the+} everything I said

Table 3: Successful and failure examples by EREF. The edits are represented by [-deletion-] and {+insertion+}. Adjacent pairs of deletion and insertion are considered as substitution.

error injection rates (from 0% to 20%). It is important to note that the number of tokens between the parser output and the oracle may be different because of error injection into the test set and $Acts_{ER}$ during parsing. To handle this mismatch, we evaluate the dependency accuracy with alignment (Favre et al., 2010) in the spirit of SParseval (Roark et al., 2006), where tokens between a hypothesis and oracle are aligned prior to calculating the dependency accuracy.

In the second experiment, we use the Treebank of Learner English (TLE) (Berzak et al., 2016) to see the grammaticality improvement in a real scenario. TLE contains 5,124 sentences and 2.69 (std 1.9) token errors per sentence. The average sentence length is 19.06 (std 9.47). TLE also provides dependency labels and POS tags on the *raw (ungrammatical)* sentences. It is important to note that TLE has dependency annotation only for the original *ungrammatical* sentences, and therefore we do not compute the accuracy of dependency parse in this experiment. Since the corpus size is small, we train EREF (E05 to E20) on 100k sentences from Annotated Gigaword (Napoles et al., 2012) and used TLE as a test set. Spelling errors are ignored because EREF can use the POS information. Grammaticality is evaluated by a regression model (Heilman et al., 2014), which scores grammaticality on the ordinal scale (from 1 to 4).

Results Table 1 shows the result of unlabeled dependency accuracy (UAS).[2] As previously pre-sented (Foster, 2007; Cahill, 2015), our experiment also shows that parser performance deteriorated as the error rate in the test corpus increased. On the error-free test set (0%), the baseline (EF pipeline) outperforms other EREF models; the accuracy is lower when the parser is trained on noisier data. The difference among the models becomes small when the test set has 10% error injection rate. As the rate increases further, the trend of parser accuracy reverses. When the test set has 15% or higher noise, the E20 is the most accurate parser. This trend is presented by the slope of deterioration $\nabla = \frac{\text{accuracy}_{20\%} - \text{accuracy}_{0\%}}{20}$ in Table 1; a parser trained on noisier training data shows smaller decline and more robustness.[3] This indicates that the EREF is more robust than the vanilla EF on ungrammatical texts by jointly parsing and correcting errors.

Table 2 demonstrates the result of grammaticality improvement (1-4 scale) on the TLE corpus, and Table 3 shows successful and failure corrections by EREF. Minimally trained models (E05 and E10) show little improvement in grammaticality because the models are too conservative to make edits. The models with higher error-injection rates (E15 and E20) achieve 0.1 to 0.3 improvements that are statistically significant. There is still room to improve regarding the amount of corrections. This is probably because TLE contains a variety of errors (e.g., collocation, punctuation) in addition to the five error types we focus. To deal with other error types, we can extend EREF by adding more actions, although it increases the search space.

From a practical perspective, the level of ungrammaticality should be realized ahead of time. This is an issue to be addressed in future research.

---

[2]Technically, it is possible to train the model with learning labels simultaneously (LAS), but there is a trade-off between search space and training time. The primary goal of this experiment is to see if the EREF is able to detect and correct grammatical errors.

[3]Baseline model *without* preprocessing always underperformed the preprocessed baseline.

4 Related Work

Our work lies at the intersection of parsing non-canonical texts and grammatical error correction.

Joint dependency parsing and disfluency detection has been pursued (Rasooli and Tetreault, 2013, 2014; Honnibal and Johnson, 2014; Wu et al., 2015; Yoshikawa et al., 2016), where a parser jointly parses and detects disfluency (e.g., reparandum and interregnum) for a given speech utterance. Our work could be considered an extension via adding SUBSTITUTE and INSERT actions, although we depend on easy-first non-directional parsing framework instead of a left-to-right strategy. Importantly, the DELETE action is easier to handle than the SUBSTITUTE and INSERT actions, because they bring us challenging issues about a process of candidate word generation and avoiding an infinite loop in derivation. We have addressed these issues as explained in §2.

In terms of the literature from grammatical error correction, this work is closely related to Dahlmeier and Ng (2012), where they show an error correction decoder with the easy-first strategy. The decoder iteratively corrects the most probable ungrammatical token by applying different classifiers for each error type. The EREF parser also depends on the easy-first strategy to find ungrammatical index to be deleted, inserted, or substituted, but it parses and corrects errors jointly whereas the decoder is designed as a grammatical error correction framework rather than a parser.

There is a line of work for parsing ungrammatical sentences (e.g., web forum) by adapting an *existing* parsing scheme on domain specific annotations (Petrov and McDonald, 2012; Cahill, 2015; Berzak et al., 2016; Nagata and Sakaguchi, 2016). Although we share an interest with respect to dealing with ungrammatical sentences, EREF focuses on the parsing scheme for repairing grammatical errors instead of adapting a parser with a domain specific annotation scheme.

More broadly, our work can also be regarded as one of the joint parsing and text normalization tasks such as joint spelling correction and POS tagging (Sakaguchi et al., 2012), word segmentation and POS tagging (Kaji and Kitsuregawa, 2014; Qian et al., 2015).

5 Conclusions

We have presented an *error-repair* variant of the *non-directional easy-first* dependency parser. We have introduced three new actions, SUBSTITUTE, INSERT, and DELETE into the parser so that it jointly parses and corrects grammatical errors in a sentence. To address the issue of parsing incompletion due to the new actions, we have proposed simple constraints that keep track of editing history for each token and the total number of edits during derivation. The experimental result has demonstrated robustness of EREF parsers against EF and grammaticality improvement. Our work is positioned at the intersection of noisy text parsing and grammatical error correction. The EREF is a flexible formalism not only for grammatical error correction but other tasks with jointly editing and parsing a given sentence.

Acknowledgments

This work was supported in part by the JHU Human Language Technology Center of Excellence (HLTCOE), and DARPA LORELEI. The U.S. Government is authorized to reproduce and distribute reprints for Governmental purposes. The views and conclusions contained in this publication are those of the authors and should not be interpreted as representing official policies or endorsements of DARPA or the U.S. Government.

References

Yevgeni Berzak, Jessica Kenney, Carolyn Spadine, Jing Xian Wang, Lucia Lam, Keiko Sophie Mori, Sebastian Garza, and Boris Katz. 2016. Universal dependencies for learner english. In *Proceedings of the 54th Annual Meeting of the Association for Computational Linguistics (Volume 1: Long Papers)*. Association for Computational Linguistics, pages 737–746.

Aoife Cahill. 2015. Parsing learner text: to shoehorn or not to shoehorn. In *Proceedings of The 9th Linguistic Annotation Workshop*. Association for Computational Linguistics, Denver, Colorado, USA, pages 144–147.

Michael Collins. 2002. Discriminative training methods for hidden markov models: Theory and experiments with perceptron algorithms. In *Proceedings of the 2002 Conference on Empirical Methods in Natural Language Processing*. Association for Computational Linguistics, pages 1–8.

Daniel Dahlmeier and Hwee Tou Ng. 2012. A beam-search decoder for grammatical error correction. In *Proceedings of the 2012 Joint Conference on Empirical Methods in Natural Language Processing and Computational Natural Language Learning*. Association for Computational Linguistics, Jeju Island, Korea, pages 568–578.

Benoit Favre, Bernd Bohnet, and Dilek Hakkani-Tür. 2010. Evaluation of semantic role labeling and dependency parsing of automatic speech recognition output. In *2010 IEEE International Conference on Acoustics, Speech and Signal Processing*. pages 5342–5345.

Jennifer Foster. 2007. Treebanks gone bad. *International Journal of Document Analysis and Recognition (IJDAR)* 10(3):129–145.

Jennifer Foster and Oistein Andersen. 2009. Generrate: Generating errors for use in grammatical error detection. In *Proceedings of the Fourth Workshop on Innovative Use of NLP for Building Educational Applications*. Association for Computational Linguistics, Boulder, Colorado, pages 82–90.

Yoav Goldberg and Michael Elhadad. 2010. An efficient algorithm for easy-first non-directional dependency parsing. In *Human Language Technologies: The 2010 Annual Conference of the North American Chapter of the Association for Computational Linguistics*. Association for Computational Linguistics, Los Angeles, California, pages 742–750.

Yoav Goldberg and Joakim Nivre. 2013. Training deterministic parsers with non-deterministic oracles. *Transactions of the Association for Computational Linguistics* 1:403–414.

Kenneth Heafield. 2011. KenLM: faster and smaller language model queries. In *Proceedings of the EMNLP 2011 Sixth Workshop on Statistical Machine Translation*. Edinburgh, Scotland, United Kingdom, pages 187–197.

Michael Heilman, Aoife Cahill, Nitin Madnani, Melissa Lopez, Matthew Mulholland, and Joel Tetreault. 2014. Predicting grammaticality on an ordinal scale. In *Proceedings of the 52nd Annual Meeting of the Association for Computational Linguistics (Volume 2: Short Papers)*. Association for Computational Linguistics, Baltimore, Maryland, pages 174–180.

Matthew Honnibal and Mark Johnson. 2014. Joint incremental disfluency detection and dependency parsing. *Transactions of the Association for Computational Linguistics* 2:131–142.

Nobuhiro Kaji and Masaru Kitsuregawa. 2014. Accurate word segmentation and pos tagging for japanese microblogs: Corpus annotation and joint modeling with lexical normalization. In *Proceedings of the 2014 Conference on Empirical Methods in Natural Language Processing (EMNLP)*. Association for Computational Linguistics, Doha, Qatar, pages 99–109.

Claudia Leacock, Martin Chodorow, Michael Gamon, and Joel Tetreault. 2014. Automated grammatical error detection for language learners. *Synthesis lectures on human language technologies* 7(1):1–170.

Mitchell P Marcus, Mary Ann Marcinkiewicz, and Beatrice Santorini. 1993. Building a large annotated corpus of english: The penn treebank. *Computational linguistics* 19(2):313–330.

Ryo Nagata and Keisuke Sakaguchi. 2016. Phrase structure annotation and parsing for learner english. In *Proceedings of the 54th Annual Meeting of the Association for Computational Linguistics (Volume 1: Long Papers)*. Association for Computational Linguistics, Berlin, Germany, pages 1837–1847.

Courtney Napoles, Matthew Gormley, and Benjamin Van Durme. 2012. Annotated gigaword. In *Proceedings of the Joint Workshop on Automatic Knowledge Base Construction and Web-scale Knowledge Extraction*. Association for Computational Linguistics, pages 95–100.

Hwee Tou Ng, Siew Mei Wu, Yuanbin Wu, Christian Hadiwinoto, and Joel Tetreault. 2013. The conll-2013 shared task on grammatical error correction. In *Proceedings of the Seventeenth Conference on Computational Natural Language Learning: Shared Task*. Association for Computational Linguistics, Sofia, Bulgaria, pages 1–12.

Joakim Nivre. 2004. Incrementality in deterministic dependency parsing. In *Proceedings of the Workshop on Incremental Parsing: Bringing Engineering and Cognition Together*. Association for Computational Linguistics, Stroudsburg, PA, USA, IncrementParsing '04, pages 50–57.

Joakim Nivre. 2009. Non-projective dependency parsing in expected linear time. In *Proceedings of the Joint Conference of the 47th Annual Meeting of the ACL and the 4th International Joint Conference on Natural Language Processing of the AFNLP*. Association for Computational Linguistics, Suntec, Singapore, pages 351–359.

Slav Petrov and Ryan McDonald. 2012. Overview of the 2012 shared task on parsing the web. *Notes of the First Workshop on Syntactic Analysis of Non-Canonical Language (SANCL)* .

Tao Qian, Yue Zhang, Meishan Zhang, Yafeng Ren, and Donghong Ji. 2015. A transition-based model for joint segmentation, pos-tagging and normalization. In *Proceedings of the 2015 Conference on Empirical Methods in Natural Language Processing*. Association for Computational Linguistics, Lisbon, Portugal, pages 1837–1846.

Mohammad Sadegh Rasooli and Joel Tetreault. 2013. Joint parsing and disfluency detection in linear time. In *Proceedings of the 2013 Conference on Empirical Methods in Natural Language Processing*. Association for Computational Linguistics, Seattle, Washington, USA, pages 124–129.

Mohammad Sadegh Rasooli and Joel Tetreault. 2014. Non-monotonic parsing of fluent umm i mean disfluent sentences. In *Proceedings of the 14th Conference of the European Chapter of the Association for*

Computational Linguistics, volume 2: Short Papers.
Association for Computational Linguistics, Gothenburg, Sweden, pages 48–53.

Brian Roark, Mary Harper, Eugene Charniak, Bonnie Dorr, Mark Johnson, Jeremy Kahn, Yang Liu, Mari Ostendorf, John Hale, Anna Krasnyanskaya, Matthew Lease, Izhak Shafran, Matthew Snover, Robin Stewart, and Lisa Yung. 2006. Sparseval: Evaluation metrics for parsing speech. In *Proceedings of the Fifth International Conference on Language Resources and Evaluation (LREC'06)*. European Language Resources Association (ELRA).

Alla Rozovskaya and Dan Roth. 2014. Building a state-of-the-art grammatical error correction system. *Transactions of the Association for Computational Linguistics* 2:414–434.

Keisuke Sakaguchi, Tomoya Mizumoto, Mamoru Komachi, and Yuji Matsumoto. 2012. Joint English spelling error correction and POS tagging for language learners writing. In *Proceedings of COLING 2012*. The COLING 2012 Organizing Committee, Mumbai, India, pages 2357–2374.

Shuangzhi Wu, Dongdong Zhang, Ming Zhou, and Tiejun Zhao. 2015. Efficient disfluency detection with transition-based parsing. In *Proceedings of the 53rd Annual Meeting of the Association for Computational Linguistics and the 7th International Joint Conference on Natural Language Processing (Volume 1: Long Papers)*. Association for Computational Linguistics, Beijing, China, pages 495–503.

Hiroyasu Yamada and Yuji Matsumoto. 2003. Statistical dependency analysis with support vector machines. In *In Proceedings of IWPT*. pages 195–206.

Masashi Yoshikawa, Hiroyuki Shindo, and Yuji Matsumoto. 2016. Joint transition-based dependency parsing and disfluency detection for automatic speech recognition texts. In *Proceedings of the 2016 Conference on Empirical Methods in Natural Language Processing*. Association for Computational Linguistics, Austin, Texas, pages 1036–1041.

Attention Strategies for Multi-Source Sequence-to-Sequence Learning

Jindřich Libovický and **Jindřich Helcl**
Charles University, Faculty of Mathematics and Physics
Institute of Formal and Applied Linguistics
Malostranské náměstí 25, 118 00 Prague, Czech Republic
{libovicky, helcl}@ufal.mff.cuni.cz

Abstract

Modeling attention in neural multi-source sequence-to-sequence learning remains a relatively unexplored area, despite its usefulness in tasks that incorporate multiple source languages or modalities. We propose two novel approaches to combine the outputs of attention mechanisms over each source sequence, *flat* and *hierarchical*. We compare the proposed methods with existing techniques and present results of systematic evaluation of those methods on the WMT16 Multimodal Translation and Automatic Post-editing tasks. We show that the proposed methods achieve competitive results on both tasks.

1 Introduction

Sequence-to-sequence (S2S) learning with attention mechanism recently became the most successful paradigm with state-of-the-art results in machine translation (MT) (Bahdanau et al., 2014; Sennrich et al., 2016a), image captioning (Xu et al., 2015; Lu et al., 2016), text summarization (Rush et al., 2015) and other NLP tasks.

All of the above applications of S2S learning make use of a single encoder. Depending on the modality, it can be either a recurrent neural network (RNN) for textual input data, or a convolutional network for images.

In this work, we focus on a special case of S2S learning with multiple input sequences of possibly different modalities and a single output-generating recurrent decoder. We explore various strategies the decoder can employ to attend to the hidden states of the individual encoders.

The existing approaches to this problem do not explicitly model different importance of the inputs to the decoder (Firat et al., 2016; Zoph and Knight, 2016). In multimodal MT (MMT), where an image and its caption are on the input, we might expect the caption to be the primary source of information, whereas the image itself would only play a role in output disambiguation. In automatic post-editing (APE), where a sentence in a source language and its automatically generated translation are on the input, we might want to attend to the source text only in case the model decides that there is an error in the translation.

We propose two interpretable attention strategies that take into account the roles of the individual source sequences explicitly—flat and hierarchical attention combination.

This paper is organized as follows: In Section 2, we review the attention mechanism in single-source S2S learning. Section 3 introduces new attention combination strategies. In Section 4, we evaluate the proposed models on the MMT and APE tasks. We summarize the related work in Section 5, and conclude in Section 6.

2 Attentive S2S Learning

The attention mechanism in S2S learning allows an RNN decoder to directly access information about the input each time before it emits a symbol. Inspired by content-based addressing in Neural Turing Machines (Graves et al., 2014), the attention mechanism estimates a probability distribution over the encoder hidden states in each decoding step. This distribution is used for computing the context vector—the weighted average of the encoder hidden states—as an additional input to the decoder.

The standard attention model as described by Bahdanau et al. (2014) defines the attention energies e_{ij}, attention distribution α_{ij}, and the con-

Proceedings of the 55th Annual Meeting of the Association for Computational Linguistics (Short Papers), pages 196–202
Vancouver, Canada, July 30 - August 4, 2017. ©2017 Association for Computational Linguistics
https://doi.org/10.18653/v1/P17-2031

text vector c_i in i-th decoder step as:

$$e_{ij} = v_a^\top \tanh(W_a s_i + U_a h_j), \qquad (1)$$

$$\alpha_{ij} = \frac{\exp(e_{ij})}{\sum_{k=1}^{T_x} \exp(e_{ik})}, \qquad (2)$$

$$c_i = \sum_{j=1}^{T_x} \alpha_{ij} h_j. \qquad (3)$$

The trainable parameters W_a and U_a are projection matrices that transform the decoder and encoder states s_i and h_j into a common vector space and v_a is a weight vector over the dimensions of this space. T_x denotes the length of the input sequence. For the sake of clarity, bias terms (applied every time a vector is linearly projected using a weight matrix) are omitted.

Recently, Lu et al. (2016) introduced *sentinel gate*, an extension of the attentive RNN decoder with LSTM units (Hochreiter and Schmidhuber, 1997). We adapt the extension for gated recurrent units (GRU) (Cho et al., 2014), which we use in our experiments:

$$\psi_i = \sigma(W_y y_i + W_s s_{i-1}) \qquad (4)$$

where W_y and W_s are trainable parameters, y_i is the embedded decoder input, and s_{i-1} is the previous decoder state.

Analogically to Equation 1, we compute a scalar energy term for the sentinel:

$$e_{\psi_i} = v_a^\top \tanh\left(W_a s_i + U_a^{(\psi)}(\psi_i \odot s_i)\right) \qquad (5)$$

where W_a, $U_a^{(\psi)}$ are the projection matrices, v_a is the weight vector, and $\psi_i \odot s_i$ is the sentinel vector. Note that the sentinel energy term does not depend on any hidden state of any encoder. The sentinel vector is projected to the same vector space as the encoder state h_j in Equation 1. The term e_{ψ_i} is added as an extra attention energy term to Equation 2 and the sentinel vector $\psi_i \odot s_i$ is used as the corresponding vector in the summation in Equation 3.

This technique should allow the decoder to choose whether to attend to the encoder or to focus on its own state and act more like a language model. This can be beneficial if the encoder does not contain much relevant information for the current decoding step.

3 Attention Combination

In S2S models with multiple encoders, the decoder needs to be able to combine the attention information collected from the encoders.

A widely adopted technique for combining multiple attention models in a decoder is concatenation of the context vectors $c_i^{(1)}, \ldots, c_i^{(N)}$ (Zoph and Knight, 2016; Firat et al., 2016). As mentioned in Section 1, this setting forces the model to attend to each encoder independently and lets the attention combination to be resolved implicitly in the subsequent network layers.

In this section, we propose two alternative strategies of combining attentions from multiple encoders. We either let the decoder learn the α_i distribution jointly over all encoder hidden states (*flat* attention combination) or factorize the distribution over individual encoders (*hierarchical* combination).

Both of the alternatives allow us to explicitly compute distribution over the encoders and thus interpret how much attention is paid to each encoder at every decoding step.

3.1 Flat Attention Combination

Flat attention combination projects the hidden states of all encoders into a shared space and then computes an arbitrary distribution over the projections. The difference between the concatenation of the context vectors and the flat attention combination is that the α_i coefficients are computed jointly for all encoders:

$$\alpha_{ij}^{(k)} = \frac{\exp(e_{ij}^{(k)})}{\sum_{n=1}^{N} \sum_{m=1}^{T_x^{(n)}} \exp\left(e_{im}^{(n)}\right)} \qquad (6)$$

where $T_x^{(n)}$ is the length of the input sequence of the n-th encoder and $e_{ij}^{(k)}$ is the attention energy of the j-th state of the k-th encoder in the i-th decoding step. These attention energies are computed as in Equation 1. The parameters v_a and W_a are shared among the encoders, and U_a is different for each encoder and serves as an encoder-specific projection of hidden states into a common vector space.

The states of the individual encoders occupy different vector spaces and can have a different dimensionality, therefore the context vector cannot be computed as their weighted sum. We project them into a single space using linear projections:

$$c_i = \sum_{k=1}^{N} \sum_{j=1}^{T_x^{(k)}} \alpha_{ij}^{(k)} U_c^{(k)} h_j^{(k)} \qquad (7)$$

where $U_c^{(k)}$ are additional trainable parameters.

The matrices $U_c^{(k)}$ project the hidden states into a common vector space. This raises a question whether this space can be the same as the one that is projected into in the energy computation using matrices $U_a^{(k)}$ in Equation 1, i.e., whether $U_c^{(k)} = U_a^{(k)}$. In our experiments, we explore both options. We also try both adding and not adding the sentinel $\alpha_i^{(\psi)} U_c^{(\psi)} (\psi_i \odot s_i)$ to the context vector.

3.2 Hierarchical Attention Combination

The hierarchical attention combination model computes every context vector independently, similarly to the concatenation approach. Instead of concatenation, a second attention mechanism is constructed over the context vectors.

We divide the computation of the attention distribution into two steps: First, we compute the context vector for each encoder independently using Equation 3. Second, we project the context vectors (and optionally the sentinel) into a common space (Equation 8), we compute another distribution over the projected context vectors (Equation 9) and their corresponding weighted average (Equation 10):

$$e_i^{(k)} = v_b^\top \tanh(W_b s_i + U_b^{(k)} c_i^{(k)}), \qquad (8)$$

$$\beta_i^{(k)} = \frac{\exp(e_i^{(k)})}{\sum_{n=1}^{N} \exp(e_i^{(n)})}, \qquad (9)$$

$$c_i = \sum_{k=1}^{N} \beta_i^{(k)} U_c^{(k)} c_i^{(k)} \qquad (10)$$

where $c_i^{(k)}$ is the context vector of the k-th encoder, additional trainable parameters v_b and W_b are shared for all encoders, and $U_b^{(k)}$ and $U_c^{(k)}$ are encoder-specific projection matrices, that can be set equal and shared, similarly to the case of flat attention combination.

4 Experiments

We evaluate the attention combination strategies presented in Section 3 on the tasks of multimodal translation (Section 4.1) and automatic post-editing (Section 4.2).

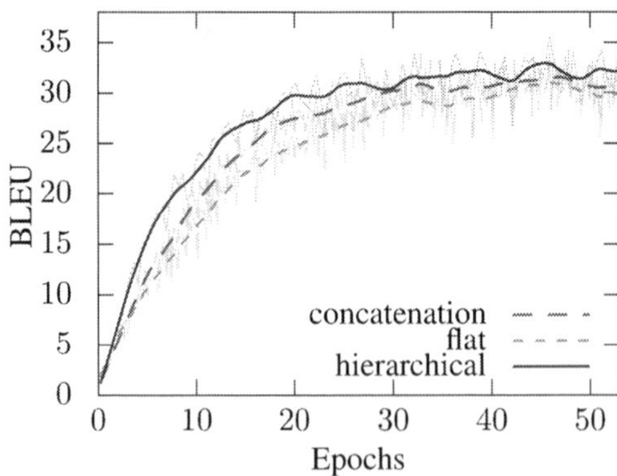

Figure 1: Learning curves on validation data for context vector concatenation (blue), flat (green) and hierarchical (red) attention combination without sentinel and without sharing the projection matrices.

The models were implemented using the Neural Monkey sequence-to-sequence learning toolkit (Helcl and Libovický, 2017).[1][2] In both setups, we process the textual input with bidirectional GRU network (Cho et al., 2014) with 300 units in the hidden state in each direction and 300 units in embeddings. For the attention projection space, we use 500 hidden units. We optimize the network to minimize the output cross-entropy using the Adam algorithm (Kingma and Ba, 2014) with learning rate 10^{-4}.

4.1 Multimodal Translation

The goal of multimodal translation (Specia et al., 2016) is to generate target-language image captions given both the image and its caption in the source language.

We train and evaluate the model on the Multi30k dataset (Elliott et al., 2016). It consists of 29,000 training instances (images together with English captions and their German translations), 1,014 validation instances, and 1,000 test instances. The results are evaluated using the BLEU (Papineni et al., 2002) and METEOR (Denkowski and Lavie, 2011).

In our model, the visual input is processed with a pre-trained VGG 16 network (Simonyan and Zisserman, 2014) without further fine-tuning. Atten-

---

[1] http://github.com/ufal/neuralmonkey
[2] The trained models can be downloaded from http://ufallab.ms.mff.cuni.cz/~libovicky/acl2017_att_models/

tion distribution over the visual input is computed from the last convolutional layer of the network. The decoder is an RNN with 500 conditional GRU units (Firat and Cho, 2016) in the recurrent layer. We use byte-pair encoding (Sennrich et al., 2016b) with a vocabulary of 20,000 subword units shared between the textual encoder and the decoder.

The results of our experiments in multimodal MT are shown in Table 1. We achieved the best results using the hierarchical attention combination without the sentinel mechanism, which also showed the fastest convergence. The flat combination strategy achieves similar results eventually. Sharing the projections for energy and context vector computation does not improve over the concatenation baseline and slows the training almost prohibitively. Multimodal models were not able to surpass the textual baseline (BLEU 33.0).

Using the conditional GRU units brought an improvement of about 1.5 BLEU points on average, with the exception of the concatenation scenario where the performance dropped by almost 5 BLEU points. We hypothesize this is caused by the fact the model has to learn the implicit attention combination on multiple places – once in the output projection and three times inside the conditional GRU unit (Firat and Cho, 2016, Equations 10-12). We thus report the scores of the introduced attention combination techniques trained with conditional GRU units and compare them with the concatenation baseline trained with plain GRU units.

4.2 Automatic MT Post-editing

Automatic post-editing is a task of improving an automatically generated translation given the source sentence where the translation system is treated as a black box.

We used the data from the WMT16 APE Task (Bojar et al., 2016; Turchi et al., 2016), which consists of 12,000 training, 2,000 validation, and 1,000 test sentence triplets from the IT domain. Each triplet contains an English source sentence, an automatically generated German translation of the source sentence, and a manually post-edited German sentence as a reference. In case of this dataset, the MT outputs are almost perfect in and only little effort was required to post-edit the sentences. The results are evaluated using the human-targeted error rate (HTER) (Snover et al., 2006) and BLEU score (Papineni et al., 2002).

	share	sent.	MMT		APE	
			BLEU	METEOR	BLEU	HTER
concat.			31.4 ± .8	48.0 ± .7	62.3 ± .5	24.4 ± .4
flat	×	×	30.2 ± .8	46.5 ± .7	62.6 ± .5	24.2 ± .4
flat	×	✓	29.3 ± .8	45.4 ± .7	62.3 ± .5	24.3 ± .4
flat	✓	×	30.9 ± .8	47.1 ± .7	62.4 ± .6	24.4 ± .4
flat	✓	✓	29.4 ± .8	46.9 ± .7	62.5 ± .6	24.2 ± .4
hierarchical	×	×	**32.1 ± .8**	**49.1 ± .7**	62.3 ± .5	24.1 ± .4
hierarchical	×	✓	28.1 ± .8	45.5 ± .7	62.6 ± .6	24.1 ± .4
hierarchical	✓	×	26.1 ± .7	42.4 ± .7	62.4 ± .5	24.3 ± .4
hierarchical	✓	✓	22.0 ± .7	38.5 ± .6	62.5 ± .5	24.1 ± .4

Table 1: Results of our experiments on the test sets of Multi30k dataset and the APE dataset. The column 'share' denotes whether the projection matrix is shared for energies and context vector computation, 'sent.' indicates whether the sentinel vector has been used or not.

Following Libovický et al. (2016), we encode the target sentence as a sequence of edit operations transforming the MT output into the reference. By this technique, we prevent the model from paraphrasing the input sentences. The decoder is a GRU network with 300 hidden units. Unlike in the MMT setup (Section 4.1), we do not use the conditional GRU because it is prone to overfitting on the small dataset we work with.

The models were able to slightly, but significantly improve over the baseline – leaving the MT output as is (HTER 24.8). The differences between the attention combination strategies are not significant.

5 Related Work

Attempts to use S2S models for APE are relatively rare (Bojar et al., 2016). Niehues et al. (2016) concatenate both inputs into one long sequence, which forces the encoder to be able to work with both source and target language. Their attention is then similar to our flat combination strategy; however, it can only be used for sequential data.

The best system from the WMT'16 competition (Junczys-Dowmunt and Grundkiewicz, 2016) trains two separate S2S models, one translating from MT output to post-edited targets and the second one from source sentences to post-edited targets. The decoders average their output distributions similarly to decoder ensembling. The biggest source of improvement in this state-of-the-art posteditor came from additional training data generation, rather than from changes in the network architecture.

Source: a man sleeping in a green room on a couch .
Reference: ein Mann schläft in einem grünen Raum auf einem Sofa .
Output with attention:

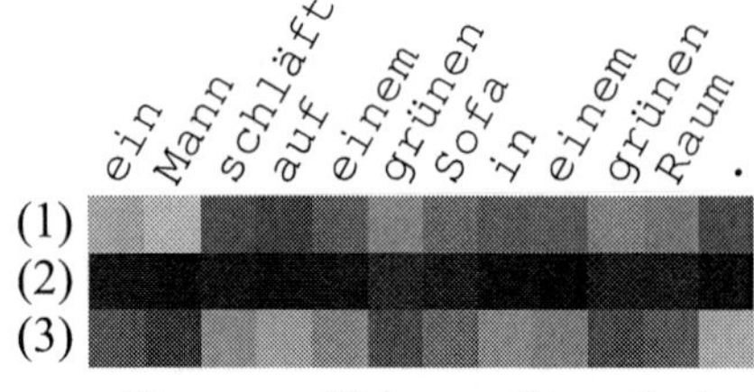

Figure 2: Visualization of hierarchical attention in MMT. Each column in the diagram corresponds to the weights of the encoders and sentinel. Note that the despite the overall low importance of the image encoder, it gets activated for the content words.

Caglayan et al. (2016) used an architecture very similar to ours for multimodal translation. They made a strong assumption that the network can be trained in such a way that the hidden states of the encoder and the convolutional network occupy the same vector space and thus sum the context vectors from both modalities. In this way, their multimodal MT system (BLEU 27.82) remained far bellow the text-only setup (BLEU 32.50).

New state-of-the-art results on the Multi30k dataset were achieved very recently by Calixto et al. (2017). The best-performing architecture uses the last fully-connected layer of VGG-19 network (Simonyan and Zisserman, 2014) as decoder initialization and only attends to the text encoder hidden states. With a stronger monomodal baseline (BLEU 33.7), their multimodal model achieved a BLEU score of 37.1. Similarly to Niehues et al. (2016) in the APE task, even further improvement was achieved by synthetically extending the dataset.

6   Conclusions

We introduced two new strategies of combining attention in a multi-source sequence-to-sequence setup. Both methods are based on computing a joint distribution over hidden states of all encoders.

We conducted experiments with the proposed strategies on multimodal translation and automatic post-editing tasks, and we showed that the flat and hierarchical attention combination can be applied to these tasks with maintaining competitive score to previously used techniques.

Unlike the simple context vector concatenation, the introduced combination strategies can be used with the conditional GRU units in the decoder. On top of that, the hierarchical combination strategy exhibits faster learning than than the other strategies.

Acknowledgments

We would like to thank Ondřej Dušek, Rudolf Rosa, Pavel Pecina, and Ondřej Bojar for a fruitful discussions and comments on the draft of the paper.

This research has been funded by the Czech Science Foundation grant no. P103/12/G084, the EU grant no. H2020-ICT-2014-1-645452 (QT21), and Charles University grant no. 52315/2014 and SVV project no. 260 453. This work has been using language resources developed and/or stored and/or distributed by the LINDAT-Clarin project of the Ministry of Education of the Czech Republic (project LM2010013).

References

Dzmitry Bahdanau, Kyunghyun Cho, and Yoshua Bengio. 2014. Neural machine translation by jointly learning to align and translate. *CoRR* abs/1409.0473. http://arxiv.org/abs/1409.0473.

Ondřej Bojar, Rajen Chatterjee, Christian Federmann, Yvette Graham, Barry Haddow, Matthias Huck, Antonio Yepes, Philipp Koehn, Varvara Logacheva, Christof Monz, Matteo Negri, Aurelie Névéol, Mariana Neves, Martin Popel, Matt Post, Raphael Rubino, Carolina Scarton, Lucia Specia, Marco Turchi, Karin Verspoor, and Marcos Zampieri. 2016. Findings of the 2016 conference on machine translation (WMT16). In *Proceedings of the First Conference on Machine Translation (WMT). Volume 2: Shared Task Papers*. Association for Computational Linguistics, Association for Computational Linguistics, Stroudsburg, PA, USA, volume 2, pages 131–198.

Ozan Caglayan, Walid Aransa, Yaxing Wang, Marc Masana, Mercedes García-Martínez, Fethi Bougares, Loïc Barrault, and Joost van de Weijer. 2016. Does multimodality help human and machine for translation and image captioning? In *Proceedings of the First Conference on Machine Translation*. Association for Computational Linguistics, Berlin, Germany, pages 627–633. http://www.aclweb.org/anthology/W16-2358.

Iacer Calixto, Qun Liu, and Nick Campbell. 2017. Incorporating global visual features into attention-based neural machine translation. *CoRR* abs/1701.06521. http://arxiv.org/abs/1701.06521.

Kyunghyun Cho, Bart van Merrienboer, Dzmitry Bahdanau, and Yoshua Bengio. 2014. On the properties of neural machine translation: Encoder–decoder approaches. In *Proceedings of SSST-8, Eighth Workshop on Syntax, Semantics and Structure in Statistical Translation*. Association for Computational Linguistics, Doha, Qatar, pages 103–111. http://www.aclweb.org/anthology/W14-4012.

Michael Denkowski and Alon Lavie. 2011. Meteor 1.3: Automatic metric for reliable optimization and evaluation of machine translation systems. In *Proceedings of the Sixth Workshop on Statistical Machine Translation*. Association for Computational Linguistics, Edinburgh, United Kingdom, pages 85–91. http://www.aclweb.org/anthology/W11-2107.

Desmond Elliott, Stella Frank, Khalil Sima'an, and Lucia Specia. 2016. Multi30k: Multilingual english-german image descriptions. *CoRR* abs/1605.00459. http://arxiv.org/abs/1605.00459.

Orhan Firat and Kyunghyun Cho. 2016. Conditional gated recurrent unit with attention mechanism. https://github.com/nyu-dl/dl4mt-tutorial/blob/master/docs/cgru.pdf. Published online, version adbaeea.

Orhan Firat, Kyunghyun Cho, and Yoshua Bengio. 2016. Multi-way, multilingual neural machine translation with a shared attention mechanism. In *Proceedings of the 2016 Conference of the North American Chapter of the Association for Computational Linguistics: Human Language Technologies*. Association for Computational Linguistics, San Diego, CA, USA, pages 866–875. http://www.aclweb.org/anthology/N16-1101.

Alex Graves, Greg Wayne, and Ivo Danihelka. 2014. Neural turing machines. *CoRR* abs/1410.5401. http://arxiv.org/abs/1410.5401.

Jindřich Helcl and Jindřich Libovický. 2017. Neural monkey: An open-source tool for sequence learning. *The Prague Bulletin of Mathematical Linguistics* (107):5–17. https://doi.org/10.1515/pralin-2017-0001.

Sepp Hochreiter and Jürgen Schmidhuber. 1997. Long short-term memory. *Neural Comput.* 9:1735–1780. https://doi.org/10.1162/neco.1997.9.8.1735.

Marcin Junczys-Dowmunt and Roman Grundkiewicz. 2016. Log-linear combinations of monolingual and bilingual neural machine translation models for automatic post-editing. In *Proceedings of the First Conference on Machine Translation*. Association for Computational Linguistics, Berlin, Germany, pages 751–758. http://www.aclweb.org/anthology/W/W16/W16-2378.

Diederik P. Kingma and Jimmy Ba. 2014. Adam: A method for stochastic optimization. *CoRR* abs/1412.6980. http://arxiv.org/abs/1412.6980.

Jindřich Libovický, Jindřich Helcl, Marek Tlustý, Ondřej Bojar, and Pavel Pecina. 2016. CUNI system for WMT16 automatic post-editing and multimodal translation tasks. In *Proceedings of the First Conference on Machine Translation*. Association for Computational Linguistics, Berlin, Germany, pages 646–654. http://www.aclweb.org/anthology/W/W16/W16-2361.

Jiasen Lu, Caiming Xiong, Devi Parikh, and Richard Socher. 2016. Knowing when to look: Adaptive attention via a visual sentinel for image captioning. *CoRR* abs/1612.01887. http://arxiv.org/abs/1612.01887.

Jan Niehues, Eunah Cho, Thanh-Le Ha, and Alex Waibel. 2016. Pre-translation for neural machine translation. *CoRR* abs/1610.05243. http://arxiv.org/abs/1610.05243.

Kishore Papineni, Salim Roukos, Todd Ward, and Wei-Jing Zhu. 2002. Bleu: a method for automatic evaluation of machine translation. In *Proceedings of 40th Annual Meeting of the Association for Computational Linguistics*. Association for Computational Linguistics, Philadelphia, Pennsylvania, USA, pages 311–318. https://doi.org/10.3115/1073083.1073135.

Alexander M. Rush, Sumit Chopra, and Jason Weston. 2015. A neural attention model for abstractive sentence summarization. In *Proceedings of the 2015 Conference on Empirical Methods in Natural Language Processing*. Association for Computational Linguistics, Lisbon, Portugal, pages 379–389. https://aclweb.org/anthology/D/D15/D15-1044.

Rico Sennrich, Barry Haddow, and Alexandra Birch. 2016a. Edinburgh neural machine translation systems for WMT 16. In *Proceedings of the First Conference on Machine Translation*. Association for Computational Linguistics, Berlin, Germany, pages 371–376. http://www.aclweb.org/anthology/W/W16/W16-2323.

Rico Sennrich, Barry Haddow, and Alexandra Birch. 2016b. Neural machine translation of rare words with subword units. In *Proceedings of the 54th Annual Meeting of the Association for Computational Linguistics (Volume*

1: Long Papers). Association for Computational Linguistics, Berlin, Germany, pages 1715–1725. http://www.aclweb.org/anthology/P16-1162.

Karen Simonyan and Andrew Zisserman. 2014. Very deep convolutional networks for large-scale image recognition. *CoRR* abs/1409.1556. http://arxiv.org/abs/1409.1556.

Matthew Snover, Bonnie Dorr, Richard Schwartz, Linnea Micciulla, and John Makhoul. 2006. A study of translation edit rate with targeted human annotation. In *Proceedings of association for machine translation in the Americas*. volume 200.

Lucia Specia, Stella Frank, Khalil Sima'an, and Desmond Elliott. 2016. A shared task on multimodal machine translation and crosslingual image description. In *Proceedings of the First Conference on Machine Translation*. Association for Computational Linguistics, Berlin, Germany, pages 543–553. http://www.aclweb.org/anthology/W16-2346.

Marco Turchi, Rajen Chatterjee, and Matteo Negri. 2016. WMT16 APE shared task data. LINDAT/CLARIN digital library at the Institute of Formal and Applied Linguistics, Charles University in Prague. http://hdl.handle.net/11372/LRT-1632.

Kelvin Xu, Jimmy Ba, Ryan Kiros, Kyunghyun Cho, Aaron Courville, Ruslan Salakhudinov, Rich Zemel, and Yoshua Bengio. 2015. Show, attend and tell: Neural image caption generation with visual attention. In David Blei and Francis Bach, editors, *Proceedings of the 32nd International Conference on Machine Learning (ICML-15)*. JMLR Workshop and Conference Proceedings, Lille, France, pages 2048–2057. http://jmlr.org/proceedings/papers/v37/xuc15.pdf.

Barret Zoph and Kevin Knight. 2016. Multi-source neural translation. In *Proceedings of the 2016 Conference of the North American Chapter of the Association for Computational Linguistics: Human Language Technologies*. Association for Computational Linguistics, San Diego, CA, USA, pages 30–34. http://www.aclweb.org/anthology/N16-1004.

Understanding and Detecting Supporting Arguments of Diverse Types

Xinyu Hua and **Lu Wang**
College of Computer and Information Science
Northeastern University
Boston, MA 02115
hua.x@husky.neu.edu   luwang@ccs.neu.edu

Abstract

We investigate the problem of sentence-level *supporting argument detection* from relevant documents for user-specified claims. A dataset containing claims and associated citation articles is collected from online debate website idebate.org. We then manually label sentence-level supporting arguments from the documents along with their types as STUDY, FACTUAL, OPINION, or REASONING. We further characterize arguments of different types, and explore whether leveraging type information can facilitate the supporting arguments detection task. Experimental results show that LambdaMART (Burges, 2010) ranker that uses features informed by argument types yields better performance than the same ranker trained without type information.

1   Introduction

Argumentation plays a crucial role in persuasion and decision-making processes. An argument usually consists of a central claim (or conclusion) and several supporting premises. Constructing arguments of high quality would require the inclusion of diverse information, such as factual evidence and solid reasoning (Rieke et al., 1997; Park and Cardie, 2014). For instance, as shown in Figure 1, the editor on idebate.org – a Wikipedia-style website for gathering pro and con arguments on controversial issues, utilizes arguments based on study, factual evidence, and expert opinion to support the anti-gun claim "legally owned guns are frequently stolen and used by criminals". However, it would require substantial human effort to collect information from diverse resources to support argument construction. In order to facilitate this process, there is a pressing need for tools that can automatically detect supporting arguments.

To date, most of the argument mining research focuses on recognizing argumentative components

- A June 2013 IOM report states that "almost all guns used in criminal acts enter circulation via initial legal transaction". [study]
- Between 2005 and 2010, 1.4 million guns were stolen from US homes during property crimes (including bulglary and car theft), a yearly average of 232,400. [factual]
- Ian Ayres, JD, PhD, ... states, "with guns being a product that can be easily carried away and quickly sold at a relatively high fraction of the initial cost, the presence of more guns can actually serve as a stimulus to burglary and theft." [expert opinion]

Figure 1: Three different types of arguments used to support the claim "Legally owned guns are frequently stolen and used by criminals".

and their structures from constructed arguments based on curated corpus (Mochales and Moens, 2011; Stab and Gurevych, 2014; Feng and Hirst, 2011; Habernal and Gurevych, 2015; Nguyen and Litman, 2016). Limited work has been done for retrieving supporting arguments from external resources. Initial effort by Rinott et al. (2015) investigates the detection of relevant factual evidence from Wikipedia articles. However, it is unclear whether their method can perform well on documents of different genres (e.g. news articles vs. blogs) for detecting distinct types of supporting information.

In this work, *we present a novel study on the task of sentence-level supporting argument detection from relevant documents for a user-specified claim.* Take Figure 2 as an example: assume we are given a claim on the topic of "banning cosmetic surgery" and a relevant article (cited for argument construction), we aim to automatically pinpoint the sentence(s) (in *italics*) among all sentences in the cited article that can be used to back up the claim. We define such tasks as *supporting argument detection.* Furthermore, another goal of

Proceedings of the 55th Annual Meeting of the Association for Computational Linguistics (Short Papers), pages 203–208
Vancouver, Canada, July 30 - August 4, 2017. ©2017 Association for Computational Linguistics
https://doi.org/10.18653/v1/P17-2032

- **Topic**: This house would ban cosmetic surgery - **Claim**: An outright ban would be easier than the partial bans that have been enacted in some places. - **Human Constructed Argument**: ...This potentially leaves difficulty drawing the line for what is allowed.[1] ...
Citation Article [1]: *"Australian State Ban Cosmetic Surgery for Teens"* - ...It is unfortunate that a parent would consider letting a 16-year-old daughter have a breast augmentation." *- But others worry that similar legislation, if it ever comes to pass in the United States, would draw a largely arbitrary line – and could needlessly restrict some teens from procedures that would help their self-esteem.* - Dr. Malcolm Z. Roth, director of plastic surgery at Maimondes Medical Center in Brooklyn, N.Y. , said he believes that some teens are intelligent and mature enough to comprehend the risks and benefits of cosmetic surgery....

Figure 2: A typical debate motion consists of a Topic, Claims, and Human Constructed Arguments. Citation article is marked at the end of sentence. Our goal is to find out supporting argument (in *italics*) from citation article that can back up the given claim.

this work is to understand and characterize different types of supporting arguments. Indeed, human editors do use different types of information to promote persuasiveness as we will show in Section 3. Prediction performance also varies among different types of supporting arguments.

Given that none of the existing datasets is suitable for our study, we collect and annotate a corpus from Idebate, which contains hundreds of debate topics and corresponding claims.[1] As is shown in Figure 2, each claim is supported with some human constructed argument, with cited articles marked on sentence level. After careful inspection on the supporting arguments, we propose to label them as STUDY, FACTUAL, OPINION, or REASONING. Substantial inter-annotator agreement rate is achieved for both supporting argument labeling (with Cohen's κ of 0.8) and argument type annotation, on 200 topics with 621 reference articles.

Based on the new corpus, we first carry out a study on characterizing arguments of different types via type prediction. We find that arguments

of STUDY and FACTUAL tend to use more concrete words, while arguments of OPINION contain more named entities of person names. We then investigate whether argument type can be leveraged to assist supporting argument detection. Experimental results based on LambdaMART (Burges, 2010) show that utilizing features composite with argument types achieves a Mean Reciprocal Rank (MRR) score of 57.65, which outperforms an unsupervised baseline and the same ranker trained without type information. Feature analysis also demonstrates that salient features have significantly different distribution over different argument types.

For the rest of the paper, we summarize related work in Section 2. The data collection and annotation process is described in Section 3, which is followed by argument type study (Section 4). Experiment on supporting argument detection is presented in Section 5. We finally conclude in Section 6.

2 Related Work

Our work is in line with argumentation mining, which has recently attracted significant research interest. Existing work focuses on argument extraction from news articles, legal documents, or online comments without given user-specified claim (Moens et al., 2007; Palau and Moens, 2009; Mochales and Moens, 2011; Park and Cardie, 2014). Argument scheme classification is also widely studied (Biran and Rambow, 2011; Feng and Hirst, 2011; Rooney et al., 2012; Stab and Gurevych, 2014; Al Khatib et al., 2016), which emphasizes on distinguishing different types of arguments. To the best of our knowledge, none of them studies the interaction between types of arguments and their usage to support a user-specified claim. This is the gap we aim to fill.

3 Data and Annotation

We rely on data from `idebate.org`, where human editors construct paragraphs of arguments, either supporting or opposing claims under controversial topics. We also extract textual citation articles as source of information used by editors during argument construction. In total we collected 383 unique debates, out of which 200 debates are randomly selected for study. After removing invalid ones, our final dataset includes 450 claims

---

[1]The labeled dataset along with the annotation guideline will be released at `xyhua.me`.

STUDY: Results and discoveries, usually quantitative, as a result of some research investment.
FACTUAL: Description of some occurred events or facts, or chapters in law or declaration.
OPINION: Quotes from some person or group, either direct or indirect. It usually contains subjective, judgemental and evaluative languages, and might reflect the position or stance of some entity.
REASONING: Logical structures. It usually can be further broken down into causal or conditional substructures.

Table 1: Annotation scheme for our dataset. Due to space limit, we do not show detailed explanations and examples.

and 621 citation articles with about 53,000 sentences.

Annotation Process. As shown in Figure 2, we first annotate which sentence(s) from a citation articles is used by the editor as supporting arguments. Then we annotate the type for each of them as STUDY, FACTUAL, OPINION, or REASONING, based on the scheme in Table 1.[2] For instance, the highlighted supporting argument in Figure 2 is labeled as REASONING.

Two experienced annotators were hired to identify supporting arguments by reading through the whole cited article and locating the sentences that best match the reference human constructed argument. This task is rather complicated since human do not just repeat or directly quote the original sentences from citation articles, they also paraphrase, summarize, and generalize. For instance, the original sentence is "The global counterfeit drug trade, a billion-dollar industry, is thriving in Africa", which is paraphrased to "This is exploited by the billion dollar global counterfeit drug trade" in human constructed argument.

The annotators were asked to annotate independently, then discuss and resolve disagreements and give feedback about current scheme. We compute inter-annotator agreement based on Cohen's κ for both supporting arguments labeling and argument type annotation. For supporting arguments we have a high degree of consensus, with Cohen's κ ranges from 0.76 to 0.83 in all rounds and 0.80 overall. For argument type annotation, we achieve Cohen's κ of 0.61 for STUDY, 0.75 for FACTUAL, 0.71 for OPINION, and 0.29 for REASONING[3]

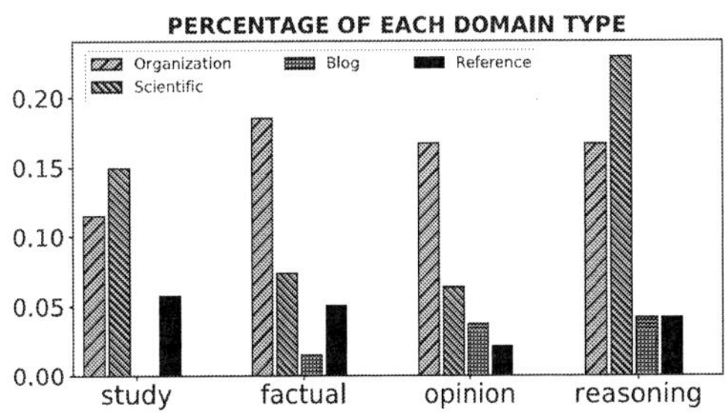

Figure 3: For each supporting argument type, from left to right shows the percentage of domain names of organizations, scientific, blog, and reference. We do not display statistics for news, because news articles take the same portion in all types (about 50%).

Statistics. In total 995 sentences are identified as supporting arguments. Among those, 95 (9.55%) are labeled as STUDY, 497 (49.95%) as FACTUAL, 363 (36.48%) as OPINION, and 40 (4.02%) as REASONING.

We further analyze the source of the supporting arguments. Domain names of the citation articles are collected based on their URL, and then categorized into "news", "organization", "scientific", "blog", "reference", and others, according to a taxonomy provided by Alexa[4] with a few edits to fit our dataset. News articles are the major source for all types, which account for roughly 50% for each. We show the distribution of other four types in Figure 3. Arguments of STUDY and REASONING are mostly from "scientific" websites (14.9% and 22.9%), whereas "organization" websites contribute a large portion of arguments of FACTUAL (18.5%) and OPINION (16.7%).

4   A Study On Argument Type Prediction

Here we characterize arguments of different types based on diverse features under the task of predicting argument types. Supporting arguments identified from previous section are utilized for experiments. We also leverage the learned classifier in this section to label the sentences that are not supporting arguments, which will be used for supporting argument detection in the next section. Four major types of features are considered.

Basic Features. We calculate frequencies of unigram and bigram words, number of four major types of part-of-speech tags (verb, noun, adjective, and adverb), number of dependency relations, and

---

[2]We end up with the four-type scheme as a trade-off between complexity and its coverage of the arguments.

[3]Many times annotators have different interpretation on REASONING, and frequently label it as OPINION. This results

in a low agreement for REASONING.

[4]http://www.alexa.com/topsites/category

	Acc	F1
Majority class	0.520	0.171
Random	0.240	0.199
Log-linear (ngrams)	0.535	0.277
Log-linear (all features)	**0.622**	**0.436**

Table 2: Results for argument type prediction. One-vs-rest classifiers are learned for Log-linear models.

number of seven types of named entities (Chinchor and Robinson, 1997).

Sentiment Features. We also compute number of positive, negative and neutral words in MPQA lexicon (Wilson et al., 2005), and number of words from a subset of semantic categories from General Inquirer (Stone et al., 1966).[5]

Discourse Features. We use the number of discourse connectives from the top two levels of Penn Discourse Tree Bank (Prasad et al., 2007).

Style Features. We measure word attributes for their concreteness (perceptible vs. conceptual), valence (or pleasantness), arousal (or intensity of emotion), and dominance (or degree of control) based on the lexicons collected by Brysbaert et al. (2014) and Warriner et al. (2013).

We utilize Log-linear model for argument type prediction with one-vs-rest setup. Three baselines are considered: (1) random guess, (2) majority class, and (3) unigrams and bigrams as features for Log-linear model. Identified supporting arguments are used for experiments, and divided into training set (50%), validation set (25%) and test set (25%). From Table 2, we can see that Log-linear model trained with all features outperforms the ones trained with ngram features. To further characterize arguments of different types, we display sample features with significant different values in Figure 4. As can be seen, arguments of STUDY and FACTUAL tend to contain more concrete words and named entities. Arguments of OPINION mention more person names, which implies that expert opinions are commonly quoted.

5 Supporting Argument Detection

We cast the sentence-level supporting argument detection problem as a ranking task.[6] Features

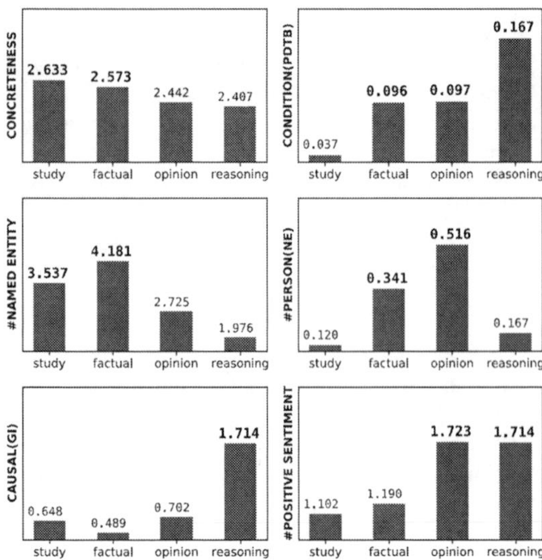

Figure 4: Average features values for different argument types. Numbers in **boldface** are significantly higher than the others based on paired t-test ($p < 0.05$).

in Section 4 are also utilized here as "Sentence features" with additional features considering the sentence position in the article. We further employ features that measure similarity between claims and sentences, and the composite features that leverage argument type information.

Similarity Features. We compute similarity between claim and candidate sentence based on TF-IDF and average word embeddings. We also consider ROUGE (Lin, 2004), a recall oriented metric for summarization evaluation. In particular, ROUGE-L, a variation based on longest common subsequence, is computed by treating claim as reference and each candidate sentence as sample summary. In similar manner we use BLEU (Papineni et al., 2002), a precision oriented metric.

Composite Features. We adopt composite features to study the interaction of other features with type of the sentence. Given claim c and sentence s with any feature mentioned above, a composite feature function $\phi_{M\text{(type, feature)}}(s, c)$ is set to the actual feature value if and only if the argument type matches. For instance, if the ROUGE-L score is 0.2, and s is of type STUDY, then $\phi_{M\text{(study, ROUGE)}}(s, c) = 0.2$. $\phi_{M\text{(factual, ROUGE)}}(s, c)$, $\phi_{M\text{(opinion, ROUGE)}}(s, c)$, $\phi_{M\text{(reasoning, ROUGE)}}(s, c)$ are all set to 0.

---

[5] Categories used: Strong, Weak, Virtue, Vice, Ovrst (Overstated), Undrst (Understated), Academ (Academic), Doctrin (Doctrine), Econ (Economic), Relig (Religious), Causal, Ought, and Perceiv (Perception).

[6] Many sentences in the citation article is relevant to the topic to various degrees. We focus on detecting the most relevant ones, and thus treat it as a ranking problem instead of a binary classification task.

Feature set	MRR	NDCG
Baselines		
TFIDF similarity	45.48	56.48
W2V similarity	47.65	59.00
Ngrams	27.26	43.83
Separate feature sets		
Sentence (Sen)	55.38*	65.09*
Similarity (Simi)	43.13	55.16
Comp(type, Sen) + Comp(type, Simi)	55.75*	64.91*
Additive Feature Test		
Sen + Ngrams + Simi	56.43*	65.79*
+ Comp(type, Sen) + Comp(type, Simi)	**57.65***	**66.51***
+ Comp(type, Claim)	56.58*	65.68*

Table 3: Supporting argument detection results. Comp(type, Sen) stands for composite features of argument type and sentence features, similarly for Comp(type,Simi). Comp(type,Claim) represents composite features of type and claim features. Results that are statistically significantly better than all three baselines are marked with $*$ (paired t-test, $p < 0.05$).

We choose LambdaMART (Burges, 2010) for experiments, which is shown to be successful for many text ranking problems (Chapelle and Chang, 2011). Our model is evaluated by Mean Reciprocal Rank (MRR) and Normalized Discounted Cumulative Gain (NDCG) using 5-fold cross validation. We compare to TFIDF and Word embedding similarity baselines, and LambdaMART trained with ngrams (unigrams and bigrams).

Results in Table 3 show that using composite features with argument type information (Comp(type, Sen) + Comp(type, Simi)) can improve the ranking performance. Specifically, the best performance is achieved by adding composite features to sentence features, similarity features, and ngram features. As can be seen, supervised methods outperform unsupervised baseline methods. And similarity features have similar performance as those baselines. The best performance is achieved by combination of sentence features, N-grams, similarity, and two composite types, which is boldfaced. Feature sets that significantly outperform all three baselines are marked with $*$.

For feature analysis, we conduct t-test for individual feature values between supporting arguments and the others. We breakdown features according to their argument types and show top salient composite features in Table 4. For all sentences of type STUDY, relevant ones tend to contain more "percentage" and more concrete words. We also notice those sentences with more hedging words are more likely to be considered. For sentences of FACTUAL, position of sentence in article

Feature	STUDY	FACTUAL	OPINION	REASONING
# PERC, NE	** ↑↑↑↑	–	–	–
# LOC, NE	–	** ↑↑	–	** ↑
position of sentence	** ↓↓	* * ** ↓↓	–	* * * * ↓↓↓↓
concreteness of sentence	* * * ↑↑	–	** ↑↑	* * * ↓
arousal of sentence	* * * ↑↑	–	** ↑↑	** ↓
# hedging word	** ↑↑↑	–	–	–
ROUGE	* * * ↑↑	* * * ↑	** ↑↑	–
concreteness of claim	* * * ↑↑	–	** ↑↑	* * * ↓
arousal of claim	* * * ↑↑	–	** ↑↑	* * * ↓

Table 4: Comparison of feature significance under composition with different types. The number of $*$ stands for the p-value based on t-test between supporting argument sentences and the others after Bonferroni correction. From one $*$ to four, the p-value scales as: 0.05, 1e-3, 1e-5, and 1e-10. When mean value of supporting argument sentences is larger, ↑ is used; otherwise, ↓ is displayed. Number of arrows represents the ratio of the larger value over smaller one. "-" indicates no significant difference.

plays an important role, as well as their similarity to the claim based on ROUGE scores. For type OPINION, unlike all other types, position of sentence seems to be insignificant. As we could imagine, opinionated information might scatter around the whole documents. For sentences of REASONING, the ones that can be used as supporting arguments tend to be less concrete and less emotional, as opposed to opinion.

6 Conclusion

We presented a novel study on the task of sentence-level supporting argument detection from relevant documents for a user-specified claim. Based on our newly-collected dataset, we characterized arguments of different types with a rich feature set. We also showed that leveraging argument type information can further improve the performance of supporting argument detection.

Acknowledgments

This work was supported in part by National Science Foundation Grant IIS-1566382 and a GPU gift from Nvidia. We thank Kechen Qin for his help on data collection. We also appreciate the valuable suggestions on various aspects of this work from three anonymous reviewers.

References

Khalid Al Khatib, Henning Wachsmuth, Johannes Kiesel, Matthias Hagen, and Benno Stein. 2016. A news editorial corpus for mining argumentation strategies. In *Proceedings of COLING 2016, the 26th International Conference on Computational Linguistics: Technical Papers*. Osaka, Japan, pages 3433–3443.

Or Biran and Owen Rambow. 2011. Identifying justifications in written dialogs by classifying text as argumentative. *International Journal of Semantic Computing* 5(04):363–381.

Marc Brysbaert, Amy Beth Warriner, and Victor Kuperman. 2014. Concreteness ratings for 40 thousand generally known english word lemmas. *Behavior research methods* 46(3):904–911.

Christopher JC Burges. 2010. From ranknet to lambdarank to lambdamart: An overview. *Learning* 11(23-581):81.

Olivier Chapelle and Yi Chang. 2011. Yahoo! learning to rank challenge overview. In *Yahoo! Learning to Rank Challenge*. pages 1–24.

Nancy Chinchor and Patricia Robinson. 1997. Muc-7 named entity task definition. In *Proceedings of the 7th Conference on Message Understanding*. volume 29.

Vanessa Wei Feng and Graeme Hirst. 2011. Classifying arguments by scheme. In *Proceedings of the 49th Annual Meeting of the Association for Computational Linguistics: Human Language Technologies-Volume 1*. Association for Computational Linguistics, pages 987–996.

Ivan Habernal and Iryna Gurevych. 2015. Exploiting debate portals for semi-supervised argumentation mining in user-generated web discourse. In *Proceedings of the 2015 Conference on Empirical Methods in Natural Language Processing*. Association for Computational Linguistics, Lisbon, Portugal, pages 2127–2137.

Chin-Yew Lin. 2004. Rouge: A package for automatic evaluation of summaries. In *Text summarization branches out: Proceedings of the ACL-04 workshop*. Barcelona, Spain, volume 8.

Raquel Mochales and Marie-Francine Moens. 2011. Argumentation mining. *Artificial Intelligence and Law* 19(1):1–22.

Marie-Francine Moens, Erik Boiy, Raquel Mochales Palau, and Chris Reed. 2007. Automatic detection of arguments in legal texts. In *Proceedings of the 11th international conference on Artificial intelligence and law*. ACM, pages 225–230.

Huy Nguyen and Diane Litman. 2016. Context-aware argumentative relation mining. In *Proceedings of the 54th Annual Meeting of the Association for Computational Linguistics (Volume 1: Long Papers)*. Association for Computational Linguistics, Berlin, Germany, pages 1127–1137.

Raquel Mochales Palau and Marie-Francine Moens. 2009. Argumentation mining: the detection, classification and structure of arguments in text. In *Proceedings of the 12th international conference on artificial intelligence and law*. ACM, pages 98–107.

Kishore Papineni, Salim Roukos, Todd Ward, and Wei-Jing Zhu. 2002. Bleu: a method for automatic evaluation of machine translation. In *Proceedings of the 40th annual meeting on association for computational linguistics*. Association for Computational Linguistics, pages 311–318.

Joonsuk Park and Claire Cardie. 2014. Identifying appropriate support for propositions in online user comments. In *Proceedings of the First Workshop on Argumentation Mining*. pages 29–38.

Rashmi Prasad, Eleni Miltsakaki, Nikhil Dinesh, Alan Lee, Aravind Joshi, Livio Robaldo, and Bonnie L Webber. 2007. The penn discourse treebank 2.0 annotation manual .

Richard D Rieke, Malcolm Osgood Sillars, and Tarla Rai Peterson. 1997. *Argumentation and critical decision making*. New York: Longman.

Ruty Rinott, Lena Dankin, Carlos Alzate Perez, Mitesh M Khapra, Ehud Aharoni, and Noam Slonim. 2015. Show me your evidence-an automatic method for context dependent evidence detection. In *EMNLP*. pages 440–450.

Niall Rooney, Hui Wang, and Fiona Browne. 2012. Applying kernel methods to argumentation mining. In *Twenty-Fifth International FLAIRS Conference*.

Christian Stab and Iryna Gurevych. 2014. Identifying argumentative discourse structures in persuasive essays. In *EMNLP*. pages 46–56.

Philip J Stone, Dexter C Dunphy, and Marshall S Smith. 1966. The general inquirer: A computer approach to content analysis. .

Amy Beth Warriner, Victor Kuperman, and Marc Brysbaert. 2013. Norms of valence, arousal, and dominance for 13,915 english lemmas. *Behavior research methods* 45(4):1191–1207.

Theresa Wilson, Janyce Wiebe, and Paul Hoffmann. 2005. Recognizing contextual polarity in phrase-level sentiment analysis. In *Proceedings of the conference on human language technology and empirical methods in natural language processing*. Association for Computational Linguistics, pages 347–354.

A Neural Model for User Geolocation and Lexical Dialectology

Afshin Rahimi   **Trevor Cohn**   **Timothy Baldwin**
School of Computing and Information Systems
The University of Melbourne
`arahimi@student.unimelb.edu.au`
`{t.cohn,tbaldwin}@unimelb.edu.au`

Abstract

We propose a simple yet effective text-based user geolocation model based on a neural network with one hidden layer, which achieves state of the art performance over three Twitter benchmark geolocation datasets, in addition to producing word and phrase embeddings in the hidden layer that we show to be useful for detecting dialectal terms. As part of our analysis of dialectal terms, we release DAREDS, a dataset for evaluating dialect term detection methods.

1 Introduction

Many services such as web search (Leung et al., 2010), recommender systems (Ho et al., 2012), targeted advertising (Lim and Datta, 2013), and rapid disaster response (Ashktorab et al., 2014) rely on the location of users to personalise information and extract actionable knowledge. Explicit user geolocation metadata (e.g. GPS tags, WiFi footprint, IP address) is not usually available to third-party consumers, giving rise to the need for geolocation based on profile data, text content, friendship graphs (Jurgens et al., 2015) or some combination of these (Rahimi et al., 2015b,a). The strong geographical bias, most obviously at the language level (e.g. Finland vs. Japan), and more subtly at the dialect level (e.g. in English used in north-west England vs. north-east USA vs. Texas, USA), clearly reflected in language use in social media services such as Twitter, has been used extensively either for geolocation of users (Eisenstein et al., 2010; Roller et al., 2012; Rout et al., 2013; Han et al., 2014; Wing and Baldridge, 2014) or dialectology (Cook et al., 2014; Eisenstein, 2015). In these methods, a user is often represented by the concatenation of their tweets, and the geolocation model is trained on a very small percentage of explicitly geotagged

tweets, noting the potential biases implicit in geotagged tweets (Pavalanathan and Eisenstein, 2015).

Lexical dialectology is (in part) the converse of user geolocation (Eisenstein, 2015): given text associated with a variety of regions, the task is to identify terms that are distinctive of particular regions. The complexity of the task is two-fold: (1) localised named entities (e.g. sporting team names) are not of interest; and (2) without semantic knowledge it is difficult to detect terms that are in general use but have a special meaning in a region.

In this paper we propose a text-based geolocation method based on neural networks. Our contributions are as follows: (1) we achieve state-of-the-art results on benchmark Twitter geolocation datasets; (2) we show that the model is less sensitive to the specific location discretisation method; (3) we release the first broad-coverage dataset for evaluation of lexical dialectology models; (4) we incorporate our text-based model into a network-based model (Rahimi et al., 2015a) and improve the performance utilising both network and text; and (5) we use the model's embeddings for extraction of local terms and show that it outperforms two baselines.

2 Related Work

Related work on Twitter user geolocation falls into two categories: text-based and network-based methods. Text-based methods make use of the geographical biases of language use, and network-based methods rely on the geospatial homophily of user–user interactions. In both cases, the assumption is that users who live in the same geographic area share similar features (linguistic or interactional). Three main text-based approaches are: (1) the use of gazetteers (Lieberman et al., 2010; Quercini et al., 2010); (2) unsupervised text clustering based on topic models or similar (Eisenstein et al., 2010; Hong et al., 2012; Ahmed et al.,

Proceedings of the 55th Annual Meeting of the Association for Computational Linguistics (Short Papers), pages 209–216
Vancouver, Canada, July 30 - August 4, 2017. ©2017 Association for Computational Linguistics
https://doi.org/10.18653/v1/P17-2033

2013); and (3) supervised classification (Ding et al., 2000; Backstrom et al., 2008; Cheng et al., 2010; Hecht et al., 2011; Kinsella et al., 2011; Wing and Baldridge, 2011; Han et al., 2012; Rout et al., 2013), which unlike gazetteers can be applied to informal text and compared to topic models, scales better. The classification models often rely on less than 1% of geotagged tweets for supervision and discretise real-valued coordinates into equal-sized grids (Serdyukov et al., 2009), administrative regions (Cheng et al., 2010; Hecht et al., 2011; Kinsella et al., 2011; Han et al., 2012, 2014), or flat (Wing and Baldridge, 2011) or hierarchical k-d tree clusters (Wing and Baldridge, 2014). Network-based methods also use either real-valued coordinates (Jurgens et al., 2015) or discretised regions (Rahimi et al., 2015a) as labels, and use label propagation over the interaction graph (e.g. @-mentions). More recent methods have focused on representation learning by using sparse coding (Cha et al., 2015) or neural networks (Liu and Inkpen, 2015), utilising both text and network information (Rahimi et al., 2015a).

Dialect is a variety of language shared by a group of speakers (Wolfram and Schilling, 2015). Our focus here is on geographical dialects which are spoken (and written in social media) by people from particular areas. The traditional approach to dialectology is to find the geographical distribution of known lexical alternatives (e.g. *you*, *yall* and *yinz*: (Labov et al., 2005; Nerbonne et al., 2008; Gonçalves and Sánchez, 2014; Doyle, 2014; Huang et al., 2015; Nguyen and Eisenstein, 2016)), the shortcoming of which is that the alternative lexical variables must be known beforehand. There have also been attempts to automatically identify such words from geotagged documents (Eisenstein et al., 2010; Ahmed et al., 2013; Cook et al., 2014; Eisenstein, 2015). The main idea is to find lexical variables that are disproportionately distributed in different locations either via model-based or statistical methods (Monroe et al., 2008). There is a research gap in evaluating the geolocation models in terms of their usability in retrieving dialect terms given a geographic region.

We use a text-based neural approach trained on geotagged Twitter messages that: (a) given a geographical region, identifies the associated lexical terms; and (b) given a text, predicts its location.

3   Data

We use three existing Twitter user geolocation datasets: (1) GEOTEXT (Eisenstein et al., 2010), (2) TWITTER-US (Roller et al., 2012), and (3) TWITTER-WORLD (Han et al., 2012). These datasets have been used widely for training and evaluation of geolocation models. They are all pre-partitioned into training, development and test sets. Each user is represented by the concatenation of their tweets, and labeled with the latitude/longitude of the first collected geotagged tweet in the case of GEOTEXT and TWITTER-US, and the centre of the closest city in the case of TWITTER-WORLD.[1] GEOTEXT and TWITTER-US cover the continental US, and TWITTER-WORLD covers the whole world, with 9k, 449k and 1.3m users, respectively as shown in Figure 1.[2]   **DAREDS** is a dialect-term dataset novel to this research, created from the Dictionary of American Regional English (DARE) (Cassidy et al., 1985). DARE consists of dialect regions, their terms and meaning.[3] It is based on dialectal surveys from different regions of the U.S., which are then postprocessed to identify dialect regions and terms. In order to construct a dataset based on DARE, we downloaded the web version of DARE, cleaned it, and removed multi-word expressions and highly-frequent words (any word which occurred in the top 50k most frequent words, based on a word frequency list (Norvig, 2009). For dialect regions that don't correspond to a single state or set of cities (e.g. *South*), we mapped it to the most populous cities within each region. For example, within the *Pacific Northwest* dialect region, we manually extracted the most populous cities (Seattle, Tacoma, Portland, Salem, Eugene) and added those cities to DAREDS as subregions.

The resulting dataset (DAREDS) consists of around 4.3k dialect terms from 99 U.S. dialect regions. DAREDS is the largest standardised dialectology dataset.

4   Methods

We use a multilayer perceptron (MLP) with one hidden layer as our location classifier, where the

---

[1]The decision as to how a given user is labeled was made by the creators of the original datasets, and has been preserved in this work, despite misgivings about the representativeness of the label for some users.

[2]The datasets can be obtained from `https://github.com/utcompling/textgrounder`

[3]`http://www.daredictionary.com/`

Figure 1: The geographical distribution of training points in GEOTEXT (left), TWITTER-US (middle) and TWITTER-WORLD (right). Each red point is a training user. The number of training users is 5.6K, 429K and 1.3M in each dataset respectively. Despite the number of training instances being higher in TWITTER-WORLD (right) compared to TWITTER-US (middle), there is greater user density in the case of the latter.

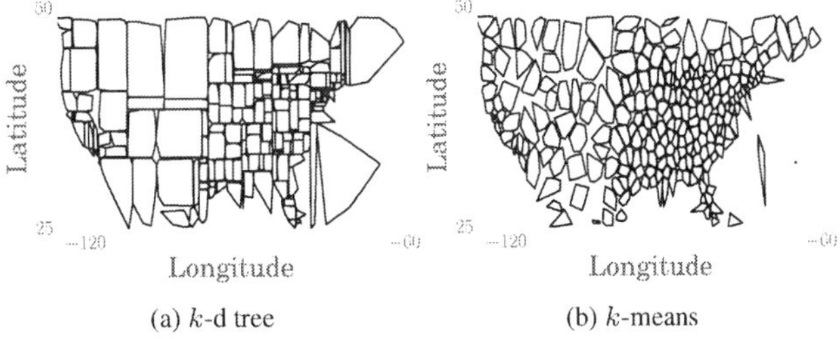

(a) k-d tree

(b) k-means

Figure 2: Discretisation of TWITTER-US training coordinates using k-d tree and k-means clustering shown by the convex hulls around the training points within each cluster.

input is l_2 normalised bag-of-words features for a given user. We exclude @-mentions, words with document frequency less than 10, and stop words. The output is either a k-d tree leaf node or k-means discretisation of real-valued coordinates of training locations, the output of which is visualised for TWITTER-US in Figure 2. The hidden layer output provides word (and phrase, as bags of words) embeddings for dialectal analysis.

The number of regions, regularisation strength, hidden layer and mini-batch size are tuned over development data and set to $(32, 10^{-5}, 896, 100)$, $(256, 10^{-6}, 2048, 10000)$ and $(930, 10^{-6}, 3720, 10000)$ for GEOTEXT, TWITTER-US and TWITTER-WORLD, respectively. The parameters are optimised using Adamx (Kingma and Ba, 2014) using Lasagne/Theano (Theano Development Team, 2016). Following Cheng (2010) and Eisenstein (2010), we evaluated the geolocation model using mean and median error in km ("Mean" and "Median" resp.) and accuracy within 161km of the actual location ("Acc@161"). Note that lower numbers are better for Mean and Median, and higher numbers better for Acc@161.

While the focus of this paper is text-based user geolocation, state-of-the-art results for the three datasets have been achieved with hybrid text+network-based models, where the predictions of the text-based model are fed into a mention network as "dongle" nodes to each user node, providing a personalised geolocation prior for each user (Rahimi et al., 2015a). Note that it would, of course, be possible to combine text and network information in a joint deep learning model (Yang et al., 2016; Kipf and Welling, 2016), which we leave to future work (noting that scalability will potentially be a major issue for the larger datasets).

To test the applicability of the model's embeddings in dialectology, we created DAREDS. The output of the hidden layer of the model is used as embeddings for both location names and dialect terms. Given a dialect region name, we retrieve its nearest neighbours in the embedding space, and compare them to dialect terms associated with that location. We also compare the quality of the embeddings with pre-trained word2vec embeddings and the embeddings from the output layer of LR (logistic regression) (Rahimi et al., 2015b) as baselines. Regions in DAREDS can be very broad (e.g. *SouthWest*), meaning that words associated with those locations will be used across a large number

---

[4] The results reported in Rahimi et al. (2015b; 2015a) for TWITTER-WORLD were over a superset of the dataset; the results reported here are based on the actual dataset.

	GEOTEXT			TWITTER-US			TWITTER-WORLD		
	Acc@161	Mean	Median	Acc@161	Mean	Median	Acc@161	Mean	Median
TEXT-BASED METHODS									
Proposed method (MLP + k-d tree)	38	844	389	54	554	120	34	1456	415
Proposed method (MLP + k-means)	40	856	380	55	581	91	36	1417	373
(Rahimi et al., 2015b) (LR)	38	880	397	50	686	159	32	1724	530
(Wing and Baldridge, 2014) (uniform)	—	—	—	49	703	170	32	1714	490
(Wing and Baldridge, 2014) (k-d tree)	—	—	—	48	686	191	31	1669	509
(Melo and Martins, 2015)	—	—	—	—	702	208	—	1507	502
(Cha et al., 2015)	—	581	425	—	—	—	—	—	—
(Liu and Inkpen, 2015)	—	—	—	—	733	377	—	—	—
NETWORK-BASED METHODS									
(Rahimi et al., 2015a) MADCEL-W	58	586	60	54	705	116	45	2525	279
TEXT+NETWORK-BASED METHODS									
(Rahimi et al., 2015a) MADCEL-W-LR	**59**	581	**57**	60	529	78	**53**	1403	111
MADCEL-W-MLP	**59**	**578**	61	**61**	**515**	**77**	**53**	**1280**	**104**

Table 1: Geolocation results over the three Twitter datasets, based on the text-based MLP with k-d tree or k-means discretisation and text+network model MADCEL-W-MLP using MLP with k-d tree for text-based predictions. We compare with state-of-the-art results for each dataset.[4] "—" signifies that no results were reported for the given metric or dataset.

of cities contained within that region. We generate a region-level embedding by simply taking the city names associated with the region, and feeding them as BoW input for LR and MLP and averaging their embeddings for word2vec. We evaluate the retrieved terms by computing recall of DAREDS terms existing in TWITTER-US (1071 terms) at $k \in \{0.05\%, 0.1\%, 0.2\%, 0.5\%, 1\%, 2\%, 5\%\}$ of vocabulary size. The code and the DAREDS dataset are available at https://github.com/afshinrahimi/acl2017.

NYC	LA	Chicago	Philadelphia
manhattan	lapd	chi	septa
ny	wiltern	uic	erked
soho	ralphs	metra	philly
mets	ucla	depaul	phillies
nycc	weho	bears	jawn
nyu	lausd	chitown	#udproblems
#electriczoo	#hollywoodbowl	cta	dickhead
yorkers	lmu	bogus	flyers
mta	asf	lbs	irked
#thingswhitepeopledo	lacma	lbvvs	erkin

Table 2: Nearest neighbours of place names.

5 Results

5.1 Geolocation

The performance of the text-based MLP model with k-d tree and k-means discretisation over the three datasets is shown in Table 1. The results are also compared with state-of-the-art text-based methods based on a flat (Rahimi et al., 2015b; Cha et al., 2015) or hierarchical (Wing and Baldridge, 2014; Melo and Martins, 2015; Liu and Inkpen, 2015) geospatial representation. Our method outperforms both the flat and hierarchical text-based models by a large margin. Comparing the two discretisation strategies, k-means outperforms k-d tree by a reasonable margin. We also incorporated the MLP predictions into a network-based model based on the method of Rahimi et al. (2015a), and improved upon their work. We analysed the Median error of MLP (k-d tree) over the development users of TWITTER-US in each of the U.S. states as shown

in Figure 3. The error is highest in states with lower training coverage (e.g. Maine, Montana, Wisconsin, Iowa and Kansas). We also randomly sampled 50 development samples from the 1000 samples with highest prediction errors to check the biases of the model. Most of the errors are the result of geolocating users from Eastern U.S. in Western U.S. particularly in Los Angeles and San Francisco.

5.2 Dialectology

We quantitatively tested the quality of the geographical embeddings by calculating the micro-average recall of the k-nearest dialect terms (in terms of the proportion of retrieved dialect terms) given a dialect region, as shown in Figure 4. Recall at 0.5% is about 3.6%, meaning that we were able to retrieve 3.6% of the dialect terms given the dialect region name in the geographical embedding space. The embeddings slightly outperform the output layer of logistic regression (LR) (Rahimi et al., 2015b)

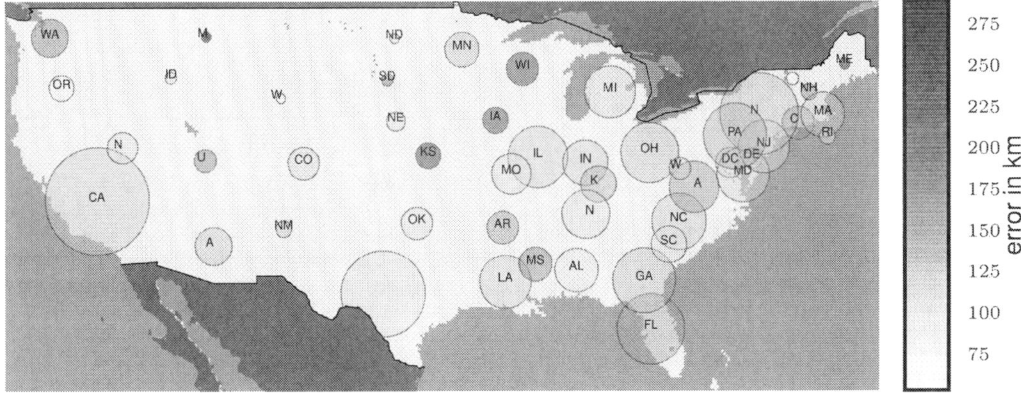

Figure 3: The geographical distribution of Median error of MLP (k-d tree) in each state over the development set of TWITTER-US. The colour indicates error and the size indicates the number of development users within the state.

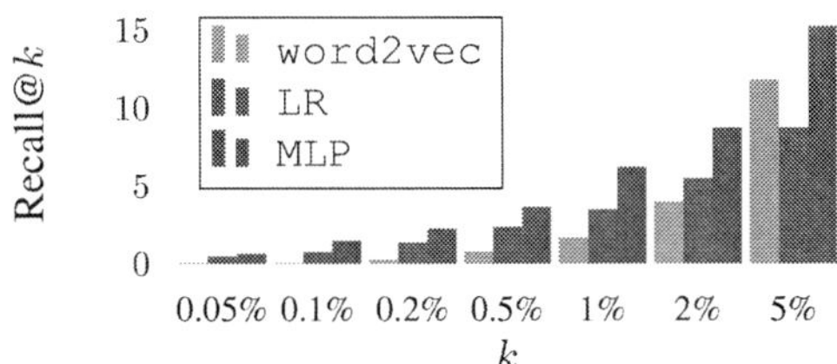

Figure 4: Micro-averaged Recall@k results for retrieving dialect terms given the dialect region name using LR embeddings, pre-trained word2vec embeddings as baselines, and our embeddings (MLP). For example at $k = 0.5\%$ of vocabulary (1292 words), recall is 3.6% for MLP compared to 2.3% for LR and less than 1% for word2vec.

and word2vec pre-trained embeddings, but there is still substantial room for improvement.

Our model is slightly better than both baselines, and can retrieve 3.6% of the correct dialect terms given the region name at 0.5% of the total vocabulary, noting the significant performance gap left for future research. It is worth noting that the retrieved terms that are not included in DAREDS are not irrelevant: many of them are toponyms (e.g. city names, rivers, companies, or companies) associated with the given region which are not of interest in dialectology. Equally, some are terms that don't exist in the DARE dictionary but might be of interest for dialectologists because language use in social media is so dynamic that they won't be captured by traditional survey-like approaches. A major shortcoming of this work is that it doesn't incorporate sense distinctions and so can't recover dialect terms that are uniformly distributed but have an idiomatic usage in a particular region.

6 Conclusion and Future Work

We proposed a new text geolocation model based on the multilayer perceptron (MLP), and evaluated it over three benchmark Twitter geolocation datasets. We achieved state-of-the-art text-based results over all datasets. We used the parameters of the hidden layer of the neural network as word and phrase embeddings. We performed a nearest neighbour search on a sample of city names and dialect terms, and showed that the embeddings can be used both to discover dialect terms from a geographic area and to find the geographic area a dialect term is spoken. To evaluate the geographical embeddings quantitatively, we created DAREDS, a machine-readable version of the DARE dictionary and compared the performance of dialect term retrieval given dialect region name in terms of recall (Figure 4), and compared the performance to the performance in pre-trained word2vec and LR embeddings.

Acknowledgments

We thank the anonymous reviewers for their insightful comments and valuable suggestions. This work was funded in part by the Australian Government Research Training Program Scholarship, and the Australian Research Council.

References

Amr Ahmed, Liangjie Hong, and Alexander J. Smola. 2013. Hierarchical geographical modeling of user locations from social media posts. In *Proceedings of the 22nd International Conference on World Wide Web (WWW 2013)*. Rio de Janeiro, Brazil, pages 25–36.

Zahra Ashktorab, Christopher Brown, Manojit Nandi, and Aron Culotta. 2014. Tweedr: Mining Twitter to inform disaster response. In *Proceedings of the 11th International Conference on Information Systems for Crisis Response and Management (IS-CRAM 2014)*. University Park, USA, pages 354–358.

Lars Backstrom, Jon Kleinberg, Ravi Kumar, and Jasmine Novak. 2008. Spatial variation in search engine queries. In *Proceedings of the 17th International Conference on World Wide Web (WWW 2008)*. Beijing, China, pages 357–366.

Frederic Gomes Cassidy et al. 1985. *Dictionary of American Regional English*. Belknap Press of Harvard University Press.

Miriam Cha, Youngjune Gwon, and HT Kung. 2015. Twitter geolocation and regional classification via sparse coding. In *Proceedings of the 9th International Conference on Weblogs and Social Media (ICWSM 2015)*. Oxford, UK, pages 582–585.

Zhiyuan Cheng, James Caverlee, and Kyumin Lee. 2010. You are where you tweet: a content-based approach to geo-locating Twitter users. In *Proceedings of the 19th ACM International Conference Information and Knowledge Management (CIKM 2010)*. Toronto, Canada, pages 759–768.

Paul Cook, Bo Han, and Timothy Baldwin. 2014. Statistical methods for identifying local dialectal terms from gps-tagged documents. *Dictionaries: Journal of the Dictionary Society of North America* 35(35):248–271.

Junyan Ding, Luis Gravano, and Narayanan Shivakumar. 2000. Computing geographical scopes of web resources. In *Proceedings of the 26th International Conference on Very Large Data Bases (VLDB 2000)*. Cairo, Egypt, pages 545–556.

Gabriel Doyle. 2014. Mapping dialectal variation by querying social media. In *Proceedings of the 14th Conference of the EACL (EACL 2014)*. Gothenburg, Sweden, pages 98–106.

Jacob Eisenstein. 2015. Written dialect variation in online social media. In Charles Boberg, John Nerbonne, and Dom Watt, editors, *Handbook of Dialectology*, Wiley.

Jacob Eisenstein, Brendan O'Connor, Noah A Smith, and Eric P Xing. 2010. A latent variable model for geographic lexical variation. In *Proceedings of the 2010 Conference on Empirical Methods in Natural Language Processing (EMNLP 2010)*. Boston, USA, pages 1277–1287.

Bruno Gonçalves and David Sánchez. 2014. Crowdsourcing dialect characterization through twitter. *PloS one* 9(11):e112074.

Bo Han, Paul Cook, and Timothy Baldwin. 2012. Geolocation prediction in social media data by finding location indicative words. In *Proceedings of the 24th International Conference on Computational Linguistics (COLING 2012)*. Mumbai, India, pages 1045–1062.

Bo Han, Paul Cook, and Timothy Baldwin. 2014. Text-based Twitter user geolocation prediction. *Journal of Artificial Intelligence Research* 49:451–500.

Brent Hecht, Lichan Hong, Bongwon Suh, and Ed H Chi. 2011. Tweets from Justin Bieber's heart: the dynamics of the location field in user profiles. In *Proceedings of the SIGCHI Conference on Human Factors in Computing Systems*. Vancouver, Canada, pages 237–246.

Shen-Shyang Ho, Mike Lieberman, Pu Wang, and Hanan Samet. 2012. Mining future spatiotemporal events and their sentiment from online news articles for location-aware recommendation system. In *Proceedings of the First ACM SIGSPATIAL International Workshop on Mobile Geographic Information Systems*. Redondo Beach, California, pages 25–32.

Liangjie Hong, Amr Ahmed, Siva Gurumurthy, Alexander J. Smola, and Kostas Tsioutsiouliklis. 2012. Discovering geographical topics in the Twitter stream. In *Proceedings of the 21st International Conference on World Wide Web (WWW 2012)*. Lyon, France, pages 769–778.

Yuan Huang, Diansheng Guo, Alice Kasakoff, and Jack Grieve. 2015. Understanding US regional linguistic variation with Twitter data analysis. *Computers, Environment and Urban Systems* 59:244–255.

David Jurgens, Tyler Finethy, James McCorriston, Yi Tian Xu, and Derek Ruths. 2015. Geolocation prediction in Twitter using social networks: A critical analysis and review of current practice. In *Proceedings of the 9th International Conference on Weblogs and Social Media (ICWSM 2015)*. Oxford, UK, pages 188–197.

Diederik Kingma and Jimmy Ba. 2014. Adam: A method for stochastic optimization. *arXiv preprint arXiv:1412.6980* .

Sheila Kinsella, Vanessa Murdock, and Neil O'Hare. 2011. "I'm eating a sandwich in Glasgow": Modeling locations with tweets. In *Proceedings of the 3rd International Workshop on Search and Mining User-generated Contents*. Glasgow, UK, pages 61–68.

Thomas N. Kipf and Max Welling. 2016. Semi-supervised classification with graph convolutional networks. *arXiv preprint arXiv:1609.02907* .

William Labov, Sharon Ash, and Charles Boberg. 2005. *The Atlas of North American English: Phonetics, Phonology and Sound Change*. Walter de Gruyter.

Kenneth Wai-Ting Leung, Dik Lun Lee, and Wang-Chien Lee. 2010. Personalized web search with location preferences. In *2010 IEEE 26th International Conference on Data Engineering (ICDE 2010)*. Long Beach, USA, pages 701–712.

Michael D Lieberman, Hanan Samet, and Jagan Sankaranarayanan. 2010. Geotagging with local lexicons to build indexes for textually-specified spatial data. In *Proceedings of the 26th International Conference on Data Engineering (ICDE 2010)*. IEEE, Long Beach, USA, pages 201–212.

Kwan Hui Lim and Amitava Datta. 2013. A topological approach for detecting Twitter communities with common interests. In Martin Atzmueller, Alvin Chin, and Denis Helic, editors, *Ubiquitous Social Media Analysis*, Springer, pages 23–43.

Ji Liu and Diana Inkpen. 2015. Estimating user location in social media with stacked denoising auto-encoders. In *Proceedings of the 2015 Conference of the North American Chapter of the Association for Computational Linguistics — Human Language Technologies (NAACL HLT 2015)*. Denver, USA, pages 201–210.

Fernando Melo and Bruno Martins. 2015. Geocoding textual documents through the usage of hierarchical classifiers. In *Proceedings of the 9th Workshop on Geographic Information Retrieval (GIR 2015)*. Paris, France, pages 7:1–7:9.

Burt L. Monroe, Michael P. Colaresi, and Kevin M. Quinn. 2008. Fightin'words: Lexical feature selection and evaluation for identifying the content of political conflict. *Political Analysis* 16(4):372–403.

John Nerbonne, Peter Kleiweg, Wilbert Heeringa, and Franz Manni. 2008. Projecting dialect distances to geography: Bootstrap clustering vs. noisy clustering. In *Proceedings of the 31st Annual Conference of the Gesellschaft für Klassifikation*. pages 647–654.

Dong Nguyen and Jacob Eisenstein. 2016. A kernel independence test for geographical language variation. *CoRR* abs/1601.06579.

Peter Norvig. 2009. Natural language corpus data. In Toby Segaran and Jeff Hammerbacher, editors, *Beautiful Data: The Stories Behind Elegant Data Solutions*, O'Reilly Media, pages 219–242.

Umashanthi Pavalanathan and Jacob Eisenstein. 2015. Confounds and consequences in geotagged Twitter data. In *Proceedings of the 2015 Conference on Empirical Methods in Natural Language Processing (EMNLP 2015)*. Lisbon, Portugal, pages 2138–2148.

Gianluca Quercini, Hanan Samet, Jagan Sankaranarayanan, and Michael D. Lieberman. 2010. Determining the spatial reader scopes of news sources using local lexicons. In *Proceedings of the 18th SIGSPATIAL International Conference on Advances in Geographic Information Systems (SIGSPATIAL 2010)*. New York, USA, pages 43–52.

Afshin Rahimi, Trevor Cohn, and Timothy Baldwin. 2015a. Twitter user geolocation using a unified text and network prediction model. *Proceedings of the 53rd Annual Meeting of the Association for Computational Linguistics — 7th International Joint Conference on Natural Language Processing (ACL-IJCNLP 2015)* pages 630–636.

Afshin Rahimi, Duy Vu, Trevor Cohn, and Timothy Baldwin. 2015b. Exploiting text and network context for geolocation of social media users. In *Proceedings of the 2015 Conference of the North American Chapter of the Association for Computational Linguistics — Human Language Technologies (NAACL HLT 2015)*. Denver, USA, pages 1362–1367.

Stephen Roller, Michael Speriosu, Sarat Rallapalli, Benjamin Wing, and Jason Baldridge. 2012. Supervised text-based geolocation using language models on an adaptive grid. In *Proceedings of the 2012 Joint Conference on Empirical Methods in Natural Language Processing and Computational Natural Language Learning (EMNLP-CONLL 2012)*. Jeju, Korea, pages 1500–1510.

Dominic Rout, Kalina Bontcheva, Daniel Preoțiuc-Pietro, and Trevor Cohn. 2013. Where's @wally?: A classification approach to geolocating users based on their social ties. In *Proceedings of the 24th ACM Conference on Hypertext and Social Media (Hypertext 2013)*. Paris, France, pages 11–20.

Pavel Serdyukov, Vanessa Murdock, and Roelof Van Zwol. 2009. Placing flickr photos on a map. In *Proceedings of the 32nd International ACM SIGIR Conference on Research and Development in Information Retrieval*. Boston, USA, pages 484–491.

Theano Development Team. 2016. Theano: A Python framework for fast computation of mathematical expressions. *arXiv e-prints* abs/1605.02688.

Benjamin P. Wing and Jason Baldridge. 2011. Simple supervised document geolocation with geodesic grids. In *Proceedings of the 49th Annual Meeting of the Association for Computational Linguistics: Human Language Technologies-Volume 1 (ACL-HLT 2011)*. Portland, USA, pages 955–964.

Benjamin P. Wing and Jason Baldridge. 2014. Hierarchical discriminative classification for text-based geolocation. In *Proceedings of the 2014 Conference on Empirical Methods in Natural Language Processing (EMNLP 2014)*. Doha, Qatar, pages 336–348.

Walt Wolfram and Natalie Schilling. 2015. *American English: Dialects and Variation*. John Wiley & Sons.

Zhilin Yang, William Cohen, and Ruslan Salakhutdinov. 2016. Revisiting semi-supervised learning with graph embeddings. *arXiv preprint arXiv:1603.08861* .

A Corpus of Natural Language for Visual Reasoning

Alane Suhr[†], Mike Lewis[‡], James Yeh[†], and Yoav Artzi[†]

[†] Dept. of Computer Science and Cornell Tech, Cornell University, New York, NY 10044
{suhr, yoav}@cs.cornell.edu, jamesclyeh@gmail.com

[‡] Facebook AI Research, Menlo Park, CA 94025
mikelewis@fb.com

Abstract

We present a new visual reasoning language dataset, containing 92,244 pairs of examples of natural statements grounded in synthetic images with 3,962 unique sentences. We describe a method of crowdsourcing linguistically-diverse data, and present an analysis of our data. The data demonstrates a broad set of linguistic phenomena, requiring visual and set-theoretic reasoning. We experiment with various models, and show the data presents a strong challenge for future research.

1 Introduction

Understanding complex compositional language in context is a challenge shared by many tasks. Visual question answering and robot instruction systems require reasoning about sets of objects, quantities, comparisons, and spatial relations; for example, when instructing home assistance or assembly-line robots to manipulate objects in cluttered environments. This reasoning requires robust language understanding, and is only partially addressed by existing datasets. VQA (Antol et al., 2015), while lexically and visually diverse, includes relatively short sentences with limited coverage of such phenomena. CLEVR (Johnson et al., 2016) and SHAPES (Andreas et al., 2016b), in contrast, display complex compositional structure, but include only synthetic language.

In this paper, we introduce the Cornell Natural Language Visual Reasoning (NLVR) corpus and task. We define the binary prediction task of judging if a statement is true for an image or not, and introduce a corpus of annotated pairs of natural language statements and synthetic images.

Collecting this kind of language presents two challenges. First, we must design environments to

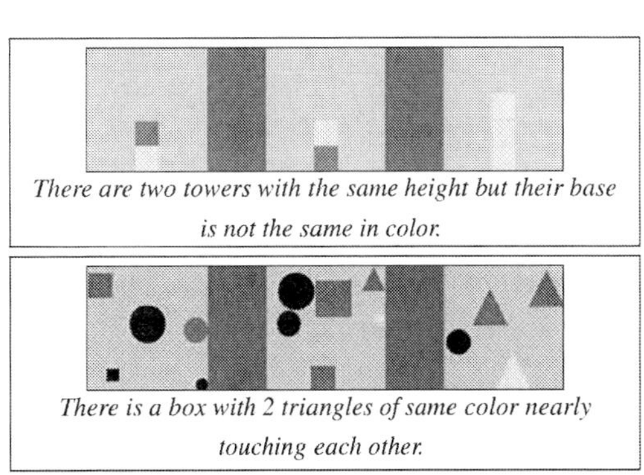

Figure 1: Example sentences and images from our corpus. Each image includes three boxes with different object types. The truth value of the top sentence is true, while the bottom is false.

support such descriptions. We use simple visual environments displaying objects with complex visual relations between them. Figure 1 shows two generated images. The second challenge is eliciting complex descriptions displaying a range of syntactic and semantic phenomena. We use a two-stage crowdsourcing process. In the first stage, we present sets of images and ask workers to write descriptive statements that distinguish them. Using synthetic images with abstract shapes allows us to control the potential distinctions between them; for example, by discouraging simple statements about object existence. In the second stage, we ask workers to label the truth value for the sentences and images generated in the first stage.

Our data includes 92,244 sentence-image pairs with 3,962 unique sentences. We include both images and the structured representation used to generate them to support research using both raw visual information and structured data. Figure 1 shows two examples. To assess the difficulty of NLVR, we experiment with multiple baselines. The best model using images achieves an accuracy of 66.12, demonstrating remaining challenges

Proceedings of the 55th Annual Meeting of the Association for Computational Linguistics (Short Papers), pages 217–223
Vancouver, Canada, July 30 - August 4, 2017. ©2017 Association for Computational Linguistics
https://doi.org/10.18653/v1/P17-2034

in the data. We also analyze the language in our data for presence of certain linguistic phenomena, and compare this analysis with related datasets. The data and leaderboard are available at `http://lic.nlp.cornell.edu/nlvr`.

2 Related Work and Datasets

Several datasets have been created to study visual reasoning and language. VQA (Antol et al., 2015; Zitnick and Parikh, 2013) includes crowd-sourced questions and answers for photographs and abstract scenes, and has been studied extensively (e.g., Lu et al., 2016; Xu and Saenko, 2016; Zhou et al., 2015; Chen et al., 2015a; Andreas et al., 2016b,a; Ray et al., 2016). In contrast to VQA, we use synthetic images and emphasize representing a broad range of language phenomena. Our motivation is similar to that of SHAPES (Andreas et al., 2016b) and CLEVR (Johnson et al., 2016). Both datasets also use synthetic images and emphasize representing diverse spatial language. However, unlike our approach, they include only automatically generated language.

Visual reasoning has also been addressed in instructional language corpora (e.g., MacMahon et al., 2006; Chen and Mooney, 2011; Bisk et al., 2016), where executable instructions are grounded in manipulable environments. The language we observe is similar to the type of language studied for understanding and generation of referential expressions (Mitchell et al., 2010; Matuszek et al., 2012; FitzGerald et al., 2013).

Our task is related to caption generation, which has been studied extensively (e.g., Pedersoli et al., 2016; Carrara et al., 2016; Chen et al., 2016) with MSCOCO (Chen et al., 2015b) and Flickr30K (Young et al., 2014; Plummer et al., 2015). In contrast to caption generation, our task does not require approximate metrics like BLEU.

Several existing datasets focus on natural language querying of structured representations, including GeoQuery (Zelle, 1995) and WikiTables (Pasupat and Liang, 2015). Our work is complementary to these resources. While our corpus was collected using images, we also provide structured representations. When used with these representations, our corpus is similar to WikiTables, where questions are paired with small web tables. Instead of web tables, we use object sets and focus on visual language.

3 Task

Statements in our data are grounded in synthetic images rendered from structured representations. Given an example, the task is to determine whether a statement is true or false for the image or structured representation. While we describe the image, the structured representation is equivalent. We provide examples of the structured representation in the supplementary material. Images are divided into three *boxes*. Figure 1 shows two images. Each box contains 1-8 *objects*. Each object has four properties: *position* (x/y coordinates), *color* (black, blue, yellow), *shape* (triangle, square, circle), and *size* (small, medium, large). Objects within a box cannot overlap and must be contained entirely in the box. We distinguish between images containing scattered objects and images containing only squares arranged in towers up to four blocks tall. The top image in Figure 1 is a tower example; the bottom is a scatter example.

This design encourages compositional language with complex visual reasoning. We divide the image into boxes to encourage set theoretic reasoning within and between boxes. We also use a relatively limited number of values for each property. While a large number of properties provides a more diverse image, it is likely to result in descriptions that refer to property differences. We find that the limited number of properties elicits descriptions with rich compositional structure.

4 Data Collection

We generate images following the structure described in Section 3, and collect grounded natural language descriptions. Data is collected in two phases: sentence writing and validation. During sentence writing, workers are asked to write contrasting descriptions about a set of images. To validate sentences, the description is paired with each of the images. We execute the collection process four times to collect training, development, and two test sets (Test-P and Test-U). We retain one test set as unreleased (Test-U).

Generating Images We generate images by rendering a randomly sampled structured representation. The number of objects in each box and their properties are sampled uniformly. We generate an equal number of scatter and tower images. To generate the sets of images presented to annotators, we generate two images independently, a third image by using the set of objects in the first im-

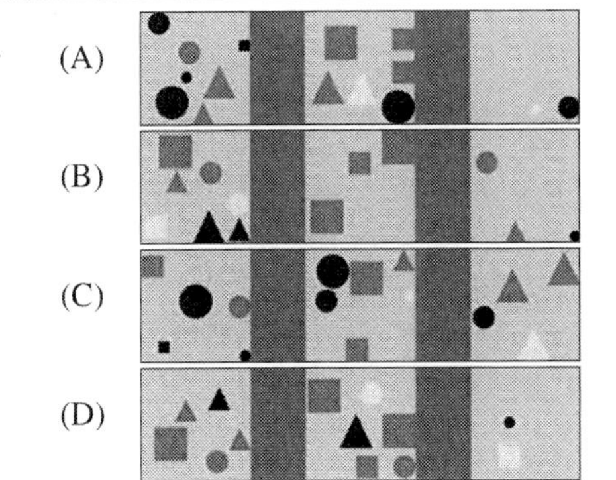

Write one sentence. This sentence must meet all of the following requirements:
- It describes A.
- It describes B.
- It does *not* describe C.
- It does *not* describe D.
- It does *not* mention the images explicitly (e.g. "In image A, ...").
- It does *not* mention the order of the light grey squares (e.g. "In the rightmost square...")

There is no one correct sentence for this image. There may be multiple sentences which satisfy the above requirements. If you can think of more than one sentence, submit only one.

Figure 2: Sentence writing prompt. The bottom sentence in Figure 1 was generated from this prompt.

age and randomly re-shuffling them between the boxes, and a fourth image by re-shuffling the objects in the second image. For images with towers, we constrain the re-shuffling to form towers.

Phase 1 – Sentence Writing Each writing task presents an annotator with four images. Figure 2 shows the sentence writing prompt, including the set of constraints, which is shown for all writing tasks. The constraints force the worker to contrast two pairs by referring to similarities and differences between the images, but not to refer to the position of the image in the prompt, or of each box in each image. These constraints are placed to elicit more set-theoretic language, and to allow us to divide the result of each task into four examples, pairing the annotator's sentence with each of the four images it was presented with.

Phase 2 – Validation In the second phase, we pair each sentence with the four images used to generate it. We re-label all sentence-image pairs as true or false, correcting for any violations of the constraints in the first phase. We do not use the original position of the image as any part of the final label to neutralize any ordering effect. In practice, 8.2% of examples had a different label than inferred from their original position in

	Unique sentences	Examples
Train	3,163	74,460
Dev	267	5,940
Test-P	266	5,934
Test-U	266	5,910
Total	3,962	92,244

Table 1: Data statistics.

the first phase. During validation, boxes are randomly permuted to ensure the last constraint was followed. We allow workers to annotate a sentence as nonsensical with regard to the image, and instruct annotators to ignore grammar errors.

Post-processing We prune pairs when their majority class is nonsensical. When collecting multiple annotations for a pair, we prune pairs if the gap between the classes is less than two votes.

5   Data Statistics and Analysis

We use the crowdsourcing platform Upwork,[1] and select ten annotators using a small set of example questions. We collect 3,974 task instances and 28,723 total validation judgments at a total cost of $5,526. From these 3,974 task instances we extract 15,896 sentence-image pairs. We prune 522 pairs in post-processing. For the training set we collect a single validation annotation for each sentence-image pair; for the rest of the data we collect five annotations each. Finally, we generate six sentence-image pairs from each sample by permuting the boxes. The validation step ensures this permutation does not change the label. Table 1 shows the number of sentences and pairs, including permutations, for each split.

We merge the development and test splits to calculate agreement statistics. We calculate Krippendorf's α and Fleiss' κ (Cocos et al., 2015) on both the full and pruned datasets. To calculate Fleiss' κ, we randomly permute the five annotations to be assigned to five "raters" and compute average kappa from 100 iterations. Before pruning, we observe $\alpha = 0.768$ and $\kappa = 0.709$, indicating substantial agreement (Landis and Koch, 1977). Pruning improves agreement to $\alpha = 0.831$ (indicating almost-perfect agreement) and $\kappa = 0.808$.

We analyze 200 development sentences to identify the distribution of semantic phenomena and syntactic ambiguity (Table 2). For comparison, we apply this analysis to 200 abstract-image and 200 real-image sentences from VQA (Antol et al., 2015). The difference in the distribution illustrates the complexity of our data. The mean sentence

---

[1] http://upwork.com

	VQA (abs)	VQA (real)	Our Data	NMN Correct	Example
Semantics					
Cardinality (hard)	12	11.5	66	63.8	*There are **exactly four objects** not touching any edge*
Cardinality (soft)	0	1	16	63.4	*There is a box with **at least one** square and **at least three** triangles.*
Existential	4.5	11.5	88	64.2	***There is a tower** with yellow base.*
Universal	1	1	7.5	67.8	*There is a black item in **every box**.*
Coordination	3	5	17	58.5	*There are 2 blue circles **and** 1 blue triangle*
Coreference	8.5	6.5	3	55.3	*There is a blue triangle touching the wall with **its** side.*
Spatial Relations	31	42.5	66	61.6	*there is one tower with a yellow block **above** a yellow block*
Comparative	1.5	1	3	73.6	*There is a box with multiple items and only one item **has a different color**.*
Presupposition[2]	79	80	19.5	54.0	*There is a box with seven items and **the three black items** are the same in shape.*
Negation	0	1	9.5	51.0	*there is exactly one black triangle **not touching** the edge*
Syntax					
Coordination	0	0	4.5	53.4	*There is a box with at least one square **and** at least three triangles.*
PP Attachment	7	3	23	70.9	*There is a black block on a black block as the base of a tower **with** three blocks.*

Table 2: Qualitative and empirical analysis of our data and VQA (Antol et al., 2015). We analyze 200 sentences for each dataset. The data is categorized to semantic and syntactic categories. We use the terms *hard* and *soft* cardinality to differentiate between language using exact numerical values and ranges. For each dataset, we show the percentage of the samples analyzed that demonstrate the phenomena. We analyze abstract (abs) and real images from VQA separately. For our data, we also include the accuracy using the NMN system (Section 6) for the subset of images we tagged with this category.

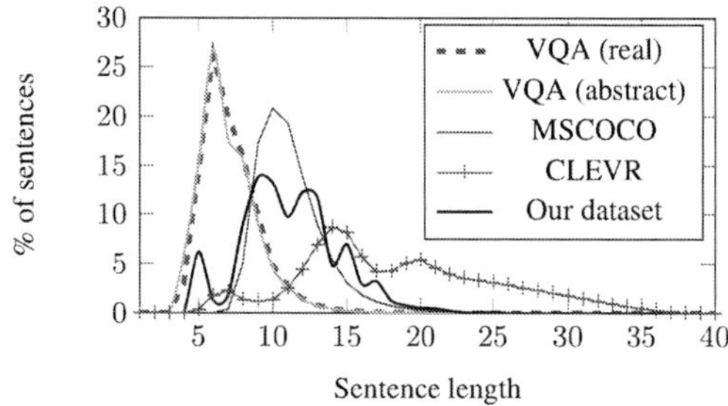

Figure 3: Distribution of sentence lengths.

length in our data is 11.22 tokens and the vocabulary size is 262. In Figure 3, we compare sentence length distribution to VQA, MSCOCO (Chen et al., 2015b), and CLEVR (Johnson et al., 2016). Our sentences are generally longer than VQA and more similar in length to MSCOCO. However, our task is more similar to VQA, where context is used to understand language, rather than to generate.

6 Methods

We evaluate multiple methods on the rendered images and structured representations. Hyperparameters and initialization details are described in the supplementary material.

6.1 Majority Class and Single Modality

We use image- and text-only models to measure how well biases in our data can be used to solve the task. If the model is able to do well on the text- or image-only baselines, this implies our data does not require the two modalities. Antol et al. (2015) performed a similar analysis of VQA with the questions only to gauge how and if background knowledge of the domain could aid performance.

Majority Assign the most common label (true) to all examples.

Text Only Encode the sentence with a recurrent neural network (RNN; Elman, 1990) with long short-term memory units (LSTM; Hochreiter and Schmidhuber, 1997) and a binary softmax computed from the final output.

Image Only Encode the image with a convolutional neural network (CNN) with three layers. The CNN output is used by a three-layer perceptron with a softmax on the final layer.[3]

6.2 Structured Representation

We use the structured representations described in Sections 3 and 4.

---

[2] We say a statement or question uses presupposition when it assumes the truth value of some proposition in order for its entire truth value to be defined. In this example, an image which does not have three black items will have no defined truth value for this statement.

[3] We also experimented using the ImageNet-trained Inception v4 model (Szegedy et al., 2017), but found it did not improve performance, possibly due to the difference between our images and ImageNet.

		Train	Dev	Test-P	Test-U
	Majority	56.37	55.31	56.16	55.43
	Text only	58.36 $\pm$0.6	56.61 $\pm$0.5	57.18 $\pm$0.6	56.21 $\pm$0.4
	Image Only	56.79 $\pm$1.3	55.35 $\pm$0.1	56.05 $\pm$0.3	55.33 $\pm$0.3
Structured representation	MaxEnt	99.99	68.04	67.68	67.82
	MLP	96.15 $\pm$1.3	67.50 $\pm$0.5	66.28 $\pm$0.4	65.32 $\pm$0.4
	Image features+RNN	59.71 $\pm$1.0	57.72 $\pm$1.4	57.62 $\pm$1.3	56.29 $\pm$0.9
Raw image	CNN+RNN	58.85 $\pm$0.2	56.59 $\pm$0.3	58.01 $\pm$0.3	56.30 $\pm$0.6
	NMN	98.37$\pm$0.6	63.06 $\pm$0.1	66.12 $\pm$0.4	61.99 $\pm$0.8

Table 3: Mean accuracy and standard deviation results. We report accuracy for the train, development, and both test sets. Three systems use the structured representation. Two systems (and Image Only) use the raw image.

MaxEnt Train a MaxEnt classifier. We use the text and structured representation to compute property- and count-based features. Property-based features trigger when some property (e.g., an object is touching a wall) is true in the structure. We create features by crossing triggered properties with each n-grams from the sentence, up to $n = 6$. Count-based features trigger when a count we observe in the image (e.g., the number of black triangles) is present in the sentence. We generate features combining the type of item counted (e.g., black triangles) with the n-grams surrounding the count in the sentence, up to $n = 6$. We provide details in the supplementary material.

MLP Train a single-layer perceptron with a softmax layer. The input to the perceptron is the mean of the feature embeddings. We use the same feature set as the MaxEnt model.

Image Features+RNN Compute features from the structure representation only, and encode the text with an LSTM RNN. The two representations are concatenated, and used as input to a two-layer perceptron and a softmax layer.

6.3 Image Representation

CNN+RNN Concatenate the CNN and RNN representations (Section 6.1) and apply a multi-layer perceptron with a softmax.

NMN The neural module networks approach of Andreas et al. (2016b). We experiment with the default maximum leaves of two, and with allowing for more expressive representations with a maximum leaves of five. We observe higher development accuracy with the trees using maximum leaves of five (63.06% vs. 62.4% with the default of two), which we use in our experiments.

7 Results

We run each experiment ten times and report mean accuracy as well as standard deviation for randomly initialized models. Table 3 shows our re-sults. NMN is the best performing model using images. Table 2 shows the NMN accuracy for each category in our qualitative analysis sample. While the number of sentences in some categories is relatively small, we observe a higher number of failures in sentences that include negations and coordinations. For models using the structured representation, the MaxEnt model provides the best performance. When ablating count-based features from the MaxEnt model, development accuracy decreases from 68.04 to 57.7. This indicates counting is an important aspect of the problem.

8 Discussion

We introduce the Cornell Natural Language Visual Reasoning dataset and task. The data includes complex compositional language grounded in images and structured representations. The task requires addressing challenges in visual and set-theoretic reasoning. We experiment with multiple systems and, in general, observe relatively low performance. Together with our qualitative analysis, this exemplifies the complexity of the data. We release our annotated training and development sets, and create two test sets. The public test set will be released along with its annotation. Computing results on the unreleased test data will require submitting trained models. Procedures for submitting models and the task leader board are available at `http://lic.nlp.cornell.edu/nlvr`.

Acknowledgments

This research was supported by a Microsoft Research Women's Fellowship, a Google Faculty Award, and an Amazon Web Services Cloud Credits for Research Grant. We thank the Cornell and University of Washington NLP groups for their support and helpful comments. We thank the anonymous reviewers for their feedback.

References

Jacob Andreas, Marcus Rohrbach, Trevor Darrell, and Dan Klein. 2016a. Learning to compose neural networks for question answering. In *Proceedings of the 2016 Conference of the North American Chapter of the Association for Computational Linguistics: Human Language Technologies*. https://doi.org/10.18653/v1/N16-1181.

Jacob Andreas, Marcus Rohrbach, Trevor Darrell, and Dan Klein. 2016b. Neural module networks. In *Conference on Computer Vision and Pattern Recognition*.

Stanislaw Antol, Aishwarya Agrawal, Jiasen Lu, Margaret Mitchell, Dhruv Batra, C. Lawrence Zitnick, and Devi Parikh. 2015. VQA: Visual question answering. In *International Journal of Computer Vision*.

Yonatan Bisk, Deniz Yuret, and Daniel Marcu. 2016. Natural language communication with robots. In *Proceedings of the 2016 Conference of the North American Chapter of the Association for Computational Linguistics: Human Language Technologies*. https://doi.org/10.18653/v1/N16-1089.

Fabio Carrara, Andrea Esuli, Tiziano Fagni, Fabrizio Falchi, and Alejandro Moreo. 2016. Picture it in your mind: Generating high level visual representations from textual descriptions. *CoRR* abs/1606.07287.

David L. Chen and Raymond J. Mooney. 2011. Learning to interpret natural language navigation instructions from observations. In *Proceedings of the National Conference on Artificial Intelligence*.

Kan Chen, Jiang Wang, Liang-Chieh Chen, Haoyuan Gao, Wei Xu, and Ramakant Nevatia. 2015a. ABC-CNN: An attention based convolutional neural network for visual question answering. *CoRR* abs/1511.05960.

Wenhu Chen, Aurélien Lucchi, and Thomas Hofmann. 2016. Bootstrap, review, decode: Using out-of-domain textual data to improve image captioning. *CoRR* abs/1611.05321.

Xinlei Chen, Hao Fang, Tsung-Yi Lin, Ramakrishna Vedantam, Saurabh Gupta, Piotr Dollár, and C. Lawrence Zitnick. 2015b. Microsoft COCO captions: Data collection and evaluation server. *CoRR* abs/1504.00325.

Anne Cocos, Aaron Masino, Ting Qian, Ellie Pavlick, and Chris Callison-Burch. 2015. Effectively crowdsourcing radiology report annotations. In *Proceedings of the Sixth International Workshop on Health Text Mining and Information Analysis*. https://doi.org/10.18653/v1/W15-2614.

Jeffrey L. Elman. 1990. Finding structure in time. *Cognitive Science* 14:179–211.

Nicholas FitzGerald, Yoav Artzi, and Luke Zettlemoyer. 2013. Learning distributions over logical forms for referring expression generation. In *Proceedings of the 2013 Conference on Empirical Methods in Natural Language Processing*. http://www.aclweb.org/anthology/D13-1197.

Sepp Hochreiter and Jürgen Schmidhuber. 1997. Long short-term memory. *Neural computation* 9:1735–1780.

Justin Johnson, Bharath Hariharan, Laurens van der Maaten, Li Fei-Fei, C. Lawrence Zitnick, and Ross B. Girshick. 2016. CLEVR: A diagnostic dataset for compositional language and elementary visual reasoning. *CoRR* abs/1612.06890.

J. Richard Landis and Gary Koch. 1977. The measurement of observer agreement for categorical data. *Biometrics* 33 1:159–74.

Jiasen Lu, Jianwei Yang, Dhruv Batra, and Devi Parikh. 2016. Hierarchical question-image co-attention for visual question answering. In *Neural Information Processing Systems*.

Matthew MacMahon, Brian Stankiewics, and Benjamin Kuipers. 2006. Walk the talk: Connecting language, knowledge, action in route instructions. In *Proceedings of the National Conference on Artificial Intelligence*.

Cynthia Matuszek, Nicholas FitzGerald, Luke Zettlemoyer, Liefeng Bo, and Dieter Fox. 2012. A joint model of language and perception for grounded attribute learning. In *Proceedings of the International Conference on Machine Learning*.

Margaret Mitchell, Kees van Deemter, and Ehud Reiter. 2010. Natural reference to objects in a visual domain. In *Proceedings of the 6th International Natural Language Generation Conference*. http://aclweb.org/anthology/W10-4210.

Panupong Pasupat and Percy Liang. 2015. Compositional semantic parsing on semi-structured tables. In *Proceedings of the 53rd Annual Meeting of the Association for Computational Linguistics and the 7th International Joint Conference on Natural Language Processing (Volume 1: Long Papers)*. https://doi.org/10.3115/v1/P15-1142.

Marco Pedersoli, Thomas Lucas, Cordelia Schmid, and Jakob Verbeek. 2016. Areas of attention for image captioning. *CoRR* abs/1612.01033.

Bryan A. Plummer, Liwei Wang, Chris M. Cervantes, Juan C. Caicedo, Julia Hockenmaier, and Svetlana Lazebnik. 2015. Flickr30k entities: Collecting region-to-phrase correspondences for richer image-to-sentence models. In *The IEEE International Conference on Computer Vision*.

Arijit Ray, Gordon Christie, Mohit Bansal, Dhruv Batra, and Devi Parikh. 2016. Question relevance in VQA: Identifying non-visual and false-premise questions. In *Proceedings of the 2016 Conference on Empirical Methods in Natural Language Processing*. http://aclweb.org/anthology/D16-1090.

Christian Szegedy, Sergey Ioffe, Vincent Vanhoucke, and Alexander A. Alemi. 2017. Inception-v4, inception-resnet and the impact of residual connections on learning. In *Association for the Advancement of Artificial Intelligence*.

Huijuan Xu and Kate Saenko. 2016. Ask, attend and answer: Exploring question-guided spatial attention for visual question answering. In *European Conference on Computer Vision*.

Peter Young, Alice Lai, Micah Hodosh, and Julia Hockenmaier. 2014. From image descriptions to visual denotations. *Transactions of the Association of Computational Linguistics* http://aclweb.org/anthology/Q14-1006.

John M. Zelle. 1995. *Using inductive logic programming to automate the construction of natural language parsers*. Ph.D. thesis, University of Texas, Austin.

Bolei Zhou, Yuandong Tian, Sainbayar Sukhbaatar, Arthur Szlam, and Rob Fergus. 2015. Simple baseline for visual question answering. *CoRR* abs/1512.02167.

C. Lawrence Zitnick and Devi Parikh. 2013. Bringing semantics into focus using visual abstraction. In *2013 IEEE Conference on Computer Vision and Pattern Recognition*.

Neural Architecture for Temporal Relation Extraction: A Bi-LSTM Approach for Detecting Narrative Containers

Julien Tourille
LIMSI, CNRS
Univ. Paris-Sud
Université Paris-Saclay
julien.tourille@limsi.fr

Olivier Ferret
CEA, LIST,
Gif-sur-Yvette,
F-91191 France.
olivier.ferret@cea.fr

Xavier Tannier
LIMSI, CNRS
Univ. Paris-Sud
Université Paris-Saclay
xavier.tannier@limsi.fr

Aurélie Névéol
LIMSI, CNRS
Université Paris-Saclay
aurelie.neveol@limsi.fr

Abstract

We present a neural architecture for containment relation identification between medical events and/or temporal expressions. We experiment on a corpus of de-identified clinical notes in English from the Mayo Clinic, namely the THYME corpus. Our model achieves an F-measure of 0.613 and outperforms the best result reported on this corpus to date.

1 Introduction

Temporal information extraction from clinical health records allows for a fine-grained analysis of patient health history. Providing medical staff with patient timelines could lead to improved diagnostic and care. Important temporal information (such as when a patient started a treatment, or when they started experiencing side effects from a treatment) can be found only within the narrative portion of records and needs the development of new Natural Language Processing methods in order to be accessed.

In this paper, we present a neural architecture for narrative container identification between medical events (EVENT) and/or temporal expressions (TIMEX3). We experiment on the THYME corpus (Styler IV et al., 2014), a corpus of de-identified clinical notes in English from the Mayo Clinic. We use the Gold Standard annotations for EVENT and TIMEX3 entities and we focus on containment relation extraction where the objective is to identify temporal relations between pairs of entities formalized as narrative container relations.

2 Related Work

SemEval has been offering a shared task related to temporal relation extraction from clinical narratives over the past two years (Bethard et al., 2015, 2016). Relying on the THYME corpus, the task challenged participants to extract EVENT and TIMEX3 entities and then to extract narrative container relations and document creation time relations. Herein, we focus on the second part of the challenge, temporal relation extraction and more specifically the narrative container relations. Different approaches have been implemented by the participants, including Support Vector Machine (SVM) classifiers (AAl Abdulsalam et al., 2016; Cohan et al., 2016; Lee et al., 2016; Tourille et al., 2016), Conditional Random Fields (CRF) and convolutional neural networks (CNNs) (Chikka, 2016). Beyond the challenges, Leeuwenberg and Moens (2017) propose a model based on a structured perceptron to jointly predict both types of temporal relations. Lin et al. (2016) performs training instance augmentation to increase the number of training examples and implement a SVM based model for containment relation extraction. Dligach et al. (2017) implement models based on CNNs and Long Short-Term Memory Networks (LSTMs) (Hochreiter and Schmidhuber, 1997) to extract containment relations from the THYME corpus.

From a more general perspective, relation extraction and classification is a task explored by many approaches, from fully unsupervised to fully supervised. Recent years have seen an increasing interest for the use of neural approaches.

Proceedings of the 55th Annual Meeting of the Association for Computational Linguistics (Short Papers), pages 224–230
Vancouver, Canada, July 30 - August 4, 2017. ©2017 Association for Computational Linguistics
https://doi.org/10.18653/v1/P17-2035

Recursive neural networks (Socher et al., 2011, 2013) have proved useful for tasks involving long-distance relations, such as semantic relation extraction (Hashimoto et al., 2013; Li et al., 2015). Convolutional networks have also been used (dos Santos et al., 2015; Zeng et al., 2014) and more recently, recurrent networks such as LSTM showed to be more robust for learning long-distance semantic information (Miwa and Bansal, 2016; Xu et al., 2015; Zhou et al., 2016).

3 Data

3.1 Corpus Presentation

The THYME corpus is a collection of clinical texts written in English from a cancer department that have been released during the Clinical TempEval campaigns (Bethard et al., 2015, 2016). This corpus contains documents annotated with medical events and temporal expressions as well as narrative container relations.

According to the annotation guidelines of the THYME corpus, a medical event is anything that could be of interest on the patient's clinical timeline. It could be for instance a medical procedure, a disease or a diagnosis. There are five attributes given to each event: *Contextual Modality*, *Degree*, *Polarity*, *Type* and *DocTimeRel*.

Temporal expressions are assigned a *Class* attribute. Possible values for these attributes are presented in Table 2.

Narrative containers can be apprehended as temporal buckets in which several events may be included. These containers are anchored by temporal expressions, medical events or other concepts. Styler IV et al. (2014) argue that the use of narrative containers instead of classical temporal relations (Allen, 1983) yields better annotation while keeping most of the useful temporal information intact. The concept of narrative container is illustrated in Figure 1 and described further in Pustejovsky and Stubbs (2011).

We identify two types of narrative container relations: relations that stay within sentence boundaries ($\approx$75% of the instances) and relations that spread over several sentences. In the rest of the paper, we will refer to them as intra- and inter-sentence relations. Descriptive statistics on the corpus are presented in Table 1.

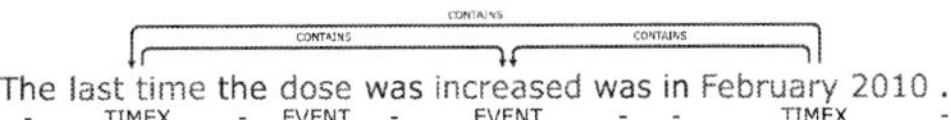

Figure 1: Examples of intra-sentence narrative container relations.

	Train	Test
EVENT	49,147	15,503
TIMEX3	5,791	1,917
Intra-sentence relations	12,855	4,365
Inter-sentence relations	4,582	1,565

Table 1: Descriptive statistics about the train and test parts of the THYME corpus.

3.2 Preprocessing

We preprocessed the corpus using cTAKES (Savova et al., 2010), an open-source natural language processing system for the extraction of information from electronic health records. We extracted sentence and token boundaries, as well as token types and semantic types of the entities that have a span overlap with a least one gold standard EVENT entity of the THYME corpus. Semantic types are a set of subject categories (organized as a tree) that are used to categorize concepts in the UMLS® (Unified Medical Language System) Metathesaurus. There are currently 135 types (Bodenreider, 2004). This information was added to the set of Gold Standard attributes available for EVENT entities in the corpus. An overview of the attributes available for each token is presented in Table 2.

4 Task Description

The container relation extraction task can be cast as a 3-class classification problem. For each combination of EVENT and/or TIMEX3 from left to right, three cases are possible:

- the first entity temporally *contains* the second entity,
- the first entity *is* temporally *contained* by the second entity,
- there is no temporal containment relation between the entities.

Intra- and inter-sentence relation detection can be seen as two different tasks with specific features. Intra-sentence relations can benefit from intra-sentential clues such as adverbs (e.g. *during*) or pronouns (e.g. *which*) which are not available at the inter-sentence level. Furthermore, past work on the topic seems to indicate that this differentia-

Source	Attribute	Values
Corpus	Contextual Modality	Actual, Hypothetical, Hedged, Generic or no-value
	Degree	Most, Little, N/A or no-value
	Polarity	Pos, Neg or no-value
	Type	Aspectual, Evidential, N/A or no-value
	DocTimeRel	Before, Before-Overlap, Overlap, After or no-value
	Entity	EVENT, TIMEX3 or no-entity
cTAKES	Entity Type[a]	DiseaseDisorderMention, LabMention, MedicationEventMention, MedicationMention, ProcedureMention, SignSymptomMention or no-value
	Semantic Type[a]	list of semantic types extracted from the training corpus or no-value

[a] If the token is not part of an EVENT entity, the value is automatically *no-value*.

Table 2: Attributes available for each token of the corpus after preprocessing.

tion improves overall performance (Tourille et al., 2016). We have adopted this approach by building two separate classifiers, one for intra-sentence relations and one for inter-sentence relations.

If we were to consider all combinations of entities within documents for inter-sentence relations, it would result in a very large training corpus with very few positive examples. In order to cope with this issue, we limit our experiments to inter-sentence relations that do not span over more than three sentences. By doing so, we obtain a manageable training corpus size with less unbalanced classes while keeping a good coverage. It results in 2,085 inter-sentences relations for the training corpus and 743 for the test corpus.

5 Neural Network Model

First, we present the main component of our model in Section 5.1. Then, we describe the word embeddings that we use as input for the model in Section 5.2. Finally, we present the parameters used for network training in Section 5.3.

5.1 Temporal Relation Extraction

Our approach relies on Long Short-Term Memory Networks (LSTMs) (Hochreiter and Schmidhuber, 1997). The architecture of our model is presented in Figure 2. For a given sequence of tokens separating two entities (EVENT and/or TIMEX3), represented as vectors, we compute a representation by going from left to right in the sequence (forward LSTM in figure 2).

As LSTMs tend to be biased toward the most recent inputs, this implementation would be biased toward the second entity of each pair processed by the network. To counteract this effect, we compute the reverse representation with an LSTM reading the sequence backwards, from right to left (backward LSTM in figure 2). By doing so, we keep as

much information as possible about the two entities.

The two final states are then concatenated and linearly transformed to a 3-dimensional vector representing the number of categories (concatenation and projection in figure 2). Finally, a softmax function is applied.

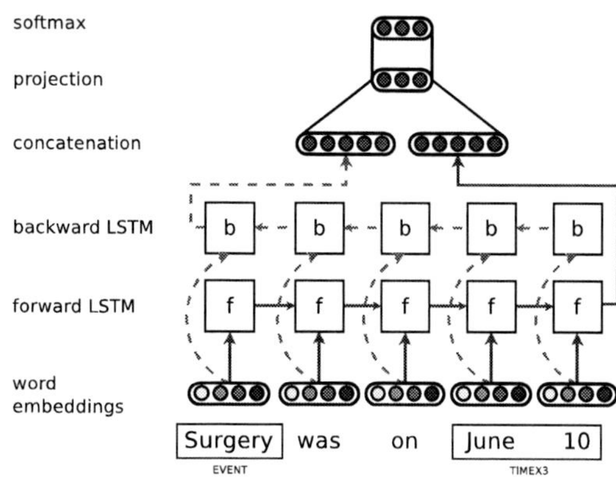

Figure 2: Neural architecture for containment relation extraction.

5.2 Input Embeddings

Vectors representing tokens are built by concatenating a character-based embedding, a word embedding, one embedding per Gold Standard attribute and one embedding per cTAKES attribute. While the word embedding is a classical option in the context of neural models, the embeddings for Gold Standard and cTAKES attributes are a way of integrating in such model features that have been demonstrated as useful in previous work. Finally, temporal clues such as verbs, and more particularly their tense, which are important in assessing if one entity temporally contains another, are taken into account by our character-based representation

	Intra-sentence classifier						Inter-sentence classifier					
	ref	pred	corr	P	R	F1	ref	pred	corr	P	R	F1
No Features	4365	4529	3035	0.670	0.681	0.675	743	895	377	0.421	**0.498**	0.456
+ GS	4365	4253	2980	**0.701**	0.661	0.680	743	692	349	**0.504**	0.462	**0.482**
+ cTAKES	4365	4780	3170	0.663	**0.704**	**0.683**	743	628	305	0.486	0.408	0.443

Table 3: Results obtained by the intra-sentence and inter-sentence classifiers for each model of this paper. We report the number of Gold Standard relations (ref), the number of relations predicted by our system (pred), the number of true positives (corr), the precision (P), the recall (R) and the F1-measure (F1).

of tokens.

An overview of the embedding computation is presented in Figure 3. Following Lample et al. (2016), the character-based representation is constructed with a Bi-LSTM. First, a random embedding is generated for every character present in the training corpus. Token characters are then processed with a forward and backward LSTM similar to the one we use in our general architecture. The final character-based representation is the result of the concatenation of the forward and backward representations.

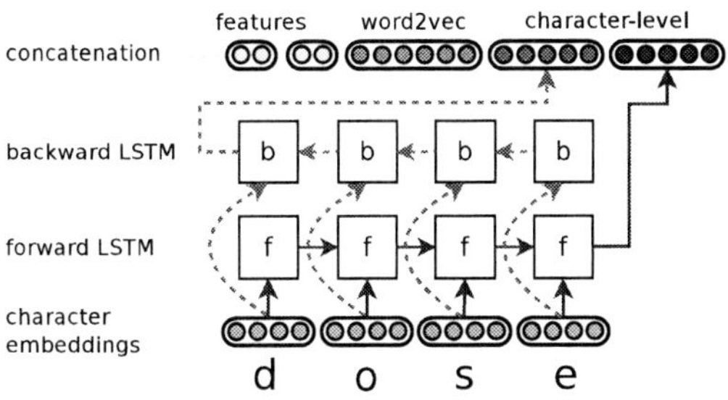

Figure 3: Neural architecture for input embeddings.

We use a character embedding size of 8 and hidden dimensions of 25 for the forward and backward LSTMs, resulting in a final representation size of 50 after concatenation. This representation is randomly initialized and incrementally defined by the training of the whole network.

For word embeddings, our vectors are pretrained by applying *word2vec* (Mikolov et al., 2013) on the Mimic 3 corpus (Johnson et al., 2016)[1]. In order to account for unknown tokens during the test phase, we train a special embedding UNK by replacing randomly some singletons with the UNK token (probability of replacement = 0.5).

In the inter-sentence relation classifier, we introduce a specific token for identifying sentence breaks. This token is composed of one distinctive character and it is associated to a specific word embedding.

Similarly to the character embeddings, we randomly initialize one embedding per token attribute value, with an embedding size of 4. All these embeddings are then concatenated in a final representation.

5.3   Network Training

We implemented the network using TensorFlow (Abadi et al., 2015). We trained our network with mini-batch Stochastic Gradient Descent using Adam (Kingma and Ba, 2014) with a batch-size of 256. The learning rate was set to 0.001. The hidden layers of our forward and backward LSTMs have a size of 512. We kept 10% of the training corpus for a development corpus and we implemented early stopping with a patience of 10 epochs without performance improvement. Finally, we used dropout training to avoid overfitting. We applied dropout on input embeddings with a rate of 0.5.

6   Experiments and Discussion

We experimented with three configurations. In the first one, we used only word embeddings and character embeddings. In the second one, we added the feature embeddings related to the Gold Standard (GS) attributes. Finally, in a third experiment, we added the feature embeddings related to cTAKES. For each experiment, we report precision (P), recall (R) and F1-measure (F1) computed with the official evaluation script[2] provided during the Clinical TempEval challenges. Results of the experiments are presented in Table 4. For comparison, we report the baseline provided as reference during the Clinical TempEval shared tasks,

---

[1] Parameters used during computation: algorithm = CBOW; min-count = 4; vector size = 100; window = 8.

[2] https://github.com/bethard/anaforatools

	P	R	F1
baseline (closest)	0.459	0.154	0.231
Lee et al. (2016)	0.588	0.559	0.573
Lin et al. (2016)	0.669	0.534	0.594
No features	0.646	0.568	0.605
+ GS features	**0.687**	0.549	0.610
+ cTAKES features	0.657	**0.575**	**0.613**

Table 4: Experimentation results. We report precision (P), recall (R) and F1-measure (F1) for each configuration of our model, for the best system of the Clinical TempEval 2016 challenge (Lee et al., 2016) and for the best result obtained so far on the corpus (Lin et al., 2016).

the results of the best system of the Clinical TempEval 2016 challenge (Lee et al., 2016) and the best scores obtained after the challenge (Lin et al., 2016) on the test portion of the corpus. Both Lee et al. (2016) and Lin et al. (2016) rely on SVM classifiers using hand-engineered linguistic features.

All three of our models perform better in terms of F1-measure than Lee et al. (2016) and Lin et al. (2016). Our two best models also outperform Leeuwenberg and Moens (2017), who report an F-measure of .608 using a structured perceptron. Interestingly, their model did not distinguish between intra- and inter- sentence relations, but instead considered that related entities had to occur within a window of 30 tokens. We see that the addition of attribute embeddings slightly improves the overall performance of our system (+0.008). Adding the embeddings of GS features contributes to the major part of this improvement but tends to increase the imbalance between recall and precision. On the contrary, while the attribute embeddings related to cTAKES seem to have little impact on the overall performance, they tend to restore more balanced precision and recall.

The results for respectively intra- and inter-sentence relations are presented in Table 3. Similarly to our global results, the intra-sentence classifier benefits from the addition of feature embeddings with a small increase for GS features and only a very little improvement for cTAKES features.

The inter-sentence classifier exhibits the same trend: GS features do improve the performance. However, adding cTAKES features degrades it slightly (-0.013).

The closest work compared to ours is clearly Dligach et al. (2017) as it also heavily relies on neural models for extracting temporal containment relations between medical events. Dligach et al. (2017) tested both CNN and LSTM models and found CNN superior to LSTM. However, this work addressed intra-sentence relations only. Moreover, its LSTM model was not a Bi-LSTM model as ours and it did not include character-based or attribute embeddings. Finally, it distinguished EVENT-TIMEX3 and EVENT-EVENT relations while we have only one model for the two types of relations.

7 Conclusion and Perspectives

From a global perspective, the work we have presented in this article shows that in accordance with a more general trend, our neural model for extracting containment relations clearly outperforms classical approaches based on feature engineering. However, it also shows that incorporating classical features in such a model is a way to improve it, even if all kinds of features do not contribute equally to such improvement. A more fine-grained study has now to be performed to determine the most meaningful features in this perspective and to measure the contribution of each feature to the overall performance, with a specific emphasis on character-based embeddings.

Beyond a further analysis of the characteristics of our model, we are interested in two main extensions. The first one will investigate whether training two models, one for EVENT-TIMEX3 relations and one for EVENT-EVENT relations, as done by Dligach et al. (2017), is a better option than training one model for all types of containment relations as presented herein. The second extension consists in transposing the model we have defined in this work for English to French, as done by Tourille et al. (2017) for a more traditional approach based on a feature engineering approach.

Acknowledgements

We thank the anonymous reviewers for their insightful comments. This work was supported by Labex Digicosme, operated by the Foundation for Scientific Cooperation (FSC) Paris-Saclay, under grant CÔT and by the French National Agency for Research under grant CABeRneT ANR-13-JS02-0009-01.

References

Abdulrahman AAl Abdulsalam, Sumithra Velupillai, and Stephane Meystre. 2016. UtahBMI at SemEval-2016 Task 12: Extracting Temporal Information from Clinical Text. In *Proceedings of the 10th International Workshop on Semantic Evaluation (SemEval-2016)*. Association for Computational Linguistics, San Diego, California, pages 1256–1262.

Martín Abadi, Ashish Agarwal, Paul Barham, Eugene Brevdo, Zhifeng Chen, Craig Citro, Greg S. Corrado, Andy Davis, Jeffrey Dean, Matthieu Devin, Sanjay Ghemawat, Ian Goodfellow, Andrew Harp, Geoffrey Irving, Michael Isard, Yangqing Jia, Rafal Jozefowicz, Lukasz Kaiser, Manjunath Kudlur, Josh Levenberg, Dan Mané, Rajat Monga, Sherry Moore, Derek Murray, Chris Olah, Mike Schuster, Jonathon Shlens, Benoit Steiner, Ilya Sutskever, Kunal Talwar, Paul Tucker, Vincent Vanhoucke, Vijay Vasudevan, Fernanda Viégas, Oriol Vinyals, Pete Warden, Martin Wattenberg, Martin Wicke, Yuan Yu, and Xiaoqiang Zheng. 2015. TensorFlow: Large-Scale Machine Learning on Heterogeneous Systems. Software available from tensorflow.org. http://tensorflow.org/.

James F. Allen. 1983. Maintaining Knowledge About Temporal Intervals. *Communications of the ACM* 26(11):832–843.

Steven Bethard, Leon Derczynski, Guergana Savova, James Pustejovsky, and Marc Verhagen. 2015. SemEval-2015 Task 6: Clinical TempEval. In *Proceedings of the 9th International Workshop on Semantic Evaluation (SemEval 2015)*. Association for Computational Linguistics, Denver, USA, pages 806–814.

Steven Bethard, Guergana Savova, Wei-Te Chen, Leon Derczynski, James Pustejovsky, and Marc Verhagen. 2016. SemEval-2016 Task 12: Clinical TempEval. In *Proceedings of the 10th International Workshop on Semantic Evaluation (SemEval-2016)*. Association for Computational Linguistics, San Diego, California, pages 1052–1062.

Olivier Bodenreider. 2004. The Unified Medical Language System (UMLS): integrating biomedical terminology. *Nucleic Acids Research* 32:267–270.

Veera Raghavendra Chikka. 2016. CDE-IIITH at SemEval-2016 Task 12: Extraction of Temporal Information from Clinical documents using Machine Learning techniques. In *Proceedings of the 10th International Workshop on Semantic Evaluation (SemEval-2016)*. Association for Computational Linguistics, San Diego, California, pages 1237–1240.

Arman Cohan, Kevin Meurer, and Nazli Goharian. 2016. GUIR at SemEval-2016 task 12: Temporal Information Processing for Clinical Narratives. In *Proceedings of the 10th International Workshop on Semantic Evaluation (SemEval-2016)*. Association for Computational Linguistics, San Diego, California, pages 1248–1255.

Dmitriy Dligach, Timothy Miller, Chen Lin, Steven Bethard, and Guergana Savova. 2017. Neural temporal relation extraction. In *Proceedings of the 15th Conference of the European Chapter of the Association for Computational Linguistics: Volume 2, Short Papers*. Association for Computational Linguistics, Valencia, Spain, pages 746–751.

Cicero dos Santos, Bing Xiang, and Bowen Zhou. 2015. Classifying Relations by Ranking with Convolutional Neural Networks. In *Proceedings of the 53rd Annual Meeting of the Association for Computational Linguistics and the 7th International Joint Conference on Natural Language Processing (Volume 1: Long Papers)*. Association for Computational Linguistics, Beijing, China, pages 626–634.

Kazuma Hashimoto, Makoto Miwa, Yoshimasa Tsuruoka, and Takashi Chikayama. 2013. Simple Customization of Recursive Neural Networks for Semantic Relation Classification. In *Proceedings of the 2013 Conference on Empirical Methods in Natural Language Processing*. Association for Computational Linguistics, Seattle, Washington, USA, pages 1372–1376.

Sepp Hochreiter and Jürgen Schmidhuber. 1997. Long short-term memory. *Neural computation* 9(8):1735–1780.

Alistair E. W. Johnson, Tom J. Pollard, Lu Shen, Liwei H. Lehman, Mengling Feng, Mohammad Ghassemi, Benjamin Moody, Peter Szolovits, Leo A. Celi, and Roger G. Mark. 2016. MIMIC-III, a freely accessible critical care database. *Scientific Data* 3.

Diederik P. Kingma and Jimmy Ba. 2014. Adam: A Method for Stochastic Optimization. *CoRR* abs/1412.6980. http://arxiv.org/abs/1412.6980.

Guillaume Lample, Miguel Ballesteros, Sandeep Subramanian, Kazuya Kawakami, and Chris Dyer. 2016. Neural Architectures for Named Entity Recognition. In *Proceedings of the 2016 Conference of the North American Chapter of the Association for Computational Linguistics: Human Language Technologies*. Association for Computational Linguistics, San Diego, California, pages 260–270.

Hee-Jin Lee, Hua Xu, Jingqi Wang, Yaoyun Zhang, Sungrim Moon, Jun Xu, and Yonghui Wu. 2016. UTHealth at SemEval-2016 Task 12: an End-to-End System for Temporal Information Extraction from Clinical Notes. In *Proceedings of the 10th International Workshop on Semantic Evaluation (SemEval-2016)*. Association for Computational Linguistics, San Diego, California, pages 1292–1297.

Artuur Leeuwenberg and Marie-Francine Moens. 2017. Structured Learning for Temporal Relation Extraction from Clinical Records. In *Proceedings* of the 15th Conference of the European Chapter of the Association for Computational Linguistics: Volume 1, Long Papers*. Association for Computational Linguistics, Valencia, Spain, pages 1150–1158.

Jiwei Li, Thang Luong, Dan Jurafsky, and Eduard Hovy. 2015. When Are Tree Structures Necessary for Deep Learning of Representations? In *Proceedings of the 2015 Conference on Empirical Methods in Natural Language Processing*. Association for Computational Linguistics, Lisbon, Portugal, pages 2304–2314.

Chen Lin, Timothy Miller, Dimitry Dligach, Steven Bethard, and Guergana Savova. 2016. Improving Temporal Relation Extraction with Training Instance Augmentation. In *Proceedings of the 15th Workshop on Biomedical Natural Language Processing*. Association for Computational Linguistics, Berlin, Germany, pages 108–113.

Tomas Mikolov, Kai Chen, Greg Corrado, and Jeffrey Dean. 2013. Efficient Estimation of Word Representations in Vector Space. *CoRR* abs/1301.3781.

Makoto Miwa and Mohit Bansal. 2016. End-to-End Relation Extraction using LSTMs on Sequences and Tree Structures. In *Proceedings of the 54th Annual Meeting of the Association for Computational Linguistics (Volume 1: Long Papers)*. Association for Computational Linguistics, Berlin, Germany, pages 1105–1116.

James Pustejovsky and Amber Stubbs. 2011. Increasing Informativeness in Temporal Annotation. In *Proceedings of the 5th Linguistic Annotation Workshop*. Association for Computational Linguistics, Stroudsburg, PA, USA, LAW V '11, pages 152–160.

Guergana K. Savova, James J. Masanz, Philip V. Ogren, Jiaping Zheng, Sunghwan Sohn, Karin C. Kipper-Schuler, and Christopher G. Chute. 2010. Mayo clinical Text Analysis and Knowledge Extraction System (cTAKES): architecture, component evaluation and applications. *Journal of the American Medical Informatics Association* 17(5):507–513.

Richard Socher, Jeffrey Pennington, Eric H. Huang, Andrew Y. Ng, and Christopher D. Manning. 2011. Semi-Supervised Recursive Autoencoders for Predicting Sentiment Distributions. In *Proceedings of the 2011 Conference on Empirical Methods in Natural Language Processing*. Association for Computational Linguistics, Edinburgh, Scotland, UK., pages 151–161.

Richard Socher, Alex Perelygin, Jean Wu, Jason Chuang, Christopher D. Manning, Andrew Ng, and Christopher Potts. 2013. Recursive Deep Models for Semantic Compositionality Over a Sentiment Treebank. In *Proceedings of the 2013 Conference on Empirical Methods in Natural Language Processing*. Association for Computational Linguistics, Seattle, Washington, USA, pages 1631–1642.

William Styler IV, Steven Bethard, Sean Finan, Martha Palmer, Sameer Pradhan, Piet de Groen, Brad Erickson, Timothy Miller, Chen Lin, Guergana Savova, and James Pustejovsky. 2014. Temporal Annotation in the Clinical Domain. *Transactions of the Association for Computational Linguistics* 2:143–154.

Julien Tourille, Olivier Ferret, Aurélie Névéol, and Xavier Tannier. 2016. LIMSI-COT at SemEval-2016 Task 12: Temporal relation identification using a pipeline of classifiers. In *Proceedings of the 10th International Workshop on Semantic Evaluation (SemEval-2016)*. Association for Computational Linguistics, San Diego, California, pages 1136–1142.

Julien Tourille, Olivier Ferret, Xavier Tannier, and Aurélie Névéol. 2017. Temporal information extraction from clinical text. In *Proceedings of the 15th Conference of the European Chapter of the Association for Computational Linguistics (EACL 2017), short paper session*. Valencia, Spain, pages 739–745.

Yan Xu, Lili Mou, Ge Li, Yunchuan Chen, Hao Peng, and Zhi Jin. 2015. Classifying Relations via Long Short Term Memory Networks along Shortest Dependency Paths. In *Proceedings of the 2015 Conference on Empirical Methods in Natural Language Processing*. Association for Computational Linguistics, Lisbon, Portugal, pages 1785–1794.

Daojian Zeng, Kang Liu, Siwei Lai, Guangyou Zhou, and Jun Zhao. 2014. Relation Classification via Convolutional Deep Neural Network. In *Proceedings of COLING 2014, the 25th International Conference on Computational Linguistics: Technical Papers*. Dublin City University and Association for Computational Linguistics, Dublin, Ireland, pages 2335–2344.

Peng Zhou, Wei Shi, Jun Tian, Zhenyu Qi, Bingchen Li, Hongwei Hao, and Bo Xu. 2016. Attention-Based Bidirectional Long Short-Term Memory Networks for Relation Classification. In *Proceedings of the 54th Annual Meeting of the Association for Computational Linguistics (Volume 2: Short Papers)*. Association for Computational Linguistics, Berlin, Germany, pages 207–212.

How to Make Context More Useful?
An Empirical Study on Context-Aware Neural Conversational Models

Zhiliang Tian,[1] Rui Yan,[2]* Lili Mou,[3] Yiping Song,[4] Yansong Feng,[2] Dongyan Zhao[2]

[1]Baidu Inc., China `tianzhiliang@baidu.com`
[2]Institute of Computer Science and Technology, Peking University, China
[3]Key Laboratory of High Confidence Software Technologies, MoE, China
Institute of Software, Peking University, China
[4]Institute of Network Computing and Information Systems, Peking University, China
`{ruiyan,songyiping,yansong,zhaody}@pku.edu.cn  doublepower.mou@gmail.com`

Abstract

Generative conversational systems are attracting increasing attention in natural language processing (NLP). Recently, researchers have noticed the importance of context information in dialog processing, and built various models to utilize context. However, there is no systematic comparison to analyze how to use context effectively. In this paper, we conduct an empirical study to compare various models and investigate the effect of context information in dialog systems. We also propose a variant that explicitly weights context vectors by context-query relevance, outperforming the other baselines.

1 Introduction

Recently, human-computer conversation is attracting increasing attention due to its promising potentials and alluring commercial values. Researchers have proposed both retrieval methods (Ji et al., 2014; Yan et al., 2016) and generative methods (Ritter et al., 2011; Shang et al., 2015) for automatic conversational systems. With the success of deep learning techniques, neural networks have demonstrated powerful capability of learning human dialog patterns; given a user-issued utterance as an input query q, the network can generate a reply r, which is usually accomplished in a sequence-to-sequence (`Seq2Seq`) manner (Shang et al., 2015).

In the literature, there are two typical research setups for dialog systems: single-turn and multi-turn. Single-turn conversation is, perhaps, the simplest setting where the model only takes q into consideration when generating r (Shang et al.,

2015; Mou et al., 2016). However, most real-world dialogs comprise multiple turns. Previous utterances (referred to as *context* in this paper) could also provide useful information about the dialog status and are the key to coherent multi-turn conversation.

Existing studies have realized the importance of context, and proposed several context-aware conversational systems. For example, Yan et al. (2016) directly concatenate context utterances and the current query; others use hierarchical models, first capturing the meaning of individual utterances and then integrating them as discourses (Serban et al., 2016). There could be several ways of combining context and the current query, e.g., pooling or concatenation (Sordoni et al., 2015). Unfortunately, previous literature lacks a systematic comparison of the above methods.

In this paper, we conduct an empirical study on context modeling in `Seq2Seq`-like conversational systems. We emphasize the following research questions:

- **RQ1.** *How can we make better use of context information?* Our study shows that hierarchical models are generally better than non-hierarchical ones. We also propose a variant of context integration that explicitly weights a context vector by its relevance measure, outperforming simple vector pooling or concatenation.
- **RQ2.** *What is the effect of context on neural dialog systems?* We find context information is useful to neural conversational models. It yields longer, more informative and diversified replies.

To sum up, the contributions of this paper are two-fold: (1) We conduct a systematic study on context modeling in neural conversational models. (2) We further propose an explicitly con-

---

*Corresponding author.

Proceedings of the 55th Annual Meeting of the Association for Computational Linguistics (Short Papers), pages 231–236
Vancouver, Canada, July 30 - August 4, 2017. ©2017 Association for Computational Linguistics
https://doi.org/10.18653/v1/P17-2036

text weighting approach, outperforming the other baselines.

2 Models

2.1 Non-Hierarchical Model

To model a few utterances before the current query, several studies directly concatenate these sentences together and use a single model to capture the meaning of context and the query (Yan et al., 2016; Sordoni et al., 2015). They are referred to as *non-hierarchical models* in our paper. Such method is also used in other NLP tasks, e.g., document-level sentiment analysis (Xu et al., 2016) and machine comprehension (Wang and Jiang, 2017).

Following the classic encode-decoder framework, we use a `Seq2Seq` network, which transforms the query and context into a fixed-length vector v_{enc} by a recurrent neural network (RNN) during encoding; then, in the decoding phase, it generates a reply r with another RNN in a word-by-word fashion. (See Figure 1a.)

In our study, we adopt RNNs with gated recurrent units (Cho et al., 2014, GRUs), which alleviates the long propagation problem of vanilla RNNs. When decoding, we apply beam search with a size of 5.

2.2 Hierarchical Model

A more complicated approach to context modeling is to build hierarchical models with a two-step strategy: an utterance-level model captures the meaning of each individual sentences, and then an inter-utterance model integrates context and query information (Figure 1b).

Researchers have tried different ways of combining information during inter-utterance modeling; this paper evaluates several prevailing methods.

Sum pooling. Sum pooling (denoted as `Sum`) integrates information over a candidate set by summing the values in each dimension (Figure 2a). Given context vectors $v_{c_1}, \cdots, v_{c_n}$ and the query vector v_q, the encoded vector v_{enc} is

$$v_{enc} = \sum_{i=1}^{n} v_{c_i} + v_q \tag{1}$$

Sum pooling is used in Sordoni et al. (2015), where bag-of-words (BoW) features of context

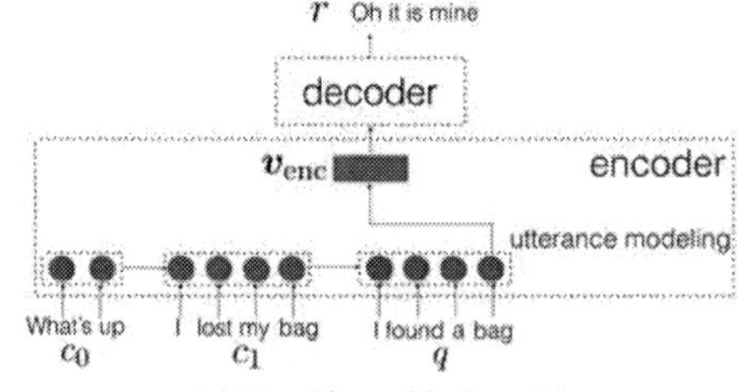

(a) Non-hierarchical model.

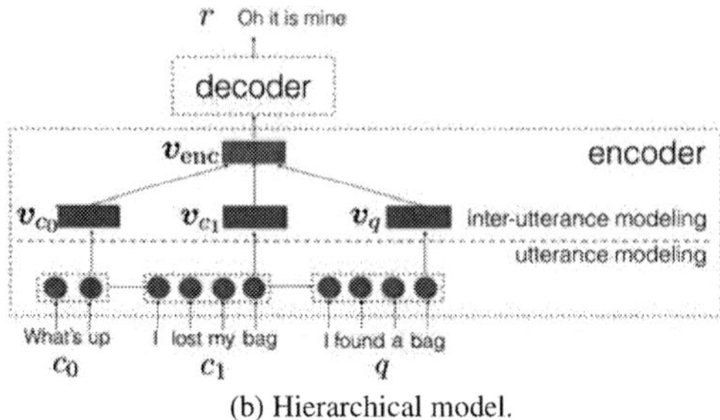

(b) Hierarchical model.

Figure 1: `Seq2Seq`-like neural networks generate a reply r based on context $\mathcal{C} = \{c_1, \ldots, c_n\}$ and the current query q with (a) non-hierarchical or (b) hierarchical models.

and the query are simply added. In our experiments, sum pooling operates on the features extracted by sentence-level RNNs of context and query utterances, as modern neural networks preserve more information than BoW features.

Concatenation. Concatenation (`Concat`) is yet another method used in Sordoni et al. (2015). This strategy concatenates every utterance-level vectors v_{c_i} and v_q as a long vector, i.e., $v_{enc} = [v_{c_0}; \ldots; v_{c_n}; v_q]$. (See Figure 2b.)

Compared with sum pooling, vector concatenation can distinguish different roles of the context and query, as this operation keeps input separately. One potential shortcoming, however, is that concatenation only works with fixed-length context.

Sequential integration. Yao et al. (2015) and Serban et al. (2015) propose hierarchical dialog systems, where an inter-utterance RNN is built upon utterance-level RNNs' features (last hidden state). Training is accomplished by end-to-end gradient propagation, and the process is illustrated in Figure 2c.

Using an RNN to integrate context and query vectors in a sequential manner enables complicated information interaction. Based on the RNN's hidden states, `Sum` and `Concat` could also be applied to obtain the encoded vector v_{enc}.

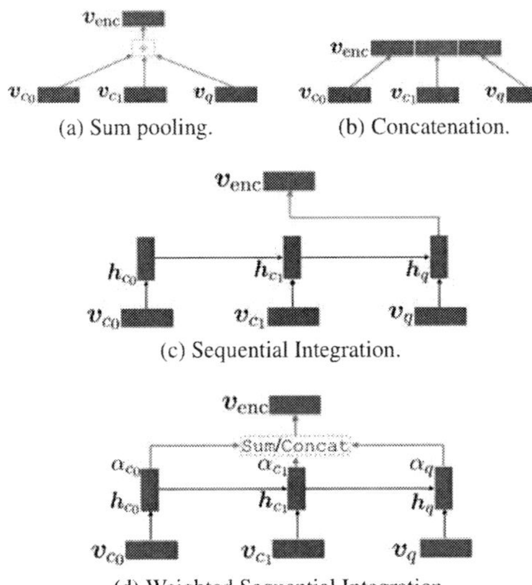

(a) Sum pooling.   (b) Concatenation.

(c) Sequential Integration.

(d) Weighted Sequential Integration.

Figure 2: The inter-utterance modeling in hierarchical models. v_{c_i} and v_q are the utterance-level vectors, h_{c_i} and h_q are the utterance-level hidden states, α_{c_i} and α_q are the explicitly weights and v_{enc} is the output of the encoder.

However, we found their performance is worse than only using the last hidden state (denoted as Seq). One plausible reason might be that the inter-sentence RNN is not long and that RNN can preserve these information well. Therefore, this variant is adopted in our experiments, as shown in Figure 2c.

2.3 Explicitly Weighting by Context-Query Relevance

In conversation, context utterances may vary in content and semantics: context utterances that are relevant to the query may be useful, while irrelevant ones may bring more about noise. Following this intuition, we propose a variant that explicitly weights the context vector by an attention score of context-query relevance.

First, we compute the similarity between the context and query by the cosine measure

$$s_{c_i} = \mathrm{sim}(c_i, q) = \frac{e_{c_i} \cdot e_q}{\|e_{c_i}\| \cdot \|e_q\|} \tag{2}$$

where

$$e_{c_i} = \sum_{w \in c_i} e_w \quad \text{and} \quad e_q = \sum_{w' \in q} e_{w'} \tag{3}$$

that is, the sentence embedding is the sum of word embeddings.

Following the spirit of attention mechanisms (Bahdanau et al., 2014), we would like to normalize these similarities by a softmax function and obtain attention probabilities:

$$\alpha_{c_i} = \frac{\exp(s_{c_i})}{\sum_{j=0}^{n} \exp(s_{c_j}) + \exp(s_q)} \tag{4}$$

$$\alpha_q = \frac{\exp(s_q)}{\sum_{j=0}^{n} \exp(s_{c_j}) + \exp(s_q)} \tag{5}$$

where s_q is computed in the same manner as s_{c_i} and is always 1, which is the cosine of two same vectors. The intuition is that, if the context is less relevant, we should mainly focus on the query itself, but if the context is relevant, we should focus more evenly across context and the query.

In other words, our explicitly weighting approach could be viewed as *heuristic attention*. Akin to Subsection 2.2, we aggregate the weighted context and query vectors by pooling and concatenation, resulting in the following two variants.

- WSeq (sum), where weighted vectors are summed together

$$v_{\text{enc}} = \sum_{i=0}^{n} \alpha_{c_i} h_{c_i} + \alpha_q h_q \tag{6}$$

- WSeq (concat), where weighted vectors are concatenated

$$v_{\text{enc}} = [\alpha_{c_0} h_{c_0}; \ldots; \alpha_{c_n} h_{c_n}; \alpha_q h_q] \tag{7}$$

Notice that the explicitly weighting approach can also be applied to sentence embeddings (without inter-sentence RNN). We denote the variants by WSum and WConcat, respectively; details are not repeated. They are included for comparison in Section 3.2.

3 Experiments

3.1 Setup

We conducted all experiments on a Chinese dataset crawled from an online free chatting platform, Baidu Tieba.[1] To facilitate the research of context's effect, we established a multi-turn conversational corpus following Sordoni et al. (2015) and Serban et al. (2015). A data sample contains three utterances, being a triple ⟨*last_context, query, reply*⟩. In total, we had

---

[1] https://tieba.baidu.com

Method		BLEU-1	BLEU-2	BLEU-3	BLEU-4
Context-Insensitive		4.611	1.488	0.657	0.311
Non-Hierarchical		4.805	1.507	0.678	0.343
Hierarchical	Sum	4.440	1.367	0.505	0.042
	WSum	5.055	1.667	0.741	0.378
	Concat	5.107	1.688	0.747	0.420
	WConcat	5.181	1.763	0.745	0.342
	Seq	**5.355**	1.771	0.916	0.387
	WSeq (sum)	5.134	1.586	0.7429	0.4359
	WSeq (concat)	5.322	**1.883**	**0.9966**	**0.6897**

Table 1: Performance of different models.

500,000 samples for training, 2000 for validation, and 4000 for testing. The hyperparameters of neural networks were mainly derived from Shang et al. (2015) and Song et al. (2016): embeddings 620d and hidden states 1000d; we used AdaDelta for optimization.

3.2 Results and Analysis

We evaluated model performance by BLEU scores. As this paper compares various models, it is unaffordable for us to hire workers to manually annotate their satisfaction. BLEU scores, albeit imperfect for open-domain dialog systems, exhibits more or less correlation with human satisfaction (Liu et al., 2016; Tao et al., 2017). We present in Table 1 the overall performance of the models introduced in Section 2, and answer our research questions as follows.

RQ1: *How can we make better use of context information?*

We first observe that context-aware methods generally outperform the context-insensitive one. This implies context is indeed useful in open-domain, chit-chat-style dialog systems. The results are consistent with previous studies (Sordoni et al., 2015; Serban et al., 2015).

Among context-aware neural conversational models, we have the following findings.

- Hierarchical structures outperform the non-hierarchical one.

Comparing the non-hierarchical and hierarchical structures, we find it obvious that (most) hierarchical models outperform the non-hierarchical one by a large margin. The results show that, dialog systems are differ-

ent from other NLP applications, e.g., comprehension (Wang and Jiang, 2017), where non-hierarchical recurrent neural networks are adopted to better integrate information across different sentences. A plausible explanation, as indicated by Meng et al. (2017), is that conversational sentences are not necessarily uttered by a same speaker, and literature shows consistent evidence of the effectiveness of hierarchical RNNs in dialog systems.

- Keeping the roles of different utterances separately is important.

As mentioned in Section 2, the concatenation operation (Concat) distinguishes the roles of different utterances, while sum pooling Sum aggregates information in a homogeneous way. We see that the former outperforms the latter in both sentence-embedding and inter-sentence RNN levels, showing that sum pooling is not suitable for treating dialog context. Our conjecture is that sum pooling buries illuminating query information under less important context. Hence, keeping them separately will generally help.

- The context-query relevance score benefits conversational systems.

Our explicitly weighting approach computes an attention probability by context-query relevance. In all variants (Sum, Concat, and Seq), explicitly weighting improves the performance by a large margin (except BLEU-1 for Seq). The results indicate that context-query relevance is useful, as it emphasizes

Method	Length	Entropy	Diversity
Context-Insensitive	4.008	7.648	0.917
Context-Aware	4.204	7.863	0.927
Ground Truth	9.735	9.277	0.949

Table 2: The length, entropy, and diversity of the replies on the context-insensitive and context-aware (`WSeq, concat`) methods.

relevant context utterances as well as weakens irrelevant contexts.

RQ2: *What is the effect of context on neural dialog systems?*

We are now curious about how context information affects neural conversational systems. In Table 2, we present three auxiliary metrics, i.e., sentence length, entropy, and diversity. The former two are used in Serban et al. (2016) and Mou et al. (2016), whereas the latter one is used in Zhang and Hurley (2008).

As shown, content-aware conversational models tend to generate longer, more meaningful and diverse replies compared with content-insensitive models, given that they also improve BLEU scores.[2]

This shows an interesting phenomenon of neural sequence generation: an encoder-decoder framework needs sufficient source information for meaningful generation of the target; it simply does not fall into meaningful content from less meaningful input. A similar phenomenon is also reported in our previous work (Mou et al., 2016); we show that, a same network will generate more meaningful sentences if it starts from a given (meaningful) keyword. These results also partially explain why a `seq2seq` neural network tends to generate short and universally relevant replies in open-domain conversation, despite its success in machine translation, abstractive summarization, etc.

4 Conclusion

In this work, we analyzed the effect of context in generative conversational models. We conducted a systematic comparison among existing methods and our newly proposed variant that explicitly weights context vectors by context-query relevance.

We show that hierarchical RNNs generally outperform non-hierarchical ones, and that explicitly weighting context information can emphasize the relevant context utterances and weaken less relevant ones.

Our experiments also reveal an interesting phenomenon: with context information, neural networks tend to generate longer, more meaningful and diverse replies, which sheds light on neural sequence generation.

Acknowledgments

We thank the reviewers for insightful comments. This research is partially supported by 863 Grant No. 2015AA015403 and NSFC Grant No. 61672058.

References

Dzmitry Bahdanau, Kyunghyun Cho, and Yoshua Bengio. 2014. Neural machine translation by jointly learning to align and translate. In *Proceedings of the International Conference on Learning Representations*.

Kyunghyun Cho, Bart Van Merriënboer, Dzmitry Bahdanau, and Yoshua Bengio. 2014. On the properties of neural machine translation: Encoder-decoder approaches. *arXiv preprint arXiv:1409.1259* .

Zongcheng Ji, Zhengdong Lu, and Hang Li. 2014. An information retrieval approach to short text conversation. *arXiv preprint arXiv:1408.6988* .

Chia-Wei Liu, Ryan Lowe, Iulian Serban, Mike Noseworthy, Laurent Charlin, and Joelle Pineau. 2016. How NOT to evaluate your dialogue system: An empirical study of unsupervised evaluation metrics for dialogue response generation. In *Proceedings of the 2016 Conference on Empirical Methods in Natural Language Processing*. pages 2122–2132. https://doi.org/10.18653/v1/D16-1230.

Zhao Meng, Lili Mou, and Zhi Jin. 2017. Hierarchical RNN with static sentence-level attention for text-based speaker change detection. *arXiv preprint arXiv:1703.07713* .

Lili Mou, Yiping Song, Rui Yan, Ge Li, Lu Zhang, and Zhi Jin. 2016. Sequence to backward and forward sequences: A content-introducing approach to generative short-text conversation. In *Proceedings of the 26th International Conference on Computational Linguistics*. pages 3349–3358. http://aclweb.org/anthology/C16-1316.

---

[2]This condition is important when we draw conclusions. The length, entropy and diversity metrics do not make sense by themselves alone, because a system can achieve very high scores by repetitively generating random words.

Alan Ritter, Colin Cherry, and William B Dolan. 2011. Data-driven response generation in social media. In *Proceedings of the Conference on Empirical Methods in Natural Language Processing*. pages 583–593. http://aclweb.org/anthology/D11-1054.

Iulian V Serban, Alessandro Sordoni, Yoshua Bengio, Aaron Courville, and Joelle Pineau. 2015. Building end-to-end dialogue systems using generative hierarchical neural network models. In *Proceedings of the 30th AAAI Conference on Artificial Intelligence*. pages 3776–3783.

Iulian Vlad Serban, Alessandro Sordoni, Ryan Lowe, Laurent Charlin, Joelle Pineau, Aaron Courville, and Yoshua Bengio. 2016. A hierarchical latent variable encoder-decoder model for generating dialogues. *arXiv preprint arXiv:1605.06069* .

Lifeng Shang, Zhengdong Lu, and Hang Li. 2015. Neural responding machine for short-text conversation. In *Proceedings of the 53rd Annual Meeting of the Association for Computational Linguistics and the 7th International Joint Conference on Natural Language Processing (Volume 1: Long Papers)*. pages 1577–1586. https://doi.org/10.3115/v1/P15-1152.

Yiping Song, Rui Yan, Xiang Li, Dongyan Zhao, and Ming Zhang. 2016. Two are better than one: An ensemble of retrieval-and generation-based dialog systems. *arXiv preprint arXiv:1610.07149* .

Alessandro Sordoni, Michel Galley, Michael Auli, Chris Brockett, Yangfeng Ji, Margaret Mitchell, Jian-Yun Nie, Jianfeng Gao, and Bill Dolan. 2015. A neural network approach to context-sensitive generation of conversational responses. In *Proceedings of the 2015 Conference of the North American Chapter of the Association for Computational Linguistics: Human Language Technologies*. pages 196–205. https://doi.org/10.3115/v1/N15-1020.

Chongyang Tao, Lili Mou, Dongyan Zhao, and Rui Yan. 2017. RUBER: An unsupervised method for automatic evaluation of open-domain dialog systems. *arXiv preprint arXiv:1701.03079* .

Shuohang Wang and Jing Jiang. 2017. Machine comprehension using match-LSTM and answer pointer. In *Proceedings of the International Conference on Learning Representations*.

Jiacheng Xu, Danlu Chen, Xipeng Qiu, and Xuanjing Huang. 2016. Cached long short-term memory neural networks for document-level sentiment classification. In *Proceedings of the Conference on Empirical Methods in Natural Language Processing*. pages 1660–1669. https://doi.org/10.18653/v1/D16-1172.

Rui Yan, Yiping Song, and Hua Wu. 2016. Learning to respond with deep neural networks for retrieval-based human-computer conversation system. In *Proceedings of the 39th International ACM SIGIR Conference on Research and Development in Information Retrieval*. pages 55–64.

Kaisheng Yao, Geoffrey Zweig, and Baolin Peng. 2015. Attention with intention for a neural network conversation model. In *NIPS Workshop*.

Mi Zhang and Neil Hurley. 2008. Avoiding monotony: Improving the diversity of recommendation lists. In *Proceedings of the 2008 ACM Conference on Recommender Systems*. pages 123–130.

Cross-lingual and cross-domain discourse segmentation of entire documents

Chloé Braud
CoAStaL DIKU
University of Copenhagen
University Park 5,
2100 Copenhagen
chloe.braud@gmail.com

Ophélie Lacroix
CoAStaL DIKU
University of Copenhagen
University Park 5,
2100 Copenhagen
lacroix@di.ku.dk

Anders Søgaard
CoAStaL DIKU
University of Copenhagen
University Park 5,
2100 Copenhagen
soegaard@di.ku.dk

Abstract

Discourse segmentation is a crucial step in building end-to-end discourse parsers. However, discourse segmenters only exist for a few languages and domains. Typically they only detect intra-sentential segment boundaries, assuming gold standard sentence and token segmentation, and relying on high-quality syntactic parses and rich heuristics that are not generally available across languages and domains. In this paper, we propose statistical discourse segmenters for five languages and three domains that do not rely on gold pre-annotations. We also consider the problem of learning discourse segmenters when no labeled data is available for a language. Our fully supervised system obtains 89.5% F_1 for English newswire, with slight drops in performance on other domains, and we report supervised and unsupervised (cross-lingual) results for five languages in total.

1 Introduction

Discourse segmentation is the first step in building a discourse parser. The goal is to identify the minimal units — called Elementary Discourse Units (EDU) — in the documents that will then be linked by discourse relations. For example, the sentences (1a) and (1b)[1] are each segmented into two EDUs, then respectively linked by a CONTRAST and an ATTRIBUTION relation. The EDUs are mostly clauses and may cover a full sentence. This step is crucial: making a segmentation error leads to an error in the final analysis. Discourse segmentation can also inform other tasks, such as argumentation

mining, anaphora resolution, or speech act assignment (Sidarenka et al., 2015).

(1) a. [Such trappings suggest a glorious past] [but give no hint of a troubled present.]

b. [He said] [the thrift will to get regulators to reverse the decision.]

We focus on the Rhetorical Structure Theory (RST) (Mann and Thompson, 1988) – and resources such as the RST Discourse Treebank (RST-DT) (Carlson et al., 2001) – in which discourse structures are trees covering the documents. Most recent works on RST discourse parsing focuses on the task of tree building, relying on a gold discourse segmentation (Ji and Eisenstein, 2014; Feng and Hirst, 2014; Li et al., 2014; Joty et al., 2013). However, discourse parsers' performance drops by 12-14% when relying on *predicted* segmentation (Joty et al., 2015), underscoring the importance of discourse segmentation. State-of-the-art performance for discourse segmentation on the RST-DT is about 91% in F_1 with predicted parses (Xuan Bach et al., 2012), but these systems rely on a gold segmentation of sentences and words, therefore probably overestimating performance *in the wild*. We propose to build discourse segmenters without making any data assumptions. Specifically, rather than segmenting sentences, our systems segment documents directly.

Furthermore, only a few systems have been developed for languages other than English and domains other than the Wall Street Journal texts from the RST-DT. We are the first to perform experiments across 5 languages, and 3 non-newswire English domains. Since our goal is to provide a system usable for low-resource languages, we only use language-independent resources: here, the Universal Dependencies (UD) (Nivre et al.,

---

[1]The examples come from the RST Discourse Treebank.

Proceedings of the 55th Annual Meeting of the Association for Computational Linguistics (Short Papers), pages 237–243
Vancouver, Canada, July 30 - August 4, 2017. ©2017 Association for Computational Linguistics
https://doi.org/10.18653/v1/P17-2037

2016) Part-of-Speech (POS) tags, for which annotations exist for about 50 languages. For the cross-lingual experiments, we also rely on cross-lingual word embeddings induced from parallel data. With a shared representation, we can transfer model parameters across languages, or learn models jointly through multi-task learning.

Contributions: We (i) propose a general statistical discourse segmenter (ii) that does not assume gold sentences and tokens, and (iii) evaluate it across 5 languages and 3 domains.

We make our code available at https://bitbucket.org/chloebt/discourse.

2 Related work

For English RST-DT, the best discourse segmentation results were presented in Xuan Bach et al. (2012) (F_1 91.0% with automatic parse, 93.7 with gold parse) – and in Joty et al. (2015) for the Instructional corpus (Subba and Di Eugenio, 2009) (F_1 80.9% on 10-fold). Segmenters based on handwritten rules have been developed for Brazilian Portuguese (Pardo and Nunes, 2008) (51.3% to 56.8%, depending on the genre), Spanish (da Cunha et al., 2010, 2012) (80%) and Dutch (van der Vliet, 2010) (73% with automatic parse, 82% with gold parse).[2]

Most statistical discourse segmenters are based on classifiers (Fisher and Roark, 2007; Joty et al., 2015). Subba and Di Eugenio (2007) were the first to use a neural network, and Sporleder and Lapata (2005) to model the task as a sequence prediction problem. In this work, we do sequence prediction using a neural network.

All these systems rely on a quite large range of lexical and syntactic features (e.g. token, POS tags, lexicalized production rules). Sporleder and Lapata (2005) present arguments for a knowledge-lean system that can be used for low-resourced languages. Their system, however, still relies on several tools and gold annotations (e.g. POS tagger, chunker, list of connectives, gold sentences). In contrast, we present what is to the best of our knowledge the first work on discourse segmentation that is directly applicable to low-resource languages, presenting results for scenarios where no labeled data is available for the target language.

Previous work, relying on gold sentence boundaries, also only considers intra-sentential segment

boundaries. We move to processing entire documents, motivated by the fact that sentence boundaries are not easily detected across all languages.

3 Discourse segmentation

Nature of the EDUs Discourse segmentation is the first step in annotating a discourse corpus. The annotation guidelines define what is the nature of the EDUs, broadly relying on lexical and syntactic clues. If sentences and independent clauses are always minimal units, some fine distinctions make the task difficult.

In the English RST-DT (Carlson and Marcu, 2001), lexical information is crucial: for instance, the presence of the discourse connective "but" in example (1a)[3] indicates the beginning of an EDU. In addition, clausal complements of verbs are generally not treated as EDUs. Exceptions are the complements of attribution verbs, as in (1b), and the infinitival clauses marking a PURPOSE relation as the second EDU in (2a). Note that, in this latter example, the first infinitival clause ("**to** cover up …") is, however, not considered as an EDU. This fine distinction corresponds to one of the main difficulties of the task. Another one is linked to coordination: coordinated clauses are generally segmented as in (2b), but not coordinated verb phrases as in (2c).

(2) a. [A grand jury has been investigating whether officials at Southern Co. accounting conspired **to** cover up their accounting for spare parts] [**to** evade federal income taxes.]

b. [they parcel out money] [so that their clients can find temporary living quarters,] [buy food] (…) [and replaster walls.]

c. [Under Superfund, those] [who owned, generated or transported hazardous waste] [are liable for its cleanup, (…)]

Finally, in a multi-lingual and multi-domain setting, note that all the corpora do not follow the same rules: for example, the relation ATTRIBUTION is only annotated in the English RST-DT and the corpora for Brazilian Portuguese, consequently, complements of attribution verbs are not segmented in the other corpora.

---

[2] For German (Sidarenka et al., 2015) propose a segmenter in clauses (that may be EDU or not).

[3] All the examples given come from (Carlson et al., 2001).

Binary task As in previous studies, we view segmentation as a binary task at the word level: a word is either an EDU boundary (label B, beginning an EDU) or not (label I, inside an EDU). This design choice is motivated by the fact that, in RST corpora, the EDUs cover the documents entirely, and that EDUs mostly are adjacent spans of text. An exception is when embedded EDUs break up another EDU, as in Example (3). The units 1 and 3 form in fact one EDU. We follow previous work on treating this as three segments, but note that this may not be the optimal solution.

(3) [But maintaining the key components (...)]$_1$
[– a stable exchange rate and high levels of imports –]$_2$
[will consume enormous amounts (...).]$_3$

Document-level segmentation Contrary to previous studies, we do not assume gold sentences: Since sentence boundaries are EDU boundaries, our system jointly predicts sentence and intra-sentential EDU boundaries.

4 Cross-lingual/-domain segmentation

Data is scarce for discourse. In order to build statistical segmenters for new, low-resourced languages and domains, we propose to combine corpora within a multi-task learning setting (Section 5) leveraging data from well-resourced languages or domains. Models are trained on several (source) languages (resp. domains) – each viewed as an auxiliary task – for building a system for a (target) language (resp. domain).

Cross-domain For cross-domain experiments, the models are trained on all the other (source) domains and parameters are tuned on data for the target domain. This allows us to improve performance when only few data points (i.e. development set) are annotated for a specific domain (semi-supervised setting).

Cross-lingual For cross-lingual experiments, we tune our system's parameters by training a system on the data for three languages with sufficient amounts of data (namely, German, Spanish and Brazilian Portuguese), and using English data as a development set. We then train a new model also using multi-task learning (with these tuned parameters) using only source training data, and report performance on the target test set. This allows us to estimate performance when no data is available for the language of interest (unsupervised adaptation).

5 Multi-task learning

Our models perform sequence labeling based on a stacked k-layer bi-directional LSTM, a variant of LSTMs (Hochreiter and Schmidhuber, 1997) that reads the input in both regular and reversed order, allowing to take into account both left and right contexts (Graves and Schmidhuber, 2005). For our task, this enables us, for example, to distinguish between coordinated nouns and clauses. This model takes as input a sequence of words (and, here, POS tags) represented by vectors (initialized randomly or, for words, using pre-trained embedding vectors). The sequence goes through an embedding layer, and we compute the predictions of the forward and backward states for the k stacked layers. At the upper level, we compute the softmax predictions for each word based on a linear transformation. We use a logistic loss.

We also investigate joint training of multiple languages and domains for discourse segmentation. We thus try to leverage languages and domains regularities by sharing the architecture and parameters through multi-task training, where an auxiliary task is a source language (resp. domain) different from the target language (resp. domain) of interest. Specifically, we train models based on hard parameters sharing (Caruana, 1993; Collobert et al., 2011; Klerke et al., 2016; Plank et al., 2016):[4] each task is associated with a specific output layer, whereas the inner layers – the stacked LSTMs – are shared across the tasks. At training time, we randomly sample data points from one task and do forward predictions. During backpropagation, we modify the weights of the shared layers and the task-specific outer layer. The model is optimized for one target task (corresponding to the development data used). Except for the outer layer, the target task model is thus regularized by the induction of auxiliary models.

6 Corpora

Table 1 summarizes statistics about the data. For English, we use four corpora, allowing us to evaluate cross-domain performance: the RST-DT (En-DT) composed of Wall Street Journal articles; the SFU review corpus[5] (En-SFU-DT) containing product reviews; the instructional corpus (En-Instr-DT) (Subba and Di Eugenio, 2009) built

---

[4]We used a modified version of (Plank et al., 2016) fixing the random seed and using standard SGD.
[5]https://www.sfu.ca/~mtaboada

Corpus	#Doc	#EDU	#Sent	#Words
En-SFU-DT	400	28,260	16,827	328,362
En-DT	385	21,789	9,074	210,584
Pt-DT	330	12,594	4,385	136,346
Es-DT	266	3,325	1,816	57,768
En-Instr-DT	176	5,754	3,090	56,197
De-DT	174	2,979	1,805	33,591
En-Gum-DT	54	3,151	2,400	44,577
Nl-DT	80	2,345	1,692	25,095

Table 1: Number of documents, EDUs, sentences and words (according to UDPipe, see Section 7).

		Mono	Cross	UDP-S	UDP-P
languages	En-DT	89.5	**62.4**	55.6	57.5
	Pt-DT	82.2	**64.0**	49.0	62.5
	Es-DT	79.3	64.3	**64.9**	53.3
	De-DT	85.1	**76.6**	69.7	68.7
	Nl-DT	-	**82.6**	80.2	76.6
domains	En-DT (news)	89.5	**63.0**	55.6	57.5
	En-SFU-DT	85.5	**81.5**	70.2	66.1
	En-Instr-DT	87.1	**77.7**	66.5	69.5
	En-Gum-DT	-	68.1	**77.2**	61.8

Table 2: Results (F_1), comparing cross-lingual and cross-domain results with UDPipe.

on instruction manuals; and the GUM corpus[6] (En-Gum-DT) containing interviews, news, travel guides and how-tos.

For cross-lingual experiments, we use annotated corpora for Spanish (Es-DT) (da Cunha et al., 2011),[7] German (De-DT) (Stede, 2004; Stede and Neumann, 2014), Dutch (Nl-DT) (Vliet et al., 2011; Redeker et al., 2012) and, for Brazilian Portuguese, we merged four corpora (Pt-DT) (Cardoso et al., 2011; Collovini et al., 2007; Pardo and Seno, 2005; Pardo and Nunes, 2003, 2004) as done in (Maziero et al., 2015).

Three other RST corpora exist, but we were not able to obtain cross-lingual word embeddings for Basque (Iruskieta et al., 2013) and Chinese (Wu et al., 2016), and could not obtain the data for Tamil (Subalalitha and Parthasarathi, 2012).

7 Experiments

Data We use the official test sets for the En-DT (38 documents) and the Es-DT (84). For the others, we randomly choose 38 documents as test set, and either keep the rest as development set (Nl-DT) or split it into a train and a development set.

Baselines As baselines at the document level, we report the scores obtained (a) when only considering the sentence boundaries predicted using UDPipe (Straka et al., 2016) (UDP-S),[8] and (b) when EDU boundaries are added after each token PoS-tagged with "PUNCT" (UDP-P), marking either an inter- or an intra-sentential boundary.

Systems As described in Section 3, our systems are either mono-lingual or mono-domain (mono), or based on a joint training across languages or domains (cross). The "mono" systems are built for the languages and domains represented by enough data (upper part of Table 1). The "cross" models are trained using multi-task learning.

Parameters The hyper-parameters are tuned on the development set: number of iterations $i \in \{10, 20, 30\}$, Gaussian noise $\sigma \in \{0.1, 0.2\}$, and number of dimensions $d \in \{50, 500\}$. We fix the number n of stacked hidden layers to 2 and the size of the hidden layers h to 100 after experimenting on the En-DT.[9] Our final models use $\sigma = 0.2$ and $d = 500$.

Representation We use tokens and POS tags as input data.[10] The aim is to build a representation considering the current word and its context, i.e. its POS and the surrounding words/POS. We use the pre-trained UDPipe models to postag the documents for all languages. We experiment with randomly initialized and pre-trained cross-lingual word embeddings built on Europarl (Levy et al., 2017), keeping either the full 500 dimensions, or the first 50 ones.

Results Our systems are evaluated using F_1 over the boundaries (B labels), disregarding the first word of each document. Our scores are summarized in Table 2.

Our supervised, monolingual systems unsurprisingly give the best performance, with F_1 above 80%. The results are generally linked to the size of the corpora, the larger the better. Only exception is the En-SFU-DT, which, however, include more varied annotation (the authors stated that the annotations "have not been checked for reliability").

The (semi-supervised) cross-domain setting allows us to present the scores one can expect when

---

[6]https://corpling.uis.georgetown.edu/gum/
[7]We only use the test set from the annotator A.
[8]http://ufal.mff.cuni.cz/udpipe

[9]With $n \in \{1, 2, 3\}$ and $h \in \{100, 200, 400\}$.
[10]A document is a sequence alternating words and POS. The tokens are labeled with a B or an I, the POS, always labeled with an I, are inserted after each token they refer to.

only 25 documents are annotated for a new domain (i.e. the development set for the target domain), and to give the first results on the En-Gum-DT, but here, our model is actually outperformed by the sentence-based baseline (UDP-S).

The (unsupervised) cross-lingual models are generally largely better than UDPipe. These are scores that one can expect when doing cross-lingual transfer to build a discourse segmenter for a new language for which no annotated data are available. The performance is still quite high, demonstrating the coherence between the annotation schemes, and the potential of cross-lingual transfer. We acknowledge that this is a small set of relatively similar Indo-European languages, however.

Note that the sentence-based baseline has a high precision (e.g. 96.6 on Es-DT against 59.8 for the cross-lingual system), but a much lower recall, since it mainly predicts the sentence boundaries. On corpora that mostly contain sentential EDUs (e.g. Nl-DT, see Table 1), this is a good strategy. Using the punctuation (UDP-P) could be a better approximation for corpora with more varied EDUs, see the large gain for the Pt-DT and the En-Instr-DT.

Our scores are not directly comparable with sentence-level state-of-the-art systems (see Section 2). However, for En-DT, our best system correctly identifies 950 sentence boundaries out of 991, but gets only 84.5% in F_1 for intra-sentential boundaries,[11] thus lower than the state-of-the-art (91.0%). This is because we consider much less information, and because the system was not optimized for this task. Interestingly, our simple system beats HILDA (Hernault et al., 2010) (74.1% in F_1), is as good as the other neural network based system (Subba and Di Eugenio, 2007), and is close to SPADE (Soricut and Marcu, 2003) (85.2% in F_1) (Joty et al., 2015), while all of these systems use parse tree information.

Finally, looking at the errors of our system on the En-DT, we found that most of them are on the tokens "to" (30 out of 94 not predicted as 'B') and "and" (24 out of 103), as expected given the annotation guidelines (see Section 3). These words are highly ambiguous regarding discourse segmentation (e.g. in the test set, 42.3% of "and" indicates a boundary). We also found errors with coordinated

verb phrases – e.g. "[when rates are rising] [**and** shift out at times]" – that should be split (Carlson et al., 2001), a distinction hard to make without syntactic trees. Finally, since we use predicted POS tags, our system learns from noisy data and makes errors due to postagging and tokenisation errors.

8   Conclusion

We proposed new discourse segmenters with good performance for many languages and domains, at the document level, within a fully predicted setting and using only language independent tools.

Acknowledgements

We would like to thank the anonymous reviewers for their comments. This research is funded by the ERC Starting Grant LOWLANDS No. 313695.

References

Paula C.F. Cardoso, Erick G. Maziero, Mara Luca Castro Jorge, Eloize R.M. Seno, Ariani Di Felippo, Lucia Helena Machado Rino, Maria das Gracas Volpe Nunes, and Thiago A. S. Pardo. 2011. CSTNews - a discourse-annotated corpus for single and multi-document summarization of news texts in Brazilian Portuguese. In *Proceedings of the 3rd RST Brazilian Meeting*. pages 88–105.

Lynn Carlson and Daniel Marcu. 2001. Discourse tagging reference manual. Technical report, University of Southern California Information Sciences Institute.

Lynn Carlson, Daniel Marcu, and Mary Ellen Okurowski. 2001. Building a discourse-tagged corpus in the framework of Rhetorical Structure Theory. In *Proceedings of the Second SIGdial Workshop on Discourse and Dialogue*.

Rich Caruana. 1993. Multitask learning: a knowledge-based source of inductive bias. In *Proceedings of ICML*.

Ronan Collobert, Jason Weston, Léon Bottou, Michael Karlen, Koray Kavukcuoglu, and Pavel Kuksa. 2011. Natural language processing (almost) from scratch. *The Journal of Machine Learning Research* 12:2493–2537.

Sandra Collovini, Thiago I Carbonel, Juliana Thiesen Fuchs, Jorge César Coelho, Lúcia Rino, and Renata Vieira. 2007. Summ-it: Um corpus anotado com informaçoes discursivas visandoa sumarizaçao automática. In *Proceedings of TIL*.

Iria da Cunha, Eric SanJuan, Juan-Manuel Torres-Moreno, Marina Lloberas, and Irene Castellón.

---

[11]This score ignores the sentences containing only one EDU (Sporleder and Lapata, 2005).

2010. DiSeg: Un segmentador discursivo automático para el español. *Procesamiento del lenguaje natural* 45:145–152.

Iria da Cunha, Eric SanJuan, Juan-Manuel Torres-Moreno, Marina Lloberes, and Irene Castellón. 2012. DiSeg 1.0: The first system for Spanish discourse segmentation. *Expert Syst. Appl.* 39(2):1671–1678.

Iria da Cunha, Juan-Manuel Torres-Moreno, and Gerardo Sierra. 2011. On the development of the RST Spanish Treebank. In *Proceedings of LAW*.

Vanessa Wei Feng and Graeme Hirst. 2014. A linear-time bottom-up discourse parser with constraints and post-editing. In *Proceedings of ACL*.

Seeger Fisher and Brian Roark. 2007. The utility of parse-derived features for automatic discourse segmentation. In *Proceedings ACL*.

Alex Graves and Jrgen Schmidhuber. 2005. Framewise phoneme classification with bidirectional lstm and other neural network architectures. *Neural Networks* pages 5–6.

Hugo Hernault, Helmut Prendinger, David A. duVerle, and Mitsuru Ishizuka. 2010. HILDA: A discourse parser using support vector machine classification. *Dialogue and Discourse* 1:1–33.

Sepp Hochreiter and Jürgen Schmidhuber. 1997. Long short-term memory. *Neural Computation* 9(8):1735–1780.

Mikel Iruskieta, María J. Aranzabe, Arantza Diaz de Ilarraza, Itziar Gonzalez-Dios, Mikel Lersundi, and Oier Lopez de la Calle. 2013. The RST Basque Treebank: an online search interface to check rhetorical relations. In *Proceedings of the 4th Workshop RST and Discourse Studies*.

Yangfeng Ji and Jacob Eisenstein. 2014. Representation learning for text-level discourse parsing. In *Proceedings of ACL*.

Shafiq Joty, Giuseppe Carenini, and Raymond T. Ng. 2015. Codra: A novel discriminative framework for rhetorical analysis. *Computational Linguistics* 41:3.

Shafiq R. Joty, Giuseppe Carenini, Raymond T. Ng, and Yashar Mehdad. 2013. Combining intra- and multi-sentential rhetorical parsing for document-level discourse analysis. In *Proceedings of ACL*.

Sigrid Klerke, Yoav Goldberg, and Anders Søgaard. 2016. Improving sentence compression by learning to predict gaze. In *Proceedings of NAACL*.

Omer Levy, Anders Søgaard, and Yoav Goldberg. 2017. A strong baseline for learning cross-lingual word embeddings from sentence alignments. In *Proceedings of EACL*.

Jiwei Li, Rumeng Li, and Eduard H. Hovy. 2014. Recursive deep models for discourse parsing. In *Proceedings of EMNLP*.

William C. Mann and Sandra A. Thompson. 1988. Rhetorical Structure Theory: Toward a functional theory of text organization. *Text* 8:243–281.

Erick G. Maziero, Graeme Hirst, and Thiago A. S. Pardo. 2015. Adaptation of discourse parsing models for Portuguese language. In *Proceedings of the Brazilian Conference on Intelligent Systems (BRACIS)*.

Joakim Nivre, Željko Agić, Lars Ahrenberg, Maria Jesus Aranzabe, Masayuki Asahara, Aitziber Atutxa, Miguel Ballesteros, John Bauer, Kepa Bengoetxea, Yevgeni Berzak, Riyaz Ahmad Bhat, Cristina Bosco, Gosse Bouma, Sam Bowman, Gülşen Cebirolu Eryiit, Giuseppe G. A. Celano, Çar Çöltekin, Miriam Connor, Marie-Catherine de Marneffe, Arantza Diaz de Ilarraza, Kaja Dobrovoljc, Timothy Dozat, Kira Droganova, Tomaž Erjavec, Richárd Farkas, Jennifer Foster, Daniel Galbraith, Sebastian Garza, Filip Ginter, Iakes Goenaga, Koldo Gojenola, Memduh Gokirmak, Yoav Goldberg, Xavier Gómez Guinovart, Berta Gonzáles Saavedra, Normunds Grūzītis, Bruno Guillaume, Jan Hajič, Dag Haug, Barbora Hladká, Radu Ion, Elena Irimia, Anders Johannsen, Hüner Kaşkara, Hiroshi Kanayama, Jenna Kanerva, Boris Katz, Jessica Kenney, Simon Krek, Veronika Laippala, Lucia Lam, Alessandro Lenci, Nikola Ljubešić, Olga Lyashevskaya, Teresa Lynn, Aibek Makazhanov, Christopher Manning, Cătălina Mărănduc, David Mareček, Héctor Martínez Alonso, Jan Mašek, Yuji Matsumoto, Ryan McDonald, Anna Missilä, Verginica Mititelu, Yusuke Miyao, Simonetta Montemagni, Keiko Sophie Mori, Shunsuke Mori, Kadri Muischnek, Nina Mustafina, Kaili Müürisep, Vitaly Nikolaev, Hanna Nurmi, Petya Osenova, Lilja Øvrelid, Elena Pascual, Marco Passarotti, Cenel-Augusto Perez, Slav Petrov, Jussi Piitulainen, Barbara Plank, Martin Popel, Lauma Pretkalnia, Prokopis Prokopidis, Tiina Puolakainen, Sampo Pyysalo, Loganathan Ramasamy, Laura Rituma, Rudolf Rosa, Shadi Saleh, Baiba Saulīte, Sebastian Schuster, Wolfgang Seeker, Mojgan Seraji, Lena Shakurova, Mo Shen, Natalia Silveira, Maria Simi, Radu Simionescu, Katalin Simkó, Kiril Simov, Aaron Smith, Carolyn Spadine, Alane Suhr, Umut Sulubacak, Zsolt Szántó, Takaaki Tanaka, Reut Tsarfaty, Francis Tyers, Sumire Uematsu, Larraitz Uria, Gertjan van Noord, Viktor Varga, Veronika Vincze, Jing Xian Wang, Jonathan North Washington, Zdeněk Žabokrtský, Daniel Zeman, and Hanzhi Zhu. 2016. Universal dependencies 1.3. LINDAT/CLARIN digital library at Institute of Formal and Applied Linguistics, Charles University in Prague. http://hdl.handle.net/11234/1-1699.

Thiago A. S. Pardo and Maria das Graças Volpe Nunes. 2003. A construção de um corpus de textos científicos em Português do Brasil e sua marcação retórica. Technical report, Universidade de São Paulo.

Thiago A. S. Pardo and Maria das Graças Volpe Nunes. 2004. Relações retóricas e seus marcadores superficiais: Análise de um corpus de textos científicos em Português do Brasil. *Relatório Técnico NILC* .

Thiago A. S. Pardo and Maria das Graças Volpe Nunes. 2008. On the development and evaluation of a Brazilian Portuguese discourse parser. *Revista de Informática Teórica e Aplicada* 15(2):43–64.

Thiago A. S. Pardo and Eloize R. M. Seno. 2005. Rhetalho: Um corpus de referência anotado retoricamente. In *Proceedings of Encontro de Corpora*.

Barbara Plank, Anders Søgaard, and Yoav Goldberg. 2016. Multilingual part-of-speech tagging with bidirectional long short-term memory models and auxiliary loss. In *Proceedings of ACL*.

Gisela Redeker, Ildik Berzlnovich, Nynke van der Vliet, Gosse Bouma, and Markus Egg. 2012. Multi-layer discourse annotation of a dutch text corpus. In *Proceedings of LREC*.

Uladzimir Sidarenka, Andreas Peldszus, and Manfred Stede. 2015. Discourse segmentation of german texts. *Journal of Language Technology and Computational Linguistics* 30(1):71–98.

Radu Soricut and Daniel Marcu. 2003. Sentence level discourse parsing using syntactic and lexical information. In *Proceedings of NAACL*.

Caroline Sporleder and Mirella Lapata. 2005. Discourse chunking and its application to sentence compression. In *Proceedings of HLT/EMNLP*.

Manfred Stede. 2004. The potsdam commentary corpus. In *Proceedings of the ACL Workshop on Discourse Annotation*.

Manfred Stede and Arne Neumann. 2014. Potsdam commentary corpus 2.0: Annotation for discourse research. In *Proceedings of LREC*.

Milan Straka, Jan Hajič, and Straková. 2016. UDPipe: Trainable Pipeline for Processing CoNLL-U Files Performing Tokenization, Morphological Analysis, POS Tagging and Parsing. In *Proceedings of LREC*.

C N Subalalitha and Ranjani Parthasarathi. 2012. An approach to discourse parsing using sangati and Rhetorical Structure Theory. In *Proceedings of the Workshop on Machine Translation and Parsing in Indian Languages (MTPIL-2012)*.

Rajen Subba and Barbara Di Eugenio. 2007. Automatic discourse segmentation using neural networks. In *Workshop on the Semantics and Pragmatics of Dialogue*.

Rajen Subba and Barbara Di Eugenio. 2009. An effective discourse parser that uses rich linguistic information. In *Proceedings of ACL-HLT*.

Nynke van der Vliet. 2010. Syntax-based discourse segmentation of Dutch text. In *15th Student Session, ESSLLI*.

Nynke Van Der Vliet, Ildikó Berzlnovich, Gosse Bouma, Markus Egg, and Gisela Redeker. 2011. Building a discourse-annotated Dutch text corpus. In *S. Dipper and H. Zinsmeister (Eds.), Beyond Semantics, Bochumer Linguistische Arbeitsberichte 3*. pages 157–171.

Yunfang Wu, Fuqiang Wan, Yifeng Xu, and Xueqiang Lü. 2016. A new ranking method for Chinese discourse tree building. *Acta Scientiarum Naturalium Universitatis Pekinensis* 52(1):65–74.

Ngo Xuan Bach, Nguyen Le Minh, and Akira Shimazu. 2012. A reranking model for discourse segmentation using subtree features. In *Proceedings of Sigdial*.

Detecting Good Arguments in a Non-Topic-Specific Way: An Oxymoron?

Beata Beigman Klebanov, Binod Gyawali, Yi Song
Educational Testing Service
660 Rosedale Road
Princeton, NJ, USA
`bbeigmanklebanov,bgyawali,ysong@ets.org`

Abstract

Automatic identification of good arguments on a controversial topic has applications in civics and education, to name a few. While in the civics context it might be acceptable to create separate models for each topic, in the context of scoring of students' writing there is a preference for a single model that applies to all responses. Given that good arguments for one topic are likely to be irrelevant for another, is a single model for detecting good arguments a contradiction in terms? We investigate the extent to which it is possible to close the performance gap between topic-specific and across-topics models for identification of good arguments.

1 Introduction & Related Work

Argumentation is an important skill in higher education and the workplace; students are expected to show sound reasoning and use relevant evidence (Council of Chief State School Officers & National Governors Association, 2010). The increase in argumentative writing tasks, in both instructional and assessment contexts, results in a high demand for automated feedback on and scoring of arguments.

Automated analysis of argumentative writing has mostly concentrated on argument structure – namely, presence of claims and premises, and relationships between them (Ghosh et al., 2016; Nguyen and Litman, 2016; Persing and Ng, 2016; Ong et al., 2014; Stab and Gurevych, 2014). Addressing the content of arguments in on-line debates, Habernal and Gurevych (2016) ranked arguments on the same topic by convincingness; they showed that convincingness can be automatically predicted, to an extent, in a cross-topics fashion, as

they trained their systems on 31 debates and tested on a new one. Swanson et al. (2015) reported that annotation of argument quality is challenging, with inter-annotator agreement (ICC) around 0.40. They also showed that automated across-topics prediction is very hard; for some topics, no effective prediction was achieved.

Song et al. (2014) developed an annotation protocol for analyzing argument critiques in students' essays, drawing on the theory of argumentation schemes (Walton et al., 2008; Walton, 1996). According to this theory, different types of arguments invite specific types of critiques. For example, an argument from authority made in the prompt – *According to X, Y is the case* – avails critiques along the lines of whether X has the necessary knowledge and is an unbiased source of information about Y. Analyzing prompts used in an assessment of argument critique skills, Song et al. (2014) identified a number of common schemes, such as arguments from policy, sample, example, and used the argumentation schemes theory to specify what critiques would count as "good" for arguments from the given scheme. Once a prompt is associated with a specific set of argumentation schemes, it follows that those critiques that count as good under one of the schemes used in the prompt would be considered as good critiques in essays responding to that prompt. The goal of the annotation was to identify all sentences in an essay that participate in making a good critique, according to the above definition. Every sentence in an essay is annotated with the label of the critique that it raises, or "generic" if none. In the current paper, we build upon this earlier work.

In practical large-scale automated scoring contexts, new essay prompts are often introduced without rebuilding the scoring system, which is typically subject to a periodic release schedule. Therefore, the assumption that the system

Proceedings of the 55th Annual Meeting of the Association for Computational Linguistics (Short Papers), pages 244–249
Vancouver, Canada, July 30 - August 4, 2017. ©2017 Association for Computational Linguistics
https://doi.org/10.18653/v1/P17-2038

will have seen essays responding to each of the prompts it could encounter at deployment time is often unwarranted. Further, not only should a system be able to handle responses to an unseen prompt, it must do it gracefully, since a large disparity in the system's performance across different prompts might raise fairness concerns.

Our practical goal is thus a development of a robust argument critique analysis system for essays. Our theoretical goal is the investigation of the extent that it is at all possible to capture aspects of argument *content* in a fashion that would *generalize across various essay topics.*

2 Annotation

We used Song et al. (2014) annotation protocol, adapting as needed to cover additional argumentation schemes. Song et al. (2017) provides a detailed exposition of the argumentation-scheme-based analysis of a number of prompts and of the annotation process. For the current study, we used a simplified version of the annotation where sentences are labeled as **non-generic** (namely, containing a good critique according to some argumentation scheme), or **generic** (all the rest of the sentences in the essay). The average inter-annotator agreement on the "generic" vs "non-generic" sentence-level classification is $k{=}0.67$.

The "non-generic" category covers all sentences that raise a good critique; everything else is "generic". The latter category thus includes, for example, sentences that rehash the argument in the prompt, provide critical but vague statements that cannot be clearly identified as a specific critique from our list (such as "The author should provide more information"), provide specific critical statements that aren't valid arguments. For example, in response to the prompt that states that the new policy led to a 10% decrease in unemployment in four years, one writer argued that "People who were unemployed could have died within the last four years and that is why there is a decrease." While trying to provide an alternative explanation to the putative effect of the policy is a reasonable move, this is not a valid argument, because it is exceedingly unlikely that unemployed people died in such disproportionate numbers to have such a big impact on the unemployment statistics.

3 Data

For this study, we use a same-topic and an across-topics sets of college-level argument critique essays. The first is used to set the bar for the performance in the context where the training and the testing essays respond to the same prompt. The second is the main dataset focused on generalization across prompts.

3.1 Same-topic

A total of 900 essays were annotated, 300 essays for each of 3 prompts. For each prompt, we train a model on 260 responses and test on 40. The training sets per prompt contain on average 2,700 sentences, of which 38% are classified as containing good argument critiques. Two of the three same-topic sets were used previously in Song et al. (2014).

3.2 Across-topics

A total of 500 essays were annotated, 50 essays for each of 10 prompts. We perform 10-fold cross validation, training on 9 prompts and testing on the 10th, modeling a scenario of generalization to an unknown topic. There are, on average, 5,492 sentences available for training, of which 3,917 (42%) are classified as containing good critiques.

4 How far do we get with pure content?

Given that making a good critique is presumably mostly about saying the right things, we expect lexical models to perform well in same-topic context and badly in the across-topics one. We evaluated 1-3grams, 1-4grams, and 1-5grams models learned using a logistic regression classifier. Differences in performance tended to be in the third or fourth decimal digit; we therefore report results for 1-3grams only. Classification accuracies are shown in row 2 of Table 1, following the majority baseline (row 1), in both same-topic and across-topics scenarios. We show average performance (**Av**) as well as the worst performance (**Min**) on 3 prompts (same-topic) and on 10 prompts (across topics). We also evaluated models built using chi-square based feature selection (**f.s.**), eliminating all features with p value above 0.05 (row 3 in Table 1).

For the same-topic context, lexical features perform at .738. As expected, lexical features are much less effective across topics, with average performance of only .645. We observe substantial gaps of 9 (.738 vs .645) and 8 (.679 vs .604) accuracy points, for average and worst case, respectively, between same-topic and across-topics scenarios for ngram models. Feature selection is ineffective in both scenarios (compare rows 2 and 3 in Table 1).

5   How far do we get with pure structure?

An approach that is perhaps better aligned with the across-topics setting is to notice that in detailing one's arguments, one tends to utilize a specially structured discourse, and that discourse role could provide a clue to the argumentative function of a sentence, without reliance on what the sentence is actually saying (beyond discourse connectives that are used to help identify the discourse role). In particular, argumentative essays often have a fairly standard structure, where a general claim (or stance, or thesis) on the issue is introduced in the beginning of the essay, followed by a sequence of main points, each elaborated using supporting statements, and finally followed by a conclusion that often re-states the thesis and provides a high-level summary of the argument. We expect the "meat" of the argument to occur mostly in the supporting statements that provide detailed exposition of the author's arguments. We use a discourse parser for argumentative essays (Burstein et al., 2003) to classify sentences into the following discourse units: Thesis, Background, MainPoint, Support, Conclusion, and Other. Row 4 (**dr**) in Table 1 shows the performance of this set of 6 binary features. Of the 6 features, Support and MainPoint have a positive weight (predict "non-generic"), the rest predict "generic".

We further hypothesize that the position of a sentence inside a discourse segment might also provide some information: A sentence surrounded by Support sentences is likely to be in the middle of exposition of an argument, as opposed to the last Supporting sentence before the next Main Point that could be summary-like, leading up to a shift to a new topic. We therefore built two sets of transition features, one for all pairs of <previous_sentence_role,current_sentence_role> (such as <Thesis,Main Point> for a sentence that is classified as Main Point and follows a Thesis sentence), and the other – for all pairs of <current_sentence_role,next_sentence_role>. We also added BeginningOfEssay and EndOfEssay

	Model	Same Topic		Across Topics	
		Av.	Min.	Av.	Min.
1	Majority	.660	.612	.580	.399[1]
2	1-3gr	.738	.679	.645	.604
3	1-3gr f.s.	.697	.635	.633	.580
4	dr	.668	.619	.678	.634
5	dr_pn	.677	.631	.687	.649
6	dr_pn+1-3gr	.741	.690	.700	.674
7	1-3gr ppos	.728	.687	.654	.616
8	dr_pn+1-3gr ppos	**.745**	**.701**	**.706**	**.686**
9	SongEtAl2014	.756	.702	.678	.642

Table 1:   Classification accuracies for generic vs non-generic sentences. Our best results for same-topic and across-topics scenarios are boldfaced.

discourse tags to handle the first and the last sentences of the essay. Table 2 shows the weights for some of the features.

	Discourse Transition Feature			Weight
	Previous	Current	Next	
1	Support	Support		0.760
2	MainPoint	Support		0.238
3	Thesis	Support		-0.028
4		Support	Support	0.716
5		Support	MainPoint	0.220
6		Support	Concl.	0.047
7		Concl.	Concl.	0.063
8		Concl.	EndOfEssay	-0.680

Table 2:   Weights of the transition features.

We observe that the likelihood of the current Support sentence to carry argumentative content is higher if it follows another Support sentence (row 1) than if it follows a Main Point (row 2); if the Support sentence follows Thesis, it is actually not likely to contain argumentative content (perhaps it is more like a Main Point sentence than like a typical Support). Likewise, being followed by another Support sentence is a good sign (row 4), but being the last Support sentence before transitioning to a new Main Point has a much lower positive weight (row 5), and being the last Support before Conclusion has a still lower positive weight (row 6). Interestingly, while being the last Conclusion sentence in the essay strongly predicts "generic" (row 8), if the next sentence is still within the Conclusion segment, the prediction is actually slightly positive (row 7), suggesting that some authors rehash their arguments in substantial detail in concluding remarks, warranting a "non-generic" designation.

---

[1]The majority baseline for one prompt is below 50% because for that prompt the majority class is actually sentences that raise appropriate arguments, differently from the other 9 prompts.

Table 1 shows the performance of the discourse role features (**dr**), the transition pairs using previous and next discourse roles (**dr_pn**),[2] and the combination of content and discourse (row 6).

We observe that transforming the discourse role features into transitional features is effective. Second, the discourse role features are inferior to the content features for same-topic, while the opposite is true for the across-topics scenario.

Discourse structure information does in fact get us quite far in the across-topics scenario, further than the lexical information on its own. Combining the two types of information further improves performance in across-topics scenario, and reduces the gap between across-topics and same-topic contexts to 4 points on average (.741 vs .700) and 1.5 points in worst case (.690 vs .674), for a combined discourse structure and content model.

6   Can we do better?

In an attempt to further improve across-topics performance, we generalized ngrams representations and adapted feature selection to reflect the across-topics dynamic more directly.

6.1   Generalized ngrams

Suppose the prompt is arguing that some entity N should do some action V. While N and V might differ across prompts, critical sentences to the end that N should not do V are likely to occur across different prompts. In the current ngrams representation, N and V differ across prompts, and are unknown for a prompt that is unseen during training. We represent all content words (nouns, verbs, adjectives, adverbs, and cardinal numbers) in the prompt as their part-of-speech labels; we should be able to capture features such as "should not VB". Rows 7 and 8 in Table 1 show the **1-3gr ppos** model; it improves over 1-3gr in both the average and the worst cases, on its own and on top of the dr_pn features, in the across-topics scenario. The improvement over dr_pn+1-3gr is marginally significant (p<0.1, Wilcoxon Signed-Ranks 2-tailed test, n=10, W=33).

The single strongest lexical predictor of a generic sentence is the first person singular pronoun *I*; such sentences are likely to express stance (*I think this is a good plan*), or contain discourse-management expressions such as *I will show that the author's arguments are flawed*. Words such as *assumptions, evidence, information, argument, statistics, idea, reasons* all have negative weight, suggesting that they typically belong to generic sentences such as *The author's argument lacks evidence* that does not raise a specific critique. Lexical features for the positive class include modality as in *might, perhaps, could, possible that, potential, necessarily, if a*; negation (*not, will not*), as well as more specific lexica that point out, for example, outcomes of a policy (*expensive, increase in, affected the, fails to*). Positive features with prompt elements include *NNS does not, NN do not, many NNS, NN NNS are, NNS who VBD, could have VBN, will not VB*.

6.2   Feature Selection

We experimented with three feature selection methods. (1) We selected features with $p<0.05$ using χ^2 test (**p0.05**). (2) We selected features with $p<0.05$ for at least two out of the 9 training prompts, to find features that are likely to generalize across prompts (**p0.05_2pr**). (3) We selected features based on their mutual information with the label conditioned on values of the dr_pn features, to encourage selection of features that augment, rather than repeat, the discourse information. We calculated for each training prompt, and took the 2nd highest of the 9 values.[3] We selected features in the top 5% of this metric (**mi5%_2pr**).

Table 3 shows the results. The p0.05 mechanism is ineffective; 0.05_2pr selection is better. The mi5%_2pr mechanism performs within .002 of the original, while reducing the number of features by two orders of magnitude.

F.s.	#Features	Av.	Min.
No f.s.	~ 200.000	.706	.686
p0.05	$\sim 3,500$	.687	.656
p0.05_2pr	< 500	.702	.678
mi5%_2pr	$\sim 1,000$	.704	.684

Table 3: Performance of feature selection, for the dr_pn+1-3gr ppos model, across topics.

7   Benchmark

We also compared our best across-topics system (dr_pn+1-3gr ppos) to the system described in

---

Song et al. (2014). The Song et al. (2014) system uses the following features: length of the sentence, parts of speech, overlap of words in the sentence with the prompt, relative position of the sentence in the essay, 1-3gr, and 1-3gr in previous and next sentences. The performance is shown in row 9 in Table 1. Our improvement over Song et al. (2014) is statistically significant in the across-topics scenario (p<0.05, Wilcoxon Signed-Ranks test, 2-tailed, n=10, W=51).

8 Conclusion

We presented experiments on classifying essay sentences as containing good argument critiques or not. While a good argument critique is a matter of content, we show that it is possible to build classifiers that are not prompt-specific, using discourse structure features and generalized lexical features that take into account reference to the text of the prompt to which the author is responding. Starting from a ngrams baseline where the performance gap between same-prompt and across-topics scenarios is 9 accuracy points on average (.738 vs .645) and 8 points in worst case (.679 vs .604), we close half the gap in average performance (.745 vs .706) and are down to only 1.5 point difference in worst case performance (.701 vs .686). This performance is preserved with only about 0.5% of the features, using a conditional mutual information criterion. The improvement in worst case performance is important for ensuring that the system does not exhibit large performance differences across different essay prompts used on the same test. We also show that our best system significantly improves over the state-of-art system for argument critique detection task on comparable essay data for the across-topics scenario.

References

Jill Burstein, Daniel Marcu, and Kevin Knight. 2003. Finding the write stuff: Automatic identification of discourse structure in student essays. *IEEE Intelligent Systems* 18(1):32–39. https://doi.org/10.1109/MIS.2003.1179191.

Debanjan Ghosh, Aquila Khanam, Yubo Han, and Smaranda Muresan. 2016. Coarse-grained argumentation features for scoring persuasive essays. In *Proceedings of the 54th Annual Meeting of the Association for Computational Linguistics (Volume 2: Short Papers)*. Association for Computational Linguistics, Berlin, Germany, pages 549–554. http://anthology.aclweb.org/P16-2089.

Ivan Habernal and Iryna Gurevych. 2016. Which argument is more convincing? Analyzing and predicting convincingness of Web arguments using bidirectional LSTM. In *Proceedings of the 54th Annual Meeting of the Association for Computational Linguistics (Volume 1: Long Papers)*. Association for Computational Linguistics, Berlin, Germany, pages 1589–1599. http://www.aclweb.org/anthology/P16-1150.

Huy Nguyen and Diane Litman. 2016. Context-aware argumentative relation mining. In *Proceedings of the 54th Annual Meeting of the Association for Computational Linguistics (Volume 1: Long Papers)*. Association for Computational Linguistics, Berlin, Germany, pages 1127–1137. http://www.aclweb.org/anthology/P16-1107.

Nathan Ong, Diane Litman, and Alexandra Brusilovsky. 2014. Ontology-based argument mining and automatic essay scoring. In *Proceedings of the First Workshop on Argumentation Mining*. Association for Computational Linguistics, Baltimore, Maryland, pages 24–28. http://www.aclweb.org/anthology/W14-2104.

Isaac Persing and Vincent Ng. 2016. End-to-end argumentation mining in student essays. In *Proceedings of the 2016 Conference of the North American Chapter of the Association for Computational Linguistics: Human Language Technologies*. Association for Computational Linguistics, San Diego, California, pages 1384–1394. http://www.aclweb.org/anthology/N16-1164.

Yi Song, Paul Deane, and Beata Beigman Klebanov. 2017. Toward the automated scoring of written arguments: Developing an innovative approach for annotation. *ETS Research Report Series* https://doi.org/10.1002/ets2.12138.

Yi Song, Michael Heilman, Beata Beigman Klebanov, and Paul Deane. 2014. Applying argumentation schemes for essay scoring. In *Proceedings of the First Workshop on Argumentation Mining*. Association for Computational Linguistics, Baltimore, Maryland, pages 69–78. http://www.aclweb.org/anthology/W14-2110.

Christian Stab and Iryna Gurevych. 2014. Identifying argumentative discourse structures in persuasive essays. In *Proceedings of the 2014 Conference on Empirical Methods in Natural Language Processing (EMNLP)*. Association for Computational Linguistics, Doha, Qatar, pages 46–56. http://www.aclweb.org/anthology/D14-1006.

Reid Swanson, Brian Ecker, and Marilyn Walker. 2015. Argument mining: Extracting arguments from online dialogue. In *Proceedings of the 16th Annual Meeting of the Special Interest Group on Discourse and Dialogue*. Association for Computational Linguistics, Prague, Czech Republic, pages 217–226. http://aclweb.org/anthology/W15-4631.

Douglas N. Walton. 1996. *Argumentation schemes for presumptive reasoning*. Mahwah, NJ: Lawrence Erlbaum.

Douglas N. Walton, Chris Reed, and Fabrizio Macagno. 2008. *Argumentation schemes.* New York, NY: Cambridge University Press.

Argumentation Quality Assessment: Theory vs. Practice

Henning Wachsmuth *   Nona Naderi **   Ivan Habernal ***   Yufang Hou ****
Graeme Hirst **   Iryna Gurevych ***   Benno Stein *
* Bauhaus-Universität Weimar, Weimar, Germany, `www.webis.de`
** University of Toronto, Toronto, Canada, `www.cs.toronto.edu/compling`
*** Technische Universität Darmstadt, Darmstadt, Germany, `www.ukp.tu-darmstadt.de`
**** IBM Research, Dublin, Ireland, `ie.ibm.com`

Abstract

Argumentation quality is viewed differently in argumentation theory and in practical
assessment approaches. This paper studies
to what extent the views match empirically.
We find that most observations on quality
phrased spontaneously are in fact adequately represented by theory. Even more, relative comparisons of arguments in practice correlate with absolute quality ratings
based on theory. Our results clarify how
the two views can learn from each other.

1 Introduction

The assessment of argumentation quality is critical
for any application built upon argument mining,
such as debating technologies (Rinott et al., 2015).
However, research still disagrees on whether quality should be assessed from a theoretical or from a
practical viewpoint (Allwood, 2016).

Theory states, among other things, that a cogent
argument has acceptable premises that are relevant
to its conclusion and sufficient to draw the conclusion (Johnson and Blair, 2006). Practitioners object that such quality dimensions are hard to assess
for real-life arguments (Habernal and Gurevych,
2016b). Moreover, the normative nature of theory
suggests *absolute* quality ratings, but in practice it
seems much easier to state which argument is more
convincing—a *relative* assessment. Consider two
debate-portal arguments for "advancing the common good is better than personal pursuit", taken
from the corpora analyzed later in this paper:

Argument A *"While striving to make advancements for the common good you can change the
world forever. Allot of people have succeded in
doing so. Our founding fathers, Thomas Edison,
George Washington, Martin Luther King jr, and
many more. These people made huge advances for
the common good and they are honored for it."*

Argument B *"I think the common good is a better
endeavor, because it's better to give then to receive.
It's better to give other people you're hand out in
help then you holding your own hand."*

In the study of Habernal and Gurevych (2016b),
annotators assessed Argument *A* as more convincing than *B*. When giving reasons for their assessment, though, they saw *A* as more credible and well
thought through; that does not seem to be too far
from the theoretical notion of cogency.

This paper gives empirical answers to the question of how different the theoretical and practical
views of argumentation quality actually are. Section 2 briefly reviews existing theories and practical
approaches. Section 3 then empirically analyzes
correlations in two recent argument corpora, one
annotated for 15 well-defined quality dimensions
taken from theory (Wachsmuth et al., 2017a) and
one with 17 reasons for quality differences phrased
spontaneously in practice (Habernal and Gurevych,
2016a). In a crowdsourcing study, we test whether
lay annotators achieve agreement on the theoretical
quality dimensions (Section 4).

We find that assessments of overall argumentation quality largely match in theory and practice.
Nearly all phrased reasons are adequately represented in theory. However, some theoretical quality
dimensions seem hard to separate in practice. Most
importantly, we provide evidence that the observed
relative quality differences are reflected in absolute quality ratings. Still, our study underpins the
fact that the theory-based argumentation quality
assessment remains complex. Our results do not
generally answer the question of what view of argumentation quality is preferable, but they clarify
where theory can learn from practice and vice versa.
In particular, practical approaches indicate what to
focus on to simplify theory, whereas theory seems
beneficial to guide quality assessment in practice.

Proceedings of the 55th Annual Meeting of the Association for Computational Linguistics (Short Papers), pages 250–255
Vancouver, Canada, July 30 - August 4, 2017. ©2017 Association for Computational Linguistics
https://doi.org/10.18653/v1/P17-2039

Quality Dimension	Short Description of Dimension
Cogency	Argument has (locally) acceptable, relevant, and sufficient premises.
Local acceptability	Premises worthy of being believed.
Local relevance	Premises support/attack conclusion.
Local sufficiency	Premises enough to draw conclusion.
Effectiveness	Argument persuades audience.
Credibility	Makes author worthy of credence.
Emotional appeal	Makes audience open to arguments.
Clarity	Avoids deviation from the issue, uses correct and unambiguous language.
Appropriateness	Language proportional to the issue, supports credibility and emotions.
Arrangement	Argues in the right order.
Reasonableness	Argument is (globally) acceptable, relevant, and sufficient.
Global acceptability	Audience accepts use of argument.
Global relevance	Argument helps arrive at agreement.
Global sufficiency	Enough rebuttal of counterarguments.
Overall quality	Argumentation quality in total.

Table 1: The 15 theory-based quality dimensions rated in the corpus of Wachsmuth et al. (2017a).

Polarity	Label	Short Description of Reason
Negative properties of Argument B	5-1	*B* is attacking / abusive.
	5-2	*B* has language/grammar issues, or uses humour or sarcasm.
	5-3	*B* is unclear / hard to follow.
	6-1	*B* has no credible evidence / no facts.
	6-2	*B* has less or insufficient reasoning.
	6-3	*B* uses irrelevant reasons.
	7-1	*B* is only an opinion / a rant.
	7-2	*B* is non-sense / confusing.
	7-3	*B* does not address the topic.
	7-4	*B* is generally weak / vague.
Positive properties of Argument A	8-1	*A* has more details/facts/examples, has better reasoning / is deeper.
	8-4	*A* is objective / discusses other views.
	8-5	*A* is more credible / confident.
	9-1	*A* is clear / crisp / well-written.
	9-2	*A* sticks to the topic.
	9-3	*A* makes you think.
	9-4	*A* is well thought through / smart.
Overall	**Conv**	*A* is more convincing than *B*.

Table 2: The 17+1 practical reason labels given in the corpus of Habernal and Gurevych (2016a).

2 Theory versus Practice

This section outlines major theories and practical approaches to argumentation quality assessment, including those we compare in the present paper.

2.1 Theoretical Views of Quality Assessment

Argumentation theory discusses logical, rhetorical, and dialectical quality. As few real-life arguments are logically sound, requiring true premises that deductively entail a conclusion, cogency (as defined in Section 1) is largely seen as the main logical quality (Johnson and Blair, 2006; Damer, 2009; Govier, 2010). Toulmin (1958) models the general structure of logical arguments, and Walton et al. (2008) analyze schemes of fallacies and strong arguments. A fallacy is a kind of error that undermines reasoning (Tindale, 2007). Strength may mean cogency but also rhetorical effectiveness (Perelman and Olbrechts-Tyteca, 1969). Rhetoric has been studied since Aristotle (2007) who developed the notion of the means of persuasion (logos, ethos, pathos) and their linguistic delivery in terms of arrangement and style. Dialectical quality dimensions resemble those of cogency, but arguments are judged specifically by their reasonableness for achieving agreement (van Eemeren and Grootendorst, 2004).

Wachsmuth et al. (2017a) point out that dialectical builds on rhetorical, and rhetorical builds on logical quality. They derive a unifying taxonomy from the major theories, decomposing quality hierarchically into cogency, effectiveness, reasonableness, and subdimensions. Table 1 lists all 15 dimensions

covered. In Section 3, we use their absolute quality ratings from 1 (low) to 3 (high) annotated by three experts for each dimension of 304 arguments taken from the *UKPConvArg1* corpus detailed below.

2.2 Practical Views of Quality Assessment

There is an application area where absolute quality ratings of argumentative text are common practice: essay scoring (Beigman Klebanov et al., 2016). Persing and Ng (2015) annotated the argumentative strength of essays composing multiple arguments with notable agreement. For single arguments, however, all existing approaches that we are aware of assess quality in relative terms, e.g., Cabrio and Villata (2012) find accepted arguments based on attack relations, Wei et al. (2016) rank arguments by their persuasiveness, and Wachsmuth et al. (2017b) rank them by their relevance. Boudry et al. (2015) argue that normative concepts such as fallacies rarely apply to real-life arguments and that they are too sophisticated for operationalization.

Based on the idea that relative assessment is easier, Habernal and Gurevych (2016b) crowdsourced the *UKPConvArg1* corpus. Argument pairs *(A, B)* from a debate portal were classified as to which argument is more convincing. Without giving any guidelines, the authors also asked for reasons as to why *A* is more convincing than *B*. In a follow-up study (Habernal and Gurevych, 2016a), these reasons were used to derive a hierarchical annotation scheme. 9111 argument pairs were then labeled with one or more of the 17 reason labels in Table 2

Quality Dimension		Negative Properties of Argument B										Positive Properties of Argument A							Conv
		5-1	5-2	5-3	6-1	6-2	6-3	7-1	7-2	7-3	7-4	8-1	8-4	8-5	9-1	9-2	9-3	9-4	
Cog	**Cogency**	.86	.74	.67	.66	.85	.43	.81	.83	.84	.75	.59	.58	.62	.70	.67	.64	**.75**	.59
LA	Local acceptability	.92	.77	.86	.49	.90	**.80**	.86	.89	.89	.74	.58	.43	.73	.64	.67	.56	.73	.58
LR	Local relevance	.87	.77	.86	.70	**.95**	.45	.84	.92	**.95**	.73	.61	.56	.68	.69	.65	.70	.66	.62
LS	Local sufficiency	.79	.69	.67	.68	.74	.38	.85	.92	.84	**.79**	.63	.67	.54	.64	.52	**.78**	.70	.61
Eff	**Effectiveness**	.84	.71	.67	.66	.85	.62	**.87**	.92	.84	.71	.59	.57	.65	.66	.58	**.78**	.72	.59
Cre	Credibility	.78	.69	.71	.52	**.95**	**.80**	.66	.81	.67	.57	.51	.44	.66	.60	.71	.39	.62	.50
Emo	Emotional appeal	.80	.50	.59	.55	.70	**.80**	.70	.80	.67	.60	.36	.35	.41	.30	.42	.73	.50	.38
Cla	Clarity	.61	.70	**.91**	.41	**.95**	.58	.61	.87	.67	.60	.41	.40	.41	.68	.71	.56	.58	.44
App	Appropriateness	.94	**.86**	**.91**	.50	**.95**	.45	**.87**	.74	.36	**.79**	.57	.59	.69	.72	**.79**	.53	.57	.59
Arr	Arrangement	.81	.75	.86	.67	.85	.40	.78	.77	.67	.68	.60	**.73**	.64	**.73**	.73	**.78**	.72	.62
Rea	**Reasonableness**	.92	**.86**	.67	**.73**	.90	.49	.85	**.94**	.84	.73	.64	.56	.70	.69	.65	**.78**	.64	.63
GA	Global acceptability	**1.00**	.80	.82	.65	.76	.62	**.87**	.86	**.95**	.71	.63	.62	**.75**	.59	.67	.72	.68	.63
GR	Global relevance	.97	**.86**	.82	.63	.82	.71	.86	.82	**.95**	.75	.61	.51	.49	.66	.46	.72	.57	.61
GS	Global sufficiency	.77	.57	.59	.62	.85	.47	.75	.72	.71	.64	.59	.69	.46	.53	.39	.71	.61	.56
OQ	**Overall quality**	.94	.85	.79	.71	.90	.53	.85	.92	.84	.72	**.65**	.58	.69	.72	.61	.73	.73	**.64**
# Pairs with label x-y		34	55	18	115	11	16	64	37	10	50	536	79	68	86	34	26	39	736

Table 3: Kendall's τ rank correlation of each of the 15 quality dimensions of all argument pairs annotated by Wachsmuth et al. (2017a) given for each of the 17+1 reason labels of Habernal and Gurevych (2016a). Bold/gray: Highest/lowest value in each column. Bottom row: The number of labels for each dimension.

by crowd workers (*UKPConvArg2*). These pairs represent the practical view in our experiments.

3 Matching Theory and Practice

We now report on experiments that we performed to examine to what extent the theory and practice of argumentation quality assessment match.[1]

3.1 Corpus-based Comparison of the Views

Several dimensions and reasons in Tables 1 and 2 seem to refer to the same or opposite property, e.g., *clarity* and *5-3 (unclear)*. This raises the question of how absolute ratings of arguments based on theory relate to relative comparisons of argument pairs in practice. We informally state three hypotheses:

Hypothesis 1 The reasons for quality differences in practice are adequately represented in theory.

Hypothesis 2 The perception of overall argumentation quality is the same in theory and practice.

Hypothesis 3 Relative quality differences are reflected by differences in absolute quality ratings.

As both corpora described in Section 2 are based on the *UKPConvArg1* corpus and thus share many arguments, we can test the hypotheses empirically.

3.2 Correlations of Dimensions and Reasons

For Hypotheses 1 and 2, we consider all 736 pairs of arguments from Habernal and Gurevych (2016a) where both have been annotated by Wachsmuth et al. (2017a). For each pair *(A, B)* with *A* being

more convincing than *B*, we check whether the ratings of *A* and *B* for each dimension (averaged over all annotators) show a concordant difference (i.e., a higher rating for *A*), a disconcordant difference (lower), or a tie. This way, we can correlate each dimension with all reason labels in Table 2 including *Conv*. In particular, we compute Kendall's τ based on all argument pairs given for each label.[2]

Table 3 presents all τ-values. The phrasing of a reason can be assumed to indicate a clear quality difference—this is underlined by the generally high correlations. Analyzing the single values, we find much evidence for Hypothesis 1: Most notably, label *5-1* perfectly correlates with *global acceptability*, fitting the intuition that abuse is not acceptable. The high τ's of *8-5 (more credible)* for *local acceptability* (.73) and of *9-4 (well thought through)* for *cogency* (.75) confirm the match assumed in Section 1. Also, the values of *5-3 (unclear)* for *clarity* (.91) and of *7-2 (non-sense)* for *reasonableness* (.94) as well as the weaker correlation of *8-4 (objective)* for *emotional appeal* (.35) makes sense.

Only the comparably low τ of *6-1 (no credible evidence)* for *local acceptability* (.49) and *credibility* (.52) seem really unexpected. Besides, the descriptions of *6-2* and *6-3* sound like *local* but cor-

---

[2]Lacking better options, we ignore pairs where a label is not given: It is indistinguishable whether the associated reason does not hold, has not been given, or is just not included in the corpus. Thus, τ is more "boosted" the fewer pairs exist for a label and, thus, its values are not fully comparable across labels. Notice, though, that *Conv* exists for all pairs. So, the values of *Conv* suggest the magnitude of τ without boosting.

Polarity	Label	Cog	LA	LR	LS	Eff	Cre	Emo	Cla	App	Arr	Rea	GA	GR	GS	OQ
Negative	5-1	1.30	1.44	1.77	1.29	1.26	1.46	1.64	1.84	1.62	1.55	1.34	1.45	1.65	1.19	1.29
properties of	5-2	1.51	1.73	1.97	1.39	1.41	1.66	1.82	1.96	1.89	1.72	1.55	1.72	1.74	1.21	1.48
Argument B	5-3	1.46	1.78	2.06	1.43	1.39	1.63	**1.96**	1.87	2.04	1.65	**1.63**	1.85	1.76	1.28	1.52
	6-1	1.54	**1.87**	2.22	1.43	1.44	**1.72**	1.85	**2.15**	2.12	1.79	1.62	**1.89**	1.89	1.27	1.55
	6-2	1.30	1.52	1.88	1.27	1.21	1.52	1.85	1.94	1.88	1.67	1.36	1.61	1.55	1.15	1.33
	6-3	**1.60**	1.85	**2.23**	**1.52**	**1.52**	1.65	1.79	2.00	**2.15**	**1.92**	**1.63**	1.85	**2.00**	**1.40**	**1.60**
	7-1	1.43	1.74	1.97	1.33	1.34	1.60	1.82	1.95	1.89	1.72	1.48	1.71	1.68	1.22	1.43
	7-2	1.45	1.68	1.97	1.41	1.39	1.53	1.86	1.84	1.95	1.67	1.53	1.68	1.70	1.25	1.48
	7-3	1.20	1.47	1.60	1.10	1.17	1.47	1.60	1.70	1.80	1.40	1.20	1.40	1.30	1.07	1.13
	7-4	1.43	1.71	2.02	1.37	1.34	1.71	1.79	1.95	1.97	1.65	1.55	1.75	1.75	1.23	1.46
Positive	8-1	1.56	1.89	2.20	1.46	1.48	1.71	1.88	2.05	2.07	1.79	1.65	1.88	1.92	1.30	1.57
properties of	8-4	1.65	1.97	2.27	1.53	1.61	1.73	1.86	2.12	2.14	1.89	1.73	1.92	1.96	1.37	1.64
Argument A	8-5	1.69	**2.07**	**2.39**	1.58	1.60	**1.81**	1.98	**2.19**	**2.25**	**1.99**	1.82	2.04	**2.11**	1.38	1.75
	9-1	1.54	1.86	2.22	1.49	1.43	1.67	1.84	2.09	2.03	1.74	1.63	1.85	1.92	1.30	1.54
	9-2	1.56	1.76	2.22	1.45	1.49	1.58	1.98	2.02	2.00	1.74	1.62	1.81	1.84	1.28	1.51
	9-3	1.55	1.78	2.31	1.42	1.49	1.68	**2.01**	2.18	2.10	1.79	1.63	1.83	1.97	1.27	1.50
	9-4	**1.78**	1.99	2.32	**1.64**	**1.68**	**1.81**	1.99	2.17	2.19	1.93	**1.86**	**2.05**	2.09	**1.44**	**1.79**
min(*Pos.*)−min(*Neg.*)		0.34	0.32	0.60	0.32	0.26	0.12	0.24	0.32	0.38	0.34	0.42	0.41	0.54	0.20	0.37
max(*Pos.*)−max(*Neg.*)		0.18	0.20	0.16	0.12	0.16	0.09	0.05	0.04	0.10	0.07	0.23	0.16	0.11	0.04	0.19

Table 4: The mean rating for each quality dimension of those arguments from Wachsmuth et al. (2017a) given for each reason label (Habernal and Gurevych, 2016a). The bottom rows show that the minimum maximum mean ratings are consistently higher for the positive properties than for the negative properties.

relate more with *global* relevance and sufficiency respectively. Similarly, *7-3 (off-topic)* correlates strongly with local *and* global relevance (both .95). So, these dimensions seem hard to separate.

In line with Hypothesis 2, the highest correlation of *Conv* is indeed given for *overall quality* (.64). Thus, argumentation quality assessment seems to match in theory and practice to a broad extent.

3.3 Absolute Ratings for Relative Differences

The correlations found imply that the relative quality differences captured are reflected in absolute differences. For explicitness, we computed the mean rating for each quality dimension of all arguments from Wachsmuth et al. (2017a) with a particular reason label from Habernal and Gurevych (2016a). As each reason refers to one argument of a pair, this reveals whether the labels, although meant to signal relative differences, indicate absolute ratings.

Table 4 compares the mean ratings of "negative labels" (*5-1* to *7-4*) and "positive" ones (*8-1* to *9-4*). For all dimensions, the maximum and minimum value are higher for the positive than for the negative labels—a clear support of Hypothesis 3.[3] Also, Table 4 reveals which reasons predict absolute differences most: The mean ratings of *7-3 (off-topic)* are very low, indicating a strong negative impact, while *6-3 (irrelevant reasons)* still shows rather

high values. Vice versa, especially *8-5 (more credible)* and *9-4 (well thought through)* are reflected in high ratings, whereas *9-2 (sticks to topic)* does not have much positive impact.

4 Annotating Theory in Practice

The results of Section 3 suggest that theory may guide the assessment of argumentation quality in practice. In this section, we evaluate the reliability of a crowd-based annotation process.

4.1 Absolute Quality Ratings by the Crowd

We emulated the expert annotation process carried out by Wachsmuth et al. (2017a) on *CrowdFlower* in order to evaluate whether lay annotators suffice for a theory-based quality assessment. In particular, we asked the crowd to rate the same 304 arguments as the experts for all 15 given quality dimensions with scores from 1 to 3 (or choose "cannot judge"). Each argument was rated 10 times at an offered price of $0.10 for each rating (102 annotators in total). Given the crowd ratings, we then performed two comparisons as detailed in the following.

4.2 Agreement of the Crowd with Experts

First, we checked to what extent lay annotators and experts agree in terms of Krippendorff's α. On one hand, we compared the mean of all 10 crowd ratings to the mean of the three ratings of Wachsmuth et al. (2017a). On the other hand, we estimated a reliable rating from the crowd ratings using MACE (Hovy et al., 2013) and compared it to the experts.

---

[3]While the differences seem not very large, this is expected, as in many argument pairs from Habernal and Gurevych (2016a) both arguments are strong or weak respectively.

Quality Dimension		(a) Crowd / Expert Mean	MACE	(b) Crowd 1 / 2 / Expert Mean	MACE	(c) Crowd 1 / Expert Mean	MACE	(d) Crowd 2 / Expert Mean	MACE
Cog	**Cogency**	.27	.38	.24	.29	.38	.37	.05	.27
LA	Local acceptability	.49	.35	.37	.27	.49	.33	.30	.25
LR	Local relevance	.42	.39	.33	.28	.41	.39	.26	.25
LS	Local sufficiency	.18	.31	.21	.21	.34	.27	−.04	.19
Eff	**Effectiveness**	.13	.31	.19	.20	.27	.28	−.06	.20
Cre	Credibility	.41	.27	.31	.20	.43	.23	.22	.19
Emo	Emotional appeal	.45	.23	.32	.13	.41	.20	.25	.10
Cla	Clarity	.42	.28	.33	.23	.39	.27	.29	.20
App	Appropriateness	**.54**	.26	**.40**	.20	.48	.24	**.43**	.17
Arr	Arrangement	.53	.30	.36	.24	.49	.27	.35	.24
Rea	**Reasonableness**	.33	.40	.27	.31	.42	**.40**	.09	.29
GA	Global acceptability	**.54**	.40	.36	.29	**.53**	.37	.33	.28
GR	Global relevance	.44	.31	.31	.20	.50	.29	.22	.18
GS	Global sufficiency	−.17	.19	.04	.11	.00	.16	−.27	.11
OQ	**Overall quality**	.43	**.43**	.38	**.33**	.43	**.40**	.28	**.33**

Table 5: Mean and MACE Krippendorff's α agreement between (a) the crowd and the experts, (b) two independent crowd groups and the experts, (c) group 1 and the experts, and (d) group 2 and the experts.

Table 5(a) presents the results. For the mean ratings, most α-values are above .40. This is similar to the study of Wachsmuth et al. (2017b), where a range of .27 to .51 is reported, meaning that lay annotators achieve similar agreement to experts. Considering the minimum of mean and MACE, we observe the highest agreement for *overall quality* (.43)—analog to Wachsmuth et al. (2017b). Also, *global sufficiency* has the lowest agreement in both cases. In contrast, the experts hardly said "cannot judge" at all, whereas the crowd chose it for about 4% of all ratings (most often for global sufficiency), possibly due to a lack of training. Still, we conclude that the crowd generally handles the theory-based quality assessment almost as well as the experts.

However, the complexity of the assessment is underlined by the generally limited agreement, suggesting that either simplification or stricter guidelines are needed. Regarding simplification, the most common practical reasons of Habernal and Gurevych (2016a) imply what to focus on.

4.3 Reliability of the Crowd Annotations

In the second comparison, we checked how many crowd annotators are needed to compete with the experts. For this purpose, we split the crowd ratings into two independent groups of 5 and treated the mean and MACE of each group as a single rating. We then computed the agreement of both groups and each group individually against the experts.

The α-values for both groups are listed in Table 5(b). On average, they are a bit lower than those of all 10 crowd annotators in Table 5(a). Hence, five crowd ratings per argument seem not enough for sufficient reliability. Tables 5(c) and 5(d) reveal the reason behind, namely, the results of crowd group 1 and group 2 differ clearly. At the same time, the values in Table 5(c) are close to those in Table 5(a), so 10 ratings might suffice. Moreover, we see that the most stable α-values in Table 5 are given for *overall quality*, indicating that the theory indeed helps assessing quality reliably.

5 Conclusion

This paper demonstrates that the theory and practice of assessing argumentation quality can learn from each other. Most reasons for quality differences phrased in practice seem well-represented in the normative view of theory and correlate with absolute quality ratings. In our study, lay annotators had similar agreement on the ratings as experts. Considering that some common reasons are quite vague, the diverse and comprehensive theoretical view of argumentation quality may guide a more insightful assessment. On the other hand, some quality dimensions remain hard to assess and/or to separate in practice, resulting in limited agreement. Simplifying theory along the most important reasons will thus improve its practical applicability.

Acknowledgments

We thank Vinodkumar Prabhakaran and Yonatan Bilu for their ongoing participation in our research on argumentation quality. Also, we acknowledge financial support of the DFG (ArguAna, AIPHES), the Natural Sciences and Engineering Research Council of Canada, and the Volkswagen Foundation (Lichtenberg-Professorship Program).

References

Jens Allwood. 2016. Argumentation, activity and culture. In *6th International Conference on Computational Models of Argument (COMMA 16)*. Potsdam, Germany, page 3.

Aristotle. 2007. *On Rhetoric: A Theory of Civic Discourse* (George A. Kennedy, translator). Clarendon Aristotle series. Oxford University Press.

Beata Beigman Klebanov, Christian Stab, Jill Burstein, Yi Song, Binod Gyawali, and Iryna Gurevych. 2016. Argumentation: Content, structure, and relationship with essay quality. In *Proceedings of the Third Workshop on Argument Mining (ArgMining2016)*. Association for Computational Linguistics, pages 70–75. https://doi.org/10.18653/v1/W16-2808.

Maarten Boudry, Fabio Paglieri, and Massimo Pigliucci. 2015. The fake, the flimsy, and the fallacious: Demarcating arguments in real life. *Argumentation* 29(4):431–456.

Elena Cabrio and Serena Villata. 2012. Combining textual entailment and argumentation theory for supporting online debates interactions. In *Proceedings of the 50th Annual Meeting of the Association for Computational Linguistics (Volume 2: Short Papers)*. Association for Computational Linguistics, pages 208–212. http://aclweb.org/anthology/P12-2041.

T. Edward Damer. 2009. *Attacking Faulty Reasoning: A Practical Guide to Fallacy-Free Arguments*. Wadsworth, Cengage Learning, 6th edition.

Trudy Govier. 2010. *A Practical Study of Argument*. Wadsworth, Cengage Learning, 7th edition.

Ivan Habernal and Iryna Gurevych. 2016a. What makes a convincing argument? Empirical analysis and detecting attributes of convincingness in web argumentation. In *Proceedings of the 2016 Conference on Empirical Methods in Natural Language Processing*. Association for Computational Linguistics, pages 1214–1223. http://aclweb.org/anthology/D16-1129.

Ivan Habernal and Iryna Gurevych. 2016b. Which argument is more convincing? Analyzing and predicting convincingness of web arguments using bidirectional lstm. In *Proceedings of the 54th Annual Meeting of the Association for Computational Linguistics (Volume 1: Long Papers)*. Association for Computational Linguistics, pages 1589–1599. https://doi.org/10.18653/v1/P16-1150.

Dirk Hovy, Taylor Berg-Kirkpatrick, Ashish Vaswani, and Eduard Hovy. 2013. Learning whom to trust with MACE. In *Proceedings of the 2013 Conference of the North American Chapter of the Association for Computational Linguistics: Human Language Technologies*. Association for Computational Linguistics, pages 1120–1130. http://aclweb.org/anthology/N13-1132.

Ralph H. Johnson and J. Anthony Blair. 2006. *Logical Self-defense*. Intern. Debate Education Association.

Chaïm Perelman and Lucie Olbrechts-Tyteca. 1969. *The New Rhetoric: A Treatise on Argumentation* (John Wilkinson and Purcell Weaver, translator). University of Notre Dame Press.

Isaac Persing and Vincent Ng. 2015. Modeling argument strength in student essays. In *Proceedings of the 53rd Annual Meeting of the Association for Computational Linguistics and the 7th International Joint Conference on Natural Language Processing (Volume 1: Long Papers)*. Association for Computational Linguistics, pages 543–552. https://doi.org/10.3115/v1/P15-1053.

Ruty Rinott, Lena Dankin, Carlos Alzate Perez, M. Mitesh Khapra, Ehud Aharoni, and Noam Slonim. 2015. Show me your evidence — An automatic method for context dependent evidence detection. In *Proceedings of the 2015 Conference on Empirical Methods in Natural Language Processing*. Association for Computational Linguistics, pages 440–450. https://doi.org/10.18653/v1/D15-1050.

Christopher W. Tindale. 2007. *Fallacies and Argument Appraisal. Critical Reasoning and Argumentation*. Cambridge University Press.

Stephen E. Toulmin. 1958. *The Uses of Argument*. Cambridge University Press.

Frans H. van Eemeren and Rob Grootendorst. 2004. *A Systematic Theory of Argumentation: The Pragma-Dialectical Approach*. Cambridge University Press.

Henning Wachsmuth, Nona Naderi, Yufang Hou, Yonatan Bilu, Vinodkumar Prabhakaran, Alberdingk Tim Thijm, Graeme Hirst, and Benno Stein. 2017a. Computational argumentation quality assessment in natural language. In *Proceedings of the 15th Conference of the European Chapter of the Association for Computational Linguistics: Volume 1, Long Papers*. Association for Computational Linguistics, pages 176–187. http://aclweb.org/anthology/E17-1017.

Henning Wachsmuth, Benno Stein, and Yamen Ajjour. 2017b. "PageRank" for argument relevance. In *Proceedings of the 15th Conference of the European Chapter of the Association for Computational Linguistics: Volume 1, Long Papers*. Association for Computational Linguistics, pages 1117–1127. http://aclweb.org/anthology/E17-1105.

Douglas Walton, Christopher Reed, and Fabrizio Macagno. 2008. *Argumentation Schemes*. Cambridge University Press.

Zhongyu Wei, Yang Liu, and Yi Li. 2016. Is this post persuasive? Ranking argumentative comments in online forum. In *Proceedings of the 54th Annual Meeting of the Association for Computational Linguistics (Volume 2: Short Papers)*. Association for Computational Linguistics, pages 195–200. https://doi.org/10.18653/v1/P16-2032.

A Recurrent Neural Model with Attention for the Recognition of Chinese Implicit Discourse Relations

Samuel Rönnqvist[1,2,*], **Niko Schenk**[2,*] and **Christian Chiarcos**[2]

[1]Turku Centre for Computer Science – TUCS, Åbo Akademi University, Turku, Finland
[2]Applied Computational Linguistics Lab, Goethe University, Frankfurt am Main, Germany
`sronnqvi@abo.fi`
`{schenk,chiarcos}@informatik.uni-frankfurt.de`

Abstract

We introduce an attention-based Bi-LSTM for Chinese implicit discourse relations and demonstrate that modeling argument pairs as a joint sequence can outperform word order-agnostic approaches. Our model benefits from a partial sampling scheme and is conceptually simple, yet achieves state-of-the-art performance on the Chinese Discourse Treebank. We also visualize its attention activity to illustrate the model's ability to selectively focus on the relevant parts of an input sequence.

1 Introduction

True text understanding is one of the key goals in Natural Language Processing and requires capabilities beyond the lexical semantics of individual words or phrases. Natural language descriptions are typically driven by an inter-sentential coherent structure, exhibiting specific *discourse* properties, which in turn contribute significantly to the global meaning of a text. Automatically detecting how meaning units are organized benefits practical downstream applications, such as question answering (Sun and Chai, 2007), recognizing textual entailment (Hickl, 2008), sentiment analysis (Trivedi and Eisenstein, 2013), or text summarization (Hirao et al., 2013).

Various formalisms in terms of semantic coherence frameworks have been proposed to account for these contextual assumptions (Mann and Thompson, 1988; Lascarides and Asher, 1993; Webber, 2004). The annotation schemata of the Penn Discourse Treebank (Prasad et al., 2008, PDTB) and the Chinese Discourse Treebank (Zhou and Xue, 2012, CDTB), for instance, define

discourse units as syntactically motivated character spans in the text, augmented with relations pointing from the second argument (*Arg2*, prototypically, a discourse unit associated with an explicit discourse marker) to its antecedent, i.e., the discourse unit *Arg1*. Relations are labeled with a relation type (its sense) and the associated discourse marker. Both, PDTB and CDTB, distinguish *explicit* from *implicit* relations depending on the presence of such a marker (e.g., *because*/ 因).[1] Sense classification for implicit relations is by far more challenging because the argument pairs lack the marker as an important feature. Consider, for instance, the following example from the CDTB as implicit CONJUNCTION:

> ***Arg1***: 会谈就一些原则和具体问题进行了深入讨论，达成了一些谅解 *In the talks, they discussed some principles and specific questions in depth, and reached some understandings*
>
> ***Arg2***: 双方一致认为会谈具有积极成果 *Both sides agree that the talks have positive results*

Motivation: Previous work on implicit sense labeling is heavily feature-rich and requires domain-specific, semantic lexicons (Pitler et al., 2009; Feng and Hirst, 2012; Huang and Chen, 2011). Only recently, resource-lean architectures have been proposed. These promising neural methods attempt to infer latent representations appropriate for implicit relation classification (Zhang et al., 2015; Ji et al., 2016; Chen et al., 2016). So far, unfortunately, these models have been evaluated *only* on four top-level senses—sometimes even with inconsistent evaluation setups.[2] Furthermore, most systems have initially been designed for the English PDTB and involve complex, task-

---

[1]The set of relation types and senses is completed by alternative lexicalizations (ALTLEX/discourse marker rephrased), and entity relations (ENTREL/anaphoric coherence).

[2]E.g., four binary classifiers vs. four-way classification.

Proceedings of the 55th Annual Meeting of the Association for Computational Linguistics (Short Papers), pages 256–262
Vancouver, Canada, July 30 - August 4, 2017. ©2017 Association for Computational Linguistics
https://doi.org/10.18653/v1/P17-2040

---

*Both first authors contributed equally to this work.

specific architectures (Liu and Li, 2016), while discourse modeling techniques for Chinese have received very little attention in the literature and are still seriously underrepresented in terms of publicly available systems. What is more, over 80% of all words in Chinese discourse relations are implicit—compared to only 52% in English (Zhou and Xue, 2012).

Recently, in the context of the CoNLL 2016 shared task (Xue et al., 2016), a first independent evaluation platform beyond class level has been established. Surprisingly, the best performing neural architectures to date are standard *feedforward* networks, cf. Wang and Lan (2016); Schenk et al. (2016); Qin et al. (2016). Even though these specific models completely ignore word order within arguments, such feedforward architectures have been claimed by Rutherford et al. (2016) to generally outperform any thoroughly-tuned recurrent architecture.

Our Contribution: In this work, we release the first attention-based *recurrent* neural sense classifier, specifically developed for Chinese implicit discourse relations. Inspired by Zhou et al. (2016), our system is a practical adaptation of the recent advances in relation modeling extended by a novel sampling scheme.

Contrary to previous assertions by Rutherford et al. (2016), our model demonstrates superior performance over traditional bag-of-words approaches with feedfoward networks by treating discourse arguments as a joint sequence. We evaluate our method within an independent framework and show that it performs very well beyond standard class-level predictions, achieving state-of-the-art accuracy on the CDTB test set.

We illustrate how our model's attention mechanism provides means to highlight those parts of an input sequence that are relevant for the classification decision, and thus, it may enable a better understanding of the implicit discourse parsing problem. Our proposed network architecture is flexible and largely language-independent as it operates only on word embeddings. It stands out due to its structural simplicity and builds a solid ground for further development towards other textual domains.

2 Approach

We propose the use of an attention-based bidirectional Long Short-Term Memory (Hochreiter

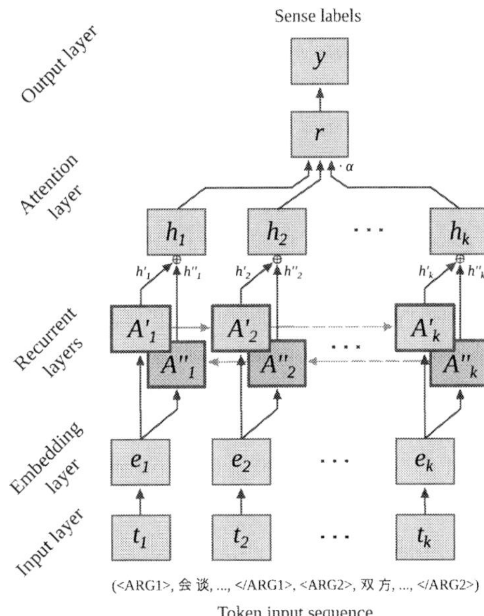

Figure 1: The attention-based bidirectional LSTM network for the task of modeling argument pairs for Chinese implicit discourse relations.

and Schmidhuber, 1997, LSTM) network to predict senses of discourse relations. The model draws upon previous work on LSTM, in particular its bidirectional mode of operation (Graves and Schmidhuber, 2005), attention mechanisms for recurrent models (Bahdanau et al., 2014; Hermann et al., 2015), and the combined use of these techniques for entity relation recognition in annotated sequences (Zhou et al., 2016). More specifically, our model is a flexible recurrent neural network with capabilities to *sequentially* inspect tokens and to highlight which parts of the input sequence are most informative for the discourse relation recognition task, using the weighting provided by the attention mechanism. Furthermore, the model benefits from a novel sampling scheme for arguments, as elaborated below. The system is learned in an end-to-end manner and consists of multiple layers, which are illustrated in Figure 1.

First, token sequences are taken as input and special markers (<ARG1>, </ARG1>, etc.) are inserted into the corresponding positions to inform the model on the start and end points of argument spans. This way, we can ensure a general flexibility in modeling discourse units and could easily extend them with additional context, for instance. In our experiments on implicit arguments, only the tokens in the respective spans are considered. Note that, unlike previous works, our approach models *Arg1-Arg2* pairs as a *joint* sequence and does not first compute intermediate representations of arguments separately.

Second, an input layer encodes tokens using one-hot vector representations (t_i for tokens at positions $i \in [1, k]$), and a subsequent embedding layer provides a dense representation (e_i) to serve as input for the recurrent layers. The embedding layer is initialized using pre-trained word vectors, in our case 300-dimensional Chinese Gigaword vectors (Graff and Chen, 2005).[3] These embeddings are further tuned as the network is trained towards the prediction task. Embeddings for unknown tokens, e.g., markers, are trained by back-propagation only. Note that, tokens, markers and the pre-trained vectors represent the only source of information for the prediction task.

For the recurrent setup, we use a layer of LSTM networks in a bidirectional manner, in order to better capture dependencies between parts of the input sequence by inspection of both left and right-hand-side contexts at each time step. The LSTM holds a state representation as a continuous vector passed to the subsequent time step, and it is capable of modeling long-range dependencies due to its gated memory. The forward (A') and backward (A'') LSTMs traverse the sequence e_i, producing sequences of vectors h_i' and h_i'' respectively, which are then summed together (indicated by $\oplus$ in Figure 1).

The resulting sequence of vectors h_i is reduced into a single vector and fed to the final softmax output layer in order to classify the sense label y of the discourse relation. This vector may be obtained either as the final vector h produced by an LSTM, or through pooling of all h_i, or by using attention, i.e., as a weighted sum over h_i. While the model may be somewhat more difficult to optimize using attention, it provides the added benefit of interpretability, as the weights highlight to what extent the classifier considers the LSTM state vectors at each token during modeling. This is particularly interesting for discourse parsing, as most previous approaches have provided little support for pinpointing the driving features in each argument span.

Finally, the attention layer contains the trainable

vector w (of the same dimensionality as vectors h_i) which is used to dynamically produce a weight vector α over time steps i by:

$$\alpha = softmax(w^T tanh(H))$$

where H is a matrix consisting of vectors h_i. The output layer r is the weighted sum of vectors in H:

$$r = H\alpha^T$$

Partial Argument Sampling: For the purpose of enlarging the instance space of training items in the CDTB, and thus, in order to improve the predictive performance of the model, we propose a novel *partial sampling* scheme of arguments, whereby the model is trained and validated on sequences containing both arguments, as well as *single* arguments. A data point (a_1, a_2, y), with a_i being the token sequence of argument i, is expanded into $\{(a_1, a_2, y), (a_1, a_2, y), (a_1, y), (a_2, y)\}$. We duplicate bi-argument samples (a_1, a_2, y) (in training and development data only) to balance their frequencies against single-argument samples.

Two lines of motivation support the inclusion of single argument training examples, grounded in linguistics and machine learning, respectively. First, it has been shown that single arguments in isolation can evoke a strong expectation towards a certain implicit discourse relation, cf. Asr and Demberg (2015) and, in particular, Rohde and Horton (2010) in their psycholinguistic study on *implicit causality verbs*. Second, the procedure may encourage the model to learn better representations of individual argument spans in support of modeling of arguments in composition, cf. LeCun et al. (2015). Due to these aspects, we believe this data augmentation technique to be effective in reinforcing the overall robustness of our model.

Implementational Details: We train the model using fixed-length sequences of 256 tokens with zero padding at the beginning of shorter sequences and truncate longer ones. Each LSTM has a vector dimensionality of 300, matching the embedding size. The model is regularized by 0.5 dropout rate between the layers and weight decay ($2.5e^{-6}$) on the LSTM inputs. We employ Adam optimization (Kingma and Ba, 2014) using the cross-entropy loss function with mini batch size of 80.[4]

---

[3] http://www.cs.brandeis.edu/~clp/conll16st/dataset.html

[4] The model is implemented in *Keras* https://keras.io/.

CDTB Development Set			CDTB Test Set		
Rank	System	% accuracy	Rank	System	% accuracy
1	Wang and Lan (2016)	73.53	1	Wang and Lan (2016)	72.42
2	Qin et al. (2016)	71.57	2	Schenk et al. (2016)	71.87
3	Schenk et al. (2016)	70.59	3	Rutherford and Xue (2016)	70.47
4	Rutherford and Xue (2016)	68.30	4	Qin et al. (2016)	67.41
5	Weiss and Bajec (2016)	66.67	5	Weiss and Bajec (2016)	64.07
6	Weiss and Bajec (2016)	61.44	6	Weiss and Bajec (2016)	63.51
7	Jian et al. (2016)	21.90	7	Jian et al. (2016)	21.73
	This Paper:	**93.52**[*]		**This Paper:**	**73.01**

Table 1: Non-explicit parser scores on the official CoNLL 2016 CDTB development and test sets. ([*]Scores on development set are obtained through partial sampling and are not directly comparable.)

Sense Label	Training	Dev't	Test
CONJUNCTION	5,174	189	228
majority class	(66.3%)	(62.8%)	(64.8%)
EXPANSION	1,188	48	40
ENTREL	1,099	50	71
CAUSATION	187	10	8
CONTRAST	66	3	1
PURPOSE	56	1	3
CONDITIONAL	26	0	1
TEMPORAL	26	0	0
PROGRESSION	7	0	0
# impl. rels	7,804	301	352

Table 2: Implicit sense labels in the CDTB.

3 Evaluation

We evaluate our recurrent model on the CoNLL 2016 shared task data[5] which include the official training, development and test sets of the CDTB; cf. Table 2 for an overview of the implicit sense distribution.[6]

In accordance with previous setups (Rutherford et al., 2016), we treat entity relations (ENTREL) as implicit and exclude ALTLEX relations. In the evaluation, we focus on the *sense-only* track, the subtask for which gold arguments are provided and a system is supposed to label a given argument pair with the correct sense. The results are shown in Table 1.

With our proposed architecture it is possible to correctly label 257/352 (73.01%) of implicit rela-

tions on the test set, outperforming the best feed-forward system of Wang and Lan (2016) and all other word order-agnostic approaches. Development and test set performances suggest the robustness of our approach and its ability to generalize to unseen data.

Ablation Study: We perform an ablation study to quantitatively assess the contribution of two of the characteristic aspects of our model. First, we compare the use of the attention mechanism against the simpler alternative of feeding the final LSTM hidden vectors (h'_k and h''_1) directly to the output layer. When attention is turned off, this yields an absolute decrease in performance of 2.70% on the test set, which is substantial and significant according to a Welch two-sample t-test ($p < .001$). Second, we independently compare the use of the partial sampling scheme against training on the standard argument pairs in the CDTB. Here, the absence of the partial sampling scheme yields an absolute decrease in accuracy of 5.74% ($p < .001$), which demonstrates its importance for achieving competitive performance on the task.

Performance on the PDTB: As a side experiment, we investigate the model's language independence by applying it to the implicit argument pairs of the English PDTB. Due to computational time constraints we do not optimize hyperparameters, but instead train the model using identical settings as for Chinese, which is expected to lead to suboptimal performance on the evaluation data. Nevertheless, we measure 27.09% accuracy on the PDTB test set (surpassing the majority class baseline of 22.01%), which shows that the model has potential to generalize across implicit discourse relations in a different language.

---

[5]http://www.cs.brandeis.edu/~clp/conll16st/

[6]Note that, in the CDTB, implicit relations appear almost *three times more often* than explicit relations. Out of these, 65% appear within the same sentence. Finally, 25 relations in the training set have two labels.

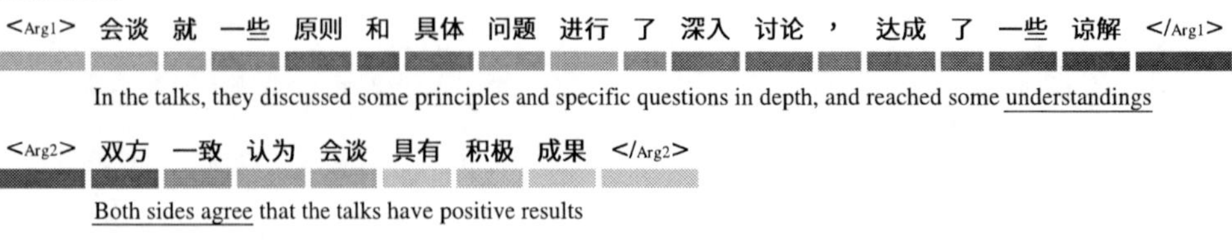

Figure 2: Visualization of attention weights for Chinese characters with high (dark blue) and low (light blue) intensities. The underlined English phrases are semantically structure-shared by the two arguments.

Visualizing Attention Weights: Finally, in Figure 2, we illustrate the learned attention weights which pinpoint important subcomponents within a given implicit discourse relation. For the implicit CONJUNCTION relation the weights indicate a peak on the transition between the argument boundary, establishing a connection between the semantically related terms *understandings–agree*. Most ENTRELs show an opposite trend: here second arguments exhibit larger intensities than *Arg1*, as most entity relations follow the characteristic writing style of newspapers by adding additional information by reference to the same entity.

4 Summary & Outlook

In this work, we have presented the first attention-based recurrent neural sense labeler specifically developed for Chinese implicit discourse relations. Its ability to model discourse units sequentially and jointly has been shown to be highly beneficial, both in terms of state-of-the-art performance on the CDTB (outperforming word order-agnostic feedforward approaches), and also in terms of insightful observations into the inner workings of the model through its attention mechanism. The architecture is structurally simple, benefits from partial argument sampling, and can be eas-ily adapted to similar relation recognition tasks. In future work, we intend to extend our approach to different languages and domains, e.g., to the recent data sets on narrative story understanding or question answering (Mostafazadeh et al., 2016; Feng et al., 2015). We believe that recurrent modeling of implicit discourse information can be a driving force in successfully handling such complex semantic processing tasks.[7]

Acknowledgments

The authors would like to thank Ayah Zirikly, Philip Schulz and Wei Ding for their very helpful suggestions on an early draft version of the paper, and also thank the anonymous reviewers for their valuable feedback and insightful comments. We are grateful to Farrokh Mehryary for technical support with the attention layer implementation. Computational resources were provided by CSC – IT Centre for Science, Finland, and Arcada University of Applied Sciences, Helsinki, Finland. Our research at Goethe University Frankfurt was supported by the project 'Linked Open Dictionaries (LiODi, 2015-2020)', funded by the German Ministry for Education and Research (BMBF).

[7]The code involved in this study is publicly available at http://www.acoli.informatik.uni-frankfurt.de/resources/.

References

Fatemeh Torabi Asr and Vera Demberg. 2015. Uniform Information Density at the Level of Discourse Relations: Negation Markers and Discourse Connective Omission. In *11th International Conference on Computational Semantics (IWCS)*. page 118. http://www.coli.uni-saarland.de/ fatemeh/iwcs2015.pdf.

Dzmitry Bahdanau, Kyunghyun Cho, and Yoshua Bengio. 2014. Neural Machine Translation by Jointly Learning to Align and Translate. *CoRR* abs/1409.0473. http://arxiv.org/abs/1409.0473.

Jifan Chen, Qi Zhang, Pengfei Liu, Xipeng Qiu, and Xuanjing Huang. 2016. Implicit Discourse Relation Detection via a Deep Architecture with Gated Relevance Network. In *Proceedings of the 54th Annual Meeting of the Association for Computational Linguistics, ACL 2016, August 7-12, 2016, Berlin, Germany, Volume 1: Long Papers*. http://aclweb.org/anthology/P/P16/P16-1163.pdf.

Minwei Feng, Bing Xiang, Michael R. Glass, Lidan Wang, and Bowen Zhou. 2015. Applying deep learning to answer selection: A study and an open task. In *2015 IEEE Workshop on Automatic Speech Recognition and Understanding, ASRU 2015, Scottsdale, AZ, USA, December 13-17, 2015*. pages 813–820. https://doi.org/10.1109/ASRU.2015.7404872.

Vanessa Wei Feng and Graeme Hirst. 2012. Text-level Discourse Parsing with Rich Linguistic Features. In *Proceedings of the 50th Annual Meeting of the Association for Computational Linguistics: Long Papers - Volume 1*. Association for Computational Linguistics, Stroudsburg, PA, USA, ACL '12, pages 60–68. http://www.aclweb.org/anthology/P12-1007.

David Graff and Ke Chen. 2005. Chinese Gigaword. LDC Catalog No.: LDC2003T09, ISBN, 1:58563-58230.

Alex Graves and Jürgen Schmidhuber. 2005. Framewise phoneme classification with bidirectional LSTM and other neural network architectures. *Neural Networks* 18(5-6):602–610. https://doi.org/10.1016/j.neunet.2005.06.042.

Karl Moritz Hermann, Tomas Kocisky, Edward Grefenstette, Lasse Espeholt, Will Kay, Mustafa Suleyman, and Phil Blunsom. 2015. Teaching machines to read and comprehend. In *Advances in Neural Information Processing Systems*. pages 1693–1701.

Andrew Hickl. 2008. Using Discourse Commitments to Recognize Textual Entailment. In *Proceedings of the 22nd International Conference on Computational Linguistics - Volume 1*. Association for Computational Linguistics, Stroudsburg, PA, USA, COLING '08, pages 337–344. http://dl.acm.org/citation.cfm?id=1599081.1599124.

Tsutomu Hirao, Yasuhisa Yoshida, Masaaki Nishino, Norihito Yasuda, and Masaaki Nagata. 2013. Single-Document Summarization as a Tree Knapsack Problem. In *Proceedings of the 2013 Conference on Empirical Methods in Natural Language Processing, EMNLP 2013, 18-21 October 2013, Grand Hyatt Seattle, Seattle, Washington, USA, A meeting of SIGDAT, a Special Interest Group of the ACL*. pages 1515–1520. http://aclweb.org/anthology/D/D13/D13-1158.pdf.

Sepp Hochreiter and Jürgen Schmidhuber. 1997. Long Short-Term Memory. *Neural Comput.* 9(8):1735–1780. https://doi.org/10.1162/neco.1997.9.8.1735.

Hen-Hsen Huang and Hsin-Hsi Chen. 2011. Chinese Discourse Relation Recognition. In *Proceedings of 5th International Joint Conference on Natural Language Processing*. Asian Federation of Natural Language Processing, Chiang Mai, Thailand, pages 1442–1446. http://www.aclweb.org/anthology/I11-1170.

Yangfeng Ji, Gholamreza Haffari, and Jacob Eisenstein. 2016. A Latent Variable Recurrent Neural Network for Discourse-Driven Language Models. In *Proceedings of the 2016 Conference of the North American Chapter of the Association for Computational Linguistics: Human Language Technologies*. Association for Computational Linguistics, San Diego, California, pages 332–342. http://www.aclweb.org/anthology/N16-1037.

Ping Jian, Xiaohan She, Chenwei Zhang, Pengcheng Zhang, and Jian Feng. 2016. Discourse Relation Sense Classification Systems for CoNLL-2016 Shared Task. In *Proceedings of the CoNLL-16 shared task*. Association for Computational Linguistics, pages 158–163. https://doi.org/10.18653/v1/K16-2022.

Diederik P. Kingma and Jimmy Ba. 2014. Adam: A method for stochastic optimization. *CoRR* abs/1412.6980. http://arxiv.org/abs/1412.6980.

Alex Lascarides and Nicholas Asher. 1993. Temporal Interpretation, Discourse Relations and Commonsense entailment. *Linguistics and Philosophy* 16(5):437–493.

Yann LeCun, Yoshua Bengio, and Geoffrey Hinton. 2015. Deep learning. *Nature* 521(7553):436–444.

Yang Liu and Sujian Li. 2016. Recognizing Implicit Discourse Relations via Repeated Reading: Neural Networks with Multi-Level Attention. In *Proceedings of the 2016 Conference on Empirical Methods in Natural Language Processing, EMNLP 2016, Austin, Texas, USA, November 1-4, 2016*. pages 1224–1233. http://aclweb.org/anthology/D/D16/D16-1130.pdf.

William C. Mann and Sandra A. Thompson. 1988. Rhetorical structure theory: Toward a functional theory of text organization. *Text* 8(3):243–281.

Nasrin Mostafazadeh, Nathanael Chambers, Xiaodong He, Devi Parikh, Dhruv Batra, Lucy Vanderwende, Pushmeet Kohli, and James Allen. 2016. A Corpus and Cloze Evaluation for Deeper Understanding of Commonsense Stories. In *Proceedings of the 2016 Conference of the North American Chapter of the Association for Computational Linguistics: Human Language Technologies*. Association for Computational Linguistics, San Diego, California, pages 839–849. http://www.aclweb.org/anthology/N16-1098.

Emily Pitler, Annie Louis, and Ani Nenkova. 2009. Automatic Sense Prediction for Implicit Discourse Relations in Text. In *Proceedings of the Joint Conference of the 47th Annual Meeting of the ACL and the 4th International Joint Conference on Natural Language Processing of the AFNLP: Volume 2 - Volume 2*. Association for Computational Linguistics, Stroudsburg, PA, USA, ACL 2009, pages 683–691. http://www.aclweb.org/anthology/P09/P09-1077.pdf.

Rashmi Prasad, Nikhil Dinesh, Alan Lee, Eleni Miltsakaki, Livio Robaldo, Aravind Joshi, and Bonnie Webber. 2008. The Penn Discourse TreeBank 2.0. In *Proceedings, 6th International Conference on Language Resources and Evaluation*. Marrakech, Morocco, pages 2961–2968.

Lianhui Qin, Zhisong Zhang, and Hai Zhao. 2016. Shallow Discourse Parsing Using Convolutional Neural Network. In *Proceedings of the CoNLL-16 shared task*. Association for Computational Linguistics, pages 70–77. https://doi.org/10.18653/v1/K16-2010.

Hannah Rohde and William Horton. 2010. Why or what next? Eye movements reveal expectations about discourse direction. Talk at the 23rd Annual CUNY Conference on Human Sentence Processing. New York, NY.

Attapol Rutherford and Nianwen Xue. 2016. Robust Non-Explicit Neural Discourse Parser in English and Chinese. In *Proceedings of the CoNLL-16 shared task*. Association for Computational Linguistics, pages 55–59. https://doi.org/10.18653/v1/K16-2007.

Attapol T. Rutherford, Vera Demberg, and Nianwen Xue. 2016. Neural Network Models for Implicit Discourse Relation Classification in English and Chinese without Surface Features. *CoRR* abs/1606.01990. http://arxiv.org/abs/1606.01990.

Niko Schenk, Christian Chiarcos, Kathrin Donandt, Samuel Rönnqvist, Evgeny Stepanov, and Giuseppe Riccardi. 2016. Do We Really Need All Those Rich Linguistic Features? A Neural Network-Based Approach to Implicit Sense Labeling. In *Proceedings of the CoNLL-16 shared task*. Association for Computational Linguistics, pages 41–49. https://doi.org/10.18653/v1/K16-2005.

Mingyu Sun and Joyce Y Chai. 2007. Discourse processing for context question answering based on linguistic knowledge. *Knowledge-Based Systems* 20(6):511–526.

Rakshit S. Trivedi and Jacob Eisenstein. 2013. Discourse connectors for latent subjectivity in sentiment analysis. In *Human Language Technologies: Conference of the North American Chapter of the Association of Computational Linguistics, Proceedings, June 9-14, 2013, Westin Peachtree Plaza Hotel, Atlanta, Georgia, USA*. pages 808–813. http://aclweb.org/anthology/N/N13/N13-1100.pdf.

Jianxiang Wang and Man Lan. 2016. Two End-to-end Shallow Discourse Parsers for English and Chinese in CoNLL-2016 Shared Task. In *Proceedings of the CoNLL-16 shared task*. Association for Computational Linguistics, pages 33–40. https://doi.org/10.18653/v1/K16-2004.

Bonnie L. Webber. 2004. D-LTAG: extending lexicalized TAG to discourse. *Cognitive Science* 28(5):751–779. http://dblp.uni-trier.de/db/journals/cogsci/cogsci28.html.

Gregor Weiss and Marko Bajec. 2016. Discourse Sense Classification from Scratch using Focused RNNs. In *Proceedings of the CoNLL-16 shared task*. Association for Computational Linguistics, pages 50–54. https://doi.org/10.18653/v1/K16-2006.

Nianwen Xue, Hwee Tou Ng, Sameer Pradhan, Bonnie Webber, Attapol Rutherford, Chuan Wang, and Hongmin Wang. 2016. The CoNLL-2016 Shared Task on Shallow Discourse Parsing. In *Proceedings of the Twentieth Conference on Computational Natural Language Learning - Shared Task*. Association for Computational Linguistics, Berlin, Germany.

Biao Zhang, Jinsong Su, Deyi Xiong, Yaojie Lu, Hong Duan, and Junfeng Yao. 2015. Shallow Convolutional Neural Network for Implicit Discourse Relation Recognition. In *Proceedings of the 2015 Conference on Empirical Methods in Natural Language Processing, EMNLP 2015, Lisbon, Portugal, September 17-21, 2015*. pages 2230–2235. http://aclweb.org/anthology/D/D15/D15-1266.pdf.

Peng Zhou, Wei Shi, Jun Tian, Zhenyu Qi, Bingchen Li, Hongwei Hao, and Bo Xu. 2016. Attention-Based Bidirectional Long Short-Term Memory Networks for Relation Classification. In *Proceedings of the 54th Annual Meeting of the Association for Computational Linguistics, ACL 2016, August 7-12, 2016, Berlin, Germany, Volume 2: Short Papers*. http://aclweb.org/anthology/P/P16/P16-2034.pdf.

Yuping Zhou and Nianwen Xue. 2012. PDTB-style Discourse Annotation of Chinese Text. In *Proceedings of the 50th Annual Meeting of the Association for Computational Linguistics (Volume 1: Long Papers)*. Association for Computational Linguistics, Jeju Island, Korea, pages 69–77. http://www.aclweb.org/anthology-new/P/P12/P12-1008.bib.

Discourse Annotation of Non-native Spontaneous Spoken Responses Using the Rhetorical Structure Theory Framework

Xinhao Wang[1], **James V. Bruno**[2], **Hillary R. Molloy**[1], **Keelan Evanini**[2], **Klaus Zechner**[2]

Educational Testing Service

[1]90 New Montgomery St #1500, San Francisco, CA 94105, USA

[2]660 Rosedale Road, Princeton, NJ 08541, USA

`xwang002, jbruno, hmolloy, kevanini, kzechner@ets.org`

Abstract

The availability of the Rhetorical Structure Theory (RST) Discourse Treebank has spurred substantial research into discourse analysis of written texts; however, limited research has been conducted to date on RST annotation and parsing of spoken language, in particular, non-native spontaneous speech. Considering that the measurement of discourse coherence is typically a key metric in human scoring rubrics for assessments of spoken language, we initiated a research effort to obtain RST annotations of a large number of non-native spoken responses from a standardized assessment of academic English proficiency. The resulting inter-annotator κ agreements on the three different levels of Span, Nuclearity, and Relation are 0.848, 0.766, and 0.653, respectively. Furthermore, a set of features was explored to evaluate the discourse structure of non-native spontaneous speech based on these annotations; the highest performing feature showed a correlation of 0.612 with scores of discourse coherence provided by expert human raters.

1 Introduction

The spread of English as the global language of education and commerce is continuing, and there is a strong interest in developing assessment systems that can automatically score spontaneous speech from non-native speakers with the goals of reducing the burden on human raters, improving reliability, and generating feedback that can be used by language learners. Discourse coherence, which refers to the conceptual relations be- tween different units within a response, is an important aspect of communicative competence, as is reflected in human scoring rubrics for assessments of non-native English (ETS, 2012). However, discourse-level features have rarely been investigated in the context of automated speech scoring. This study aims to construct a discourse-level annotation of non-native spontaneous speech in the framework of Rhetorical Structure Theory (RST) (Mann and Thompson, 1988), which can then be used in automated discourse analysis and coherence measurement for non-native spoken responses, thereby improving the validity of the automated scoring systems.

RST is a descriptive framework that has been widely used in the analysis of discourse organization of written texts (Taboada and Mann, 2006b), and has been applied to various natural language processing tasks, including language generation, text summarization, and machine translation (Taboada and Mann, 2006a). In particular, the availability of RST annotations on a selection of 385 Wall Street Journal articles from the Penn Treebank[1] (Carlson et al., 2001) has facilitated RST-based discourse analysis of written texts, since it provides a standard benchmark for comparing the performance of different techniques for document-level discourse parsing (Joty et al., 2013; Feng and Hirst, 2014).

Another important application of RST closely related to our research is the automated evaluation of discourse in student essays. For example, one study used features for each sentence in an essay to reflect the status of its parent node as well as its rhetorical relation based on automatically parsed RST trees with the goal of providing feedback to students about the discourse structure in the essay (Burstein et al., 2003). Another study compared

---

[1]`https://catalog.ldc.upenn.edu/`
`LDC2002T07`

263

Proceedings of the 55th Annual Meeting of the Association for Computational Linguistics (Short Papers), pages 263–268
Vancouver, Canada, July 30 - August 4, 2017. ©2017 Association for Computational Linguistics
https://doi.org/10.18653/v1/P17-2041

features derived from deep hierarchical discourse relations based on RST parsing and features derived from shallow discourse relations based on Penn Discourse Treebank (PDTB) (Prasad et al., 2008) parsing in the task of essay scoring and demonstrated the effectiveness of deep discourse structure in better differentiation of text coherence (Feng et al., 2014).

Related work has also been conducted to annotate discourse relations in spoken language, which is produced and processed differently from written texts (Rehbein et al., 2016), and often lacks explicit discourse connectives that are more frequent in written language. Instead of the rooted-tree structure that is employed in RST, the annotation scheme with shallow discourse structure and relations from the PDTB (Prasad et al., 2008) has been generally used for spoken language (Demirahin and Zeyrek, 2014; Stoyanchev and Bangalore, 2015). For example, Tonelli et al. adapted the PDTB annotation scheme to annotate discourse relations in spontaneous conversations in Italian (Tonelli et al., 2010) and Rehbein et al. compared two frameworks, PDTB and CCR (Cognitive approach to Coherence Relations) (Sanders et al., 1992), for the annotation of discourse relations in spoken language (Rehbein et al., 2016).

In contrast to these previous studies, this study focuses on monologic spoken responses produced by non-native speakers within the context of a language proficiency assessment. A discourse annotation scheme based on the RST framework was selected due to the fact that it can effectively demonstrate the deep hierarchical discourse structure across an entire response, rather than focusing on the local coherence of adjacent units.

2 Data

This study obtained manual RST annotations on a corpus of 600 spoken responses drawn from a large-scale, high-stakes standardized assessment of English for non-native speakers, the TOEFL® Internet-based Test (TOEFL® iBT), which assesses English communication skills for academic purposes (ETS, 2012). The speaking section of the TOEFL iBT assessment contains six tasks, each of which requires the test taker to provide an unscripted spoken response 45 or 60 seconds in duration. The corpus used in this study includes 100 responses from each of six different test questions that comprise two different speaking tasks:

1) Independent questions: providing an opinion based on personal experience (N = 200 responses) and 2) Integrated questions: summarizing or discussing material provided in a reading and/or listening passage (N = 400 responses). The spoken responses were all manually transcribed using standard punctuation and capitalization. The average number of words per response is 104.4 (st. dev. = 34.4) and the average number of sentences is 5.5 (st. dev. = 2.1).

The spoken responses were all provided with holistic English proficiency scores on a scale of 1 to 4 by expert human raters in the context of operational, high-stakes scoring for the spoken language assessment. The scoring rubrics address the following three main aspects of speaking proficiency: delivery (pronunciation, fluency, prosody), language use (grammar and lexical choice), and topic development (content and coherence). In order to ensure a sufficient quantity of responses from each proficiency level, 25 responses were selected randomly from each of the 4 score points for each of the 6 test questions.

The current study builds on a previous study that investigated approaches for modeling discourse coherence in non-native spontaneous speech (but which did not consider the hierarchical rhetorical structure of speech) (Wang et al., 2013). In that study, each spoken response in the same corpus that was used for the current study was provided with global discourse coherence scores. Two expert annotators (not drawn from the pool of expert human raters who provided the holistic scores) provided each response with a score on a scale of 1 to 3 based on the orthographic transcriptions of the spoken response. The three score points were defined as follows: 3 = highly coherent (contains no instances of confusing arguments or examples), 2 = somewhat coherent (contains some awkward points in which the speaker's line of argument is unclear), 1 = barely coherent (the entire response was confusing and hard to follow). In addition, the annotators were specifically required to ignore disfluencies and grammatical errors as much as possible. The inter-annotator agreement for these coherence scores was $\kappa = 0.68$. These discourse coherence scores are reused in the current study (along with the holistic profiency scores presented above) to evaluate the performance of features measuring discourse coherence based on the RST annotations.

3 Annotation

3.1 Guidelines

We used a modified version of the tagging reference manual for the RST Discourse Treebank (Carlson and Marcu, 2001) for this study. According to these guidelines, annotators segment a transcribed spoken response into Elementary Discourse Unit (EDU) spans of text (corresponding to clauses or clause-like units), and indicate rhetorical relations between non-overlapping spans which typically consist of a nucleus (the most essential information in the rhetorical relation) and a satellite (supporting or background information). In contrast to well-formed written text, non-native spontaneous speech frequently contains ungrammatical sentences, disfluencies, fillers, hesitations, false starts, and unfinished utterances. In some cases, these spoken responses do not constitute coherent, well-formed discourse. On the other hand, spoken responses are relatively shorter and comprise simpler discourse structures with fewer relations, which simplifies the RST annotation task in comparison to written text. In order to account for these differences, we created an addendum to the RST Discourse Treebank manual introducing the following additional relations: Disfluency relations (in which the disfluent span is the satellite and the corresponding fluent span is the nucleus), Awkward relations (corresponding to portions of the response where the speaker's discourse structure is infelicitous; awkward relations are based on pre-existing relations, such as *awkward-Reason*, if the intended relation is clear but is expressed incoherently or are labeled as *awkward-Other* if there is no clear relation between the awkward EDU and the surrounding discourse), Unfinished Utterance relations (representing EDUs at the end of a response that are incomplete because the test taker ran out of time in which the incomplete span is the satellite and the root node of the discourse tree is the nucleus), and Discourse Particle relations (such as *you know* and *right*, which are satellites of adjacent spans).

The discourse annotation tool used in the RST Discourse Treebank[2] was also adopted for this study. Using this tool, annotators incrementally build hierarchical discourse trees in which the leaves are the EDUs and the internal nodes correspond to contiguous spans of text. When the annotators assign the rhetorical relation for a node of the tree, they provide the relation's label (drawn from the pre-defined set of relations in the annotation guidelines) and also indicate whether the spans that comprise the relation are nuclei or satellites. Figure 1 shows an example of an annotated RST tree for a response with a proficiency score of 1. This response includes three disfluencies (EDUs 3, 6, and 9), which are satellites of the corresponding repair nuclei. In addition, the response also includes an awkward Comment-Topic relation between EDU 2 and the node combining EDUs 3-11, indicated by *awkward-Comment-Topic-2*; in this multinuclear relation, the annotator judged that the second branch of the relation was awkward, which is indicated by the *2* that was appended to the relation label.

3.2 Pilot Annotation

The manual annotations were provided by two experts with prior experience in various types of data annotation on both text and speech. First, a pilot annotation was conducted to train and calibrate the annotators based on 48 training samples drawn from the TOEFL® Practice Online (TPO) product[3], which offers practice tests simulating the TOEFL iBT testing experience with authentic test questions. The training samples were selected from a TPO test form with 6 test questions and were balanced according to test question and proficiency score, i.e., 2 responses from each score level for each question.

Human annotators were trained in a two-step process: 1) after a comprehensive study of the annotation guidelines described in Section 3.1, the two annotators were initially trained with 16 TPO responses (8 responses from an Independent question and 8 responses from an Integrated question) by first performing independent annotation and then resolving all disagreements through a discussion of the guidelines; 2) another round of training was conducted on an additional set of 32 TPO responses (8 responses from an Independent question and 24 responses from an Integrated question). Each annotator first annotated this set of 32 responses independently; the two annotators subsequently conducted a thorough joint review and discussion of each other's annotations in order to resolve all disagreements on this set.

In order to measure the human agreement on

Figure 1: Example of an annotated RST tree on a response with a proficiency score of 1.

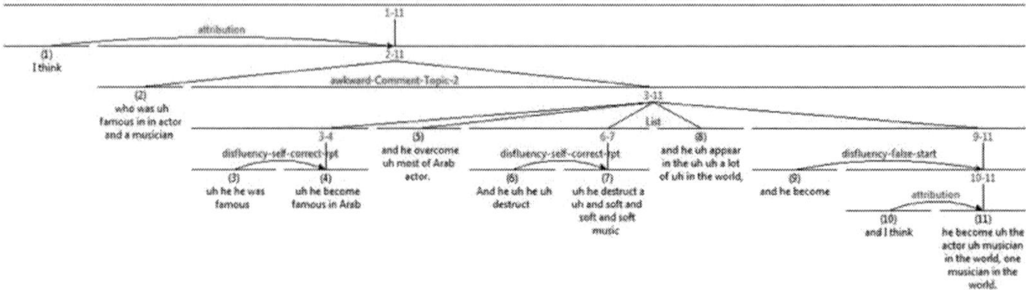

the EDU segmentation task, we first converted the segmentation sequences into 0/1 sequences: for each word in a response, 1 is assigned if a segment boundary exists after the word; otherwise, 0 is assigned. The inter-annotator agreement rate on the EDU segmentations of the 32 pilot samples (from stage 2) was $\kappa = 0.876$. On the hierarchical tree building task, inter-annotator agreement was evaluated on the levels of Span (assignment of discourse segment), Nuclearity (assignment of nucleus vs. satellite), and Relation (assignment of rhetorical relation) using κ, as described in (Marcu et al., 1999); on the 32 samples, the κ values are 0.861, 0.769, and 0.631 for the three levels, respectively.

3.3 Formal Annotation

For the formal annotation on the full set of 600 TOEFL spoken responses, 120 responses from 6 test questions (5 responses from each score level from each question) were selected for double annotation, and the remaining 480 responses received a single annotation.

The 120 double-annotated responses were split into two batches of equal size and the two annotators each performed EDU segmentation independently on one of the batches. Subsequently, the annotators reviewed each other's EDU segmentations and adjudicated all disagreements to obtain gold-standard EDU segmentation for the 120 responses in the double-annotation set. The average number of EDUs per response in the two batches in this set of 120 responses were 15.1 and 14.1. The annotators subsequently performed the remaining steps of RST annotation (assigning the relations, nuclearity, and hierarchical structure) independently on all 120 responses using the adjudicated EDU segmentations. Table 1 shows that the κ agreements on the three levels of Span, Nucle-

Table 1: Human agreement on RST annotations in terms of κ and F1-Measure.

	Span	Nuclearity	Relation
κ	0.848	0.766	0.653
F1-Measure	0.872	0.724	0.522

Table 2: The average number of awkward relations appearing in responses from each of the four proficiency score levels.

	1	2	3	4
Annotator 1	3.2	1.1	1.1	0.3
Annotator 2	2.1	1.2	0.7	0.3

arity, and Relation are 0.848, 0.766, and 0.653, respectively. Besides the κ evaluation, the standard ways of F1-Measure on three levels of Span, Nuclearity, and Relation (Marcu, 2000), commonly used to evaluate the performance of RST parsers, are also reported in Table 1. The F1-measures were calculated according to each pair of trees from two annotators on the same sample and then averaged across all samples, i.e., a macroaveraged F1-measure.

The human agreement results also indicate that two annotators tend to agree better on responses from speakers with higher speaking proficiency levels. This is demonstrated by positive correlations between the F1 agreement scores and the human proficiency ratings: 0.197 for Span annotations, 0.210 for Nuclearity, and 0.188 for Relation.

In addition, we also examined the distribution of the manually identified awkward relations. As shown in Table 2, awkward points occur with higher frequency in responses with lower proficiency scores.

4 Discourse Features

The ultimate aim of this line of research is to use an RST-annotated corpus to investigate features for automatically assessing discourse structure in spontaneous non-native speech. Using the annotated discourse trees, we extracted several different features based on the distribution of relations and the structure of the trees, including the number of EDUs (n_edu), the number of relations (n_rel), the number of awkward relations (n_awk_rel), the number of rhetorical relations, i.e., relations that were neither classified as awkward nor as a disfluency (n_rhe_rel), the number of different types of rhetorical relations (n_rhe_relTypes), the percentage of rhetorical relations (perc_rhe_rel) out of all relations, the depth of the RST trees (tree_depth), and the ratio between n_edu and tree_depth (ratio_nedu_depth). Table 3 lists the Pearson correlation coefficients of these features with both the holistic proficiency scores and the discourse coherence scores and demonstrates the effectiveness of these features. The n_rhe_rel feature achieves the highest correlation of 0.691 with the holistic proficiency scores, and the normalized feature perc_rhe_rel achieves the highest correlation of 0.612 with the discourse coherence scores. It is interesting to note that RST-based discourse features generally have higher correlations with the holistic speaking proficiency scores than with the more specific discourse coherence scores. This result is somewhat unexpected, since the holistic proficiency scores are based only partially on discourse coherence and also cover other aspects of speaking proficiency, such as pronunciation, fluency, grammar, and vocabulary. One potential explanation for the higher correlations could be the difference in score range (1-4 for the holistic proficiency scores and 1-3 for the discourse scores). In addition, as described in Section 2, the data set used in this study was created using a stratified random sample with an even distribution of holistic scores (which may increase the features' correlations with holistic scores), but this constraint does not apply to the discourse coherence scores.

5 Conclusion and Future Work

In this study, we obtained discourse coherence annotations based on Rhetorical Structure Theory for a corpus of 600 non-native spontaneous spoken responses drawn from a standardized assess-

Table 3: Pearson correlation coefficients (r) of discourse features with both the holistic proficiency scores as well as the discourse coherence scores. For the 120 double-annotated responses, the averaged feature values were used.

Features	Proficiency	Coherence
n_edu	0.58	0.397
n_rel	0.584	0.396
n_awk_rel	-0.396	-0.509
n_rhe_rel	0.691	0.541
n_rhe_relTypes	0.64	0.557
perc_rhe_rel	0.589	0.612
tree_depth	0.365	0.25
ratio_nedu_depth	0.529	0.367

ment of non-native English. The RST annotation results show that the annotators achieved similar inter-annotator agreement rates as have been reported in previous studies that investigated well-formed written text (Marcu et al., 1999). In addition, we demonstrate the potential of using features derived from these RST annotations for assessing non-native spoken English through moderately high correlations with both holistic speaking proficiency scores and discourse coherence scores; the highest performing feature when evaluated on the discourse coherence scores provided by expert raters was the percentage of rhetorical relations in the entire spoken response (perc_rhe_rel), with a correlation of 0.612.

In the future, we will continue this work by addressing the following main research questions: a) how can we develop additional effective features from the discourse trees; b) how well can an automatic discourse parser trained on the obtained annotations perform; c) how well will the proposed features perform when extracted using an automatic RST parser; d) how well will the features perform when using an automated speech recognizer (rather than human transcribers) to obtain textual transcriptions of a spoken response.

References

Jill Burstein, Daniel Marcu, and Kevin Knight. 2003. Finding the write stuff: Automatic identification of discourse structure in student essays. *IEEE Intelligent Systems* 18(1):32–39.

Lynn Carlson and Daniel Marcu. 2001. Discourse tagging reference manual. Technical Report ISI-TR-545, ISI Technical Report.

Lynn Carlson, Daniel Marcu, and Mary Ellen Okurows. 2001. Building a discourse-tagged corpus in the framework of rhetorical structure theory. In *2nd SIGDIAL Workshop on Discourse and Dialogue*. Aalborg, Denmark, pages 1–10.

In Demirahin and Deniz Zeyrek. 2014. Annotating discourse connectives in spoken Turkish. In *The 8th Liguistic Annotation Workshop*. Dublin, Ireland, pages 105–109.

ETS. 2012. The official guide to the TOEFL® test. *Fourth Edition, McGraw-Hill* .

Vanessa Wei Feng and Graeme Hirst. 2014. A linear-time bottom-up discourse parser with constraints and post-editing. In *Proceedings of the 52nd Annual Meeting of the Association for Computational Linguistics*. Baltimore, Maryland, pages 511–521.

Vanessa Wei Feng, Ziheng Lin, and Graeme Hirst. 2014. The impact of deep hierarchical discourse structures in the evaluation of text coherence. In *Proceedings of COLING 2014, the 25th International Conference on Computational Linguistics: Technical Papers*. Dublin, Ireland, pages 940–949.

Shafiq Joty, Giuseppe Carenini, Raymond Ng, and Yashar Mehdad. 2013. Combining intra- and multi-sentential rhetorical parsing for document-level discourse analysis. In *Proceedings of the 51st Annual Meeting of the Association for Computational Linguistics*. Sofia, Bulgaria, pages 486–496.

William C. Mann and Sandra A. Thompson. 1988. Rhetorical structure theory: Toward a functional theory of text organization. *Text - Interdisciplinary Journal for the Study of Discourse (Text)* 8(3):243–281.

Daniel Marcu. 2000. *The Theory and Practice of Discourse Parsing and Summarization*. MIT Press.

Daniel Marcu, Estibaliz Amorrortu, and Magdalena Romera. 1999. Experiments in constructing a corpus of discourse trees. In *ACL Workshop on Standards and Tools for Discourse Tagging*. College Park, Maryland, pages 48–57.

Rashmi Prasad, Nikhil Dinesh, Alan Lee, Eleni Miltsakaki, and Livio Robaldo. 2008. The Penn Discourse TreeBank 2.0. In *The 6th International Conference on Language Resources and Evaluation (LREC)*. Marrakech, Morocco, pages 2961–2968.

Ines Rehbein, Merel Scholman, and Vera Demberg. 2016. Annotating discourse relations in spoken language: A comparison of the PDTB and CCR frameworks. In *The Tenth International Conference on Language Resources and Evaluation (LREC 2016)*. Portorož, Slovenia, pages 1039–1046.

Ted J. M. Sanders, Wilbert P. M. Spooren, and Leo G. M. Noordman. 1992. Toward a taxonomy of coherence relations. *Discourse Processes* 15(1):1–35.

Svetlana Stoyanchev and Srinivas Bangalore. 2015. Discourse in customer care dialogues. Poster presented at the Workshop of Identification and Annotation of Discourse Relations in Spoken Language. Saarbrücken, Germany.

Maite Taboada and William C. Mann. 2006a. Applications of Rhetorical Structure Theory. *Discourse Studies* 8(4):567–588.

Maite Taboada and William C. Mann. 2006b. Rhetorical Structure Theory: Looking back and moving ahead. *Discourse Studies* 8(3):423–459.

Sara Tonelli, Giuseppe Riccardi, Rashmi Prasad, and Aravind Joshi. 2010. Annotation of discourse relations for conversational spoken dialogs. In *The Seventh International Conference on Language Resources and Evaluation (LREC'10)*. Valetta, Malta, pages 2084–2090.

Xinhao Wang, Keelan Evanini, and Klaus Zechner. 2013. Coherence modeling for the automated assessment of spontaneous spoken responses. In *Proceedings of the 2013 Conference of the North American Chapter of the Association for Computational Linguistics: Human Language Technologies*. Atlanta, Georgia, pages 814–819.

Improving Implicit Discourse Relation Recognition with Discourse-specific Word Embeddings

Changxing Wu[1,2], Xiaodong Shi[1,2]*, Yidong Chen[1,2], Jinsong Su[3], Boli Wang[1,2]

Fujian Key Lab of the Brain-like Intelligent Systems, Xiamen University, China[1]
School of Information Science and Technology, Xiamen University, China[2]
Xiamen University, China[3]

wcxnlp@163.com   boliwang@stu.xmu.edu.cn
{mandel, ydchen, jssu}@xmu.edu.cn

Abstract

We introduce a simple and effective method to learn discourse-specific word embeddings (*DSWE*) for implicit discourse relation recognition. Specifically, *DSWE* is learned by performing connective classification on massive explicit discourse data, and capable of capturing discourse relationships between words. On the PDTB data set, using *DSWE* as features achieves significant improvements over baselines.

1 Introduction

Recognizing discourse relations (e.g., *Contrast, Conjunction*) between two sentences is a crucial subtask of discourse structure analysis. These relations can benefit many downstream NLP tasks, including question answering, machine translation and so on. A discourse relation instance is usually defined as a discourse connective (e.g., *but, and*) taking two arguments (e.g., *clause, sentence*). For explicit discourse relation recognition, using only connectives as features achieves more than 93% in accuracy (Pitler and Nenkova, 2009). Without obvious clues like connectives, implicit discourse relation recognition is still challenging.

The earlier researches usually develop linguistically informed features and use supervised learning method to perform the task (Pitler et al., 2009; Lin et al., 2009; Louis et al., 2010; Rutherford and Xue, 2014; Braud and Denis, 2015). Among these features, word pairs occurring in argument pairs are considered as important features, since they can partially catch discourse relationships between two arguments. For example, synonym word pairs like *(good, great)* may indicate a *Conjunction* relation, while antonym word pairs like *(good, bad)*

may mean a *Contrast* relation. However, classifiers based on word pairs in previous work do not work well because of the data sparsity problem. To address this problem, recent researches use word embeddings (aka distributed representations) instead of words as input features, and design various neural networks to capture discourse relationships between arguments (Zhang et al., 2015; Ji and Eisenstein, 2015; Qin et al., 2016; Chen et al., 2016; Liu and Li, 2016). While these researches achieve promising results, they are all based on pre-trained word embeddings ignoring discourse information (e.g., *good, great,* and *bad* are often mapped into close vectors). Intuitively, using word embeddings sensitive to discourse relations would further boost the performance.

In this paper, we propose to learn discourse-specific word embeddings (*DSWE*) from explicit data for implicit discourse relation recognition. Our method is inspired by the observation that synonym (antonym) word pairs tend to appear around the discourse connective *and (but)*. Other connectives can also provide some discourse clues. We expect to encode these discourse clues into the distributed representations of words, to capture discourse relationships between them. To this end, we use a simple neural network to perform connective classification on massive explicit data. Explicit data can be considered to be automatically labeled by connectives. While they cannot be directly used as training data for implicit discourse relation recognition and contain some noise, they are effective enough to provide weakly supervised signals for training the discourse-specific word embeddings.

We apply *DSWE* as features in a supervised neural network for implicit discourse relations recognition. On the PDTB (Prasad et al., 2008), using *DSWE* yields significantly better performance than using off-the-shelf word embeddings,

---

*Corresponding author.

Proceedings of the 55th Annual Meeting of the Association for Computational Linguistics (Short Papers), pages 269–274
Vancouver, Canada, July 30 - August 4, 2017. ©2017 Association for Computational Linguistics
https://doi.org/10.18653/v1/P17-2042

or recent systems incorporating explicit data. We detail our method in Section 2 and evaluate it in Section 3. Conclusions are given in Section 4. Our learned *DSWE* is publicly available at here.

2 Discourse-specific Word Embeddings

In this section, we first introduce the neural network model for learning discourse-specific word embeddings (*DSWE*), and then the way of collecting explicit discourse data for training. Finally, we highlight the differences between our work and the related researches.

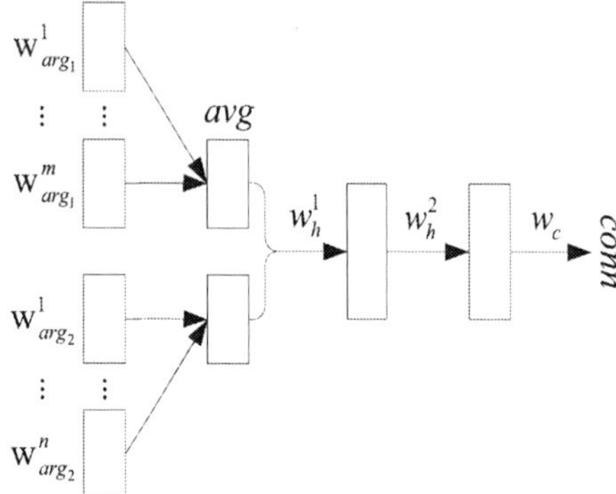

Figure 1: Neural network model for learning *DSWE*. An explicit instance is denoted as $(arg_1, arg_2, conn)$. $w^1_{arg_1}$, ..., $w^m_{arg_1}$ mean the words in arg_1. Two arguments are concatenated as input and the number of hidden layers is not limited to two.

We induce *DSWE* based on explicit data by performing connective classification. The connective classification task predicts which discourse connective is suitable for combining two given arguments. It is essentially similar to implicit relation recognition, just with different output labels. Therefore, any existing neural network model for implicit relation recognition can be easily used for connective classification. We adapt the model in (Wu et al., 2016) for connective classification because it is simple enough to enable us to train on massive data. As illustrated in Figure 1, an argument is first represented as the average of distributed representations of words in it. On the concatenation of two arguments, multiple non-linear hidden layers are then used to capture the interactions between them. Finally, a *softmax* layer is stacked for classification. We combine the cross-entropy error and regularization error multiplied

by the coefficient λ as the objective function. During training, we initialize distributed representations of all words randomly and tune them to minimize the objective function. The finally obtained distributed representations of all words are our discourse-specific word embeddings.

Collecting explicit discourse data includes two steps: 1) distinguish whether a connective occurring reflects a discourse relation. For example, the connective *and* can either function as a discourse connective to join two *Conjunction* arguments, or be just used to link two nouns in a phrase. 2) identify the positions of two arguments. According to (Prasad et al., 2008), arg_2 is defined as the argument following a connective, however, arg_1 can be located within the same sentence as the connective, in some previous or following sentence. Lin et al. (2014) show that the accuracy of distinguishing connectives is more than 97%, while identifying arguments is below than 80%. Therefore, we use the existing toolkit[1] to find discourse connectives, and just collect explicit instances using patterns like [$arg1\ because\ arg2$], where two arguments are in the same sentence, to decrease noise. We believe these simple patterns are enough when using a very large corpus. Note that there are 100 discourse connectives in the PDTB, we ignore four parallel connectives (e.g., *if...then*) for simplicity. The way of collecting explicit data can be easily generalized to other languages, one just need to train a classifier to find discourse connectives following (Lin et al., 2014).

Some aspects of this work are similar to (Biran and McKeown, 2013; Braud and Denis, 2016). Based on massive explicit instances, they first build a word-connective co-occurrence frequency matrix[2], and then weight these raw frequencies. In this way, they represent words in the space of connectives to directly encode their discourse function. The major limitation of their approach is that the dimension of the word representations must be less than or equal to the number of connectives. By comparison, we learn *DSWE* by predicting connectives conditioning on arguments, which yields better performance and has no such dimension limitation. Some researchers use explicit data as additional training data via multi-task learning (Lan et al., 2013; Liu et al., 2016) or data selection (Rutherford and Xue, 2015; Wu et al., 2016).

---

[1] https://github.com/linziheng/pdtb-parser.
[2] Biran and McKeown (2013) calculate co-occurrences between word pairs and connectives.

In both cases, explicit data are directly used to estimate the parameters of implicit relation classifiers. As a result, it is hard for them to incorporate massive explicit data because of the noise problem. By contrast, we leverage massive explicit data by learning word embeddings from them.

3 Experiments

3.1 Data and Settings

We collect explicit data from the *Xin* and *Ltw* parts of the English Gigaword Corpus (3rd edition), and get about 4.92M explicit instances. We randomly sample 20,000 instances as the development set and the others as the training set for *DSWE*. After discarding words occurring less than 5 times, the size of the vocabulary is 185,048. For the connective classification task, we obtain an accuracy of about 53% on the development set.

We adapt the neural network model described in Figure 1 as the classifier for implicit discourse relation recognition (*CDRR*). Specifically, we concatenate some surface features with the last hidden layer as the input of the *softmax* layer to predict discourse relations. We choose 500 *Production rule* (Lin et al., 2009) and 500 *Brown Cluster Pair* (Rutherford and Xue, 2014) features based on mutual information using the toolkit provided by Peng et al. (2005). Our learned *DSWE* is used as the pre-trained word embeddings for *CDRR*, and fixed during training.

Hyper-parameters for training *DSWE* and *CDRR* are selected based on their corresponding development set, and listed in Table 1.

Hyper-parameter	DSWE	CDRR
$wdim$	300	300
$hsizes$	[200]	[200, 50]
lr	1.0	0.005
λ	0.0001	0.0001
$update$	SGD	AdaGrad
f	ReLU	ReLU

Table 1: Hyper-parameters for training *DSWE* and *CDRR*. $wdim$ means the dimension of word embeddings, $hsizes$ the sizes of hidden layers, lr the learning rate, λ the regularization coefficient, $update$ the parameter update strategy and f the nonlinear function. Note that [200, 50] means that *CDRR* uses two layers with the sizes of 200 and 50, respectively. And the learning rate for training *DSWE* is decayed by a factor of 0.8 per epoch.

Following Liu et al. (2016), we perform a 4-way classification on the four top-level relations in the PDTB: $Temporal$ ($Temp$), $Comparison$ ($Comp$), $Contingency$ ($Cont$) and $Expansion$ ($Expa$). The PDTB is split into the training set (Sections 2-20), development set (Sections 0-1) and test set (Sections 21-22). Table 2 lists the statistics of these data sets. Due to the small and uneven test data set, we run our method 10 times with different random seeds (therefore different initial parameters), and report the results (of a run) which are closest to the average results. Finally, we use both $Accuracy$ and $Macro\ F_1$ (macro-averaged F_1) to evaluate our method.

Relation	Train	Dev	Test
$Temp$	582	48	55
$Comp$	1855	189	145
$Cont$	3235	281	273
$Expa$	6673	638	538

Table 2: Statistics of data sets on the PDTB.

3.2 Results

We compare our learned discourse-specific word embeddings (*DSWE*) with two publicly available embeddings[3]:

1) *GloVe*[4]: trained on 6B words from *Wikipedia 2014* and *Gigaword 5* using the count based model in (Pennington et al., 2014), with a vocabulary of 400K and a dimensionality of 300.

2) *word2vec*[5]: trained on 100B words from *Google News* using the CBOW model in (Mikolov et al., 2013), with a vocabulary of 3M and a dimensionality of 300.

Results in Table 3 show that using *DSWE* gains significant improvements (one-tailed t-test with $p<0.05$) over using *GloVe* or *word2vec*, on both $Accuracy$ and $Macro\ F_1$. Furthermore, using *DSWE* achieves better performance across all relations on the F_1 score, especially for minority relations ($Temp$, $Comp$ and $Cont$). Overall, our *DSWE* can effectively incorporate discourse infor-

---

[3]The reasons for using those publicly available word embeddings are: 1) They are both trained on massive data. 2) It will be convenient for other people to reproduce our experiments. 3) Using *GloVe* or *word2vec* word embeddings trained on the same corpus as *DSWE* achieves worse performance than using these two public ones.

[4]http://nlp.stanford.edu/projects/glove/glove.6B.zip

[5]https://code.google.com/archive/p/word2vec/GoogleNews-vectors-negative300.bin.gz

CDRR		+GloVe	+word2vec	+DSWE
$Temp$	P	36.00	27.03	31.58
	R	16.36	18.18	21.82
	F_1	22.50	21.74	25.81
$Comp$	P	53.97	50.00	43.00
	R	23.45	20.00	29.66
	F_1	32.69	28.57	35.10
$Cont$	P	44.90	51.81	55.29
	R	40.29	36.63	42.12
	F_1	42.47	42.92	47.82
$Expa$	P	60.47	60.72	63.91
	R	76.21	81.60	79.00
	F_1	67.43	69.63	70.66
$Accuracy$		55.68	57.17	**58.85**
$Macro\ F_1$		41.27	40.71	**44.84**

Table 3: Results of using different word embeddings. We also list the Precision, Recall and F_1 score for each relation.

mation in explicit data, and thus benefits implicit discourse relation recognition.

We also compare our method with three recent systems which also use explicit data to boost the performance:

1) *R&X2015*: Rutherford and Xue (2015) construct weakly labeled data from explicit data based on the chosen connectives, to enlarge the training data directly.

2) *B&D2016*: Braud and Denis (2016) learn connective-based word representations and build a logistic regression model based on them[6].

3) *Liu2016*: Liu et al. (2016) use a multi-task neural network to incorporate several discourse-related data, including explicit data and the RST-DT corpus (William and Thompson, 1988).

System	$Accuracy$	$Macro\ F_1$
$R\&X2015$	57.10	40.50
$B\&D2016$	52.81	42.27
$Liu2016$	57.27	**44.98**
$CDRR+DSWE$	**58.85**	44.84

Table 4: Comparison with recent systems.

Results in Table 4 show the superiority of our method. Although *Liu2016* performs slightly better on $Macro\ F_1$, it uses the additional labeled RST-DT corpus. For *R&X2015* and *Liu2016*, they

---

[6]We carefully reproduce their model since they adopt a different setting in preprocessing the PDTB.

both incorporate relatively small explicit data because of the noise problem, for example, 20,000 and 40,000 instances respectively. By contrast, our method benefits from about 4.9M explicit instances. While *B&D2016* uses massive explicit data, it is limited by the fact that the maximum dimension of word representations is restricted to the number of connectives, for example 96 in their work. Overall, our method can effectively utilize massive explicit data, and thus is more powerful than baselines.

not		*good*	
word2vec	*DSWE*	*word2vec*	*DSWE*
do	no	great	great
did	n't	bad	lot
anymore	never	terrific	very
necessarily	nothing	decent	better
anything	neither	nice	success
anyway	none	excellent	well
does	difficult	fantastic	happy
never	nor	better	certainly
want	refused	solid	respect
neither	impossible	lousy	fine
if	limited	wonderful	import
know	declined	terrible	positive
anybody	nobody	Good	help
yet	little	tough	useful
either	denied	best	welcome

Table 5: Top 15 closest words of *not* and *good* in both *word2vec* and *DSWE*.

To give an intuition of what information is encoded into the learned *DSWE*, we list in Table 5 the top 15 closest words of *not* and *good*, according to the cosine similarity. We can find that, in *DSWE*, words similar to *not* to some extent have negative meanings. And since *declined* is similar to *not*, a classifier may easily identify the implicit instance [*A network spokesman would* **not** *comment. ABC Sports officials* **declined** *to be interviewed.*] as the *Conjunction* relation. For *good* in *DSWE*, the similar words no longer include words like *bad*. Furthermore, the similar score between *good* and *great* is 0.54 while the score between *good* and *bad* is just 0.33, which may make a classifier easier to distinguish word pairs *(good, great)* and *(good, bad)*, and thus is helpful for predicting the *Conjunction* relation. This qualitative analysis demonstrates the ability of our *DSWE* to capture the discourse relationships between words.

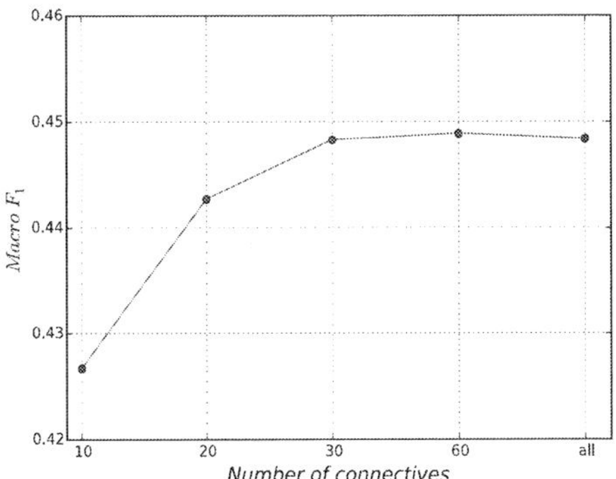

Figure 2: Impact of connectives used in training *DSWE*.

Finally, we conduct experiments to investigate the impact of connectives used in training *DSWE* on our results. Specifically, we use the explicit discourse instances with the top 10, 20, 30, 60 most frequent or all connectives to learn *DSWE*, accounting for 78.9%, 91.9%, 95.8%, 99.4% or 100% of total instances, respectively. The top 10 most frequent connectives are: *and*, *but*, *also*, *while*, *as*, *when*, *after*, *if*, *however* and *because*, which cover all four top-level relations defined in the PDTB. As illustrated in Figure 2, with only the top 10 connectives, the learned *DSWE* achieves better performance than the common word embeddings. We observe a significant improvement when using top 20 connectives, almost the best performance with top 30 connectives, and no further substantial improvement with more connectives. These results indicate that we can use only top n most frequent connectives to collect explicit discourse data for *DSWE*, which is very convenient for most languages.

4   Conclusion

In this paper, we learn discourse-specific word embeddings from massive explicit data for implicit discourse relation recognition. Experiments on the PDTB show that using the learned word embeddings as features can significantly boost the performance. We also show that our method can use explicit data more effectively than previous work. Since most of neural network models for implicit discourse relation recognition use pre-trained word embeddings as input, we hope that our learned word embeddings would benefit them.

Acknowledgments

We would like to thank all the reviewers for their constructive and helpful suggestions on this paper. This work is partially supported by the Natural Science Foundation of China (Grant Nos. 61573294, 61672440, 61075058), the Ph.D. Programs Foundation of Ministry of Education of China (Grant No. 20130121110040), the Foundation of the State Language Commission of China (Grant No. WT135-10), the Natural Science Foundation of Fujian Province (Grant No. 2016J05161).

References

Or Biran and Kathleen McKeown. 2013. Aggregated Word Pair Features for Implicit Discourse Relation Disambiguation. In *Proceedings of ACL*. Sofia, Bulgaria, pages 69–73.

Chloé Braud and Pascal Denis. 2015. Comparing Word Representations for Implicit Discourse Relation Classification. In *Proceedings of EMNLP*. Lisbon, Portugal, pages 2201–2211.

Chloé Braud and Pascal Denis. 2016. Learning Connective-based Word Representations for Implicit Discourse Relation Identification. In *Proceedings of EMNLP*. Austin, Texas, pages 203–213.

Jifan Chen, Qi Zhang, Pengfei Liu, Xipeng Qiu, and Xuanjing Huang. 2016. Implicit Discourse Relation Detection via a Deep Architecture with Gated Relevance Network. In *Proceedings of ACL*. Berlin, Germany, pages 1726–1735.

Yangfeng Ji and Jacob Eisenstein. 2015. One Vector is Not Enough: Entity-Augmented Distributed Semantics for Discourse Relations. *Transactions of the Association for Computational Linguistics* 3:329–344.

Man Lan, Yu Xu, and Zhengyu Niu. 2013. Leveraging Synthetic Discourse Data via Multi-task Learning for Implicit Discourse Relation Recognition. In *Proceedings of ACL*. Sofia, Bulgaria, pages 476–485.

Ziheng Lin, Min-Yen Kan, and Hwee Tou Ng. 2009. Recognizing Implicit Discourse Relations in the Penn Discourse Treebank. In *Proceedings of EMNLP*. PA, USA, pages 343–351.

Ziheng Lin, Hwee Tou Ng, and Min-Yen Kan. 2014. A PDTB-styled End-to-end Discourse Parser. *Natural Language Engineering* 20(02):151–184.

Yang Liu and Sujian Li. 2016. Recognizing Implicit Discourse Relations via Repeated Reading: Neural Networks with Multi-Level Attention. In *Proceedings of EMNLP*. Austin, Texas, pages 1224–1233.

Yang Liu, Sujian Li, Xiaodong Zhang, and Zhifang Sui. 2016. Implicit Discourse Relation Classification via Multi-Task Neural Networks. In *Proceedings of AAAI*. Arizona, USA, pages 2750–2756.

Annie Louis, Aravind Joshi, Rashmi Prasad, and Ani Nenkova. 2010. Using Entity Features to Classify Implicit Discourse Relations. In *Proceedings of SIGDIAL*. PA, USA, pages 59–62.

Tomas Mikolov, Kai Chen, Greg Corrado, and Jeffrey Dean. 2013. Efficient Estimation of Word Representations in Vector Space. *arXiv:1301.3781 [cs]* .

H. Peng, Fulmi Long, and C. Ding. 2005. Feature Selection Based on Mutual Information Criteria of Max-dependency, Max-relevance, and Min-redundancy. *IEEE Transactions on PAMI* 27(8):1226–1238.

Jeffrey Pennington, Richard Socher, and Christopher Manning. 2014. Glove: Global Vectors for Word Representation. In *Proceedings of EMNLP*. Doha, Qatar, pages 1532–1543.

Emily Pitler, Annie Louis, and Ani Nenkova. 2009. Automatic Sense Prediction for Implicit Discourse Relations in Text. In *Proceedings of ACL-IJCNLP*. PA, USA, pages 683–691.

Emily Pitler and Ani Nenkova. 2009. Using Syntax to Disambiguate Explicit Discourse Connectives in Text. In *Proceedings of ACL-IJCNLP*. PA, USA, pages 13–16.

Rashmi Prasad, Nikhil Dinesh, Alan Lee, Eleni Miltsakaki, Livio Robaldo, Aravind Joshi, and Bonnie Webber. 2008. The Penn Discourse TreeBank 2.0. In *Proceedings of LREC*. volume 24, pages 2961–2968.

Lianhui Qin, Zhisong Zhang, and Hai Zhao. 2016. A Stacking Gated Neural Architecture for Implicit Discourse Relation Classification. In *Proceedings of EMNLP*. Austin, Texas, pages 2263–2270.

Attapol Rutherford and Nianwen Xue. 2014. Discovering Implicit Discourse Relations Through Brown Cluster Pair Representation and Coreference Patterns. In *Proceedings of EACL*. Gothenburg, Sweden, pages 645–654.

Attapol Rutherford and Nianwen Xue. 2015. Improving the Inference of Implicit Discourse Relations via Classifying Explicit Discourse Connectives. In *Proceedings of NAACL*. Denver, Colorado, pages 799–808.

Mann William and Sandra Thompson. 1988. Rhetorical Structure Theory: Towards a Functional Theory of Text Organization. *Text* 8(3):243–281.

Changxing Wu, Xiaodong Shi, Yidong Chen, Yanzhou Huang, and Jinsong Su. 2016. Bilingually-constrained Synthetic Data for Implicit Discourse Relation Recognition. In *Proceedings of EMNLP*. Austin, Texas, pages 2306–2312.

Biao Zhang, Jinsong Su, Deyi Xiong, Yaojie Lu, Hong Duan, and Junfeng Yao. 2015. Shallow Convolutional Neural Network for Implicit Discourse Relation Recognition. In *Proceedings of EMNLP*. Lisbon, Portugal, pages 2230–2235.

Oracle Summaries of Compressive Summarization

Tsutomu Hirao and **Masaaki Nishino** and **Masaaki Nagata**
NTT Communication Science Laboratories, NTT Corporation
2-4 Hikaridai, Seika-cho, Soraku-gun, Kyoto, 619-0237, Japan
`{hirao.tsutomu,nishino.masaaki,nagata.masaaki}@lab.ntt.co.jp`

Abstract

This paper derives an Integer Linear Programming (ILP) formulation to obtain an oracle summary of the *compressive summarization* paradigm in terms of ROUGE. The oracle summary is essential to reveal the upper bound performance of the paradigm. Experimental results on the DUC dataset showed that ROUGE scores of compressive oracles are significantly higher than those of extractive oracles and state-of-the-art summarization systems. These results reveal that compressive summarization is a promising paradigm and encourage us to continue with the research to produce informative summaries.

1 Introduction

Compressive summarization, a joint model integrating sentence extraction and sentence compression within a unified framework, has been attracting attention in recent years (Martins and Smith, 2009; Berg-Kirkpatrick et al., 2011; Almeida and Martins, 2013; Qian and Liu, 2013; Kikuchi et al., 2014; Yao et al., 2015). Since compressive summarization methods can use a sub-sentence as an atomic unit, they can pack more information into summaries than extractive methods, which employ sentences as atomic units. Thus, compressive summarization is essential when we want to produce summaries under tight length constraints. There are two approaches to compress entire document(s) to be grammatical; one is trimming the phrase structure trees (Berg-Kirkpatrick et al., 2011) and the other is trimming the dependency trees obtained from the document(s) (Martins and Smith, 2009; Almeida and Martins, 2013; Qian and Liu, 2013; Kikuchi et al., 2014; Yao et al.,

2015). This paper focuses on the latter approach because recently it has been receiving much attention.

To measure the performance of compressive summarization methods, ROUGE (Lin, 2004), an automatic evaluation metric, is widely used. ROUGE evaluates a system summary by exploiting a set of human-made reference summaries to give a score in the range [0,1]. When n-gram occurrences of the system summary agree with those in a set of reference summaries, the value is 1. However, system summaries cannot achieve ROUGE=1 since summarization systems cannot reproduce reference summaries in most cases. In other words, the maximum ROUGE score that can be achieved by compressive summarization is unclear. As a result, researchers cannot know how much room for further improvement is left. Thus, it is beneficial to reveal the upper bound summary that achieves the maximum ROUGE score and can be produced by the systems. The upper bound summary is known as the oracle summary. To obtain the oracle summary on extractive summarization paradigms, several approaches have been proposed. Sipos et al. (2012) utilized a greedy algorithm, and Kubina et al. (2013) utilized exhaustive search based on heuristics. However, their oracle summaries do not always retain the optimal (maximum) ROUGE score. Recently, Hirao et al. (2017) derived an Integer Linear Programming (ILP) formulation to obtain the optimal oracle summary. Their oracle summary can help researchers to comprehend the strict limitation of the extractive summarization paradigm. However, their method cannot be applied to obtain compressive oracle summaries.

To reveal the ultimate limitation of the compressive summarization paradigm, we propose an ILP formulation to obtain a compressive oracle summary that maximizes the ROUGE score. We con-

Proceedings of the 55th Annual Meeting of the Association for Computational Linguistics (Short Papers), pages 275–280
Vancouver, Canada, July 30 - August 4, 2017. ©2017 Association for Computational Linguistics
https://doi.org/10.18653/v1/P17-2043

ducted experimental evaluation on the Document Understanding Conference (DUC) 2004 dataset. The result demonstrated that ROUGE scores of compressive oracle summaries completely outperformed those of extractive oracle summaries and those of state-of-the-art summarization methods. This indicates that compressive summarization is a promising paradigm for leveraging research resources.

2 Definition of Compressive Oracle Summaries

Before defining compressive oracle summary, we briefly describe ROUGE_n. Given K reference summaries $\boldsymbol{R}=\{R_1,\ldots,R_K\}$ and a system summary S. Let $G=\{g_1^n,\ldots,g_M^n\}$ be the set of all n-grams appearing in reference summaries. Let $|G|=M$. ROUGE_n is defined as follows:

$$\text{ROUGE}_n(\boldsymbol{R},S) =$$
$$\frac{\sum_{k=1}^{K}\sum_{j=1}^{M}\min\{N(g_j^n,R_k),N(g_j^n,S)\}}{\sum_{k=1}^{K}\sum_{j=1}^{M}N(g_j^n,R_k)} \quad (1)$$

g_j^n represents the j-th n-gram appearing in reference summaries. $N(g_j^n,R_k)$ and $N(g_j^n,S)$ are the number of occurrences of n-gram g_j^n in R_k and S, respectively. Thus, compressive oracle summaries are defined as follows:

$$O = \underset{S\subseteq T}{\arg\max}\ \text{ROUGE}_n(\boldsymbol{R},S) \quad (2)$$
$$\text{s.t.}\ \ \ell(S) \leq L_{\max}.$$

T is the set of all valid word subsequences[1] obtained from sentences contained in the input document(s), and $L_{\max}$ is the length limitation of the oracle summary. $\ell(S)$ indicates the number of words in the summary. Neither approximation nor exact algorithms are known for solving this problem.

3 ILP Formulation to Obtain the Compressive Oracle Summary

3.1 Dependency Structure of a Sentence

In this paper, we follow the dependency tree trimming approach proposed by Filippova et al. (2008; 2013). They proposed rules that transform a tree that represents dependency relation between

---

[1]Word subsequences can be regarded as grammatical sentences. We regard rooted subtrees of dependency trees as valid word subsequences. For details, see Section 3.1.

words into a tree that represents dependency relation between chunks (consisting of a word or word sequence). Since we can trim their dependency trees without loss of grammatical consistency, Thus, we employ the trees in our compressive summarization framework. Figure 1 shows examples.

3.2 ILP Formulation

$$\text{maximize} \quad \sum_{k=1}^{K}\sum_{j=1}^{M} z_{k,j} \quad (3)$$

$$\text{s.t.} \quad \sum_{i=1}^{|D|}\sum_{u=1}^{E_i} \ell_{i,u}b_{i,u} \leq L_{\max} \quad (4)$$

$$\forall j: \quad \sum_{\tau\in\mathcal{T}(g_j^n)} m_\tau \geq z_{k,j} \quad (5)$$

$$\forall j: \quad N(g_j^n,R_k) \geq z_{k,j} \quad (6)$$

$$\forall i,u: \quad b_{i,\text{parent}(i,u)} \geq b_{i,u} \quad (7)$$

$$\forall i,v,q \in V_i(w_{i,v}): \quad b_{i,q} \geq m_{i,v} \quad (8)$$

$$\forall i,v,p \in U_i(w_{i,v}): \quad b_{i,p} \leq 1 - m_{i,v} \quad (9)$$

$$\forall i,u: \quad m_{i,v} \in \{0,1\} \quad (10)$$

$$\forall i,v: \quad b_{i,u} \in \{0,1\} \quad (11)$$

$$\forall k,j: \quad z_{k,j} \in \mathbb{Z}_+. \quad (12)$$

Since the denominator of equation (1) is constant for a given set of reference summaries, we can find an oracle summary by maximizing the numerator of equation (1). Equation (3) is the objective function that corresponds to maximization of the numerator of equation (1). $z_{k,j}$ is the count of the j-th n-gram that is contained in both the k-th reference summary and the oracle summary. Equation (4) ensures that the length of the oracle summary is less than $L_{\max}$. $b_{i,u}$ is a binary decision variable indicating whether u-th chunk in i-th sentence is contained in an oracle summary or not. $\ell_{i,u}$ indicates the number of the words in u-th chunk in the i-th sentence. D is a set of sentences and E_i is the number of chunks in the i-th sentence. Equations (5) and (6) represent min operation in equation (1). $w_{i,v}$ is the v-th possible word sequence whose length is n and that is contained in the i-th sentence, and $m_{i,v}$ is a binary decision variable indicating whether $w_{i,v}$ is contained in the oracle summary or not. $\mathcal{T}(g_j^n)$ is a set of tuples consisting of indices (i,v) whose word sequence corresponds to g_j^n, i.e., $\mathcal{T}(g_j^n)=\{(i,v)|w_{i,v}=g_j^n\}$. Thus, $z_{k,j}=\min\{N(g_j^n,R_k),N(g_j^n,S)\}$. Equation (7) ensures that an oracle summary consists

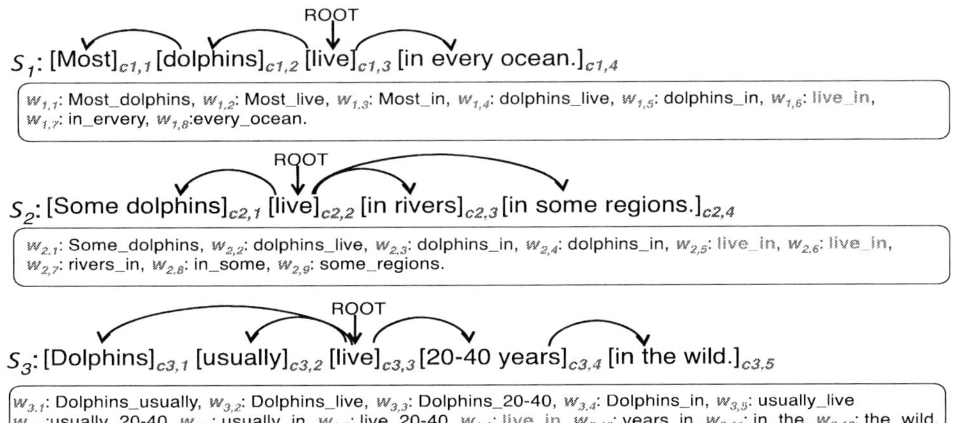

Figure 1: Examples of trees that represent dependency relations between chunks, and word sequences (whose length is 2). Chunks are enclosed in square brackets. Note that we disregard word sequences that are generated by destroying the structure of chunks such as "live_every" in S_1, "dolphins_in" in S_2, "live_wild" in S_3.

of a set of rooted subtrees of the sentences in the entire document(s). Function parent (i, u) returns the index of the parent chunk of the u-th chunk in the dependency tree obtained from the i-th sentence. Equations (8) and (9) represent the dependency relation between n-grams and chunks. When we include $w_{i,v}$ in the oracle summary, we have to include all chunks that contain the words in $w_{i,v}$. In addition, when the above chunks have gap(s), we have to drop chunk(s) within the gap(s). Here, $V_i(w_{i,v})$ is a set of indices of chunks that includes words in $w_{i,v}$, and $U_i(w_{i,v})$ is a set of indices of chunks within the gap(s), defined as $\{h \mid \min(V_i(w_{i,v})) < h < \max(V_i(w_{i,v}))\}$ and $h \notin V_i(w_{i,v})$.

We give an example to show how chunks and word sequences are related. When we pack a bigram "live_in" in an oracle summary, there are four candidates in the source document (Fig. 1). Word subsequences, $w_{1,6}, w_{2,5}, w_{2,6}$ and $w_{3,9}$ match "live_in". Thus, $\mathcal{T}(\text{live\_in}) = \{(1, 6), (2, 5), (2, 6), (3, 9)\}$. Here, when we want to pack $w_{2,6}$ into the oracle summary, we have to pack both chunks $c_{2,2}$ and $c_{2,4}$ ($b_{2,2} = b_{2,4} = 1$) because $U_2(w_{2,6}) = \{2, 4\}$. Then, we have to drop chunk $c_{2,3}(b_{2,3} = 0)$ because $c_{2,3}$ is within the gap between chunks $c_{2,2}$ and $c_{2,4}$ ($V_2(w_{2,6}) = 3$). Similarly, when we pack $w_{3,9}$ into an oracle summary, we have to pack both chunks $c_{3,3}$ and $c_{3,5}$ and drop chunk $c_{3,4}$. However, this compres-

sion is not allowed since there is no dependency relationship between $c_{3,3}$ and $c_{3,5}$.

After solving the ILP problem, we can obtain compressive oracle summaries by collecting chunks according to $b_{i,u}=1$.

4 Experiments

To investigate the potential limitation of the compressive summarization paradigm, we compare ROUGE scores of compressive oracle summaries with those of extractive oracle summaries and those obtained from state-of-the-art summarization systems. Extractive oracle summaries are obtained by solving the ILP formulation proposed by (Hirao et al., 2017). System summaries are extracted from a public repository[2] (Hong et al., 2014).

4.1 Settings

We conducted experimental evaluation on the DUC-2004 dataset for multiple document summarization evaluation, a widely used benchmark test set for generic multiple document summarization tasks. The dataset consists of 50 topics, each of which contains 10 newspaper articles. To obtain oracle summaries based on the ILP formulation described in section 3.2, first, we applied the Stanford parser (de Marneffe et al., 2006) to all

---

[2] http://www.cis.upenn.edu/~nlp/corpora/sumrepo.html

Method	Metric			
	$n=1$	$n=2$	$n=1+2$	Sent.
Ext. $n=1$	**42.6**	13.1	24.1	5.34
Ext. $n=2$	36.6	**16.9**	24.3	5.06
Ext. $n=1+2$	40.9	16.1	**25.4**	5.24
Comp. $n=1$	**50.9**	13.8	27.7	10.6
Comp. $n=2$	40.9	**21.3**	28.6	7.82
Comp. $n=1+2$	47.9	19.7	**30.3**	8.48
RegSum	33.1	10.2	18.8	4.9
ICSISumm	31.0	10.3	18.0	4.2

Table 1: ROUGE scores and the number of sentences of extractive and compressive oracle summaries and those obtained from state-of-the-art summarization systems, RegSum and ICSISumm. $n=1$ corresponds to ROUGE_1, $n=2$ corresponds to ROUGE_2, $n=1+2$ corresponds to ROUGE-SU0. "Sent." indicates the average number of sentences in the summaries.

sentences in the dataset to obtain dependency relations between words, and then we transformed them into trees that represent the dependency relations between chunks by applying Filippova's rules (Filippova and Strube, 2008; Filippova and Altun, 2013). To solve the ILP problem, we utilized `CPLEX version 12.5.1.0`.

We obtained and evaluated oracle summaries based on three variants of ROUGE, ROUGE_1, ROUGE_2 and ROUGE-SU0, with the following conditions[3]: (1) ROUGE_1, utilizing unigrams excluding stopwords (2) ROUGE_2, utilizing bigrams with stopwords, and (3) ROUGE-SU0, which is an extension of ROUGE_n, utilizing unigram and bigram (excluding skip-bigram) statistics.

4.2 Results and Discussion

Table 1 shows ROUGE scores of compressive and extractive oracle summaries and those of RegSum (Hong and Nenkova, 2014) that achieved the best ROUGE_1 and ICSISumm (Gillick and Favre, 2009; Gillick et al., 2009) that achieved the best ROUGE_2 on the DUC-2004 dataset, respectively.

We compare ROUGE scores of compressive oracle summaries with extractive oracle summaries. The best scores are obtained when we use the same ROUGE variant for both computation and evaluation (see bolded scores in Table 1). There are large differences between the best scores of ex-

---

[3] With stop words: options "-n 2 -s -m -x" are used. Without stop words: options "-n 2 -m -x" are used.

Method		Score
Ext.	$n=1$	4.55
Ext.	$n=2$	4.58
Comp.	$n=1$	3.88
Comp.	$n=2$	4.07

Table 2: Readability evaluation by human subjects

tractive method and compressive method. The differences are 8.3 points, 4.4 points and 4.9 points for ROUGE_1, ROUGE_2, ROUGE-SU0, respectively. As one of the reasons for the above results, compressive oracle summaries have a much larger number of (sub-)sentences than extractive oracle summaries for the same length limitation. This is an advantage of compressive summarization over extractive summarization.

However, we have to note that compressive oracle summaries optimized to ROUGE_1 may not be desirable since they are produced by compressing sentences by ignoring contexts. In fact, they obtained remarkable gain for ROUGE_1 score (8.3 points), while they obtained modest gains in ROUGE_2 and ROUGE-SU0 (0.7 and 3.6 points, respectively). This may suggest that the resultant summaries overfit to the unigrams in the reference summaries.

We compare ROUGE scores of compressive oracle summaries with those of system summaries, ROUGE scores of compressive oracle summaries completely outperformed those of state-of-the-art systems. The differences are in a range from 11 to 17 points.

The results demonstrated that compressive summarization is a promising approach to produce more informative summaries, and room still exists for further improvement. Thus, compressive summarization is important research topic to leverage our resources.

4.3 Readability evaluation

We conducted human evaluation to compare readability of extractive oracle summaries to that of compressive oracle summaries. We presented the oracle summaries to five human subjects and asked them to rate the summaries using an integer scale from 1 (very poor) to 5 (very good). Table 2 shows the results. Extractive oracle summaries achieved near perfect scores. Although the scores of compressive oracle summaries are inferior to those of extractive oracle summaries, they achieved good

---

Reference:
The Wye River accord has not been implemented. As the Israeli cabinet was considering the agreement, Islamic Jihad militants exploded a car bomb in nearby Mahane Yehuda market. The cabinet suspended ratification of the agreement, demanding the Palestinian Authority take steps against terrorism. Further, after the bombing, Israeli Prime Minister Netanyahu announced the resumption of construction of a new settlement, Har Homa, in a traditionally Arab area east of Jerusalem. Israel also demands that Arafat outlaw the military wings of Islamic Jihad and Hamas. The attack injured 24 Israelis, but only the two assailants, Sughayer and Tahayneh, were killed.

Extractive oracle summary $n = 1$:
The procedure is part of the Wye River agreement negotiated last month. The radical group Islamic Jihad claimed responsibility Saturday for the market bombing and vowed more attacks to try to block the new peace accord. Most recently, Israel's Cabinet put off a vote to ratify the accord after a suicide bombing Friday in Jerusalem that killed the two assailants and injured 21 Israelis. David Bar-Illan, a top aide to Israeli Prime Minister Benjamin Netanyahu, said Sunday that Israel expects Palestinian leader Yasser Arafat to formally outlaw the military wings of Islamic Jihad and the larger militant group Hamas.

Compressive oracle summary $n = 1$:
The Israeli cabinet suspended ratification of the Wye agreement. A Prime Minister Benjamin Netanyahu said that Israel would continue to build Jewish neighborhoods throughout Jerusalem including at a site in the Arab sector of the city. Netanyahu's Cabinet delayed action on the peace accord. The radical group Islamic Jihad claimed responsibility for the bombing and vowed attacks. Implementation of the Israeli-Palestinian land-for-security accord was to have begun. David Bar-Illan said that Israel expects Palestinian Yasser Arafat to outlaw the military wings of Islamic Jihad and the Hamas. Their car-bomb blew in a Jerusalem market killing men and wounding 24 people.

Extractive oracle summary $n = 2$:
In response to the attack, the Israeli cabinet suspended ratification of the Wye agreement until there " is verification that the Palestinian authority is indeed fighting terrorism." The radical group Islamic Jihad claimed responsibility Saturday for the market bombing and vowed more attacks to try to block the new peace accord. Most recently, Israel's Cabinet put off a vote to ratify the accord after a suicide bombing Friday in Jerusalem that killed the two assailants and injured 21 Israelis. Their car-bomb blew apart two hours later in a Jerusalem market, killing both men and wounding 24 people. I'm going to Paradise. "

Compressive oracle summary $n = 2$:
The Israeli cabinet suspended ratification of the agreement. Hassan Asfour said the Palestinian Authority condemned the attack. Two people were killed. The procedure is part of the Wye River agreement. The radical group Islamic Jihad claimed responsibility for the bombing and vowed more attacks. Israel is demanding that the military wings of two radical Islamic groups be outlawed. Implementation of the land-for-security accord was to have begun. Israel's Cabinet put off a vote to ratify the accord after a bombing in Jerusalem that killed the two assailants and injured 21 Israelis. Their car-bomb blew in a Jerusalem market killing men.

Figure 2: Summaries obtained from topic:D30010

enough score, around 4. The results support that our trimming approach based on chunk is effective. We show examples of oracle summaries in Figure 2.

5 Conclusion

To reveal the ultimate limitations of the compressive summarization paradigm, this paper proposed an Integer Linear Programming (ILP) formulation to obtain compressive oracle summaries in terms of ROUGE. Evaluation results obtained from the DUC 2004 dataset demonstrated that ROUGE scores of compressive summaries are significantly superior to those of extractive oracle summaries and those of the state-of-the-art systems. These results imply that the compressive summarization paradigm is a promising direction to produce informative summaries and encourage leveraging of further resources for the research.

References

Miguel B. Almeida and André F.T. Martins. 2013. Fast and robust compressive summarization with dual decomposition and multi-task learning. In *Proc. of the 51st Annual Meeting of the Association for Computational Linguistics (ACL)*. pages 196–206.

Taylor Berg-Kirkpatrick, Dan Gillick, and Dan Klein. 2011. Jointly learning to extract and compress. In *Proc. of the 49th Annual Meeting of the Association for Computational Linguistics (ACL)*. pages 481–490.

Marie-Catherine de Marneffe, Bill MacCartney, and Christopher D. Manning. 2006. Generating typed dependency parses from phrase structure parses. In *In Proceedings of International Conference on Language Resources and Evaluation (LREC)*. pages 449–454.

Katja Filippova and Yasemin Altun. 2013. Overcoming the lack of parallel data in sentence compression. In *Proc. of the 2013 Conference on Empirical Methods in Natural Language Processing (EMNLP)*. pages 1481–1491.

Katja Filippova and Michael Strube. 2008. Dependency tree based sentence compression. In *Proc. of* the 5th International Natural Language Generation Conference (INLG). pages 25–32.

Dan Gillick and Benoit Favre. 2009. A scalable global model for summarization. In *Proc. of the Workshop on Integer Linear Programming for Natural Language Processing*. pages 10–18.

Dan Gillick, Benoit Favre, Dilek Hakkani-Tur, Berndt Bohnet, Yang Liu, and Shasha Xie. 2009. The ICSI/UTD summarization system at TAC 2009. In *Proc. of the Text Analysis Conference (TAC)*.

Tsutomu Hirao, Masaaki Nishino, Jun Suzuki, and Masaaki Nagata. 2017. Enumeration of extractive oracle summaries. In *Proc. of the 15th Conference of the European Chapter of the Association for Computational Linguistics (EACL)*. pages 386–396.

Kai Hong, John Conroy, Benoit Favre, Alex Kulesza, Hui Lin, and Ani Nenkova. 2014. A repository of state of the art and competitive baseline summaries for generic news summarization. In *Proc. of the Ninth International Conference on Language Resources and Evaluation (LREC'14)*. pages 1608–1616.

Kai Hong and Ani Nenkova. 2014. Improving the estimation of word importance for news multi-document summarization. In *Proc. of the 14th Conference of the European Chapter of the Association for Computational Linguistics (EACL)*. pages 712–721.

Yuta Kikuchi, Tsutomu Hirao, Hiroya Takamura, Manabu Okumura, and Masaaki Nagata. 2014. Single document summarization based on nested tree structure. In *Proc. of the 52nd Annual Meeting of the Association for Computational Linguistics (ACL)*. pages 315–320.

Jeff Kubina, John Conroy, and Judith Schlesinger. 2013. ACL 2013 multiling pilot overview. In *Proc. of the MultiLing 2013 Workshop on Multilingual Multi-document Summarization*. pages 29–38.

Chin-Yew Lin. 2004. ROUGE: A Package for Automatic Evaluation of Summaries. In *Proc. of Workshop on Text Summarization Branches Out*. pages 74–81.

Andre Martins and Noah A. Smith. 2009. Summarization with a joint model for sentence extraction and compression. In *Proc. of the Workshop on Integer Linear Programming for Natural Language Processing*. pages 1–9.

Xian Qian and Yang Liu. 2013. Fast joint compression and summarization via graph cuts. In *Proc. of the 2013 Conference on Empirical Methods in Natural Language Processing (EMNLP)*. pages 1492–1502.

Ruben Sipos, Pannaga Shivaswamy, and Thorsten Joachims. 2012. Large-margin learning of submodular summarization models. In *Proc. of the 13th Conference of the European Chapter of the Association for Computational Linguistics (EACL)*. pages 224–233.

Jin-ge Yao, Xiaojun Wan, and Jianguo Xiao. 2015. Compressive document summarization via sparse optimization. In *Proc. of the 24th International Joint Conference on Artificial Intelligence (IJCAI 2015)*. pages 1376–1382.

Japanese Sentence Compression with a Large Training Dataset

Shun Hasegawa
Tokyo Institute of Technology, Japan
`hasegawa.s@lr.pi.titech.ac.jp`

Yuta Kikuchi
Preferred Networks, Inc., Japan
`kikuchi@preferred.jp`

Hiroya Takamura
Tokyo Institute of Technology, Japan
`takamura@pi.titech.ac.jp`

Manabu Okumura
Tokyo Institute of Technology, Japan
`oku@pi.titech.ac.jp`

Abstract

In English, high-quality sentence compression models by deleting words have been trained on automatically created large training datasets. We work on Japanese sentence compression by a similar approach. To create a large Japanese training dataset, a method of creating English training dataset is modified based on the characteristics of the Japanese language. The created dataset is used to train Japanese sentence compression models based on the recurrent neural network.

1 Introduction

Sentence compression is the task of shortening a sentence while preserving its important information and grammaticality. Robust sentence compression systems are useful by themselves and also as a module in an extractive summarization system (Berg-Kirkpatrick et al., 2011; Thadani and McKeown, 2013). In this paper, we work on Japanese sentence compression by deleting words. One advantage of compression by deleting words as opposed to abstractive compression lies in the small search space. Another one is that the compressed sentence is more likely to be free from incorrect information not mentioned in the source sentence.

There are many sentence compression models for Japanese (Harashima and Kurohashi, 2012; Hirao et al., 2009; Hori and Furui, 2004) and for English (Knight and Marcu, 2000; Turner and Charniak, 2005; Clarke and Lapata, 2006). In recent years, a high-quality English sentence compression model by deleting words was trained on a large training dataset (Filippova and Altun, 2013; Filippova et al., 2015). While it is impractical to create a large

training dataset by hand, one can be created automatically from news articles (Filippova and Altun, 2013). The procedure is as follows (where S, H, and C respectively denote the first sentence of an article, the headline, and the created compressed sentence of S). Firstly, to restrict the training data to grammatical and informative sentences, only news articles satisfying certain conditions are used. Then, nouns, verbs, adjectives, and adverbs (i.e., content words) shared by S and H are identified by matching word lemmas, and a rooted dependency subtree that contains all the shared content words is regarded as C.

However, their method is designed for English, and cannot be applied to Japanese as it is. Thus, in this study, their method is modified based on the following three characteristics of the Japanese language: (a) Abbreviation of nouns and nominalization of verbs frequently occur in Japanese. (b) Words that are not verbs can also be the root node especially in headlines. (c) Subjects and objects that can be easily estimated from the context are often omitted.

The created training dataset is used to train three models. The first model is the original Filippova et al.'s model, an encoder-decoder model with a long short-term memory (LSTM), which we extend in this paper to make the other two models that can control the output length (Kikuchi et al., 2016), because controlling the output length makes a compressed sentence more informative under the desired length.

2 Creating training dataset for Japanese

Filippova et al.'s method of creating training data consists of the conditions imposed on news articles and the following three steps: (1) identification of shared content words, (2) transformation of a dependency tree, and (3) extraction of the min-

Proceedings of the 55th Annual Meeting of the Association for Computational Linguistics (Short Papers), pages 281–286
Vancouver, Canada, July 30 - August 4, 2017. ©2017 Association for Computational Linguistics
https://doi.org/10.18653/v1/P17-2044

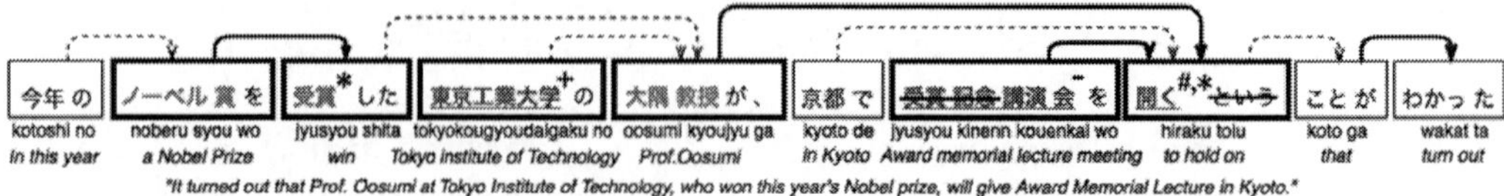

Figure 1: Dependency tree of S^1. Squares and arrows respectively indicate chunks and dependency relations. Bold arrows mean that chunks are merged into a single node. Bold squares are extracted as C.

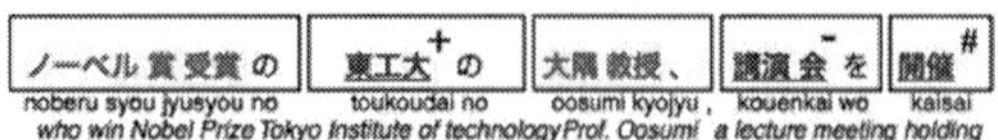

Figure 2: A sequence of chunks of H^1

imum rooted subtree. We modified their method based on the characteristics of the Japanese language as follows. To explain our method, a dependency tree of S and a sequence of *bunsetsu* chunks of H in Japanese are shown in Figures 1 and 2. Note that nodes of dependency trees in Japanese are *bunsetsu* chunks each consisting of content words followed by function words.

2.1 Identification of shared content words

Content words shared by S and H are identified by matching lemmas and pronominal anaphora resolution in Filippova et al.'s method. Abbreviation of nouns and nominalization of verbs frequently occur in Japanese (characteristic (a) in Introduction), and it is difficult to identify these transformations simply by matching lemmas. Thus, after the identification by matching lemmas, two identification methods (described below) using character-level information are applied. Note that pronominal anaphora resolution is not used, because pronouns are often omitted in Japanese.

Abbreviation of nouns: There are two types of abbreviations of nouns in Japanese. One is the abbreviation of a proper noun, which shortens the form by deleting characters (e.g., the pair with "+" in Figures 1 and 2). The other is the abbreviation of consecutive nouns, which deletes nouns that behave as adjectives (e.g., the pair with "-"). To deal with such cases, if the character sequence of the noun sequence in a chunk in H is identical to a subsequence of characters composing the noun sequence in a chunk in S, the noun sequences in H and S are regarded as shared.

Nominalization of verbs: Many verbs in Japanese have corresponding nouns with similar meanings (e.g., the pair with # in Figures 1 and

2). Such pairs often share the same Chinese character, *kanji*. Kanji is an ideogram and is more informative than the other types of Japanese letters. Thus, if a noun in H and a verb in S^2 share one kanji, the noun and the verb are regarded as shared.

2.2 Transformation of a dependency tree

Some edges in dependency trees cannot be cut without changing the meaning or losing the grammaticality of the sentence. In Filippova et al.'s method, the nodes linked by such an edge are merged into a single node before extraction of the subtree. The method is adapted to Japanese as follows. If the function word of a chunk is one of the specific particles[3], which often make obligatory cases, the chunk and its modifiee are merged into a single node. In Figure 1, the chunks at the start and end of a bold arrow are merged into a single node.

2.3 Extraction of the minimum rooted subtree

In Filippova et al.'s method, the minimum rooted subtree that contains all the shared content words is extracted from the transformed tree. We modify their method to take into account the characteristics (a) and (b).

Deleting the global root: In English, only verbs can be the root node of a subtree. However, in Japanese, words with other parts-of-speech can also be the root node in headlines (characteristics (b)). Therefore, the global root, which is the root node of S, and the chunks including a word that can be located at the end of a sentence[4], are the candidates for the root node of a subtree. Then, if the root node is not the global root, words succeeding the word that can be located at the end are removed from the root node. In Figure 1, among the two words with "*" that can be located at the

---

[2] Candidates are restricted to verbs consisting of one kanji and some following hiragana.

[3] "を (wo)", "に (ni)", "が (ga)" and "は (ha)"

[4] An auxiliary verb, a noun, or a verb of which next word is not a noun, an auxiliary verb, or "の (no)"

end, the latter is extracted as the root, and the succeeding word is removed from the chunk.

Reflecting abbreviated forms: Abbreviation of nouns frequently occurs in Japanese (characteristic (a)). Thus, in C, original forms are replaced by their abbreviated forms obtained as explained in Section 2.1 (e.g., the pair with "-" in Figures 1 and 2). However, we do not allow the head of a chunk to be deleted to keep the grammaticality. We also restrict here ourselves to word-level deletion and do not allow character-level deletion, because our purpose is to construct a training dataset for compression by word deletion. In the example of Figure 1, chunks in bold squares are extracted as C.

2.4 Conditions imposed on news articles

Filippova et al.'s method imposed eight conditions on news articles to restrict the training data to grammatical and informative sentences. In our method, these conditions are modified to adapt to Japanese. Firstly, the condition "S should include content words of H in the same order" is removed, because word order in Japanese is relatively free. Secondly, the condition "S should include all content words of H" is relaxed to "the ratio of shared content words to content words in H is larger than threshold θ" because in Japanese, subjects and objects that can be easily estimated from the context are often omitted (characteristics (c)). In addition, two conditions "H should have a verb" and "H must not begin with a verb" are removed, leaving four conditions[5].

3 Sentence compression with LSTM

Three models are used for sentence compression. Each model predicts a label sequence, where the label for each word is either "retain" or "delete" (Filippova et al., 2015). The first is an encoder-decoder model with LSTM (*lstm*) (Sutskever et al., 2014). Given an input sequence $\mathbf{x} = (x_1, x_2, \ldots, x_n)$, y_t in label sequence $\mathbf{y} = (y_1, y_2, \ldots, y_n)$ is computed as follows:

$$s_0 = encoder(\mathbf{x})$$
$$(s_t, m_t) = decoder(s_{t-1}, m_{t-1}, e_1(x_t) \oplus e_l(y_{t-1}))$$
$$y_t = softmax(W * s_t + b),$$

threshold θ	0.1	0.2	0.3	0.4	0.5	0.6	0.7	0.8	0.9	1.0
size(10k)	202	189	172	154	134	106	81	59	35	27
vocab(k)	105	102	98	94	90	81	72	62	48	42
ROUGE-2	54.6	54.4	54.0	54.3	55.3	54.0	55.1	54.4	53.0	53.3

Table 1: Created training data with each θ. ROUGE-2 is the score of compressed sentence generated by the model trained on each training data to target.

where $\oplus$ indicates concatenation, s_t and m_t are respectively a hidden state and a memory cell at time t, and $e_1(word)$ is embedding of $word$. If $label$ is "retain", $e_l(label)$ is $(1; 0)$; otherwise, $(0; 1)$. m_0 is a zero vector.

As the second and the third models, we extend the first model to control the output length (Kikuchi et al., 2016). The second model, *lstm+leninit*, initializes the memory cell of the decoder as follows: $m_0 = tarlen * b_{len}$ where $tarlen$ is the desired output length, and b_{len} is a trainable parameter. The third model, *lstm+lenemb*, uses the embedding of the potential desired length $e_2(length)$ as an additional input. In this case, $e_1(x_t) \oplus e_l(y_{t-1}) \oplus e_2(l_t)$ is used as the input of the decoder where l_t is the potential desired length at time t.

4 Experiments

The created training datasets were used to train three models for sentence compression. To see the effect of the modified subtree extraction method (Section 2.3), two training datasets were tested: *rooted* and *multi-root+*. *rooted* includes only deletion of the leafs in a dependency tree. In contrast, *multi-root+* includes deleting the global root and reflecting abbreviated forms besides it.

Setting: Training datasets were created from seven million, 35-years' worth of news articles from the Mainichi, Nikkei, and Yomiuri newspapers, from which duplicate sentences and sentences in test data were filtered out. Gold-standard data were composed of the first sentences of the 1,000 news articles from Mainichi, each of which has 5 compressed sentences separately created by five human annotators. 100 sentences of the gold-standard data were used as development data, while the other sentences were used as test data. The three models were trained on datasets created with each value of threshold θ[6], which is the parameter used in the condition (introduced in Sec-

---

[5]"H is not a question", "both H and S are not less than four words.", "S is more than 1.5 times longer than H", and "S is more than 1.5 times longer than C".

[6]In Table 2, the thresholds for our models are 0.7, 0.5, 0.3, 0.6, 0.4, and 0.2, respectively, from the top.

dataset	model	R-1	ROUGE-2			R-L	CR
			R(R-2)	P	F		
	prop-w-dpnd	73.8	56.5	51.5	53.7	32.7	60.5
	tree-base	68.6	52.6	50.4	51.4	34.4	59.1
rooted	*lstm*	66.3	51.5	59.3	54.6	36.1	51.8
rooted	*lstm+leninit*	70.8	55.2	57.1	55.9	36.0	56.8
rooted	*lstm+lenemb*	71.0	55.2	56.7	55.7	35.9	57.8
multi-root+	*lstm*	60.8	50.6	60.5	54.1	33.7	47.9
multi-root+	*lstm+leninit*	71.7	56.0	57.8	56.7	36.3	57.8
multi-root+	*lstm+lenemb*	72.6	56.2	56.4	56.1	35.8	59.4

Table 2: Automatic evaluation. R-1, R-2, and R-L are ROUGE-1, ROUGE-2, and ROUGE-L score. R, P and F are recall, precision and F-measure.

tion 2.4). The properties of the dataset in relation to θ are shown in Table 1. θ is tuned for ROUGE-2 score on the development data. In Table 1, we show the tendency of the ROUGE-2 scores when *lstm+leninit* was trained on created *rooted* with each θ. From Table 1, we chose 0.5 as θ. All models are three stacked LSTM layers[7]. Words with frequency lower than five are regarded as unknown words. ADAM[8] was used as the optimization method. The desired length was set to the bytes of a compressed sentence randomly chosen from the five human-generated sentences. In the test step, beam-search was used (beam size: 20) and candidates exceeding the desired length were truncated.

tree-base and prop-w-dpnd: Existing methods for Japanese sentence compression are not based on the training on a large dataset. Therefore, the proposed method is compared with two methods, *tree-base*, (Filippova and Strube, 2008) and *prop-w-dpnd* (Harashima and Kurohashi, 2012), which are not based on supervised learning. *tree-base* is implemented as an integer linear programming problem that finds a subtree of a dependency tree. *prop-w-dpnd* is also implemented as an integer linear programming problem, but modified based on characteristics of the Japanese language. *prop-w-dpnd* allows the deletion inside the chunks.

4.1 Automatic evaluation

Table 2 shows the ROUGE score of each model. We used ROUGE-1, ROUGE-2, and ROUGE-L (R-1, R-2, and R-L) for evaluation. In addition, we also show the precision and F-measure of ROUGE-2 because the output length of each model is not same. Compression ratio (CR) is the ratio of the bytes of the compressed sentence to the bytes of the source sentence. Average

CR of the test data is approximately 61.0%. We think we should focus on F-measure of ROUGE-2 because of the different CR of the models. The models trained on a large training dataset achieved higher F-measure than the unsupervised models. Moreover, F-measure of *lstm+leninit* and *lstm+lenemb*, which were trained on either *multi-root+* or *rooted*, is significantly better than *prop-w-dpnd* (p < 0.001). *lstm* achieved lower R-1 and R-2 than the other models trained on a large training dataset, probably because it tends to generate too short sentences, as indicated by low CR. It is also noteworthy that CRs of *lstm+leninit* and *lstm+lenemb* are mostly closer to the average CR of the test data than *lstm*. Furthermore, *lstm+leninit* and *lstm+lenemb* trained on *multi-root+* instead of *rooted* worked better in terms of F-measure. We consider it is because various types of deletion make the compression model more flexible, as indicated by closer CR of the model trained on *multi-root+* instead of *rooted* to the average CR of the test data.

4.2 Human evaluation

The difference between *lstm+leninit* and *lstm+lenemb* trained on *multi-root+* was investigated first. With *lstm+leninit*, 2 out of 100 sentences, chosen randomly, ended with a word that cannot be located at the end of a sentence. In contrast, with *lstm+lenemb*, 24 sentences ended with such words and therefore are ungrammatical, although *lenemb* has shown to be effective in abstractive sentence summarization (Kikuchi et al., 2016). This result suggests that *lstm+lenemb* is excessively affected by the desired length because *lenemb* receives the potential desired length at each time of decoding. In fact, 21 out of the 24 sentences are as long as the desired length.

Then, *lstm+leninit* trained on *multi-root+* was evaluated by crowdsourcing in comparison with the gold-standard and *tree-base*. Each crowd-

---

[7]Dimension of word embedding and hidden layer:256, dropout:20%

[8]α:0.001, β_1:0.9, β_2:0.999, eps:1e-8, batchsize:180

model	read	info
gold-standard	4.22	3.76
lstm+leninit	3.99	3.09
prop-w-dpnd	3.55	2.81

Table 3: Human absolute evaluation

model	read	info	training data	read	info
lstm+leninit	78	108	*multi-root+*	55	85
lstm	47	47	*rooted*	57	33
tie	125	95	*tie*	138	132

Table 4: Human relative evaluation

sourcing worker reads each source sentence and a set of the compressed sentences, reordered randomly, and gives a score from 1 to 5 (where 5 is best) to each compressed sentence in terms of informativeness (*info*) and readability (*read*). As shown in Table 3, in terms of both *read* and *info*, *lstm+leninit* archived higher scores than *prop-w-dpnd*, and the difference is significant ($p < 0.001$).

Next, *lstm+leninit* was compared with *lstm* (both are trained on *multi-root+*), and *multi-root+* was compared with *rooted* (*lstm+leninit* was used as the model), by human relative evaluation. In this evaluation, each worker votes for one of *lstm+leninit*, *lstm*, or tie, and for one of *multi-root+*, *rooted*, or tie. 250 votes in total were received (50 sentences $\times$ 5 votes). The results are shown in Table 4. *lstm+leninit* is better than *lstm* in terms of *read*, which is not directly related to the output length, as well as of *info*. It is also clear that *multi-root+* achieves much higher *info* with a negligible reduction in *read* than *rooted*.

5 Conclusion

Filippova et al.'s method of creating training data for English sentence compression was modified to create a training dataset for Japanese sentence compression. The effectiveness of the created Japanese training dataset was verified by automatic and human evaluation. Our method can refine the created dataset by giving more flexibility in compression and achieved better informativeness with negligible reduction in readability. Furthermore, it has been shown that controlling the output length improves the performance of the sentence compression models.

Acknowledgment

This work was supported by Google Research Award, JSPS KAKENHI Grant Number JP26280080, and JPMJPR1655.

References

Taylor Berg-Kirkpatrick, Dan Gillick, and Dan Klein. 2011. Jointly learning to extract and compress. In *Proceedings of the 49th Annual Meeting of the Association for Computational Linguistics: Human Language Technologies - Volume 1*. pages 481–490.

James Clarke and Mirella Lapata. 2006. Models for sentence compression: A comparison across domains, training requirements and evaluation measures. In *Proceedings of the 21st International Conference on Computational Linguistics and the 44th Annual Meeting of the Association for Computational Linguistics*. pages 377–384.

Katja Filippova, Enrique Alfonseca, Carlos A. Colmenares, Lukasz Kaiser, and Oriol Vinyals. 2015. Sentence compression by deletion with lstms. In *Proceedings of the 2015 Conference on Empirical Methods in Natural Language Processing*. pages 360–368.

Katja Filippova and Yasemin Altun. 2013. Overcoming the lack of parallel data in sentence compression. In *Proceedings of the 2013 Conference on Empirical Methods in Natural Language Processing*. pages 1481–1491.

Katja Filippova and Michael Strube. 2008. Dependency tree based sentence compression. In *Proceedings of the Fifth International Natural Language Generation Conference*. pages 25–32.

Jun Harashima and Sadao Kurohashi. 2012. Flexible Japanese sentence compression by relaxing unit constraints. In *Proceedings of COLING 2012*. pages 1097–1112.

Tsutomu Hirao, Jun Suzuki, and Hideki Isozaki. 2009. A syntax-free approach to japanese sentence compression. In *Proceedings of the Joint Conference of the 47th Annual Meeting of the ACL and the 4th International Joint Conference on Natural Language Processing of the AFNLP*. pages 826–833.

Chiori Hori and Sadaoki Furui. 2004. Speech summarization : An approach through word extraction and a method for evaluation (¡special section¿the 2002 ieice excellent paper award). *IEICE transactions on information and systems* pages 15–25.

Yuta Kikuchi, Graham Neubig, Ryohei Sasano, Hiroya Takamura, and Manabu Okumura. 2016. Controlling output length in neural encoder-decoders. In *Proceedings of the 2016 Conference on Empirical Methods in Natural Language Processing*. pages 1328–1338.

Kevin Knight and Daniel Marcu. 2000. Statistics-based summarization - step one: Sentence compression. In *Proceedings of the Seventeenth National Conference on Artificial Intelligence and Twelfth Conference on Innovative Applications of Artificial Intelligence*. pages 703–710.

Ilya Sutskever, Oriol Vinyals, and Quoc V. Le. 2014. Sequence to sequence learning with neural networks. In *Proceedings of the 27th International Conference on Neural Information Processing Systems*. pages 3104–3112.

Kapil Thadani and Kathleen McKeown. 2013. Sentence compression with joint structural inference. In *Proceedings of the Seventeenth Conference on Computational Natural Language Learning*. pages 65–74.

Jenine Turner and Eugene Charniak. 2005. Supervised and unsupervised learning for sentence compression. In *Proceedings of the 43rd Annual Meeting on Association for Computational Linguistics*. pages 290–297.

A Neural Architecture for Generating Natural Language Descriptions from Source Code Changes

Pablo Loyola, Edison Marrese-Taylor and Yutaka Matsuo
Graduate School of Engineering
The University of Tokyo
Tokyo, Japan
`{pablo,emarrese,matsuo}@weblab.t.u-tokyo.ac.jp`

Abstract

We propose a model to automatically describe changes introduced in the source code of a program using natural language. Our method receives as input a set of code commits, which contains both the modifications and message introduced by an user. These two modalities are used to train an encoder-decoder architecture. We evaluated our approach on twelve real world open source projects from four different programming languages. Quantitative and qualitative results showed that the proposed approach can generate feasible and semantically sound descriptions not only in standard in-project settings, but also in a cross-project setting.

1 Introduction

Source code, while conceived as a set of structured and sequential instructions, inherently reflects human intent: it encodes the way we command a machine to perform a task. In that sense, it is expected that it follows to some extent the same distributional regularities that a proper natural language manifests (Hindle et al., 2012). Moreover, the unambiguous nature of source code, comprised in plain and human-readable format, allows an indirect way of communication between developers, a phenomenon boosted in recent years given the current software development paradigm, where billions of lines code are written in a distributed and asynchronous way (Gousios et al., 2014).

The scale and complexity of software systems these days has naturally led to explore automated ways to support developers' code comprehension (Letovsky, 1987) from a linguistic perspective. One of these attempts is automatic summarization, which aims to generate a compact representation of the source code in a portion of natural language (Haiduc et al., 2010).

While existing code summarization methods are able to provide relevant insights about the purpose and functional features of the code, their scope is inherently static. In contrast, software development can be seen as a sequence of incremental changes, intended to either generate a new functionality or to repair an existing one. Source code changes are critical for understanding program evolution, which motivated us to explore if it is possible to extend the notion of summarization to encode code changes into natural language representations, i.e., develop a model able to *explain* a source code level modification. With this, we envision a tool for developers that is able to *i)* ease the comprehension of the dynamics of the system, which could be useful for debugging and repairing purposes and *ii)* automate the documentation of source code changes.

To this end, we rely on the concept of code commit, the standard contribution procedure implemented in modern subversion systems (Gousios et al., 2014), which provides both the actual change and a short explanatory paragraph. Our model consists of an encoder-decoder architecture which is trained on a set of triples conformed by the version of a system before and after the change, along with the comment. Given the high heterogeneity of the modalities involved, we rely on an attention mechanism to efficiently learn the parts of the sequences that are more expressive and have more explanatory power.

We performed an empirical study on twelve real world software systems, from which we obtained the commit activity to evaluate our model. Our experiments explored in-project and cross-project scenarios, and our results showed that the proposed model is able to generate semantically sound descriptions.

Proceedings of the 55th Annual Meeting of the Association for Computational Linguistics (Short Papers), pages 287–292
Vancouver, Canada, July 30 - August 4, 2017. ©2017 Association for Computational Linguistics
https://doi.org/10.18653/v1/P17-2045

2 Related Work

The use natural language processing to support software engineering tasks has increased consistently over the years, mainly in terms of source code search, traceability and program feature location (Panichella et al., 2013; Asuncion et al., 2010).

The emergence of unifying paradigms that explicitly relate programming and natural languages in distributional terms (Hindle et al., 2012) and the availability of large corpus mainly from open source software opened the door for the use of language modeling for several tasks (Raychev et al., 2015). Examples of this are approaches for learning program representations (Mou et al., 2016), bug localization (Huo et al.), API suggestion (Gu et al., 2016) and code completion (Raychev et al., 2014).

Source code summarization has received special attention, ranging from the use of information retrieval techniques to the addition of physiological features such as eye tracking (Rodeghero et al., 2014). In recent years several representation learning approaches have been proposed, such as (Allamanis et al., 2016), where the authors employ a convolutional architecture embedded inside an attention mechanism to learn an efficient mapping between source code tokens and natural language keywords.

More recently, (Iyer et al., 2016) proposed a encoder-decoder model that learns to summarize from Stackoverflow data, which contains snippet of code along with descriptions. Both approaches share the use of attention mechanisms (Bahdanau et al., 2014) to overcome the natural disparity between the modalities when finding relevant token alignments. Although we also use an attention mechanism, we differ from them in the sense we are targeting the changes in the code rather than the description of a file.

In terms of specifically working on code change summarization, Cortés-Coy et al. (2014); Linares-Vásquez et al. (2015) propose a method based on a set of rules that considers the type and impact of the changes, and (Buse and Weimer, 2010) combines summarization with symbolic execution. To the best of our knowledge, our approach represents the first attempt to generate natural language descriptions from code changes without the use of hand-crafted features, a desirable setting given the heterogeneity of the data involved.

3 Proposed Model

Our model assumes the existence of T versions of a given project $\{v_1, \ldots, v_T\}$. Given a pair of consecutive versions (v_{t-1}, v_t), we define the tuple (C_t, N_t), where $C_t = \Delta_{t-1}^t(v)$ represents a code snippet associated to changes over v in time t and N_t represents its corresponding natural language (NL) description. Let $\mathbb{C}$ be the set of all source code snippets and $\mathbb{N}$ be the set of all descriptions in NL. We consider a training corpus with T code snippets and summary pairs (C_t, N_t), $1 \leq t \leq T$, $C_t \in \mathbb{C}$, $N_t \in \mathbb{N}$. Then, for a given code snippet $C_k \in \mathbb{C}$, the goal of our model is to produce the most likely NL description $N^\star$.

Concretely, similarly to (Iyer et al., 2016), we use an attention-augmented encoder-decoder architecture. The encoder can be seen as a lookup layer, which simply reads through the source input sequence and returns the embedded tokens. The decoder is a RNN that reads this representation and generates NL words one at a time based on its current hidden state and guided by a global attention model (Luong et al., 2015). We model the probability of a description as a product of the conditional next-word probabilities. More formally, for each NL token $n_i \in N_t$ we define,

$$h_i = f(n_{i-1}E, h_{i-1}) \quad (1)$$
$$p(n_i|n_1, ..., n_{i-1}) \propto W \tanh(W_1 h_i + W_2 a_i) \quad (2)$$

where E is the embedding matrix for NL tokens, $\propto$ denotes a softmax operation, h_i represents the hidden state and a_i is the contribution from the attention model on the source code. W, W_1 and W_2 are trainable combination matrices. The decoder repeats the recurrence until a fixed number of words or a special *END* token is generated. The attention contribution a_i is defined as $a_i = \sum_{j=1}^{k} \alpha_{i,j} \cdot c_j F$, where $c_j \in C_t$ is a source code token, F is the source code token embedding matrix and $\alpha_{i,j}$ is:

$$\alpha_{i,j} = \frac{\exp\left(h_i^\top c_j F\right)}{\sum_{c_j \in C_t} \exp\left(h_i^\top c_j F\right)} \quad (3)$$

We use a dropout-regularized LSTM cell for the decoder (Zaremba et al., 2015) and also add dropout at the NL embeddings and at the output softmax layer, to prevent over-fitting. We added special *START* and *END* tokens to our training sequences and replaced all tokens and output words occurring less than 2 and 3 times, respectively, with a special *UNK* token. We set the maximum code and NL length to be 100 tokens. For decoding, we approximate $N^\star$ by performing a beam search on the space of all possible summaries using the model output, with a beam size of 10 and a maximum summary length of 20 words.

To evaluate the quality of our generated descriptions we use both METEOR (Lavie and Agarwal, 2007) and sentence level BLEU-4 (Papineni et al., 2002). Since the training objective does not directly optimize for these scores, we compute METEOR on our validation set after every epoch and save the intermediate model that gives the maximum score as the final model. For evaluation on our test set we used the BLEU-4 score.

4 Empirical Study

Data and pre-processing: We captured historical data from twelve open source projects hosted on Github based on their popularity and maturity, selecting 3 projects for each of the following languages: *python*, *java*, *javascript* and *c++*. For each project, we downloaded diff files and metadata of the full commit history. Diff files encode per-line differences between two files or sets of files in a standard format, allowing us to recover source code changes in each commit at the line level. On the other hand, medatada allows us to recover information such as the author and message of each commit.

The extracted commit messages were processed using the Penn Treebank tokenizer (Marcus et al., 1993), which nicely deals with punctuation and other text marks. To obtain a source code representation of each commit, we parsed the diff files and used a lexer (Brandl, 2016) to tokenize their contents in a per-line fashion allowing us to maximize the amount of source code recovered from the diff files. Data and source code available[1].

Experimental Setup: Given the flat structure of the diff file, source code in contiguous lines might not necessarily correspond to originally neighboring code lines. Moreover, they might come from different files in the project. To deal with this issue, we first worked only with those commits that modify a single file in the project; we call this the *atomicity* assumption. By using only *atomic* commits we reduced our training data by an average of roughly 50%, but in exchange we made sure all the extracted code lines came from

---

Language	Project	Full	Atomic	Added	Rem.
python	Theano	24,200	65.40%	11.43%	2,83%
	keras	2,855	66.02%	11.07%	3,01%
	youtube-dl	13,968	74.49%	11.52%	2,59%
javascript	node	15,811	53.17%	11.87%	3,21%
	angular	6,204	32.90%	5.59%	1,72%
	react	7,806	53.29%	12.67%	2,72%
c++	opencv	20,480	50.08%	8.83%	1,66%
	CNTK	10,792	38.36%	6.00%	2,23%
	bitcoin	12,596	48.11%	9.84%	2,56%
java	CoreNLP	9,149	42.77%	7.84%	1,98%
	elasticsearch	25,764	43.77%	9.02%	2,61%
	guava	3,821	38.63%	8.90%	2,64%
Average		12,787	50.58%	9.55%	2,48%

Table 1: Summary of our collected data.

the same file. At the same time, we expect to maximize the likelihood of observing a direct relation between the commit message and the lines altered.

We then relaxed our *atomicity* assumption and experimented with the *full* commit history. Given our maximum sequence length constrain of 100 tokens, we only observed an average of 1,97% extra data on each project. Since source code lines may come from different files, we added a delimiting token *NEW_FILE* when corresponding.

We were also interested in studying the performance of the model in a cross-project setting. Given the additional challenges that this involves, we designed a more controlled experiment. Starting from the *atomic* dataset, we selected commits that only add or only remove code lines, conforming a derived dataset that we call *uni-action*. We chose the *python* language to maximize the available data. See Table 1.

Results and Discussion: We begin by training our model on the *atomic* dataset. As baseline we used MOSES (Koehn et al., 2007) which although is designed as a phrase-based machine translation system, was previously used by Iyer et al. (2016) to generate text from source code. Concretely, we treated the tokenized code snippet as the source language and the NL description as the target. We trained a 3-gram language model using KenLM (Heafield et al., 2013) and used mGiza to obtain alignments. For validation, we use minimum error rate training (Bertoldi et al., 2009; Och, 2003) in our validation set.

As Table 3 shows, our model trained on *atomic* data outperforms the baseline in all but one project with an average gain of 5 BLEU points. In particular, we observe bigger gains for java projects such as *CoreNLP* and *guava*. We hypothesize this is because program differences in Java tend to be longer than the rest. While this impacts on training time, at the same time it allows the model to work with a larger vocabulary space. On the other hand, our model performs similarly to MOSES for the *node* and slightly worse for the *youtube-dl*. A detailed inspection of the NL messages for *node* showed that many of them exhibit a fixed pattern in their structure. We believe this rigidity restrains the generation capabilities of the decoder, making it more prone to memorization.

Table 2 shows examples of generated descriptions for real changes and their references. Results suggest that our model is able to generate semantically sound descriptions for the changes. We can also visualize the summarizing power of the model, as seen in the *Theano* and *bitcoin* examples. We observe a tendency to choose more general terms over too specific ones meanwhile also avoiding irrelevant words such as numbers or names. Results also suggest the emergence of rephrasing capabilities, specifically in the second example from *Theano*. Finally, our generated descriptions are, in most cases, semantically well correlated to the reference descriptions. We also report not so successful results, such as case of *youtube-dl*, where we can see signs of memorization on the generated descriptions.

Regarding the cross-project setting experiments on *python*, we obtained BLEU scores of 14.6 and 18.9 for only-adding and only-removing instances in the *uni-action* dataset, respectively. We also obtained validation accuracies up to 43.94%, suggesting feasibility in this more challenging scenario. Moreover, as the generated descriptions from the *keras* project in Table 2 show, the model is still able to generate semantically sound descriptions.

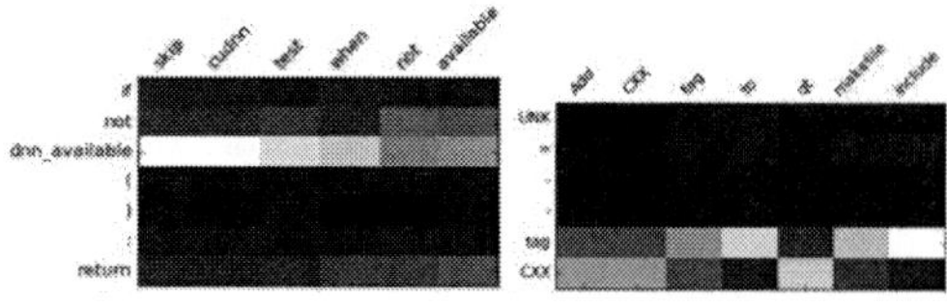

Figure 1: Heatmaps of attention weights $\alpha_{i,j}$.

Despite the small data increase, we also trained our model on *full* datasets as a way to confirm the generative power of our model. In particular, we wanted to test the model is able leverage on *atomic* data to also capture and compress multi-file changes. As shown in Table 3, results in terms of BLEU and validation accuracy manifest reasonable consistency, despite the higher disparity be-

	Reference	Generated
keras	Fix image resizing in preprocessing/image	Fixed image preprocessing .
keras	Fix test flakes	Fix flaky test
Theano	fix crash in the new warning message .	Better warning message .
Theano	remove var not used .	remove not used code .
Theano	Better error msg	better error message .
bitcoin	Merge pull request 4486 45abeb2 Update Debian packaging description for new bitcoin-cli (Johnathan Corgan)	Update Debian packaging description for new bitcoin-cli
bitcoin	Add two unittest-related files to .gitignore	Add : Minor files to .gitignore
CoreNLP	Add a bunch of verbs which are more likely to be xcomp than vmod	Add a bunch of verbs which are more to be xcomp than vmod
CoreNLP	Add a brief test for optional nodes	make this test do something
youtube-dl	[crunchyroll] Fix uploader and upload date extraction	[crunchyroll] Fix uploader extraction
youtube-dl	[extractor/common] Improve base url construction	[extractor/common] Improve extraction
youtube-dl	[mixcloud] Use unicode_literals	[common] Use unicode_literals
opencv	fixed gcc compilation	fixed compile under linux
opencv	remove unused variables in OCL_PERF_TEST_P ( )	remove unused variable in the module

Table 2: Examples of generated natural language passages v/s original ones taken from the test set.

tween source code and natural language on this dataset, which means the model was able to learn representations with more compressive power.

Soft alignments derived from Figure 1, which shows examples of attention heatmaps, illustrate how the model effectively associates source code tokens with meaningful words.

Dataset	atomic			full	
	Val. acc	BLEU	Moses	Val. acc	BLEU
Theano	36.81%	9.5	7.1	39.88%	10.9
keras	45.76%	13.7	7.8	59.30%	8.8
youtube-dl	50.84%	16.4	17.5	53.65%	17.7
node	52.46%	7.8	7.7	53.70%	7.2
angular	44.39%	13.9	11.7	45.06%	15.3
react	49.44%	11.4	10.7	48.61%	12.1
opencv	50.77%	11.2	9.0	49.00%	8.4
CNTK	48.88%	17.9	11.8	44.85%	9.3
bitcoin	50.04%	17.9	13.0	55.03%	15.1
CoreNLP	63.20%	28.5	10.1	62.25%	26.7
elasticsearch	36.53%	11.8	5.2	35.98%	6.4
guava	65.52%	29.8	19.5	67.15%	34.3

Table 3: Results on the *atomic* and *full* datasets.

5   Conclusion and Future work

We proposed an encoder-decoder model for automatically generating natural descriptions from source code changes. We believe our current results suggest that the idea is feasible and, if improved, could represent a contribution for the understanding of software evolution from a linguistic perspective. As future work, we will consider improving the model by allowing feature learning from richer inputs, such as abstract syntax trees and also functional data, such as execution traces.

References

Miltiadis Allamanis, Hao Peng, and Charles Sutton. 2016. A convolutional attention network for extreme summarization of source code. *arXiv preprint arXiv:1602.03001* .

Hazeline U. Asuncion, Arthur U. Asuncion, and Richard N. Taylor. 2010. Software traceability with topic modeling. In *Proceedings of the 32Nd ACM/IEEE International Conference on Software Engineering - Volume 1*. ACM, New York, NY, USA, ICSE '10, pages 95–104. https://doi.org/10.1145/1806799.1806817.

Dzmitry Bahdanau, Kyunghyun Cho, and Yoshua Bengio. 2014. Neural machine translation by jointly learning to align and translate. *arXiv preprint arXiv:1409.0473* .

Nicola Bertoldi, Haddow Barry, and Jean-Baptiste Fouet. 2009. Improved minimum error rate training in moses. *The Prague Bulletin of Mathematical Linguistics* pages 1–11.

Georg Brandl. 2016. Pygments: Python syntax highlighter. http://pygments.org.

Raymond P.L. Buse and Westley R. Weimer. 2010. Automatically documenting program changes. In *Proceedings of the IEEE/ACM International Conference on Automated Software Engineering*. ACM, New York, NY, USA, ASE '10, pages 33–42. https://doi.org/10.1145/1858996.1859005.

Luis Fernando Cortés-Coy, Mario Linares Vásquez, Jairo Aponte, and Denys Poshyvanyk. 2014. On automatically generating commit messages via summarization of source code changes. In *SCAM*. volume 14, pages 275–284.

Georgios Gousios, Martin Pinzger, and Arie van Deursen. 2014. An exploratory study of the pull-based software development model. In *Proceedings of the 36th International Conference on Software Engineering*. ACM, pages 345–355.

Xiaodong Gu, Hongyu Zhang, Dongmei Zhang, and Sunghun Kim. 2016. Deep api learning. In *Proceedings of the 2016 24th ACM SIGSOFT International Symposium on Foundations of Software Engineering*. ACM, New York, NY, USA, FSE 2016, pages 631–642. https://doi.org/10.1145/2950290.2950334.

Sonia Haiduc, Jairo Aponte, and Andrian Marcus. 2010. Supporting program comprehension with source code summarization. In *Proceedings of the 32nd ACM/IEEE International Conference on Software Engineering-Volume 2*. ACM, pages 223–226.

Kenneth Heafield, Ivan Pouzyrevsky, Jonathan H. Clark, and Philipp Koehn. 2013. Scalable modified Kneser-Ney language model estimation. In *Proceedings of the 51st Annual Meeting of the Association for Computational Linguistics*. Sofia, Bulgaria, pages 690–696.

Abram Hindle, Earl T Barr, Zhendong Su, Mark Gabel, and Premkumar Devanbu. 2012. On the naturalness of software. In *2012 34th International Conference on Software Engineering (ICSE)*. IEEE, pages 837–847.

Xuan Huo, Ming Li, and Zhi-Hua Zhou. ???? Learning unified features from natural and programming languages for locating buggy source code .

Srinivasan Iyer, Ioannis Konstas, Alvin Cheung, and Luke Zettlemoyer. 2016. Summarizing source code using a neural attention model. In *Proceedings of the 54th Annual Meeting of the Association for Computational Linguistics (Volume 1: Long Papers)*. Association for Computational Linguistics, Berlin, Germany, pages 2073–2083. http://www.aclweb.org/anthology/P16-1195.

Philipp Koehn, Hieu Hoang, Alexandra Birch, Chris Callison-Burch, Marcello Federico, Nicola Bertoldi, Brooke Cowan, Wade Shen, Christine Moran, Richard Zens, Chris Dyer, Ondrej Bojar, Alexandra Constantin, and Evan Herbst. 2007. Moses: Open source toolkit for statistical machine translation. In *Proceedings of the 45th Annual Meeting of the Association for Computational Linguistics Companion Volume Proceedings of the Demo and Poster Sessions*. Association for Computational Linguistics, Prague, Czech Republic, pages 177–180. http://www.aclweb.org/anthology/P07-2045.

Alon Lavie and Abhaya Agarwal. 2007. Meteor: An automatic metric for mt evaluation with high levels of correlation with human judgments. In *Proceedings of the Second Workshop on Statistical Machine Translation*. Association for Computational Linguistics, Stroudsburg, PA, USA, StatMT '07, pages 228–231. http://dl.acm.org/citation.cfm?id=1626355.1626389.

Stanley Letovsky. 1987. Cognitive processes in program comprehension. *Journal of Systems and software* 7(4):325–339.

Mario Linares-Vásquez, Luis Fernando Cortés-Coy, Jairo Aponte, and Denys Poshyvanyk. 2015. Changescribe: A tool for automatically generating commit messages. In *Proceedings of the 37th International Conference on Software Engineering-Volume 2*. IEEE Press, pages 709–712.

Thang Luong, Hieu Pham, and Christopher D. Manning. 2015. Effective approaches to attention-based neural machine translation. In *Proceedings of the 2015 Conference on Empirical Methods in Natural Language Processing*. Association for Computational Linguistics, Lisbon, Portugal, pages 1412–1421. http://aclweb.org/anthology/D15-1166.

Mitchell P Marcus, Mary Ann Marcinkiewicz, and Beatrice Santorini. 1993. Building a large annotated corpus of english: The penn treebank. *Computational linguistics* 19(2):313–330.

Lili Mou, Ge Li, Lu Zhang, Tao Wang, and Zhi Jin. 2016. Convolutional neural networks over tree structures for programming language processing. In *Proc. AAAI*. AAAI Press, pages 1287–1293.

Franz Josef Och. 2003. Minimum error rate training in statistical machine translation. In *Proceedings of the 41st Annual Meeting of the Association for Computational Linguistics*. Association for Computational Linguistics, Sapporo, Japan, pages 160–167. https://doi.org/10.3115/1075096.1075117.

Annibale Panichella, Bogdan Dit, Rocco Oliveto, Massimiliano Di Penta, Denys Poshyvanyk, and Andrea De Lucia. 2013. How to effectively use topic models for software engineering tasks? an approach based on genetic algorithms. In *Proceedings of the 2013 International Conference on Software Engineering*. IEEE Press, Piscataway, NJ, USA, ICSE '13, pages 522–531. http://dl.acm.org/citation.cfm?id=2486788.2486857.

Kishore Papineni, Salim Roukos, Todd Ward, and Wei-Jing Zhu. 2002. Bleu: a method for automatic evaluation of machine translation. In *Proceedings of 40th Annual Meeting of the Association for Computational Linguistics*. Association for Computational Linguistics, Philadelphia, Pennsylvania, USA, pages 311–318. https://doi.org/10.3115/1073083.1073135.

Veselin Raychev, Martin Vechev, and Andreas Krause. 2015. Predicting program properties from big code. In *ACM SIGPLAN Notices*. ACM, volume 50, pages 111–124.

Veselin Raychev, Martin Vechev, and Eran Yahav. 2014. Code completion with statistical language models. In *ACM SIGPLAN Notices*. ACM, volume 49, pages 419–428.

Paige Rodeghero, Collin McMillan, Paul W McBurney, Nigel Bosch, and Sidney D'Mello. 2014. Improving automated source code summarization via an eye-tracking study of programmers. In *Proceedings of the 36th International Conference on Software Engineering*. ACM, pages 390–401.

Wojciech Zaremba, Ilya Sutskever, and Vinyals Oriol. 2015. Recurrent neural network regularization. In *Proceedings of the 3rd International Conference on Learning Representations*.

English Event Detection With Translated Language Features

Sam Wei
School of IT
University of Sydney
Sydney, Australia
swei4829@uni.sydney.edu.au

Igor Korostil
TEG Analytics
Sydney, Australia

Joel Nothman
Sydney Informatics Hub
University of Sydney
Sydney, Australia

Ben Hachey
School of IT
University of Sydney
Sydney, Australia

{eeghor,joel.nothman,ben.hachey}@gmail.com

Abstract

We propose novel radical features from automatic translation for event extraction. Event detection is a complex language processing task for which it is expensive to collect training data, making generalisation challenging. We derive meaningful subword features from automatic translations into target language. Results suggest this method is particularly useful when using languages with writing systems that facilitate easy decomposition into subword features, e.g., logograms and Cangjie. The best result combines logogram features from Chinese and Japanese with syllable features from Korean, providing an additional 3.0 points f-score when added to state-of-the-art generalisation features on the TAC KBP 2015 Event Nugget task.

1 Introduction

Event trigger detection is the task of identifying the mention that predicates the occurrence of an event and assigning it an event type (e.g., attack). Typical training data for event trigger detection includes fewer than 200 annotated documents (Ellis et al., 2015). Yet systems attempt to identify many event types (e.g., 38 for the data used here), making data sparsity a particular challenge (Ji, 2009; Zhu et al., 2014).

Existing approaches use two main strategies for handling data sparsity. One strategy is to use lexical databases. Lexical databases have become a standard feature set for event detection. They make it easy to include synonyms and word-class information through hypernym relations. However, they require substantial human effort to build and can have low coverage. Another approach is to induce word-class information through cluster-ing. Here cluster co-membership can be used to find synonyms and cluster identifiers provide abstracted word-class information.

We propose novel semantic features for English event detection derived from automatic translations into thirteen languages. In particular, we explore the use of Cangjie[1] radicals in Chinese and Japanese. Where characters represent concepts, they have often been composed of smaller pictographic units, called radicals. For example: 明(bright) is composed of two radicals 日,月 (sun, moon) with corresponding Latin letter sequence "AB". While this composition is often not productive, we hypothesise that the recurrence of some radicals among related concepts' logograms may be exploited to identify semantic affinity.

Results suggest that (1) translated language features are especially useful if the target language has a writing system facilitating easy decomposition into useful subword features; (2) logograms (e.g., Chinese, Japanese), radicals (e.g., Chinese, Japanese) and syllables (e.g., Japanese, Korean) prove beneficial and complementary; and (3) Chinese characters are particularly useful, comparable to WordNet. Adding the best translated language features to the final system improves F1 by 3.0 points over a state-of-the-art feature set on the TAC KBP 2015 nugget type detection task.

2 Background

Multilingual resources have been successfully applied to various NLP tasks such as named entity recognition (Klementiev and Roth, 2006), paraphrasing (Bannard and Callison-Burch, 2005), sentiment analysis (Wan, 2008), and word sense disambiguation (Lefever and Hoste, 2010).

---

[1] https://en.wikipedia.org/wiki/Cangjie_input_method

Proceedings of the 55th Annual Meeting of the Association for Computational Linguistics (Short Papers), pages 293–298
Vancouver, Canada, July 30 - August 4, 2017. ©2017 Association for Computational Linguistics
https://doi.org/10.18653/v1/P17-2046

Ji (2009) reports significantly improved event trigger extraction via cross-lingual clusters of English translations to Chinese trigger words over large corpora. At runtime, these are used to replace low-confidence event triggers with other high-confidence predicates from the same cluster. We describe an approach leveraging cross-lingual information not only from words, but also at the level of characters and radicals. Like Zhu et al. (2014), we use Google Translate and build bilingual feature vectors from the translations as well as original English sentences. While they address event trigger type classification only, we address both trigger detection and classification. We use new translated language features and evaluate with a range of languages.

Li et al. (2012) show that monolingual Chinese event trigger extraction benefits from using compositional semantics inferred from Chinese characters. We use similar Chinese character information as features for English event trigger detection also using maximum entropy modelling. Furthermore, we introduce new radical features that take advantage of semantic compositionality of Chinese characters.

2.1 Task

We address the event nugget detection task from the Text Analysis Conference Knowledge Base Population (TAC KBP) 2015 shared task (Mitamura and Hovy, 2015), which includes trigger detection and classification. An event trigger is the smallest extent of text (usually a word or short continuous phrase) that predicates the occurrence of an event (LDC, 2015). The task defines 9 event types and and 38 subtypes. Like most task participants, we formulate event trigger detection as a token-level classification task. We use a maximum entropy classifier here, with IOB encoding (Sang and Veenstra, 1999) to represent multi-word mentions.

For comparison, we implement the baseline and lexical generalisation features from Hong et al. (2015). This was the best-performing system in the TAC 2015 nugget type detection task, with an F1 of 58.3. We do not replicate their semi-supervised techniques here as we want to isolate the comparison of translated language features to other generalisation features. Since translated language features leverage off-the-shelf automatic translation, we believe the results here will gener-

alise to semi-supervised learning as well.

Baseline Features (BASE) Our baseline system uses standard surface features used for event extraction. Features of the current token include the full word token as it appears in the sentence, its lemma, its part of speech (POS), its entity type, and a feature that indicates whether the first character of the token is capitalised. Context features are computed for a window of one token on either side of the current token. They include lemma bigrams, POS bigrams and entity type bigrams. Finally, grammatical features are computed based on a dependency parse of the sentence. These include dependency relation types for the governor and any dependents, conjoined relation type and lemma, conjoined relation type and POS, and conjoined relation type and entity type.

Lexical generalisation Features (LEX) We include three generalisation feature sets from the literature as a benchmark. The first lexical resource we use is Nomlex (Macleod et al., 1998) – a dictionary of nouns that are generated from another verb class, usually verbs. We also use Brown clusters trained on the Reuters corpus (Brown et al., 1992; Turian et al., 2010). Brown clusters group words into classes by performing a hierarchical clustering over distributional representations of the contexts in which they appear. Finally, we use WordNet (Miller, 1995) – a lexical database that includes synonym relations and semantic type-of/hypernym relationships. These relations have been used to extend feature sets beyond observed tokens which can help with identification of rare or unseen event triggers.

3 Approach

We use machine translation (MT) service to obtain translated text. The translation is done at sentence level. We cache the translation results on files to ensure the experiments are repeatable. Below are example sentences translated from English into Chinese and Spanish.

> **EN** *The attack by insurgents happened yesterday.*
> **ZH** 叛亂分子的襲擊發生在昨天。 (1)
> **ES** *El ataque de los insurgentes pasó ayer.*

3.1 Translated Language Features (TRANS)

We generate three types of logogram features and use stem features for non-logogram languages.

Word features (word) Different words in English can be translated into the same word in another language. For example there are 201 unique

Chinese Character	Radical Symbol	Latin Radical	English Word
打	手一弓	QMN	hit
擊	十水手	JEQ	strike
投	手竹弓水	QHNE	throw
擲	手廿大中	QTKL	throw
折(磨)	手竹一中	QHML	torture
拆	手竹一卜	QHMY	demolish
拷(打)	手十大尸	QJKS	torture
割	十口中弓	JRLN	cut
刺	木月中弓	DBLN	stab

Table 1: Attack event triggers. The radical "手" (Q, hand) frequently appears in the attack event triggers. Radicals "中 弓(刀)" (LN, knife) appear frequently when events are associated with actions that are performed with a knife

English trigger words for attack events and only 160 unique words in their Chinese translations. Therefore if an English trigger word is not in the training data, the model might still recognise the trigger if it has seen the Chinese translation before.

Logogram character features (char) Chinese and Japanese logograms are compositions of one or more characters defining their meanings. Therefore, different words representing the same event often contain similar characters. There are 195 unique Chinese characters for the attack event triggers in the corpus. The most frequently appearing characters are "擊" (strike, attack), "戰" (war, fight), "殺" (kill), "爭" (fight, dispute), and "炸" (bomb, explode).

Logogram Cangjie features (Cangjie) Chinese and Japanese characters can be further decomposed to smaller components called radicals. Certain radicals are more commonly found for a particular event type (Table 1). Cangjie is one of the methods to decompose Chinese characters. It was designed to use on computers with QWERTY keyboards so the radicals can be easily stored, indexed and searched by most computer systems. In addition to word and character features, we compute Cangjie features for logographic languages.

Stem features (stem) For many languages character and radical features cannot be generated. We generate stem features in addition to the word features where available. We use the NLTK Snowball stemmer for German, Spanish, Finnish, Hungarian, Dutch and Russian; and the NLTK ISRI stemmer for Arabic. By including a range of languages, we hope to separate the effect of syllabic from semantic components of logograms.

3.2 Translation Alignment

Translated language features require each English word to be aligned to one in the translated sentence. We use the translation service obtain all possible translations of a given English word, e.g.:

$$
\begin{aligned}
&\textbf{EN} \quad \textit{attack} \\
&\textbf{ZH} \quad \text{進攻, 砰擊, 發作, \underline{攻擊}, 攻打, 捣擊, 抨擊, ...} \quad (2) \\
&\textbf{ES} \quad \textit{acometida, \underline{ataque contra}, agresión, ...}
\end{aligned}
$$

If one of these is in the translated sentence, then an alignment is made. If not, then we use the most likely word translation (underlined above).

4 Experiments

We use the TAC KBP 2015 English event nugget data (Ellis et al., 2015) for the experiments. Development experiments use the training data (LDC2015E73) and the evaluation data (LDC2015R26) is held out for final results. The development corpus contains a total of 158 documents from two genres: 81 newswire documents and 77 discussion forum documents. We split this into 80% for training and 20% for development testing. We use Google Translate to obtain sentence and word translations into target languages and derive translated language features to help with the English task. Evaluation uses the official scorer from the shared task, where a trigger is counted as correct if both the trigger span and its event subtype are correctly identified.

Comparing languages First, we explore how translated language features perform across the thirteen languages. Figure 1 shows how much each target language improves BASE on development data. We include all word, stem, character and Cangjie features as available for each language. Chinese, Japanese and Korean stand out, with improvements as high as 19.17 points f-score due mostly to large increases in recall. These results suggest that languages with writing systems that facilitate easy decomposition into meaningful subword features are particularly useful.

Combining languages Next, we test whether system performance can be further improved using TRANS features from multiple languages. We add target languages one at a time in order of individual performance, and find that Traditional Chinese, Japanese and Korean to Simplified Chinese together improve F1 by 2.5 points. This combined feature set is used in the remaining analysis and experimental results.

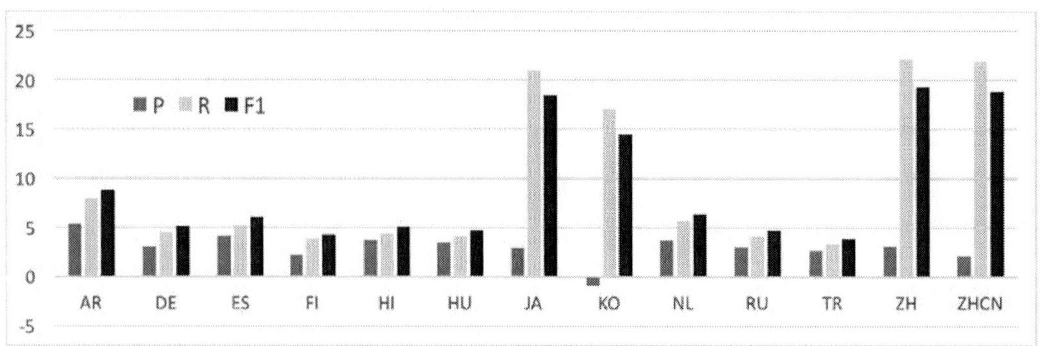

Figure 1: Effect of individual languages on development data, showing the difference in precision, recall and F1 compared to the BASE scores of 55.16, 20.62 and 30.02. AR:Arabic, DE:German, ES:Spanish, FI:Finnish, HI:Hindi, HU:Hungarian, JA:Japanese, KO:Korean, NL:Dutch, RU:Russian, TR:Turkish, ZH:Chinese (Simplified), ZHCN:Chinese (Traditional).

Error analysis We explore characteristic errors for BASE+LEX versus BASE+TRANS for the attack event on evaluation data. We randomly sample twenty instances where one is correct and the other is incorrect. Of six LEX FN errors, two are triggers not seen in the training data, e.g., 'wages' (*Transfer-Money*), and 'resignation' (*End-Position*). In other cases, there seem to be too few training instances, e.g., 'pardoning' (*Pardon*) only appears once in the training data. The TRANS FN error is due to a bad translation in which 'strike' (*Attack*) is a translated to the 'work stoppage' sense instead of the 'forceful hit' sense.

For both systems, most FP errors correspond to cases with challenging ambiguity. For instance, both systems label 'appeal' as *Justice.Appeal* event in two sentences where the word 'appeal' means 'ask for aid', instead of 'taking a court case to a higher court'. The translation was incorrect in this case. Similarly, 'report' appears six times in the training data as three different event types (*Broadcast*, *Correspondence*, *Move-Person*).

Long-tail generalisation Table 2 shows type-level results for BASE+LEX and BASE+TRANS compared to BASE alone. The generalisation feature sets outperform the baseline for all but three of the 38 event types. For *Pardon*, BASE obtains 97 F1 so there is little room for improvement. For *Execute*, LEX features have no effect while TRANS doubles BASE F1. *Contact* is the only type where generalisation features are harmful. Ignoring ties, BASE+TRANS performs best on more types (13) than BASE+LEX (11). TRANS appears to help more with long-tail entity types that have fewer training instances (e.g., *Bankruptcy*, *Appeal*, *Born*). Encouragingly, this

Type	Trn	Tst	BA	LX	TR
Attack	547	253	29	**60**	58
Move-Person	390	127	15	**37**	33
Transfer-Money	366	185	18	35	**49**
Die	357	157	45	63	**66**
Broadcast	305	112	14	**20**	16
Contact	260	77	**29**	24	23
Transfer-Ownership	234	46	9	20	**34**
Meet	221	23	15	**44**	38
Pardon	221	18	97	97	95
Arrest-Jail	208	79	54	70	**71**
Convict	173	49	71	74	**81**
End-Position	130	79	18	51	**55**
Extradite	62	1	0	0	**100**
Execute	51	15	12	12	**24**
Release-Parole	45	28	0	87	**95**
Bankruptcy	30	3	0	50	**89**
Appeal	25	12	0	57	**92**
Born	13	6	0	22	**40**

Table 2: Comparing instance count in training (Trn) and test (Tst) to F1 for BASE (BA), LEX (LX) and TRANS (TR).

analysis also suggests that LEX and TRANS can be complementary, with LEX doing particularly well on some types (e.g., *Trial-Hearing*, *Correspond*) and TRANS doing particularly well on others (e.g., *Transfer-Money*, *Release-Parole*).

5 Final Results and Discussion

Table 3 contains final results on the held-out evaluation data. The final translated language feature set (TRANS) comprises word, character and Cangjie features from Traditional Chinese, Simplified Chinese, Japanese and Korean. TRANS features provide a large F1 improvement of 17.4 over the baseline (BASE), similar to the benchmark lexical generalisation features (LEX). They differ in precision-recall tradeoff, with higher recall but lower precision from TRANS. LEX and TRANS are complementary, giving F1 of 55.0.

System	P	R	F
BASE	60.4	24.1	34.4
BASE+LEX	66.8	42.6	52.0
BASE+TRANS	59.6	45.8	51.8
BASE+LEX+TRANS	67.9	46.2	**55.0**
TAC 2015 medians	61.7	40.7	48.8
TAC 2015 #1	75.2	47.7	**58.4**

Table 3: Final results comparing translated language features (TRANS) to benchmark lexical generalisation features (LEX). BASE+LEX is our implementation of the core Hong et al. classifier. TAC KPB 2015 #1 corresponds to reported results for Hong et al. including semi-supervised learning. TAC KPB 2015 shared task has 38 runs submitted from 14 teams.

This is 20.6 points higher than the baseline features alone, and improves both the precision of LEX and the recall of TRANS.

The main appeal of the approach here is that translated character and radical features are easy to obtain using off-the-shelf tools. This provides a simple technique to capture semantic information and leverage the word sense disambiguation encoded in translation models trained over very large datasets. Given the positive results here, we plan to explore translation and alignment strategies to improve precision. We also plan to quantify the effect of different translation systems and system change over time.

6 Conclusion

We described an event detection system leveraging features from off-the-shelf automatic translation to improve generalisation to new data. Chinese, Japanese and Korean prove especially useful as they provide natural decomposition into informative subword features, i.e., characters (Chinese and Japanese), radicals (Chinese and Japanese) and syllables (Korean). None of the nine other languages explored provide similar levels of natural decomposition and none provided additional benefit. The best system includes Chinese, Japanese and Korean character features. These translated language features improve f-score by 3 points on top of the English-only generalisation features from WordNet, Nomlex and Brown clusters.

Acknowledgments

We wish to thank Will Radford and the anonymous reviewers for their helpful feedback. This research is funded by the Capital Markets Co-operative Research Centre. Ben Hachey is the recipient of an Australian Research Council Discovery Early Career Researcher Award (DE120102900).

References

Colin Bannard and Chris Callison-Burch. 2005. Paraphrasing with bilingual parallel corpora. In *Annual Meeting of the Association for Computational Linguistics*. pages 597–604. https://doi.org/10.3115/1219840.1219914.

Peter F. Brown, Peter V. deSouza, Robert L. Mercer, Vincent J. Della Pietra, and Jenifer C. Lai. 1992. Class-based n-gram models of natural language. *Computational Linguistics* 18(4):467–479. http://www.aclweb.org/anthology/J/J92/J92-4003.pdf.

Joe Ellis, Jeremy Getman, Dana Fore, Neil Kuster, Zhiyi Song, Ann Bies, and Stephanie Strassel. 2015. Overview of linguistic resources for the TAC KBP 2015 evaluations: Methodologies and results. In *Text Analysis Conference*.

Yu Hong, Di Lu, Dian Yu, Xiaoman Pan, Xiaobin Wang, Yadong Chen, Lifu Huang, and Heng Ji. 2015. RPI BLENDER TAC-KBP2015 system description. In *Text Analysis Conference*.

Heng Ji. 2009. Cross-lingual predicate cluster acquisition to improve bilingual event extraction by inductive learning. In *NAACL Workshop on Unsupervised and Minimally Supervised Learning of Lexical Semantics*. pages 27–35. http://www.aclweb.org/anthology/W09-1704.

Alexandre Klementiev and Dan Roth. 2006. Weakly supervised named entity transliteration and discovery from multilingual comparable corpora. In *International Conference on Computational Linguistics and Annual Meeting of the Association for Computational Linguistics*. pages 817–824. https://doi.org/10.3115/1220175.1220278.

LDC. 2015. *Rich ERE Annotation Guidelines Overview*. Linguistic Data Consortium. Version 4.1. Accessed 14 November 2015 from `http://cairo.lti.cs.cmu.edu/kbp/2015/event/summary_rich_ere_v4.1.pdf`.

Els Lefever and Veronique Hoste. 2010. SemEval-2010 task 3: Cross-lingual word sense disambiguation. In *International Workshop on Semantic Evaluation*. pages 15–20. http://www.aclweb.org/anthology/S10-1003.

Peifeng Li, Guodong Zhou, Qiaoming Zhu, and Libin Hou. 2012. Employing compositional semantics and discourse consistency in chinese event extraction. In *Joint Conference on Empirical Methods in Natural Language Processing and Computational Natural Language Learning*. pages 1006–1016. http://www.aclweb.org/anthology/D12-1092.

Catherine Macleod, Ralph Grishman, Adam Meyers, Leslie Barrett, and Ruth Reeves. 1998. Nomlex: A lexicon of nominalizations. In *Euralex International Congress*. pages 187–193.

George A. Miller. 1995. Wordnet: A lexical database for english. *Commun. ACM* 38(11):39–41. https://doi.org/10.1145/219717.219748.

Teruko Mitamura and Eduard Hovy. 2015. *TAC KBP Event Detection and Coreference Tasks for English*. Version 1.0. Accessed 14 November 2015 from `http://cairo.lti.cs.cmu.edu/kbp/2015/event/Event_Mention_Detection_and_Coreference-2015-v1.1.pdf`.

Erik F. Tjong Kim Sang and Jorn Veenstra. 1999. Representing text chunks. In *Conference of the European Chapter of the Association for Computational Linguistics*. pages 173–179. https://doi.org/10.3115/977035.977059.

Joseph Turian, Lev-Arie Ratinov, and Yoshua Bengio. 2010. Word representations: A simple and general method for semi-supervised learning. In *Annual Meeting of the Association for Computational Linguistics*. pages 384–394. http://www.aclweb.org/anthology/P10-1040.

Xiaojun Wan. 2008. Using bilingual knowledge and ensemble techniques for unsupervised Chinese sentiment analysis. In *Proceedings of the Conference on Empirical Methods in Natural Language Processing*. pages 553–561. http://www.aclweb.org/anthology/D08-1058.

Zhu Zhu, Shoushan Li, Guodong Zhou, and Rui Xia. 2014. Bilingual event extraction: a case study on trigger type determination. In *Annual Meeting of the Association for Computational Linguistics*. pages 842–847. http://www.aclweb.org/anthology/P14-2136.

EviNets: Neural Networks for Combining Evidence Signals for Factoid Question Answering

Denis Savenkov
Emory University
denis.savenkov@emory.edu

Eugene Agichtein
Emory University
eugene.agichtein@emory.edu

Abstract

A critical task for question answering is the final answer selection stage, which has to combine multiple signals available about each answer candidate. This paper proposes *EviNets*: a novel neural network architecture for factoid question answering. *EviNets* scores candidate answer entities by combining the available supporting evidence, *e.g.,* structured knowledge bases and unstructured text documents. *EviNets* represents each piece of evidence with a dense embeddings vector, scores their relevance to the question, and aggregates the support for each candidate to predict their final scores. Each of the components is generic and allows plugging in a variety of models for semantic similarity scoring and information aggregation. We demonstrate the effectiveness of *EviNets* in experiments on the existing TREC QA and WikiMovies benchmarks, and on the new Yahoo! Answers dataset introduced in this paper. *EviNets* can be extended to other information types and could facilitate future work on combining evidence signals for joint reasoning in question answering.

1 Introduction

Most of the recent works in Question Answering (QA) have focused on the problem of semantic matching between a question and candidate answer sentences (He and Lin, 2016; Rao et al., 2016; Yang et al., 2016). The datasets used in these works, such as Answer Sentence Selection Dataset (Wang et al., 2007) and WikiQA (Yang et al., 2015), typically contain a relatively small set of sentences, and the task is to select those that state the answer to the question. However, for many questions, a single sentence does not pro-

vide sufficient information, and it may not be reliable in isolation. At the same time, the redundancy of information in large corpora, such as the Web, has been shown useful to improve information retrieval approaches to QA (Clarke et al., 2001).

This work focuses on factoid questions, which can be answered with an entity, *i.e.,* an object in a Knowledge Base (KB) such as Freebase. Knowledge Base Question Answering (KBQA) techniques, such as Berant et al. (2013); Yih et al. (2015); Bast and Haussmann (2015), can be used to answer some of the user questions directly from a KB. However, KBs are inherently incomplete (Dong et al., 2014), and do not have sufficient information to answer many other questions (Fader et al., 2014).

Previous, feature-engineering, approaches for combining different data sources to improve answer retrieval were shown to be quite effective for QA (Sun et al., 2015; Xu et al., 2016; Savenkov and Agichtein, 2016). Alternatively, Memory Networks (Sukhbaatar et al., 2015) and their extensions (Miller et al., 2016) use embeddings to represent relevant data as memories, and summarize them into a single vector, therefore losing information about answers provenances.

In this paper, we introduce *EviNets*, a novel neural network architecture for factoid question answering, which provides a unified framework for aggregating evidence, supporting answer candidates. Given a question, *EviNets* retrieves a set of relevant pieces of information, *e.g.,* sentences from a corpora or knowledge base triples, and extracts mentioned entities as candidate answers. All the evidence signals are then embedded into the same vector space, scored and aggregated using multiple strategies for each answer candidate. Experiments on the TREC QA, WikiMovies and new Yahoo! Answers datasets demonstrate the effectiveness of *EviNets*, and its ability to handle both unstructured text and structured KB triples.

299

Proceedings of the 55th Annual Meeting of the Association for Computational Linguistics (Short Papers), pages 299–304
Vancouver, Canada, July 30 - August 4, 2017. ©2017 Association for Computational Linguistics
https://doi.org/10.18653/v1/P17-2047

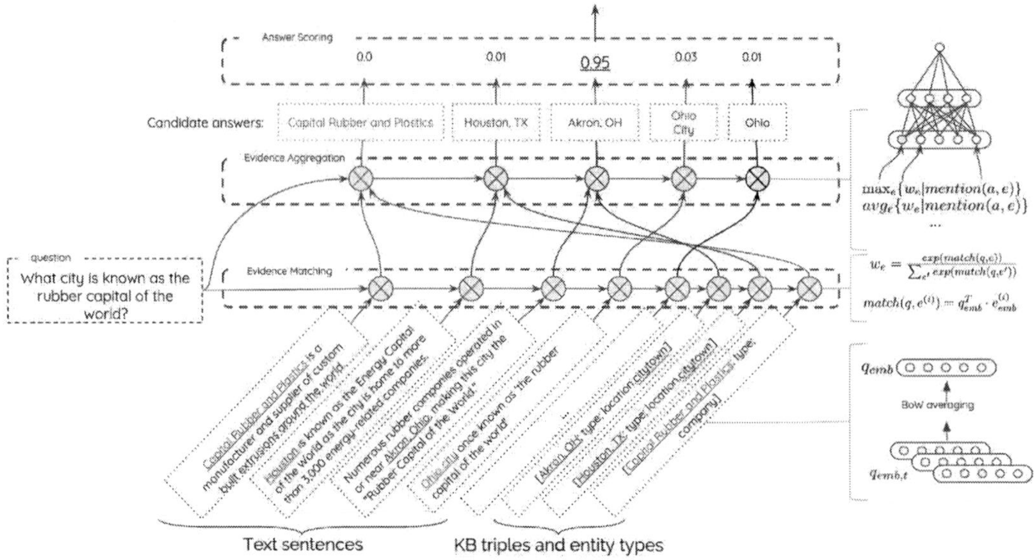

Figure 1: The EviNets neural network architecture for combining evidence in factoid question answering.

2 *EviNets* Question Answering Model

The high level architecture of *EviNets* is illustrated in Figure 1. For a given question, we extract potentially relevant information, *e.g.,* sentences from documents retrieved from text corpora using a search system. Next, we can use an entity linking system, such as TagMe (Ferragina and Scaiella, 2010), to identify entities mentioned in the extracted information, which become candidate answers. *EviNets* can further incorporate additional supporting evidence, *e.g.,* textual description of candidate answer entities, and potentially useful KB triples, such as types (Sun et al., 2015). Finally, question, answer candidates and supporting evidence are given as input to the *EviNets* neural network.

Let us denote a question by q, and $\{q_t \in R^{|V|}\}$, as a one-hot encoding of its tokens from a fixed vocabulary V. a_i is a candidate answer from the set A, and we will assume, that each answer is represented as a single entity. For each question, we have a fixed set $E = E_{text} \cup E_{KB}$ of evidence statements $e^{(i)}, i = 1..M$, and their tokens $e_t^{(i)}$. A boolean function $mention : A \times E \rightarrow \{0, 1\}$ provides the information about which answer candidates are mentioned in which evidences. Individual tokens $q_t, a_i, e_t^{(i)}$ are translated into the embedding space using a matrix $W_{D \times |V|}$, where D is the dimension of the embeddings, *i.e.,* $q_{emb,t} = W q_t$,

$a_{emb,i} = W a_t$ and $e_{emb,t}^{(i)} = W e_t^{(i)}$. In our experiments, we use the same matrix for questions, evidence, and answers. KB entities are considered to be individual tokens, while predicates and type names are tokenized into constituent words.

2.1 Memory Matching Module

Evidence matching is responsible for estimating the relevance of each of the pieces of evidence to the question, *i.e.,* $w_e = softmax(match(q, e))$. The function *match(q, e)* can be implemented using any of the recently proposed semantic similarity estimation architectures[1]. One of the simplest approaches is to average question and each evidence token embeddings and score the similarity using the dot product: $q_{emb} = \frac{1}{L_q} \sum_t q_{emb,t}$ and $e_{emb}^{(i)} = \frac{1}{L_e} \sum_t e_{emb,t}^{(i)}$ and $match(q, e^{(i)}) = q_{emb}^T \cdot e_{emb}^{(i)}$.

2.2 Evidence Aggregation Module

After all the evidence signals have been scored, *EviNets* aggregates the support for each answer candidate. Table 1 summarizes the evidence signals used. With these features, *EviNets* captures different aspects, *i.e.,* how well individual sentences match the question, how frequently the candidate is mentioned and how well a set of answer

---

[1]https://goo.gl/6gWrgA

Evidence Feature	Description
Maximum evidence score mentioning the answer	$\max_e\{w_e\|mention(a,e)\}, e \in E, E_{text} \text{ or } E_{KB}$
Average evidence score mentioning the answer	$avg_e\{w_e\|mention(a,e)\}, e \in E, E_{text} \text{ or } E_{KB}$
Sum of evidence scores mentioning the answer	$\sum_e\{w_e\|mention(a,e)\}, e \in E, E_{text} \text{ or } E_{KB}$
Number of mentions	$\sum_e\{1\|mention(a,e)\}, e \in E_{text}$
Weighted memory similarity to the question	$(\frac{1}{M}\sum_i w_e e_{emb}^{(i)}) \cdot q_{emb}$
Weighted memory similarity to the answer (Sukhbaatar et al., 2015)	$(\frac{1}{M}\sum_i w_e e_{emb}^{(i)}) \cdot a_{emb}$ or $R^T(\frac{1}{M}\sum_i w_e e_{emb}^{(i)} + q_{emb}) \cdot a_{emb}$, where $R_{D \times D}$ is a rotation matrix
Weighted memory answer mentions similarity to the answer (Miller et al., 2016)	$(\frac{1}{M}\sum_e w_e[\sum_a a_{emb} \| mention(e,a)]) \cdot a_{emb}$

Table 1: Signals we used to aggregate evidence in support for each of the answer candidates a.

Dataset	Example Questions
TREC QA	Where is the highest point in Japan?
1236 train	What is the coldest place on earth?
202 test	Who was the first U.S. president to appear on TV?
WikiMovies	what films did Ira Sachs write?
96185 train	what films does Claude Akins appear in?
10000 dev	the movie Victim starred who?
9952 test	what type of film is Midnight Run?
Y! Answers	What is Elvis's hairstyle called?
1898 train	Who is this kid in Mars Attacks?
271 dev	who invented denim jeans?
542 test	who's the woman on the progressive.com commercials?

Table 2: Description of TREC QA, WikiMovies and Yahoo! Answers factoid QA datasets.

evidences covers the information requested in the question.

2.3 Answer Scoring Module

Finally, *EviNets* uses the aggregated signals to predict the answer scores, to rank them, and to return the best candidate as the final answer to the question. For this purpose, we use two fully-connected neural network layers with the ReLU activation function, with 32 and 8 hidden units respectively. The model was trained end-to-end by optimizing the cross entropy loss function using the Adam algorithm (Kingma and Ba, 2014).

3 Experimental Evaluation

To test our framework we used TREC QA (Sun et al., 2015), WikiMovies (Miller et al., 2016) benchmarks and the new Yahoo! Answers dataset[2] derived from factoid questions posted on the CQA website (Table 2). In all experiments, embeddings were initialized with 300-dimensional vectors pre-trained with Glove (Pennington et al., 2014). Embeddings for multi-word entity names were obtained by averaging the word vectors of constituent words.

3.1 Baselines

As baselines for different experiments depending on availability and specifics of a dataset we considered the following methods:

- IR-based QA systems: *AskMSR* (Brill et al., 2002) and *AskMSR+* (Tsai et al., 2015), which select the best answer based on the frequency of entity mentions in retrieved text snippets.
- KBQA systems: *SemPre* (Berant et al., 2013) and *Aqqu* (Bast and Haussmann, 2015), which identify possible topic entities of the question, and select the answer from the candidates in the neighborhood of these entities in a KB.
- Hybrid system *QuASE* (Sun et al., 2015) detects mentions of knowledge base entities in text passages, and uses the types and description information from the KB to support answer selection.
- Hybrid system *Text2KB* (Savenkov and Agichtein, 2016), which uses textual resources to improve different stages of the KBQA pipeline.
- Memory Networks: *MemN2N* (Sukhbaatar et al., 2015) and *KV MemN2N* (Miller et al., 2016) represent relevant information with embeddings, and summarize the memories into a single vector using the soft attention mechanism. Additionally, KV MemN2N splits memories into key-value pairs, where keys are used for matching against the question, and values are used to summarize the memories.

[2]available for research purposes at http://ir.mathcs.emory.edu/software-data/

Method	P	R	F1
SemPre	0.157	0.104	0.125
Text2KB	0.287	0.287	0.288
AskMSR+	0.493	0.490	0.491
QuASE (text)	0.550	0.550	0.550
QuASE (text+kb)	0.579	**0.579**	**0.579**
MemN2N	0.333	0.328	0.330
KV MemN2N	0.517	0.500	0.508
EviNets (text)	0.580	0.560	0.569
EviNets (text+kb)	**0.585**	0.564	0.574

Table 3: Precision, Recall and F1 of different methods on TREC QA dataset. Improvements over KV MemN2N are statistically significant.

3.2 TREC QA dataset

The TREC QA dataset is composed of factoid questions, which can be answered with an entity, and were used in TREC 8-12 question answering tracks. Similarly to Sun et al. (2015) we used web search (using the Microsoft Bing Web Search API) to retrieve top 50 documents, parsed them, extracted sentences and ranked them using tf-idf similarity to the question. To compare our results with the existing state-of-the-art, we used the same set of candidate entities as used by the QuASE model. We note that the extracted evidence differs between the models, and we were unable to match some of the candidates to our sentences. For text+kb experiment, just as QuASE, we used entity descriptions and types from Freebase knowledge base. Table 3 summarizes the results. *EviNets* achieves competitive results on the dataset, beating KV MemN2N by 13% in F1 score, and, unlike QuASE, does not rely on expensive feature engineering and does not require any external resources to train.

3.3 WikiMovies dataset

The WikiMovies dataset contains questions in the movies domain along with relevant Wikipedia passages and OMDb knowledge base. Since KVMemN2N already achieves an almost perfect result answering the questions using the KB, we focus on using the provided movie articles from Wikipedia. We followed the preprocessing procedures described in Miller et al. (2016). Unlike TREC QA, where there are often multiple relevant supporting pieces of evidence, answers in the WikiMovies dataset usually have a single relevant sentence, which, however, mentions multi-

Method	Accuracy
MemN2N (wiki windows)	0.699*
KV MemN2N (wiki windows)	0.762*
AskMSR (entities)	0.314
KV MemN2N (wiki sentences)	0.524
EviNets (wiki)	0.616
EviNets (wiki + entity types)	**0.667**

Table 4: Accuracy of EviNets and baseline models on the WikiMovies dataset. The results marked * are obtained using a different setup, *i.e.,* they use pre-processed entity window memories, and the whole set of entities as candidates.

ple entities. To help the model distinguish the correct answer, and explore its abilities to encode structured and unstructured data, we generated additional *entity type* triples. For example, if an entity E appears as an object of the predicate `directed_by` in OMDb, we added the `[E, type, director]` triple. As baselines, we used MemN2N and KV MemN2N models, and the results are presented in Table 4. As we can see, with the same setup using individual sentences as evidence/memories *EviNets* significantly outperforms the KV MemN2N model by 27%. It is important to emphasize that the best-reported results of memory networks were obtained using *entity-centered windows* as memories, which requires special pre-processing and increases the number of memories. Additionally, these models used *all* of the KB entities as candidate answers, whereas *EviNets* relies only on the mentioned ones, which is a more scalable scenario for open-domain question answering, where it is not realistic to score millions of candidate answers in real-time.

3.4 Yahoo! Answers dataset

Yahoo! recently released a dataset with search queries, which lead to clicks on factoid Yahoo! Answers questions, identified as questions with the best answer containing less than 3 words and a Wikipedia page as the specified source of information[3]. This dataset contains 15K queries, which correspond to 4725 unique Yahoo! Answers questions (Table 2). We took these questions, and mapped answers to KB entities using the TagMe entity linking library (Ferragina and Scaiella, 2010). We filtered out questions, for

---

[3]L27 dataset https://webscope.sandbox.yahoo.com

Method	P	R	F1
Aqqu	0.116	0.117	0.116
Text2KB	0.170	0.170	0.170
AskMSR (entities)	0.175	0.319	0.226
MemN2N	0.072	0.131	0.092
KV MemN2N	0.126	0.228	0.162
EviNets (text)	0.210	0.383	0.271
EviNets (text+kb)	**0.226**	**0.409**	**0.291**
Oracle	0.622	1.0	0.767

Table 5: Precision, Recall and F1 of different methods on Yahoo! Answers factoid QA dataset. The Oracle assumes candidate answers are ranked perfectly and its performance is limited by the initial retrieval step.

which no answer entities with a good confidence[4] were identified, *e.g.,* date answers, and randomly split the rest into training, development and test sets, with 2711 questions in total. Similarly to the TREC QA experiments, we extracted textual evidence using Bing Web Search API, by retrieving top 50 relevant documents, extracting the main content blocks, and splitting them into sentences. We applied the TagMe entity linker to the extracted sentences, and considered all entities of mentions with the confidence score above the 0.2 threshold as candidate answers. For candidate entities we also retrieved relevant KB triples, such as entity types and descriptions, which extended the original pool of evidences.

Table 5 summarizes the results of *EviNets* and some baseline methods on the created Yahoo! Answers dataset. As we can see, knowledge base data is not enough to answer most of these questions, and a state-of-the-art KBQA system Aqqu gets only 0.116 precision. Adding textual data helps significantly, and Text2KB improves the precision to 0.17, which roughly matches the results of the AskMSR system, that ranks candidate entities by their popularity in the retrieved documents. Using text along with KB evidence gave higher performance metrics, boosting F1 from 0.271 to 0.291. EviNets significantly improves over the baseline approaches, beating AskMSR by 28% and KV MemN2N by almost 80% in F1 score.

4 Related Work

The success of deep neural network architectures in computer vision and NLP applications mo-

tivated researchers to investigate applying these techniques for answer sentence selection, evaluated on TREC QA (Wang et al., 2007), WikiQA (Yang et al., 2015) and other datasets. A number of models proposed in recent years explore different ways of matching questions and answer sentences (He and Lin, 2016; Yang et al., 2016; Rao et al., 2016). Our *EviNets* architecture allows to easily plug these sentence matching networks into the evidence matching module, and provides the aggregation layer, which helps to make a decision based on all available information.

Our evidence representation module is based on the ideas of memory networks (Sukhbaatar et al., 2015; Kumar et al., 2015; Miller et al., 2016), which also embed relevant information into a vector space. However, they use soft attention mechanism to retrieve the memories, and do not use links from memories to the corresponding answer candidates, which means that all relevant information is squeezed into a fixed dimensional vector. This limitation has been partially addressed in Wang et al. (2016) and Henaff et al. (2016), which accumulate evidence for each answer separately using a recurrent neural network. In contrast, the evidence aggregation in our *EviNets* model uses multiple different features, which is more flexible and can be extended with other signals.

5 Conclusions

We presented *EviNets*, a neural network for question answering, which encodes and aggregates multiple evidence signals to select answers. Experiments on TREC QA, WikiMovies and Yahoo! Answers datasets demonstrate that *EviNets* can be trained end-to-end to use both the available textual and knowledge base information. EviNets improves over the baselines, both in cases when there are many or just a few relevant pieces of evidence, by helping build an aggregate picture and distinguish between candidates, mentioned together in a relevant memory, as is the case for WikiMovies dataset. The results of our experiments also demonstrate that EviNets can incorporate signals from different data sources, *e.g.,* adding KB triples helps to improve the performance over text-only setup. As a limitation of this work and a direction for future research, *EviNets* could be extended to support dynamic evidence retrieval, which would allow retrieving additional answer candidates and evidence as needed.

---

[4]A minimum ρ score of 0.2 from TagMe was required.

References

Hannah Bast and Elmar Haussmann. 2015. More accurate question answering on freebase. In *Proceedings of the 24th ACM International on Conference on Information and Knowledge Management*.

Jonathan Berant, Andrew Chou, Roy Frostig, and Percy Liang. 2013. Semantic parsing on freebase from question-answer pairs. In *Proceedings of the 2013 Conference on Empirical Methods in Natural Language Processing*.

Eric Brill, Susan Dumais, and Michele Banko. 2002. An analysis of the askmsr question-answering system. In *Proceedings of the ACL-02 conference on Empirical methods in natural language processing-Volume 10*.

Charles LA Clarke, Gordon V Cormack, and Thomas R Lynam. 2001. Exploiting redundancy in question answering. In *Proceedings of the 24th annual international ACM SIGIR conference*.

Xin Dong, Evgeniy Gabrilovich, Geremy Heitz, Wilko Horn, Ni Lao, Kevin Murphy, Thomas Strohmann, Shaohua Sun, and Wei Zhang. 2014. Knowledge vault: A web-scale approach to probabilistic knowledge fusion. In *Proceedings of the 20th ACM SIGKDD*.

Anthony Fader, Luke Zettlemoyer, and Oren Etzioni. 2014. Open question answering over curated and extracted knowledge bases. In *Proceedings of the 20th ACM SIGKDD international conference on Knowledge discovery and data mining*.

Paolo Ferragina and Ugo Scaiella. 2010. Tagme: on-the-fly annotation of short text fragments (by wikipedia entities). In *Proceedings of the 19th ACM ICKM*.

Hua He and Jimmy Lin. 2016. Pairwise word interaction modeling with deep neural networks for semantic similarity measurement. In *Proceedings of NAACL-HLT*.

Mikael Henaff, Jason Weston, Arthur Szlam, Antoine Bordes, and Yann LeCun. 2016. Tracking the world state with recurrent entity networks. *arXiv preprint arXiv:1612.03969* .

Diederik P. Kingma and Jimmy Ba. 2014. Adam: A method for stochastic optimization. *CoRR* abs/1412.6980. http://arxiv.org/abs/1412.6980.

Ankit Kumar, Ozan Irsoy, Jonathan Su, James Bradbury, Robert English, Brian Pierce, Peter Ondruska, Ishaan Gulrajani, and Richard Socher. 2015. Ask me anything: Dynamic memory networks for natural language processing. *CoRR, abs/1506.07285* .

Alexander Miller, Adam Fisch, Jesse Dodge, Amir-Hossein Karimi, Antoine Bordes, and Jason Weston. 2016. Key-value memory networks for directly reading documents. *arXiv preprint arXiv:1606.03126* .

Jeffrey Pennington, Richard Socher, and Christopher D. Manning. 2014. Glove: Global vectors for word representation. In *Empirical Methods in Natural Language Processing (EMNLP)*. http://www.aclweb.org/anthology/D14-1162.

Jinfeng Rao, Hua He, and Jimmy Lin. 2016. Noise-contrastive estimation for answer selection with deep neural networks. In *Proceedings of the 25th ACM International on Conference on Information and Knowledge Management*.

Denis Savenkov and Eugene Agichtein. 2016. When a knowledge base is not enough: Question answering over knowledge bases with external text data. In *Proceedings of the 39th ACM SIGIR conference*.

Sainbayar Sukhbaatar, Jason Weston, Rob Fergus, et al. 2015. End-to-end memory networks. In *Advances in neural information processing systems*. pages 2440–2448.

Huan Sun, Hao Ma, Wen-tau Yih, Chen-Tse Tsai, Jingjing Liu, and Ming-Wei Chang. 2015. Open domain question answering via semantic enrichment. In *Proceedings of the 24th International Conference on World Wide Web*.

C Tsai, Wen-tau Yih, and C Burges. 2015. Web-based question answering: Revisiting askmsr. Technical report, Technical Report MSR-TR-2015-20, Microsoft Research.

Mengqiu Wang, Noah A Smith, and Teruko Mitamura. 2007. What is the jeopardy model? a quasi-synchronous grammar for qa. In *EMNLP-CoNLL*. volume 7, pages 22–32.

Xun Wang, Katsuhito Sudoh, Masaaki Nagata, Tomohide Shibata, Kawahara Daisuke, and Kurohashi Sadao. 2016. Reading comprehension using entity-based memory network. *arXiv preprint arXiv:1612.03551* .

Kun Xu, Siva Reddy, Yansong Feng, Songfang Huang, and Dongyan Zhao. 2016. Question answering on freebase via relation extraction and textual evidence. *arXiv preprint arXiv:1603.00957* .

Liu Yang, Qingyao Ai, Jiafeng Guo, and W Bruce Croft. 2016. anmm: Ranking short answer texts with attention-based neural matching model. In *Proceedings of the 25th ACM International on Conference on Information and Knowledge Management*.

Yi Yang, Scott Wen-tau Yih, and Chris Meek. 2015. Wikiqa: A challenge dataset for open-domain question answering. In *Proceedings of the 2015 Conference on Empirical Methods in Natural Language Processing*.

Scott Wen-tau Yih, Ming-Wei Chang, Xiaodong He, and Jianfeng Gao. 2015. Semantic parsing via staged query graph generation: Question answering with knowledge base. In *Proceedings of the 53rd Annual Meeting of the ACL*.

Pocket Knowledge Base Population

Travis Wolfe   **Mark Dredze**   **Benjamin Van Durme**
Human Language Technology Center of Excellence
Johns Hopkins University

Abstract

Existing Knowledge Base Population methods extract relations from a closed relational schema with limited coverage, leading to sparse KBs. We propose *Pocket Knowledge Base Population (PKBP)*, the task of dynamically constructing a KB of entities related to a query and finding the best characterization of relationships between entities. We describe novel Open Information Extraction methods which leverage the PKB to find informative trigger words. We evaluate using existing KBP shared-task data as well as new annotations collected for this work. Our methods produce high quality KBs from just text with many more entities and relationships than existing KBP systems.

1   Introduction

Much of human knowledge is contained in text in books, encyclopedias, the internet, and written communications. Building knowledge bases to store, search, and reason over this information is an important problem in natural language understanding. A lot of work in knowledge base population (KBP) has focused on the NIST Text Analysis Conference track of the same name, and specifically the slot filling task. Slot Filling (SF) defines a relational schema similar to Wikipedia infoboxes. SF KBP systems extract facts from text corresponding to an entity called the query.

This work addresses two issues concerning SF KBP. First, the SF schema has strict semantics for the relations which can be extracted, and thus no SF relation can be extracted for most related entities, leading to sparse KBs. Second, because SF has a small static schema, most research has focused on batch processing for a single schema,

limiting downstream usefulness. This means KBs built by slot filling have limited applicability in some real world settings of interest.

We address these issues by proposing *Pocket Knowledge Base Population*. Pocket KBs (PKBs) are dense entity-centric KBs dynamically constructed for a query. In both SF and pocket KBP, a query is an entity of interest and a document mentioning that entity. However, in PKB the primary goal is to populate the KB with nodes for all entities related to the query, irrespective of any prior beliefs about relations. PKB edges store representations of mentions referring to the entities connected by that edge, and thus may better serve downstream tasks which don't perfectly align to a particular schema.

We describe a PKBP system which builds KBs from text corpora. This includes unsupervised methods for finding related entities and mentions of them and the query with accuracies of 89.5 and 93.1 respectively when evaluated on SF queries. We also propose novel entity-centric Open IE (Banko et al., 2007) methods for characterizing the relationship between entities which perform twice as well as a syntactically-informed baseline. Our contributions also include a comparison between pocket and SF KBs constructed on SF queries, showing our KBs are multiple times larger while remaining high quality. We make our system publicly available.[1]

2   Pocket Knowledge Base Population

The defining characteristic of pocket KBs is they are small, entity-centric, and dynamically generated according to a query. Most work in KBP is centered around batch processing with a relation extractor, whereas PKBP is based on entity men-

---

[1] https://hub.docker.com/r/hltcoe/pocket-knowledge-base-population

305

Proceedings of the 55th Annual Meeting of the Association for Computational Linguistics (Short Papers), pages 305–310
Vancouver, Canada, July 30 - August 4, 2017. ©2017 Association for Computational Linguistics
https://doi.org/10.18653/v1/P17-2048

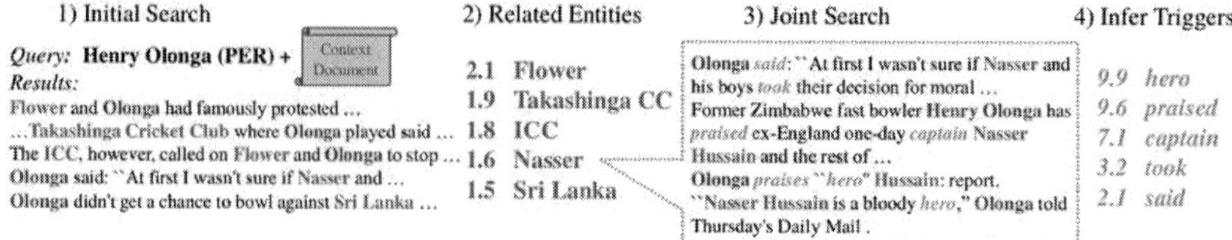

Figure 1: High level steps of the PKB construction process. Example PKBs can be found in Table 3. The first two steps of initial search and related entities are described in §3.1, the third step of joint searching in §3.2, and finally extracting triggers in §3.3.

tion search and ad-hoc trigger extraction. PKBs resemble a hub and spoke graph where the hub is the query and nodes on the outside are related entities. The spokes represent mentions proving that an entity is related to the query. Traversing this graph by crossing a spoke is akin to building a new PKB with that related entity as the new hub.

PKBs are aids for "knowledge-based" search over a document collection. KBs are useful for question answering (Yao, 2014) and PKBs serve this goal because related entities are good answer candidates for questions about a query. SF KBs are specialized to the case where you know the questions ahead of time, like "Where does Mary work?" and "Who is ACME's parent company?". PKBs offer a set of answers for queries with clues as to their relationship, like Marc Bolland and Stuart Rose are related because of events described using the word *replaced*. KBs are also useful information retrieval (IR) tools (Dietz and Schuhmacher, 2015) for human guided corpus exploration. PKBs serve this goal by providing ranked lists of related entities and over the mentions describing their relationship to the query.

We describe a system which achieves the goals of PKBP using low-resource and unsupervised methods. We discuss how PKBs are built in §3 and evaluate their quality in §4 on SF queries.

3   Construction

There are three steps to PKB construction: §3.1 discovering related entities, §3.2 finding mentions of the query and related entities, and §3.3 extracting trigger word explanations.

3.1   Discovering Related Entities

Candidate related entities are collected by searching for mentions of the query and taking other mentions which appear in the results. This process is similar to cross document entity coreference and

we adopt the vector space model (Bagga and Baldwin, 1998). First, **triage features** are used to locate sentences in an inverted index, including the mention headword and all word unigrams and bigrams (case sensitive and insensitive).

Next, we use **context features**: a word unigram tf-idf vector. We implement a compromise between Cucerzan (2007) (used sentences before, after, and containing a mention) and Bagga and Baldwin (1998) (used any sentence in a coreference chain). Instead of running a coreference resolver, we use the high-precision heuristic of linking mentions with the same headword and NER type. Terms are weighted as $\frac{2}{1+d}$ where d is the distance in sentences to the nearest mention.

Our **attribute features** are a generalization of Mann and Yarowsky (2003). They train a few ad-hoc relation extractors like `birth_year` and `occupation` from seed facts. Their extractions provide high-precision signal for merging entity mentions. We found extracting all NNP$*$ or capitalized JJ$*$ words within 4 edges in a dependency tree was less sparse, requires no seeds, and produced similar quality attributes. We union these attributes across mentions found by the headword and NER type coreference heuristic to build a fine-grain tf-idf vector. We use the same $\frac{2}{1+d}$ re-weighting for attributes, except where d is the distance in dependency edges to the entity mention head. The closest attributes are descriptors within a noun phrase like `HEAD-nn-Dr.`. We include the NER type of the headword to distinguish between attributes like `PERSON-nn-American` and `ORGANIZATION-nn-American`.

Given the triage features $t(m)$, context features $c(m)$, and attribute features $a(m)$, we search for mentions m which maximize

$$(1 + \alpha_t \cos\theta_t)(1 + \alpha_c \cos\theta_c)(1 + \alpha_a \theta_a)$$

where $\cos\theta_t$ is the cosine similarity between

$t(m_{query})$ and $t(m)$. We only consider the subset of mentions that have $\cos \theta_t > 0$, which can be efficiently retrieved via an inverted index.

Any mention with a score higher than τ is considered coreferent with the query. We extract mentions in the same sentences as the query as candidate related entities if they have an NER type of PER, ORG, or LOC. We link candidate mentions against entities in the PKB using the same coreference score used to retrieve query mentions. If a candidate's best link has a score $s < \tau$, we promote it to an entity and add it to the PKB with probability $1 - \frac{s}{\tau}$.[2]

3.2 Joint Linking of Related Entities

At this point there are on the order of 100 mentions of the query and 20 to 50 related entities.[3] For each entity, we perform a joint search for it and the query. These entity co-occurrences will form the spokes in the PKB and be used to characterize the relationship between and relatedness to the query.

Joint entity searches are similar to single-mention searches in §3.1 with two differences. First, instead of having a single mention to compute feature vectors from, there are multiple. Feature vectors for entities are built up from mentions, where the weight of a mention $w(m) = \rho^b$ for $\rho \in (0, 1)$ and b is how many mentions were linked before m. Second, we are scoring mention pairs (with both mentions in the same sentence) as the geometric mean of the coreference scores of both links. The coreference score function does not need to change, but the triage step does: we only consider sentences which have $\cos \theta_t > 0$ for both the query and the related entity and use the same τ. Entity relatedness is a function of how often entities are mentioned together. We modeled it as the sum of the joint entity linking probabilities, where the probability of a link is $\text{logit}^{-1}(\frac{s}{\tau})$.

3.3 Trigger Word Analysis

At this stage we have found on the order of 2 to 20 sentences which mention the query and a related entity which will be used to determine the relation between them. There is work on rule-based (Banko et al., 2007; Fader et al., 2011; Angeli et al., 2015), supervised (Mausam et al., 2012),

and distantly-supervised (Mintz et al., 2009) methods for characterizing relations in text. Our method is similar to distant supervision, where a KB of known facts is used to infer how relations are expressed, but we use supervision from the KB being constructed. We cast the problem of characterizing a relation as a search for *trigger words*. We state our priors on trigger words and condition on the data to find likely triggers.

Predicate (triggers) and arguments are syntactically close together. Assuming the related entity mention heads are arguments, we compute the probability that these two random walks in a dependency tree end up at the same token. This serves as a weak syntactically informed prior.

Information is conveyed as a surprisal under a background distribution (codebook). We compute a unigram distribution over words which are likely under our syntactic prior for triggers (conditioned on the NER type of the two arguments). We use this marginal distribution as a codebook. We divide out this codebook probability in every pair of related entity mentions in the PKB giving a cost in bits (log probability ratio) of each trigger word.

Repetition indicates importance. We sum the costs for each trigger across sentences. We weaken this assumption by averaging the max and the sum for each trigger for the final score.

This process yields a score for every trigger word, and we use the top k triggers to characterize the relationship between entities. For each trigger we keep, we also maintain provenance information for mentions using a given trigger.

4 Experiments

We use the TAC SF13 query entities to evaluate our methods; 50 person and 50 organization entities are used as queries to construct 100 PKBs. 70 of the 100 query entities were NIL (26/60 PER and 44/50 ORG), meaning that they do not appear in the TAC KB, though our methods aren't in principle sensitive to this because they create entities on the fly. We use annotated versions of Gigaword 5 (Parker et al., 2011; Ferraro et al., 2014) and English Wikipedia (February 24, 2016 dump) to construct our PKBs.[4] We use Amazon Mechanical Turk workers as annotators. We generated our PKBs with $\tau = 15$, $\rho = 0.5$, $\alpha_t = 40$, $\alpha_c = 20$, and $\alpha_a = 10$. These constants were tuned by hand

---

[2]Mentions with a score near τ may be coreferent, so we prefer low scoring mentions to avoid over-splitting entities.

[3]These values depend on the query (which are more or less rare in a corpus) and pruning thresholds (for our experiments we stop at 100 query mentions)

[4]We do not use the coreference annotations provided by Annotated Gigaword, only the features described in §3.1.

and are not sensitive to small changes. We take a subset of the PKB which covers the 15 most related entities and the one-best trigger for each. We call these "explanations" where each is a sentence with three labels: a) a mention of the query m_q, b) a mention of the a related entity m_r, and c) a trigger word t.

Entity Linking and Relatedness For each explanation, we ask: COREF: Does the query mention refer to the same entity as m_q? RELATED: Is the query entity meaningfully related to the referent of m_r? These annotations are not done by the same annotators to avoid confirmation bias. Worried annotators might be lulled into thinking all COREF instances were true, we made the task ternary by adding an intruder entity (randomly drawn from SF13 queries). Annotators were shown m_q and could choose coreference with the query, the intruder, or neither.[5] We drop annotations from annotators who chose an intruder[6] because we know these to be incorrect, and compute accuracy as proportion of the remaining annotations which chose the query.

RELATED was posed as a binary task of whether m_r is more related to the query or the intruder (without highlighting m_q). In positive cases, the annotator should observe that sentence shown contains a mention of the query entity and explains why they are related. The results are in Table 1.

Our system retrieves coreferent and related mentions with high accuracy. For coreference, mistakes usually happen when there is significant lexical overlap but some distinguishing feature that proves too subtle for our system to doubt the match, like Midwest High Speed Rail Association vs U.S. High Speed Rail Association or [English] Nationwide Building Society vs Irish Nationwide Building Society.

For relatedness, the biggest source of errors are news organizations listed as related entities because it is common to see sentences like *"Mohammed Sobeih, Moussa's deputy, told The Associated Press on Monday that..."*. Future work might address this problem by using normalized measures of statistical relatedness like PMI rather than raw co-occurrence counts.

Trigger Words To evaluate the informativeness of chosen triggers, we present annotators with m_q,

	PER	ORG	All
COREF	94.6	91.5	93.1
RELATED	90.7	88.2	89.5
COREF and RELATED	86.6	80.9	83.9

Table 1: PKB entity accuracy.

	System	Intruder	Neither
Person	29.4	12.4	58.2
Organization	29.1	17.3	53.7
All	29.2	14.7	56.1

Table 2: Related entity trigger identification.

m_r, and two potential trigger words highlighted. One trigger is chosen according to §3.3 and the other is an NN★ | VB★ | JJ★ | RB★ word in the projection of the dependency node dominating both entities.[7] The annotator may choose either trigger as a good characterization of the situation involving m_q and m_r, or label neither as sufficient. Note that this baseline is strong: it shares the entity linking (§3.2), trigger sentence selection (§3.3), and dependency parse tree as our system. We report the results in Table 2.

Our method is chosen about twice as often as a syntactically informed baseline, but fails to find a high quality trigger word more than half of the time. Some mistakes are caused by rare but oft-repeated words like "50" in: *"Bolland, 50, ... will replace Briton Stuart Rose"*. "50" has nothing to do with the relationship between Bolland and Rose, but it's repeated in 4 sentences about both of them, a stylistic coincidence our system cannot ignore. In other cases there is no word in situ which can explain entities' relatedness, like "... *the day after Wimbledon concludes, Montcourt must serve a five-week ban and ...*". The author and the reader can likely infer that Montcourt *competed* at Wimbledon, but this fact is not explicitly committed to, limiting our systems ability to extract a trigger.

Related Entities vs Slot Fillers There is no fair way to evaluate systems without a common schema, but we offer some extraction statistics. On SF13 queries our system generated 17.6 relevant entities/query,[8] each having 4.6 trigger words/pair, 2.1 mentions/trigger word, and 9.8

---

[5]The order of the intruder and the query were randomized.
[6]This affected 6.1% of COREF annotations.

[7]If no nodes match this, we walk up the tree until we find a node which has at least one allowed descendant.
[8]This is given a cap of 20 relevant entities per query to avoid a skewed average and keep construction time down.

Query Entity		Related Entity		Triggers
Marc Bolland	PER	Dalton Philips	PER	*appointed, departure, following, move*
Marc Bolland	PER	Stuart Rose	PER	*replace, 50, Briton*
Marc Bolland	PER	Marks & Spencer	ORG	*departure, CEO, become, following*
Henry Olonga	PER	Givemore Makoni	PER	*club, president, done, played*
Henry Olonga	PER	England	LOC	*cricketer, asylum, hiding, quit*
Henry Olonga	PER	Harare	LOC	*hiding, armbands, wore*
Mohammad Oudeh	PER	Munich	LOC	*massacre, briefed, defended*
Mohammad Oudeh	PER	Fatah Revolutionary Council	ORG	*faction, belonged, return*
Mohammad Oudeh	PER	Gaza Strip	LOC	*allows, asked, host*
A123 Systems LLC	ORG	Fisker	ORG	*supplier, struck, recall, owns*
A123 Systems LLC	ORG	Watertown, Massachusetts	LOC	*produces, batteries, company*
A123 Systems LLC	ORG	Obama	PER	*plant, opening, Granholm*
United Steelworkers of America	ORG	Curt Brown	PER	*spokesman, rejected, contracts*
United Steelworkers of America	ORG	Wayne Fraser	PER	*negotiator, spokesman, union*
United Steelworkers of America	ORG	Jerry Fallos	PER	*boss, broke, shut, local*
BNSF	ORG	Santa Fe	LOC	*asked, vote*
BNSF	ORG	Chapman	ORG	*venture, help, transition, joint*
BNSF	ORG	Robert Krebs	PER	*Burlington, chairman*

Table 3: Examples of slices of PKBs for the three most related entities for six queries and the best triggers for each pair. Supporting sentences for related entities and trigger words are not shown.

mentions/pair. In extractions from *all* systems in the SF13 evaluation (pooling answers, filtering out incorrect), they filled 6.0 slots/query with 14.2 fillers/query and 38.3 mentions/query as provenance. Some slots have string-valued fillers, but many could be related entities in the PKB sense. In these cases, we found 2.2 entities/query overlapping, 1.7 fillers not in their corresponding PKB and 10.8 related entities which weren't fillers.

5 Related Work

Blanco and Zaragoza (2010) study the information retrieval problem of finding *support sentences* which explain the relationship between a query and an entity, which is similar to this work. Our work addresses two new aspects of this problem: 1) how to automatically find related entities, which are assumed given in that work and 2) how to find the salient parts of support sentences (trigger words) by aggregating evidence across sentences.

This work shares goals with Dalton and Dietz (2013) and Dietz and Schuhmacher (2015), who create "knowledge sketches": distributions over documents, entities, and relations related to a query. The primary difference is that our work creates a KB instead of returning results from an existing one. They use Freebase for relations and Wikipedia for anchor text and links. Our approach uses parsed and NER tagged text.

Open vocabulary characterization of entities was investigated by Raghavan et al. (2004). They found intersecting entity language models yields common descriptors. Their notion of similarity (e.g. **Ronald Reagan** and **Richard Nixon** are both *presidents*) is different from our notion of relatedness (e.g. **Alexander Haig** and **Princeton, NJ** are related via *Meredith* – Haig's sister).

Finally other work has used Open IE for SF KBP. Soderland et al. (2013) and Finin et al. (2015) manually created a mapping between the Ollie (Mausam et al., 2012) and SF schemas. Angeli et al. (2015) perform OpenIE and then map between their schema and SF with PMI[2].

6 Conclusion

We propose *Pocket Knowledge Base Population* for dynamically building dense entity-centric KBs. We evaluate our methods on SF queries and find high accuracies of related entity discovery and coreference. We propose novel Open Information Extraction methods which leverage the PKB to identify trigger words and show they are effective at explaining related entities. In future work we hope to use PKBs for tasks like QA and IR.

Acknowledgments

This research was supported by the Human Language Technology Center of Excellence (HLT-COE) and Bloomberg L.P. The views and conclusions contained in this publication are those of the authors.

References

Gabor Angeli, Melvin Jose Johnson Premkumar, and Christopher D. Manning. 2015. Leveraging linguistic structure for open domain information extraction. In *Proceedings of the 53rd Annual Meeting of the Association for Computational Linguistics and the 7th International Joint Conference on Natural Language Processing (Volume 1: Long Papers)*. Association for Computational Linguistics, Beijing, China, pages 344–354. http://www.aclweb.org/anthology/P15-1034.

Amit Bagga and Breck Baldwin. 1998. Entity-based cross-document coreferencing using the vector space model. In *Proceedings of the 36th Annual Meeting of the Association for Computational Linguistics and 17th International Conference on Computational Linguistics - Volume 1*. Association for Computational Linguistics, Stroudsburg, PA, USA, ACL '98, pages 79–85. https://doi.org/10.3115/980845.980859.

Michele Banko, Michael J. Cafarella, Stephen Soderland, Matt Broadhead, and Oren Etzioni. 2007. Open information extraction from the web. In *Proceedings of the 20th International Joint Conference on Artifical Intelligence*. Morgan Kaufmann Publishers Inc., San Francisco, CA, USA, IJCAI'07, pages 2670–2676. http://dl.acm.org/citation.cfm?id=1625275.1625705.

Roi Blanco and Hugo Zaragoza. 2010. Finding support sentences for entities. In *Proceedings of the 33rd International ACM SIGIR Conference on Research and Development in Information Retrieval*. ACM, New York, NY, USA, SIGIR '10, pages 339–346. https://doi.org/10.1145/1835449.1835507.

Silviu Cucerzan. 2007. Large-scale named entity disambiguation based on Wikipedia data. In *Proceedings of the 2007 Joint Conference on Empirical Methods in Natural Language Processing and Computational Natural Language Learning (EMNLP-CoNLL)*. Association for Computational Linguistics, Prague, Czech Republic, pages 708–716. http://www.aclweb.org/anthology/D/D07/D07-1074.

Jeffrey Dalton and Laura Dietz. 2013. Constructing query-specific knowledge bases. In *Proceedings of the 2013 Workshop on Automated Knowledge Base Construction*. ACM, New York, NY, USA, AKBC '13, pages 55–60. https://doi.org/10.1145/2509558.2509568.

Laura Dietz and Michael Schuhmacher. 2015. An interface sketch for queripidia: Query-driven knowledge portfolios from the web. In Krisztian Balog, Jeffrey Dalton, Antoine Doucet, and Yusra Ibrahim, editors, *Proceedings of the Eighth Workshop on Exploiting Semantic Annotations in Information Retrieval, ESAIR 2015, Melbourne, Australia, October 23, 2015*. ACM, pages 43–46. https://doi.org/10.1145/2810133.2810145.

Anthony Fader, Stephen Soderland, and Oren Etzioni. 2011. Identifying relations for open information extraction. In *Proceedings of the Conference on Empirical Methods in Natural Language Processing*. Association for Computational Linguistics, Stroudsburg, PA, USA, EMNLP '11, pages 1535–1545. http://dl.acm.org/citation.cfm?id=2145432.2145596.

Francis Ferraro, Max Thomas, Matthew R. Gormley, Travis Wolfe, Craig Harman, and Benjamin Van Durme. 2014. Concretely annotated corpora. In *The NIPS 2014 AKBC Workshop*.

Tim Finin, Dawn Lawrie, Paul McNamee, James Mayfield, Douglas Oard, Nanyun Peng, Ning Gao, Yiu-Chang Lin, Josh MacLin, and Tim Dowd. 2015. Hltcoe participation in tac kbp 2015: Cold start and tedl. In *Text Analytics Conference (TAC)*.

Gideon S. Mann and David Yarowsky. 2003. Unsupervised personal name disambiguation. In *Proceedings of the Seventh Conference on Natural Language Learning at HLT-NAACL 2003 - Volume 4*. Association for Computational Linguistics, Stroudsburg, PA, USA, CONLL '03, pages 33–40. https://doi.org/10.3115/1119176.1119181.

Mausam, Michael Schmitz, Robert Bart, Stephen Soderland, and Oren Etzioni. 2012. Open language learning for information extraction. In *Proceedings of the 2012 Joint Conference on Empirical Methods in Natural Language Processing and Computational Natural Language Learning*. Association for Computational Linguistics, Stroudsburg, PA, USA, EMNLP-CoNLL '12, pages 523–534. http://dl.acm.org/citation.cfm?id=2390948.2391009.

Mike Mintz, Steven Bills, Rion Snow, and Dan Jurafsky. 2009. Distant supervision for relation extraction without labeled data. In *Proceedings of the Joint Conference of the 47th Annual Meeting of the ACL and the 4th International Joint Conference on Natural Language Processing of the AFNLP: Volume 2-Volume 2*. Association for Computational Linguistics, pages 1003–1011.

Robert Parker, David Graff, Junbo Kong, Ke Chen, and Kazuaki Maeda. 2011. English gigaword fifth edition, linguistic data consortium. Technical report, Technical report, Technical Report. Linguistic Data Consortium, Philadelphia.

Hema Raghavan, James Allan, and Andrew McCallum. 2004. An exploration of entity models, collective classification and relation description .

Stephen Soderland, John Gilmer, Robert Bart, Oren Etzioni, and Daniel S Weld. 2013. Open information extraction to kbp relations in 3 hours. In *TAC*.

Xuchen Yao. 2014. *Feature-driven Question Answering with Natural Language Alignment*. Ph.D. thesis.

Answering Complex Questions Using Open Information Extraction

Tushar Khot and **Ashish Sabharwal** and **Peter Clark**
Allen Institute for Artificial Intelligence, Seattle, WA, U.S.A.
{tushark,ashishs,peterc}@allenai.org

Abstract

While there has been substantial progress in factoid question-answering (QA), answering complex questions remains challenging, typically requiring both a large body of knowledge and inference techniques. Open Information Extraction (Open IE) provides a way to generate semi-structured knowledge for QA, but to date such knowledge has only been used to answer simple questions with retrieval-based methods. We overcome this limitation by presenting a method for reasoning with Open IE knowledge, allowing more complex questions to be handled. Using a recently proposed support graph optimization framework for QA, we develop a new inference model for Open IE, in particular one that can work effectively with multiple short facts, noise, and the relational structure of tuples. Our model significantly outperforms a state-of-the-art structured solver on complex questions of varying difficulty, while also removing the reliance on manually curated knowledge.

1 Introduction

Effective question answering (QA) systems have been a long-standing quest of AI research. Structured curated KBs have been used successfully for this task (Berant et al., 2013; Berant and Liang, 2014). However, these KBs are expensive to build and typically domain-specific. Automatically constructed open vocabulary *(subject; predicate; object)* style tuples have broader coverage, but have only been used for simple questions where a single tuple suffices (Fader et al., 2014; Yin et al., 2015).

Our goal in this work is to develop a QA system that can perform reasoning with Open IE (Banko et al., 2007) tuples for complex multiple-choice questions that require tuples from multiple sentences. Such a system can answer complex questions in resource-poor domains where curated knowledge is unavailable. Elementary-level science exams is one such domain, requiring complex reasoning (Clark, 2015). Due to the lack of a large-scale structured KB, state-of-the-art systems for this task either rely on shallow reasoning with large text corpora (Clark et al., 2016; Cheng et al., 2016) or deeper, structured reasoning with a small amount of automatically acquired (Khot et al., 2015) or manually curated (Khashabi et al., 2016) knowledge.

Consider the following question from an Alaska state 4th grade science test:

> *Which object in our solar system reflects light and is a satellite that orbits around one planet? (A) Earth (B) Mercury (C) the Sun (D) the Moon*

This question is challenging for QA systems because of its complex structure and the need for multi-fact reasoning. A natural way to answer it is by combining facts such as *(Moon; is; in the solar system)*, *(Moon; reflects; light)*, *(Moon; is; satellite)*, and *(Moon; orbits; around one planet)*.

A candidate system for such reasoning, and which we draw inspiration from, is the TABLEILP system of Khashabi et al. (2016). TABLEILP treats QA as a search for an optimal subgraph that connects terms in the question and answer via rows in a set of curated tables, and solves the optimization problem using Integer Linear Programming (ILP). We similarly want to search for an optimal subgraph. However, a large, automatically extracted tuple KB makes the reasoning context different on three fronts: (a) unlike reasoning with tables, chaining tuples is less important and reliable as join rules aren't

Proceedings of the 55th Annual Meeting of the Association for Computational Linguistics (Short Papers), pages 311–316
Vancouver, Canada, July 30 - August 4, 2017. ©2017 Association for Computational Linguistics
https://doi.org/10.18653/v1/P17-2049

available; (b) conjunctive evidence becomes paramount, as, unlike a long table row, a single tuple is less likely to cover the entire question; and (c) again, unlike table rows, tuples are noisy, making combining redundant evidence essential. Consequently, a table-knowledge centered inference model isn't the best fit for noisy tuples.

To address this challenge, we present a new ILP-based model of inference with tuples, implemented in a reasoner called TUPLEINF. We demonstrate that TUPLEINF significantly outperforms TABLEILP by 11.8% on a broad set of over 1,300 science questions, without requiring manually curated tables, using a substantially simpler ILP formulation, and generalizing well to higher grade levels. The gains persist even when both solvers are provided identical knowledge. This demonstrates for the first time how Open IE based QA can be extended from simple lookup questions to an effective system for complex questions.

2   Related Work

We discuss two classes of related work: retrieval-based web question-answering (simple reasoning with large scale KB) and science question-answering (complex reasoning with small KB).

Web QA: There exist several systems for retrieval-based Web QA problems (Ferrucci et al., 2010; Brill et al., 2002). While structured KBs such as Freebase have been used in many (Berant et al., 2013; Berant and Liang, 2014; Kwiatkowski et al., 2013), such approaches are limited by the coverage of the data. QA systems using semi-structured Open IE tuples (Fader et al., 2013, 2014; Yin et al., 2015) or automatically extracted web tables (Sun et al., 2016; Pasupat and Liang, 2015) have broader coverage but are limited to simple questions with a single query.

Science QA: Elementary-level science QA tasks require reasoning to handle complex questions. Markov Logic Networks (Richardson and Domingos, 2006) have been used to perform probabilistic reasoning over a small set of logical rules (Khot et al., 2015). Simple IR techniques have also been proposed for science tests (Clark et al., 2016) and Gaokao tests (equivalent to the SAT exam in China) (Cheng et al., 2016).

The work most related to TUPLEINF is the aforementioned TABLEILP solver. This approach focuses on building inference chains using man-ually defined join rules for a small set of curated tables. While it can also use open vocabulary tuples (as we assess in our experiments), its efficacy is limited by the difficulty of defining reliable join rules for such tuples. Further, each row in some complex curated tables covers all relevant contextual information (e.g., each row of the *adaptation* table contains (animal, adaptation, challenge, explanation)), whereas recovering such information requires combining multiple Open IE tuples.

3   Tuple Inference Solver

We first describe the tuples used by our solver. We define a tuple as *(subject; predicate; objects)* with zero or more objects. We refer to the subject, predicate, and objects as the fields of the tuple.

3.1   Tuple KB

We use the text corpora (S) from Clark et al. (2016) to build our tuple KB. S contains 5×10^{10} tokens (280 GB of plain text) extracted from Web pages as well as around 80,000 sentences from various domain-targeted sources. For each test set, we use the corresponding training questions Q_{tr} to retrieve domain-relevant sentences from S. Specifically, for each multiple-choice question $(q, A) \in Q_{tr}$ and each choice $a \in A$, we use all non-stopword stemmed tokens in q and a as an ElasticSearch[1] query against S. We take the top 200 hits, run Open IE v4,[2] and aggregate the resulting tuples over all $a \in A$ and over all questions in Q_{tr} to create the tuple KB (T).[3]

3.2   Tuple Selection

Given a multiple-choice question qa with question text q and answer choices A=$\{a_i\}$, we select the most relevant tuples from T and S as follows.

Selecting from Tuple KB: We use an inverted index to find the 1,000 tuples that have the most overlapping tokens with question tokens $tok(qa)$.[4] We also filter out any tuples that overlap only with $tok(q)$ as they do not support any answer. We compute the normalized TF-IDF score by treating the question, q, as a query and each tuple, t, as a

---

[1] https://www.elastic.co/products/elasticsearch
[2] http://knowitall.github.io/openie
[3] Available at *http://allenai.org/data.html*
[4] All tokens are stemmed and stop-word filtered.

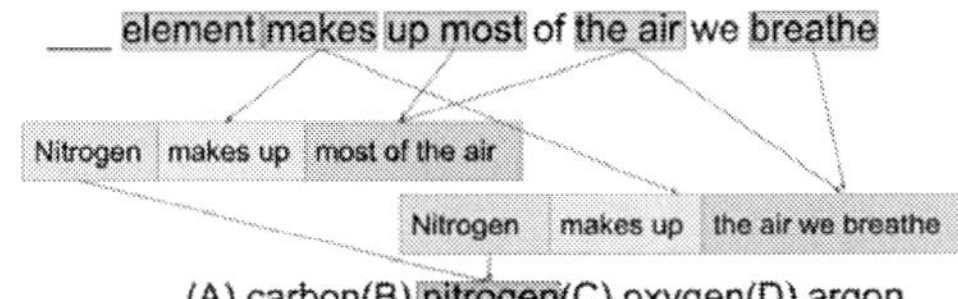

Figure 1: An example support graph linking a question (top), two tuples from the KB (colored) and an answer option (nitrogen).

document:

$$tf(x, q) = 1 \text{ if } x \in q, \ 0 \text{ otherwise}$$
$$idf(x) = \log\left(1 + N/n_x\right)$$
$$tf\text{-}idf(t, q) = \sum_{x \in t \cap q} idf(x)$$

where N is the total number of tuples in the KB and n_x is the number of tuples containing x. We normalize the *tf-idf* score by the number of tokens in t and q, and take the 50 top-scoring tuples T_{qa}.

On-the-fly tuples from text: To handle questions from new domains not covered by the training set, we extract additional tuples *on the fly* from S (similar to Sharma et al. (2015)). We perform the same ElasticSearch query described earlier for building T. We ignore sentences that cover none or all answer choices as they are not discriminative. We also ignore long sentences (>300 characters) and sentences with negation[5] as they tend to lead to noisy inference. We then run Open IE on these sentences and re-score the resulting tuples using the Jaccard score[6] due to the lossy nature of Open IE, and finally take the 50 top-scoring tuples T'_{qa}.

3.3 Support Graph Search

Similar to TABLEILP, we view the QA task as searching for a graph that best connects the terms in the question (qterms) with an answer choice via the knowledge; see Figure 1 for a simple illustrative example. Unlike standard alignment models used for tasks such as Recognizing Textual Entailment (RTE) (Dagan et al., 2010), however, we must score alignments between a set $T_{qa} \cup T'_{qa}$ of structured tuples and a (potentially multi-sentence) multiple-choice question qa.

The qterms, answer choices, and tuples fields form the set of possible vertices, $\mathcal{V}$, of the support graph. Edges connecting qterms to tuple fields and tuple fields to answer choices form the set of possible edges, $\mathcal{E}$. The support graph, $G(V, E)$, is a

subgraph of $\mathcal{G}(\mathcal{V}, \mathcal{E})$ where V and E denote "active" nodes and edges, resp. We define an ILP optimization model to search for the best support graph (i.e., the active nodes and edges) as follows.

Variables

The ILP has a binary variable for each qterm (x_q), tuple (x_t), tuple field (x_f), and answer choice (x_a), indicating whether the corresponding graph node is active. There is a binary activity variable (x_e) for each edge $e \in \mathcal{E}$. For efficiency, we only create a qterm→field edge and a field→choice edge if the corresponding coefficient is no smaller than a certain threshold (0.1 and 0.2, resp.).

Objective Function

The objective function coefficient c_e of each edge $e(t, h)$ is determined by a word-overlap score.[7] While TABLEILP used WordNet (Miller, 1995) paths to compute the edge weight, this measure results in unreliable scores when faced with longer phrases found in Open IE tuples.

Compared to a curated KB, it is easy to find Open IE tuples that match irrelevant parts of the questions. To mitigate this issue, we scale the coefficients c_q of qterms in our ILP objective to focus on important terms. Since the later terms in a question tend to provide the most critical information, we scale qterm coefficients based on their position in the question. Also, qterms that appear in almost all of the selected tuples tend not to be discriminative as any tuple would support such a qterm. Hence we scale qterm coefficients inversely by the frequency with which they occur in the selected tuples. Appendix A describes the coefficient for qterm as well as other variables in detail.

Constraints

Since Open IE tuples do not come with schema and join rules, we can define a substantially simpler model compared to TABLEILP. This reduces the reasoning capability but also eliminates the reliance on hand-authored join rules and regular expressions used in TABLEILP. We discovered (see empirical evaluation) that this simple model can achieve the same score as TABLEILP on the Regents test (target test set used by TABLEILP) and generalizes better to different grade levels.

We start with a few constraints defining what is an active node or edge, shown as the first groups of constraints in Table 1. To avoid positive edge coefficients in the objective function resulting in

---

[5] containing not, 'nt, or except
[6] $| \ tok(t) \cap tok(qa) \ | \ / \ | \ tok(t) \cup tok(qa) \ |$

[7] $w(t, h) = | \ tok(t) \cap tok(h) \ | \ / \ | \ tok(h) \ |$

| Active variable must have an active edge |
| Active edge must have an active source node |
| Active edge must have an active target node |
| Exactly one answer choice must be active |
| Active field implies tuple must be active |
| Active field must have $< w_1$ connected edges |
| Active choice must have $< w_2$ edges |
| Active qterm must have $< w_3$ edges |
| Support graph must have $< w_4$ active tuples |
| Active tuple must have $\geq w_5$ active fields |
| Active tuple must have an edge to some qterm |
| Active tuple must have an edge to some choice |
| Active tuple must have active subject |
| If a tuple predicate aligns to q, the subject (object) must align to a term preceding (following, resp.) q |

Table 1: High-level ILP constraints; we report results for $\vec{w} = (2, 4, 4, 4, 2)$; the model can be improved with more careful parameter selection

spurious edges in the support graph, we limit the number of active edges from an active tuple, question choice, tuple fields, and qterms (second group of constraints in Table 1). Our model is also capable of using multiple tuples to support different parts of the question as illustrated in Figure 1. To avoid spurious tuples that only connect with the question (or choice) or ignore the relation being expressed in the tuple, we add constraints that require each tuple to connect a qterm with an answer choice (third group of constraints in Table 1).

We also define new constraints based on the Open IE tuple structure. Since an Open IE tuple expresses a fact about the tuple's subject, we require that the subject must be active. To avoid issues such as *(Planet; orbit; Sun)* matching the sample question in the introduction ("Which object...orbits around a planet"), we also add an ordering constraint (fourth group in Table 1).

We note that TUPLEINF only combines parallel evidence, i.e., each tuple must individually connect words in the question to the answer choice. For reliable multi-hop reasoning using OpenIE tuples, one can add inter-tuple connections to the support graph search, controlled by a small number of rules over Open IE predicates. Learning such rules for the Science domain is an open problem and potential avenue for future work.

4 Experiments

Comparing our method with two state-of-the-art systems for 4th and 8th grade science exams, we demonstrate that (a) TUPLEINF with only automatically extracted tuples significantly outperforms TABLEILP with its original curated knowl-

Solvers	4th Grade	8th Grade
TABLEILP(C)	39.9	34.1
TUPLEINF(T+T')	**51.7**	**51.6**
TABLEILP(C+T)	42.1	37.9
TUPLEINF(C+T)	**47.5**	**48.0**

Table 2: TUPLEINF is significantly better at structured reasoning than TABLEILP.[9]

edge as well as with additional tuples, and (b) TUPLEINF's complementary approach to IR leads to an improved ensemble. Numbers in bold indicate statistical significance based on the Binomial exact test (Howell, 2012) at $p = 0.05$.

We consider two question sets. (1) **4th Grade set** (1220 train, 1304 test) is a 10x larger superset of the NY Regents questions (Clark et al., 2016), and includes professionally written licensed questions. (2) **8th Grade set** (293 train, 282 test) contains 8th grade questions from various states.[8]

We consider two knowledge sources:

(1) The **Sentence corpus** (S) consists of domain-targeted 80K sentences and 280 GB of plain text extracted from web pages used by Clark et al. (2016). This corpus is used as a collection of sentences by the IR solver. It is also used to create the tuple KB T (Sec. 3.1) and on-the-fly question-specific tuples T'_{qa} (Sec. 3.2) for TUPLEINF.

(2) TABLEILP uses ~70 **Curated tables** (C) containing about 7,600 rows, designed for 4th grade NY Regents exams.

We compare TUPLEINF with two state-of-the-art baselines. **IR** is a simple yet powerful information-retrieval baseline (Clark et al., 2016) that selects the answer option with the best matching sentence in a corpus. **TABLEILP** is the state-of-the-art structured inference baseline (Khashabi et al., 2016) developed for science questions.

4.1 Results

Table 2 shows that TUPLEINF, with no curated knowledge, outperforms TABLEILP on both question sets by more than 11%. The lower half of the table shows that even when both solvers are given

---

[8] See the *Middle School Without Diagrams* set from AI2 Science Questions v1 (Feb 2016) at http://allenai.org/data/science-exam-questions.html for the 8th Grade set. For future comparisons, we also report our score on their smaller 4th Grade set: *Elementary School Without Diagrams* (432 train, 339 test).

[9] TUPLEINF(T+T') achieves a score of 56.1% on the *Elementary School Without Diagrams* test set (cf. Footnote 8) compared to TABLEILP(C)'s score of 46.7%.

Solvers	4th Grade	8th Grade
IR(S)	52.0	52.8
IR(S) + TABLEILP(C)	53.3	54.5
IR(S) + TUPLEINF(T+T')	**55.3**	55.1

Table 3: TUPLEINF is complementarity to IR, resulting in a strong ensemble

the same knowledge (C+T),[10] the improved selection and simplified model of TUPLEINF[11] results in a statistically significant improvement. Our simple model, TUPLEINF(C + T), also achieves scores comparable to TABLEILP on the latter's target Regents questions (61.4% vs TABLEILP's reported 61.5%) without any specialized rules.

Table 3 shows that while TUPLEINF achieves similar scores as the IR solver, the approaches are complementary (structured lossy knowledge reasoning vs. lossless sentence retrieval). The two solvers, in fact, differ on 47.3% of the training questions. To exploit this complementarity, we train an ensemble system (Clark et al., 2016) which, as shown in the table, provides a substantial boost over the individual solvers. Further, IR + TUPLEINF is consistently better than IR + TABLEILP.

Finally, in combination with IR and the statistical association based PMI solver (which scores 54.1% by itself) of Clark et al. (2016), TUPLEINF achieves a score of 58.2% on the 4th grade set. This compares favorably to TABLEILP's ensemble score of 56.7%, again attesting to TUPLEINF's strength.[12]

5 Error Analysis

We describe four classes of failure of TUPLEINF, and the future work they suggest.

Missing Important Words: *Which material will spread out to completely fill a larger container? (A) air (B) ice (C) sand (D) water*
In this question, we have tuples that support that water will spread out and fill a larger container, but miss the critical word "completely". A method for detecting salient question words would help here.

Lossy IE: *Which action is the best method to separate a mixture of salt and water? . . .*
The IR solver correctly answers this question by using the sentence: *Separate the salt and water mixture by evaporating the water.* However, TUPLEINF is not able to answer this question as Open IE is unable to extract tuples from this imperative sentence. While the additional structure from Open IE is generally helpful for more robust matching, the conversion to tuples sometimes loses important bits of information.

Bad Alignment: *Which of the following gases is necessary for humans to breathe in order to live? (A) Oxygen (B) Carbon dioxide (C) Helium (D) Water vapor*
TUPLEINF returns "Carbon dioxide" as the answer because of the tuple *(humans; breathe out; carbon dioxide).* The chunk "to breathe" in the question has a high alignment score to the "breathe out" relation in the tuple, even though they have completely different meaning. An improved phrase alignment module can mitigate this issue.

Out of Scope: *Deer live in forest for shelter. If the forest was cut down, which situation would most likely happen? . . .*
Such questions require modeling a state presented in the question and reasoning over this state, which is out of scope of our solver.

6 Conclusion

We presented a new QA system, TUPLEINF, that can reason over a large, potentially noisy knowledge base of (subject, predicate, object) style tuples, in order to answer complex questions. Our results establish TUPLEINF as a new state-of-the-art structured reasoning solver for elementary-level science that does not rely on curated knowledge and generalizes to higher grade levels. Our error analysis points to lossy IE and textual misalignments as two main causes of failure, suggesting future work around incorporating tuple context and distributional similarity measures.

Acknowledgments

The authors would like to thank Oren Etzioni for valuable feedback on an early draft of this paper, and Colin Arenz and Michal Guerquin for helping us develop this system.

---

[10] See Appendix B for how tables (and tuples) are used by TUPLEINF (and TABLEILP).

[11] On average, TABLEILP (TUPLEINF) has 3,403 (1,628, resp.) constraints and 982 (588, resp.) variables. TUPLEINF's ILP can be solved in half the time taken by TABLEILP, reducing the overall question answering time by 68.6%.

[12] We observed no difference in scores on the 8th grade set.

References

Tobias Achterberg. 2009. SCIP: solving constraint integer programs. *Math. Prog. Computation* 1(1):1–41.

Michele Banko, Michael J. Cafarella, Stephen Soderland, Matthew Broadhead, and Oren Etzioni. 2007. Open information extraction from the web. In *IJCAI*.

Jonathan Berant, Andrew Chou, Roy Frostig, and Percy Liang. 2013. Semantic parsing on Freebase from question-answer pairs. In *Empirical Methods in Natural Language Processing (EMNLP)*.

Jonathan Berant and Percy Liang. 2014. Semantic parsing via paraphrasing. In *ACL*.

Eric Brill, Susan Dumais, and Michele Banko. 2002. An analysis of the AskMSR question-answering system. In *Proceedings of EMNLP*. pages 257–264.

Gong Cheng, Weixi Zhu, Ziwei Wang, Jianghui Chen, and Yuzhong Qu. 2016. Taking up the Gaokao Challenge: An information retrieval approach. In *IJCAI*.

Peter Clark. 2015. Elementary school science and math tests as a driver for AI: take the Aristo challenge! In *29th AAAI/IAAI*. Austin, TX, pages 4019–4021.

Peter Clark, Oren Etzioni, Tushar Khot, Ashish Sabharwal, Oyvind Tafjord, Peter Turney, and Daniel Khashabi. 2016. Combining retrieval, statistics, and inference to answer elementary science questions. In *30th AAAI*.

Ido Dagan, Bill Dolan, Bernardo Magnini, and Dan Roth. 2010. Recognizing textual entailment: Rational, evaluation and approaches–erratum. *Natural Language Engineering* 16(01):105–105.

Anthony Fader, Luke S. Zettlemoyer, and Oren Etzioni. 2013. Paraphrase-driven learning for open question answering. In *ACL*.

Anthony Fader, Luke S. Zettlemoyer, and Oren Etzioni. 2014. Open question answering over curated and extracted knowledge bases. In *KDD*.

David Ferrucci, Eric Brown, Jennifer Chu-Carroll, James Fan, David Gondek, Aditya A Kalyanpur, Adam Lally, J William Murdock, Eric Nyberg, John Prager, et al. 2010. Building Watson: An overview of the DeepQA project. *AI Magazine* 31(3):59–79.

David Howell. 2012. *Statistical methods for psychology*. Cengage Learning.

Daniel Khashabi, Tushar Khot, Ashish Sabharwal, Peter Clark, Oren Etzioni, and Dan Roth. 2016. Question answering via integer programming over semi-structured knowledge. In *IJCAI*.

Tushar Khot, Niranjan Balasubramanian, Eric Gribkoff, Ashish Sabharwal, Peter Clark, and Oren Etzioni. 2015. Exploring Markov logic networks for question answering. In *EMNLP*.

Tom Kwiatkowski, Eunsol Choi, Yoav Artzi, and Luke S. Zettlemoyer. 2013. Scaling semantic parsers with on-the-fly ontology matching. In *EMNLP*.

George Miller. 1995. WordNet: a lexical database for english. *Communications of the ACM* 38(11):39–41.

Panupong Pasupat and Percy Liang. 2015. Compositional semantic parsing on semi-structured tables. In *ACL*.

Matthew Richardson and Pedro Domingos. 2006. Markov logic networks. *Machine learning* 62(1–2):107–136.

Arpit Sharma, Nguyen Ha Vo, Somak Aditya, and Chitta Baral. 2015. Towards addressing the winograd schema challenge - building and using a semantic parser and a knowledge hunting module. In *IJCAI*.

Huan Sun, Hao Ma, Xiaodong He, Wen tau Yih, Yu Su, and Xifeng Yan. 2016. Table cell search for question answering. In *WWW*.

Pengcheng Yin, Nan Duan, Ben Kao, Jun-Wei Bao, and Ming Zhou. 2015. Answering questions with complex semantic constraints on open knowledge bases. In *CIKM*.

Bootstrapping for Numerical Open IE

Swarnadeep Saha
Department of CSE
I.I.T. Delhi
writetoswarna@gmail.com

Harinder Pal[*]
Microsoft Corporation
hapal@microsoft.com

Mausam
Department of CSE
I.I.T. Delhi
mausam@cse.iitd.ac.in

Abstract

We design and release BONIE, the first open *numerical* relation extractor, for extracting Open IE tuples where one of the arguments is a number or a quantity-unit phrase. BONIE uses bootstrapping to learn the specific dependency patterns that express numerical relations in a sentence. BONIE's novelty lies in task-specific customizations, such as inferring *implicit* relations, which are clear due to context such as units (for e.g., 'square kilometers' suggests area, even if the word 'area' is missing in the sentence). BONIE obtains 1.5x yield and 15 point precision gain on numerical facts over a state-of-the-art Open IE system.

1   Introduction

Open Information Extraction (Open IE) systems extract relational tuples from text, without requiring a pre-specified vocabulary (Etzioni et al., 2008; Mausam, 2016), by constructing the relation phrases and arguments from within the sentences themselves. Early works on Open IE such as REVERB (Etzioni et al., 2011) extract verb-mediated relations via a handful of human-defined patterns. OLLIE improves recall by learning dependency patterns, using bootstrapping over REVERB extractions (Mausam et al., 2012). Open IE 4.2, a state-of-the-art open information extractor, is based on a combination of SRLIE, a verb-mediated extractor over SRL frames (Christensen et al., 2011), and RELNOUN 2.0, which performs special linguistic processing for extraction from complex noun phrases (Pal and Mausam, 2016).[1]

---

[*]Most work was done when the author was a graduate student at IIT Delhi.

[1] *https://github.com/knowitall/openie*

1. Sentence: *Hong Kong's labour force is 3.5 million.*
Open IE 4.2: (Hong Kong's labour force; is; 3.5 million)
BONIE: (Hong Kong; has labour force of; 3.5 million)
2. Sentence: *Microsoft has 100,000 employees.*
Open IE 4.2: (Microsoft; has; 100,000 employees)
BONIE: (Microsoft; has number of employees; 100,000)
3. Sentence: *James Valley is nearly 600 miles long.*
Open IE 4.2: (James Valley; is; nearly 600 miles long)
BONIE: (James Valley; has length of; nearly 600 miles)
4. Sentence: *Donald Trump is 70 years old.*
Open IE 4.2: (Donald Trump; is; 70 years old)
BONIE: (Donald Trump; has age of; 70 years)
5. Sentence: *James Valley has 5 sq kms of fruit orchards.*
Open IE 4.2: (James Valley; has; 5 sq kms of fruit orchards)
BONIE: (James Valley; has area of fruit orchards; 5 sq kms)

Table 1: Comparison of Open IE 4.2 and BONIE

In this work, we present and release[2] the first system for open numerical extraction, which we name BONIE for **B**ootstrapping-based **O**pen **N**umerical **I**nformation **E**xtractor. It is important to note that existing Open IE systems, like Open IE 4.2, may also extract numerical facts. However, they are oblivious to the presence of numbers in arguments. Therefore, they may miss important extractions and may not always output the best numerical facts. Table 1 compares extractions generated by Open IE 4.2 and BONIE on some of the sample sentences.

At a high level BONIE follows OLLIE's design of identifying seed facts, constructing training data by bootstrapping sentences that may mention a seed fact, pattern learning and ranking. Madaan et al (2016) note that bootstrapping for numerical IE is challenging; it can lead to high noise and missed recall, since numbers can easily match out of context, and numbers may not match due to approximations. In response, similar to most previous works (e.g., LUCHS (Hoffmann et al., 2010)) BONIE matches a number if it is within a percentage threshold. Additionally, BONIE uses a quantity extractor (Roy et al., 2015), which provides

---

[2] Available at *https://github.com/Open-NRE*

Proceedings of the 55th Annual Meeting of the Association for Computational Linguistics (Short Papers), pages 317–323
Vancouver, Canada, July 30 - August 4, 2017. ©2017 Association for Computational Linguistics
https://doi.org/10.18653/v1/P17-2050

the units mentioned in the sentence – BONIE bootstraps a sentence only when the units match.

When compared to OLLIE, BONIE contributes several numerical IE specific customizations. (1) Since no open facts are available for this task, we first manually define a set of high-precision seed patterns, which are run over a large corpus to generate seed facts. (2) Not all seeds are fit for bootstrapping – many don't even have an entity as first argument. We develop heuristics to identify an informative subset from these. After bootstrapping and pattern learning, we find that we are missing important tuples. E.g., sentence #3 in Table 1 above has no explicit relation word – the relation "has length of" is implicit via the adjective 'long'. And, sentence #5 expresses the relation 'area' via the units. (3) BONIE identifies implicit relations using additional processing of units and adjectives. (4) Finally, BONIE can tag a quantity as *count* and prepends "number of" in the relation phrase (sentence #2).

2 Related Work

One of the first Open IE systems to obtain substantial recall is OLLIE (Mausam et al., 2012), which is a pattern learning approach based on a bootstrapped training data using high precision verb-based extractions. Other methods augment the linguistic knowledge in the systems – Exemplar (de Sá Mesquita et al., 2013) adds new rules over dependency parses, SRLIE develops extraction logic over SRL frames (Christensen et al., 2011). Several works identify clauses and operate over restructured sentences (Schmidek and Barbosa, 2014; Corro and Gemulla, 2013; Bast and Haussmann, 2013). Other approaches use tree kernels (Xu et al., 2013), qualia-based patterns (Xavier et al., 2015), and simple within-sentence inference (Bast and Haussmann, 2014). However, none of them handle numbers specifically, and hence do not work for our problem.

Numerical Relations: Numbers play an important role in extracting information from text. Early works have seen people working on understanding numbers that express temporal information (Ling and Weld, 2010). More recently, the focus has been on numbers that express physical quantities or measures, either mentioned in text (Chaganty and Liang, 2016) or in the context of web tables (Ibrahim et al., 2016; Neumaier et al., 2016), or on numbers that represent cardinalities of relations (Mirza et al., 2017).

One of the prior works that applies to generic numerical relations is LUCHS (Hoffmann et al., 2010), where the system uses distant supervision to create 5,000 relation extractors, which included numerical relations as well. Researchers have also specifically developed *numerical relation* extractors to extract those relations where one of the arguments is a quantity (Vlachos and Riedel, 2015; Intxaurrondo et al., 2015; Madaan et al., 2016). However, all of them extract only an ontology relation, and hence are not directly applicable to Open IE.

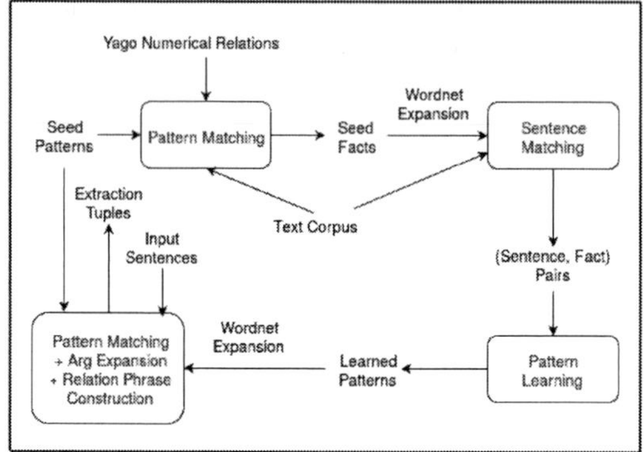

Figure 1: BONIE flow diagram

3 Open Numerical Relation Extraction

The goal of Open Numerical Relation Extraction is to process a sentence that has a quantity mention in it, and extract any tuple of the form (Arg1, relation phrase, Arg2) where Arg2 (or Arg1) is a quantity. As a first step, BONIE learns patterns where Arg2 is a quantity, as most English sentences tend to express numerical facts in active voice. Figure 1 outlines BONIE's algorithm, which operates in two phases: training and extraction. BONIE's training includes creation of seed facts, generation of training data via bootstrapping, and pattern learning over dependency parses. In the extraction phrase, BONIE performs pattern matching and parse-based expansion to construct numerical tuples. These numerical tuples are made more coherent by a novel relation construction step.

As an example, the sentence *"India has a population of 1.2 billion"* matches seed pattern #2 (from Figure 2) to create a seed fact (India; population; 1.2 billion; null). This 'null' represents that the quantity needs no unit. While bootstrapping, this seed fact may match a sentence *"India is the second most populous country in the world, with a population of 1.25 billion."* in the corpus.

318

```
Seed Dependency Patterns
1. <(#is|are|was|were|been|be#verb)<(nsubj#{rel}#nnp|nn)<(prep#of|for#in)<(pobj#{arg}#nnp|nn|prp)>>(attr#{quantity}#.+)>>
2. <(#has|have|had|having#verb)<(dobj#{rel}#nnp|nn)<(prep##in)<(pobj#{quantity}#.+)>>(nsubj#{arg}#nnp|nn|prp)>>
3. <(#is|are|was|were|been|be#verb)<(nsubj#{arg}#nnp|nn|prp)(acomp|advmod#{rel}#jj|rb)<(npadvmod#{quantity}#.+)>>>
4. <(#has|have|had|having#verb)<(nsubj#arg#nnp|nn|prp)(dobj#quantity#.+)<(prep#of#in)<(pobj#{rel}#nnp|nn)>>>>
5. <(##verb)<(attr|acomp#{quantity}#.+)(nsubj#{rel}#nnp|nn)<(poss#{arg}#nnp|nn)>>>
6. <(#{rel}#verb)<(auxpass#is|are|was|were|been|be#verb)(nsubjpass#{arg}#nnp|nn|prp)(prep##in)<(pobj#{quantity}#.+)>>
```

Figure 2: Seed Dependency Patterns in BONIE

This training example will help learn a new pattern.[3] This pattern, when applied to the sentence *"Microsoft Windows is the most popular operating system, with a customer base of 300 million users"*, will extract (Microsoft Windows; has customer base of; 300 million users).

While BONIE's skeleton broadly resembles that of OLLIE's (Mausam et al., 2012), it brings in customizations specific to the problem of numerical extraction such as a modified pattern language, heuristics for generating high quality seed set and training data, special processing for non-noun relations, and a novel relation construction step. We now describe BONIE's algorithm in detail.

3.1 Generation of Seed Facts

Since open numerical facts are not readily available, we first write a handful of high-precision dependency patterns (see Figure 2 for a list). Each dependency pattern encodes the minimal sub-tree of the dependency parse connecting the relation, quantity and argument in that sentence. BONIE encodes a node in a pattern via '$<depLabel>\#<word>\#<POSTag>$', where 'depLabel' is the edge connecting the node to its parent, 'word' is the word at the node, 'POSTag' is its part of speech tag; '#' is a delimiter separating them. {rel}, {arg} and {quantity} in the patterns are placeholders for relation, argument and quantity headwords, respectively. BONIE generates seed facts by parsing the corpus and matching seed patterns with the parse. In case of a successful match, a seed fact of the form (arg headword; relation headword; quantity; unit) is generated. Argument and relation headwords are extracted directly from the parse. For the other two, it uses Illinois Quantifier (Roy et al., 2015), which returns both the quantity and unit separately.

Since seed facts form the basis of our training task, they must be as clean as possible – BONIE

adds several filters to reduce noise. It considers a seed fact as valid only when the quantity node in the pattern is within some quantity span given by Illinois Quantifier. It also rejects any fact whose argument is not a proper noun.

After these filters it gets high-precision extractions, but not necessarily good seeds – many seeds are generic, which may easily match unrelated sentences. E.g., (Michael; drove; 20; kms) isn't a good seed, since 'Michael' isn't specific, and could erroneously match sentences mentioning another Michael with some unrelated reference of a 20 km drive. To improve the set, BONIE checks for the presence of a seed fact in Yago KB (Hoffart et al., 2013) and keeps only those that are common. Since Yago has many numerical facts for height, area, latitude, GDP, etc., this gives BONIE a diverse set of clean facts for further training.

Finally, some numerical facts may be expressed without using a nominal relation word. BONIE uses WordNet (Miller, 1995) to generate new seeds from such seed facts using the derivationally related noun form of the relation headword. For example, (Brown ; tall ; 13 ; inches) gets transformed to (Brown; height; 13; inches), which gets added as a seed fact.

3.2 Bootstrapping

Similar to OLLIE, BONIE finds sentences that contain all words in a seed fact and generates *(sentence, fact)* pairs. But unlike OLLIE, BONIE has quantities and units, and matching them as words isn't appropriate. Illinois Quantifier performs an internal normalization for both, e.g, changes 'dollars' and '$' to 'US$', and '%' to 'percent'. Since seed facts also have normalized units, we run Illinois quantifier on candidate sentences and match normalized units directly. Moreover, BONIE maintains a percentage threshold δ to control the amount of allowed difference between quantities in the sentence and seed fact. Once all constituents of a fact match with a sentence, BONIE generates the *(sentence, fact)* pair.

---

[3] `<(#is#verb)<(nsubj#{arg}#nnp|nn)(prep#with#in)<(pobj#{rel}#nnp|nn)<(prep#of#in)<(pobj#{quantity}#.+)>>>>>`

3.3 Open Pattern Learning

For each *(sentence, fact)* pair, BONIE parses the sentence, and replaces the argument and relation words of the fact with '{arg}' and '{rel}' placeholders. For quantity and unit words, BONIE replaces the one at a higher level in the parse with '{quantity}'. The minimal path containing '{arg}', '{rel}' and '{quantity}' is learned as a pattern. Since quantity and unit are typically expected to remain close to each other in a sentence, BONIE rejects all such patterns where the distance between them exceeds a certain threshold value.

Some patterns are learned with specific words such as 'contains' in example (partial) <(#contains#verb)<(dobj#{quantity}#.+)<... We believe that this pattern should work with all inflections and synonyms of 'contain', BONIE uses WordNet to expand the pattern by including all inflections and synset synonyms. Each pattern is scored based on the number of times it is learned from the data.

3.4 Constructing Extractions

After matching a pattern to a new sentence, similar to OLLIE, arg/rel phrases are completed by expanding the extracted headnouns on poss, det, num, neg, amod, quantmod, nn, and pobj edges. If one of the children of the argument headword is a prep, rcmod or partmod edge, the whole subtree under that is extracted. Quantity phrase is extracted by Illinois quantifier, but if any sibling node of the quantity node is connected by a prep edge, with the word 'of', BONIE expands the entire subtree below it. This allows *"10 percent of 100 dollars"* to be included in the quantity phrase.

Relation Phrase Construction: Whenever the relation headword is an adjective or an adverb, BONIE uses WordNet to get its derivationally related noun form and that becomes the new relation. This transforms the tuple (Donald Trump ; old ; about 70 years) to (Donald Trump ; has age of ; about 70 years).

Sometimes, sentences don't use a numerical relation word – it is obvious from the units. E.g., sentence #4 on page 1 expresses the 'area' relation implicitly. BONIE infers these implicit relations using the unit analysis in UnitTagger (Sarawagi and Chakrabarti, 2014). Whenever BONIE sees a unit (sq kms) getting mistreated as a relation it uses UnitTagger to infer relations from units and postprocesses the extraction accordingly. The ex-

traction, as a result changes from (James Valley; has sq kms of ; 5 of fruit orchards) to (James Valley ; has area of fruit orchards ; 5 sq kms).

Finally, in cases when a plural noun relation word also appears as a unit in the quantifier, BONIE hypothesizes that it is a count extraction, and prepends 'number of' to the relation headword and removes the unit from the quantity phrase. E.g., (Microsoft; has employees; 100,000 employees) from sentence #2 becomes (Microsoft; has number of employees; 100,000).

4 Experiments

We build BONIE over data from ClueWeb12,[4] filtered so as to keep only the sentences that contain numbers. We further remove those where quantity represents a date, time, or duration, and where the quantity is accompanied by document words like 'Section', 'Table', or 'Figure'. We use the dependency parser from ClearNLP[5]. We generate about 21,000 seed facts from roughly 20 million numerical sentences. These are matched against 7 million numerical sentences obtaining about 18,500 (sentence, fact) pairs.

We tried different values of δ (the matching threshold) and found results to not be sensitive as long as δ varies in the range of 2% to 5%. So we set δ=2% during the final evaluation. The distance threshold between the quantity and unit mentioned in Section 2.3 is set to 3 and is based on our general understanding of parse trees.

BONIE learns around 7,000 new patterns. Since pattern frequency is a good indicator of pattern quality (Wu and Weld, 2010), we rank the patterns on the basis of frequency and take the top 1,000 patterns for further analysis. We find that almost all patterns beyond the top 1,000 are learned only once or twice on our training set. Our decision to ignore all patterns beyond the top 1,000 is so that we have a support of at least three for each pattern.

We sample a random testset of 2,000 numerical sentences from ClueWeb12 (not used in training). Two annotators with NLP experience annotate each extraction for correctness. We obtain an inter-annotator agreement of 97%, and report the results on the subset where both annotators agree.

Since there are no open numerical extractors available, we compare BONIE against an Open IE system and another closed numerical IE system.

---

[4] *http://www.lemurproject.org/clueweb12.php/*
[5] *https://github.com/clir/clearnlp*

Setting	Precision	Yield
NumberRule	50.00	6
Open IE 4.2	62.50	296
BONIE (seed patterns only)	85.71	72
+ learned patterns	13.88	362
+ fact filters	55.27	351
+ Yago + WordNet expansion on facts	72.69	418
+ Relation phrase construction	77.91	448
+ WordNet expansion on patterns	77.23	458

Table 2: Precision and Yield (#correct numerical extractions) on a dataset of 2000 ClueWeb12 numerical sentences.

Table 2 reports the precisions and yields of all systems. We first compare against numerical tuples from Open IE 4.2,[6] a publicly available state-of-the-art Open IE system that combines SRLIE and RELNOUN. BONIE outputs a much higher precision and yield on numerical facts, as compared to Open IE 4.2. We also compare against Number-Rule, a state-of-the-art closed numerical IE system (Madaan et al., 2016). NumberRule[7] can be quickly re-targeted to any new semantic relation by inputting keywords. We feed all of Yago numerical relation words as keywords to Number-Rule, but still find that it was able to generate only 12 extractions on our testset.

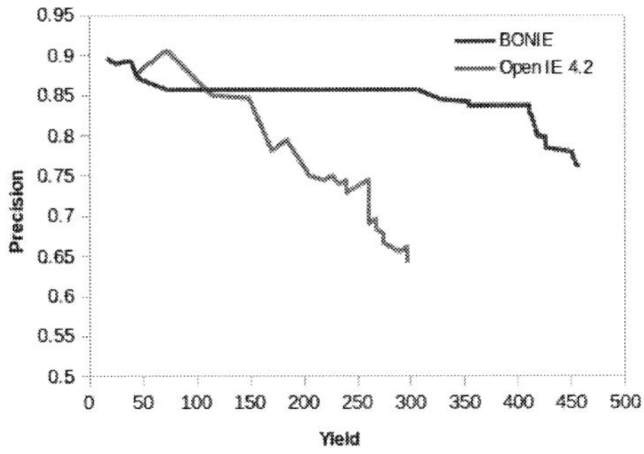

Figure 3: Comparison of Precision-Yield curves for BONIE and Open IE 4.2. BONIE achieves substantially larger area under the curve than Open IE 4.2.

We also perform additional ablation study to evaluate the value of each component. Just the seed patterns themselves have a significantly higher precision but much smaller yield. This is expected, since the seeds must be highly precise for bootstrapping. If Yago matching and other seed filtering heuristics are turned off, the precision of the system goes down drastically due to a very noisy bootstrapped set. If the post-processing of relation phrase construction is turned off, there is a 5 point precision loss and about 7% yield reduction due to some incorrect extracted tuples, which are corrected by post-processing. Finally,

Wordnet-based expansion has marginal increase in yield and slight precision loss.

Open IE 4.2 associates a confidence value with each extraction - ranking against which generates a precision-yield curve. For BONIE, we rank the patterns in such a way that the seed patterns are at the top, followed by the learned patterns. The learned patterns are ordered based on their frequencies. Figure 3 reports the curves for both the systems and we find that BONIE has a larger area under the curve as compared to Open IE 4.2.

Estimating recall in Open IE is difficult since it requires annotators to exhaustively tag all open extractions in a sentence. To get an estimate, an author manually tagged 100 sentences with all numerical extractions. We find that BONIE's recall is about 48%. Two-thirds of missed recall is because of missing conjuncts. E.g., it misses the tuple relating retirement age with 68 years in *"The retirement age for men is 65 years and 68 years for women."* Other missed recall is due to complexity of sentences or inaccuracy of parsers.

5 Conclusions

We release BONIE [8], the first open numerical relation extractor and other resources for further research. BONIE is based on bootstrapping and pattern learning and follows previous similar works such as OLLIE. However, for effective bootstrapping and training, it implements various customizations specific to numerical relations in curation of seed fact set, matching of sentences, and construction of relation phrase at the time of extraction. BONIE significantly outperforms both open non-numerical IE, and closed numerical IE systems with 1.5x yield and 15 point precision gain over a state-of-the-art Open IE system. We find that better conjunction processing is an important future step for improving BONIE's recall even further.

Acknowledgements

This work is supported by Google language understanding and knowledge discovery focused research grants, a Bloomberg award, a Visvesvaraya faculty award by Govt. of India and an IRD seed grant at I.I.T, Delhi. We also thank Microsoft for the Microsoft Azure sponsorship and a Microsoft Travel grant in support of the work.

---

[6] *https://github.com/knowitall/openie*

[7] *https://github.com/NEO-IE*

[8] Available at *https://github.com/Open-NRE*

References

Hannah Bast and Elmar Haussmann. 2013. Open information extraction via contextual sentence decomposition. In *2013 IEEE Seventh International Conference on Semantic Computing, Irvine, CA, USA, September 16-18, 2013*. pages 154–159.

Hannah Bast and Elmar Haussmann. 2014. More informative open information extraction via simple inference. In *Advances in Information Retrieval - 36th European Conference on IR Research, ECIR 2014, Amsterdam, The Netherlands, April 13-16, 2014. Proceedings*. pages 585–590.

Arun Tejasvi Chaganty and Percy Liang. 2016. How much is 131 million dollars? putting numbers in perspective with compositional descriptions. In *Proceedings of the 54th Annual Meeting of the Association for Computational Linguistics, ACL 2016, August 7-12, 2016, Berlin, Germany, Volume 1: Long Papers*.

Janara Christensen, Mausam, Stephen Soderland, and Oren Etzioni. 2011. An analysis of open information extraction based on semantic role labeling. In *Proceedings of the 6th International Conference on Knowledge Capture (K-CAP 2011), June 26-29, 2011, Banff, Alberta, Canada*. pages 113–120.

Luciano Del Corro and Rainer Gemulla. 2013. Clausie: clause-based open information extraction. In *22nd International World Wide Web Conference, WWW '13, Rio de Janeiro, Brazil, May 13-17, 2013*. pages 355–366.

Filipe de Sá Mesquita, Jordan Schmidek, and Denilson Barbosa. 2013. Effectiveness and efficiency of open relation extraction. In *Proceedings of the 2013 Conference on Empirical Methods in Natural Language Processing, EMNLP 2013, 18-21 October 2013, Grand Hyatt Seattle, Seattle, Washington, USA, A meeting of SIGDAT, a Special Interest Group of the ACL*. pages 447–457.

Oren Etzioni, Michele Banko, Stephen Soderland, and Daniel S. Weld. 2008. Open information extraction from the web. *Commun. ACM* 51(12):68–74.

Oren Etzioni, Anthony Fader, Janara Christensen, Stephen Soderland, and Mausam. 2011. Open information extraction: The second generation. In *IJCAI 2011, Proceedings of the 22nd International Joint Conference on Artificial Intelligence, Barcelona, Catalonia, Spain, July 16-22, 2011*. pages 3–10.

Johannes Hoffart, Fabian M. Suchanek, Klaus Berberich, and Gerhard Weikum. 2013. YAGO2: A spatially and temporally enhanced knowledge base from wikipedia. *Artif. Intell.* 194:28–61.

Raphael Hoffmann, Congle Zhang, and Daniel S. Weld. 2010. Learning 5000 relational extractors. In *ACL 2010, Proceedings of the 48th Annual Meeting of the Association for Computational Linguistics, July 11-16, 2010, Uppsala, Sweden*. pages 286–295.

Yusra Ibrahim, Mirek Riedewald, and Gerhard Weikum. 2016. Making sense of entities and quantities in web tables. In *Proceedings of the 25th ACM International on Conference on Information and Knowledge Management, CIKM 2016, Indianapolis, IN, USA, October 24-28, 2016*. pages 1703–1712.

Ander Intxaurrondo, Eneko Agirre, Oier Lopez de Lacalle, and Mihai Surdeanu. 2015. Diamonds in the rough: Event extraction from imperfect microblog data. In *NAACL HLT 2015, The 2015 Conference of the North American Chapter of the Association for Computational Linguistics: Human Language Technologies, Denver, Colorado, USA, May 31 - June 5, 2015*. pages 641–650.

Xiao Ling and Daniel S. Weld. 2010. Temporal information extraction. In *Proceedings of the Twenty-Fourth AAAI Conference on Artificial Intelligence, AAAI 2010, Atlanta, Georgia, USA, July 11-15, 2010*.

Aman Madaan, Ashish Mittal, Mausam, Ganesh Ramakrishnan, and Sunita Sarawagi. 2016. Numerical relation extraction with minimal supervision. In *Proceedings of the Thirtieth AAAI Conference on Artificial Intelligence, February 12-17, 2016, Phoenix, Arizona, USA.*. pages 2764–2771.

Mausam. 2016. Open information extraction systems and downstream applications. In *Proceedings of the Twenty-Fifth International Joint Conference on Artificial Intelligence, IJCAI 2016, New York, NY, USA, 9-15 July 2016*. pages 4074–4077.

Mausam, Michael Schmitz, Stephen Soderland, Robert Bart, and Oren Etzioni. 2012. Open language learning for information extraction. In *Proceedings of the 2012 Joint Conference on Empirical Methods in Natural Language Processing and Computational Natural Language Learning, EMNLP-CoNLL 2012, July 12-14, 2012, Jeju Island, Korea*. pages 523–534.

George A. Miller. 1995. Wordnet: A lexical database for english. *Commun. ACM* 38(11):39–41.

Paramita Mirza, Simon Razniewski, Fariz Darari, and Gerhard Weikum. 2017. Cardinal virtues: Extracting relation cardinalities from text.

Sebastian Neumaier, Jürgen Umbrich, Josiane Xavier Parreira, and Axel Polleres. 2016. Multi-level semantic labelling of numerical values. In *The Semantic Web - ISWC 2016 - 15th International Semantic Web Conference, Kobe, Japan, October 17-21, 2016, Proceedings, Part I*. pages 428–445.

Harinder Pal and Mausam. 2016. Demonyms and compound relational nouns in nominal open IE. In *Proceedings of the 5th Workshop on Automated Knowledge Base Construction, AKBC@NAACL-HLT 2016, San Diego, CA, USA, June 17, 2016*. pages 35–39.

Subhro Roy, Tim Vieira, and Dan Roth. 2015. Reasoning about quantities in natural language. *TACL* 3:1–13.

Sunita Sarawagi and Soumen Chakrabarti. 2014. Open-domain quantity queries on web tables: annotation, response, and consensus models. In *The 20th ACM SIGKDD International Conference on Knowledge Discovery and Data Mining, KDD '14, New York, NY, USA - August 24 - 27, 2014.* pages 711–720.

Jordan Schmidek and Denilson Barbosa. 2014. Improving open relation extraction via sentence restructuring. In *Proceedings of the Ninth International Conference on Language Resources and Evaluation (LREC-2014), Reykjavik, Iceland, May 26-31, 2014.*. pages 3720–3723.

Andreas Vlachos and Sebastian Riedel. 2015. Identification and verification of simple claims about statistical properties. In *Proceedings of the 2015 Conference on Empirical Methods in Natural Language Processing, EMNLP 2015, Lisbon, Portugal, September 17-21, 2015.* pages 2596–2601.

Fei Wu and Daniel S. Weld. 2010. Open information extraction using wikipedia. In *ACL 2010, Proceedings of the 48th Annual Meeting of the Association for Computational Linguistics, July 11-16, 2010, Uppsala, Sweden.* pages 118–127.

Clarissa Castellã Xavier, Vera Lúcia Strube de Lima, and Marlo Souza. 2015. Open information extraction based on lexical semantics. *J. Braz. Comp. Soc.* 21(1):4:1–4:14.

Ying Xu, Mi-Young Kim, Kevin Quinn, Randy Goebel, and Denilson Barbosa. 2013. Open information extraction with tree kernels. In *Human Language Technologies: Conference of the North American Chapter of the Association of Computational Linguistics, Proceedings, June 9-14, 2013, Westin Peachtree Plaza Hotel, Atlanta, Georgia, USA.* pages 868–877.

Feature-Rich Networks for Knowledge Base Completion

Alexandros Komninos
Department of Computer Science
University of York
York, YO10 5GH
United Kingdom
ak1153@york.ac.uk

Suresh Manandhar
Department of Computer Science
University of York2
York, YO10 5GH
United Kingdom
suresh@cs.york.ac.uk

Abstract

We propose jointly modelling Knowledge Bases and aligned text with Feature-Rich Networks. Our models perform Knowledge Base Completion by learning to represent and compose diverse feature types from partially aligned and noisy resources. We perform experiments on Freebase utilizing additional entity type information and syntactic textual relations. Our evaluation suggests that the proposed models can better incorporate side information than previously proposed combinations of bilinear models with convolutional neural networks, showing large improvements when scoring the plausibility of unobserved facts with associated textual mentions.

1 Introduction

Knowledge Bases (KB) are an important resource for many applications such as question answering (Reddy et al., 2014), relation extraction (Mintz et al., 2009) and named entity recognition (Ling and Weld, 2012). While large collaborative KBs like Freebase (Bollacker et al., 2008) and DBpedia (Auer et al., 2007) contain facts about million of entities, they are mostly incomplete and contain errors. A large amount of research has been dedicated to automatically extend knowledge bases, a task called Entity Linking or Knowledge Base Completion (KBC). Proposed approaches to KBC either reason about the internal structure of the KB, or utilize external data sources that indicate relations between the entities in the KB.

A very successful approach to KBC is latent feature models (Nickel et al., 2011; Bordes et al., 2013; Socher et al., 2013; Nickel et al., 2016). Such models embed the symbols of the KB into

a low dimensional space and assign a score to unseen triples as a function of the latent feature representations. Most approaches define a scoring function as a linear or bilinear operator. Latent feature models have shown good performance when considering the internal structure of KBs and are scalable to very large datasets.

Utilizing textual data or other external resources for KBC is a challenging task but has the potential of constantly updating KBs as new information becomes available. A line of work uses the KB as a means to obtain distant supervision to train relation extraction systems that classify textual mentions into one of the KBs relations (Mintz et al., 2009; Hoffmann et al., 2011; Surdeanu et al., 2012). State-of-the-art approaches for KBC with external textual data are obtained by latent feature models that jointly embed the KB symbols and text relations into the same space (Riedel et al., 2013; Toutanova et al., 2015). The benefit of such models over relation extraction systems is that they can combine both the internal structure of the KB and textual information to reason about the plausibility of unobserved facts.

A commonly used approach for augmenting a KBC given an aligned text corpus is by adopting a Universal Schema (Riedel et al., 2013), where extracted textual relations between entities are directly added to the knowledge graph and treated the same as KB relations. This allows application of any latent variable model defined over triples to jointly embed the KB and text relations to the same space. An extension to the Universal Schema approach was proposed by (Toutanova et al., 2015), where representations of text relations are formed compositionally by Convolutional Neural Networks (CNNs) and then composed with entity vectors by a bilinear model to score a fact. However, these models show only moderate improvement when incorporating tex-

324

Proceedings of the 55th Annual Meeting of the Association for Computational Linguistics (Short Papers), pages 324–329
Vancouver, Canada, July 30 - August 4, 2017. ©2017 Association for Computational Linguistics
https://doi.org/10.18653/v1/P17-2051

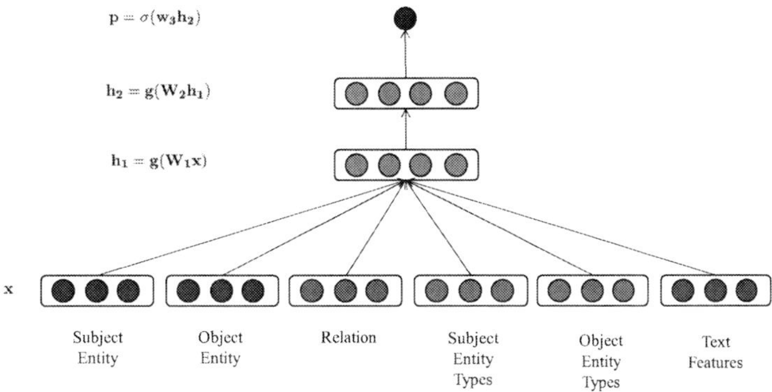

Figure 1: Feature-Rich Network with all the aligned feature types associated with a fact.

tual relations.

A limitation of the Universal Schema approach for joint embedding of KBs and text is that information about the correspondence between KB and text relations is only implicitly available through their co-occurrence with entities. Text relations can often be noisy and pairs of entities can co-occur in the same sentence without sharing a semantic relation. In addition, there is usually a mismatch in the relations found in the KB and those expressed in text. The model has to learn the alignment between KB and text relations without explicit evidence of co-occurrence between the two, and then propagate that information through the entity embeddings in order to score unseen KB triples.

We propose a different approach to combine KB and textual evidence, where the textual relations are not part of the same graph but are treated as side evidence. In our setting, a fact does not necessarily consist of a (sbj, rel, obj) triple, but as an n-tuple where extra elements are formed by extracting additional information from the KB and aligned side resources such as text. We score the probability of the tuple being true by learning latent representations for each element of the tuple, and then learning a composition and scoring function parameterized by a Multilayer Perceptron (MLP). We choose MLPs as they are a generic method to model interactions between latent features without having to specify the form of a composition operator for tuples of different arity. When scoring the plausibility of unseen facts, all the side evidence associated with that fact becomes explicit through the n-tuple.

We evaluate the ability of the proposed Feature-Rich Networks (FRN) for KBC on the challenging FB15k-237 (Toutanova et al., 2015). We compare the performance of bilinear models to an MLP when facts are represented as simple triples, and the contribution of two additional types of aligned information: entity types and textual relation mentions from a side corpus. We also evaluate the contribution of initializing feature representations from external models. Evaluation suggests that while MLPs and bilinear models perform similarly when treating facts as triples of KB symbols, the proposed approach can better utilize additional textual data than a combination of CNNs with bilinear models, showing large improvements in predicting unseen facts when they have linked relation mentions in text.

2 Model Definition

Knowledge Bases can be represented as a directed graph where nodes are entities $e \in E$ and edges are typed relations $r \in R$. A fact in the KB is encoded as a triple (e_s, r, e_o), where e_s is the subject entity and e_o is the object entity. Starting with an existing KB consisting of a set of observed facts, our goal is to reason about the plausibility of unobserved facts, given some additional external resource. In our proposed model, we expand the representation of a fact to an n-tuple by considering alignments of the additional resource with elements of the triple. Our most expressive model encodes a fact as $\mathcal{X} = (e_s, r, e_o, t_s, t_o, T_{o,s})$, where t_s, t_o are associated representation of types of the two entities, and $T_{o,s}$ is the aligned textual evidence associated with a pair of entities from a side corpus. Representations of entities and entity types are shared between subjects and objects.

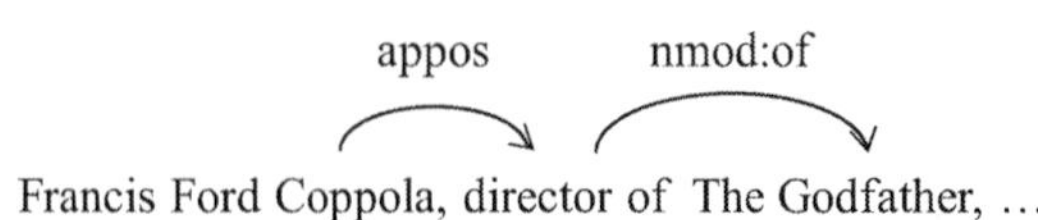

subject entity	`/m/02vyw`
object entity	`/m/07g1sm`
relation	`/film/director/film`
subject entity types	`/people/person /film/director/ /award/award_winner`
object entity types	`/film/film /award/award_winning_work`
text features	`appos⁻¹_Esbj director appos_director of nmod:of⁻¹_director nmod:of_Eobj`

Extracted features for a KB fact with a single associated textual relation mention.

2.0.1 Feature Rich Networks

We model the probability of an n-tuple being true with an MLP that learns to compose and score the compatibility of the features associated with it. Features for each individual element of the tuple are assigned low dimensional embeddings which are concatenated to form the input to the MLP. The embeddings are jointly learned with the composition and scoring model through back-propagation. The probability of a fact being true is given by:

$$p(\mathcal{X} = 1) = \sigma(\mathbf{w_3} \cdot g(\mathbf{W_2} \cdot g(\mathbf{W_1} \cdot \mathbf{x}))) \quad (1)$$

$$\mathbf{x} = v(e_s); v(r); v(e_o); v(t_s); v(t_o); v(T_{s,o}) \quad (2)$$

where W_1, W_2, w_3 are the weights of the network, $g(\bullet)$ is a non-linear function applied element-wise, $\sigma(\bullet)$ is the sigmoid function and $v(\bullet)$ are latent feature representations of each element of the tuple. We use Rectified Linear Units as non-linearities (Nair and Hinton, 2010).

2.1 Additional Features

We create compositional representations for the entity types and textual relation mentions with simple aggregation functions of their feature embeddings. Although not considered in this work, the overall approach is highly modular allowing for each component to be modelled by a different kind of network.

Freebase Entity Types

Entities in Freebase can have multiple types assigned to them. While entity types are explicitly provided in Freebase, we instead learn type representations by considering observed relations in the training set. Each relation in Freebase is encoded as a `domain/type/property` of the subject entity. We extract the set of all triples where an entity takes the subject position, and keep the `domain/type` part as a type feature of that entity. We aggregate embeddings of all the observed discrete features using summation followed by L2-normalization to create the final representation of an entity's type. We use a special UNKNOWN symbol for entities with no observed types in the training set (i.e., entities that do not appear as subject of a triple). We create entity type representations for both subject and object entities and concatenate them to the input vector of the network.

Text Relations

We use a side corpus where pairs of entities are linked to the KB and take the shortest dependency path connecting them as a textual relation mention. Since textual relations are tied to entity pairs, we collect all mentions for a given entity pair and associate them with a fact. This results in a set of phrases that act as textual evidence for relations of an entity pair.

We create a representation of the associated text for each entity pair by using a Neural Bag of Words model augmented with dependency features. A dependency feature is a symbol for a word having a specific dependency relation, such as `compound_knowledge`, `compound⁻¹_base` for the `knowledge base` noun compound. Similar to the Entity Type representations, embeddings of words and dependency features are aggregated by summation followed by L2-normalization, and a special UNKNOWN symbol is assigned to tuples whose pair of entities does

| | All | | With Mentions | | Without Mentions | |
Model	MRR	H@10	MRR	H@10	MRR	H@10
KB only						
F	16.9	24.5	26.4	49.1	13.3	15.5
E	33.2	47.6	25.5	37.8	36.0	51.2
DistMult	35.7	52.3	26.0	39.0	39.3	57.2
E + DistMult	37.3	55.2	28.6	42.9	**40.5**	59.8
FRN trp	35.8	55.3	28.7	44.3	38.6	59.7
FRN trp + types	36.0	56.0	28.2	45.0	39.0	60.3
FRN trp + types + init	**37.6**	**57.5**	**30.5**	**48.3**	40.4	**61.1**
KB and text						
Conv-F	19.2	28.4	34.9	63.7	13.3	15.4
Conv-E	33.2	47.6	25.5	37.8	36.0	51.2
Conv-DistMult	36.6	53.5	28.3	43.4	39.7	57.2
Conv-E + Conv-DistMult	40.1	58.1	33.9	49.9	**42.2**	**61.1**
FRN trp + types + text	38.1	58.3	**45.4**	**68.8**	35.2	54.2
FRN trp + types + text + init	**40.3**	**62.0**	44.1	68.3	38.7	59.5

Table 1: Evaluation results on the FB15k-237 dataset. Results for F,E,DistMult and their CNN versions are reported from (Toutanova et al., 2015). With/Without Mentions indicates KB facts with/without aligned textual relations for their entity pair.

not have textual relation mentions. While our text representation component is quite simple, similar models have shown competitive performance on modelling short text (Komninos and Manandhar, 2016).

Initialization with Pre-trained Embeddings

We experiment with pre-trained embeddings to initialize the entity vectors and text feature embeddings of our model. Text feature embeddings are initialized from an available dependency based skip-gram model trained on Wikipedia (Komninos and Manandhar, 2016). Features that are not included in the vocabulary of the pre-trained model are initialized with a random vector from a normal distribution with zero mean and same variance as the set of pre-trained embeddings. For entity vectors, we retrieve the English name of the entity from Freebase and construct a representation by averaging the embeddings of the words appearing in the name. Entities that do not have a name property are initialized randomly.

2.2 Training

The network weights are optimized by minimizing the binary cross-entropy loss over minibatches using the AdaM optimizer (Kingma and Ba, 2014). To avoid the large computational cost of training with all possible unobserved facts, we make use of negative sampling. The loss function is:

$$L(\Theta) = -\sum_{|\mathcal{X}_p|} \log p(\mathcal{X}_p) - \sum_{|\mathcal{X}_n|} \log(1 - p(\mathcal{X}_n))$$

(3)

where Θ are all the parameters of the network including the feature embeddings, $\mathcal{X}_p$ are the observed facts in the training set and $\mathcal{X}_n$ are randomly drawn unobserved facts. We construct the negative samples by fixing the subject entity and relation, and uniformly sampling an object entity with the restriction that the resulting triple is not included in the training set. We then expand the triple with entity type and text alignments. This negative sampling schedule follows the evaluation procedure, where the network has to rank triples that only differ in the object entity position. Experiments in the validation set indicated that for a fixed number of negative samples, only considering negative samples that differ in the object position performs better than also including negative samples for the subject position.

3 Evaluation

3.1 Dataset and Evaluation Protocol

The FB15k237 dataset consists of about 15k entities and 237 relations derived from the FB15k dataset (Toutanova et al., 2015). This subset of relations does not contain redundant relations that can be easily inferred, resulting in a more challenging task compared to the original FB15k dataset. There are 310,116 triples in the dataset split into 272,115/17,535/20,466 for training/validation/testing. In addition to the KB, the dataset includes dependency paths of approximately 2.7 million relation instances of linked entity mentions extracted from the ClueWeb corpus (Gabrilovich et al., 2013).

Evaluation follows the procedure of (Toutanova et al., 2015). Given a positive fact in the test set, the subject entity and relation are fixed and models have to rank all facts formed by the object entities appearing in the training set. The reported metrics are mean reciprocal rank (MRR) and hits@10. Hits@10 is the fraction of positive facts ranked in the top 10 positions. Positive facts in the training, validation and test set are removed before ranking.

3.2 Implementation Details

Hyperparameters of the model were chosen by maximizing MRR on the validation set. We use two 300-dimensional hidden layers for the MLP, and dimensions of feature embeddings are: 300 for entity and text features, 100 for relations and 20 for entity type features. The number of negative samples was set to 20 as increasing their number only resulted in minor gains, and the batch size was set to 420. Best models were chosen among 20 epochs of training by monitoring validation MRR. Models with embedding initializations converged within the first 10 epochs. Initialization in the text model includes initializing entity and relation embeddings from a model without text mentions.

3.3 Results

We compare our Feature-Rich Networks with the bilinear models F and E (Riedel et al., 2013), model DistMult (Yang et al., 2014) and their CNN augmented versions (Toutanova et al., 2015). Results can be seen in Table 1.

We first observe that when modelling just KB triples, the MLP model outperforms individual bilinear formulations, performing similarly to the best combination of DistMult + E. This shows that an additive combination of bilinear models is a strong baseline even though it does not use additional parameters other than embeddings to compose and score triples. The addition of entity type information has a positive but small contribution to performance. This is not surprising as entity type information is extracted from observed relations, and latent feature models can effectively learn that during training. On the other hand, initializing entity embeddings with averaged word embeddings of their names results in a substantial performance gain of about 1.5 points in both MRR and hits@10. In general, we observe that all models perform worse on facts with textual relation mentions when they have not access to such mentions.

When textual relation mentions are added, we observe that our proposed model increases its performance score about 3 points in MRR and 4.5 in hits@10 compared to the best model that does not include text. Contrary to the conv-bilinear models, the performance gain is much larger for facts with textual mentions, reaching an additional 15/20 in MRR/hits@10 respectively. We attribute this gain to the explicitly represented textual relation alignments with the KB symbols as encoded by the expanded tuple representations, and the non-linear composition of its elements by the MLP. We also notice that embedding initialization performs better overall.

4 Conclusion

In this paper, we propose joint modelling of Knowledge Bases and text with Feature-Rich Networks. Our models can learn to combine information from different sources and better utilize noisy information from text than bilinear models augmented with convolutional neural networks. Besides text, we experiment with entity types and initialization with pre-trained embeddings, getting positive gains in performance. An interesting direction for future work is to combine our models with additional aligned information, such as multiple KBs and to experiment with different components such as CNNs or LSTMs for text encoding.

Acknowledgements

Alexandros Komninos was supported by EPSRC via an Engineering Doctorate in LSCITS. Suresh Manandhar was supported by EPSRC grant EP/I037512/1, A Unified Model of Compositional & Distributional Semantics: Theory and Application.

References

Sören Auer, Christian Bizer, Georgi Kobilarov, Jens Lehmann, Richard Cyganiak, and Zachary Ives. 2007. Dbpedia: A nucleus for a web of open data. In *The semantic web*, Springer, pages 722–735.

Kurt Bollacker, Colin Evans, Praveen Paritosh, Tim Sturge, and Jamie Taylor. 2008. Freebase: a collaboratively created graph database for structuring human knowledge. In *Proceedings of the 2008 ACM SIGMOD international conference on Management of data*. AcM, pages 1247–1250.

Antoine Bordes, Nicolas Usunier, Alberto Garcia-Duran, Jason Weston, and Oksana Yakhnenko. 2013. Translating embeddings for modeling multi-relational data. In *Advances in neural information processing systems*. pages 2787–2795.

Evgeniy Gabrilovich, Michael Ringgaard, and Amarnag Subramanya. 2013. Facc1: Freebase annotation of clueweb corpora, version 1 (release date 2013-06-26, format version 1, correction level 0). *Note: http://lemurproject. org/clueweb09/FACC1/Cited by 5.*

Raphael Hoffmann, Congle Zhang, Xiao Ling, Luke Zettlemoyer, and Daniel S Weld. 2011. Knowledge-based weak supervision for information extraction of overlapping relations. In *Proceedings of the 49th Annual Meeting of the Association for Computational Linguistics: Human Language Technologies-Volume 1*. Association for Computational Linguistics, pages 541–550.

Diederik Kingma and Jimmy Ba. 2014. Adam: A method for stochastic optimization. *arXiv preprint arXiv:1412.6980* .

Alexandros Komninos and Suresh Manandhar. 2016. Dependency based embeddings for sentence classification tasks. In *Proceedings of NAACL:HLT*. Association for Computational Linguistics, pages 1490–1500.

Xiao Ling and Daniel S Weld. 2012. Fine-grained entity recognition. In *AAAI*. Citeseer.

Mike Mintz, Steven Bills, Rion Snow, and Dan Jurafsky. 2009. Distant supervision for relation extraction without labeled data. In *Proceedings of the Joint Conference of the 47th Annual Meeting of the ACL and the 4th International Joint Conference on Natural Language Processing of the AFNLP: Volume 2-Volume 2*. Association for Computational Linguistics, pages 1003–1011.

Vinod Nair and Geoffrey E Hinton. 2010. Rectified linear units improve restricted boltzmann machines. In *Proceedings of the 27th international conference on machine learning (ICML-10)*. pages 807–814.

Maximilian Nickel, Kevin Murphy, Volker Tresp, and Evgeniy Gabrilovich. 2016. A review of relational machine learning for knowledge graphs. *Proceedings of the IEEE* 104(1):11–33.

Maximilian Nickel, Volker Tresp, and Hans-Peter Kriegel. 2011. A three-way model for collective learning on multi-relational data. In *Proceedings of the 28th international conference on machine learning (ICML-11)*. pages 809–816.

Siva Reddy, Mirella Lapata, and Mark Steedman. 2014. Large-scale semantic parsing without question-answer pairs. *Transactions of the Association for Computational Linguistics* 2:377–392.

Sebastian Riedel, Limin Yao, Andrew McCallum, and Benjamin M Marlin. 2013. Relation extraction with matrix factorization and universal schemas .

Richard Socher, Danqi Chen, Christopher D Manning, and Andrew Ng. 2013. Reasoning with neural tensor networks for knowledge base completion. In *Advances in neural information processing systems*. pages 926–934.

Mihai Surdeanu, Julie Tibshirani, Ramesh Nallapati, and Christopher D Manning. 2012. Multi-instance multi-label learning for relation extraction. In *Proceedings of the 2012 joint conference on empirical methods in natural language processing and computational natural language learning*. Association for Computational Linguistics, pages 455–465.

Kristina Toutanova, Danqi Chen, Patrick Pantel, Hoifung Poon, Pallavi Choudhury, and Michael Gamon. 2015. Representing text for joint embedding of text and knowledge bases. In *EMNLP*. Citeseer, volume 15, pages 1499–1509.

Bishan Yang, Wen-tau Yih, Xiaodong He, Jianfeng Gao, and Li Deng. 2014. Embedding entities and relations for learning and inference in knowledge bases. *arXiv preprint arXiv:1412.6575* .

Fine-Grained Entity Typing with High-Multiplicity Assignments

Maxim Rabinovich and **Dan Klein**
Computer Science Division
University of California, Berkeley
{rabinovich,klein}@cs.berkeley.edu

Abstract

As entity type systems become richer and more fine-grained, we expect the number of types assigned to a given entity to increase. However, most fine-grained typing work has focused on datasets that exhibit a low degree of type multiplicity. In this paper, we consider the high-multiplicity regime inherent in data sources such as Wikipedia that have semi-open type systems. We introduce a set-prediction approach to this problem and show that our model outperforms unstructured baselines on a new Wikipedia-based fine-grained typing corpus.

1 Introduction

Motivated by potential applications to information retrieval, coreference resolution, question answering, and other downstream tasks, recent work on entity typing has moved beyond coarse-grained systems towards richer ontologies with much more detailed information, and therefore correspondingly more specific types (Ling and Weld, 2012; Gillick et al., 2014; Yogatama et al., 2015).

As types become more specific, entities will tend to belong to more types (i.e. there will tend to be higher type multiplicity). However, most data used in previous work exhibits an extremely *low* degree of multiplicity.

In this paper, we focus on the high multiplicity case, which we argue naturally arises in large-scale knowledge resources. To illustrate this point, we construct a corpus of entity mentions paired with higher-multiplicity type assignments. Our corpus is based on mentions and categories drawn from Wikipedia, but we generalize and denoise the raw Wikipedia categories to provide more coherent supervision. Table 1 gives examples of type

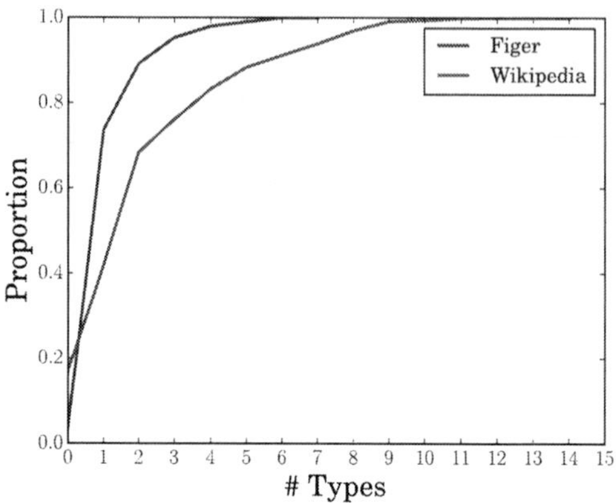

Figure 1: Comparison of type set size CDFs for the our Wikipedia corpus and the prior FIGER corpus (Ling and Weld, 2012). The figure illustrates that our corpus exhibits much greater type assignment multiplicity.

assignments from our dataset.

As type multiplicity grows, it is natural to consider type prediction as an inherently set-valued problem and ask questions about how such sets might be modeled. To this end, we develop a structured prediction approach in which the sets of assigned types are predicted as first-class objects, including a preliminary consideration of how to efficiently search over them. The resulting model captures type correlations and ultimately outperforms a strong unstructured baseline.

Related work The fine-grained entity typing problem was first investigated in detail by Ling and Weld (2012). Subsequently, Gillick et al. (2014) introduced a larger evaluation corpus for this task and introduced methods for training predictors based on multiclass classification. Both used the Freebase typing system, coarsened to approximately 100 types, and subsequent work

330

Proceedings of the 55th Annual Meeting of the Association for Computational Linguistics (Short Papers), pages 330–334
Vancouver, Canada, July 30 - August 4, 2017. ©2017 Association for Computational Linguistics
https://doi.org/10.18653/v1/P17-2052

David Foster Wallace	`novelist suicide sportswriter writer alumnus ...`
Albert Einstein	`physicist agnostic emigrant people pacifist ...`
NATO	`organization treaty document organisation alliance ...`
Federal Reserve	`agency authorities banks institution organization ...`
Industrial Revolution	`concept history evolution revolution past ...`
Black Death	`concept epidemic pandemic disaster ...`

Table 1: With types from a large corpus like Wikipedia, large type set assignments become common.

Entity	Raw Type	Projected Type
	`Short_story_writers`	`writer`
	`Amherst_alumni`	`alumnus`
David Foster Wallace	`Illinois_State_faculty`	`faculty`
	`People_from_New_York`	`people`
	`Essayists`	`essayist`

Table 2: Example of an entity and its types, before and after projection. The projection operation collapses related types that would be very difficult to learn in their original, highly specific forms.

has mostly followed this lead (Yaghoobzadeh and Schütze, 2016; Yogatama et al., 2015), although types based on WordNet have recently also been investigated (Corro et al., 2015).

Most prior work has focused on unstructured predictors using some form of multiclass logistic regression (Ling and Weld, 2012; Gillick et al., 2014; Shimaoka et al., 2016; Yaghoobzadeh and Schütze, 2016; Yogatama et al., 2015). Some of these approaches implicitly incorporate structure during decoding by enforcing hierarchy constraints (Gillick et al., 2014), while neural approaches can encode correlations in a soft manner via shared hidden layers (Shimaoka et al., 2016; Yaghoobzadeh and Schütze, 2016).

Our work differs from these lines of work in two respects: its use of a corpus exhibiting high type multiplicity with types derived from a semi-open inventory and its use of a fully structured model and decoding procedure, one that can in principle be integrated with neural models if desired. Previously, most results focused on the low-multiplicity Freebase-based FIGER corpus. The only work we are aware of that uses a type system similar to ours used a rule-based system and evaluated on their own newswire- and Twitter-based evaluation corpora (Corro et al., 2015).

2 Model

Our structured prediction framework is based on modeling type assignments as sets. Each entity e is assigned a set of types T^* drawn from the overall set of types $\mathcal{T}$. Our goal is thus to predict, given an input sentence-entity pair, the set of types associated with that entity.

We take the commonly-used linear model approach to this structured prediction problem. Given a featurizer φ that takes an input sentence x and entity e, we seek to learn a weight vector w such that

$$f(x, e) = \operatorname{argmax}_T w^\top \varphi(x, e, T) \quad (1)$$

predicts T correctly with high accuracy.

Our approach stands in contrast to prior work, which deployed several techniques, of similar efficacy, to port single-type learning and inference strategies to the multi-type setting (Gillick et al., 2014). Provided type interactions can be neglected, equation (1) can be simplified to

$$f_{\text{single}}(x, e) = \left\{ t \in \mathcal{T}: w^\top \varphi(x, e, t) \geq r \right\}.$$

This simplification corresponds to expanding each multi-type example triple (x, e, T^*) into a set of single-type example triples $\left\{ (x, e, t^*)_{t^* \in T^*} \right\}$. Learning can then be done using any technique for multiclass logistic regression, and inference can be carried out by specifying a threshold r and predicting all types that score above that threshold: In prior work, a simple $r = 0$ threshold was used (Ling and Weld, 2012).

In this paper, we focus on the more general specification (1), though in Section 2.2, we explain a simplification that can be used to speed up inference if desired.

2.1 Features

Modeling type assignments as sets in principle opens the door to non-decomposable set features (a simple instance of which would be set size). For reasons of tractability, we assume our features factor along type pairs:

$$\varphi\left(x,\ e,\ T\right) = \sum_{t \in T} \varphi\left(x,\ e,\ t\right) + \sum_{t,\ t' \in T} \varphi\left(t,\ t'\right) \tag{2}$$

Note that in addition to enforcing factorization over type pairs, the specification (2) requires that any features linking the type assignment to the observed entity mention depend only on a single type at a time. We investigated non-decomposable features, but found they did not lead to improved performance.

We use entity mention features very similar to those in previous work:

1. **Context unigrams and bigrams.** Indicators on all uni- and bigrams within a certain window of the entity mention.

2. **Dependency parse features.** Indicators on the lexical parent of the entity mention head, as well as the corresponding dependency type. Separately, indicators on the lexical children of the entity mention head and their dependency types.

3. **Entity head and non-head tokens.** Indicators on the syntactic head of the entity mention and on its non-head tokens.

4. **Word shape features.** Indicators on the shape of each token in the entity mention.

We combine these features with type-based features to obtain the features our model actually uses:

1. **Conjunction features.** These are simple conjunctions of mention features with indicators on type membership in the predicted set. Using only these features results in an unstructured model.

2. **Type pair features.** These are indicators on pairs of types appearing in the predicted set.

3. **Graph-based features.** As we discuss in Section 3, the type system in our corpus comes with a graph structure. We add indicators on certain patterns occurring within the

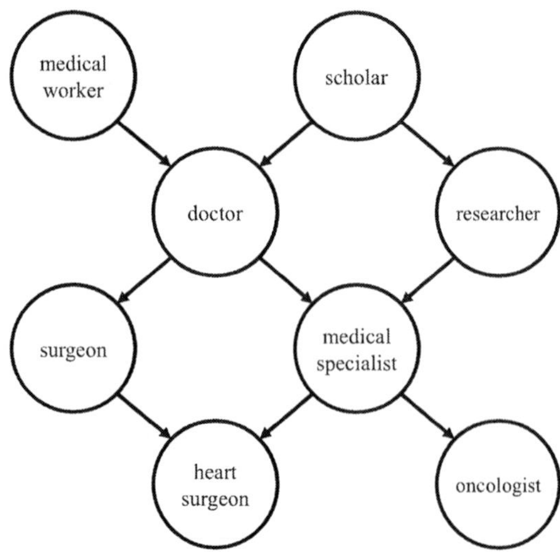

Figure 2: Fragment of the graph underlying our type system.

set—e.g. a parent-child type pair, sibling type pairs, and so on, abstracting away the specific types.

2.2 Learning and Inference

We train our system using structured max-margin (Tsochantaridis et al., 2005). Optimization is performed via AdaGrad on the primal (Kummerfeld et al., 2015). We use set-F1 as our loss function.

Inference, for both prediction and loss-augmented decoding, poses a greater challenge, as solving the maximization problem (1) exactly requires iterating over all subsets of the type system.

Fortunately, we find a simple greedy algorithm is effective. Our decoder begins by choosing the type that scores highest individually, taking only single-type features into account. It then proceeds by iteratively adding new types into the set until doing so would decrease the score.

At the cost of restricting the permissible type sets slightly, we can speed up the greedy procedure further. Specifically, we can require that the predicted type set T be *connected* in some constraint graph over the types—either the co-occurrence graph, the complete graph, or the graph underlying the type system. If we denote by C the set of all such connected sets, the corresponding predictor would be

$$f_{\mathrm{conn}}\left(x,\ e\right) = \mathrm{argmax}_{T \in C}\ w^\top \varphi\left(x,\ e,\ T\right)$$

Level	Features	P	R	F1
Entity	Unstructured	50.0	**67.2**	52.9
	+ Pairs	53.3	64.1	54.3
	+ Graph	**53.9**	63.9	**54.5**
Sentence	Unstructured	42.6	**58.9**	44.4
	+ Pairs	46.5	54.1	**45.6**
	+ Graph	**47.0**	53.6	**45.6**

Table 3: Results on our corpus. All quantities are macro-averaged.

The greedy decoding procedure for this predictor is faster because at each step, it need only consider adding types that are adjacent to some type that has already been included.

3 Corpus

Our corpus construction methodology involves three key stages: mention identification, type system construction, and type assignment.[1] We explain each of these in turn.

Mention identification. We follow prior work on entity linking (Durrett and Klein, 2014) and take all mentions that occur as anchor text. We filter the resulting collection of mentions down to those that pass a heuristic filter that removes mentions of common nouns, as well as spurious sentences representing Wikipedia formatting.

Type system construction. Prior work on fine-grained entity typing has derived its type system from Freebase (Ling and Weld, 2012; Gillick et al., 2014). The resulting ontologies thus inherit the coverage and specificity limitations of Freebase, somewhat exacerbated by manual coarsening.

Motivated by efforts to inject broader coverage, more complex knowledge resources into NLP systems, we instead derive our types from the Wikipedia category and WordNet graphs, in a manner similar to that of Ponzetto and Strube (2007).

Our base type set consists of all Wikipedia categories. By following back-pointers in articles for categories, we derive a base underlying directed graph. To eliminate noise, we filter down to all categories whose syntactic heads can be found in WordNet and keep directed edges only when the head of the parent is a WordNet ancestor of the head of the child. We conclude by projecting each type down to its syntactic head.

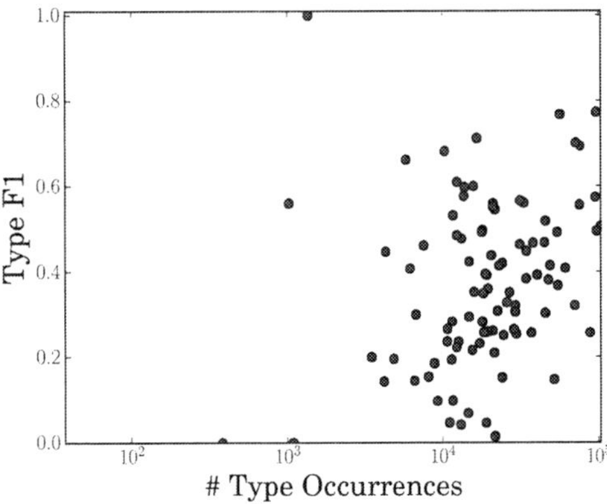

Figure 3: Per-type F1 scores plotted by type frequency in the training corpus.

head of the child. We conclude by projecting each type down to its syntactic head.

Type assignment. The type set for an entity is obtained by taking its Wikipedia category assignments, augmenting these with their ancestors in the category graph above, and then projecting these down to their syntactic heads.

4 Experiments

We evaluate our method on the dataset described in Section 3. For these experiments, we restrict to the 100 most frequent types and downsample to 750K mentions. We use a baseline that closely replicates the FIGER system (Ling and Weld, 2012). Within our framework, this can be thought of as a model that sets all type pair features in (2) to zero.

Table 3 summarizes our results. Starting with the baseline, we incrementally add the type pair, graph-based, and set size features discussed in 2.1. Adding type pair features results in an appreciable performance gain, while the graph features bring little benefit—potentially because pairwise correlations suffice to summarize the set structure when the number of types is moderately low.

A concern when studying multiclass problems with large numbers of classes, whether predicting sets or individual labels, is that performance on instances associated with common classes will dominate the performance metric. Figure 3 shows micro-averaged F1 for the binary prediction task associated with predicting the presence or absence of each type, demonstrating that our performance is strong even for many rare types.

---

[1] Our corpus will be released at `http://people.eecs.berkeley.edu/~rabinovich/`.

5 Conclusion

We have highlighted the issue of multiplicity in fine-grained entity typing. Whereas most prior work has focused on corpora with low multiplicity assignments, we denoised the Wikipedia type system to construct a realistic corpus with high multiplicity type assignments. Using this corpus as a testbed, we showed that an approach based on structured prediction of sets can outperform unstructured baselines when type assignments have high multiplicity. Our approach may therefore be preferable in such contexts.

References

Luciano del Corro, Abdalghani Abujabal, Rainer Gemulla, and Gerhard Weikum. 2015. Finet: Context-aware fine-grained named entity typing. Assoc. for Computational Linguistics.

Greg Durrett and Dan Klein. 2014. A joint model for entity analysis: Coreference, typing, and linking. *Transactions of the Association for Computational Linguistics* 2:477–490.

Dan Gillick, Nevena Lazic, Kuzman Ganchev, Jesse Kirchner, and David Huynh. 2014. Context-dependent fine-grained entity type tagging. *arXiv preprint arXiv:1412.1820* .

Jonathan K Kummerfeld, Taylor Berg-Kirkpatrick, and Dan Klein. 2015. An empirical analysis of optimization for max-margin NLP. In *Proceedings of the Conference on Empirical Methods in Natural Language Processing*. volume 273, page 279.

Xiao Ling and Daniel S Weld. 2012. Fine-grained entity recognition. In *Twenty-Sixth AAAI Conference on Artificial Intelligence*.

Simone Paolo Ponzetto and Michael Strube. 2007. Deriving a large scale taxonomy from wikipedia.

Sonse Shimaoka, Pontus Stenetorp, Kentaro Inui, and Sebastian Riedel. 2016. An attentive neural architecture for fine-grained entity type classification. *arXiv preprint arXiv:1604.05525* .

Ioannis Tsochantaridis, Thorsten Joachims, Thomas Hofmann, and Yasemin Altun. 2005. Large margin methods for structured and interdependent output variables. *Journal of Machine Learning Research* 6(Sep):1453–1484.

Yadollah Yaghoobzadeh and Hinrich Schütze. 2016. Corpus-level fine-grained entity typing using contextual information. *arXiv preprint arXiv:1606.07901* .

Dani Yogatama, Dan Gillick, and Nevena Lazic. 2015. Embedding methods for fine grained entity type classification. In *Proceedings of the 53rd Annual Meeting of the Association for Computational Linguistics and the 7th International Joint Conference on Natural Language Processing of the Asian Federation of Natural Language Processing, ACL.*

Group Sparse CNNs for Question Classification with Answer Sets

Mingbo Ma   Liang Huang
School of EECS
Oregon State University
Corvallis, OR 97331, USA
{mam,liang.huang}@oregonstate.edu

Bing Xiang   Bowen Zhou
IBM Watson Group
T. J. Watson Research Center
Yorktown Heights, NY 10598, USA
{bingxia,zhou}@us.ibm.com

Abstract

Question classification is an important task with wide applications. However, traditional techniques treat questions as general sentences, ignoring the corresponding answer data. In order to consider answer information into question modeling, we first introduce novel group sparse autoencoders which refine question representation by utilizing group information in the answer set. We then propose novel group sparse CNNs which naturally learn question representation with respect to their answers by implanting group sparse autoencoders into traditional CNNs. The proposed model significantly outperform strong baselines on four datasets.

1   Introduction

Question classification has applications in many domains ranging from question answering to dialog systems, and has been increasingly popular in recent years. Several recent efforts (Kim, 2014; Kalchbrenner et al., 2014; Ma et al., 2015) treat questions as general sentences and employ Convolutional Neural Networks (CNNs) to achieve remarkably strong performance in the TREC question classification task.

We argue, however, that those general sentence modeling frameworks neglect two unique properties of question classification. First, different from the flat and coarse categories in most sentence classification tasks (i.e. sentimental classification), question classes often have a hierarchical structure such as those from the New York State DMV FAQ[1] (see Fig. 1). Another unique aspect of question classification is the well prepared answers for each question or question category. These answer

---

[1] Crawled from http://nysdmv.custhelp.com/app/home. This data and our code will be at http://github.com/cosmmb.

1: Driver License/Permit/Non-Driver ID	
a: *Apply for original*	(49 questions)
b: *Renew or replace*	(24 questions)
...	
2: Vehicle Registrations and Insurance	
a: *Buy, sell, or transfer a vehicle*	(22 questions)
b: *Reg. and title requirements*	(42 questions)
...	
3: Driving Record / Tickets / Points	
...	

Figure 1: Examples from NYDMV FAQs. There are 8 top-level categories, 47 sub-categories, and 537 questions (among them 388 are *unique*; many questions fall into multiple categories).

sets generally cover a larger vocabulary (than the questions themselves) and provide richer information for each class. We believe there is a great potential to enhance question representation with extra information from corresponding answer sets.

To exploit the hierarchical and overlapping structures in question categories and extra information from answer sets, we consider dictionary learning (Candès and Wakin, 2008; Rubinstein et al., 2010) which is a common approach for representing samples from many correlated groups with external information. This learning procedure first builds a dictionary with a series of grouped bases. These bases can be initialized randomly or from external data (from the answer set in our case) and optimized during training through Sparse Group Lasso (SGL) (Simon et al., 2013).

To apply dictionary learning to CNN, we first develop a neural version of SGL, *Group Sparse Autoencoders* (GSAs), which to the best of our knowledge, is the first full neural model with group sparse constraints. The encoding matrix of GSA (like the dictionary in SGL) is grouped into different categories. The bases in different groups can be either initialized randomly or by

Proceedings of the 55th Annual Meeting of the Association for Computational Linguistics (Short Papers), pages 335–340
Vancouver, Canada, July 30 - August 4, 2017. ©2017 Association for Computational Linguistics
https://doi.org/10.18653/v1/P17-2053

the sentences in corresponding answer categories. Each question sentence will be reconstructed by a few bases within a few groups. GSA can use either linear or nonlinear encoding or decoding while SGL is restricted to be linear. Eventually, to model questions with sparsity, we further propose novel *Group Sparse Convolutional Neural Networks* (GSCNNs) by implanting the GSA onto CNNs, essentially enforcing group sparsity between the convolutional and classification layers. This framework is a jointly trained neural model to learn question representation with group sparse constraints from both question and answer sets.

2 Group Sparse Autoencoders

2.1 Sparse Autoencoders

Autoencoder (Bengio et al., 2007) is an unsupervised neural network which learns the hidden representations from data. When the number of hidden units is large (e.g., bigger than input dimension), we can still discover the underlying structure by imposing sparsity constraints, using sparse autoencoders (SAE) (Ng, 2011):

$$J_{\text{sparse}}(\rho) = J + \alpha \sum_{j=1}^{s} KL(\rho \| \hat{\rho}_j) \qquad (1)$$

where J is the autoencoder reconstruction loss, ρ is the desired sparsity level which is small, and thus $J_{\text{sparse}}(\rho)$ is the sparsity-constrained version of loss J. Here α is the weight of the sparsity penalty term defined below:

$$KL(\rho \| \hat{\rho}_j) = \rho \log \frac{\rho}{\hat{\rho}_j} + (1 - \rho) \log \frac{1 - \rho}{1 - \hat{\rho}_j} \qquad (2)$$

where

$$\hat{\rho}_j = \frac{1}{m} \sum_{i=1}^{m} h_j^i$$

represents the average activation of hidden unit j over m examples (SAE assumes the input features are correlated).

As described above, SAE has a similar objective to traditional sparse coding which tries to find sparse representations for input samples. Besides applying simple sparse constraints to the network, group sparse constraints is also desired when the class categories are structured and overlapped. Inspired by group sparse lasso (Yuan and Lin, 2006) and sparse group lasso (Simon et al., 2013), we propose a novel architecture below.

2.2 Group Sparse Autoencoders

Group Sparse Autoencoder (GSA), unlike SAE, categorizes the weight matrix into different groups. For a given input, GSA reconstructs the input signal with the activations from only a few groups. Similar to the average activation $\hat{\rho}_j$ for sparse autoencoders, GSA defines each grouped average activation for the hidden layer as follows:

$$\hat{\eta}_p = \frac{1}{mg} \sum_{i=1}^{m} \sum_{l=1}^{g} \|h_{p,l}^i\|_2 \qquad (3)$$

where g represents the size of each group, and $\hat{\eta}_j$ first sums up all the activations within p^{th} group, then computes the average p^{th} group respond across different samples' hidden activations.

Similar to Eq. 2, we also use KL divergence to measure the difference between estimated intra-group activation and global group sparsity:

$$KL(\eta \| \hat{\eta}_p) = \eta \log \frac{\eta}{\hat{\eta}_p} + (1 - \eta) \log \frac{1 - \eta}{1 - \hat{\eta}_p} \qquad (4)$$

where G is the number of groups. Then the objective function of GSA is:

$$J_{\text{groupsparse}}(\rho, \eta) = J + \alpha \sum_{j=1}^{s} KL(\rho \| \hat{\rho}_j)$$
$$+ \beta \sum_{p=1}^{G} KL(\eta \| \hat{\eta}_p) \qquad (5)$$

where ρ and η are constant scalars which are our target sparsity and group-sparsity levels, resp. When α is set to zero, GSA only considers the structure between difference groups. When β is set to zero, GSA is reduced to SAE.

2.3 Visualizing Group Sparse Autoencoders

In order to have a better understanding of GSA, we use the MNIST dataset to visualize GSA's internal parameters. Fig. 2 and Fig. 3 illustrate the projection matrix and the corresponding hidden activations. We use 10,000 training samples. We set the size of the hidden layer to 500 with 10 groups. Fig. 2(a) visualizes the input image for hand written digit 0.

In Fig. 2(b), we find similar patterns within each group. For example, group 8 has different forms of digit 0, and group 9 includes different forms of digit 7. However, it is difficult to see any meaningful patterns from the projection matrix of basic autoencoders in Fig. 2(c).

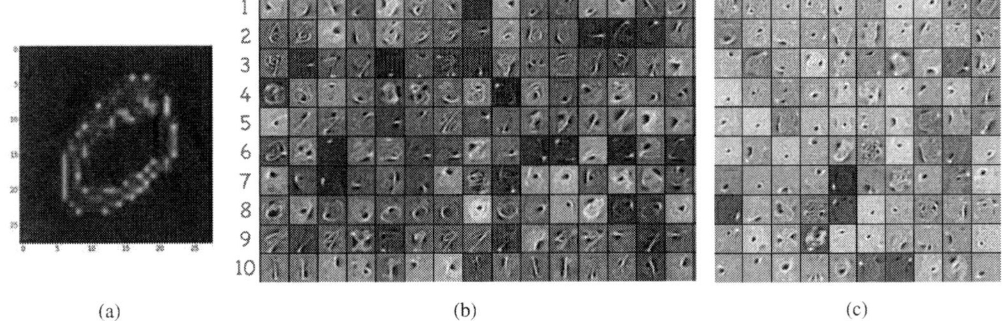

(a)   (b)   (c)

Figure 2: The input figure with hand written digit 0 is shown in (a). Figure (b) is the visualization of trained projection matrix $\mathbf{W}$ on MNIST dataset. Different rows represent different groups of $\mathbf{W}$ in Eq. 5. For each group, we only show the first 15 (out of 50) bases. The red numbers on the left side are the indices of 10 different groups. Figure (c) is the projection matrix from basic autoencoders.

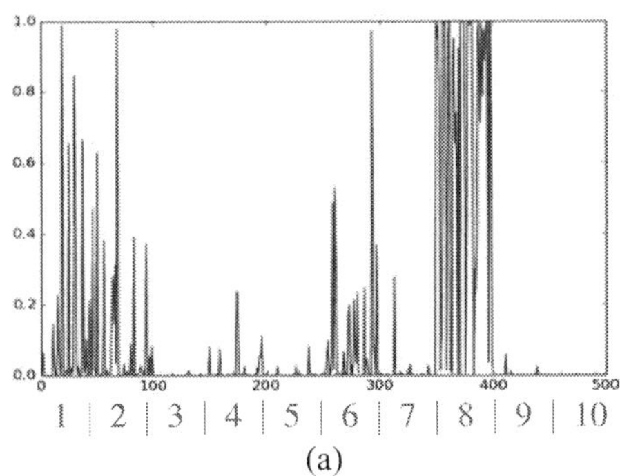

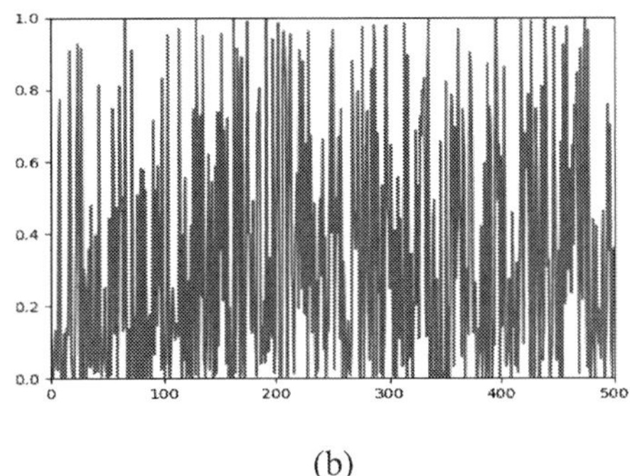

(a)   (b)

Figure 3: (a): the hidden activations $\mathbf{h}$ for the input image in Fig. 2(a). The red numbers corresponds to the index in Fig. 2(b). (b): the hidden activations $\mathbf{h}$ for the same input image from basic autoencoders.

Fig. 3(a) shows the hidden activations with respect to the input image of digit 0. The patterns of the 10th row in Fig. 2(b) are very similar to digit 1 which is very different from digit 0 in shape. Therefore, there is no activation in group 10 in Fig. 3(a). The majority of hidden layer activations are in groups 1, 2, 6 and 8, with group 8 being the most significant. When compared to the projection matrix visualization in Fig. 2(b), these results are reasonable since the 8th row has the most similar patterns of digit 0. However, we could not find any meaningful pattern from the hidden activations of basic autoencoder as shown in Fig. 3(b).

GSA could be directly applied to small image data (e.g. MINIST dataset) for pre-training. However, in tasks which prefer dense semantic representations (e.g. sentence classification), we still need CNNs to learn the sentence representation automatically. In order to combine advantages from GSA and CNNs, we propose Group Sparse

Convolutional Neural Networks below.

3 Group Sparse CNNs

CNNs were first proposed by (LeCun et al., 1995) in computer vision and adapted to NLP by (Collobert et al., 2011). Recently, many CNN-based techniques have achieved great successes in sentence modeling and classification (Kim, 2014; Kalchbrenner et al., 2014).

Following sequential CNNs, one dimensional convolutions operate the convolution kernel in sequential order $\mathbf{x}_{i,j} = \mathbf{x}_i \oplus \mathbf{x}_{i+1} \oplus \cdots \oplus \mathbf{x}_{i+j}$, where $\mathbf{x}_i \in \mathbb{R}^e$ represents the e dimensional word representation for the i-th word in the sentence, and $\oplus$ is the concatenation operator. Therefore $\mathbf{x}_{i,j}$ refers to concatenated word vector from the i-th word to the $(i + j)$-th word in sentence.

A convolution operates a filter $\mathbf{w} \in \mathbb{R}^{n \times e}$ to a window of n words $\mathbf{x}_{i,i+n}$ with bias term b' by $a_i = \sigma(\mathbf{w} \cdot \mathbf{x}_{i,i+n} + b')$ with non-linear activation

337

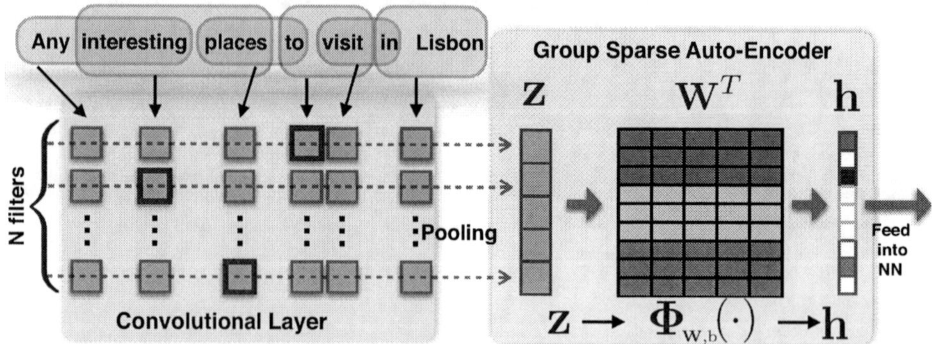

Figure 4: Group Sparse CNN. We add an extra dictionary learning layer between sentence representation $\mathbf{z}$ and the final classification layer. $\mathbf{W}$ is the projection matrix (functions as a dictionary) that converts $\mathbf{z}$ to the group sparse representation $\mathbf{h}$ (Eq. 5). Different colors in the projection matrix represent different groups. We show $\mathbf{W}^\mathsf{T}$ instead of $\mathbf{W}$ for presentation purposes. Darker colors in $\mathbf{h}$ mean larger values and white means zero.

function σ to produce a new feature. The filter $\mathbf{w}$ is applied to each word in the sentence, generating the feature map $\mathbf{a} = [a_1, a_2, \cdots, a_L]$ where L is the sentence length. We then use $\hat{a} = \max\{\mathbf{a}\}$ to represent the entire feature map after max-pooling.

In order to capture different aspects of patterns, CNNs usually randomly initialize a set of filters with different sizes and values. Each filter will generate a feature as described above. To take all the features generated by N different filters into count, we use $\mathbf{z} = [\hat{a_1}, \cdots, \hat{a_N}]$ as the final representation. In conventional CNNs, this $\mathbf{z}$ will be directly fed into classifiers after the sentence representation is obtained, e.g. fully connected neural networks (Kim, 2014). There is no easy way for CNNs to explore the possible hidden representations with underlaying structures.

In order to exploit these structures, we propose Group Sparse Convolutional Neural Networks (GSCNNs) by placing one extra layer between the convolutional and the classification layers. This extra layer mimics the functionality of GSA from Section 2. Shown in Fig. 4, after the conventional convolutional layer, we get the feature map $\mathbf{z}$ for each sentence. In stead of directly feeding it into a fully connected neural network for classification, we enforce the group sparse constraint on $\mathbf{z}$ in a way similar to the group sparse constraints on hidden layer in GSA from Sec. 2. Then, we use the sparse hidden representation $\mathbf{h}$ in Eq. 5 as the new sentence representation, which is then fed into a fully connected neural network for classification. The parameters $\mathbf{W}$ in Eq. 5 will

also be fine tunned during the last step.

Different ways of initializing the projection matrix in Eq. 5 can be summarized below:

- **Random Initialization**: When there is no answer corpus available, we first randomly initialize N vectors to represent the group information from the answer set. Then we cluster these N vectors into G categories with g centroids for each category. These centroids from different categories will be the initialized bases for projection matrix $\mathbf{W}$ which will be learned during training.

- **Initialization from Questions**: Instead of using random initialized vectors, we can also use question sentences for initializing the projection matrix when the answer set is not available. We need to pre-train the sentences with CNNs to get the sentence representation. We then select G largest categories in terms of number of question sentences. Then we get g centroids from each category by k-means. We concatenate these $G \times g$ vectors to form the projection matrix.

- **Initialization from Answers**: This is the most ideal case. We follow the same procedure as above, with the only difference being using the answer sentences in place of question sentences to pre-train the CNNs.

4 Experiments

Since there is little effort to use answer sets in question classification, we did not find any suit-

Datasets	C_t	C_s	N_{data}	N_{test}	N_{ans}	Multi-label
TREC	6	50	5952	500	-	No
INSURANCE	-	319	1580	303	2176	Yes
DMV	8	47	388	50	2859	Yes
YAHOO Ans	27	678	8871	3027	10365	No

Table 1: Summary of datasets. C_t and C_s are the numbers of top-level and sub- categories, resp. N_{data}, N_{test}, N_{ans} are the sizes of data set, test set, and answer set, resp. Multilabel means each question can belong to multiple categories.

	TREC	INSUR.	DMV	YAHOO dataset		
				sub	top	unseen
CNN†	93.6	51.2	60	20.8	53.9	47
+sparsity‡	93.2	51.4	62	20.2	54.2	46
$\mathbf{W}_R$	93.8	53.5	62	21.8	54.5	48
$\mathbf{W}_Q$	**94.2**	53.8	64	22.1	54.1	48
$\mathbf{W}_A$	-	**55.4**	**66**	**22.2**	**55.8**	**53**

Table 2: Experimental results. Baselines: †sequential CNNs ($\alpha = \beta = 0$ in Eq. 5), ‡CNNs with global sparsity ($\beta = 0$). $\mathbf{W}_R$: randomly initialized projection matrix. $\mathbf{W}_Q$: question-initialized projection matrix. $\mathbf{W}_A$: answer set-initialized projection matrix. There are three different classification settings for YAHOO: subcategory, top-level category, and top-level accuracies on unseen sub-labels.

able datasets which are publicly available. We collected two datasets ourselves and also used two other well-known ones. These datasets are summarized in Table 1. INSURANCE is a private dataset we collected from a car insurance company's website. Each question is classified into 319 classes with corresponding answer data. All questions which belong to the same category share the same answers. The DMV dataset is collected from New York State the DMV's FAQ website. The YAHOO Ans dataset is only a subset of the original publicly available YAHOO Answers dataset (Fleming et al., 2012; Shah and Pomerantz, 2010). Though not very suitable for our framework, we still included the frequently used TREC dataset (factoid question type classification) for comparison.

We only compare our model's performance with CNNs for two following reasons: we consider our "group sparsity" as a modification to the general CNNs for grouped feature selection. This idea is orthogonal to any other CNN-based models and can be easily applied to them; in addition, as discussed in Sec. 1, we did not find any other model in comparison with solving question classification tasks with answer sets.

There is crucial difference between the INSURANCE and DMV datasets on one hand and the YAHOO set on the other. In INSURANCE and DMV, all questions in the same (sub)category share the same answers, whereas YAHOO provides individual answers to each question.

For multi-label classification (INSURANCE and DMV), we replace the softmax layer in CNNs with a sigmoid layer which predicts each category independently while softmax is not.

All experimental results are summarized in Table 2. The improvements are substantial for INSURANCE and DMV, but not as significant for YAHOO and TREC. One reason for this is the questions in YAHOO/TREC are shorter, which makes the group information harder to encode. Another reason is that each question in YAHOO/TREC has a single label, and thus can not fully benefit from group sparse properties.

Besides the conventional classification tasks, we also test our proposed model on an unseen-label case. In these experiments, there are a few sub-category labels that are not included in the training data. However, we still hope that our model could still return the correct parent category for these unseen subcategories at test time. In the testing set of YAHOO dataset, we randomly add 100 questions whose subcategory labels are unseen in training set. The classification results of YAHOO-unseen in Table 2 are obtained by mapping the predicted subcategories back to top-level categories. The improvements are substantial due to the group information encoding.

5 Conclusions

In order to better represent question sentences with answer sets and group structure, we first presented a novel GSA framework, a neural version of dictionary learning. We then proposed group sparse convolutional neural networks by embedding GSA into CNNs, which result in significantly better question classification over strong baselines.

Acknowledgment

We thank the anonymous reviewers for their suggestions. This work is supported in part by NSF IIS-1656051, DARPA FA8750-13-2-0041 (DEFT), DARPA XAI, a Google Faculty Research Award, and an HP Gift.

References

Yoshua Bengio, Pascal Lamblin, Dan Popovici, and Hugo Larochelle. 2007. Greedy layer-wise training of deep networks. In *Advances in Neural Information Processing Systems 19*.

Emmanuel J. Candès and Michael B. Wakin. 2008. An Introduction To Compressive Sampling. In *Signal Processing Magazine, IEEE*. volume 25. http://dx.doi.org/10.1109/msp.2007.914731.

R. Collobert, J. Weston, L. Bottou, M. Karlen, K. Kavukcuoglu, and P. Kuksa. 2011. Natural language processing (almost) from scratch. In *Journal of Machine Learning Research*. volume 12, pages 2493–2537.

Simon Fleming, Dan Chalmers, and Ian Wakeman. 2012. A deniable and efficient question and answer service over ad hoc social networks. In *Information Retrieval*.

Nal Kalchbrenner, Edward Grefenstette, and Phil Blunsom. 2014. A convolutional neural network for modelling sentences. In *Proceedings of the 52nd Annual Meeting of the Association for Computational Linguistics*. Association for Computational Linguistics.

Yoon Kim. 2014. Convolutional neural networks for sentence classification. In *Proceedings of the 2014 Conference on Empirical Methods in Natural Language Processing (EMNLP)*. Association for Computational Linguistics, Doha, Qatar, pages 1746–1751. http://www.aclweb.org/anthology/D14-1181.

Y. LeCun, L. Jackel, L. Bottou, A. Brunot, C. Cortes, J. Denker, H. Drucker, I. Guyon, U. Mller, E. Sckinger, P. Simard, and V. Vapnik. 1995. Comparison of learning algorithms for handwritten digit recognition. In *International Conference on Artificial Neural Networks*. pages 53–60.

Mingbo Ma, Liang Huang, Bing Xiang, and Bowen Zhou. 2015. Dependency-based convolutional neural networks for sentence embedding. In *Proceedings of ACL 2015*.

Andrew Ng. 2011. Sparse autoencoder. In *CS294A Lecture notes*. Stanford University, page 72.

R. Rubinstein, A. M. Bruckstein, and M. Elad. 2010. Dictionaries for sparse representation modeling. In *Neural Computation*.

Chirag Shah and Jefferey Pomerantz. 2010. Evaluating and predicting answer quality in community qa. In *Proceedings of the 33rd International ACM SIGIR Conference on Research and Development in Information Retrieval*. ACM, New York, NY, USA.

Noah Simon, Jerome Friedman, Trevor Hastie, and Rob Tibshirani. 2013. A sparse-group lasso. In *Journal of Computational and Graphical Statistics*.

Ming Yuan and Yi Lin. 2006. Model selection and estimation in regression with grouped variables. In *Journal of the Royal Statistical Society*. volume 68, pages 49–67.

Multi-Task Learning of Keyphrase Boundary Classification

Isabelle Augenstein *
Department of Computer Science
University College London
i.augenstein@ucl.ac.uk

Anders Søgaard *
Department of Computer Science
University of Copenhagen
soegaard@di.ku.dk

Abstract

Keyphrase boundary classification (KBC) is the task of detecting keyphrases in scientific articles and labelling them with respect to predefined types. Although important in practice, this task is so far underexplored, partly due to the lack of labelled data. To overcome this, we explore several auxiliary tasks, including semantic super-sense tagging and identification of multi-word expressions, and cast the task as a multi-task learning problem with deep recurrent neural networks. Our multi-task models perform significantly better than previous state of the art approaches on two scientific KBC datasets, particularly for long keyphrases.

1 Introduction

The scientific keyphrase boundary classification (KBC) task consists of a) determining keyphrase boundaries, and b) labelling keyphrases with their types according to a predefined schema. KBC is motivated by the need to efficiently search scientific literature, which can be summarised by their keyphrases. Several companies are working on keyphrase-based recommender systems for scientific literature or search interfaces where scientific articles decorate graphs, in which nodes are keyphrases. Such keyphrases must be dynamically retrieved from the articles, because important scientific concepts emerge on a daily basis, and the most recent concepts are typically the ones of interest to scientists.

KBC is not a common task in NLP, and there are only few small annotated datasets for inducing supervised KBC models, made available recently

(QasemiZadeh and Schumann, 2016; Augenstein et al., 2017). Typical KBC approaches therefore rely on hand-crafted gazetteers (Hasan and Ng, 2014) or reduce the task to extracting a list of keyphrases for each document (Kim et al., 2010) instead of identifying mentions of keyphrases in sentences. For related more common NLP tasks such as named entity recognition and identification of multi-word expressions, neural sequence labelling methods have been shown to be useful (Lample et al., 2016). In order to overcome the small data problem, we study using more widely available data for tasks related to KBC and exploit their synergies in a deep multi-task learning setup.

Multi-task learning has become popular within natural language processing and machine learning over the last few years; in particular, *hard* parameter sharing of hidden layers in deep learning models. This approach to multi-task learning has three advantages: a) It significantly reduces Rademacher complexity (Baxter, 2000; Maurer, 2007), i.e., the risk of over-fitting, b) it is space-efficient, reducing the number of parameters, and c) it is easy to implement.

This paper shows how hard parameter sharing can be used to improve gazetteer-free keyphrase boundary classification models, by exploiting different syntactically and semantically annotated corpora, as well as more readily available data such as hyperlinks.

Contributions We study the so far widely underexplored, though in practice important task of scientific keyphrase boundary classification, for which only a small amount of training data is available. We overcome this by identifying good auxiliary tasks and cast it as a multi-task learning problem. We evaluate our models across two new, manually annotated corpora of scientific articles and outperform single-task approaches by up

---

*Both authors contributed equally

Proceedings of the 55th Annual Meeting of the Association for Computational Linguistics (Short Papers), pages 341–346
Vancouver, Canada, July 30 - August 4, 2017. ©2017 Association for Computational Linguistics
https://doi.org/10.18653/v1/P17-2054

to 9.64% F1, mostly due to better performance for long keyphrases.

2 Keyphrase Boundary Classification

Consider the following sentence from a scientific paper:

(1) We find that simple interpolation methods, like log-linear and linear interpolation, improve the performance but fall short of the performance of an oracle.

This sentence occurs in the ACL RD-TEC 2.0 corpus. Here, *interpolation methods* and *log-linear and linear interpolation* are annotated as technical keyphrases, *performance* as a keyphrase related to measurements, and *oracle* is a keyphrase labelled as miscellaneous. Below, we are interested in predicting the boundaries *and* the types of all keyphrases.

3 Multi-Task Learning

Multi-task learning is an approach to learning, in which generalisation is improved by taking advantage of the inductive bias in training signals of related tasks. When abundant labelled data is available for an auxiliary task, but little data for the target task, multi-task learning can act as a form of semi-supervised learning combined with a distant supervision signal. Inducing a model from only the sparse target task data may lead to overfitting to random noise in the data, but relying on auxiliary data helps the model generalise, making it easier to abstract away from noise, as well as leveraging the marginal distribution of auxiliary input data. From a representation learning perspective, auxiliary tasks can be used to induce representations that may be beneficial for the target task. Caruana (1993) also suggests that the auxiliary task can help focus attention in the induction of the target task model. Finally, multi-task learning can be cast as a regulariser as studies show reductions in Rademacher complexity in multi-task architectures over single-task architectures (Baxter, 2000; Maurer, 2007).

Here, we follow the probably most common approach to multi-task learning, known as *hard parameter sharing*. This was introduced in Caruana (1993) in the context of deep neural networks, in which hidden layers can be shared among tasks. We assume T different training set, $D_1, \cdots, D_T$,

where each D_t contains pairs of input-output sequences $(w_{1:n}, y_{1:n}^t)$, $w_i \in V$, $y_i^t \in L^t$. The input vocabulary V is shared across tasks, but the output vocabularies (tagset) L^t are task dependent. At each step in the training process we choose a random task t, followed by a random training instance $(w_{1:n}, y_{1:n}^t) \in D_t$. We use the tagger to predict the labels $\hat{y}_i^t$, suffer a loss with respect to the true labels y_i^t and update the model parameters. The parameters are trained jointly for a sentence, i.e. cross-entropy loss over each sentence is employed. Each task is associated with an independent classification function, but all tasks share the hidden layers. Note that for our experiments, we only consider one auxiliary task at a time.

4 Experiments

Experimental Setup We perform experiments for both keyphrase boundary identification (*unlabelled*), and keyphrase boundary identification and classification (*labelled*). Metrics measured are token-level precision, recall and F1, which are micro-average results across keyphrase types. Types are defined by the two datasets studied.

Auxiliary tasks We experiment with five auxiliary tasks: (1) syntactic chunking using annotations extracted from the English Penn Treebank, following Søgaard and Goldberg (2016); (2) frame target annotations from FrameNet 1.5 (corresponding to the target identification and classification tasks in Das et al. (2014)); (3) hyperlink prediction using the dataset from Spitkovsky et al. (2010), (4) identification of multi-word expressions using the Streusle corpus (Schneider and Smith, 2015); and (5) semantic super-sense tagging using the Semcor dataset, following Johannsen et al. (2014). We train our models on the main task with one auxiliary task at a time. Note that the datasets for the auxiliary tasks are not annotated with keyphrase boundary identification or classification labels.

Datasets We evaluate on the SemEval 2017 Task 10 dataset (Augenstein et al., 2017) and the the ACL RD-TEC 2.0 dataset (QasemiZadeh and Schumann, 2016). The SemEval 2017 dataset is annotated with three keyphrase types, the ACL RD-TEC dataset with seven. For the former, we test on the development portion of the dataset, as the test set is not released yet. We randomly split ACL RD-TEC into a training and test set, reserv-

	SemEval 2017 Task 10	ACL RD-TEC
Labels	Material, Process, Task	Technology and Method, Tool and Library, Language Resource, Language Resource Product, Measures and Measurements, Models, Other
Topics	Computer Science, Physics, Material Science	Natural Language Processing
Number all keyphrases	5730	2939
Proportion singleton keyphrases	31%	83%
Proportion single-word mentions	18%	23%
Proportion mentions with word length $>= 2$	82%	77%
Proportion mentions with word length $>= 3$	51%	33%
Proportion mentions with word length $>= 5$	22%	8%

Table 1: Characteristics of SemEval 2017 Task 10 and ACL-RD-TEC corpora, statistics of training sets

ing 1/3 for testing. Key dataset characteristics are summarised in Table 1. One important observation is that the SemEval 2017 dataset contains a significantly higher proportion of long keyphrases than the ACL dataset.

Models Our single- and multi-task networks are three-layer, bi-directional LSTMs (Graves and Schmidhuber, 2005) with pre-trained SENNA embeddings.[1] For the multi-task networks, we follow the training procedure outlined in Section 3. The dimensionality of the embeddings is 50, and we follow Søgaard and Goldberg (2016) in using the same dimensionality for the hidden layers. We add a dropout of 0.1 to the input and train these architectures with momentum SGD with initial learning rate of 0.001 and momentum of 0.9 for 10 epochs.

Baselines Our baselines are Finkel et al. (2005)[2] and Lample et al. (2016)[3], in order to compare to a lexicalised and a state-of-the-art neural method. We use the implementations released by the authors and re-train models on our data.

5   Results and Analysis

Results for SemEval 2017 Task 10 corpus are presented in Table 2, and for the ACL RD-TEC corpus in Table 3. For the SemEval corpus, all five labelled multi-task learning models outperform both examples of previous work, as well as our single-task BiLSTM baseline, by some margin. For ACL RD-TEC, three of out five multi-task learning labelled labelled perform better than the single-task BiLSTM baseline.

On the SemEval corpus, the F1 error reduction of of the best labelled model over the Stanford tagger is 9.64%. The lexicalised Finkel et al. (2005) model shows a surprisingly competitive performance on the ACL RD-TEC corpus, where it is only 2 points in F1 behind our best performing labelled model and on par with our best-performing unlabelled model. Results with Lample et al. (2016), on the other hand, are lower than the Finkel et al. (2005) baseline. This might be due to the model having a large set of parameters to model state transitions which poses a difficulty for small training datasets.

Overall, multi-task models show bigger improvements over baselines for the SemEval corpus, and all models achieve better results on ACL RD-TEC. Statistics shown in Table 1 help to explain this. Most noticeably, the SemEval dataset contains a significantly higher proportion of long keyphrases than the ACL dataset. Interestingly, ACL RD-TEC contains a large proportion of keyphrases which only appear once in the training set (singletons), significantly fewer keyphrases and more keyphrase type, but that does not seem to impact results as much as a high proportion of long keyphrases.

All models struggle with semantically vague or broad keyphrases (e.g. 'items', 'scope', 'key') and long keyphrases, especially those containing clauses (e.g. 'complete characterisation of the oxide particles', 'earley deduction proof procedure for definite clauses'). The multi-task models generally outperform the BiLSTM baseline for long phrases (e.g. 'language-independent system for

[1]http://ronan.collobert.com/senna/
[2]http://nlp.stanford.edu/software/
  CRF-NER.shtml
[3]https://github.com/clab/
  stack-lstm-ner

Method	Unlabelled			Labelled		
	Precision	Recall	F1	Precision	Recall	F1
Finkel et al. (2005)	77.89	50.27	61.10	49.90	27.97	35.85
Lample et al. (2016)	71.92	49.37	58.55	41.36	28.47	33.72
BiLSTM	81.58	57.86	67.71	45.80	32.48	38.01
BiLSTM + Chunking	82.88	52.08	63.96	55.54	34.90	42.86
BiLSTM + Framenet	77.86	56.05	65.18	54.04	38.91	45.24
BiLSTM + Hyperlinks	76.59	60.53	67.62	46.99	44.09	41.13
BiLSTM + Multi-word	74.80	70.18	**72.42**	46.99	44.09	**45.49**
BiLSTM + Super-sense	83.70	51.76	63.93	56.94	35.25	43.54

Table 2: Results for keyphrase boundary classification on the SemEval 2017 Task 10 corpus

Method	Unlabelled			Labelled		
	Precision	Recall	F1	Precision	Recall	F1
Finkel et al. (2005)	84.16	80.08	**82.07**	59.97	53.86	56.75
Lample et al. (2016)	65.60	86.06	74.45	31.30	41.07	35.53
BiLSTM	83.40	80.36	81.85	59.62	57.45	58.51
BiLSTM + Chunking	83.36	79.46	81.37	59.26	57.24	57.84
BiLSTM + Framenet	84.11	79.39	81.68	60.64	57.24	58.89
BiLSTM + Hyperlinks	83.94	79.12	81.46	60.18	56.73	58.40
BiLSTM + Multi-word	84.86	76.92	80.69	59.81	54.21	56.87
BiLSTM + Super-sense	84.67	78.29	81.36	61.35	56.73	**58.95**

Table 3: Results for keyphrase boundary classification on the ACL RD-TEC corpus

automatic discovery of text in parallel translation', 'honeycomb network of graphite bricks'). Being able to recognise long keyphrases correctly is part of the reason our multi-task models outperform the baselines, especially on the SemEval dataset, which contains many such long keyphrases.

6 Related Work

Multi-Task Learning Hard sharing of all hidden layers was introduced in Caruana (1993), and popularised in NLP by Collobert et al. (2011a). Several variants have been introduced, including hard sharing of selected layers (Søgaard and Goldberg, 2016) and sharing of parts (subspaces) of layers (Liu et al., 2015). Søgaard and Goldberg (2016) show that hard parameter sharing is an effective regulariser, also on heterogeneous tasks such as the ones considered here. Hard parameter sharing has been studied for several tasks, including CCG super tagging (Søgaard and Goldberg, 2016), text normalisation (Bollman and Søgaard, 2016), neural machine translation (Dong et al., 2015; Luong et al., 2016), and super-sense tagging (Martínez Alonso and Plank, 2017). Sharing of information can further be achieved by extending LSTMs with an external memory shared across tasks (Liu et al., 2016). A further instance of multi-task learning is to optimise a supervised training objective jointly with an unsupervised training objective, as shown in Yu et al. (2016) for natural language generation and auto-encoding, and in Rei (2017) for different sequence labelling tasks and language modelling.

Boundary Classification KBC is very similar to named entity recognition (NER), though arguably harder. Deep neural networks have been applied to NER in Collobert et al. (2011b); Lample et al. (2016). Other successful methods rely on conditional random fields, thereby modelling the probability of each output label conditioned on the label at the previous time step. Lample et al. (2016), currently state-of-the-art for NER, stack CRFs on top of recurrent neural networks. We leave exploring such models in combination with multi-task learning for future work.

Keyphrase detection methods specific to the scientific domain often use keyphrase gazetteers as features or exploit citation graphs (Hasan and Ng, 2014). However, previous methods relied on corpora annotated for type-level identification, not for mention-level identification (Kim et al., 2010; Sterckx et al., 2016). While most applications rely on extracting keyphrases (as types), this has the unfortunate consequence that previous work ignores acronyms and other short-hand forms referring to methods, metrics, etc. Further, relying on gazetteers makes overfitting likely, obtaining lower scores on out-of-gazetteer keyphrases.

7 Conclusions and Future Work

We present a new state of the art for keyphrase boundary classification, using data from related, auxiliary tasks; in particular, super-sense tagging and identification of multi-word expressions. Deep multi-task learning improves significantly on previous approaches to KBC, with error reductions of up to 9.64%, mostly due to better identification and labelling of long keyphrases.

In future work, we want to explore alternative multi-task learning regimes to hard parameter sharing and experiment with additional auxiliary tasks. The auxiliary tasks considered here are standard NLP tasks, hyperlink prediction aside. Other tasks may be more directly relevant such as predicting the layout of calls for papers for scientific conferences, or predicting hashtags in tweets by scientists, since both data sources contain scientific keyphrases.

Acknowledgments

We would like to thank Elsevier for supporting this work.

References

Isabelle Augenstein, Mrinal Das, Sebastian Riedel, Lakshmi Vikraman, and Andrew McCallum. 2017. SemEval-2017 Task 10 : Extracting Keyphrases and Relations from Scientific Publications. In *Proceedings of SemEval, to appear*.

Jonathan Baxter. 2000. A model of inductive bias learning. *Journal of Artificial Intelligence Research* 12:149–198.

Marcel Bollman and Anders Søgaard. 2016. Improving historical spelling normalization with bi-directional LSTMs and multi-task learning. In *Proceedings of COLING*.

Rich Caruana. 1993. Multitask Learning: A Knowledge-Based Source of Inductive Bias. In *Proceedings of ICML*.

Ronan Collobert, Jason Weston, Léon Bottou, Michael Karlen, Koray Kavukcuoglu, and Pavel Kuksa. 2011a. Natural language processing (almost) from scratch. *The Journal of Machine Learning Research* 12:2493–2537.

Ronan Collobert, Jason Weston, Léon Bottou, Michael Karlen, Koray Kavukcuoglu, and Pavel Kuksa. 2011b. Natural language processing (almost) from scratch. *The Journal of Machine Learning Research* 12:2493–2537.

Dipanjan Das, Desai Chen, Andre Martins, Nathan Schneider, and Noah Smith. 2014. Frame-semantic parsing. *Computational linguistics* 40(1):9–56.

Daxiang Dong, Hua Wu, Wei He, Dianhai Yu, and Haifeng Wang. 2015. Multi-Task Learning for Multiple Language Translation. In *Proceedings of ACL*.

Jenny Finkel, Trond Grenager, and Christopher Manning. 2005. Incorporating non-local information into information extraction systems by Gibbs sampling. In *Proceedings of ACL*.

Alex Graves and Jürgen Schmidhuber. 2005. Framewise Phoneme Classification with Bidirectional LSTM and other Neural Network Architectures. *Neural Networks* 18(5):602–610.

Kazi Saidul Hasan and Vincent Ng. 2014. Automatic Keyphrase Extraction: A Survey of the State of the Art. In *Proceedings of ACL*.

Anders Johannsen, Dirk Hovy, Héctor Martínez, Barbara Plank, and Anders Søgaard. 2014. More or less supervised supersense tagging of Twitter. In *Proceedings of *SEM*.

Su Nam Kim, Olena Medelyan, Min-Yen Kan, and Timothy Baldwin. 2010. SemEval-2010 Task 5 : Automatic Keyphrase Extraction from Scientific Articles. In *Proceedings of SemEval*.

Guillaume Lample, Miguel Ballesteros, Sandeep Subramanian, Kazuya Kawakami, and Chris Dyer. 2016. Neural Architectures for Named Entity Recognition. In *Proceedings of NAACL-HLT*. pages 260–270.

Pengfei Liu, Shafiq Joty, and Helen Meng. 2015. Fine-grained Opinion Mining with Recurrent Neural Networks and Word Embeddings. In *Proceedings of EMNLP*.

Pengfei Liu, Xipeng Qiu, and Xuanjing Huang. 2016. Deep Multi-Task Learning with Shared Memory for Text Classification. In *Proceedings of EMNLP*.

Minh-Thang Luong, Quoc V. Le, Ilya Sutskever, Oriol Vinyals, and Lukasz Kaiser. 2016. Multi-task Sequence to Sequence Learning. In *Proceedings of ICLR*.

Héctor Martínez Alonso and Barbara Plank. 2017. When is multitask learning effective? Semantic sequence prediction under varying data conditions. In *Proceedings of EACL*.

Andreas Maurer. 2007. Bounds for Linear Multi Task Learning. *Journal of Machine Learning Research* 7:117–139.

Behrang QasemiZadeh and Anne-Kathrin Schumann. 2016. The ACL RD-TEC 2.0: A Language Resource for Evaluating Term Extraction and Entity Recognition Methods. In *Proceedings of LREC*.

Marek Rei. 2017. Semi-supervised Multitask Learning for Sequence Labeling. In *Proceedings of ACL, to appear*.

Nathan Schneider and Noah Smith. 2015. A Corpus and Model Integrating Multiword Expressions and Supersenses. *Proceedings of NAACL-HLT* .

Anders Søgaard and Yoav Goldberg. 2016. Deep multi-task learning with low level tasks supervised at lower layers. In *Proceedings of ACL*.

Valentin Spitkovsky, Daniel Jurafsky, and Hiyan Alshawi. 2010. Profiting from Mark-Up: Hyper-Text Annotations for Guided Parsing. In *Proceedings of ACL*.

Lucas Sterckx, Cornelia Caragea, Thomas Demeester, and Chris Develder. 2016. Supervised Keyphrase Extraction as Positive Unlabeled Learning. In *Proceedings of EMNLP*.

Lei Yu, Jan Buys, and Phil Blunsom. 2016. Online Segment to Segment Neural Transduction. In *Proceedings of EMNLP*.

Cardinal Virtues: Extracting Relation Cardinalities from Text

Paramita Mirza[1], Simon Razniewski[2], Fariz Darari[2], Gerhard Weikum[1]

[1] Max Planck Institute for Informatics
[2] Free University of Bozen-Bolzano
{paramita, weikum}@mpi-inf.mpg.de
{razniewski, darari}@inf.unibz.it

Abstract

Information extraction (IE) from text has largely focused on relations between individual entities, such as who has won which award. However, some facts are never fully mentioned, and no IE method has perfect recall. Thus, it is beneficial to also tap contents about the cardinalities of these relations, for example, how many awards someone has won. We introduce this novel problem of extracting cardinalities and discuss specific challenges that set it apart from standard IE. We present a distant supervision method using conditional random fields. A preliminary evaluation results in precision between 3% and 55%, depending on the difficulty of relations.

1 Introduction

Motivation Information extraction (IE) can infer relations between named entities from text (e.g., (Mitchell et al., 2015; Del Corro and Gemulla, 2013; Mausam et al., 2012)), yielding for example which awards an athlete has won, or instances of family relations like spouses, children, etc. These methods can be harnessed for summarization, question answering (QA), and more. For populating knowledge bases (KBs), the IE output is usually cast into subject-predicate-object (SPO) triples, such as ⟨*BarackObama, hasChild, Malia*⟩, or sometimes n-ary tuples such as ⟨*MichaelPhelps, hasWon, OlympicGold, 200mButterfly, 2016*⟩.

IE has focused on capturing full SPO triples (or n-ary facts) with all arguments bound to entities for relation P. However, news, biographies or discussion forums often contain numeric expressions that reveal cardinalities of relations. Phrases such as "her two children" or "his 28th medal" are valuable cues for quantifying the *hasChild* and *hasWon* relations. This can be harnessed in QA for cases like "Who won the most Olympic medals?"

An important application of relation cardinalities is KB curation. KBs are notoriously incomplete, contain erroneous triples, and are limited in keeping up with the pace of real-world changes. For example, a KB may contain only 10 of the 28 Olympic medals that Phelps has won, or may incorrectly list 3 children for Obama. Extracting the cardinalities of relations for given subject entities can address all of these issues.

Relation cardinalities are disregarded by virtually all IE methods. Open IE methods (Mausam et al., 2012; Del Corro and Gemulla, 2013) capture triples (or quadruples) such as ⟨*Obama, has, two children*⟩. However, there is no way to interpret the numeric expression in the O slot of this triple. While IE methods that hinge on prespecified relations for KB population (e.g., NELL (Mitchell et al., 2015)) can already capture numeric values for explicitly stated attributes such as ⟨*Berlin2016attack, hasNumOfVictims, 32*⟩, they are currently not able to learn them.

This paper addresses the novel task of extracting relation cardinalities. For a given subject entity s and predicate p, we aim to infer the cardinality $|\{\langle S, P, O \rangle \mid S = s, P = p\}|$ directly from text, without having to observe any O entities. This task poses several challenges:

- *IE Training.* Most IE methods build on seed-based distant supervision. However, if the underlying KB is not complete, taking the counts of SPO triples for a given SP pair may result in wrong seeds, which can lead to poor patterns.
- *Compositionality.* The cardinality of an SP pair for a relation may depend on several cardinality mentions. For example, when observing "Angelina has *two* sons and *three* daughters", one could infer the children cardinality by summing.

Proceedings of the 55th Annual Meeting of the Association for Computational Linguistics (Short Papers), pages 347–351
Vancouver, Canada, July 30 - August 4, 2017. ©2017 Association for Computational Linguistics
https://doi.org/10.18653/v1/P17-2055

- *Linguistic Variance.* In addition to cardinal numbers, cardinality IE should also pay attention to number-related terms, e.g., "Angelina gives birth to *twins*", or ordinal information, e.g., "Angelina's *fourth* child", which can reveal lower bounds on relation cardinalities.

Approach and Contribution Our method learns patterns of phrases that contain cardinal numbers, relying on the distant supervision approach by counting facts for given SP pairs. Our technical contributions are as follows: *(i)* we provide a statistical analysis of numeric information in Wikipedia articles; *(ii)* we develop a CRF-based extraction method for relation cardinalities that achieves precision scores of up to 55%; *(iii)* we analyze further challenges in this research and outline possible solutions.

2 Related Work

Knowledge Bases and Information Extraction Automated KB construction is a major effort for quite a while. Some approaches, such as YAGO (Suchanek et al., 2007) or DBpedia (Auer et al., 2007), focus on structured parts of Wikipedia, while other approaches such as OLLIE (Mausam et al., 2012), ClauseIE (Del Corro and Gemulla, 2013) or NELL (Mitchell et al., 2015), focus on unstructured contents across the whole Web. In the latter, usually the schema is also not predefined, thus such approaches are called Open IE. Most state-of-the-art systems now rely on distant supervision (Craven and Kumlien, 1999; Mintz et al., 2009).

Despite all efforts, KBs are immensely incomplete. For instance, the average number of children per person in Wikidata (Vrandečić and Krötzsch, 2014) is just 0.02 (Razniewski et al., 2016).

Numbers and Relation Cardinalities Numbers in text are an important source of information. Much work has been done on understanding numbers that express temporal information (Ling and Weld, 2010; Strötgen and Gertz, 2010), and more recently, on numbers that express physical quantities or measures, either mentioned in text (Chaganty and Liang, 2016) or in the context of web tables (Ibrahim et al., 2016; Neumaier et al., 2016).

In contrast, numbers that express relation cardinalities have received little attention so far. State-of-the-art Open-IE systems either hardly extract cardinality information or fail to extract cardinal-

NE Tag	Frequency
DATE, TIME, DURATION, SET (temporal)	54.28%
NUMBER	40.13%
Relation cardinality	*18.86%*
PERCENT	2.92%
MONEY	2.25%
PERSON, LOCATION, ORGANIZATION	0.26%
ORDINAL	0.16%

Table 1: NE-tags of numbers in Wikipedia.

ities at all. While NELL, for instance, knows 13 relations about the number of casualties and injuries in disasters, they all contain only seed facts and no learned facts. The only prior work we are aware of is of Mirza et al. (2016), who use manually created patterns to mine children cardinalities from Wikipedia. It is shown that with 30 manually crafted patterns and simple filters it is possible to extract 86,227 children-cardinality-assertions with a precision of 94.3%.

3 Relation Cardinalities

Definition We define a mention that expresses relation cardinalities as the following: *"A cardinal number that states the number of objects that stand in a specific relation with a certain subject."*

Using this definition, we analyzed how often relation cardinalities occur in Wikipedia. Relying on the part-of-speech (PoS) tagger of Stanford CoreNLP (Manning et al., 2014), we extracted numbers–i.e., words tagged as CD (cardinal number)–from 10,000 random Wikipedia articles. The distribution of their named-entity (NE) tags, according to Stanford NE-tagger, is shown in Table 1. While temporal-related numbers are the most frequent, around 40% are classified only as unspecific NUMBER. By manually checking 100 random NUMBERs, we observed that 47 are relation cardinalities,[1] i.e., approximately 18.86% of all numbers in Wikipedia are relation cardinalities.

We also analyzed the nouns frequently modified by NUMBERs, based on their dependency paths, finding *people*, *games*, *children*, *times*, *members* and *seasons* among the top nouns. Coarse topic-grouping of the nouns shows that most NUMBERs are about sport (*games*, *goals*), followed by artwork (*seasons*, *books*), politics and organization (*members*, *countries*), and family (*children*).

---

[1] Among the others are measures, age, or expressions like "*one* of the...".

4 Relation Cardinality Extraction

Ideally, we would like to make sense of all cardinality statements found in text. However, this would require us to resolve the meaning of a large set of vague predicates, which is in general a difficult task. We thus turn the problem around: given a well defined relation/predicate p, a subject s and a corresponding text about s, we now try to estimate the relation cardinality (i.e., the count of $\langle s, p, * \rangle$ triples), based on cardinality assertions found in the text. We chose four Wikidata predicates that span various domains, *child* (P40), *spouse* (P26), *has part* (P527) of a series of creative works (restricted to novel, book and film series), and *contains administrative territorial entity* (P150). As the text source for subjects of each predicate, we consider sentences containing numbers taken from their respective English Wikipedia articles.

Methodology We approach the problem via sequence labelling, i.e., given a sentence containing at least one number, we aim to determine whether each number in the sentence corresponds to the cardinality of a certain relation. We build a Conditional Random Field (CRF) based model with CRF++ (Kudo, 2005) for each relation, taking as features the context lemmas (window size of 5) around the observed token t, along with bigrams and trigrams containing t.

To generate the training data, we rely on distant supervision, annotating *candidate numbers*[2] in the text as correct cardinalities whenever they correspond to the exact triple count (count > 0) found in the knowledge base. Otherwise, they are labelled as O (for Others), like the rest of non-number tokens. Table 2 contains for each considered relation (p), the number of subjects (#s) in Wikidata, which have links to English Wikipedia pages and have at least one $\langle s, p, * \rangle$ triple.

We predict the relation cardinality of a given $\langle s, p \rangle$ pair by selecting the number positively annotated with marginal probability–resulting from forward-backward inference–higher than 0.1, and choosing the one with the highest probability if there are several.

Experiments Two experimental settings are considered: *vanilla* refers to the distant supervision approach explained above, while for *only-*

nummod, we only annotate a candidate number as correct cardinality if it modifies a noun, i.e., there is an incoming dependency relation of label *nummod* according to the Stanford Dependency Parser. This is to exclude numbers as in "*one of the reasons...*" from training examples. We also considered a naive baseline, which chooses a random number from a pool of numbers existing in each text about a certain subject.

Furthermore, to estimate how well KB counts are suited as ground truth, we compare them on the the child relation with the manually-created *number of children* (P1971) property from Wikidata.

Evaluation Results We manually annotated the evaluation data with the true relation counts, since the knowledge base is highly incomplete, and thus, the triple counts are often incorrect. Whenever the cardinality matches the true count, we also manually inspected how relevant the textual evidence–the context surrounding the cardinal number–is for the observed relation. Table 2 shows the performance of our CRF-based method in finding the correct relation cardinality, evaluated on manually annotated 20 (*has part*), 100 (*admin. terr. entity*) and 200 (*child* and *spouse*) randomly selected subjects that have at least one object.

The random-number baseline achieves a precision of 5% (*has part*), 3.5% (*admin. territ. entity*), 0% (*spouse*) and 11.2% (*child*). Compared to that, especially using *only-nummod*, our method gives encouraging results for *has part, admin. territ. entity and child*, with 30-50% precision and around 30% F1-score. For *spouse*, the performance is significantly lower, reasons are discussed below. Furthermore, we can observe that using manual ground truth as training data for the *child* relation can boost performance considerably. Still, the performance is significantly below the state-of-the-art in fact extraction, where *child* triples can be extracted from Wikipedia text with 96% precision (Palomares et al., 2016).

5 Analysis

A qualitative analysis of the training data and evaluation results revealed three aspects that make extracting relation cardinalities difficult.

Quality of Training Data Unlike training data for normal fact extraction, which is generally highly correct (e.g., YAGO claims 95% precision (Suchanek et al., 2007)), taking triple counts

---

[2]Numbers that are not labelled as DATE, TIME, DURATION, SET, MONEY and PERCENT by Stanford NE-tagger.

p	#s	baseline	vanilla			only-nummod		
		P	P	R	F1	P	R	F1
has part (creative work series)	261	.050	.333	.316	.324	.353	.316	.333
contains admin. terr. entity	18,000	.034	.390	.188	.254	.548	.200	.293
spouse	45,917	0	.014	.011	.013	.028	.017	.021
child	35,057	.112	.151	.129	.139	.320	.219	.260
child (manual ground truth)	6,408		0.374	0.309	0.338	0.452	0.315	0.371

Table 2: Number of Wikidata entities as subjects (#s) of each predicate (p), and evaluation results on manually annotated randomly selected subjects that have at least an object.

found in knowledge bases as ground truth generally gives wrong results. For example, our manual evaluation of *child* shows that the triple count from Wikidata is 46% lower than what the texts assert.

As shown by the last row of Table 2, higher quality of training data can considerably boost the performance of cardinality extraction. Unfortunately, manually curated data is generally difficult to obtain. We see two avenues to tackle training data quality:

1. *Filtering ground truth.* Instead of taking the counts of all entities as ground truth, one might trade size for quality, e.g., using popular entities only, as for these there are chances that KBs are more complete.
2. *Incompleteness-resilient distant supervision.* Triple counts in KBs are often lower than what is correct, but rarely too high. Thus, an avenue might be to label all numbers equal or higher than the KB count as correct, instead of only considering the equal ones. Given that different cardinalities could then be labelled as correct, this would require a postprocessing step in which conflicting counts are consolidated.

Compositionality Around 16% of false positives in extracting *child* cardinalities can be attributed to failures in identifying the correct count for, e.g., "They have *two* sons and *one* daughter together; he has *four* children from an earlier relationship." This was also observed for other relations, e.g., "The Qidong county has *4* subdistricts, *17* towns and *3* townships under its juridiction." We see two avenues to tackle this problem:

1. *Aggregating numbers.* In training data generation, one could label a sequence of number as correct cardinalities if the sum of the numbers is equal to the relation count. In the prediction step, one might sum up all consecutive cardinalities that are labelled with sufficient confidence.

2. *Learning composition rules.* One may try to learn the composition of counts, for instance, that children are composed of sons and daughters, then try to extract the composing cardinalities.

Linguistic Variance We observe that for the *spouse* relation, expressing the count with cardinal numbers ("He has married *four* times") is only found for 4% of subjects. It is more common to express the count with ordinal numbers, e.g., "John's *first* wife, Mary, ...", which allows us to conclude that the spouse-count for John is at least–and most probably more than–one. An approach to such relations might be to identify ordinals numbers that express lower bounds of relations. Subsequently, one could reason over these bounds and try to infer relation counts.

Our initial motivation was to make sense of the so far ignored large fraction of numbers that express relation cardinalities. However, we noticed quickly that relation cardinalities are frequently also expressed without numbers at all. This is especially true for the case of count zero, which is mostly expressed using negation ("He never married"), and the count one, which is expressed using indefinite articles ("They have a child") or the signal-word *only* ("Their only child, James"). Terms such as *twins* or *trilogy* are also ways to express domain-specific relation cardinalities. We see two avenues to approach this variance:

1. *Translation to numbers.* For the 0's and 1's, a possible approach is to translate certain kinds of negation and indefinite articles into explicit numbers (e.g., "do *not* have *any* children" → "have 0 children").
2. *Word similarity with cardinals.* If a word bears high similarity with cardinal numbers, possibly also in other languages such as Latin or Greek, one might consider it as a candidate number.

6 Conclusion

In this paper we have introduced the problem of relation cardinality extraction. We believe that relation cardinalities can be useful in a variety of tasks. Our next goal is to make distant supervision incompleteness-resilient and to deal with compositionality, hoping that these can improve the precision of our approach. We also aim to take ordinals into account and to experiment with linguistic transformation for the cases of cardinalities 0 and 1, hoping that these could boost the recall.

A limitation of our work is also that we only focus on Wikipedia articles, assume that all statements are about the article's subject, and just take the statement with the highest confidence. In future work we aim to include a larger article base in combination with named entity recognition, coreference resolution and a truth consolidation step.

Acknowledgments

We thank Werner Nutt and Sebastian Rudolph for their feedback on an earlier version of this work. We thank the anonymous reviewers for their helpful comments. This work has been partially supported by the project "The Call for Recall", funded by the Free University of Bozen-Bolzano.

References

Sören Auer, Christian Bizer, Georgi Kobilarov, Jens Lehmann, Richard Cyganiak, and Zachary Ives. 2007. *DBpedia: A nucleus for a web of open data.* Springer.

Arun Chaganty and Percy Liang. 2016. How much is 131 million dollars? putting numbers in perspective with compositional descriptions. In *ACL*. pages 578–587.

Mark Craven and Johan Kumlien. 1999. Constructing biological knowledge bases by extracting information from text sources. In *Proceedings of the Seventh International Conference on Intelligent Systems for Molecular Biology*. pages 77–86.

Luciano Del Corro and Rainer Gemulla. 2013. ClausIE: clause-based open information extraction. In *WWW*. ACM, pages 355–366.

Yusra Ibrahim, Mirek Riedewald, and Gerhard Weikum. 2016. Making sense of entities and quantities in web tables. In *CIKM*. pages 1703–1712.

Taku Kudo. 2005. CRF++: Yet another CRF toolkit. *Software available at http://crfpp. sourceforge.net .*

Xiao Ling and Daniel S Weld. 2010. Temporal information extraction. In *AAAI*. volume 10, pages 1385–1390.

Christopher D Manning, Mihai Surdeanu, John Bauer, Jenny Rose Finkel, Steven Bethard, and David McClosky. 2014. The Stanford CoreNLP natural language processing toolkit. *ACL (System Demonstrations)* pages 55–60.

Mausam, Michael Schmitz, Stephen Soderland, Robert Bart, and Oren Etzioni. 2012. Open language learning for information extraction. In *EMNLP*. pages 523–534.

Mike Mintz, Steven Bills, Rion Snow, and Daniel Jurafsky. 2009. Distant supervision for relation extraction without labeled data. In *ACL*. pages 1003–1011.

Paramita Mirza, Simon Razniewski, and Werner Nutt. 2016. Expanding Wikidatas parenthood information by 178%, or how to mine relation cardinalities. *ISWC Posters & Demos* .

Tom M. Mitchell, William W. Cohen, Estevam R. Hruschka Jr., Partha Pratim Talukdar, Justin Betteridge, Andrew Carlson, Bhavana Dalvi Mishra, Matthew Gardner, Bryan Kisiel, Jayant Krishnamurthy, Ni Lao, Kathryn Mazaitis, Thahir Mohamed, Ndapandula Nakashole, Emmanouil Antonios Platanios, Alan Ritter, Mehdi Samadi, Burr Settles, Richard C. Wang, Derry Tanti Wijaya, Abhinav Gupta, Xinlei Chen, Abulhair Saparov, Malcolm Greaves, and Joel Welling. 2015. Never-ending learning. In *AAAI*. pages 2302–2310.

Sebastian Neumaier, Jürgen Umbrich, Josiane Xavier Parreira, and Axel Polleres. 2016. Multi-level semantic labelling of numerical values. In *ISWC*. pages 428–445.

Thomas Palomares, Youssef Ahres, Juhana Kangaspunta, and Christopher Ré. 2016. Wikipedia knowledge graph with DeepDive. In *ICWSM*. pages 65–71.

Simon Razniewski, Fabian M. Suchanek, and Werner Nutt. 2016. But what do we actually know? *Proceedings of AKBC* pages 40–44.

Jannik Strötgen and Michael Gertz. 2010. Heideltime: High quality rule-based extraction and normalization of temporal expressions. In *SemEval Workshop*. pages 321–324.

Fabian M. Suchanek, Gjergji Kasneci, and Gerhard Weikum. 2007. YAGO: a core of semantic knowledge. *WWW* pages 697–706.

Denny Vrandečić and Markus Krötzsch. 2014. Wikidata: a free collaborative knowledgebase. *Communications of the ACM* 57(10):78–85.

Integrating Deep Linguistic Features in Factuality Prediction over Unified Datasets

Gabriel Stanovsky[1]**, Judith Eckle-Kohler**[2]**, Yevgeniy Puzikov**[2]**,
Ido Dagan**[1] **and Iryna Gurevych**[2]

[1]Bar-Ilan University Computer Science Department, Ramat Gan, Israel
[2]Ubiquitous Knowledge Processing Lab (UKP), Technische Universitat Darmstadt, Germany
gabriel.stanovsky@gmail.com
www.ukp.tu-darmstadt.de
dagan@cs.biu.ac.il

Abstract

Previous models for the assessment of commitment towards a predicate in a sentence (also known as factuality prediction) were trained and tested against a specific annotated dataset, subsequently limiting the generality of their results. In this work we propose an intuitive method for mapping three previously annotated corpora onto a single factuality scale, thereby enabling models to be tested across these corpora. In addition, we design a novel model for factuality prediction by first extending a previous rule-based factuality prediction system and applying it over an abstraction of dependency trees, and then using the output of this system in a supervised classifier. We show that this model outperforms previous methods on all three datasets. We make both the unified factuality corpus and our new model publicly available.

1 Introduction

Factuality prediction is the task of determining the level of commitment towards a predicate in a sentence according to a specific source, e.g., the author (Saurí and Pustejovsky, 2009). For instance, the author uses linguistic cues to mark the embedded proposition as factual in (1) (cue: *surprising*), as uncertain in (2) and (3) (cues: *risk*, *might*), and as counterfactual (cue: *did not manage*) or uncertain (cue: *will not manage*) in (4).

(1) *It is not **surprising** that they work.*

(2) *She takes the **risk** to find out the truth.*

(3) *She **might** find out the truth.*

(4) *He **did/will not** manage to be in time.*

Detecting factuality is hard as the linguistic means used to express it closely interact. For example, lexical cues, such as the proposition-embedding predicates in (1) and (4) interact with negation (in (1), (4)) and tense (in (4)).

Detecting factuality has many potential applications. For instance, in knowledge base population, only propositions marked as factual should be admitted into the knowledge base, while hypothetical or negated ones should be left out. Similarly, for argumentation analysis and question answering, factuality can play a major role in backing a specific claim or supporting evidence for an answer to a question at hand.

Recent research efforts have approached the factuality task from two complementing directions: automatic prediction and large scale annotation. Previous attempts for automatic factuality prediction either took a rule-based, deep syntactic approach (Lotan et al., 2013; Saurí and Pustejovsky, 2012) or a machine learning approach over more shallow features (Lee et al., 2015). In terms of annotation, each effort was largely carried out independently of the others, picking up different factuality flavors and different annotation scales.

In correlation, the proposed algorithms have targeted a single annotated resource which they aim to recover. Subsequently, this separation between annotated corpora has prevented a comparison across datasets. Further, the models are nonportable, inhibiting advancements in one dataset to carry over to any of the other annotations.

Our contribution in this work is twofold. First, we suggest that the task can benefit from a unified representation. We exemplify this by mapping the representation of two recent datasets (FactBank (Saurí and Pustejovsky, 2009) and MEANTIME (Minard et al., 2016)) onto the $[-3, +3]$ scale, as annotated by (Lee et al., 2015). This unification allows us to test the generality of mod-

Proceedings of the 55th Annual Meeting of the Association for Computational Linguistics (Short Papers), pages 352–357
Vancouver, Canada, July 30 - August 4, 2017. ©2017 Association for Computational Linguistics
https://doi.org/10.18653/v1/P17-2056

els which were previously applicable on a single dataset. Second, we design a new model for factuality prediction that extends TruthTeller (Lotan et al., 2013), which employed implicative signatures (MacCartney and Manning, 2009; Karttunen, 2012) over dependency trees using a large predicate lexicon. We first extend TruthTeller's lexicon by about 40% through a semi-automatic process (following Eckle-Kohler (2016)). We then apply TruthTeller's rules over an abstraction of dependency trees (Stanovsky et al., 2016), which represents predicate-argument structures more consistently, thereby allowing TruthTeller rules to apply on a wider range of syntactic constructions. Finally, we surpass previous methods by using the output from TruthTeller as deep linguistically-informed features in a supervised classifier, thus successfully integrating a rule-based approach in a machine learning framework.

Overall, we hope that our unified representation will enable training and testing on larger, more diverse datasets, and that the good performance of our new model indicates its usability across different flavors of factuality prediction. We make both the unified factuality corpus and the new model publicly available.[1]

2 Background

Factuality prediction requires the identification of uncertainty, a concept which largely corresponds to the linguistic notion of *modality* (Hacquard, 2011). Modality expresses possibilities and necessities by means of negation, modal verbs (*may, might, can*), main verbs (*agree, refuse*), adjectives (*dishonest*), future tense (*will, won't*), and more. Looking at the numerous and varied possibilities language offers to express all the different shades of modality, it is clear that factuality does not assume any fixed set of discrete values either. Instead, the underlying linguistic system forms a continuous spectrum ranging from factual to counterfactual (Saurí and Pustejovsky, 2009).

While linguistic theory assigns a spectrum of factuality values, recent years have seen many practical efforts to capture the notion of factuality in a consistent annotation (Saurí and Pustejovsky, 2009; Nissim et al., 2013; Lee et al., 2015; OGorman et al., 2016; Minard et al., 2016; Ghia et al., 2016). Each of these make certain deci-

sions regarding the granularity of factuality that they aim to extract. In the course of this work we chose to set our focus on three of these annotations: FactBank (Saurí and Pustejovsky, 2009), MEANTIME (Minard et al., 2016) and the UW corpus (Lee et al., 2015). We use these specific corpora as they represent recent efforts, display a range of different design choices (e.g., in their notion of factuality and method of annotation), and are made publicly available which ensures the ease of the reproducibility of our experiments. Table 1 sums the properties and variations of these corpora. For example, we can see that: (1) the UW corpus uses a continuous scale and is annotated by crowdsourcing, while MEANTIME and FactBank were annotated discretely by experts, (2) FactBank annotates factuality from different perspectives, and (3) MEANTIME is significantly smaller compared to the other corpora.

In parallel with the creation of these annotated resources, several efforts were made to predict factuality in an automatic manner. The methods for doing so can be largely divided into rule-based systems which examine deep linguistic features, and machine learning algorithms which generally extract more shallow features. The De Facto factuality profiler (Saurí and Pustejovsky, 2012) and TruthTeller algorithms (Lotan et al., 2013) take the rule-based approach and assign a discrete annotation of factuality (following the values assigned by FactBank) using a deterministic rule-based top-down approach on dependency trees, changing the factuality assessment when encountering factuality affecting predicates or modality and negation cues (following implicative signatures by Karttunen (2012)). In addition to a factuality assessment, TruthTeller assigns three values per predicate in the sentence: (1) implicative signature from a hand-coded lexicon indicating how this predicate changes the factuality of its embedded clause, in positive and negative contexts, (2) clause truth, marking the factuality assessment of the entire clause, and (3) negation and uncertainty, indicating whether this predicate is affected by negation or modality. Both of these algorithms rely on a hand-written lexicon of predicates, indicating how they modify the factuality status of their embedded predicates (e.g., **refuse** negates while **assure** asserts it). In this work we will make use of the more recent TruthTeller which uses a much larger lexicon of 1,700 predicates (verbs, adjectives and

---

Corpus	#Tokens/Sentences	Factuality Values		Type	Annotators	Perspective
		Original	Our mapping			
FactBank	77231 / 3839	Factual (CT+/-)	+3.0 / -3.0	Discrete	Experts	Author's and discourse-internal sources
		Probable (PR+/-)	+2.0 / -2.0			
		Possible (PS+/-)	+1.0 / -1.0			
		Unknown (Uu/CTu)	0.0			
MEANTIME[†]	9743 / 631	Fact / Counterfact	+3.0 / -3.0	Discrete	Experts	Author's
		Possibility (uncertain)	+1.5 / -1.5			
		Possibility (future)	+0.5 / -0.5			
UW	106371 / 4234	[-3.0, 3.0]		Continuous	Crowdsource	Author's

Table 1: Factuality annotation statistics and mappings used in this paper - the number of tokens and sentences in each corpus, the original factuality value with the corresponding converted value to UW scale, the type of annotation (discrete or continuous), the annotators' proficiency, and the perspective to which the annotation refers. [†]This is an abstraction over the original MEANTIME annotation (suggested by the MEANTIME authors), which is composed of polarity, certainty and temporality.

nouns) compared to De Facto's lexicon, which contains 646 predicates.

In a separate attempt which we will call *UW system*, Lee et al. (2015) have used SVM regression techniques to predict a *continuous* factuality value from lexical and syntactic features (lemma, part of speech, and dependency paths). Similarly to the TruthTeller approach, they also predict a single factuality value pertaining to the author's commitment towards the predicate.

3 Unified Factuality Representation

We achieve a unified representation by mapping FactBank and MEANTIME onto the UW $[-3, +3]$ range in a simple automatic rule-based manner.

Table 1 describes these rules (see column "Our mapping"), which were hand-written by consulting the annotation guidelines of each of the corpora. Specifically, in converting FactBank we take only the author's perspective annotations as these comply with the annotations of the other corpora, and for MEANTIME we use their proposed abstraction into factual, uncertain and possible (in the future). We map from the discrete values (MEANTIME and FactBank) to the continuous scale (UW) since this conversion is *lossless*: if two events receive different factuality values in the original annotation, they will also differ in the unified representation, and vice versa. Furthermore, since FactBank and MEANTIME are both discrete, it is not clear a priori how to map between them.

Label distribution Given the above conversion, we can plot the label distribution of all three corpora on the same scale (Figure 1). This analysis

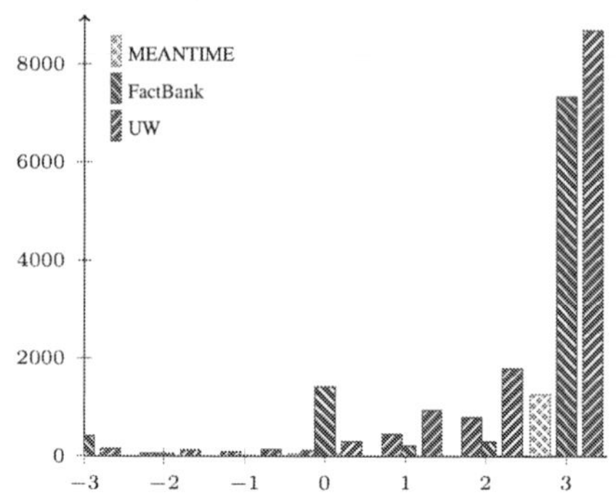

Figure 1: Histogram of factuality values in FactBank(red), UW (blue), and MEANTIME(green).

reveals that all corpora are significantly skewed towards the factual end of the scale, where the majority of the annotation mass is located. In particular, we find that MEANTIME is especially biased, assigning the factual value (+3) to 90% of its event annotations. Overall, we suspect that this is an inherent trait of the news domain which tends to be more factual than other text types (e.g., educational texts or opinion pieces).

4 Model

Following the automatic conversion which achieves a unified representation for our three datasets, we devise a factuality prediction model composed of three main components: (1) augmentation of the TruthTeller lexicon with about 800 adjectival, nominal and verbal predicates, (2) syntactic re-ordering with PropS (Stanovsky et al., 2016), (3) application of TruthTeller on top of PropS trees (Lotan et al., 2013). In the following we describe these components.

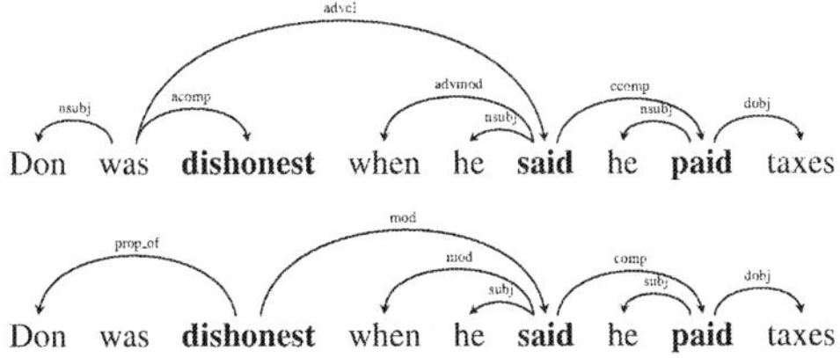

Figure 2: Dependency tree (top, obtained with spaCy) versus PropS representation (bottom, obtained via the online demo). Note that PropS posits *dishonest* as the head of *said*, while the dependency tree obstructs this relation.

Extending TruthTeller's lexicon We extended the TruthTeller lexicon of single-word predicates by integrating a large resource of modality markers. Following the approach of Eckle-Kohler (2016), we first induced the modality status of English adjectives and nouns from the subcategorization frames of their German counterparts listed in a large valency lexicon (using the "IMSLex German Lexicon" (Fitschen, 2004) and Google Translate for obtaining the translations[2]). We focused on four modality classes (the classes *wh-factual* and *wh/if-factual* indicating factuality, and the two classes *future-orientation* and *non-factual*, indicating uncertainty)[3] and semi-automatically mapped them to the signatures used in TruthTeller. We performed the same kind of mapping for the modality classes of English verbs provided by Eckle-Kohler (2016). The result of this process extended TruthTeller's lexicon by roughly 40% (265 adjectives, 281 nouns, and 133 verbs).

Integrating PropS with TruthTeller PropS was recently presented as an abstraction over dependency trees. Most convenient in our case is its re-ordering of non-verbal predicates (adjectival, conditional, non-lexical, etc.) such that each predicate is the direct head of its respective arguments. For example, for adjectival predication, compare the different parses in Figure 2. PropS positions *dishonest* as the head of *said*, which is subsequently the head of *paid*. This chain allows the implicative signature encoded in TruthTeller to capture this complex relation. The dependency syntax, in contrast, obstructs this relation by positing *dishonest* as a leaf node under *when*. The overall consistency of PropS annotation allows the top-down approach of TruthTeller to apply to predicates beyond the verbal case.

Finally, we take as features all four TruthTeller annotations (see Section 2) of the target predicate, its PropS head and its children (padding or truncating to 4 children). For a fair comparison with the UW system, we use these features to train an SVM regression (Basak et al., 2007) model to predict the final factuality value.

5 Evaluation

In this section we describe the experiments we carried out on the three unified datasets (FactBank, MEANTIME, and UW). For a fair comparison, we use the same train, development, test split of the datasets for all systems. We preprocess the data with the spaCy Python library.[4] In all our experiments we compute the metrics used in Lee et al. (2015): (1) *Mean Absolute Error*[5] (MAE), which computes the absolute fit of the model and (2) *Pearson correlation coefficient* between automatic predictions and gold labels, especially informative in biased test sets as it assesses how well the model captures the variability in the gold data.

5.1 Baselines

We test the performance of our model on the unified factuality corpus against that of several algorithms, representing the state-of-the-art (SoA) in competing approaches.

Rule-based approach For a SoA rule-based approach we use TruthTeller with extended lexicon as described in Section 4. We convert its discrete predictions to the [-3, +3] scale using a handwritten conversion table, similarly to our mapping of FactBank annotations.

Supervised approach The SoA for supervised learning is represented by the features from the UW system. We note that for practical issues, we did not use the same solver[6], but instead used support vector regression (SVR) model with a linear kernel (as implemented in the *scikit-learn* Python

---

[2]We used the translation function available as part of Google Sheets. https://www.google.com/sheets and removed all translation pairs with English multi-words.

[3]In Eckle-Kohler (2016), these are the classes containing the majority of the verb types.

[4]https://spacy.io

[5]Note that in our case this ranges between 0 (perfect performance) and 6 (worst performance).

[6]UW used the IBM CPLEX Optimizer

library[7]). All hyperparameters were tuned on the development set.

Semantic representation approach In addition to the rule-based and supervised approaches, we experimented with a semantic abstraction of the sentence. For that end, we extracted features inspired by the UW system on the popular AMR formalism (Banarescu et al., 2013) using a SoA parser (Pust et al., 2015). Our hope was that this would improve performance by focusing on the more semantically-significant portions of the predicate-argument structure. In particular, we extracted the following features from the predicted AMR structures: immediate parents, grandparents and siblings of the target node, lemma and POS tag of the target and preceding token in the sentence, and a Boolean feature based on the AMR *polarity* role (indicating semantic negation).

All-factual approach Finally, we compare against an **all-factual** baseline which assigns +3.0 to all predicates. Since the task is by nature heavily biased towards the factual label, it is interesting to compare against such a simple (yet strong) lower bound. See the supplemental material for a technical elaboration on the baselines implementation.

5.2 Results

Several observations can be made following the results on our test sets (Table 2).

Rule-based baseline is a good starting point The rule-based performance is well correlated with the gold predictions on FactBank and UW, showing its off-the-shelf usability.

Supervised setting improves performance Adding our features provided a predictive signal for factuality assessment on all test sets. More significant improvement is observed in the larger FactBank and UW corpora.

UW achieves good correlation UW gives a more diverse annotation thanks to its richer feature set (including lemma and dependency path). While this hurts MAE in some scenarios, it overall leads to good correlation with the gold data.

MEANTIME proves especially hard None of the systems were able to surpass the all-factual baseline in terms of MAE on MEANTIME. This

Dataset	FactBank		UW		MEANTIME	
	MAE	r	MAE	r	MAE	r
All-factual	.80	0	.78	0	**.31**	0
UW feat.[†]	.81	.66	.51	**.71**	.56	.33
AMR	.66	.66	.64	.58	.44	.30
Rule-based	.75	.62	.72	.63	.35	.23
Supervised	**.59**	**.71**	**.42**	.66	.34	**.47**

Table 2: Performance of the baselines against our new supervised model (bottom). [†]The performance of UW features on MEANTIME and FactBank uses a different solver from that in Lee et al. (2015). See Section 5 for details.

is due to its much smaller size and heavy factual bias (assigning +3.0 to 90% of the predicates).

AMR models achieve comparable performance While AMR provides a more abstract representation, many aspects of factuality (interaction of verb tenses, modal verbs, negation) are not modeled. Noisy automatic parses also diminish the positive effect of richer feature representation.

6 Conclusions and Future Work

We presented an intuitive method for mapping FactBank and MEANTIME onto the UW scale, and presented a novel factuality model which extends TruthTeller and applies it over PropS' abstraction of dependency trees. An interesting direction for future work is to address the inherent bias in the data towards the factual end of the scale by uniformly bucketing the factuality values, which will affect the way the evaluation is carried out on top of these annotations.

We made both the unified representation and the trained model publicly available[8], hoping that it will enable factuality research across larger, more diverse datasets.

Acknowledgments

We would like to thank the anonymous reviewers for their helpful comments. This work was supported in part by grants from the MAGNET program of the Israeli Office of the Chief Scientist (OCS) and by the German Research Foundation through the German-Israeli Project Cooperation (DIP, grant DA 1600/1-1).

---

[7]http://scikit-learn.org/

[8]https://github.com/gabrielStanovsky/unified-factuality

References

Laura Banarescu, Claire Bonial, Shu Cai, Madalina Georgescu, Kira Griffitt, Ulf Hermjakob, Kevin Knight, Philipp Koehn, Martha Palmer, and Nathan Schneider. 2013. Abstract meaning representation for sembanking .

Debasish Basak, Srimanta Pal, and Dipak Chandra Patranabis. 2007. Support vector regression. *Neural Information Processing-Letters and Reviews* 11(10):203–224.

Judith Eckle-Kohler. 2016. Verbs taking clausal and non-finite arguments as signals of modality revisiting the issue of meaning grounded in syntax. In *Proceedings of the 54th Annual Meeting of the Association for Computational Linguistics (ACL 2016)*. Association for Computational Linguistics, volume Volume 1: Long Papers, pages 811–822.

Arne Fitschen. 2004. Ein Computerlinguistisches Lexikon als komplexes System. PhD Thesis, Universität Stuttgart, Germany.

Elisa Ghia, Lennart Kloppenburg, Malvina Nissim, Paola Pietrandrea, and Valerio Cervoni. 2016. A construction-centered approach to the annotation of modality. In Nicoletta Calzolari (Conference Chair), Khalid Choukri, Thierry Declerck, Sara Goggi, Marko Grobelnik, Bente Maegaard, Joseph Mariani, Helene Mazo, Asuncion Moreno, Jan Odijk, and Stelios Piperidis, editors, *Proceedings of the 12thISO Workshop on Interoperable Semantic Annotation*. European Language Resources Association (ELRA).

Valentine Hacquard. 2011. Modality. In Claudia Maienborn, Klaus von Heusinger, and Paul Portner, editors, *Semantics: An International Handbook of Natural Language Meaning. HSK 33.2*, Berlin: Mouton de Gruyter, pages 1484–1515.

Lauri Karttunen. 2012. Simple and Phrasal Implicatives. In **SEM 2012: The First Joint Conference on Lexical and Computational Semantics*. Montréal, Canada, pages 124–131.

Kenton Lee, Yoav Artzi, Yejin Choi, and Luke Zettlemoyer. 2015. Event detection and factuality assessment with non-expert supervision. In *Proceedings of the 2015 Conference on Empirical Methods in Natural Language Processing (EMNLP)*. Association for Computational Linguistics, Lisbon, Portugal.

Amnon Lotan, Asher Stern, and Ido Dagan. 2013. Truthteller: Annotating predicate truth. In *HLT-NAACL*. pages 752–757.

Bill MacCartney and Christopher D. Manning. 2009. An extended model of natural logic. In *Proceedings of the Eighth International Conference on Computational Semantics*. Tilburg, The Netherlands, IWCS-8 '09, pages 140–156.

Anne-Lyse Minard, Manuela Speranza, Ruben Urizar, Begona Altuna, Marieke van Erp, Anneleen Schoen, and Chantal van Son. 2016. Meantime, the newsreader multilingual event and time corpus. *Proceedings of LREC2016* .

Malvina Nissim, Paola Pietrandrea, Andrea Sanso, and Caterina Mauri. 2013. Cross-Linguistic Annotation of Modality: a Data-Driven Hierarchical Model. In *Proceedings of the 9th Joint ISO - ACL SIGSEM Workshop on Interoperable Semantic Annotation*. Potsdam, Germany, pages 7–14.

Tim OGorman, Kristin Wright-Bettner, and Martha Palmer. 2016. Richer event description: Integrating event coreference with temporal, causal and bridging annotation. *Computing News Storylines* page 47.

Michael Pust, Ulf Hermjakob, Kevin Knight, Daniel Marcu, and Jonathan May. 2015. Parsing english into abstract meaning representation using syntax-based machine translation. In *Proceedings of the 2015 Conference on Empirical Methods in Natural Language Processing*. Association for Computational Linguistics, Lisbon, Portugal, pages 1143–1154.

Roser Saurí and James Pustejovsky. 2009. Factbank: a corpus annotated with event factuality. *Language resources and evaluation* 43(3):227.

Roser Saurí and James Pustejovsky. 2012. Are You Sure That This Happened? Assessing the Factuality Degree of Events in Text. *Computational Linguistics* 38(2):261–299.

Gabriel Stanovsky, Jessica Ficler, Ido Dagan, and Yoav Goldberg. 2016. Getting more out of syntax with props. *arXiv preprint* .

Question Answering on Knowledge Bases and Text
using Universal Schema and Memory Networks

Rajarshi Das[*♠]   **Manzil Zaheer**[*♡]   **Siva Reddy**[♣] and **Andrew McCallum**[♠]
♠College of Information and Computer Sciences, University of Massachusetts Amherst
♡School of Computer Science, Carnegie Mellon University
♣School of Informatics, University of Edinburgh
{rajarshi, mccallum}@cs.umass.edu, manzilz@cs.cmu.edu
siva.reddy@ed.ac.uk

Abstract

Existing question answering methods infer answers either from a knowledge base or from raw text. While knowledge base (KB) methods are good at answering compositional questions, their performance is often affected by the incompleteness of the KB. Au contraire, web text contains millions of facts that are absent in the KB, however in an unstructured form. *Universal schema* can support reasoning on the union of both structured KBs and unstructured text by aligning them in a common embedded space. In this paper we extend universal schema to natural language question answering, employing *memory networks* to attend to the large body of facts in the combination of text and KB. Our models can be trained in an end-to-end fashion on question-answer pairs. Evaluation results on SPADES fill-in-the-blank question answering dataset show that exploiting universal schema for question answering is better than using either a KB or text alone. This model also outperforms the current state-of-the-art by 8.5 F_1 points.

1   Introduction

Question Answering (QA) has been a long-standing goal of natural language processing. Two main paradigms evolved in solving this problem: 1) answering questions on a knowledge base; and 2) answering questions using text.

Knowledge bases (KB) contains facts expressed in a fixed schema, facilitating compositional reasoning. These attracted research ever since the early days of computer science, e.g., BASEBALL (Green Jr et al., 1961). This problem has matured into learning semantic parsers from parallel question and logical form pairs (Zelle and Mooney,

1996; Zettlemoyer and Collins, 2005), to recent scaling of methods to work on very large KBs like Freebase using question and answer pairs (Berant et al., 2013). However, a major drawback of this paradigm is that KBs are highly incomplete (Dong et al., 2014). It is also an open question whether KB relational structure is expressive enough to represent world knowledge (Stanovsky et al., 2014; Gardner and Krishnamurthy, 2017)

The paradigm of exploiting text for questions started in the early 1990s (Kupiec, 1993). With the advent of web, access to text resources became abundant and cheap. Initiatives like TREC QA competitions helped popularizing this paradigm (Voorhees et al., 1999). With the recent advances in deep learning and availability of large public datasets, there has been an explosion of research in a very short time (Rajpurkar et al., 2016; Trischler et al., 2016; Nguyen et al., 2016; Wang and Jiang, 2016; Lee et al., 2016; Xiong et al., 2016; Seo et al., 2016; Choi et al., 2016). Still, text representation is unstructured and does not allow the compositional reasoning which structured KB supports.

An important but under-explored QA paradigm is where KB and text are exploited together (Ferrucci et al., 2010). Such combination is attractive because text contains millions of facts not present in KB, and a KB's generative capacity represents infinite number of facts that are never seen in text. However QA inference on this combination is challenging due to the structural non-uniformity of KB and text. *Distant supervision* methods (Bunescu and Mooney, 2007; Mintz et al., 2009; Riedel et al., 2010; Yao et al., 2010; Zeng et al., 2015) address this problem partially by means of aligning text patterns with KB. But the rich and ambiguous nature of language allows a fact to be expressed in many different forms which these models fail to capture. *Universal schema* (Riedel et al., 2013) avoids the alignment problem by jointly embedding KB facts

Proceedings of the 55th Annual Meeting of the Association for Computational Linguistics (Short Papers), pages 358–365
Vancouver, Canada, July 30 - August 4, 2017. ©2017 Association for Computational Linguistics
https://doi.org/10.18653/v1/P17-2057

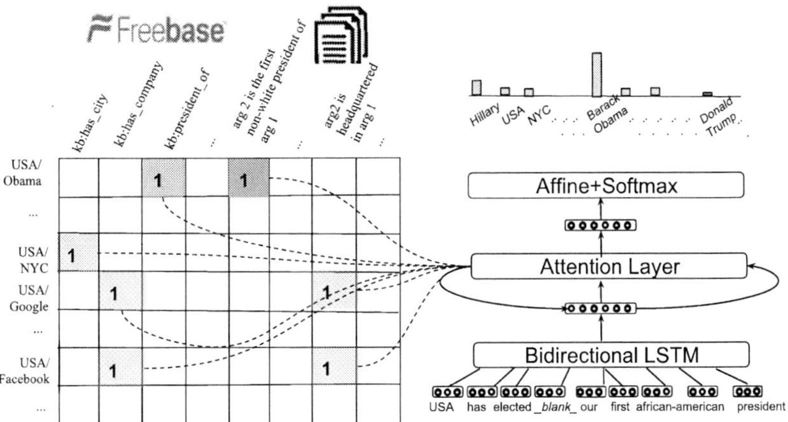

Figure 1: Memory network attending the facts in the universal schema (matrix on the left). The color gradients denote the attention weight on each fact.

and text into a uniform structured representation, allowing interleaved propagation of information. Figure 1 shows a universal schema matrix which has pairs of entities as rows, and Freebase and textual relations in columns. Although universal schema has been extensively used for relation extraction, this paper shows its applicability to QA. Consider the question *USA has elected _blank_, our first african-american president* with its answer *Barack Obama*. While Freebase has a predicate for representing presidents of USA, it does not have one for 'african-american' presidents. Whereas in text, we find many sentences describing the presidency of Barack Obama and his ethnicity at the same time. Exploiting both KB and text makes it relatively easy to answer this question than relying on only one of these sources.

Memory networks (MemNN; Weston et al. 2015) are a class of neural models which have an external memory component for encoding short and long term context. In this work, we define the memory components as observed cells of the universal schema matrix, and train an end-to-end QA model on question-answer pairs.

The contributions of the paper are as follows (a) We show that universal schema representation is a better knowledge source for QA than either KB or text alone, (b) On the SPADES dataset (Bisk et al., 2016), containing real world fill-in-the-blank questions, we outperform state-of-the-art semantic parsing baseline, with 8.5 F_1 points. (c) Our analysis shows how individual data sources help fill the weakness of the other, thereby improving overall performance.

2 Background

Problem Definition Given a question q with words $w_1, w_2, \ldots, w_n$, where these words contain one _blank_ and at least one entity, our goal is to fill in this _blank_ with an answer entity q_a using a knowledge base $\mathcal{K}$ and text $\mathcal{T}$. Few example question answer pairs are shown in Table 2.

Universal Schema Traditionally universal schema is used for relation extraction in the context of knowledge base population. Rows in the schema are formed by entity pairs (e.g. USA, NYC), and columns represent the relation between them. A relation can either be a KB relation, or it could be a pattern of text that exist between these two entities in a large corpus. The embeddings of entities and relation types are learned by low-rank matrix factorization techniques. Riedel et al. (2013) treat textual patterns as static symbols, whereas recent work by Verga et al. (2016) replaces them with distributed representation of sentences obtained by a RNN. Using distributed representation allows reasoning on sentences that are similar in meaning but different on the surface form. We too use this variant to encode our textual relations.

Memory Networks MemNNs are neural attention models with external and differentiable memory. MemNNs decouple the memory component from the network thereby allowing it store external information. Previously, these have been successfully applied to question answering on KB where the memory is filled with distributed representation of KB triples (Bordes et al., 2015), or for reading comprehension (Sukhbaatar et al., 2015; Hill et al., 2016), where the memory consists of distributed representation of sentences in the comprehension. Recently, key-value MemNN are introduced (Miller et al., 2016) where each memory slot consists of a key and value. The attention weight is computed only by comparing the question with the key memory, whereas the value is used to compute the contextual representation to predict the answer. We use this variant of MemNN for our model. Miller et al. (2016), in their experiments, store either KB triples or sentences as memories but they do not explicitly model multiple memories containing distinct data sources like we do.

3 Model

Our model is a MemNN with universal schema as its memory. Figure 1 shows the model architecture.

Memory: Our memory $\mathcal{M}$ comprise of both KB and textual triples from universal schema. Each memory cell is in the form of key-value pair. Let $(s, r, o) \in \mathcal{K}$ represent a KB triple. We represent this fact with distributed key $\mathbf{k} \in \mathbb{R}^{2d}$ formed by concatenating the embeddings $\mathbf{s} \in \mathbb{R}^d$ and $\mathbf{r} \in \mathbb{R}^d$ of subject entity s and relation r respectively. The embedding $\mathbf{o} \in \mathbb{R}^d$ of object entity o is treated as its value $\mathbf{v}$.

Let $(s, [w_1, \ldots, arg_1, \ldots, arg_2, w_n], o) \in \mathcal{T}$ represent a textual fact, where arg_1 and arg_2 correspond to the positions of the entities 's' and 'o'. We represent the key as the sequence formed by replacing arg_1 with 's' and arg_2 with a special '_blank_' token, i.e., $k = [w_1, \ldots, s, \ldots, \_blank\_, w_n]$ and value as just the entity 'o'. We convert k to a distributed representation using a bidirectional LSTM (Hochreiter and Schmidhuber, 1997; Graves and Schmidhuber, 2005), where $\mathbf{k} \in \mathbb{R}^{2d}$ is formed by concatenating the last states of forward and backward LSTM, i.e., $\mathbf{k} = \left[\overrightarrow{\text{LSTM}}(k); \overleftarrow{\text{LSTM}}(k) \right]$. The value $\mathbf{v}$ is the embedding of the object entity o. Projecting both KB and textual facts to $\mathbb{R}^{2d}$ offers a unified view of the knowledge to reason upon. In Figure 1, each cell in the matrix represents a memory containing the distributed representation of its key and value.

Question Encoder: A bidirectional LSTM is also used to encode the input question q to a distributed representation $\mathbf{q} \in \mathbb{R}^{2d}$ similar to the key encoding step above.

Attention over cells: We compute attention weight of a memory cell by taking the dot prod-

uct of its key $\mathbf{k}$ with a contextual vector $\mathbf{c}$ which encodes most important context in the current iteration. In the first iteration, the contextual vector is the question itself. We only consider the memory cells that contain at least one entity in the question. For example, for the input question in Figure 1, we only consider memory cells containing USA. Using the attention weights and values of memory cells, we compute the context vector $\mathbf{c_t}$ for the next iteration t as follows:

$$\mathbf{c_t} = \mathbf{W_t} \left(\mathbf{c_{t-1}} + \mathbf{W_p} \sum_{(k,v) \in \mathcal{M}} (\mathbf{c_{t-1}} \cdot \mathbf{k})\mathbf{v} \right)$$

where $\mathbf{c_0}$ is initialized with question embedding $\mathbf{q}$, $\mathbf{W_p}$ is a projection matrix, and $\mathbf{W_t}$ represents the weight matrix which considers the context in previous hop and the values in the current iteration based on their importance (attention weight). This multi-iterative context selection allows multi-hop reasoning without explicitly requiring a symbolic query representation.

Answer Entity Selection: The final contextual vector c_t is used to select the answer entity q_a (among all 1.8M entities in the dataset) which has the highest inner product with it.

4 Experiments

4.1 Evaluation Dataset

We use Freebase (Bollacker et al., 2008) as our KB, and ClueWeb (Gabrilovich et al., 2013) as our text source to build universal schema. For evaluation, literature offers two options: 1) datasets for text-based question answering tasks such as answer sentence selection and reading comprehension; and 2) datasets for KB question answering.

Although the text-based question answering datasets are large in size, e.g., SQuAD (Rajpurkar et al., 2016) has over 100k questions, answers to these are often not entities but rather sentences which are not the focus of our work. Moreover these texts may not contain Freebase entities at all, making these skewed heavily towards text. Coming to the alternative option, WebQuestions (Berant et al., 2013) is widely used for QA on Freebase. This dataset is curated such that all questions can be answered on Freebase alone. But since our goal is to explore the impact of universal schema, testing on a dataset completely answerable on a KB is not ideal. WikiMovies dataset (Miller et al., 2016) also has similar properties. Gardner and Krishnamurthy (2017) created a dataset with motivations similar to

Model	Dev. F_1	Test F_1
Bisk et al. (2016)	32.7	31.4
ONLYKB	39.1	38.5
ONLYTEXT	25.3	26.6
ENSEMBLE.	39.4	38.6
UNISCHEMA	**41.1**	**39.9**

Table 1: QA results on SPADES.

ours, however this is not publicly released during the submission time.

Instead, we use SPADES (Bisk et al., 2016) as our evaluation data which contains fill-in-the-blank cloze-styled questions created from ClueWeb. This dataset is ideal to test our hypothesis for following reasons: 1) it is large with 93K sentences and 1.8M entities; and 2) since these are collected from Web, most sentences are natural. A limitation of this dataset is that it contains only the sentences that have entities connected by at least one relation in Freebase, making it skewed towards Freebase as we will see (§ 4.4). We use the standard train, dev and test splits for our experiments. For text part of universal schema, we use the sentences present in the training set.

4.2 Models

We evaluate the following models to measure the impact of different knowledge sources for QA.

ONLYKB: In this model, MemNN memory contains only the facts from KB. For each KB triple (e_1, r, e_2), we have two memory slots, one for (e_1, r, e_2) and the other for its inverse (e_2, r^i, e_1).

ONLYTEXT: SPADES contains sentences with blanks. We replace the blank tokens with the answer entities to create textual facts from the training set. Using every pair of entities, we create a memory cell similar to as in universal schema.

ENSEMBLE This is an ensemble of the above two models. We use a linear model that combines the scores from, and use an ensemble to combine the evidences from individual models.

UNISCHEMA This is our main model with universal schema as its memory, i.e., it contains memory slots corresponding to both KB and textual facts.

4.3 Implementation Details

The dimensions of word, entity and relation embeddings, and LSTM states were set to $d = 50$. The word and entity embeddings were initialized with word2vec (Mikolov et al., 2013) trained on 7.5

Question	Answer
1. USA have elected _blank_, our first african-american president.	Obama
2. Angelina has reportedly been threatening to leave _blank_.	Brad_Pitt
3. Spanish is more often a second and weaker language among many _blank_.	Latinos
4. _blank_ is the third largest city in the United_States.	Chicago
5. _blank_ was Belshazzar 's father.	Nabonidus

Table 2: A few questions on which ONLYKB fails to answer but UNISCHEMA succeeds.

million ClueWeb sentences containing entities in Freebase subset of SPADES. The network weights were initialized using Xavier initialization (Glorot and Bengio, 2010). We considered up to a maximum of 5k KB facts and 2.5k textual facts for a question. We used Adam (Kingma and Ba, 2015) with the default hyperparameters (learning rate=1e-3, β_1=0.9, β_2=0.999, ε=1e-8) for optimization. To overcome exploding gradients, we restricted the magnitude of the ℓ_2 norm of the gradient to 5. The batch size during training was set to 32.

To train the UNISCHEMA model, we initialized the parameters from a trained ONLYKB model. We found that this is crucial in making the UNISCHEMA to work. Another caveat is the need to employ a trick similar to *batch normalization* (Ioffe and Szegedy, 2015). For each minibatch, we normalize the mean and variance of the textual facts and then scale and shift to match the mean and variance of the KB memory facts. Empirically, this stabilized the training and gave a boost in the final performance.

4.4 Results and Discussions

Table 1 shows the main results on SPADES. UNISCHEMA outperforms all our models validating our hypothesis that exploiting universal schema for QA is better than using either KB or text alone. Despite SPADES creation process being friendly to Freebase, exploiting text still provides a significant improvement. Table 2 shows some of the questions which UNISCHEMA answered but ONLYKB failed. These can be broadly classified into (a) relations that are not expressed in Freebase (e.g., african-american presidents in sentence 1); (b) intentional facts since curated databases only represent concrete facts rather than intentions (e.g., threating to leave in sentence 2); (c) comparative predicates like first, second, largest, smallest (e.g., sentences 3 and 4); and (d) providing addi-

Model	Dev. F_1
ONLYKB correct	39.1
ONLYTEXT correct	25.3
UNISCHEMA correct	41.1
ONLYKB or ONLYTEXT got it correct	45.9
Both ONLYKB and ONLYTEXT got it correct	18.5
ONLYKB got it correct and ONLYTEXT did not	20.6
ONLYTEXT got it correct and ONLYKB did not	6.80
Both UNISCHEMA and ONLYKB got it correct	34.6
UNISCHEMA got it correct and ONLYKB did not	6.42
ONLYKB got it correct and UNISCHEMA did not	4.47
Both UNISCHEMA and ONLYTEXT got it correct	19.2
UNISCHEMA got it correct and ONLYTEXT did not	21.9
ONLYTEXT got it correct and UNISCHEMA did not	6.09

Table 3: Detailed results on SPADES.

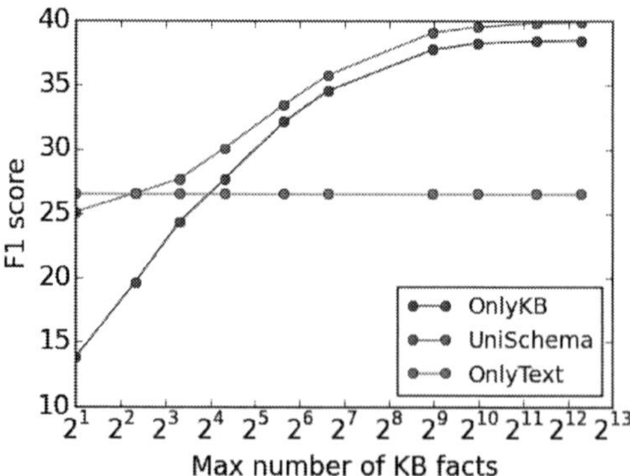

Figure 2: Performance on varying the number of available KB facts during test time. UNISCHEMA model consistently outperforms ONLYKB

tional type constraints (e.g., in sentence 5, Freebase does not have a special relation for *father*. It can be expressed using the relation *parent* along with the type constraint that the answer is of gender *male*).

We have also anlalyzed the nature of UNIS-CHEMA attention. In 58.7% of the cases the attention tends to prefer KB facts over text. This is as expected since KBs facts are concrete and accurate than text. In 34.8% of cases, the memory prefers to attend text even if the fact is already present in the KB. For the rest (6.5%), the memory distributes attention weight evenly, indicating for some questions, part of the evidence comes from text and part of it from KB. Table 3 gives a more detailed quantitative analysis of the three models in comparison with each other.

To see how reliable is UNISCHEMA, we gradually increased the coverage of KB by allowing only a fixed number of randomly chosen KB facts for each entity. As Figure 2 shows, when the KB coverage is less than 16 facts per entity, UNISCHEMA outperforms ONLYKB by a wide-margin indicating UNISCHEMA is robust even in resource-scarce scenario, whereas ONLYKB is very sensitive to the coverage. UNISCHEMA also outperforms EN-SEMBLE showing joint modeling is superior to ensemble on the individual models. We also achieve the state-of-the-art with 8.5 F_1 points difference. Bisk et al. use graph matching techniques to convert natural language to Freebase queries whereas even without an explicit query representation, we outperform them.

5 Related Work

A majority of the QA literature that focused on exploiting KB and text either improves the infer-ence on the KB using text based features (Krishnamurthy and Mitchell, 2012; Reddy et al., 2014; Joshi et al., 2014; Yao and Van Durme, 2014; Yih et al., 2015; Neelakantan et al., 2015b; Guu et al., 2015; Xu et al., 2016b; Choi et al., 2015; Savenkov and Agichtein, 2016) or improves the inference on text using KB (Sun et al., 2015).

Limited work exists on exploiting text and KB jointly for question answering. Gardner and Krishnamurthy (2017) is the closest to ours who generate a open-vocabulary logical form and rank candidate answers by how likely they occur with this logical form both in Freebase and text. Our models are trained on a weaker supervision signal without requiring the annotation of the logical forms.

A few QA methods infer on curated databases combined with OpenIE triples (Fader et al., 2014; Yahya et al., 2016; Xu et al., 2016a). Our work differs from them in two ways: 1) we do not need an explicit database query to retrieve the answers (Neelakantan et al., 2015a; Andreas et al., 2016); and 2) our text-based facts retain complete sentential context unlike the OpenIE triples (Banko et al., 2007; Carlson et al., 2010).

6 Conclusions

In this work, we showed universal schema is a promising knowledge source for QA than using KB or text alone. Our results conclude though KB is preferred over text when the KB contains the fact of interest, a large portion of queries still attend to text indicating the amalgam of both text and KB is superior than KB alone.

Acknowledgments

We sincerely thank Luke Vilnis for helpful insights. This work was supported in part by the Center for Intelligent Information Retrieval and in part by DARPA under agreement number FA8750-13-2-0020. The U.S. Government is authorized to reproduce and distribute reprints for Governmental purposes notwithstanding any copyright notation thereon. Any opinions, findings and conclusions or recommendations expressed in this material are those of the authors and do not necessarily reflect those of the sponsor.

References

Jacob Andreas, Marcus Rohrbach, Trevor Darrell, and Dan Klein. 2016. Learning to Compose Neural Networks for Question Answering. In *NAACL*.

Michele Banko, Michael J Cafarella, Stephen Soderland, Matthew Broadhead, and Oren Etzioni. 2007. Open Information Extraction from the Web. In *IJ-CAI*.

Jonathan Berant, Andrew Chou, Roy Frostig, and Percy Liang. 2013. Semantic Parsing on Freebase from Question-Answer Pairs. In *EMNLP*.

Yonatan Bisk, Siva Reddy, John Blitzer, Julia Hockenmaier, and Mark Steedman. 2016. Evaluating Induced CCG Parsers on Grounded Semantic Parsing. In *EMNLP*.

Kurt Bollacker, Colin Evans, Praveen Paritosh, Tim Sturge, and Jamie Taylor. 2008. Freebase: A collaboratively created graph database for structuring human knowledge. In *ICDM*.

Antoine Bordes, Nicolas Usunier, Sumit Chopra, and Jason Weston. 2015. Large-scale simple question answering with memory networks. *CoRR* .

Razvan C. Bunescu and Raymond J. Mooney. 2007. Learning to extract relations from the web using minimal supervision. In *ACL*.

Andrew Carlson, Justin Betteridge, Bryan Kisiel, Burr Settles, Jr. Estevam R. Hruschka, and Tom M. Mitchell. 2010. Toward an Architecture for Never-ending Language Learning. In *AAAI*.

Eunsol Choi, Daniel Hewlett, Alexandre Lacoste, Illia Polosukhin, Jakob Uszkoreit, and Jonathan Berant. 2016. Hierarchical question answering for long documents. *arXiv preprint arXiv:1611.01839* .

Eunsol Choi, Tom Kwiatkowski, and Luke Zettlemoyer. 2015. Scalable Semantic Parsing with Partial Ontologies. In *ACL*.

Xin Dong, Evgeniy Gabrilovich, Geremy Heitz, Wilko Horn, Ni Lao, Kevin Murphy, Thomas Strohmann, Shaohua Sun, and Wei Zhang. 2014. Knowledge Vault: A Web-scale Approach to Probabilistic Knowledge Fusion. New York, NY, USA, KDD '14.

Anthony Fader, Luke Zettlemoyer, and Oren Etzioni. 2014. Open question answering over curated and extracted knowledge bases. In *KDD*. ACM, pages 1156–1165.

David Ferrucci, Eric Brown, Jennifer Chu-Carroll, James Fan, David Gondek, Aditya A Kalyanpur, Adam Lally, J William Murdock, Eric Nyberg, John Prager, and others. 2010. Building Watson: An overview of the DeepQA project. *AI magazine* .

Evgeniy Gabrilovich, Michael Ringgaard, and Amarnag Subramanya. 2013. Facc1: Freebase annotation of clueweb corpora. (http://lemurproject.org/clueweb09/.

Matt Gardner and Jayant Krishnamurthy. 2017. Open-Vocabulary Semantic Parsing with both Distributional Statistics and Formal Knowledge. In *AAAI*.

Xavier Glorot and Yoshua Bengio. 2010. Understanding the difficulty of training deep feedforward neural networks. In *AISTATS*.

Alex Graves and Jürgen Schmidhuber. 2005. Framewise phoneme classification with bidirectional lstm and other neural network architectures. *Neural Networks* .

Bert F Green Jr, Alice K Wolf, Carol Chomsky, and Kenneth Laughery. 1961. Baseball: an automatic question-answerer. In *Papers presented at the May 9-11, 1961, western joint IRE-AIEE-ACM computer conference*. ACM, pages 219–224.

K. Guu, J. Miller, and P. Liang. 2015. Traversing knowledge graphs in vector space. In *EMNLP*.

Felix Hill, Antoine Bordes, Sumit Chopra, and Jason Weston. 2016. The goldilocks principle: Reading children's books with explicit memory representations. *ICLR* .

Sepp Hochreiter and Jürgen Schmidhuber. 1997. Long short-term memory. *Neural Computation* .

Sergey Ioffe and Christian Szegedy. 2015. Batch normalization: Accelerating deep network training by reducing internal covariate shift. In *ICML*. JMLR Workshop and Conference Proceedings.

Mandar Joshi, Uma Sawant, and Soumen Chakrabarti. 2014. Knowledge Graph and Corpus Driven Segmentation and Answer Inference for Telegraphic Entity-seeking Queries. In *EMNLP*.

Diederik P. Kingma and Jimmy Ba. 2015. Adam: A method for stochastic optimization. *ICLR* .

Jayant Krishnamurthy and Tom Mitchell. 2012. Weakly Supervised Training of Semantic Parsers. In *EMNLP*.

Julian Kupiec. 1993. MURAX: A robust linguistic approach for question answering using an on-line encyclopedia. In *SIGIR*. ACM.

Kenton Lee, Tom Kwiatkowski, Ankur Parikh, and Dipanjan Das. 2016. Learning recurrent span representations for extractive question answering. *arXiv preprint arXiv:1611.01436* .

Tomas Mikolov, Ilya Sutskever, Kai Chen, Greg S Corrado, and Jeff Dean. 2013. Distributed representations of words and phrases and their compositionality. In *NIPS*.

Alexander H. Miller, Adam Fisch, Jesse Dodge, Amir-Hossein Karimi, Antoine Bordes, and Jason Weston. 2016. Key-value memory networks for directly reading documents. *In EMNLP* .

Mike Mintz, Steven Bills, Rion Snow, and Dan Jurafsky. 2009. Distant supervision for relation extraction without labeled data. In *ACL*.

Arvind Neelakantan, Quoc V Le, and Ilya Sutskever. 2015a. Neural programmer: Inducing latent programs with gradient descent. *arXiv preprint arXiv:1511.04834* .

Arvind Neelakantan, Benjamin Roth, and Andrew McCallum. 2015b. Compositional vector space models for knowledge base completion. In *ACL*.

Tri Nguyen, Mir Rosenberg, Xia Song, Jianfeng Gao, Saurabh Tiwary, Rangan Majumder, and Li Deng. 2016. MS MARCO: A Human Generated MAchine Reading COmprehension Dataset. *CoRR* abs/1611.09268.

Pranav Rajpurkar, Jian Zhang, Konstantin Lopyrev, and Percy Liang. 2016. SQuAD: 100,000+ Questions for Machine Comprehension of Text. In *EMNLP*. Austin, Texas.

Siva Reddy, Mirella Lapata, and Mark Steedman. 2014. Large-scale semantic parsing without question-answer pairs. *TACL 2*.

Sebastian Riedel, Limin Yao, and Andrew McCallum. 2010. Modeling relations and their mentions without labeled text. In *ECML PKDD*.

Sebastian Riedel, Limin Yao, Andrew McCallum, and Benjamin M. Marlin. 2013. Relation extraction with matrix factorization and universal schemas. In *NAACL*.

Denis Savenkov and Eugene Agichtein. 2016. When a knowledge base is not enough: Question answering over knowledge bases with external text data. In *SIGIR*. ACM.

Minjoon Seo, Sewon Min, Ali Farhadi, and Hannaneh Hajishirzi. 2016. Query-reduction networks for question answering. *arXiv preprint arXiv:1606.04582* .

Gabriel Stanovsky, Omer Levy, and Ido Dagan. 2014. Proposition Knowledge Graphs. *COLING 2014* .

Sainbayar Sukhbaatar, Arthur Szlam, Jason Weston, and Rob Fergus. 2015. End-to-end memory networks. In *NIPS*.

Huan Sun, Hao Ma, Wen-tau Yih, Chen-Tse Tsai, Jingjing Liu, and Ming-Wei Chang. 2015. Open domain question answering via semantic enrichment. In *WWW*. ACM.

Adam Trischler, Tong Wang, Xingdi Yuan, Justin Harris, Alessandro Sordoni, Philip Bachman, and Kaheer Suleman. 2016. NewsQA: A Machine Comprehension Dataset. *CoRR* abs/1611.09830.

Patrick Verga, David Belanger, Emma Strubell, Benjamin Roth, and Andrew McCallum. 2016. Multilingual relation extraction using compositional universal schema .

Ellen M Voorhees et al. 1999. The trec-8 question answering track report. In *Trec*. volume 99, pages 77–82.

Shuohang Wang and Jing Jiang. 2016. Machine comprehension using match-lstm and answer pointer. *arXiv preprint arXiv:1608.07905* .

Jason Weston, Sumit Chopra, and Antoine Bordes. 2015. Memory networks. *In ICLR* .

Caiming Xiong, Victor Zhong, and Richard Socher. 2016. Dynamic Coattention Networks For Question Answering. *arXiv preprint arXiv:1611.01604* .

Kun Xu, Yansong Feng, Songfang Huang, and Dongyan Zhao. 2016a. Hybrid Question Answering over Knowledge Base and Free Text. In *COLING*.

Kun Xu, Siva Reddy, Yansong Feng, Songfang Huang, and Dongyan Zhao. 2016b. Question Answering on Freebase via Relation Extraction and Textual Evidence. In *ACL*.

Mohamed Yahya, Denilson Barbosa, Klaus Berberich, Qiuyue Wang, and Gerhard Weikum. 2016. Relationship queries on extended knowledge graphs. In *Proceedings of the Ninth ACM International Conference on Web Search and Data Mining*. ACM, pages 605–614.

Limin Yao, Sebastian Riedel, and Andrew McCallum. 2010. Collective cross-document relation extraction without labelled data. In *EMNLP*.

Xuchen Yao and Benjamin Van Durme. 2014. Information Extraction over Structured Data: Question Answering with Freebase. In *ACL*.

Wen-tau Yih, Ming-Wei Chang, Xiaodong He, and Jianfeng Gao. 2015. Semantic Parsing via Staged Query Graph Generation: Question Answering with Knowledge Base. In *ACL*.

John M Zelle and Raymond J Mooney. 1996. Learning to parse database queries using inductive logic programming. In *AAAI*. Portland, Oregon.

Daojian Zeng, Kang Liu, Yubo Chen, and Jun Zhao. 2015. Distant supervision for relation extraction via piecewise convolutional neural networks. In *EMNLP*.

Luke S. Zettlemoyer and Michael Collins. 2005. Learning to Map Sentences to Logical Form: Structured Classification with Probabilistic Categorial Grammars. In *UAI*. Edinburgh, Scotland.

Differentiable Scheduled Sampling for Credit Assignment

Kartik Goyal
Carnegie Mellon University
Pittsbrugh, PA, USA
kartikgo@cs.cmu.edu

Chris Dyer
DeepMind
London, UK
cdyer@google.com

Taylor Berg-Kirkpatrick
Carnegie Mellon University
Pittsburgh, PA, USA
tberg@cs.cmu.edu

Abstract

We demonstrate that a continuous relaxation of the argmax operation can be used to create a differentiable approximation to greedy decoding for sequence-to-sequence (seq2seq) models. By incorporating this approximation into the scheduled sampling training procedure (Bengio et al., 2015)–a well-known technique for correcting exposure bias–we introduce a new training objective that is continuous and differentiable everywhere and that can provide informative gradients near points where previous decoding decisions change their value. In addition, by using a related approximation, we demonstrate a similar approach to sampled-based training. Finally, we show that our approach outperforms cross-entropy training and scheduled sampling procedures in two sequence prediction tasks: named entity recognition and machine translation.

1 Introduction

Sequence-to-Sequence (seq2seq) models have demonstrated excellent performance in several tasks including machine translation (Sutskever et al., 2014), summarization (Rush et al., 2015), dialogue generation (Serban et al., 2015), and image captioning (Xu et al., 2015). However, the standard cross-entropy training procedure for these models suffers from the well-known problem of exposure bias: because cross-entropy training always uses gold contexts, the states and contexts encountered during training do not match those encountered at test time. This issue has been addressed using several approaches that try to incorporate awareness of decoding choices into the training optimization. These include reinforcement learning (Ranzato et al., 2016; Bahdanau et al., 2017), imitation learning (Daumé et al., 2009; Ross et al., 2011; Bengio et al., 2015), and beam-based approaches (Wiseman and Rush, 2016; Andor et al., 2016; Daumé III and Marcu, 2005). In this paper, we focus on one the simplest to implement and least computationally expensive approaches, *scheduled sampling* (Bengio et al., 2015), which stochastically incorporates contexts from previous decoding decisions into training.

While scheduled sampling has been empirically successful, its training objective has a drawback: because the procedure directly incorporates greedy decisions at each time step, the objective is discontinuous at parameter settings where previous decisions change their value. As a result, gradients near these points are non-informative and scheduled sampling has difficulty assigning credit for errors. In particular, the gradient does not provide information useful in distinguishing between local errors without future consequences and cascading errors which are more serious.

Here, we propose a novel approach based on scheduled sampling that uses a differentiable approximation of previous greedy decoding decisions inside the training objective by incorporating a continuous relaxation of argmax. As a result, our end-to-end relaxed greedy training objective is differentiable everywhere and fully continuous. By making the objective continuous at points where previous decisions change value, our approach provides gradients that can respond to cascading errors. In addition, we demonstrate a related approximation and reparametrization for sample-based training (another training scenario considered by scheduled sampling (Bengio et al., 2015)) that can yield stochastic gradients with lower variance than in standard scheduled sampling. In our experiments on two different tasks, machine translation (MT) and named entity recognition (NER), we show that our approach outperforms both cross-entropy training and standard

366

Proceedings of the 55th Annual Meeting of the Association for Computational Linguistics (Short Papers), pages 366–371
Vancouver, Canada, July 30 - August 4, 2017. ©2017 Association for Computational Linguistics
https://doi.org/10.18653/v1/P17-2058

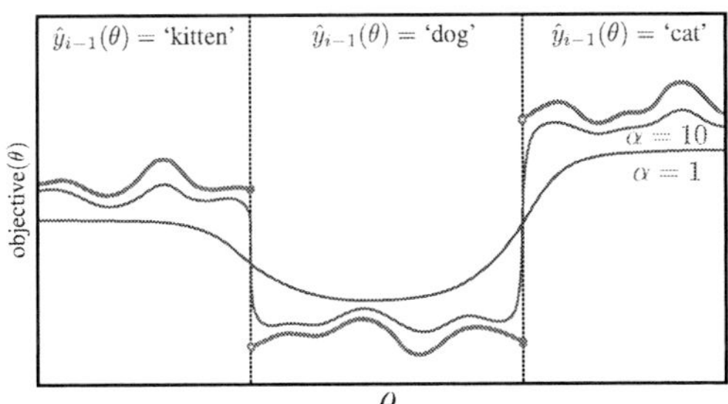

Figure 1: Discontinuous scheduled sampling objective (red) and continuous relaxations (blue and purple).

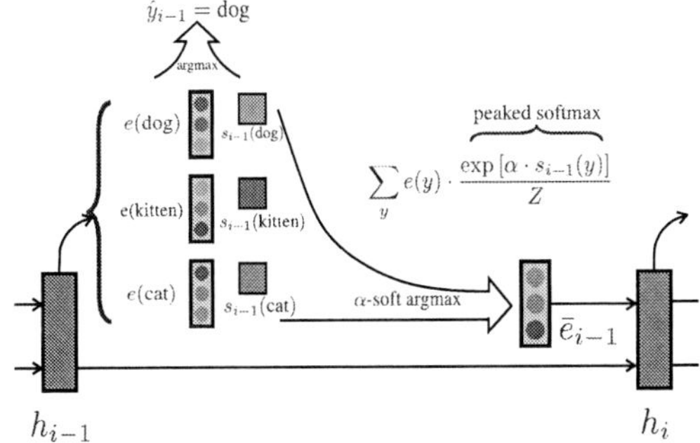

Figure 2: Relaxed greedy decoder that uses a continuous approximation of argmax as input to the decoder state at next time step.

2 Discontinuity in Scheduled Sampling

While scheduled sampling (Bengio et al., 2015) is an effective way to rectify exposure bias, it cannot differentiate between cascading errors, which can lead to a sequence of bad decisions, and local errors, which have more benign effects. Specifically, scheduled sampling focuses on learning optimal behavior in the current step given the fixed decoding decision of the previous step. If a previous bad decision is largely responsible for the current error, the training procedure has difficulty adjusting the parameters accordingly. The following machine translation example highlights this credit assignment issue:

Ref: The cat purrs .   Pred: The dog barks .

At step 3, the model prefers the word 'barks' after incorrectly predicting 'dog' at step 2. To correct this error, the scheduled sampling procedure would increase the score of 'purrs' at step 3, conditioned on the fact that the model predicted (incorrectly) 'dog' at step 2, which is not the ideal learning behaviour. Ideally, the model should be able to backpropagate the error from step 3 to the source of the problem which occurred at step 2, where 'dog' was predicted instead of 'cat'.

The lack of credit assignment during training is a result of discontinuity in the objective function used by scheduled sampling, as illustrated in Figure 1. We denote the ground truth target symbol at step i by y_i^*, the embedding representation of word y by $e(y)$, and the hidden state of a seq2seq decoder at step i as h_i. Standard cross-entropy training defines the loss at each step to be $\log p(y_i^*|h_i(e(y_{i-1}^*), h_{i-1}))$, while scheduled sampling uses loss $\log p(y_i^*|h_i(e(\hat{y}_{i-1}), h_{i-1}))$, where

$\hat{y}_{i-1}$ refers the model's prediction at the previous step.[1] Here, the model prediction $\hat{y}_{i-1}$ is obtained by argmaxing over the output softmax layer. Hence, in addition to the intermediate hidden states and final softmax scores, the previous model prediction, $\hat{y}_{i-1}$, itself depends on the model parameters, θ, and ideally, should be back-propagated through, unlike the gold target symbol y_{i-1}^* which is independent of model parameters. However, the argmax operation is discontinuous, and thus the training objective (depicted in Figure 1 as the red line) exhibits discontinuities at parameter settings where the previous decoding decisions change value (depicted as changes from 'kitten' to 'dog' to 'cat'). Because these change points represent discontinuities, their gradients are undefined and the effect of correcting an earlier mistake (for example 'dog' to 'cat') as the training procedure approaches such a point is essentially hidden.

In our approach, described in detail in the next section, we attempt to fix this problem by incorporating a continuous relaxation of the argmax operation into the scheduled sampling procedure in order to form an approximate but fully continuous objective. Our relaxed approximate objective is depicted in Figure 1 as blue and purple lines, depending on temperature parameter α which trades-off smoothness and quality of approximation.

3 Credit Assignment via Relaxation

In this section we explain in detail the continuous relaxation of greedy decoding that we will use to build a fully continuous training objective. We also introduce a related approach for sample-based training.

---

[1] For the sake of simplicity, the 'always sample' variant of scheduled sampling is described (Bengio et al., 2015).

3.1 Soft Argmax

In scheduled sampling, the embedding for the best scoring word at the previous step is passed as an input to the current step. This operation[2] can be expressed as

$$\hat{e}_{i-1} = \sum_{y} e(y)\mathbf{1}[\forall y' \neq y \ \ s_{i-1}(y) > s_{i-1}(y')]$$

where y is a word in the vocabulary, $s_{i-1}(y)$ is the output score of that word at the previous step, and $\hat{e}_{i-1}$ is the embedding passed to the next step. This operation can be relaxed by replacing the indicator function with a *peaked softmax function* with hyperparameter α to define a soft argmax procedure:

$$\bar{e}_{i-1} = \sum_{y} e(y) \cdot \frac{\exp\left(\alpha \ s_{i-1}(y)\right)}{\sum_{y'} \exp\left(\alpha \ s_{i-1}(y')\right)}$$

As $\alpha \to \infty$, the equation above approaches the true argmax embedding. Hence, with a finite and large α, we get a linear combination of all the words (and therefore a continuous function of the parameters) that is dominated heavily by the word with maximum score.

3.2 Soft Reparametrized Sampling

Another variant of scheduled sampling is to pass a sampled embedding from the softmax distribution at the previous step to the current step instead of the argmax. This is expected to enable better exploration of the search space during optimization due to the added randomness and hence result in a more robust model. In this section, we discuss and review an approximation to the Gumbel reparametrization trick that we use as a module in our sample-based decoder. This approximation was proposed by Maddison et al. (2017) and Jang et al. (2016), who showed that the same soft argmax operation introduced above can be used for reducing variance of stochastic gradients when sampling from softmax distributions. Unlike soft argmax, this approach is not a fully continuous approximation to the sampling operation, but it does result in much more informative gradients compared to naive scheduled sampling procedure.

The Gumbel reparametrization trick shows that sampling from a categorical distribution can be refactored into sampling from a simple distribution followed by a deterministic transformation as follows: (i) sampling an independent Gumbel noise G for each element in the categorical distribution, typically done by transforming a sample from the uniform distribution: $U \sim Uniform(0, 1)$ as $G = -log(-log\ U)$, then (ii) adding it componentwise to the unnormalized score of each element, and finally (iii) taking an argmax over the vector. Using the same argmax softening procedure as above, they arrive at an approximation to the reparametrization trick which mitigates some of the gradient's variance introduced by sampling. The approximation is[3]:

$$\tilde{e}_{i-1} = \sum_{y} e(y) \cdot \frac{\exp\left(\alpha\left(s_{i-1}(y) + G_y\right)\right)}{\sum_{y'} \exp\left(\alpha\left(s_{i-1}(y') + G_{y'}\right)\right)}$$

We will use this 'concrete' approximation of softmax sampling in our relaxation of scheduled sampling with a sample-based decoder. We discuss details in the next section. Note that our original motivation based on removing discontinuity does not strictly apply to this sampling procedure, which still yields a stochastic gradient due to sampling from the Gumbel distribution. However, this approach is conceptually related to greedy relaxations since, here, the soft argmax reparametrization reduces gradient variance which may yield a more informative training signal. Intuitively, this approach results in the gradient of the loss to be more aware of the sampling procedure compared to naive scheduled sampling and hence carries forward information about decisions made at previous steps. The empirical results, discussed later, show similar gains to the greedy scenario.

3.3 Differentiable Relaxed Decoders

With the argmax relaxation introduced above, we have a recipe for a fully differentiable greedy decoder designed to produce informative gradients near change points. Our final training network for scheduled sampling with relaxed greedy decoding is shown in Figure 2. Instead of conditioning the current hidden state, h_i, on the argmax embedding from the previous step, $\hat{e}_{i-1}$, we use the α-soft argmax embedding, $\bar{e}_{i-1}$, defined in Section 3.1. This removes the discontinuity in the original greedy scheduled sampling objective by passing a linear combination of embeddings, dominated by the argmax, to the next step. Figure 1

---

[2] Assuming there are no ties for the sake of simplicity.

[3] This is different from using the expected softmax embedding because our approach approximates the actual sampling process instead of linearly weighting the embeddings by their softmax probabilities

illustrates the effect of varying α. As α increases, we more closely approximate the greedy decoder.

As in standard scheduled sampling, here we minimize the cross-entropy based loss at each time step. Hence the computational complexity of our approach is comparable to standard seq2seq training. As we discuss in Section 5, mixing model predictions randomly with ground truth symbols during training (Bengio et al., 2015; Daumé et al., 2009; Ross et al., 2011), while annealing the probability of using the ground truth with each epoch, results in better models and more stable training. As a result, training is reliant on the *annealing schedule* of two important hyperparameters: i) ground truth mixing probability and ii) the α *parameter* used for approximating the argmax function. For output prediction, at each time step, we can still output the hard argmax, depicted in Figure 2.

For the case of scheduled sampling with sample-based training–where decisions are sampled rather than chosen greedily (Bengio et al., 2015)–we conduct experiments using a related training procedure. Instead of using soft argmax, we use the soft sample embedding, $\tilde{e}_{i-1}$, defined in Section 3.2. Apart from this difference, training is carried out using the same procedure.

4 Related Work

Gormley et al. (2015)'s approximation-aware training is conceptually related, but focuses on variational decoding procedures. Hoang et al. (2017) also propose continuous relaxations of decoders, but are focused on developing better inference procedures. Grefenstette et al. (2015) successfully use a soft approximation to argmax in neural stack mechanisms. Finally, Ranzato et al. (2016) experiment with a similarly motivated objective that was not fully continuous, but found it performed worse than the standard training.

5 Experimental Setup

We perform experiments with machine translation (MT) and named entity recognition (NER).

Data: For MT, we use the same dataset (the German-English portion of the IWSLT 2014 machine translation evaluation campaign (Cettolo et al., 2014)), preprocessing and data splits as Ranzato et al. (2016). For named entity recognition, we use the CONLL 2003 shared task data (Tjong Kim Sang and De Meulder, 2003) for German language and use the provided data splits. We perform no preprocessing on the data.The output vocabulary length for MT is 32000 and 10 for NER.

Implementation details: For MT, we use a seq2seq model with a simple attention mechanism (Bahdanau et al., 2015), a bidirectional LSTM encoder (1 layer, 256 units), and an LSTM decoder (1 layer, 256 units). For NER, we use a seq2seq model with an LSTM encoder (1 layer, 64 units) and an LSTM decoder (1 layer, 64 units) with a fixed attention mechanism that deterministically attends to the ith input token when decoding the ith output, and hence does not involve learning of attention parameters. [4]

Hyperparameter tuning: We start by training with actual ground truth sequences for the first epoch and decay the probability of selecting the ground truth token as an inverse sigmoid (Bengio et al., 2015) of epochs with a decay strength parameter k. We also tuned for different values of α and explore the effect of varying α exponentially (annealing) with the epochs. In table 1, we report results for the best performing configuration of decay parameter and the α parameter on the validation set. To account for variance across randomly started runs, we ran multiple random restarts (RR) for all the systems evaluated and always used the RR with the best validation set score to calculate test performance.

Comparison We report validation and test metrics for NER and MT tasks in Table 1, F1 and BLEU respectively. 'Greedy' in the table refers to scheduled sampling with soft argmax decisions (either soft or hard) and 'Sample' refers the corresponding reparametrized sample-based decoding scenario. We compare our approach with two baselines: standard cross-entropy loss minimization for seq2seq models ('Baseline CE') and the standard scheduled sampling procedure (Bengio et al. (2015)). We report results for two variants of our approach: one with a fixed α parameter throughout the training procedure (α-soft fixed), and the other in which we vary α exponentially with the number of epochs (α-soft annealed).

---

[4]*Fixed attention* refers to the scenario when we use the bidirectional LSTM encoder representation of the source sequence token at time step t while decoding at time step t instead of using a linear combination of all the input sequences weighted according to the attention parameters in the standard attention mechanism based models.

Table 1: Result on NER and MT. We compare our approach (α-soft argmax with fixed and annealed temperature) with standard cross entropy training (Baseline CE) and discontinuous scheduled sampling (Bengio et al. (2015)). 'Greedy' and 'Sample' refer to Section 3.1 and Section 3.2.

Training procedure	NER (F1)				MT (BLEU)			
	Dev		Test		Dev		Test	
Baseline CE	49.43		53.32		20.35		19.11	
	Greedy		Sample		Greedy		Sample	
	Dev	Test	Dev	Test	Dev	Test	Dev	Test
Bengio et al. (2015)	49.75	54.83	50.90	54.60	20.52	19.85	20.40	19.69
α-soft fixed	51.65	55.88	51.13	56.25	21.32	20.28	20.48	19.69
α-soft annealed	51.43	**56.33**	50.99	54.20	21.28	20.18	21.36	**20.60**

6 Results

All three approaches improve over the standard cross-entropy based seq2seq training. Moreover, both approaches using continuous relaxations (greedy and sample-based) outperform standard scheduled sampling (Bengio et al., 2015). The best results for NER were obtained with the relaxed greedy decoder with annealed α which yielded an F1 gain of +3.1 over the standard seq2seq baseline and a gain of +1.5 F1 over standard scheduled sampling. For MT, we obtain the best results with the relaxed sample-based decoder, which yielded a gain of +1.5 BLEU over standard seq2seq and a gain of +0.75 BLEU over standard scheduled sampling.

We observe that the reparametrized sample-based method, although not fully continuous end-to-end unlike the soft greedy approach, results in good performance on both the tasks, particularly MT. This might be an effect of stochastic exploration of the search space over the output sequences during training and hence we expect MT to benefit from sampling due to a much larger search space associated with it. We also observe that annealing α results in good performance which suggests that a smoother approximation to the loss function in the initial stages of training is helpful in guiding the learning in the right direction. However, in our experiments we noticed that the performance while annealing α was sensitive to the hyperparameter associated with the annealing schedule of the mixing probability in scheduled sampling during training.

The computational complexity of our approach is comparable to that of standard seq2seq training. However, instead of a vocabulary-sized max and lookup, our approach requires a matrix multiplication. Practically, we observed that on GPU hardware, all the models for both the tasks had similar speeds which suggests that our approach leads to accuracy gains without compromising run-time. Moreover, as shown in Table 2, we observe that a gradual decay of mixing probability consistently compared favorably to more aggressive decay schedules. We also observed that the 'always sample' case of relaxed greedy decoding, in which we never mix in ground truth inputs (see Bengio et al. (2015)), worked well for NER but resulted in unstable training for MT. We reckon that this is an effect of large difference between the search space associated with NER and MT.

7 Conclusion

Our positive results indicate that mechanisms for credit assignment can be useful when added to the models that aim to ameliorate exposure bias. Further, our results suggest that continuous relaxations of the argmax operation can be used as effective approximations to hard decoding during training.

Acknowledgements

We thank Graham Neubig for helpful discussions. We also thank the three anonymous reviewers for their valuable feedback.

k	100	10	1	*Always*
NER (F1)	56.33	55.88	55.30	54.83

Table 2: Effect of different schedules for scheduled sampling on NER. k is the decay strength parameter. Higher k corresponds to gentler decay schedules. *Always* refers to the case when predictions at the previous predictions are always passed on as inputs to the next step.

References

Daniel Andor, Chris Alberti, David Weiss, Aliaksei Severyn, Alessandro Presta, Kuzman Ganchev, Slav Petrov, and Michael Collins. 2016. Globally normalized transition-based neural networks. In *Association for Computational Linguistics*.

Dzmitry Bahdanau, Philemon Brakel, Kelvin Xu, Anirudh Goyal, Ryan Lowe, Joelle Pineau, Aaron Courville, and Yoshua Bengio. 2017. An actor-critic algorithm for sequence prediction. In *International Conference on Learning Representations*.

Dzmitry Bahdanau, Kyunghyun Cho, and Yoshua Bengio. 2015. Neural machine translation by jointly learning to align and translate. In *International Conference on Learning Representations*.

Samy Bengio, Oriol Vinyals, Navdeep Jaitly, and Noam Shazeer. 2015. Scheduled sampling for sequence prediction with recurrent neural networks. In *Advances in Neural Information Processing Systems*. pages 1171–1179.

Mauro Cettolo, Jan Niehues, Sebastian Stüker, Luisa Bentivogli, and Marcello Federico. 2014. Report on the 11th iwslt evaluation campaign, iwslt 2014. In *Proceedings of the International Workshop on Spoken Language Translation, Hanoi, Vietnam*.

Hal Daumé, John Langford, and Daniel Marcu. 2009. Search-based structured prediction. *Machine learning* 75(3):297–325.

Hal Daumé III and Daniel Marcu. 2005. Learning as search optimization: Approximate large margin methods for structured prediction. In *Proceedings of the 22nd international conference on Machine learning*. ACM, pages 169–176.

Matthew R. Gormley, Mark Dredze, and Jason Eisner. 2015. Approximation-aware dependency parsing by belief propagation. *Transactions of the Association for Computational Linguistics (TACL)* .

Edward Grefenstette, Karl Moritz Hermann, Mustafa Suleyman, and Phil Blunsom. 2015. Learning to transduce with unbounded memory. In *Advances in Neural Information Processing Systems*. pages 1828–1836.

Cong Duy Vu Hoang, Gholamreza Haffari, and Trevor Cohn. 2017. Decoding as continuous optimization in neural machine translation. *arXiv preprint arXiv:1701.02854* .

Eric Jang, Shixiang Gu, and Ben Poole. 2016. Categorical reparameterization with gumbel-softmax. In *International Conference on Learning Representations*.

Chris J Maddison, Andriy Mnih, and Yee Whye Teh. 2017. The concrete distribution: A continuous relaxation of discrete random variables. In *International Conference on Learning Representations*.

Marc'Aurelio Ranzato, Sumit Chopra, Michael Auli, and Wojciech Zaremba. 2016. Sequence level training with recurrent neural networks. In *International Conference on Learning Representations*.

Stéphane Ross, Geoffrey J Gordon, and Drew Bagnell. 2011. A reduction of imitation learning and structured prediction to no-regret online learning. In *AISTATS*. volume 1, page 6.

Alexander M Rush, Sumit Chopra, and Jason Weston. 2015. A neural attention model for abstractive sentence summarization. In *Empirical Methods in Natural Language Processing*.

Iulian V Serban, Alessandro Sordoni, Yoshua Bengio, Aaron Courville, and Joelle Pineau. 2015. Building end-to-end dialogue systems using generative hierarchical neural network models. In *AAAI'16 Proceedings of the Thirtieth AAAI Conference on Artificial Intelligence*.

Ilya Sutskever, Oriol Vinyals, and Quoc V Le. 2014. Sequence to sequence learning with neural networks. In *Advances in neural information processing systems*. pages 3104–3112.

Erik F Tjong Kim Sang and Fien De Meulder. 2003. Introduction to the conll-2003 shared task: Language-independent named entity recognition. In *Proceedings of the seventh conference on Natural language learning at HLT-NAACL 2003-Volume 4*. Association for Computational Linguistics, pages 142–147.

Sam Wiseman and Alexander M Rush. 2016. Sequence-to-sequence learning as beam-search optimization. In *Empirical Methods in Natural Language Processing*.

Kelvin Xu, Jimmy Ba, Ryan Kiros, Kyunghyun Cho, Aaron C Courville, Ruslan Salakhutdinov, Richard S Zemel, and Yoshua Bengio. 2015. Show, attend and tell: Neural image caption generation with visual attention. In *ICML*. volume 14, pages 77–81.

A Deep Network with Visual Text Composition Behavior

Hongyu Guo

National Research Council Canada

1200 Montreal Road, Ottawa, Ontario, K1A 0R6

hongyu.guo@nrc-cnrc.gc.ca

Abstract

While natural languages are compositional, how state-of-the-art neural models achieve compositionality is still unclear. We propose a deep network, which not only achieves competitive accuracy for text classification, but also exhibits compositional behavior. That is, while creating hierarchical representations of a piece of text, such as a sentence, the lower layers of the network distribute their layer-specific attention weights to individual words. In contrast, the higher layers compose meaningful phrases and clauses, whose lengths increase as the networks get deeper until fully composing the sentence.

1 Introduction

Deep neural networks leverage task-specific architectures to develop hierarchical representations of the input, where higher level representations are derived from lower level features (Conneau et al., 2016). Such hierarchical representations have visually demonstrated compositionality in image processing, i.e., pixels combine to form shapes and then contours (Farabet et al., 2013; Zeiler and Fergus, 2014). Natural languages are also compositional, i.e., words combine to form phrases and then sentences. Yet unlike in vision, how deep neural models in NLP, which mainly operate on distributed word embeddings, achieve compositionality, is still unclear (Li et al., 2015, 2016).

We propose an Attention Gated Transformation (AGT) network, where each layer's feature generation is gated by a layer-specific attention mechanism (Bahdanau et al., 2014). Specifically, through distributing its attention to the original given text, each layer of the networks tends to *in-*

crementally retrieve new words and phrases from the original text. The new knowledge is then combined with the previous layer's features to create the current layer's representation, thus resulting in composing longer or new phrases and clauses while creating higher layers' representations of the text.

Experiments on the Stanford Sentiment Treebank (Socher et al., 2013) dataset show that the AGT method not only achieves very competitive accuracy, but also exhibits compositional behavior via its layer-specific attention. We empirically show that, given a piece of text, e.g., a sentence, the lower layers of the networks select individual words, e.g, negative and conjunction words *not* and *though*, while the higher layers aim at composing meaningful phrases and clauses such as negation phrase *not so much*, where the phrase length increases as the networks get deeper until fully composing the whole sentence. Interestingly, after composing the sentence, the compositions of different sentence phrases compete to become the dominating features of the end task.

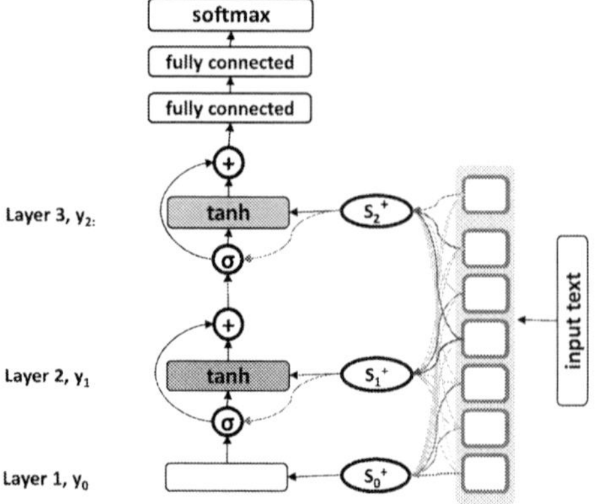

Figure 1: An AGT network with three layers.

Proceedings of the 55th Annual Meeting of the Association for Computational Linguistics (Short Papers), pages 372–377

Vancouver, Canada, July 30 - August 4, 2017. ©2017 Association for Computational Linguistics

https://doi.org/10.18653/v1/P17-2059

2 Attention Gated Transformation Network

Our AGT network was inspired by the Highway Networks (Srivastava et al., 2015a,b), where each layer is equipped with a *transform gate*.

2.1 Transform Gate for Information Flow

Consider a feedforward neural network with multiple layers. Each layer l typically applies a non-linear transformation f (e.g., $tanh$, parameterized by W_l^f), on its input, which is the output of the most recent previous layer (i.e., y_{l-1}), to produce its output y_l. Here, $l = 0$ indicates the first layer and y_0 is equal to the given input text x, namely $y_0 = x$:

$$y_l = f(y_{l-1}, W_l^f) \qquad (1)$$

While in a highway network (the left column of Figure 1), an additional non-linear transform gate function T_l is added to the $l^{th}(l > 0)$ layer:

$$y_l = f(y_{l-1}, W_l^f)T_l + y_{l-1}(1 - T_l) \qquad (2)$$

where the function T_l expresses how much of the representation y_l is produced by transforming the y_{l-1} (first term in Equation 2), and how much is just carrying from y_{l-1} (second term in Equation 2). Here T_l is typically defined as:

$$T_l = \sigma(W_l^t y_{l-1} + b_l^t) \qquad (3)$$

where W_l^t is the weight matrix and b_l^t the bias vector; σ is the non-linear activation function.

With transform gate T, the networks learn to decide if a feature transformation is needed at each layer. Suppose σ represents a sigmoid function. In such case, the output of T lies between zero and one. Consequently, when the transform gate is one, the networks pass through the transformation f over y_{l-1} and block the pass of input y_{l-1}; when the gate is zero, the networks pass through the unmodified y_{l-1}, while the transformation f over y_{l-1} is suppressed.

The left column of Figure 1 reflects the highway networks as proposed by (Srivastava et al., 2015b). Our AGT method adds the right two columns of Figure 1. That is, 1) the transform gate T_l now is not a function of y_{l-1}, but a function of the selection vector s_l^+, which is determined by the attention distributed to the given input x by the lth layer (will be discussed next), and 2) the function f takes as input the concatenation of y_{l-1} and s_l^+

to create feature representation y_l. These changes result in an attention gated transformation when forming hierarchical representations of the text.

2.2 Attention Gated Transformation

In AGT, the activation of the transform gate at each layer depends on a layer-specific attention mechanism. Formally, given a piece of text x, such as a sentence with N words, it can be represented as a matrix $B \in \mathbb{R}^{N \times d}$. Each row of the matrix corresponds to one word, which is represented by a d-dimensional vector as provided by a learned word embedding table. Consequently, the selection vector s_l^+, for the lth layer, is the softmax weighted sum over the N word vectors in B:

$$s_l^+ = \sum_{n=1}^{N} d_{l,n} B[n : n] \qquad (4)$$

with the weight (i.e., attention) $d_{l,n}$ computed as:

$$d_{l,n} = \frac{exp(m_{l,n})}{\sum_{n=1}^{N} exp(m_{l,n})} \qquad (5)$$

$$m_{l,n} = w_l^m \tanh(W_l^m(B[n : n])) \qquad (6)$$

here, w_l^m and W_l^m are the weight vector and weight matrix, respectively. By varying the attention weight $d_{l,n}$, the s_l^+ can focus on different rows of the matrix B, namely different words of the given text x, as illustrated by different color curves connecting to s^+ in Figure 1. Intuitively, one can consider s^+ as a learned word selection component: choosing different sets of words of the given text x by distributing its distinct attention.

Having built one s^+ for each layer from the given text x, the activation of the transform gate for layer l ($l > 0$) (i.e., Equation 3) is calculated:

$$T_l = \sigma(W_l^t s_l^+ + b_l^t) \qquad (7)$$

To generate feature representation y_l, the function f takes as input the concatenation of y_{l-1} and s_l^+. That is, Equation 2 becomes:

$$y_l = \begin{cases} s_l^+, & l = 0 \\ f([y_{l-1}; s_l^+], W_l^f)T_l + y_{l-1}(1 - T_l), & l > 0 \end{cases} \qquad (8)$$

where [...;...] denotes concatenation. Thus, at each layer l, the gate T_l can regulate either passing through y_{l-1} to form y_l, or retrieving novel knowledge from the input text x to augment y_{l-1} to create a better representation for y_l.

Finally, as depicted in Figure 1, the feature representation of the last layer of the AGT is fed into two fully connected layers followed by a softmax function to produce a distribution over the possible target classes. For training, we use multi-class cross entropy loss.

Note that, Equation 8 indicates that the representation y_l depends on both s_l^+ and y_{l-1}. In other words, although Equation 7 states that the gate activation at layer l is computed by s_l^+, the gate activation is also affected by y_{l-1}, which embeds the information from the layers below l.

Intuitively, the AGT networks are encouraged to consider new words/phrases from the input text at higher layers. Consider the fact that the s_0^+ at the bottom layer of the AGT only deploys a linear transformation of the bag-of-words features. If no new words are used at higher layers of the networks, it will be challenge for the AGT to sufficiently explore different combinations of word sets of the given text, which may be important for building an accurate classifier. In contrast, through tailoring its attention for new words at different layers, the AGT enables the words selected by a layer to be effectively combined with words/phrases selected by its previous layers to benefit the accuracy of the classification task (more discussions are presented in Section 3.2).

3 Experimental Studies

3.1 Main Results

The Stanford Sentiment Treebank data contains 11,855 movie reviews (Socher et al., 2013). We use the same splits for training, dev, and test data as in (Kim, 2014) to predict the fine-grained 5-class sentiment categories of the sentences. For comparison purposes, following (Kim, 2014; Kalchbrenner et al., 2014; Lei et al., 2015), we trained the models using both phrases and sentences, but only evaluate sentences at test time. Also, we initialized all of the word embeddings (Cherry and Guo, 2015; Chen and Guo, 2015) using the 300 dimensional pre-trained vectors from GloVe (Pennington et al., 2014). We learned 15 layers with 200 dimensions each, which requires us to project the 300 dimensional word vectors; we implemented this using a linear transformation, whose weight matrix and bias term are shared across all words, followed by

a tanh activation. For optimization, we used Adadelta (Zeiler, 2012), with learning rate of 0.0005, mini-batch of 50, transform gate bias of 1, and dropout (Srivastava et al., 2014) rate of 0.2. All these hyperparameters were determined through experiments on the validation-set.

AGT	50.5
high-order CNN	**51.2**
tree-LSTM	51.0
DRNN	49.8
PVEC	48.7
DCNN	48.5
DAN	48.2
CNN-MC	47.4
CNN	47.2
RNTN	45.7
NBoW	44.5
RNN	43.2
SVM	38.3

Table 1: Test-set accuracies obtained; results except the AGT are drawn from (Lei et al., 2015).

Figure 2: Soft attention distribution (top) and phrase length distribution (bottom) on the test set.

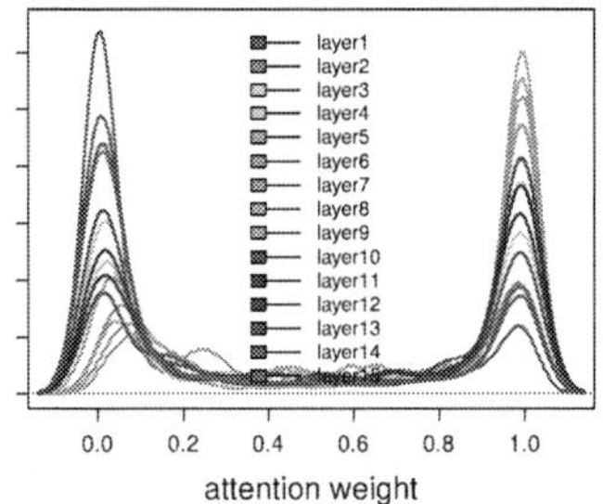

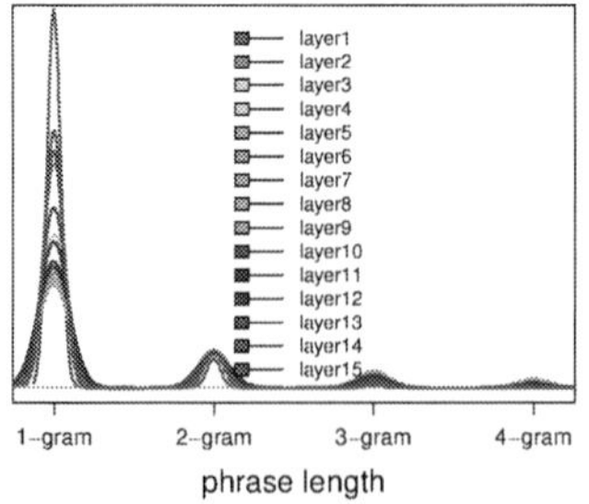

Table 1 presents the test-set accuracies obtained by different strategies. Results in Table 1 indicate that the AGT method achieved very competitive accuracy (with 50.5%), when compared to the state-of-the-art results obtained by the tree-LSTM (51.0%) (Tai et al., 2015; Zhu et al., 2015) and high-order CNN approaches (51.2%) (Lei et al., 2015).

Top subfigure in Figure 2 depicts the distribu-

Figure 3: Transform gate activities of the test-set (top) and the first sentence in Figure 4 (bottom).

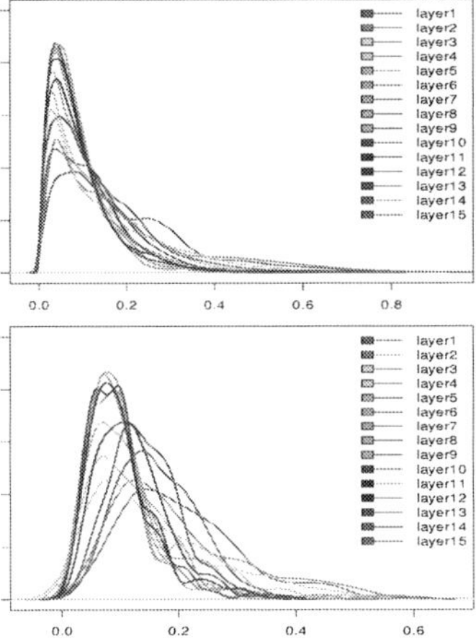

tions of the attention weights created by different layers on all test data, where the attention weights of all words in a sentence, i.e., $d_{l,n}$ in Equation 4, are normalized to the range between 0 and 1 within the sentence. The figure indicates that AGT generated very spiky attention distribution. That is, most of the attention weights are either 1 or 0. Based on these narrow, peaked bell curves formed by the normal distributions for the attention weights of 1 and 0, we here consider a word has been *selected* by the networks if its attention weight is larger than 0.95, i.e., receiving more than 95% of the full attention, and a phrase has been *composed and selected* if a set of consecutive words all have been selected.

In the bottom subfigure of Figure 2 we present the distribution of the phrase lengths on the test set. This figure indicates that the middle layers of the networks e.g., 8th and 9th, have longer phrases (green and blue curves) than others, while the layers at the two ends contain shorter phrases (red and pink curves).

In Figure 3, we also presented the transform gate activities on all test sentences (top) and that of the first example sentence in Figure 4 (bottom). These curves suggest that the transform gates at the middle layers (green and blue curves) tended to be close to zero, indicating the pass-through of lower layers' representations. On the contrary, the gates at the two ends (red and pink curves) tended to be away from zero with large tails, implying the retrieval of new knowledge from the input text. These are consistent with the results below.

Figure 4 presents three sentences with various lengths from the test set, with the attention weights numbered and then highlighted in heat map. Figure 4 suggests that the lower layers of the networks selected individual words, while the higher layers aimed at phrases. For example, the first and second layers seem to *select* individual words carrying strong sentiment (e.g., *predictable*, *bad*, *never* and *delicate*), and conjunction and negation words (e.g., *though* and *not*). Also, meaningful phrases were *composed and selected* by later layers, such as *not so much, not only... but also, bad taste, bad luck, emotional development*, and *big screen*. In addition, in the middle layer, i.e., the 8th layer, the whole sentences were composed by filtering out uninformative words, resulting in concise versions, as follows (selected words and phrases are highlighted in color blocks).

1) *though* plot *predictable* movie never feels formulaic *attention* nuances *emotional development* delicate characters
2) *bad company leaves* bad taste *not only* bad luck *but also* staleness *script*
3) *not so much* movie *picture* big screen

Interestingly, if relaxing the word selection criteria, e.g., including words receiving more than the median, rather than 95%, of the full attention, the sentences recruited more conjunction and modification words, e.g., *because, for, a, its* and *on*, thus becoming more readable and fluent:

1) *though* plot is predictable *movie never feels formulaic* because *attention is on* nuances *emotional development* delicate characters
2) *bad company leaves a bad taste* not only because *its bad luck timing* but also *staleness* its script
3) *not so much a movie* a picture book for *big screen*

Now, consider the AGT's compositional behavior for a specific sentence, e.g., the last sentence in Figure 4. The first layer solely *selected* the word *not* (with attention weight of 1 and all other words with weights close to 0), but the 2nd to 4th layers gradually pulled out new words *book, screen* and *movie* from the given text. Incrementally, the 5th and 6th layers further *selected* words to form phrases *not so much, picture book*, and *big screen*. Finally, the 7th and 8th layers added some

Figure 4: Three sentences from the test set and their attention received from the 15 layers (L1 to L15).

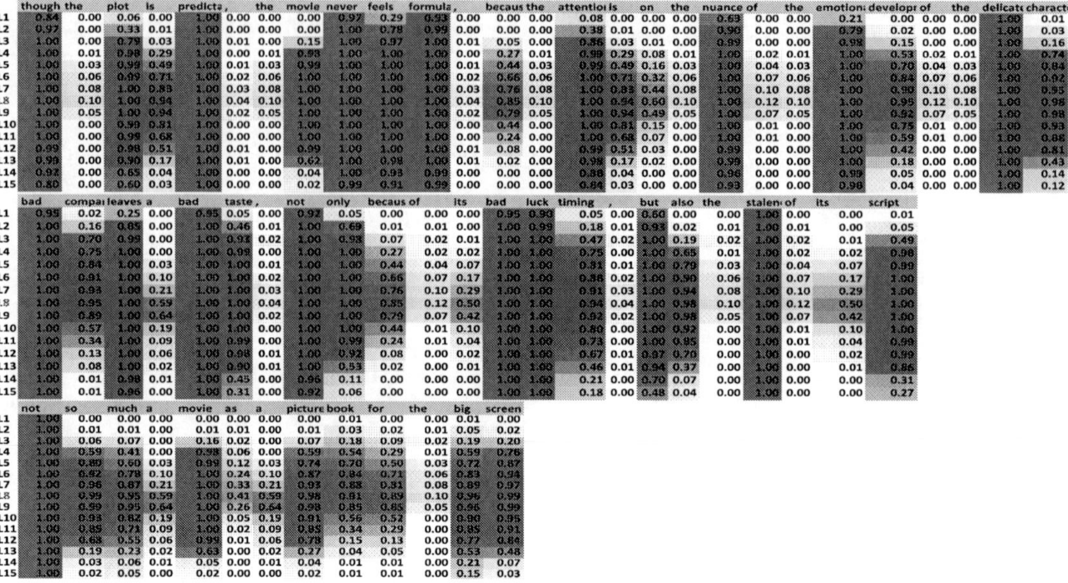

conjunction and quantification words *a* and *for* to make the sentence more fluent. This recursive composing process resulted in the sentence "*not so much a movie a picture book for big screen*".

Interestingly, Figures 4 and 2 also imply that, after composing the sentences by the middle layer, the AGT networks shifted to re-focus on shorter phrases and informative words. Our analysis on the transform gate activities suggests that, during this re-focusing stage the compositions of sentence phrases competed to each others, as well as to the whole sentence composition, for the dominating task-specific features to represent the text.

3.2 Further Observations

As discussed at the end of Section 2.2, intuitively, including new words at different layers allows the networks to more effectively explore different combinations of word sets of the given text than that of using all words only at the bottom layer of the networks. Empirically, we observed that, if with only s_0^+ in the AGT network, namely removing s_i^+ for $i > 0$, the test-set accuracy dropped from 50.5% to 48.5%. In other words, transforming a linear combination of the bag-of-words features was insufficient for obtaining sufficient accuracy for the classification task. For instance, if being augmented with two more selection vectors s_i^+, namely removing s_i^+ for $i > 2$, the AGT was able to improve its accuracy to 49.0%.

Also, we observed that the AGT networks tended to select informative words at the lower layers. This may be caused by the recursive form of Equation 8, which suggests that the words retrieved by s_0^+ have more chance to combine with and influence the selection of other feature words. In our study, we found that, for example, the top 3 most frequent words selected by the first layer of the AGT networks were all negation words: *n't*, *never*, and *not*. These are important words for sentiment classification (Zhu et al., 2014).

In addition, like the transform gate in the Highway networks (Srivastava et al., 2015a) and the forget gate in the LSTM (Gers et al., 2000), the attention-based transform gate in the AGT networks is sensitive to its bias initialization. We found that initializing the bias to one encouraged the compositional behavior of the AGT networks.

4 Conclusion and Future Work

We have presented a novel deep network. It not only achieves very competitive accuracy for text classification, but also exhibits interesting text compositional behavior, which may shed light on understanding how neural models work in NLP tasks. In the future, we aim to apply the AGT networks to incrementally generating natural text (Guo, 2015; Hu et al., 2017).

References

Dzmitry Bahdanau, Kyunghyun Cho, and Yoshua Bengio. 2014. Neural machine translation by jointly learning to align and translate. In *ICLR 2015*.

Boxing Chen and Hongyu Guo. 2015. Representation based translation evaluation metrics. In *ACL (2)*. pages 150–155.

Colin Cherry and Hongyu Guo. 2015. The unreasonable effectiveness of word representations for twitter named entity recognition. In *HLT-NAACL*. pages 735–745.

Alexis Conneau, Holger Schwenk, Loïc Barrault, and Yann LeCun. 2016. Very deep convolutional networks for natural language processing. *CoRR* abs/1606.01781.

Clément Farabet, Camille Couprie, Laurent Najman, and Yann LeCun. 2013. Learning hierarchical features for scene labeling. *IEEE Trans. Pattern Anal. Mach. Intell.* 35(8):1915–1929.

Felix A. Gers, Jürgen A. Schmidhuber, and Fred A. Cummins. 2000. Learning to forget: Continual prediction with lstm. *Neural Comput.* 12(10):2451–2471.

Hongyu Guo. 2015. Generating text with deep reinforcement learning. In *NIPS2015 Deep Reinforcement Learning Workshop*.

Zhiting Hu, Zichao Yang, Xiaodan Liang, Ruslan Salakhutdinov, and Eric P Xing. 2017. Controllable text generation. *arXiv preprint arXiv:1703.00955* .

Nal Kalchbrenner, Edward Grefenstette, and Phil Blunsom. 2014. A convolutional neural network for modelling sentences. *CoRR* abs/1404.2188.

Yoon Kim. 2014. Convolutional neural networks for sentence classification. *CoRR* abs/1408.5882.

Tao Lei, Regina Barzilay, and Tommi S. Jaakkola. 2015. Molding cnns for text: non-linear, nonconsecutive convolutions. *CoRR* abs/1508.04112.

Jiwei Li, Xinlei Chen, Eduard H. Hovy, and Dan Jurafsky. 2015. Visualizing and understanding neural models in NLP. *CoRR* abs/1506.01066.

Jiwei Li, Will Monroe, and Dan Jurafsky. 2016. Understanding neural networks through representation erasure. *arXiv preprint arXiv:1612.08220* .

Jeffrey Pennington, Richard Socher, and Christopher D Manning. 2014. Glove: Global vectors for word representation. In *EMNLP*. volume 14, pages 1532–43.

Richard Socher, Alex Perelygin, Jean Y. Wu, Jason Chuang, Christopher D. Manning, Andrew Y. Ng, and Christopher Potts. 2013. Recursive deep models for semantic compositionality over a sentiment treebank. In *EMNLP '13*.

Nitish Srivastava, Geoffrey Hinton, Alex Krizhevsky, Ilya Sutskever, and Ruslan Salakhutdinov. 2014. Dropout: A simple way to prevent neural networks from overfitting. *J. Mach. Learn. Res.* 15(1).

Rupesh Kumar Srivastava, Klaus Greff, and Jürgen Schmidhuber. 2015a. Highway networks. *CoRR* abs/1505.00387.

Rupesh Kumar Srivastava, Klaus Greff, and Jürgen Schmidhuber. 2015b. Training very deep networks. In *Proceedings of the 28th International Conference on Neural Information Processing Systems*. NIPS'15, pages 2377–2385.

Kai Sheng Tai, Richard Socher, and Christopher D. Manning. 2015. Improved semantic representations from tree-structured long short-term memory networks. *CoRR* abs/1503.00075.

Matthew D. Zeiler. 2012. ADADELTA: an adaptive learning rate method. *CoRR* abs/1212.5701.

Matthew D. Zeiler and Rob Fergus. 2014. Visualizing and understanding convolutional networks. In *Computer Vision - ECCV 2014 - 13th European Conference, Zurich, Switzerland, September 6-12, 2014, Proceedings, Part I*. pages 818–833.

Xiaodan Zhu, Hongyu Guo, Saif Mohammad, and Svetlana Kiritchenko. 2014. An empirical study on the effect of negation words on sentiment. In *ACL (1)*. pages 304–313.

Xiaodan Zhu, Parinaz Sobhani, and Hongyu Guo. 2015. Long short-term memory over recursive structures. In *ICML*. pages 1604–1612.

Neural System Combination for Machine Translation

Long Zhou[†], Wenpeng Hu[†], Jiajun Zhang[†*], Chengqing Zong[††]
[†]University of Chinese Academy of Sciences, Beijing, China
National Laboratory of Pattern Recognition, CASIA, Beijing, China
[‡]CAS Center for Excellence in Brain Science and Intelligence Technology, Shanghai, China
{long.zhou,wenpeng.hu,jjzhang,cqzong}@nlpr.ia.ac.cn

Abstract

Neural machine translation (NMT) becomes a new approach to machine translation and generates much more fluent results compared to statistical machine translation (SMT). However, SMT is usually better than NMT in translation adequacy. It is therefore a promising direction to combine the advantages of both NMT and SMT. In this paper, we propose a neural system combination framework leveraging multi-source NMT, which takes as input the outputs of NMT and SMT systems and produces the final translation. Extensive experiments on the Chinese-to-English translation task show that our model archives significant improvement by 5.3 BLEU points over the best single system output and 3.4 BLEU points over the state-of-the-art traditional system combination methods.

1 Introduction

Neural machine translation has significantly improved the quality of machine translation in recent several years (Kalchbrenner and Blunsom, 2013; Sutskever et al., 2014; Bahdanau et al., 2015; Junczys-Dowmunt et al., 2016a). Although most sentences are more fluent than translations by statistical machine translation (SMT) (Koehn et al., 2003; Chiang, 2005), NMT has a problem to address translation adequacy especially for the rare and unknown words. Additionally, it suffers from over-translation and under-translation to some extent (Tu et al., 2016). Compared to N-MT, SMT, such as phrase-based machine translation (PBMT, (Koehn et al., 2003)) and hierarchical phrase-based machine translation (HPMT,

(Chiang, 2005)), does not need to limit the vocabulary and can guarantee translation coverage of source sentences. It is obvious that NMT and SMT have different strength and weakness. In order to take full advantages of both NMT and SMT, system combination can be a good choice.

Traditionally, system combination has been explored respectively in sentence-level, phrase-level, and word-level (Kumar and Byrne, 2004; Feng et al., 2009; Chen et al., 2009). Among them, word-level combination approaches that adopt confusion network for decoding have been quite successful (Rosti et al., 2007; Ayan et al., 2008; Freitag et al., 2014). However, these approaches are mainly designed for SMT without considering the features of NMT results. NMT opts to produce diverse words and free word order, which are quite different from SMT. And this will make it hard to construct a consistent confusion network. Furthermore, traditional system combination approaches cannot guarantee the fluency of the final translation results.

In this paper, we propose a neural system combination framework, which is adapted from the multi-source NMT model (Zoph and Knight, 2016). Different encoders are employed to model the semantics of the source language input and each best translation produced by different NMT and SMT systems. The encoders produce multiple context vector representations, from which the decoder generates the final output word by word. Since the same training data is used for NMT, SMT and neural system combination, we further design a smart strategy to simulate the real training data for neural system combination.

Specifically, we make the following contributions in this paper:

- We propose a neural system combination method, which is adapted from multi-source

---

[*]Corresponding author.

Proceedings of the 55th Annual Meeting of the Association for Computational Linguistics (Short Papers), pages 378–384
Vancouver, Canada, July 30 - August 4, 2017. ©2017 Association for Computational Linguistics
https://doi.org/10.18653/v1/P17-2060

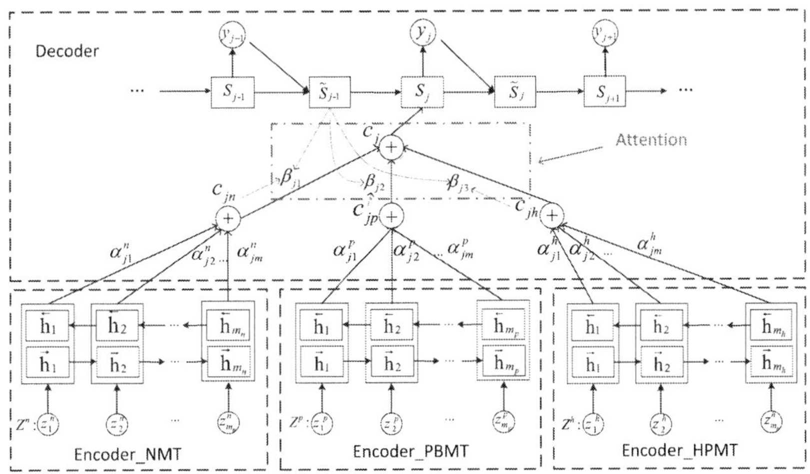

Figure 1: The architecture of Neural System Combination Model.

NMT model and can accommodate both source inputs and different system translations. It combines the fluency of NMT and adequacy (especially the ability to address rare words) of SMT.

- We design a good strategy to construct appropriate training data for neural system combination.

- The extensive experiments on Chinese-English translation show that our model archives significant improvement by 3.4 BLEU points over the state-of-the-art system combination methods and 5.3 BLEU points over the best individual system output.

2 Neural Machine Translation

The encoder-decoder NMT with an attention mechanism (Bahdanau et al., 2015) has been proposed to softly align each decoder state with the encoder states, and computes the conditional probability of the translation given the source sentence.

The encoder is a bidirectional neural network with gated recurrent units (GRU) (Cho et al., 2014) which reads an input sequence $X = (x_1, x_2, ..., x_m)$ and encodes it into a sequence of hidden states $H = h_1, h_2, ..., h_m$.

The decoder is a recurrent neural network that predicts a target sequence $Y = (y_1, y_2, ..., y_n)$. Each word y_j is predicted based on a recurrent hidden state s_j, the previously predicted word y_{j-1}, and a context vector c_j. c_j is obtained from the weighted sum of the annotations h_i. We use the latest implementation of attention-based NMT[1].

3 Neural System Combination for Machine Translation

Macherey and Och (2007) gave empirical evidence that these systems to be combined need to be almost uncorrelated in order to be beneficial for system combination. Since NMT and SMT are two kinds of translation models with large differences, we attempt to build a neural system combination model, which can take advantage of the different systems.

Model: Figure 1 illustrates the neural system combination framework, which can take as input the source sentence and the results of MT systems. Here, we use MT results as inputs to detail the model.

Formally, given the result sequences $Z(Z^n, Z^p,$ and $Z^h)$ of three MT systems for the same source sentence and previously generated target sequence $Y_{<j} = (y_1, y_2, ..., y_{j-1})$, the probability of the next target word y_j is

$$p(y_j|Y_{<j}, Z) = softmax(f(c_j, y_{j-1}, s_j)) \quad (1)$$

Here $f(.)$ is a non-linear function, y_{j-1} represents the word embedding of the previous prediction word, and s_j is the state of decoder at time step j, calculated by

$$s_j = GRU(\tilde{s}_{j-1}, c_j) \quad (2)$$

---

[1] https://github.com/nyu-dl/dl4mt-tutorial

System	MT03	MT04	MT05	MT06	Ave
PBMT	37.47	41.20	36.41	36.03	37.78
HPMT	**38.05**	**41.47**	**36.86**	36.04	**38.10**
NMT	37.91	38.95	36.02	**36.65**	37.38
Jane (Freitag et al., 2014)	39.83	42.75	38.63	39.10	40.08
Multi	40.64	44.81	38.80	38.26	40.63
Multi+Source	42.16	45.51	40.28	39.03	41.75
Multi+Ensemble	41.67	45.95	40.37	39.02	41.75
Multi+Source+Ensemble	**43.55**	**47.09**	**42.02**	**41.10**	**43.44**

Table 1: Translation results (BLEU score) for different machine translation and system combination methods. Jane is a open source machine translation system combination toolkit that uses confusion network decoding. **Best** and **important** results per category are highlighted.

$$\tilde{s}_{j-1} = GRU(s_{j-1}, y_{j-1}) \tag{3}$$

where s_{j-1} is previous hidden state, $\tilde{s}_{j-1}$ is an intermediate state. And c_j is the context vector of system combination obtained by attention mechanism, which is computed as weighted sum of the context vectors of three MT systems, just as illustrated in the middle part of Figure 1.

$$c_j = \sum_{k=1}^{K} \beta_{jk} c_{jk} \tag{4}$$

where K is the number of MT systems, and β_{jk} is a normalized item calculated as follows:

$$\beta_{jk} = \frac{exp(\tilde{s}_{j-1} \cdot c_{jk})}{\sum_{k'} exp(\tilde{s}_{j-1} \cdot c_{jk'})} \tag{5}$$

Here, we calculate kth MT system context c_{jk} as a weighted sum of the source annotations:

$$c_{jk} = \sum_{i=1}^{m} \alpha_{ji}^{k} h_i \tag{6}$$

where $h_i = [\overrightarrow{h}_i; \overleftarrow{h}_i]$ is the annotation of z_i from a bi-directional GRU, and its weight α_{ji}^{k} is computed by

$$\alpha_{ji}^{k} = \frac{exp(e_{ji})}{\sum_{l=1}^{m} exp(e_{jl})} \tag{7}$$

where $e_{ji} = v_a^T tanh(W_a \tilde{s}_{j-1} + U_a h_i)$ scores how well $\tilde{s}_{j-1}$ and h_i match.

Training Data Simulation: The neural system combination framework should be trained on the outputs of multiple translation systems and the gold target translations. In order to keep consistency in training and testing, we design a strategy to simulate the real scenario. We randomly divide the training corpus into two parts, then reciprocally train the MT system on one half and translate the source sentences of the other half into target translations. The MT translations and the gold target reference can be available.

4 Experiments

We perform our experiments on the Chinese-English translation task. The MT systems participating in system combination are PBMT, HPMT and NMT. The evaluation metric is case-insensitive BLEU (Papineni et al., 2002).

4.1 Data preparation

Our training data consists of 2.08M sentence pairs extracted from LDC corpus. We use NIST 2003 Chinese-English dataset as the validation set, NIST 2004-2006 datasets as test sets. We list all the translation methods as follows:

- **PBMT**: It is the start-of-the-art phrase-based SMT system. We use its default setting and train a 4-gram language model on the target portion of the bilingual training data.

- **HPMT**: It is a hierarchical phrase-based SMT system, which uses its default configuration as PBMT in Moses.

- **NMT**: It is an attention-based NMT system, with the same setting given in section 2.

4.2 Training Details

The hyper-parameters used in our neural combination system are described as follows. We limit both Chinese and English vocabulary to 30k in our experiments. The number of hidden units is 1000

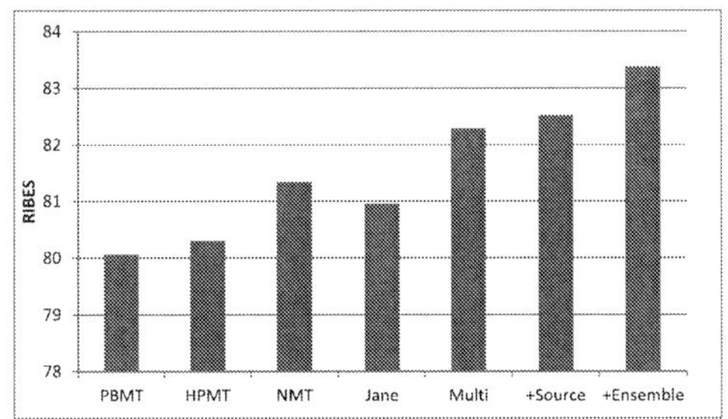

Figure 2: Translation results (RIBES score) for different machine translation and system combination methods.

System	MT03	MT04	MT05	MT06	Ave
NMT	1086	1145	1020	708	989.8
Ours	**869**	**1023**	**909**	**609**	**852.5**

Table 2: The number of unknown words in the results of NMT and our model.

System	MT03	MT04	MT05	MT06	Ave
E-NMT	39.14	40.78	37.31	37.89	38.78
Jane	40.61	43.28	39.05	39.18	40.53
Ours	**43.61**	**47.65**	**42.02**	**41.17**	**43.61**

Table 3: Translation results (BLEU score) when we replace original NMT with strong E-NMT, which uses ensemble strategy with four NMT models. All results of system combination are based on strong outputs of E-NMT.

and the word embedding dimension is 500 for all source and target word. The network parameters are updated with Adadelta algorithm. We adopt beam search with beam size b=10 at test time.

As to confusion-network-based system Jane, we use its default configuration and train a 4-gram language model on target data and 10M Xinhua portion of Gigaword corpus.

4.3 Main Results

We compare our neural combination system with the best individual engines, and the state-of-the-art traditional combination system Jane (Freitag et al., 2014). Table 1 shows the BLEU of different models on development data and test data. The BLEU score of the multi-source neural combination model is 2.53 higher than the best single model H-PMT. The source language input gives a further improvement of +1.12 BLEU points.

As shown in Table 1, Jane outperforms the best single MT system by 1.92 BLEU points. However, our neural combination system with source language gets an improvement of 1.67 BLEU points over Jane. Furthermore, when augmenting our neural combination system with ensemble decoding [2], it leads to another significant boost of +1.69 BLEU points.

4.4 Word Order of Translation

We evaluate word order by the automatic evaluation metrics RIBES (Isozaki et al., 2010), whose score is a metric based on rank correlation coefficients with word precision. RIBES is known to have stronger correlation with human judgements than BLEU for English as discussed in Isozaki et al. (2010).

Figure 2 illustrates experimental results of RIBES scores, which demonstrates that our neural combination model outperforms the best result of single MT system and Jane. Additionally, although BLEU point of Jane is higher than single NMT system, the word order of Jane is worse in terms of RIBES.

4.5 Rare and Unknown Words Translation

It is difficult for NMT systems to handle rare words, because low-frequency words in training data cannot capture latent translation mappings in neural network model. However, we do not need to limit the vocabulary in SMT, which are often able to translate rare words in training data. As shown in Table 2, the number of unknown words of our proposed model is 137 fewer than original NMT model.

Table 4 shows an example of system combination. The Chinese word zǔzhīwǎng is an out-of-vocabulary(OOV) for NMT and the baseline N-MT cannot correctly translate this word. Although PBMT and HPMT translate this word well, they does not conform to the grammar. By combining the merits of NMT and SMT, our model gets the correct translation.

4.6 Effect of Ensemble Decoding

The performance of candidate systems is very important to the result of system combination, and we use ensemble strategy with four NMT models to improve the performance of original NMT system. As shown in Table 3, the E-NMT with

---

[2]We use four neural combination models in ensemble model.

Source	海珊 也 与 恐怖 组织网 建立 了 联系 。
Pinyin	*hǎnshān yě yǔ kǒngbù zǔzhīwǎng jiànlì le liánxì* 。
Reference	hussein has also established ties with terrorist networks .
PBMT	hussein also has established relations and terrorist group .
HPMT	hussein also and terrorist group established relations .
NMT	hussein also established relations with UNK .
Jane	hussein also has established relations with .
Multi	hussein also has established relations with the terrorist group .

Table 4: Translation examples of single system, Jane and our proposed model.

ensemble strategy outperforms the original NMT system by +1.40 BLEU points, and it has become the best sytem in all MT systems, which is +0.68 BLEU points higher than HPMT.

After replacing original NMT with strong E-NMT , Jane outperforms original result by +0.45 BLEU points, and our model gets an improvement of +3.08 BLEU points over Jane. Experiments further demonstrate that our proposed model is effective and robust for system combination.

5 Related Work

The recently proposed neural machine translation has drawn more and more attention. Most of the existing approaches and models mainly focus on designing better attention models (Luong et al., 2015a; Mi et al., 2016a,b; Tu et al., 2016; Meng et al., 2016), better strategies for handling rare and unknown words (Luong et al., 2015b; Li et al., 2016; Zhang and Zong, 2016a; Sennrich et al., 2016b) , exploiting large-scale monolingual data (Cheng et al., 2016; Sennrich et al., 2016a; Zhang and Zong, 2016b), and integrating SMT techniques (Shen et al., 2016; Junczys-Dowmunt et al., 2016b; He et al., 2016).

Our focus in this work is aiming to take advantage of NMT and SMT by system combination, which attempts to find consensus translations among different machine translation systems. In past several years, word-level, phrase-level and sentence-level system combination methods were well studied (Bangalore et al., 2001; Rosti et al., 2008; Li and Zong, 2008; Li et al., 2009; Heafield and Lavie, 2010; Freitag et al., 2014; Ma and Mckeown, 2015; Zhu et al., 2016), and reported state-of-the-art performances in benchmarks for SMT. Here, we propose a neural system combination model which combines the advantages of NMT and SMT efficiently.

Recently, Niehues et al. (2016) use phrase-based SMT to pre-translate the inputs into target translations. Then a NMT system generates the final hypothesis using the pre-translation. Moreover, multi-source MT has been proved to be very effective to combine multiple source languages (Och and Ney, 2001; Zoph and Knight, 2016; Firat et al., 2016a,b; Garmash and Monz, 2016). Unlike previous works, we adapt multi-source NMT for system combination and design a good strategy to simulate the real training data for our neural system combination.

6 Conclusion and Future Work

In this paper, we propose a novel neural system combination framework for machine translation. The central idea is to take advantage of NMT and SMT by adapting the multi-source NMT model. The neural system combination method cannot only address the fluency of NMT and the adequacy of SMT, but also can accommodate the source sentences as input. Furthermore, our approach can further use ensemble decoding to boost the performance compared to traditional system combination methods.

Experiments on Chinese-English datasets show that our approaches obtain significant improvements over the best individual system and the state-of-the-art traditional system combination methods. In the future work, we plan to encode n-best translation results to further improve the system combination quality. Additionally, it is interesting to extend this approach to other tasks like sentence compression and text abstraction.

Acknowledgments

The research work has been funded by the Natural Science Foundation of China under Grant No. 61333018 and No. 61673380, and it is also supported by the Strategic Priority Research Program of the CAS under Grant No. XDB02070007.

References

Necip Fazil Ayan, Jing Zheng, and Wen Wang. 2008. *Improving alignments for better confusion networks for combining machine translation systems*. In Proceedings of COLING 2008.

Dzmitry Bahdanau, Kyunghyun Cho, and Yoshua Bengio. 2015. *Nuural machine translation by jointly learning to align and translate*. In Proceedings of ICLR 2015.

Srinivas Bangalore, German Bordel, and Giuseppe Richardi. 2001. *Computing consensus translation from multiple machine translation systems*. In Proceedings of IEEE ASRU.

Boxing Chen, Min Zhang, Haizhou Li, and Aiti Aw. 2009. *A comparative study of hypothesis alignment and its improvement for machine translation system combination*. In Proceedings of ACL 2009.

Yong Cheng, Wei Xu, Zhongjun He, Wei He, Hua Wu, Maosong Sun, and Yang Liu. 2016. *Semi-supervised learning for neural machine translation*. In Proceedings of ACL 2016.

David Chiang. 2005. *A hierarchical phrase-based model for statistical machine translation*. In Proceedings of ACL 2005.

Kyunghyun Cho, Bart van Merrienboer, Caglar Gulcehre, Dzmitry Bahdanau, Fethi Bougares, Holger Schwenk, and Yoshua Bengio. 2014. *Learning phrase representations using RNN encoder – decoder for statistical machine translation*. In Proceedings of EMNLP 2014.

Yang Feng, Yang Liu, Haitao Mi, Qun Liu, and Yajuan Lu. 2009. *Lattice-based system combination for statistical machine translation*. In Proceedings of ACL 2009.

Orhan Firat, Kyunghyun Cho, and Yoshua Bengio. 2016a. *Multi-way, multilingual neural machine translation with a shared attention mechanism*. In Proceedings of NAACL-HLT 2016.

Orhan Firat, Baskaran Sankaran, Yaser Al-Onaizan, Fatos T. Yarman Vural, and Kyunghyun Cho. 2016b. *Zero-resource translation with multi-lingual neural machine translation*. In Proceedings of EMNLP 2016.

Markus Freitag, Matthias Huck, and Hermann Ney. 2014. *Jane: open source machine translation system combiantion*. In Proceedings of EACL 2014.

Ekaterina Garmash and Christof Monz. 2016. *Ensemble learning for multi-source neural machine translation*. In Proceedings of COLING 2016.

Wei He, Zhongjun He, Hua Wu, and Haifeng Wang. 2016. *Improved neural machine translation with SMT features*. In Proceedings of AAAI 2016.

Kenneth Heafield and Alon Lavie. 2010. *Combining machine translation output with open source*. The Prague Bulletin of Machematical Linguistics.

Hideki Isozaki, Tsutomu Hirao, Kevin Duh, Katsuhito Sudoh, and Hajime Tsukada. 2010. *Automatic e-valuation of translation quality for distant language pairs*. In Proceedings of EMNLP 2010.

Marcin Junczys-Dowmunt, Tomasz Dwojak, and Hieu Hoang. 2016a. *Is neural machine translation ready for deployment? A case study on 30 translation directions*. In Proceedings of IWSLT 2016.

Marcin Junczys-Dowmunt, Tomasz Dwojak, and Rico Sennrich. 2016b. *The AMU-UEDIN submission to the WMT16 news translation task: attention-based NMT models as feature functions in phrase-based SMT*. In Proceedings of WMT 2016.

Nal Kalchbrenner and Phil Blunsom. 2013. *Recurrent continuous translation models*. In Proceedings of EMNLP 2013.

Philipp Koehn, Franz J. Och, and Daniel Marcu. 2003. *Statistical phrase-based translation*. In Proceedings of ACL NAACL 2013.

Shankar Kumar and William Byrne. 2004. *Minimum bayes-risk decoding for statistical machine translation*. In Proceedings of HLT-NAACL 2004.

Maoxi Li, Jiajun Zhang, Yu Zhou, and Chengqing Zong. 2009. *The CASIA statistical machine translation system for IWSLT 2009*. In Proceedings of IWSLT2009.

Maoxi Li and Chengqing Zong. 2008. *Word reordering alignment for combination of statistical machine translation systems*. In Proceedings of the International Symposium on Chinese Spoken Language Processing.

Xiaoqing Li, Jiajun Zhang, and Chengqing Zong. 2016. *Towards zero unknown word in neural machine translation*. In Proceedings of IJCAI 2016.

Minh-Thang Luong, Hieu Pham, and Christopher D. Manning. 2015a. *Effective approaches to attention-based neural machine translation*. In Proceedings of EMNLP 2015.

Minh-Thang Luong, Ilya Sutskever, Quoc V Le, Oriol Vinyals, and Wojciech Zaremba. 2015b. *Addressing the rare word problem in neural machine translation*. In Proceedings of ACL 2015.

Wei-Yun Ma and Kathleen Mckeown. 2015. *System combination for machine translation through paraphrasing*. In Proceedings of EMNLP 2015.

Wolfgang Macherey and Franz Josef Och. 2007. *An empirical study on computing consensus translations from multiple machine translation systems*. In Proceedings of EMNLP 2007.

Fandong Meng, Zhengdong Lu, Hang Li, and Qun Liu. 2016. *Interactive attention for neural machine translation*. In Proceedings of COLING 2016.

Haitao Mi, Baskaran Sankaran, Zhiguo Wang, Niyu Ge, and Abe Ittycheriah. 2016a. *A coverage embedding model for neural machine translation*. In Proceedings of EMNLP 2016.

Haitao Mi, Zhiguo Wang, Niyu Ge, and Abe Ittycheriah. 2016b. *Supervised attentions for neural machine translation*. In Proceedings of EMNLP 2016.

Jan Niehues, Eunah Cho, Thanh-Le Ha, and Alex Waibel. 2016. *Pre-translation for neural machine translation*. In Proceedings of COLING 2016.

Franz Josef Och and Hermann Ney. 2001. *Statistical multi-source translation*. In Proceedings of MT Summit.

Kishore Papineni, Salim Roukos, Todd Ward, and Wei-Jing Zhu. 2002. *Bleu: a methof for automatic evaluation of machine translation*. In Proceedings of ACL 2002.

Antti-Veikko I. Rosti, Spyros Matsoukas, and Richard Schwartz. 2007. *Improved word-level system combination for machine translation*. In Proceedings of ACL 2007.

Antti-Veikko I. Rosti, Bing Zhang, Spyros Matsoukas, and Richard Schwartz. 2008. *Incremental hypothesis alignment for building confusion networks with appplication to machine translation systems combination*. In Proceedings of the Third ACL Workshop on Statistical Machine Translation.

Rico Sennrich, Barry Haddow, and Alexandra Birch. 2016a. *Improving neural machine translation models with monolingual data*. In Proceedings of ACL 2016.

Rico Sennrich, Barry Haddow, and Alexandra Birch. 2016b. *Neural machine translation of rare words with subword units*. In Proceedings of ACL 2016.

Shiqi Shen, Yong Cheng, Zhongjun He, Wei He, Hua Wu, Maosong Sun, and Yang Liu. 2016. *Minimum risk training for neural machine translation*. In Proceedings of ACL 2016.

Ilya Sutskever, Oriol Vinyals, and Quoc VV Le. 2014. *Sequence to sequence learning with neural networks*. In Proceedings of NIPS 2014.

Zhaopeng Tu, Zhengdong Lu, Yang Liu, Xiaohua Liu, and Hang Li. 2016. *Modeling coverage for neural machine translation*. In Proceedings of ACL 2016.

Jiajun Zhang and Chengqing Zong. 2016a. *Bridging neural machine translation and bilingual dictionaries*. arXiv preprint arXiv:1610.07272.

Jiajun Zhang and Chengqing Zong. 2016b. *Exploiting source-side monolingual data in neural machine translation.*. In Proceedings of EMNLP 2016.

Junguo Zhu, Muyun Yang, Sheng Li, and Tiejun Zhao. 2016. *Sentence-level paraphrasing for machine translation system combination*. In Proceedings of ICYCSEE 2016.

Barret Zoph and Kevin Knight. 2016. *Multi-source neural translation*. In Proceedings of NAACL-HLT 2016.

An Empirical Comparison of Domain Adaptation Methods for Neural Machine Translation

Chenhui Chu[1]*, **Raj Dabre**[2], and **Sadao Kurohashi**[2]
[1]Institute for Datability Science, Osaka University
[2]Graduate School of Informatics, Kyoto University
`chu@ids.osaka-u.ac.jp, {raj, kuro}@nlp.ist.i.kyoto-u.ac.jp`

Abstract

In this paper, we propose a novel domain adaptation method named *"mixed fine tuning"* for neural machine translation (NMT). We combine two existing approaches namely *fine tuning* and *multi domain* NMT. We first train an NMT model on an out-of-domain parallel corpus, and then fine tune it on a parallel corpus which is a mix of the in-domain and out-of-domain corpora. All corpora are augmented with artificial tags to indicate specific domains. We empirically compare our proposed method against fine tuning and multi domain methods and discuss its benefits and shortcomings.

1 Introduction

One of the most attractive features of neural machine translation (NMT) (Bahdanau et al., 2015; Cho et al., 2014; Sutskever et al., 2014) is that it is possible to train an end to end system without the need to deal with word alignments, translation rules and complicated decoding algorithms, which are a characteristic of statistical machine translation (SMT) systems. However, it is reported that NMT works better than SMT only when there is an abundance of parallel corpora. In the case of low resource domains, vanilla NMT is either worse than or comparable to SMT (Zoph et al., 2016).

Domain adaptation has been shown to be effective for low resource NMT. The conventional domain adaptation method is *fine tuning*, in which an out-of-domain model is further trained on in-domain data (Luong and Manning, 2015; Sennrich et al., 2016b; Servan et al., 2016; Freitag and Al-Onaizan, 2016). However, fine tuning

tends to overfit quickly due to the small size of the in-domain data. On the other hand, *multi domain* NMT (Kobus et al., 2016) involves training a single NMT model for multiple domains. This method adds tags "<2domain>" to the source sentences in the parallel corpora to indicate domains without any modifications to the NMT system architecture. However, this method has not been studied for domain adaptation in particular.

Motivated by these two lines of studies, we propose a new domain adaptation method called *"mixed fine tuning,"* where we first train an NMT model on an out-of-domain parallel corpus, and then fine tune it on a parallel corpus that is a mix of the in-domain and out-of-domain corpora. Fine tuning on the mixed corpus instead of the in-domain corpus can address the overfitting problem. All corpora are augmented with artificial tags to indicate specific domains. We tried two different corpora settings on two different language pairs:

- Manually created resource poor corpus (Chinese-to-English translation): Using the NTCIR data (patent domain; resource rich) (Goto et al., 2013) to improve the translation quality for the IWSLT data (TED talks; resource poor) (Cettolo et al., 2015).

- Automatically extracted resource poor corpus (Chinese-to-Japanese translation): Using the ASPEC data (scientific domain; resource rich) (Nakazawa et al., 2016) to improve the translation quality for the Wiki data (resource poor). The parallel corpus of the latter domain was automatically extracted (Chu et al., 2016a).

We observed that "mixed fine tuning" works significantly better than methods that use fine tuning

---

This work was done when the first author was a researcher of Japan Science and Technology Agency.

Proceedings of the 55th Annual Meeting of the Association for Computational Linguistics (Short Papers), pages 385–391
Vancouver, Canada, July 30 - August 4, 2017. ©2017 Association for Computational Linguistics
https://doi.org/10.18653/v1/P17-2061

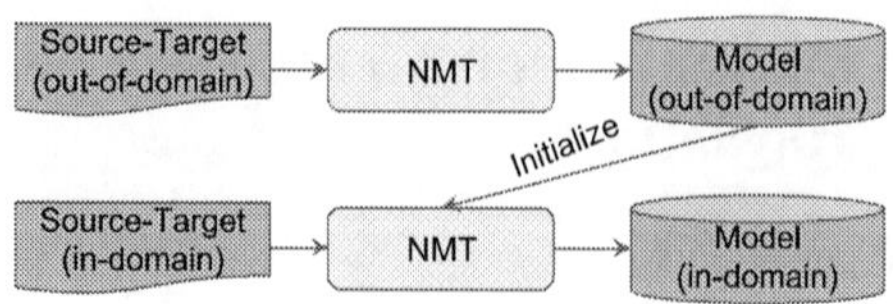

Figure 1: Fine tuning for domain adaptation.

and domain tag based approaches separately. Our contributions are twofold:

- We propose a novel method that combines the best of existing approaches and show that it is effective.

- To the best of our knowledge this is the first work on an empirical comparison of various domain adaptation methods.

2 Related Work

Fine tuning has also been explored for various NLP tasks using neural networks such as sentiment analysis and paraphrase detection (Mou et al., 2016). Tag based NMT has also been shown to be effective for control the politeness of translations (Sennrich et al., 2016a) and multilingual NMT (Johnson et al., 2016).

Besides fine tuning and multi domain NMT using tags, another direction of domain adaptation for NMT is using in-domain monolingual data. Either training an in-domain recurrent neural network (RNN) language model for the NMT decoder (Gülçehre et al., 2015) or generating synthetic data by back translating target in-domain monolingual data (Sennrich et al., 2016b) have been studied.

3 Methods for Comparison

All the methods that we compare are simple and do not need any modifications to the NMT system.

3.1 Fine Tuning

Fine tuning is the conventional way for domain adaptation, and thus serves as a baseline in this study. In this method, we first train an NMT system on a resource rich out-of-domain corpus till convergence, and then fine tune its parameters on a resource poor in-domain corpus (Figure 1).

3.2 Multi Domain

The *multi domain* method is originally motivated by (Sennrich et al., 2016a), which uses tags to control the politeness of NMT translations. The overview of this method is shown in the dotted section in Figure 2. In this method, we simply concatenate the corpora of multiple domains with two small modifications:

- Appending the domain tag "<2domain>" to the source sentences of the respective corpora.[1] This primes the NMT decoder to generate sentences for the specific domain.

- Oversampling the smaller corpus so that the training procedure pays equal attention to each domain.

We can further fine tune the multi domain model on the in-domain data, which is named as "multi domain + fine tuning."

3.3 Mixed Fine Tuning

The proposed *mixed fine tuning* method is a combination of the above methods (shown in Figure 2). The training procedure is as follows:

1. Train an NMT model on out-of-domain data till convergence.

2. Resume training the NMT model from step 1 on a mix of in-domain and out-of-domain data (by oversampling the in-domain data) till convergence.

By default, we utilize domain tags, but we also consider settings where we do not use them (i.e., "w/o tags"). We can further fine tune the model from step 2 on the in-domain data, which is named as "mixed fine tuning + fine tuning."

Note that in the "fine tuning" method, the vocabulary obtained from the out-of-domain data is used for the in-domain data; while for the "multi domain" and "mixed fine tuning" methods, we use a vocabulary obtained from the mixed in-domain and out-of-domain data for all the training stages. Regarding development data, for fine tuning, an out-of-domain development set is first used for training the out-of-domain NMT model, then an in-domain development set is used for fine tuning; For multi-domain, a mix of in-domain and out-of-domain development sets are used; For mixed fine tuning, an out-of-domain development set is first used for training the out-of-domain NMT model, then a mix of in-domain and out-of-domain development sets are used for mixed fine tuning.

---

[1] We verified the effectiveness of the domain tags by comparing against a setting that does not use them, see the "w/o tags" settings in Tables 1 and 2.

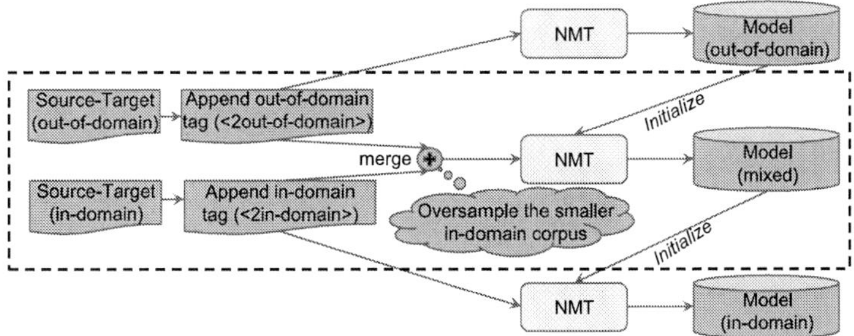

Figure 2: Mixed fine tuning with domain tags for domain adaptation (The section in the dotted rectangle denotes the multi domain method).

4 Experimental Settings

We conducted NMT domain adaptation experiments in two different settings as follows:

4.1 High Quality In-domain Corpus Setting

Chinese-to-English translation was the focus of the high quality in-domain corpus setting. We utilized the resource rich patent out-of-domain data to augment the resource poor spoken language in-domain data. The patent domain MT was conducted on the Chinese-English subtask (NTCIR-CE) of the patent MT task at the NTCIR-10 workshop[2] (Goto et al., 2013). The NTCIR-CE task uses 1M, 2k, and 2k sentences for training, development, and testing, respectively. The spoken domain MT was conducted on the Chinese-English subtask (IWSLT-CE) of the TED talk MT task at the IWSLT 2015 workshop (Cettolo et al., 2015). The IWSLT-CE task contains 209,491 sentences for training. We used the dev 2010 set for development, containing 887 sentences. We evaluated all methods on the 2010, 2011, 2012, and 2013 test sets, containing 1570, 1245, 1397, and 1261 sentences, respectively.

4.2 Low Quality In-domain Corpus Setting

Chinese-to-Japanese translation was the focus of the low quality in-domain corpus setting. We utilized the resource rich scientific out-of-domain data to augment the resource poor Wikipedia (essentially open) in-domain data. The scientific domain MT was conducted on the Chinese-Japanese paper excerpt corpus (ASPEC-CJ)[3] (Nakazawa et al., 2016), which is one subtask of the workshop on Asian translation (WAT)[4] (Nakazawa et al., 2015). The ASPEC-CJ task uses 672315, 2090, and 2107 sentences for training, development, and testing, respectively. The Wikipedia domain task was conducted on a Chinese-Japanese corpus automatically extracted from Wikipedia (WIKI-CJ) (Chu et al., 2016a) using the ASPEC-CJ corpus as a seed. The WIKI-CJ task contains 136013, 198, and 198 sentences for training, development, and testing, respectively.

4.3 MT Systems

For NMT, we used the KyotoNMT system[5] (Cromieres et al., 2016). The NMT settings were the same as (Cromieres et al., 2016) except that we used a vocabulary size of 32k for all the experiments, and did not ensemble independently trained parameters. The sizes of the source and target vocabularies, the source and target side embeddings, the hidden states, the attention mechanism hidden states, and the deep softmax output with a 2-maxout layer were set to 32,000, 620, 1000, 1000, and 500, respectively. We used 2-layer LSTMs for both the source and target sides. ADAM was used as the learning algorithm, with a dropout rate of 20% for the inter-layer dropout, and L2 regularization with a weight decay coefficient of 1e-6. The mini batch size was 64, and sentences longer than 80 tokens were discarded. We early stopped the training process when we observed that the BLEU score of the development set converges. For testing, we ensembled the three parameters of the best development loss, the best development BLEU, and the final parameters in a single training run. Beam size was set to 100. The maximum length of the translation was set to 2, and 1.5 times of the source sentences for Chinese-to-English, and Chinese-to-Japanese, respectively.

---

[2]http://ntcir.nii.ac.jp/PatentMT-2/
[3]http://lotus.kuee.kyoto-u.ac.jp/ASPEC/
[4]http://orchid.kuee.kyoto-u.ac.jp/WAT/
[5]https://github.com/fabiencro/knmt

System	NTCIR-CE	IWSLT-CE				
		test 2010	test 2011	test 2012	test 2013	average
IWSLT-CE SMT	-	12.73	16.27	14.01	14.67	14.31
IWSLT-CE NMT	-	6.75	9.08	9.05	7.29	7.87
NTCIR-CE SMT	29.54	3.57	4.70	4.21	4.74	4.33
NTCIR-CE NMT	37.11	2.23	2.83	2.55	2.85	2.60
Fine tuning	17.37	13.93	18.99	16.12	17.12	16.41
Multi domain	36.40	13.42	19.07	16.56	17.54	16.34
Multi domain w/o tags	37.32	12.57	17.40	15.02	15.96	14.97
Multi domain + Fine tuning	14.47	13.18	18.03	16.41	16.80	15.82
Mixed fine tuning	37.01	**15.04**	**20.96**	**18.77**	**18.63**	**18.01**
Mixed fine tuning w/o tags	**39.67**	14.47	**20.53**	18.10	17.97	17.43
Mixed fine tuning + Fine tuning	32.03	14.40	19.53	17.65	17.94	17.11

Table 1: Domain adaptation results (BLEU-4 scores) for IWSLT-CE using NTCIR-CE.

For performance comparison, we also conducted experiments on phrase based SMT (PB-SMT). We used the Moses PBSMT system (Koehn et al., 2007) for all of our MT experiments. For the respective tasks, we trained 5-gram language models on the target side of the training data using the KenLM toolkit[6] with interpolated Kneser-Ney discounting, respectively. In all of our experiments, we used the GIZA++ toolkit[7] for word alignment; tuning was performed by minimum error rate training (Och, 2003), and it was re-run for every experiment.

For both MT systems, we preprocessed the data as follows. For Chinese, we used KyotoMorph[8] for segmentation, which was trained on the CTB version 5 (CTB5) and SCTB (Chu et al., 2016b). For English, we tokenized and lowercased the sentences using the *tokenizer.perl* script in Moses. Japanese was segmented using JUMAN[9] (Kurohashi et al., 1994).

For NMT, we further split the words into sub-words using byte pair encoding (BPE) (Sennrich et al., 2016c), which has been shown to be effective for the rare word problem in NMT. Another motivation of using sub-words is making the different domains share more vocabulary, which is important especially for the resource poor domain. For the Chinese-to-English tasks, we trained two BPE models on the Chinese and English vocabularies, respectively. For the Chinese-to-Japanese tasks, we trained a joint BPE model on both of the Chinese and Japanese vocabularies, because Chinese and Japanese could share some vocabularies of Chinese characters. The number of merge operations was set to 30k for all the tasks.

[6]https://github.com/kpu/kenlm/

[7]http://code.google.com/p/giza-pp

[8]https://bitbucket.org/msmoshen/kyotomorph-beta

[9]http://nlp.ist.i.kyoto-u.ac.jp/EN/index.php?JUMAN

System	ASPEC-CJ	WIKI-CJ
WIKI-CJ SMT	-	36.83
WIKI-CJ NMT	-	18.29
ASPEC-CJ SMT	36.39	17.43
ASPEC-CJ NMT	**42.92**	20.01
Fine tuning	22.10	**37.66**
Multi domain	42.52	35.79
Multi domain w/o tags	40.78	33.74
Multi domain + Fine tuning	22.78	34.61
Mixed fine tuning	**42.56**	**37.57**
Mixed fine tuning w/o tags	41.86	**37.23**
Mixed fine tuning + Fine tuning	31.63	**37.77**

Table 2: Domain adaptation results (BLEU-4 scores) for WIKI-CJ using ASPEC-CJ.

5 Results

Tables 1 and 2 show the translation results on the Chinese-to-English and Chinese-to-Japanese tasks, respectively. The entries with SMT and NMT are the PBSMT and NMT systems, respectively; others are the different methods described in Section 3. In both tables, the numbers in bold indicate the best system and all systems that were not significantly different from the best system. The significance tests were performed using the bootstrap resampling method (Koehn, 2004) at $p < 0.05$.

We can see that without domain adaptation, the SMT systems perform significantly better than the NMT system on the resource poor domains, i.e., IWSLT-CE and WIKI-CJ; while on the resource rich domains, i.e., NTCIR-CE and ASPEC-CJ, NMT outperforms SMT. Directly using the SMT/NMT models trained on the out-of-domain data to translate the in-domain data shows bad performance. With our proposed "Mixed fine tuning" domain adaptation method, NMT significantly outperforms SMT on the in-domain tasks.

Comparing different domain adaptation methods, "Mixed fine tuning" shows the best performance. We believe the reason for this is that "Mixed fine tuning" can address the over-fitting problem of "Fine tuning." We observed that both fine-tuning and mixed fine-tuning tends to converge after 1 epoch of training, and thus we early stopped training soon after 1 epoch. After 1 epoch of training, fine-tuning overfitted very quickly, while mixed fine-tuning did not overfit. In addition, "Mixed fine tuning" does not worsen the quality of out-of-domain translations, while "Fine tuning" and "Multi domain" do. One shortcoming of "Mixed fine tuning" is that compared to "Fine tuning," it took a longer time for the fine tuning process, as the time until convergence is essentially proportional to the size of the data used for fine tuning. Note that training as long as "Mixed fine tuning" is not helpful for "Fine tuning" due to overfitting.

"Multi domain" performs either as well as (IWSLT-CE) or worse than (WIKI-CJ) "Fine tuning," but "Mixed fine tuning" performs either significantly better than (IWSLT-CE) or is comparable to (WIKI-CJ) "Fine tuning." We believe the performance difference between the two tasks is due to their unique characteristics. As WIKI-CJ data is of relatively poorer quality, mixing it with out-of-domain data does not have the same level of positive effects as those obtained by the IWSLT-CE data.

The domain tags are helpful for both "Multi domain" and "Mixed fine tuning." Essentially, further fine tuning on in-domain data does not help for both "Multi domain" and "Mixed fine tuning." We believe that there are two reasons for this. Firstly, the "Multi domain" and "Mixed fine tuning" methods already utilize the in-domain data used for fine tuning. Secondly, fine tuning on the small in-domain data overfits very quickly. Actually, we observed that adding fine-tuning on top of both "Multi domain" and "Mixed fine tuning" overfits at the beginning of training.

Mixed fine tuning performs significantly better on the out-domain NTCIR-CE test set without tags as compared to with tags (39.67 v.s. 37.01). We believe the reason for this is that without tags the IWSLT-CE in-domain data can contribute more to the out-of-domain NTCIR-CE data. With tags, the NMT training tends to learn a model that pays equal attention to each domain. Without tags, the NMT training pays more attention to the NTCIR-CE data as it contains much longer sentences, al-though we oversampled the IWSLT-CE data. As the IWSLT-CE data is TED talks, there could be some vocabulary and content overlaps between the IWSLT-CE the NTCIR-CE data, and thus appending the IWSLT-CE data to the NTCIR-CE data can benefit for the NTCIR-CE translation. In the case of WIKI-CJ and ASPEC-CJ, due to the low quality of WIKI-CJ, appending WIKI-CJ to ASPEC-CJ does not improve the ASPEC-CJ translation.

6 Conclusion

In this paper, we proposed a novel domain adaptation method named "mixed fine tuning" for NMT. We empirically compared our proposed method against fine tuning and multi domain methods, and have shown that it is effective but is sensitive to the quality of the in-domain data used. The presented methods are language and domain independent, and thus we believe that the general observations also hold on other languages and domains. Furthermore, we believe the contribution in this paper can be helpful for domain adaptation of other NN based natural language processing tasks.

In the future, we plan to incorporate an RNN model into our architecture to leverage abundant in-domain monolingual corpora. We also plan on exploring the effects of synthetic data by back translating large in-domain monolingual corpora.

Acknowledgments

This work was partly supported by JSPS and DST under the Japan-India Science Cooperative Program. We are very appreciated to Prof. Daisuke Kawahara, Dr. Toshiaki Nakazawa, and Dr. Fabien Cromieres for helping improving the writing quality of this paper. We also thank the anonymous reviewers for their insightful comments.

References

Dzmitry Bahdanau, Kyunghyun Cho, and Yoshua Bengio. 2015. Neural machine translation by jointly learning to align and translate. In *In Proceedings of the 3rd International Conference on Learning Representations (ICLR 2015)*. International Conference on Learning Representations, San Diego, USA.

M Cettolo, J Niehues, S Stüker, L Bentivogli, R Cattoni, and M Federico. 2015. The iwslt 2015 evaluation campaign. In *Proceedings of the Twelfth International Workshop on Spoken Language Translation (IWSLT)*.

Kyunghyun Cho, Bart van Merriënboer, Çalar Gülçehre, Dzmitry Bahdanau, Fethi Bougares, Holger Schwenk, and Yoshua Bengio. 2014. Learning phrase representations using rnn encoder–decoder for statistical machine translation. In *Proceedings of the 2014 Conference on Empirical Methods in Natural Language Processing (EMNLP)*. Association for Computational Linguistics, Doha, Qatar, pages 1724–1734. http://www.aclweb.org/anthology/D14-1179.

Chenhui Chu, Raj Dabre, and Sadao Kurohashi. 2016a. Parallel sentence extraction from comparable corpora with neural network features. In *Proceedings of the Tenth International Conference on Language Resources and Evaluation (LREC 2016)*. European Language Resources Association (ELRA), Paris, France.

Chenhui Chu, Toshiaki Nakazawa, Daisuke Kawahara, and Sadao Kurohashi. 2016b. SCTB: A Chinese treebank in scientific domain. In *Proceedings of the 12th Workshop on Asian Language Resources (ALR12)*. The COLING 2016 Organizing Committee, Osaka, Japan, pages 59–67. http://aclweb.org/anthology/W16-5407.

Fabien Cromieres, Chenhui Chu, Toshiaki Nakazawa, and Sadao Kurohashi. 2016. Kyoto university participation to wat 2016. In *Proceedings of the 3rd Workshop on Asian Translation (WAT2016)*. The COLING 2016 Organizing Committee, Osaka, Japan, pages 166–174. http://aclweb.org/anthology/W16-4616.

Markus Freitag and Yaser Al-Onaizan. 2016. Fast domain adaptation for neural machine translation. *arXiv preprint arXiv:1612.06897* .

Isao Goto, Ka-Po Chow, Bin Lu, Eiichiro Sumita, and Benjamin K. Tsou. 2013. Overview of the patent machine translation task at the ntcir-10 workshop. In *Proceedings of the 10th NTCIR Conference*. National Institute of Informatics (NII), Tokyo, Japan, pages 260–286.

Çaglar Gülçehre, Orhan Firat, Kelvin Xu, Kyunghyun Cho, Loïc Barrault, Huei-Chi Lin, Fethi Bougares, Holger Schwenk, and Yoshua Bengio. 2015. On using monolingual corpora in neural machine translation. *CoRR* abs/1503.03535. http://arxiv.org/abs/1503.03535.

Melvin Johnson, Mike Schuster, Quoc V. Le, Maxim Krikun, Yonghui Wu, Zhifeng Chen, Nikhil Thorat, Fernanda B. Viégas, Martin Wattenberg, Greg Corrado, Macduff Hughes, and Jeffrey Dean. 2016. Google's multilingual neural machine translation system: Enabling zero-shot translation. *CoRR* abs/1611.04558. http://arxiv.org/abs/1611.04558.

Catherine Kobus, Josep Crego, and Jean Senellart. 2016. Domain control for neural machine translation. *arXiv preprint arXiv:1612.06140* .

Philipp Koehn. 2004. Statistical significance tests for machine translation evaluation. In *Proceedings of EMNLP 2004*. Association for Computational Linguistics, Barcelona, Spain, pages 388–395.

Philipp Koehn, Hieu Hoang, Alexandra Birch, Chris Callison-Burch, Marcello Federico, Nicola Bertoldi, Brooke Cowan, Wade Shen, Christine Moran, Richard Zens, Chris Dyer, Ondrej Bojar, Alexandra Constantin, and Evan Herbst. 2007. Moses: Open source toolkit for statistical machine translation. In *Proceedings of the 45th Annual Meeting of the Association for Computational Linguistics Companion Volume Proceedings of the Demo and Poster Sessions*. Association for Computational Linguistics, Prague, Czech Republic, pages 177–180. http://www.aclweb.org/anthology/P/P07/P07-2045.

Sadao Kurohashi, Toshihisa Nakamura, Yuji Matsumoto, and Makoto Nagao. 1994. Improvements of Japanese morphological analyzer JUMAN. In *Proceedings of the International Workshop on Sharable Natural Language*. pages 22–28.

Minh-Thang Luong and Christopher D Manning. 2015. Stanford neural machine translation systems for spoken language domains. In *Proceedings of the 12th International Workshop on Spoken Language Translation*. Da Nang, Vietnam, pages 76–79.

Lili Mou, Zhao Meng, Rui Yan, Ge Li, Yan Xu, Lu Zhang, and Zhi Jin. 2016. How transferable are neural networks in nlp applications? In *Proceedings of the 2016 Conference on Empirical Methods in Natural Language Processing*. Association for Computational Linguistics, Austin, Texas, pages 479–489. https://aclweb.org/anthology/D16-1046.

Toshiaki Nakazawa, Hideya Mino, Isao Goto, Graham Neubig, Sadao Kurohashi, and Eiichiro Sumita. 2015. Overview of the 2nd Workshop on Asian Translation. In *Proceedings of the 2nd Workshop on Asian Translation (WAT2015)*. Kyoto, Japan, pages 1–28.

Toshiaki Nakazawa, Manabu Yaguchi, Kiyotaka Uchimoto, Masao Utiyama, Eiichiro Sumita, Sadao Kurohashi, and Hitoshi Isahara. 2016. Aspec: Asian scientific paper excerpt corpus. In *Proceedings of the Tenth International Conference on Language Resources and Evaluation (LREC 2016)*. European Language Resources Association (ELRA), Paris, France.

Franz Josef Och. 2003. Minimum error rate training in statistical machine translation. In *Proceedings of the 41st Annual Meeting of the Association for Computational Linguistics*. Association for Computational Linguistics, Sapporo, Japan, pages 160–167. http://www.aclweb.org/anthology/P03-1021.

Rico Sennrich, Barry Haddow, and Alexandra Birch. 2016a. Controlling politeness in neural machine translation via side constraints. In *Proceedings of the 2016 Conference of the*

North American Chapter of the Association for Computational Linguistics: Human Language Technologies. Association for Computational Linguistics, San Diego, California, pages 35–40. http://www.aclweb.org/anthology/N16-1005.

Rico Sennrich, Barry Haddow, and Alexandra Birch. 2016b. Improving neural machine translation models with monolingual data. In *Proceedings of the 54th Annual Meeting of the Association for Computational Linguistics (Volume 1: Long Papers)*. Association for Computational Linguistics, Berlin, Germany, pages 86–96. http://www.aclweb.org/anthology/P16-1009.

Rico Sennrich, Barry Haddow, and Alexandra Birch. 2016c. Neural machine translation of rare words with subword units. In *Proceedings of the 54th Annual Meeting of the Association for Computational Linguistics (Volume 1: Long Papers)*. Association for Computational Linguistics, Berlin, Germany, pages 1715–1725. http://www.aclweb.org/anthology/P16-1162.

Christophe Servan, Josep Crego, and Jean Senellart. 2016. Domain specialization: a post-training domain adaptation for neural machine translation. *arXiv preprint arXiv:1612.06141* .

Ilya Sutskever, Oriol Vinyals, and Quoc V. Le. 2014. Sequence to sequence learning with neural networks. In *Proceedings of the 27th International Conference on Neural Information Processing Systems*. MIT Press, Cambridge, MA, USA, NIPS'14, pages 3104–3112. http://dl.acm.org/citation.cfm?id=2969033.2969173.

Barret Zoph, Deniz Yuret, Jonathan May, and Kevin Knight. 2016. Transfer learning for low-resource neural machine translation. In *Proceedings of the 2016 Conference on Empirical Methods in Natural Language Processing, EMNLP 2016, Austin, Texas, USA, November 1-4, 2016*. pages 1568–1575. http://aclweb.org/anthology/D/D16/D16-1163.pdf.

Efficient Extraction of Pseudo-Parallel Sentences
from Raw Monolingual Data Using Word Embeddings

Benjamin Marie   **Atsushi Fujita**

National Institute of Information and Communications Technology

3-5 Hikaridai, Seika-cho, Souraku-gun, Kyoto, 619-0289, Japan

{bmarie, atsushi.fujita}@nict.go.jp

Abstract

We propose a new method for extracting *pseudo-parallel* sentences from a pair of large monolingual corpora, without relying on any document-level information. Our method first exploits word embeddings in order to efficiently evaluate trillions of candidate sentence pairs and then a classifier to find the most reliable ones. We report significant improvements in domain adaptation for statistical machine translation when using a translation model trained on the sentence pairs extracted from in-domain monolingual corpora.

1 Introduction

Parallel corpus is an indispensable resource for statistical and neural machine translation. Generally, using more sentence pairs to train a translation system makes it able to produce better translations. However, for most language pairs and domains, parallel corpora remain scarce due mainly to the cost of their creation (Germann, 2001).

In the last two decades, numerous methods have been proposed to extract parallel sentences from comparable corpora. In addition to comparable corpora in large quantity, to the best of our knowledge, all previous methods heavily rely on document-level information and/or lexical translation models, such as those for statistical machine translation (SMT) systems (Zhao and Vogel, 2002; Fung and Cheung, 2004; Munteanu and Marcu, 2005; Tillmann and Xu, 2009) and manually-created bilingual lexicon (Utiyama and Isahara, 2003). The most successful approaches use cross-lingual information retrieval techniques (Abdul Rauf and Schwenk, 2011; Ştefănescu et al., 2012) to extract sentence pairs from comparable documents. Using such document pairs

has the strong advantage that it drastically reduces the search space; we need to consider only sentence pairs in each document pair instead of scoring all sentence pairs in the two monolingual corpora. However, in many cases, we do not have access to document-level information. Only Tillmann and Xu (2009) have explored this scenario using efficient caching strategies to extract useful sentence pairs from nearly one trillion candidates in comparable data. Yet, their approach is tightly related to the exploitation of accurate lexical translation models and does not allow us to introduce other features. The reliance on lexical translation models implies that we must have already access to parallel data sufficiently large for obtaining accurate estimates. Nevertheless, the most useful sentence pairs for SMT are actually the ones that contain infrequent or even unseen tokens in these parallel data. Relying only on lexical translation models thus seems rather inadequate to extract sentence pairs containing numerous infrequent or unseen tokens, and may actually be more prone to extract sentence pairs that contain words and phrases for which we already have accurate translation probability estimates.

This paper proposes a new method that exploits word embeddings to efficiently extract *pseudo-parallel* sentences[1] from raw monolingual data without using any document-level information. We report significant improvements of translation quality in a domain adaptation scenario for SMT.

2 Sentence pair extraction

During the sentence pair extraction, we do not assume an access to document-level information. Our method thus has to be efficient in evaluating

---

[1] As in previous work, we regard the sentence pairs extracted by our method as "pseudo-parallel" because they are not necessarily parallel. As shown by Goutte et al. (2012), even very noisy parallel corpora may be useful for SMT.

Proceedings of the 55th Annual Meeting of the Association for Computational Linguistics (Short Papers), pages 392–398

Vancouver, Canada, July 30 - August 4, 2017. ©2017 Association for Computational Linguistics

https://doi.org/10.18653/v1/P17-2062

trillions of sentence pairs hypothesized from two monolingual corpora, each containing millions of sentences. To achieve this computationally challenging task, we need a fast way to compute some similarity between the source and target sentences, without relying on large lexical translation models that may not be available or accurate enough in some low-resourced conditions.

2.1 Step 1: Filtering with sentence embeddings

Assuming the availability of large-scale monolingual data, our method exploits word embeddings (Mikolov et al., 2013b) that are fast to estimate. First, word embeddings for each language are learned from the given monolingual data. This enables us to evaluate arbitrary sentence pair given all the words it contains, which is not fully guaranteed by a lexical translation model as some tokens may be out-of-vocabulary (OOV). We then proceed to the projection of all the source word embeddings to the target embedding space, following Mikolov et al. (2013a),[2] in order to represent both source and target words in the same space.

To compute the similarity between arbitrary sentence pairs, we represent each sentence by averaging the embeddings of its constituent words.[3]

As a result of this first step, our method keeps for each source sentence the n closest target sentences (n being small, for instance with a value of 100) according to the similarity score.

2.2 Step 2: Refining with a classifier

Given a far smaller search space, this second step evaluates and re-ranks the remaining sentence pairs, incorporating more complex features to train a classifier. We use a total of five features.

For each sentence pair, we use the score computed in the first step and a more accurate similarity score based on alignments between word embeddings, following the work in Kajiwara and

---

[2]Despite the availability of more accurate methods (Coulmance et al., 2015; Duong et al., 2016) we choose this method considering its low computational cost and its reasonable need of external resources to estimate the translation matrix, i.e., only a small bilingual dictionary.

[3]As shown by Adi et al. (2016), this can be effective to encode sentence-level information such as content and length, while being computationally more efficient than other methods, such as inducing paragraph vectors (Le and Mikolov, 2014) and using LSTM auto-encoders (Li et al., 2015). Our decision also relies on the promising accuracy of linear projection of word (not sentence) embeddings across different languages (Mikolov et al., 2013a).

Komachi (2016). They found out that the average of the cosine similarity between all the best word pairs, for each source word, taken from the sentence pair, shown in Eq. (1), was a good indicator of similarity between two sentences.

$$S(\mathbf{x}, \mathbf{y}) = \frac{1}{|\mathbf{x}|} \sum_{i=1}^{|\mathbf{x}|} \max_j \phi(x_i^{emb}, y_j^{emb}) \qquad (1)$$

where $\mathbf{x}$ and $\mathbf{y}$ are respectively the source and target sentences, $|\mathbf{x}|$ the length of $\mathbf{x}$, and ϕ the cosine similarity between the embeddings in the target language space of the i-th word in $\mathbf{x}$, i.e., x_i^{emb}, and the j-th word in $\mathbf{y}$, i.e., y_j^{emb}. The computation of this score can be highly costly, depending on the sentence length and the number of dimensions of the word embeddings. Thus, we compute this score only for the source to target direction, unlike Kajiwara and Komachi (2016).

In many situations, we may also have an access to a lexical translation model trained on some parallel data. We therefore incorporate the scores proposed by Tillmann and Xu (2009), but considering one probability for each translation direction, instead of summing them up, so that our classifier can optimize their weight separately.

$$P(\mathbf{x}|\mathbf{y}) = \sum_{i=1}^{|\mathbf{x}|} \frac{1}{|\mathbf{x}|} \log(\frac{1}{|\mathbf{y}|} \sum_{j=1}^{|\mathbf{y}|} p(x_i^{tok}|y_j^{tok})) \quad (2)$$

$$P(\mathbf{y}|\mathbf{x}) = \sum_{j=1}^{|\mathbf{y}|} \frac{1}{|\mathbf{y}|} \log(\frac{1}{|\mathbf{x}|} \sum_{i=1}^{|\mathbf{x}|} p(y_j^{tok}|x_i^{tok})) \quad (3)$$

where x_i^{tok} is the i-th token in $\mathbf{x}$, y_j^{tok} the j-th token in $\mathbf{y}$ and p the probability given by an already estimated lexical translation model.

Our last feature is the length ratio of the source and target sentences (Munteanu and Marcu, 2005).

To assign a real-valued score to each sentence pair in order to filter and rank them, we train a Maximum Entropy (ME) classifier, following Munteanu and Marcu (2005). ME classifier suits particularly well our situation, since we deal with a small number of dense features and have hundred millions of sentence pairs to classify quickly.

Positive examples for training the classifier can be obtained straightforwardly: we use true sentence pairs sampled from parallel data, different from the one used to train the lexical translation model. As for negative examples, Munteanu and Marcu (2005) randomly paired sentences from their parallel data using two constraints: a length ratio not greater than two, and a coverage constraint that considers a negative example only if more than half of the words of the source sentence has a translation in the given target sentence according to some bilingual lexicon. However, from a large parallel corpus, one can easily retrieve another target sentence, almost identical, containing most of the words that the true target sentence also contains. In this case, the negative example will be almost as semantically close as the positive one, weakening the discriminative power of the features based on word embeddings. To circumvent this problem, we generate negative examples, as many as positive examples, without using this coverage constraint.

Having assigned a score for each sentence pair, we make a pseudo-parallel corpus selecting the target sentence with the best score for each source sentence and retaining only the sentence pairs with a score above some threshold, *th*. This pseudo-parallel corpus can then be used to train a new phrase table.

3 Experiments

We evaluated our method in a scenario of domain adaptation for phrase-based SMT (PBSMT). In this scenario, we assumed a lot of general-domain parallel data to train a general-domain phrase table and a lot of in-domain monolingual data as our source of in-domain pseudo-parallel sentences.

3.1 Data and SMT system

We experimented with the French–English language pair, both translation directions, on the medical domain. We used `Moses` (Koehn et al., 2007) to train, tune, and test our PBSMT systems. The general-domain phrase table was trained on Europarl V7[4] (1.99M sentences). The in-domain monolingual data were prepared by applying the NLTK[5] sentence segmenter to the concatenation of all the monolingual corpora provided for the WMT'14 medical translation task.[6] As the source of extracting in-domain sentence pairs, we randomly sampled 1M sentences (33M tokens) from the French data and 5M sentences (164M tokens) from the English data. Given pseudo-parallel sentences extracted by our method from these data

(see Section 3.2), we trained an in-domain phrase table. `Moses` exploits the two phrase tables, i.e., general-domain and in-domain ones, with its multiple decoding path ability. The PBSMT systems used one language model trained on the entire target in-domain monolingual data concatenated to the target side of Europarl and News Crawl data provided by WMT'15.[7] The development and test data used to tune and evaluate the PBSMT systems were excerpts of the EMEA parallel corpus (Carpuat et al., 2012).

3.2 Parameters for sentence pair extraction

We used `word2vec`[8] to learn word embeddings with the parameters `-cbow 1 -window 10 -negative 15 -sample 1e-4 -iter 15 -min-count 1`, specifying 800 and 300 dimensions for the source and target languages, respectively,[9] on the same data used to train the language models. The translation matrix used to project the source word embeddings to the target embedding space was trained on a bilingual lexicon containing the 5k[10] most frequent French tokens,[11] from Europarl, and their most probable single token in English given by the Europarl phrase table. The first step of our method evaluated five trillion (1M×5M) sentence pairs and retained the 100 closest target sentences for each source sentence.

The second step then dealt with only 100M (1M×100) sentence pairs. The lexical translation probabilities used to compute our features were given by the Europarl lexical translation models. We used `Scikit-learn`[12] to train the ME classifier, with default parameters, on 5k positive and 5k negative examples[13] randomly generated from the MultiUn corpus.[14] According to the classifier's score, only the 1-best target sentence for each source sentence was retained. We discarded sentence pairs having a score lower than a thresh-

---

[4] `http://statmt.org/europarl/`

[5] `http://www.nltk.org/`

[6] `http://statmt.org/wmt14/medical-task/`

[7] `http://statmt.org/wmt15/`

[8] `http://word2vec.googlecode.com/`

[9] Mikolov et al. (2013a) observed that a more accurate projection is obtained when using a greater number of dimensions on the source side than that for the target side.

[10] Vulić and Korhonen (2016) demonstrated that 5k word pairs is enough to train a useful translation matrix.

[11] We extracted sentence pairs regarding French and English as source and target languages, respectively, but used the resulted parallel corpus for both translation directions.

[12] `http://scikit-learn.org/`

[13] We chose this number empirically through observing the classification accuracy on a set of held-out sentence pairs.

[14] `http://opus.lingfil.uu.se/MultiUN.php`

| System | Fr→En | | En→Fr | | #extracted | speed |
	BLEU	#OOV	BLEU	#OOV	pairs	(#pairs/sec)
Only general-domain phrase table	25.9	3,134	23.1	3,099	-	-
Baseline (Tillmann and Xu (2009))	27.2	2,729	24.7	2,661	121k	1.22M
Proposed method ($th = 0.955$)	**28.0**	2,607	**25.4**	2,533	121k	14.46M
Proposed method ($th = 0.700$)	**28.6**	1,985	**26.4**	1,955	361k	14.46M
Proposed method w/ cov. constraint ($th = 0.600$)	26.1	3,064	23.2	3,077	11k	19.21M

Table 1: BLEU scores (Papineni et al., 2002) averaged over 3 tuning runs, obtained when added an in-domain phrase table to the system, created either by the baseline method or by our work with or without the coverage constraint activated (denoted "w/ cov. constraint"). Bold scores indicate statistical significance (p < 0.01) of the score over the baseline system, measured by approximate randomization using `MultEval` (Clark et al., 2011). We also present the number of OOV tokens in the test set and the number of sentence pairs actually used to train the in-domain phrase table. The speed of the method to evaluate sentence pairs from monolingual data was measured with 100 CPU threads (Xeon E5-2600) on 1 trillion sentence pairs randomly sampled.

old value. We examined {0.5, 0.6, 0.7, 0.8, 0.9} as the threshold value through tuning PBSMT systems, and determined 0.7 to be optimal.

We regarded the method proposed by Tillmann and Xu (2009) as a baseline, because it does not rely on document-level information, as ours. Unlike our method, in addition to the constraint based on length ratio, this method also used the coverage constraint. As discussed in Section 2.2, this constraint speeds up the extraction, but sacrifices source sentences with numerous OOV due to its heavy reliance on a bilingual lexicon learned from parallel data. To measure the effect of the coverage constraint, we also activated it in some of our experiments using our method. Then, as for our method, we discarded sentence pairs having a score lower than a threshold value and found the threshold value of -10 to be the best among {-15, -12, -10, -7}.

3.3 Results

Table 1 presents the results. Both the baseline and our methods outperformed the system using only the general-domain phrase table in both translation directions. This may be explained by the presence of highly parallel sentences in the in-domain monolingual data, from Wikipedia articles for instance, that can be retrieved by both methods.

Our method significantly outperformed the baseline, with 1.4 and 1.7 BLEU points gains respectively for Fr→En and En→Fr. Our method, with the optimal threshold of 0.7, extracted 361k sentence pairs from the in-domain monolingual data, while the baseline method extracted only 121k sentence pairs due presumably to the use of the coverage constraint that might remove source sentences with a high OOV ratio. Less OOV tokens remained with the system using our method, highlighting the positive effect of exploiting word embeddings in addition to lexical translation models. Activating the coverage constraint on our method was harmful and was significantly worse than the baseline. This constraint excludes candidate sentence pairs by relying only on general-domain lexical translation models, while our classifier is trained to use word embeddings that are more robust but unhelpful to discriminate the remaining candidates. Therefore, the optimal threshold value allowed the extraction of only 11k sentence pairs. In contrast, without this constraint, even with a high threshold value of 0.955 that retrieved as many sentence pairs as the baseline method, the extracted sentence pairs resulted in a significantly higher BLEU score than the baseline method, with a slightly better lexical coverage. Last but not least, our method is 11.9 times faster than the baseline method.

4 Feature contribution

To evaluate the impact of the features used during classification, we performed a feature ablation experiment. The results for the EMEA translation

Feature set	th	Fr→En	En→Fr
all	0.7	28.6	26.4
-avg. emb.	0.7	28.8	26.1
-max. al. emb.	0.7	29.0	26.1
-max. al. emb.	0.8	28.4	25.6
-lex. prob.	0.8	28.3	26.0
-length	0.6	28.9	26.4

Table 2: Results (BLEU) obtained without using some of the features during the classification (see Section 2.2). The features removed, independently, are the following: averaged word embeddings (avg. emb.), maximum alignment between embeddings (max. al. emb.), lexical translation probabilities (lex. prob.) and the length ratio of the source and target sentences (length). The "th" column indicates the threshold value for the classifier's score above which we retain the sentence pairs. This value was selected among the values $\{0.5, 0.6, 0.7, 0.8, 0.9\}$ with respect to the BLEU score on the development data, through the tuning of the PBSMT system, for each configuration.

task are reported in Table 2.

For both translation directions, the features that have the most important were the ones based on lexical translaiton probabilities and alignments between embeddings. For instance, in En→Fr translation, removing them led to a significant drop of 0.4 and 0.8 BLEU points, respectively.

For the Fr→En translation direction, surprisingly, we observed improvements on the test set for all configurations, except when removing either of the above two types of features. However, we did not observe such improvements for the En→Fr translation direction; removing any feature(s) consistently led to a lower or equal BLEU score. Feature ablation did not improve the performance on the development set for both translation directions, neither.

5 Classifier accuracy

To better understand the performance of our method, we also evaluated the accuracy of the classifier used in step 2 (see Section 2.2). Note that this evaluation does not intend to show how well the classifier retrieves useful pseudo-parallel sentences. We cannot directly evaluate it, as we do not have an evaluation data set that contains *gold pseudo-parallel sentences* at hand.

A set of in-domain *truly parallel sentences* was used for our evaluation. We selected the 50k first source sentences from the held-out in-domain EMEA parallel corpus,[15] and used each one of them to make two sentence pairs in order to obtain a positive and a negative example. For the positive example, the source sentence is associated to its correct translation from the EMEA corpus, while for the negative example, we associated the source sentence with a target sentence randomly extracted from the EMEA corpus. The classifier has then to decide if the sentence pair is correct or incorrect.

The classifier is the same one that was presented in Section 3.2 and trained on the MultiUn parallel data. On our EMEA evaluation data set, this classifier achieves an accuracy of 85.98%. This high accuracy highlights the potential of our method in retrieving highly, or truly, parallel sentences if such kinds of sentence pairs exist in the monolingual data exploited by our approach.

6 Conclusion and future work

We presented a method for extracting pseudo-parallel sentences from a pair of large monolingual corpora, without relying on any document-level information. Our domain adaptation experiments showed that our method outperformed the state-of-the-art method by more efficiently extracting more useful sentence pairs from in-domain monolingual data. In addition to the improved BLEU scores, our method provides a better handling of OOV, ignored by other methods that strongly rely on already trained lexical translation models.

Our method can further be speeded up by some approximation, such as local sensitive hashing, or by using a smaller number of dimensions for word embeddings. We leave the study of their impact to our future work. We believe that our work is also useful for other downstream tasks that need comparable or pseudo-parallel sentences, such as parallel phrase extraction (Hewavitharana and Vogel, 2016) and adaptation of neural machine translation systems (Luong and Manning, 2015; Freitag and Al-Onaizan, 2016).

Acknowledgments

We would like to thank all the reviewers for their valuable comments and suggestions.

---

[15] We used the EMEA training data provided by the same workshop on domain adaptation (Carpuat et al., 2012) that released the development and test data used in our experiments.

References

Sadaf Abdul Rauf and Holger Schwenk. 2011. Parallel sentence generation from comparable corpora for improved smt. *Machine Translation* 25(4):341–375. https://doi.org/10.1007/s10590-011-9114-9.

Yosshi Adi, Einat Kermany, Yonatan Belinkov, Ofer Lavi, and Yoav Goldberg. 2016. Fine-grained analysis of sentence embeddings using auxiliary prediction tasks. In *Proceedings of ICLR 2017*. https://arxiv.org/pdf/1608.04207v3.pdf.

Marine Carpuat, Hal Daumé III, Alexander Fraser, Chris Quirk, Fabienne Braune, Ann Clifton, Ann Irvine, Jagadeesh Jagarlamudi, John Morgan, Majid Razmara, Aleš Tamchyna, Katharine Henry, and Rachel Rudinger. 2012. Domain adaptation in machine translation: Final report. In *2012 Johns Hopkins Summer Workshop Final Report*. http://hal3.name/damt/.

Jonathan H. Clark, Chris Dyer, Alon Lavie, and Noah A. Smith. 2011. Better hypothesis testing for statistical machine translation: Controlling for optimizer instability. In *Proceedings of ACL-HLT*. Portland, Oregon. http://aclweb.org/anthology/P11-2031.

Jocelyn Coulmance, Jean-Marc Marty, Guillaume Wenzek, and Amine Benhalloum. 2015. Transgram, fast cross-lingual word-embeddings. In *Proceedings of EMNLP*. Lisbon, Portugal. https://doi.org/10.18653/v1/D15-1131.

Long Duong, Hiroshi Kanayama, Tengfei Ma, Steven Bird, and Trevor Cohn. 2016. Learning crosslingual word embeddings without bilingual corpora. In *Proceedings of EMNLP*. Austin, Texas. http://aclweb.org/anthology/D16-1136.

Markus Freitag and Yaser Al-Onaizan. 2016. Fast domain adaptation for neural machine translation. *CoRR* abs/1612.06897. https://arxiv.org/abs/1612.06897.

Pascale Fung and Percy Cheung. 2004. Mining very-non-parallel corpora: Parallel sentence and lexicon extraction via bootstrapping and em. In *Proceedings of EMNLP*. Barcelona, Spain. http://aclweb.org/anthology/W04-3208.

Ulrich Germann. 2001. Building a statistical machine translation system from scratch: How much bang for the buck can we expect? In *Proceedings of the ACL Workshop on Data-Driven Methods in Machine Translation*. Toulouse, France. http://aclweb.org/anthology/W01-1409.

Cyril Goutte, Marine Carpuat, and George Foster. 2012. The impact of sentence alignment errors on phrase-based machine translation performance. In *Proceedings of AMTA*. San Diego, USA. http://www.mt-archive.info/AMTA-2012-Goutte.pdf.

Sanjika Hewavitharana and Stephan Vogel. 2016. Extracting parallel phrases from comparable data for machine translation. *Natural Language Engineering* 22(4):549–573. https://doi.org/10.1017/S1351324916000139.

Tomoyuki Kajiwara and Mamoru Komachi. 2016. Building a monolingual parallel corpus for text simplification using sentence similarity based on alignment between word embeddings. In *Proceedings of COLING*. Osaka, Japan. http://aclweb.org/anthology/C16-1109.

Philipp Koehn, Hieu Hoang, Alexandra Birch, Chris Callison-Burch, Marcello Federico, Nicola Bertoldi, Brooke Cowan, Wade Shen, Christine Moran, Richard Zens, Chris Dyer, Ondřej Bojar, Alexandra Constantin, and Evan Herbst. 2007. Moses: Open source toolkit for statistical machine translation. In *Proceedings of ACL*. Prague, Czech Republic. http://aclweb.org/anthology/P07-2045.

Quoc V. Le and Tomas Mikolov. 2014. Distributed representations of sentences and documents. *CoRR* abs/1405.4053. https://arxiv.org/abs/1405.4053.

Jiwei Li, Minh-Thang Luong, and Dan Jurafsky. 2015. A hierarchical neural autoencoder for paragraphs and documents. *CoRR* abs/1506.01057. https://arxiv.org/abs/1506.01057.

Minh-Thang Luong and Christopher D. Manning. 2015. Stanford neural machine translation systems for spoken language domains. In *Proceedings of IWSLT*. Da Nang, Vietnam. http://www.mt-archive.info/15/IWSLT-2015-luong.pdf.

Tomas Mikolov, Quoc V. Le, and Ilya Sutskever. 2013a. Exploiting similarities among languages for machine translation. *CoRR* abs/1309.4168. http://arxiv.org/abs/1309.4168.

Tomas Mikolov, Ilya Sutskever, Kai Chen, Greg S Corrado, and Jeff Dean. 2013b. Distributed representations of words and phrases and their compositionality. In *Proceedings of NIPS*. https://papers.nips.cc/paper/5021-distributed-representations-of-words-and-phrases-and-their-compositionality.pdf.

Dragos Stefan Munteanu and Daniel Marcu. 2005. Improving machine translation performance by exploiting non-parallel corpora. *Computational Linguistics* 31(4):477–504. http://aclweb.org/anthology/J05-4003.

Kishore Papineni, Salim Roukos, Todd Ward, and Wei-Jing Zhu. 2002. Bleu: a method for automatic evaluation of machine translation. In *Proceedings of ACL*. Philadelphia, USA. http://aclweb.org/anthology/P02-1040.

Dan Ştefănescu, Radu Ion, and Sabine Hunsicker. 2012. Hybrid parallel sentence mining from comparable corpora. In *Proceedings of EAMT*. Trento, Italy. http://www.mt-archive.info/EAMT-2012-Stefanescu.pdf.

Christoph Tillmann and Jian-ming Xu. 2009. A simple sentence-level extraction algorithm for comparable data. In *Proceedings of HLT-NAACL*. Boulder, Colorado. http://aclweb.org/anthology/N09-2024.

Masao Utiyama and Hitoshi Isahara. 2003. Reliable measures for aligning japanese-english news articles and sentences. In *Proceedings of ACL*. Sapporo, Japan. http://aclweb.org/anthology/P03-1010.

Ivan Vulić and Anna Korhonen. 2016. On the role of seed lexicons in learning bilingual word embeddings. In *Proceedings of ACL*. Berlin, Germany. http://aclweb.org/anthology/P16-1024.

Bing Zhao and Stephan Vogel. 2002. Adaptive parallel sentences mining from web bilingual news collection. In *Proceedings of IEEE ICDM*. Maebashi, Japan. http://dl.acm.org/citation.cfm?id=844380.844785.

Feature Hashing for Language and Dialect Identification

Shervin Malmasi
Harvard Medical School, Boston, MA
Macquarie University, Australia
shervin.malmasi@mq.edu.au

Mark Dras
Macquarie University
Sydney, Australia
mark.dras@mq.edu.au

Abstract

We evaluate feature hashing for language
identification (LID), a method not previously used for this task. Using a standard
dataset, we first show that while feature
performance is high, LID data is highly
dimensional and mostly sparse ($>99.5\%$)
as it includes large vocabularies for many
languages; memory requirements grow as
languages are added. Next we apply hashing using various hash sizes, demonstrating that there is no performance loss with
dimensionality reductions of up to 86%.
We also show that using an ensemble of
low-dimension hash-based classifiers further boosts performance. Feature hashing
is highly useful for LID and holds great
promise for future work in this area.

1 Introduction

Language Identification (LID) is the task of determining the language of a text, at the document,
sub-document or even sentence level. LID is a
fundamental preprocessing task in NLP and is also
used in lexicography, machine translation and information retrieval. It is widely used for filtering
to select documents in a specific language; *e.g.*
LID can filter webpages or tweets by language.

Although LID has been widely studied, several
open issues remain (Hughes et al., 2006). Current
goals include developing models that can identify thousands of languages; extending the task to
more fine-grained dialect identification; and making LID functionality more readily available to
users/developers. A common challenge among
these goals is dealing with high dimensional feature spaces. LID differs from traditional text categorization tasks in some important aspects. Standard tasks, such as topic classification, are usually
performed within a single language, and the maximum feature space size is a function of the single
language's vocabulary. However, LID must deal
with vocabulary from many languages and the feature space grows prodigiously.

This raises immediate concerns about memory
requirements for such systems and portends implementation issues for applying the systems to
dozens, hundreds or even thousands of languages.
Recent LID work has reported results on datasets
including over 1,300 languages (Brown, 2014), albeit using small samples. Such models are going
to include an extraordinarily large feature space,
and individual vectors for each sample are going
to be extremely sparse. LID is usually done using
n-grams and as the number of languages and/or
n gets larger, the feature space will become prohibitively large or impractical for real-world use.

For high dimensional input, traditional dimensionality reduction methods (*e.g.* PCA, LDA) can
be computationally expensive. Feature selection
methods, *e.g.* those using entropy, are simpler but
still expensive. Recently, feature hashing has been
shown to be a very effective dimensionality reduction method (Weinberger et al., 2009). It has
proven to be useful in numerous machine learning
applications, particularly for handling extremely
high dimensional data. It also provides numerous
other benefits, which we describe in §2.1.

Although hashing could be tremendously useful for LID, to our knowledge no such experiments
have been reported to date. It is unclear how collisions of features from different languages would
affect its application for LID. Accordingly, the
aims of the present work are to: (1) evaluate the
effectiveness of hashing for LID; (2) compare its
performance to the standard n-gram approach; (3)
assess the role of hash size (and collision rate) on
accuracy for different feature types; and (4) determine if ensemble methods can boost performance.

Proceedings of the 55th Annual Meeting of the Association for Computational Linguistics (Short Papers), pages 399–403
Vancouver, Canada, July 30 - August 4, 2017. ©2017 Association for Computational Linguistics
https://doi.org/10.18653/v1/P17-2063

2 Related Work

2.1 Language and Dialect Identification

Work in language identification (LID) dates back to the seminal work of Beesley (1988), Dunning (1994) and Cavnar and Trenkle (1994). Automatic LID methods have since been widely used in NLP research and applications. Recently, attention has turned to discriminating between close languages, such as Malay-Indonesian and Croatian-Serbian (Ljubešić et al., 2007), or even dialects/varieties of one language, *e.g.* Arabic dialects (Malmasi et al., 2015). This has been the focus of the "Discriminating Similar Language" (DSL) shared task series in recent years. In this work we use data from the 2016 task (Malmasi et al., 2016).

The 2016 task used data from 12 different languages/dialects. A training and development set consisting of 20,000 sentences from each language and an unlabelled test set of 1,000 sentences per language was used for evaluation. Most participants relied on multi-class discriminative classifiers trained with word unigrams and character n-grams (Malmasi et al., 2016).

2.2 Feature Hashing

Feature hashing is a method for mapping a high-dimensional input to a low-dimensional space using hashing (Weinberger et al., 2009). Hashing has proven to be simple, efficient and effective. It has been applied to various tasks including protein sequence classification (Caragea et al., 2012), sentiment analysis (Da Silva et al., 2014), and malware detection (Jang et al., 2011).

This method uses a hash function $h(x)$ to arbitrarily map input to a hash key of a specified size. The hash size, *e.g.* 2^{18}, determines the size of the mapped feature space. Hash functions are many-to-one mappings. Collision occur when distinct inputs yield the same output, *i.e.* $h(a) = h(b)$. The collision rate is affected by the hash size. From a learning perspective, collisions cause random clustering of features and introduce noise; unrelated features map to the same vector index and may degrade the learner's accuracy. However, it has been shown that "the interference between independently hashed subspaces is negligible with high probability" (Weinberger et al., 2009).

A positive by-product of hashing is that it eliminates the need for a feature dictionary. In NLP, bag-of-words models require a full pass over the data to identify the vocabulary for each feature type (*e.g.* n-grams) and build a feature index.

Eliminating this has many benefits: it simplifies implementation of feature extraction methods, reduces memory overhead, and facilitates distributed computing. Global statistics, *e.g.* totals and per-class feature counts, are usually required for feature selection and dimensionality reduction methods. Feature hashing may eliminate the need for full processing of the data to calculate these.

3 Data and Experimental Setup

Our methodology is based on the results of 2016 DSL Shared Task (Malmasi et al., 2016) and we use their dataset. The DSL task is performed at the sentence level, making it more challenging.

3.1 Data

A key shortcoming in LID research has been the absence of a common dataset for evaluation (Hughes et al., 2006), a need that has been met by the corpora released as part of the DSL shared task series. We use the DSLCC 3.0 corpus from the 2016 DSL task.[1] This allows us to compare our findings to that of the 17 participants. Using a standard, publicly available dataset also facilitates replicability of our results. The 2016 task used data from 12 different languages and varieties,[2] including training/development sets composed of 20,000 sentences per language. An unlabelled test set of 1,000 sentences per language was used for evaluation. The total sentences for training and testing are 240k and 12k, respectively. We report our results on the standard test set.

3.2 Classifier and Evaluation

Participants applied various methods, but the task organizers note that linear classifiers, particularly SVMs, were the most successful (Malmasi et al., 2016). This is unsurprising as SVMs have been very successful for text classification and we adopt this method. The data is balanced across classes, so accuracy is used as the evaluation metric.

3.3 Features

Most DSL entries use surface features, with words and high-order character n-grams being particularly successful. We apply character n-grams of order 1–6 (`CH1-6`) and word unigrams (`WD1`).

---

[1] http://ttg.uni-saarland.de/resources/DSLCC/

[2] Bosnian (BS), Argentine Spanish (ES_AR), Peninsular Spanish (ES_ES), Mexican Spanish (ES_MX), Canadian French (FR_CA), Hexagonal French (FR_FR), Croatian (HR), Indonesian (ID), Malay (MY), Brazilian Portuguese (PT_BR), European Portuguese (PT_PT) and Serbian (SR).

4 Feature Performance & Dimensionality

In our first experiment we examine the feature space in our dataset and establish the memory requirements and accuracy of the feature types we use (character 1–6 n-grams and word unigrams).

For each feature type we extract the training vectors and use it to train a linear SVM model which is used to classify the standard test set. We report the feature's accuracy on the test set along with some statistics about the data: the number of features in the training data, the number of out-of-vocabulary (OOV) features[3] in the test data, and the sparsity[4] of the training data matrix. These results are shown in Figure 1.

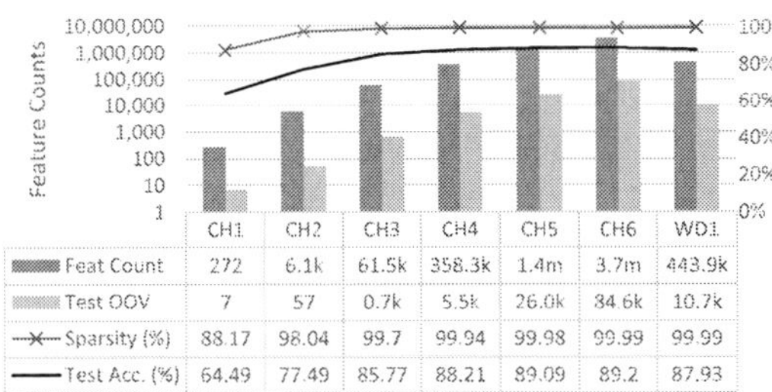

Figure 1: Details of our feature spaces. Training set feature counts and test set OOV counts are shown as bars (left axis, logarithmic scale). Training data sparsity and test set accuracy are shown as lines (in %, right axis).

These results reveal a number of interesting patterns. Character n-grams perform better than word unigrams. The winner of the 2016 DSL task combined various character n-grams into an SVM model to obtain 89.4% accuracy on the test set. We obtain the best result of 89.2% using character 6-grams alone. The character n-gram feature grow rapidly, from 61k trigrams to 3.7m 6-grams. While accuracy plateaus at 6-grams, there is only a 1% improvement from 4- to 6-grams, but a huge feature space increase. The number of OOV test features also increases, but is relatively small.

The sparsity analysis is also revealing, showing that for many features only around 0.1% of the training matrix contains non-zero values. We can expect that this sparsity will rapidly grow with the addition of more classes to the dataset. This poses a huge problem for practical applications of LID for discriminating large number of languages.

In this regard, we can also assess how the dimensionality cumulatively increases as languages

are added, shown in Figure 2. Features increase even as similar languages are added; we expect this trend to continue if more classes are added.

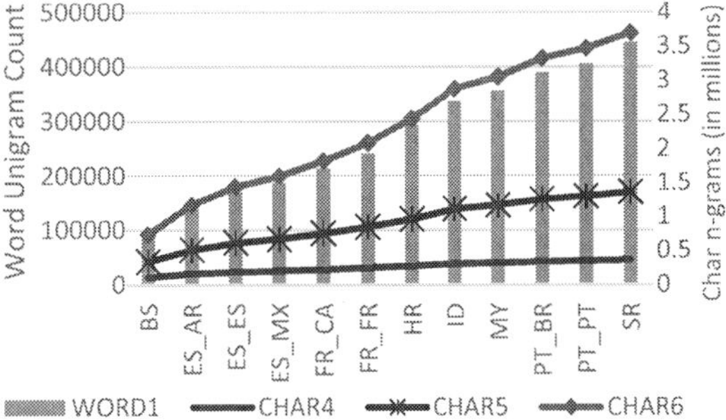

Figure 2: Feature growth rate as classes are added. Words (bars, left axis) and character n-grams (lines, right axis) grow as languages are added.

5 Feature Hashing Performance

Having established baseline performance for our features using the standard approach, we now experiment with applying feature hashing to the same data in order to evaluate its effectiveness for this task and compare it to the standard approach.

We also assess the effect of hash size on the feature collision rate, and in turn, on classification accuracy. To do this we test each feature[5] using hash sizes in the range 2^{10} (1024) to 2^{22} (2.1m) features, which covers most of our feature types. Our hash function is implemented using the signed 32-bit version of MurmurHash3.[6]

We report each feature's accuracy at every hash size, with the smallest hash that yields maximal accuracy considered to be the best result. Each feature is compared against its performance using the full feature space (baseline). These results, along with the reduction in the feature space for the best results, are listed in Table 1.

Our first observation is that every feature matches baseline performance at a hash size smaller than its full feature space. This demonstrates that feature hashing is useful for LID.

We can also assess the effect of feature collisions using the results, which we plot in Figure 3. We note that at the same hash size, features with a larger space perform worse. That is, with a 2^{12} hash size, CHAR4 outperforms 5- and 6-grams. This is evidence of performance degradation due to hash collision. However, we see that when using an appropriately sized hash, feature collisions between languages do not degrade performance.

---

[3] *i.e.* features present in the test set but not the training set.
[4] Matrix sparsity is the proportion of zero-valued elements.
[5] Except character unigrams which only have 272 features.
[6] https://github.com/aappleby/smhasher

Feature	Baseline	Hash Size													Δ feats
		2^{10}	2^{11}	2^{12}	2^{13}	2^{14}	2^{15}	2^{16}	2^{17}	2^{18}	2^{19}	2^{20}	2^{21}	2^{22}	
CHAR2	0.77	0.74	0.76	**0.77**	0.77	0.77	0.77	0.77	0.77	0.77	0.77	0.77	0.77	0.77	-33%
CHAR3	0.86	0.74	0.79	0.82	0.84	0.85	**0.86**	0.86	0.86	0.86	0.86	0.86	0.86	0.86	-47%
CHAR4	0.88	0.70	0.76	0.80	0.83	0.86	0.86	**0.88**	0.88	0.88	0.88	0.88	0.88	0.88	-82%
CHAR5	0.89	0.65	0.72	0.77	0.81	0.84	0.86	0.87	0.88	**0.89**	0.89	0.89	0.89	0.89	-81%
CHAR6	0.89	0.58	0.67	0.73	0.78	0.82	0.84	0.87	0.87	0.88	**0.89**	0.89	0.89	0.89	-86%
WORD1	0.88	0.70	0.74	0.78	0.81	0.83	0.85	0.86	0.87	**0.88**	0.88	0.88	0.88	0.88	-41%

Table 1: Test set accuracy for hashed features at each hash size. Baseline is accuracy without hashing. Best result (w/ smallest hash) per row in bold. Last column is the best result's reduction in dimensionality. We observe that every feature matches its baseline at a hash size smaller than its full feature space.

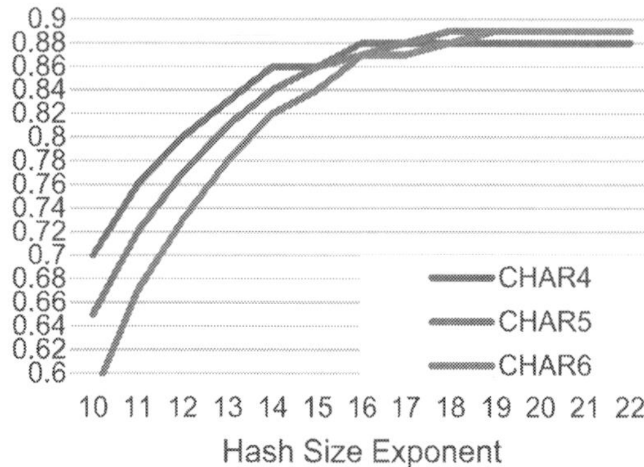

Figure 3: Performance (left axis) of 3 features at different hash sizes. Higher order n-grams perform worse at lower hash sizes due to collisions.

We also analyze the memory reduction achieved via hashing by calculating the relative difference in dimensionality between the best result and the full feature set, listed in the last column of Table 1. We see very significant reductions of up to 86% in dimensionality without any performance loss. Character 4-grams yield very competitive results (0.88) with a large feature space reduction of 82% using a hash size of 2^{16}.

6 Hashing-based Ensemble Classifier

Ensemble classifiers combine multiple learners with the aim of improving accuracy through enhanced decision making. They have been applied to many tasks and shown to achieve better results compared to single-classifier methods (Oza and Tumer, 2008). By aggregating the outputs of multiple classifiers their outputs are generally considered to be more robust. Ensembles have been successfully used for LID, *e.g.* winning the 2015 task (Malmasi and Dras, 2015a). They also achieve state-of-the-art performance for Native Language Identification (Malmasi and Dras, 2017). Could an ensemble composed of low-dimension hash-based classifiers achieve competitive performance?

In order to assess this we created an ensemble of our features with a hash size of 2^{16}. Evaluating against the test set, a hard voting ensemble achieved 88.7% accuracy while a probability-based combination obtained 89.2%. Comparing to the winning shared task accuracy of 89.4%, this is an excellent result given that only 65,536 features were used by our system. Ensemble combination boosted our best single-model 2^{16} hash size result by 1.1%. This highlights the utility of ensemble methods for hashing-based feature spaces. It also shows that model combination can compensate for small performance losses caused by hashing.

7 Discussion and Conclusion

We presented the first application of feature hashing for language identification. Results show that hashing is highly effective for LID and can ameliorate the dimensionality issues that can impose prohibitive memory requirements for some LID tasks. We further showed that reduced feature spaces with as few as 65k features can be combined in ensemble classifiers to boost performance. We also demonstrated the effect of hash collision on accuracy, and outlined the type of analysis needed to choose the correct hash size for a given feature.

Hashing provided dimensionality reductions of up to 86% without performance degradation. This is impressive considering that no feature selection or analysis was performed, making it highly efficient. This reduction facilitates model loading and training as we also showed that LID data is extremely sparse, with over 99% of our training matrix cells containing zeros. This is particularly useful for limited memory scenarios (*e.g.* handheld or embedded devices). It may also enable the use of methods requiring dense data representations, something often infeasible for large datasets.

Another key advantage of hashing is that it eliminates the need for maintaining a feature dictionary, making it easy to develop feature extraction modules. This greatly simplifies parallelization, lending itself to online learning and distributed systems, which are important issues for LID systems in our experience.

Hashing also holds promise for facilitating the use of deep learning methods for LID. In the 2016 DSL task, such systems performed "poorly compared to traditional classifiers"; participants cited "memory requirements and long training times" spanning several days (Malmasi et al., 2016). Feature hashing has recently been used to compress neural networks (Chen et al., 2015) and its application for deep learning-based text classification may provide insightful results.

There are also downsides to hashing, including the inability to interpret feature weights and model parameters, and some minor performance loss.

Future work in this area includes evaluation on larger datasets, as well as cross-corpus experiments, which may also be insightful. The application of these methods to other text classification tasks, particularly those dealing with language varieties such as Native Language Identification (Malmasi and Dras, 2015b), could also provide a deeper understanding about how they work.

References

Kenneth R Beesley. 1988. Language identifier: A computer program for automatic natural-language identification of on-line text. In *Proceedings of the 29th Annual Conference of the American Translators Association*. page 54.

Ralf D Brown. 2014. Non-linear Mapping for Improved Identification of 1300+ Languages. In *EMNLP*.

Cornelia Caragea, Adrian Silvescu, and Prasenjit Mitra. 2012. Protein sequence classification using feature hashing. *Proteome science* 10(1):S14.

William B. Cavnar and John M. Trenkle. 1994. N-Gram-Based Text Categorization. In *Proceedings of SDAIR-94*. Las Vegas, US, pages 161–175.

Wenlin Chen, James T Wilson, Stephen Tyree, Kilian Q Weinberger, and Yixin Chen. 2015. Compressing neural networks with the hashing trick. In *ICML*. pages 2285–2294.

Nadia FF Da Silva, Eduardo R Hruschka, and Estevam R Hruschka. 2014. Tweet sentiment analysis with classifier ensembles. *Decision Support Systems* 66:170–179.

Ted Dunning. 1994. *Statistical identification of language*. Computing Research Laboratory, New Mexico State University.

Baden Hughes, Timothy Baldwin, Steven Bird, Jeremy Nicholson, and Andrew MacKinlay. 2006. Reconsidering language identification for written language resources .

Jiyong Jang, David Brumley, and Shobha Venkataraman. 2011. Bitshred: feature hashing malware for scalable triage and semantic analysis. In *Proceedings of the 18th ACM conference on Computer and communications security*. ACM, pages 309–320.

Nikola Ljubešić, Nives Mikelić, and Damir Boras. 2007. Language indentification: How to distinguish similar languages? In *Information Technology Interfaces*. pages 541–546.

Shervin Malmasi and Mark Dras. 2015a. Language Identification using Classifier Ensembles. In *Proceedings of LT4VarDial 2015*.

Shervin Malmasi and Mark Dras. 2015b. Multilingual Native Language Identification. In *Natural Language Engineering*.

Shervin Malmasi and Mark Dras. 2017. Native Language Identification using Stacked Generalization. *arXiv preprint arXiv:1703.06541* .

Shervin Malmasi, Eshrag Refaee, and Mark Dras. 2015. Arabic Dialect Identification using a Parallel Multidialectal Corpus. In *Proceedings of PACLING 2015*. pages 209–217.

Shervin Malmasi, Marcos Zampieri, Nikola Ljubešić, Preslav Nakov, Ahmed Ali, and Jörg Tiedemann. 2016. Discriminating between Similar Languages and Arabic Dialect Identification: A Report on the Third DSL Shared Task. In *Proceedings of the 3rd Workshop on Language Technology for Closely Related Languages, Varieties and Dialects (VarDial)*. Osaka, Japan, pages 1–14.

Nikunj C Oza and Kagan Tumer. 2008. Classifier ensembles: Select real-world applications. *Information Fusion* 9(1):4–20.

Kilian Weinberger, Anirban Dasgupta, John Langford, Alex Smola, and Josh Attenberg. 2009. Feature hashing for large scale multitask learning. In *Proceedings of the 26th Annual International Conference on Machine Learning*. ACM, pages 1113–1120.

Detection of Chinese Word Usage Errors for Non-Native Chinese Learners with Bidirectional LSTM

Yow-Ting Shiue, Hen-Hsen Huang and Hsin-Hsi Chen
Department of Computer Science and Information Engineering
National Taiwan University
No. 1, Sec. 4, Roosevelt Road, Taipei, 10617 Taiwan
`orina1123@gmail.com,hhhuang@nlg.csie.ntu.edu.tw,hhchen@ntu.edu.tw`

Abstract

Selecting appropriate words to compose a sentence is one common problem faced by non-native Chinese learners. In this paper, we propose (bidirectional) LSTM sequence labeling models and explore various features to detect word usage errors in Chinese sentences. By combining CWINDOW word embedding features and POS information, the best bidirectional LSTM model achieves accuracy 0.5138 and MRR 0.6789 on the HSK dataset. For 80.79% of the test data, the model ranks the ground-truth within the top two at position level.

1 Introduction

Recently, more and more people around the world choose Chinese as their second language. That results in an increasing need for automatic grammatical error detection and correction (GEC) tools. To measure the performance of GEC systems in a standardized manner, several shared tasks have been conducted for English (Dale and Kilgarriff, 2011; Dale et al., 2012; Ng et al., 2013, 2014) and Chinese (Yu et al., 2014; Lee et al., 2015, 2016).

In Chinese sentences, a word usage error (WUE) is a grammatically or semantically incorrect token which is written in a wrong form itself, or is an existent word but is improper for its context (refer to example (E1)). In fact, many Chinese WUEs result from subtle semantic unsuitability instead of violation of syntactic constraints. In example (E1), both 權力 (power) and 權利 (right) are nouns in Chinese, and both versions are grammatically correct. It is difficult to formulate an explicit rule for recognizing this kind of errors.

(E1) 人們 有 (*權力,權利) 吃 安全 的 食品 。
(People have the (*power, right) to enjoy safe food.)

Shiue and Chen (2016) adopted the HSK corpus, a dynamic composition corpus built by Beijing Language and Culture University, to study the detection of WUEs. Instead of specific position information, their model only determines whether a sentence segment contains WUEs. Huang et al. (2016) used the HSK corpus to study the preposition selection problem. They proposed gated recurrent unit (GRU)-based models to select the most suitable one from a closed set of Chinese prepositions given the sentential context. Although their approach can be utilized to detect and correct preposition errors, it is still worth investigating how to recognize WUEs involving other types of words such as verbs and nouns.

In the past few years, distributed word representations derived from neural network models (Mikolov et al., 2013a; Pennington et al., 2014) have become popular among various studies in natural language processing. Beyond surface forms, these low-dimensional vector representations can encode syntactic and semantic information implicitly (Mikolov et al., 2013b). Because WUEs involve syntactic or semantic problems, vector representations could be promising for finding the erroneous tokens.

One challenging aspect of dealing with grammatical errors is that the errors usually do not stand on their own, but are dependent on the context (Chollampatt et al., 2016). Therefore, we need a model that considers the sequence of words in a sentence as a whole to determine which position needs correction. One possible model for this task is the Long Short-Term Memory (LSTM) model (Hochreiter and Schmidhuber, 1997), which processes sequential data and generates the output based not only on the information of the current time step, but also on the past information stored in the memory layer. Rei and Yannakoudakis (2016) adopted neural network models, including

404

Proceedings of the 55th Annual Meeting of the Association for Computational Linguistics (Short Papers), pages 404–410
Vancouver, Canada, July 30 - August 4, 2017. ©2017 Association for Computational Linguistics
https://doi.org/10.18653/v1/P17-2064

LSTM, to detect errors in English learner writing. However, they mainly focused on comparing different composition architectures under the same word representation, so it remained unclear to what extent pre-trained word embeddings can help. Huang and Wang (2016) used LSTM for Chinese grammatical error diagnosis, but their models are trained only on learner data, without external well-formed text. That means the performance might be limited by the relatively small amount of annotated sentences written by foreign learners.

This paper utilizes LSTM and its extension (Bidirectional LSTM) along with the information derived from external resources to deal with Chinese WUE detection. Several types of pre-trained word embeddings and additional token-level features are considered. Each token in a sentence will be labeled correct or incorrect. Experimental results show that our models can rank the ground-truth error position toward the top of the candidate list.

2 WUE Detection Based on Bidirectional LSTM

We formulate the Chinese WUE detection task as a sequence labeling problem. Each token, the fundamental unit after word segmentation, is labeled either correct (0) or incorrect (1).

We utilize the LSTM model for labeling. LSTM models long sequences better than simple recurrent neural network (RNN) does, since it is equipped with input, output and forget gates to control how much information is used. The ability of LSTM to capture longer dependencies among time steps makes it suitable for modeling the complex dependencies of the erroneous token on the other parts of the sentence.

We train the LSTM model with the Adam optimizer (Kingma and Ba, 2014) implemented in Keras (Chollet, 2015). The loss function is binary cross entropy. The batch size and the initial learning rate is set to 32 and 0.001 respectively. The training process is stopped when the validation accuracy does not increase for two consecutive epochs. The model with the highest validation accuracy is selected as the final model.

We apply a sigmoid activation function before the output layer, so the output score of each token, which is between 0 and 1, can be interpreted as the predicted level of incorrectness. With these scores,

our system can output a ranked list of candidate error positions. The positions with the highest incorrectness scores will be marked as incorrect. In (E2) we show an example labeling result of our system. The tokens 差 (bad) and 知識 (knowledge), with the highest scores, are most likely to be incorrect.

(E2) 學習　的　　知識　也　　很　　差
　　0.056　0.035　**0.153**　0.039　0.030　**0.429**
(The **knowledge** learned is also very **bad**.)

Bidirectional LSTM (Schuster and Paliwal, 1997) is an extension of LSTM which includes a backward LSTM layer. Both information before and after the current time step are taken into consideration. We need the "future" information to detect the error in example (E3). The incorrectness of the token 留在 (left at) cannot be determined without considering its object 我們 (us).

(E3) 店 是 爸爸 (*留在,留給) 我們 的 。
(The store is our father left (*at,to) us.)

3 Sequence Embedding Features

We consider the word sequence in a sentence and the corresponding POS tag sequence. They are mapped to sequences of real-valued vectors through an embedding layer. These vectors are also updated during the training process.

3.1 Word Embeddings

We set the word embedding size to 400. Besides randomly initialized embedding, we also tried several types of pre-trained word vectors. To train the word embeddings, we utilize the Chinese part of the ClueWeb09 dataset[1]. The Chinese part was extracted and segmented by Yu et al. (2012).

CBOW/Skip-gram Word Embeddings

We trained word vectors with the two architectures included in the word2vec software (Mikolov et al., 2013a). The continuous bag-of-words model (CBOW) uses the words in a context window to predict the target word, while the skip-gram model (SG) uses the target word to predict every word in the context window.

CWINDOW/Structured Skip-gram Word Embeddings

Taking the order of the context words into consideration, we also employ the continuous window model (CWIN) and the structured skip-gram

---

[1]http://lemurproject.org/clueweb09.php

405

model (Struct-SG) (Ling et al., 2015). The former replaces the summation of context word vectors in CBOW with a concatenation operation, and the latter applies different projection matrices for predicting context words in different relative position with the target word.

3.2 POS Embeddings

The POS embeddings are randomly initialized. We set the embedding size to 20, which is slightly smaller than the number of different POS tags (30) in our dataset.

4 Token Features

In addition to representing each token as a real-valued vector, we also incorporate some abstract features. These features are derived from the Google Chinese Web 5-gram corpus (Liu et al., 2010) and will be referred to as "n-gram features".

4.1 Out-of-Vocabulary Indicator

This feature is simply a bit indicating whether a word is an out-of-vocabulary word or not. If a token never appears in the Web 5-gram corpus, the bit is set to 1; otherwise it is set to 0.

4.2 N-gram Probability Features

We compute the n-gram probability of each token using the occurrence count in the Web 5-gram corpus. We consider only up to trigrams since the probabilities are mostly zero when $n > 3$. Given the limited amount of available learner data, these probabilities may serve as useful features indicating how likely an expression is valid in Chinese.

5 Experiments

5.1 Dataset

We obtain the "wrong" part of the HSK dataset used in (Shiue and Chen, 2016). Each sentence segment has exactly one token-level position that is erroneous. Word segmentation and POS tagging are performed with the Stanford CoreNLP toolkit (Manning et al., 2014). We filter out any sentence segment whose corrected version differs from it by more than one token due to segmentation issue. That is, we only focus on the cases in which the error can be corrected by replacing one single token. After filtering, we end up with 10,510 sentence segments. We use 10% data for validation and testing respectively, and the remaining 80% data as the training set.

5.2 Evaluation

Accuracy

We use the detection accuracy as our main evaluation metric. A test instance is regarded as correct only if our system gives the highest score of incorrectness for the ground-truth position. This metric is relatively strict as the average length of the sentence segments in our dataset is 9.24. The McNemar's test is adopted to perform statistical significance test.

Mean Reciprocal Rank (MRR)

The mean reciprocal rank rewards the test instances for which the model ranks the ground-truth near the top of the candidate list. MRR is defined as $\frac{1}{N}\sum_{i=1}^{N}\frac{1}{rank(i)}$, where N is the total number of test instances and $rank(i)$ is the rank of the ground-truth position of test instance i.

Hit@k Rate

The Hit@k rate regards a test instance as correct if the answer is ranked within the top k places. In the experiments, k is set to 2. We report this metric since one of the most common types of WUEs is collocation error. In example (E2), the problem involves a pair of words, i.e., the adjective 差 (bad) is not a suitable modifier of the noun 知識 (knowledge). (E4) and (E5) are both acceptable.

(E4) 學習 的 知識 也 很 不足
(The knowledge learned is also **insufficient**.)
(E5) 學習 的 態度 也 很 差
(The **attitude** of learning is also very bad.)

Which correction is better highly depends on the context or even the intended meaning in the writer's mind. If the model proposes two potentially erroneous tokens which are closely related to each other, it can be useful for Chinese learners.

Hit@r% Rate

Finding the exact position of the error could be more challenging in a longer sentence segment. We propose another hit rate measure which takes the segment length (len) into account. Specifically, we regard one test instance as correct if the answer is ranked within the top $\max(1, \lfloor len * r\% \rfloor)$ candidates. We report hit@20%. That is, for segments shorter than 10 tokens, the system is allowed to propose one candidate; for those whose length is between 10 and 14, the system is allowed to propose two, and so on. Equivalently, this measure judges whether our system can rank the ground-truth error position within the top 20%

Model	Features	Accuracy	MRR	Hit@2	Hit@20%
Random Baseline	-	0.1239	0.3312	0.2478	0.1611
LSTM	Rand. Init. Word Embedding	0.4186	0.6010	0.7222	0.6565
	CBOW	0.4072	0.5923	0.7155	0.6432
	CBOW + POS	0.4263	0.6150	0.7564	0.6908
	CBOW + POS + n-gram	0.4386	0.6204	0.7526	0.6755
	SG	0.4072	0.5910	0.7146	0.6365
	SG + POS	0.4301	0.6170	0.7593	0.6965
	SG + POS + n-gram	0.4386	0.6205	0.7507	0.6755
	CWIN	0.4853	0.6537	0.7774	0.7031
	CWIN + POS	0.4681	0.6435	0.7783	0.7022
	CWIN + POS + n-gram	0.4700	0.6502	0.7945	0.7269
	Struct-SG	0.4710	0.6412	0.7650	0.6889
	Struct-SG + POS	0.4757	0.6441	0.7593	0.6822
	Struct-SG + POS + n-gram	0.4881	0.6577	0.7840	0.7184
Bi-LSTM	CWIN	0.4795	0.6547	0.7840	0.7174
	CWIN + POS	**0.5138**	**0.6789**	0.8097	0.7479
	CWIN + POS + n-gram	0.4948	0.6719	**0.8173**	**0.7507**
	Struct-SG	0.4710	0.6412	0.7650	0.6889
	Struct-SG + POS	0.4757	0.6441	0.7593	0.6822
	Struct-SG + POS + n-gram	0.4948	0.6658	0.8040	0.7374

Table 1: Performance of the LSTM/Bi-LSTM sequence labeling models with different sets of features.

of the candidate list. This metric compromises Accuracy and Hit@k.

6   Results and Analysis

Table 1 shows the performance of our WUE detection models with different input features. The random baseline is a system randomly choosing one token as the incorrect position. The LSTM model using only randomly initialized word embeddings largely outperforms the random baseline. The pre-trained CBOW/SG word embeddings seem not very useful, leading to detection performance slightly lower than the model with random initial word embeddings. For both CBOW and SG, introducing the POS sequence improves the detection accuracy by about 2% and also improves all other measurements. The n-gram features further increase the accuracy by about 1%.

On the other hand, the CWIN and Struct-SG embeddings themselves are very powerful. Incorporating the POS and n-gram features leads to only slight improvements in terms of accuracy. Despite the small impact on accuracy, the n-gram features bring obvious improvements on hit@2 and hit@20% rates, indicating that they do facilitate the model in promoting the rank of the ground-truth position. Under the same set of features, all models with CWIN/Struct-SG significantly outperform their CBOW/SG counterparts ($p < 0.05$).

Bidirectional LSTM (Bi-LSTM) further enhance the performance of LSTM. The Bi-LSTM with CWIN+POS features achieves the best accuracy and MRR, and significantly outperforms its LSTM counterpart ($p < 0.005$). Bi-LSTM with CWIN+POS+n-gram features achieves the best Hit@2 and Hit@20%. To take a closer look, we analyze the performance of the two types of models on different length of segments in Table 2. We use the versions with all set of features and report hit@20% rates. Using Bi-LSTM leads to some improvement on short (≤ 9 tokens) segments, and larger improvement on mid-length (10~14 tokens) ones. Even longer (≥ 15 tokens) segments are relatively rare since foreign learners seldom construct complex sentences.

In Section 5.2 we justify the use of the hit@2 metric by pointing out that a WUE usually involves a pair of words dependent on each other. We can verify whether the top two candidates proposed by our model are closely related by examining the dependency distance. We take the output of the Bi-LSTM model with CWIN+POS+n-gram features and analyze the error cases where the model ranks the ground-truth error position second. We use the dependency parsing output of CoreNLP to construct an undirected graph, where

Length (# tests)	# proposed	LSTM	Bi-LSTM
≤ 9 (645)	1	0.7426	**0.7659**
10~14 (317)	2	0.6908	**0.7319**
≥ 15 (89)	≥ 3	**0.7416**	0.7079

Table 2: Hit@20% rates of LSTM and Bi-LSTM on segments with different lengths.

# correct ($c_1 = a$)		520 (49.48%)
# tests where $c_2 = a$		339 (32.25%)
Average $dis(c_1, c_2)$ when $c_2 = a$		2.07
# tests where $c_2 = a$ and $dis(c_1, c_2) = 1$		129 (12.27%)

Table 3: Summary of the analysis of the dependency between the top two candidates proposed by the CWIN+POS+n-gram Bi-LSTM model. a denotes the ground-truth error position. c_1 and c_2 denote the first and the second candidate positions proposed by the model. $dis(c_1, c_2)$ is the distance between c_1 and c_2 on the dependency graph.

POS (# tests)	CWIN	CWIN+POS
VV (325)	0.8123	**0.8185**
NN (282)	0.6879	**0.7447**
AD (134)	0.6194	**0.7015**

Table 4: Hit@20% rates of Bi-LSTM models with or without POS features on three most frequent POS tags of the erroneous token.

each dependency corresponds to an edge, and calculate the shortest distance between the top two candidates in these cases. The results are summarized in Table 3. The average distance (2.07) is small compared to the average length of the segments (9.24), indicating that our model can consider the dependencies among words when ranking the candidate positions.

A factor that might limit the effectiveness of POS features is that the POS tagger trained on well-formed text may not perform well on noisy learner data. In fact, for 26.7% of the test data, the POS tag of the original erroneous token differs from that of its corrected version. We compare the performance of the model with or without POS features on three most frequent POS tags in Table 4. As can be seen, the POS information of the erroneous segment, which potentially contains errors, can still be helpful for detecting anomaly of the segment. In example (E6) we show the scores of incorrectness predicted by models with or without POS features. The "DEC + AD" construction is invalid in Chinese, so in this case the error can be detected more easily if POS information is available.

(E6)	應該	有	別人	的	*盡力
POS tag	VV	VE	NN	DEC	**AD**
w/o POS	0.048	**0.226**	0.030	0.016	0.042
w/ POS	0.010	0.066	0.031	0.071	**0.077**

(There should be someone else's **utmost**.)

Word	Error rate	Precision	Recall
產生 (generate)	0.571 (8/14)	0.700 (7/10)	0.875 (7/8)
經驗 (experience)	0.500 (5/10)	0.667 (4/6)	0.800 (4/5)
發生 (happen)	0.455 (5/11)	0.571 (4/7)	0.800 (4/5)
而 (so)	0.417 (20/48)	0.550 (11/20)	0.550 (11/20)

Table 5: Precision/recall of Bi-LSTM models with CWIN+POS features on four most commonly misused ($err\_rate(w) > 0.4$) words.

In Table 5 we show the precision/recall of the Bi-LSTM model with CWIN+POS features on four most commonly misused words. The error rate of a word w is calculated on the test set by $err\_rate(w) = \frac{\text{\# segments in which } w \text{ is misused}}{\text{\# segments containing } w}$. We exclude words that occur in less than 10 segments regardless of their error rates. In general, our model achieves high recall and fair precision. Discriminating correct and wrong usage of the conjunction 而 (so), which often connects more than one segment, seems to be the most difficult. For example, in (E7) the inappropriateness of 而 cannot be recognized unless we consider the wider context of this segment.

(E7) (*而,並) 當成 此生 做人 的 道理
(..., (*so,and) take it as a lifelong way to behave around others.)

7 Conclusion

In this paper we propose an LSTM-based sequence labeling model for detecting WUEs in sentences written by non-native Chinese learners. The experimental results suggest that the CWIN/Struct-SG embeddings, which consider word orders, are better word features for Chinese WUE detection. Moreover, Bi-LSTM is more preferred than LSTM. While a wrong usage often involves more than one token, making it difficult to determine which one should be corrected, the best model can rank the ground-truth error position within the top two in 80.97% of the cases.

One possible future direction is to exploit more sophisticated structural information such as dependency paths. Moreover, it is also worth studying how to extend our system to cope with the correction task.

Acknowledgments

This research was partially supported by Ministry of Science and Technology, Taiwan, under grants MOST-104-2221-E-002-061-MY3 and MOST-105-2221-E-002-154-MY3.

References

Shamil Chollampatt, Kaveh Taghipour, and Hwee Tou Ng. 2016. Neural network translation models for grammatical error correction. In *Proceedings of the Twenty-Fifth International Joint Conference on Artificial Intelligence*. pages 2768–2774.

François Chollet. 2015. Keras. `https://github.com/fchollet/keras`.

Robert Dale, Ilya Anisimoff, and George Narroway. 2012. Hoo 2012: A report on the preposition and determiner error correction shared task. In *Proceedings of the Seventh Workshop on Building Educational Applications Using NLP*. Association for Computational Linguistics, pages 54–62. http://aclweb.org/anthology/W12-2006.

Robert Dale and Adam Kilgarriff. 2011. Helping our own: The hoo 2011 pilot shared task. In *Proceedings of the 13th European Workshop on Natural Language Generation*. Association for Computational Linguistics, pages 242–249. http://aclweb.org/anthology/W11-2838.

Sepp Hochreiter and Jürgen Schmidhuber. 1997. Long short-term memory. *Neural computation* 9(8):1735–1780.

Hen-Hsen Huang, Yen-Chi Shao, and Hsin-Hsi Chen. 2016. Chinese preposition selection for grammatical error diagnosis. In *Proceedings of COLING 2016, the 26th International Conference on Computational Linguistics: Technical Papers*. The COLING 2016 Organizing Committee, pages 888–899. http://aclweb.org/anthology/C16-1085.

Shen Huang and Houfeng Wang. 2016. Bi-lstm neural networks for chinese grammatical error diagnosis. In *Proceedings of the 3rd Workshop on Natural Language Processing Techniques for Educational Applications (NLPTEA 2016)*. The COLING 2016 Organizing Committee, pages 148–154. http://aclweb.org/anthology/W16-4919.

Diederik Kingma and Jimmy Ba. 2014. Adam: A method for stochastic optimization. *arXiv preprint arXiv:1412.6980* .

Lung-Hao Lee, Gaoqi Rao, Liang-Chih Yu, Endong Xun, Baolin Zhang, and Li-Ping Chang. 2016. Overview of nlp-tea 2016 shared task for chinese grammatical error diagnosis. In *Proceedings of the 3rd Workshop on Natural Language Processing Techniques for Educational Applications (NLPTEA 2016)*. The COLING 2016 Organizing Committee, pages 40–48. http://aclweb.org/anthology/W16-4906.

Lung-Hao Lee, Liang-Chih Yu, and Li-Ping Chang. 2015. Overview of the nlp-tea 2015 shared task for chinese grammatical error diagnosis.

In *Proceedings of the 2nd Workshop on Natural Language Processing Techniques for Educational Applications (NLPTEA 2015)*. Association for Computational Linguistics, pages 1–6. https://doi.org/10.18653/v1/W15-4401.

Wang Ling, Chris Dyer, W. Alan Black, and Isabel Trancoso. 2015. Two/too simple adaptations of word2vec for syntax problems. In *Proceedings of the 2015 Conference of the North American Chapter of the Association for Computational Linguistics: Human Language Technologies (HLT-NAACL)*. Association for Computational Linguistics, pages 1299–1304. https://doi.org/10.3115/v1/N15-1142.

Fang Liu, Meng Yang, and Dekang Lin. 2010. Chinese web 5-gram version 1. *Linguistic Data Consortium, Philadelphia* .

Christopher Manning, Mihai Surdeanu, John Bauer, Jenny Finkel, Steven Bethard, and David McClosky. 2014. The stanford corenlp natural language processing toolkit. In *Proceedings of 52nd Annual Meeting of the Association for Computational Linguistics: System Demonstrations*. Association for Computational Linguistics, pages 55–60. https://doi.org/10.3115/v1/P14-5010.

Tomas Mikolov, Kai Chen, Greg Corrado, and Jeffrey Dean. 2013a. Efficient estimation of word representations in vector space. *arXiv preprint arXiv:1301.3781* .

Tomas Mikolov, Wen-tau Yih, and Geoffrey Zweig. 2013b. Linguistic regularities in continuous space word representations. In *Proceedings of the 2013 Conference of the North American Chapter of the Association for Computational Linguistics: Human Language Technologies (HLT-NAACL)*. Association for Computational Linguistics, pages 746–751. http://aclweb.org/anthology/N13-1090.

Tou Hwee Ng, Mei Siew Wu, Ted Briscoe, Christian Hadiwinoto, Hendy Raymond Susanto, and Christopher Bryant. 2014. The conll-2014 shared task on grammatical error correction. In *Proceedings of the Eighteenth Conference on Computational Natural Language Learning: Shared Task*. Association for Computational Linguistics, pages 1–14. https://doi.org/10.3115/v1/W14-1701.

Tou Hwee Ng, Mei Siew Wu, Yuanbin Wu, Christian Hadiwinoto, and Joel Tetreault. 2013. The conll-2013 shared task on grammatical error correction. In *Proceedings of the Seventeenth Conference on Computational Natural Language Learning: Shared Task*. Association for Computational Linguistics, pages 1–12. http://aclweb.org/anthology/W13-3601.

Jeffrey Pennington, Richard Socher, and Christopher Manning. 2014. Glove: Global vectors for word representation. In *Proceedings of the 2014 Conference on Empirical Methods in Natural Language Processing (EMNLP)*. Association for Computational Linguistics, pages 1532–1543. https://doi.org/10.3115/v1/D14-1162.

Marek Rei and Helen Yannakoudakis. 2016. Compositional sequence labeling models for error detection in learner writing. In *Proceedings of the 54th Annual Meeting of the Association for Computational Linguistics (Volume 1: Long Papers)*. Association for Computational Linguistics, pages 1181–1191. https://doi.org/10.18653/v1/P16-1112.

Mike Schuster and Kuldip K Paliwal. 1997. Bidirectional recurrent neural networks. *IEEE Transactions on Signal Processing* 45(11):2673–2681.

Yow-Ting Shiue and Hsin-Hsi Chen. 2016. Detecting word usage errors in chinese sentences for learning chinese as a foreign language. In *Proceedings of the Tenth International Conference on Language Resources and Evaluation (LREC 2016)*. European Language Resources Association (ELRA), pages 220–224.

Chi-Hsin Yu, Yi jie Tang, and Hsin-Hsi Chen. 2012. Development of a web-scale chinese word n-gram corpus with parts of speech information. In *Proceedings of the Eighth International Conference on Language Resources and Evaluation (LREC 2012)*. European Language Resources Association (ELRA), pages 320–324.

Liang-Chih Yu, Lung-Hao Lee, and Li-Ping Chang. 2014. Overview of grammatical error diagnosis for learning chinese as a foreign language. In *Proceedings of the 1st Workshop on Natural Language Processing Techniques for Educational Applications (NLPTEA 2014)*. pages 42–47.

Automatic Compositor Attribution in the First Folio of Shakespeare

Maria Ryskina* **Hannah Alpert-Abrams†** **Dan Garrette‡** **Taylor Berg-Kirkpatrick***

* Language Technologies Institute, Carnegie Mellon University, {mryskina,tberg}@cs.cmu.edu
†Comparative Literature Program, University of Texas at Austin, halperta@gmail.com
‡ Google, dhgarrette@google.com

Abstract

Compositor attribution, the clustering of pages in a historical printed document by the individual who set the type, is a bibliographic task that relies on analysis of orthographic variation and inspection of visual details of the printed page. In this paper, we introduce a novel unsupervised model that jointly describes the textual and visual features needed to distinguish compositors. Applied to images of Shakespeare's *First Folio*, our model predicts attributions that agree with the manual judgements of bibliographers with an accuracy of 87%, even on text that is the output of OCR.

1 Introduction

Within literary studies, the field of bibliography has an unusually long tradition of quantitative analysis. One particularly relevant area is that of *compositor attribution*—the clustering of pages in a historical printed document by the individual (the *compositor*) who set the type. Like stylometry, a long-standing area of NLP that has largely focused on attributing the authorship of text (Holmes, 1994; Hope, 1994; Juola, 2006; Koppel et al., 2009; Jockers and Witten, 2010), the analysis of *orthographic* patterns is fundamental to compositor attribution. Additionally, compositor attribution often makes use of *visual* features, such as whitespace layout, introducing new challenges. These analyses have traditionally been done by hand, but efforts are painstaking due to the difficulty of manually recording these features.

In this paper, we present an unsupervised model specifically designed for compositor attribution that incorporates both textual and visual sources of evidence traditionally used by bibliographers (Hinman, 1963; Taylor, 1981; Blayney, 1991).

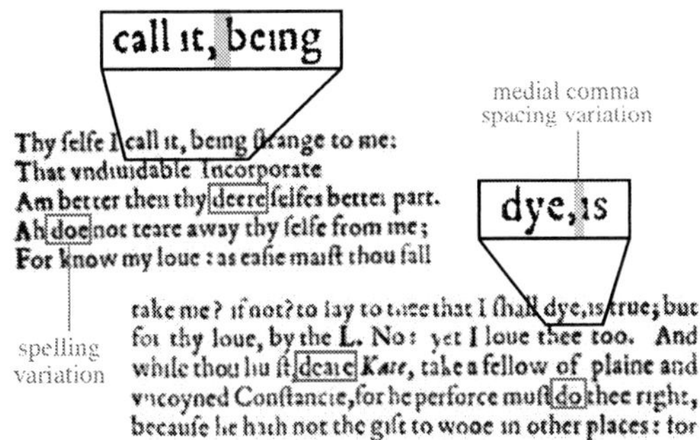

Figure 1: The compositor of the left page tended to use the spellings doe and deere, while the compositor for the right page used spellings do and deare, indicating these pages were likely set by different people. The varying width of the medial comma whitespace also distinguishes the typesetters.

Our model jointly describes the patterns of variation both in orthography and in the whitespace between glyphs, allowing us to cluster pages by discovering patterns of similarity and difference. When applied to digital scans of historical printed documents, our approach learns orthographic and whitespace preferences of individual compositors and predicts groupings of pages set by the same compositor.[1] This is, to our knowledge, the first attempt to perform compositor attribution automatically. Prior work has proposed automatic approaches to authorship attribution—which is typically viewed as the supervised problem of identifying a particular author given samples of their writing. In contrast, compositor attribution lacks supervision because compositors are unknown and, in addition, focuses on different linguistic patterns. We explain spellings of words conditioned on word choice, not the word choice itself.

---

[1] The validity of compositor attribution has sparked an ongoing and heated debate among bibliographers (McKenzie, 1969, 1984; Rizvi, 2016); while some reject parts or all of this approach, it continues to be cited in authoritative bibliographical texts (Gaskell, 2007; Blayney, 1996). Without taking a position in this debate, we seek only to automate the methods that remain in use by particular bibliographers (Blayney, 1996; Burrows, 2013).

Proceedings of the 55th Annual Meeting of the Association for Computational Linguistics (Short Papers), pages 411–416
Vancouver, Canada, July 30 - August 4, 2017. ©2017 Association for Computational Linguistics
https://doi.org/10.18653/v1/P17-2065

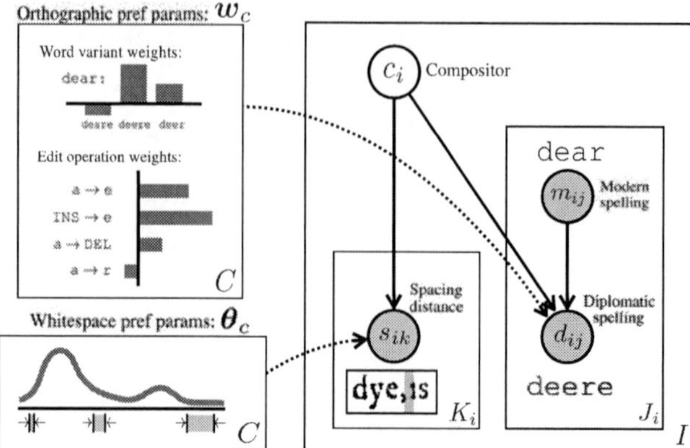

Figure 2: In our model, a compositor c_i is generated for page i from a multinomial prior. Then, each diplomatic word, d_{ij}, is generated conditioned on c_i and the corresponding modern word, m_{ij}, from a distribution parameterized by weight vector w_c. Finally, each medial comma spacing width (measured in pixels), s_{ik}, is generated conditioned on c_i from a distribution parameterized by θ_c.

To evaluate our approach, we fit our model to digital scans of Shakespeare's *First Folio* (1623)— a document with well established manual judgements of compositor attribution. We find that even when relying on noisy OCR transcriptions of textual content, our model predicts compositor attributions that agree with manual annotations 87% of the time, outperforming several simpler baselines. Our approach opens new possibilities for considering patterns across a larger vocabulary of words and at a higher visual resolution than has been possible historically. Such a tool may enable scalable first-pass analysis in understudied domains as a complement to humanistic studies of composition.

2 Background

In this paper we focus on modeling the same types of observations made by scholars and demonstrate agreement with authoritative attributions. We use compositor studies of Shakespeare's *First Folio* to inform our approach, drawing on the methods proposed by Hinman (1963), Howard-Hill (1973), and Taylor (1981). Hinman's landmark 1963 study clustered the pages of the *First Folio* according to five different compositors based on variations in spelling among three common words. Figure 1, for example, shows portions of two pages of the *First Folio* with different spelling variants for the words dear and do: one compositor used deere and doe, while the other used deare and do. Hinman relied on the assumption that each compositor was consistent in their preferences for the sake of convenience in the typesetting process (Blayney, 1991). Subsequent studies looked at larger sets of words and more general orthographic preferences (e.g. the preference to terminate words with -ie instead of -y), leading to modifications of Hinman's original analysis

(Howard-Hill, 1973; Taylor, 1981). In this paper we propose a probabilistic model designed to capture both word-specific preferences and general orthographic patterns. To separate the effect of the compositor from the choices made by the author or editor, we condition on a modernized (collated) version of Shakespeare's text as was done by scholars.

Visual features, including typeface usage and whitespace layout, also inform compositor attribution. For example, the highlighted spacing in Figure 1 shows different choices after medial commas (commas that occur before the end of the line). Bibliographers produced new hypotheses about how many compositors were involved in production based on the analysis of the use of spaces before and after punctuation (Howard-Hill, 1973; Taylor, 1981). We additionally incorporate this source of evidence into to our automatic approach by modeling pixel-level whitespace distances.

Bibliographers also use contextual information to inform their analyses, including copy text orthography, printing house records, collation, type case usage, and the use of type with cast-on spaces. In our model, we restrict our analysis to only those features that can be derived from the OCR output and simple visual analysis.

3 Model

Our computational approach to compositor attribution operates on the sources of evidence that have been considered by bibliographers. In particular, we focus on jointly modeling patterns of orthographic variation and spacing preferences across pages of a document, treating compositor assignments as latent variables in a generative model. We assume access to a diplomatic transcription of the document (a transcription faithful to the original orthography), which we automatically align with a modernized version.[2] We experiment with both manually and automatically (OCR) produced transcriptions, and assume access to pixel-level spacing information on each page, which can be extracted using OCR as described in Section 4.

Figure 2 shows the generative process. In our model, each of I total pages is generated independently. The compositor assignment for the ith page is represented by the variable $c_i \in \{1, \ldots, C\}$ and is generated from a multinomial prior. For page i, each diplomatic word, d_{ij}, is generated conditioned on the corresponding modern word, m_{ij}, and the compositor who set the page, c_i. Finally, the model produces the pixel width of the space after each medial comma, s_{ik}, again conditioned on the compositor, c_i. The joint distribution for page i, conditioned on modern text, takes the following form:

$$
\begin{aligned}
P(\{d_{ij}\}, \{s_{ik}\}, c_i | \{m_{ij}\}) = \\
\quad P(c_i) \qquad\qquad \text{[Prior on compositors]} \\
\quad \cdot \prod_{j=1}^{J_i} P(d_{ij} | m_{ij}, c_i; \boldsymbol{w}_{c_i}) \quad \text{[Orthographic model]} \\
\quad \cdot \prod_{k=1}^{K_i} P(s_{ik} | c_i; \boldsymbol{\theta}_{c_i}) \qquad \text{[Whitespace model]}
\end{aligned}
$$

3.1 Orthographic Preference Model

We choose the parameterization of the distribution of diplomatic words in order to capture two types of spelling preference: (1) general preferences for certain character groups (such as $-\texttt{ie}$) and (2) preferences that only pertain to a particular word and do not indicate a larger pattern. Since it is unknown which of the two behaviors is dominant, we let the model describe both and learn to separate their effects. Using a log-linear parameterization,

$$
P(d|m, c; \boldsymbol{w}) \propto \exp(\boldsymbol{w}_c^\top \mathbf{f}(m, d))
$$

we introduce features to capture both effects. Here, $\mathbf{f}(m, d)$ is a feature function defined on modern word m paired with diplomatic word d, while $\boldsymbol{w}_c$ is a weight vector corresponding to compositor c.

To capture word-specific preferences we add an indicator feature for each pair of modern word m and diplomatic spelling d. We refer to these as WORD features below. To capture general orthographic preferences we introduce an additional set of features based on the edit operations involved in the computation of Levenshtein distance between m and d. In particular, each operation is added as a separate feature, both with and without local context (previous or next character of the modern word). We refer to this group as EDIT features. The weight vector for each compositor represents their unique biases, as shown in the depiction of these parameters in Figure 2.

3.2 Whitespace Preference Model

Manual analysis of spacing has revealed differences across pages. In particular, the choice of spaced or non-spaced punctuation marks is hypothesized by biobliographers to be indicative of compositor preference and specific typecase. We add whitespace distance to our model to capture those observations. While bibliographers only made a coarse distinction between spaced or non-spaced commas, in our model we generate medial comma spacing widths, s_{ik}, that are measured in pixels to enable finer-grained analysis. We use a simple multinomial parameterization where each pixel width is treated as a separate outcome up to some maximum allowable width:

$$
s_{ik} | c_i \sim Mult(\boldsymbol{\theta}_{c_i})
$$

Here, $\boldsymbol{\theta}_c$ represents the vector of multinomial spacing parameters corresponding to compositor c. We choose this parameterization because it can capture non-unimodal whitespace preference distributions, as depicted in Figure 2, and it makes learning simple.

3.3 Learning and Inference

Modern and diplomatic words and spacing variables are observed, while compositor assignments are latent. In order to fit the model to an input document we estimate the orthographic preference parameters, $\boldsymbol{w}_c$, and spacing preference parameters, $\boldsymbol{\theta}_c$, for each compositor using EM. The E-step is accomplished via a tractable sum over compositor assignments, while the M-step for $\boldsymbol{w}_c$ is accomplished via gradient ascent (Berg-Kirkpatrick et al., 2010). The M-step for spacing parameters, $\boldsymbol{\theta}_c$, uses the standard multinomial update. Predicting compositor groups is accomplished via an

---

[2]Modern editions are common for many books that are of interest to bibliographers, though future work could consider how to cope with their absence.

| Model Setup | Bodleian Transcription | | | | Ocular OCR Transcription | | | |
| | Hinman Attr | | Blayney Attr | | Hinman Attr | | Blayney Attr | |
	1-to-1	M-to-1	1-to-1	M-to-1	1-to-1	M-to-1	1-to-1	M-to-1
RANDOM	22.5	49.6	16.7	49.6	22.5	49.6	16.7	49.6
BASIC w/ HINMAN	67.9	71.8	60.4	67.3	66.6	70.5	47.1	63.8
w/ AUTO	64.3	81.0	58.8	81.3	64.9	81.1	53.7	80.7
FEAT w/ EDIT	75.3	79.1	77.1	83.1	76.8	77.4	76.1	76.0
w/ EDIT + WORD	81.1	81.1	80.7	80.6	75.1	75.0	74.4	74.4
w/ EDIT + SPACE	**87.6**	**87.5**	**87.3**	**87.2**	**86.7**	**86.6**	**85.9**	**85.8**
w/ ALL	83.8	83.7	83.5	83.4	82.5	82.4	82.4	82.2

Table 1: The experimental results for all setups of the model. In the experiments with BASIC model, we compare the short HINMAN word list with the automatically filtered AUTO word list. We show results for several variants of our full model, labeled as FEAT, both with and without spacing generation. A random baseline is included for comparison.

independent argmax over each c_i. In all experiments we run 75 iterations of EM with 100 random restarts, choosing the learned parameters corresponding the best model likelihood.

4 Experiments

Data: To evaluate our model when it has access to perfectly transcribed historical text, we use the Bodleian diplomatic transcription of the *First Folio*.[3] To test whether our approach can also work with untranscribed books, we ran the Ocular OCR system (Berg-Kirkpatrick et al., 2013) on the Bodleian facsimile images to create an automatic diplomatic transcription. In both cases, we used Ocular's estimates of glyph bounding boxes on the complete *First Folio* images to extract spacing information. The modern text was taken from MIT Complete Works of Shakespeare[4] and was aligned with diplomatic transcriptions by running a word-level edit distance calculation. The extracted substitutions form the model's observed modern-diplomatic word pairs.

Evaluation: To compare the recovered attribution with those proposed by bibliographers, we evaluate against an authoritative attribution compiled by Peter Blayney (1996) which includes the work of various scholars (Hinman, 1963; Howard-Hill, 1973, 1976, 1980; Taylor, 1981; O'Connor, 1975; Werstine, 1982). We also evaluate our system against an earlier, highly influential model proposed by Hinman (1963), which we approximate by reverting certain compositor divisions in Blayney's attribution. Hinman's attribution posited five compositors, while Blayney's posited eight. In experiments, we set the model's maximum number of compositors to $C = 5$ when evaluating on Hinman's attribution, and use $C = 8$

[3] http://firstfolio.bodleian.ox.ac.uk/
[4] http://shakespeare.mit.edu/

with Blayney's. We compute the one-to-one and many-to-one accuracy, mapping the recovered page groups to the gold compositors to maximize accuracy, as is standard for many unsupervised clustering tasks, e.g. POS induction (see Christodoulopoulos et al. (2010)).

BASIC model variant: We evaluate a simple baseline model that uses a multinomial parameterization for generating diplomatic words and does not incorporate spacing information. We use two different options for selection of spelling variants to be considered by the model. First, we consider only the three words selected by Hinman: do, go and here (referred to as HINMAN). Second, we use a larger, automatically selected, word list (referred to as AUTO). Here, we select all modern words with frequency greater than 70 that are not names and that exhibit sufficient variance in diplomatic spellings (most common diplomatic spelling occurs in less than 80% of aligned tokens). For our full model, described in the next section, we always use the larger AUTO word list.

FEAT model variant: We run experiments with several variants of our full model, described in Section 3 (referred to as FEAT since they use a feature-based parameterization of diplomatic word generation.) We try ablations of WORD and EDIT features, as well as model variants with and without the spacing generation component (referred to as SPACE.) We refer to the full model that includes both types of features and spacing generation as ALL.

5 Results

Our experimental results are presented in Table 1. The BASIC variant, modeled after Hinman's original procedure, substantially outperforms the random baseline, with the HINMAN word list outperforming the larger AUTO word list. However, use

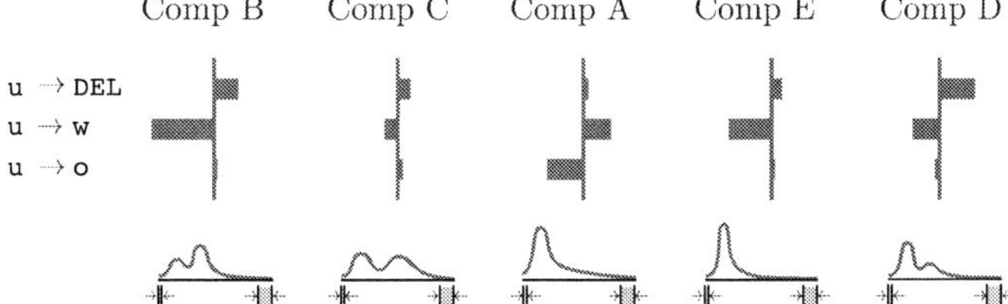

Figure 3: Learned behaviors of the Folio compositors. Our model only detected the presence of five compositors (ranked according to number of pages the compositor set in our model's prediction). Compositor D's habit of omitting u (yong vs. young) and compositor C's usage of spaced medial commas were also noticed in Taylor (1981).

of the larger word list with feature-based models yields large gains in all scenarios, including evaluation on Hinman's original attributions and while using OCR diplomatic transcriptions. The best-performing model for both manually transcribed and OCR text uses EDIT features in conjunction with spacing generation and achieves an accuracy of up to 87%. Including WORD features on top of this leads to slightly reduced performance, perhaps as a result of the substantially increased number of free parameters. In the OCR scenario, the addition of WORD features on top of EDIT decreases accuracy, unlike the same experiment with the manual transcription. This is possibly a result of the reduced reliability of full word forms due to mistakes in OCR.

Particularly interesting is the result that spacing, rarely a factor considered in NLP models, improves the accuracy significantly for our system when compared with EDIT features alone. Because pixel-level visual information and arbitrary orthographic patterns are also the most difficult features to measure manually, our results give strong evidence to the assertion that NLP-style models can aid bibliographers.

6 Discussion

The results on OCR (character error rate for most plays $\approx 10 - 15\%$) transcripts are only marginally worse than those on manual transcripts, which shows that our approach can be generalized for the common case where manual diplomatic transcriptions are not available. For our experiments, we also chose a common modern edition of Shakespeare instead of more carefully produced modernized transcription of the facsimile—our goal being to again show that this approach can be generalized, perhaps to documents where careful modernizations of the facsimile are not available. Together, these results suggest that our model may be sufficiently robust to aid bibliographers in their analysis of less studied texts.

Figure 3 shows an example of the feature weights and spacing parameters learned by the FEAT w/ ALL model. Our statistical approach is able to successfully explain some of the observations scholars made. For example, Taylor (1981) notices that compositors C and D prefer to omit u in young but A does not. Our model reflects this by giving u → DEL high weight for D and low weight for A. However, the weight of a single feature is difficult to interpret in isolation. This might be the reason why our model only moderately agrees in case of compositor C. Another example can be seen in spacing patterns: according to Taylor (1981), compositor C uses spaced medial commas unlike A and D. Our model learns the same behavior.

7 Conclusion

Our primary goal is to scale the methods of compositor attribution, including both textual and visual modes of evidence, for use across books and corpora. By using principled statistical techniques and considering evidence at a larger scale, we offer a more robust approach to compositor identification than has previously been possible. The fact that our system works well on OCR texts means that we are not restricted to only those documents for which we have manually produced transcriptions, opening up the possibility for bibliographic study on a much larger class of texts. Though we are unable to incorporate the kinds of world knowledge used by bibliographers, our ability to include more information and more fine-grained information allows us to recreate their results. Having validated these techniques on the *First Folio*, where historical claims are well established, we hope future work can extend these methods and their application.

Acknowledgements

We thank the three anonymous reviewers for their valuable feedback. This project is funded in part by the NSF under grant 1618044.

References

Taylor Berg-Kirkpatrick, Alexandre Bouchard-Côté, John DeNero, and Dan Klein. 2010. Painless unsupervised learning with features. In *Proceedings of the North American Chapter of the Association for Computational Linguistics: Human Language Technologies*.

Taylor Berg-Kirkpatrick, Greg Durrett, and Dan Klein. 2013. Unsupervised transcription of historical documents. In *Proceedings of the Association for Computational Linguistics*.

Peter W. M. Blayney. 1991. *The First Folio of Shakespeare: In Conjunction with the Exhibition at the Folger Shakespeare Library, Washington, DC, April 1, 1991-September 21, 1991*. Folger Shakespeare Library.

Peter W. M. Blayney, editor. 1996. *The First Folio of Shakespeare: The Norton Facsimile*. Norton.

Ian R. Burrows. 2013. "The peryod of my blisse": Commas, ends and utterance in Solyman and Perseda. *Textual Cultures: Texts, Contexts, Interpretation* 8(2):95–120.

Christos Christodoulopoulos, Sharon Goldwater, and Mark Steedman. 2010. Two decades of unsupervised POS induction: How far have we come? In *Proceedings of the Conference on Empirical Methods in Natural Language Processing*.

Philip Gaskell. 2007. *A New Introduction to Bibliography*. Oak Knoll Press.

Charlton Hinman. 1963. *The printing and proofreading of the First Folio of Shakespeare*, volume 1. Oxford: Clarendon Press.

David I. Holmes. 1994. Authorship attribution. *Computers and the Humanities* 28(2):87–106.

Jonathan Hope. 1994. *The authorship of Shakespeare's plays: A socio-linguistic study*. Cambridge University Press.

Trevor H. Howard-Hill. 1973. The compositors of Shakespeare's Folio Comedies. *Studies in bibliography* 26:61–106.

Trevor H. Howard-Hill. 1976. *Compositors B and E in the Shakespeare First Folio and Some Recent Studies*. Self-published.

Trevor H. Howard-Hill. 1980. New light on compositor E of the Shakespeare First Folio. *The Library* 6(2):156–178.

Matthew L. Jockers and Daniela M. Witten. 2010. A comparative study of machine learning methods for authorship attribution. *Literary and Linguistic Computing* 25(2):215–223.

Patrick Juola. 2006. Authorship attribution. *Foundations and Trends in Information Retrieval* 1(3):233–334.

Moshe Koppel, Jonathan Schler, and Shlomo Argamon. 2009. Computational methods in authorship attribution. *J. Am. Soc. Inf. Sci. Technol.* 60(1):9–26. https://doi.org/10.1002/asi.v60:1.

D. F. McKenzie. 1969. Printers of the mind: Some notes on bibliographical theories and printing-house practices. *Studies in Bibliography* 22:1–75.

D. F. McKenzie. 1984. Stretching a point: Or, the case of the spaced-out comps. *Studies in Bibliography* 37:106–121.

John O'Connor. 1975. Compositors D and F of the Shakespeare First Folio. *Studies in Bibliography* 28:81–117.

Pervez Rizvi. 2016. Use of spellings for compositor attribution in the First Folio. *The Papers of the Bibliographical Society of America* 110:1–53.

Gary Taylor. 1981. The shrinking compositor A of the Shakespeare First Folio. *Studies in Bibliography* 34:96–117.

Paul Werstine. 1982. Cases and compositors in the Shakespeare First Folio Comedies. *Studies in Bibliography* 35:206–234.

STAIR Captions:
Constructing a Large-Scale Japanese Image Caption Dataset

Yuya Yoshikawa   **Yutaro Shigeto**   **Akikazu Takeuchi**

Software Technology and Artificial Intelligence Research Laboratory (STAIR Lab)
Chiba Institute of Technology
2-17-1, Tsudanuma, Narashino, Chiba, Japan.
{yoshikawa,shigeto,takeuchi}@stair.center

Abstract

In recent years, automatic generation of image descriptions (captions), that is, *image captioning*, has attracted a great deal of attention. In this paper, we particularly consider generating Japanese captions for images. Since most available caption datasets have been constructed for English language, there are few datasets for Japanese. To tackle this problem, we construct a large-scale Japanese image caption dataset based on images from MS-COCO, which is called *STAIR Captions*. STAIR Captions consists of 820,310 Japanese captions for 164,062 images. In the experiment, we show that a neural network trained using STAIR Captions can generate more natural and better Japanese captions, compared to those generated using English-Japanese machine translation after generating English captions.

1 Introduction

Integrated processing of natural language and images has attracted attention in recent years. The Workshop on Vision and Language held in 2011 has since become an annual event[1]. In this research area, methods to automatically generate image descriptions (captions), that is, *image captioning*, have attracted a great deal of attention (Karpathy and Fei-Fei, 2015; Donahue et al., 2015; Vinyals et al., 2015; Mao et al., 2015) .

Image captioning is to automatically generate a caption for a given image. By improving the quality of image captioning, image search using natural sentences and image recognition support for

---

[1] In recent years it has been held as a joint workshop such as EMNLP and ACL; https://vision.cs.hacettepe.edu.tr/vl2017/

visually impaired people by outputting captions as sounds can be made available. Recognizing various images and generating appropriate captions for the images necessitates the compilation of a large number of image and caption pairs.

In this study, we consider generating image captions in Japanese. Since most available caption datasets have been constructed for English language, there are few datasets for Japanese. A straightforward solution is to translate English captions into Japanese ones by using machine translation such as Google Translate. However, the translated captions may be literal and unnatural because image information cannot be reflected in the translation. Therefore, in this study, we construct a Japanese image caption dataset, and for given images, we aim to generate more natural Japanese captions than translating the generated English captions into the Japanese ones.

The contributions of this paper are as follows:

- We constructed a large-scale Japanese image caption dataset, *STAIR Captions*, which consists of Japanese captions for all the images in MS-COCO (Lin et al., 2014) (Section 3).

- We confirmed that quantitatively and qualitatively better Japanese captions than the ones translated from English captions can be generated by applying a neural network-based image caption generation model learned on STAIR Captions (Section 5).

STAIR Captions is available for download from http://captions.stair.center.

2 Related Work

Some English image caption datasets have been proposed (Krishna et al., 2016; Kuznetsova et al., 2013; Ordonez et al., 2011; Vedantam et al.,

Proceedings of the 55th Annual Meeting of the Association for Computational Linguistics (Short Papers), pages 417–421
Vancouver, Canada, July 30 - August 4, 2017. ©2017 Association for Computational Linguistics
https://doi.org/10.18653/v1/P17-2066

2015; Isola et al., 2014). Representative examples are PASCAL (Rashtchian et al., 2010), Flickr3k (Rashtchian et al., 2010; Hodosh et al., 2013), Flickr30k (Young et al., 2014) —an extension of Flickr3k—, and MS-COCO (Microsoft Common Objects in Context) (Lin et al., 2014).

As detailed in Section 3, we annotate Japanese captions for the images in MS-COCO. Note that when annotating the Japanese captions, we did not refer to the original English captions in MS-COCO.

MS-COCO is a dataset constructed for research on image classification, object recognition, and English caption generation. Since its release, MS-COCO has been used as a benchmark dataset for image classification and caption generation. In addition, many studies have extended MS-COCO by annotating additional information about the images in MS-COCO[2].

Recently, a few caption datasets in languages other than English have been constructed (Miyazaki and Shimizu, 2016; Grubinger et al., 2006; Elliott et al., 2016). In particular, the study of Miyazaki and Shimizu (2016) is closest to the present study. As in our study, they constructed a Japanese caption dataset called YJ Captions. The main difference between STAIR Captions and YJ Captions is that STAIR Captions provides Japanese captions for a greater number of images. In Section 3, we highlight this difference by comparing the statistics of STAIR Captions and YJ Captions.

3 STAIR Captions

3.1 Annotation Procedure

This section explains how we constructed STAIR Captions. We annotated all images (164,062 images) in the 2014 edition of MS-COCO. For each image, we provided five Japanese captions. Therefore, the total number of captions was 820,310. Following the rules for publishing datasets created based on MS-COCO, the Japanese captions we created for the test images are excluded from the public part of STAIR Captions.

To annotate captions efficiently, we first developed a web system for caption annotation. Figure 1 shows the example of the annotation screen in the web system. Each annotator looks at the displayed image and writes the corresponding Japanese description in the text box under the image. By

Figure 1: Example of annotation screen of web system for caption annotation.

pressing the send (送信) button, a single task is completed and the next task is started.

To concurrently and inexpensively annotate captions by using the above web system, we asked part-time job workers and crowd-sourcing workers to perform the caption annotation. The workers annotated the images based on the following guidelines. (1) A caption must contain more than 15 letters. (2) A caption must follow the da/dearu style (one of writing styles in Japanese). (3) A caption must describe only what is happening in an image and the things displayed therein. (4) A caption must be a single sentence. (5) A caption must not include emotions or opinions about the image. To guarantee the quality of the captions created in this manner, we conducted sampling inspection of the annotated captions, and the captions not in line with the guidelines were removed. The entire annotation work was completed by about 2,100 workers in about half a year.

3.2 Statistics

This section introduces the quantitative characteristics of STAIR Captions. In addition, we compare it to YJ Captions (Miyazaki and Shimizu, 2016), a dataset with Japanese captions for the images in MS-COCO like in STAIR Captions.

Table 1 summarizes the statistics of the datasets. Compared with YJ Captions, overall, the numbers of Japanese captions and images in STAIR Captions are 6.23x and 6.19x, respectively. In the public part of STAIR Captions, the numbers of images and Japanese captions are 4.65x and 4.67x greater than those in YJ Captions, respectively. That the numbers of images and captions are large in STAIR Captions is an important point in image caption

---

[2]http://mscoco.org/external/

Table 1: Comparison of dataset specifications. Numbers in the brackets indicate statistics of public part of STAIR Captions.

	Ours	YJ Captions
# of images	164,062 (123,287)	26,500
# of captions	820,310 (616,435)	131,740
Vocabulary size	35,642 (31,938)	13,274
Avg. # of chars	23.79 (23.80)	23.23

generation because it reduces the possibility of unknown scenes and objects appearing in the test images. The vocabulary of STAIR Captions is 2.69x larger than that of YJ Captions. Because of the large vocabulary of STAIR Captions, it is expected that the caption generation model can learn and generate a wide range of captions. The average numbers of characters per a sentence in STAIR Captions and in YJ Captions are almost the same.

4 Image Caption Generation

In this section, we briefly review the caption generation method proposed by Karpathy and Fei-Fei (2015), which is used in our experiments (Section 5).

This method consists of a convolutional neural network (CNN) and long short-term memory (LSTM)[3]. Specifically, CNN first extracts features from a given image, and then, LSTM generates a caption from the extracted features.

Let I be an image, and the corresponding caption be $Y = (y_1, y_2, \cdots, y_n)$. Then, caption generation is defined as follows:

$$\mathbf{x}^{(im)} = \mathrm{CNN}(I),$$
$$\mathbf{h}_0 = \tanh\left(\mathbf{W}^{(im)}\mathbf{x}^{(im)} + \mathbf{b}^{(im)}\right),$$
$$\mathbf{c}_0 = \mathbf{0},$$
$$\mathbf{h}_t, \mathbf{c}_t = \mathrm{LSTM}\left(\mathbf{x}_t, \mathbf{h}_{t-1}, \mathbf{c}_{t-1}\right) \qquad (t \geq 1),$$
$$y_t = \mathrm{softmax}\left(\mathbf{W}_o\mathbf{h}_t + \mathbf{b}_o\right),$$

where $\mathrm{CNN}(\cdot)$ is a function that outputs the image features extracted by CNN, that is, the final layer of CNN, and y_t is the tth output word. The input $\mathbf{x}_t$ at time t is substituted by a word embedding vector corresponding to the previous output, that is, y_{t-1}. The generation process is repeated until LSTM outputs the symbol that indicates the end of sentence.

---

[3] Although their original paper used RNN, they reported in the appendix that LSTM performed better than RNN. Thus, we used LSTM.

In the training phase, given the training data, we train $\mathbf{W}^{(im)}$, $\mathbf{b}^{(im)}$, $\mathbf{W}_*$, $\mathbf{b}_*$, CNN, and LSTM parameters, where $*$ represents wild card.

5 Experiments

In this section, we perform an experiment which generates Japanese captions using STAIR Captions. The aim of this experiment is to show the necessity of a Japanese caption dataset. In particular, we evaluate quantitatively and qualitatively how fluent Japanese captions can be generated by using a neural network-based caption generation model trained on STAIR Captions.

5.1 Experimental Setup

5.1.1 Evaluation Measure

Following the literature (Chen et al., 2015; Karpathy and Fei-Fei, 2015), we use BLEU (Papineni et al., 2002), ROUGE (Lin, 2004), and CIDEr (Vedantam et al., 2015) as evaluation measures. Although BLEU and ROUGE were developed originally for evaluating machine translation and text summarization, we use them here because they are often used for measuring the quality of caption generation.

5.1.2 Comparison Methods

In this experiment, we evaluate the following caption generation methods.

- En-generator $\rightarrow$ MT: A pipeline method of English caption generation and English-Japanese machine translation. This method trains a neural network, which generates English captions, with MS-COCO. In the test phase, given an image, we first generate an English caption to the image by the trained neural network, and then translate the generated caption into Japanese one by machine translation. Here, we use Google translate[4] for machine translation. This method is the baseline.

- Ja-generator: This method trains a neural network using STAIR Captions. Unlike MS-COCO $\rightarrow$ MT, this method directly generate a Japanese caption from a given image .

As mentioned in Section 4, we used the method proposed by Karpathy and Fei-Fei (2015) as caption generation models for both En-generator $\rightarrow$ MT and Ja-generator.

---

[4] https://translate.google.com/

Table 2: Experimental results of Japanese caption generation. The numbers in boldface indicate the best score for each evaluation measure.

	BLEU-1	BLEU-2	BLEU-3	BLEU-4	ROUGE_L	CIDEr
En-generator → MT	0.565	0.330	0.204	0.127	0.449	0.324
Ja-generator	**0.763**	**0.614**	**0.492**	**0.385**	**0.553**	**0.833**

Table 3: Examples of generated image captions. En-generator denotes the caption generator trained with MS-COCO. En-generator → MT is the pipeline method: it first generates English caption and performs machine translation subsequently. Ja-generator was trained with Japanese captions.

In both the methods, following Karpathy and Fei-Fei, we only trained LSTM parameters, while CNN parameters were fixed. We used VGG with 16 layers as CNN, where the VGG parameters were the pre-trained ones[5]. With the optimization of LSTM, we used mini-batch RMSProp, and the batch size was set to 20.

5.1.3 Dataset Separation

Following the experimental setting in the previous studies (Chen et al., 2015; Karpathy and Fei-Fei, 2015), we used 123,287 images included in the MS-COCO training and validation sets and their corresponding Japanese captions. We divided the dataset into three parts, i.e., 113,287 images for the training set, 5,000 images for the validation set, and 5,000 images for the test set.

The hyper-parameters of the neural network were tuned based on CIDEr scores by using the validation set. As preprocessing, we applied morphological analysis to the Japanese captions using MeCab[6].

---

[5]http://www.robots.ox.ac.uk/~vgg/research/very_deep/

[6]http://taku910.github.io/mecab/

5.2 Results

Table 2 summarizes the experimental results. The results show that Ja-generator, that is, the approach in which Japanese captions were used as training data, outperformed En-generator → MT, which was trained without Japanese captions.

Table 3 shows two examples where Ja-generator generated appropriate captions, whereas En-generator → MT generated unnatural ones. In the example at the top in Table 3, En-generator first generated the term, "*A double decker bus.*" MT translated the term into as "二重デッカーバス", but the translation is word-by-word and inappropriate as a Japanese term. By contrast, Ja-generator generated "二階建てのバス (*two-story bus*)," which is appropriate as the Japanese translation of *A double decker bus*. In the example at the bottom of the table, En-generator → MT yielded the incorrect caption by translating "*A bunch of food*" as "食べ物の束 (*A bundle of food*)." By contrast, Ja-generator correctly recognized that the food pictured in the image is a donut, and expressed it as "ドーナツがたくさん (*A bunch of donuts*)."

6 Conclusion

In this paper, we constructed a new Japanese image caption dataset called STAIR Captions. In STAIR Captions, Japanese captions are provided for all the images of MS-COCO. The total number of Japanese captions is 820,310. To the best of our knowledge, STAIR Captions is currently the largest Japanese image caption dataset.

In our experiment, we compared the performance of Japanese caption generation by a neural network-based model with and without STAIR Captions to highlight the necessity of Japanese captions. As a result, we showed the necessity of STAIR Captions. In addition, we confirmed that Japanese captions can be generated simply by adapting the existing caption generation method.

In future work, we will analyze the experimental results in greater detail. Moreover, by using both Japanese and English captions, we will develop multi-lingual caption generation models.

References

Xinlei Chen, Hao Fang, Tsung-Yi Lin, Ramakrishna Vedantam, Saurabh Gupta, Piotr Dollár, and C. Lawrenc Zitnick. 2015. Microsoft COCO captions: Data collection and evaluation server. *arXiv preprint* 1504.00325.

Jeff Donahue, Lisa Anne Hendricks, Sergio Guadarrama, Marcus Rohrbach, Subhashini Venugopalan, Kate Saenko, and Trevor Darrell. 2015. Long-term recurrent convolutional networks for visual recognition and description. In *Proceedings of the IEEE Computer Society Conference on Computer Vision and Pattern Recognition (CVPR)*.

D. Elliott, S. Frank, K. Sima'an, and L. Specia. 2016. Multi30k: Multilingual english-german image descriptions. In *Workshop on Vision and Language*. pages 70–74.

Michael Grubinger, Paul Clough, Henning Müller, and Thomas Deselaers. 2006. The IAPR Benchmark: A new evaluation resource for visual information systems. In *Proceedings of the Fifth International Conference on Language Resources and Evaluation (LREC)*.

Micah Hodosh, Peter Young, and Julia Hockenmaier. 2013. Framing image description as a ranking task: Data, models and evaluation metrics. *Journal of Artificial Intelligence Research* 47:853–899.

Phillip Isola, Jianxiong Xiao, Devi Parikh, and Antonio Torralba. 2014. What makes a photograph memorable? *IEEE Transactions on Pattern Analysis and Machine Intelligence* 36(7):1469–1482.

Andrej Karpathy and Li Fei-Fei. 2015. Deep visual-semantic alignments for generating image descriptions. In *Proceedings of the IEEE Computer Society Conference on Computer Vision and Pattern Recognition (CVPR)*. pages 3128–3137.

Ranjay Krishna, Yuke Zhu, Oliver Groth, Justin Johnson, Kenji Hata, Joshua Kravitz, Stephanie Chen, Yannis Kalanditis, Li-Jia Li, David A. Shamma, Michael S. Bernstein, Li Fei-Fei, Yannis Kalantidis, Li-Jia Li, David A. Shamma, Michael S. Bernstein, and Fei-Fei Li. 2016. Visual Genome: Connecting language and vision using crowdsourced dense image annotations. *arXiv preprint arXiv:602.07332* .

Polina Kuznetsova, Vicente Ordonez, Alexander Berg, Tamara Berg, and Yejin Choi. 2013. Generalizing image captions for image-text parallel corpus. In *Proceedings of the 51st Annual Meeting of the Association for Computational Linguistics (ACL)*. pages 790–796.

Chin-Yew Lin. 2004. Rouge: A package for automatic evaluation of summaries. In *Proceedings of the Workshop on Text Summarization Branches Out*. pages 25–26.

TY Lin, M Maire, S Belongie, J Hays, and P Perona. 2014. Microsoft COCO: Common objects in context. In *European Conference on Computer Vision (ECCV)*. pages 740–755.

Junhua Mao, Wei Xu, Yi Yang, Jiang Wang, Zhiheng Huang, and Alan Yuille. 2015. Deep captioning with multimodal recurrent neural networks (M-RNN). In *International Conference on Learning Representations (ICLR)*.

Takashi Miyazaki and Nobuyuki Shimizu. 2016. Cross-lingual image caption generation. In *Proceedings of the 54th Annual Meeting of the Association for Computational Linguistics (ACL)*. pages 1780–1790.

Vicente Ordonez, Girish Kulkarni, and Tamara L Berg. 2011. Im2Text: Describing images using 1 million captioned dhotographs. In *Advances in Neural Information Processing Systems (NIPS)*. pages 1143–1151.

Kishore Papineni, Salim Roukos, Todd Ward, and Wei-Jing Zhu. 2002. BLEU: A method for automatic evaluation of machine translation. In *Proceedings of the 40th Annual Meeting of the Association of Computational Linguistics (ACL)*. pages 311–318.

Cyrus Rashtchian, Peter Young, Micah Hodosh, and Julia Hockenmaier. 2010. Collecting image annotations using Amazon's mechanical turk. In *NAACL HLT Workshop on Creating Speech and Language Data with Amazon's Mechanical Turk*. pages 139–147.

Ramakrishna Vedantam, C. Lawrence Zitnick, and Devi Parikh. 2015. CIDEr: Consensus-based image description evaluation. In *Proceedings of the IEEE Computer Society Conference on Computer Vision and Pattern Recognition (CVPR)*. pages 4566–4575.

Oriol Vinyals, Alexander Toshev, Samy Bengio, and Dumitru Erhan. 2015. Show and tell: A neural image caption generator. In *Proceedings of the IEEE Computer Society Conference on Computer Vision and Pattern Recognition (CVPR)*. pages 3156–3164.

Peter Young, Alice Lai, Micah Hodosh, and Julia Hockenmaier. 2014. From image descriptions to visual denotations: New similarity metrics for semantic inference over event descriptions. *Transactions of the Association for Computational Linguistics* 2:67–78.

"Liar, Liar Pants on Fire":
A New Benchmark Dataset for Fake News Detection

William Yang Wang
Department of Computer Science
University of California, Santa Barbara
Santa Barbara, CA 93106 USA
`william@cs.ucsb.edu`

Abstract

Automatic fake news detection is a challenging problem in deception detection, and it has tremendous real-world political and social impacts. However, statistical approaches to combating fake news has been dramatically limited by the lack of labeled benchmark datasets. In this paper, we present LIAR: a new, publicly available dataset for fake news detection. We collected a decade-long, 12.8K manually labeled short statements in various contexts from POLITIFACT.COM, which provides detailed analysis report and links to source documents for each case. This dataset can be used for fact-checking research as well. Notably, this new dataset is an order of magnitude larger than previously largest public fake news datasets of similar type. Empirically, we investigate automatic fake news detection based on surface-level linguistic patterns. We have designed a novel, hybrid convolutional neural network to integrate metadata with text. We show that this hybrid approach can improve a text-only deep learning model.

1 Introduction

In this past election cycle for the 45th President of the United States, the world has witnessed a growing epidemic of fake news. The plague of fake news not only poses serious threats to the integrity of journalism, but has also created turmoils in the political world. The worst real-world impact is that fake news seems to create real-life fears: last year, a man carried an AR-15 rifle and walked in a Washington DC Pizzeria, because he recently read online that "this pizzeria was harbor-

ing young children as sex slaves as part of a child-abuse ring led by Hillary Clinton"[1]. The man was later arrested by police, and he was charged for firing an assault rifle in the restaurant (Kang and Goldman, 2016).

The broadly-related problem of deception detection (Mihalcea and Strapparava, 2009) is not new to the natural language processing community. A relatively early study by Ott et al. (2011) focuses on detecting deceptive review opinions in sentiment analysis, using a crowdsourcing approach to create training data for the positive class, and then combine with truthful opinions from TripAdvisor. Recent studies have also proposed stylometric (Feng et al., 2012), semi-supervised learning (Hai et al., 2016), and linguistic approaches (Pérez-Rosas and Mihalcea, 2015) to detect deceptive text on crowdsourced datasets. Even though crowdsourcing is an important approach to create labeled training data, there is a mismatch between training and testing. When testing on real-world review datasets, the results could be suboptimal since the positive training data was created in a completely different, simulated platform.

The problem of fake news detection is more challenging than detecting deceptive reviews, since the political language on TV interviews, posts on Facebook and Twitters are mostly short statements. However, the lack of manually labeled fake news dataset is still a bottleneck for advancing computational-intensive, broad-coverage models in this direction. Vlachos and Riedel (2014) are the first to release a public fake news detection and fact-checking dataset, but it only includes 221 statements, which does not permit machine learning based assessments.

To address these issues, we introduce the LIAR

---

[1] http://www.nytimes.com/2016/12/05/business/media/comet-ping-pong-pizza-shooting-fake-news-consequences.html

Proceedings of the 55th Annual Meeting of the Association for Computational Linguistics (Short Papers), pages 422–426
Vancouver, Canada, July 30 - August 4, 2017. ©2017 Association for Computational Linguistics
https://doi.org/10.18653/v1/P17-2067

dataset, which includes 12,836 short statements labeled for truthfulness, subject, context/venue, speaker, state, party, and prior history. With such volume and a time span of a decade, LIAR is an order of magnitude larger than the currently available resources (Vlachos and Riedel, 2014; Ferreira and Vlachos, 2016) of similiar type. Additionally, in contrast to crowdsourced datasets, the instances in LIAR are collected in a grounded, more natural context, such as political debate, TV ads, Facebook posts, tweets, interview, news release, etc. In each case, the labeler provides a lengthy analysis report to ground each judgment, and the links to all supporting documents are also provided.

Empirically, we have evaluated several popular learning based methods on this dataset. The baselines include logistic regression, support vector machines, long short-term memory networks (Hochreiter and Schmidhuber, 1997), and a convolutional neural network model (Kim, 2014). We further introduce a neural network architecture to integrate text and meta-data. Our experiment suggests that this approach improves the performance of a strong text-only convolutional neural networks baseline.

2 LIAR: a New Benchmark Dataset

The major resources for deceptive detection of reviews are crowdsourced datasets (Ott et al., 2011; Pérez-Rosas and Mihalcea, 2015). They are very useful datasets to study deception detection, but the positive training data are collected from a simulated environment. More importantly, these datasets are not suitable for fake statements detection, since the fake news on TVs and social media are much shorter than customer reviews.

Vlachos and Riedel (2014) are the first to construct fake news and fact-checking datasets. They obtained 221 statements from CHANNEL 4[2] and POLITIFACT.COM[3], a Pulitzer Prize-winning website. In particular, PolitiFact covers a wide-range of political topics, and they provide detailed judgments with fine-grained labels. Recently, Ferreira and Vlachos (2016) have released the Emergent dataset, which includes 300 labeled rumors from PolitiFact. However, with less than a thousand samples, it is impractical to use these datasets as benchmarks for developing and evaluating machine learning algorithms for fake news detection.

Statement: *"The last quarter, it was just announced, our gross domestic product was below zero. Who ever heard of this? Its never below zero."*
Speaker: Donald Trump
Context: presidential announcement speech
Label: Pants on Fire
Justification: According to Bureau of Economic Analysis and National Bureau of Economic Research, the growth in the gross domestic product has been below zero 42 times over 68 years. Thats a lot more than "never." We rate his claim Pants on Fire!

Statement: *"Newly Elected Republican Senators Sign Pledge to Eliminate Food Stamp Program in 2015."*
Speaker: Facebook posts
Context: social media posting
Label: Pants on Fire
Justification: More than 115,000 social media users passed along a story headlined, "Newly Elected Republican Senators Sign Pledge to Eliminate Food Stamp Program in 2015." But they failed to do due diligence and were snookered, since the story came from a publication that bills itself (quietly) as a "satirical, parody website." We rate the claim Pants on Fire.

Statement: *"Under the health care law, everybody will have lower rates, better quality care and better access."*
Speaker: Nancy Pelosi
Context: on 'Meet the Press'
Label: False
Justification: Even the study that Pelosi's staff cited as the source of that statement suggested that some people would pay more for health insurance. Analysis at the state level found the same thing. The general understanding of the word "everybody" is every person. The predictions dont back that up. We rule this statement False.

Figure 1: Some random excerpts from the LIAR dataset.

---

[2] http://blogs.channel4.com/factcheck/
[3] http://www.politifact.com/

Dataset Statistics	
Training set size	10,269
Validation set size	1,284
Testing set size	1,283
Avg. statement length (tokens)	17.9
Top-3 Speaker Affiliations	
Democrats	4,150
Republicans	5,687
None (e.g., FB posts)	2,185

Table 1: The LIAR dataset statistics.

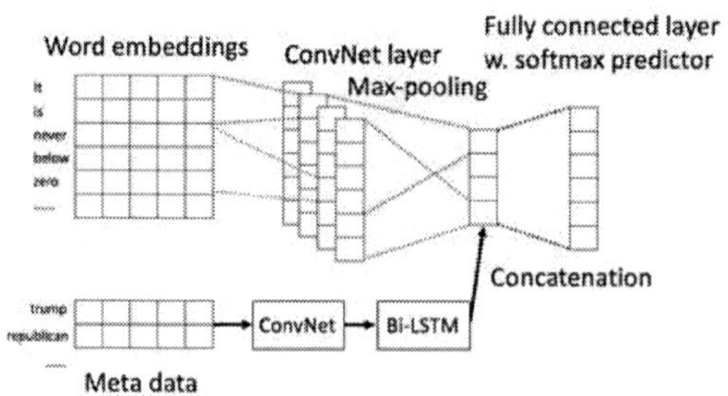

Figure 2: The proposed hybrid Convolutional Neural Networks framework for integrating text and meta-data.

Therefore, it is of crucial significance to introduce a larger dataset to facilitate the development of computational approaches to fake news detection and automatic fact-checking.

We show some random snippets from our dataset in Figure 1. The LIAR dataset[4] includes 12.8K human labeled short statements from POLITIFACT.COM's API[5], and each statement is evaluated by a POLITIFACT.COM editor for its truthfulness. After initial analysis, we found duplicate labels, and merged the full-flop, half-flip, no-flip labels into false, half-true, true labels respectively. We consider six fine-grained labels for the truthfulness ratings: *pants-fire, false, barely-true, half-true, mostly-true, and true*. The distribution of labels in the LIAR dataset is relatively well-balanced: except for 1,050 pants-fire cases, the instances for all other labels range from 2,063 to 2,638. We randomly sampled 200 instances to examine the accompanied lengthy analysis reports and rulings. Not that fact-checking is not a classic labeling task in NLP. The verdict requires extensive training in journalism for finding relevant evidence. Therefore, for second-stage verifications, we went through a randomly sampled subset of the analysis reports to check if we agreed with the reporters' analysis. The agreement rate measured by Cohens kappa was 0.82. We show the corpus statistics in Table 1. The statement dates are primarily from 2007-2016.

The speakers in the LIAR dataset include a mix of democrats and republicans, as well as a significant amount of posts from online social media. We include a rich set of meta-data for each speaker—in addition to party affiliations, current job, home state, and credit history are also provided. In particular, the credit history includes the historical counts of inaccurate statements for each speaker. For example, Mitt Romney has a credit history vector $h = \{19, 32, 34, 58, 33\}$, which corresponds to his counts of "pants on fire", "false", "barely true", "half true", "mostly true" for historical statements. Since this vector also includes the count for the current statement, it is important to subtract the current label from the credit history when using this meta data vector in prediction experiments.

These statements are sampled from various of contexts/venues, and the top categories include *news releases, TV/radio interviews, campaign speeches, TV ads, tweets, debates, Facebook posts, etc.* To ensure a broad coverage of the topics, there is also a diverse set of subjects discussed by the speakers. The top-10 most discussed subjects in the dataset are *economy, healthcare, taxes, federal-budget, education, jobs, state-budget, candidates-biography, elections, and immigration.*

3 Automatic Fake News Detection

One of the most obvious applications of our dataset is to facilitate the development of machine learning models for automatic fake news detection. In this task, we frame this as a 6-way multi-class text classification problem. And the research questions are:

- Based on surface-level linguistic realizations only, how well can machine learning algorithms classify a short statement into a fine-grained category of fakeness?

- Can we design a deep neural network architecture to integrate speaker related meta-data

---

[4] https://www.cs.ucsb.edu/~william/data/liar_dataset.zip

[5] http://static.politifact.com/api/v2apidoc.html

with text to enhance the performance of fake news detection?

Since convolutional neural networks architectures (CNNs) (Collobert et al., 2011; Kim, 2014; Zhang et al., 2015) have obtained the state-of-the-art results on many text classification datasets, we build our neural networks model based on a recently proposed CNN model (Kim, 2014). Figure 2 shows the overview of our hybrid convolutional neural network for integrating text and meta-data.

We randomly initialize a matrix of embedding vectors to encode the metadata embeddings. We use a convolutional layer to capture the dependency between the meta-data vector(s). Then, a standard max-pooling operation is performed on the latent space, followed by a bi-directional LSTM layer. We then concatenate the max-pooled text representations with the meta-data representation from the bi-directional LSTM, and feed them to fully connected layer with a softmax activation function to generate the final prediction.

4   LIAR: Benchmark Evaluation

In this section, we first describe the experimental setup, and the baselines. Then, we present the empirical results and compare various models.

4.1   Experimental Settings

We used five baselines: a majority baseline, a regularized logistic regression classifier (LR), a support vector machine classifier (SVM) (Crammer and Singer, 2001), a bi-directional long short-term memory networks model (Bi-LSTMs) (Hochreiter and Schmidhuber, 1997; Graves and Schmidhuber, 2005), and a convolutional neural network model (CNNs) (Kim, 2014). For LR and SVM, we used the LIBSHORTTEXT toolkit[6], which was shown to provide very strong performances on short text classification problems (Wang and Yang, 2015). For Bi-LSTMs and CNNs, we used TensorFlow for the implementation. We used pre-trained 300-dimensional word2vec embeddings from Google News (Mikolov et al., 2013) to warm-start the text embeddings. We strictly tuned all the hyperparameters on the validation dataset. The best filter sizes for the CNN model was (2,3,4). In all cases, each size has 128 filters. The dropout keep probabilities was optimized to 0.8,

---

[6]https://www.csie.ntu.edu.tw/~cjlin/libshorttext/

Models	Valid.	Test
Majority	0.204	0.208
SVMs	0.258	0.255
Logistic Regress0ion	0.257	0.247
Bi-LSTMs	0.223	0.233
CNNs	0.260	0.270
Hybrid CNNs		
Text + Subject	0.263	0.235
Text + Speaker	**0.277**	0.248
Text + Job	0.270	0.258
Text + State	0.246	0.256
Text + Party	0.259	0.248
Text + Context	0.251	0.243
Text + History	0.246	0.241
Text + All	0.247	**0.274**

Table 2: The evaluation results on the LIAR dataset. The top section: text-only models. The bottom: text + meta-data hybrid models.

while no L_2 penalty was imposed. The batch size for stochastic gradient descent optimization was set to 64, and the learning process involves 10 passes over the training data for text model. For the hybrid model, we use 3 and 8 as filter sizes, and the number of filters was set to 10. We considered 0.5 and 0.8 as dropout probabilities. The hybrid model requires 5 training epochs.

We used grid search to tune the hyperparameters for LR and SVM models. We chose accuracy as the evaluation metric, since we found that the accuracy results from various models were equivalent to f-measures on this balanced dataset.

4.2   Results

We outline our empirical results in Table 2. First, we compare various models using text features only. We see that the majority baseline on this dataset gives about 0.204 and 0.208 accuracy on the validation and test sets respectively. Standard text classifier such as SVMs and LR models obtained significant improvements. Due to overfitting, the Bi-LSTMs did not perform well. The CNNs outperformed all models, resulting in an accuracy of 0.270 on the heldout test set. We compare the predictions from the CNN model with SVMs via a two-tailed paired t-test, and CNN was significantly better ($p < .0001$). When considering all meta-data and text, the model achieved the best result on the test data.

5 Conclusion

We introduced LIAR, a new dataset for automatic fake news detection. Compared to prior datasets, LIAR is an order of a magnitude larger, which enables the development of statistical and computational approaches to fake news detection. LIAR's authentic, real-world short statements from various contexts with diverse speakers also make the research on developing broad-coverage fake news detector possible. We show that when combining meta-data with text, significant improvements can be achieved for fine-grained fake news detection. Given the detailed analysis report and links to source documents in this dataset, it is also possible to explore the task of automatic fact-checking over knowledge base in the future. Our corpus can also be used for stance classification, argument mining, topic modeling, rumor detection, and political NLP research.

References

Ronan Collobert, Jason Weston, Léon Bottou, Michael Karlen, Koray Kavukcuoglu, and Pavel Kuksa. 2011. Natural language processing (almost) from scratch. *Journal of Machine Learning Research* 12(Aug):2493–2537.

Koby Crammer and Yoram Singer. 2001. On the algorithmic implementation of multiclass kernel-based vector machines. *Journal of machine learning research* 2(Dec):265–292.

Song Feng, Ritwik Banerjee, and Yejin Choi. 2012. Syntactic stylometry for deception detection. In *Proceedings of the 50th Annual Meeting of the Association for Computational Linguistics: Short Papers-Volume 2*. Association for Computational Linguistics, pages 171–175.

William Ferreira and Andreas Vlachos. 2016. Emergent: a novel data-set for stance classification. In *Proceedings of the 2016 Conference of the North American Chapter of the Association for Computational Linguistics: Human Language Technologies*. ACL.

Alex Graves and Jürgen Schmidhuber. 2005. Framewise phoneme classification with bidirectional lstm and other neural network architectures. *Neural Networks* 18(5):602–610.

Zhen Hai, Peilin Zhao, Peng Cheng, Peng Yang, Xiao-Li Li, Guangxia Li, and Ant Financial. 2016. Deceptive review spam detection via exploiting task relatedness and unlabeled data. In *EMNLP*.

Sepp Hochreiter and Jürgen Schmidhuber. 1997. Long short-term memory. *Neural computation* 9(8):1735–1780.

Cecilia Kang and Adam Goldman. 2016. In washington pizzeria attack, fake news brought real guns. In *the New York Times*.

Yoon Kim. 2014. Convolutional neural networks for sentence classification. In *Proceedings of the 2014 Conference on Empirical Methods in Natural Language Processing (EMNLP)*.

Rada Mihalcea and Carlo Strapparava. 2009. The lie detector: Explorations in the automatic recognition of deceptive language. In *Proceedings of the ACL-IJCNLP 2009 Conference Short Papers*.

Tomas Mikolov, Kai Chen, Greg Corrado, and Jeffrey Dean. 2013. Efficient estimation of word representations in vector space. *arXiv preprint arXiv:1301.3781* .

Myle Ott, Yejin Choi, Claire Cardie, and Jeffrey T Hancock. 2011. Finding deceptive opinion spam by any stretch of the imagination. In *Proceedings of the 49th Annual Meeting of the Association for Computational Linguistics: Human Language Technologies-Volume 1*. Association for Computational Linguistics, pages 309–319.

Verónica Pérez-Rosas and Rada Mihalcea. 2015. Experiments in open domain deception detection. In *EMNLP*. pages 1120–1125.

Andreas Vlachos and Sebastian Riedel. 2014. Fact checking: Task definition and dataset construction. *Proceedings of the ACL 2014 Workshop on Language Technology and Computational Social Science* .

William Yang Wang and Diyi Yang. 2015. That's so annoying!!!: A lexical and frame-semantic embedding based data augmentation approach to automatic categorization of annoying behaviors using #petpeeve tweets. In *Proceedings of the 2015 Conference on Empirical Methods in Natural Language Processing (EMNLP 2015)*. ACL, Lisbon, Portugal.

Xiang Zhang, Junbo Zhao, and Yann LeCun. 2015. Character-level convolutional networks for text classification. In *Advances in neural information processing systems*. pages 649–657.

English Multiword Expression-aware Dependency Parsing Including Named Entities

Akihiko Kato and **Hiroyuki Shindo** and **Yuji Matsumoto**

Graduate School of Information and Science
Nara Institute of Science and Technology
8916-5, Takayama, Ikoma, Nara, 630-0192, Japan
{kato.akihiko.ju6, shindo, matsu} @is.naist.jp

Abstract

Because syntactic structures and spans of multiword expressions (MWEs) are independently annotated in many English syntactic corpora, they are generally inconsistent with respect to one another, which is harmful to the implementation of an aggregate system. In this work, we construct a corpus that ensures consistency between dependency structures and MWEs, including named entities. Further, we explore models that predict both MWE-spans and an MWE-aware dependency structure. Experimental results show that our joint model using additional MWE-span features achieves an MWE recognition improvement of 1.35 points over a pipeline model.

1 Introduction

To solve complex Natural Language Processing (NLP) tasks that require deep syntactic analysis, various levels of annotation such as parse trees and named entities (NEs) must be consistent with one another (Finkel and Manning, 2009). Otherwise, it is usually impossible to combine these pieces of information effectively.

However, the standard syntactic corpus of English, Penn Treebank, is not concerned with consistency between syntactic trees and spans of multiword expressions (MWEs). In Penn Treebank, that is, an MWE-span does not always correspond to a span dominated by a single non-terminal node. Therefore, word-based dependency structures converted from Penn Treebank are generally inconsistent with MWE-spans (Figure 1a). To mitigate this inconsistency, Kato et al. (2016) estab-

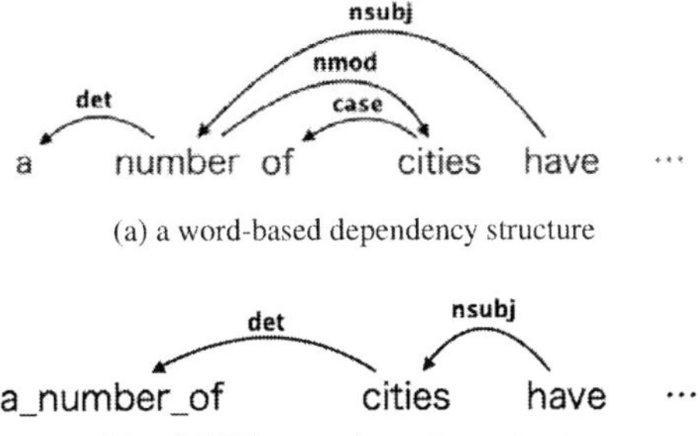

(a) a word-based dependency structure

(b) an MWE-aware dependency structure

Figure 1: A word-based and an MWE-aware dependency structure. In the former, a span of an MWE ("a number of") does not correspond to any subtree. The MWE is represented as a single node in the latter structure.

lishes each span of functional MWEs [1] as a subtree of a phrase structure in the Wall Street Journal portion of Ontonotes (Pradhan et al., 2007).

To pursue this direction further, we construct a corpus such that dependency structures are consistent with MWEs, by extending Kato et al. (2016)'s corpus [2]. As is the case with their corpus, each MME is a syntactic unit in an MWE-aware dependency structure from our corpus (Figure 1b). Moreover, our corpus includes not only functional MWEs but also NEs. Because NEs are highly productive and occur more frequently than functional MWEs, they are difficult to cover in a dictionary.

Consistency between NE-spans and phrase structures is not guaranteed because they are independently annotated in most syntactic corpora.

---

[1] By functional MWEs, we mean MWEs that function either as prepositions, conjunctions, determiners, pronouns, or adverbs.

[2] We release our dependency corpus at https://github.com/naist-cl-parsing/mwe-aware-dependency. MWE-aware phrase structures will be distributed from LDC as a part of LDC2017T01.

Proceedings of the 55th Annual Meeting of the Association for Computational Linguistics (Short Papers), pages 427–432
Vancouver, Canada, July 30 - August 4, 2017. ©2017 Association for Computational Linguistics
https://doi.org/10.18653/v1/P17-2068

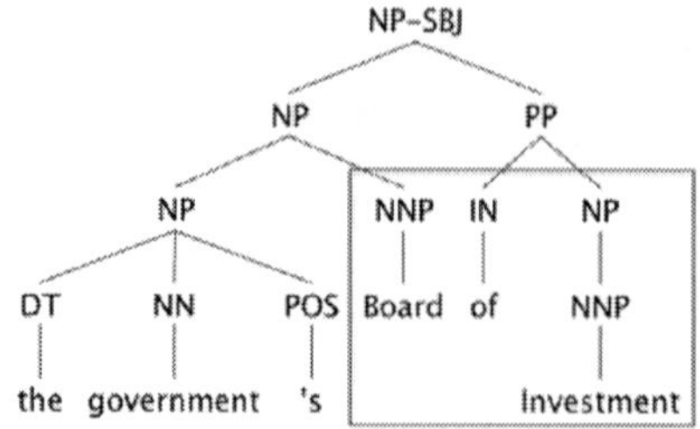

Figure 2: Example of inconsistency between NE-spans and phrase structures. A rectangle shows an NE-span.

MWE_POS	NNP	RB	IN	others
MWE Instances	20,992	3,796	2,424	737
MWE Types	11,875	377	92	52

Table 1: Corpus statistics.

For instance, in Figure 2, an NE-span is "Board of Investment," which is inconsistent with the syntactic tree. Therefore, we resolve this inconsistency by modifying phrase structures locally and establishing each NE as a subtree.

Furthermore, to evaluate the constructed corpus, we explore pipeline and joint models that predict both MWE-spans and an MWE-aware dependency tree [3]. Our experimental results show that the proposed joint model with additional MWE-span features achieves an MWE recognition improvement of 1.35 points over the pipeline model.

2   MWE-aware Dependency Corpus

To ensure consistency between MWE annotations and dependency structures, we first integrate NE annotations on Ontonotes [4] into phrase structures such that functional MWEs are established as subtrees. Subsequently, we convert phrase structures to dependency structures. We construct our corpus by extending Kato et al. (2016)'s corpus [5], which is itself built on a corpus by Shigeto et al. (2013). Regarding MWE annotations, Shigeto et al. (2013) first constructed an MWE dictionary by extracting functional MWEs from the English-language Wiktionary [6], and classified their occurrences in Ontonotes into either MWE or literal usage. Kato et al. (2016) integrated these MWE annotations into phrase structures and established functional MWEs as subtrees.

Next, we describe the establishment of each NE as a subtree. If an NE-span does not correspond to any non-terminal in a phrase structure, there are two possibilities: (A) the NE-span corresponds to multiple contiguous children of a subtree, or (B) the NE-span has crossing brackets with the spans in the parse tree (Finkel and Manning, 2009; Kato et al., 2016). In Case (A), we insert a new non-terminal ("MWE_NNP") that governs the NE-span [7]. In Case (B), many instances correspond to a noun phrase (NP) comprised of a nested NP and a prepositional phrase (Figure 2). In the main NP, a modifier, such as a determiner, an adjective, or a possessive NP, precedes an NE. For these instances, according to Finkel and Manning (2009), we reduce Case (B) to Case (A) by moving the modifier from the nested NP to the main NP. Then, we establish each NE as a subtree by inserting an MWE-specific non-terminal. Furthermore, in some instances it is more reasonable to enlarge NE-spans than to modify phrase structures. As a typical example, there is an NE annotation that covers only part of a coordination structure, such as "Peter and Edward Bronfman," where "Edward Bronfman" is annotated as an NE. In this case, we extend an original NE-span to the whole coordination structure. We show the statistics for the corpus in Table 1 [8]. This corpus has 27,949 MWE instances in 37,015 sentences. A histogram

Type of MWEs	Non-terminal	Contiguous children	Crossing brackets
Functional MWEs	3,466	1,663	1,799
NEs	18,625	2,252	144

Table 2: Histogram tabling the consistency between MWE-spans and phrase structures.

---

[3] Although Kato et al. (2016) conducts experiments regarding MWE-aware dependency parsing, they use gold MWE-spans. This is not a realistic scenario. By contrast, our parsing models do not use gold MWE-spans.

[4] We exploit NE annotations on Ontonotes Release 5.0 (LDC2013T19). We address traditional NEs, such as persons, locations, and organizations, while omitting the following: DATE, TIME, PERCENT, MONEY, QUANTITY, ORDINAL, and CARDINAL. Note that we only focus on multiword NEs.

[5] https://catalog.ldc.upenn.edu/LDC2017T01

[6] https://en.wiktionary.org

[7] We do not require manual annotations for Case (A).

[8] NEs have NNP as an MWE-level POS tag.

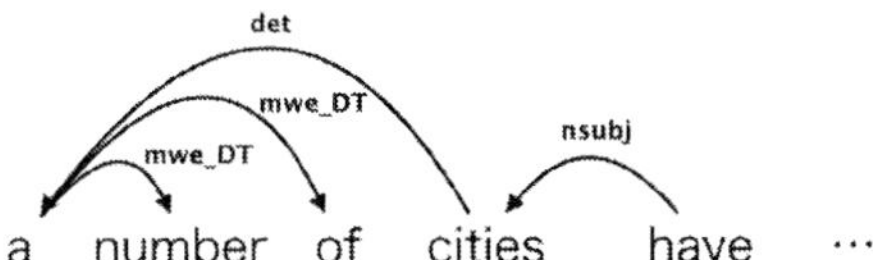

Figure 3: In the joint model, we directly infer an MWE-aware dependency tree in which an MWE ("a number of") is represented as a head-initial structure by a dependency parser.

tabling the consistency between MWE-spans and phrase structures is shown in Table 2. For tree-to-dependency conversion, we first replace a sub-tree corresponding to an MWE by a preterminal node and its child node. The preterminal node has an MWE-level POS (MWE_POS) tag. The child node is generated by joining all components of the MWE with underscores. We then convert a phrase structure into a Stanford-style dependency structure (Marneffe and Manning, 2008) (Figure 1b).

3   Models for MWE identification and MWE-aware dependency parsing

In this section, we explore models that predict both MWE-spans and an MWE-aware dependency structure (Figure 1b).

3.1   Pipeline Model

The pipeline model involves the following three steps. First, BIO tags encoding MWE-spans and MWE_POS tags, such as "B_NNP" and "I_DT" are predicted by a sequential labeler based on Conditional Random Fields (CRFs) (Lafferty et al., 2001). Second, tokens belonging to each predicted MWE-span are concatenated into a single node. Finally, an MWE-based dependency structure (Figure 1b) is predicted by an arc-eager transition-based parser. For the CRFs, in addition to word-form and character-based features, we use 1- to 3-gram features based on dictionaries of functional MWEs and NEs within 5-word windows from a target token. For a dictionary of functional MWEs, we use the dictionary by Shigeto et al. (2013) (Section 2). Meanwhile, we create a dictionary of NEs from a title list of English Wikipedia articles, excepting stop words, provided by UniNE [9]. Regarding parsing features, we use

baseline features and rich non-local features proposed by Zhang and Nivre (2011).

3.2   Joint Model

In the proposed joint model, MWE-spans and MWE_POS tags are encoded as dependency labels, and conventional word-based dependency parsing is performed by an arc-eager transition-based parser. We use the same parsing features used in the pipeline model. We convert MWEs in MWE-aware dependency structures (Figure 1b) to head-initial structures (Figure 3) that encode MWE-spans and MWE_POS tags. Note that this representation is similar to Universal Dependency (McDonald et al., 2013). When parsing, we use constraints based on a history of transitions and the dictionary of functional MWEs. This is done to avoid invalid dependency trees. Because NEs are highly productive, we do not use a constraint regarding NEs.

Joint(+dict)

We designed additional features based on matches with dictionaries of NEs and functional MWEs. Hereafter, we refer to the joint model coupled with these additional features as joint(+dict). For instance, given a sentence that starts with "a number of cities," the additional features are as follows: a / B_DT, number / I_DT, of / I_DT, cities / O. Based on these additional features, we extend the baseline features proposed by Zhang and Nivre (2011) to develop MWE-specific features whose atomic features include not only words and word-level POS tags, but also BIO tags encoding MWE-spans and MWE_POS tags.

Joint(+pred_span)

Because dictionary matching is not concerned with context, in this setting, we use MWE-spans and MWE_POS tags predicted by CRF, rather than dictionary matching. Hereafter, we refer to this as joint(+pred_span). By using features extracted from CRF predictions, we can mitigate error propagation from sequential labeling and consider information from a full sentence. Moreover, we can alleviate difficulties in predicting MWE-spans and MWE_POS tags encoded as head-initial structures (Figure 3) by the parser.

4   Experimental Setting

We split the Wall Street Journal (WSJ) portion of Ontonotes, using sections 2-21 for training, and section 23 for testing. For all models, we used

---

[9] http://members.unine.ch/jacques.savoy/clef/englishST.txt

Model	Dependency Parsing				MWE Recognition	
	All sentences		**First tokens of MWEs**			
	UAS	LAS	UAS	LAS	FUM	FTM
Pipeline	91.39	89.42	84.06	78.22	91.40	91.32
Joint	91.15	89.18	81.93	77.74	89.03	88.79
Joint(+dict)	91.36	89.37	84.45	80.74	91.93	91.78
Joint(+pred_span)	91.50	89.51	84.85	81.29	92.75	92.60

Table 3: Experimental results on the test set.

Model	Dependency Parsing (First tokens of MWEs)				MWE Recognition		
	Functional MWEs		**NEs**		**Functional MWEs**		**NEs**
	UAS	LAS	UAS	LAS	FUM	FTM	FUM
Pipeline	78.89	64.01	85.58	82.41	96.76	96.42	89.81
Joint	71.28	65.05	85.07	81.49	91.01	89.93	88.47
Joint(+dict)	79.93	73.70	85.79	82.82	97.94	97.25	90.16
Joint(+pred_span)	81.31	74.74	85.89	83.23	97.59	96.91	91.32

Table 4: Breakdown of experimental results by type of MWE. Note that UAS / LAS are calculated regarding first tokens of MWEs. For NEs, the FTM is the same as the FUM because each NE always takes NNP as an MWE-level POS tag, and is not repeated.

the POS tags predicted by the Stanford POS tagger (Toutanova et al., 2003) [10]. For the pipeline model and joint(+pred_span), we used MWE-spans and MWE_POS tags predicted by CRF [11]. For dependency parsing, we used Redshift (Honnibal et al., 2013) for all models, with a beam size of 16 for decoding. For training, we removed non-projective dependency trees. For testing, we parsed all sentences. To evaluate parsing, we used unlabeled and labeled attachment scores (UAS/LAS) [12]. For the pipeline model, we converted each concatenated token corresponding to an MWE into a head-initial structure and compared this with the gold tree. For the joint model, we directly compared a predicted tree with the gold tree. To evaluate MWE recognition, we used the F-measure for untagged / tagged MWEs (FUM/FTM) [13]. For the pipeline model, we compared the gold MWEs with predictions by CRF. For the proposed joint model, we compared the gold MWEs with predicted MWE-spans and

MWE_POS tags represented as dependency labels.

5 Experimental Results and Discussion

We present the experimental results in Table 3. Comparing the joint model with the pipeline model, there is not much difference between these models regarding UAS / LAS for all sentences. However, the former is 2.13 / 0.48 points worse than the latter in terms of UAS / LAS regarding the first tokens of MWEs (1269 in 34,526 tokens), and 2.37 / 2.53 points worse than the latter regarding FUM / FTM. These results suggest that the performance of the joint model with no additional features at predicting dependencies inside and around MWEs is worse than the pipeline model. One of the reasons for this is that the exploitation of head-initial structures in the joint model (Figure 3) involves the addition of MWE-specific labels. This results in an increase in the total number of dependency labels from 41 to 50. Because of this broader output space, more search errors can occur in the joint model compared with the pipeline model. Moreover, a breakdown by type of MWE (Table 4) shows that most differences in performance between these two models are related to functional MWEs. These results suggest that constraints regarding functional MWEs during parsing (3.2) are harmful to the joint model with no additional features in terms of its performance with

---

[10] We used 20-way jackknifing for the training split. The test split was automatically tagged by the POS tagger trained on the training split.

[11] We used 20-way jackknifing for the training split. The test split was automatically tagged by the sequential labeler trained on the training split.

[12] When calculating UAS/LAS, we removed punctuation.

[13] FUM only focuses on MWE-spans, whereas FTM focuses on both MWE-spans and MWE_POS tags.

respect to functional MWEs.

By adding MWE-specific features to the joint model, however, we observe at least a 2.52 / 3.00 point improvement in terms of UAS / LAS regarding the first tokens of MWEs, and a 2.90 / 2.99 point improvement regarding FUM / FTM. As a result, we obtain a 1.35 / 1.28 point improvement with joint(+pred_span) compared with the pipeline model in terms of FUM / FTM. A breakdown by type of MWE shows that the addition of MWE-specific features leads to a performance improvement, especially for functional MWEs (Table 4). These results suggest that MWE-specific features are effective at both MWE recognition through dependency parsing and the prediction of dependencies connecting inside and outside of MWEs.

Comparing the joint(+pred_span) with the joint(+dict), the former is 0.40 / 0.55 points better than the latter in terms of UAS / LAS regarding the first tokens of MWEs, and 0.82 / 0.82 points better than the latter regarding FUM / FTM. We can attribute this gain in performance to the additional features extracted from more accurate predictions of MWE-spans and MWE_POS tags by CRF than those by dictionary matching.

6 Related Work

Whereas French Treebank is available for French MWEs (Abeillé et al., 2003), there have been only limited corpora for English MWE-aware dependency parsing. Schneider et al. (2014) constructs an MWE-annotated corpus on English Web Treebank (Bies et al., 2012). However, this corpus is relatively small as training data for a parser, and its MWE annotations are not consistent with syntactic trees. By contrast, our corpus covers the whole of the WSJ portion of Ontonotes and ensures consistency between MWE annotations and parse trees.

Korkontzelos and Manandhar (2010) reports an improvement in base-phrase chunking by pre-grouping MWEs as words-with-spaces. They focus on compound nouns, adjective-noun constructions, and named entities. However, they use gold MWE-spans, and this is not a realistic setting. By contrast, we use predicted MWE-spans.

Three works concerned with a French MWE-aware syntactic parsing are relevant. First, Green et al. (2013) proposes a method for recognizing contiguous MWEs as a part of constituency parsing by using MWE-specific non-terminals. They

investigate a CFG-based model and a model based on tree-substitution grammars. Second, Candito and Constant (2014) compares several architectures for graph-based dependency parsing and MWE recognition, in which MWE recognition is conducted before, during, and after parsing. Finally, Nasr et al. (2015) explores a joint model of MWE recognition and dependency parsing. They focus on complex function words. In terms of data representation, they adopt one similar to ours, insofar as the components of an MWE are linked by dependency edges whose labels are MWE-specific.

7 Conclusion

We constructed a corpus that ensures consistency in Ontonotes between dependency structures and English MWEs, including named entities. Furthermore, we explored models that can predict both MWE-spans and an MWE-aware dependency structure. Our experiments show that by using additional MWE-span features, our joint model achieves an MWE recognition improvement of 1.35 points over the pipeline model.

Acknowledgments

This work was partially supported by JST CREST Grant Number JPMJCR1513 and JSPS KAKENHI Grant Number 15K16053. We are grateful to members of the Computational Linguistics Laboratory at NAIST, and to the anonymous reviewers for their valuable feedback. Regarding the preparation of a title list from English-language Wikipedia articles, we are particularly grateful for the assistance given by Motoki Sato.

References

Anne Abeillé, Lionel Clément, and François Toussenel. 2003. *Building a Treebank for French*, Springer Netherlands, Dordrecht, pages 165–187.

Ann Bies, Justin Mott, Colin Warner, and Seth Kulick. 2012. English web treebank. *Technical Report LDC2012T13, Linguistic Data Consortium, Philadelphia, Pennsylvania, USA.* .

Marie Candito and Matthieu Constant. 2014. Strategies for contiguous multiword expression analysis and dependency parsing. In *Proceedings of the 52nd Annual Meeting of the Association for Computational Linguistics (Volume 1: Long Papers)*. Association for Computational Linguistics, pages 743–753. https://doi.org/10.3115/v1/P14-1070.

Rose Jenny Finkel and D. Christopher Manning. 2009. Joint parsing and named entity recognition. In *Proceedings of Human Language Technologies: The 2009 Annual Conference of the North American Chapter of the Association for Computational Linguistics*. Association for Computational Linguistics, pages 326–334. http://aclweb.org/anthology/N09-1037.

Spence Green, Marie-Catherine de Marneffe, and Christopher D Manning. 2013. Parsing models for identifying multiword expressions. *Computational Linguistics* 39(1):195–227.

Matthew Honnibal, Yoav Goldberg, and Mark Johnson. 2013. *Proceedings of the Seventeenth Conference on Computational Natural Language Learning*, Association for Computational Linguistics, chapter A Non-Monotonic Arc-Eager Transition System for Dependency Parsing, pages 163–172. http://aclweb.org/anthology/W13-3518.

Akihiko Kato, Hiroyuki Shindo, and Yuji Matsumoto. 2016. Construction of an english dependency corpus incorporating compound function words. In Nicoletta Calzolari (Conference Chair), Khalid Choukri, Thierry Declerck, Sara Goggi, Marko Grobelnik, Bente Maegaard, Joseph Mariani, Helene Mazo, Asuncion Moreno, Jan Odijk, and Stelios Piperidis, editors, *Proceedings of the Tenth International Conference on Language Resources and Evaluation (LREC 2016)*. European Language Resources Association (ELRA), Paris, France.

Ioannis Korkontzelos and Suresh Manandhar. 2010. Can recognising multiword expressions improve shallow parsing? In *Human Language Technologies: The 2010 Annual Conference of the North American Chapter of the Association for Computational Linguistics*. Association for Computational Linguistics, Los Angeles, California, pages 636–644. http://www.aclweb.org/anthology/N10-1089.

John Lafferty, Andrew McCallum, and Fernando Pereira. 2001. Conditional random fields: Probabilistic models for segmenting and labeling sequence data. In *Proc. 18th International Conf. on Machine Learning*. Morgan Kaufmann, San Francisco, CA, pages 282–289. citeseer.ist.psu.edu/lafferty01conditional.html.

Marie-Catherine Marneffe and D. Christopher Manning. 2008. *Coling 2008: Proceedings of the workshop on Cross-Framework and Cross-Domain Parser Evaluation*, Coling 2008 Organizing Committee, chapter The Stanford Typed Dependencies Representation, pages 1–8. http://aclweb.org/anthology/W08-1301.

Ryan McDonald, Joakim Nivre, Yvonne Quirmbach-Brundage, Yoav Goldberg, Dipanjan Das, Kuzman Ganchev, Keith Hall, Slav Petrov, Hao Zhang, Oscar Täckström, Claudia Bedini, Núria Bertomeu Castelló, and Jungmee Lee. 2013. Universal dependency annotation for multilingual parsing. In *Proceedings of the 51st Annual Meeting of the Association for Computational Linguistics (Volume 2: Short Papers)*. Association for Computational Linguistics, pages 92–97. http://aclweb.org/anthology/P13-2017.

Alexis Nasr, Carlos Ramisch, José Deulofeu, and André Valli. 2015. Joint dependency parsing and multiword expression tokenization. In *Proceedings of the 53rd Annual Meeting of the Association for Computational Linguistics and the 7th International Joint Conference on Natural Language Processing (Volume 1: Long Papers)*. Association for Computational Linguistics, Beijing, China, pages 1116–1126. http://www.aclweb.org/anthology/P15-1108.

Sameer S. Pradhan, Eduard H. Hovy, Mitchell P. Marcus, Martha Palmer, Lance A. Ramshaw, and Ralph M. Weischedel. 2007. Ontonotes: A unified relational semantic representation. In *Proceedings of the First IEEE International Conference on Semantic Computing (ICSC 2007), September 17-19, 2007, Irvine, California, USA*. pages 517–526. https://doi.org/10.1109/ICSC.2007.83.

Nathan Schneider, Spencer Onuffer, Nora Kazour, Emily Danchik, Michael T. Mordowanec, Henrietta Conrad, and Noah A. Smith. 2014. Comprehensive annotation of multiword expressions in a social web corpus. In Nicoletta Calzolari, Khalid Choukri, Thierry Declerck, Hrafn Loftsson, Bente Maegaard, Joseph Mariani, Asuncion Moreno, Jan Odijk, and Stelios Piperidis, editors, *Proceedings of the Ninth International Conference on Language Resources and Evaluation (LREC'14)*. European Language Resources Association (ELRA), Reykjavik, Iceland, pages 455–461. ACL Anthology Identifier: L14-1433.

Yutaro Shigeto, Ai Azuma, Sorami Hisamoto, Shuhei Kondo, Tomoya Kouse, Keisuke Sakaguchi, Akifumi Yoshimoto, Frances Yung, and Yuji Matsumoto. 2013. *Proceedings of the 9th Workshop on Multiword Expressions*, Association for Computational Linguistics, chapter Construction of English MWE Dictionary and its Application to POS Tagging, pages 139–144. http://aclweb.org/anthology/W13-1021.

Kristina Toutanova, Dan Klein, Christopher D. Manning, and Yoram Singer. 2003. Feature-rich part-of-speech tagging with a cyclic dependency network. In *Proceedings of the 2003 Human Language Technology Conference of the North American Chapter of the Association for Computational Linguistics*. http://aclweb.org/anthology/N03-1033.

Yue Zhang and Joakim Nivre. 2011. Transition-based dependency parsing with rich non-local features. In *Proceedings of the 49th Annual Meeting of the Association for Computational Linguistics: Human Language Technologies*. Association for Computational Linguistics, pages 188–193. http://aclweb.org/anthology/P11-2033.

Improving Semantic Composition with Offset Inference

Thomas Kober, Julie Weeds, Jeremy Reffin and **David Weir**
TAG laboratory, Department of Informatics, University of Sussex
Brighton, BN1 9RH, UK
{t.kober, j.e.weeds, j.p.reffin, d.j.weir}@sussex.ac.uk

Abstract

Count-based distributional semantic models suffer from sparsity due to unobserved but plausible co-occurrences in any text collection. This problem is amplified for models like Anchored Packed Trees (APTs), that take the grammatical type of a co-occurrence into account. We therefore introduce a novel form of distributional inference that exploits the rich type structure in APTs and infers missing data by the same mechanism that is used for semantic composition.

1 Introduction

Anchored Packed Trees (APTs) is a recently proposed approach to distributional semantics that takes distributional composition to be a process of lexeme contextualisation (Weir et al., 2016). A lexeme's meaning, characterised as knowledge concerning co-occurrences involving that lexeme, is represented with a higher-order dependency-typed structure (the APT) where paths associated with higher-order dependencies connect vertices associated with weighted lexeme multisets. The central innovation in the compositional theory is that the APT's type structure enables the precise alignment of the semantic representation of each of the lexemes being composed. Like other count-based distributional spaces, however, it is prone to considerable data sparsity, caused by not observing all plausible co-occurrences in the given data. Recently, Kober et al. (2016) introduced a simple unsupervised algorithm to infer missing co-occurrence information by leveraging the distributional neighbourhood and ease the sparsity effect in count-based models.

In this paper, we generalise distributional inference (DI) in APTs and show how precisely the same mechanism that was introduced to support distributional composition, namely "offsetting" APT representations, gives rise to a novel form of distributional inference, allowing us to infer co-occurrences from neighbours of these representations. For example, by transforming a representation of *white* to a representation of "things that can be white", inference of unobserved, but plausible, co-occurrences can be based on finding near neighbours (which will be nouns) of the "things that can be white" structure. This furthermore exposes an interesting connection between distributional inference and distributional composition. Our method is unsupervised and maintains the intrinsic interpretability of APTs[1].

2 Offset Representations

The basis of how composition is modelled in the APT framework is the way that the co-occurrences are structured. In characterising the distributional semantics of some lexeme w, rather than just recording a co-occurrence between w and w' within some context window, we follow Padó and Lapata (2007) and record the dependency path from w to w'. This syntagmatic structure makes it possible to appropriately offset the semantic representations of each of the lexemes being composed in some phrase. For example many nouns will have distributional features starting with the type `amod`, which cannot be observed for adjectives or verbs. Thus, when composing the adjective *white* with the noun *clothes*, the feature spaces of the two lexemes need to be aligned first. This can be achieved by offsetting one of the constituents, which we will explain in more detail in this section.

We will make use of the following nota-

---

[1] We release our code and data at `https://github.com/tttthomasssss/acl2017`

Proceedings of the 55th Annual Meeting of the Association for Computational Linguistics (Short Papers), pages 433–440
Vancouver, Canada, July 30 - August 4, 2017. ©2017 Association for Computational Linguistics
https://doi.org/10.18653/v1/P17-2069

tion throughout this work. A typed distributional feature consists of a path and a lexeme such as in `amod`:*white*. Inverse paths are denoted by a horizontal bar above the dependency relation such as in $\overline{\texttt{dobj}}$:*prefer* and higher-order paths are separated by a dot such as in $\overline{\texttt{amod}}$`.compound`:*dress*.

Offset representations are the central component in the composition process in the APT framework. Figure 1 shows the APT representations for the adjective *white* (left) and the APT for the noun *clothes* (right), as might have been observed in a text collection. Each node holds a multiset of lexemes and the anchor of an APT reflects the current perspective of a lexeme at the given node. An offset representation can be created by shifting the anchor along a given path. For example the lexeme *white* is at the same node as other adjectives such as *black* and *clean*, whereas nouns such as *shoes* or *noise* are typically reached via the $\overline{\texttt{amod}}$ edge.

Offsetting in APTs only involves a change in the anchor, the underlying structure remains unchanged. By offsetting the lexeme *white* by `amod` the anchor is shifted along the $\overline{\texttt{amod}}$ edge, which results in creating a noun view for the adjective *white*. We denote the offset view of a lexeme for a given path by superscripting the offset path, for example the `amod` offset of the adjective *white* is denoted as *white*$^{\texttt{amod}}$. The offsetting procedure changes the starting points of the paths as visible in Figure 1 between the anchors for *white* and *white*$^{\texttt{amod}}$, since paths always begin at the anchor. The red dashed line in Figure 1 reflects that anchor shift. The lexeme *white*$^{\texttt{amod}}$ represents a prototypical "white thing", that is, a noun that has been modified by the adjective *white*. We note that all edges in the APT space are bi-directional as exemplified in the coloured `amod` and $\overline{\texttt{amod}}$ edges in the APT for *white*, however for brevity we only show uni-directional edges in Figure 1.

By considering the APT representations for the lexemes *white* and *clothes* in Figure 1, it becomes apparent that lexemes with different parts of speech are located in different areas of the semantic space. If we want to compose the adjective-noun phrase *white clothes*, we need to offset one of the two constituents to align the feature spaces in order to leverage their distributional commonalities. This can be achieved by either creating a noun offset view of *white*, by shift-

ing the anchor along the $\overline{\texttt{amod}}$ edge, or by creating an adjective offset representation of *clothes* by shifting its anchor along `amod`. In this work we follow Weir et al. (2016) and always offset the dependent in a given relation. Table 1 shows a subset of the features of Figure 1 as would be represented in a vectorised APT. Vectorising the whole APT lexicon results in a very high-dimensional and sparse typed distributional space. The features for *white*$^{\texttt{amod}}$ (middle column) highlight the change in feature space caused by offsetting the adjective *white*. The features of the offset view *white*$^{\texttt{amod}}$, are now aligned with the noun *clothes* such that the two can be composed. Composition can be performed by either selecting the *union* or *intersection* of the aligned features.

white	*white*$^{\texttt{amod}}$	*clothes*
`:`*clean*	`amod:`*clean*	`amod:`*wet*
`amod:`*shoes*	`:`*shoes*	`:`*dress*
`amod.dobj:`*wear*	`dobj:`*wear*	`dobj:`*wear*
`amod.nsubj.`*earn*	`nsubj:`*earn*	`nsubj:`*admit*

Table 1: Sample of vectorised features for the APTs shown in Figure 1. Offsetting *white* by `amod` creates an offset view, *white*$^{\texttt{amod}}$, representing a noun, and has the consequence of aligning the feature space with *clothes*.

2.1 Qualitative Analysis of Offset Representations

Any offset view of a lexeme is behaviourally identical to a "normal" lexeme. It has an associated part of speech, a distributional representation which locates it in semantic space, and we can find neighbours for it in the same way that we find neighbours for any other lexeme. In this way, a single APT data structure is able to provide many different views of any given lexeme. These views reflect the different ways in which the lexeme is used. For example *law*$^{\overline{\texttt{nsubj}}}$ is the $\overline{\texttt{nsubj}}$ offset representation of the noun *law*. This lexeme is a verb and represents an action carried out by the *law*. This contrasts with *law*$^{\overline{\texttt{dobj}}}$, which is the $\overline{\texttt{dobj}}$ offset representation of the noun *law*. It is also a verb, however represents actions done to the *law*. Table 2 lists the 10 nearest neighbours for a number of lexemes, offset by `amod`, $\overline{\texttt{dobj}}$ and $\overline{\texttt{nsubj}}$ respectively.

For example, the neighbourhood of the lexeme *ancient* in Table 2 shows that the offset view for *ancient*$^{\texttt{amod}}$ is a prototypical representation of an "ancient thing", with neighbours easily associated with the property *ancient*. Furthermore, Table 2

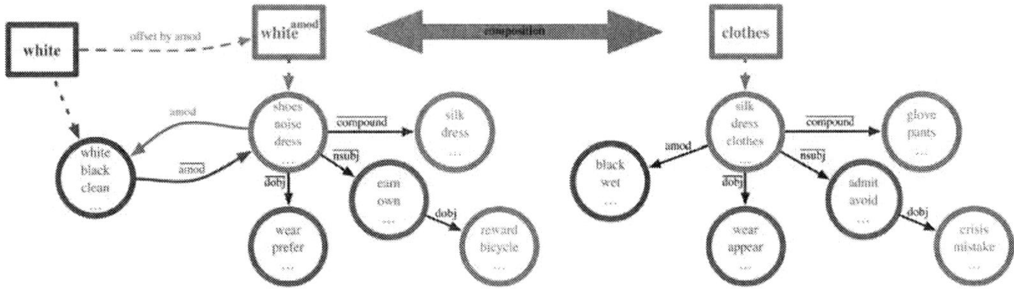

Figure 1: Structured distributional APT space. Different colours reflect different parts of speech. Boxes denote the current anchor of the APT, circles represent nodes in the APT space, holding lexemes, and edges represent their relationship within the space.

illustrates that nearest neighbours of offset views are often other offset representations. This means that for example actions carried out by a *mother* tend to be similar to actions carried out by a *father* or a *parent*.

2.2 Offset Inference

Our approach generalises the unsupervised algorithm proposed by Kober et al. (2016), henceforth "standard DI", as a method for inferring missing knowledge into an APT representation. Rather than simply inferring potentially plausible, but unobserved co-occurrences from near distributional neighbours, inferences can be made involving offset APTs. For example, the adjective *white* can be offset so that it represents a noun — a prototypical "white thing". This allows inferring plausible co-occurrences from other "things that can be white", such as *shoes* or *shirts*. Our algorithm therefore reflects the contextualised use of a word. This has the advantage of being able to make flexible and fine grained distinctions in the inference process. For example if the noun *law* is used as a subject, our algorithm allows inferring plausible co-occurrences from "other actions carried out by the law". This contrasts the use of *law* as an object, where offset inference is able to find co-occurrences on the basis of "other actions done to the law". This is a crucial advantage over the method of Kober et al. (2016) which only supports inference on uncontextualised lexemes.

A sketch of how offset inference for a lexeme w works is shown in Algorithm 1. Our algorithm requires a distributional model M, an APT representation for the lexeme w for which to perform offset inference, a dependency path p, describing the offset for w, and the number of neighbours k.

The offset representation of w' is then enriched with the information from its distributional neighbours by some merge function. We note that if the offset path p is the empty path, we would recover the algorithm presented by Kober et al. (2016). Our algorithm is unsupervised, and agnostic to the input distributional model and the neighbour retrieval function.

Algorithm 1 Offset Inference

1: **procedure** OFFSET_INFERENCE(M, w, p, k)
2: $\quad$ $w' \leftarrow$ offset(w, p)
3: $\quad$ **for all** n in neighbours(M, w', k) **do**
4: $\quad\quad$ $w'' \leftarrow$ merge(w'', n)
5: $\quad$ **end for**
6: $\quad$ **return** w''
7: **end procedure**

Connection to Distributional Composition

An interesting observation is the similarity between distributional inference and distributional composition, as both operations are realised by the same mechanism — an offset followed by inferring plausible co-occurrence counts for a single lexeme in the case of distributional inference, or for a phrase in the case of composition. The merging of co-occurrence dimensions for distributional inference can also be any of the operations commonly used for distributional composition such as pointwise minimum, maximum, addition or multiplication.

This relation creates an interesting dynamic between distributional inference and composition when used in a complementary manner as in this work. The former can be used as a process of *co-occurrence embellishment* which is adding miss-

Offset Representation	Nearest Neighbours
$ancient^{amod}$	civilzation, mythology, tradition, ruin, monument, trackway, tomb, antiquity, folklore, deity
red^{amod}	$blue^{amod}$, $black^{amod}$, $green^{amod}$, $dark^{amod}$, onion, pepper, red, tomato, carrot, garlic
$economic^{amod}$	$political^{amod}$, $societal^{amod}$, cohabiting, economy, growth, cohabitant, globalisation, competitiveness, globalization, prosperity
$government^{\overline{dobj}}$	overthrow, $party^{\overline{dobj}}$, $authority^{\overline{dobj}}$, $leader^{\overline{dobj}}$, $capital^{\overline{dobj}}$, $force^{\overline{dobj}}$, $state^{\overline{dobj}}$, $official^{\overline{dobj}}$, $minister^{\overline{dobj}}$, oust
$problem^{\overline{dobj}}$	$difficulty^{\overline{dobj}}$, solve, coded, $issue^{\overline{dobj}}$, $injury^{\overline{dobj}}$, overcome, $question^{\overline{dobj}}$, think, $loss^{\overline{dobj}}$, relieve
$law^{\overline{dobj}}$	violate, $rule^{\overline{dobj}}$, enact, repeal, $principle^{\overline{dobj}}$, unmake, enforce, $policy^{\overline{dobj}}$, obey, flout
$researcher^{\overline{nsubj}}$	$physician^{\overline{nsubj}}$, $writer^{\overline{nsubj}}$, theorize, thwart, theorise, hypothesize, surmise, $student^{\overline{nsubj}}$, $worker^{\overline{nsubj}}$, apprehend
$mother^{\overline{nsubj}}$	$wife^{\overline{nsubj}}$, $father^{\overline{nsubj}}$, $parent^{\overline{nsubj}}$, $woman^{\overline{nsubj}}$, re-married, remarry, $girl^{\overline{nsubj}}$, breastfeed, $family^{\overline{nsubj}}$, disown
$law^{\overline{nsubj}}$	$rule^{\overline{nsubj}}$, $principle^{\overline{nsubj}}$, $policy^{\overline{nsubj}}$, criminalize, $case^{\overline{nsubj}}$, $contract^{\overline{nsubj}}$, prohibit, proscribe, enjoin, $charge^{\overline{nsubj}}$

Table 2: List of the 10 nearest neighbours of amod, $\overline{dobj}$ and $\overline{nsubj}$ offset representations.

ing information, however with the risk of introducing some noise. The latter on the other hand can be used as a process of *co-occurrence filtering*, that is leveraging the enriched representations, while also sieving out the previously introduced noise.

3 Experiments

For our experiments we re-implemented the standard DI method of Kober et al. (2016) for a direct comparison. We built an order 2 APT space on the basis of the concatenation of ukWaC, Wackypedia and the BNC (Baroni et al., 2009), pre-parsed with the Malt parser (Nivre et al., 2006). We PPMI transformed the raw co-occurrence counts prior to composition, using a negative SPPMI shift of $\log 5$ (Levy and Goldberg, 2014b). We also experimented with composing normalised counts and applying the PPMI transformation after composition as done by Weeds et al. (2017), however found composing PPMI scores to work better for this task.

We evaluate our offset inference algorithm on two popular short phrase composition benchmarks by Mitchell and Lapata (2008) and Mitchell and Lapata (2010), henceforth ML08 and ML10 respectively. The ML08 dataset consists of 120 distinct verb-object (VO) pairs and the ML10 dataset contains 108 adjective-noun (AN), 108 noun-noun (NN) and 108 verb-object pairs. The goal is to compare a model's similarity estimates to human provided judgements. For both tasks, each phrase pair has been rated by multiple human annotators on a scale between 1 and 7, where 7 indicates maximum similarity. Comparison with human judgements is achieved by calculating Spearman's ρ between the model's similarity estimates and the scores of each human annotator individually. We performed composition by *intersection* and tuned the number of neighbours by a grid search over {0, 10, 30, 50, 100, 500, 1000} on the ML10 develop-

ment set, selecting 10 neighbours for NNs, 100 for ANs and 50 for VOs for both DI algorithms. We calculate statistical significance using the method of Steiger (1980).

Effect of the number of neighbours

Figure 2 shows the effect of the number of neighbours for AN, NN and VO phrases, using offset inference, on the ML10 development set. Interestingly, NN compounds exhibit an early saturation effect, while VOs and ANs require more neighbours for optimal performance. One explanation for the observed behaviour is that up to some threshold, the neighbours being added contribute actually missing co-occurrence events, whereas past that threshold distributional inference degrades to just generic smoothing that is simply compensating for sparsity, but overwhelming the representations with non-plausible co-occurrence information. A similar effect has also been observed by Erk and Pado (2010) in an exemplar-based model.

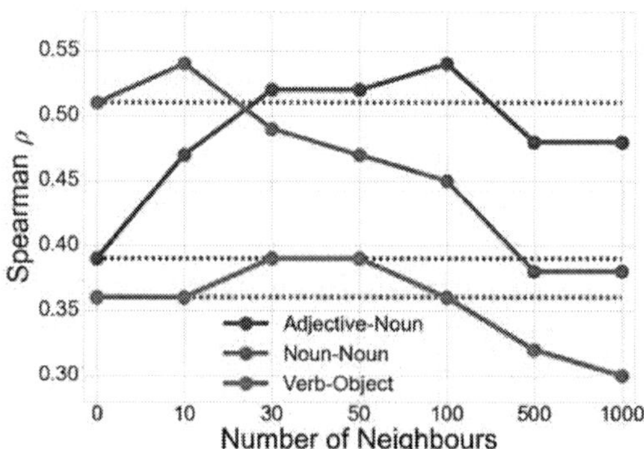

Figure 2: Effect of the number of neighbours on the ML10 development set.

Results

Table 3 shows that both forms of distributional inference significantly outperform a baseline without DI. On average, offset inference outperforms the method of Kober et al. (2016) by a statistically significant margin on both datasets.

APT configuration	ML10				ML08
	AN	NN	VO	Avg	VO
None	0.35	0.50	0.39	0.41	0.22
Standard DI	0.48[‡]	0.51	0.43[‡]	0.47[‡]	0.29[‡]
Offset Inference	**0.49[‡]**	**0.52**	**0.44[‡]**	**0.48[*‡]**	**0.31[†‡]**

Table 3: Comparison of DI algorithms. ‡ denotes statistical significance at $p < 0.01$ in comparison to the method without DI, * denotes statistical significance at $p < 0.01$ in comparison to standard DI and † denotes statistical significance at $p < 0.05$ in comparison to standard DI.

Table 4 shows that offset inference substantially outperforms comparable sparse models by Dinu et al. (2013) on ML08, achieving a new state-of-the-art, and matches the performance of the state-of-the-art neural network model of Hashimoto et al. (2014) on ML10, while being fully interpretable.

Model	ML10 - Average	ML08
Our work	**0.48**	**0.31**
Blacoe and Lapata (2012)	0.44	-
Hashimoto et al. (2014)	**0.48**	-
Weir et al. (2016)	0.43	0.26
Dinu et al. (2013)	-	$0.23 - 0.26$
Erk and Padó (2008)	-	0.27

Table 4: Comparison with existing methods.

4   Related Work

Distributional inference has its roots in the work of Dagan et al. (1993, 1994), who aim to find probability estimates for unseen words in bigrams, and Schütze (1992, 1998) who leverages the distributional neighbourhood through clustering of contexts for word-sense discrimination. Recently Kober et al. (2016) revitalised the idea for compositional distributional semantic models.

Composition with distributional semantic models has become a popular research area in recent years. Simple, yet competitive methods, are based on pointwise vector addition or multiplication (Mitchell and Lapata, 2008, 2010). However, these approaches neglect the structure of the text defining composition as a commutative operation.

A number of approaches proposed in the literature attempt to overcome this shortcoming by introducing weighted additive variants (Guevara, 2010, 2011; Zanzotto et al., 2010). Another popular strand of work models semantic composition on the basis of ideas arising in formal semantics. Composition in such models is usually implemented as operations on higher-order tensors (Ba-

roni and Zamparelli, 2010; Baroni et al., 2014; Coecke et al., 2011; Grefenstette et al., 2011; Grefenstette and Sadrzadeh, 2011; Grefenstette et al., 2013; Kartsaklis and Sadrzadeh, 2014; Paperno et al., 2014; Tian et al., 2016; Van de Cruys et al., 2013). Another widespread approach to semantic composition is to use neural networks (Bowman et al., 2016; Hashimoto et al., 2014; Hill et al., 2016; Mou et al., 2015; Socher et al., 2012, 2014; Wieting et al., 2015; Yu and Dredze, 2015), or convolutional tree kernels (Croce et al., 2011; Zanzotto and Dell'Arciprete, 2012; Annesi et al., 2014) as composition functions.

The above approaches are applied to untyped distributional vector space models where untyped models contrast with typed models (Baroni and Lenci, 2010) in terms of whether structural information is encoded in the representation as in the models of Erk and Padó (2008); Gamallo and Pereira-Fariña (2017); Levy and Goldberg (2014a); Padó and Lapata (2007); Thater et al. (2010, 2011); Weeds et al. (2014).

The perhaps most popular approach in the literature to evaluating compositional distributional semantic models is to compare human word and phrase similarity judgements with similarity estimates of composed meaning representations, under the assumption that better distributional representations will perform better at these tasks (Blacoe and Lapata, 2012; Dinu et al., 2013; Erk and Padó, 2008; Hashimoto et al., 2014; Hermann and Blunsom, 2013; Kiela et al., 2014; Turney, 2012).

5   Conclusion

In this paper we have introduced a novel form of distributional inference that generalises the method introduced by Kober et al. (2016). We have shown its effectiveness for semantic composition on two benchmark phrase similarity tasks where we achieved state-of-the-art performance while retaining the interpretability of our model. We have furthermore highlighted an interesting connection between distributional inference and distributional composition.

In future work we aim to apply our novel method to improve modelling selectional preferences, lexical inference, and scale up to longer phrases and full sentences.

References

Paolo Annesi, Danilo Croce, and Roberto Basili. 2014. Semantic compositionality in tree kernels. In *Proceedings of the 23rd ACM International Conference on Conference on Information and Knowledge Management*. ACM, New York, NY, USA, CIKM '14, pages 1029–1038. https://doi.org/10.1145/2661829.2661955.

Marco Baroni, Raffaella Bernardi, and Roberto Zamparelli. 2014. Frege in space: A program for compositional distributional semantics. *Linguistic Issues in Language Technology* 9(6):5–110.

Marco Baroni, Silvia Bernardini, Adriano Ferraresi, and Eros Zanchetta. 2009. The wacky wide web: a collection of very large linguistically processed web-crawled corpora. *Language Resources and Evaluation* 43(3):209–226. https://doi.org/10.1007/s10579-009-9081-4.

Marco Baroni and Alessandro Lenci. 2010. Distributional memory: A general framework for corpus-based semantics. *Computational Linguistics* 36(4):673–721.

Marco Baroni and Roberto Zamparelli. 2010. Nouns are vectors, adjectives are matrices: Representing adjective-noun constructions in semantic space. In *Proceedings of the 2010 Conference on Empirical Methods in Natural Language Processing*. Association for Computational Linguistics, Cambridge, MA, pages 1183–1193. http://www.aclweb.org/anthology/D10-1115.

William Blacoe and Mirella Lapata. 2012. A comparison of vector-based representations for semantic composition. In *Proceedings of the 2012 Joint Conference on Empirical Methods in Natural Language Processing and Computational Natural Language Learning*. Association for Computational Linguistics, Jeju Island, Korea, pages 546–556. http://www.aclweb.org/anthology/D12-1050.

Samuel R. Bowman, Jon Gauthier, Abhinav Rastogi, Raghav Gupta, Christopher D. Manning, and Christopher Potts. 2016. A fast unified model for parsing and sentence understanding. In *Proceedings of the 54th Annual Meeting of the Association for Computational Linguistics (Volume 1: Long Papers)*. Association for Computational Linguistics, Berlin, Germany, pages 1466–1477. http://www.aclweb.org/anthology/P16-1139.

Bob Coecke, Mehrnoosh Sadrzadeh, and Stephen Clark. 2011. Mathematical foundations for a compositional distributed model of meaning. *Linguistic Analysis* 36(1-4):345–384.

Danilo Croce, Alessandro Moschitti, and Roberto Basili. 2011. Structured lexical similarity via convolution kernels on dependency trees. In *Proceedings of the 2011 Conference on Empirical Methods in Natural Language Processing*. Association for Computational Linguistics, Edinburgh, Scotland, UK., pages 1034–1046. http://www.aclweb.org/anthology/D11-1096.

Ido Dagan, Shaul Marcus, and Shaul Markovitch. 1993. Contextual word similarity and estimation from sparse data. In *Proceedings of the 31st Annual Meeting on Association for Computational Linguistics*. Association for Computational Linguistics, Stroudsburg, PA, USA, ACL '93, pages 164–171. https://doi.org/10.3115/981574.981596.

Ido Dagan, Fernando Pereira, and Lillian Lee. 1994. Similarity-based estimation of word cooccurrence probabilities. In *Proceedings of the 32nd Annual Meeting of the Association for Computational Linguistics*. Association for Computational Linguistics, Las Cruces, New Mexico, USA, pages 272–278. https://doi.org/10.3115/981732.981770.

Georgiana Dinu, Nghia The Pham, and Marco Baroni. 2013. General estimation and evaluation of compositional distributional semantic models. In *Proceedings of the Workshop on Continuous Vector Space Models and their Compositionality*. Association for Computational Linguistics, Sofia, Bulgaria, pages 50–58. http://www.aclweb.org/anthology/W13-3206.

Katrin Erk and Sebastian Padó. 2008. A structured vector space model for word meaning in context. In *Proceedings of the 2008 Conference on Empirical Methods in Natural Language Processing*. Association for Computational Linguistics, Honolulu, Hawaii, pages 897–906. http://www.aclweb.org/anthology/D08-1094.

Katrin Erk and Sebastian Pado. 2010. Exemplar-based models for word meaning in context. In *Proceedings of the ACL 2010 Conference Short Papers*. Association for Computational Linguistics, Uppsala, Sweden, pages 92–97. http://www.aclweb.org/anthology/P10-2017.

Pablo Gamallo and Martín Pereira-Fariña. 2017. Compositional semantics using feature-based models from wordnet. In *Proceedings of the 1st Workshop on Sense, Concept and Entity Representations and their Applications*. Association for Computational Linguistics, Valencia, Spain, pages 1–11. http://www.aclweb.org/anthology/W17-1901.

E. Grefenstette, G. Dinu, Y. Zhang, M. Sadrzadeh, and M. Baroni. 2013. Multi-step regression learning for compositional distributional semantics. In *Proceedings of the 10th International Conference on Computational Semantics (IWCS 2013) – Long Papers*. Association for Computational Linguistics, Potsdam, Germany, pages 131–142. http://www.aclweb.org/anthology/W13-0112.

Edward Grefenstette and Mehrnoosh Sadrzadeh. 2011. Experimental support for a categorical compositional distributional model of meaning. In *Proceedings of the 2011 Conference on Empirical Methods in Natural Language Processing*. Association for Computational Linguistics,

Edinburgh, Scotland, UK., pages 1394–1404. http://www.aclweb.org/anthology/D11-1129.

Edward Grefenstette, Mehrnoosh Sadrzadeh, Stephen Clark, Bob Coecke, and Stephen Pulman. 2011. Concrete sentence spaces for compositional distributional models of meaning. *Proceedings of the 9th International Conference on Computational Semantics (IWCS 2011)* pages 125–134.

Emiliano Guevara. 2010. A regression model of adjective-noun compositionality in distributional semantics. In *Proceedings of the 2010 Workshop on GEometrical Models of Natural Language Semantics*. Association for Computational Linguistics, Uppsala, Sweden, pages 33–37. http://www.aclweb.org/anthology/W10-2805.

Emiliano Guevara. 2011. Computing semantic compositionality in distributional semantics. In *Proceedings of the Ninth International Conference on Computational Semantics*. Association for Computational Linguistics, Stroudsburg, PA, USA, IWCS '11, pages 135–144.

Kazuma Hashimoto, Pontus Stenetorp, Makoto Miwa, and Yoshimasa Tsuruoka. 2014. Jointly learning word representations and composition functions using predicate-argument structures. In *Proceedings of the 2014 Conference on Empirical Methods in Natural Language Processing (EMNLP)*. Association for Computational Linguistics, Doha, Qatar, pages 1544–1555. http://www.aclweb.org/anthology/D14-1163.

Karl Moritz Hermann and Phil Blunsom. 2013. The role of syntax in vector space models of compositional semantics. In *Proceedings of the 51st Annual Meeting of the Association for Computational Linguistics (Volume 1: Long Papers)*. Association for Computational Linguistics, Sofia, Bulgaria, pages 894–904. http://www.aclweb.org/anthology/P13-1088.

Felix Hill, KyungHyun Cho, Anna Korhonen, and Yoshua Bengio. 2016. Learning to understand phrases by embedding the dictionary. *Transactions of the Association for Computational Linguistics* 4:17–30. http://www.aclweb.org/anthology/Q/Q16/Q16-1002.pdf.

Dimitri Kartsaklis and Mehrnoosh Sadrzadeh. 2014. A study of entanglement in a categorical framework of natural language. In *Proceedings of the 11th Workshop on Quantum Physics and Logic (QPL)*.

Douwe Kiela, Felix Hill, Anna Korhonen, and Stephen Clark. 2014. Improving multi-modal representations using image dispersion: Why less is sometimes more. In *Proceedings of the 52nd Annual Meeting of the Association for Computational Linguistics (Volume 2: Short Papers)*. Association for Computational Linguistics, Baltimore, Maryland, pages 835–841. http://www.aclweb.org/anthology/P14-2135.

Thomas Kober, Julie Weeds, Jeremy Reffin, and David Weir. 2016. Improving sparse word representations with distributional inference for semantic composition. In *Proceedings of the 2016 Conference on Empirical Methods in Natural Language Processing*. Association for Computational Linguistics, Austin, Texas, pages 1691–1702. https://aclweb.org/anthology/D16-1175.

Omer Levy and Yoav Goldberg. 2014a. Dependency-based word embeddings. In *Proceedings of the 52nd Annual Meeting of the Association for Computational Linguistics (Volume 2: Short Papers)*. Association for Computational Linguistics, Baltimore, Maryland, pages 302–308. http://www.aclweb.org/anthology/P14-2050.

Omer Levy and Yoav Goldberg. 2014b. Neural word embedding as implicit matrix factorization. In Z. Ghahramani, M. Welling, C. Cortes, N.D. Lawrence, and K.Q. Weinberger, editors, *Advances in Neural Information Processing Systems 27*, Curran Associates, Inc., pages 2177–2185.

Jeff Mitchell and Mirella Lapata. 2008. Vector-based models of semantic composition. In *Proceedings of ACL-08: HLT*. Association for Computational Linguistics, Columbus, Ohio, pages 236–244. http://www.aclweb.org/anthology/P/P08/P08-1028.

Jeff Mitchell and Mirella Lapata. 2010. Composition in distributional models of semantics. *Cognitive Science* 34(8):1388–1429. https://doi.org/10.1111/j.1551-6709.2010.01106.x.

Lili Mou, Hao Peng, Ge Li, Yan Xu, Lu Zhang, and Zhi Jin. 2015. Discriminative neural sentence modeling by tree-based convolution. In *Proceedings of the 2015 Conference on Empirical Methods in Natural Language Processing*. Association for Computational Linguistics, Lisbon, Portugal, pages 2315–2325. http://aclweb.org/anthology/D15-1279.

Joakim Nivre, Johan Hall, and Jens Nilsson. 2006. Maltparser: A data-driven parser-generator for dependency parsing. Technical report, Växjö University.

Sebastian Padó and Mirella Lapata. 2007. Dependency-based construction of semantic space models. *Computational Linguistics* 33(2):161–199. https://doi.org/10.1162/coli.2007.33.2.161.

Denis Paperno, Nghia The Pham, and Marco Baroni. 2014. A practical and linguistically-motivated approach to compositional distributional semantics. In *Proceedings of the 52nd Annual Meeting of the Association for Computational Linguistics (Volume 1: Long Papers)*. Association for Computational Linguistics, Baltimore, Maryland, pages 90–99. http://www.aclweb.org/anthology/P14-1009.

Hinrich Schütze. 1992. Dimensions of meaning. In *Proceedings of ACM/IEEE Conference on Supercomputing*. IEEE Computer Society Press, pages 787–796. http://dl.acm.org/citation.cfm?id=147877.148132.

Hinrich Schütze. 1998. Automatic word sense discrimination. *Computational Linguistics* 24(1):97–123.

Richard Socher, Brody Huval, Christopher D. Manning, and Andrew Y. Ng. 2012. Semantic compositionality through recursive matrix-vector spaces. In *Proceedings of the 2012 Joint Conference on Empirical Methods in Natural Language Processing and Computational Natural Language Learning*. Association for Computational Linguistics, Jeju Island, Korea, pages 1201–1211. http://www.aclweb.org/anthology/D12-1110.

Richard Socher, Andrej Karpathy, Quoc Le, Christopher Manning, and Andrew Ng. 2014. Grounded compositional semantics for finding and describing images with sentences. *Transactions of the Association for Computational Linguistics* 2:207–218.

James H Steiger. 1980. Tests for comparing elements of a correlation matrix. *Psychological Bulletin* 87(2):245.

Stefan Thater, Hagen Fürstenau, and Manfred Pinkal. 2010. Contextualizing semantic representations using syntactically enriched vector models. In *Proceedings of the 48th Annual Meeting of the Association for Computational Linguistics*. Association for Computational Linguistics, Uppsala, Sweden, pages 948–957. http://www.aclweb.org/anthology/P10-1097.

Stefan Thater, Hagen Fürstenau, and Manfred Pinkal. 2011. Word meaning in context: A simple and effective vector model. In *Proceedings of 5th International Joint Conference on Natural Language Processing*. Asian Federation of Natural Language Processing, Chiang Mai, Thailand, pages 1134–1143. http://www.aclweb.org/anthology/I11-1127.

Ran Tian, Naoaki Okazaki, and Kentaro Inui. 2016. Learning semantically and additively compositional distributional representations. In *Proceedings of the 54th Annual Meeting of the Association for Computational Linguistics (Volume 1: Long Papers)*. Association for Computational Linguistics, Berlin, Germany, pages 1277–1287. http://www.aclweb.org/anthology/P16-1121.

Peter D. Turney. 2012. Domain and function: A dual-space model of semantic relations and compositions. *Journal of Artificial Intelligence Research* 44(1):533–585.

Tim Van de Cruys, Thierry Poibeau, and Anna Korhonen. 2013. A tensor-based factorization model of semantic compositionality. In *Proceedings of the 2013 Conference of the North American Chapter of the Association for Computational Linguistics: Human Language Technologies*. Association for Computational Linguistics, Atlanta, Georgia, pages 1142–1151. http://www.aclweb.org/anthology/N13-1134.

Julie Weeds, Thomas Kober, Jeremy Reffin, and David Weir. 2017. When a red herring in not a red herring: Using compositional methods to detect non-compositional phrases. In *Proceedings of the 15th Conference of the European Chapter of the Association for Computational Linguistics: Volume 2, Short Papers*. Association for Computational Linguistics, Valencia, Spain, pages 529–534. http://www.aclweb.org/anthology/E17-2085.

Julie Weeds, David Weir, and Jeremy Reffin. 2014. Distributional composition using higher-order dependency vectors. In *Proceedings of the 2nd Workshop on Continuous Vector Space Models and their Compositionality (CVSC)*. Association for Computational Linguistics, Gothenburg, Sweden, pages 11–20. http://www.aclweb.org/anthology/W14-1502.

David Weir, Julie Weeds, Jeremy Reffin, and Thomas Kober. 2016. Aligning packed dependency trees: a theory of composition for distributional semantics. *Computational Linguistics, special issue on Formal Distributional Semantics* 42(4):727–761.

John Wieting, Mohit Bansal, Kevin Gimpel, and Karen Livescu. 2015. From paraphrase database to compositional paraphrase model and back. *Transactions of the Association for Computational Linguistics* 3:345–358. http://www.aclweb.org/anthology/Q/Q15/Q15-1025.pdf.

Mo Yu and Mark Dredze. 2015. Learning composition models for phrase embeddings. *Transactions of the Association for Computational Linguistics* 3:227–242. http://aclweb.org/anthology/Q/Q15/Q15-1017.pdf.

Fabio Massimo Zanzotto and Lorenzo Dell'Arciprete. 2012. Distributed tree kernels. In John Langford and Joelle Pineau, editors, *Proceedings of the 29th International Conference on Machine Learning (ICML-12)*. Omnipress, New York, NY, USA, ICML '12, pages 193–200.

Fabio Massimo Zanzotto, Ioannis Korkontzelos, Francesca Fallucchi, and Suresh Manandhar. 2010. Estimating linear models for compositional distributional semantics. In *Proceedings of Coling*. pages 1263–1271. http://www.aclweb.org/anthology/C10-1142.

Learning Topic-Sensitive Word Representations

Marzieh Fadaee   **Arianna Bisazza**   **Christof Monz**
Informatics Institute, University of Amsterdam
Science Park 904, 1098 XH Amsterdam, The Netherlands
`{m.fadaee,a.bisazza,c.monz}@uva.nl`

Abstract

Distributed word representations are widely used for modeling words in NLP tasks. Most of the existing models generate one representation per word and do not consider different meanings of a word. We present two approaches to learn multiple topic-sensitive representations per word by using Hierarchical Dirichlet Process. We observe that by modeling topics and integrating topic distributions for each document we obtain representations that are able to distinguish between different meanings of a given word. Our models yield statistically significant improvements for the lexical substitution task indicating that commonly used single word representations, even when combined with contextual information, are insufficient for this task.

1 Introduction

Word representations in the form of dense vectors, or word embeddings, capture semantic and syntactic information (Mikolov et al., 2013a; Pennington et al., 2014) and are widely used in many NLP tasks (Zou et al., 2013; Levy and Goldberg, 2014; Tang et al., 2014; Gharbieh et al., 2016). Most of the existing models generate one representation per word and do not distinguish between different meanings of a word. However, many tasks can benefit from using multiple representations per word to capture polysemy (Reisinger and Mooney, 2010). There have been several attempts to build repositories for word senses (Miller, 1995; Navigli and Ponzetto, 2010), but this is laborious and limited to few languages. Moreover, defining a universal set of word senses is challenging as polysemous words can exist at many levels of granularity (Kilgarriff, 1997; Navigli, 2012).

In this paper, we introduce a model that uses a nonparametric Bayesian model, Hierarchical Dirichlet Process (HDP), to learn multiple topic-sensitive representations per word. Yao and van Durme (2011) show that HDP is effective in learning topics yielding state-of-the-art performance for sense induction. However, they assume that topics and senses are interchangeable, and train individual models per word making it difficult to scale to large data. Our approach enables us to use HDP to model senses effectively using large unannotated training data. We investigate to what extent distributions over word senses can be approximated by distributions over topics without assuming these concepts to be identical. The contributions of this paper are: (i) We propose three unsupervised, language-independent approaches to approximate senses with topics and learn multiple topic-sensitive embeddings per word. (ii) We show that in the Lexical Substitution ranking task our models outperform two competitive baselines.

2 Topic-Sensitive Representations

In this section we describe the proposed models. To learn topics from a corpus we use HDP (Teh et al., 2006; Lau et al., 2014). The main advantage of this model compared to non-hierarchical methods like the Chinese Restaurant Process (CRP) is that each document in the corpus is modeled using a mixture model with topics shared between all documents (Teh et al., 2005; Brody and Lapata, 2009). HDP yields two sets of distributions that we use in our methods: distributions over topics for words in the vocabulary, and distributions over topics for documents in the corpus.

Similarly to Neelakantan et al. (2014), we use neighboring words to detect the meaning of the context, however, we also use the two HDP dis-

Proceedings of the 55th Annual Meeting of the Association for Computational Linguistics (Short Papers), pages 441–447
Vancouver, Canada, July 30 - August 4, 2017. ©2017 Association for Computational Linguistics
https://doi.org/10.18653/v1/P17-2070

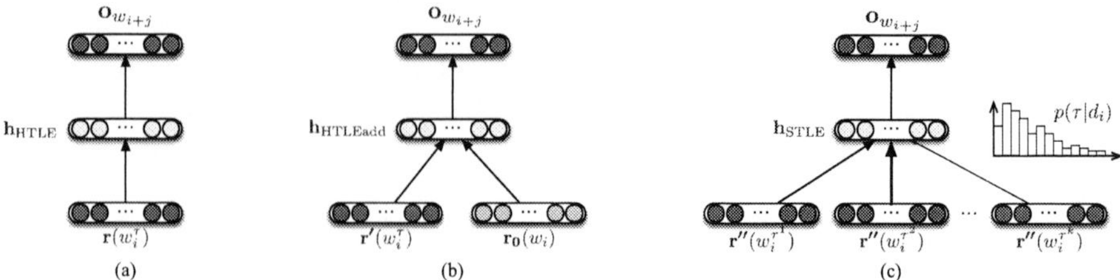

Figure 1: Illustration of our topic-sensitive representation models: (a) hard-topic labeled representations (HTLE), (b) hard topic-labeled representations plus generic word representation (HTLEadd), (c) soft topic-labeled representations (STLE).

tributions. By doing so, we take advantage of the topic of the document beyond the scope of the neighboring words, which is helpful when the immediate context of the target word is not sufficiently informative. We modify the Skipgram model (Mikolov et al., 2013a) to obtain multiple topic-sensitive representations per word type using topic distributions. In addition, we do not cluster context windows and train for different senses of the words individually. This reduces the sparsity problem and provides a better representation estimation for rare words. We assume that meanings of words can be determined by their contextual information and use the distribution over topics to differentiate between occurrences of a word in different contexts, i.e., documents with different topics. We propose three different approaches (see Figure 1): two methods with hard topic labeling of words and one with soft labeling.

2.1 Hard Topic-Labeled Representations

The trained HDP model can be used to hard-label a new corpus with one topic per word through sampling. Our first model variant (Figure 1(a)) relies on hard labeling by simply considering each word-topic pair as a separate vocabulary entry. To reduce sparsity on the context side and share the word-level information between similar contexts, we use topic-sensitive representations for target words (input to the network) and standard, i.e., unlabeled, word representations for context words (output). Note that this results in different input and output vocabularies. The training objective is then to maximize the log-likelihood of context words w_{i+j} given the target word-topic pair w_i^τ:

$$\mathcal{L}_{HardT\text{-}SG} = \frac{1}{I} \sum_{i=1}^{I} \sum_{\substack{-c \leqslant j \leqslant c \\ j \neq 0}} \log p(w_{i+j}|w_i^\tau)$$

where I is the number of words in the training corpus, c is the context size and τ is the topic assigned to w_i by HDP sampling. The embedding of a word in context $\mathbf{h}(w_i)$ is obtained by simply extracting the row of the input lookup table ($\mathbf{r}$) corresponding to the HDP-labeled word-topic pair:

$$\mathbf{h}_{\text{HTLE}}(w_i) = \mathbf{r}(w_i^\tau) \tag{1}$$

A possible shortcoming of the HTLE model is that the representations are trained separately and information is not shared between different topic-sensitive representations of the same word. To address this issue, we introduce a model variant that learns multiple topic-sensitive word representations and generic word representations simultaneously (Figure 1(b)). In this variant (HTLEadd), the target word embedding is obtained by adding the word-topic pair representation ($\mathbf{r}'$) to the generic representation of the corresponding word ($\mathbf{r_0}$):

$$\mathbf{h}_{\text{HTLEadd}}(w_i) = \mathbf{r}'(w_i^\tau) + \mathbf{r_0}(w_i) \tag{2}$$

2.2 Soft Topic-Labeled Representations

The model variants above rely on the hard labeling resulting from HDP sampling. As a soft alternative to this, we can directly include the topic distributions estimated by HDP for each document (Figure 1(c)). Specifically, for each update, we use the topic distribution to compute a weighted sum over the word-topic representations ($\mathbf{r}''$):

$$\mathbf{h}_{\text{STLE}}(w_i) = \sum_{k=1}^{T} p(\tau_k|d_i)\, \mathbf{r}''(w_i^{\tau_k}) \tag{3}$$

where T is the total number of topics, d_i the document containing w_i, and $p(\tau_k|d_i)$ the probability assigned to topic τ_k by HDP in document d_i. The training objective for this model is:

$$\mathcal{L}_{SoftT\text{-}SG} = \frac{1}{I} \sum_{i=1}^{I} \sum_{\substack{-c \leqslant j \leqslant c \\ j \neq 0}} \log p(w_{i+j}|w_i, \tau)$$

word	**bat**	
Pre-trained w2v	bats, batting, Pinch_hitter_Brayan_Pena, batsman, batted, Hawaiian_hoary, Batting	
Pre-trained GloVe	bats, batting, Bat, catcher, fielder, hitter, outfield, hitting, batted, catchers, balls	
SGE on Wikipedia	uroderma, magnirostrum, sorenseni, miniopterus, promops, luctus, micronycteris	
TSE on Wikipedia	τ_1	ball, pitchout, batter, toss-for, umpire, batting, bowes, straightened, fielder, flies
	τ_2	vespertilionidae, heran, hipposideros, sorenseni, luctus, coxi, kerivoula, natterer
word	**jaguar**	
Pre-trained w2v	jaguars, Macho_B, panther, lynx, rhino, lizard, tapir, tiger, leopard, Florida_panther	
Pre-trained GloVe	jaguars, panther, mercedes, Jaguar, porsche, volvo, ford, audi, mustang, bmw, biuck	
SGE on Wikipedia	electramotive, viper, roadster, saleen, siata, chevrolet, camaro, dodge, nissan, escort	
TSE on Wikipedia	τ_1	ford, bmw, chevrolet, honda, porsche, monza, nissan, dodge, marauder, peugeot, opel
	τ_2	wiedii, puma, margay, tapirus, jaguarundi, yagouaroundi, vison, concolor, tajacu
word	**appeal**	
Pre-trained w2v	appeals, appealing, appealed, Appeal, rehearing, apeal, Appealing, ruling, Appeals	
Pre-trained GloVe	appeals, appealed, appealing, Appeal, court, decision, conviction, plea, sought	
SGE on Wikipedia	court, appeals, appealed, carmody, upheld, verdict, jaruvan, affirmed, appealable	
TSE on Wikipedia	τ_1	court, case, appeals, appealed, decision, proceedings, disapproves, ruling
	τ_2	sfa, steadfast, lackadaisical, assertions, lack, symbolize, fans, attempt, unenthusiastic

Table 1: Nearest neighbors of three examples in different representation spaces using cosine similarity. **w2v** and **GloVe** are pre-trained embeddings from (Mikolov et al., 2013a) and (Pennington et al., 2014) respectively. **SGE** is the Skipgram baseline and **TSE** is our topic-sensitive Skipgram (cf. Equation (1)), both trained on Wikipedia. τ_k stands for HDP-inferred topic k.

where τ is the topic of document d_i learned by HDP. The STLE model has the advantage of directly applying the distribution over topics in the Skipgram model. In addition, for each instance, we update all topic representations of a given word with non-zero probabilities, which has the potential to reduce the sparsity problem.

2.3 Embeddings for Polysemous Words

The representations obtained from our models are expected to capture the meaning of a word in different topics. We now investigate whether these representations can distinguish between different word senses. Table 1 provides examples of nearest neighbors. For comparison we include our own baseline, i.e., embeddings learned with Skipgram on our corpus, as well as Word2Vec (Mikolov et al., 2013b) and GloVe embeddings (Pennington et al., 2014) pre-trained on large data.

In the first example, the word *bat* has two different meanings: animal or sports device. One can see that the nearest neighbors of the baseline and pre-trained word representations either center around one primary, i.e., most frequent, meaning of the word, or it is a mixture of different meanings. The topic-sensitive representations, on the other hand, correctly distinguish between the two different meanings. A similar pattern is observed for the word *jaguar* and its two meanings: car

or animal. The last example, *appeal*, illustrates a case where topic-sensitive embeddings are not clearly detecting different meanings of the word, despite having some correct words in the lists. Here, the meaning *attract* does not seem to be captured by any embedding set.

These observations suggest that topic-sensitive representations capture different word senses to some extent. To provide a systematic validation of our approach, we now investigate whether topic-sensitive representations can improve tasks where polysemy is a known issue.

3 Evaluation

In this section we present the setup for our experiments and empirically evaluate our approach on the context-aware word similarity and lexical substitution tasks.

3.1 Experimental setup

All word representations are learned on the English Wikipedia corpus containing 4.8M documents (1B tokens). The topics are learned on a 100K-document subset of this corpus using the HDP implementation of Teh et al. (2006). Once the topics have been learned, we run HDP on the whole corpus to obtain the word-topic labeling (see Section 2.1) and the document-level topic distributions (Section 2.2). We train each model vari-

Model	Dimension		
	100	300	600
SGE + C (Mikolov et al., 2013a)	0.59	0.59	0.62
MSSG (Neelakantan et al., 2014)	0.60	0.61	**0.64**
HTLE	**0.63**	0.56	0.55
HTLEadd	0.61	**0.61**	0.58
STLE	0.59	0.58	0.55

Table 2: Spearman's rank correlation performance for the Word Similarity task on SCWS.

ant with window size $c = 10$ and different embedding sizes (100, 300, 600) initialized randomly.

We compare our models to several baselines: Skipgram (SGE) and the best-performing multi-sense embeddings model per word type (MSSG) (Neelakantan et al., 2014). All model variants are trained on the same training data with the same settings, following suggestions by Mikolov et al. (2013a) and Levy et al. (2015). For MSSG we use the best performing similarity measure (avgSimC) as proposed by Neelakantan et al. (2014).

3.2 Context-Aware Word Similarity Task

Despite its shortcomings (Faruqui et al., 2016), word similarity remains the most frequently used method of evaluation in the literature. There are multiple test sets available but in almost all of them word pairs are considered out of context. To the best of our knowledge, the only word similarity data set providing word context is SCWS (Huang et al., 2012). To evaluate our models on SCWS, we run HDP on the data treating each word's context as a separate document. We compute the similarity of each word pair as follows:

$$Sim(w_1, w_2) = cos(\mathbf{h}(w_1), \mathbf{h}(w_2))$$

where $\mathbf{h}(w_i)$ refers to any of the topic-sensitive representations defined in Section 2. Note that w_1 and w_2 can refer to the same word.

Table 2 provides the Spearman's correlation scores for different models against the human ranking. We see that with dimensions 100 and 300, two of our models obtain improvements over the baseline. The MSSG model of Neelakantan et al. (2014) performs only slightly better than our HLTE model by requiring considerably more parameters (600 vs. 100 embedding size).

3.3 Lexical Substitution Task

This task requires one to identify the best replacements for a word in a sentential context. The pres-

Model	Infer.	LS-SE07			LS-CIC		
		Dimension			Dimension		
		100	300	600	100	300	600
SGE		36.2	40.5	41.1	30.4	32.1	32.3
SGE + C	n/a	36.6	40.9	41.6	32.8	36.1	36.8
MSSG		37.8	41.1	42.9	33.9	37.8	39.1
HTLE		39.8▲	42.5▲	43.0▲	32.1	32.7	33.0
HTLEadd	Smp	39.4△	41.3▲	41.8	30.4	31.5	31.7
STLE		35.2	36.7	39.0	32.9	32.3	33.9
HTLE		**40.3▲**	**42.8▲**	**43.4▲**	36.6▲	**40.9▲**	**41.3▲**
HTLEadd	Exp	39.9▲	41.8▲	42.2	35.5△	37.9△	38.6
STLE		38.7△	41.0	41.0	**36.8▲**	36.8	37.1

Table 3: GAP scores on LS-SE07 and LS-CIC sets. For SGE + C we use the *context* embeddings to disambiguate the substitutions. Improvements over the best baseline (MSSG) are marked ▲ at $p < .01$ and △ at $p < .05$.

ence of many polysemous target words makes this task more suitable for evaluating sense embedding. Following Melamud et al. (2015) we pool substitutions from different instances and rank them by the number of annotators that selected them for a given context. We use two evaluation sets: LS-SE07 (McCarthy and Navigli, 2007), and LS-CIC (Kremer et al., 2014).

Unlike previous work (Szarvas et al., 2013; Kremer et al., 2014; Melamud et al., 2015) we do not use any syntactic information, motivated by the fact that high-quality parsers are not available for most languages. The evaluation is performed by computing the Generalized Average Precision (GAP) score (Kishida, 2005). We run HDP on the evaluation set and compute the similarity between target word w_t and each substitution w_s using two different inference methods in line with how we incorporate topics during training:

Sampled (Smp): $Sim_{\mathrm{TSE}}(w_s, w_t) =$
$$cos(\mathbf{h}(w_s^\tau), \mathbf{h}(w_t^{\tau'})) + \frac{\sum_c cos(\mathbf{h}(w_s^\tau), \mathbf{o}(w_c))}{C}$$

Expected (Exp): $Sim_{\mathrm{TSE}}(w_s, w_t) = \sum_{\tau, \tau'} p(\tau)\, p(\tau')$
$$cos(\mathbf{h}(w_s^\tau), \mathbf{h}(w_t^{\tau'})) + \frac{\sum_{\tau, c} cos(\mathbf{h}(w_s^\tau), \mathbf{o}(w_c))\, p(\tau)}{C}$$

where $\mathbf{h}(w_s^\tau)$ and $\mathbf{h}(w_t^{\tau'})$ are the representations for substitution word s with topic τ and target word t with topic τ' respectively (cf. Section 2), w_c are context words of w_t taken from a sliding window of the same size as the embeddings, $\mathbf{o}(w_c)$ is the context (i.e., output) representation of w_c, and C is the total number of context words. Note

Model	Dim = 100					Dim = 300					Dim = 600				
	n.	v.	adj.	adv.	All	n.	v.	adj.	adv.	All	n.	v.	adj.	adv.	All
SGE + C	37.2	31.6	37.1	42.2	36.6	39.2	35.0	39.0	**55.4**	40.9	39.7	35.7	39.9	**56.2**	41.6
HTLE	**42.4**	**33.9**	**38.1**	**49.7**	**40.3**	**44.9**	**37.0**	**41.0**	50.9	**42.8**	**45.2**	**37.2**	**42.1**	51.9	**43.4**

Table 4: GAP scores on the candidate ranking task on LS-SE07 for different part-of-speech categories.

that these two methods are consistent with how we train HTLE and STLE.

The *sampled* method, similar to HTLE, uses the HDP model to assign topics to word occurrences during testing. The *expected* method, similar to STLE, uses the HDP model to learn the probability distribution of topics of the context sentence and uses the entire distribution to compute the similarity. For the Skipgram baseline we compute the similarity $Sim_{\text{SGE+C}}(w_s, w_t)$ as follows:

$$cos(\mathbf{h}(w_s), \mathbf{h}(w_t)) + \frac{\sum_c cos(\mathbf{h}(w_s), \mathbf{o}(w_c))}{C}$$

which uses the similarity between the substitution word and all words in the context, as well as the similarity of target and substitution words.

Table 3 shows the GAP scores of our models and baselines.[1] One can see that all models using multiple embeddings per word perform better than SGE. Our proposed models outperform both SGE and MSSG in both evaluation sets, with more pronounced improvements for LS-CIC. We further observe that our *expected* method is more robust and performs better for all embedding sizes.

Table 4 shows the GAP scores broken down by the main word classes: noun, verb, adjective, and adverb. With 100 dimensions our best model (HTLE) yields improvements across all POS tags, with the largest improvements for adverbs and smallest improvements for adjectives. When increasing the dimension size of embeddings the improvements hold up for all POS tags apart from adverbs. It can be inferred that larger dimension sizes capture semantic similarities for adverbs and context words better than other parts-of-speech categories. Additionally, we observe for both evaluation sets that the improvements are preserved when increasing the embedding size.

4   Related Work

While the most commonly used approaches learn one embedding per word type (Mikolov et al.,

---

[1] We use the nonparametric rank-based Mann-Whitney-Wilcoxon test (Sprent and Smeeton, 2016) to check for statistically significant differences between runs.

2013a; Pennington et al., 2014), recent studies have focused on learning multiple embeddings per word due to the ambiguous nature of language (Qiu et al., 2016). Huang et al. (2012) cluster word contexts and use the average embedding of each cluster as word sense embeddings, which yields improvements on a word similarity task. Neelakantan et al. (2014) propose two approaches, both based on clustering word contexts: In the first, they fix the number of senses manually, and in the second, they use an ad-hoc greedy procedure that allocates a new representation to a word if existing representations explain the context below a certain threshold. Li and Jurafsky (2015) used a CRP model to distinguish between senses of words and train vectors for senses, where the number of senses is not fixed. They use two heuristic approaches for assigning senses in a context: 'greedy' which assigns the locally optimum sense label to each word, and 'expectation' which computes the expected value for a word in a given context with probabilities for each possible sense.

5   Conclusions

We have introduced an approach to learn topic-sensitive word representations that exploits the document-level context of words and does not require annotated data or linguistic resources. Our evaluation on the lexical substitution task suggests that topic distributions capture word senses to some extent. Moreover, we obtain statistically significant improvements in the lexical substitution task while not using any syntactic information. The best results are achieved by our hard topic-labeled model which learns topic-sensitive representations by assigning topics to target words.

Acknowledgments

This research was funded in part by the Netherlands Organization for Scientific Research (NWO) under project numbers 639.022.213 and 639.021.646, and a Google Faculty Research Award. We thank the anonymous reviewers for their helpful comments.

References

Samuel Brody and Mirella Lapata. 2009. Bayesian word sense induction. In *Proceedings of the 12th Conference of the European Chapter of the ACL (EACL 2009)*. Association for Computational Linguistics, Athens, Greece, pages 103–111. http://www.aclweb.org/anthology/E09-1013.

Manaal Faruqui, Yulia Tsvetkov, Pushpendre Rastogi, and Chris Dyer. 2016. Problems with evaluation of word embeddings using word similarity tasks. In *Proc. of the 1st Workshop on Evaluating Vector Space Representations for NLP*. http://arxiv.org/pdf/1605.02276v1.pdf.

Waseem Gharbieh, Virendra C Bhavsar, and Paul Cook. 2016. A word embedding approach to identifying verb–noun idiomatic combinations. In *Proc. of the 12th Workshop on Multiword Expressions MWE 2016*. page 112. https://www.aclweb.org/anthology/W/W16/W16-1817.pdf.

Eric Huang, Richard Socher, Christopher Manning, and Andrew Ng. 2012. Improving word representations via global context and multiple word prototypes. In *Proceedings of the 50th Annual Meeting of the Association for Computational Linguistics (Volume 1: Long Papers)*. Association for Computational Linguistics, Jeju Island, Korea, pages 873–882. http://www.aclweb.org/anthology/P12-1092.

Adam Kilgarriff. 1997. I don't believe in word senses. *Computers and the Humanities* 31(2):91–113.

Kazuaki Kishida. 2005. *Property of average precision and its generalization: An examination of evaluation indicator for information retrieval experiments*. National Institute of Informatics Tokyo, Japan.

Gerhard Kremer, Katrin Erk, Sebastian Padó, and Stefan Thater. 2014. What substitutes tell us - analysis of an "all-words" lexical substitution corpus. In *Proceedings of the 14th Conference of the European Chapter of the Association for Computational Linguistics*. Association for Computational Linguistics, Gothenburg, Sweden, pages 540–549. http://www.aclweb.org/anthology/E14-1057.

Jey Han Lau, Paul Cook, Diana McCarthy, Spandana Gella, and Timothy Baldwin. 2014. Learning word sense distributions, detecting unattested senses and identifying novel senses using topic models. In *Proceedings of the 52nd Annual Meeting of the Association for Computational Linguistics (Volume 1: Long Papers)*. Association for Computational Linguistics, Baltimore, Maryland, pages 259–270. http://www.aclweb.org/anthology/P14-1025.

Omer Levy and Yoav Goldberg. 2014. Dependency-based word embeddings. In *Proceedings of the 52nd Annual Meeting of the Association for Computational Linguistics (Volume 2: Short Papers)*. Association for Computational Linguistics, Baltimore, Maryland, pages 302–308. http://www.aclweb.org/anthology/P14-2050.

Omer Levy, Yoav Goldberg, and Ido Dagan. 2015. Improving distributional similarity with lessons learned from word embeddings. *Transactions of the Association for Computational Linguistics* 3:211–225. https://transacl.org/ojs/index.php/tacl/article/view/570.

Jiwei Li and Dan Jurafsky. 2015. Do multi-sense embeddings improve natural language understanding? In *Proceedings of the 2015 Conference on Empirical Methods in Natural Language Processing*. Association for Computational Linguistics, Lisbon, Portugal, pages 1722–1732. http://aclweb.org/anthology/D15-1200.

Diana McCarthy and Roberto Navigli. 2007. Semeval-2007 task 10: English lexical substitution task. In *Proceedings of the Fourth International Workshop on Semantic Evaluations (SemEval-2007)*. Association for Computational Linguistics, Prague, Czech Republic, pages 48–53. http://www.aclweb.org/anthology/S/S07/S07-1009.

Oren Melamud, Omer Levy, and Ido Dagan. 2015. A simple word embedding model for lexical substitution. In *Proceedings of the 1st Workshop on Vector Space Modeling for Natural Language Processing*. Association for Computational Linguistics, Denver, Colorado, pages 1–7. http://www.aclweb.org/anthology/W15-1501.

Tomas Mikolov, Kai Chen, Greg Corrado, and Jeffrey Dean. 2013a. Efficient estimation of word representations in vector space. *arXiv preprint arXiv:1301.3781* .

Tomas Mikolov, Ilya Sutskever, Kai Chen, Greg S Corrado, and Jeff Dean. 2013b. Distributed representations of words and phrases and their compositionality. In *Advances in Neural Information Processing Systems 26*, Curran Associates, Inc., pages 3111–3119. http://papers.nips.cc/paper/5021-distributed-representations-of-words-and-phrases-and-their-compositionality.pdf.

George A. Miller. 1995. Wordnet: A lexical database for english. *Commun. ACM* 38(11):39–41.

Roberto Navigli. 2012. *SOFSEM 2012: Theory and Practice of Computer Science: 38th Conference on Current Trends in Theory and Practice of Computer Science, Špindlerův Mlýn, Czech Republic, January 21-27, 2012. Proceedings*, Springer Berlin Heidelberg, Berlin, Heidelberg, chapter A Quick Tour of Word Sense Disambiguation, Induction and Related Approaches, pages 115–129.

Roberto Navigli and Simone Paolo Ponzetto. 2010. Babelnet: Building a very large multilingual semantic network. In *Proceedings of the 48th Annual Meeting of the Association for Computational Linguistics*. Association for Computational Linguistics, Uppsala, Sweden, pages 216–225. http://www.aclweb.org/anthology/P10-1023.

Arvind Neelakantan, Jeevan Shankar, Alexandre Passos, and Andrew McCallum. 2014. Efficient nonparametric estimation of multiple embeddings per word in vector space. In *Proceedings of the 2014 Conference on Empirical Methods in Natural Language Processing (EMNLP)*. Association for Computational Linguistics, Doha, Qatar, pages 1059–1069. http://www.aclweb.org/anthology/D14-1113.

Jeffrey Pennington, Richard Socher, and Christopher Manning. 2014. Glove: Global vectors for word representation. In *Proceedings of the 2014 Conference on Empirical Methods in Natural Language Processing (EMNLP)*. Association for Computational Linguistics, Doha, Qatar, pages 1532–1543. http://www.aclweb.org/anthology/D14-1162.

Lin Qiu, Kewei Tu, and Yong Yu. 2016. Context-dependent sense embedding. In *Proceedings of the 2016 Conference on Empirical Methods in Natural Language Processing*. Association for Computational Linguistics, Austin, Texas, pages 183–191. https://aclweb.org/anthology/D16-1018.

Joseph Reisinger and Raymond J. Mooney. 2010. Multi-prototype vector-space models of word meaning. In *Human Language Technologies: The 2010 Annual Conference of the North American Chapter of the Association for Computational Linguistics*. Association for Computational Linguistics, Los Angeles, California, pages 109–117. http://www.aclweb.org/anthology/N10-1013.

Peter Sprent and Nigel C Smeeton. 2016. *Applied nonparametric statistical methods*. CRC Press.

György Szarvas, Róbert Busa-Fekete, and Eyke Hüllermeier. 2013. Learning to rank lexical substitutions. In *Proceedings of the 2013 Conference on Empirical Methods in Natural Language Processing*. Association for Computational Linguistics, Seattle, Washington, USA, pages 1926–1932. http://www.aclweb.org/anthology/D13-1198.

Duyu Tang, Furu Wei, Nan Yang, Ming Zhou, Ting Liu, and Bing Qin. 2014. Learning sentiment-specific word embedding for twitter sentiment classification. In *Proceedings of the 52nd Annual Meeting of the Association for Computational Linguistics (Volume 1: Long Papers)*. Association for Computational Linguistics, Baltimore, Maryland, pages 1555–1565. http://www.aclweb.org/anthology/P14-1146.

Yee W. Teh, Michael I. Jordan, Matthew J. Beal, and David M. Blei. 2005. Sharing clusters among related groups: Hierarchical dirichlet processes. In L. K. Saul, Y. Weiss, and L. Bottou, editors, *Advances in Neural Information Processing Systems 17*, MIT Press, pages 1385–1392. http://papers.nips.cc/paper/2698-sharing-clusters-among-related-groups-hierarchical-dirichlet-processes.pdf.

Yee Whye Teh, Michael I. Jordan, Matthew J. Beal, and David M. Blei. 2006. Hierarchical dirichlet processes. *Journal of the American Statistical Association* 101(476):1566–1581.

Xuchen Yao and Benjamin van Durme. 2011. Nonparametric bayesian word sense induction. In *Graph-based Methods for Natural Language Processing*. The Association for Computer Linguistics, pages 10–14.

Will Y. Zou, Richard Socher, Daniel Cer, and Christopher D. Manning. 2013. Bilingual word embeddings for phrase-based machine translation. In *Proceedings of the 2013 Conference on Empirical Methods in Natural Language Processing*. Association for Computational Linguistics, Seattle, Washington, USA, pages 1393–1398. http://www.aclweb.org/anthology/D13-1141.

Temporal Word Analogies: Identifying Lexical Replacement with Diachronic Word Embeddings

Terrence Szymanski

Insight Centre for Data Analytics

University College Dublin

`terrence.szymanski@insight-centre.org`

Abstract

This paper introduces the concept of temporal word analogies: pairs of words which occupy the same semantic space at different points in time. One well-known property of word embeddings is that they are able to effectively model traditional word analogies ("word w_1 is to word w_2 as word w_3 is to word w_4") through vector addition. Here, I show that temporal word analogies ("word w_1 at time t_α is like word w_2 at time t_β") can effectively be modeled with diachronic word embeddings, provided that the independent embedding spaces from each time period are appropriately transformed into a common vector space. When applied to a diachronic corpus of news articles, this method is able to identify temporal word analogies such as "*Ronald Reagan* in 1987 is like *Bill Clinton* in 1997", or "*Walkman* in 1987 is like *iPod* in 2007".

1 Background

The meanings of utterances change over time, due both to changes within the linguistic system and to changes in the state of the world. For example, the meaning of the word *awful* has changed over the past few centuries from something like "awe-inspiring" to something more like "very bad", due to a process of semantic drift. On the other hand, the phrase *president of the United States* has meant different things at different points in time due to the fact that different people have occupied that same position at different times. These are very different types of changes, and the latter may not even be considered a linguistic phenomenon, but both types of change are relevant to the concept of temporal word analogies.

I define a temporal word analogy (TWA) as a pair of words which occupy a similar semantic space at different points in time. For example, assuming that there is a semantic space associated with "President of the USA", this space was occupied by Ronald Reagan in the 1980s, and by Bill Clinton in the 1990s. So a temporal analogy holds: "*Ronald Reagan* in 1987 is like *Bill Clinton* in 1997".

Distributional semantics methods, particularly vector-space models of word meanings, have been employed to study both semantic change and word analogies, and as such are well-suited for the task of identifying TWAs. The principle behind these models, that the meaning of words can be captured by looking at the contexts in which they appear (i.e. other words), is not a recent idea, and is generally attributed to Harris (1954) or Firth (1957). The modern era of applying this principle algorithmically began with latent semantic analysis (LSA) (Landauer and Dumais, 1997), and the recent explosion in popularity of word embeddings is largely due to the very effective *word2vec* neural network approach to computing word embeddings (Mikolov et al., 2013a). In these types of vector space models (VSMs), the meaning of a word is represented as a multi-dimensional vector, and semantically-related words tend to have vectors that relate to one another in regular ways (e.g. by occupying nearby points in the vector space). One factor in word embeddings' recent popularity is their eye-catching ability to model word analogies using vector addition, as in the well-known example $king + man - woman = queen$ (Mikolov et al., 2013b).

Sagi et al. (2011) were the first to advocate the use of distributional semantics methods (specifically LSA) to automate and quantify large-scale studies of semantic change, in contrast to a more traditional approach in which a researcher inspects

Proceedings of the 55th Annual Meeting of the Association for Computational Linguistics (Short Papers), pages 448–453
Vancouver, Canada, July 30 - August 4, 2017. ©2017 Association for Computational Linguistics
https://doi.org/10.18653/v1/P17-2071

a handful of selected words by hand. While not using a VSM approach, Mihalcea and Nastase (2012) used context words as features to perform "word epoch disambiguation", effectively capturing changes in word meanings over time. And several recent papers have combined neural embedding methods with large-scale diachronic corpora (e.g. the Google Books corpus) to study changes in word meanings over time. Kim et al. (2014) measured the drift (as cosine similarity) of a word's vector over time to identify words like *cell* and *gay* whose meaning changed over the past 100 years. Kulkarni et al. (2015) used a similar approach, combined with word frequencies and changepoint detection, to plot a word's movement through different lexical neighborhoods over time. Most recently, Hamilton et al. (2016) employed this methodology to discover and support two laws of semantic change, noting that words with higher frequency or higher levels of polysemy are more likely to experience semantic changes.

While the study of word meanings over time using diachronic text corpora is a relatively niche subject with little commercial applicability, it has recently gained attention in the broader computational linguistics community. A 2015 SemEval task was dedicated to Diachronic Text Evaluation (Popescu and Strapparava, 2015); while systems submitted to the task successfully predicted the date of a text using traditional machine learning algorithms (Szymanski and Lynch, 2015), none of the submissions employed distributional semantics methods. Also in 2015, the president of the ACL singled out recent work (cited in the previous paragraph) using word embeddings to study semantic change as valuable examples of "more scientific uses of distributed representations and Deep Learning" in computational linguistics (Manning, 2015).

The present work is inspired by this line of research, and is a continuation on the same theme with a twist: whereas past work has investigated specific words whose meanings have changed over time, the present work investigates specific meanings whose words have changed over time.

2 Method for Discovering Temporal Word Analogies

In general, work using diachronic word embeddings to study semantic change follows a common procedure: first, train independent VSMs for each time period in the diachronic corpus; second, transform those VSMs into a common space; and finally, compare a word's vectors from different VSMs to identify patterns of change over time. This paper follows a similar methodology.

Algorithm 1 Calculating temporal word analogies

$V_A \leftarrow Word2Vec(CorpusA)$
$V_B \leftarrow Word2Vec(CorpusB)$
$T \leftarrow FitTransform(V_B, V_A)$
$V_{B^*} \leftarrow ApplyTransform(T, V_B)$
$vec_1 \leftarrow LookupVector(V_A, word_1)$
$vec_2 \leftarrow NearestNeighbor(vec_1, V_{B^*})$
$word_2 \leftarrow LookupWord(V_{B^*}, vec_2)$

The general process of calculating a TWA is given in Algorithm 1. For example, if Corpus A is the 1987 texts, and Corpus B is the 1997 texts, and $word_1$ is *reagan*, then $word_2$ will be *clinton*. Crucially, it is only by applying the transformation to the B vector space that it becomes possible to directly compare the B^* space with vectors from the A space. The Python code used in this paper to implement this method is available to download.[1]

1. Training Independent VSMs: The data used in this analysis is a corpus of New York Times articles spanning the years 1987 through 2007, containing roughly 50 million words per year. The texts were lowercased and tokenized, and common bigrams were re-tokenized by a single pass of *word2phrase*. A separate embedding model was trained for each year in the corpus using *word2vec* with default-like parameters.[2] This resulted in 21 independent vector space models, each with a vocabulary of roughly 100k words.

2. Aligning Independent VSMs: Because training word embeddings typically begins with a random initial state, and the training itself is stochastic, the embeddings from different runs (even on the same dataset) are not comparable with one another. (Many properties of the embedding space, such as the distances between points, are consistent, but the actual values of the vectors are random.) This poses a challenge to work on diachronic word embeddings, which requires the ability to compare the vectors of the same word in different, independently-trained, VSMs. Previous work has employed different approaches to this problem:

---
[1] https://github.com/tdszyman/twapy.
[2] Example parameters: CBOW model, vector size 200, window size 8, negative samples 5.

Non-random initialization. In this approach, used by Kim et al. (2014), the values for the VSM are not randomly initialized, but instead are initialized with the values from a previously-trained model, e.g. training of the 1988 model would begin with values from the 1987 model.

Local linear regression. This approach, used by Kulkarni et al. (2015), assumes that two VSMs are equivalent under a linear transformation, and that most words' meanings do not change over time. A linear regression model is fit to a sample of vectors from the neighborhood of a word (hence "local"), minimizing the mean squared error, i.e. minimizing the distance between the two vectors of a given word in the two vector spaces. A potential drawback of this approach is that it must be applied separately for each focal word.

Orthogonal Procrustes. This approach, used by Hamilton et al. (2016), is similar to linear regression in that it aims to learn a transformation of one embedding space onto another, minimizing the distance between pairs of points, but uses a different mathematical method and is applied globally to the full space.

A thorough investigation into the relative benefits of the different methods listed above would be a valuable contribution to future work in this area. In the present work, I take a global linear regression approach, broadly similar to that used by Kulkarni et al. (2015). However, I use a large sample of points to fit the model, and I apply the transformation globally to the entire VSM. Experiments showed that the accuracy of the transformation (measured by the mean Euclidean distance between pairs of points) increases as the sample size increases: using 10% of the total vocabulary shared by the two models (i.e. roughly 10k out of 100k tokens) produces good results, but there is little reason not to use all of the points (perhaps excluding the specific words that are the target of study, although even this does not make much practical difference in the outputs).

3. Solving Temporal Word Analogies: Once the independent VSMs have been transformed, it is possible to compare vectors from one VSM with vectors from another VSM. Solving a TWA is then simply a matter of loading the vector of word w_1 from the VSM V_A, and then finding the point in the transformed VSM V_2^* closest to that vector. That point corresponds to word w_2, the solution to the analogy. It is also possible to align a series of VSMs to a single "root" VSM, and thereby trace the analogues of a word over time. The results of applying this method are discussed next.

3 Example Outputs and Analysis

Using the New York Times corpus, each of the 20 VSMs from 1998 to 2007 were aligned to the 1987 VSM, making it possible to trace a series of analogies over time (e.g. "Which words in 1988, 1989, 1990 ... are like *reagan* in 1987?"). A set of illustrative words from 1987 was chosen, and their vectors from the 1987 VSM were extracted. Then, for each subsequent year, the nearest word in that years' transformed VSM was found. The outputs are displayed in Table 1.

One way to interpret Table 1 is to think of each column as representing a single semantic concept, and the words in that column illustrate the different words embodying that concept at different points in time. So column 1 represents "President of the USA" and column 2 represents "mayor of New York City". The outputs of the TWA system perfectly reflect the names of the people holding these offices; likely due to the fact that these concepts are discussed in the corpus with high frequency and a well-defined lexical neighborhood (e.g. *White House, Oval Office, president*).

While the other columns do not produce quite as clean analogies, they do tell interesting stories. The breakup of the Soviet Union is visible in the transition from *soviet* to *russian* in 1992, and later that concept (something like "geopolitical foe of the United States") is taken up in the 2000s by North Korea and Iran, two members of George W. Bush's "Axis of Evil" . Changes in technology can be observed, with the 1987 vector for *Walkman* (representing something like "portable listening device") passing through *CD player* and *MP3 player* ultimately to *iPod* in 2007. Cultural changes can also be observed: the TWA "*yuppie* in 1987 is like *hipster* in 2003", is validated by reports in the media (Bergstein, 2016).

It is not easy to pin a precise meaning to each of these columns, and the "right" answer to any given TWA is to some degree a subjective judgment. Any given entity may fill multiple roles at once: which role should be the focus of the analogy? Each vector in the VSM can be thought of as combining multiple components: for example, the vectors for *reagan* include a component having to do with Ronald Reagan himself (based on words

1987	reagan	koch	soviet	iran_contra	navratilova	yuppie	walkman
1988	reagan	koch	soviet	iran_contra	sabatini	yuppie	tape_deck
1989	bush	koch	soviet	iran_contra	navratilova	yuppie	walkman
1990	bush	dinkins	soviet	iran_contra	navratilova	yuppie	headphones
1991	bush	dinkins	soviet	iran_contra	navratilova	yuppie	cassette_player
1992	bush	dinkins	russian	iran_contra	sabatini	yuppie	walkman
1993	clinton	dinkins	russian	iran_contra	navratilova	yuppie	cd_player
1994	clinton	mr_giuliani	russian	iran_contra	sanchez_vicario	yuppie	walkman
1995	clinton	giuliani	russian	white_house	graf	yuppie	cassette_player
1996	clinton	giuliani	russian	whitewater	graf	yuppie	walkman
1997	clinton	giuliani	russian	iran_contra	hingis	yuppie	headphones
1998	clinton	giuliani	russian	lewinsky	hingis	yuppie	headphones
1999	clinton	mayor_giuliani	russian	white_house	hingis	yuppie	buttons
2000	clinton	giuliani	russian	white_house	hingis	yuppie	headset
2001	bush	giuliani	russian	iran_contra	capriati	yuppie	headset
2002	bush	bloomberg	russian	white_house	hingis	gen_x	mp3_player
2003	bush	bloomberg	russian	white_house	agassi	hipsters	walkman
2004	bush	bloomberg	north_korean	iran_contra	federer	gen_x	headphones
2005	bush	bloomberg	north_korean	white_house	roddick	geek	ear_buds
2006	bush	bloomberg	iranian	white_house	hingis	teen	headset
2007	bush	bloomberg	iranian	capitol_hill	federer	dads	ipod

Table 1: Examples of words from 1987 and their analogues over time. Each column corresponds to a single point in vector space, and each row shows the word closest to that point in a given year.

relating to his personal attributes or names of family members) as well as a component having to do with the presidency (based on words like *president*, *veto* or *White House*). The analogies based on the 1987 *reagan* vector produce the names of other presidents over time (as in Table 1); however, if the 1999 *reagan* vector is used as the starting point, then 17 of the 20 analogies produced are either *reagan* or *ronald_reagan*. This illustrates how the vector from 1999 contains a stronger component of the individual man rather than the presidency, due to the change in how he was written about when no longer in office. Similarly, the *Iran Contra* vector can be viewed as a mixture of 'the Iran Contra crisis itself' and a more generic "White House scandal" concept. This second component causes Clinton-era scandals like *Whitewater* and *Lewinsky* to briefly appear in that space, while the first causes *Iran Contra* to continue to appear over time.

4 Evaluation

Standard evaluation sets of word analogies exist and are commonly used as a measure of the quality of word embeddings (but see Linzen (2016) for why this can be problematic and misleading). No data set of manually-verified TWAs currently exists, so a small evaluation set was assembled by hand: ten TWA categories were selected which could be expected to be both newsworthy and unambiguous, and values for each year in the corpus were identified using encyclopedic sources. When all pairs of years are considered, this yields a total of 4,200 individual TWAs. This data set, including the prediction outputs, is available online.

For comparison, a baseline system which always predicts the output w_2 to be the same as the input w_1 was implemented. (A system based on word co-occurrence counts was also implemented, but produced no usable output.[3]) Table 2 shows the accuracy of the embedding-based system and the baseline for each category. Accuracy is determined by exact match, so *mayor_giuliani* is incorrect for *giuliani*. Some categories are clearly much more difficult than others: prediction accuracy is 96% for "President of the USA", but less than 1% for "Best Actress". The names of Oscar Best Actress winners change every year with very little repetition, and it may be that an actress' role as an award winner only constitutes a small part of her overall news coverage.

Accuracy is a useful metric, but it is not necessarily the best way to evaluate TWAs. Due to the nature of the data (the U.S. President, for example, only changes every four or eight years), the baseline system works quite well when the time depth of the analogy ($\delta_t = |t_\alpha - t_\beta|$) is small. However,

---

[3]The co-occurrence matrices were expensive to construct due to the volume of data, and despite efforts to smooth the distributions, the analogy outputs were noisy, dominated by low-frequency tokens with relatively few non-zero components and high cosine similarities. But it is possible that with more careful engineering this approach could be effective.

	Baseline	Embeddings
CEO of Goldman Sachs	17.6	1.7
Governor of New York	44.8	62.4
Mayor of NYC	24.8	85.0
NFL MVP	1.9	1.4
Oscar Best Actress	1.0	0.5
President of the USA	40.0	96.4
Prime Minister of the UK	37.6	33.6
Secretary of State of USA	11.9	21.9
Super Bowl Champions	5.7	32.6
WTA Top-ranked Player	16.2	26.4
$\delta_t <= 5$ years	37.8	40.8
$\delta_t > 5$ years	6.9	32.7
Overall	20.1	36.2

Table 2: Analogy prediction accuracy.

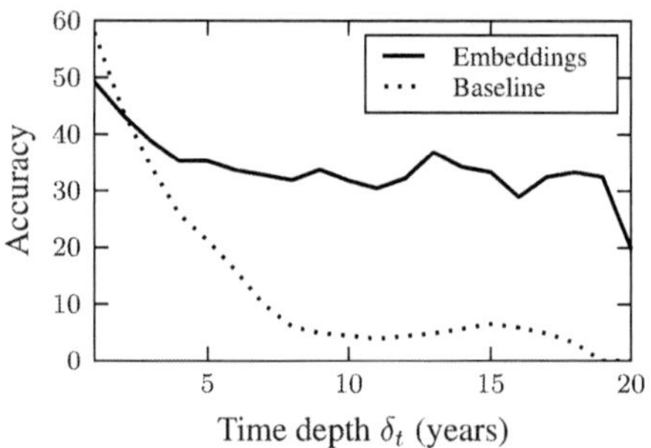

Figure 1: Accuracy as function of time depth.

as time depth increases, its accuracy drops sharply, while the embedding-based method remains effective, as illustrated in Figure 1. And even when the embedding-based system makes the "wrong" prediction, the output may still be insightful for data exploration, which is a more likely application for this method rather than prediction.

The analogies evaluated here have the benefits of being easy to compile and evaluate, but they represent only one specific subset of TWAs. Other, less-clearly-defined, types of analogies (like the *yuppie* and *walkman* examples) would require a less rigid (and more expensive), form of evaluation, such as obtaining human acceptability judgments of the automatically-produced analogies.

5 Conclusion

In this paper I have presented the concept of temporal word analogies and a method for identifying them using diachronic word embeddings. The method presented here is effective at solving TWAs, as shown in the evaluation, but its greater strength may be as a tool for data exploration. The small set of examples included in this paper illustrate political and social changes that unfold over time, and in the hands of users with diverse corpora and research questions, many more interesting analogies would likely be discovered using this same method.

The method presented in this paper is not the only way that TWAs could be predicted. If the VSMs could somehow be trained jointly, rather than independently, this would eliminate the need for transformation and the noise it introduces. Or perhaps it is sufficient to look at lexical neighborhoods, rather the vectors themselves. One limitation of the embedding approach is that it requires vast amounts of data from each time period: tens of millions of words are required to train a model with *word2vec*. This makes it impractical for many historical corpora, which tend to be much smaller than the corpus used here. If a simpler, count-based approach could be made to work, this might be more applicable to smaller corpora. A method which incorporates word frequency (Kulkarni et al., 2015) might be effective at identifying when one word drops from common usage and another word appears. And assigning a measure of confidence to the proposed TWAs could help automatically identify meaningful analogies from the vast combinations of words and years that exist.

In a domain where large quantities of real-time text are available, this method could potentially be applied as a form of event detection, identifying new entrants into a semantic space. And the same method described here could potentially be applied to other, non-diachronic, types of corpora. For example, given corpora of British English and American English, this methodology might be used to identify dialectal analogies, e.g. *"elevator* in US English is like *lift* in British English."* Indeed, this general approach of comparing words in multiple embedding spaces could have many applications outside of diachronic linguistics.

Acknowledgments

I would like to thank all the participants at the Insight Centre for Data Analytics special interest group meeting on NLP at NUI Galway for their encouraging and insightful feedback. Thanks also to the anonymous ACL reviewers, for encouraging the addition of a quantitative evaluation. This work was partially supported by Science Foundation Ireland through the Insight Centre for Data Analytics under grant number SFI/12/RC/2289.

References

Rachelle Bergstein. 2016. Are hipsters the new yuppies? *forbes.com* October 12, 2016.

J. R. Firth. 1957. A synopsis of linguistic theory 1930-1955. In *Studies in Linguistic Analysis*. Philological Society.

William L. Hamilton, Jure Leskovec, and Dan Jurafsky. 2016. Diachronic word embeddings reveal historical laws of semantic change. In *Proceedings of the 54th Annual Meeting of the Association for Computational Linguistics (Volume 1: Long Papers)*.

Zellig Harris. 1954. Distributional structure. *Word* 10(23):146–162.

Yoon Kim, Yi-I Chiu, Kentaro Hanaki, Darshan Hegde, and Slav Petrov. 2014. Temporal analysis of language through neural language models. In *Proceedings of the ACL 2014 Workshop on Language Technologies and Computational Social Science*. pages 61–65.

Vivek Kulkarni, Rami Al-Rfou, Bryan Perozzi, and Steven Skiena. 2015. Statistically significant detection of linguistic change. In *Proceedings of the 24th International Conference on World Wide Web*. pages 625–635.

Thomas K. Landauer and Susan T. Dumais. 1997. A solution to Plato's problem: The latent semantic analysis theory of the acquisition, induction, and representation of knowledge. *Psychological Review* 104(2):211–140.

Tal Linzen. 2016. Issues in evaluating semantic spaces using word analogies. In *Proceedings of the 1st Workshop on Evaluating Vector-Space Representations for NLP*. pages 13–18.

Christopher D. Manning. 2015. Computational linguistics and deep learning. *Computational Linguistics* 41(4).

Rada Mihalcea and Vivi Nastase. 2012. Word epoch disambiguation: Finding how words change over time. In *Proceedings of the 50th Annual Meeting of the Association for Computational Linguistics (Volume 2: Short Papers)*.

Tomas Mikolov, Kai Chen, Greg Corrado, and Jeffrey Dean. 2013a. Efficient estimation of word representations in vector space. In *International Conference on Learning Representations Workshop*.

Tomas Mikolov, Wen tau Yih, and Geoffrey Zweig. 2013b. Linguistic regularities in continuous space word representations. In *Proceedings of the 2013 Conference of the North American Chapter of the Association for Computational Linguistics: Human Language Technologies*. pages 746–751.

Octavian Popescu and Carlo Strapparava. 2015. Semeval 2015, task 7: Diachronic text evaluation. In *Proceedings of the 9th International Workshop on Semantic Evaluation (SemEval 2015)*.

Eyal Sagi, Stefan Kaufmann, and Brady Clark. 2011. Tracing semantic change with latent semantic analysis. In *Current Methods in Historical Semantics*. De Gruyter Mouton.

Terrence Szymanski and Gerard Lynch. 2015. UCD: Diachronic text classification with character, word, and syntactic n-grams. In *Proceedings of the 9th International Workshop on Semantic Evaluation (SemEval 2015)*.

Methodical Evaluation of Arabic Word Embeddings

Mohammed Elrazzaz
Computer Science and Engineering Department
Qatar University
Doha, Qatar
`mohammed.elrazzaz@qu.edu.qa`

Shady Elbassuoni
Computer Science Department
American University of Beirut
Beirut, Lebanon
`se58@aub.edu.lb`

Khaled Shaban
Computer Science and Engineering Department
Qatar University
Doha, Qatar
`khaled.shaban@qu.edu.qa`

Chadi Helwe
Computer Science Department
American University of Beirut
Beirut, Lebanon
`cth05@aub.edu.lb`

Abstract

Many unsupervised learning techniques
have been proposed to obtain meaningful representations of words from text. In
this study, we evaluate these various techniques when used to generate Arabic word
embeddings. We first build a benchmark
for the Arabic language that can be utilized
to perform intrinsic evaluation of different
word embeddings. We then perform additional extrinsic evaluations of the embeddings based on two NLP tasks.

1 Introduction

Distributed word representations, commonly referred to as word embeddings, represent words as
vectors in a low-dimensional space. The goal of
this deep representation of words is to capture syntactic and semantic relationships between words.
These word embeddings have been proven to be
very useful in various NLP applications, particularly those employing deep learning.

Word embeddings are typically learned using
unsupervised learning techniques on large text
corpora. Many techniques have been proposed to
learn such embeddings (Pennington et al., 2014;
Mikolov et al., 2013; Mnih and Kavukcuoglu,
2013). While most of the work has focused on
English word embeddings, few attempts have been
carried out to learn word embeddings for other languages, mostly using the above mentioned techniques.

In this paper, we focus on Arabic word embeddings. Particularly, we provide a thorough evaluation of the quality of four Arabic word embeddings that have been generated by previous work

(Zahran et al., 2015; Al-Rfou et al., 2013). We use
both intrinsic and extrinsic evaluation methods to
evaluate the different embeddings. For the intrinsic evaluation, we build a benchmark consisting of
over 115,000 word analogy questions for the Arabic language. Unlike previous attempts to evaluate Arabic embeddings, which relied on translating existing English benchmarks, our benchmark
is the first specifically built for the Arabic language and is publicly available for future work in
this area [1]. Translating an English benchmark is
not the best strategy to evaluate Arabic embeddings for the following reasons. First, the currently available English benchmarks are specifically designed for the English language and some
of the questions there are not applicable to Arabic.
Second, Arabic has more relations compared to
English and these should be included in the benchmark as well. Third, translating an English benchmark is subject to errors since it is usually carried
out in an automatic fashion.

In addition to the new benchmark, we also extend the basic analogy reasoning task by taking
into consideration more than two word pairs when
evaluating a relation, and by considering the top-5
words rather than only the top-1 word when answering an analogy question. Finally, we perform
an extrinsic evaluation of the different embeddings
using two different NLP tasks, namely Document
Classification and Named Entity Recognition.

2 Related Work

There is a wealth of research on evaluating unsupervised word embeddings, which can be can be
broadly divided into intrinsic and extrinsic evalu-

---

[1] `http://oma-project.com/res_home`

Proceedings of the 55th Annual Meeting of the Association for Computational Linguistics (Short Papers), pages 454–458
Vancouver, Canada, July 30 - August 4, 2017. ©2017 Association for Computational Linguistics
https://doi.org/10.18653/v1/P17-2072

Relation	(a, b)		(c, d)		#pairs	#tuples
Capital	Egypt مصر	Cairo القاهرة	Qatar قطر	Doha الدوحة	124	15252
Currency	Egypt مصر	Pound الجنيه	Qatar قطر	Riyal الريال	155	23870
Male-Female	boy ولد	girl بنت	husband زوج	wife زوجة	101	10100
Opposite	male ذكر	female أنثى	woke up أصبح	slept أمسى	110	11990
Comparative	big كبير	bigger أكبر	small صغير	smaller أصغر	100	9900
Nationality	Holland هولندا	Dutch هولندي	India الهند	Indian هندي	100	9900
Past Tense	travel سفر	traveled سافر	fight قتال	fought قاتل	110	11990
Plural	man رجل	men رجال	house بيت	houses بيوت	111	12210
Pair	man رجل	2 men رجلان	house بيت	2 houses بيتان	100	9900
ALL					1011	115112

Table 1: Summary of the Arabic Word Analogy Benchmark

ations. Intrinsic evaluations mostly rely on word analogy questions and measure the similarity of words in the low-dimensional embedding space (Mikolov et al., 2013; Gao et al., 2014; Schnabel et al., 2015). Extrinsic evaluations assess the quality of the embeddings as features in models for other tasks, such as semantic role labeling and part-of-speech tagging (Collobert et al., 2011), or noun-phrase chunking and sentiment analysis (Schnabel et al., 2015). However, all of these tasks and benchmarks are build for English and thus cannot be used to assess the quality of Arabic word embeddings, which is the main focus here.

To the best of our knowledge, only a handful of recent studies attempted evaluating Arabic word embeddings. Zahran et al. (Zahran et al., 2015) translated the English benchmark in (Mikolov et al., 2013) and used it to evaluate different embedding techniques when applied on a large Arabic corpus. However, as the authors themselves point out, translating an English benchmark is not the best strategy to evaluate Arabic embeddings. Zahran et al. also consider extrinsic evaluation on two NLP tasks, namely query expansion for IR and short answer grading.

Dahou et al. (Dahou et al., 2016) used the analogy questions from (Zahran et al., 2015) after correcting some Arabic spelling mistakes resulting from the translation and after adding new analogy questions to make up for the inadequacy of the English questions for the Arabic language. They also performed an extrinsic evaluation using sentiment analysis. Finally, Al-Rfou et al. (Al-Rfou et al., 2013) generated word embeddings for 100 different languages, including Arabic, and evaluated the embeddings using part-of-speech tagging, however the evaluation was done only for a handful of European languages.

3 Benchmark

Our benchmark is the first specifically designed for the Arabic language. It consists of nine relations, each consisting of over 100 word pairs. An Arabic linguist who was properly introduced to the word-analogy task provided the list of relations. Once the nine relations were defined, two different people collectively generated the word pairs. The two people are native Arabic speakers, and one of them is a co-author and the other is not. Table 1 displays the list of all relations in our benchmark as well as two example word pairs for each relation. The full benchmark and the evaluation tool can be obtained from the following link: `http://oma-project.com/res_home`.

Translating an English benchmark is not adequate for many reasons. First, the currently available English benchmarks contain many questions that are not applicable to Arabic. For example, comparative and superlative relations are the same in Arabic, except that the superlatives are usually prefixed with the Arabic equivalent of "the". Another example is the opposite relation, where some words in Arabic do not have antonyms, in which case the antonym is typically expressed by prefixing the word with "not". Second, Arabic has more relations compared to English. For instance, in Arabic there is the pair relation (see Table 1 for an example). Third, translating an English benchmark is considerably difficult due to the high ambiguity of the Arabic language.

Given our benchmark, we generate a test bank consisting of over 100,000 tuples. Each tuple consists of two word pairs (a, b) and (c, d) from the same relation. For each of our nine relations, we generate a tuple by combining two different word pairs from the same relation. Once tuples have been generated, they can be used as word analogy questions to evaluate different word embeddings as defined by Mikolov et al. (Mikolov et al., 2013). A word analogy question for a tuple consisting of two word pairs (a, b) and (c, d) can be formulated as follows: "a to b is like c to ?". Each such question will then be answered by calculating a target vector $t = b - a + c$. We then calculate the cosine similarity between the target vector t and the vector representation of each word w in a given word embeddings V. Finally, we retrieve the most similar word w to t, i.e., $argmax_{w \in V \& w \notin \{a,b,c\}} \frac{w \cdot t}{||w||||t||}$. If $w = d$ (i.e., the same word) then we assume that the word embeddings V has answered the question correctly.

We also use our benchmark to generate additional analogy questions by using more than two word pairs per question. This provides a more accurate representation of a relation as mentioned in (Mikolov et al., 2013). For each relation, we generate a question per word pair consisting of the word pair plus 10 random word pairs from the same relation. Thus, each question would consist of 11 word pairs (a_i, b_i) where $1 \leq i \leq 11$. We then use the average of the first 10 word pairs to generate the target vector t as follows: $t = \frac{1}{10} \sum_i^{10} (b_i - a_i) + a_{11}$. Finally we retrieve the closest word w to the target vector t using cosine similarity as in the previous case. The question is considered to be answered correctly if the answer word w is the same as b_{11}.

Moreover, we also extend the traditional word analogy task by taking into consideration if the correct answer is among the top-5 closest words in the embedding space to the target vector t, which allows us to more leniently evaluate the embeddings. This is particularly important in the case of Arabic since many forms of the same word exist, usually with additional prefixes or suffixes such as the equivalent of the article "the" or possessive determiners such as "her", "his", or "their". For example, consider one question which asks "ولد to بِنت is like ملك to ?", i.e., "man to woman is

like king to ?", with the answer being "ملكة" or "queen". Now, if we rely only on the top-1 word and it happens to be "ملكته", which means "his queen" in English, the question would be considered to be answered wrongly. To relax this and ensure that different forms of the same word will not result in a mismatch, we use the top-5 words for evaluation rather than the top-1.

4 Evaluation

We compare four different Arabic word embeddings that have been generated by previous work. The first three are based on a large corpus of Arabic documents constructed by Zahran et al. (Zahran et al., 2015), which consists of 2,340,895 words. Using this corpus, the authors generated three different word embeddings using three different techniques, namely the Continuous Bag-of-Words (CBOW) model (Mikolov et al., 2013), the Skip-gram model (Mikolov et al., 2013) and GloVe (Pennington et al., 2014). The fourth word embeddings we evaluate in this paper is the Arabic part of the Polyglot word embeddings, which was trained on the Arabic Wikipedia by Al-Rfou et al and consists of over 100,000 words (Al-Rfou et al., 2013). To the best of our knowledge, these are the only available word embeddings that have been constructed for the Arabic language.

4.1 Intrinsic Evaluation

As we mentioned in the previous section, we use our word analogy benchmark to evaluate the embeddings using four different criteria, namely using top-1 and top-5 words when representing relations using two versus 11 word pairs. Tables 2 displays the accuracy of each embedding technique for the four evaluation criteria. Note that we consider a question to be answered wrongly if at least one of the words in the question are not present in the word embeddings. That is, we take into consideration the coverage of the embeddings as well (Gao et al., 2014).

As can be seen in Table 2, the CBOW model consistently outperforms all other compared models for all four evaluation criteria. The performance of Polyglot is particularly low since the embeddings were trained on a much smaller corpus (Arabic portion of Wikipedia), and thus both its coverage and the quality of the embeddings are much lower. As can also be seen from the table, the accuracies of all the methods are boosted when

Model	CBOW	Skip-gram	GloVe	Polyglot	CBOW	Skip-gram	Glove	Polyglot
Relation	top-1 two pairs				top-5 two pairs			
Capital	31%	26.6%	31.7%	0.4%	42.9%	40.8%	47%	1.8%
Currency	3.15%	2%	0.8%	0.4%	4.9%%	3.9%	3.7%	1.6%
Male-Female	29%	24.8%	30.8%	3.8%	45.6%	40.6	52.4%	8.3%
Opposite	7.6%	4.41%	7.3%	2.3%	15.75%	10.65%	19.8%	5.4%
Comparative	23.9%	15.7%	21.7%	1.4%	39.61%	30.95%	38.3%	4%
Nationality	29%	29.91%	25.8%	0.8%	34.65%	39.6%	32.4%	3%
Past Tense	4.3%	2.7%	4.5%	0.4%	11.4%	9.6%	16.7%	1.5%
Plural	23.3%	13.28%	19%	2.9%	45.12%	37.9%	41.9%	7.2%
Pair	8.6%	7.6%	1.8%	0.02%	23%	21.3%	5.3%	0.07%
ALL	16.3%	12.8%	14.5%	1.3%	26.6%	23.8%	26.4%	3.4%
Relation	top-1 11 pairs				top-5 11 pairs			
Capital	28.2%	28.2%	33.8	0%	48.38%	40.3%	50.8%	0.8%
Currency	3.8%	3.8%	0.64%	0.6%	7%	4.5%	2.5%	0.6%
Male-Female	29.7%	25.7%	26.7%	4.9%	48.5%	39.6%	52.4%	7.9%
Opposite	5.4%	3.6%	5.4%	2.7%	16.3%	8.1%	15.4%	3.6%
Comparative	31%	23%	25%	1%	49%	36%	39%	2%
Nationality	35%	32%	34%	1%	41%	43%	39%	4%
Past Tense	1.8%	0%	3.6%	1.8%	15.4%	9%	17.2%	3.6%
Plural	20.7%	11.7%	18%	4.5%	48.6%	39.6%	44.2%	6.3%
Pair	8%	11%	3%	0%	21%	18%	9%	0%
ALL	17.4%	14.8%	16%	1.9%	31.1%	25.4%	28.8%	2.5%

Table 2: Intrinsic evaluation of the word embeddings using different criteria

Model	Document Classification	NER
CBOW	0.948	0.800
Skip-gram	0.954	0.799
GloVe	0.946	0.816
Polyglot	0.882	0.649

Table 3: F-measure for two NLP tasks

representing a relation using 11 pairs rather just two pairs. This validates that it is indeed more appropriate to use more than two pairs to represent relations in word analogy tasks.

When considering the top-5 matches, the accuracies of the embeddings are boosted drastically, which indeed shows that relying on just the top-1 word to assess the quality of embeddings might be unduly harsh, particularly in the case of Arabic.

4.2 Extrinsic Evaluation

We perform extrinsic evaluation of the four word embeddings using two NLP tasks, namely: Arabic Document Classification and Arabic Named Entity Recognition (NER). In the Document Classification task, the goal is to classify Arabic Wikipedia articles into four different classes (person (PER), organization (ORG), location (LOC), or miscellaneous (MISC)). To do this, we relied on a neural network with a Long Short-Term Memory (LSTM) layer (Hochreiter and Schmidhuber, 1997), which is fed from the word embeddings. The LSTM layer is followed by two fully-connected layers, which in turn are followed by a softmax layer that predicts class-assignment probabilities. The model was trained for 150 epochs on 8,000 articles, validated on 1,000 articles, and tested on another 1,000 articles.

In the NER task, the goal is to label each word in a given sequence using one of the following labels: PER, LOC, ORG, and MISC, which represent different Named Entity classes. The same architecture as in the Document Classification task was used for this task as well. The model was trained for 150 epochs on 3,852 sentences and tested on 963 sentence using Columbia's University Arabic Named Entity Recognition Corpus (Columbia University, 2016). We used an LSTM neural network for both tasks since they flexibly make use of contextual data and thus are commonly used in NLP tasks such as Document Classification and NER.

As can be seen in Table 3, the first three methods CBOW, Skip-gram and GloVe seem to perform relatively well for both the Document Classification task as well as the NER task with very comparable performance in terms of F-measure. They also clearly outperform Polyglot when it comes to both tasks as well.

4.3 Discussion

Our experimental results indicate the superiority of CBOW and SKip-gram as word embeddings compared to Polyglot. This can be mainly attributed to the fact that the first two embeddings were trained using a much larger corpus and thus had both better coverage and higher accuracies when it comes to the word analogy task. This is also evident in the case of the extrinsic evaluation. Thus, when training word embeddings, it is crucial to use large training data to obtain meaningful embeddings.

Moreover, when performing the intrinsic evaluation of the different embeddings, we observed that relying on just the top-1 word is unduly harsh for Arabic. This is mainly attributed to the fact that for Arabic, and unlike other languages such as English, different forms of the same word exist and these must be taken into consideration when evaluating the embeddings. Thus, it is advised to use the top-k matches to perform the evaluation, where k is 5 for instance. It is also advisable to represent a relation with multiple word pairs, rather than just two as is currently done in most similar studies, to guarantee that the relation is well represented.

5   Conclusion

In this paper, we described the first word analogy benchmark specifically designed for the Arabic language. We used our benchmark to evaluate available Arabic word embeddings using the basic analogy reasoning task as well as extensions of it. In addition, we also evaluated the quality of the various embeddings using two NLP tasks, namely Document Classification and NER.

Acknowledgments

This work was made possible by NPRP 6-716-1-138 grant from the Qatar National Research Fund (a member of Qatar Foundation). The statements made herein are solely the responsibilty of the authors.

References

Rami Al-Rfou, Bryan Perozzi, and Steven Skiena. 2013. Polyglot: Distributed word representations for multilingual nlp. *arXiv preprint arXiv:1307.1662* .

Ronan Collobert, Jason Weston, Léon Bottou, Michael Karlen, Koray Kavukcuoglu, and Pavel Kuksa. 2011. Natural language processing (almost) from scratch. *The Journal of Machine Learning Research* 12:2493–2537.

Columbia University. 2016. Arabic Named Entity Recognition Task. `http://www1.ccls.columbia.edu/~ybenajiba/downloads.html`.

Abdelghani Dahou, Shengwu Xiong, Junwei Zhou, Mohamed Houcine Haddoud, and Pengfei Duan. 2016. Word embeddings and convolutional neural network for arabic sentiment classification. In *International Conference on Computational Linguistics*. pages 2418–2427.

Bin Gao, Jiang Bian, and Tie-Yan Liu. 2014. Wordrep: A benchmark for research on learning word representations. *arXiv preprint arXiv:1407.1640* .

Sepp Hochreiter and Jürgen Schmidhuber. 1997. Long short-term memory. *Neural computation* 9(8):1735–1780.

Tomas Mikolov, Kai Chen, Greg Corrado, and Jeffrey Dean. 2013. Efficient estimation of word representations in vector space. *arXiv preprint arXiv:1301.3781* .

Andriy Mnih and Koray Kavukcuoglu. 2013. Learning word embeddings efficiently with noise-contrastive estimation. In *Advances in Neural Information Processing Systems*. pages 2265–2273.

Jeffrey Pennington, Richard Socher, and Christopher Manning. 2014. Glove: Global Vectors for Word Representation. In *Proceedings of the 2014 Conference on Empirical Methods in Natural Language Processing (EMNLP)*. Association for Computational Linguistics, Doha, Qatar, pages 1532–1543.

Tobias Schnabel, Igor Labutov, David M Mimno, and Thorsten Joachims. 2015. Evaluation methods for unsupervised word embeddings. In *EMNLP*. pages 298–307.

Mohamed A Zahran, Ahmed Magooda, Ashraf Y Mahgoub, Hazem Raafat, Mohsen Rashwan, and Amir Atyia. 2015. Word representations in vector space and their applications for arabic. In *International Conference on Intelligent Text Processing and Computational Linguistics*. Springer, pages 430–443.

Multilingual Connotation Frames: A Case Study on Social Media for Targeted Sentiment Analysis and Forecast

Hannah Rashkin[†]   **Eric Bell**[‡]   **Yejin Choi**[†]   **Svitlana Volkova**[‡]

[†]Paul G. Allen School of Computer Science & Engineering, University of Washington
{hrashkin,yejin}@cs.washington.edu
[‡]Data Sciences and Analytics, Pacific Northwest National Laboratory
{eric.bell,svitlana.volkova}@pnnl.gov

Abstract

People around the globe respond to major real world events through social media. To study targeted public sentiments across many languages and geographic locations, we introduce *multilingual connotation frames*: an extension from English connotation frames of Rashkin et al. (2016) with 10 additional European languages, focusing on the implied sentiments among event participants engaged in a frame. As a case study, we present large scale analysis on targeted public sentiments toward salient events and entities using 1.2 million multilingual connotation frames extracted from Twitter.

1 Introduction

People around the globe use social media to express their reflections and opinions on major real world events (Atefeh and Khreich, 2015; Radinsky and Horvitz, 2013). In order to facilitate multilingual public sentiment tracking on social media, we introduce *multilingual connotation frames*,[1] a multilingual extension from English connotation frames of Rashkin et al. (2016) with 10 additional European languages, including low-resource languages such as Polish, Finnish, and Russian.

Definition 1.1. Connotation Frames: A framework for encoding predicate-specific connotative relationships implied by a predicate towards its arguments.

Figure 1 shows a selected subset of the connotation frames that is relevant in our study. See Rashkin et al. (2016) for the full description of the connotation frames.

---

[1]Publicly available at homes.cs.washington.edu/~hrashkin/multicf.html.

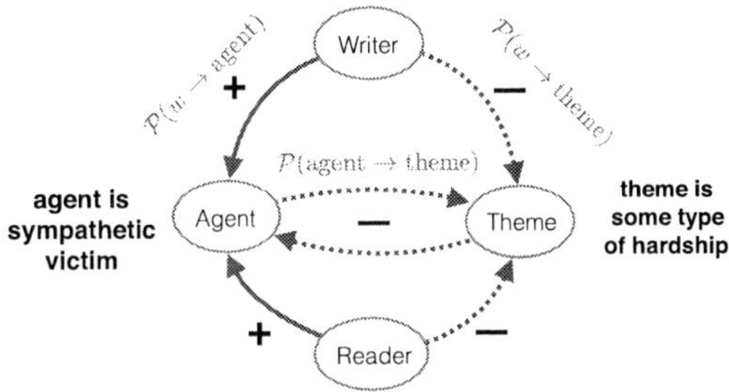

Figure 1: The connotation frame of *"survive"* with respect to directional sentiments among *"writer"*, *"agent"*, *"theme"*, and *"reader"*. The tweet examples show automatically induced multilingual connotation frames.

There are two important benefits to develop multilingual connotation frames. First, they serve as a unique lexical resource to enable *targeted* sentiment analysis, which rarely exists for most languages.

Definition 1.2. Targeted Sentiment: A sentiment label indicating how a source entity feels about a target entity.

In the example shown in Figure 1, *"teenager survived Boston Marathon bombing"*, the connotation frame allows us to correctly interpret (implied) targeted sentiments including:

1. sentiment(teenager → bombing) = −
2. sentiment(writer → bombing) = −
3. sentiment(writer → teenager) = +

Second, they allow us to study a broad spectrum of sentiments including nuanced ones; in the ex-

Proceedings of the 55th Annual Meeting of the Association for Computational Linguistics (Short Papers), pages 459–464
Vancouver, Canada, July 30 - August 4, 2017. ©2017 Association for Computational Linguistics
https://doi.org/10.18653/v1/P17-2073

Lang	# Tuples	Examples
EN	643,004	(korea, fires, missile)
ES	305,310	(acuerdo, vulnera, derecho)
FR	85,286	(obama, quitte, cuba)
PT	76,849	(valentino, renova, contrato)
RU	28,511	(путин, обсуди, моста)
DE	23,197	(seehofer, lösen, flüchtlingskrise)
NL	14,091	(artiesten, bevestigd, komst)
IT	13,586	(conte, lascia, nazionale)
FI	2,859	(hans, tekemään, valintansa)
SV	2,229	(rubio, avslutar, kampanj)
PL	2,226	(papież, wyrazi, zgodę)

Table 1: The number and the example of (agent, verb, theme) tuples extracted from tweets across languages.

amples discussed above, connotation frames allow us to infer (1) the likely sentiment among the event participants (e.g., a surviving teenager is likely to be negative toward the Boston bombing), and (2) the likely sentiment of the author towards events and entities (e.g., the writer is likely to be sympathetic toward the teenager while negative toward the incident), even though none of these sentiment implications are overtly expressed.

To validate the empirical utility of the new multilingual connotation lexicon, we present a successful case study of large scale connotation analysis (Section 4.1) and forecast (Section 4.2) based on connotation frames extracted from 1.2 million tweets in 10 different European languages spanning over a 15 day period.

2   Multilingual Twitter Dataset

We obtained multilingual geo-located tweets spanning Mar 15 – Mar 29, 2016. This 15 day duration covers Brussels attacks on Mar 22 as well as one whole week before and after, allowing us to study the public sentiment dynamics in response to a major terrorist event. We focus on tweets that are likely to be about "news-worthy" topics by selecting tweets that came from trusted sources such as twitter-verified accounts or known news accounts, or contained hashtags #breaking or #news.[2] We used SyntaxNet dependency parser (Andor et al., 2016) and trained additional SyntaxNet models for 10 non-English languages using Universal Dependencies annotations.[3] We extracted 1.2 million agent-verb-theme tuples as listed in Table 1.

---

[2] We experimented with other automatic ways of finding news sources by identifying popular hashtags, but this method did not translate well to other languages.

[3] http://universaldependencies.org/

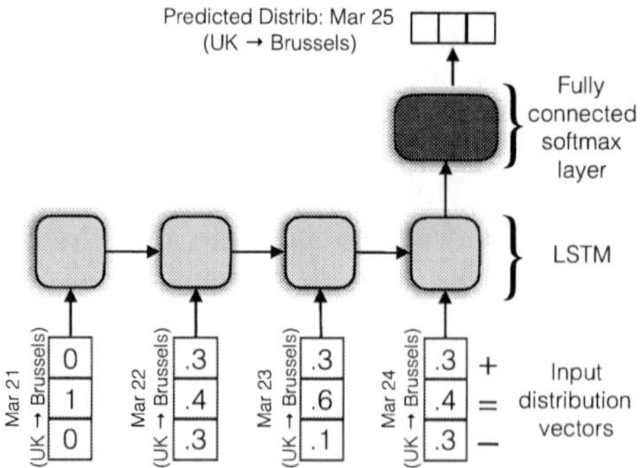

Figure 2: Diagram of LSTM model for predicting the distribution of perspectives from a location (e.g., UK) towards an entity (e.g., Brussels) on a given day (e.g., March 25), based on the previous days.

3   Methods

3.1   Multilingual Connotation Frames

We perform context-based projection of English connotation frames to 10 additional European languages using large parallel corpora. Since connotation of a word arises from the context in which the word is used, we want to ensure the translated connotation frames are used in similar contexts. We use existing parallel corpora with automatic word-alignment: the Opus Corpus (Tiedemann, 2012) using Multi-UN parallel data (Eisele and Chen, 2010) for Russian and EuroParl parallel data (Koehn, 2005) for all other languages.

More concretely, for each non-English verb, v' (e.g., *assassiner* in French), we compute the probability of it being translated to English verb v by counting the alignments.

We then define the connotation frame of v', $\mathcal{F}(v')$, by transferring the connotation frame of the English verb $v*$, $\mathcal{F}(v*)$, that has the highest translation probability:

$$v* = \mathrm{argmax}_v p(v|v')$$

$$\mathcal{F}(v') = \mathcal{F}(v*)$$

For example, the connotation frame for *assassiner* is propagated from *murder*, the English word that it is aligned with the most.

3.2   Extracting Targeted Sentiments

Using the connotation frame lexicon, we compute the distribution of targeted sentiments towards most-frequently-mentioned named entities. We also compute sentiments expressed by each

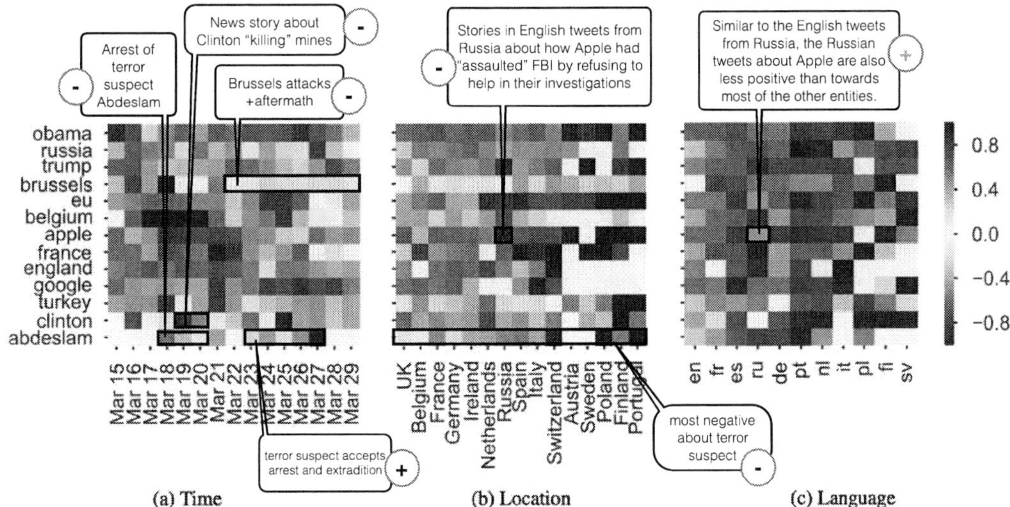

Figure 3: Heatmap of expected perspectives towards 13 named entities over 2 week period using only English tweets from European countries. Red is more positive, blue is more negative.

country by aggregating all sentiments of the writers located in that country (e.g., the distribution of positive, neutral, and negative perspectives expressed towards Obama in British tweets). The aggregated polarities can be represented as a 3-dimensional probability vector, $p = [p^+ p^= p^-]$, as will be used in the sentiment forecast task below. For other analysis, we summarize this polarity distribution as a scalar score by taking the expected value of the polarity: $E[p] = p^+ - p^-$.

3.3 Forecasting Sentiment Dynamics

We also study forecasting sentiment dynamics: predicting the sentiment distribution of the next day given the sentiment trend of previous days. For this task, we track the distribution of directional sentiments from each country towards the hundred most-frequently-mentioned named entities. At test-time, each model is given directional sentiment distributions for the previous 4 days as input and predicts tomorrow's distribution (e.g., forecasting 1 day ahead). We also train models for predicting the distribution half a week later (forecasting 4 days ahead).

We performed an additional experiment for English (EN_J) where the perspectives of all countries are aggregated together in order to predict the global perspective. For all experiments, we use 10-fold cross-validation and measure the symmetric Kullback-Leibler (KL) divergence between the true distribution and the predicted one.

We experiment with Long Short-term Memory

models (LSTMs) (Hochreiter and Schmidhuber, 1997) to integrate the dynamic contextual information from the past, as depicted in 2. Hidden dimension is 16, and we use ADAM optimization with KL divergence as the objective. For implementation, we use Keras[4] on top of Theano.[5]

Baselines We use two baselines. The first is MEAN, the average distribution seen in the training data. The second are SVMs with linear kernels, which worked well in predicting influenza activity in a similar set-up (Santillana et al., 2015). For the baselines, we encode the distributions from the 4 previous days as a flattened 12-dim. vector, and each portion of the distribution is predicted separately.

4 Results

4.1 Connotation Analysis

For the most frequently mentioned named entities, we compute heatmaps of the expected perspective being expressed towards that entity.

In Figure 3A, we use the English tweets from European countries to plot the change in connotative polarity towards these entities over the course of the 15 day period. Generally, the changes in polarity from day-to-day seem to be gradual and frequently are similar to the day before. There are a couple of exceptions e.g., the polarity towards

---

[4]`https://keras.io`
[5]`https://deeplearning.net/software/theano`

Brussels changes abruptly on March 22 (the day of the Brussels attacks), reflecting the change in tone of all tweets related to Brussels at that time.

Overall, there are mostly positive polarities expressed. This may reflect people's tendency to avoid phrasing stories too harshly, choosing to be more euphemistic even when they discuss bad news.

In Figure 3B, we aggregated the polarities of these tweets by country of origin. While most of the polarities are positive-strongly positive, the tweets about Brussels and Belgium are more neutral or even slightly negative.

Lastly, in Figure 3C, we used all of the tweets from European countries to aggregate expected polarities in 11 different languages. Non-English languages show a much higher tendency towards positive scores, particularly the languages with less tweets (Polish, Finnish, Swedish).

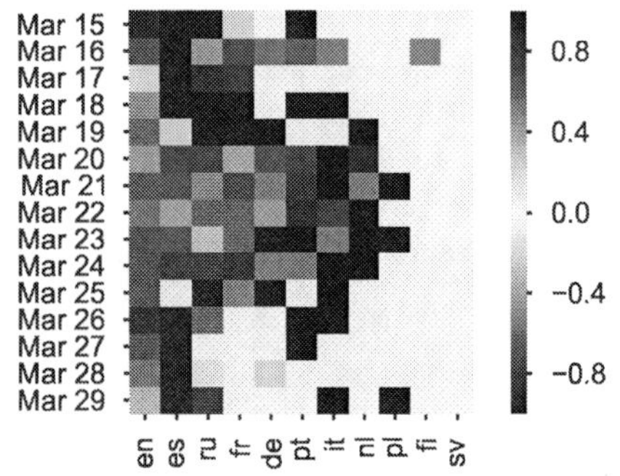

Figure 4: Heatmap of perspectives towards Obama over time in 11 different languages.

As a more detailed analysis, Figure 4 shows a heatmap of how the connotation expressed towards Obama shifts over time across different languages. Obama was not discussed much in Finnish or Swedish, whereas he was discussed everyday in English, Spanish, and Russian. In the middle of the two week period, the perspective towards Obama drops slightly, most notably in Spanish, which overlaps with his controversial trip to Cuba (March 20 – 22).

4.2 Sentiment Dynamics

In Table 2, we summarize the results of our experiments for predicting targeted sentiment dynamics. For each language, we report the average Kullback-Leibler divergence for the baselines and the LSTM model (higher scores are worse). We show prediction results in two settings: predicting

Data	Forecast + 1 day			Forecast + 4 days		
	Mean	SVM	LSTM	Mean	SVM	LSTM
EN$_J$	1.96	1.76	1.67	2.03	2.14	2.02
EN	4.88	1.94	1.79	5.12	3.91	3.91
RU	4.27	1.72	1.34	4.50	3.11	2.74
FR	2.23	1.80	1.76	4.33	3.24	3.12
ES	3.57	2.02	1.82	3.74	3.22	2.98
DE	4.43	2.24	1.77	4.73	3.61	3.55
NL	3.69	2.62	2.05	3.83	3.71	3.41
PT	3.84	1.97	2.04	3.94	3.03	3.11
IT	4.56	2.08	1.97	4.67	3.48	3.28
PL	4.01	1.67	1.46	4.06	3.37	3.32
SV	4.01	1.92	0.76	4.17	2.70	2.23
FI	4.90	2.04	1.84	4.99	4.14	4.20

Table 2: Average Kullback-Leibler divergence of output of the LSTM in predicting the distribution of writers' perspectives per entity for 11 different languages. In the first row, the perspectives from all countries are aggregated together.

the distribution one day ahead vs. four days ahead.

The LSTM outperforms the baselines in most languages with a few exceptions, such as Portuguese. All models perform worse at forecasting 4 days into the future than one day ahead, demonstrating how much connotation can vary over time as news events change, even in a small time period. On average, the LSTM achieves KL-divergence of 1.7 when predicting one day ahead and 3.26 when predicting 4 days ahead, lower than any of the baselines.

4.3 Error Analysis

For error analysis, we removed entities from Figure 3 from the training data and used them as a small test set for an LSTM trained on the remaining data in English with aggregation over all countries. In Figure 5, we have plotted the predicted marginal probabilities of four entities with the positive portion of the distribution (blue line) on the top half of the y-axis and the negative portion (red line) flipped onto the negative half of the axis.

The LSTM follows the general shape of the true curves, but frequently misses sudden spikes (e.g., the spike in negative polarity towards Russia on March 27th). In Table 3, we also report the KL divergences on predictions towards these entities. The model tends to perform less well at predicting sentiment towards entities where there were sudden spikes in sentiment based on news stories.

5   Related Work

There have been substantial studies for sentiment analysis on twitter (Agarwal et al., 2011; Kouloumpis et al., 2011; Pak and Paroubek, 2010;

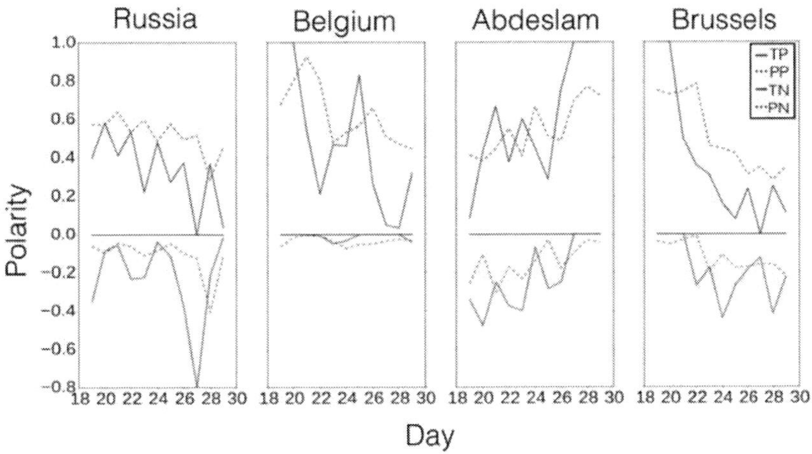

Figure 5: True versus predicted polarity distributions over time on three specific entities (TP: True Positive, PP: Predicted Positive, TN: True Negative, PN: Predicted Negative).

Entity	KL	Entity	KL	Entity	KL
Trump	0.12	England	0.14	EU	0.22
Obama	0.25	Turkey	0.30	Google	0.32
apple	0.37	Russia	0.76	Belgium	0.95
Clinton	1.13	Brussels	1.14	Abdeslam	1.79

Table 3: Error analysis on held-out entities.

Liu and Zhang, 2012), as well as targetted sentiment (Deng and Wiebe, 2015), implicit sentiment (Deng and Wiebe, 2014; Feng et al., 2013; Greene and Resnik, 2009) and specific aspects of subjective language (Mohammad and Turney, 2010; Choi and Wiebe, 2014) in other domains. Previous investigations include using targetted sentiment to predict international relations (Chambers et al., 2015), analyzing stylistic elements to predict tweet popularity (Tan et al., 2014), and exploring the re-phrasing of social media posts referencing specific news articles (Tan et al., 2016). Compared to most prior studies that focused on overt sentiment in English-only tweets, our work aims to study targeted implied sentiments across temporal, spatial, and linguistic borders.

Some work (Tsytsarau et al., 2014; O'Connor et al., 2010; De et al., 2016) has analyzed the transition of overt sentiment over a period of time and related the shifts in sentiment to news events. A body of work has also used predictive signals in Twitter to track and sense upcoming unrest and protests in specific countries (Ramakrishnan et al., 2014; Goode et al., 2015), and the future progression of flu activity based on multiple text sources (Santillana et al., 2015). In contrast, we focus on predicting the sentiment dynamics in social media based on previous trends.

6 Conclusions

When reporting news, people write with their own implicit and explicit biases and judgments. An author's choice of language reveals connotations towards entities, which can be captured within the connotation frames that we have extended to 10 European languages.

This work is one of the first to present a large scale analysis of multilingual connotation dynamics, and helps explore multiple perspectives on diverse issues across languages, time and countries – a critical piece in understanding journalistic portrayal and biases.

7 Acknowledgments

This research was conducted at Pacific Northwest National Laboratory, a multiprogram national laboratory operated by Battelle for the U.S. We would like to thank Josh Harrison, Jill Schroeder and Justin Day for their contribution. We would also like to thank anonymous reviewers for providing insightful feedback. This material is based upon work supported by the National Science Foundation Graduate Research Fellowship Program under Grant No. DGE-1256082, in part by NSF grants IIS-1408287, IIS-1524371, and gifts by Google and Facebook.

References

Apoorv Agarwal, Boyi Xie, Ilia Vovsha, Owen Rambow, and Rebecca Passonneau. 2011. Sentiment analysis of twitter data. In *Proceedings of the workshop on languages in social media*. ACL, pages 30–38.

Daniel Andor, Chris Alberti, David Weiss, Aliaksei Severyn, Alessandro Presta, Kuzman Ganchev, Slav Petrov, and Michael Collins. 2016. Globally normalized transition-based neural networks. In *Proceedings of ACL*.

Farzindar Atefeh and Wael Khreich. 2015. A survey of techniques for event detection in twitter. *Computational Intelligence* 31(1):132–164.

Nathanael Chambers, Victor Bowen, Ethan Genco, Xisen Tian, Eric Young, Ganesh Harihara, and Eugene Yang. 2015. Identifying political sentiment between nation states with social media. In *Proceedings of EMNLP*. pages 65–75.

Yoonjung Choi and Janyce Wiebe. 2014. +/-effectwordnet: Sense-level lexicon acquisition for opinion inference. In *EMNLP*. pages 1181–1191.

Abir De, Isabel Valera, Niloy Ganguly, Sourangshu Bhattacharya, and Manuel Gomez Rodriguez. 2016. Learning and forecasting opinion dynamics in social networks. In *Proceedings of NIPS*.

Lingjia Deng and Janyce Wiebe. 2014. Sentiment propagation via implicature constraints. In *EACL*. pages 377–385.

Lingjia Deng and Janyce Wiebe. 2015. Mpqa 3.0: An entity/event-level sentiment corpus. In *HLT-NAACL*. pages 1323–1328.

Andreas Eisele and Yu Chen. 2010. Multiun: A multilingual corpus from united nation documents. In *Proceedings of LREC*. pages 2868–2872.

Song Feng, Jun Seok Kang, Polina Kuznetsova, and Yejin Choi. 2013. Connotation lexicon: A dash of sentiment beneath the surface meaning. In *ACL*. pages 1774–1784.

Brian J Goode, Siddharth Krishnan, Michael Roan, and Naren Ramakrishnan. 2015. Pricing a protest: Forecasting the dynamics of civil unrest activity in social media. *PloS one* 10(10):e0139911.

Stephan Greene and Philip Resnik. 2009. More than words: Syntactic packaging and implicit sentiment. In *Proceedings of NAACL-HLT*. ACL, pages 503–511.

Sepp Hochreiter and Jürgen Schmidhuber. 1997. Long short-term memory. *Neural computation* 9(8):1735–1780.

Philipp Koehn. 2005. Europarl: A parallel corpus for statistical machine translation. In *MT summit*. volume 5, pages 79–86.

Efthymios Kouloumpis, Theresa Wilson, and Johanna D Moore. 2011. Twitter sentiment analysis: The good the bad and the omg! In *Proceedings of ICWSM*. AAAI.

Bing Liu and Lei Zhang. 2012. A survey of opinion mining and sentiment analysis. In *Mining text data*, Springer, pages 415–463.

Saif M Mohammad and Peter D Turney. 2010. Emotions evoked by common words and phrases: Using mechanical turk to create an emotion lexicon. In *Proceedings of the NAACL HLT 2010 workshop on computational approaches to analysis and generation of emotion in text*. Association for Computational Linguistics, pages 26–34.

Brendan O'Connor, Ramnath Balasubramanyan, Bryan Routledge, and Noah Smith. 2010. From tweets to polls: Linking text sentiment to public opinion time series. In *Proceedings of ICWSM*. 122-129, pages 1–2.

Alexander Pak and Patrick Paroubek. 2010. Twitter as a corpus for sentiment analysis and opinion mining. In *Proceedings of LREC*. volume 10, pages 1320–1326.

Kira Radinsky and Eric Horvitz. 2013. Mining the web to predict future events. In *Proceedings of WSDM*. ACM, pages 255–264.

Naren Ramakrishnan, Patrick Butler, Sathappan Muthiah, Nathan Self, Rupinder Khandpur, Parang Saraf, Wei Wang, Jose Cadena, Anil Vullikanti, Gizem Korkmaz, et al. 2014. 'beating the news' with embers: forecasting civil unrest using open source indicators. In *Proceedings of KDD*. ACM, pages 1799–1808.

Hannah Rashkin, Sameer Singh, and Yejin Choi. 2016. Connotation frames: A data-driven investigation. In *Proceedings of ACL*.

Mauricio Santillana, André T Nguyen, Mark Dredze, Michael J Paul, Elaine O Nsoesie, and John S Brownstein. 2015. Combining search, social media, and traditional data sources to improve influenza surveillance. *PLoS Comput Biol* 11(10):e1004513.

Chenhao Tan, Adrien Friggeri, Menlo Park, and Menlo Park. 2016. Lost in Propagation? Unfolding News Cycles from the Source. In *Proceedings of AAAI*.

Chenhao Tan, Lillian Lee, and Bo Pang. 2014. The effect of wording on message propagation: Topic- and author-controlled. In *Proceedings of ACL*.

Jörg Tiedemann. 2012. Parallel data, tools and interfaces in opus. In *LREC*. pages 2214–2218.

Mikalai Tsytsarau, Themis Palpanas, and Malu Castellanos. 2014. Dynamics of news events and social media reaction. In *Proceedings of KDD*. ACM, pages 901–910.

Best–Worst Scaling More Reliable than Rating Scales:
A Case Study on Sentiment Intensity Annotation

Svetlana Kiritchenko and **Saif M. Mohammad**
National Research Council Canada
{svetlana.kiritchenko, saif.mohammad}@nrc-cnrc.gc.ca

Abstract

Rating scales are a widely used method for data annotation; however, they present several challenges, such as difficulty in maintaining inter- and intra-annotator consistency. Best–worst scaling (BWS) is an alternative method of annotation that is claimed to produce high-quality annotations while keeping the required number of annotations similar to that of rating scales. However, the veracity of this claim has never been systematically established. Here for the first time, we set up an experiment that directly compares the rating scale method with BWS. We show that with the same total number of annotations, BWS produces significantly more reliable results than the rating scale.

1 Introduction

When manually annotating data with quantitative or qualitative information, researchers in many disciplines, including social sciences and computational linguistics, often rely on *rating scales (RS)*. A rating scale provides the annotator with a choice of categorical or numerical values that represent the measurable characteristic of the rated data. For example, when annotating a word for sentiment, the annotator can be asked to choose among integer values from 1 to 9, with 1 representing the strongest negative sentiment, and 9 representing the strongest positive sentiment (Bradley and Lang, 1999; Warriner et al., 2013). Another example is the Likert scale, which measures responses on a symmetric agree–disagree scale, from 'strongly disagree' to 'strongly agree' (Likert, 1932). The annotations for an item from multiple respondents are usually averaged to obtain a real-valued score for that item. Thus, for an N-item set, if each item is to be annotated by five respondents, then the number of annotations required is $5N$.

While frequently used in many disciplines, the rating scale method has a number of limitations (Presser and Schuman, 1996; Baumgartner and Steenkamp, 2001). These include:

- *Inconsistencies in annotations by different annotators*: one annotator might assign a score of 7 to the word *good* on a 1-to-9 sentiment scale, while another annotator can assign a score of 8 to the same word.
- *Inconsistencies in annotations by the same annotator*: an annotator might assign different scores to the same item when the annotations are spread over time.
- *Scale region bias*: annotators often have a bias towards a part of the scale, for example, preference for the middle of the scale.
- *Fixed granularity:* in some cases, annotators might feel too restricted with a given rating scale and may want to place an item in-between the two points on the scale. On the other hand, a fine-grained scale may overwhelm the respondents and lead to even more inconsistencies in annotation.

Paired Comparisons (Thurstone, 1927; David, 1963) is a comparative annotation method, where respondents are presented with pairs of items and asked which item has more of the property of interest (for example, which is more positive). The annotations can then be converted into a ranking of items by the property of interest, and one can even obtain real-valued scores indicating the degree to which an item is associated with the property of interest. The paired comparison method does not suffer from the problems discussed above for the rating scale, but it requires a large number of annotations—order N^2, where N is the number of items to be annotated.

Proceedings of the 55th Annual Meeting of the Association for Computational Linguistics (Short Papers), pages 465–470
Vancouver, Canada, July 30 - August 4, 2017. ©2017 Association for Computational Linguistics
https://doi.org/10.18653/v1/P17-2074

Best–Worst Scaling (BWS) is a less-known, and more recently introduced, variant of comparative annotation. It was developed by Louviere (1991), building on some groundbreaking research in the 1960s in mathematical psychology and psychophysics by Anthony A. J. Marley and Duncan Luce. Annotators are presented with n items at a time (an n-tuple, where $n > 1$, and typically $n = 4$). They are asked which item is the *best* (highest in terms of the property of interest) and which is the *worst* (lowest in terms of the property of interest). When working on 4-tuples, best–worst annotations are particularly efficient because by answering these two questions, the results for five out of six item–item pair-wise comparisons become known. All items to be rated are organized in a set of m 4-tuples ($m \geq N$, where N is the number of items) so that each item is evaluated several times in diverse 4-tuples. Once the m 4-tuples are annotated, one can compute real-valued scores for each of the items using a simple counting procedure (Orme, 2009). The scores can be used to rank items by the property of interest.

BWS is claimed to produce high-quality annotations while still keeping the number of annotations small ($1.5N$–$2N$ tuples need to be annotated) (Louviere et al., 2015; Kiritchenko and Mohammad, 2016a). However, the veracity of this claim has never been systematically established. In this paper, we pit the widely used rating scale squarely against BWS in a quantitative experiment to determine which method provides more reliable results. We produce real-valued sentiment intensity ratings for 3,207 English terms (words and phrases) using both methods by aggregating responses from several independent annotators. We show that BWS ranks terms more reliably, that is, when comparing the term rankings obtained from two groups of annotators for the same set of terms, the correlation between the two sets of ranks produced by BWS is significantly higher than the correlation for the two sets obtained with RS. The difference in reliability is more marked when about $5N$ (or less) total annotations are obtained, which is the case in many NLP annotation projects (Strapparava and Mihalcea, 2007; Socher et al., 2013; Mohammad and Turney, 2013). Furthermore, the reliability obtained by rating scale when using ten annotations per term is matched by BWS with only $3N$ total annotations (two annotations for each of the $1.5N$ 4-tuples).

The sparse prior work in natural language annotations that uses BWS involves the creation of datasets for relational similarity (Jurgens et al., 2012), word-sense disambiguation (Jurgens, 2013), and word–sentiment intensity (Kiritchenko and Mohammad, 2016a). However, none of these works has systematically compared BWS with the rating scale method. We hope that our findings will encourage the use of BWS more widely to obtain high-quality NLP annotations. All data from our experiments as well as scripts to generate BWS tuples, to generate item scores from BWS annotations, and for assessing reliability of the annotations are made freely available.[1]

2 Complexities of Comparative Evaluation

Both rating scale and BWS are less than perfect ways to capture the true word–sentiment intensities in the minds of native speakers of a language. Since the "true" intensities are not known, determining which approach is better is non-trivial.[2]

A useful measure of quality is reproducibility— if repeated independent manual annotations from multiple respondents result in similar sentiment scores, then one can be confident that the scores capture the true sentiment intensities. Thus, we set up an experiment that compares BWS and RS in terms of how similar the results are on repeated independent annotations.

It is expected that reproducibility improves with the number of annotations for both methods. (Estimating a value often stabilizes as the sample size is increased.) However, in rating scale annotation, each item is annotated individually whereas in BWS, groups of four items (4-tuples) are annotated together (and each item is present in multiple different 4-tuples). To make the reproducibility evaluation fair, we ensure that the term scores are inferred from the same total number of annotations for both methods. For an N-item set, let k_{rs} be the number of times each item is annotated via a rating scale. Then the total number of rating scale annotations is $k_{rs}N$. For BWS, let the same N-item set be converted into m 4-tuples that are each annotated k_{bws} times. Then the total number of BWS annotations is $k_{bws}m$. In our experiments, we compare results across BWS and rating scale at points when $k_{rs}N = k_{bws}m$.

---

[1] www.saifmohammad.com/WebPages/BestWorst.html

[2] Existing sentiment lexicons are a result of one or the other method and so cannot be treated as the truth.

The cognitive complexity involved in answering a BWS question is different from that in a rating scale question. On the one hand, for BWS, the respondent has to consider four items at a time simultaneously. On the other hand, even though a rating scale question explicitly involves only one item, the respondent must choose a score that places it appropriately with respect to other items.[3] Quantifying the degree of cognitive load of a BWS annotation vs. a rating scale annotation (especially in a crowdsourcing setting) is particularly challenging, and beyond the scope of this paper. Here we explore the extent to which the rating scale method and BWS lead to the same resulting scores when the annotations are repeated, controlling for the total number of annotations.

3 Annotating for Sentiment

We annotated 3,207 terms for sentiment intensity (or degree of positive or negative valence) with both the rating scale and best–worst scaling. The annotations were done by crowdsourcing on CrowdFlower.[4] The workers were required to be native English speakers from the USA.

3.1 Terms

The term list includes 1,621 positive and negative single words from Osgood's valence subset of the General Inquirer (Stone et al., 1966). It also included 1,586 high-frequency short phrases formed by these words in combination with simple negators (e.g., *no*, *don't*, and *never*), modals (e.g., *can*, *might*, and *should*), or degree adverbs (e.g., *very* and *fairly*). More details on the term selection can be found in (Kiritchenko and Mohammad, 2016b).

3.2 Annotating with Rating Scale

The annotators were asked to rate each term on a 9-point scale, ranging from -4 (extremely negative) to 4 (extremely positive). The middle point (0) was marked as 'not at all positive or negative'. Example words were provided for the two extremes (-4 and 4) and the middle (0) to give the annotators a sense of the whole scale.

Each term was annotated by twenty workers for the total number of annotations to be $20N$ ($N =$

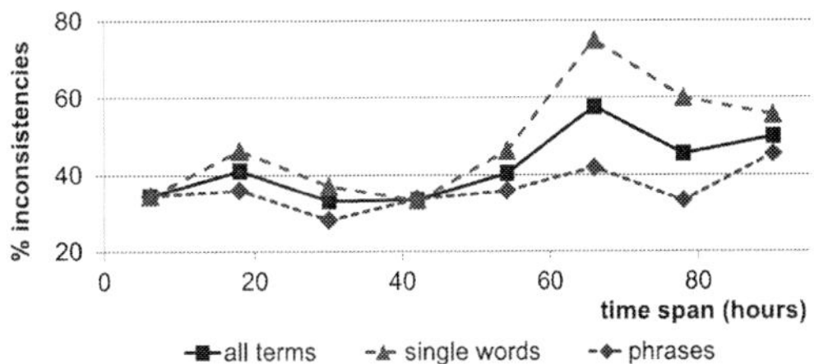

Figure 1: The inconsistency rate in repeated annotations by same workers using rating scale.

$3,207$ is the number of terms). A small portion (5%) of terms were internally annotated by the authors. If a worker's accuracy on these check questions fell below 70%, that worker was refused further annotation, and all of their responses were discarded. The final score for each term was set to the mean of all ratings collected for this term.[5] On average, the ratings of a worker correlated well with the mean ratings of the rest of the workers (average Pearson's $r = 0.9$, min $r = 0.8$). Also, the Pearson correlation between the obtained mean ratings and the ratings from similar studies by Warriner et al. (2013) and by Dodds et al. (2011) were 0.94 (on 1,420 common terms) and 0.96 (on 998 common terms), respectively.[6]

To determine how consistent individual annotators are over time, 180 terms (90 single words and 90 phrases) were presented for annotation twice with intervals ranging from a few minutes to a few days. For 37% of these instances, the annotations for the same term by the same worker were different. The average rating difference for these inconsistent annotations was 1.27 (on a scale from -4 to 4). Fig. 1 shows the inconsistency rate in these repeated annotations as a function of time interval between the two annotations. The inconsistency rate is averaged over 12-hour periods. One can observe that intra-annotator inconsistency increases with the increase in time span between the annotations. Single words tend to be annotated with higher inconsistency than phrases. However, when annotated inconsistently, phrases have larger average difference between the scores (1.28 for phrases vs. 1.21 for single words). Twelve out of 90 phrases (13%) have the average difference greater than or equal to 2 points. This shows that it is difficult for annotators to remain consistent when using the rating scale.

---

[3] A somewhat straightforward example is that *good* cannot be given a sentiment score less than what was given to *okay*, and it cannot be given a score greater than that given to *great*. Often, more complex comparisons need to be considered.

[4] The full set of annotations as well as the instructions to annotators for both methods are available at http://www.saifmohammad.com/WebPages/BestWorst.html.

[5] When evaluated as described in Sections 4 and 5, median and mode produced worse results than mean.

[6] Warriner et al. (2013) list a correlation of 0.95 on 1029 common terms with the lexicon by Bradley and Lang (1999).

3.3 Annotating with Best–Worst Scaling

The annotators were presented with four terms at a time (a 4-tuple) and asked to select the most positive term and the most negative term. The same quality control mechanism of assessing a worker's accuracy on internally annotated check questions (discussed in the previous section) was employed here as well. $2N$ (where $N = 3,207$) distinct 4-tuples were randomly generated in such a manner that each term was seen in eight different 4-tuples, and no term appeared more than once in a tuple.[7] Each 4-tuple was annotated by 10 workers. Thus, the total number of annotations obtained for BWS was $20N$ (just as in RS). We used the partial sets of $1N$, $1.5N$, and the full set of $2N$ 4-tuples to investigate the impact of the number of unique 4-tuples on the quality of the final scores.

We applied the *counting procedure* to obtain real-valued term–sentiment scores from the BWS annotations (Orme, 2009; Flynn and Marley, 2014): the term's score was calculated as the percentage of times the term was chosen as most positive minus the percentage of times the term was chosen as most negative. The scores range from -1 (most negative) to 1 (most positive). This simple and efficient procedure has been shown to produce results similar to ones obtained with more sophisticated statistical models, such as multinomial logistic regression (Louviere et al., 2015).

In a separate study, we use the resulting dataset of 3,207 words and phrases annotated with real-valued sentiment intensity scores by BWS, which we call Sentiment Composition Lexicon for Negators, Modals, and Degree Adverbs (SCL-NMA), to analyze the effect of different modifiers on sentiment (Kiritchenko and Mohammad, 2016b).

4 How different are the results obtained by rating scale and BWS?

The difference in final outcomes of BWS and RS can be determined in two ways: by directly comparing term scores or by comparing term ranks. To compare scores, we first linearly transform the BWS and rating scale scores to scores in the range 0 to 1. Table 1 shows the differences in scores, differences in rank, Spearman rank correlation ρ, and Pearson correlation r for $3N$, $5N$, and $20N$ annotations. Observe that the differences are markedly larger for commonly used annotation scenarios

---

[7]The script used to generate the 4-tuples is available at http://www.saifmohammad.com/WebPages/BestWorst.html.

# annotations	Δ score	Δ rank	ρ	r
$3N$	0.11	397	0.85	0.85
$5N$	0.10	363	0.87	0.88
$20N$	0.08	264	0.93	0.93

Table 1: Differences in final outcomes of BWS and RS, for different total numbers of annotations.

Term set	# terms	ρ	r
all terms	3,207	.93	.93
single words	1621	.94	.95
all phrases	1586	.92	.91
negated phrases	444	.74	.79
pos. phrases that have a negator	83	-.05	-.05
neg. phrases that have a negator	326	.46	.46
modal phrases	418	.75	.82
pos. phrases that have a modal	272	.44	.45
neg. phrases that have a modal	95	.57	.56
adverb phrases	724	.91	.95

Table 2: Correlations between sentiment scores produced by BWS and rating scale.

where only $3N$ or $5N$ total annotations are obtained, but even with $20N$ annotations, the differences across RS and BWS are notable.

Table 2 shows Spearman (ρ) and Pearson (r) correlation between the ranks and scores produced by RS and BWS on the full set of $20N$ annotations. Notice that the scores agree more on single terms and less so on phrases. The correlation is noticeably lower for phrases involving negations and modal verbs. Furthermore, the correlation drops dramatically for positive phrases that have a negator (e.g., *not hurt, nothing wrong*).[8] The annotators also showed greater inconsistencies while scoring these phrases on the rating scale (std. dev. $\sigma = 1.17$ compared to $\sigma = 0.81$ for the full set). Thus it seems that the outcomes of rating scale and BWS diverge to a greater extent when the complexity of the items to be rated increases.

5 Annotation Reliability

To assess the reliability of annotations produced by a method (BWS or rating scale), we calculate average *split-half reliability (SHR)* over 100 trials. SHR is a commonly used approach to determine consistency in psychological studies, that we employ as follows. All annotations for a term or a tuple are randomly split into two halves. Two sets

---

[8]A term was considered positive (negative) if the scores obtained for the term with rating scale and BWS are both greater than or equal to zero (less than zero). Some terms were rated inconsistently by the two methods; therefore, the number of the positive and negative terms for a category (negated phrases and modal phrases) does not sum to the total number of terms in the category.

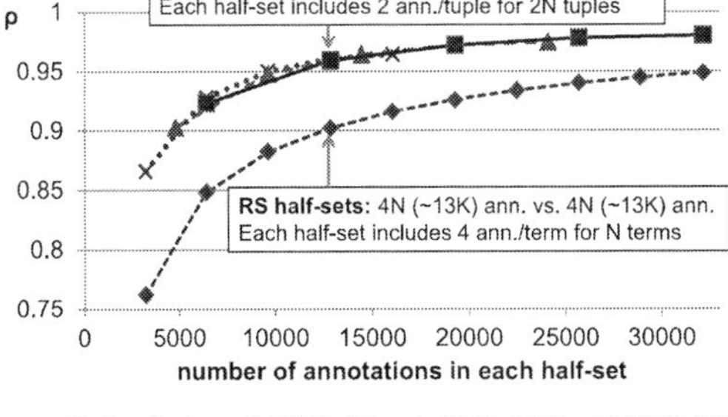

Figure 2: SHR for RS and BWS (for $N = 3207$).

Term set	# terms	BWS	RS
all terms	3,207	.98	.95
single words	1621	.98	.96
all phrases	1586	.98	.94
negated phrases	444	.91	.78
pos. phrases that have a negator	83	.79	.17
neg. phrases that have a negator	326	.81	.49
modal phrases	418	.96	.80
pos. phrases that have a modal	272	.89	.53
neg. phrases that have a modal	95	.83	.63
adverb phrases	724	.97	.92

Table 3: Average SHR for BWS and rating scale (RS) on different subsets of terms.

of scores are produced independently from the two halves. Then the correlation between the two sets of scores is calculated. If a method is more reliable, then the correlation of the scores produced by the two halves will be high. Fig. 2 shows the Spearman rank correlation (ρ) for half-sets obtained from rating scale and best–worst scaling data as a function of the available annotations in each half-set. It shows for each annotation set the split-half reliability using the full set of annotations ($10N$ per half-set) as well as partial sets obtained by choosing k_{rs} annotations per term for rating scale (where k_{rs} ranges from 1 to 10) or k_{bws} annotations per 4-tuple for BWS (where k_{bws} ranges from 1 to 5). The graph also shows BWS results obtained using $1N$, $1.5N$, and $2N$ unique 4-tuples. In each case, the x-coordinate represents the total number of annotations in each half-set. Recall that the total number of annotations for rating scale equals $k_{rs}N$, and for BWS it equals $k_{bws}m$, where m is the number of 4-tuples. Thus, for the case where $m = 2N$, the two methods are compared at points where $k_{rs} = 2k_{bws}$.

There are two important observations we can make from Fig. 2. First, we can conclude that the reliability of the BWS annotations is very similar on the sets of $1N$, $1.5N$, and $2N$ annotated 4-tuples as long as the total number of annotations is the same. This means that in practice, in order to improve annotation reliability, one can increase either the number of unique 4-tuples to annotate or the number of independent annotations for each 4-tuple. Second, annotations produced with BWS are more reliable than annotations obtained with rating scales. The difference in reliability is especially large when only a small number of annotations ($\leq 5N$) are available. For the full set of more than 64K annotations ($10N = {\sim}32K$ in

each half-set) available for both methods, the average split-half reliability for BWS is $\rho = 0.98$ and for the rating scale method the reliability is $\rho = 0.95$ (the difference is statistically significant, $p < .001$). One can obtain a reliability of $\rho = 0.95$ with BWS using just $3N$ ($\sim$10K) annotations in a half-set (30% of what is needed for rating scale).[9]

Table 3 shows the split-half reliability (SHR) on different subsets of terms. Observe that positive phrases that include a negator (the class that diverged most across BWS and rating scale), is also the class that has an extremely low SHR when annotated by rating scale. The drop in SHR for the same class when annotated with BWS is much less. Similar pattern is observed for other phrase classes as well, although to a lesser extent. All of the results shown in this section, indicate that BWS surpasses rating scales on the ability to reliably rank items by sentiment, especially for phrasal items that are linguistically more complex.

6   Conclusions

We presented an experiment that directly compared the rating scale method of annotation with best–worst scaling. We showed that, controlling for the total number of annotations, BWS produced significantly more reliable results. The difference in reliability was more marked when about $5N$ (or less) total annotations for an N-item set were obtained. BWS was also more reliable when used to annotate linguistically complex items such as phrases with negations and modals. We hope that these findings will encourage the use of BWS more widely to obtain high-quality annotations.

Acknowledgments

We thank Eric Joanis and Tara Small for discussions on best–worst scaling and rating scales.

[9]Similar trends are observed with Pearson's coefficient though the gap between BWS and RS results is smaller.

References

Hans Baumgartner and Jan-Benedict E.M. Steenkamp. 2001. Response styles in marketing research: A cross-national investigation. *Journal of Marketing Research* 38(2):143–156.

Margaret M. Bradley and Peter J. Lang. 1999. Affective norms for English words (ANEW): Instruction manual and affective ratings. Technical report, The Center for Research in Psychophysiology, University of Florida.

Herbert Aron David. 1963. *The method of paired comparisons*. Hafner Publishing Company, New York.

Peter Sheridan Dodds, Kameron Decker Harris, Isabel M. Kloumann, Catherine A. Bliss, and Christopher M. Danforth. 2011. Temporal patterns of happiness and information in a global social network: Hedonometrics and Twitter. *PloS One* 6(12):e26752.

T. N. Flynn and A. A. J. Marley. 2014. Best-worst scaling: theory and methods. In Stephane Hess and Andrew Daly, editors, *Handbook of Choice Modelling*, Edward Elgar Publishing, pages 178–201.

David Jurgens. 2013. Embracing ambiguity: A comparison of annotation methodologies for crowdsourcing word sense labels. In *Proceedings of the Annual Conference of the North American Chapter of the Association for Computational Linguistics: Human Language Technologies (NAACL)*. Atlanta, Georgia, pages 556–562. http://aclweb.org/anthology/N13-1062.

David Jurgens, Saif M. Mohammad, Peter Turney, and Keith Holyoak. 2012. SemEval-2012 Task 2: Measuring degrees of relational similarity. In *Proceedings of the International Workshop on Semantic Evaluation (SemEval)*. Montréal, Canada, pages 356–364. http://www.aclweb.org/anthology/S12-1047.

Svetlana Kiritchenko and Saif M. Mohammad. 2016a. Capturing reliable fine-grained sentiment associations by crowdsourcing and best–worst scaling. In *Proceedings of the Annual Conference of the North American Chapter of the Association for Computational Linguistics: Human Language Technologies (NAACL)*. San Diego, California, pages 811–817. https://doi.org/10.18653/v1/N16-1095.

Svetlana Kiritchenko and Saif M. Mohammad. 2016b. The effect of negators, modals, and degree adverbs on sentiment composition. In *Proceedings of the 7th Workshop on Computational Approaches to Subjectivity, Sentiment and Social Media Analysis*. San Diego, California, pages 43–52. http://www.aclweb.org/anthology/W16-0410.

Rensis Likert. 1932. A technique for the measurement of attitudes. *Archives of psychology* .

Jordan J. Louviere. 1991. Best-worst scaling: A model for the largest difference judgments. Working Paper.

Jordan J. Louviere, Terry N. Flynn, and A. A. J. Marley. 2015. *Best–Worst Scaling: Theory, Methods and Applications*. Cambridge University Press.

Saif M. Mohammad and Peter D. Turney. 2013. Crowdsourcing a word–emotion association lexicon. *Computational Intelligence* 29(3):436–465.

Bryan Orme. 2009. Maxdiff analysis: Simple counting, individual-level logit, and HB. Sawtooth Software, Inc.

Stanley Presser and Howard Schuman. 1996. *Questions and Answers in Attitude Surveys: Experiments on Question Form, Wording, and Context*. SAGE Publications, Inc.

Richard Socher, Alex Perelygin, Jean Y. Wu, Jason Chuang, Christopher D. Manning, Andrew Y. Ng, and Christopher Potts. 2013. Recursive deep models for semantic compositionality over a sentiment treebank. In *Proceedings of the Conference on Empirical Methods in Natural Language Processing (EMNLP)*. Seattle, USA.

Philip Stone, Dexter C. Dunphy, Marshall S. Smith, Daniel M. Ogilvie, and associates. 1966. *The General Inquirer: A Computer Approach to Content Analysis*. The MIT Press.

Carlo Strapparava and Rada Mihalcea. 2007. Semeval-2007 task 14: Affective text. In *Proceedings of the Fourth International Workshop on Semantic Evaluations (SemEval-2007)*. Association for Computational Linguistics, Prague, Czech Republic, pages 70–74. http://www.aclweb.org/anthology/S/S07/S07-1013.

Louis L. Thurstone. 1927. A law of comparative judgment. *Psychological review* 34(4):273.

Amy Beth Warriner, Victor Kuperman, and Marc Brysbaert. 2013. Norms of valence, arousal, and dominance for 13,915 English lemmas. *Behavior Research Methods* 45(4):1191–1207.

Demographic Inference on Twitter using Recursive Neural Networks

Sunghwan Mac Kim, Qiongkai Xu, Lizhen Qu, Stephen Wan and **Cécile Paris**

Data61, CSIRO, Australia

{Mac.Kim, Qiongkai.Xu, Lizhen.Qu, Stephen.Wan, Cecile.Paris}@data61.csiro.au

Abstract

In social media, demographic inference is a critical task in order to gain a better understanding of a cohort and to facilitate interacting with one's audience. Most previous work has made independence assumptions over topological, textual and label information on social networks. In this work, we employ recursive neural networks to break down these independence assumptions to obtain inference about demographic characteristics on Twitter. We show that our model performs better than existing models including the state-of-the-art.

1 Introduction

Social media is a popular public platform for communicating, sharing information and expressing opinions. Millions of users discuss a variety of topics such as politics or sports. Valuable insights can be obtained by analysing social media content (e.g., mining consumer preferences), and, consequently, social media data is now a valuable resource. Accordingly, social media analytics have received much attention among researchers and companies (Wan and Paris, 2014; Valdes et al., 2015; Zubiaga et al., 2016).

Inferring demographic characteristics from social media is a useful mechanism to gain a better understanding of a cohort and one's audience, and to facilitate interacting with that audience. Many researchers have studied ways to infer demographic attributes of Twitter users, such as age (Mislove et al., 2011; Mohammady Ardehaly and Culotta, 2015), gender (Filippova, 2012; Taniguchi et al., 2015), occupation (Preoţiuc-Pietro et al., 2015; Kim et al., 2016), location (Jurgens et al., 2015; Jayasinghe et al., 2016) or political preferences (Volkova et al., 2014; McCormick et al., 2015).

A common approach to infer demographic characteristics is the use of supervised classifiers trained on textual features. The main limitation of this approach is that it makes little use of the network topology. Several network embedding methods have been proposed to learn distributed dense representations for vertices in graphs: Deep-Walk (Perozzi et al., 2014) or LINE (Tang et al., 2015). While these two models can capture the topological structure of social networks, their performances are still limited, as the text features associated with vertices are not considered. For instance, text messages that Twitter users post, tweets, can offer great potential to enhance the vertex embeddings. Yang et al. (2015) proposed the Text-Associated DeepWalk (TADW) to enhance the discriminative power of the vertex embeddings by incorporating the text information into the embedding generation process. Although this matrix factorisation framework is effective on the vertex classification task, it can produce suboptimal embeddings. This is because the label information is not exploited in the unsupervised framework. More recently, Pan et al. (2016) proposed the Tri-Party Deep Network Representation (TriDNR), a method that incorporates the label information in addition to the text and topological information. However, in TriDNR, the text in a vertex is assumed to be independent of neighbour vertices. Furthermore, the two optimisation problems (learning vertex embeddings and training discriminative classifiers) are tackled separately. This is also true of TADW.

In this paper, we tackle the problem of inferring demographic characteristics from social networks as a vertex classification task on graphs. We employ recursive neural networks (RNNs) to infer three demographic attributes of Twitter users

Proceedings of the 55th Annual Meeting of the Association for Computational Linguistics (Short Papers), pages 471–477
Vancouver, Canada, July 30 - August 4, 2017. ©2017 Association for Computational Linguistics
https://doi.org/10.18653/v1/P17-2075

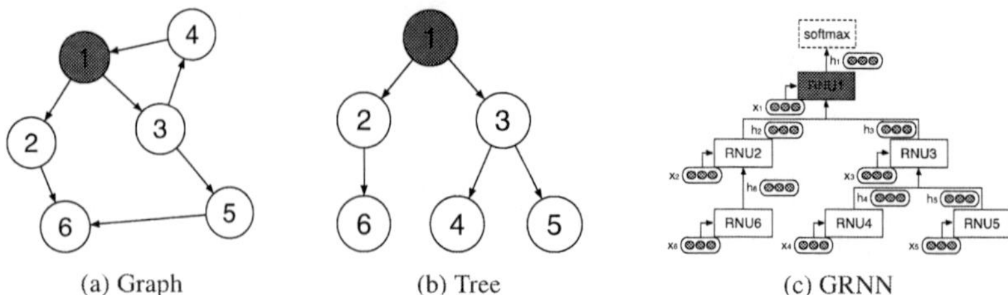

(a) Graph   (b) Tree   (c) GRNN

Figure 1: An illustration of GRNN construction steps: (a) The graph consisting of six vertices; (b) The tree converted from the graph using breadth-first search; (c) The GRNN constructed from the tree. The target vertex is marked in red.

(age, gender and user type) based on network topology, text content and label information. Our model breaks down the independence assumption by leveraging RNNs on paths in graphs. We show that our model achieves better performance compared to existing models including the state-of-the-art. While high performance is achieved using solely neural network models, more importantly, we find that different demographic inference tasks benefit to varying the topological size of RNNs. To our knowledge, there has been little previous work applying neural network based methods to the problem of inferring social media demographics.

2 Graph Recursive Neural Networks

RNNs are deep learning models that recursively compose the vector of a parent unit from those of child units over a given structure in topological order (Pollack, 1990). They have shown to be very effective for various natural language processing (NLP) tasks, capturing syntactic and semantic composition (Socher et al., 2011; Qian et al., 2015). In this section, we describe the framework of Graph RNNs (GRNNs) (Xu et al., 2017) to classify the vertices of a graph. This framework allows us to infer the demographic characteristics of social media users.

We formally define the problem of Twitter vertex classification as follows: A Twitter social network is defined as $G = (V, E)$, where V is the set of vertices (users) and E is the set of edges (relationships) between the vertices. Each edge $e \in E$ is an ordered pair $e = (v_i, v_j)$, where $v_i, v_j \in V$, that is unweighted[1] ($w_{ij} = 0$) but di-

rected ($(i, j) \not\equiv (j, i)$). Each v_i is associated with a pair of (x_i, y_i), where $x_i \in \mathcal{X}$ is a feature vector and $y_i \in \mathcal{Y}$ is a particular label that depends on x_i. $\mathcal{X}$ and $\mathcal{Y}$ thus denote a set of feature vectors and a set of possible predicted labels in G, respectively. Our goal is then to predict the most likely label $\hat{y}_t \in \mathcal{Y}$ for $v_t \in V$, which is the target vertex to be classified: $\hat{y}_t = \text{argmax}_{y_t \in \mathcal{Y}} P_\theta(y_t | v_t, G, \mathcal{X})$ using a RNN with parameters θ.

GRNNs contain five components that will be presented in this section: 1) Graph-to-Tree Conversion, 2) Word Embedding layer, 3) Recursive Neural Unit layer and 4) Softmax Output layer, as illustrated in Figure 1.

2.1 Graph-to-Tree Conversion

A graph is converted to tree structures before constructing a RNN for each tree. Specifically, we construct a tree $T = (V_T, E_T)$ of depth d rooted at v_t using a breadth-first search algorithm from G. V_T and E_T are the sets of vertices and edges in the tree. $(v, w) \in E_T$ denotes an edge from a parent vertex v to a child vertex w.

2.2 Word Embeddings

Let $S_i = \{w_1, w_2, ..., w_R\}$ be texts (e.g., tweets) consisting of R words, which are associated with a vertex v_i. Every word w_r is converted into a real-valued vector e_r by looking up the embedding matrix $E \in \mathbb{R}^{d_w |V|}$, where d_w is the size of word embedding and $|V|$ is a vocabulary size. The matrix E is initialised using the Skip-gram model (Mikolov et al., 2013). S_i is then fed into the next layer as a real-valued feature vector $x_i = \{e_1, e_2, ..., e_R\}$.

2.3 Recursive Neural Units

Once we construct a tree from a graph, we build a RNN using one of two types of recursive neural units (RNUs) for each vertex $v_k \in T$: Naive

---

[1] While the edges in the Twitter social network can be weighted (e.g., based on the importance of relationship), we only take into account an unweighted social network in this study.

Recursive Neural Unit (NRNU) and Long Short-Term Memory Unit (LSTMU).

2.3.1 Graph Naive Recursive Neural Net

Each NRNU for a vertex v_k take its feature vector x_k and a hidden state $\tilde{h}_k$ as input. Max pooling produces $\tilde{h}_k$ from all hidden state vectors h_r of the child vertices v_r of v_k.[2] A hidden state vector h_k of v_k is obtained using weight matrices, followed by a non-linear function tanh:

$$\tilde{h}_k = \max_{v_r \in C(v_k)} \{h_r\}$$
$$h_k = \tanh(W^{(h)}x_k + U^{(h)}\tilde{h}_k + b^{(h)})$$

where $C(v_k)$ is the set of child vertices of v_k ($v_r \in C(v_k)$) and h_r is a hidden state of a child vertex v_r. $W^{(h)}$ and $U^{(h)}$ are weight matrices, and $b^{(h)}$ is a bias vector for model parameters. In this paper, we refer to Graph Naive Recursive Neural Network as GNRNN incorporating NRNU as a RNU.

2.3.2 Graph Long Short-Term Memory Net

LSTMU (Hochreiter and Schmidhuber, 1997) was originally proposed to tackle a sequential labelling problem and it is able to model long-range dependencies by incorporating gated memory cells. At each time step, LSTMU takes the sequential input vector and the previous hidden state vector to produce the next hidden state. In this study, LSTMU is employed as a RNU to represent a vertex in a tree, and it naturally captures the relationships between vertices.

For a vertex v_k, LSTMU takes x_k and $\tilde{h}_k$ as input, and generates the input, forget and output gate signals, denoted as i_k, f_k and o_k respectively. It produces a memory cell state c_k and hidden state h_k with respect to a vertex v_k:

$$\tilde{h}_k = \max_{v_r \in C(v_k)} \{h_r\}$$
$$\tilde{c}_k = \tanh(W^{(c)}x_k + U^{(c)}\tilde{h}_k + b^{(c)})$$
$$i_k = \sigma(W^{(i)}x_k + U^{(i)}\tilde{h}_k + b^{(i)})$$
$$f_{kr} = \sigma(W^{(f)}x_k + U^{(f)}h_r + b^{(f)})$$
$$o_k = \sigma(W^{(o)}x_k + U^{(o)}\tilde{h}_k + b^{(o)})$$
$$c_k = i_k \odot \tilde{c}_k + \sum_{v_r \in C(v_k)} f_{kr} \odot c_r$$
$$h_k = o_k \odot \tanh(c_k)$$

where $\odot$ refers to element-wise product and σ indicates the sigmoid function. $W^{(*)}$, $U^{(*)}$ and $b^{(*)}$

---

[2]Our preliminary results demonstrated that the max pooling strategy achieved better performance than sum and average poolings.

Dataset	Gender	Age	UserType
Users $|V|$	5,367	6,482	3,017
Relationships $|E|$	5,088	6,514	38,785
Labels $|Y|$	2	2	3
Avg. degree	1.90	2.01	25.71
Num. texts	383,425	701,889	3,017
Vocab size	12,558	20,946	615

Table 1: Statistics of the three Twitter social networks. Num. texts indicates the number of tweets for Gender and Age, and the number of profile descriptions for UserType.

are LSTM parameters. We call a tree-structured network topology consisting of LSTMUs as Graph Long Short-Term Memory Net (GLSTMN).

2.4 Softmax Output

At the end, the hidden state h_t is fed into a softmax classifier to predict the label y_t of the target vertex v_t after calculating the hidden states of all vertices in T: $P_\theta(y_t|v_t, G, \mathcal{X}) = softmax(W^{(s)}h_t + b^{(s)})$
$\hat{y}_t = \text{argmax}_{y_t \in \mathcal{Y}} P_\theta(y_t|v_t, G, \mathcal{X})$.

3 Experimental Setup

In this section, we provide an overview of datasets and the models that are evaluated in the experiments.

3.1 Datasets

We evaluate the effectiveness of our model on three types of social networks: gender, age and user type classification. Twitter users follow others or are followed, and two types of relationships are used to build the social networks: *friend* and *follower*. A user is associated with others via the following relationship, the user's *friend* in Twitter's terminology. *Follower* relationships indicate that a user receives all the tweets from those the user follows.

- **Gender** (Volkova, 2014) is a Twitter social network encoding *friend* relationships between users. The labels of this network are *Male* and *Female*.

- **Age** (Volkova, 2014) is a Twitter social network encoding *friend* relationships between users. The labels of this network are *Young* (18-23 years old) and *Old* (25-30 years old).

- **UserType** (Kim et al., 2017) is a Twitter social network encoding *follower* relationships between users. The labels represent the types of Twitter users: *Individual*, *Organisation* and *other*.

To generate text features of vertices, up to 1K tweets per user are used in Gender and Age, whereas Twitter user profile descriptions are used in UserType. All words are stemmed, and then stop words and words with document frequency less than 10 are removed. The statistics of the datasets are summarised in Table 1.

3.2 Evaluated Models

We compare the GRNN model with several existing models to assess vertex classification performance.

- **Lexica (LX)** (Sap et al., 2014): a lexicon-based method produced from Twitter to calculate the scores of gender and age. These scores are used to predict their labels for users.

- **Logistic Regression (LR)** (Hosmer Jr et al., 2013): a commonly used linear model in the NLP community, only using textual contents in vertices. Bag-of-words feature vectors are generated without incorporating any topological information of a network.

- **Label Propagation (LP)** (Wang and Zhang, 2006): a graph-based semi-supervised learning model, where label probabilities are propagated to all unlabelled neighbours. The probability derivation steps are terminated for the remaining vertices when all label probabilities converge.

- **Text-Associated DeepWalk (TADW)** (Yang et al., 2015): an unsupervised vertex embedding learning method. Low-dimensional representations of vertices are induced both from their texts and graph relationships based on inductive matrix factorisation.

- **Tri-Party Deep Network Representation (TriDNR)** (Pan et al., 2016): two neural networks incorporating the texts, relationships and labels of vertices in graphs. As in TADW, unlabelled vertices are classified using Support Vector Machines (SVMs) (Cortes and Vapnik, 1995) trained on learned vertex embeddings.

3.3 Experiment Settings

In our experiments, we follow the standard experimental protocol for vertex classification task. More specifically, we evaluate classification ac-

Labelled Nodes	20%	40%	60%	80%
LX	50.72	50.35	53.29	57.37
LR	57.37	59.91	61.97	62.37
LP	55.92	60.53	60.39	61.05
TADW	53.07	50.93	54.04	51.47
TriDNR	50.99	49.56	48.03	56.58
GNRNN_d0	57.37	61.67	63.03	65.79
GNRNN_d1	57.76	61.84	63.55	66.05
GNRNN_d2	57.76	61.84	63.55	66.05
GLSTMN_d0	**58.29**	**63.68**	**64.21**	**68.16**
GLSTMN_d1	57.37	62.46	63.95	**68.16**
GLSTMN_d2	57.37	62.46	63.95	**68.16**

Table 2: Vertex classification results on Gender (e.g., GNRNN with depth 1 is represented by GNRNN_d1). Numbers in bold represent the highest performance in each column in all tables.

Labelled Nodes	20%	40%	60%	80%
LX	50.10	50.69	46.76	47.95
LR	67.75	71.15	72.97	73.70
LP	67.47	71.61	71.86	73.97
TADW	66.81	68.80	69.31	68.89
TriDNR	58.13	57.60	49.66	57.53
GNRNN_d0	72.46	74.56	74.62	74.79
GNRNN_d1	72.53	71.61	76.69	75.89
GNRNN_d2	72.46	71.98	76.14	76.44
GLSTMN_d0	73.49	74.47	75.86	77.53
GLSTMN_d1	**73.91**	**75.02**	77.93	**80.82**
GLSTMN_d2	73.43	74.65	**78.48**	80.27

Table 3: Vertex classification results on Age.

curacy[3] with different training ratios, increasing from 20% to 80%. For each training ratio, we randomly generate 5 different training datasets. For each training dataset, we run 10 trials and record the highest accuracy on each testing dataset. We then report the average accuracy for the same ratio of training datasets.

We test six different model architectures using NRNU and LSTMU with three different tree depths ($d = 0$, $d = 1$, $d = 2$). The tree depth corresponds to the number of hops between users in a social network. For all the GRNN models, the size of the hidden units is set to 200. We use Adagrad (Duchi et al., 2011) with a batch size of 20 as the optimisation method that automatically adapts the learning rate in training. The initial learning rate is set to 0.1 for LR and LP, and 0.01 for all GRNNs.

4 Results and Analysis

In this section, we present the experimental results and analysis on vertex classification for the three

---

[3] We report accuracy following previous work for Age and Gender datasets, consisting of balanced label distributions. Although UserType is imbalanced, accuracy is reported in this paper for simplicity and consistency. Previous work also reports classification accuracy for this task.

Labelled Nodes	20%	40%	60%	80%
LR	74.76	76.18	76.98	77.91
LP	73.41	74.50	75.99	75.33
TADW	72.62	75.67	76.43	75.69
TriDNR	74.90	77.91	**80.37**	**81.62**
GNRNN_d0	77.02	77.96	78.51	79.21
GNRNN_d1	73.97	77.10	78.66	79.37
GNRNN_d2	NA	NA	NA	NA
GLSTMN_d0	**77.16**	**78.63**	79.40	79.77
GLSTMN_d1	72.41	76.51	78.53	80.46
GLSTMN_d2	NA	NA	NA	NA

Table 4: Vertex classification results on UserType. NA stands for "Not Available".

networks. Numbers in bold represent the highest performance in each column in all tables.

As shown in Table 2, GNRNN and GLSTMN perform better than the evaluated models for the task of gender prediction, with no performance gain when the depth of the tree is increased. Namely, GLSTMN_d0 is the best performing model for this task. Table 3 shows that GLSTMN also achieves the best performance for age prediction. For this task, however, performance increases with the depth of the tree. For the task of user type classification, Table 4 shows that we attain the best performance with tree depth $d = 1$ for GLSTMN for the training ratio of 80%. Note that we could not train the GRNN models with tree depth 2 (GNRNN_d2 and GLSTMN_d2) on the UserType dataset on our Linux server with 64G memory due to the lack of memory. As shown in Table 1, the average degree of UserType is roughly 10 times larger than that of Gender or Age. The degree of a vertex in a graph indicates the number of edges connected to adjacent vertices. It means that the GRNN models could have approximately 625 ($= 25 \times 25$) vertices in average for the tree depth of 2. Our experiments show that a dense graph consisting of high degree vertices is intractable under the GRNN model.

Interestingly, LR and LP are effective methods for Gender and Age compared to TADW and TriDNR. In particular, TADW performs poorly on Gender, and TriDNR marginally outperforms GLSTMN on the dense social network, UserType.

To summarise, we observed four findings:

1. The GRNN models (GNRNN and GLSTMN) overall outperform the existing models by a noticeable margin in most cases (except for UserType), showing the benefit of RNNs for social network inferences on vertices.

2. The LSTM unit in GLSTMN gives superior performance over the NRN unit in GNRNN regardless of datasets. Our results are in line with other findings, showing that the LSTM works consistently better than the standard recurrent neural network.

3. GRNNs have different optimal tree depths for each demographic inference task. Tree depth does not improve inference performance for Gender, indicating that only text information is sufficient without incorporating network information. For age, tree depth allows GRNNs to be more effective although its increase does not consistently lead to better performance for GLSTMN. Similarly, tree depth increases the performance of GRNNs for UserType. We hypothesise this may be related to the nature of social interactions (e.g., Twitter users in the similar age group are more likely to interact).

4. The matrix factorisation-based methods (TADW and TriDNR) relatively work well on datasets having high degree vertices, whereas the GRNN models achieve relatively good performance on graphs containing low degree vertices.

5   Conclusions and Future Work

In this paper we tackled the demographic inference problem on Twitter as vertex classification on a graph using GRNNs, demonstrating their effectiveness against strong models for selected datasets. The RNN framework provides an effective way to incorporate network, text and label information for Twitter demographic inference. However, different demographic inference tasks benefit to varying the tree depth of GRNN models.

As our future work, we plan to employ other state-of-the-art deep learning models (Yang et al., 2016; Kipf and Welling, 2017) that vary in the nature of the dependency between network, text and label information for demographic inference to confirm the effectiveness of our proposals.

Acknowledgments

The authors are grateful to three anonymous ACL reviewers. We would also like to thank Brian Jin, who ran the data collection for this study.

References

Corinna Cortes and Vladimir Vapnik. 1995. Support-vector networks. *Machine Learning* 20(3):273–297.

John Duchi, Elad Hazan, and Yoram Singer. 2011. Adaptive subgradient methods for online learning and stochastic optimization. *Machine Learning Research* 12:2121–2159.

Katja Filippova. 2012. User demographics and language in an implicit social network. In *Proceedings of the 2012 Joint Conference on Empirical Methods in Natural Language Processing and Computational Natural Language Learning*. Association for Computational Linguistics, Jeju Island, Korea, pages 1478–1488.

Sepp Hochreiter and Jürgen Schmidhuber. 1997. Long short-term memory. *Neural Computation* 9(8):1735–1780.

David W Hosmer Jr, Stanley Lemeshow, and Rodney X Sturdivant. 2013. *Applied logistic regression*, volume 398. John Wiley & Sons.

Gaya Jayasinghe, Brian Jin, James Mchugh, Bella Robinson, and Stephen Wan. 2016. CSIRO Data61 at the WNUT geo shared task. In *Proceedings of the 2nd Workshop on Noisy User-generated Text (WNUT)*. The COLING 2016 Organizing Committee, Osaka, Japan, pages 218–226.

David Jurgens, Tyler Finethy, James McCorriston, Yi Tian Xu, and Derek Ruths. 2015. Geolocation prediction in Twitter using social networks: A critical analysis and review of current practice. In *Proceedings of the Ninth International Conference on Web and Social Media, ICWSM 2015, University of Oxford, Oxford, UK, May 26-29, 2015*. pages 188–197.

Sunghwan Mac Kim, Cécile Paris, Robert Power, and Stephen Wan. 2017. Distinguishing individuals from organisations on Twitter. In *Proceedings of the 26th International Conference on World Wide Web*. International World Wide Web Conferences Steering Committee, Perth, Australia, WWW '17, pages 805–806.

Sunghwan Mac Kim, Stephen Wan, and Cécile Paris. 2016. Occupational representativeness in Twitter. In *Proceedings of the 21st Australasian Document Computing Symposium, ADCS 2016, Caulfield, VIC, Australia, December 5-7, 2016*. pages 57–64.

Thomas N Kipf and Max Welling. 2017. Semi-supervised classification with graph convolutional networks. In *Proceedings of the International Conference on Learning Representations (ICLR)*.

Tyler H. McCormick, Hedwig Lee, Nina Cesare, Ali Shojaie, and Emma S. Spiro. 2015. Using Twitter for demographic and social science research: Tools for data collection and processing. *Sociological Methods & Research* .

Tomas Mikolov, Kai Chen, Greg Corrado, and Jeffrey Dean. 2013. Efficient estimation of word representations in vector space. *CoRR* abs/1301.3781.

Alan Mislove, Sune Lehmann, Yong-Yeol Ahn, Jukka-Pekka Onnela, and J. Niels Rosenquist. 2011. Understanding the demographics of Twitter users. In *Proceedings of the Fifth International Conference on Weblogs and Social Media, ICWSM 2011, Barcelona, Catalonia, Spain, July 17-21, 2011*. The AAAI Press, pages 554–557.

Ehsan Mohammady Ardehaly and Aron Culotta. 2015. Inferring latent attributes of Twitter users with label regularization. In *Proceedings of the 2015 Conference of the North American Chapter of the Association for Computational Linguistics: Human Language Technologies*. Association for Computational Linguistics, Denver, Colorado, pages 185–195.

Shirui Pan, Jia Wu, Xingquan Zhu, Chengqi Zhang, and Yang Wang. 2016. Tri-party deep network representation. In *Proceedings of the 25th International Joint Conference on Artificial Intelligence, IJCAI 2016, New York, NY, USA, 9-15 July 2016*. pages 1895–1901.

Bryan Perozzi, Rami Al-Rfou, and Steven Skiena. 2014. Deepwalk: Online learning of social representations. In *Proceedings of the 20th ACM SIGKDD International Conference on Knowledge Discovery and Data Mining*. ACM, New York, NY, USA, KDD '14, pages 701–710.

Jordan B. Pollack. 1990. Recursive distributed representations. *Artificial Intelligence* 46(1-2):77–105.

Daniel Preoţiuc-Pietro, Vasileios Lampos, and Nikolaos Aletras. 2015. An analysis of the user occupational class through Twitter content. In *Proceedings of the 53rd Annual Meeting of the Association for Computational Linguistics and the 7th International Joint Conference on Natural Language Processing (Volume 1: Long Papers)*. Association for Computational Linguistics, Beijing, China, pages 1754–1764.

Qiao Qian, Bo Tian, Minlie Huang, Yang Liu, Xuan Zhu, and Xiaoyan Zhu. 2015. Learning tag embeddings and tag-specific composition functions in recursive neural network. In *Proceedings of the 53rd Annual Meeting of the Association for Computational Linguistics and the 7th International Joint Conference on Natural Language Processing (Volume 1: Long Papers)*. Association for Computational Linguistics, Beijing, China, pages 1365–1374.

Maarten Sap, Gregory Park, Johannes Eichstaedt, Margaret Kern, David Stillwell, Michal Kosinski, Lyle Ungar, and Hansen Andrew Schwartz. 2014. Developing age and gender predictive lexica over social media. In *Proceedings of the 2014 Conference on Empirical Methods in Natural Language Processing (EMNLP)*. Association for Computational Linguistics, Doha, Qatar, pages 1146–1151.

Richard Socher, Eric H. Huang, Jeffrey Pennington, Andrew Y. Ng, and Christopher D. Manning. 2011. Dynamic pooling and unfolding recursive autoencoders for paraphrase detection. In *Proceedings of the 24th International Conference on Neural Information Processing Systems*. Curran Associates Inc., USA, NIPS'11, pages 801–809.

Jian Tang, Meng Qu, Mingzhe Wang, Ming Zhang, Jun Yan, and Qiaozhu Mei. 2015. Line: Large-scale information network embedding. In *Proceedings of the 24th International Conference on World Wide Web*. International World Wide Web Conferences Steering Committee, Republic and Canton of Geneva, Switzerland, WWW '15, pages 1067–1077.

Tomoki Taniguchi, Shigeyuki Sakaki, Ryosuke Shigenaka, Yukihiro Tsuboshita, and Tomoko Ohkuma. 2015. A weighted combination of text and image classifiers for user gender inference. In *Proceedings of the Fourth Workshop on Vision and Language*. Association for Computational Linguistics, Lisbon, Portugal, pages 87–93.

Jose Manuel Delgado Valdes, Jacob Eisenstein, and Munmun De Choudhury. 2015. Psychological effects of urban crime gleaned from social media. In *Proceedings of the 9th International Conference on Web and Social Media, ICWSM 2015, University of Oxford, Oxford, UK, May 26-29, 2015*. AAAI Press, Menlo Park, California, pages 598–601.

Svitlana Volkova. 2014. Twitter data collection: Crawling users, neighbors and their communication for personal attribute prediction in social media. *Center for Language and Speech Processing, Johns Hopkins University* .

Svitlana Volkova, Glen Coppersmith, and Benjamin Van Durme. 2014. Inferring user political preferences from streaming communications. In *Proceedings of the 52nd Annual Meeting of the Association for Computational Linguistics (Volume 1: Long Papers)*. Association for Computational Linguistics, Baltimore, Maryland, pages 186–196.

Stephen Wan and Cécile Paris. 2014. Improving government services with social media feedback. In *Proceedings of the 19th International Conference on Intelligent User Interfaces*. ACM, New York, NY, USA, IUI '14, pages 27–36.

Fei Wang and Changshui Zhang. 2006. Label propagation through linear neighborhoods. In *Proceedings of the 23rd International Conference on Machine Learning*. ACM, New York, NY, USA, ICML '06, pages 985–992.

Qiongkai Xu, Qing Wang, Chenchen Xu, and Lizhen Qu. 2017. Collective vertex classification using recursive neural network. *arXiv preprint arXiv:1701.06751* .

Cheng Yang, Zhiyuan Liu, Deli Zhao, Maosong Sun, and Edward Y. Chang. 2015. Network representation learning with rich text information. In *Proceedings of the 24th International Joint Conference on Artificial Intelligence*. AAAI Press, IJCAI'15, pages 2111–2117.

Zhilin Yang, William W. Cohen, and Ruslan Salakhutdinov. 2016. Revisiting semi-supervised learning with graph embeddings. In *Proceedings of the 33nd International Conference on Machine Learning, ICML 2016, New York City, NY, USA, June 19-24, 2016*. pages 40–48.

Arkaitz Zubiaga, Maria Liakata, Rob Procter, Geraldine Wong Sak Hoi, and Peter Tolmie. 2016. Analysing how people orient to and spread rumours in social media by looking at conversational threads. *PloS one* 11(3):e0150989.

Twitter Demographic Classification Using Deep Multi-modal Multi-task Learning

Prashanth Vijayaraghavan[*]
MIT
Cambridge, MA, USA
pralav@mit.edu

Soroush Vosoughi[*]
MIT
Cambridge, MA, USA
soroush@mit.edu

Deb Roy
MIT
Cambridge, MA, USA
dkroy@media.mit.edu

Abstract

Twitter should be an ideal place to get a fresh read on how different issues are playing with the public, one that's potentially more reflective of democracy in this new media age than traditional polls. Pollsters typically ask people a fixed set of questions, while in social media people use their own voices to speak about whatever is on their minds. However, the demographic distribution of users on Twitter is not representative of the general population. In this paper, we present a demographic classifier for gender, age, political orientation and location on Twitter. We collected and curated a robust Twitter demographic dataset for this task. Our classifier uses a deep multi-modal multi-task learning architecture to reach a state-of-the-art performance, achieving an F1-score of 0.89, 0.82, 0.86, and 0.68 for gender, age, political orientation, and location respectively.

1 Introduction

While the most ambitious polls are based on standardized interviews with a few thousand people, millions are tweeting freely and publicly in their own voices about issues they care about. This data offers a vibrant 24/7 snapshot of people's response to various events and topics.

However, the people using Twitter are not representative of the general US population (Greenwood et al., 2016). Therefore, if one is to use Twitter to understand the public's views on various, it is essential to understand the demographic of the users on Twitter. A robust demographic classification algorithm can also be utilized for detection of non-human account, especially in the context of bots involved in the spread of rumors and false information on Twitter (Vosoughi, 2015).

In this paper, we present a state-of-the-art demographic classifier for Twitter. We focus on four different demographic categories: (a) Gender, (b) Age, (c) Political Orientation and (d) Location. We implement different variants of the deep multi-modal multi-task learning architecture to infer these demographic categories.

2 Features

Our deep multi-modal multi-task learning models (DMT-Demographic Models) use features extracted from the users' Twitter profile (such as name, profile picture, and description), the users following network and the users historical tweets (what they have said in the past). Below, we explain how these features are extracted and used.

2.1 Name

The name specified by users in their profile is mainly used for gender prediction. We used three datasets for gender associations of common names:

- We used the data from US Census Bureau data which contains male and female[1] first names along with frequency of names for the sample male and female population with respect to 1990 census.

- We obtained yearly data for the 100 most popular female and male names between 1960 and 2010 and calculate the overall frequency of a name being used in each list.

- We also have a list of European names and popular first from other countries associated

---

[*] The first two authors contributed equally to this work.

[1] https://www2.census.gov/topics/genealogy/1990surnames/

Proceedings of the 55th Annual Meeting of the Association for Computational Linguistics (Short Papers), pages 478–483
Vancouver, Canada, July 30 - August 4, 2017. ©2017 Association for Computational Linguistics
https://doi.org/10.18653/v1/P17-2076

with gender information[2].

Using the above datasets, we associate each name with a vector of size 2 representing the probability that the name occurs in male list and female list based on frequency available in the datasets.

2.2 Following Network

Network Features can be a signal in prediction of some of the demographic parameters. But it is difficult to utilize the complete list of followers and following information of each and every user due to curse of dimensionality. Therefore, we build an binary vector of size N_{dim} for each user with each index of the vector representing a popular Twitter profiles associated with age, political orientation or location and the value (1, 0) represents if the user is following the profile or not. These profiles are short-listed based on the following techniques:

- We search for user accounts on Twitter for task specific keywords like teenager, 80s, 90s for Age prediction; Democrat, Republican for political orientation and state names for location prediction.

- We take advantage of the data collected from our earlier work (Vijayaraghavan et al., 2016) in processing news stories, classifying named entities into various categories and mapping them to Twitter handles. We use the political personalities mapped onto Twitter to the list of twitter profiles that can potentially act as a signal for our prediction tasks.

Sample Twitter handles associated with each of the tasks are given in Table 1. For gender, the handles were too generic, so we expect that there are inherent latent features that can contribute towards gender prediction based on the shortlisted Twitter handles. We experiment with one or two fully-connected layers and compress the information to a N_{emb}-sized vector.

2.3 Profile Description

The profile description can be really useful to predict all the demographic parameters. Since, GRU is computationally less expensive than LSTM and performs better than standard RNN, we use a gated recurrent network (GRU) (Cho et al., 2014; Chung et al., 2014). At each time step t, GRU unit takes a

word embedding x_t and a hidden state h_t as input. The internal transition operations of the GRU are defined as follows:

$$z_t = \sigma(W^{(z)}x_t + U^{(z)}h_{t-1} + b^{(z)}) \qquad (1)$$

$$r_t = \sigma(W^{(r)}x_t + U^{(r)}h_{t-1} + b^{(r)}) \qquad (2)$$

$$\tilde{h}_t = tanh(Wx_t + r_t \cdot U_{t-1}^h + b^{(}h) \qquad (3)$$

$$h_t = z_t \cdot h_{t-1} + (1 - z_t)\tilde{h}_t \qquad (4)$$

where $W^{(z)}, W^{(r)}, W \in \mathbb{R}^{d_h \times d_i}, U^{(z)}, U^{(r)}, U \in \mathbb{R}^{d_h \times d_h}$ and $\cdot$ is an element-wise product. The dimensions d_h and d_i are hyperparameters representing the hidden state size and input embedding size respectively. In our experiments, we represent the description as a (a) vector using GRU's final hidden state i.e. the hidden state representation (referred as $D_F \in \mathbb{R}^{d_h}$) at the last time step (b) matrix using all the time steps of hidden state, represented as $D_M \in \mathbb{R}^{L \times d_h}$, where L is the sequence length of the user description.

2.4 Profile Picture

Age and gender prediction can exploit the features extracted from profile picture. We extract dense feature representation from the image using the Inception architecture (Szegedy et al., 2015). Since we deal with multiple tasks, we experiment with two different layers ($pool_3$ and $mixed_1 0$) representations from the Inception architecture. The output vector sizes are $I_V = 2048$ and $I_M = 64 \times 2048$ respectively.

2.5 Tweets

Finally, we also use tweets for our multitask learning problem. In our experiments, we restrict it to user's recent K tweets. The list of tweets, each of which is word sequence ($S_i = [w_1^i, w_2^i, ..., w_N^i]$), are encoded using a positional encoding scheme as used in (Sukhbaatar et al., 2015). (For a more sophisticated encoding of the tweets, one can use the Tweet2Vec by Vosoughi et al. (Vosoughi et al., 2016), however the algorithm requires a massive training dataset, which might not be available to everyone) For the positional encoding scheme, the sentence representation is computed by

$$P_i = \sum_{j=1}^{N} l_j \cdot w_j^i \qquad (5)$$

---

[2]https://hackage.haskell.org/package/gender-
0.1.1.0/src/data/nam_dict.txt.UTF8

Task	Sample Twitter Handles
Age	@80s_Kidz, @The1980sGirl, @60s70sKids, @IL0VEthe80s, @90syears, @The90sLife
Pol-Orien	@realDonaldTrump, @HillaryClinton, @youngdemocrat, @GOP, @NancyPelosi
Location	@california, @UWBadgers, @UtahGov, @UMichFootball, @PureMichigan

Table 1: Sample Twitter handles used to create the network features for each task.

N is the maximum number of words in a sentence and l_j is a column vector with structure

$$l_j^p = (1 - j/N) - (p/q)(1 - 2j/N) \quad (6)$$

where p is the embedding index and q is the dimension of the embedding. The tweet representation obtained from the positional encoding summarizes the word tokens in the sentence. We explore tweet features as (1) a vector by summing up all the K-tweet embeddings $T_q \in \mathbb{R}^q$, (2) a matrix by concatenating all the K-tweet embeddings $T_{Kq} \in \mathbb{R}^{K \times q}$

3 DMT-Demographic Models

Some of the latent information from one task can be useful to predict another task. Therefore, we propose three variants of deep multi-modal multi-task learning demographic models to leverage the multi-modal nature of data. Figure 1 gives an illustration of our proposed models. In this section, we explain the single task output layer followed by the various models.

3.1 Vanilla DMT-Demographic Model

This model takes vector features extracted from various user details (explained in section 2) represented by D_F, T_q, N_{emb}, I_V for description, tweet, network and image features respectively. The feature vectors are concatenated and passed through a fully-connected layer. The output of the fully-connected layer is a compressed latent feature vector of size h. This shared latent vector is given to a task-specific output layer explained in Section 4. For gender prediction task, name features are concatenated with latent vector before feeding it to the output layer.

3.2 Attention-based DMT-Demographic Model

All the modalities do not contribute equally to each of our tasks. Hence, for each task, we concatenate the weighted modal feature representations obtained through attention mechanism and then pass it through a fully-connected layer to get

a latent feature vector. Formally, the extracted features vectors represented by D_F, T_q, N_{emb}, I_V are concatenated to get a matrix $M \in \mathbb{R}^{d \times 4}$ where d is the dimension of each feature. If the extracted features are not of the same dimension d, then we introduce a fully-connected layer and transform it to a d-sized vector. The attention over different modal features are computed as follows.

$$\alpha = softmax(W^{(2)}tanh(W^{(1)}M + b^{(1)}) + b^{(2)}) \quad (7)$$

where $\alpha \in \mathbb{R}^{1 \times d}$. We multiply each of the feature vectors by their corresponding α value to get a weighted feature representation. These weighted representation are concatenated before passing it through a fully-connected layer. The latent vector obtained from the fully connected layer is now task-specific and not shared between tasks. The latent vector is given to a task-specific output layer.

3.3 Hierarchical Attention-based DMT - Demographic Model

This model is a slight variant of the previous model. In this model, we introduce another level of attention mechanism over the extracted features. The main intuition behind this approach is to have more attention on individual features based on their importance for a task. For example, certain words like 'male','husband' in user's description might be more suitable for gender prediction than any other task. So we weigh such words higher than the other words in the description during gender prediction task. However, these weights might not be applicable for a location prediction task. Hence, we implement a hierarchical attention mechanism that has task-specific weighted feature extraction followed by task-specific attention over the modalities. The rest of the architecture is similar to the attention-based model.

This model uses the matrix representation associated with each of the features like description (D_M), tweets (T_{Kq}) and profile picture (I_M). However, the network features (N_{emb}) remain unchanged. The attention applied over the extracted features is similar to Equation 7 where the dimen-

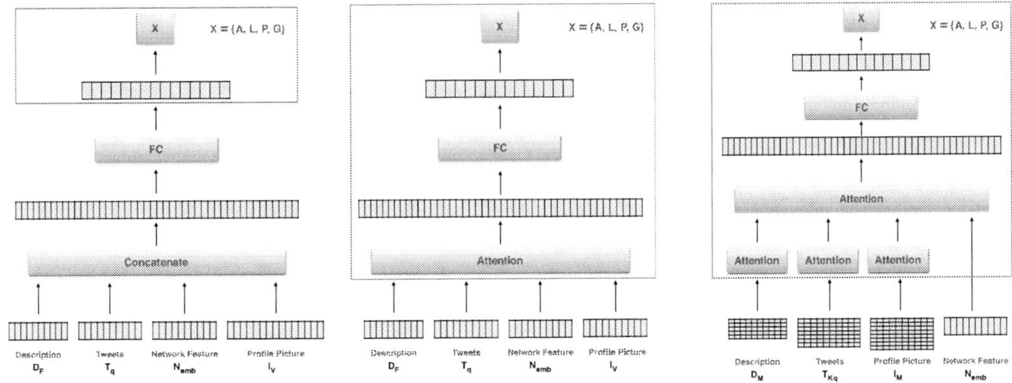

Figure 1: Illustration of variants of the DMT-Demographic Model. Left: Vanilla DMT-Demographic Model; Center: Attention-based DMT-Demographic Model; Right: Hierarchical Attention-based DMT-Demographic Model.

sions of weight parameters are feature-specific. For the sake of convenience, let $\beta^{(F)}$ be the weights similar to α associated with a feature F. For each feature F, we perform a weighted sum over the extracted representation matrix to obtain a vector representation. Let $M^{(F)}$ denote the matrix representation of an extracted feature F, then the vector representation $V^{(F)}$ of the feature F can be computed as follows.

$$V^{(F)} = \sum_{r=1}^{r_F} \beta_r^{(F)} M_r^{(F)} \qquad (8)$$

where r_F is the maximum number of rows in the representation matrix $M^{(F)}$ associated with feature F. These vector representations of all the features are fed to layers similar to attention-based DMT model.

It is important to note that all the models incorporate name features with the final latent vector representation for gender prediction task.

4 Output Layer

Given a specific task A, we feed the latent feature vector $h^{(A)}$, obtained after applying any of the explained models, to a softmax layer depending on the classification task. So the task-specific representations are fed to task-specific output layers.

$$\tilde{y}^{(A)} = softmax(W^{(A)}h^{(A)} + b^{(A)}), \quad (9)$$

where $\tilde{y}^{(A)}$ is a distribution over various categories associated with task A.

For each task A, we minimize the cross-entropy of the predicted and true distributions.

$$L^{(A)}(\tilde{y}^{(A)}, y^{(A)}) = \sum_{i=1}^{N} \sum_{j=1}^{C^{(A)}} y_i^{j(A)} log(\tilde{y}_i^{j(A)})$$

$$(10)$$

where $y_i^{j(A)}$ and $\tilde{y}_i^{j}(A)$ are the true label and prediction probabilities for task A, N denotes the total number of training samples and $C^{(A)}$ is the total number of classes associated with the task A. Thus, the parameters of our network are optimized for global objective function given by:

$$\eta = \sum_{A \in X} L^{(A)}(\tilde{y}^{(A)}, y^{(A)}) \qquad (11)$$

where X={Age, Location, Political Orientation, Gender}

5 Data Collection & Evaluation

We agglomerated data based on user tweets and their profile description. With access to Twitter API, we were able to get the timeline and profile information of a subset of users. We perform simple analysis of tweets and user description and those that contain phrases like "I'm a girl / woman / guy / man / husband / wife / mother/ father", "I am a democrat / republican / liberal / conservative" or "I support hillary / trump", "Happy 30th birthday to me","I'm 30 years old", "Born in 1980" etc. and their variants are shortlisted. These phrases act as indicators of gender, political orientation and age. For location prediction task, we used a combination of two different Twitter fields to collect

481

Task	Test Data Size	Majority Classifier (%)
Gender	9,960	53%
Age	6,580	43%
Pol-Orien	5,255	52%
Location	16,956	9%

Table 2: Task-specific details of test data.

data: (a) latitude, longitude from geo-tagged user tweets, (b) Location field in user profile information. The various categories associated with each of the tasks are: (a) Gender: M,F (b) Age: < 30, $30 - 60$, > 60 (c) Political Orientation: Democrat, Republican (d) Location: All states in USA.

In order to avoid selection bias in the dataset collected, we introduce some noise in the training set by randomly removing the terms (from tweet or description) used for shortlisting the user profile. The total size of the training set is 50,859. We evaluate our models on task-specific annotated (mechanical turk) data or data collected based on different phrase indicators from user's tweet or description that was not a part of training set. The details of the test set are given in Table 2. The macro F1-score of different DMT-Demographic models (plus two baseline non-neural network based models) on the test data can be seen in Table 3. Hierarchical-Attention model performs well ahead of the other two models for almost all the tasks. However, the performance of all the models fall flat for location prediction task. Location-specific feature augmentation can be explored to improve its performance further.

6 Related Work

The main distinctions of several of these models with DMT-Demographic models are that (a) most previous literature use only tweet content analysis to predict demographic information (Nguyen et al., 2013) while our model leverages different modals of user information including profile picture, (b) though some of the works use interesting network information they do not leverage other user details as potential signals (Colleoni et al., 2014; Culotta et al., 2015), (c) many of the models involve a lot of feature engineering like extracting location indicative words for geolocation prediction, etc. (Han et al., 2014; Sloan et al., 2015), (d) our model learns shared and task-specific layer parameters as we handle the demographic prediction

Task	Model	Macro F1
Gender	Random Forrest	0.817
	SVM	0.828
	Vanilla DMT	0.866
	Attention DMT	0.875
	Hierarchical-Attention DMT	**0.890**
Age	Random Forrest	0.724
	SVM	0.733
	Vanilla DMT	0.792
	Attention DMT	0.805
	Hierarchical-Attention DMT	**0.819**
Political Orientation	Random Forrest	0.785
	SVM	0.772
	Vanilla DMT	0.825
	Attention DMT	0.847
	Hierarchical-Attention DMT	**0.859**
Location	Random Forrest	0.668
	SVM	0.665
	Vanilla DMT	0.678
	Attention DMT	0.674
	Hierarchical-Attention DMT	**0.680**

Table 3: Task-specific Macro F1-score for different DMT-Demographic models.

problem as a multi-task learning problem using different modalities like image (profile picture), text (tweets and user description) and network features (following).

7 Conclusion

In this paper, we presented a state-of-the-art demographic classifier for identifying the gender, age, political orientation and the location of users on Twitter. We also collected and curated a novel Twitter demographic dataset and explored different variants of deep multi-modal multi-task learning architectures, settling on the Hierarchical-Attention DMT as the top performing model, achieving an F1-score of $0.89, 0.82, 0.86$, and 0.68 for gender, age, political orientation, and location respectively.

In the future, we intend to use the demographic classifier presented in this paper to study the demographic biases present on Twitter.

References

Kyunghyun Cho, Bart Van Merriënboer, Dzmitry Bahdanau, and Yoshua Bengio. 2014. On the properties of neural machine translation: Encoder-decoder approaches. *arXiv preprint arXiv:1409.1259* .

Junyoung Chung, Caglar Gulcehre, KyungHyun Cho, and Yoshua Bengio. 2014. Empirical evaluation of gated recurrent neural networks on sequence modeling. *arXiv preprint arXiv:1412.3555* .

Elanor Colleoni, Alessandro Rozza, and Adam Arvidsson. 2014. Echo chamber or public sphere? predicting political orientation and measuring political homophily in twitter using big data. *Journal of Communication* 64(2):317–332.

Aron Culotta, Nirmal Ravi Kumar, and Jennifer Cutler. 2015. Predicting the demographics of twitter users from website traffic data. In *AAAI*. pages 72–78.

Shannon Greenwood, Andrew Perrin, and Maeve Duggan. 2016. Demographics of social media users in 2016. `http://www.pewinternet.org/2016/11/11/social-media-update-2016/`. Accessed: 2017-01-07.

Bo Han, Paul Cook, and Timothy Baldwin. 2014. Text-based twitter user geolocation prediction. *Journal of Artificial Intelligence Research* 49:451–500.

Dong-Phuong Nguyen, Rilana Gravel, RB Trieschnigg, and Theo Meder. 2013. " how old do you think i am?" a study of language and age in twitter .

Luke Sloan, Jeffrey Morgan, Pete Burnap, and Matthew Williams. 2015. Who tweets? deriving the demographic characteristics of age, occupation and social class from twitter user meta-data. *PloS one* 10(3):e0115545.

Sainbayar Sukhbaatar, Jason Weston, Rob Fergus, et al. 2015. End-to-end memory networks. In *Advances in neural information processing systems*. pages 2440–2448.

Christian Szegedy, Vincent Vanhoucke, Sergey Ioffe, Jonathon Shlens, and Zbigniew Wojna. 2015. Rethinking the inception architecture for computer vision. *arXiv preprint arXiv:1512.00567* .

Prashanth Vijayaraghavan, Soroush Vosoughi, and Deb Roy. 2016. Automatic detection and categorization of election-related tweets. In *Tenth International AAAI Conference on Web and Social Media*.

Soroush Vosoughi. 2015. *Automatic detection and verification of rumors on Twitter*. Ph.D. thesis, Massachusetts Institute of Technology.

Soroush Vosoughi, Prashanth Vijayaraghavan, and Deb Roy. 2016. Tweet2vec: Learning tweet embeddings using character-level cnn-lstm encoder-decoder. In *Proceedings of the 39th International ACM SIGIR conference on Research and Development in Information Retrieval*. ACM, pages 1041–1044.

A Network Framework for Noisy Label Aggregation in Social Media

Xueying Zhan[1], **Yaowei Wang**[1], **Yanghui Rao**[1,*],
Haoran Xie[2], **Qing Li**[3], **Fu Lee Wang**[4], **Tak-Lam Wong**[2]

[1] School of Data and Computer Science, Sun Yat-sen University, Guangzhou, China
[2] Department of Mathematics and Information Technology,
The Education University of Hong Kong, Hong Kong SAR
[3] Department of Computer Science, City University of Hong Kong, Hong Kong SAR
[4] Caritas Institute of Higher Education, Hong Kong SAR
{zhanxy5, wangyw7}@mail2.sysu.edu.cn, raoyangh@mail.sysu.edu.cn,
hrxie2@gmail.com, qing.li@cityu.edu.hk, pwang@cihe.edu.hk, tlwong@eduhk.hk

Abstract

This paper focuses on the task of noisy label aggregation in social media, where users with different social or culture backgrounds may annotate invalid or malicious tags for documents. To aggregate noisy labels at a small cost, a network framework is proposed by calculating the matching degree of a document's topics and the annotators' meta-data. Unlike using the back-propagation algorithm, a probabilistic inference approach is adopted to estimate network parameters. Finally, a new simulation method is designed for validating the effectiveness of the proposed framework in aggregating noisy labels.

1 Introduction

Social media allows users to share their views, opinions, emotion tendencies, and other personal information online. It is quite valuable to analyze and predict user opinions from these materials (Wang and Pal, 2015), in which supervised learning is one of the effective paradigms (Xu et al., 2015). However, the performance of a supervised learning algorithm relies heavily on the quality of training labels (Song et al., 2015). In social media, many training data are collected via simple heuristic rules or online crowdsourcing systems, such as Amazon's Mechanical Turk (www.mturk.com) which allows multiple labelers to annotate the same object (Zhang et al., 2013). Due to the lack

---

*The corresponding author.

of quality control, it can be hard for a model to reconcile such noise in training labels.

This study aims to aggregate noisy labels by matching annotators and documents. Unlike other noisy label aggregation and integration tasks (or algorithms), such as Learning to Rank (LtR) and integrating crowdsourced labels which rely on accurate instance sources (Ustinovskiy et al., 2016) or confidence scores (Oyama et al., 2013), we only need features that can be obtained with a small cost (*i.e.*, topics). Compared with acquiring accurate instance sources or confidence scores, which is very hard, extracting topics can be done conveniently by many existing topic models. Note that label noise is not always random, as *adversarial noise* may occur in real-world environments when a malicious agent is permitted to select labels for certain instances (Auer and Cesa-Bianchi, 1998). For example, a fake annotator is purchased to promote defective goods by giving high ratings. Noisy labels in such a manner are extremely difficult to be handled (Nicholson et al., 2015). To validate the effectiveness of aggregating the aforementioned noisy labels, we propose to design a new simulation method in Section 4.

2 Related Work

To aggregate or refine noisy labels, several approaches have been proposed recently. Whitehill et al. (Whitehill et al., 2009) explored a probabilistic model to combine labels from both human labelers and automatic classifiers in image classification. Raykar et al. (Raykar et al., 2010) used a Bayesian approach for supervised learning over

484

Proceedings of the 55th Annual Meeting of the Association for Computational Linguistics (Short Papers), pages 484–490
Vancouver, Canada, July 30 - August 4, 2017. ©2017 Association for Computational Linguistics
https://doi.org/10.18653/v1/P17-2077

noisy labels from multiple annotators. Oyama et al. (Oyama et al., 2013) proposed to integrate labels of crowdsourcing workers using their confidence scores. Song et al. (Song et al., 2015) developed a single-label refinement algorithm to adjust noisy and missing labels. Ustinovskiy et al. (Ustinovskiy et al., 2016) proposed an optimization framework via remapping and reweighting methods to solve the problem of LtR with the existence of noisy labels.

Different from the previous study that modeled the difficulties of instances and the user's authority (Whitehill et al., 2009), we target at integrating multiple labels for each instance by estimating the *matching degree* of documents and annotators. Consequently, our work is applicable to aggregating individual sentiment labels in social media, where users under various scenarios (*e.g.*, character and preference) may express invalid or noisy sentiments to different topics.

3 Noisy Label Aggregation Framework

3.1 Problem Definition

The problem of noisy label aggregation is defined as follows: Given N documents (instances) annotated by M users (annotators) over C kinds of labels, we generate D topics by existing unsupervised topic models. Let $\mathbf{T} \in \mathbb{R}^{N \times D}$ be topics of all instances, where the i-th row of $\mathbf{T}$ (*i.e.*, $\mathbf{T}_i$) is the topic distribution of document i, and the size of $\mathbf{T}_i$ (*i.e.*, $|\mathbf{T}_i|$) is D. Let $\mathbf{F} \in \mathbb{R}^{M \times U}$ be features (*e.g.*, age and gender) of all annotators, where $\mathbf{F}_j$ is the feature distribution of user j and $|\mathbf{F}_j| = U$. To model different dimensions of document topics (D) and annotator features (U) jointly, we map $\mathbf{T}_i$ and $\mathbf{F}_j$ to K latent factors denoted as $\mathbf{S}_i$ and $\mathbf{A}_j$, *i.e.*, $|\mathbf{S}_i| = |\mathbf{A}_j| = K$.

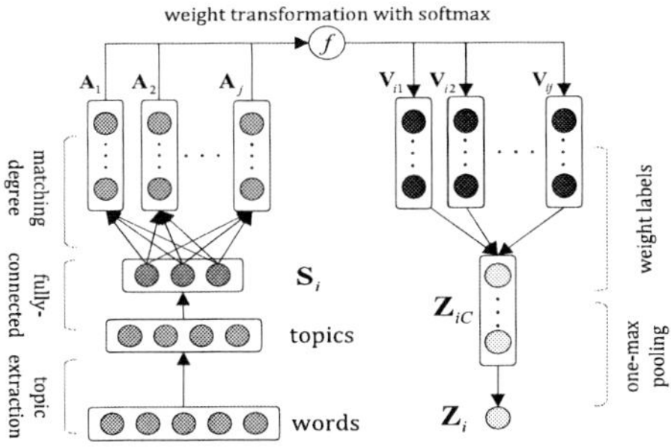

Figure 1: Our proposed network framework.

To estimate the ground truth label Z_i, we propose a novel network framework via aggregating the observable labels $\mathbf{V}_i$, as shown in Fig. 1. In our framework, the correctness of V_{ij} depends on whether annotator j *matches* document i.

3.2 Detailed Steps

Topic Extraction (TE): For document features, it is rough to use *tf* or *tf-idf* since they ignore the versatility of semantics among various contexts. Without considering the semantic units called topics, the accurate category of each document may be hard to access (Song et al., 2016). Short messages (*e.g.*, tweets) are prevalent in social media, which differ from normal documents insofar as the number of words is fewer and most words only occur once in each instance. To extract topics from such a sparse word space, we employ the Biterm Topic Model (BTM) by breaking each document into biterms and leveraging the information of the whole corpus (Yan et al., 2013).

Fully-connected Operation (FcO): There can be a large difference between dimensions of document topics and annotator features, so we need convert $\mathbf{T}$ and $\mathbf{F}$ to the same latent space. This step conducts linear transformation by introducing fully-connected weights $\mathbf{W_T} \in \mathbb{R}^{D \times K}$ and $\mathbf{W_F} \in \mathbb{R}^{U \times K}$, as follows: $\mathbf{S} = \mathbf{TW_T}$ and $\mathbf{A} = \mathbf{FW_F}$. The values of $\mathbf{S}$ and $\mathbf{A}$ are proportional to the label correctness probability.

Since more cohesive topics may indicate that the document's category is more concentrated and can be correctly annotated by more users, the topic distribution embeds key information on the document factors $\mathbf{S}$. To map $\mathbf{T}$ to $\mathbf{S}$ well, we propose the concept of *topic entropy* that acts as the constraint factor, by calculating the centralization of each document's topics: $H(d_i) = -\sum_{z=1}^{D} p(t_z|d_i) \, log_D\big(p(t_z|d_i)\big)$, where $p(t_z|d_i)$ is the probability of the z-th topic conditioned to document i, and D constrains the values ranging from 0 to 1. The lower $H(d_i)$, the higher the concentration of topics and the label correctness for document i. We thus infer the relationship between $\mathbf{S}_i$ and $H(d_i)$ as $||\mathbf{S}_i||_2 \propto 1/H(d_i)$, where $||\mathbf{S}_i||_2$ is the Euclidean norm of $\mathbf{S}_i$.

Matching Degree Calculation (MDC): This step calculates the *matching degree* of document i and annotator j, which is denoted as g_{ij} by the similarity/distance between latent factors $\mathbf{S}_i$ and $\mathbf{A}_j$. Intuitively, a basketball enthusiast j matches close to a document i that contains the "basket-ball" topic, which indicates that the "matching degree" of i and j is high with a large similarity. The inner product is used here, and it can be replaced by distance measures.

Weight Transformation (WT): We employ transformation to distinguish different scores effectively. The activation function is *sigmoid* (softmax) or *tanh*. Since most document labels are assumed to be discrete independent variables, we encode V_{ij} as a binary vector. The higher g_{ij} of a label, the closer it is to the ground truth. Namely, we should weight these labels in such a way that if a label has high g_{ij}, its weight will be increased; meanwhile, other labels should be punished. For *sigmoid* and *tanh*, the punishment is $1 - w_{ij}$ and $-w_{ij}$, respectively. Take four labels, the transformation weight w_{ij} and $V_{ij} = (1, 0, 0, 0)$ as an example, the label weight via *sigmoid* is $V_{ij}^{new} = (w_{ij}, 1 - w_{ij}, 1 - w_{ij}, 1 - w_{ij})$.

Label Weighting (LW) and One-max Pooling: The final step is to output by integrating weighted labels, where the multiplicative combination is used in aggregation, and the output is the maximum one of aggregated labels $\mathbf{Z}_{iC}$.

3.3 Parameter Estimation

Since training labels may contain noise, it is inaccurate to employ the back-propagation method which uses the error between predicted and training labels as feedback for parameter estimation. Thus, we turn the estimation of model parameters $\mathbf{W_T}$ and $\mathbf{W_F}$ into a probabilistic problem. The graphical representation is illustrated in Fig. 2.

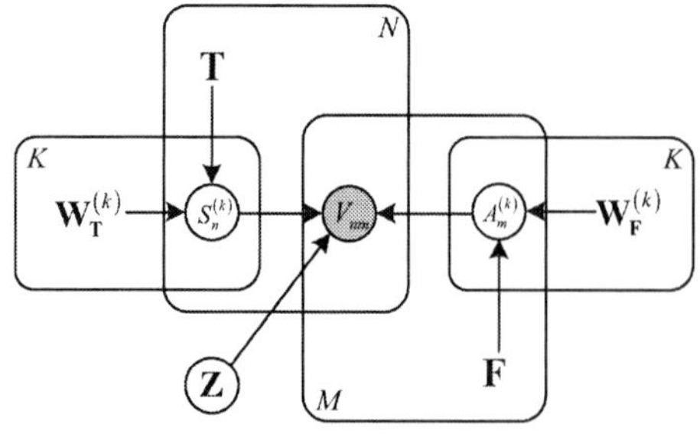

Figure 2: Probabilistic graphical representation.

Firstly, we define $\mathbf{W} = \{\mathbf{W_T}, \mathbf{W_F}\}$ for simplicity. Secondly, the parameter distribution is determined by the Maximum A Posteriori (MAP) principal: $\mathbf{W}^* = \arg\max_{\mathbf{W}} Pr(\mathbf{W}|\mathbf{V}, \mathbf{T}, \mathbf{F}) = \arg\max_{\mathbf{W}} \sum_{\mathbf{Z}} Pr(\mathbf{Z})Pr(\mathbf{W}|\mathbf{V}, \mathbf{T}, \mathbf{F}, \mathbf{Z})$.

Finally, the following Expectation Maximization (EM) algorithm is used to estimate $\mathbf{W}^*$.

Initialization: We first initialize $\mathbf{W}$ randomly. The prior of ground truth $\mathbf{Z}$ can be set to $1/C$ or the frequency of each observable label.

Expectation (E): We then compute the expectation of the joint log-likelihood of observable and hidden variables given $\mathbf{W}$ (*i.e.*, the Q function), as follows: $Q(\mathbf{W}) = E[\ln Pr(\mathbf{V}, \mathbf{Z}, \mathbf{T}, \mathbf{F}|\mathbf{W})] = E[\ln Pr(\mathbf{V}|\mathbf{Z}, \mathbf{T}, \mathbf{F}, \mathbf{W})] + E[\ln Pr(\mathbf{Z}, \mathbf{T}, \mathbf{F}|\mathbf{W})]$.

Maximization (M): According to the Q function, the maximum likelihood of hidden variables is estimated by the gradient ascent method.

Alternation: The above E and M steps are alternately performed until the likelihood converges.

4 Experiments

4.1 Datasets and Baselines

As sentiment and emotion detection are widely studied in social media analysis (Wang and Pal, 2015), we test model performance based on the Stanford Twitter Sentiment (STS) and the International Survey on Emotion Antecedents and Reactions (ISEAR) corpus. The original STS dataset (Go et al., 2009) contains 1.6 million tweets that were automatically labeled as positive or negative using emoticons as labels, in which $80K$ (5%) randomly selected tweets were used to speed up the training process, $16K$ (1%) randomly selected tweets were used as the validation set, and 359 tweets were manually annotated as the testing set (dos Santos and Gatti, 2014). ISEAR is composed of $7,666$ sentences annotated by $1,096$ participants with different culture backgrounds (Scherer and Wallbott, 1994). These participants completed questionnaires about their 34 kinds of personal information (*e.g.*, age, gender, city, country, and religion), as well as their experiences and reactions over seven emotions. For the ISEAR corpus, we randomly selected 60% of sentences as the training set, 20% as the validation set, and the remaining 20% as the testing set.

We use the following models for comparison: Majority Voting (MV) (Sheng et al., 2008), Maximum Likelihood Estimator (MLE) (Raykar et al., 2010), and Generative model of Labels, Abilities and Difficulties (GLAD) (Whitehill et al., 2009). The baselines of MV and MLE are implemented by following (Sheng et al., 2008; Raykar et al., 2010), and GLAD is run by the software that is available in public at (Whitehill et al., 2009). We also implement the multivariate version of GLAD, called MGLAD as the baseline for the ISEAR corpus with seven emotions. Although there are some more recent models on label aggregation (Oyama et al., 2013) or refinement (Song et al., 2015; Ustinovskiy et al., 2016), they either require additional features like users' reported confidence scores, or are only suitable to a corpus with one label for each document. To compare sentiment and emotion classification performance using the aggregated labels for training, we further apply the above noisy label aggregation models to a linear Support Vector Machine (SVM) with squared hinge loss (Chang and Lin, 2011). As shown in the existing studies with refined labels, the linear SVM performed well on sentiment classification of reviews (Pang et al., 2002) and tweets (Vo and Zhang, 2015).

4.2 Experimental Design

To evaluate the performance of noisy label aggregation models, each instance should be annotated by multiple users. Unlike previous studies which introduced a parameter to disturb ground truth labels (Sheng et al., 2008) or employed online crowdsourcing systems (Whitehill et al., 2009; Raykar et al., 2010) to generate noisy annotations, we design a new simulation approach by following the process of Profile Injection Attack in Collaborative Recommender Systems (Williams and Mobasher, 2006). This is because the existing methods can not assign multiple labels to each instance, or are difficult to generate virtual users and access their information ($e.g.$, age and gender). In particular, the following steps have been performed. First, we generate virtual users with different features, making them the neighbors of existing (actual) annotators. For each dimension of the actual annotators' features, we take the mean value if the attribute is continuous. For discrete attributes, we randomly select one type from the existing attribute values. If the dataset has no user features, we set it as a unit vector. Second, we generate document annotating vectors for virtual users. Each annotating vector is composed of three parts: annotating for filler instances (I_F), which is a set of randomly chosen filler instances drawn from the whole dataset, untagged instances ($I_\emptyset$), and the target instance (i_t). The purpose of setting I_F and $I_\emptyset$ is to make the virtual user looks like an ordinary annotator. We

select three simulation types from Profile Injection Attack (Williams and Mobasher, 2006), $i.e.$, random, average, and love/hate. In the random method, the label for each instance $i \in I_F$ is drawn from a normal distribution around the annotations across the whole dataset, and the probability of labeling correctly to i is $1/C$. The corresponding probabilities are 0.5 and 1 for the average and love/hate methods, respectively. In all these methods, the annotation for i_t is randomly selected from wrong labels.

We tune the number of topics D and annotator features U by performing a grid search over all D and U values, with $D \in \{2, 3, 4, ..., 10\}$ on both datasets, $U = 34$ on ISEAR, and $U \in \{1, 10, 100, 500, 1000\}$ on STS that contains user ID only. The value of K is set to the maximum of D and U. Based on the performance on the validation set, we set $D = 6, U = 1000, K = 1000$ for STS, and $D = 2, U = 34, K = 34$ for ISEAR. For the sum of $|I_F|$ and $|i_t|$ ($i.e.$, attack size) for each virtual user, we set it as the mean number of annotations in actual users. The sum of selecting i_t in each simulation is called the profile size, and the percentage of the profile size is denoted as o. Following the previous criterion of choosing the noise rate (Auer and Cesa-Bianchi, 1998), we set $o \in \{0.05, 0.1, 0.2, 0.5\}$. According to (Ustinovskiy et al., 2016), each target instance except for those in I_F is annotated by three users. Thus, the number of virtual users is set to $2oN$. We set the parameter values of MV, MLE, and M/GLAD according to (Sheng et al., 2008; Raykar et al., 2010; Whitehill et al., 2009), and apply the grid search method to obtain the optimal parameters for SVM.

4.3 Results and Analysis

Firstly, we evaluate the noisy label aggregation performance of different models by comparing the proportion of estimated labels which match the actual categories ($i.e.$, accuracy). The results are shown in Fig. 3, which indicates that our model performs the best under various conditions. From the aspect of simulation methods, the accuracy of the random one is the lowest and the Love/Hate one is the highest, which is consistent to the correctly labeling probability for each method. The results of the random and average ones over STS are similar, because $C = 2$ on STS.

Particularly, our model performs better than

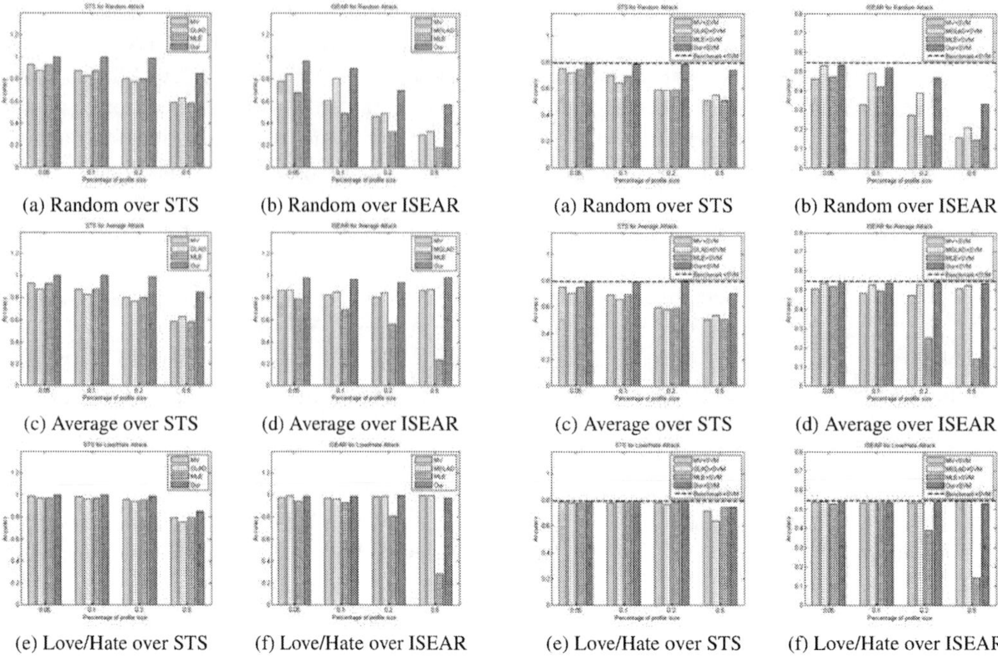

(a) Random over STS	(b) Random over ISEAR
(c) Average over STS	(d) Average over ISEAR
(e) Love/Hate over STS	(f) Love/Hate over ISEAR

Figure 3: Label aggregation performance.

(a) Random over STS	(b) Random over ISEAR
(c) Average over STS	(d) Average over ISEAR
(e) Love/Hate over STS	(f) Love/Hate over ISEAR

Figure 4: Classification performance.

baselines in aggregating noisy labels, especially when the noise scale becomes large. For instance, our model achieves 85% and 57% accuracies on STS and ISEAR when using the random method and $o = 0.5$, which indicates that our model has higher capability of recognizing adversarial noise (i_t). In the random method, we can also observe that the performance differences are more significant on ISEAR than STS. This is because ISEAR has more elaborate, $i.e.$, 34 kinds of observable user information, which validates the joint influence of users and documents on noisy label aggregation. To evaluate the performance differences statistically, we use the 12 groups of results over all methods and o values based on the conventional significance level ($i.e.$, p value) of 0.05. The p values of t-tests between our model and MV, M/GLAD, MLE are 0.0087, 0.0009, 0.0067 over STS, and 0.0535, 0.1037, 0.0007 over ISEAR, which indicates that the performance differences between our model and baselines are statistically significant on both datasets, except for MV and MGLAD in the love/hate method over ISEAR. The reason may be that each virtual user annotates around seven instances on ISEAR, and only one label is incorrect for the love/hate method, which makes the simple MV perform competitively.

Secondly, we compare the classification perfor-mance of SVM using labels from different noisy label aggregation models for training. The accuracies are shown in Fig. 4, in which dotted lines represent results on benchmark datasets without conducting the Profile Injection Attack process. Compared to other methods, the performance of SVM based on the aggregated labels from our model is almost closer to that of SVM using benchmark datasets. For the average method and $o = 0.2$ over STS, we can observe that SVM in conjunction with our model performs even better than that on the benchmark dataset. This is because emoticons are used as annotations for STS, which may introduce errors to the original labels.

5 Conclusions

In this paper, we proposed a network framework for noisy label aggregation by calculating the *matching degree* of documents and annotators. Experiments using a new simulation method of generating noisy labels validated the effectiveness of the proposed framework. As our model is linear in feature transformation, it is flexible to handle large-scale datasets. In the future, we plan to compare the model performance using different topic models, improve our model by exploiting the feedback of a small proportion of refined labels, and recruit actual participants to provide noisy labels.

Acknowledgments

The authors are thankful to the reviewers for their constructive comments and suggestions on this paper. The work described in this paper was supported by the National Natural Science Foundation of China (61502545), a grant from the Research Grants Council of the Hong Kong Special Administrative Region, China (UGC/FDS11/E03/16), the Start-Up Research Grant (RG 37/2016-2017R), and the Internal Research Grant (RG 66/2016-2017) of The Education University of Hong Kong.

References

P. Auer and N. Cesa-Bianchi. 1998. On-line learning with malicious noise and the closure algorithm. *Annals of Mathematics and Artificial Intelligence* 23(1-2):83–99.

C.-C. Chang and C.-J. Lin. 2011. LIBSVM: A library for support vector machines. *Journal of ACM Transactions on Intelligent Systems and Technology* 2(3):27:1–27:27.

C.N. dos Santos and M. Gatti. 2014. Deep convolutional neural networks for sentiment analysis of short texts. In *Proceedings of the 25th International Conference on Computational Linguistics (COLING)*. pages 69–78.

A. Go, R. Bhayani, and L. Huang. 2009. Twitter sentiment classification using distant supervision. *Cs224n Project Report* .

B. Nicholson, J. Zhang, V.S. Sheng, and Z. Wang. 2015. Label noise correction methods. In *IEEE International Conference on Data Science and Advanced Analytics (DSAA)*. pages 1–9.

S. Oyama, Y. Baba, Y. Sakurai, and H. Kashima. 2013. Accurate integration of crowdsourced labels using workers' self-reported confidence scores. In *Proceedings of the 23rd International Joint Conference on Artificial Intelligence (IJCAI)*. pages 2554–2560.

B. Pang, L. Lee, and S. Vaithyanathan. 2002. Thumbs up? sentiment classification using machine learning techniques. In *Proceedings of the Conference on Empirical Methods in Natural Language Processing (EMNLP)*. pages 79–86.

V.C. Raykar, S. Yu, L.H. Zhao, G.H. Valadez, C. Florin, L. Bogoni, and L. Moy. 2010. Learning from crowds. *Journal of Machine Learning Research* 11:1297–1322.

K.R. Scherer and H.G. Wallbott. 1994. Evidence for universality and cultural variation of differential emotion response patterning. *Journal of Personality & Social Psychology* 66(2):310–328.

V.S. Sheng, F. Provost, and P.G. Ipeirotis. 2008. Get another lable? improving data quality and data mining using multiple, noisy labelers. In *Proceedings of the 14th ACM SIGKDD International Conference on Knowledge Discovery and Data Mining (SIGKDD)*. pages 614–622.

K. Song, W. Gao, L. Chen, S. Feng, D. Wang, and C. Zhang. 2016. Build emotion lexicon from the mood of crowd via topic-assisted joint non-negative matrix factorization. In *Proceedings of the 39th International ACM SIGIR conference on Research and Development in Information Retrieval (SIGIR)*. pages 773–776.

Y. Song, C. Wang, M. Zhang, H. Sun, and Q. Yang. 2015. Spectral label refinement for noisy and missing text labels. In *Proceedings of the 29th AAAI Conference on Artificial Intelligence (AAAI)*. pages 2972–2978.

Y. Ustinovskiy, V. Fedorova, G. Gusev, and P. Serdyukov. 2016. An optimization framework for remapping and reweighting noisy relevance labels. In *Proceedings of the 39th International ACM SIGIR Conference on Research and Development in Information Retrieval (SIGIR)*. pages 105–114.

D. Vo and Y. Zhang. 2015. Target-dependent twitter sentiment classification with rich automatic features. In *Proceedings of the 24th International Joint Conference on Artificial Intelligence (IJCAI)*. pages 1347–1353.

Y. Wang and A. Pal. 2015. Detecting emotions in social media: A constrained optimization approach. In *Proceedings of the 24th International Joint Conference on Artificial Intelligence (IJCAI)*. pages 996–1002.

J. Whitehill, P. Ruvolo, T. Wu, J. Bergsma, and J.R. Movellan. 2009. Whose vote should count more: Optimal integration of labels from labelers of unknown expertise. In *Proceedings of the 23rd Annual Conference on Neural Information Processing Systems (NIPS)*. pages 2035–2043.

C.A. Williams and B. Mobasher. 2006. Thesis: Profile injection attack detection for securing collaborative recommender systems. *Service Oriented Computing & Applications* 1(3):157–170.

R. Xu, T. Chen, Y. Xia, Q. Lu, B. Liu, and X. Wang. 2015. Word embedding composition for data imbalances in sentiment and emotion classification. *Cognitive Computation* 7(2):226–240.

X. Yan, J. Guo, Y. Lan, and X. Cheng. 2013. A biterm topic model for short texts. In *Proceedings of the 22nd International Conference on World Wide Web (WWW)*. pages 1445–1456.

J. Zhang, X. Wu, and V.S. Sheng. 2013. Imbalanced multiple noisy labeling for supervised learning. In *Proceedings of the 27th AAAI Conference on Artificial Intelligence (AAAI)*. pages 1080–1085.

A ISEAR's Annotator Features

The ISEAR corpus contains 34 kinds of personal information of participants. For clarity, the total set of annotator features is given below.

- Subject's backgrounds: (1) city, (2) Country, (3) ID suffix, (4) gender, (5) age, (6) religion, (7) practising religion, (8) father's job, (9) mother's job, and (10) field of study.

- Questionnaire: (11) when did the situation or event happen? (12) how long did you feel the emotion? (13) how intense was this feeling?

- Physiological symptoms of participants: (14) ergotropic arousal, (15) trophotropic arousal, and (16) felt temperature.

- Expressive behavior and other features of participants: (17) movement behavior, (18) laughing or smiling, (19) crying or sobbing, (20) nonverbal activity, (21) paralinguistic activity, (22) verbal activity, (23) moving against people or things, aggression, (24) did you expect the situation or event that caused your emotion to occur? (25) did you try to hide or to control your feelings so that nobody would know how you really felt? (26) did you find the event itself pleasant or unpleasant? (27) would you say that the situation or event that caused your emotion was unjust or unfair? (28) did the event help or hinder you to follow your plans or to achieve your aims? (29) who do you think was responsible for the event in the first place? (30) how did you evaluate your ability to act on or to cope with the event and its consequences when you were first confronted with this situation? (31) if the event was caused by your own or someone else's behavior, would this behavior itself be judged as improper or immoral by your acquaintances? (32) how did this event affect your feelings about yourself, such as your self-esteem or your self confidence? (33) how did this event change your relationships with the people involved? and (34) the "NEUTRO" attribute.

B Noisy Label Aggregation Algorithm

In our method of noisy label aggregation as shown in Algorithm 1, the cost of calculating $\mathbf{S}$ and $\mathbf{A}$ by FcO (line 6) is linear to the number of

---

Algorithm 1 Noisy Label Aggregation

Input:
    $\mathbf{V}$: Observable labels;
    $\mathbf{F}$: Features of users;
    ω: Words of documents;
    δ: Threshold of convergence.

Output:
    Aggregated labels.

1:   $\mathbf{T} \leftarrow TE(\omega)$;
2:   Initialize parameter $\mathbf{W}$ randomly;
3:   $Q \leftarrow 0$;
4:   **repeat**
5:      $lastQ \leftarrow Q$;
6:      $\{\mathbf{S}, \mathbf{A}\} \leftarrow FcO(\mathbf{W}, \mathbf{T}, \mathbf{F})$;
7:      **for** each $i \in [1, N]$ **do**
8:        **for** each $j \in [1, M]$ **do**
9:          $g_{ij} = MDC(\mathbf{S}_i, \mathbf{A}_j)$;
10:        $V_{ij}^{new} = WT(g_{ij}, V_{ij}, sigmoid)$;
11:      **end for**
12:      $\mathbf{Z}_{iC} = LW(\mathbf{V}_i^{new})$;
13:      **end for**
14:      $Q \leftarrow \text{E-Step}(\mathbf{Z}_{iC})$;
15:      $\mathbf{W} \leftarrow \text{M-Step}(Q, \mathbf{W})$;
16: **until** $|Q - lastQ| < \delta$;
17: **return** Z_i, *i.e.*, the maximum one of $\mathbf{Z}_{iC}$.

---

instances, *i.e.*, $O(NDK)$, and the total number of users, *i.e.*, $O(MUK)$, respectively. Before the EM iteration (lines 7 to 13), it takes $O(NM(K + C))$ to weigh all labels $\mathbf{V}$. For each iteration of EM (lines 14 to 15), the optimization with stochastic gradient descent takes $O(NMC + NK + MK)$ when each user annotates all documents. Assume that our algorithm converges after t iterations ($t < 10$ in our experiments), the overall time complexity is $O(NM(K + C)t)$, which is linear to the numbers of instances and users.

C Gradient Derivation

Given the estimated value of $\mathbf{Z}_{iC}$, the Q function can be calculated by $Q(\mathbf{W}) = \sum_{ij} \mathbf{Z}_{iC} \ln V_{ij}^{new} + const$. Since the vector V_{ij}^{new} has two possible values when using *sigmoid* (*i.e.*, w_{ij} and $1 - w_{ij}$), the gradient of $\ln V_{ij}^{new}$ on parameter $W_T^{i,k}$ is $(V_{ij} - w_{ij})A_{jk}$, *i.e.*, $[w_{ij}(1 - w_{ij})]/w_{ij}A_{jk}$ and $[-w_{ij}(1 - w_{ij})]/(1 - w_{ij})A_{jk}$, respectively. Then, the gradient of Q on parameter $W_T^{i,k}$ can be derived as $\partial Q/\partial W_T^{i,k} = \sum_j \mathbf{Z}_{iC}(V_{ij} - w_{ij})A_{jk}$. Similarly, the gradient of Q on parameter $W_F^{j,k}$ is given by $\partial Q/\partial W_F^{j,k} = \sum_i \mathbf{Z}_{iC}(V_{ij} - w_{ij})S_{ik}$.

Parser Adaptation for Social Media by Integrating Normalization

Rob van der Goot
University of Groningen
`r.van.der.goot@rug.nl`

Gertjan van Noord
University of Groningen
`g.j.m.van.noord@rug.nl`

Abstract

This work explores normalization for parser adaptation. Traditionally, normalization is used as separate pre-processing step. We show that integrating the normalization model into the parsing algorithm is beneficial. This way, multiple normalization candidates can be leveraged, which improves parsing performance on social media. We test this hypothesis by modifying the Berkeley parser; out-of-the-box it achieves an F1 score of 66.52. Our integrated approach reaches a significant improvement with an F1 score of 67.36, while using the best normalization sequence results in an F1 score of only 66.94.

1 Introduction

The non-canonical language use on social media introduces many difficulties for existing NLP models. For some NLP tasks, there has already been an effort to annotate enough data to train models, e.g. named entity recognition (Baldwin et al., 2015), sentiment analysis (Nakov et al., 2016) and paraphrase detection (Xu et al., 2015). For parsing social media texts, such a resource is not available yet, although there are some small treebanks that can be used for development/testing purposes (Foster et al., 2011; Kong et al., 2014; Kaljahi et al., 2015; Daiber and van der Goot, 2016). To the best of our knowledge, the only treebank big enough to train a supervised parser for user generated content is the English Web Treebank (Petrov and McDonald, 2012). This treebank consists of constituency trees from five different web domains, not including the domain of social media.

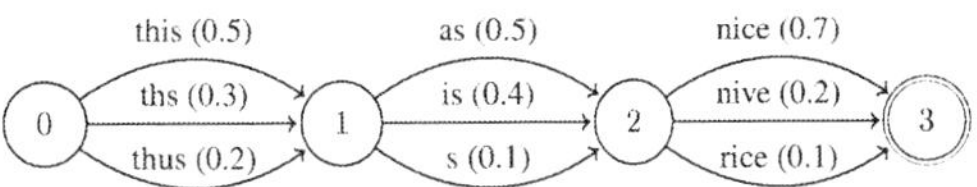

Figure 1: A possible output of the normalization model for the sentence 'ths s nice'.

The magnitude of domain adaptation problems for the social media domain becomes clear when training the Berkeley parser on newswire text, and comparing its in-domain performance with performance on the Twitter domain. The Berkeley parser achieves an F1 score above 90 on newswire text (Petrov and Klein, 2007). An empirical experiment that we carried out on a Twitter treebank shows that the F1 score drops below 70 for this domain.

Annotating a new training treebank for this domain would not only be an expensive solution, the ever-changing nature of social media makes this approach less effective over time. We propose an approach in which we integrate normalization into the parsing model. The normalization model provides the parser with different normalization candidates for each word in the input sentence. Existing algorithms can then be used to find the optimal parse tree over this lattice (Bar-Hillel et al., 1961). A possible normalization lattice for the sentence 'this is nice' is shown in Figure 1. In this example output, the probability of 'as' is higher than the probability of 'is', whereas the most fluent word sequence would be 'this is nice'. The parser can disambiguate this word graph because it has access to the syntactic context: 'is' is usually tagged as VBZ, while 'as' is mostly tagged as IN. This example shows the main motivation for using an integrated approach; the extra information from the normalization can be useful for parsing.

Proceedings of the 55th Annual Meeting of the Association for Computational Linguistics (Short Papers), pages 491–497
Vancouver, Canada, July 30 - August 4, 2017. ©2017 Association for Computational Linguistics
https://doi.org/10.18653/v1/P17-2078

2   Related Work

SANCL 2012 hosted a shared task on parsing the English Web Treebank (EWT) (Petrov and Mc-Donald, 2012). A wide variety of different approaches were used: ensemble parsers, product grammars, self/up-training, word clustering, genre classification and normalization. The teams that used normalization often used simple rule-based systems, and the actual effect of normalization on the final parser performance was not tested. Foster (2010) experiment with rule-based normalization on forum data in isolation and report a performance gain of 2% in F1 score.

A theoretical exploration of the effect of normalization on forum data is done by Kaljahi et al. (2015). They released the Foreebank, a treebank consisting of forum texts, annotated with normalization and constituency trees. They show that parsing manually normalized sentences results in a 2% increase of F1 score. Baldwin and Li (2015) evaluate the effect of different normalization actions on dependency parsing performance for the social media domain. They conclude that a variety of different normalization actions is useful for parsing.

A more practical exploration of the effect of normalization for the social media domain is done by Zhang et al. (2013). They test the effect of automatic normalization on dependency parsing by using automatically derived parse trees of the normalized sentences as reference. Other work that uses automatic normalization is Daiber and van der Goot (2016), which compare the effect of lexical normalization with machine translation on a manually annotated dependency treebank. All previous work uses only the best normalization sequence; errors in this pre-processing step are directly propagated to the parser.

For POS tagging, however, a joint approach is proposed by Li and Liu (2015). They use the n-best output of different normalization systems to generate a Viterbi encoding, based on all possible pairs of normalization candidates and their possible POS tags. Using this joint approach, they improve on both POS tagging and normalization.

3   Method

We first describe how an existing normalization model is modified for this specific use. Then we discuss how we integrate this normalization into the parsing model.

3.1   Normalization

We use an existing normalization model (van der Goot, 2016). This model generates candidates using the Aspell spell checker[1] and a word embeddings model trained on Twitter data (Godin et al., 2015). Features from this generation are complemented with n-gram probability features of canonical text (Brants and Franz, 2006) and the Twitter domain. A random forest classifier (Breiman, 2001) is exploited for the ranking of the generated candidates.

Van der Goot (2016) focused on finding the correct normalization candidate for erroneous tokens, gold error detection was assumed. Therefore, the model was trained only on the words that were normalized in the training data. Since we do not know in advance which words should be normalized, we can not use this model. Instead, we train the model on all words in the training data, including words that do not need normalization. Accordingly, we add the original token as a normalization candidate and add a binary feature to indicate this. These adaptations enable the model to learn which words should be normalized.

We compare the traditional approach of only using the best normalization sequence with an integrated approach, in which the parsing model has access to multiple normalization candidates for each word. Within the integrated approach, we compare normalizing only the words unknown to the parser against normalizing all words. We refer to these approaches as 'UNK' and 'ALL', respectively. Figure 1 shows a possible output when using ALL. When using UNK, the word 'nice' would not have any normalization candidates.

3.2   Parsing

We adapt the state-of-the-art PCFG Berkeley Parser (Petrov and Klein, 2007) to fit our needs. The main strength of this PCFG-LA parser is that it automatically learns to split constituents into finer categories during training, and thus learns a more refined grammar than a raw treebank grammar. It maintains efficiency by using a coarse-to-fine parsing setup. Unknown words are clustered by prefixes, suffixes, the presence of special characters or capitals and their position in the sentence.

Parsing word lattices is not a new problem. The parsing as intersection algorithm (Bar-Hillel et al., 1961) laid the theoretical background for ef-

---

[1] www.aspell.net

ficiently deriving the best parse tree of a word lattice given a context-free grammar. Previous work on parsing a word lattice in a PCFG-LA setup includes Constant et al. (2013), and Goldberg and Elhadad (2011) for the Berkeley Parser. However, these models do not support probabilities, which are naturally provided by the normalization in our setup. Another problem is the handling of word ambiguities, which is crucial in our model.

Our adaptations to the Berkeley Parser resemble the adaptations done by Goldberg and Elhadad (2011). In addition, we allow multiple words on the same position. For every POS tag in every position we only keep the highest scoring word. This suffices, since there is no syntactic ambiguity possible with only unary rules from POS tags to words, and therefore it is impossible for the lower scoring words to end up in the final parse tree.

To incorporate the probability from the normalization model (P_{norm}) into the chart, we combine it with the probability from the POS tag assigned by the built-in tagger of the Berkeley parser (P_{pos}) using the weighted harmonic mean (Rijsbergen, 1979):

$$P_{chart} = (1 + \beta^2) * \frac{P_{norm} * P_{pos}}{(\beta^2 * P_{norm}) + P_{pos}} \quad (1)$$

Here, β is the relative weight we give to the normalization and P_{chart} is the probability used in the parsing chart. We use this formula because it allows us to have a weighted average, in which we reward the model if both probabilities are more balanced.

4   Data

The normalization model we use is supervised, i.e. it needs annotated training data from the target domain. This is readily available for Twitter; we use 2,000 manually normalized Tweets from Li and Liu (2014) as training data.

We use the treebank from Foster et al. (2011) as develop and test data for our parser. It comprises 269 trees for developing and 250 trees for testing, all annotated using the annotation guidelines for the Penn Treebank (Bies et al., 1995) with some small adaptations for the Twitter domain (usernames, hashtags and urls are annotated as an NNP under an NP). For training, we use the English Web Treebank (EWT) concatenated with the standard training sections (2-21) of the Wall Street Journal (WSJ) part of the Penn treebank (Marcus et al., 1993).

Corpus	Sents	Words/ sent	Unk%
WSJ (2-21)	39,832	23.9	4.4
EWT	16,520	15.3	3.7
Foster et al. (2011)[*]	269	11.1	9.3
Li and Liu (2014)	2,577	15.7	14.1

Table 1: Some basic statistics for our training and development corpora. % of unknown words (Unk) calculated against the Aspell dictionary ignoring capitalization. [*]Only the development part.

Some basic statistics of our training and development data can be found in Table 1. Perhaps surprisingly, the percentage of unknown words in the EWT is lower than in the WSJ. This can be explained by the fact that the WSJ texts contains lots of jargon and named entities which are not present in the Aspell dictionary. The difference in percentage of unknown words between the normalization training data and the development treebank data might be an obstacle at first sight, but this can be overcome by tuning the weight (β) when combining the normalization and parse probabilities (Equation 1). Nevertheless, the effect of normalization will be smaller when there is less noise in the data.

5   Results

The parser is evaluated using the F1 score as implemented by EVALB[2]. All results in this section are averaged over 10 runs, using different seeds for the normalization model, unless mentioned otherwise.

The performance of our model depends on two parameters: the number of normalization candidates per word α and the weight given to the normalization β. We tuned these parameters on the development data using $\alpha \in [1\text{-}10]$ and $\beta \in [0.125, 0.25, 0.5, 1, 2, 4, 8, 16]$ to find the optimal values. The best performance is achieved using $\alpha = 6$ and $\beta = 2$. From this optimal setting, we will compare the effects of these variables for both the UNK and the ALL normalization strategies.

Figure 2 shows the effect of using different numbers of candidates and our baseline: the vanilla Berkeley parser. Using only the single best normalization sequence ($\alpha = 1$) we can obtain an improvement of 1.7% when normalizing all tokens. If we only normalize the unknown tokens

---

[2]nlp.cs.nyu.edu/evalb

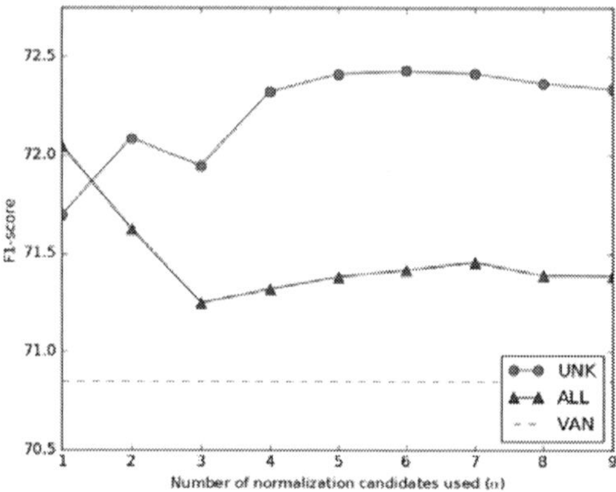

Figure 2: F1 scores on the development data when using multiple candidates while normalizing ALL words or only the UNKnown words (*beta* = 2), compared to a VANilla Berkeley parser.

the performance is slightly worse, but it still outperforms the baseline.

If we use more normalization candidates, performance increases; it converges around $\alpha = 6$. At this optimal setting, the baseline is outperformed by 2.2%. However, if more than only the first candidate is used, it is not beneficial to normalize all words anymore. This is probably an effect of creating too much distance between the original sentence and the normalization. The F1 score converges for higher number of candidates, because lower ranked candidates have very low normalization probabilities and are thus unlikely to affect the final parse.

The normalization model seldomly finds a correct candidate beyond $\alpha > 2$, at $\alpha = 2$ the recall for unknown words is 89.4% on the LexNorm corpus (Han and Baldwin, 2011), whereas the accuracy at $\alpha = 6$ is 91.7%. Perhaps surprisingly, the parser performance still improves when increasing α. Manual evaluation reveals that these improvements are obtained by using incorrect normalization candidates. Because these normalization candidates share some syntactic properties with the original word, they can still help in deriving a better syntactic parse. Figure 3 shows an example of this phenomenon; "Bono" is normalized to Bono's, and is therefore tagged as an NNS, even though this tag is still not correct, the head gets tagged correctly as NP. Combined with the normalization of "NOT", this results in a much better parse tree.

Table 2 shows the results using different

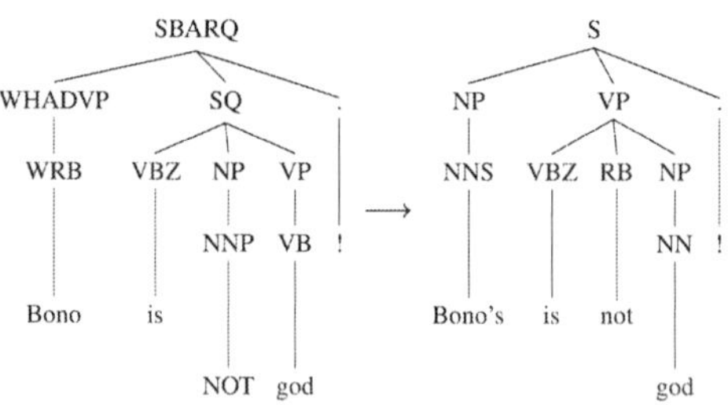

Figure 3: An example parse from the development corpus; left is the output of the vanilla Berkeley parser, right is the output with the integrated normalization.

weights. We compare the non-integrated approach ($\alpha = 1$) with the optimal number of candidates ($\alpha = 6$). The best results are achieved when β is 2, meaning that the normalization should get a higher weight than the POS tagger. The integrated model scores higher with almost all weights, the difference between ALL and UNK is similar as in Figure 2.

For the test data, we use the parameter settings that performed best on the development treebank (UNK, $\alpha = 6$, $\beta = 2$), and the best performing seed for the normalization model. The results on the test data are compared to the traditional approach of only using the best normalization sequence, the vanilla Berkeley parser, and the Stanford PCFG parser (Petrov and Klein, 2007) in Table 3. The integrated approach significantly outperforms the Berkeley parser as well as the traditional approach. It becomes apparent that the test part of the treebank is more difficult than the development part. Although the increase is smaller,

Cands(α)	1		6	
Weight(β)	UNK	ALL	UNK	ALL
0.125	70.79	71.12	70.88	69.45
0.25	70.79	71.12	70.99	62.97
0.5	70.86	71.18	71.21	70.51
1.0	71.19	71.52	71.78	71.08
2.0	**71.77**	**72.10**	**72.21**	**71.46**
4.0	71.73	72.01	72.02	71.43
8.0	71.12	71.33	71.69	71.26
16.0	70.29	70.32	70.50	70.09

Table 2: F1 scores on the development data using different weights, comparing only using the best candidate versus using 6 candidates.

Parser	dev	test
Stanford parser	66.05	61.95
Berkeley parser	70.85	66.52
Best norm. seq.	72.04	66.94
Integrated norm.	**72.77**	**67.36**[*]
Gold POS tags	74.98	71.80

Table 3: F1 scores of our proposed models and previous work on the test set, trained on the EWT and WSJ. [*]Statistical significant against Berkeley-parser at $P < 0.01$ and at $P < 0.05$ against the best normalization sequence using a paired t-test.

Parse level	Berkeley	Integrated Norm.
3	756	765
6	3,086	3,115

Table 4: The average number of constituents in the chart per sentence for the middle parsing level (3) and the final level (6) on our development set.

normalization still improves parser performance. On the development set, 46% of the errors which can be accounted to mistakes made by the POS tagger are solved, whereas on the test set, we only solve 16% of this theoretical upper bound.

6 Discussion

The addition of multiple words on one position in the chart will probably lead to less pruning in the Berkeley parser, because more constituents in the tree will have a relatively high probability. To test if performance improvements are simply an effect of less pruning, we perform two additional experiments. Firstly, we use the vanilla Berkeley parser with lower pruning thresholds[3] on the Twitter development treebank. This results in a decrease in F1 score from 70.85 to 70.64, showing that our normalization model has a different effect. Secondly, we run our proposed parsing model on the standard development part of the more canonical WSJ data (section 24). The vanilla Berkeley parser achieves an F1 score of 89.15, whereas our best performing model scores 89.12 due to over-normalization. This shows that our model does not improve performance across all domains.

To test the effect of the normalization on the search space, we simply count the number of surviving constituents in the chart in the middle and final parse level. Results can be found in Table 4. There is a slight increase in the number of constituents when using normalization. A similar effect can be found for the parsing time; averaged over 10 runs, the vanilla Berkeley parser took 24.3 seconds on the development set, whereas our

model took 24.5 seconds on the same machine.

7 Conclusion

We have shown that we can significantly improve the parsing of out-of domain data by using normalization. If we use normalization as a simple pre-processing step, we observe a small improvement in performance, while higher improvements can be achieved by using an integrated approach. Improvements in parsing performance are not only an effect of using correct normalization candidates, but are also due to wrong normalization candidates which share syntactic properties with the original word. Additionally, we show that when using only the best normalization sequence, it is better to normalize all words instead of only the unknown words. However, when using an integrated approach it is better to only consider unknown words for normalization.

Potential directions for future work include: allowing multiword replacements, normalization driven by the parsing model, and using lexicalized parsing so that the normalization candidates are used for more decisions in the parsing process than just assigning POS tags. To further improve the F1-score for the parsing of Tweets, complementary methods can be used: reranking, uptraining or ensembling parsers and grammars are some obvious next steps.

The source code of our experiments has been made publicly available [4].

Acknowledgements

We would like to thank our colleagues, especially Barbara Plank and Antonio Toral , and the anonymous reviewers for their valuable feedback. Furthermore we would like to thank Jennifer Foster for sharing the Twitter treebank. This work is part of the Parsing Algorithms for Uncertain Input project, funded by the Nuance Foundation.

---

[3]Tested by running the parser with `--accurate`. We also tried to tune the thresholds even further manually, but this had similar effects.

[4]`https://bitbucket.org/robvanderg/berkeleygraph`

References

Timothy Baldwin, Marie-Catherine de Marneffe, Bo Han, Young-Bum Kim, Alan Ritter, and Wei Xu. 2015. Shared tasks of the 2015 workshop on noisy user-generated text: Twitter lexical normalization and named entity recognition. In *Proceedings of the Workshop on Noisy User-generated Text*. Association for Computational Linguistics, Beijing, China, pages 126–135. http://www.aclweb.org/anthology/W15-4319.

Tyler Baldwin and Yunyao Li. 2015. An in-depth analysis of the effect of text normalization in social media. In *Proceedings of the 2015 Conference of the North American Chapter of the Association for Computational Linguistics: Human Language Technologies*. Association for Computational Linguistics, Denver, Colorado, pages 420–429. http://www.aclweb.org/anthology/N15-1045.

Yehoshua Bar-Hillel, Micha Perles, and Eliahu Shamir. 1961. On formal properties of simple phrase structure grammars. *Sprachtypologie und Universalienforschung* 14:143–172.

Ann Bies, Mark Ferguson, Karen Katz, Robert MacIntyre, Victoria Tredinnick, Grace Kim, Mary Ann Marcinkiewicz, and Britta Schasberger. 1995. Bracketing guidelines for Treebank II style Penn Treebank project. Technical report, University of Pennsylvania.

Thorsten Brants and Alex Franz. 2006. Web 1T 5-gram version 1. Technical report, Google.

Leo Breiman. 2001. Random forests. *Machine learning* 45(1):5–32.

Matthieu Constant, Joseph Le Roux, and Anthony Sigogne. 2013. Combining compound recognition and pcfg-la parsing with word lattices and conditional random fields. *ACM Transactions on Speech and Language Processing (TSLP)* 10(3):8.

Joachim Daiber and Rob van der Goot. 2016. The denoised web treebank: Evaluating dependency parsing under noisy input conditions. In *Proceedings of the Tenth International Conference on Language Resources and Evaluation (LREC 2016)*. European Language Resources Association (ELRA), Paris, France. http://www.lrec-conf.org/proceedings/lrec2016/pdf/86_Paper.pdf.

Jennifer Foster. 2010. "cba to check the spelling": Investigating parser performance on discussion forum posts. In *Human Language Technologies: The 2010 Annual Conference of the North American Chapter of the Association for Computational Linguistics*. Association for Computational Linguistics, Los Angeles, California, pages 381–384. http://www.aclweb.org/anthology/N10-1060.

Jennifer Foster, Özlem Çetinoglu, Joachim Wagner, Joseph Le Roux, Stephen Hogan, Joakim Nivre, Deirdre Hogan, and Josef Van Genabith. 2011. #hardtoparse: POS Tagging and parsing the Twitterverse. In *AAAI 2011 Workshop On Analyzing Microtext*. United States, pages 20–25.

Fréderic Godin, Baptist Vandersmissen, Wesley De Neve, and Rik Van de Walle. 2015. Multimedia Lab @ ACL WNUT NER shared task: Named entity recognition for Twitter microposts using distributed word representations. In *Proceedings of the Workshop on Noisy User-generated Text*. Association for Computational Linguistics, Beijing, China, pages 146–153. http://www.aclweb.org/anthology/W15-4322.

Yoav Goldberg and Michael Elhadad. 2011. Joint hebrew segmentation and parsing using a pcfgla lattice parser. In *Proceedings of the 49th Annual Meeting of the Association for Computational Linguistics: Human Language Technologies*. Association for Computational Linguistics, Portland, Oregon, USA, pages 704–709. http://www.aclweb.org/anthology/P11-2124.

Bo Han and Timothy Baldwin. 2011. Lexical normalisation of short text messages: Makn sens a #twitter. In *Proceedings of the 49th Annual Meeting of the Association for Computational Linguistics: Human Language Technologies*. Association for Computational Linguistics, Portland, Oregon, USA, pages 368–378. http://www.aclweb.org/anthology/P11-1038.

Rasoul Kaljahi, Jennifer Foster, Johann Roturier, Corentin Ribeyre, Teresa Lynn, and Joseph Le Roux. 2015. Foreebank: Syntactic analysis of customer support forums. In *Proceedings of the 2015 Conference on Empirical Methods in Natural Language Processing*. Association for Computational Linguistics, Lisbon, Portugal, pages 1341–1347. http://aclweb.org/anthology/D15-1157.

Lingpeng Kong, Nathan Schneider, Swabha Swayamdipta, Archna Bhatia, Chris Dyer, and Noah A. Smith. 2014. A dependency parser for Tweets. In *Proceedings of the 2014 Conference on Empirical Methods in Natural Language Processing (EMNLP)*. Association for Computational Linguistics, Doha, Qatar, pages 1001–1012. http://www.aclweb.org/anthology/D14-1108.

Chen Li and Yang Liu. 2014. Improving text normalization via unsupervised model and discriminative reranking. In *Proceedings of the ACL 2014 Student Research Workshop*. Association for Computational Linguistics, Baltimore, Maryland, USA, pages 86–93. http://www.aclweb.org/anthology/P14-3012.

Chen Li and Yang Liu. 2015. Joint POS tagging and text normalization for informal text. In *Proceedings of the Twenty-Fourth International Joint Conference on Artificial Intelligence, IJCAI 2015, Buenos Aires, Argentina, July 25-31, 2015*. pages 1263–1269. http://ijcai.org/Proceedings/15/Papers/182.pdf.

Mitchell P Marcus, Mary Ann Marcinkiewicz, and Beatrice Santorini. 1993. Building a large annotated corpus of English: The Penn Treebank. *Computational linguistics* 19(2):313–330.

Preslav Nakov, Alan Ritter, Sara Rosenthal, Fabrizio Sebastiani, and Veselin Stoyanov. 2016. Semeval-2016 task 4: Sentiment analysis in Twitter. In *Proceedings of the 10th International Workshop on Semantic Evaluation (SemEval-2016)*. Association for Computational Linguistics, San Diego, California, pages 1–18. http://www.aclweb.org/anthology/S16-1001.

Slav Petrov and Dan Klein. 2007. Improved inference for unlexicalized parsing. In *Human Language Technologies 2007: The Conference of the North American Chapter of the Association for Computational Linguistics; Proceedings of the Main Conference*. Association for Computational Linguistics, Rochester, New York, pages 404–411. http://aclweb.org/anthology/N07-1051.

Slav Petrov and Ryan McDonald. 2012. Overview of the 2012 shared task on parsing the web. In *Notes of the First Workshop on Syntactic Analysis of Non-Canonical Language (SANCL)*. volume 59.

CJ Rijsbergen. 1979. *Information Retrieval*, volume 2. University of Glasgow.

Rob van der Goot. 2016. Normalizing social media texts by combining word embeddings and edit distances in a random forest regressor. In *Normalisation and Analysis of Social Media Texts (NormSoMe)*. http://www.let.rug.nl/rob/doc/normsome2016.pdf.

Wei Xu, Chris Callison-Burch, and Bill Dolan. 2015. Semeval-2015 task 1: Paraphrase and semantic similarity in twitter (pit). In *Proceedings of the 9th International Workshop on Semantic Evaluation (SemEval 2015)*. Association for Computational Linguistics, Denver, Colorado, pages 1–11. http://www.aclweb.org/anthology/S15-2001.

Congle Zhang, Tyler Baldwin, Howard Ho, Benny Kimelfeld, and Yunyao Li. 2013. Adaptive parser-centric text normalization. In *Proceedings of the 51st Annual Meeting of the Association for Computational Linguistics (Volume 1: Long Papers)*. Association for Computational Linguistics, Sofia, Bulgaria, pages 1159–1168. http://www.aclweb.org/anthology/P13-1114.

AliMe Chat: A Sequence to Sequence and Rerank based Chatbot Engine

Minghui Qiu, Feng-Lin Li, Siyu Wang, Xing Gao, Yan Chen,
Weipeng Zhao, Haiqing Chen, Jun Huang, Wei Chu
Alibaba Group, Hangzhou, China
`{minghui.qmh, fenglin.lfl}@alibaba-inc.com`

Abstract

We propose *AliMe Chat*, an open-domain chatbot engine that integrates the joint results of Information Retrieval (IR) and Sequence to Sequence (Seq2Seq) based generation models. *AliMe Chat* uses an attentive Seq2Seq based rerank model to optimize the joint results. Extensive experiments show our engine outperforms both IR and generation based models. We launch *AliMe Chat* for a real-world industrial application and observe better results than another public chatbot.

1 Introduction

Chatbots have boomed during the last few years, e.g., Microsoft's XiaoIce, Apple's Siri, Google's Google Assistant. Unlike traditional apps where users interact with them through simple and structured language (e.g., "submit", "cancel", "order", etc.), chatbots allow users to interact with them using natural language, text or speech (even image).

We are working on enabling bots to answer customer questions in the E-commerce industry. Currently, our bot serves millions of customer questions per day (mainly Chinese, also some English). The majority of them is business-related, but also around 5% of them is chat-oriented (several hundreds of thousands in number). To offer better user experience, it is necessary to build an open-domain chatbot engine.

Commonly used techniques for building open-domain chatbots include IR model (Ji et al., 2014; Yan et al., 2016b) and generation model (Bahdanau et al., 2015; Sutskever et al., 2014; Vinyals and Le, 2015). Given a question, the former retrieves the nearest question in a Question-Answer (QA) knowledge base and takes the paired answer, the latter generates an answer based on a pre-trained Seq2Seq model. Often, IR models fail to handle long-tail questions that are not close to those in a QA base, and generation models may generate inconsistent or meaningless answers (Li et al., 2016; Serban et al., 2016).

To alleviate these problems, we propose a hybrid approach that integrates both IR and generation models. In our approach, we use an attentive Seq2Seq rerank model to optimize the joint results. Specifically, for a question, we first use an IR model to retrieve a set of QA pairs and use them as candidate answers, and then rerank the candidate answers using an attentive Seq2Seq model: if the top candidate has a score higher than a certain threshold, it will be taken as the answer; otherwise the answer will be offered by a generation based model (see Fig. 1 for the detailed process).

Our paper makes the following contributions:

- We propose a novel hybrid approach that uses an attentive Seq2Seq model to optimize the joint results of IR and generation models.

- We conducted a set of experiments to assess the approach. Results show that our approach outperforms both IR and generation.

- We compared our chatbot engine with a public chatbot. Evidence suggests that our engine has a better performance.

- We launched *AliMe Chat* for a real-world industrial application.

The rest of the paper is structured as follows: Section 2 presents our hybrid approach, followed by experiments in Section 3, related work is in Section 4, and Section 5 concludes our work.

2 A Seq2Seq based Rerank Approach

We present an overview of our approach in Fig. 1. At first, we construct a QA knowledge base from the chat log of our online customer service cen-

Proceedings of the 55th Annual Meeting of the Association for Computational Linguistics (Short Papers), pages 498–503
Vancouver, Canada, July 30 - August 4, 2017. ©2017 Association for Computational Linguistics
https://doi.org/10.18653/v1/P17-2079

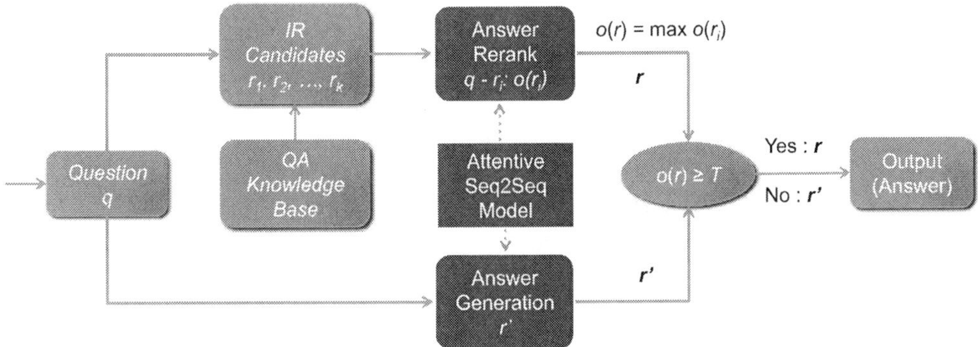

Figure 1: Overview of our hybrid approach.

ter. Based on this QA knowledge base, we then develop three models: an IR model, a generation based model and a rerank model. There are two points to be noted: (1) all the three models are based on words (i.e., word segmentation is needed): the input features of IR model are words, while those of generation model and rerank model are word embeddings, which are pre-trained using fasttext (Bojanowski et al., 2016) and further fine-tuned in the two models; (2) our generation based model and rerank model are built on the same Seq2Seq structure, the former is to generate an output while the latter is to score the candidate answers with regarding to an input question.

Given an input question q and a threshold T, the procedure of our approach is as follows:

- First, we use the IR model to retrieve a set of k candidate QA pairs $\langle q_{\mathrm{kb}_i}, r_i \rangle_{i=1}^{k}$ ($k = 10$).

- Second, we pair q with each candidate answer r_i and calculate a confidence score $o(r_i) = s(q, r_i)$ for each pair using the scoring function in Eqn. 2 of the rerank model.

- Third, we consider the answer r with the maximal score $o(r) = \max o(r_i)$: if $o(r) \geq T$, take the answer r; otherwise output a reply r' from the generation based model.

Here, the threshold T is obtained through an empirical study, to be discussed in Section 3.2.

2.1 QA Knowledge Base

We use the chat log of our online customer service center between 2016-01-01 and 2016-06-01 as our original data source (the conversations are taken between customers and staff). We construct QA pairs from conversations by pairing each question with an adjacent answer. When needed, we flatten consecutive questions (resp. answers) by concate-

nating them. After that, we filter out QA pairs that contain business related keywords. Finally, we obtained 9,164,834 QA pairs.

2.2 IR Model

Our retrieval model employs search technique to find the most similar question for each input and then obtain the paired answer. With word segmentation, we build an inverted index for the set of all 9,164,834 questions by mapping each word to a set of questions that contain that word. Given a question, we segment it into a set of words, remove stop words, extend the set with their synonyms, and use the refined set to call back a set of QA candidate pairs. We then employ BM25 (Robertson et al., 2009) to calculate similarities between the input question and the retrieved questions, and take the paired answer of the most similar one as the answer.

2.3 Generation based Model

Our generation based model is built on the attentive Seq2Seq structure (Bahdanau et al., 2015).

Let $\theta_i = \{y_1, y_2, \cdots, y_{i-1}, c_i\}$, the probability of generating a word y_i at position i is given by Eqn. 1, where f is a nonlinear function that computes the probability, s_{i-1} is the hidden state of the output at position $i - 1$, c_i is a context vector that depends on $(h_1, h_2, \cdots, h_m)$, the hidden states of the input sequence: $c_i = \sum_{j=1}^{m} \alpha_{ij} h_j$, $\alpha_{ij} = a(s_{i-1}, h_j)$ is given by an alignment model that scores how well the input at position j matches to the output at $i - 1$ (Bahdanau et al., 2015). An example is shown in Fig. 2, where $i = 3$ and $m = 4$.

$$p(y_i = w_i | \theta_i) = p(y_i = w_i | y_1, y_2, \ldots, y_{i-1}, c_i)$$
$$= f(y_{i-1}, s_{i-1}, c_i) \quad (1)$$

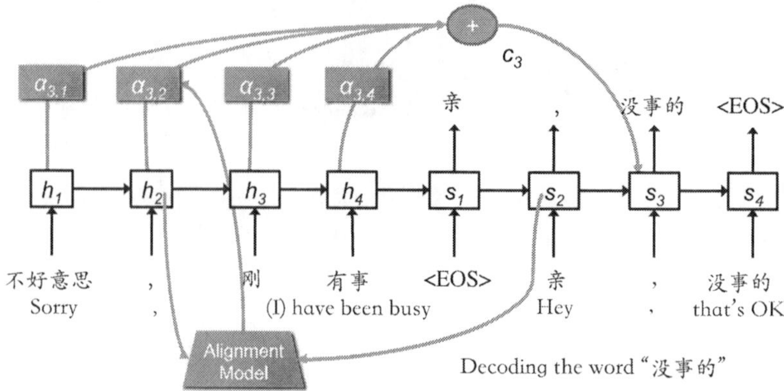

Figure 2: Attentive Seq2Seq model. Our model is mainly for Chinese.

We choose Gated Recurrent Units (GRU) as our Recurrent Neural Network (RNN) unit. A few important implementations are discussed below.

Bucketing and padding. To handle questions and answers of different lengths, we employ the bucket mechanism proposed in Tensorflow [1]. We use five buckets $(5, 5)$, $(5, 10)$, $(10, 15)$, $(20, 30)$, $(45, 60)$ to accommodate QA pairs of different length, e.g., a question of length 4 and an answer of length 8 will be put in bucket $(5, 10)$, and pad questions and answers with a special symbol "_PAD" when needed.

Softmax over sampled words. To speed up the training process, we apply softmax to a set of sampled vocabulary words (the target word and 512 random ones) rather than the whole set. The idea is similar with the importance sampling strategy in (Jean et al., 2014).

Beam search decoder. In the decode phase, we use beam search, which maintains top-k ($k = 10$) output sequences at each moment t, instead of greedy search, which keeps only one at each time t, to make our generation more reasonable.

2.4 Attentive Seq2Seq Rerank Model

Our rerank model uses the same attentive Seq2Seq model to score candidate answers with regarding to an input question. Specifically, we choose *mean probability*, denoted as $s^{\text{Mean-Prob}}$ in Eqn. 2, as our scoring function (a candidate answer is treated as a word sequence $w_1, w_2, \cdots, w_n$). We have also tried *inverse of averaged cross-entropy* and *harmonic mean*, but they had a poorer performance.

$$s^{\text{Mean-Prob}} = \frac{1}{n} \sum_{i=1}^{n} p(y_i = w_i | \theta_i) \quad (2)$$

---

[1] https://www.tensorflow.org/tutorials/seq2seq

3 Experiments

In our experiments, we first examined the effectiveness of attentive Seq2Seq model with the scoring criterion *mean probability*; we then evaluated the effectiveness of IR, Generation, IR + Rerank, IR + Rerank + Generation (our approach); we also conducted an online A/B test on our approach and a baseline chatbot engine; lastly, we compared our engine with a publicly available chatbot.

For evaluation, we have business analysts go through the answer of each testing question (two analysts for the experiment comparing with another public chatbot, and one for the other experiments), and mark them with three graded labels: "0" for unsuitable, "1" means that the answer is only suitable in certain contexts, "2" indicates that the answer is suitable. To determine whether an answer is suitable or not, we define five evaluation rules, namely "right in grammar", "semantically related", "well-spoken language", "context independent" and "not overly generalized". An answer will be labeled as suitable only if it satisfies all the rules, neutral if it satisfies the first three and breaks either of the latter two, and unsuitable otherwise.

We use top-1 accuracy (P_{top_1}) as the criterion because the output of some approaches can be more than one (e.g., IR). This indicator measures whether the top-1 candidate is suitable or neutral, and is calculated as follows: $P_{top_1} = (N_{suitable} + N_{neutral})/N_{total}$, where $N_{suitable}$ means the number of questions marked as suitable (other symbols are defined similarly).

3.1 Evaluating Rerank Models

We first compared two Seq2Seq models (the basic one proposed in (Cho et al., 2014), the attentive one presented in Section 2.4), on three scoring criteria (*mean probability, inverse of averaged cross-entropy* and *harmonic mean*) using a set of randomly sampled 500 questions. We show the P_{top_1} result in Table 1, which suggests that the attentive Seq2Seq model with $s^{\text{Mean-Prob}}$ has the best performance. We use it in our rerank model.

	IR+Rerank			IR
	$s^{\text{Mean-Prob}}$	$s^{\text{Cross-Ent}}$	s^{HM}	
Basic	0.48	0.48	0.47	0.47
Attentive	**0.54**	0.53	0.53	

Table 1: Comparison of different rerank models.

3.2 Evaluating Candidate Approaches

We then evaluated the effectiveness of the following four approaches with another set of 600 questions: IR, Generation, IR + Rerank, IR + Rerank + Generation. We present the result in Fig. 3. Clearly the proposed approach (IR + Rerank + Generation) has the best top-1 accuracy: with a confidence score threshold $T = 0.19$, $P_{top_1} = 60.01\%$. Here, questions with a score higher than 0.19 (the left of the dashed line, 535 out of 600), are answered using rerank, and the rest is handled by generation. The P_{top_1} for the other three alternatives are 47.11%, 52.02%, and 56.23%, respectively. Note that a narrowly higher P_{top_1} can be achieved if a higher threshold is used (e.g., 0.48), or, put differently, rerank less and generate more. We use the lower threshold because of the uncontrollability and poor interpretability of Seq2Seq generation: with an elegant decrease at the P_{top_1}, we gain more controllability and interpretability.

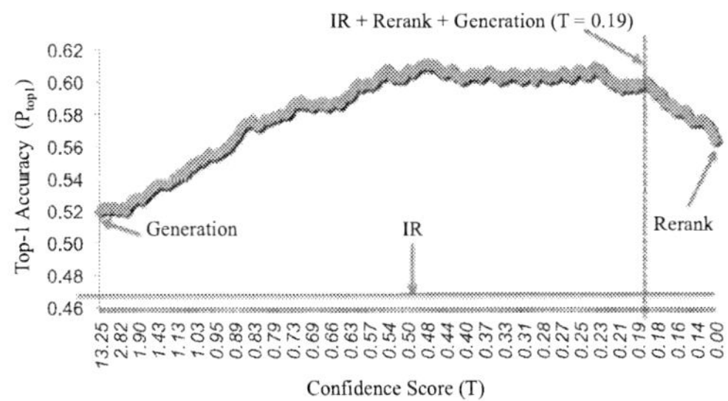

Figure 3: Top-1 accuracy of candidate approaches.

3.3 Online A/B Test

We implemented the proposed method in *AliMe Chat*, our online chatbot engine, and conducted an A/B test on the new and the existing IR method (questions are equally distributed to the two approaches). We randomly sampled 2136 QA pairs, with 1089 questions answered by IR and 1047 handled by our hybrid approach, and compared

their top-1 accuracies. As shown in Table 2, the new approach has a P_{top_1} of 60.36%, which is much higher than that of the IR baseline (40.86%).

Model	N_{total}	$N_{unsuitable}$	$N_{neutral}$	$N_{suitable}$	P_{top_1}
IR	1089	644	384	61	40.86%
Hybrid	1047	415	504	128	60.36%

Table 2: Comparison with IR model in A/B test.

3.4 Comparing with a Public Chatbot

To further evaluate our approach, we compared it with a publicly available chatbot [2]. We select 878 out of the 1047 testing questions (used in the A/B test) by removing questions relevant to our chatbot, and use it to test the public one. To compare their answers with ours, two business analysts were asked to choose a better response for each testing question. Table 3 shows the averaged results from the two analysts, clearly our chatbot has a better performance (better on 37.64% of the 878 questions and worse on 18.84%). The Kappa measure between the analysts is 0.71, which shows a substantial agreement.

	Win	Equal	Lose
Number	330	382	165
Percentage	37.64%	43.52%	18.84%

Table 3: Comparison with another chatbot.

3.5 Online Serving

We deployed our approach in our chatbot engine. For online serving, reranking is of key importance to run time performance: if k candidate QA pairs are ranked *asynchronously*, the engine has to wait for the last reranker and it will get worse when QPS (questions per second) is high. Our solution is to bundle each k QA pairs together and transform it into a $k \times n$ matrix (n is the maximal length of the concatenation of the k QA pairs, padding is used when needed), and then make use of parallel matrix multiplication in the rerank model to accelerate the computation. In our experiments, the batch approach helps to save 41% of the processing time when comparing with the *asynchronous* way. Specifically, more than 75% of questions take less than 150ms with rerank and less than 200ms with generation. Moreover, our engine is able to support a peak QPS of 42 on a cluster of 5 service instances, with each reserving 2 cores and 4G memory on an Intel Xeon E5-2430 server. This makes our approach applicable to industrial bots.

---

[2] http://www.tuling123.com/

We launched *AliMe Chat* as an online service and integrated it into *AliMe Assist*, our intelligent assistant in the E-commerce field that supports not only chatting but also customer service (e.g., sales return), shopping guide and life assistance (e.g., book flight). We show an example chat dialog generated by our chat service [3] in Fig 4

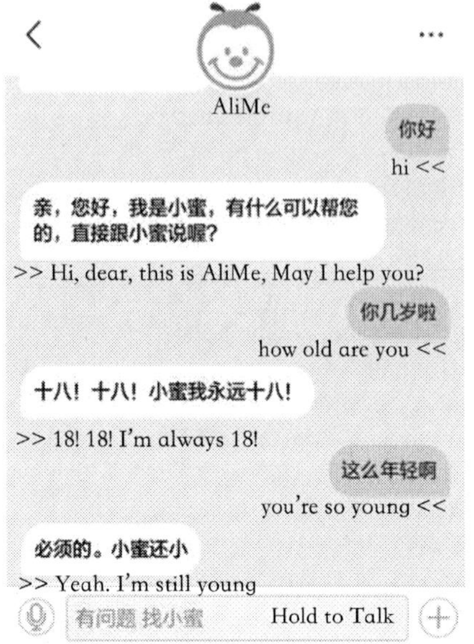

Figure 4: An example chat dialog of *AliMe Chat*.

4 Related Work

Closed-domain dialog systems typically use rule- or template- based methods (Williams and Zweig, 2016; Wen et al., 2016), and dialog state tracking (Henderson, 2015; Wang and Lemon, 2013; Mrksic et al., 2015). Differently, *open-domain* chatbots often adopt data-driven techniques. Commonly used include *IR* and *Seq2Seq generation*.

IR based techniques mainly focus on finding the nearest question(s) from a QA knowledge base for an input question, e.g., (Isbell et al., 2000), (Ji et al., 2014), (Yan et al., 2016b). A recent work (Yan et al., 2016a) has tried a neural network based method for matching. Usually, IR based models have difficulty in handling long-tail questions.

Seq2Seq based generation models are typically trained on a QA knowledge base or conversation corpus, and used to generate an answer for each input. In this direction, RNN based Seq2Seq models are shown to be effective (Cho et al., 2014;

Sutskever et al., 2014; Ritter et al., 2011; Shang et al., 2015; Sordoni et al., 2015; Serban et al., 2016). A basic Seq2Seq model is proposed in (Sutskever et al., 2014), and enhanced with attention by (Bahdanau et al., 2015). Further, Sordoni et al. (2015) considered context information, Li et al. (2016) tried to let Seq2Seq models generate diversified answers by attaching a diversity-promoting objective function. Despite many efforts, Seq2Seq generation models are still likely to generate inconsistent or meaningless answers.

Our work combines both IR based and generation based models. Our work differs from another recent combinational approach (Song et al., 2016) in that they use an IR model to rerank the union of retrieved and generated answers. Furthermore, we found that our attentive Seq2Seq rerank approach helps to improve the IR results significantly.

5 Conclusion

In this paper, we proposed an attentive Seq2Seq based rerank approach that combines both IR and generation based model. We have conducted a series of evaluations to assess the effectiveness of our proposed approach. Results show that our hybrid approach outperforms both the two models. We implemented this new method in an industrial chatbot and released an online service.

There are many interesting problems to be further explored. One is *context*, which is of key importance to multi-round interaction in dialog system. Currently, we use a simple strategy to incorporate context: given a question, if less than three candidates are retrieved by the IR model, we enhance it with its previous question and sent the concatenation to the IR engine again. We have tried other context-aware techniques, e.g. context sensitive model (Sordoni et al., 2015), neural conversation model (Sutskever et al., 2014), but they do not scale up well in our scenario. We are still exploring scalable context-aware methods. Also, we are working on *personification*, i.e., empowering our chatbot with characters and emotions.

Acknowledgments

The authors would like to thank Juwei Ren, Lanbo Li, Zhongzhou Zhao, Man Yuan, Qingqing Yu, Jun Yang and other members of Alibaba Cloud for helpful discussions and comments. We would also like to thank reviewers for their valuable comments.

---

[3]Interested readers can access *AliMe Assist* through the Taobao App by following the path "(My Taobao)→(My AliMe)".

References

Dzmitry Bahdanau, Kyunghyun Cho, and Yoshua Bengio. 2015. Neural machine translation by jointly learning to align and translate. *In Proceedings of ICLR 2015* .

Piotr Bojanowski, Edouard Grave, Armand Joulin, and Tomas Mikolov. 2016. Enriching word vectors with subword information. *arXiv preprint arXiv:1607.04606* .

Kyunghyun Cho, Bart van Merrienboer, Caglar Gulcehre, Dzmitry Bahdanau, Fethi Bougares, Holger Schwenk, and Yoshua Bengio. 2014. Learning phrase representations using rnn encoder–decoder for statistical machine translation. In *Proceedings of EMNLP*. pages 1724–1734.

Matthew Henderson. 2015. Machine learning for dialog state tracking: A review. In *Proceedings of The First International Workshop on Machine Learning in Spoken Language Processing*.

Charles Lee Isbell, Jr. Michael Kearns, Dave Kormann, Satinder Singh, and Peter Stone. 2000. Cobot in lambdamoo: A social statistics agent. In *Proceedings of the Seventeenth National Conference on Artificial Intelligence*. AAAI Press, pages 36–41.

Sébastien Jean, Kyunghyun Cho, Roland Memisevic, and Yoshua Bengio. 2014. On using very large target vocabulary for neural machine translation. *CoRR abs/1412.2007*.

Zongcheng Ji, Zhengdong Lu, and Hang Li. 2014. *An information retrieval approach to short text conversation*. arXiv preprint.

Jiwei Li, Michel Galley, Chris Brockett, Jianfeng Gao, and Bill Dolan. 2016. A diversity-promoting objective function for neural conversation models. In *the Proceedings of the NAACL HLT 2016*. pages 110–119.

Nikola Mrksic, Diarmuid Ó Séaghdha, Blaise Thomson, Milica Gasic, Pei-hao Su, David Vandyke, Tsung-Hsien Wen, and Steve J. Young. 2015. Multidomain dialog state tracking using recurrent neural networks. *CoRR abs/1506.07190*.

Alan Ritter, Colin Cherry, and William B. Dolan. 2011. Data-driven response generation in social media. In *Proceedings of EMNLP 2011*. pages 583–593.

Stephen Robertson, Hugo Zaragoza, et al. 2009. The probabilistic relevance framework: Bm25 and beyond. *FTIR* 3(4):333–389.

Iulian Vlad Serban, Alessandro Sordoni, Yoshua Bengio, Aaron C. Courville, and Joelle Pineau. 2016. Building end-to-end dialogue systems using generative hierarchical neural network models. In *the Proceedings of the Thirtieth AAAI 2016*. pages 3776–3784.

Lifeng Shang, Zhengdong Lu, and Hang Li. 2015. Neural responding machine for short-text conversation. In *the Proceedings of ACL 2015*. pages 1577–1586.

Yiping Song, Rui Yan, Xiang Li, Dongyan Zhao, and Ming Zhang. 2016. Two are better than one: An ensemble of retrieval- and generation-based dialog systems. volume abs/1610.07149.

Alessandro Sordoni, Michel Galley, Michael Auli, Chris Brockett, Yangfeng Ji, Margaret Mitchell, Jian-Yun Nie, Jianfeng Gao, and Bill Dolan. 2015. A neural network approach to context-sensitive generation of conversational responses. In *the Proceedings of NAACL HLT 2015*. pages 196–205.

Ilya Sutskever, Oriol Vinyals, and Quoc V. Le. 2014. Sequence to sequence learning with neural networks. In *the Proceedings of NIPS 2014*. pages 3104–3112.

Oriol Vinyals and Quoc V. Le. 2015. A neural conversational model. *ICML Deep Learning Workshop 2015* CoRR,abs/1506.05869.

Zhuoran Wang and Oliver Lemon. 2013. A simple and generic belief tracking mechanism for the dialog state tracking challenge: On the believability of observed information. In *the Proceedings of the SIGDIAL 2013*. pages 423–432.

Tsung-Hsien Wen, Milica Gasic, Nikola Mrksic, Lina M Rojas-Barahona, Pei-Hao Su, Stefan Ultes, David Vandyke, and Steve Young. 2016. *A network-based end-to-end trainable task-oriented dialogue system*. arXiv preprint.

Jason Williams and Geoffrey Zweig. 2016. End-to-end lstm-based dialog control optimized with supervised and reinforcement learning. Technical report.

Rui Yan, Yiping Song, and Hua Wu. 2016a. Learning to respond with deep neural networks for retrieval-based human-computer conversation system. In Proceedings of SIGIR '16, pages 55–64.

Zhao Yan, Nan Duan, Jun-Wei Bao, Peng Chen, Ming Zhou, Zhoujun Li, and Jianshe Zhou. 2016b. Docchat: An information retrieval approach for chatbot engines using unstructured documents. In *the Proceedings of ACL 2016*.

A Conditional Variational Framework for Dialog Generation

Xiaoyu Shen[1]*, Hui Su[2]*, Yanran Li[3], Wenjie Li[3], Shuzi Niu[2], Yang Zhao[4]
Akiko Aizawa[4] and Guoping Long[2]
[1]Saarland University, Saarbrücken, Germany
[2]Institute of Software, Chinese Academy of Science, China
[3]The Hong Kong Polytechnic University, Hong Kong
[4]National Institute of Informatics, Tokyo, Japan

Abstract

Deep latent variable models have been shown to facilitate the response generation for open-domain dialog systems. However, these latent variables are highly randomized, leading to uncontrollable generated responses. In this paper, we propose a framework allowing conditional response generation based on specific attributes. These attributes can be either manually assigned or automatically detected. Moreover, the dialog states for both speakers are modeled separately in order to reflect personal features. We validate this framework on two different scenarios, where the attribute refers to genericness and sentiment states respectively. The experiment result testified the potential of our model, where meaningful responses can be generated in accordance with the specified attributes.

1 Introduction

Seq2seq neural networks, ever since the successful application in machine translation (Sutskever et al., 2014), have demonstrated impressive results on dialog generation and spawned a great deal of variants (Vinyals and Le, 2015; Yao et al., 2015; Sordoni et al., 2015; Shang et al., 2015). The vanilla seq2seq models suffer from the problem of generating too many generic responses (generic denotes safe, commonplace responses like "I don't know"). One major reason is that the element-wise prediction models stochastical variations only at the token level, seducing the system to gain immediate short rewards and neglect the long-term structure. To

cope with this problem, (Serban et al., 2017) proposed a variational hierarchical encoder-decoder model (VHRED) that brought the idea of variational auto-encoders (VAE) (Kingma and Welling, 2013; Rezende et al., 2014) into dialog generation. For each utterance, VHRED samples a latent variable as a holistic representation so that the generative process will learn to maintain a coherent global sentence structure. However, the latent variable is learned purely in an unsupervised way and can only be explained vaguely as higher level decisions like topic or sentiment. Though effective in generating utterances with more information content, it lacks the ability of explicitly controlling the generating process.

This paper presents a conditional variational framework for generating specific responses, inspired by the semi-supervised deep generative model (Kingma et al., 2014). The principle idea is to generate the next response based on the dialog context, a stochastical latent variable and an external label. Furthermore, the dialog context for both speakers is modeled separately because they have different talking styles, personality and sentiment. The whole network structure functions like a conditional VAE (Sohn et al., 2015; Yan et al., 2016). We test our framework on two scenarios. For the first scenario, the label serves as a signal to indicate whether the response is generic or not. By assigning different values to the label, either generic or non-generic responses can be generated. For the second scenario, the label represents an imitated sentiment tag. Before generating the next response, the appropriate sentiment tag is predicted to direct the generating process.

Our framework is expressive and extendable. The generated responses agree with the predefined labels while maintaining meaningful. By changing the definition of the label, our framework can

*Authors contributed equally. Correspondence should be sent to H. Su (suhui15@iscas.ac.cn) and X. Shen (xshen@lsv.uni-saarland.de)

Proceedings of the 55th Annual Meeting of the Association for Computational Linguistics (Short Papers), pages 504–509
Vancouver, Canada, July 30 - August 4, 2017. ©2017 Association for Computational Linguistics
https://doi.org/10.18653/v1/P17-2080

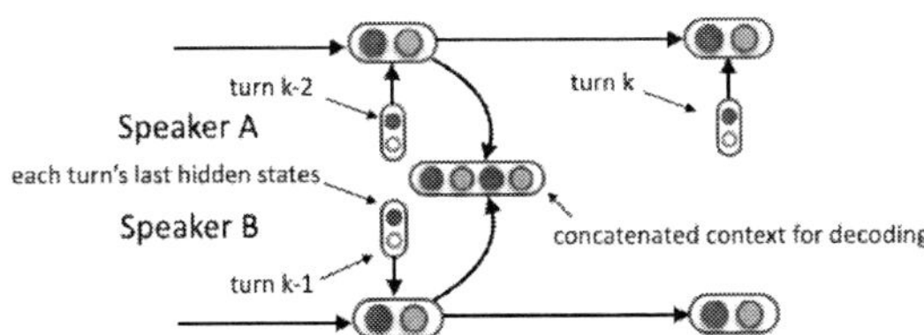

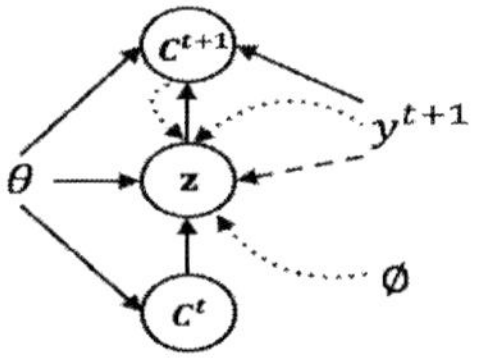

Figure 1: Computational graph for SPHRED structure. The status vector for Speaker A and Speaker B is modeled by separate RNNs then concatenated to represent the dialog context.

Figure 2: Graphical model for the conditional variational framework. Solid lines denote generative model $P_\theta(\mathbf{z}_n|\mathbf{y}_n, \mathbf{w}_1^{n-1})$ and $P_\theta(\mathbf{w}_n \mid \mathbf{y}_n, \mathbf{z}_n, \mathbf{w}_1^{n-1})$. When y^{t+1} is known, there exists an additional link from y^{t+1} to z (dashed line). C^t encodes context information up to time t. Dotted lines are posterior approximation $Q_\phi(\mathbf{z}_n|\mathbf{y}_n, \mathbf{w}_1^n)$.

be easily applied to other specific areas.

2 Models

To provide a better dialog context, we build a hierarchical recurrent encoder-decoder with separated context models (SPHRED). This section first introduces the concept of SPHRED, then explains the conditional variational framework and two application scenarios.

2.1 SPHRED

We decomposes a dialog into two levels: sequences of utterances and sub-sequences of words, as in (Serban et al., 2016). Let $\mathbf{w}_1, \ldots, \mathbf{w}_N$ be a dialog with N utterances, where $\mathbf{w}_n = (w_{n,1}, \ldots, w_{n,M_n})$ is the n-th utterance. The probability distribution of the utterance sequence factorizes as:

$$\prod_{n=1}^{N} \prod_{m=1}^{M_n} P_\theta(\mathbf{w}_{m,n}|\mathbf{w}_{m,<n}, \mathbf{w}_{<n}) \qquad (1)$$

where θ represents the model parameters and $\mathbf{w}_{<n}$ encodes the dialog context until step n.

If we model the dialog context through a single recurrent neural network (RNN), it can only represent a general dialog state in common but fail to capture the respective status for different speakers. This is inapplicable when we want to infer implicit personal attributes from it and use them to influence the sampling process of the latent variable, as we will see in Section 2.4. Therefore, we model the dialog status for both speakers separately. As displayed in Figure 1, SPHRED contains an encoder RNN of tokens and two status RNNs of utterances, each for one speaker. When modeling turn k in a dialog, each status RNN takes as input the last encoder RNN state of turn $k - 2$. The

higher-level context vector is the concatenation of both status vectors.

We will show later that SPHRED not only well keeps individual features, but also provides a better holistic representation for the response decoder than normal HRED.

2.2 Conditional Variational Framework

VAEs have been used for text generation in (Bowman et al., 2015; Semeniuta et al., 2017), where texts are synthesized from latent variables. Starting from this idea, we assume every utterance $\mathbf{w}_n$ comes with a corresponding label $\mathbf{y}_n$ and latent variable $\mathbf{z}_n$. The generation of $\mathbf{z}_n$ and $\mathbf{w}_n$ are conditioned on the dialog context provided by SPHRED, and this additional class label $\mathbf{y}_n$. This includes 2 situations, where the label of the next sequence is known (like for Scenario 1 in Section 2.3) or not (Section 2.4). For each utterance, the latent variable $\mathbf{z}_n$ is first sampled from a prior distribution. The whole dialog can be explained by the generative process:

$$P_\theta(\mathbf{z}_n|\mathbf{y_n}, \mathbf{w}_1^{n-1}) = \mathcal{N}(\boldsymbol{\mu}_{\text{prior}}, \Sigma_{\text{prior}}) \qquad (2)$$

$$P_\theta(\mathbf{w}_n \mid \mathbf{y}_n, \mathbf{z}_n, \mathbf{w}_1^{n-1}) =$$
$$\prod_{m=1}^{M_n} P_\theta(w_{n,m} \mid \mathbf{y}_n, \mathbf{z}_n, \mathbf{w}_1^{n-1}, w_{n,1}^{n,m-1}) \qquad (3)$$

When the label $\mathbf{y}_n$ is unknown, a suitable classifier is implemented to first predict it from the context vector. This classifier can be designed as, but not restricted to, multilayer perceptrons (MLP) or support vector machines (SVM).

Similarly, the posterior distribution of $\mathbf{z}_n$ is approximated as in Equation 4, where the context and label of the next utterance is provided. The graphical model is depicted in Figure 2.

$$Q_\phi(\mathbf{z}_n|\mathbf{y}_n, \mathbf{w}_1^n) = \mathcal{N}(\boldsymbol{\mu}_{\text{posterior}}, \Sigma_{\text{posterior}}) \quad (4)$$

The training objective is derived as in Formula 5, which is a lower bound of the logarithm of the sequence probability. When the label is to be predicted ($\bar{\mathbf{y}}_n$), an additional classification loss (first term) is added such that the distribution $q_\phi(\mathbf{y}_n|\mathbf{w}_1^{n-1})$ can be learned together with other parameters.

$$\log P_\theta(\mathbf{w}_1, \ldots, \mathbf{w}_N) \geq \mathbb{E}_{p(\mathbf{w}_n, \mathbf{y}_n)}\left[q_\phi(\mathbf{y}_n|\mathbf{w}_1^{n-1})\right]$$
$$- \sum_{n=1}^{N} \text{KL}\left[Q_\psi(\mathbf{z}_n \mid \mathbf{w}_1^n, \mathbf{y}_n) \| P_\theta(\mathbf{z}_n \mid \mathbf{w}_1^{n-1}, \bar{\mathbf{y}}_n)\right]$$
$$+ \mathbb{E}_{Q_\psi(\mathbf{z}_n|\mathbf{w}_1^n, \mathbf{y}_n)}[\log P_\theta(\mathbf{w}_n \mid \mathbf{z}_n, \mathbf{w}_1^{n-1}, \mathbf{y}_n)]$$
$$(5)$$

2.3 Scenario 1

A major focus in the current research is to avoid generating generic responses, so in the first scenario, we let the label $\mathbf{y}$ indicate whether the corresponding sequence is a generic response, where $y = 1$ if the sequence is generic and $y = 0$ otherwise. To acquire these labels, we manually constructed a list of generic phrases like "I have no idea", "I don't know", etc. Sequences containing any one of such phrases are defined as generic, which in total constitute around 2 percent of the whole corpus. At test time, if the label is fixed as 0, we expect the generated response should mostly belong to the non-generic class.

No prediction is needed, thus the training cost does not contain the first item in Formula 5. This scenario is designed to demonstrate our framework can explicitly control which class of responses to generate by assigning corresponding values to the label.

2.4 Scenario 2

In the second scenario, we experiment with assigning imitated sentiment tags to generated responses. The personal sentiment is simulated by appending :), :(or :P at the end of each utterance, representing positive, negative or neutral sentiment respectively. For example, if we append ":)" to the original "OK", the resulting "OK :)" becomes positive. The initial utterance of every speaker is randomly tagged. We consider two rules for the tags of next utterances. Rule 1 confines the sentiment tag to stay constant for both

speakers. Rule 2 assigns the sentiment tag of next utterance as the average of the preceding two ones. Namely, if one is positive and the other is negative, the next response would be neutral.

The label $\mathbf{y}$ represents the sentiment tag, which is unknown at test time and needs to be predicted from the context. The probability $q_\phi(\mathbf{y}_n|\mathbf{w}_1^{n-1})$ is modeled by feedforward neural networks. This scenario is designed to demonstrate our framework can successfully learn the manually defined rules to predict the proper label and decode responses conforming to this label.

3 Experiments

We conducted our experiments on the Ubuntu dialog Corpus (Lowe et al., 2015), which contains about 500,000 multi-turn dialogs. The vocabulary was set as the most frequent 20,000 words. All the letters are transferred to lowercase and the Out-of-Vocabulary (OOV) words were preprocessed as <unk> tokens.

3.1 Training Procedures

Model hyperparameters were set the same as in VHRED model except that we reduced by half the context RNN dimension. The encoder, context and decoder RNNs all make use of the Gated Recurrent Unit (GRU) structure (Cho et al., 2014). Labels were mapped to embeddings with size 100 and word vectors were initialized with the pubic Word2Vec embeddings trained on the Google News Corpus[1]. Following (Bowman et al., 2015), 25% of the words in the decoder were randomly dropped. We multiplied the KL divergence and classification error by a scalar which starts from zero and gradually increases so that the training would initially focus on the stochastic latent variables. At test time, we outputted responses using beam search with beam size set to 5 (Graves, 2012) and <unk> tokens were prevented from being generated. We implemented all the models with the open-sourced Python library Tensorflow (Abadi et al., 2016) and optimized using the Adam optimizer (Kingma and Ba, 2014). Dialogs are cut into set of slices with each slice containing 80 words then fed into the GPU memory. All models were trained with batch size 128. We use the learning rate 0.0001 for our framework and 0.0002 for other models. Every model is tested on the val-

---

[1] https://code.google.com/archive/p/word2vec/

idation dataset once every epoch and stops until it gains nothing more within 5 more epochs.

3.2 Evaluation

Accurate automatic evaluation of dialog generation is difficult (Galley et al., 2015; Pietquin and Hastie, 2013). In our experiment, we conducted three embedding-based evaluations (average, greedy and extrema) (Liu et al., 2016) on all our models, which map responses into vector space and compute the cosine similarity. Though not necessarily accurate, the embedding-based metrics can to a large extent measure the semantic similarity and test the ability of successfully generating a response sharing a similar topic with the golden answer. The results of a GRU language model (LM), HRED and VHRED were also provided for comparison. For the two scenarios of our framework, we further measured the percentage of generated responses matching the correct labels (accuracy). In (Liu et al., 2016), current popular metrics are shown to be not well correlated with human judgements. Therefore, we also carried out a human evaluation. 100 examples were randomly sampled from the test dataset. The generated responses from the models were shuffled and randomly distributed to 5 volunteers[2]. People were requested to give a binary score to the response from 3 aspects, grammaticality, coherence with history context and diversity. Every response was evaluated 3 times and the result agreed by most people was adopted.

3.3 Results of Metric-based Evaluation

As can be seen from Table 1, SPHRED outperforms both HRED and LM over all the three embedding-based metrics. This implies separating the single-line context RNN into two independent parts can actually lead to a better context representation. It is worth mentioning the size of context RNN hidden states in SPHRED is only half of that in HRED, but it still behaves better with fewer parameters. Hence it is reasonable to apply this context information to our framework.

The last 4 rows in Table 1 display the results of our framework applied in two scenarios mentioned in Section 2.3 and 2.4. SCENE1-A and SCENE1-B correspond to Scenario 1 with the label fixed as 1 and 0. 90.9% of generated responses

---

[2] All volunteers are well-educated students who have received a Bachelor's degree on computer science or above.

in SCENE1-A are generic and 86.9% in SCENE1-B are non-generic according to the manually-built rule, which verified the proper effect of the label. SCENE2-A and SCENE2-B correspond to rule 1 and 2 in Scenario 2. Both successfully predict the sentiment with very minor mismatches (0.2% and 0.8%). The high accuracy further demonstrated SPHRED's capability of maintaining individual context information. We also experimented by substituting the encoder with a normal HRED, the resulting model cannot predict the correct sentiment at all because the context information is highly mingled for both speakers. The embedding based scores of our framework are still comparable with SPHRED and even better than VHRED. Imposing an external label didn't bring any significant quality decline.

Model	Average	Greedy	Extrema	Accuracy
LM	0.360	0.348	0.310	-
HRED	0.429	0.466	0.383	-
SPHRED	**0.468**	**0.478**	**0.434**	-
VHRED	0.403	0.432	0.374	-
SCENE1-A	-	-	-	90.9%
SCENE1-B	0.426	0.432	0.396	86.9%
SCENE2-A	0.465	0.440	0.428	99.8%
SCENE2-B	0.463	0.437	0.420	99.2%

Table 1: Metric-based Evaluation. SCENE1-A is set to generate generic responses, so it makes no sense to measure it with embedding-based metrics

3.4 Results of Human Evaluation

We conducted human evaluations on VHRED and our framework (Table 3). All models share similar scores, except SCENE1-A receiving lower scores with respect to coherence. This can be explained by the fact that SCENE1-A is trained to generate only generic responses, which limits its power of taking coherence into account. VHRED and Scenario 2 perform close to each other. Scenario 1, due to the effect of the label, receives extreme scores for diversity.

In general, the statistical results of human evaluations on sentence quality are very similar between the VHRED model and our framework. This agrees with the metric-based results and supports the conclusion drawn in Section 3.3. Though the sample size is relatively small and human judgements can be inevitably disturbed by subjective factors, we believe these results can shed some light on the understanding of our framework.

A snippet of the generated responses can be

Context	Response
anybody in the house ?????_eou_ how to change the default ubuntu wall paper ? _eou_ how to change the default ubuntu wallpaper ? _eou_ _eot_ Is there an echo in your head ? Is there an echo in your head ? _eou_ _eot_ what do you mean ? _eou_ _eot_ Repeating = Bad . _eou_ _eot_ no body is answering me _eou_ _eot_	**LM:** What do you want to do with it ? **HRED:** I don't know . **SPHRED:** If you want to change the default wallpaper , you can change the default theme
How can I install seamonkey ? _eou_ To save me the pastebin _eou_ I am looking to install seamonkey , anyone ? _eou_ _eot_ http://www.seamonkey-project.org/ _eou_ _eot_ It i snot in the ubuntu repository any more _eou_ _eot_	**SCENE1-A:** sorry i have no idea . **SCENE1-B:** you need to find the package that you can use .
hey guys , how can I add an extra xsession to ubuntu 10.04 ? :) _eou_ that is , I dont want GNOME :) _eou_ _eot_ try this : https://wiki.ubuntu. com/CustomXSession :(_eou_ _eot_	**SCENE2-A:** ok thanks :)
hey guys , how can I add an extra xsession to ubuntu 10.04 ? :(_eou_ that is , I dont want GNOME :(_eou_ _eot_ try this : https://wiki.ubuntu. com/CustomXSession :) _eou_ _eot_	**SCENE2-B:** thank you for the help ! :P

Table 2: Examples of context-response pairs for the neural network models. _eou_ denotes end-of-utterance and _eot_ denotes end-of-turn token

Model	G	CD	C¬D	¬CD	¬C¬D
VHRED	97%	41%	12 %	24%	23%
SCENE1-A	96%	3%	37%	1%	59%
SCENE1-B	96%	47%	9%	40%	4%
SCENE2-A	97%	40%	14 %	23%	23%
SCENE2-B	95%	38%	20%	31%	11%

Table 3: Human Judgements, G refers to Grammaticality and the last four columns is the confusion matrix with respect to coherence and diversity

seen in Table 2. Generally speaking, SPHRED better captures the intentions of both speakers, while HRED updates the common context state and the main topic might gradually vanish for the different talking styles of speakers. SCENE1-A and SCENE1-B are designed to reply to a given context in two different ways. We can see both responses are reasonable and fit into the right class. The third and fourth rows are the same context with different appended sentiment tags and rules, both generate a suitable response and append the correct tag at the end.

4   Discussion and future work

In this work, we propose a conditional variational framework for dialog generation and verify it on two scenarios. To model the dialog state for both speakers separately, we first devised the SPHRED structure to provide the context vector for our framework. Our evaluation results show that SPHRED can itself provide a better context representation than HRED and help generate higher-quality responses. In both scenarios, our framework can successfully learn to generate responses in accordance with the predefined labels. Though with the restriction of an external label, the score of generated responses didn't significantly decreased, meaning that we can constrain the generation within a specific class while still maintaining the quality.

The manually-defined rules, though primitive, represent two most common sentiment shift conditions in reality. The results demonstrated the potential of our model. To apply to real-world scenarios, we only need to adapt the classifier to detect more complex sentiments, which we leave for future research. External models can be used for detecting generic responses or classifying sentiment categories instead of rule or symbol-based approximations. We focused on the controlling ability of our framework, future research can also experiment with bringing external knowledge to improve the overall quality of generated responses.

5   Acknowledgement

This work was supported by the National Natural Science of China under Grant No. 61602451, 61672445 and JSPS KAKENHI Grant Numbers 15H02754, 16K12546.

References

Martín Abadi, Ashish Agarwal, Paul Barham, Eugene Brevdo, Zhifeng Chen, Craig Citro, Greg S Corrado, Andy Davis, Jeffrey Dean, Matthieu Devin, et al. 2016. Tensorflow: Large-scale machine learning on heterogeneous distributed systems. *arXiv preprint arXiv:1603.04467* .

Samuel R Bowman, Luke Vilnis, Oriol Vinyals, Andrew M Dai, Rafal Jozefowicz, and Samy Bengio. 2015. Generating sentences from a continuous space. *arXiv preprint arXiv:1511.06349* .

Kyunghyun Cho, Bart Van Merriënboer, Caglar Gulcehre, Dzmitry Bahdanau, Fethi Bougares, Holger Schwenk, and Yoshua Bengio. 2014. Learning phrase representations using rnn encoder-decoder for statistical machine translation. *arXiv preprint arXiv:1406.1078* .

Michel Galley, Chris Brockett, Alessandro Sordoni, Yangfeng Ji, Michael Auli, Chris Quirk, Margaret Mitchell, Jianfeng Gao, and Bill Dolan. 2015. deltableu: A discriminative metric for generation tasks with intrinsically diverse targets. *arXiv preprint arXiv:1506.06863* .

Alex Graves. 2012. Sequence transduction with recurrent neural networks. *arXiv preprint arXiv:1211.3711* .

Diederik Kingma and Jimmy Ba. 2014. Adam: A method for stochastic optimization. *arXiv preprint arXiv:1412.6980* .

Diederik P Kingma, Shakir Mohamed, Danilo Jimenez Rezende, and Max Welling. 2014. Semi-supervised learning with deep generative models. In *Advances in Neural Information Processing Systems*. pages 3581–3589.

Diederik P Kingma and Max Welling. 2013. Auto-encoding variational bayes. *arXiv preprint arXiv:1312.6114* .

Chia-Wei Liu, Ryan Lowe, Iulian V Serban, Michael Noseworthy, Laurent Charlin, and Joelle Pineau. 2016. How not to evaluate your dialogue system: An empirical study of unsupervised evaluation metrics for dialogue response generation. *arXiv preprint arXiv:1603.08023* .

Ryan Lowe, Nissan Pow, Iulian Serban, and Joelle Pineau. 2015. The ubuntu dialogue corpus: A large dataset for research in unstructured multi-turn dialogue systems. *arXiv preprint arXiv:1506.08909* .

Olivier Pietquin and Helen Hastie. 2013. A survey on metrics for the evaluation of user simulations. *The knowledge engineering review* 28(01):59–73.

Danilo Jimenez Rezende, Shakir Mohamed, and Daan Wierstra. 2014. Stochastic backpropagation and approximate inference in deep generative models. *arXiv preprint arXiv:1401.4082* .

Stanislau Semeniuta, Aliaksei Severyn, and Erhardt Barth. 2017. A hybrid convolutional variational autoencoder for text generation. *arXiv preprint arXiv:1702.02390* .

Iulian V Serban, Alessandro Sordoni, Yoshua Bengio, Aaron Courville, and Joelle Pineau. 2016. Building end-to-end dialogue systems using generative hierarchical neural network models. *AAAI* .

Iulian Vlad Serban, Alessandro Sordoni, Ryan Lowe, Laurent Charlin, Joelle Pineau, Aaron Courville, and Yoshua Bengio. 2017. A hierarchical latent variable encoder-decoder model for generating dialogues. *AAAI* .

Lifeng Shang, Zhengdong Lu, and Hang Li. 2015. Neural responding machine for short-text conversation. *arXiv preprint arXiv:1503.02364* .

Kihyuk Sohn, Honglak Lee, and Xinchen Yan. 2015. Learning structured output representation using deep conditional generative models. In *Advances in Neural Information Processing Systems*. pages 3483–3491.

Alessandro Sordoni, Michel Galley, Michael Auli, Chris Brockett, Yangfeng Ji, Margaret Mitchell, Jian-Yun Nie, Jianfeng Gao, and Bill Dolan. 2015. A neural network approach to context-sensitive generation of conversational responses. *arXiv preprint arXiv:1506.06714* .

Ilya Sutskever, Oriol Vinyals, and Quoc V Le. 2014. Sequence to sequence learning with neural networks. In *Advances in neural information processing systems*. pages 3104–3112.

Oriol Vinyals and Quoc Le. 2015. A neural conversational model. *arXiv preprint arXiv:1506.05869* .

Xinchen Yan, Jimei Yang, Kihyuk Sohn, and Honglak Lee. 2016. Attribute2image: Conditional image generation from visual attributes. In *European Conference on Computer Vision*. Springer, pages 776–791.

Kaisheng Yao, Geoffrey Zweig, and Baolin Peng. 2015. Attention with intention for a neural network conversation model. *arXiv preprint arXiv:1510.08565* .

Question Answering through Transfer Learning
from Large Fine-grained Supervision Data

Sewon Min*
Seoul National University
shmsw25@snu.ac.kr

Minjoon Seo
University of Washington
minjoon@uw.edu

Hannaneh Hajishirzi
University of Washington
hannaneh@uw.edu

Abstract

We show that the task of question answering (QA) can significantly benefit from the transfer learning of models trained on a different large, fine-grained QA dataset. We achieve the state of the art in two well-studied QA datasets, WikiQA and SemEval-2016 (Task 3A), through a basic transfer learning technique from SQuAD. For WikiQA, our model outperforms the previous best model by more than 8%. We demonstrate that finer supervision provides better guidance for learning lexical and syntactic information than coarser supervision, through quantitative results and visual analysis. We also show that a similar transfer learning procedure achieves the state of the art on an entailment task.

1 Introduction

Question answering (QA) is a long-standing challenge in NLP, and the community has introduced several paradigms and datasets for the task over the past few years. These paradigms differ from each other in the type of questions and answers and the size of the training data, from a few hundreds to millions of examples.

We are particularly interested in the context-aware QA paradigm, where the answer to each question can be obtained by referring to its accompanying context (paragraph or a list of sentences). Under this setting, the two most notable types of supervisions are coarse *sentence-level* and fine-grained *span-level*. In sentence-level QA, the task is to pick sentences that are most relevant to the question among a list of candidates (Yang et al., 2015). In span-level QA, the task is to locate the

smallest span in the given paragraph that answers the question (Rajpurkar et al., 2016).

In this paper, we address coarser, sentence-level QA through a standard transfer learning[1] technique of a model trained on a large, span-supervised QA dataset. We demonstrate that the target task not only benefits from the scale of the source dataset but also the capability of the fine-grained span supervision to better learn syntactic and lexical information.

For the source dataset, we pretrain on SQuAD (Rajpurkar et al., 2016), a recently-released, span-supervised QA dataset. For the source and target models, we adopt BiDAF (Seo et al., 2017), one of the top-performing models in the dataset's leaderboard. For the target datasets, we evaluate on two recent QA datasets, WikiQA (Yang et al., 2015) and SemEval 2016 (Task 3A) (Nakov et al., 2016), which possess sufficiently different characteristics from that of SQuAD. Our results show 8% improvement in WikiQA and 1% improoevement in SemEval. In addition, we report state-of-the-art results on recognizing textual entailment (RTE) in SICK (Marelli et al., 2014) with a similar transfer learning procedure.

2 Background and Data

Modern machine learning models, especially deep neural networks, often significantly benefit from transfer learning. In computer vision, deep convolutional neural networks trained on a large image classification dataset such as ImageNet (Deng et al., 2009) have proved to be useful for initializing models on other vision tasks, such as object detection (Zeiler and Fergus, 2014). In nat-

---

* All work was done while the author was an exchange student at University of Washington.

[1] The borderline between transfer learning and domain adaptation is often ambiguous (Mou et al., 2016). We choose the term "transfer learning" because we also adapt the pretrained QA model to an entirely different task, RTE.

510

Proceedings of the 55th Annual Meeting of the Association for Computational Linguistics (Short Papers), pages 510–517
Vancouver, Canada, July 30 - August 4, 2017. ©2017 Association for Computational Linguistics
https://doi.org/10.18653/v1/P17-2081

Span-level QA		Sentence-level QA				RTE	
	SQuAD		*WikiQA*		*SemEval-2016 Task 3A*		*SICK*
Q	Which company made Spectre?	**Q**	Who made airbus		I saw an ad, data entry jobs online. It req-uired we give a fee and they promise fixed amount every month. Is this a scam?	**P**	Four kids are doing backbends in the park.
C	Spectre (2015) is the 24th James Bond film produced by Eon Productions. It features (...)	**C1**	Airbus SAS is an aircraft manufacturing subsi-diary of EADS, a European aerospace company.		well probably is so i be more careful if i were u. Why you looking for online jobs	**H**	Four girls are doing backbends and playing outdoors.
		C2	Airbus began as an union of aircraft companies.		SCAM!!!!!!!!!!!!!!!!!!!!!!		
		C3	Aerospace companies allowed the establishment of a joint-stock company, owned by EADS.		Bcoz i got a baby and iam nt intrested to sent him in a day care. thats y iam (...)		
A	"Eon Productions"	**A**	C1(Yes), C2(No), C3(No)		C1(Good), C2(Good), C3(Bad)	**A**	Entailment

Table 1: Examples of question-context pairs from QA datasets and premise-hypothesis pair from RTE dataset. **Q** indicates question, **C** indicates context, **A** indicates answer, **P** indicates premise and **H** indicates hypothesis.

ural language processing, domain adaptation has traditionally been an important topic for syntactic parsing (McClosky et al., 2010) and named entity recognition (Chiticariu et al., 2010), among others. With the popularity of distributed representation, pre-trained word embedding models such as word2vec (Mikolov et al., 2013b,a) and glove (Pennington et al., 2014) are also widely used for natural language tasks (Karpathy and Fei-Fei, 2015; Kumar et al., 2016). Instead of these, we initialize our models from a QA dataset and show how standard transfer learning can achieve state-of-the-art in target QA datasets.

There have been several QA paradigms in NLP, which can be categorized by the context and supervision used to answer questions. This context can range from structured and confined knowledge bases (Berant et al., 2013) to unstructured and unbounded natural language form (e.g., documents on the web (Voorhees and Tice, 2000)) and unstructured, but restricted in size (e.g., a paragraph or multiple sentences (Hermann et al., 2015)). The recent advances in neural question answering lead to numerous datasets and successful models in these paradigms (Rajpurkar et al., 2016; Yang et al., 2015; Nguyen et al., 2016; Trischler et al., 2016). The answer types in these datasets are largely divided into three categories: sentence-level, in-context span, and generation. In this paper, we specifically focus on the former two and show that span-supervised models can better learn syntactic and lexical features. Among these datasets, we briefly describe three QA datasets to be used for the experiments in this paper. We also give the description of an RTE dataset for an example of a non-QA task. Refer to Table 1 to see the examples of the datasets.

SQuAD (Rajpurkar et al., 2016) is a recent span-based QA dataset, containing 100k/10k train/dev examples. Each example is a pair of context para-graph from Wikipedia and a question created by a human, and the answer is a span in the context.

SQUAD-T is our modification of SQuAD dataset to allow for sentence selection QA. ('T' for sen*T*ence). We split the context paragraph into sentences and formulate the task as classifying whether each sentence contains the answer. This enables us to make a fair comparison between pretraining with span-supervised and sentence-supervised QA datasets.

WikiQA (Yang et al., 2015) is a sentence-level QA dataset, containing 1.9k/0.3k train/dev answerable examples. Each example consists of a real user's Bing query and a snippet of a Wikipedia article retrieved by Bing, containing 18.6 sentences on average. The task is to classify whether each sentence provides the answer to the query.

SemEval 2016 (Task 3A) (Nakov et al., 2016) is a sentence-level QA dataset, containing 1.8k/0.2k/0.3k train/dev/test examples. Each example consists of a community question by a user and 10 comments. The task is to classify whether each comment is relevant to the question.

SICK (Marelli et al., 2014) is a dataset for recognizing textual entailment (RTE), containing 4.5K/0.5K/5.0K train/dev/test examples. Each example consists of a hypothesis and a premise, and the goal is to determine if the premise is entailed by, contradicts, or is neutral to the hypothesis (hence classification problem). We also report results on SICK to show that span-supervised QA dataset can be also useful for non-QA datasets.

3 Model

Among numerous models proposed for span-level QA tasks (Xiong et al., 2017; Wang and Jiang, 2017b), we adopt an open-sourced model, BiDAF[2] (Seo et al., 2017).

---

[2]`https://allenai.github.io/bi-att-flow`

BiDAF. The inputs to the model are a question q, and a context paragraph x. Then the model selects the best answer span, which is $\arg\max_{(i,j)} \mathbf{y}_i^{\mathrm{start}} \mathbf{y}_j^{\mathrm{end}}$, where $i <= j$. Here, $\mathbf{y}_i^{\mathrm{start}}$ and $\mathbf{y}_i^{\mathrm{end}}$ are start and end position probabilities of i-th element, respectively.

Here, we briefly describe the answer module which is important for transfer learning to sentence-level QA. The input to the answer module is a sequence of vectors $\{\mathbf{h}_i\}$ each of which encodes enough information about the i-th context word and its relationship with its surrounding words and the question words. Then the role of the answer module is to map each vector $\mathbf{h}_i$ to its start and end position probabilities, $\mathbf{y}_i^{\mathrm{start}}$ and $\mathbf{y}_i^{\mathrm{end}}$.

BiDAF-T refers to the modified version of BiDAF to make it compatible with sentence-level QA. ('T' for sen*T*ence). In this task, the inputs are a question q and a list of sentences, $x_1, \ldots, x_T$, where T is the number of the sentences. Note that, unlike BiDAF, which outputs single answer per example, Here we need to output a C-way classification for each k-th sentence.

Since BiDAF is a span-selection model, it cannot be directly used for sentence-level classification. Hence we replace the original answer module of BiDAF with a different answer module, and keep the other modules identical to those of BiDAF. Given the input to the new answer module, $\{\mathbf{h}_1^k, \ldots, \mathbf{h}_N^k\}$, where the superscript is the sentence index ($1 \leq k \leq T$), we obtain the C–way classification scores for the k-th sentence, $\tilde{\mathbf{y}}^k \in [0, 1]^C$ via max-pooling method:

$$\tilde{\mathbf{y}}^k = \mathrm{softmax}(\mathbf{W} \max(\mathbf{h}_1^k, \ldots, \mathbf{h}_N^k) + \mathbf{b}) \quad (1)$$

where $\mathbf{W} \in \mathbb{R}^{C \times d}, \mathbf{b} \in \mathbb{R}^C$ are trainable weight matrix and bias, respectively, and $\max()$ function is applied elementwise.

For WikiQA and SemEval 2016, the number of classes (C) is 2, i.e. each sentence (or comment) is either relevant or not relevant. Since some of the metrics used for these datasets require full ranking, we use the predicted probability for "relevant" label to rank the sentences.

Note that BiDAF-T can be also used for the RTE dataset, where we can consider the hypothesis as a question and the premise as a context sentence ($T = 1$), and classify each example into 'entailment', 'neutral', or 'contradiction' ($C = 3$).

Transfer Learning. Transfer learning between the same model architectures[3] is straightforward: we first initialize the weights of the target model with the weights of the source model pretrained on the source dataset, and then we further train (finetune) on the target model with the target dataset. To transfer from BiDAF (on SQuAD) to BiDAF-T, we transfer all the weights of the identical modules, and initialize the new answer module in BiDAF-T with random values. For more training details, refer to Appendix A.

4   Experiments

Pretrained dataset	Fine-tuned	WikiQA			SemEval-2016		
		MAP	MRR	P@1	MAP	MRR	AvgR
-	-	62.96	64.47	49.38	76.40	82.20	86.51
SQuAD-T	No	75.22	76.40	62.96	47.23	49.31	60.01
SQuAD	No	75.19	76.31	62.55	57.80	66.10	71.13
SQuAD-T	Yes	76.44	77.85	64.61	76.30	82.51	86.64
SQuAD	Yes	79.90	82.01	70.37	78.37	85.58	87.68
SQuAD*	Yes	**83.20**	**84.58**	**75.31**	**80.20**	**86.44**	**89.14**
Rank 1		74.33	75,45	-	79.19	86.42	88.82
Rank 2		74.17	75.88	64.61	77.66	84.93	88.05
Rank 3		70.69	72.65	-	77.58	85.21	88.14

Table 2: Results on WikiQA and SemEval-2016 (Task 3A). The first row is a result from non-pretrained model, and * indicates ensemble method. Metrics used are Mean Average Precision (MAP), Mean Reciprocal Rank (MRR), Precision at rank 1 (P@1), and Average Recall (AvgR). Rank 1,2,3 indicate the results by previous works, ordered by MAP. For WikiQA, they are from Wang and Jiang (2017a); Tymoshenko et al. (2016); Miller et al. (2016), respectively. For SemEval-2016, they are from Filice et al. (2016); Joty et al. (2016); Mihaylov and Nakov (2016). SQuAD*&Yes sets the new state of the art on both datasets.

Question Answering Results. Table 2 reports the state-of-the-art results of our transfer learning on WikiQA and SemEval-2016 and the performance of previous models as well as several ablations that use no pretraining or no finetuning. There are multiple interesting observations from Table 2 as follows:

(a) If we only train the BiDAF-T model on the target datasets with no pretraining (first row of Table 2), the results are poor. This shows the importance of both pretraining and finetuning.

(b) Pretraining on SQuAD and SQuAD-T with no finetuning (second and third row) achieves results close to the state-of-the-art in the WikiQA dataset, but not in SemEval-2016. Interestingly, our result on SemEval-2016 is not better than only training without transfer learning. We conjecture that this is due to the significant difference between the domain of SemEval-2016 and

---

[3] Strictly speaking, this is a domain adaptation scenario.

that of SQuAD, which are from community and Wikipedia, respectively.

(c) Pretraining on SQuAD and SQuAD-T with finetuning (fourth and fifth row) significantly outperforms (by more than 5%) the highest-rank systems on WikiQA. It also outperforms the second ranking system in SemEval-2016 and is only 1% behind the first ranking system.

(d) Transfer learning models achieve better results with pretraining on span-level supervision (SQuAD) than coarser sentence-level supervision (SQuAD-T).[4]

Finally, we also use the ensemble of 12 different training runs on the same BiDAF architecture, which obtains the state of the art in both datasets. This system outperforms the highest-ranking system in WikiQA by more than 8% and the best system in SemEval-2016 by 1% in every metric. It is important to note that, while we definitely benefit from the scale of SQuAD for transfer learning to smaller WikiQA, given the gap between SQuAD-T and SQuAD ($> 3\%$), we see a clear sign that span-supervision plays a significant role well.

Varying the size of pretraining dataset. We vary the size of SQuAD dataset used during pretraining, and test on WikiQA with finetuning. Results are shown in Table 3. As expected, MAP on WikiQA drops as the size of SQuAD decreases. It is worth noting that pretraining on SQuAD-T (Table 2) yields 0.5 point lower MAP than pretraining on 50% of SQuAD. In other words, roughly speaking, span-level supervision data is worth more than twice the size of sentence-level supervision data for the purpose of pretraining. Also, even a small size of fine-grained supervision data helps; pretraining with 12.5% of SQuAD gives an advantage of more than 7 points than no pretraining.

Analysis. Figure 1 shows the latently-learned attention maps between the question and one of the context sentences from a WikiQA example in Table 1. The top map is pretrained on SQuAD-T (corresponding to SQuAD-T&Yes in Table 2) and the bottom map is pretrained on SQuAD (SQuAD&Yes). The more red the color, the higher

<hr>

[4]We additionally perform Mann-Whitney U Test and Mc-Nemars Test to show the statistical significance of the advantage of span-level pretraining over sentence-level pretraining. For WikiQA, the advantage is statistically significant with the confidence levels of 97.1% and 99.6%, respectively. For SemEval, we obtain the confidence levels of 97.8% and 99.9%, respectively.

Percentage of used SQuAD dataset	MAP
100%	79.90
50%	76.94
25%	74.39
12.5%	70.76

Table 3: Results with varying sizes of SQuAD dataset used during pretraining. All of them are finetuned and tested on WikiQA.

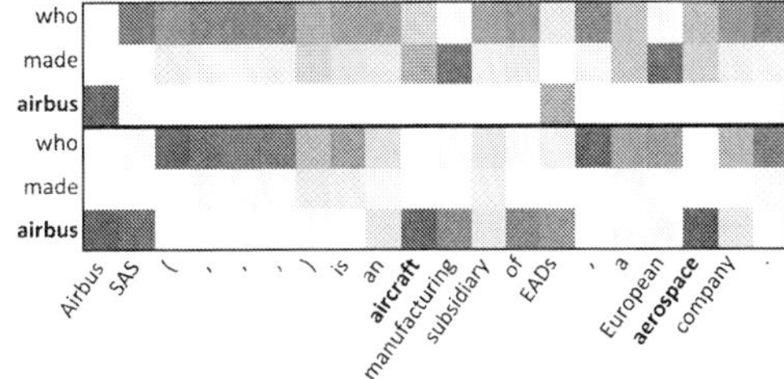

Figure 1: Attention maps showing correspondence between the words of a question (vertical) and the subset of its context (horizontal) in WikiQA for (top) SQuAD-T-pretrained model and (bottom) SQuAD-pretrained model. The more red, the higher the correspondence.

the relevance between the words. There are two interesting observations here.

First, in SQuAD-pretrained model (bottom), we see a high correspondence between question's `airbus` and context's `aircraft` and `aerospace`, but the SQuAD-T-pretrained model fails to learn such correspondence.

Second, we see that the attention map of the SQuAD-pretrained model is more sparse, indicating that it is able to more precisely localize correspondence between question and context words. In fact, we compare the sparsity of WikiQA test examples in SQuAD&Y and SQuAD-T&Y. Following Hurley and Rickard (2009), the sparsity of an attention map is defined by

$$\text{sparsity} = \frac{|\{x \in \mathbb{V}|x \le \epsilon\}|}{|\mathbb{V}|} \qquad (2)$$

where $\mathbb{V}$ is a set of values between 0 and 1 in attention map, and ϵ is a small value which we define 0.01 for here. A histogram of the sparsity is shown in Figure 2. There is a large gap in the average sparsity of WikiQA test examples between SQuAD&Yes and SQuAD-T&Yes, which are 0.84 and 0.56, respectively.

More analyses including error analysis and more visualizations are shown in Appendix B.

Entailment Results. In addition to QA experiments, we also show that the models trained on span-supervised QA can be useful for textual entailment task (RTE). Table 4 shows the trans-

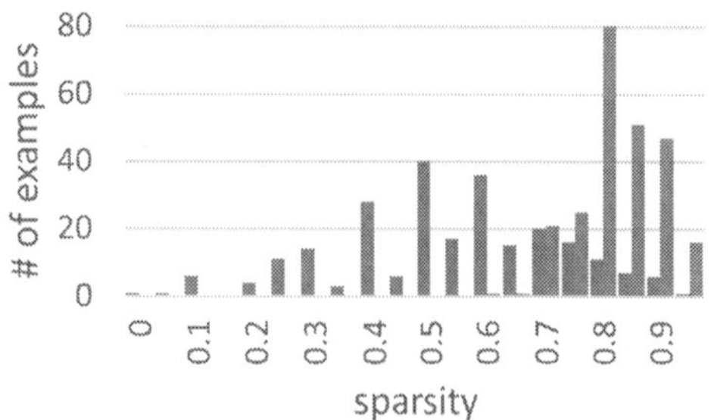

Figure 2: Histogram of the sparsity (Equation 2) of the attention maps of SQuAD-T-pretrained model (SQuAD-T&Yes, blue) and SQuAD-pretrained model (SQuAD&Yes, red). Mean sparsity of SQuAD-pretrained model (0.84) is clearly higher than that of SQuAD-T-pretrained model (0.56).

Pretrained dataset / Previous work	Accuracy
-	77.96
SQuAD-T	81.49
SQuAD	82.86
SQuAD*	84.38
SNLI	83.20
SQuAD-T + SNLI	85.00
SQuAD + SNLI	86.63
SQuAD + SNLI*	**88.22**
Yin et al. (2016)	86.2
Lai and Hockenmaier (2014)	84.57
Zhao et al. (2014)	83.64
Jimenez et al. (2014)	83.05
Mou et al. (2016)	70.9
Mou et al. (2016) (pretrained on SNLI)	77.6

Table 4: Results on SICK after finetuning. The first row is only trained on SICK. * indicates ensemble method.

fer learning results of BiDAF-T on SICK dataset (Marelli et al., 2014), with various pretraining routines. Note that SNLI (Bowman et al., 2015) is a similar task to SICK and is significantly larger (150K/10K/10K train/dev/test examples). Here we highlight three observations:

(a) BiDAF-T pretrained on SQuAD outperforms that without any pretraining by 6% and that pretrained on SQuAD-T by 2%, which demonstrates that the transfer learning from large span-based QA gives a clear improvement.

(b) Pretraining on SQuAD+SNLI outperforms pretraining on SNLI only. Given that SNLI is larger than SQuAD, the difference in their performance is a strong indicator that we are benefiting from not only the scale of SQuAD, but also the fine-grained supervision that it provides.

(c) We outperform the previous state of the art by 2% with the ensemble of SQuAD+SNLI pretraining routine.

It is worth noting that Mou et al. (2016) also shows improvement on SICK by pretraining on SNLI.

5 Conclusion

In this paper, we show state-of-the-art results on WikiQA and SemEval-2016 (Task 3A) as well as an entailment task, SICK, outperforming previous results by 8%, 1%, and 2%, respectively. We show that question answering with sentence-level supervision can greatly benefit from standard transfer learning of a question answering model trained on a large, span-level supervision. We additionally show that such transfer learning can be applicable in other NLP tasks such as textual entailment.

Acknowledgments

This research was supported by the NSF (IIS 1616112), Allen Institute for AI (66-9175), Allen Distinguished Investigator Award, and Google Research Faculty Award. We thank the anonymous reviewers for their helpful comments.

References

Jonathan Berant, Andrew Chou, Roy Frostig, and Percy Liang. 2013. Semantic parsing on freebase from question-answer pairs. In *EMNLP*.

Samuel R Bowman, Gabor Angeli, Christopher Potts, and Christopher D Manning. 2015. A large annotated corpus for learning natural language inference. In *EMNLP*.

Laura Chiticariu, Rajasekar Krishnamurthy, Yunyao Li, Frederick Reiss, and Shivakumar Vaithyanathan. 2010. Domain adaptation of rule-based annotators for named-entity recognition tasks. In *EMNLP*.

Jia Deng, Wei Dong, Richard Socher, Li-Jia Li, Kai Li, and Li Fei-Fei. 2009. Imagenet: A large-scale hierarchical image database. In *CVPR*.

Simone Filice, Danilo Croce, Alessandro Moschitti, and Roberto Basili. 2016. Kelp at semeval-2016 task 3: Learning semantic relations between questions and answers. *SemEval* 16:1116–1123.

Karl Moritz Hermann, Tomas Kocisky, Edward Grefenstette, Lasse Espeholt, Will Kay, Mustafa Suleyman, and Phil Blunsom. 2015. Teaching machines to read and comprehend. In *NIPS*.

Niall Hurley and Scott Rickard. 2009. Comparing measures of sparsity. *IEEE Transactions on Information Theory* 55(10):4723–4741.

Sergio Jimenez, George Duenas, Julia Baquero, Alexander Gelbukh, Av Juan Dios Bátiz, and Av Mendizábal. 2014. Unal-nlp: Combining soft cardinality features for semantic textual similarity, relatedness and entailment. In *SemEval Workshop*.

Shafiq Joty, Alessandro Moschitti, Fahad A Al Obaidli, Salvatore Romeo, Kateryna Tymoshenko, and Antonio Uva. 2016. Convkn at semeval-2016 task 3: Answer and question selection for question answering on arabic and english fora. *SemEval* pages 896–903.

Andrej Karpathy and Li Fei-Fei. 2015. Deep visual-semantic alignments for generating image descriptions. In *CVPR*.

Ankit Kumar, Ozan Irsoy, Jonathan Su, James Bradbury, Robert English, Brian Pierce, Peter Ondruska, Ishaan Gulrajani, and Richard Socher. 2016. Ask me anything: Dynamic memory networks for natural language processing. In *ICML*.

Alice Lai and Julia Hockenmaier. 2014. Illinois-lh: A denotational and distributional approach to semantics. *SemEval* .

Marco Marelli, Stefano Menini, Marco Baroni, Luisa Bentivogli, Raffaella Bernardi, and Roberto Zamparelli. 2014. A sick cure for the evaluation of compositional distributional semantic models. In *LREC*.

David McClosky, Eugene Charniak, and Mark Johnson. 2010. Automatic domain adaptation for parsing. In *NAACL-HLT*.

Todor Mihaylov and Preslav Nakov. 2016. Semanticz at semeval-2016 task 3: Ranking relevant answers in community question answering using semantic similarity based on fine-tuned word embeddings. *SemEval* pages 879–886.

Tomas Mikolov, Kai Chen, Greg Corrado, and Jeffrey Dean. 2013a. Efficient estimation of word representations in vector space. In *ICLR*.

Tomas Mikolov, Ilya Sutskever, Kai Chen, Greg S Corrado, and Jeff Dean. 2013b. Distributed representations of words and phrases and their compositionality. In *NIPS*.

Alexander Miller, Adam Fisch, Jesse Dodge, Amir-Hossein Karimi, Antoine Bordes, and Jason Weston. 2016. Key-value memory networks for directly reading documents. In *EMNLP*.

Lili Mou, Zhao Meng, Rui Yan, Ge Li, Yan Xu, Lu Zhang, and Zhi Jin. 2016. How transferable are neural networks in nlp applications? In *EMNLP*.

Preslav Nakov, Llus Mrquez, Alessandro Moschitti, Walid Magdy Mubarak Hamdy Hamdy, abed Alhakim Freihat, Jim Glass, and Bilal Randeree. 2016. Semeval-2016 task 3: Community question answering. *SemEval* pages 525–545.

Tri Nguyen, Mir Rosenberg, Xia Song, Jianfeng Gao, Saurabh Tiwary, Rangan Majumder, and Li Deng. 2016. Ms marco: A human generated machine reading comprehension dataset. In *NIPS Workshop*.

Jeffrey Pennington, Richard Socher, and Christopher D. Manning. 2014. Glove: Global vectors for word representation. In *EMNLP*.

Pranav Rajpurkar, Jian Zhang, Konstantin Lopyrev, and Percy Liang. 2016. Squad: 100,000+ questions for machine comprehension of text. In *EMNLP*.

Minjoon Seo, Aniruddha Kembhavi, Ali Farhadi, and Hannaneh Hajishirzi. 2017. Bidirectional attention flow for machine comprehension. In *ICLR*.

Adam Trischler, Tong Wang, Xingdi Yuan, Justin Harris, Alessandro Sordoni, Philip Bachman, and Kaheer Suleman. 2016. Newsqa: A machine comprehension dataset. *arXiv preprint arXiv:1611.09830* .

Kateryna Tymoshenko, Daniele Bonadiman, and Alessandro Moschitti. 2016. Convolutional neural networks vs. convolution kernels: Feature engineering for answer sentence reranking. In *NAACL-HLT*.

Ellen M Voorhees and Dawn M Tice. 2000. Building a question answering test collection. In *ACM SIGIR*.

Shuohang Wang and Jing Jiang. 2017a. A compare-aggregate model for matching text sequences. In *ICLR*.

Shuohang Wang and Jing Jiang. 2017b. Machine comprehension using match-lstm and answer pointer. In *ICLR*.

Zhiguo Wang, Wael Hamza, and Radu Florian. 2017. Bilateral multi-perspective matching for natural language sentences. *arXiv preprint arXiv:1702.03814* .

Caiming Xiong, Victor Zhong, and Richard Socher. 2017. Dynamic coattention networks for question answering. In *ICLR*.

Yi Yang, Wen-tau Yih, and Christopher Meek. 2015. Wikiqa: A challenge dataset for open-domain question answering. In *EMNLP*.

Wenpeng Yin, Hinrich Schütze, Bing Xiang, and Bowen Zhou. 2016. Abcnn: Attention-based convolutional neural network for modeling sentence pairs. *TACL* .

Matthew D Zeiler. 2012. Adadelta: an adaptive learning rate method. *arXiv preprint arXiv:1212.5701* .

Matthew D Zeiler and Rob Fergus. 2014. Visualizing and understanding convolutional networks. In *ECCV*.

Jiang Zhao, Tian Tian Zhu, and Man Lan. 2014. Ecnu: One stone two birds: Ensemble of heterogenous measures for semantic relatedness and textual entailment. *SemEval* pages 271–277.

A Training details

Parameters. For pretraining BiDAF on SQuAD, we follow the exact same procedure in Seo et al. (2017). For pretraining BiDAF-T on SQuAD-T, we use the same hyperparameters for all modules except the answer module, for which we use the hidden state size of 200. The learning rate is controlled by AdaDelta (Zeiler, 2012) with the initial learning rate of 0.5 and minibatch size of 50. We maintain the moving averages of all weights of the model with the exponential decay rate of 0.999 during training and use them at test. The loss function is the cross entropy between $\tilde{\mathbf{y}}^k$ and the one-hot vector of the correct classification.

Convergence. For all settings, we train models until performance on development set continue to decrease for 5k steps. Table 5 shows the median selected step on each setting.

Dataset	Pretrained	selected step
SQuAD	-	18k
SQuAD-T	-	50k
WikiQA	-	6k
WikiQA	SQuAD-T	6k
WikiQA	SQuAD	3k
SemEval-2016	-	9k
SemEval-2016	SQuAD-T	4k
SemEval-2016	SQuAD	3k
SICK	-	13k
SNLI	-	55k
SICK	SQuAD-T	9k
SNLI	SQuAD-T	31k
SICK	SQuAD	18k
SNLI	SQuAD	49k
SICK	SQuAD-T + SNLI	7k
SICK	SQuAD + SNLI	7k

Table 5: Median global step, which has the best performance on development set.

B More Analysis

Attention maps. We show some more examples of attention maps in Figure 3. (Top) We see high correspondence between same word from question and context such as `senator` and `john`, in SQuAD-pretrained model, but the SQuAD-T-pretrained model fails to learn such correspondence. (Bottom) We see high correspondence between `stems` from question and `stem` from context (left) as well as `plant` from question and `plants` from context (right), in SQuAD-pretrained model, but the SQuAD-T-pretrained model fails to learn such correspondence.

Error Analysis. Table 7 shows the comparison between answers by SQuAD-T-pretrained model and SQuAD-pretrained model on the example

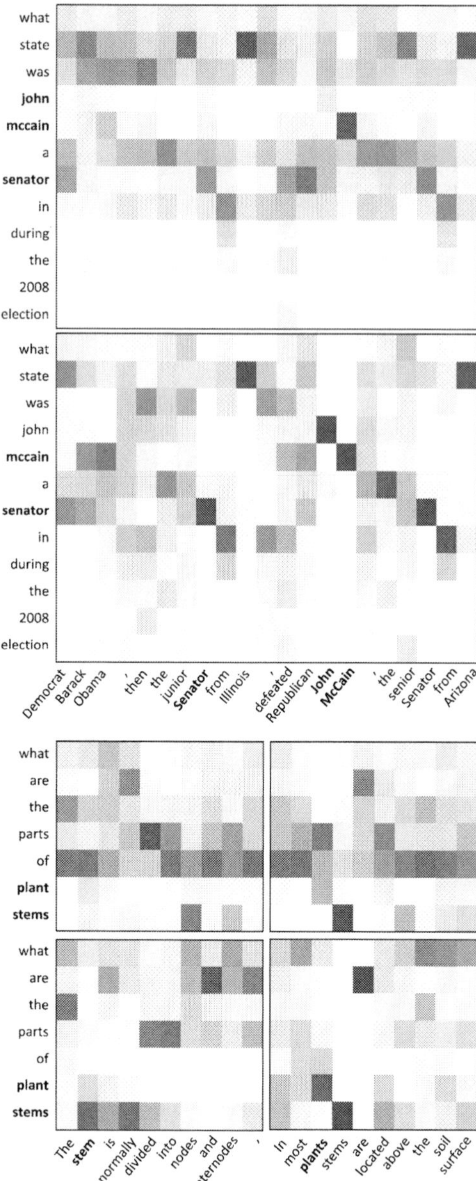

Figure 3: More attention maps showing correspondence between the words of a question (vertical) and one of candidate sentences (horizontal) in WikiQA for (top in each subfigure) SQuAD-MC-pretrained model and (bottom in each subfigure) SQuAD-pretrained model. The more red, the higher the correspondence.

of WikiQA and SemEval-2016 from Table 1. On WikiQA, SQuAD-T-pretrained model selects C2 instead of the groundtruth answer C1. On SemEval-2016, SQuAD-pretrained model ranks C3 (bad comment) higher than C2 (good comment).

In addition, we sampled 100 example randomly

Category Id	Category	Example Question	Relevant Sentence
1	Exact Match	When did SpongeBob first air?	The pilot episode of SpongeBob SquarePants first aired in the United States on May 1, 1999, following the ...
2	Paraphrase	When was How the West Was Won filmed?	How the West Was Won is a 1962 American epic Western film.
3	No Clear Clue	When was Mary Anderson born?	Mary Anderson (1866-1953) was a real estate developer, ...
4	Need prior sentence (pronoun)	When did Texas become a state?	In 1845, it joined the United States as the 28th state.
5	Need prior sentence (context)	How do you play spades?	Its major difference as compared to other Whist variants is that, instead of trump being decided by the highest bidder or at random, the Spade suit is always trump, hence the name.
6	Hard to answer	How kimberlite pipes form?	Volcanic pipes are relatively rare.

Category Id	Category	Example Question Id	Example Question
1	Asking information	Q347_R25	hi all is there any IKEA showroom in and around DOHA? Kindly reply thank you
2	Asking opinion or recommendation in specific situation	Q326_R90	Salam I am mechanical Eng. 15 years experience i got a job for Rasgas co. direct hire I am married and i have 2 kids 5 and 3 years old.my life style is average. Is 8.000 QR enough as a basic salary? (...)
3	Asking feelings in specific situation	Q348_R67	oh i wish they will build Disneyland in Qatar :) how do you think guys? It will be perfect for Qatar :)
4	Asking abstract thing	Q341_R11	id like to get to know more about Al Jazeera International from anyone on QATAR LIVING who works at Al Jazeera.
5	Not Asking	Q337_R21	I just stumbled across this news article about the the American university campuses at Education City and thought some of you may also find it interesting.
6	Asking a lot of things at once	Q337_R16	How good are Karwa services? Are they : 1. Courteous/Rude? 2. Taking the correct route/Longer route? (...) 7. A pleasure/displeasure to ride?

Table 6: Examples from each category on (top) WikiQA and (bottom) SemEval-2016 (Task 3A).

	WikiQA	SemEval-2016
SQuAD-T&Yes	C2 > C1 > C3	C1 > C3 > C2
SQuAD&Yes	C1 > C2 > C3	C2 > C1 > C3
Groundtruth	C1(Y), C2(N), C3(N)	C1(Good), C2(Good), C3(Bad)

Table 7: Comparison of ranked answers by SQuAD-T-pretrained model (SQuAD-T&Yes) and SQuAD-pretrained model (SQuAD&Yes) of examples from WikiQA and SemEval-2016 (Task 3A) in Table 1.

Pretrained dataset		total	Category Id					
SQuAD-T-Y	SQuAD-Y		1	2	3	4	5	6
total		100	37	38	6	15	2	2
Correct	Correct	49	28	14	3	4	0	0
Wrong	Correct	**26**	8	**14**	1	3	0	0
Correct	Wrong	9	1	4	1	3	0	0
Wrong	Wrong	16	0	6	1	5	2	2

Table 8: Comparison of performance of SQuAD-T-pretrained model (SQuAD-T-Y) and SQuAD-pretrained model (SQuAD-Y) on WikiQA.

Pretrained dataset		total	Category Id					
No Pretrain	SQuAD-Y		1	2	3	4	5	6
total		100	29	38	7	12	9	5
Correct	Correct	30	12	11	2	5	0	0
Wrong	Correct	**22**	6	**10**	0	2	2	2
Correct	Wrong	5	0	1	2	1	0	1
Wrong	Wrong	43	11	16	3	4	7	2

Table 9: Comparison of performance of model without pretraining (No Pretrain) and SQuAD-pretrained model (SQuAD-Y) on SemEval-2016 (Task 3A).

from WikiQA and SemEval-2016, and classified them into 6 categories(Table 6). In Table 8, we compare the performance on these WikiQA examples by SQuAD-T-pretrained model and SQuAD-pretrained model. It shows that span supervision clearly helps answering questions on Category 1 and 2, which are easier to answer, with answering correctly on most of the questions in Category 1. Similarly, we show the comparison of the performance on classified examples of the model without pretraining and SQuAD-pretrained model on SemEval-2016. It also shows that span supervision helps answering questions asking information or opinion/recommendation.

C   More Results

SQuAD-T. To better understand SQuAD-T dataset, we show the performance BiDAF-T with different training routines. We get MAP 89.46 and accuracy 85.34% with SQuAD-trained BiDAF model, and MAP 90.18 and accuracy 84.69% with SQuAD-T-trained BiDAF-T model. There is no large gap between the two models, as each paragraph of SQuAD-T has 5 sentences on average, which makes the classification problem easier than WikiQA.

SNLI. Other larger RTE datasets such as SNLI also benefit from transfer learning, although the improvement is smaller. We confirm the improvement by showing that the result on SNLI when pretraining on SQuAD with BiDAF is 82.6%, which is slightly higher than that of the model pretrained on SQuAD-T (81.6%). This, however, did not outperform the state of the art (88.8%) by Wang et al. (2017). This is mostly because BiDAF (or BiDAF-T) is a QA model, which is not designed for RTE tasks.

Self-Crowdsourcing Training for Relation Extraction

Azad Abad[†], Moin Nabi[†], Alessandro Moschitti
†DISI, University of Trento, 38123 Povo (TN), Italy
Qatar Computing Research Institute, HBKU, 34110, Doha, Qatar
{azad.abad,moin.nabi}@unitn.it
amoschitti@gmail.com

Abstract

One expensive step when defining crowd-sourcing tasks is to define the examples and control questions for instructing the crowd workers. In this paper, we introduce a self-training strategy for crowd-sourcing. The main idea is to use an automatic classifier, trained on weakly supervised data, to select examples associated with high confidence. These are used by our automatic agent to explain the task to crowd workers with a question answering approach. We compared our relation extraction system trained with data annotated (i) with distant supervision and (ii) by workers instructed with our approach. The analysis shows that our method relatively improves the relation extraction system by about 11% in F1.

1 Introduction

Recently, the Relation Extraction (RE) task has attracted the attention of many researchers due to its wide range of applications such as question answering, text summarization and bio-medical text mining. The aim of this task is to identify the type of relation between two entities in a given text. Most work on RE has mainly regarded the application of supervised methods, which require costly annotation, especially for large-scale datasets.

To overcome the annotation problem, Craven et al. (1999) firstly proposed to collect automatic annotation through Distant Supervision (DS). In the DS setting, the training data for RE is often automatically annotated utilizing an external Knowledge-Base (KB) such as Wikipedia or Freebase (Hoffmann et al., 2010; Riedel et al., 2010; Nguyen and Moschitti, 2011). Although DS has

shown to be promising for RE, it also produces many noisy labels in the automatic annotated data, which deteriorate the performance of the system trained on it.

Hoffmann et al. (2011) showed that by simply adding a small set of high quality labeled instances (i.e., human-annotated training data) to a larger set of instances annotated by DS, makes the overall precision of the system significantly increases. Such level of quality of the labels usually can be obtained at low cost via crowdsourcing.

However, this finding does not hold for more complex tasks, where the annotators[1] need to have some expertise on them. For instance in RE, several works have shown that only a marginal improvement can be achieved via crowdsourcing the data (Angeli et al., 2014; Zhang et al., 2012; Pershina et al., 2014). In such papers, the well-known Gold Standard quality control mechanism was used without annotators being trained.

Very recently, despite the previous results, Liu et al. (2016) showed a larger improvement for the RE task when training crowd workers in an interactive tutorial procedure called "Gated Instruction". This approach, however, requires a set of high-quality labeled data (i.e., the Gold Standard) for providing the instruction and feedback to the crowd workers. However, acquiring such data requires a considerable amount of human effort.

In this paper, we propose to alternatively use *Silver Standard*, i.e., a high-quality automatic annotated data, to train the crowd workers. Specifically, we introduce a self-training strategy for crowd-sourcing, where the workers are first trained with simpler examples (which we assume to be less noisy) and then gradually presented with more difficult ones. This is biologically inspired by the common human process of gradual learn-

---

[1]From now, the both entities *annotators* and *crowd workers* refer to the same concept.

Proceedings of the 55th Annual Meeting of the Association for Computational Linguistics (Short Papers), pages 518–523
Vancouver, Canada, July 30 - August 4, 2017. ©2017 Association for Computational Linguistics
https://doi.org/10.18653/v1/P17-2082

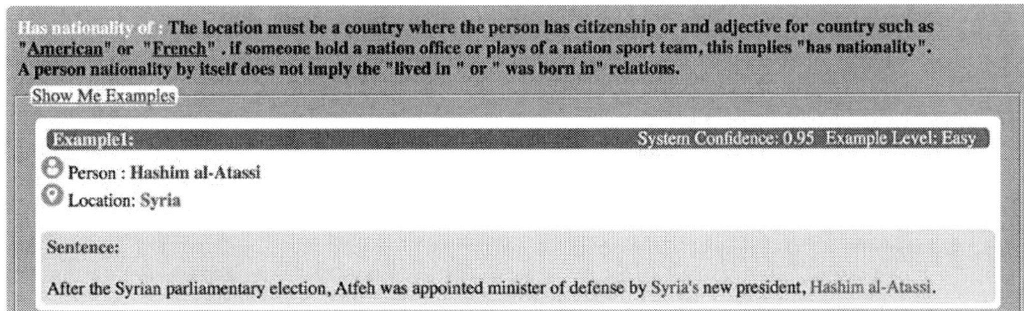

Figure 1: User Interface of crowd worker training: instruction phase

ing, starting from the simplest concepts.

Moreover, we propose an iterative human-machine co-training framework for the task of RE. The main idea is (i) to automatically select a subset of *less-noisy* examples applying an automatic classifier, (ii) training the annotators with such subset, and (iii) iterating this process after retraining the classifiers using the annotated data. That is, the educated crowd workers can provide higher quality annotations, which can be used by the system in the next iteration to improve the quality of its classification. In other words, this cycle gradually improves both system and human annotators. This is in line with the studies in human-based computational approaches, which showed that the crowd intelligence can effectively alleviate the drifting problem in auto-annotation systems (Sun et al., 2014; Russakovsky et al., 2015).

Our study shows that even without using any gold standard, we can still train workers and their annotations can achieve results comparable with the more costly state-of-the-art methods. In summary our contributions are the following:

- we introduce a self-training strategy for crowdsourcing;

- we propose an iterative human-machine co-training framework for the task of RE; and

- we test our approach on a standard benchmark, obtaining a slightly lower performance compared to the state-of-the-art methods based on Gold Standard data.

This study opens up avenues for exploiting inexpensive crowdsourcing solutions similar to ours to achieve performance gain in NLP tasks.

2 Background Work

There is a large body of work on DS for RE, but we only discuss the most related to our work and refer the reader to other recent work (Wu and Weld, 2007; Mintz et al., 2009; Bunescu, 2007; Hoffmann et al., 2010; Riedel et al., 2010; Surdeanu et al., 2012; Nguyen and Moschitti, 2011).

Many researchers have exploited the techniques of combining the DS data with small human annotated data collected via crowdsourcing, to improve the relation extractor accuracy (Liu et al., 2016; Angeli et al., 2014; Zhang et al., 2012). Angeli et al. (2014) reported a minor improvement using active learning methods to select the best instances to be crowdsourced.

In the same direction, Zhang et al. (2012) studied the effect of providing human feedback in crowdsourcing tasks and observed a minor improvement in terms of F1. At high level, our work may be viewed as employing crowdsourcing for RE. In that spirit, we are similar to these works, but with the main difference of training crowd workers to obtain higher quality annotations.

The most related paper to our work is by Liu et al. (2016), who trained the crowd workers via "Gated Instruction". They also showed that collecting higher-quality annotations can be achieved through training the workers. The produced data also improved the performance of the RE systems trained on it. Our study confirms their finding. However, unlike them, we do not employ any Gold Standard (annotated by experts) for training the annotators and instead we propose a self-training strategy to select a set of high-quality automatic annotated data (namely, Silver Standard).

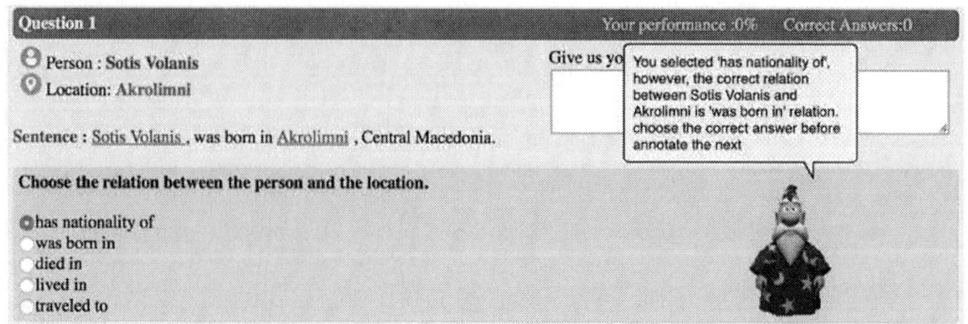

Figure 2: User Interface of crowd worker training: interactive QA phase

3 Self-Crowdsourcing Training

In this section we first explain, our proposed method for automatically identifying high-quality examples (i.e., Silver Standard) to train the crowd workers and collect annotations for the lower-quality examples. We then explain the scheme designed for crowd worker training and annotation collection.

3.1 Silver Standard Mining

The main idea of our approach to Self-Crowdsourcing training is to use the classifier's score for gradually training the crowd workers, such that the examples and labels associated with the highest prediction values (i.e., the most reliable) will be used as Silver Standard.

More in detail, our approach is based on a noisy-label dataset, DS, whose labels are extracted in a distant supervision fashion and CS a dataset to be labeled by the crowd. The first step is to divide CS into three parts: CS_I, which is used to create the instructions for the crowd workers; CS_Q, which is used for asking questions about sentence annotations; and CS_A, which is used to collect the labels from annotators, after they have been trained.

To select CS_I, we train a classifier C on DS, and then used it to label CS examples. In particular, we used MultiR framework (Hoffmann et al., 2011) to train C, as it is a widely used framework for RE. Then, we sort CS in a descending order according to the classifier prediction scores and select the first N_i elements, obtaining CS_I.

Next, we select the N_q examples of $CS \setminus CS_I$ with the highest score to create the set CS_Q. Note that the latter contains highly-reliable classifier annotations but since the scores are lower than for

CS_I examples, we conjecture that they may be more difficult to be annotated by the crowd workers.

Finally, CS_A is assigned with the remaining examples, i.e., $CS \setminus CS_I \setminus CS_Q$. These have the lowest confidence and should therefore be annotated by crowd workers. N_i and N_q can be tuned on the task, we set both to 10% of the data.

3.2 Training Schema

We conducted *crowd worker training* and *annotation collection* using the well-known Crowdflower platform[2]. Given CS_I and CS_Q (see Section 3.1), we train the annotators in two steps:

(i) **User Instruction**: first, a definition of each relation type (borrowed from TAC-KBP official guideline) is shown to the annotators. This initial training step provides the crowd workers with a big picture of the task. We then train the annotators showing them a set of examples from CS_I (see Fig. 1). The latter are presented in the reverse order of difficulty. The ranked list of examples provided by our self-training strategy facilitates the gradual education of the annotators (Nosofsky, 2011). This gives us the benefit of training the annotators with any level of expertise, which is a crucial property of crowdsourcing when there is no clue about the workers' expertise in advance.

(ii) **Interactive QA**: after the initial step, we challenge the workers in an interactive QA task with multiple-choice questions over the sentence annotation (see Fig. 2). To accomplish that, we designed an artificial agent that interacts with the crowd workers: it corrects their mistakes and makes them reasoning on why their answer was wrong. Note that, to have a better control of the

---

[2]www.crowdflower.com

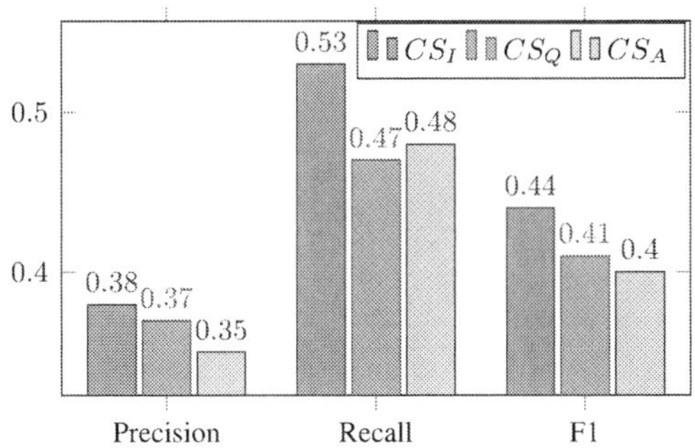

Figure 3: Accuracy of different CS partitions

Model	Pr.	Rec.	F1
DS-only	0.43	0.52	0.47
Our Method	0.50	0.54	0.52
Gated Instruction	0.53	0.57	0.55

Table 1: Evaluation of the impact of the CS_A label quality in the RE task.

worker training, we perform a selection of the sentences in CS_Q to be used for questioning in a category-wise fashion. Meaning that, we select the subsets of examples for each class of relation separately. We observed in practice that initially a lot of examples are classified as "No Relation". This is due to a difficulty of the task for the DS-based model. Thus, we used them in CS_A.

4 Experimental Setup

In this section, we first introduce the details of the used corpora, then explain the feature extraction and RE pipeline and finally present the experiments and discuss the results in detail.

4.1 Corpora

We used TAC-KBP newswires, one of the most well-known corpora for RE task. As DS, we selected 700K sentences automatically annotated using Freebase as an external KB. We used the active learning framework proposed by Angeli et al. (2014) to select CS. This allowed us to select the best sentences to be annotated by humans (sampleJS). As a result, we obtained 4,388 sentences. We divided the CS sentences in CS_I, CS_Q and CS_A, with 10%, 10% and 80% split, respectively. We requested at least 5 annotations for each sentence.

Similarly to Liu et al. (2016), we restricted our attention to 5 relations between *person* and *location*[3]. For both DS and CS, we used the publicly available data provided by Liu et al. (2016). Ultimately, 221 crowd workers participated to the task with minimum 2 and maximum 400 annotations per crowd worker. To evaluate our model, we randomly selected 200 sentences as test set and had

---

[3]*Nationality, Place-of-birth, Place-of-resident, Place-of-death, Traveled-to*

a domain expert to manually tag them using the TAC-KBP annotation guidelines.

4.2 Relation Extraction Pipeline

We used the relation extractor, MultiR (Hoffmann et al., 2010) along with lexical and syntactic features proposed by Mintz et al. (2009) such as: (i) Part of Speech (POS); (ii) windows of k words around the matched entities; (iii) the sequences of words between them; and (iv) finally, dependency structure patterns between entity pairs. These yield low-Recall as they appear in conjunctive forms but at the same time they produce a high Precision.

4.3 Experimental Results

In the first set of experiments, we verified the quality of our Silver Standard set used in our self-training methods. For this purpose, we trained MultiR on CS_I, CS_Q and CS_A and evaluate them on our test set. Figure 3 illustrates the results in terms of Precision, Recall and F1 for each partition separately. They suggest that, the extractors trained on CS_I and CS_Q are significantly better than the extractor trained on the lower part of CS, i.e., CS_A, even if the latter is much larger than the other two (80% vs. 10%).

In the next set of experiments, we evaluated the impact of adding a small set of crowdsourced data to a large set of instances annotated by Distant Supervision. We conducted the RE experiments in this setting, as this allowed us to directly compare with Liu et al. (2016). Thus, we used CS_A annotated by our proposed method along with the noisy annotated DS to train the extractor.

We compared our method with (i) the *DS-only* baseline and (ii) the state of the art, *Gated Instruction* (GI) strategy (Liu et al., 2016). We emphasize that the same set of examples (both DS and CS) are used in this experiment and just replaced the GI annotations with the annotations collected using our proposed framework.

Models	DS-only	Our Model	GI
Accuracy	56%	82%	91%

Table 2: Annotation Accuracy of crowd workers

The results are shown in Table 1. Our method improves the *DS-only* baseline by 7%, 5% and 2% (absolute) in Precision, Recall and F1, respectively. This improvement clearly confirms the benefit of our fully automatic approach to crowdsourcing in RE task.

Additionally, our model is just 3% lower than the GI method in terms of F1. In both our method and GI, the crowd workers are trained before enrolling in the main task. However, GI trains annotators using Gold Standard data, which involves a higher level of supervision with respect to our method. Thus our self-training method is potentially effective and an inexpensive alternative to GI.

We also analyzed the accuracy of the crowd workers in terms of the quality of their annotations. For this purpose, we randomly selected 100 sentences from CS_A and then had them manually annotated by an expert. We compared the accuracy of the annotations collected with our proposed approach with those provided by DS-only baseline and the GI method. Table 2 shows the results: the annotations performed by workers trained with our method are just slightly less accurate than the annotations produced by annotators trained with GI. This outcome is inline with the positive impact of our good quality annotation on the RE performance.

5 Conclusion

In this paper, we have proposed a self-training strategy for crowdsourcing as an effective alternative to train annotators with Gold Standard. Our experimental results show that the annotations of workers trained with our method are accurate and produce a good performance when used in learning algorithms for RE. Our study suggests that automatically training annotators can replace the popular consensus-based filtering scheme. Our method achieves this goal through an inexpensive training procedure.

In the future, it would be interesting to study if our method generalizes to other difficult or even simpler tasks. In particular, our approach opens up many research directions on how to best train workers or best select data for them, similarly to what active learning methods have been doing for training machines.

Acknowledgement

This work has been partially supported by the EC project CogNet, 671625 (H2020-ICT-2014-2, Research and Innovation action). Many thanks to the anonymous reviewers for their valuable suggestions.

References

Gabor Angeli, Julie Tibshirani, Jean Y. Wu, and Christopher D. Manning. 2014. Combining distant and partial supervision for relation extraction. In *In Proceedings of EMNLP*. pages 1556–1567.

Razvan C. Bunescu. 2007. Learning to extract relations from the web using minimal supervision. In *In Proceedings of the 45th Annual Meeting of the Association for Computational Linguistics (ACL07)*.

Mark Craven and Johan Kumlien. 1999. Constructing biological knowledge bases by extracting information from text sources. In *Proceedings of the Seventh International Conference on Intelligent Systems for Molecular Biology*. AAAI Press, pages 77–86. http://dl.acm.org/citation.cfm?id=645634.663209.

Raphael Hoffmann, Congle Zhang, Xiao Ling, Luke Zettlemoyer, and Daniel S. Weld. 2011. Knowledge-based weak supervision for information extraction of overlapping relations. In *Proceedings of the 49th Annual Meeting of the Association for Computational Linguistics: Human Language Technologies - Volume 1*. Association for Computational Linguistics, Stroudsburg, PA, USA, HLT '11, pages 541–550. http://dl.acm.org/citation.cfm?id=2002472.2002541.

Raphael Hoffmann, Congle Zhang, and Daniel S. Weld. 2010. Learning 5000 relational extractors. In *Proceedings of the 48th Annual Meeting of the Association for Computational Linguistics*. Association for Computational Linguistics, Stroudsburg, PA, USA, ACL '10, pages 286–295. http://dl.acm.org/citation.cfm?id=1858681.1858711.

Angli Liu, Jonathan Bragg Xiao Ling Stephen Soderland, and Daniel S Weld. 2016. Effective crowd annotation for relation extraction. In *Association for Computational Linguistics*. NAACL-HLT 2016.

Mike Mintz, Steven Bills, Rion Snow, and Dan Jurafsky. 2009. Distant supervision for relation extraction without labeled data. In *Proceedings of the Joint Conference of the 47th Annual Meeting of the ACL and the 4th International Joint Conference on Natural Language Processing of the AFNLP: Volume 2 - Volume*

2. Association for Computational Linguistics, Stroudsburg, PA, USA, ACL '09, pages 1003–1011. http://dl.acm.org/citation.cfm?id=1690219.1690287.

Truc-Vien T. Nguyen and Alessandro Moschitti. 2011. End-to-end relation extraction using distant supervision from external semantic repositories. In *Proceedings of the 49th Annual Meeting of the Association for Computational Linguistics: Human Language Technologies: Short Papers - Volume 2*. Association for Computational Linguistics, Stroudsburg, PA, USA, HLT '11, pages 277–282. http://dl.acm.org/citation.cfm?id=2002736.2002794.

Robert M Nosofsky. 2011. The generalized context model: An exemplar model of classification. *Formal approaches in categorization* pages 18–39.

Maria Pershina, Bonan Min, Wei Xu, and Ralph Grishman. 2014. Infusion of labeled data into distant supervision for relation extraction. In *Proceedings of the 2014 Conference of the Association for Computational Linguistics (ACL 2014)*. Association for Computational Linguistics, Baltimore, US.

Sebastian Riedel, Limin Yao, and Andrew McCallum. 2010. Modeling relations and their mentions without labeled text. In *Proceedings of the 2010 European Conference on Machine Learning and Knowledge Discovery in Databases: Part III*. Springer-Verlag, Berlin, Heidelberg, ECML PKDD'10, pages 148–163. http://dl.acm.org/citation.cfm?id=1889788.1889799.

Olga Russakovsky, Li-Jia Li, and Li Fei-Fei. 2015. Best of both worlds: Human-machine collaboration for object annotation. In *The IEEE Conference on Computer Vision and Pattern Recognition (CVPR)*.

Chong Sun, Narasimhan Rampalli, Frank Yang, and AnHai Doan. 2014. Chimera: Large-scale classification using machine learning, rules, and crowdsourcing. *Proc. VLDB Endow.* 7(13):1529–1540. https://doi.org/10.14778/2733004.2733024.

Mihai Surdeanu, Julie Tibshirani, Ramesh Nallapati, and Christopher D. Manning. 2012. Multi-instance multi-label learning for relation extraction. In *Proceedings of the 2012 Joint Conference on Empirical Methods in Natural Language Processing and Computational Natural Language Learning*. Association for Computational Linguistics, Stroudsburg, PA, USA, EMNLP-CoNLL '12, pages 455–465. http://dl.acm.org/citation.cfm?id=2390948.2391003.

Fei Wu and Daniel S. Weld. 2007. Autonomously semantifying wikipedia. In *Proceedings of the Sixteenth ACM Conference on Conference on Information and Knowledge Management*. ACM, New York, NY, USA, CIKM '07, pages 41–50. https://doi.org/10.1145/1321440.1321449.

Ce Zhang, Feng Niu, Christopher Ré, and Jude Shavlik. 2012. Big data versus the crowd: Looking for relationships in all the right places. In *Proceedings of the 50th Annual Meeting of the Association for Computational Linguistics: Long Papers - Volume 1*. Association for Computational Linguistics, Stroudsburg, PA, USA, ACL '12, pages 825–834. http://dl.acm.org/citation.cfm?id=2390524.2390640.*

A Generative Attentional Neural Network Model for Dialogue Act Classification

Quan Hung Tran and **Ingrid Zukerman** and **Gholamreza Haffari**
Faculty of Information Technology
Monash University, Australia
`hung.tran,ingrid.zukerman,gholamreza.haffari@monash.edu`

Abstract

We propose a novel generative neural network architecture for Dialogue Act classification. Building upon the Recurrent Neural Network framework, our model incorporates a new attentional technique and a label-to-label connection for sequence learning, akin to Hidden Markov Models. Our experiments show that both of these innovations enable our model to outperform strong baselines for dialogue-act classification on the MapTask and Switchboard corpora. In addition, we analyse empirically the effectiveness of each of these innovations.

1 Introduction

Dialogue Act (DA) classification is a sequence-to-sequence learning task where a sequence of utterances is mapped into a sequence of DAs. Some works in DA classification treat each utterance as an independent instance (Julia et al., 2010; Gambäck et al., 2011), which leads to ignoring important long-range dependencies in the dialogue history. Other works have captured inter-utterance relationships using models such as Hidden Markov Models (HMMs) (Stolcke et al., 2000; Surendran and Levow, 2006) or Recurrent Neural Networks (RNNs) (Kalchbrenner and Blunsom, 2013; Ji et al., 2016), where RNNs have been particularly successful.

In this paper, we present a generative model of utterances and dialogue acts which conditions on the relevant part of the dialogue history. To this effect, we use the *attention* mechanism (Bahdanau et al., 2014) developed originally for sequence-to-sequence models, which has proven effective in Machine Translation (Bahdanau et al., 2014; Luong et al., 2015) and DA classification (Shen and

Lee, 2016). The intuition is that different parts of an input sequence have different levels of importance with respect to the objective, and this mechanism enables the selection of the important parts. However, the traditional attention mechanism suffers from the *attention-bias* problem (Wang et al., 2016), where the attention mechanism tends to favor the inputs at the end of a sequence. To address this problem, we propose a *gated attention* mechanism, where the attention signal is represented as a gate over the input vector.

In addition, when generating a dialogue act, we capture its direct dependence on the previous dialogue act — a reasonable source of information, which, surprisingly, has not been explored in the RNN literature for DA classification.

Our experiments show that our model significantly outperforms variants that do not have our innovations, i.e., the gated attention mechanism and direct label-to-label dependency.

2 Model Description

Assume that we have a training dataset $\mathcal{D}$ comprising a collection of dialogues, where each dialogue consists of a sequence of utterances $\{y_t\}_{t=1}^T$ and the corresponding sequence of dialogue acts $\{z_t\}_{t=1}^T$. Each utterance y_t is a sequence of tokens, and its n-th token is denoted $y_{t,n}$.

We propose a generative neural model for dialogue $P_\Theta(y_{1:T}, z_{1:T})$, which specifies a joint probability distribution over a sequence of utterances $y_{1:T}$ and the corresponding sequence of dialogue acts $z_{1:T}$. This generative model is then trained discriminatively by maximising the conditional log-likelihood $\sum_{(z_{1:T}, y_{1:T}) \in \mathcal{D}} \log P_\Theta(z_{1:T} | y_{1:T})$:

$$\arg\max_\Theta \sum_{(y_{1:T}, z_{1:T}) \in \mathcal{D}} \log \frac{P_\Theta(y_{1:T}, z_{1:T})}{\sum_{z'_{1:T}} P_\Theta(y_{1:T}, z'_{1:T})}$$

Proceedings of the 55th Annual Meeting of the Association for Computational Linguistics (Short Papers), pages 524–529
Vancouver, Canada, July 30 - August 4, 2017. ©2017 Association for Computational Linguistics
https://doi.org/10.18653/v1/P17-2083

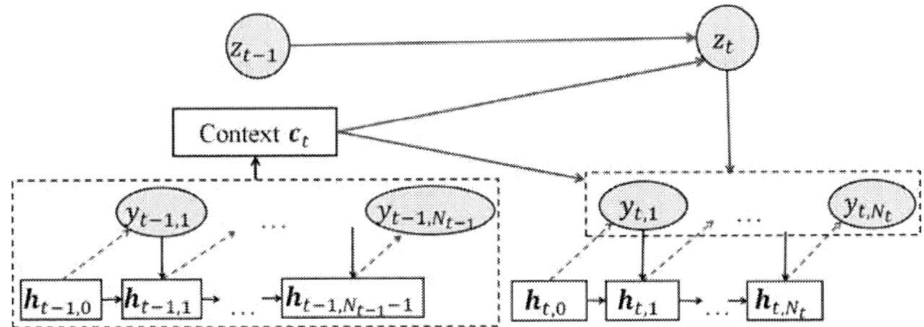

Figure 1: Graphical model representation of our model. Red connections depict dialogue-act generation (1); purple connections (dashed and continuous) depict utterance generation (2).

where Θ represents all neural network parameters. Discriminative training is employed in order to match the use of the model for predicting dialogue acts during test time, using $\arg\max_{z'_{1:T}} P_\Theta(z'_{1:T}|y_{1:T})$.

The generative story of our model is as follows: (1) generate the dialogue act of the current dialogue turn conditioned on the previous dialogue act and the previous utterance $P_\Theta(z_t|z_{t-1}, y_{t-1})$; and (2) generate the current utterance conditioned on the previous utterance and the current dialogue act $P_\Theta(y_t|z_t, y_{t-1})$. In other words, $P_\Theta(z_{1:T}, y_{1:T})$ is decomposed as:

$$\prod_{t=1}^{T} P_\Theta(z_t|z_{t-1}, y_{t-1})P_\Theta(y_t|z_t, y_{t-1}). \quad (1)$$

Furthermore, each utterance is generated by a sequential process whereby each token $y_{t,n}$ is conditioned on all the previously generated tokens $y_{t,<n}$, as well as the external conditioning context consisting of the dialogue act z_t and the previous turn's utterance y_{t-1}, i.e.,

$$P_\Theta(y_t|z_t, y_{t-1}) = \prod_{n=1}^{|y_t|} P_\Theta(y_{t,n}|y_{t,<n}, z_t, y_{t-1}). \quad (2)$$

Importantly, the decomposition of the joint distribution in Equation 1 allows dynamic programming for exact decoding (§2.2). One possible extension of our framework is to investigate a higher-order Markov model, although one needs to be conscious about the trade-off between the increase in the computational complexity of training/decoding with higher-order Markov models versus the potential gain in classification quality.

We now turn our attention to the neural architecture used to realise the components of our probabilistic model (Figure 1). We define the neural model for the conditional probability of the next dialogue act as follows:

$$P_\Theta(z_t|z_{t-1}, y_{t-1}) = \\ \text{softmax}(W_{cz}^{(z_{t-1})}c_t + b_z^{(z_{t-1})}), \quad (3)$$

where c_t is the *context* vector summarising the information from the previous utterance y_{t-1}, and $W_{cz}^{(z_{t-1})}$ and $b_z^{(z_{t-1})}$ are the softmax parameter *gated* on the previous dialogue act z_{t-1}. Due to gating, the number of parameters of the model may increase significantly; therefore, we have also explored a variant where only the bias term $b_z^{(z_{t-1})}$ is gated. We define the neural model for generating the tokens of the current utterance as follows:

$$P_\Theta(y_{t,n}|y_{t,<n}, z_t, y_{t-1}) = \\ \text{softmax}(W_{hy}^{(z_t)}h_{t,n-1} + W_c c_t + b_y), \quad (4)$$

where the weight matrix $W_{hy}^{(z_t)}$ is gated based on z_t, c_t summarises the previous utterance, and $h_{t,n-1}$ is the state of an utterance-level RNN summarising all the previously generated tokens:

$$h_{t,n-1} = f(h_{t,n-2}, E_{y_{t,n-1}}), \quad (5)$$

where $E_{y_{t,n-1}}$ provides the embedding of the token $y_{t,n-1}$ from the embedding table E, and f can be any non-linear function, i.e., the simple *sigmoid* applied to elements of a vector, or the more complex Long-Short-Term-Memory unit (*LSTM*) (Graves, 2013; Hochreiter and Schmidhuber, 1997), or the Gated-Recurrent-Unit (*GRU*) (Chung et al., 2014; Cho et al., 2014).

In what follows, we elaborate on how to best summarise the information from the previous utterance in c_t, and how to decode for the best sequence of dialogue acts given a trend model.

2.1 The Gated Attention Mechanism

Given a sequence of words in an utterance $\{y_1, \ldots, y_n\}$, we would like to compress its information in c, which is then used in the conditioning contexts of other components of the model. Typically, the last hidden state of the utterance-level RNN is taken to be the summary vector: $c = h_n$. However, it has been shown that *attending* to all RNN states is more effective.

The traditional attention mechanism (Bahdanau et al., 2014) employs a probability vector a over the words of the input utterance to summarise it. The attention elements in a are typically calculated from the current input y_n, and the previous hidden state h_{n-1}:

$$\alpha_n = g(h_{n-1}, E_{y_n}) \quad , \quad a_n = \frac{e^{\alpha_n}}{\sum_{n'=1}^{n} e^{\alpha_{n'}}},$$

where g is a non-linear function. Once the attention is defined, the representation of the input is constructed as

$$c = \sum_n a_n h_n. \tag{6}$$

The problem with this traditional attention model is that the final hidden state is a function of all the inputs, hence it is usually more "informative" than the earlier hidden states due to semantic accumulation (Wang et al., 2016). Thus, most of the attention signal is assigned to the hidden states toward the end of a sequence. In DA classification, this may not be desirable, since an important token with respect to a dialogue act can appear anywhere in an utterance. We call this the *attention bias* problem.

We propose a novel gated attention mechanism, which is inspired by the gating mechanism in LSTMs, to fix the *attention bias* problem. Similar to the forget gate of LSTMs, we use the available information to calculate an attention gate that learns whether to allow the whole *input signal* to pass through or to forget all or a part of the input signal:

$$a_n = g(h_{n-1}, E_{y_n}) \tag{7}$$
$$x_n = a_n \odot E_{y_n} \tag{8}$$
$$h_n = f(h_{n-1}, x_n) \tag{9}$$

where $\odot$ represents element-wise multiplication.

After filtering the important signal from the input token, the information from our tokens is accumulated in the last hidden state of the RNN, which we take as the summary vector $c = h_n$. Note that since the gated attention is applied to the input before the RNN calculations, it is not affected by the attention bias.

2.2 Inference: Viterbi Decoding

For prediction, we choose the sequence of dialogue acts with the highest posterior probability:

$$\arg\max_{z'_{1:T}} P_\Theta(z'_{1:T}|y_{1:T}) = \arg\max_{z'_{1:T}} P_\Theta(z'_{1:T}, y_{1:T})$$

Since the joint probability is decomposed further according to Equation 1, we can make use of dynamic programming to find the highest probability sequence of dialogue acts. Specifically, the model endows each latent variable z_t with a unary potential $P_\Theta(y_t|z_t, y_{t-1})$ and binary potential $P_\Theta(z_t|z_{t-1}, y_{t-1})$ functions. $P_\Theta(y_t|z_t, y_{t-1})$ and $P_\Theta(z_t|z_{t-1}, y_{t-1})$ are akin to the *emission* and *transition* functions of an HMM, and are calculated using Equations 2 and 3 respectively. Furthermore, the model has been carefully designed so that the hidden states in the RNNs encoding the utterances to form the context vector c_t (the representation of the previous utterance) are *not* affected by the sequence of dialogue acts, which is crucial to making the inference amenable to dynamic programming. The resulting inference algorithm is akin to the Viterbi algorithm for HMMs.

3 Experiments

Datasets. We conduct our experiments on the MapTask and Switchboard corpora. The MapTask Dialog Act corpus (Anderson et al., 1991) consists of 128 conversations and more than 27000 utterances in an instruction-giving scenario. There are 13 DA types in this corpus. For the experiments, the available data is split into three parts, train/test/validation with 103, 13 and 12 conversations respectively.

The Switchboard Dialog Act corpus (Jurafsky et al., 1997) consists of 1155 transcribed telephone conversations with around 205000 utterances. In contrast with the MapTask conversations, which are task-oriented, the Switchboard corpus consists mostly of general topic conversations. The Switchboard tag set has 42 DAs.[1]

---

[1]The original size of the tag set for Switchboard is 226, which was then collapsed into 42

	without HMM	gate bias HMM	gate all HMM
no attn.	60.97%	64.60%	63.55%
traditional	61.72%	64.73%	65.19%
gated attn.	62.21%	**65.94%**	**65.94%**

Table 1: Comparison of our model variants on the MapTask corpus.

Baselines. On MapTask, to the best of our knowledge, there is no standard data split, thus, we make the comparison against our implementation of strong baselines such as HMM-trigram (Stolcke et al., 2000) and instance-based random forest classifier (1/2/3-gram features). Ji *et al.*'s (2016) results for this corpus are obtained by running their publicly available code with the same hyper parameters as those used by our models. We also report the results of Julia *et al.* (2010)[2] and Surendran *et al.* (2006). However, the experimental setup of these two works differs from ours, hence their results are not directly comparable to ours.

On Switchboard, we compare our results with strong baselines using the experimental setup from Kalchbrenner and Blunsom (2013) and Stolcke *et al.* (2000).[3]

Our Model Configurations. We experiment with several variants of our model to explore the effectiveness of our two improvements: the HMM-like connection and the gated attention mechanism. For the HMM connection, we consider three choices: gating all parameters (Equation 3), gating only the bias, and no connection. For the attention, we consider three choices: our new gated attention mechanism, the traditional attention, and no attention. Thus, in total, we explore nine model variants.

All the model variants are implemented with the CNN package[4] and trained with Adagrad (Duchi et al., 2011) using dropout (Srivastava et al., 2014). They share the same word-embedding size (128) and hidden vector size (64).[5]

Models	Accuracy
Julia *et al.* (2010)	55.40%
Surendran *et al.* (2006)	59.10%
HMM (Stolcke *et al.* (2000))	51.40%
Random Forest (n-gram)	55.72%
Ji *et al.* (2016)	60.97%
Our model	
gated attn. + gated HMM bias	**65.94%**
gated attn. + gated HMM all	**65.94%**

Table 2: Results on MapTask data.

Models	Accuracy
Stolcke *et al.* (2000)	71.0%
Kalchbrenner and Blunsom (2013)	73.9%
Ji *et al.* (2016)	72.5%
Shen and Lee (2016)	72.6%
our model	
gated attn. + gated HMM bias	**74.2%**
gated attn. + gated HMM all	74.0%

Table 3: Results on Switchboard data.

Results and Analysis. Table 1 shows the classification accuracy of the nine variants of our model on the MapTask corpus. The classification accuracy of the two best variants of our model and the baselines appears in Tables 2 and 3 for MapTask and Switchboard respectively. The bold numbers in each table show the best accuracy achieved by the systems. As seen in these tables, our best models outperform strong baselines for both corpora.[6]

Table 1 shows that adding the attention mechanism is beneficial, as the traditional attention models always outperform their non-attention counterparts. The gated attention configurations, in turn, outperform those with the traditional attention mechanism by 0.49%-1.21%. Interestingly, the accuracy of Shen and Lee's (2016) classifier, which employs an attention mechanism, is lower than that obtained by Kalchbrenner and Blunsom (2013), whose mechanism does not use attention. We believe that the difference in performance is not due to the attention mechanism being ineffective, but because Shen and Lee (2016) treat the classification of each utterance independently. In contrast, Kalchbrenner and Blunsom (2013) take

---

[2]Julia *et al.* (2010) employed both text transcription and audio signal. Here, we report the results obtained with the transcription.

[3]There have been other works with different experimental setups (Gambäck et al., 2011; Webb and Ferguson, 2010) that obtained accuracies ranging from 77.85% to 80.72%. However, these results are not directly comparable to ours.

[4]https://github.com/clab/cnn-v1.

[5]The experiments were executed on an Intel Xeon E5-2667 CPU with 16GB of RAM. The training time for each MapTask model is less than a day, the training time for each Switchboard model takes up to four weeks.

[6]Ji *et al.* (2016) reported an accuracy of 77.0% on the Switchboard corpus, but their paper does not provide enough information about the experimental setup to replicate this result (hyper-parameters, train/test/development split). Thus, we ran the paper's publicly available code with our experimental settings, and report the result in our comparison.

the sequential nature of dialog acts into account, and run an RNN across the conversation, which conditions the generation of a dialogue act on the dialogue acts and utterances in all the previous dialogue turns.

As seen in Table 1, the performance gain from the HMM connection is larger than the gain from the attention mechanism. Without the attention mechanism, the HMM connection brings an increase of 3.63% with the gated bias HMM configuration and 2.58% with the fully gated HMM configuration. With the use of traditional attention, the improvement is 3.01% for the bias HMM configuration and 3.47% for the gated HMM configuration. Finally with the gated attention in place, the two HMM configurations improve the accuracy by 3.73%.

We used McNemar's test to determine the statistical significance between the predictions of different models, and found that our model with both innovations (HMM connections and gated attention) is statistically significantly better than the variant without these innovations with $\alpha < 0.01$.

4 Conclusions

In this work, we have proposed a new gated attention mechanism and a novel HMM-like connection in a generative model of utterances and dialogue acts. Our experiments show that these two innovations significantly improve the accuracy of DA classification on the MapTask and Switchboard corpora. In the future, we plan to apply these two innovations to other sequence-to-sequence learning tasks. Furthermore, DA classification itself can be seen as a preprocessing step in a dialogue system's pipeline. Thus, we also plan to investigate the effect of improvements in DA classification on the downstream components of a dialogue system.

References

Anne H Anderson, Miles Bader, Ellen Gurman Bard, Elizabeth Boyle, Gwyneth Doherty, Simon Garrod, Stephen Isard, Jacqueline Kowtko, Jan McAllister, Jim Miller, et al. 1991. The HCRC map task corpus. *Language and speech* 34(4):351–366.

Dzmitry Bahdanau, Kyunghyun Cho, and Yoshua Bengio. 2014. Neural machine translation by jointly learning to align and translate. *arXiv preprint arXiv:1409.0473* .

Kyunghyun Cho, Bart Van Merriënboer, Dzmitry Bahdanau, and Yoshua Bengio. 2014. On the properties of neural machine translation: Encoder-decoder approaches. *arXiv preprint arXiv:1409.1259* .

Junyoung Chung, Caglar Gulcehre, KyungHyun Cho, and Yoshua Bengio. 2014. Empirical evaluation of gated recurrent neural networks on sequence modeling. *arXiv preprint arXiv:1412.3555* .

John Duchi, Elad Hazan, and Yoram Singer. 2011. Adaptive subgradient methods for online learning and stochastic optimization. *Journal of Machine Learning Research* 12(Jul):2121–2159.

Björn Gambäck, Fredrik Olsson, and Oscar Täckström. 2011. Active learning for dialogue act classification. In *Interspeech 2011 – Proceedings of the International Conference on Spoken Language Processing*. pages 1329–1332.

Alex Graves. 2013. Generating sequences with recurrent neural networks. *arXiv preprint arXiv:1308.0850* .

Sepp Hochreiter and Jürgen Schmidhuber. 1997. Long short-term memory. *Neural computation* 9(8):1735–1780.

Yangfeng Ji, Gholamreza Haffari, and Jacob Eisenstein. 2016. A latent variable recurrent neural network for discourse-driven language models. In *Proceedings of the 2016 Conference of the North American Chapter of the Association for Computational Linguistics: Human Language Technologies*. pages 332–342. http://www.aclweb.org/anthology/N16-1037.

Fatema N Julia, Khan M Iftekharuddin, and ATIQ U ISLAM. 2010. Dialog act classification using acoustic and discourse information of maptask data. *International Journal of Computational Intelligence and Applications* 9(04):289–311.

Daniel Jurafsky, Elizabeth Shriberg, and Debra Biasca. 1997. Switchboard SWBD-DAMSL Shallow-Discourse-Function Annotation Coders Manual, Draft 13. Technical report, University of Colorado.

Nal Kalchbrenner and Phil Blunsom. 2013. Recurrent convolutional neural networks for discourse compositionality. *arXiv preprint arXiv:1306.3584* .

Minh-Thang Luong, Hieu Pham, and Christopher D. Manning. 2015. Effective approaches to attention-based neural machine translation. In *Proceedings of the 2015 Conference on Empirical Methods in Natural Language Processing*. pages 1412–1421. http://aclweb.org/anthology/D15-1166.

Sheng-syun Shen and Hung-yi Lee. 2016. Neural attention models for sequence classification: Analysis and application to key term extraction and dialogue act detection. *arXiv preprint arXiv:1604.00077* .

Nitish Srivastava, Geoffrey Hinton, Alex Krizhevsky, Ilya Sutskever, and Ruslan Salakhutdinov. 2014. Dropout: A simple way to prevent neural networks from overfitting. *Journal of Machine Learning Research* 15(1):1929–1958. http://dl.acm.org/citation.cfm?id=2627435.2670313.

Andreas Stolcke, Noah Coccaro, Rebecca Bates, Paul Taylor, Carol Van Ess-Dykema, Klaus Ries, Elizabeth Shriberg, Daniel Jurafsky, Rachel Martin, and Marie Meteer. 2000. Dialogue act modeling for automatic tagging and recognition of conversational speech. *Computational linguistics* 26(3):339–373.

Dinoj Surendran and Gina-Anne Levow. 2006. Dialog act tagging with support vector machines and hidden markov models. In *Interspeech 2006 – Proceedings of the International Conference on Spoken Language Processing*. pages 1950–1953.

Bingning Wang, Kang Liu, and Jun Zhao. 2016. Inner attention based recurrent neural networks for answer selection. In *Proceedings of the 54th Annual Meeting of the Association for Computational Linguistics (Volume 1: Long Papers)*. pages 1288–1297. http://www.aclweb.org/anthology/P16-1122.

Nick Webb and Michael Ferguson. 2010. Automatic extraction of cue phrases for cross-corpus dialogue act classification. In *Proceedings of the 23rd International Conference on Computational Linguistics: Posters*. pages 1310–1317.

Salience Rank: Efficient Keyphrase Extraction with Topic Modeling

Nedelina Teneva[*]
The University of Chicago
nteneva@uchicago.edu

Weiwei Cheng
Amazon
weiweic@amazon.de

Abstract

Topical PageRank (TPR) uses latent topic distribution inferred by Latent Dirichlet Allocation (LDA) to perform ranking of noun phrases extracted from documents. The ranking procedure consists of running PageRank K times, where K is the number of topics used in the LDA model. In this paper, we propose a modification of TPR, called *Salience Rank*. Salience Rank only needs to run PageRank once and extracts comparable or better keyphrases on benchmark datasets. In addition to quality and efficiency benefits, our method has the flexibility to extract keyphrases with varying tradeoffs between topic specificity and corpus specificity.

1 Introduction

Automatic keyphrase extraction consists of finding a set of terms in a document that provides a concise summary of the text content (Hasan and Ng, 2014). In this paper we consider unsupervised keyphrase extraction, where no human labeled corpus of documents is used for training a classifier (Grineva et al., 2009; Pasquier, 2010; Liu et al., 2009b; Zhao et al., 2011; Liu et al., 2009a). This is a scenario often arising in practical applications as human annotation and tagging is both time and resource consuming. Unsupervised keyphrase extraction is typically casted as a ranking problem – first, candidate phrases are extracted from documents, typically noun phrases identified by part-of-speech tagging; then these candidates are ranked. The performance of unsupervised keyphrase extraction algorithms is evaluated by comparing the most highly ranked keyphrases with keyphrases assigned by annotators.

______
[*] Work done as an intern at Amazon.

This paper proposes *Salience Rank*, a modification of Topical PageRank algorithm by Liu et al. (2010). Our method is close in spirit to Single Topical PageRank by Sterckx et al. (2015) and includes it as a special case. The advantages of Salience Rank are twofold:

Performance: The algorithm extracts high-quality keyphrases that are comparable to, and sometimes better than, the ones extracted by Topical PageRank. Salience Rank is more efficient than Topical PageRank as it runs PageRank once, rather than multiple times.

Configurability: The algorithm is based on the concept of "word salience" (hence its name), which is described in Section 3 and can be used to balance topic specificity and corpus specificity of the extracted keyphrases. Depending on the use case, the output of the Salience Rank algorithm can be tuned accordingly.

2 Review of Related Models

Below we introduce some notation and discuss approaches that are most related to ours.

Let $W = \{w_1, w_2, \ldots, w_N\}$ be the set of all the words present in a corpus of documents. Let $G = (W, E)$ denote a word graph, whose vertices represent words and an edge $e(w_i, w_j) \in E$ indicates the relatedness between words w_i and w_j in a document (measured, e.g., by co-occurrence or number of co-occurrences between the two words). The outdegree of vertex w_i is given by $Out(w_i) = \sum_{i:w_i \to w_j} e(w_i, w_j)$.

2.1 Topical PageRank

The main idea behind Topical PageRank (TPR) (Liu et al., 2010) is to incorporate topical information by performing Latent Dirichlet Allocation (LDA) (Blei et al., 2003) on a corpus of documents. TPR constructs a word graph $G = (W, E)$ based on the word co-occurrences within documents. It uses LDA to find the latent topics of the

Proceedings of the 55th Annual Meeting of the Association for Computational Linguistics (Short Papers), pages 530–535
Vancouver, Canada, July 30 - August 4, 2017. ©2017 Association for Computational Linguistics
https://doi.org/10.18653/v1/P17-2084

document, reweighs the word graph according to each latent topic, and runs PageRank (Page et al., 1998) once per topic.

In LDA each word w of a document d is assumed to be generated by first sampling a topic $t \in T$ (where T is a set of K topics) from d's topic distribution θ^d and then sampling a word from the distribution over words ϕ^t of topic t. Both θ^d and ϕ^t are drawn from conjugate Dirichlet priors α and β, respectively. Thus, the probability of word w, given document d and the priors α and β, is

$$p(w \mid d, \alpha, \beta) = \sum_{t \in T} p(w \mid t, \beta)\, p(t \mid d, \alpha)\,. \quad (1)$$

After running LDA, TPR ranks each word $w_i \in W$ of G by

$$R_t(w_i) = \lambda \sum_{j:\, w_j \to w_i} \frac{e(w_i, w_j)}{Out(w_j)} R_t(w_j) + (1-\lambda)p(t \mid w_i)\,, \quad (2)$$

for $t \in T$, where $p(t \mid w)$ is estimated via LDA.

TPR assigns a topic specific preference value $p(t \mid w)$ to each $w \in W$ as the jump probability at each vertex depending on the underlying topic. Intuitively, $p(t \mid w)$ indicates how much the word w focuses on topic t.[1]

At the next step of TPR, the word scores (2) are accumulated into keyphrase scores. In particular, for each topic t, a candidate keyphrase is ranked by the sum of the word scores

$$R_t(\text{phrase}) = \sum_{w_i \in \text{phrase}} R_t(w_i)\,. \quad (3)$$

By combining the topic specific keyphrase scores $R_t(\text{phrase})$ with the probability $p(t \mid d)$ derived from the LDA we can compute the final keyphrase scores across all K topics:

$$R(\text{phrase}) = \sum_{t \in T} R_t(\text{phrase})\, p(t \mid d)\,. \quad (4)$$

2.2 Single Topical PageRank

Single Topical PageRank (STPR) was recently proposed by Sterckx et al. (2015). It aims to reduce the runtime complexity of TPR and at the same time maintain its predictive performance. Similar to Salience Rank, it runs PageRank once. STPR is based on the idea of "topical word importance" $TWI(w)$, which is defined as the cosine similarity between the vector of

word-topic probabilities $[p(w \mid t_1), \ldots, p(w \mid t_K)]$ and the vector of document-topic probabilities $[p(t_1 \mid d), \ldots, p(t_K \mid d)]$, for each word w given the document d. STPR then uses PageRank to rank each word $w_i \in W$ by replacing $p(t \mid w_i)$ in (2) with $\frac{TWI(w_i)}{\sum_{w_k \in W} TWI(w_k)}$.

STPR can be seen as a special case of Salience Rank, where topic specificity of a word is considered when constructing the random walk, but corpus specificity is neglected. In practice, however, balancing these two concepts is important. It may explain why Salience Rank outperforms STPR in our experiments.

3 Salience Rank

In order to achieve performance and configurability, the Salience Rank (SR) algorithm combines the K latent topics estimated by LDA into a word metric, called *word salience*, and uses it as a preference value for each $w_i \in W$. Thus, SR needs to perform only a single run of PageRank on the word graph G in order to obtain a ranking of the words in each document.

3.1 Word Salience

In the following we provide quantitative measures for topic specificity and corpus specificity, and define word salience.

Definition 3.1 *The topic specificity of a word w is*

$$\begin{aligned} TS(w) &= \sum_{t \in T} p(t \mid w) \log \frac{p(t \mid w)}{p(t)} \\ &= KL\left(p(t \mid w) \,\|\, p(t)\right)\,. \end{aligned} \quad (5)$$

The definition of topic specificity of a word w is equivalent to Chuang et al. (2012)'s proposal of the *distinctiveness* of a word w, which is in turn equivalent to the Kullback-Leibler (KL) divergence from the marginal probability $p(t)$, i.e., the likelihood that any randomly selected word is generated by topic t, to the conditional probability $p(t \mid w)$, i.e., the likelihood that an observed word w is generated by a latent topic t. Intuitively, topic specificity measures how much a word is shared across topics: The less w is shared across topics, the higher its topic specificity $TS(w)$.

As $TS(w)$ is non-negative and unbounded, we can empirically normalize it to $[0, 1]$ by

$$\frac{TS(w) - \min_u TS(u)}{\max_u TS(u) - \min_u TS(u)}$$

---

[1] Liu et al. (2010) proposed two other quantities to bias the random walk, $p(w \mid t)$ and $p(w \mid t)p(w \mid w)$, and showed that $p(t \mid w)$ achieves the best empirical result. We therefore adopt the use of $p(t \mid w)$ here.

531

with the minimum and maximum topic specificity values in the corpus. In what follows, we always use normalized topic specificity values, unless explicitly stated otherwise.

We apply a straightforward definition for corpus specificity.

Definition 3.2 *The corpus specificity of a word w is*

$$CS(w) = p(w \mid corpus). \qquad (6)$$

The corpus specificity $CS(w)$ of a word w can be estimated by counting word frequencies in the corpus of interest. Finally, a word's salience is defined as a linear combination of its topic specificity and corpus specificity.

Definition 3.3 *The salience of a word w is*

$$S(w) = (1 - \alpha)CS(w) + \alpha TS(w), \qquad (7)$$

where $\alpha \in [0, 1]$ is a parameter controlling the tradeoff between the corpus specificity and the topic specificity of w.

On one hand, we aim to extract keyphrases that are relevant to one or more topics while, on the other hand, the extracted keyphrases as a whole should have a good coverage of the topics in the document. Depending on the downstream applications, it is often useful to be able to control the balance between these two competing principles. In other words, sometimes keyphrases with high topic specificity (i.e., phrases that are representative exclusively for certain topics) are more appropriate, while other times keyphrases with high corpus specificity (i.e., phrases that are representative of the corpus as a whole) are more appropriate. Intuitively, it is advantageous for a keyphrase extraction algorithm to have an internal "switch" tuning the extent to which extracted keyphrases are skewed towards particular topics and, conversely, the extent to which keyphrases generalize across different topics.

It needs to be emphasized that the choice of quantitative measures for topic specificity and corpus specificity used above is just one among many possibilities. For example, for topic specificity, one can make use of the topical word importance by Sterckx et al. (2015), or the several other alternatives mentioned in Section 2.1 proposed by Liu et al. (2010). For corpus specificity, alternatives besides vanilla term frequencies, such as augmented frequency (to discount

longer documents) and logarithmically scaled frequency, quickly come into mind.

Taking word salience into account, we modify (2) as follow:

$$R(w_i) = \lambda \sum_{j:w_j \to w_i} \frac{e(w_j, w_i)}{Out(w_j)} R(w_j) + (1 - \lambda)S(w_i). \qquad (8)$$

The substantial efficiency boost of SR comparing to TPR lies in the fact that in (2) K PageRanks are required to calculate $R_t(w_i), t = 1 \ldots K$ before obtaining $R(w_i)$, while in (8) $R(w_i)$ is obtained with a single PageRank.

3.2 Algorithm Description

First, SR performs LDA to estimate the latent topics $p(t)$ presented in the corpus and the probability $p(t \mid w)$, which are used to calculate the topic specificity and the salience of each word w.

Similarly to TPR, SR is performed on the word co-occurrence graph $G = (W, E)$. We use undirected graphs: When sliding a window of size s through the document, a link between two vertices is added if these two words appear within the window. It was our observation that the edge direction does not affect the keyphrase extraction performance much. The same observation was noted by Mihalcea and Tarau (2004) and Liu et al. (2010).

We then run the updated version of PageRank derived in (8) and compute the scores of the candidate keyphrases similarly to the way TPR does using (4). For a fair comparison, noun phrases with the pattern `(adjective)*(noun)+` are chosen as candidate keyphrases, which represents zero or more adjectives followed by one or more nouns. It is the same pattern suggested by Liu et al. (2010) in the original TPR paper. SR combines the K PageRank runs in TPR into a single one using salience as a preference value in the word graph.

4 Results

Our experiments are conducted on two widely used datasets in the keyphrase extraction literature, *500N-KPCrowd* (Marujo et al., 2013) and *Inspec* (Hulth, 2003). The *500N-KPCrowd* dataset consists of 500 news articles, 50 stories for each of 10 categories, manually annotated with keyphrases by 20 Amazon Mechanical Turk workers. The *Inspec* dataset is a collection of 2000 paper abstracts of Computer Science & Information Technology journal with manually assigned

dataset	algorithm	precision	recall	F measure
500N-KPCrowd	TPR	0.254	0.222	0.229 ($\pm$0.010)
	STPR	0.252	0.221	0.228 ($\pm$0.011)
	SR	0.253	0.222	0.229 ($\pm$0.010)
Inspec	TPR	0.225	0.255	0.227 ($\pm$0.007)
	STPR	0.222	0.254	0.224 ($\pm$0.007)
	SR	0.265	0.298	0.266 ($\pm$0.007)

Table 1: Comparison of the algorithms on *500N-KPCrowd* and *Inspec*. On both datasets, TPR, STPR and SR were run with 50 LDA topics. In all experiments we used a damping factor $\lambda = 0.85$ in PageRank, as in the original PageRank algorithm, and a window size $s = 2$ to construct the word graphs. Changing the window size s from 2 to 20 does not influence the results much, as also observed in Liu et al. (2010). The convergence of PageRank is achieved when the l^2 norm of the vector containing $R(w_i)$ changes smaller than 10^{-6}. The tradeoff parameter α in SR is fixed at 0.4. The 95% confidence interval for the F measure is shown in the last column.

# topics	precision	recall	F measure
5	0.249	0.218	0.225 ($\pm$0.011)
50	0.253	0.222	0.229 ($\pm$0.010)
250	0.247	0.216	0.223 ($\pm$0.011)
500	0.247	0.216	0.223 ($\pm$0.011)

Table 2: Effect of the number of LDA topics when the top 50 keyphrases were used for evaluating SR on *500N-KPCrowd*. The 95% confidence interval for the F measure is shown in the last column.

α	precision	recall	F measure
1.0	0.247	0.216	0.223 ($\pm$0.011)
0.7	0.248	0.216	0.223 ($\pm$0.011)
0.4	0.248	0.217	0.224 ($\pm$0.011)
0.1	0.254	0.222	0.229 ($\pm$0.010)
0.0	0.248	0.217	0.224 ($\pm$0.011)

Table 3: Effect of the α parameter in SR on *500N-KPCrowd*. SR was run with 50 LDA topics and the top 50 keyphrases were used for the evaluation. The 95% confidence interval for the F measure is shown in the last column.

keyphrases by the authors. Following the evaluation process described in Mihalcea and Tarau (2004), we use only the uncontrolled set of annotated keyphrases for our analysis. Since our approach is completely unsupervised, we combine the training, testing, and validation datasets. Top 50 and 10 keyphrases were used for evaluation on *500N-KPCrowd* and *Inspec*, respectively.[2]

We compare the performance of Salience Rank (SR), Topical PageRank (TPR), and Single Topical PageRank (STPR) in terms of precision, recall and F measure on *500N-KPCrowd* and *Inspec*. The results are summarized in Table 1. Details on parametrization are given in the caption. In terms of the F measure, SR achieves the best results on both datasets. It ties TPR and outperforms STPR on *500N-KPCrowd*, and outperforms both TPR and STPR on *Inspec*. The source code is available at `https://github.com/methanet/saliencerank.git`.

We further experiment with varying the number of topics K used for fitting the LDA model in SR. Table 2 shows how the F measures change on *500N-KPCrowd* as the number of topics varies. Overall, the impact of topic size is mild, with $K = 50$ being the optimal value. The impact of K on TPR can be found in Liu et al. (2010). In our approach, the random walk derived in (8) depends on the word salience, which in turn depends on K; In TPR, not only the individual random walk (2) depends on K, but the final aggregation of rankings of keyphrases also depends on K.

We also experiment with varying the tradeoff parameter α of SR. With *500N-KPCrowd*, Table 3 illustrates that different α can have a considerable impact on various performance measures. To complement the quantitative results in Table 3, Table 4 presents a concrete example, showing that varying α can lead to qualitative changes in the top ranked keyphrases. In particular, when $\alpha = 0$ the corpus specificity of the keyphrases SR extracts is high. This is demonstrated by the fact that words such as "theory" and "function" are among

---

[2]There are two common ways to set the number of output keyphrases: using a fixed value a priori as we do (Turney, 1999) or deciding a value with heuristics at runtime (Mihalcea and Tarau, 2004).

Input: Individual rationality, or doing what is best for oneself, is a standard model used to explain and predict human behavior, and von Neumann-Morgenstern game theory is the classical mathematical formalization of this theory in multiple-agent settings. Individual rationality, however, is an inadequate model for the synthesis of artificial social systems where cooperation is essential, since it does not permit the accommodation of group interests other than as aggregations of individual interests. Satisficing game theory is based upon a well-defined notion of being good enough, and does accommodate group as well as individual interests through the use of conditional preference relationships, whereby a decision maker is able to adjust its preferences as a function of the preferences, and not just the options, of others. This new theory is offered as an alternative paradigm to construct artificial societies that are capable of complex behavior that goes beyond exclusive self interest.	
Unique top keyphrases with $\alpha = 0$: classical mathematical formalization preferences theory options function multiple agent settings	**Unique top keyphrases with $\alpha = 1$:** individual interests group interests artificial social systems individual rationality conditional preference relationships standard model

Table 4: An example of running SR on an *Inspec* abstract with a minimum and maximum value of α. Unique keyphrases among the top 10 are shown.

the top keyphrases SR selects, which are highly common words in scientific papers. On the other hand, when $\alpha = 1$ these keyphrases are not presented among the top. This toy example illustrates the relevance of balancing topic and corpus specificity in practice: When presenting the keyphrases to a layman, high corpus specificity is suitable as it conveys more high-level information; when presenting to an expert in the area, high topic specificity is suitable as it dives deeper into topic specific details.

5   Conclusions & Remarks

In this paper, we propose a new keyphrase extraction method, called Salience Rank. It improves upon the Topical PageRank algorithm by Liu et al. (2010) and the Single Topical PageRank algorithm by Sterckx et al. (2015). The key advantages of this new method are twofold: (i) While maintaining and sometimes improving the quality of extracted keyphrases, it only runs PageRank once instead of K times as in Topical PageRank, therefore leads to lower runtime; (ii) By constructing the underlying word graph with newly proposed word salience, it allows the user to balance topic and corpus specificity of the extracted keyphrases.

These three methods rely only on the input corpus. They can be benefited by external resources like Wikipedia and WordNet, as indicated by, e.g., Medelyan et al. (2009), Grineva et al. (2009), Martinez-Romo et al. (2016).

In the keyphrase extraction literature, LDA is the most commonly used topic modeling method. Other methods, such as probabilistic latent semantic indexing (Hofmann, 1999), nonnegative matrix factorization (Sra and Inderjit, 2006), are viable alternatives. However, it is hard to tell in general if the keyphrase quality improves with these alternatives. We suspect that strongly depends on the domain of the dataset and a choice may be made depending on other practical considerations.

We have fixed the tradeoff parameter α throughout the experiments for a straightforward comparison to other methods. In practice, one should search the optimal value of α for the task at hand. An open question is how to theoretically quantify the relationship between α and various performance measures, such as the F measure.

Acknowledgments

We would like to thank Matthias Seeger, Cedric Archambeau, Jan Gasthaus, Alex Klementiev, Ralf Herbrich, and the anonymous ACL reviewers for their valuable inputs.

References

David M Blei, Andrew Y Ng, and Michael I Jordan. 2003. Latent Dirichlet allocation. *Journal of Machine Learning Research* 3(1):993–1022.

Jason Chuang, Christopher D Manning, and Jeffrey Heer. 2012. Termite: Visualization techniques for assessing textual topic models. In *Proceedings of the International Working Conference on Advanced Visual Interfaces*. pages 74–77.

Maria Grineva, Maxim Grinev, and Dmitry Lizorkin. 2009. Extracting key terms from noisy and multi-theme documents. In *Proceedings of the 18th International Conference on World Wide Web*. WWW, pages 661–670.

Kazi Saidul Hasan and Vincent Ng. 2014. Automatic keyphrase extraction: A survey of the state of the art. In *Proceedings of the 52nd Annual Meeting of the Association for Computational Linguistics*. ACL, pages 1262–1273.

Thomas Hofmann. 1999. Probabilistic latent semantic indexing. In *Proceedings of the 22nd Annual International ACM SIGIR Conference on Research and Development in Information Retrieval*. SIGIR, pages 50–57.

Anette Hulth. 2003. Improved automatic keyword extraction given more linguistic knowledge. In *Proceedings of the 2003 Conference on Empirical Methods in Natural Language Processing*. EMNLP, pages 216–223.

Feifan Liu, Deana Pennell, Fei Liu, and Yang Liu. 2009a. Unsupervised approaches for automatic keyword extraction using meeting transcripts. In *Proceedings of the 2009 Annual Conference of the North American Chapter of the Association for Computational Linguistics*. NAACL, pages 620–628.

Zhiyuan Liu, Wenyi Huang, Yabin Zheng, and Maosong Sun. 2010. Automatic keyphrase extraction via topic decomposition. In *Proceedings of the 2010 Conference on Empirical Methods in Natural Language Processing*. EMNLP, pages 366–376.

Zhiyuan Liu, Peng Li, Yabin Zheng, and Maosong Sun. 2009b. Clustering to find exemplar terms for keyphrase extraction. In *Proceedings of the 2009 Conference on Empirical Methods in Natural Language*. EMNLP, pages 257–266.

Juan Martinez-Romo, Lourdes Araujo, and Andres Duque Fernandez. 2016. Semgraph: Extracting keyphrases following a novel semantic graph-based approach. *Journal of the Association for Information Science and Technology* 67(1):71–82.

Luís Marujo, Anatole Gershman, Jaime Carbonell, Robert Frederking, and João P Neto. 2013. Supervised topical key phrase extraction of news stories using crowdsourcing, light filtering and co-reference normalization. *arXiv preprint arXiv:1306.4886* .

Olena Medelyan, Eibe Frank, and Ian Witten. 2009. Human-competitive tagging using automatic keyphrase extraction. In *Proceedings of the 2009 Conference on Empirical Methods in Natural Language Processing*. EMNLP, pages 1318–1327.

Rada Mihalcea and Paul Tarau. 2004. Textrank: Bringing order into texts. In *Proceedings of the 2004 Conference on Empirical Methods in Natural Language Processing*. EMNLP, pages 404–411.

Lawrence Page, Sergey Brin, Rajeev Motwani, and Terry Winograd. 1998. The PageRank citation ranking: Bringing order to the web. Technical report, Stanford University.

Claude Pasquier. 2010. Single document keyphrase extraction using sentence clustering and latent Dirichlet allocation. In *Proceedings of the 5th International Workshop on Semantic Evaluation*. pages 154–157.

Suvrit Sra and Dhillon Inderjit. 2006. Generalized non-negative matrix approximations with Bregman divergences. In *Advances in Neural Information Processing Systems 18*. NIPS, pages 283–290.

Lucas Sterckx, Thomas Demeester, Johannes Deleu, and Chris Develder. 2015. Topical word importance for fast keyphrase extraction. In *Proceedings of the 24th International Conference on World Wide Web*. WWW, pages 121–122.

Peter Turney. 1999. Learning to extract keyphrases from text. Technical report, National Research Council Canada, Institute for Information Technology.

Wayne Xin Zhao, Jing Jiang, Jing He, Yang Song, Palakorn Achananuparp, Ee-Peng Lim, and Xiaoming Li. 2011. Topical keyphrase extraction from Twitter. In *Proceedings of the 49th Annual Meeting of the Association for Computational Linguistics*. ACL, pages 379–388.

List-only Entity Linking

Ying Lin[1] *, Chin-Yew Lin[2], Heng Ji[1]
[1] Computer Science Department,
Rensselaer Polytechnic Institute, Troy, NY, USA
{liny9,jih}@rpi.edu
[2] Microsoft Research, Beijing, China
cyl@microsoft.com

Abstract

Traditional Entity Linking (EL) technologies rely on rich structures and properties in the target knowledge base (KB). However, in many applications, the KB may be as simple and sparse as lists of names of the same type (e.g., lists of products). We call it as *List-only Entity Linking* problem. Fortunately, some mentions may have more cues for linking, which can be used as *seed mentions* to bridge other mentions and the uninformative entities. In this work, we select the most linkable mentions as seed mentions and disambiguate other mentions by comparing them with the seed mentions rather than directly with the entities. Our experiments on linking mentions to seven automatically mined lists show promising results and demonstrate the effectiveness of our approach.[1]

1 Introduction

Traditional Entity Linking (EL) methods usually rely on rich structures and properties in the target knowledge base (KB). These methods may not be effective in applications where detailed descriptions and properties of target entities are absent in the KB. Consider the following situations:

Disaster Response and Recovery. When a disaster strikes, people rush to the web and post tweets about the damage and casualties. Performing EL to extract key information, such as devastated towns and donor agencies, can help us monitor the situation and coordinate rescue and recovery efforts. Although many involved entities are not well-known and usually absent in general KBs, we may be able to acquire lists of these entities from the local government as the target KB.

Voice of the Customer. EL also plays an important role in mining customer opinions from data generated on social platforms and e-commerce websites, thereby helping companies better understand the needs and expectations of their customers. However, the target products are often not covered by general KBs. For example, (Cao et al., 2015) tested 32 names of General Motors car models and only found 4 in Wikipedia. Although some companies may choose to maintain a comprehensive product KB, it will be much more practical and less costly to provide only lists of product names.

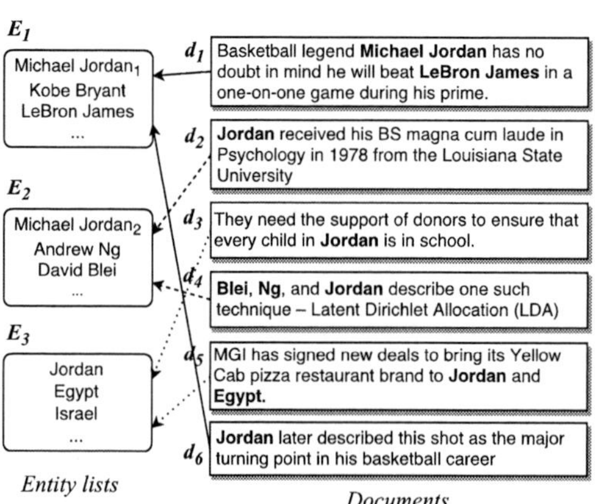

Figure 1: Link mentions to target entities in different entity lists.

Under such circumstances, we need the ability to perform EL to ad-hoc name lists instead of a comprehensive KB, namely List-only Entity Linking. Take Figure 1 as an example. For a human reader, it is not difficult to figure out the referent entities of mentions in each document based on

---

*Part of this work was done when the first author was on an internship at Microsoft Research Asia.

[1]The data set is available at: http://nlp.cs.rpi.edu/data/
link-only-entity-linking.html

Proceedings of the 55th Annual Meeting of the Association for Computational Linguistics (Short Papers), pages 536–541
Vancouver, Canada, July 30 - August 4, 2017. ©2017 Association for Computational Linguistics
https://doi.org/10.18653/v1/P17-2085

clues such as "basketball" and "LDA", whereas we will not be able to make such inference without the knowledge of the target entities. However, even if we lack the minimal knowledge (*e.g.*, Jordan is a country), we are more confident to link mentions in d_1, d_4, and d_5 because they co-occur with other entities in the same list. We consider such mentions that we are confident to link as *seed mentions*, and use them to construct contextual and non-contextual information of the target entities to enhance entity disambiguation.

Therefore, in this work, we propose to tackle the problem of List-only Entity Linking through *seed mentions*. We automatically identify seed mentions for each list using a two-step method based on the occurrence of entities and similarity between mentions. After that, in the entity disambiguation phase, we utilize the selected mentions as a bridge between uninformative entities and other mentions. Specifically, we comparing features of a non-seed mention to those of seed mentions of its entity candidates to determine which entity it should be linked to.

2   Problem Definition

Given a mention m and the entity e that it refers to, we call e the *referent entity* of m and m the *referential mention* of e. In Figure 1, for example, Michael Jordan$_1$ is the referent entity of "Jordan" in document d_6, while "Jordan" in document d_2 is an non-referential mention for Michael Jordan$_1$.

As Figure 1 shows, in the setting of List-only Entity Linking, there are a set of manually or automatically generated entity lists $\mathcal{E} = \{E_1, E_2, ..., E_l\}$ and a set of documents $D = \{d_1, d_2, ..., d_n\}$. Entities in the same list are homogeneous and share some common properties. In our experiment, each document d_i contains a mention m_i to link. Our goal is to link m_i to its referent entity $e_{i,j} \in E_j$ or returns NIL if it is unlinkable to any entities.

3   Approach

Our framework has two modules, *entity candidate retrieval* and *entity disambiguation* as Figure 2 shows. For a mention "Jordan," we retrieve two candidate entities, Michael Jordan$_1$ and Michael Jordan$_2$, from the entity lists. Next, we select a set of seed mentions for each entity from all documents. To determine the referent en-

tity of "Jordan", we compare it with seed mentions of each candidate instead of the entity itself.

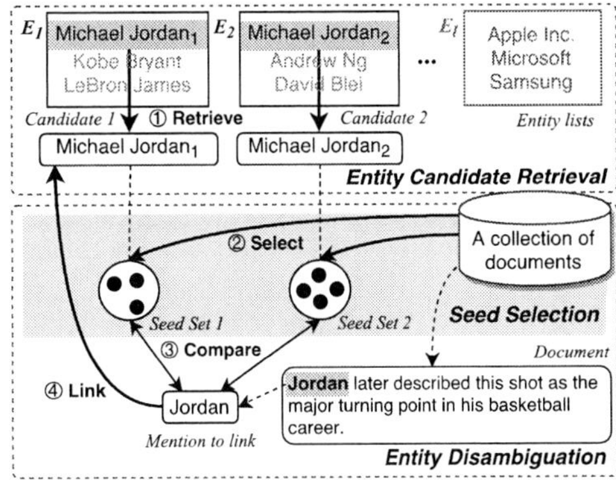

Figure 2: List-only Entity Linking Framework.

3.1   Entity Candidate Retrieval

For each mention m_i, we first locate a set of entity candidates $C_i = \{e_{i,j} | e_{i,j} \in E_j\}$ that it possibly refers to. A mention and its referent entity may have different surface forms (*e.g.*, "BMW" and Bayerische Motoren Werke). For this reason, we design a set of matching rules to improve the recall as shown in Table 1.

Category	Rule	Examples
Abbreviation	Acronym	USDOD/USDD (United States Department of Defense),
	Initial Letters	corp. (corporation), univ. (university)
	First and Last Letters	Dr. (Doctor), PA (Pennsylvania)
	Omission	Address a person by his/her given name or surname rather than full name
Substitution	Numeral	7-11 (7-Eleven)
	Symbol	AT&T (American Telephone and Telegraph Company)
	Accent Mark	hermes.com (Hermès)

Table 1: Alternative form matching rules.

3.2   Entity Disambiguation

Next, we proceed to score each candidate $e_{i,j}$ and determine which one m_i should be linked to. However, we have no knowledge of the target entities except for names and thus can't directly compare m_i with them. Rather, we propose to bridge the gap between mentions and entities through *seed mentions*.

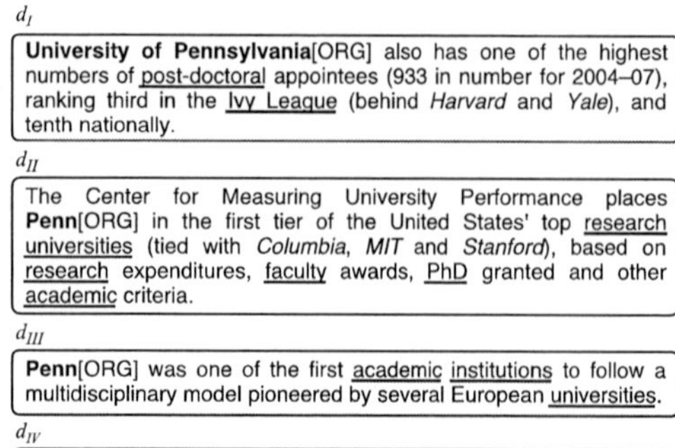

Figure 3: Bridging the gap between uncertain mentions and target entities using seed mentions.

We illustrate the idea in Figure 3. University of Pennsylvania is retrieved as an entity candidate for mentions "University of Pennsylvania", "Penn", and "Pennsylvania." We are more confident to link "University of Pennsylvania" in d_I and "Penn" in d_{II} to University of Pennsylvania because other entities in the *University* list, such as "Harvard" and "MIT," also appear in the same document. Thus, we select mentions in d_I and d_{II} as seed mentions. From d_I and d_{II}, we can extract both contextual features (*e.g.*, "academic" and "research") and non-contextual features (*e.g.*, the entity type is ORG). After that, we compare mentions in other documents with the seeds. We link "Penn" in d_{III} to University of Pennsylvania because its entity type and context are consistent with the seeds. "Pennsylvania" in d_{IV}, however, is not linked because it is recognized as a location. To capture richer contextual information and minimize the effect of noise, we select more than one seed mention using a two-step approach as follows.

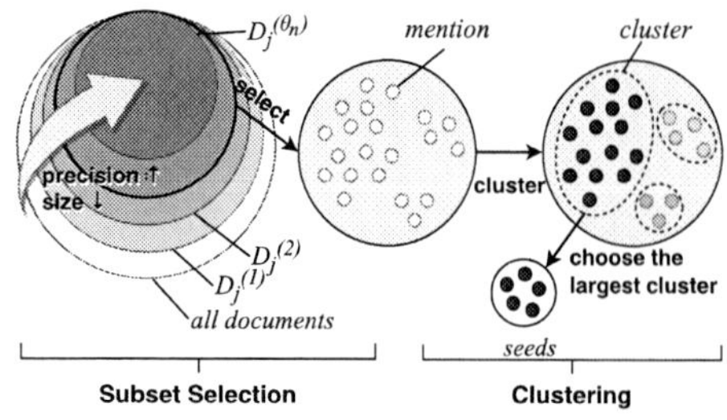

Figure 4: Seed selection.

1. **Subset Selection**. We assume that if multiple names in the same list co-occur within a docu-

ment, they are all likely to be referential mentions of this list, such as "Michael Jordan" and "LeBron James" in d_1. Hence, to identify seed mentions of list E_j, we first narrow the scope down to a subset $D_j^{(n)}$ of documents containing more than n mentions matching names in E_j. We gradually increase the n until $\theta_{\text{size}}^- \leq |D_j^{(n)}| \leq \theta_{\text{size}}^+$. θ_{size}^- and θ_{size}^+ are set to 50 and 300 in our experiments.

2. **Clustering**. We expect most mentions in the selected subset are referential of list E_j, while in fact the subset is likely to contain a small number of non-referential mentions. We need to eliminate them from the subset, otherwise they will introduce misleading features differing from the real seed mentions, hence hurting the performance of entity disambiguation. To separate referential and non-referential mentions in the selected subset, we make two assumptions: (1) Most mentions in the subset are referential, and (2) Referential mentions should be similar to each other while dissimilar from non-referential ones. Due to the lack of annotated data, we approach this problem by performing clustering, which works in an unsupervised fashion. Specifically, we represent features (described later in this section) of each mention as a vector and measure the distance between two mentions using cosine distance. After that, we run the K-means++ algorithm on the subset to separate referential and non-referential mentions, and pick mentions in the largest cluster as seed mentions.

To determine the referent entity of mention m_i, we calculate the confidence score of linking m_i to $e_{i,j} \in E_j$ using the average cosine similarity between m_i and seed mentions of list E_j:

$$c(m_i, e_{i,j}) = \frac{1}{|S_j|} \sum_{p=1}^{|S_j|} \text{sim}(m_i, m_s), m_s \in S_j$$

where S_j is the seed set of E_j. Lastly, we link m_i to the candidate with the highest confidence score.

In this work, we use the following features.

Entity Type. The entity type of a mention can be inferred from the text and used for disambiguation. For example, if most seed mentions for the *University* list are recognized as ORG, while "Harvard" in the sentence "Harvard was born and raised in Southwark, Surrey, England" is tagged as PER, it is unlikely to refer to Harvard University.

Textual Context. We also assume that referential mentions of the same entity should share

538

similar local contexts. We represent textual context using the average embedding of words within a window around the mention.

Punctuation. Punctuations preceding or following a mention may help resolve ambiguity. For example, "MA" preceded by a comma is possible to refer to a state, since states are usually the last component of an address, such as "Boston, MA".

4 Experiments

4.1 Data set

In our experiment, the construction of data set consists of two steps: collecting name lists from NeedleSeek[2] (Shi et al., 2010) and extracting documents from Wikipedia. NeedleSeek is a project aiming to mine semantic concepts from tera-scale data (ClueWeb09) and classify them into a wide range of semantic categories. For example, "KFC" is mined as a concept in the restaurant category, along with key sentences and attributes, such as employee number and founder.

To obtain target name lists, we select 7 semantic categories (see Table 2) generated by NeedleSeek as target domains, and take the top concepts in each category as target entities. We manually map each name to its pertinent Wikipedia page as a target entity (e.g., Starbucks → enwiki:Starbucks[3]). Thus, we collect lists containing 139 target entities in total. Note that category names are only for result presentation purpose and not taken as input to our model.

Category	Name Examples
President	Barack Obama, Ronald Reagan
Company	Microsoft, Apple, Adobe, IBM
University	Harvard University, Yale University
State	Washington, Florida, California, Texas
Character	Gandalf, Aragorn, Legolas, Gimli, Frodo
Brand	Prada, Chanel, Burberry, Gucci, Cartier
Restaurant	Subway, McDonald's, KFC, Starbucks

Table 2: Semantic categories from NeedleSeek.

Next, we derive a data set from Wikipedia articles through wikilinks[4], which are links to pages within English Wikipedia. For example, a wikilink [[Harvard University|Harvard]] appears as "Harvard" in text and links to the page enwiki:Harvard_University. Thus, we can consider "Harvard" as a name mention and

---

enwiki:Harvard_University as its referent entity. Consider the following sentences:

* *... then left toattend graduate school on a scholarship at* [[Harvard University|Harvard University]]...
* *On October 6, 2012,* [[Allison Harvard|Harvard]] *made an appearance in an episode of...*

Because enwiki:Harvard_University is in the *University* list, the first mention will be considered as referential, whereas the second one is non-referential. We also apply matching rules in Table 1 to obtain more non-referential mentions. After that, we extract sentences around wikilinks as a document.

Category	#Referential	#Referential (balanced)	#Non-referential
President	51, 412	14, 722	14, 818
Company	13, 312	3, 604	3, 642
University	79, 285	30, 101	30, 187
State	86, 743	9, 602	9, 106
Character	729	483	476
Brand	5, 138	1, 739	1, 781
Restaurant	4, 261	4, 261	4, 850
Total	240, 588	64, 512	61, 632

Table 3: Data set stats.

From Table 3, we can see that referential entities overwhelm non-referential ones in the extracted corpus. In order to evaluate our model fairly, we perform downsampling to balance referential and non-referential mentions, otherwise we can achieve high scores even if we link all mention to the target entities. In the balanced data set, there are 11, 065 unique entities.

4.2 Entity Linking Results

Category	Complete			Balanced Subset		
	R	P	F	R	P	F
President	94.6	89.9	92.2	87.2	80.4	83.7
Company	86.6	95.8	91.0	90.8	85.1	87.9
University	96.7	96.4	96.5	96.9	92.0	94.4
State	96.2	92.1	94.1	95.0	<u>58.6</u>	72.5
Character	92.5	61.3	73.7	92.8	<u>52.2</u>	66.8
Brand	89.6	90.2	89.9	86.7	83.2	84.9
Restaurant	87.0	81.4	84.1	86.9	88.1	87.5
Overall	95.2	93.4	94.3	93.1	81.6	87.0

Table 4: Overall performance (%). R, P, and F represent recall, precision, and F1 score, respectively.

As Table 4 demonstrates, our method shows promising results (87.0 F1 score) on the balanced data set. Nevertheless, we notice the low linking precisions for entities in the *Character* and *State* lists, which are caused by different reasons. For the *Character* list, mentions do not suffice to select

---

[2]http://needleseek.msra.cn
[3]enwiki: is short for https://en.wikipedia.org/wiki/
[4]https://en.wikipedia.org/wiki/Help:Link

high-quality seeds, whereas for the *State* list, features of referential and non-referential mentions are usually similar. Consider the following sentence:

∗ She witnessed his fatal shooting when they were together in the President's Box at Ford's Theatre on Tenth Street in Washington.

The mention "Washington" refers to "Washington, D.C.", which has the same entity type, LOCATION, as our target entity "Washington (state)". In addition, we see no obvious textual clue that indicates whether it refers to the State of Washington or not. Traditional EL approaches usually disambiguate such mentions through collective inference. They link "Ford's Theatre" and "Washington" to the KB simultaneously. Since there exists an explicit relation between "Ford's Theatre" and "Washington, D.C.", these two entities receive high confidence scores and thus are determined as the referents. Unfortunately, we cannot employ the knowledge-rich approach in the List-only Entity Linking scenario.

5 Related Work

In this paper, we define and study the List-only Entity Linking problem based on previous studies on Target Entity Disambiguation (Wang et al., 2012; Cao et al., 2015). The key difference is that they target at the disambiguation of a single list of entities, whereas we focus on entity linking to an arbitrary number of lists. Another similar problem is Named Entity Disambiguation with Linkless Knowledge Bases (LNED) (Li et al., 2016). It assumes that entities are isolated in the "linkless" KB, while each entity still has a description.

Our idea of selecting seed mentions based on co-occurrence is similar to collective inference. Most state-of-the-art EL methods utilize collective inference to link a set of coherent mentions simultaneously by selecting the most coherent set of entity candidates on the KB side (Pan et al., 2015; Huang et al., 2014; Cheng and Roth, 2013; Cassidy et al., 2012; Xu et al., 2012). In this work, without explicit relations between entities in different lists, we only take the co-occurrence of mentions in the same list into consideration. Therefore, our method is unable to benefit from the co-occurrence of John Lennon and Give Peace a Chance although they are actually strongly connected.

6 Conclusions and Future Work

In this paper, we proposed a novel framework to tackle the problem of List-only Entity Linking. The core of this framework is selecting seed mentions for each entity list to bridge the gap between mentions and non-informative target entities. Our results show this EL framework works well for this task. At present, in the seed selection step, we simply consider all co-occurring mentions of entities in the same list. In the future, we will employ more precise approaches to choose co-occurring mentions and mine relations between entities in separate lists to improve seed selection and entity disambiguation.

Acknowledgments

This work was supported by the DARPA DEFT No.FA8750-13-2-0041, U.S. DARPA LORELEI Program No. HR0011-15-C-0115, U.S. ARL NS-CTA No. W911NF-09-2-0053, and NSF IIS-1523198. The views and conclusions contained in this document are those of the authors and should not be interpreted as representing the official policies, either expressed or implied, of the U.S. Government. The U.S. Government is authorized to reproduce and distribute reprints for Government purposes notwithstanding any copyright notation here on.

References

Yixin Cao, Juanzi Li, Xiaofei Guo, Shuanhu Bai, Heng Ji, and Jie Tang. 2015. Name list only? target entity disambiguation in short texts. In *EMNLP*. https://doi.org/10.18653/v1/D15-1077.

Taylor Cassidy, Heng Ji, Lev-Arie Ratinov, Arkaitz Zubiaga, and Hongzhao Huang. 2012. Analysis and enhancement of wikification for microblogs with context expansion. In *COLING*. http://aclweb.org/anthology/C12-1028.

Xiao Cheng and Dan Roth. 2013. Relational inference for wikification. In *EMNLP*. http://aclweb.org/anthology/D13-1184.

Hongzhao Huang, Yunbo Cao, Xiaojiang Huang, Heng Ji, and Chin-Yew Lin. 2014. Collective tweet wikification based on semi-supervised graph regularization. In *ACL*. https://doi.org/10.3115/v1/P14-1036.

Yang Li, Shulong Tan, Huan Sun, Jiawei Han, Dan Roth, and Xifeng Yan. 2016. Entity disambiguation with linkless knowledge bases. In *WWW*.

Xiaoman Pan, Taylor Cassidy, Ulf Hermjakob, Heng Ji, and Kevin Knight. 2015. Unsupervised entity linking with abstract meaning representation. In *NAACL*. https://doi.org/10.3115/v1/N15-1119.

Shuming Shi, Huibin Zhang, Xiaojie Yuan, and Ji-Rong Wen. 2010. Corpus-based semantic class mining: Distributional vs. pattern-based approaches. In *COLING*. http://aclweb.org/anthology/C10-1112.

Chi Wang, Kaushik Chakrabarti, Tao Cheng, and Surajit Chaudhuri. 2012. Targeted disambiguation of ad-hoc, homogeneous sets of named entities. In *WWW*. https://doi.org/10.1145/2187836.2187934.

Jian Xu, Qin Lu, Jie Liu, and Ruifeng Xu. 2012. NLP-comp in TAC 2012 entity linking and slot-filling. In *TAC*. https://tac.nist.gov//publications/2012/papers.html.

Improving Native Language Identification by Using Spelling Errors

Lingzhen Chen
DISI
University of Trento
Trento, Italy
lzchen.cs@gmail.com

Carlo Strapparava
HLT
Fondazione Bruno Kessler
Trento, Italy
strappa@fbk.eu

Vivi Nastase
Inst. for Computational Linguistics
University of Heidelberg
Heidelberg, Germany
nastase@cl.uni-heidelberg.de

Abstract

In this paper, we explore spelling errors as a source of information for detecting the native language of a writer, a previously under-explored area. We note that character n-grams from misspelled words are very indicative of the native language of the author. In combination with other lexical features, spelling error features lead to 1.2% improvement in accuracy on classifying texts in the TOEFL11 corpus by the author's native language, compared to systems participating in the NLI shared task[1].

1 Introduction

Native Language Identification (NLI) aims to determine the native language (L1) of a writer based on his or her writings in a second language (L2). Though initially motivated by the study of cross-linguistics influence, the value of NLI is not limited to education. Potentially, it is also very valuable in academic, marketing, security and law enforcement fields. Identifying the native language is based on the assumption that the L1 of an individual impacts his or her writing in L2 due to the language transfer effect.

We focus here on the influences from L1 that surface as spelling errors in L2. Crossley and Mc-Namara (2011) showed that syntactic patterns and lexical preferences from L1 appear in L2 systematically, and are very informative for identifying the writer's native language. Texts written by authors with the same L1 also exhibit similarities with respect to the errors within.

In terms of spelling, in particular, both the sound of the words in different languages and the mapping from sounds to letters in L2 vs. L1, as well as the particular conventions of writing can

have a visible impact. In Italian, for example, each vowel has only one pronunciation, so it is very common for Italian writers to confuse the use of vowels in English: the English e can correspond to the sounds written either as i or e in Italian. In Arabic, on the other hand, vowels are rarely written, and this could cause writers to miss vowels when writing in English. In Chinese, since it uses a completely different writing system compared to English, there might be a higher probability for authors to make spelling errors when it comes to complicated words, because the mapping from English sounds to letters of the Roman alphabet is not one-to-one. We test whether we are able to capture some of these phenomena by going below the word level to character level and testing their usefulness as features for identifying the native language of the author.

Spelling errors have been used as features for NLI since Koppel et al. (2005). They considered syntax errors and eight types of spelling errors such as repeated letters, missing letters, and inversion of letters. The relative frequency of each error type with regard to the length of the document is used as feature values. By combining these with common features such as function words, they obtained a classification accuracy of 80.2% on a sub-corpora of ICLE$v1$ that consists of five languages. More recently, Nicolai et al. (2013) focused on the misspelled part of a word rather than the type of spelling errors. They used pairs of correct and misspelled parts in a word as features. Lavergne et al. (2013) adopted a similar approach to represent the spelling errors by the inner-most misspelled substring compared to the correct word. Combined with other features, they obtained a test accuracy of 75.29% on the TOEFL11 dataset.

Character n-grams have been explored, but not particularly for representing spelling errors. Brooke and Hirst (2012) showed that using char-

---

[1]https://sites.google.com/site/nlisharedtask2013/home

Proceedings of the 55th Annual Meeting of the Association for Computational Linguistics (Short Papers), pages 542–546
Vancouver, Canada, July 30 - August 4, 2017. ©2017 Association for Computational Linguistics
https://doi.org/10.18653/v1/P17-2086

acter unigrams, bigrams, and trigrams, the test accuracy can reach 37.4% for 7-class NLI on a subset of ICLE*v2* corpus. For the NLI 2013 shared task, Lahiri and Mihalcea (2013) used as features character trigrams represented by their raw frequencies. It leads to a test accuracy of 57.77%, which shows that how often character combinations are used is indicative of the L1 of an author.

Using complete words to represent spelling errors would not capture regularities that go beyond a single misspelled instance – like the preference of using i instead of e by Italian writers. We investigate the representation of spelling errors through character n-grams with size up to 3. We assess the effectiveness of using such feature representation for NLI and its contribution when combined with word and lemma n-grams, whose effectiveness has already been established (Gyawali et al., 2013; Jarvis et al., 2013). We report high classification results when using only spelling errors, and an improvement of 1.2 percentage points in accuracy, compared to the best results obtained in NLI shared task, when using spelling errors in combination with word and lemma features.

2 Data

The experiments are performed on the TOEFL11 corpus (Blanchard et al., 2013) of English essays written by non-native English learners as part of the *Test of English as a Foreign Language* (TOEFL). We also use the ICLE*v2* corpus (Granger et al., 2009) for extracting additional spelling errors. The TOEFL11 corpus is not the most recent corpus for the NLI task, but is by far one of the largest learner corpora that is balanced in terms of both topics and L1 languages.

The TOEFL11 corpus contains 4 million tokens in 12,100 essays written by authors whose native language (L1) is one of: Arabic (ARA), Chinese (ZHO), French (FRA), German (DEU), Hindi (HIN), Italian (ITA), Japanese (JPN), Korean (KOR), Spanish (SPA), Telugu (TEL) or Turkish (TUR). For each target L1, the number of essays is equal (900 in the train set, 100 in the development set and 100 in the test set). The distribution of the number of essays per topic is not perfectly balanced across different L1s, but they are rather close: the average number of essays per topic is 1,513 and the standard deviation is 229.

3 Methods

We aim to analyze the impact of spelling errors on identifying the native language of the author. We will analyze them separately and in combination with commonly used features.

3.1 Features

Word n-grams Previous work on NLI avoided lexical features due to the topic bias in the dataset. This is not an issue with the TOEFL11 corpus, since the topic distribution over the different L1s is quite balanced, as described in the previous section. Hence we can use as features the word unigrams, bigrams and trigrams. We filter out those that do not appear in at least two texts in the corpus. In the extraction of word n-grams, we ignore the use of all punctuations. Word n-gram features have as value their weighted frequencies using the Log-Entropy weighting technique. (Dumais, 1991)

Lemma n-grams This feature represents the lexical choice of a writer, regardless of the inflected form of a word. We use the n-grams of lemma produced by the TreeTagger tool (Schmid, 1994) with size up to 3. The feature extraction rule and the feature weighting scheme is the same as for word n-grams.

Character n-grams The frequency of character or character sequence usage captures information about the preference of an author in using certain sounds, combinations of sounds, prefixes or suffixes. We represent texts using character n-grams and assign them the value v_i – their relative frequency with respect to the set of n-grams (unigram, bigram, trigram) that they belong to:

$$v_i = \frac{count(i)}{\sum_{j \in S_i} count(j)}$$

where S_i is the collection of n-grams that have the same gram size as n-gram i.

Spelling errors The errors made by a writer while writing in their L2 may result from sound-to-character mappings in L1, writing preferences or other biases. These could be strong indicators for an author's L1. We extract spelling errors using the *spell* shell command. There are 34,233 unique spelling errors in the TOEFL11 corpus. We looked for additional sources of spelling errors, and extracted a list of 12,488 unique misspelled words from the ICLE*v2* corpus that are produced by writers with the common L1 as in the TOEFL11 corpus (namely Spanish, French,

Italian, German, Turkish, Chinese and Japanese). They are referred to here as *Spelling_error_ICLE* and *Spelling_error_TOEFL* in the later part of this paper. Spelling errors are binary features.

Spelling errors as character n-grams Every misspelled word in a text will be represented as character n-grams, where $n = 1..3$. Special characters marking the start and end of a word will be part of the n-grams. The value of these features is their relative frequencies, as for character n-grams.

3.2 Classifiers

Following the proven effectiveness of Support Vector Machine (SVM) by numerous experiments on text classification tasks, we adopt the use of linear SVM for NLI. In particular, we use linear SVM implemented by `scikit-learn` package (Pedregosa et al., 2011) to perform the multi-class classification.

3.3 Experiment Setup

The data is pre-processed by lower casing the tokenized version of the corpus. Each text is represented through the sets of features described above. The feature size of word n-grams up to size 3 are over 500,000 and that of lemma n-grams up to size 3 are over 400,000. The combination of the two is over 600,000. The hyper-parameter C of the linear SVM is set to 100, an optimal setting obtained by cross-validation on the train set. The performance is evaluated by classification accuracy, as was done in the NLI shared task. We test the performance of the used feature sets through a 10-fold cross-validation on the train+development set before the final run on the test set.

4 Results

The classification accuracies obtained by using different features and feature combinations are presented in Table 1. The feature sets include the word, lemma, character n-grams up to size 3 (denoted as *word_ngrams*, *lemma_ngrams*, *char_ngrams* respectively), the misspelled words in *Spelling_error_ICLE* or in *Spelling_error_TOEFL* (denoted as *word_error_icle* or *word_error_toefl*), and the character n-grams up to size 3 extracted from *Spelling_error_ICLE* or *Spelling_error_TOEFL* (denoted as *char_error_icle* or *char_error_toefl*).

In terms of classifying by a single type of feature, word n-grams are the most indicative one,

Type of Feature	10 Fold	Test
(1) *word_ngrams*	83.63 ($\pm$1.38)	84.16
(2) *lemma_ngrams*	83.18 ($\pm$1.46)	84.00
(3) *word_error_toefl*	35.05 ($\pm$1.42)	32.55
(4) *word_error_icle*	24.42 ($\pm$1.12)	26.45
(5) *char_ngrams*	66.27 ($\pm$0.93)	67.27
(6) *char_error_icle*	65.03 ($\pm$1.14)	65.73
(7) *char_error_toefl*	65.27 ($\pm$1.21)	66.45
(1) + (2)	83.91 ($\pm$1.50)	84.32
(1) + (2) + (3)	83.82 ($\pm$1.53)	84.27
(1) + (2) + (4)	83.90 ($\pm$1.49)	84.73
(1) + (2) + (5)	83.92 ($\pm$1.31)	84.64
(1) + (2) + (6)	83.85 ($\pm$1.26)	**84.82**
(1) + (2) + (7)	83.81 ($\pm$1.26)	**84.82**
Jarvis et al. (2013)	**84.50**	83.60
Nicolai et al. (2013)	58.50	81.70

Table 1: Classification accuracy of using different features by 10-fold cross-validation on the train+development set and test on the test set, the accuracy scores are in %. The values in bracket are the standard deviation of accuracy scores in 10-fold cross-validation.

which is consistent with the results reported by other researchers (Jarvis et al., 2013; Nicolai et al., 2013). Using the combination of word n-grams and lemma n-grams improves the performance of using only word n-grams by less than 0.2%. It is not a significant improvement, mainly because there is a big overlap in the features in these two categories. Word-level spelling errors when used on their own do not perform well, with one of the causes being sparseness. When combining them with other features (word n-grams and lemma n-grams), *word_error_toefl* does not seem to provide any additional information for improving classification accuracy. By combining the *word_error_icle* with lemma n-grams and word n-grams, however, we observe a small increase in classification accuracy of 0.4%. Main reason for this is that by using *word_error_icle*, we incorporate errors that are more common (since they occurred in two different corpora – ICLE*v*2 and TOEFL11 corpus).

From the classification results obtained by using feature (5), (6) and (7), it is also worth noting that by using only the character n-grams extracted from the spelling errors in *Spelling_error_TOEFL* (feature size: 5797), or even filtered by those that also appear in *Spelling_error_ICLE* (feature size:

3907), the accuracy is almost as the same as the one obtained by using all character n-grams (feature size: 12601). It shows that the character n-grams in the spelling errors are a most indicative part in all the character n-grams when it comes to identifying the L1 of an author.

Using character n-grams extracted from spelling errors works better than directly using misspelled words. It further implies that while the misspelled words might differ from one another in the text, the misspelled parts share similarities. The classifier trained by combining word n-grams, lemma n-grams and character n-grams extracted from *Spelling_error_ICLE* or from *Spelling_error_TOEFL* both reach the best test accuracy in our experiments - 84.82%, which is 1.2% better than the best result reported by Jarvis et al. (2013) in the NLI 2013 shared task. We note that including only the character n-grams extracted from the spelling errors ((1)+(2)+(6) or (1)+(2)+(7)) leads to better results than including all the character n-grams ((1)+(2)+(5)). It supports the hypothesis that spelling errors capture relevant information about the writer's native language at a character level.

Table 2 includes some of the most informative spelling errors made by writers with different L1s. They were selected based on their weights after training the SVM with word n-grams, lemma n-grams and spelling errors (as word). They seem to confirm our starting hypothesis regarding the various phenomena of language – and script – transfer that can influence spelling errors.

As shown in the table, the informative errors for each target language are quite different. French writers tend to double the character in the word, for example, they misspell *"personally"* as *"personnaly"* and *"developed"* as *"developped"*. It is also apparent that Japanese writers and Italian writers tend to misspell the vowels in a word. This may be the result of rules of word pronunciations in their own languages, and sound to letter mappings in their L1. Arabic writers tend to omit vowels. It could be due to the fact that vowels are rarely written in Arabic language and the writers carry this habit in their writing in English.

The results confirm the usefulness of features representing spelling errors, particularly at a subword level. On their own, they perform on a par with character level representation of the document. They also bring improvement in perfor-

L1	Word
ARA	*evry, experince, diffrent, advertisment, statment*
DEU	*knowlegde, advertisment, successfull, freetime, neccessary*
FRA	*generaly, personnaly, litterature, independant, developped*
HIN	*theoritical, sucess, enviornment, sucessful, gandhi*
ITA	*indipendent, specialistic, tecnology, studing, istance*
JPN	*actualy, youg, shoud, peple, convinient*
KOR	*poors, newpaper, eventhough, becaus, thesedays*
SPA	*conclution, consecuences, succesful, responsabilities, enviroment*
TEL	*oppurtunities, hardwork, intrested, atleast, donot*
TUR	*altough, spesific, easly, succesful, turkish*
ZHO	*sociaty, knowlege, easiler, sucessful, improtant*

Table 2: Most informative spelling errors made by writers with different L1

mance when combined with word and lemma n-grams, indicating that they provide at least partly complementary information to the frequently used word n-grams or lemma n-grams, which on their own have high performance.

5 Conclusion

In this work, we investigate the usefulness of spelling errors for the native language identification task. The experiments show that representing spelling errors through character n-grams captures interesting phenomena of language transfer. Both on their own and combined with customarily used word n-grams, they have high performance in terms of accuracy, when tested on the TOEFL11 corpus and compared to participating systems in the NLI shared task. In future work, it would be interesting to characterize the spelling errors with respect to similarity to specific L1s, and further explore the hints that they provide with respect to the author's native language.

Acknowledgments

We would like to thank EST for making the TOEFL11 dataset public and Fondazione Bruno Kessler for providing the facilities to conduct the related experiments. We also thank the anonymous reviewers for their detailed and insightful comments.

References

Daniel Blanchard, Joel Tetreault, Derrick Higgins, Aoife Cahill, and Martin Chodorow. 2013. Toefl11: A corpus of non-native english. *ETS Research Report Series* 2013(2):i–15. https://doi.org/10.1002/j.2333-8504.2013.tb02331.x.

Julian Brooke and Graeme Hirst. 2012. Robust, lexicalized native language identification. In *COLING 2012, 24th International Conference on Computational Linguistics, Proceedings of the Conference: Technical Papers, 8-15 December 2012, Mumbai, India.* pages 391–408. http://aclweb.org/anthology/C/C12/C12-1025.pdf.

Scott A. Crossley and Danielle S. McNamara. 2011. Shared features of l2 writing: Intergroup homogeneity and text classification. *Journal of Second Language Writing* 20(4):271–285. https://doi.org/10.1016/j.jslw.2011.05.007.

Susan T. Dumais. 1991. Improving the retrieval of information from external sources. *Behavior Research Methods, Instruments, & Computers* 23(2):229–236. https://doi.org/10.3758/BF03203370.

Sylviane Granger, Estelle Dagneaux, Fanny Meunier, and Magali Paquot. 2009. *The International Corpus of Learner English: Handbook and CD-ROM, version 2.* Presses universitaires de Louvain, Louvain-la-Neuve, Belgium. https://doi.org/10.1017/S0272263110000641.

Binod Gyawali, Gabriela Ramírez-de-la-Rosa, and Thamar Solorio. 2013. Native language identification: a simple n-gram based approach. In *Proceedings of the Eighth Workshop on Innovative Use of NLP for Building Educational Applications, BEA@NAACL-HLT 2013, June 13, 2013, Atlanta, Georgia, USA.* pages 224–231. http://aclweb.org/anthology/W/W13/W13-1729.pdf.

Scott Jarvis, Yves Bestgen, and Steve Pepper. 2013. Maximizing classification accuracy in native language identification. In *Proceedings of the Eighth Workshop on Innovative Use of NLP for Building Educational Applications, BEA@NAACL-HLT 2013, June 13, 2013, Atlanta, Georgia, USA.* pages 111–118. http://aclweb.org/anthology/W/W13/W13-1714.pdf.

Moshe Koppel, Jonathan Schler, and Kfir Zigdon. 2005. Determining an author's native language by mining a text for errors. In *Proceedings of the Eleventh ACM SIGKDD International Conference on Knowledge Discovery in Data Mining.* ACM, New York, NY, USA, KDD '05, pages 624–628. https://doi.org/10.1145/1081870.1081947.

Shibamouli Lahiri and Rada Mihalcea. 2013. Using n-gram and word network features for native language identification. In *Proceedings of the Eighth Workshop on Innovative Use of NLP for Building Educational Applications, BEA@NAACL-HLT 2013, June 13, 2013, Atlanta, Georgia, USA.* pages 251–259. http://aclweb.org/anthology/W/W13/W13-1732.pdf.

Thomas Lavergne, Gabriel Illouz, Aurélien Max, and Ryo Nagata. 2013. Limsi's participation to the 2013 shared task on native language identification. In *Proceedings of the Eighth Workshop on Innovative Use of NLP for Building Educational Applications, BEA@NAACL-HLT 2013, June 13, 2013, Atlanta, Georgia, USA.* pages 260–265. http://aclweb.org/anthology/W/W13/W13-1733.pdf.

Garrett Nicolai, Bradley Hauer, Mohammad Salameh, Lei Yao, and Grzegorz Kondrak. 2013. Cognate and misspelling features for natural language identification. In *Proceedings of the Eighth Workshop on Innovative Use of NLP for Building Educational Applications, BEA@NAACL-HLT 2013, June 13, 2013, Atlanta, Georgia, USA.* pages 140–145. http://aclweb.org/anthology/W/W13/W13-1718.pdf.

Fabian Pedregosa, Gaël Varoquaux, Alexandre Gramfort, Vincent Michel, Bertrand Thirion, Olivier Grisel, Mathieu Blondel, Peter Prettenhofer, Ron Weiss, Vincent Dubourg, Jake Vanderplas, Alexandre Passos, David Cournapeau, Matthieu Brucher, Matthieu Perrot, and Édouard Duchesnay. 2011. Scikit-learn: Machine learning in python. *Journal of Machine Learning Research* 12:2825–2830. http://dl.acm.org/citation.cfm?id=1953048.2078195.

Helmut Schmid. 1994. Probabilistic Part-of-Speech Tagging Using Decision Trees. In *Proceedings of International Conference on New Methods in Language Processing.* http://www.cis.uni-muenchen.de/ schmid/tools/TreeTagger/data/tree-tagger1.pdf.

Disfluency Detection using a Noisy Channel Model and a Deep Neural Language Model

Paria Jamshid Lou
Department of Computing
Macquarie University
Sydney, Australia
paria.jamshid-lou@hdr.mq.edu.au

Mark Johnson
Department of Computing
Macquarie University
Sydney, Australia
mark.johnson@mq.edu.au

Abstract

This paper presents a model for disfluency detection in spontaneous speech transcripts called *LSTM Noisy Channel Model*. The model uses a Noisy Channel Model (NCM) to generate n-best candidate disfluency analyses and a Long Short-Term Memory (LSTM) language model to score the underlying fluent sentences of each analysis. The LSTM language model scores, along with other features, are used in a MaxEnt reranker to identify the most plausible analysis. We show that using an LSTM language model in the reranking process of noisy channel disfluency model improves the state-of-the-art in disfluency detection.

1 Introduction

Disfluency is a characteristic of spontaneous speech which is not present in written text. Disfluencies are informally defined as interruptions in the normal flow of speech that occur in different forms, including false starts, corrections, repetitions and filled pauses. According to Shriberg's (1994) definition, the basic pattern of speech disfluencies contains three parts: *reparandum*[1], *interregnum* and *repair*. Example 1 illustrates a disfluent structure, where the reparandum *to Boston* is the part of the utterance that is replaced, the interregnum *uh, I mean* is an optional part of a disfluent structure that consists of a filled pause *uh* and a discourse marker *I mean* and the repair *to Denver* replaces the reparandum. The fluent version of Example 1 is obtained by deleting reparandum and interregnum words.

$$
\begin{array}{c}
\overbrace{\textit{I want a flight to Boston,}}^{\text{reparandum}} \\
\underbrace{\textit{uh, I mean}}_{\text{interregnum}} \underbrace{\textit{to Denver on Friday}}_{\text{repair}}
\end{array} \tag{1}
$$

While disfluency rate varies with the context, age and gender of speaker, Bortfeld et al. (2001) reported disfluencies once in every 17 words. Such frequency is high enough to reduce the readability of speech transcripts. Moreover, disfluencies pose a major challenge to natural language processing tasks, such as dialogue systems, that rely on speech transcripts (Ostendorf et al., 2008). Since such systems are usually trained on fluent, clean corpora, it is important to apply a speech disfluency detection system as a pre-processor to find and remove disfluencies from input data. By disfluency detection, we usually mean identifying and deleting reparandum words. Filled pauses and discourse markers belong to a closed set of words, so they are trivial to detect (Johnson and Charniak, 2004).

In this paper, we introduce a new model for detecting restart and repair disfluencies in spontaneous speech transcripts called *LSTM Noisy Channel Model (LSTM-NCM)*. The model uses a Noisy Channel Model (NCM) to generate n-best candidate disfluency analyses, and a Long Short-Term Memory (LSTM) language model to rescore the NCM analyses. The language model scores are used as features in a MaxEnt reranker to select the most plausible analysis. We show that this novel approach improves the current state-of-the-art.

2 Related Work

Approaches to disfluency detection task fall into three main categories: sequence tagging, parsing-based and noisy channel model. The sequence

---

[1]Reparandum is sometimes called *edit*.

Proceedings of the 55th Annual Meeting of the Association for Computational Linguistics (Short Papers), pages 547–553
Vancouver, Canada, July 30 - August 4, 2017. ©2017 Association for Computational Linguistics
https://doi.org/10.18653/v1/P17-2087

tagging models label words as fluent or disfluent using a variety of different techniques, including conditional random fields (Ostendorf and Hahn, 2013; Zayats et al., 2014; Ferguson et al., 2015), hidden Markov models (Liu et al., 2006; Schuler et al., 2010) or recurrent neural networks (Hough and Schlangen, 2015; Zayats et al., 2016). Although sequence tagging models can be easily generalized to a wide range of domains, they require a specific state space for disfluency detection, such as begin-inside-outside (BIO) style states that label words as being inside or outside of a reparandum word sequence. The parsing-based approaches refer to parsers that detect disfluencies, as well as identifying the syntactic structure of the sentence (Rasooli and Tetreault, 2013; Honnibal and Johnson, 2014; Yoshikawa et al., 2016). Training a parsing-based model requires large annotated tree-banks that contain both disfluencies and syntactic structures. Noisy channel models (NCMs) use the similarity between reparandum and repair as an indicator of disfluency. However, applying an effective language model (LM) inside an NCM is computationally complex. To alleviate this problem, some researchers use more effective LMs to rescore the NCM disfluency analyses. Johnson and Charniak (2004) applied a syntactic parsing-based LM trained on the fluent version of the Switchboard corpus to rescore the disfluency analyses. Zwarts and Johnson (2011) trained external n-gram LMs on a variety of large speech and non-speech corpora to rank the analyses. Using the external LM probabilities as features into the reranker improved the baseline NCM (Johnson and Charniak, 2004). The idea of applying external language models in the reranking process of the NCM motivates our model in this work.

3 LSTM Noisy Channel Model

We follow Johnson and Charniak (2004) in using an NCM to find the n-best candidate disfluency analyses for each sentence. The NCM, however, lacks an effective language model to capture more complicated language structures. To overcome this problem, our idea is to use different LSTM language models to score the underlying fluent sentences of the analyses proposed by the NCM and use the language model scores as features to a MaxEnt reranker to select the best analysis. In the following, we describe our model and its components in detail.

In the NCM of speech disfluency, we assume that there is a well-formed source utterance X to which some noise is added and generates a disfluent utterance Y as follows.

$$X = \text{a flight to Denver}$$
$$Y = \text{a flight } \textit{to Boston uh I mean } \text{to Denver}$$

Given Y, the goal of the NCM is to find the most likely source sentence $\hat{X}$ such that:

$$\hat{X} = \arg\max_{X} P(Y|X)P(X) \qquad (2)$$

As shown in Equation 2, the NCM contains two components: the channel model $P(Y|X)$ and the language model $P(X)$. Calculating the channel model and language model probabilities, the NCM generates 25-best candidate disfluency analyses as follows.

1. a ~~flight~~ to Boston uh I mean to Denver
2. a flight ~~to Boston~~ uh I mean to Denver
3. a flight to Boston ~~uh I mean~~ to Denver

$$\cdots \qquad (3)$$

Example 3 shows sample outputs of the NCM, where potential reparandum words are specified with strikethrough text. The MaxEnt reranker is applied on the candidate analyses of the NCM to select the most plausible one.

3.1 Channel Model

We assume that X is a substring of Y, so the source sentence X is obtained by deleting words from Y. For each sentence Y, there are only a finite number of potential source sentences. However, with the increase in the length of Y, the number of possible source sentences X grows exponentially, so it is not feasible to do exhaustive search. Moreover, since disfluent utterances may contain an unbounded number of crossed dependencies, a context-free grammar is not suitable for finding the alignments. The crossed dependencies refer to the relation between repair and reparandum words which are usually the same or very similar words in roughly the same order as in Example 4.

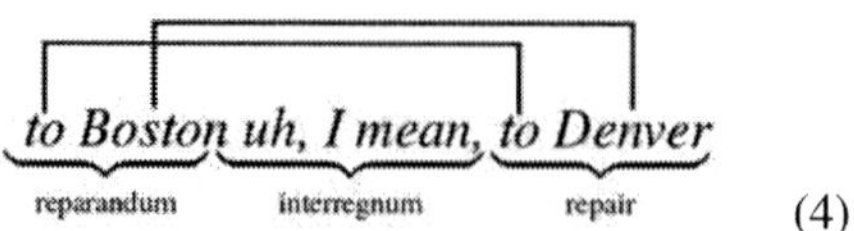

$$(4)$$

We apply a Tree Adjoining Grammar (TAG) based transducer (Johnson and Charniak, 2004) which is a more expressive formalism and provides a systematic way of formalising the channel model. The TAG channel model encodes the crossed dependencies of speech disfluency, rather than reflecting the syntactic structure of the sentence. The TAG transducer is effectively a simple first-order Markov model which generates each word in the reparandum conditioned on the preceding word in the reparandum and the corresponding word in the repair. Further detail about the TAG channel model can be found in (Johnson and Charniak, 2004).

3.2 Language Model

The language model of the NCM evaluates the fluency of the sentence with disfluency removed. The language model is expected to assign a very high probability to a fluent sentence X (e.g. *a flight to Denver*) and a lower probability to a sentence Y which still contains disfluency (e.g. *a flight to Boston uh I mean to Denver*). However, it is computationally complex to use an effective language model within the NCM. The reason is the polynomial-time dynamic programming parsing algorithms of TAG can be used to search for likely repairs if they are used with simple language models such as a bigram LM (Johnson and Charniak, 2004). The bigram LM within the NCM is too simple to capture more complicated language structure. In order to alleviate this problem, we follow Zwarts and Johnson (2011) by training LMs on different corpora, but we apply state-of-the-art recurrent neural network (RNN) language models.

LSTM

We use a long short-term memory (LSTM) neural network for training language models. LSTM is a particular type of recurrent neural networks which has achieved state-of-the-art performance in many tasks including language modelling (Mikolov et al., 2010; Jozefowicz et al., 2016). LSTM is able to learn long dependencies between words, which can be highly beneficial for the speech disfluency detection task. Moreover, it allows for adopting a distributed representation of words by constructing word embedding (Mikolov et al., 2013).

We train forward and backward (i.e. input sentences are given in reverse order) LSTM language models using truncated backpropagation through time algorithm (Rumelhart et al., 1986) with mini-batch size 20 and total number of epochs 13. The LSTM model has two layers and 200 hidden units. The initial learning rate for stochastic gradient optimizer is chosen to 1 which is decayed by 0.5 for each epoch after maximum epoch 4. We limit the maximum sentence length for training our model due to the high computational complexity of longer histories in the LSTM. In our experiments, considering maximum 50 words for each sentence leads to good results. The size of word embedding is 200 and it is randomly initialized for all LSTM LMs[2].

Using each forward and backward LSTM language model, we assign a probability to the underlying fluent parts of each candidate analysis.

3.3 Reranker

In order to rank the the 25-best candidate disfluency analyses of the NCM and select the most suitable one, we apply the MaxEnt reranker proposed by Johnson et al. (2004). We use the feature set introduced by Zwarts and Johnson (2011), but instead of n-gram scores, we apply the LSTM language model probabilities. The features are so good that the reranker without any external language model is already a state-of-the-art system, providing a very strong baseline for our work. The reranker uses both model-based scores (including NCM scores and LM probabilities) and surface pattern features (which are boolean indicators) as described in Table 1. Our reranker optimizes the expected f-score approximation described in Zwarts and Johnson (2011) with L2 regularisation.

4 Corpora for Language Modelling

In this work, we train forward and backward LSTM language models on Switchboard (Godfrey and Holliman, 1993) and Fisher (Cieri et al., 2004) corpora. Fisher consists of 2.2×10^7 tokens of transcribed text, but disfluencies are not annotated in it. Switchboard is the largest available corpus (1.2×10^6 tokens) in which disfluencies are annotated according to Shriberg's (1994) scheme. Since the bigram language model of the NCM is trained on this corpus, we cannot directly use Switchboard to build LSTM LMs. The reason is that if the training data of Switchboard is used both for predicting language fluency and optimizing the loss function, the reranker will overestimate the

---

[2] All code is written in TensorFlow (Abadi et al., 2015)

model-based features
1-2. forward & backward LSTM LM scores
3-7. log probability of the entire NCM
8. sum of the log LM probability & the log channel model probability plus number of edits in the sentence
9. channel model probability
surface pattern features
10. CopyFlags_X_Y: if there is an exact copy in the input text of length X $(1 \leq X \leq 3)$ and the gap between the copies is Y $(0 \leq Y \leq 3)$
11. WordsFlags_L_n_R: number of flags to the left (L) and to the right (R) of a 3-gram area $(0 \leq L, R \leq 1)$
12. SentenceEdgeFlags_B_L: it captures the location and length of disfluency. The Boolean B sentence initial or sentence final disfluency, L $(1 \leq L \leq 3)$ records the length of the flags.

Table 1: The features used in the reranker. They, except for the first and second one, were applied by Zwarts and Johnson (2011).

weight related to the LM features extracted from Switchboard. This is because the fluent sentence itself is part of the language model (Zwarts and Johnson, 2011). As a solution, we apply a k-fold cross-validation ($k = 20$) to train the LSTM language models when using Switchboard corpus.

We follow Charniak and Johnson (2001) in splitting Switchboard corpus into training, development and test set. The training data consists of all sw[23]*.dps files, development training consists of all sw4[5-9]*.dps files and test data consists of all sw4[0-1]*.dps files. Following Johnson and Charniak (2004), we remove all partial words and punctuation from the training data. Although partial words are very strong indicators of disfluency, standard speech recognizers never produce them in their outputs, so this makes our evaluation both harder and more realistic.

5   Results and Discussion

We assess the proposed model for disfluency detection with all MaxEnt features described in Table 1 against the baseline model. The noisy channel model with exactly the same reranker features except the LSTM LMs forms the baseline model.

To evaluate our system, we use two metrics *f-score* and *error rate*. Charniak and Johnson (2001) used the f-score of labelling reparanda

or "edited" words, while Fiscus et al (2004) defined an "error rate" measure, which is the number of words falsely labelled divided by the number of reparanda words. Since only 6% of words are disfluent in Switchboard corpus, accuracy is not a good measure of system performance. F-score, on the other hand, focuses more on detecting "edited" words, so it is a decent metric for highly skewed data.

According to Tables 2 and 3, the LSTM noisy channel model outperforms the baseline. The experiment on Switchboard and Fisher corpora demonstrates that the LSTM LMs provide information about the global fluency of an analysis that the local features of the reranker do not capture. The LSTM language model trained on Switchboard corpus results in the greatest improvement. Switchboard is in the same domain as the test data and it is also disfluency annotated. Either or both of these might be the reason why Switchboard seems to be better in comparison with Fisher which is a larger corpus and might be expected to make a better language model. Moreover, the backward LSTMs have better performance in comparison with the forward ones. It seems when sentences are fed in reverse order, the model can more easily detect the unexpected word order associated with the reparandum to detect disfluencies. In other words, that the disfluency is observed "after" the fluent repair in a backward language model is helpful for recognizing disfluencies.

baseline	85.3		
corpus	**forward**	**backward**	**both**
Switchboard	86.1	86.6	86.8
Fisher	86.2	86.5	86.3

Table 2: F-scores on the dev set for a variety of LSTM language models.

baseline	27.0		
corpus	**forward**	**backward**	**both**
Switchboard	25.5	24.8	24.3
Fisher	25.6	25.0	25.3

Table 3: Expected error rates on the dev set for a variey of LSTM language models.

We compare the performance of Kneser-Ney

smoothed 4-gram language models with the LSTM corresponding on the reranking process of the noisy channel model. We estimate the 4-gram models and assign probabilities to the fluent parts of disfluency analyses using the SRILM toolkit (Stolcke, 2002). As Tables 4 and 5 show including scores from a conventional 4-gram language model does not improve the model's ability to find disfluencies, suggesting that the LSTM model contains all the useful information that the 4-gram model does. In order to give a more general idea on the performance of LSTM over standard LM, we evaluate our model when the language model scores are used as the only features of the reranker. The f-score for the NCM alone without applying the reranker is 78.7, while using 4-gram language model scores in the reranker increases the f-score to 81.0. Replacing the 4-gram scores with LSTM language model probabilities leads to further improvement, resulting an f-score 82.3.

baseline	85.3		
corpus	**4-gram**	**LSTM**	**both**
Switchboard	85.1	86.8	86.1
Fisher	85.6	86.3	86

Table 4: F-score for 4-gram, LSTM and combination of both language models.

baseline	27.0		
corpus	**4-gram**	**LSTM**	**both**
Switchboard	27.5	24.3	26
Fisher	26.6	25.3	26

Table 5: Expected error rates for 4-gram, LSTM and combination of both language models.

We also compare our best model on the development set to the state-of-the-art methods in the literature. As shown in Table 6, the LSTM noisy channel model outperforms the results of prior work, achieving a state-of-the-art performance of 86.8. It also has better performance in comparison with Ferguson et al. (2015) and Zayat et al.'s (2016) models, even though they use richer input that includes prosodic features or partial words.

6 Conclusion and Future Work

In this paper, we present a new model for disfluency detection from spontaneous speech tran-

Model	f-score
Yoshikawa et al. (2016)	62.5
Johnson and Charniak (2004)	79.7
Johnson et al. (2004)	81.0
Rasooli and Tetreault (2013)	81.4
Qian and Liu (2013)	82.1
Honnibal and Johnson (2014)	84.1
Ferguson et al. (2015) *	85.4
Zwarts and Johnson (2011)	85.7
Zayats et al. (2016) *	85.9
LSTM-NCM	**86.8**

Table 6: Comparison of the LSTM-NCM to state-of-the-art methods on the dev set. *Models have used richer input.

scripts. It uses a long short-term memory neural network language model to rescore the candidate disfluency analyses produced by a noisy channel model. The LSTM language model scores as features in a MaxEnt reranker improves the model's ability to detect restart and repair disfluencies. The model outperforms other models reported in the literature, including models that exploit richer information from the input. As future work, we apply more complex LSTM language models such as sequence-to-sequence on the reranking process of the noisy channel model. We also intend to investigate the effect of integrating LSTM language models into other kinds of disfluency detection models, such as sequence labelling and parsing-based models.

Acknowledgements

We would like to thank the anonymous reviewers for their insightful comments and suggestions. This research was supported by a Google award through the Natural Language Understanding Focused Program, and under the Australian Research Councils Discovery Projects funding scheme (project number DP160102156).

References

Martin Abadi, Ashish Agarwal, Paul Barham, Eugene Brevdo, Zhifeng Chen, Craig Citro, Greg S. Corrado, Andy Davis, Jeffrey Dean, Matthieu Devin, Sanjay Ghemawat, Ian Goodfellow, Andrew Harp, Geoffrey Irving, Michael Isard, Yangqing Jia, Rafal Jozefowicz, Lukasz Kaiser, Manjunath Kudlur, Josh Levenberg, Dan Mane, Rajat Monga, Sherry Moore, Derek Murray, Chris Olah, Mike Schuster, Jonathon

Shlens, Benoit Steiner, Ilya Sutskever, Kunal Talwar, Paul Tucker, Vincent Vanhoucke, Vijay Vasudevan, Fernanda Viegas, Oriol Vinyals, Pete Warden, Martin Wattenberg, Martin Wicke, Yuan Yu, and Xiaoqiang Zheng. 2015. TensorFlow: Large-scale machine learning on heterogeneous systems. Software available from tensorflow.org.

Heather Bortfeld, Silvia Leon, Jonathan Bloom, Michael Schober, and Susan Brennan. 2001. Disfluency rates in conversation: Effects of age, relationship, topic, role, and gender. *Language and Speech* 44(2):123–147.

Eugene Charniak and Mark Johnson. 2001. Edit detection and parsing for transcribed speech. In *Proceedings of the 2nd Meeting of the North American Chapter of the Association for Computational Linguistics on Language Technologies.* Stroudsburg, USA, NAACL'01, pages 118–126. http://aclweb.org/anthology/N01-1016.

Christopher Cieri, David Miller, and Kevin Walker. 2004. Fisher English training speech part 1 transcripts LDC2004T19. Published by: Linguistic Data Consortium, Philadelphia, USA.

James Ferguson, Greg Durrett, and Dan Klein. 2015. Disfluency detection with a semi-Markov model and prosodic features. In *Proceedings of the Conference of the North American Chapter of the Association for Computational Linguistics: Human Language Technologies.* Denver, USA, NAACL'15, pages 257–262.

Jonathan Fiscus, John Garofolo, Audrey Le, Alvin Martin, David Pallet, Mark Przybocki, and Greg Sanders. 2004. Results of the fall 2004 STT and MDE evaluation. In *Proceedings of Rich Transcription Fall Workshop.*

John Godfrey and Edward Holliman. 1993. Switchboard-1 release 2 LDC97S62. Published by: Linguistic Data Consortium, Philadelphia, USA.

Matthew Honnibal and Mark Johnson. 2014. Joint incremental disfluency detection and dependency parsing. *Transactions of the Association for Computational Linguistics* 2(1):131–142. http://www.aclweb.org/anthology/Q14-1011.

Julian Hough and David Schlangen. 2015. Recurrent neural networks for incremental disfluency detection. In *Proceedings of the 16th Annual Conference of the International Speech Communication Association (INTERSPEECH).* Dresden, Germany, pages 845–853.

Mark Johnson and Eugene Charniak. 2004. A TAG-based noisy channel model of speech repairs. In *Proceedings of the 42nd Annual Meeting on Association for Computational Linguistics.* Barcelona, Spain, ACL'04, pages 33–39. http://aclweb.org/anthology/P04-1005.

Mark Johnson, Eugene Charniak, and Matthew Lease. 2004. An improved model for recognizing disfluencies in conversational speech. In *Proceedings of Rich Transcription Workshop.*

Rafal Jozefowicz, Oriol Vinyals, Mike Schuster, Noam Shazeer, and Yonghui Wu. 2016. Exploring the limits of language modeling. *CoRR* abs/1602.02410.

Yang Liu, Elizabeth Shriberg, Andreas Stolckeand, Dustin Hillard, Mari Ostendorf, and Mary Harper. 2006. Enriching speech recognition with automatic detection of sentence boundaries and disfluencies. *IEEE/ACM Transactions on Audio, Speech, and Language Processing* 14(5):1526–1540.

Tomas Mikolov, Martin Karafiat, Lukas Burget, Jan Cernocky, and Sanjeev Khudanpur. 2010. Recurrent neural network based language model. In *Proceedings of the 11th Annual Conference of the International Speech Communication Association (INTERSPEECH).* Makuhari, Japan, pages 1045–1048.

Tomas Mikolov, Ilya Sutskever, Kai Chen, Greg Corrado, and Jeffrey Dean. 2013. Distributed representations of words and phrases and their compositionality. In *Proceedings of the 27th Annual Conference on Neural Information Processing Systems (NIPS).* Curran Associates Inc., pages 3111–3119.

Mari Ostendorf, Benoit Favre, Ralph Grishman, Dilek Hakkani-Tur, Mary Harper, Dustin Hillard, Julia Hirschberg, Heng Ji, Jeremy G. Kahn, Yang Liu, Sameer Maskey, Evgeny Matusov, Hermann Ney, Andrew Rosenberg, Elizabeth Shriberg, Wen Wang, and Chuck Wooters. 2008. Speech segmentation and its impact on spoken document processing. *IEEE Signal Processing Magazine* 25(3):59–69.

Mari Ostendorf and Sangyun Hahn. 2013. A sequential repetition model for improved disfluency detection. In *Proceedings of the 14th Annual Conference of the International Speech Communication Association (INTERSPEECH).* Lyon, France, pages 2624–2628.

Xian Qian and Yang Liu. 2013. Disfluency detection using multi-step stacked learning. In *Proceedings of the Conference of the North American Chapter of the Association for Computational Linguistics: Human Language Technologies.* Atlanta, USA, NAACL'13, pages 820–825. http://aclweb.org/anthology/N13-1102.

Mohammad Sadegh Rasooli and Joel Tetreault. 2013. Joint parsing and disfluency detection in linear time. In *Proceedings of the 2013 Conference on Empirical Methods in Natural Language Processing.* Association for Computational Linguistics, Seattle, USA, pages 124–129. http://aclweb.org/anthology/D13-1013.

David Rumelhart, James McClelland, and PDP Research Group. 1986. *Parallel Distributed Processing: Explorations in the Microstructure of Cognition,* volume 1. MIT Press.

William Schuler, Samir AbdelRahman, Tim Miller, and Lane Schwartz. 2010. Broad-coverage parsing using human-like memory constraints. *Computational Linguistics* 36(1):1–30.

Elizabeth Shriberg. 1994. *Preliminaries to a theory of speech disfluencies*. Ph.D. thesis, University of California, Berkeley, USA.

Andreas Stolcke. 2002. SRILM: An extensible language modeling toolkit. In *Proceedings of International Conference on Spoken Language Processing*. Association for Computational Linguistics, Denver, Colorado, USA, volume 2, pages 901–904.

Masashi Yoshikawa, Hiroyuki Shindo, and Yuji Matsumoto. 2016. Joint transition-based dependency parsing and disfluency detection for automatic speech recognition texts. In *Proceedings of the Conference on Empirical Methods in Natural Language Processing (EMNLP)*. pages 1036–1041. http://aclweb.org/anthology/D16-1109.

Victoria Zayats, Mari Ostendorf, and Hannaneh Hajishirzi. 2014. Multi-domain disfluency and repair detection. In *Proceedings of the 15th Annual Conference of the International Speech Communication Association (INTERSPEECH)*. Singapore, pages 2907–2911.

Victoria Zayats, Mari Ostendorf, and Hannaneh Hajishirzi. 2016. Disfluency detection using a bidirectional LSTM. In *Proceedings of the 16th Annual Conference of the International Speech Communication Association (INTERSPEECH)*. San Francisco, USA, pages 2523–2527.

Simon Zwarts and Mark Johnson. 2011. The impact of language models and loss functions on repair disfluency detection. In *Proceedings of the 49th Annual Meeting of the Association for Computational Linguistics: Human Language Technologies*. Association for Computational Linguistics, Portland, USA, volume 1 of *HLT'11*, pages 703–711. http://aclweb.org/anthology/P11-1071.

On the Equivalence of Holographic and Complex Embeddings for Link Prediction

Katsuhiko Hayashi

NTT Communication Science Laboratories, Seika-cho, Kyoto 619 0237, Japan
hayashi.katsuhiko@lab.ntt.co.jp

Masashi Shimbo

Nara Institute of Science and Technology, Ikoma, Nara 630 0192, Japan
shimbo@is.naist.jp

Abstract

We show the equivalence of two state-of-the-art models for link prediction/knowledge graph completion: Nickel et al's holographic embeddings and Trouillon et al.'s complex embeddings. We first consider a spectral version of the holographic embeddings, exploiting the frequency domain in the Fourier transform for efficient computation. The analysis of the resulting model reveals that it can be viewed as an instance of the complex embeddings with a certain constraint imposed on the initial vectors upon training. Conversely, any set of complex embeddings can be converted to a set of equivalent holographic embeddings.

1 Introduction

Recently, there have been efforts to build and maintain large-scale knowledge bases represented in the form of a graph (*knowledge graph*) (Auer et al., 2007; Bollacker et al., 2008; Suchanek et al., 2007). Although these knowledge graphs contain billions of relational facts, they are known to be incomplete. *Knowledge graph completion* (KGC) (Nickel et al., 2015) aims at augmenting missing knowledge in an incomplete knowledge graph automatically. It can be viewed as a task of *link prediction* (Liben-Nowell and Kleinberg, 2003; Hasan and Zaki, 2011) studied in the field of statistical relational learning (Getoor and Taskar, 2007). In recent years, methods based on vector embeddings of graphs have been actively pursued as a scalable approach to KGC (Bordes et al., 2011; Socher et al., 2013; Guu et al., 2015; Yang et al., 2015; Nickel et al., 2016; Trouillon et al., 2016b).

In this paper, we investigate the connection between two models of graph embeddings that have emerged along this line of research: The *holographic embeddings* (Nickel et al., 2016) and the *complex embeddings* (Trouillon et al., 2016b). These models are simple yet achieve the current state-of-the-art performance in KGC.

We begin by showing that holographic embeddings can be trained entirely in the frequency domain induced by the Fourier transform, thereby reducing the time needed to compute the scoring function from $O(n \log n)$ to $O(n)$, where n is the dimension of the embeddings.

The analysis of the resulting training method reveals that the Fourier transform of holographic embeddings can be regarded as an instance of the complex embeddings, with a specific constraint (viz. conjugate symmetry property) cast on on the initial values.

Conversely, we also show that every set of complex embeddings has a set of holographic embeddings (with real vectors) that is equivalent, in the sense that their scoring functions are equal up to scaling.

2 Preliminaries

Let i denote the imaginary unit, $\mathbb{R}$ be the set of real values, and $\mathbb{C}$ the set of complex values. We write $[\mathbf{v}]_j$ to denote the jth component of vector $\mathbf{v}$. A superscript T (e.g., $\mathbf{v}^{\mathrm{T}}$) represents vector/matrix transpose. For a complex scalar z, vector $\mathbf{z}$, and matrix $\mathbf{Z}$, $\bar{z}$, $\bar{\mathbf{z}}$, and $\overline{\mathbf{Z}}$ represent their complex conjugate, and $\mathrm{Re}(z)$, $\mathrm{Re}(\mathbf{z})$, and $\mathrm{Re}(\mathbf{Z})$ denote their real parts, respectively.

Let $\mathbf{x} = [x_0 \cdots x_{n-1}]^{\mathrm{T}} \in \mathbb{R}^n$ and $\mathbf{y} = [y_0 \cdots y_{n-1}]^{\mathrm{T}} \in \mathbb{R}^n$. Note that the vector indices start from 0 for notational convenience. The *circular convolution* of $\mathbf{x}$ and $\mathbf{y}$, denoted by $\mathbf{x} * \mathbf{y}$, is

Proceedings of the 55th Annual Meeting of the Association for Computational Linguistics (Short Papers), pages 554–559
Vancouver, Canada, July 30 - August 4, 2017. ©2017 Association for Computational Linguistics
https://doi.org/10.18653/v1/P17-2088

defined by

$$[\mathbf{x} * \mathbf{y}]_j = \sum_{k=0}^{n-1} x_{[(j-k) \bmod n]} y_k, \tag{1}$$

where mod denotes modulus. Likewise, *circular correlation* $\mathbf{x} \star \mathbf{y}$ is defined by

$$[\mathbf{x} \star \mathbf{y}]_j = \sum_{k=0}^{n-1} x_{[(k-j) \bmod n]} y_k. \tag{2}$$

While circular convolution is commutative, circular correlation is not; i.e., $\mathbf{x} * \mathbf{y} = \mathbf{y} * \mathbf{x}$, but $\mathbf{x} \star \mathbf{y} \neq \mathbf{y} \star \mathbf{x}$ in general. As it can be verified with Eqs. (1) and (2), $\mathbf{x} \star \mathbf{y} = \text{flip}(\mathbf{x}) * \mathbf{y}$, where $\text{flip}(\mathbf{x}) = [x_{n-1} \cdots x_0]^\mathrm{T}$ is a vector obtained by arranging the components of $\mathbf{x}$ in reverse.

For n-dimensional vectors, naively computing circular convolution/correlation by Eqs. (1) and (2) requires $O(n^2)$ multiplications. However, we can take advantage of the Fast Fourier Transform (FFT) algorithm to accelerate the computation: For circular convolution, first compute the discrete Fourier transform (DFT) of $\mathbf{x}$ and $\mathbf{y}$, and then compute the inverse DFT of their elementwise vector product, i.e.,

$$\mathbf{x} * \mathbf{y} = \mathfrak{F}^{-1}(\mathfrak{F}(\mathbf{x}) \odot \mathfrak{F}(\mathbf{y})),$$

where $\mathfrak{F} : \mathbb{R}^n \to \mathbb{C}^n$ and $\mathfrak{F}^{-1} : \mathbb{C}^n \to \mathbb{R}^n$ respectively denote the DFT and inverse DFT, and $\odot$ denotes the elementwise product. DFT and inverse DFT can be computed in $O(n \log n)$ time with the FFT algorithm, and thus the computation time for circular convolution is also $O(n \log n)$. The same can be said of circular correlation. Since $\mathfrak{F}(\text{flip}(\mathbf{x})) = \overline{\mathfrak{F}(\mathbf{x})}$, we have

$$\mathbf{x} \star \mathbf{y} = \mathfrak{F}^{-1}(\overline{\mathfrak{F}(\mathbf{x})} \odot \mathfrak{F}(\mathbf{y})). \tag{3}$$

By analogy to how the Fourier transform is used in signal processing, the original real space $\mathbb{R}^n$ is called the "time" domain, and the complex space $\mathbb{C}^n$ where DFT vectors reside is called the "frequency" domain.

3 Holographic embeddings for knowledge graph completion

3.1 Knowledge graph completion

Let $\mathcal{E}$ and $\mathcal{R}$ be the finite sets of *entities* and *(binary) relations* over entities, respectively. For each relation $r \in \mathcal{R}$ and each pair $s, o \in \mathcal{E}$ of entities,

Table 1: Correspondence between operations in time and frequency domains. $\mathbf{r} \leftrightarrow \boldsymbol{\rho}$ indicates $\boldsymbol{\rho} = \mathfrak{F}(\mathbf{r})$ (and also $\mathbf{r} = \mathfrak{F}^{-1}(\boldsymbol{\rho})$).

operation	time		frequency
scalar mult.	$\alpha \mathbf{x}$	$\longleftrightarrow$	$\alpha \, \mathfrak{F}(\mathbf{x})$
summation	$\mathbf{x} + \mathbf{y}$	$\longleftrightarrow$	$\mathfrak{F}(\mathbf{x}) + \mathfrak{F}(\mathbf{y})$
flip	$\text{flip}(\mathbf{x})$	$\longleftrightarrow$	$\overline{\mathfrak{F}(\mathbf{x})}$
convolution	$\mathbf{x} * \mathbf{y}$	$\longleftrightarrow$	$\mathfrak{F}(\mathbf{x}) \odot \mathfrak{F}(\mathbf{y})$
correlation	$\mathbf{x} \star \mathbf{y}$	$\longleftrightarrow$	$\overline{\mathfrak{F}(\mathbf{x})} \odot \mathfrak{F}(\mathbf{y})$
dot product	$\mathbf{x} \cdot \mathbf{y}$	$=$	$\frac{1}{n} \mathfrak{F}(\mathbf{x}) \cdot \mathfrak{F}(\mathbf{y})$

we are interested in whether $r(s, o)$ holds[1] or not; we write $r(s, o) = +1$ if it holds, and $r(s, o) = -1$ if not. To be precise, given a *training set* $\mathcal{D} = \mathcal{R} \times \mathcal{E} \times \mathcal{E} \times \{-1, +1\}$ such that $(r, s, o, y) \in \mathcal{D}$ indicates $y = r(s, o)$, our task is to design a *scoring function* $f : \mathcal{R} \times \mathcal{E} \times \mathcal{E} \to \mathbb{R}$ such that for each of the triples (r, s, o) not observed in $\mathcal{D}$, function f should give a higher value if $r(s, o) = +1$ is more likely, and a smaller value for those that are less likely. If necessary, $f(r, s, o)$ can be converted to probability by $P[r(s, o) = +1] = \sigma(f(r, s, o))$, where $\sigma : \mathbb{R} \to (0, 1)$ is a sigmoid function.

Dataset $\mathcal{D}$ can be regarded as a directed graph in which nodes represent entities $\mathcal{E}$ and edges are labeled by relations $\mathcal{R}$. Thus, the task is essentially that of *link prediction* (Liben-Nowell and Kleinberg, 2003; Hasan and Zaki, 2011). Often, it is also called *knowledge graph completion*.

3.2 Holographic embeddings (HolE)

Nickel et al. (2016) proposed *holographic embeddings* (HolE) for knowledge graph completion. Using training data $\mathcal{D}$, this method learns the vector embeddings $\mathbf{e}_k \in \mathbb{R}^n$ of entities $k \in \mathcal{E}$ and the embeddings $\mathbf{w}_r \in \mathbb{R}^n$ of relations $r \in \mathcal{R}$. The score for triple (r, s, o) is then given by

$$f_{\text{HolE}}(r, s, o) = \mathbf{w}_r \cdot (\mathbf{e}_s \star \mathbf{e}_o). \tag{4}$$

Eq. (4) can be evaluated in time $O(n \log n)$ if $\mathbf{e}_s \star \mathbf{e}_o$ is computed by Eq. (3).

4 Spectral training of HolE

To compute the circular correlation in the scoring function of Eq. (4) efficiently, Nickel et al. (2016) used Eq. (3) in Section 2 and FFT. In this section, we extend this technique further, and con-

---

[1] Depending on the context, letter r is used either as an index to an element in $\mathcal{R}$ or the binary relation it signifies.

sider training HolE solely in the frequency domain. That is, real-valued embeddings $\mathbf{e}_k, \mathbf{w}_r \in \mathbb{R}^n$ in the original "time" domain are abolished, and instead we train their DFT counterparts $\boldsymbol{\varepsilon}_k = \mathfrak{F}(\mathbf{e}_k) \in \mathbb{C}^n$ and $\boldsymbol{\omega}_k = \mathfrak{F}(\mathbf{w}_r) \in \mathbb{C}^n$ in the frequency domain. This formulation eliminates the need of FFT and inverse FFT, which are the major computational bottleneck in HolE. As a result, Eq. (4) can be computed in time $O(n)$ directly from $\boldsymbol{\varepsilon}_k$ and $\boldsymbol{\omega}_k$.

Indeed, equivalent counterparts in the frequency domain exist for not only convolution/correlation but all other computations needed for HolE: scalar multiplication, summation (needed when vectors are updated by stochastic gradient descent), and dot product (used in Eq. (4)). The frequency-domain equivalents for these operations are summarized in Table 1. All of these can be performed efficiently (in linear time) in the frequency domain.

In particular, the following relation holds for the dot product between any "time" vectors $\mathbf{x}, \mathbf{y} \in \mathbb{R}^n$.

$$\mathbf{x} \cdot \mathbf{y} = \frac{1}{n}\, \mathfrak{F}(\mathbf{x}) \cdot \mathfrak{F}(\mathbf{y}), \tag{5}$$

where the dot product on the right-hand side is the complex inner product defined by $\mathbf{a} \cdot \mathbf{b} = \overline{\mathbf{a}}^{\mathrm{T}} \mathbf{b}$. Eq. (5) is known as Parseval's theorem (also called the *power theorem* in (Smith, 2007)), and it states that dot products in two domains are equal up to scaling.

After embeddings $\boldsymbol{\varepsilon}_k, \boldsymbol{\omega}_r \in \mathbb{C}^n$ are learned in the frequency domain, their time-domain counterparts $\mathbf{e}_k = \mathfrak{F}^{-1}(\boldsymbol{\varepsilon}_k)$ and $\mathbf{w}_r = \mathfrak{F}^{-1}(\boldsymbol{\omega}_r)$ can be recovered if needed, but this is not required as far as computation of the scoring function is concerned. Thanks to Parseval's theorem, Eq. (4) can be directly computed from the frequency vectors $\boldsymbol{\varepsilon}_k, \boldsymbol{\omega}_r \in \mathbb{C}^n$ by

$$f_{\mathrm{HolE}}(r, s, o) = \frac{1}{n}\, \boldsymbol{\omega}_r \cdot (\overline{\boldsymbol{\varepsilon}_s} \odot \boldsymbol{\varepsilon}_o). \tag{6}$$

4.1 Conjugate symmetry of spectral components

A complex vector $\boldsymbol{\xi} = [\xi_0 \cdots \xi_{n-1}]^{\mathrm{T}} \in \mathbb{C}^n$ is said to be *conjugate symmetric* (or *Hermitian*) if $\xi_j = \overline{\xi_{[(n-j) \bmod n]}}$ for $j = 0, \ldots, n-1$, or, in other words, if it can be written in the form

$$\boldsymbol{\xi} = \begin{cases} \left[\xi_0 \quad \boldsymbol{\gamma} \quad \mathrm{flip}(\overline{\boldsymbol{\gamma}})\right]^{\mathrm{T}}, & \text{if } n \text{ is odd,} \\ \left[\xi_0 \quad \boldsymbol{\gamma} \quad \xi_{n/2} \quad \mathrm{flip}(\overline{\boldsymbol{\gamma}})\right]^{\mathrm{T}}, & \text{if } n \text{ is even,} \end{cases}$$

for some $\boldsymbol{\gamma} \in \mathbb{C}^{\lceil n/2 \rceil - 1}$ and $\xi_0, \xi_{n/2} \in \mathbb{R}$.

The DFT $\mathfrak{F}(\mathbf{x})$ is conjugate symmetric if and only if $\mathbf{x}$ is a real vector. Thus, maintaining conjugate symmetry of "frequency" vectors is the key to ensure their "time" counterparts remain in real space. Below, we verify that this property is indeed preserved with stochastic gradient descent. Moreover, conjugate symmetry provides a sufficient condition under which dot product takes a real value. It also has implications on space requirement. These topics are covered in the rest of this section.

4.2 Vector initialization and update in frequency domain

Typically, at the beginning of training HolE, each individual embedding is initialized by a random vector. When we train HolE in the frequency domain, we could first generate a random real vector, regard them as a HolE vector in the time domain, and compute its DFT as the initial value in the frequency domain. An alternative, easier approach is to directly generate a random complex vector that is conjugate symmetric, and use it as the initial frequency vector. This guarantees the inverse DFT to be a real vector, i.e., there exists a valid corresponding image in the time domain.

Given a training set $\mathcal{D}$ (see Section 3.1), HolE is trained by minimizing the following objective function over parameter matrix $\boldsymbol{\Theta} = [\mathbf{e}_1 \cdots \mathbf{e}_{|\mathcal{E}|} \; \mathbf{w}_1 \cdots \mathbf{w}_{|\mathcal{R}|}] \in \mathbb{R}^{n \times (|\mathcal{E}| + |\mathcal{R}|)}$:

$$\sum_{(r,s,o,y) \in \mathcal{D}} \log\{1 + \exp(-y f_{\mathrm{HolE}}(r, s, o))\} + \lambda \|\boldsymbol{\Theta}\|_{\mathrm{F}}^2 \tag{7}$$

where $\lambda \in \mathbb{R}$ is the hyperparameter controlling the degree of regularization, and $\|\cdot\|_F$ denotes the Frobenius norm.

In our version of spectral training of HolE, the parameters matrix consists of frequency vectors $\boldsymbol{\varepsilon}_k$ and $\boldsymbol{\omega}_r$ instead of $\mathbf{e}_k$ and $\mathbf{w}_r$, i.e., $\boldsymbol{\Theta} = [\boldsymbol{\varepsilon}_1 \cdots \boldsymbol{\varepsilon}_{|\mathcal{E}|} \; \boldsymbol{\omega}_1 \cdots \boldsymbol{\omega}_{|\mathcal{R}|}] \in \mathbb{C}^{n \times (|\mathcal{E}| + |\mathcal{R}|)}$. Let us discuss the stochastic gradient descent (SGD) update with respect to these frequency vectors. In particular, we are interested in whether conjugate symmetry of vectors is preserved by the update.

Suppose vectors $\boldsymbol{\omega}_r, \boldsymbol{\varepsilon}_s, \boldsymbol{\varepsilon}_o$ are conjugate symmetric. Neglecting the contribution from the regularization term[2] in Eq. (7), we see that in

---

[2] It can be easily verified that the contribution from the regularization term to SGD update do not violate conjugate symmetry.

an SGD update step, $\alpha\partial f_{\text{HolE}}/\partial\boldsymbol{\omega}_r$, $\alpha\partial f_{\text{HolE}}/\partial\boldsymbol{\varepsilon}_s$, and $\alpha\partial f_{\text{HolE}}/\partial\boldsymbol{\varepsilon}_o$ are respectively subtracted from $\boldsymbol{\omega}_r, \boldsymbol{\varepsilon}_s, \boldsymbol{\varepsilon}_o$, where $\alpha \in \mathbb{R}$ is a factor not depending on these parameters. Noting the equalities

$$\mathbf{w}_r \cdot (\mathbf{e}_s \star \mathbf{e}_o) = \mathbf{e}_s \cdot (\mathbf{w}_r \star \mathbf{e}_o) = \mathbf{e}_o \cdot (\mathbf{w}_r * \mathbf{e}_s)$$

(see (Nickel et al., 2016, Eq. (12), p. 1958)) and their frequency counterparts

$$\boldsymbol{\omega}_r \cdot (\overline{\boldsymbol{\varepsilon}_s} \odot \boldsymbol{\varepsilon}_o) = \boldsymbol{\varepsilon}_s \cdot (\overline{\boldsymbol{\omega}_r} \odot \boldsymbol{\varepsilon}_o) = \boldsymbol{\varepsilon}_o \cdot (\boldsymbol{\omega}_r \odot \boldsymbol{\varepsilon}_s),$$

obtained through the translation of Table 1, we can derive

$$\frac{\partial f_{\text{HolE}}}{\partial\boldsymbol{\omega}_r} = \overline{\boldsymbol{\varepsilon}_s} \odot \boldsymbol{\varepsilon}_o,$$

$$\frac{\partial f_{\text{HolE}}}{\partial\boldsymbol{\varepsilon}_s} = \overline{\boldsymbol{\omega}_r} \odot \boldsymbol{\varepsilon}_o,$$

$$\frac{\partial f_{\text{HolE}}}{\partial\boldsymbol{\varepsilon}_o} = \boldsymbol{\omega}_r \odot \boldsymbol{\varepsilon}_s.$$

As seen from above, conjugation, scalar multiplication, summation, and elementwise product are used in the SGD update. And it is straightforward to verify that all these operations preserve conjugate symmetry. It follows that if $\boldsymbol{\omega}_r, \boldsymbol{\varepsilon}_s, \boldsymbol{\varepsilon}_o$ are initially conjugate symmetric, they will remain so during the course of training, which assures that the inverse DFTs of the learned embeddings are real vectors.

4.3 Real-valued dot product

In the scoring function of HolE (Eq. (4)), dot product is used for generating a real-valued "score" out of two vectors, $\mathbf{w}_r$ and $\mathbf{e}_s \odot \mathbf{e}_o$. Likewise, in Eq. (6), the dot product is applied to $\boldsymbol{\omega}_r$ and $\boldsymbol{\varepsilon}_s \odot \boldsymbol{\varepsilon}_o$, which are complex-valued. However, provided that the conjugate symmetry of these vectors is maintained, their dot product is always real. This follows from Parseval's theorem; the inverse DFTs of these frequency vectors are real, and thus their dot product is also real. Therefore, the dot product of the corresponding frequency vectors is real as well, according to Eq. (5).

4.4 Space requirement

A general complex vector $\boldsymbol{\xi} \in \mathbb{C}^n$ can be stored in memory as $2n$ floating-point numbers, i.e., one each for the real and imaginary part of a component. In our spectral representation of HolE, however, the first $\lfloor n/2 \rfloor$ components suffice to specify the frequency vector $\boldsymbol{\xi}$, since the vector is conjugate symmetric. Moreover, ξ_0 (and $\xi_{n/2}$ if n

is even) are real values. Thus, a spectral representation of HolE can be specified with exactly n floating-point numbers, which can be stored in the same amount of memory as needed by the original HolE.

5 Relation to Trouillon et al.'s complex embeddings

5.1 Complex embeddings (ComplEx)

Trouillon et al. (2016b) proposed a model of embedding-based knowledge graph completion, called *complex embeddings* (ComplEx). The objective is similar to Nickel et al.'s; the embeddings $\mathbf{e}_k$ of entities and $\mathbf{w}_r$ of relations are to be learned. In their model, however, these vectors are complex-valued, and are based on the eigendecomposition of complex matrix $\mathbf{X}_r = \mathbf{E}\mathbf{W}_r\overline{\mathbf{E}}^{\mathrm{T}}$ that encodes relation $r \in \mathcal{R}$ over pairs of entities, where $\mathbf{X}_r \in \mathbb{C}^{|\mathcal{E}|\times|\mathcal{E}|}$, $\mathbf{E} = [\mathbf{e}_1,\ldots,\mathbf{e}_{|\mathcal{E}|}]^{\mathrm{T}} \in \mathbb{C}^{|\mathcal{E}|\times n}$, and $\mathbf{W}_r = \mathrm{diag}(\mathbf{w}_r) \in \mathbb{C}^{n\times n}$ is a diagonal matrix (with diagonal elements $\mathbf{w}_r \in \mathbb{C}^n$). In practice, $\mathbf{X}_r$ needs to be a real matrix, because its (r, s)-component must define the score for $r(s, o)$. To this end, Trouillon et al. simply extracted the real part; i.e., $\mathbf{X}_r = \mathrm{Re}(\mathbf{E}\mathbf{W}_r\overline{\mathbf{E}}^{\mathrm{T}})$. Trouillon et al. (2016a) advocated this approach, by showing that any real matrix $\mathbf{X}_r$ can be expressed in this form.

With this formulation, the score for triple (r, s, o) is given by

$$f_{\text{ComplEx}}(r, s, o) = \mathrm{Re}\left(\sum_{j=0}^{n-1}[\mathbf{w}_r]_j[\mathbf{e}_s]_j\overline{[\mathbf{e}_o]_j}\right). \quad (8)$$

5.2 Equivalence of holographic and complex embeddings

Now let us rewrite Eq. (8). Noting the definition of complex dot product, i.e., $\mathbf{a} \cdot \mathbf{b} = \overline{\mathbf{a}}^{\mathrm{T}}\mathbf{b}$, we have

$$\sum_{j=0}^{n-1}[\mathbf{w}_r]_j[\mathbf{e}_s]_j\overline{[\mathbf{e}_o]_j} = (\mathbf{e}_s \odot \overline{\mathbf{e}_o})^{\mathrm{T}}\mathbf{w}_r$$

$$= \overline{(\mathbf{e}_s \odot \overline{\mathbf{e}_o})} \cdot \mathbf{w}_r \quad (\because \mathbf{a} \cdot \mathbf{b} = \overline{\mathbf{a}}^{\mathrm{T}}\mathbf{b})$$

$$= (\overline{\mathbf{e}_s} \odot \mathbf{e}_o) \cdot \mathbf{w}_r$$

$$= \overline{\mathbf{w}_r \cdot (\overline{\mathbf{e}_s} \odot \mathbf{e}_o)} \quad (\because \mathbf{a} \cdot \mathbf{b} = \overline{\mathbf{b} \cdot \mathbf{a}})$$

and since $\mathrm{Re}(\mathbf{z}) = \mathrm{Re}(\overline{\mathbf{z}})$,

$$\mathrm{Re}(\overline{\mathbf{w}_r \cdot (\overline{\mathbf{e}_s} \odot \mathbf{e}_o)}) = \mathrm{Re}(\mathbf{w}_r \cdot (\overline{\mathbf{e}_s} \odot \mathbf{e}_o)).$$

Thus, Eq. (8) can be written as

$$f_{\text{ComplEx}}(r, s, o) = \mathrm{Re}\left(\mathbf{w}_r \cdot (\overline{\mathbf{e}_s} \odot \mathbf{e}_o)\right). \quad (9)$$

Here, a marked similarity is noticeable between Eq. (9) and Eq. (6), the scoring function of our spectral version of HolE (spectral HolE); ComplEx extracts the real part of complex dot product, whereas in the spectral HolE, dot product is guaranteed to be real because all embeddings satisfy conjugate symmetry. Indeed, Eq. (6) can be equally written as

$$f_{\mathrm{HolE}}(r, s, o) = \frac{1}{n} \operatorname{Re}\left(\boldsymbol{\omega}_r \cdot (\overline{\boldsymbol{\varepsilon}_s} \odot \boldsymbol{\varepsilon}_o)\right). \qquad (10)$$

although the operator $\operatorname{Re}(\cdot)$ in this formula is redundant, since the inner product is guaranteed to be real-valued. Nevertheless, Eq. (10) elucidates the fact that the spectral HolE can be viewed as an instance of ComplEx, with the embeddings constrained to be conjugate symmetric to make the inner product in Eq. (10) real-valued.

Conversely, given a set of complex embeddings for entities and relations, we can construct their equivalent holographic embeddings, in the sense that $f_{\mathrm{ComplEx}}(r, s, o) = c f_{\mathrm{HolE}}(r, s, o)$ for every r, s, o, where $c > 0$ is a constant. For each n-dimensional complex embeddings $\mathbf{x} \in \{\mathbf{e}_k\}_{k \in \mathcal{E}} \cup \{\mathbf{w}_r\}_{r \in \mathcal{R}} \subset \mathbb{C}^n$ computed by ComplEx, we make a corresponding HolE $\mathfrak{h}(\mathbf{x}) \in \mathbb{R}^{2n+1}$ as follows: For a given complex embedding $\mathbf{x} = [x_0 \cdots x_{n-1}] \in \mathbb{C}^n$, first compute $\mathfrak{s}(\mathbf{x}) \in \mathbb{C}^{2n+1}$ by

$$\mathfrak{s}(\mathbf{x}) = \begin{bmatrix} 0 & x_0 & \cdots & x_{n-1} & \overline{x_{n-1}} & \cdots & \overline{x_0} \end{bmatrix}^{\mathrm{T}}$$
$$= \begin{bmatrix} 0 & \mathbf{x} & \mathrm{flip}(\overline{\mathbf{x}}) \end{bmatrix}^{\mathrm{T}} \qquad (11)$$

and then define $\mathfrak{h}(\mathbf{x}) = \mathfrak{F}^{-1}(\mathfrak{s}(\mathbf{x}))$. Since $\mathfrak{s}(\mathbf{x})$ is conjugate symmetric, $\mathfrak{h}(\mathbf{x})$ is a real vector.

To verify if this conversion defines an equivalent scoring function for any triple (r, s, o), let us now suppose complex embeddings $\mathbf{w}_r \in \mathbb{C}^n$ and $\mathbf{e}_s, \mathbf{e}_o \in \mathbb{C}^n$ are given. Since we regard real vectors $\mathfrak{h}(\mathbf{w}_r), \mathfrak{h}(\mathbf{e}_s), \mathfrak{h}(\mathbf{e}_o) \in \mathbb{R}^{2n+1}$ as the holographic embeddings of r, s and o, respectively, the HolE score for the triple (r, s, o) is given as

$$f_{\mathrm{HolE}}(r, s, o)$$
$$= \mathfrak{h}(\mathbf{w}_r) \cdot (\mathfrak{h}(\mathbf{e}_s) \star \mathfrak{h}(\mathbf{e}_o))$$
$$= \frac{1}{n} \mathfrak{s}(\mathbf{w}_r) \cdot (\overline{\mathfrak{s}(\mathbf{e}_s)} \odot \mathfrak{s}(\mathbf{e}_o)) \qquad (\because \text{Eq. (6)})$$
$$= \frac{1}{n} \mathfrak{s}(\mathbf{w}_r) \cdot \begin{bmatrix} 0 & \overline{\mathbf{e}_s} \odot \mathbf{e}_o & \mathrm{flip}(\overline{\overline{\mathbf{e}_s} \odot \mathbf{e}_o}) \end{bmatrix}^{\mathrm{T}} \qquad (\because \text{Eq. (11)})$$
$$= \frac{1}{n} \begin{bmatrix} 0 & \mathbf{w}_r & \mathrm{flip}(\overline{\mathbf{w}_r}) \end{bmatrix}^{\mathrm{T}} \cdot \begin{bmatrix} 0 & \overline{\mathbf{e}_s} \odot \mathbf{e}_o & \mathrm{flip}(\overline{\overline{\mathbf{e}_s} \odot \mathbf{e}_o}) \end{bmatrix}^{\mathrm{T}}$$
$$= \frac{1}{n} \left(\mathbf{w}_r \cdot (\overline{\mathbf{e}_s} \odot \mathbf{e}_o) + \mathrm{flip}(\overline{\mathbf{w}_r}) \cdot \mathrm{flip}(\overline{\overline{\mathbf{e}_s} \odot \mathbf{e}_o})\right)$$
$$= \frac{1}{n} \left(\mathbf{w}_r \cdot (\overline{\mathbf{e}_s} \odot \mathbf{e}_o) + \overline{\mathbf{w}_r} \cdot \overline{(\overline{\mathbf{e}_s} \odot \mathbf{e}_o)}\right)$$
$$= \frac{1}{n} \left(\mathbf{w}_r \cdot (\overline{\mathbf{e}_s} \odot \mathbf{e}_o) + \overline{\mathbf{w}_r \cdot (\overline{\mathbf{e}_s} \odot \mathbf{e}_o)}\right)$$
$$= \frac{2}{n} \operatorname{Re}\left(\mathbf{w}_r \cdot (\overline{\mathbf{e}_s} \odot \mathbf{e}_o)\right)$$
$$= \frac{2}{n} f_{\mathrm{ComplEx}}(r, s, o),$$

which shows that $\mathfrak{h}(\cdot)$ (or $\mathfrak{s}(\cdot)$) gives the desired conversion from ComplEx to HolE.

6 Conclusion

In this paper, we have shown that the holographic embeddings (HolE) can be trained entirely in the frequency domain. If stochastic gradient descent is used for training, the conjugate symmetry of frequency vectors is preserved, which ensures the existence of the corresponding holographic embedding in the original real space (time domain). Also, this training method eliminates the need of FFT and inverse FFT, thereby reducing the computation time of the scoring function from $O(n \log n)$ to $O(n)$.

Moreover, we have established the equivalence of HolE and the complex embeddings (ComplEx): The spectral version of HolE is subsumed by ComplEx as a special case in which conjugate symmetry is imposed on the embeddings. Conversely, every set of complex embeddings can be converted to equivalent holographic embeddings.

Many systems for natural language processing, such as those for semantic parsing and question answering, benefit from access to information stored in knowledge graphs. We plan to further investigate the property of spectral HolE and ComplEx in these applications.

Acknowledgments

We thank the anonymous reviewers for helpful comments. This work was partially supported by JSPS Kakenhi Grants 26730126 and 15H02749.

References

Sören Auer, Christian Bizer, Georgi Kobilarov, Jens Lehmann, Richard Cyganiak, and Zachary Ives. 2007. DBpedia: A nucleus for a web of open data. In *The Semantic Web: Proceedings of the 6th International Semantic Web Conference and the 2nd Asian Semantic Web Conference (ISWC '07/ASWC '07)*. Springer, Lecture Notes in Computer Science 4825, pages 722–735.

Kurt Bollacker, Colin Evans, Praveen Paritosh, Tim Sturge, and Jamie Taylor. 2008. Freebase: A collaboratively created graph database for structuring human knowledge. In *Proceedings of the 2008 ACM SIGMOD International Conference on Management of Data (SIGMOD '08)*. pages 1247–1250.

Antoine Bordes, Jason Weston, Ronan Collobert, and Yoshua Bengio. 2011. Learning structured embeddings of knowledge bases. In *Proceedings of the 25th AAAI Conference on Artificial Intelligence (AAAI '11)*. pages 301–306.

Lise Getoor and Ben Taskar. 2007. *Introduction to Statistical Relational Learning*. Adaptive Computation and Machine Learning. The MIT Press.

Kelvin Guu, John Miller, and Percy Liang. 2015. Traversing knowledge graphs in vector space. In *Proceedings of the 2015 Conference on Empirical Methods in Natural Language Processing (EMNLP '15)*. pages 318–327.

Mohammad Al Hasan and Mohammed J. Zaki. 2011. A survey of link prediction in social networks. In Charu C. Aggarwal, editor, *Social Network Data Analytics*, Springer, chapter 9, pages 243–275.

David Liben-Nowell and Jon Kleinberg. 2003. The link prediction problem for social networks. In *Proceedings of the 12nd Annual ACM International Conference on Information and Knowledge Management (CIKM '03)*. pages 556–559.

Maximilian Nickel, Kevin Murphy, Volker Tresp, and Evgeniy Gabrilovich. 2015. A review of relational machine learning for knowledge graphs. *Proceedings of the IEEE* pages 1–18.

Maximilian Nickel, Lorenzo Rosasco, and Tomaso Poggio. 2016. Holographic embeddings of knowledge graphs. In *Proceedings of the 30th AAAI Conference on Artificial Intelligence (AAAI '16)*. pages 1955–1961.

III Julius O. Smith. 2007. *Mathematics of the Discrete Fourier Transform (DFT): with Audio Applications*. W3K Publishing, 2nd edition.

Richard Socher, Danqi Chen, Christopher D. Manning, and Andrew Y. Ng. 2013. Reasoning with neural tensor networks for knowledge base completion. In *Advances in Neural Information Processing Systems 26 (NIPS '13)*. pages 926–934.

Fabian M. Suchanek, Gjergji Kasneci, and Gerhard Weikum. 2007. YAGO: A core of semantic knowledge unifying Wordnet and Wikipedia. In *Proceedings of the 16th International Conference on World Wide Web (WWW '07)*. pages 697–706.

Théo Trouillon, Christopher R. Dance, Éric Gaussier, and Guillaume Bouchard. 2016a. Decomposing real square matrices via unitary diagonalization. arXiv.math eprint 1605.07103, arXiv.

Théo Trouillon, Johannes Welbl, Sebastian Riedel, Éric Gaussier, and Guillaume Bouchard. 2016b. Complex embeddings for simple link prediction. In *Proceedings of the 33rd International Conference on Machine Learning (ICML '16)*. pages 2071–2080.

Bishan Yang, Wen tau Yih, Xiaodong He, Jianfeng Gao, and Li Deng. 2015. Embedding entities and relations for learning and inference in knowledge bases. In *Proceedings of the 3rd International Conference on Learning Representations (ICLR '15)*.

Sentence Embedding for Neural Machine Translation Domain Adaptation

Rui Wang, Andrew Finch, Masao Utiyama and Eiichiro Sumita
National Institute of Information and Communications Technology (NICT)
3-5 Hikari-dai, Seika-cho, Soraku-gun, Kyoto, Japan
{wangrui,andrew.finch,mutiyama,eiichiro.sumita}@nict.go.jp

Abstract

Although new corpora are becoming increasingly available for machine translation, only those that belong to the same or similar domains are typically able to improve translation performance. Recently Neural Machine Translation (NMT) has become prominent in the field. However, most of the existing domain adaptation methods only focus on phrase-based machine translation. In this paper, we exploit the NMT's internal embedding of the source sentence and use the sentence embedding similarity to select the sentences which are close to in-domain data. The empirical adaptation results on the IWSLT English-French and NIST Chinese-English tasks show that the proposed methods can substantially improve NMT performance by 2.4-9.0 BLEU points, outperforming the existing state-of-the-art baseline by 2.3-4.5 BLEU points.

1 Introduction

Recently, Neural Machine Translation (NMT) has set new state-of-the-art benchmarks on many translation tasks (Cho et al., 2014; Bahdanau et al., 2015; Jean et al., 2015; Tu et al., 2016; Mi et al., 2016; Zhang et al., 2016). An ever increasing amount of data is becoming available for NMT training. However, only the in-domain or related-domain corpora tend to have a positive impact on NMT performance. Unrelated additional corpora, known as out-of-domain corpora, have been shown not to benefit some domains and tasks for NMT, such as TED-talks and IWSLT tasks (Luong and Manning, 2015).

To the best of our knowledge, there are only a few works concerning NMT adaptation (Luong and Manning, 2015; Freitag and Al-Onaizan, 2016). Most traditional adaptation methods focus on Phrase-Based Statistical Machine Translation (PBSMT) and they can be broken down broadly into two main categories namely *model adaptation* and *data selection* (Joty et al., 2015) as follows.

For model adaptation, several PBSMT models, such as language models, translation models and reordering models, individually corresponding to each corpus, are trained. These models are then combined to achieve the best performance (Sennrich, 2012; Sennrich et al., 2013; Durrani et al., 2015). Since these methods focus on the internal models within a PBSMT system, they are not applicable to NMT adaptation. Recently, an NMT adaptation method (Luong and Manning, 2015) was proposed. The training is performed in two steps: first the NMT system is trained using out-of-domain data, and then further trained using in-domain data. Empirical results show their method can improve NMT performance, and this approach provides a natural baseline.

For adaptation through data selection, the main idea is to score the out-domain data using models trained from the in-domain and out-of-domain data and select training data from the out-of-domain data using a cut-off threshold on the resulting scores. A language model can be used to score sentences (Moore and Lewis, 2010; Axelrod et al., 2011; Duh et al., 2013; Wang et al., 2015), as well as joint models (Hoang and Sima'an, 2014a,b; Durrani et al., 2015), and more recently Convolutional Neural Network (CNN) models (Chen et al., 2016). These methods select useful sentences from the whole corpus, so they can be directly applied to NMT. However, these methods are specifically designed for PBSMT and nearly all of them use the models or criteria which do not have a direct relationship with the neural

560

Proceedings of the 55th Annual Meeting of the Association for Computational Linguistics (Short Papers), pages 560–566
Vancouver, Canada, July 30 - August 4, 2017. ©2017 Association for Computational Linguistics
https://doi.org/10.18653/v1/P17-2089

translation process.

For NMT sentences selection, our hypothesis is that the NMT system itself can be used to score each sentence in the training data. Specifically, an NMT system embeds the source sentence into a vector representation[1] and we can use these vectors to measure a sentence pair's similarity to the in-domain corpus. In comparison with the CNN or other sentence embedding methods, this method can directly make use of information induced by the NMT system information itself. In addition, the proposed sentence selection method can be used in conjunction with the NMT further training method (Luong and Manning, 2015).

2 NMT Background

An attention-based NMT system uses a Bidirectional RNN (BiRNN) as an encoder and a decoder that emulates searching through a source sentence during decoding (Bahdanau et al., 2015). The encoder's BiRNN consists of forward and backward RNNs. Each word x_i is represented by concatenating the forward hidden state $\overrightarrow{h_i}$ and the backward one $\overleftarrow{h_i}$ as $h_i = [\overrightarrow{h_i}; \overleftarrow{h_i}]^\top$. In this way, the source sentence $\mathbf{X} = \{x_1, ..., x_{T_x}\}$ can be represented as annotations $\mathbf{H} = \{h_1, ..., h_{T_x}\}$. In the decoder, an RNN hidden state s_j for time j is computed by:

$$s_j = f(s_{j-1}, y_{j-1}, c_j). \tag{1}$$

The context vector c_j is then, computed as a weighted sum of these annotations $\mathbf{H} = \{h_1, ..., h_{T_x}\}$, by using alignment weight α_{ji}:

$$c_j = \sum_{j=1}^{T_x} \alpha_{ji} h_i. \tag{2}$$

3 Sentence Embedding and Selection

3.1 Sentence Embedding

A source sentence can be represented as the annotations $\mathbf{H}$. However the length of $\mathbf{H}$ depends on the sentence length T_x. To represent a sentence as a fixed-length vector, we adopt the initial hidden

layer state s_{init} for the decoder as this vector:

$$s_{init}(\mathbf{X}) = tanh(\mathbf{W}\frac{\sum_{i=1}^{T_x} h_i}{T_x} + \mathbf{b}), h_i \in \mathbf{H}, \tag{3}$$

where an average pooling layer averages the annotation h_i for each source word into a fixed-length source sentence vector, and a nonlinear transition layer (weights $\mathbf{W}$ and bias $\mathbf{b}$ are jointly trained with all the other components of NMT system) transforms this embedded source sentence vector into the initial hidden state s_{init} for the decoder (Bahdanau et al., 2015).

3.2 Sentence Selection

We employ the data selection method, which is inspired by (Moore and Lewis, 2010; Axelrod et al., 2011; Duh et al., 2013). As Axelrod et al. (2011) mentioned, there are some pseudo in-domain data in out-of-domain data, which are close to in-domain data. Our intuition is to select the sentences whose embeddings are similar to the average in-domain ones, while being dis-similar to the average out-of-domain ones:

- 1) We train a French-to-English NMT system $\mathbf{N_{FE}}$ using the in-domain and out-of-domain data together as training data.[2]

- 2) Each sentence f in the training data F (both in-domain F_{in} and out-of-domain F_{out}) is embedded as a vector $v_f = s_{init}(f)$ by using $\mathbf{N_{FE}}$.

- 3) The sentence pairs (f, e) in the out-of-domain corpus F_{out} are classified into two sets: the sentences close to in-domain sentences, and those that are distant.

That is, we firstly calculate the vector centers of in-domain $C_{F_{in}}$ and out-of-domain $C_{F_{out}}$ corpora, respectively.

$$C_{F_{in}} = \frac{\sum_{f \in F_{in}} v_f}{|F_{in}|},$$
$$C_{F_{out}} = \frac{\sum_{f \in F_{out}} v_f}{|F_{out}|}. \tag{4}$$

Then we measure the Euclidean distance d between each sentence vector v_f and in-domain

---

[1]Li et al. (2016)'s fine-tuned NMT systems apply a similar sentence representation. In comparison, we adopt a transition layer between the source and target layers and don't use test data.

[2]It is possible to use a sample of the out-of-domain data. In this paper, we use all of them.

vector center $C_{F_{in}}$ as $d(v_f, C_{F_{in}})$ and out-of-domain vector center $C_{F_{out}}$ as $d(v_f, C_{F_{out}})$, respectively. We use the difference δ of these two distances to classify each sentence:

$$\delta_f = d(v_f, C_{F_{in}}) - d(v_f, C_{F_{out}}). \quad (5)$$

By using an English-to-French NMT system $\mathbf{N_{EF}}$, we can obtain a target sentence embedding v_e, in-domain target vector center $C_{E_{in}}$ and out-of-domain target vector center $C_{E_{out}}$. Corresponding distance difference δ_e is,

$$\delta_e = d(v_e, C_{E_{in}}) - d(v_e, C_{E_{out}}). \quad (6)$$

δ_f, δ_e and $\delta_{fe} = \delta_f + \delta_e$ can be used to select sentences. That is, the sentence pairs (f, e) with δ_f (or δ_e, δ_{fe}) less than a threshold are the new selected in-domain corpus. This threshold is tuned by using the development data.

4 Experiments

4.1 Data sets

The proposed methods were evaluated on two data sets as shown in Table 1.

- IWSLT 2014 English (EN) to French (FR) corpus[3] was used as in-domain training data and dev2010 and test2010/2011 (Cettolo et al., 2014), were selected as development (dev) and test data, respectively. Out-of-domain corpora contained Common Crawl, Europarl v7, News Commentary v10 and United Nation (UN) EN-FR parallel corpora.[4]

- NIST 2006 Chinese (ZH) to English corpus[5] was used as the in-domain training corpus, following the settings of (Wang et al., 2014). Chinese-to-English UN data set (LDC2013T06) and NTCIR-9 (Goto et al., 2011) patent data set were used as out-of-domain data. NIST MT 2002-2004 and NIST MT 2005/2006 were used as the development and test data, respectively. We are aware of that there are additional NIST corpora in a similar domain, but because this task was for domain adaptation, we only selected a small subset, which is mainly focused on news and

blog texts. The statistics on data sets were shown in Table 1.

These adaptation corpora settings were nearly the same as that used in (Wang et al., 2016). The differences were:

- For IWSLT, they chose FR-EN translation task, which is popular in PBSMT. We chose EN-FR, which is more popular in NMT;

- For NIST, they chose 02-05 as dev set, and we chose 02-04. Because we would report results on two test sets (MT05 and MT06) in comparison with only one (MT06).

IWSLT EN-FR	Sentences	Tokens
TED training (in-domain)	178.1K	3.5M
WMT training (out-of-domain)	17.8M	450.0M
TED dev2010	0.9K	20.1K
TED test2010	1.6K	31.9K
TED test2011	0.8K	15.6K
NIST ZH-EN	Sentences	Tokens
NIST in-domain training	430.8K	12.6M
out-of-domain training	8.8M	249.4M
dev (MT02-04)	3.4K	106.4K
test (MT05)	1.0K	34.7K
test (MT06)	1.6K	46.7K

Table 1: Statistics on data sets.

4.2 NMT System

We implemented the proposed method in Groundhog[6] (Bahdanau et al., 2015), which is one of the state-of-the-art NMT frameworks. The default settings of Groundhog were applied for all NMT systems: the word embedding dimension was 620 and the size of a hidden layer was 1000, the batch size was 64, the source and target side vocabulary sizes were 30K, the maximum sequence length were 50, and the beam size for decoding was 10. Default dropout were applied. We used a mini-batch Stochastic Gradient Descent (SGD) algorithm together with ADADELTA optimizer (Zeiler, 2012). Training was conducted on a single Tesla K80 GPU. Each NMT model was trained for 500K batches, taking 7-10 days. For sentence embedding and selection, it only took several hours to process all of sentences in the training data, because decoding was not necessary.

---

[3] https://wit3.fbk.eu/mt.php?release=2014-01
[4] http://statmt.org/wmt15/translation-task.html
[5] http://www.itl.nist.gov/iad/mig/tests/mt/2006/
[6] `https://github.com/lisa-groundhog/GroundHog`

4.3 Baselines

Along with the standard NMT baseline system, we also compared the proposed methods to the recent state-of-the-art NMT adaptation method of Luong and Manning (2015)[7] as described in Section 1. Two typical sentence selection methods for PBSMT were also used as baselines: Axelrod et al. (2011) used language model-based cross-entropy difference as criterion; Chen et al. (2016) used a CNN to classify the sentences as either in-domain or out-of-domain. In addition, we randomly sampled out-of-domain data to create a corpus the same size as that used for the best performing proposed system. We tried our best to re-implement the baseline methods using the same basic NMT setting as the proposed method.

4.4 Results and Analyses

In Tables 2 and 3, the in, out and $in + out$ indicate that the in-domain, out-of-domain and their mixture were used as the NMT training corpora. δ_f, δ_e and δ_{fe} indicate that corresponding criterion was used to select sentences, and these selected sentences were added to in-domain corpus to construct the new training corpora. $+fur$ indicates that the selected sentences were used to train an initial NMT system, and then this initial system was further trained by in-domain data (Luong and Manning, 2015). The threshold for the sentence selection method was selected on development data. That is, we selected the top ranked 10%, 20%,...,90% out-of-domain data to be added into the in-domain data, and the best performing models on development data were used in the evaluation on test data.

The vocabulary was built by using the selected corpus and in-domain corpus.[8] Translation performance was measured by case-insensitive BLEU (Papineni et al., 2002). Since the proposed method is a sentence selection approach, we can also show the effect on standard PBSMT (Koehn et al., 2007).

In the IWSLT task, the observations were as follows:

- Adding out-of-domain to in-domain data, or directly using out-of-domain data, degraded PBSMT and NMT performance.

Methods	Sent. No.	SMT tst10	SMT tst11	NMT tst10	NMT tst11
in	178.1K	31.06	32.50	29.23	30.00
out	17.7M	30.04	29.29	27.30	28.48
in+out	17.9 M	30.00	30.26	28.89	28.55
Random	5.5M	31.22	33.85	30.53	32.37
Luong	17.9 M	N/A	N/A	32.21	35.03
Axelrod	9.0M	32.06	34.81	32.26	35.54
Chen	7.3M	31.42	33.78	30.32	33.81
δ_f	7.3M	31.46	33.13	32.13	34.81
δ_e	3.7M	**32.08**	35.94	32.84	36.56
δ_{fe}	5.5M	31.79	**35.66**	32.67	36.64
δ_f+fur	7.3M	N/A	N/A	34.04	37.18
δ_e+fur	3.7M	N/A	N/A	33.88	38.04
δ_{fe}+fur	5.5M	N/A	N/A	**34.52**	**39.02**

Table 2: IWSLT EN-FR results. Luong and Manning (2015)'s **fur**ther (shorted as fur in Tables 2 and 3) training method can only be applied to NMT.

Methods	Sent. No.	SMT MT05	SMT MT06	NMT MT05	NMT MT06
in	430.8K	29.66	30.73	27.28	26.82
out	8.8M	29.91	30.13	28.67	27.79
in+out	9.3M	30.23	30.11	28.91	28.22
Random	5.7M	29.90	30.18	28.02	27.49
Luong	9.3M	N/A	N/A	29.91	29.61
Axelrod	2.2M	30.52	30.96	28.41	28.75
Chen	4.8M	30.64	31.05	28.39	28.06
δ_f	4.8M	30.90	**31.96**	29.21	30.14
δ_e	2.2M	**30.94**	31.33	30.00	30.63
δ_{fe}	5.7M	30.72	31.43	30.13	31.07
δ_f+fur	4.8M	N/A	N/A	30.80	31.54
δ_e+fur	2.2M	N/A	N/A	30.49	31.13
δ_{fe}+fur	5.7M	N/A	N/A	**31.35**	**31.80**

Table 3: NIST ZH-EN results.

- Adding data selected by δ_f, δ_e and δ_{fe} substantially improved NMT performance (3.9 to 6.6 BLEU points), and gave rise to a modest improvement in PBSMT performance (0.4 to 3.1 BLEU points). This method also outperformed the best existing baselines by up to 1.1 BLEU points for NMT and 0.8 BLEU for PBSMT.

- The proposed method worked synergistically with Luong's further training method, and the combination was able to add up to an additional 2-3 BLEU points, indicating that the proposed method and Luong's method are essentially orthogonal.

- The performance by using both sides of sentence embeddings δ_{fe} was slightly better

[7] Freitag and Al-Onaizan (2016)'s method is quite similar to Luong and Manning (2015)'s, so we did not compare to them.

[8] According to our empirical comparison, the performance did not significantly change if we used $in + out$ to build the vocabulary for all of the systems.

than using monolingual sentence embedding δ_f and δ_e.

In the NIST task, the observations were similar to the IWSLT task, except:

- Adding out-of-domain slightly improved PBSMT and NMT performance.

- The proposed method improved both PBSMT and NMT performance, but not as substantially as in IWSLT.

These observations suggest that the out-of-domain data was closer to the in-domain than in IWSLT.

5 Discussions

5.1 Selected Size Effect

We show experimental results on varying the size of additional data selected from the out-of-domain dataset, in Figure 1. It shows that the proposed method δ_{fe} reached the highest performance on dev set, when top 30% out-of-domain sentences are selected as pseudo in-domain data. δ_{fe} outperforms the other methods in most of the cases on development data.

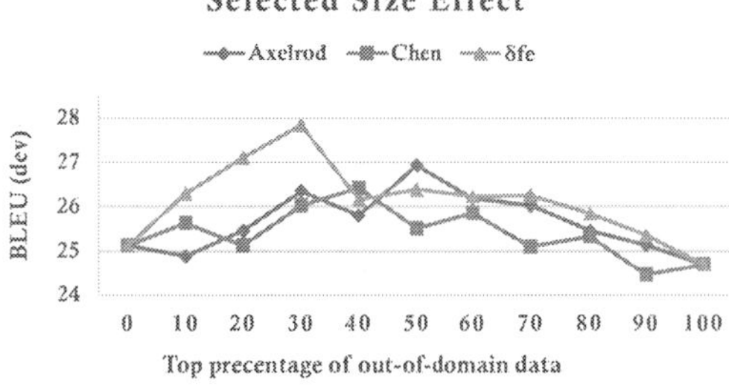

Figure 1: Selected size tuning on IWSLT.

5.2 Training Time Effect

We also show the relationship between BLEU and batches of training in Figure 2.

Most of the methods (without further training) converged after similar batches training. Specifically, in researched the highest BLEU performance on dev faster than other methods (without further training), then decreased and finally converged.

The further training methods, which firstly trained the models using out-of-domain data and then in-domain data, converged very soon after

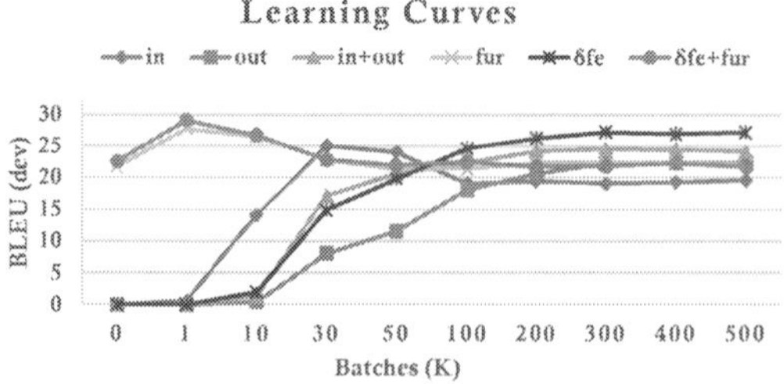

Figure 2: Training time on IWSLT.

in-domain data were introduced. In further training, the out-of-domain trained system could be considered as a pre-trained NMT system. Then the in-domain data training help NMT system overfit at in-domain data and gained around two BLEU improvement.

6 Conclusion and Future Work

In this paper, we proposed a straightforward sentence selection method for NMT domain adaptation. Instead of the existing external selection criteria, we applied the internal NMT sentence embedding similarity as the criterion. Empirical results on IWSLT and NIST tasks showed that the proposed method can substantially improve NMT performances and outperform state-of-the-art existing NMT adaptation methods on NMT (even PBSMT) performances.

In addition, we found that the combination of sentence selection and further training has an additional effect, with a fast convergence. In our further work, we will investigate the effect of training data order and batch data selection on NMT training.

Acknowledgments

Thanks a lot for the helpful discussions with Dr. Lemao Liu, Kehai Chen and Dr. Atsushi Fujita. We also appreciate the insightful comments from three anonymous reviewers.

References

Amittai Axelrod, Xiaodong He, and Jianfeng Gao. 2011. Domain adaptation via pseudo in-domain data selection. In *Proceedings of the 2011 Conference on Empirical Methods in Natural Language Processing*. Edinburgh, Scotland, U.K., pages 355–362. http://www.aclweb.org/anthology/D11-1033.

Dzmitry Bahdanau, Kyunghyun Cho, and Yoshua Bengio. 2015. Neural machine translation by jointly learning to align and translate. In *International Conference on Learning Representations*. San Diego. http://arxiv.org/abs/1409.0473.

Mauro Cettolo, Jan Niehues, Sebastian Stüker, Luisa Bentivogli, and Marcello Federico. 2014. Report on the 11th IWSLT evaluation campaign. In *Proceedings of the International Workshop on Spoken Language Translation*. Lake Tahoe, CA, USA, pages 2–17. http://workshop2014.iwslt.org/64.php.

Boxing Chen, Roland Kuhn, George Foster, Colin Cherry, and Fei Huang. 2016. Bilingual methods for adaptive training data selection for machine translation. In *The Twelfth Conference of The Association for Machine Translation in the Americas*. Austin, Texas, pages 93–106. https://amtaweb.org/amta-2016-in-austin-tx/.

Kyunghyun Cho, Bart van Merrienboer, Caglar Gulcehre, Dzmitry Bahdanau, Fethi Bougares, Holger Schwenk, and Yoshua Bengio. 2014. Learning phrase representations using RNN encoder–decoder for statistical machine translation. In *Proceedings of the 2014 Conference on Empirical Methods in Natural Language Processing*. Doha, Qatar, pages 1724–1734. http://www.aclweb.org/anthology/D14-1179.

Kevin Duh, Graham Neubig, Katsuhito Sudoh, and Hajime Tsukada. 2013. Adaptation data selection using neural language models: Experiments in machine translation. In *Proceedings of the 51st Annual Meeting of the Association for Computational Linguistics (Volume 2: Short Papers)*. Sofia, Bulgaria, pages 678–683. http://www.aclweb.org/anthology/P13-2119.

Nadir Durrani, Hassan Sajjad, Shafiq Joty, Ahmed Abdelali, and Stephan Vogel. 2015. Using joint models for domain adaptation in statistical machine translation. In *Proceedings of MT Summit XV*. Miami, FL, USA, pages 117–130. https://amtaweb.org/mt-summit-xv-proceedings/.

Markus Freitag and Yaser Al-Onaizan. 2016. Fast domain adaptation for neural machine translation. *arXiv preprint arXiv:1612.06897* http://arxiv.org/abs/1612.06897.

Isao Goto, Bin Lu, Ka Po Chow, Eiichiro Sumita, and Benjamin K. Tsou. 2011. Overview of the patent machine translation task at the NTCIR-9 workshop. In *Proceedings of NTCIR-9 Workshop Meeting*. Tokyo, Japan, pages 559–578. http://research.nii.ac.jp/ntcir/.

Cuong Hoang and Khalil Sima'an. 2014a. Latent domain phrase-based models for adaptation. In *Proceedings of the 2014 Conference on Empirical Methods in Natural Language Processing*. Doha, Qatar, pages 566–576. http://www.aclweb.org/anthology/D14-1062.

Cuong Hoang and Khalil Sima'an. 2014b. Latent domain translation models in mix-of-domains haystack. In *Proceedings of the 25th International Conference on Computational Linguistics: Technical Papers*. Dublin, Ireland, pages 1928–1939. http://www.aclweb.org/anthology/C14-1182.

Sébastien Jean, Kyunghyun Cho, Roland Memisevic, and Yoshua Bengio. 2015. On using very large target vocabulary for neural machine translation. In *Proceedings of the 53rd Annual Meeting of the Association for Computational Linguistics and the 7th International Joint Conference on Natural Language Processing (Volume 1: Long Papers)*. Beijing, China, pages 1–10. http://www.aclweb.org/anthology/P15-1001.

Shafiq Joty, Hassan Sajjad, Nadir Durrani, Kamla Al-Mannai, Ahmed Abdelali, and Stephan Vogel. 2015. How to avoid unwanted pregnancies: Domain adaptation using neural network models. In *Proceedings of the 2015 Conference on Empirical Methods in Natural Language Processing*. Lisbon, Portugal, pages 1259–1270. http://aclweb.org/anthology/D15-1147.

Philipp Koehn, Hieu Hoang, Alexandra Birch, Chris Callison-Burch, Marcello Federico, Nicola Bertoldi, Brooke Cowan, Wade Shen, Christine Moran, Richard Zens, Chris Dyer, Ondrej Bojar, Alexandra Constantin, and Evan Herbst. 2007. Moses: Open source toolkit for statistical machine translation. In *Proceedings of the 45th Annual Meeting of the Association for Computational Linguistics Companion Volume Proceedings of the Demo and Poster Sessions*. Prague, Czech Republic, pages 177–180. http://www.aclweb.org/anthology/P07-2045.

Xiaoqing Li, Jiajun Zhang, and Chengqing Zong. 2016. One sentence one model for neural machine translation. *arXiv preprint* http://arxiv.org/abs/1609.06490.

Minh-Thang Luong and Christopher D Manning. 2015. Stanford neural machine translation systems for spoken language domains. In *Proceedings of the International Workshop on Spoken Language Translation*. Da Nang, Vietnam, pages 76–79. https://nlp.stanford.edu/pubs/luong-manning-iwslt15.pdf.

Haitao Mi, Zhiguo Wang, and Abe Ittycheriah. 2016. Vocabulary manipulation for neural machine translation. In *Proceedings of the 54th Annual Meeting of the Association for Computational Linguistics (Volume 2: Short Papers)*. Berlin, Germany, pages 124–129. http://anthology.aclweb.org/P16-2021.

Robert C Moore and William Lewis. 2010. Intelligent selection of language model training data. In *Proceedings of the 48th Annual Meeting of the Association for Computational Linguistics (Volume 2: Short Papers)*. Uppsala, Sweden, pages 220–224. http://www.aclweb.org/anthology/P10-2041.

Kishore Papineni, Salim Roukos, Todd Ward, and Wei-Jing Zhu. 2002. BLEU: a method for automatic evaluation of machine translation. In *Proceedings of the 40th Annual Meeting on Association for Computational Linguistics*. Philadelphia, Pennsylvania, pages 311–318. http://www.aclweb.org/anthology/P02-1040.

Rico Sennrich. 2012. Perplexity minimization for translation model domain adaptation in statistical machine translation. In *Proceedings of the 13th Conference of the European Chapter of the Association for Computational Linguistics*. Avignon, France, pages 539–549. http://www.aclweb.org/anthology/E12-1055.

Rico Sennrich, Holger Schwenk, and Walid Aransa. 2013. A multi-domain translation model framework for statistical machine translation. In *Proceedings of the 51st Annual Meeting of the Association for Computational Linguistics (Volume 1: Long Papers)*. Sofia, Bulgaria, pages 832–840. http://www.aclweb.org/anthology/P13-1082.

Zhaopeng Tu, Zhengdong Lu, Yang Liu, Xiaohua Liu, and Hang Li. 2016. Modeling coverage for neural machine translation. In *Proceedings of the 54th Annual Meeting of the Association for Computational Linguistics (Volume 1: Long Papers)*. Berlin, Germany, pages 76–85. http://www.aclweb.org/anthology/P16-1008.

Rui Wang, Hai Zhao, Bao-Liang Lu, Masao Utiyama, and Eiichiro. Sumita. 2015. Bilingual continuous-space language model growing for statistical machine translation. *IEEE/ACM Transactions on Audio, Speech, and Language Processing* 23(7):1209–1220. https://doi.org/10.1109/TASLP.2015.2425220.

Rui Wang, Hai Zhao, Bao-Liang Lu, Masao Utiyama, and Eiichiro Sumita. 2016. Connecting phrase based statistical machine translation adaptation. In *Proceedings of the 26th International Conference on Computational Linguistics: Technical Papers*. Osaka, Japan, pages 3135–3145. http://aclweb.org/anthology/C16-1295.

Xiaolin Wang, Masao Utiyama, Andrew Finch, and Eiichiro Sumita. 2014. Empirical study of unsupervised Chinese word segmentation methods for SMT on large-scale corpora. In *Proceedings of the 52nd Annual Meeting of the Association for Computational Linguistics (Volume 2: Short Papers)*. Baltimore, Maryland, pages 752–758. http://www.aclweb.org/anthology/P14-2122.

Matthew D Zeiler. 2012. ADADELTA: an adaptive learning rate method. *arXiv preprint arXiv:1212.5701* http://arxiv.org/abs/1212.5701.

Biao Zhang, Deyi Xiong, jinsong su, Hong Duan, and Min Zhang. 2016. Variational neural machine translation. In *Proceedings of the 2016 Conference on Empirical Methods in Natural Language Processing*. Austin, Texas, pages 521–530. https://aclweb.org/anthology/D16-1050.

Data Augmentation for Low-Resource Neural Machine Translation

Marzieh Fadaee   **Arianna Bisazza**   **Christof Monz**

Informatics Institute, University of Amsterdam

Science Park 904, 1098 XH Amsterdam, The Netherlands

{m.fadaee,a.bisazza,c.monz}@uva.nl

Abstract

The quality of a Neural Machine Translation system depends substantially on the availability of sizable parallel corpora. For low-resource language pairs this is not the case, resulting in poor translation quality. Inspired by work in computer vision, we propose a novel data augmentation approach that targets low-frequency words by generating new sentence pairs containing rare words in new, synthetically created contexts. Experimental results on simulated low-resource settings show that our method improves translation quality by up to 2.9 BLEU points over the baseline and up to 3.2 BLEU over back-translation.

1 Introduction

In computer vision, data augmentation techniques are widely used to increase robustness and improve learning of objects with a limited number of training examples. In image processing the training data is augmented by, for instance, horizontally flipping, random cropping, tilting, and altering the RGB channels of the original images (Krizhevsky et al., 2012; Chatfield et al., 2014). Since the content of the new image is still the same, the label of the original image is preserved (see top of Figure 1). While data augmentation has become a standard technique to train deep networks for image processing, it is not a common practice in training networks for NLP tasks such as Machine Translation.

Neural Machine Translation (NMT) (Bahdanau et al., 2015; Sutskever et al., 2014; Cho et al., 2014) is a sequence-to-sequence architecture where an encoder builds up a representation of the source sentence and a decoder, using the previous

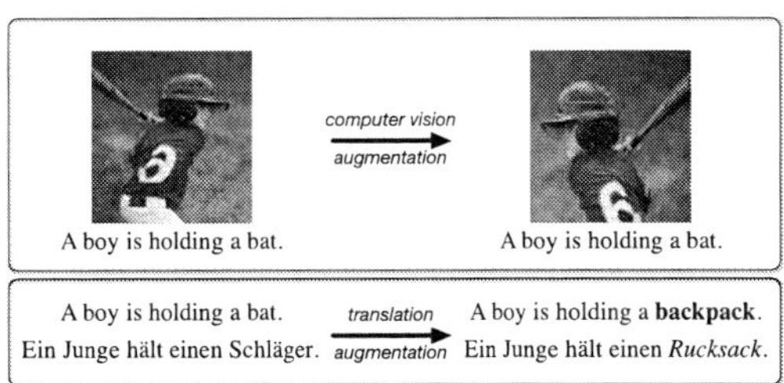

Figure 1: Top: flip and crop, two label-preserving data augmentation techniques in computer vision. Bottom: Altering one sentence in a parallel corpus requires changing its translation.

LSTM hidden states and an attention mechanism, generates the target translation.

To train a model with reliable parameter estimations, these networks require numerous instances of sentence translation pairs with words occurring in diverse contexts, which is typically not available in low-resource language pairs. As a result NMT falls short of reaching state-of-the-art performances for these language pairs (Zoph et al., 2016). The solution is to either manually annotate more data or perform unsupervised data augmentation. Since manual annotation of data is time-consuming, data augmentation for low-resource language pairs is a more viable approach. Recently Sennrich et al. (2016a) proposed a method to back-translate sentences from monolingual data and augment the bitext with the resulting pseudo parallel corpora.

In this paper, we propose a simple yet effective approach, translation data augmentation (TDA), that augments the training data by altering existing sentences in the parallel corpus, similar in spirit to the data augmentation approaches in computer vision (see Figure 1). In order for the augmentation process in this scenario to be label-preserving, any change to a sentence in one language must pre-

567

Proceedings of the 55th Annual Meeting of the Association for Computational Linguistics (Short Papers), pages 567–573

Vancouver, Canada, July 30 - August 4, 2017. ©2017 Association for Computational Linguistics

https://doi.org/10.18653/v1/P17-2090

serve the meaning of the sentence, requiring sentential paraphrasing systems which are not available for many language pairs. Instead, we propose a weaker notion of label preservation that allows to alter both source and target sentences at the same time as long as they remain translations of each other.

While our approach allows us to augment data in numerous ways, we focus on augmenting instances involving low-frequency words, because the parameter estimation of rare words is challenging, and further exacerbated in a low-resource setting. We simulate a low-resource setting as done in the literature (Marton et al., 2009; Duong et al., 2015) and obtain substantial improvements for translating English→German and German→English.

2 Translation Data Augmentation

Given a source and target sentence pair (S,T), we want to alter it in a way that preserves the semantic equivalence between S and T while diversifying as much as possible the training examples. A number of ways to do this can be envisaged, as for example paraphrasing (parts of) S or T. Paraphrasing, however, is by itself a difficult task and is not guaranteed to bring useful new information into the training data. We choose instead to focus on a subset of the vocabulary that we know to be poorly modeled by our baseline NMT system, namely words that occur rarely in the parallel corpus. Thus, the goal of our data augmentation technique is to provide novel contexts for rare words. To achieve this we search for contexts where a common word can be replaced by a rare word and consequently replace its corresponding word in the other language by that rare word's translation:

original pair	augmented pair
$S : s_1, ..., s_i, ..., s_n$	$S' : s_1, ..., s'_i, ..., s_n$
$T : t_1, ..., t_j, ..., t_m$	$T' : t_1, ..., t'_j, ..., t_m$

where t_j is a translation of s_i and word-aligned to s_i. Plausible substitutions are those that result in a fluent and grammatical sentence but do not necessarily maintain its semantic content. As an example, the rare word *motorbike* can be substituted in different contexts:

Sentence [original / **substituted**]	Plausible
My sister drives a [car / **motorbike**]	yes
My uncle sold his [house / **motorbike**]	yes
Alice waters the [plant / **motorbike**]	no (semantics)
John bought two [shirts / **motorbike**]	no (syntax)

Implausible substitutions need to be ruled out during data augmentation. To this end, rather than relying on linguistic resources which are not available for many languages, we rely on LSTM language models (LM) (Hochreiter and Schmidhuber, 1997; Jozefowicz et al., 2015) trained on large amounts of monolingual data in both forward and backward directions.

Our data augmentation method involves the following steps:

Targeted words selection: Following common practice, our NMT system limits its vocabulary V to the v most common words observed in the training corpus. We select the words in V that have fewer than R occurrences and use this as our targeted rare word list V_R.

Rare word substitution: If the LM suggests a rare substitution in a particular context, we replace that word and add the new sentence to the training data. Formally, given a sentence pair (S, T) and a position i in S we compute the probability distribution over V by the forward and backward LMs and select rare word substitutions C as follows:

$$\overrightarrow{C} = \{s'_i \in V_R : \text{topK } P_{ForwardLM_S}(s'_i \mid s_1^{i-1})\}$$
$$\overleftarrow{C} = \{s'_i \in V_R : \text{topK } P_{BackwardLM_S}(s'_i \mid s_n^{i+1})\}$$
$$C = \{s'_i \mid s'_i \in \overrightarrow{C} \wedge s'_i \in \overleftarrow{C}\}$$

where topK returns the K words with highest conditional probability according to the context. The selected substitutions s'_i, are used to replace the original word and generate a new sentence.

Translation selection: Using automatic word alignments[1] trained over the bitext, we replace the translation of word s_i in T by the translation of its substitution s'_i. Following a common practice in statistical MT, the optimal translation t'_j is chosen by multiplying direct and inverse lexical translation probabilities with the LM probability of the translation in context:

$$t'_j = \underset{t \in trans(s'_i)}{\arg \max} P(s'_i \mid t)P(t \mid s'_i)P_{LM_T}(t \mid t_1^{j-1})$$

If no translation candidate is found because the word is unaligned or because the LM probability

---

[1] We use fast-align (Dyer et al., 2013) to extract word alignments and a bilingual lexicon with lexical translation probabilities from the low-resource bitext.

is less than a certain threshold, the augmented sentence is discarded. This reduces the risk of generating sentence pairs that are semantically or syntactically incorrect.

Sampling: We loop over the original parallel corpus multiple times, sampling substitution positions, i, in each sentence and making sure that each rare word gets augmented at most N times so that a large number of rare words can be affected. We stop when no new sentences are generated in one pass of the training data.

Table 1 provides some examples resulting from our augmentation procedure. While using a large LM to substitute words with rare words mostly results in grammatical sentences, this does not mean that the meaning of the original sentence is preserved. Note that meaning preservation is not an objective of our approach.

Two translation data augmentation (TDA) setups are considered: only one word per sentence can be replaced (TDA$_{r=1}$), or multiple words per sentence can be replaced, with the condition that any two replaced words are at least five positions apart (TDA$_{r\geqslant1}$). The latter incurs a higher risk of introducing noisy sentences but has the potential to positively affect more rare words within the same amount of augmented data. We evaluate both setups in the following section.

En:	I had been told that you would [not / **voluntarily**] be speaking today.
De:	mir wurde signalisiert, sie würden heute [nicht / *freiwillig*] sprechen.
En:	the present situation is [indefensible / **confusing**] and completely unacceptable to the commission.
De:	die situation sei [unhaltbar / *verwirrend*] und für die kommission gänzlich unannehmbar.
En:	... agree wholeheartedly with the institution of an ad hoc delegation of parliament on the turkish [prison / **missile**] system.
De:	... ad-hoc delegation des parlaments für das regime in den türkischen [gefängnissen / *flugwaffen*] voll und ganz zustimmen.

Table 1: Examples of augmented data with highlighted [original / **substituted**] and [original / *translated*] words.

3 Evaluation

In this section we evaluate the utility of our approach in a simulated low-resource NMT scenario.

3.1 Data and experimental setup

To simulate a low-resource setting we randomly sample 10% of the English↔German WMT15 training data and report results on newstest 2014, 2015, and 2016 (Bojar et al., 2016). For reference we also provide the result of our baseline system on the full data.

As NMT system we use a 4-layer attention-based encoder-decoder model as described in (Luong et al., 2015) trained with hidden dimension 1000, batch size 80 for 20 epochs. In all experiments the NMT vocabulary is limited to the most common 30K words in both languages. Note that data augmentation does not introduce new words to the vocabulary. In all experiments we preprocess source and target language data with Byte-pair encoding (BPE) (Sennrich et al., 2016b) using 30K merge operations. In the augmentation experiments BPE is performed after data augmentation.

For the LMs needed for data augmentation, we train 2-layer LSTM networks in forward and backward directions on the monolingual data provided for the same task (3.5B and 0.9B tokens in English and German respectively) with embedding size 64 and hidden size 128. We set the rare word threshold R to 100, top K words to 1000 and maximum number N of augmentations per rare word to 500. In all experiments we use the English LM for the rare word substitutions, and the German LM to choose the optimal word translation in context. Since our approach is not label preserving we only perform augmentation during training and do not alter source sentences during testing.

We also compare our approach to Sennrich et al. (2016a) by back-translating monolingual data and adding it to the parallel training data. Specifically, we back-translate sentences from the target side of WMT'15 that are not included in our low-resource baseline with two settings: keeping a one-to-one ratio of back-translated versus original data $(1 : 1)$ following the authors' suggestion, or using three times more back-translated data $(3 : 1)$.

We measure translation quality by single-reference case-insensitive BLEU (Papineni et al., 2002) computed with the `multi-bleu.perl` script from Moses.

3.2 Results

All translation results are displayed in Table 2. As expected, the low-resource baseline performs much worse than the full data system, re-iterating

		De-En			En-De		
Model	Data	test2014	test2015	test2016	test2014	test2015	test2016
Full data (ceiling)	3.9M	21.1	22.0	26.9	17.0	18.5	21.7
Baseline	371K	10.6	11.3	13.1	8.2	9.2	11.0
Back-translation$_{1:1}$	731K	11.4 (+0.8)[▲]	12.2 (+0.9)[▲]	14.6 (+1.5)[▲]	9.0 (+0.8)[▲]	10.4 (+1.2)[▲]	12.0 (+1.0)[▲]
Back-translation$_{3:1}$	1.5M	11.2 (+0.6)	11.2 (−0.1)	13.3 (+0.2)	7.8 (−0.4)	9.4 (+0.2)	10.7 (−0.3)
TDA$_{r=1}$	4.5M	11.9 (+1.3)[▲,⁻]	13.4 (+2.1)[▲,▲]	15.2 (+2.1)[▲,▲]	10.4 (+2.2)[▲,▲]	11.2 (+2.0)[▲,▲]	13.5 (+2.5)[▲,▲]
TDA$_{r\geq1}$	6M	**12.6** (+2.0)[▲,▲]	**13.7** (+2.4)[▲,▲]	**15.4** (+2.3)[▲,▲]	**10.7** (+2.5)[▲,▲]	**11.5** (+2.3)[▲,▲]	**13.9** (+2.9)[▲,▲]
Oversampling	6M	11.9 (+1.3)[▲,⁻]	12.9 (+1.6)[▲,△]	15.0 (+1.9)[▲,⁻]	9.7 (+1.5)[▲,△]	10.7 (+1.5)[▲,⁻]	12.6 (+1.6)[▲,⁻]

Table 2: Translation performance (BLEU) on German-English and English-German WMT test sets (newstest2014, 2015, and 2016) in a simulated low-resource setting. Back-translation refers to the work of Sennrich et al. (2016a). Statistically significant improvements are marked [▲] at the $p < .01$ and [△] at the $p < .05$ level, with the first superscript referring to baseline and the second to back-translation$_{1:1}$.

the importance of sizable training data for NMT. Next we observe that both back-translation and our proposed TDA method significantly improve translation quality. However TDA obtains the best results overall and significantly outperforms back-translation in all test sets. This is an important finding considering that our method involves only minor modifications to the original training sentences and does not involve any costly translation process. Improvements are consistent across both translation directions, regardless of whether rare word substitutions are first applied to the source or to the target side.

We also observe that altering multiple words in a sentence performs slightly better than altering only one. This indicates that addressing more rare words is preferable even though the augmented sentences are likely to be noisier.

To verify that the gains are actually due to the rare word substitutions and not just to the repetition of part of the training data, we perform a final experiment where each sentence pair selected for augmentation is added to the training data *unchanged* (Oversampling in Table 2). Surprisingly, we find that this simple form of sampled data replication outperforms both baseline and back-translation systems,[2] while TDA$_{r\geq1}$ remains the best performing system overall.

We also observe that the system trained on augmented data tends to generate longer translations. Averaging on all test sets, the length of translations generated by the baseline is 0.88 of the average reference length, while for TDA$_{r=1}$ and TDA$_{r\geq1}$ it is 0.95 and 0.94, respectively. We attribute this effect to the ability of the TDA-trained system to generate translations for rare words that were left

untranslated by the baseline system.

4 Analysis of the Results

A desired effect of our method is to increase the number of correct rare words generated by the NMT system at test time.

To examine the impact of augmenting the training data by creating contexts for rare words on the target side, Table 3 provides an example for German→English translation. We see that the baseline model is not able to generate the rare word *centimetres* as a correct translation of the German word *zentimeter* . However, this word is not rare in the training data of the TDA$_{r\geq1}$ model after augmentation and is generated during translation. Table 3 also provides several instances of augmented training sentences targeting the word *centimetres*. Note that even though some augmented sentences are nonsensical (e.g. *the speed limit is five centimetres per hour*), the NMT system still benefits from the new context for the rare word and is able to generate it during testing.

Figure 2 demonstrates that this is indeed the case for many words: the number of rare words occurring in the reference translation ($V_R \cap V_{ref}$) is three times larger in the TDA system output than in the baseline output. One can also see that this increase is a direct effect of TDA as most of the rare words are not 'rare' anymore in the augmented data, i.e., they were augmented sufficiently many times to occur more than 100 times (see hatched pattern in Figure 2). Note that during the experiments we did not use any information from the evaluation sets.

To gauge the impact of augmenting the contexts for rare words on the source side, we examine normalized attention scores of these words before and after augmentation. When translating

---

[2]Note that this effect cannot be achieved by simply continuing the baseline training for up to 50 epochs.

Source	der tunnel hat einen querschnitt von 1,20 meter höhe und 90 zentimeter breite .
Baseline translation	the wine consists of about 1,20 m and 90 of the canal .
TDA$_{r\geqslant 1}$ translation	the tunnel has a UNK measuring meters 1.20 metres high and 90 **centimetres** wide .
Reference	the tunnel has a cross - section measuring 1.20 metres high and 90 centimetres across .
Examples of augmented data for the word *centimetres*	• the average speed of cars and buses is therefore around 20 [kilometres / **centimetres**] per hour . • grab crane in special terminals for handling capacities of up to 1,800 [tonnes / **centimetres**] per hour . • all suites and rooms are very spacious and measure between 50 and 70 [m / **centimetres**] • all we have to do is lower the speed limit everywhere to five [kilometers / **centimetres**] per hour .

Table 3: An example from newstest2014 illustrating the effect of augmenting rare words on generation during test time. The translation of the baseline does not include the rare word *centimetres*, however, the translation of our TDA model generates the rare word and produces a more fluent sentence. Instances of the augmentation of the word *centimetres* in training data are also provided.

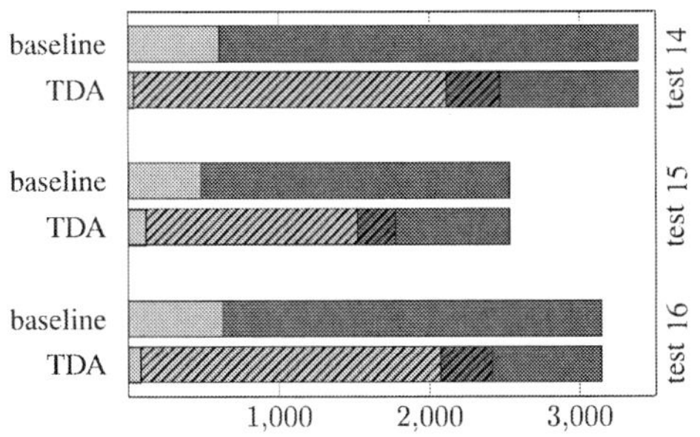

Words in $V_R \cap V_{ref}$ generated during translation
Words in $V_R \cap V_{ref}$ not generated during translation
Words in $V_R \cap V_{ref}$ affected by augmentation

Figure 2: Effect of TDA on the number of unique rare words generated during De→En translation. V_R is the set of rare words targeted by TDA$_{r\geqslant 1}$ and V_{ref} the reference translation vocabulary.

English→German with our TDA model, the attention scores for rare words on the source side are on average 8.8% higher than when translating with the baseline model. This suggests that having more accurate representations of rare words increases the model's confidence to attend to these words when encountered during test time.

En:	registered users will receive the UNK newsletter free [of / **yearly**] charge.
De:	registrierte user erhalten zudem regelmäßig [den / *jährlich*] markenticker newsletter.
En:	the personal contact is [essential / **entrusted**] to us
De:	persönliche kontakt ist uns sehr [wichtig / *betraut*]

Table 4: Examples of incorrectly augmented data with highlighted [original / **substituted**] and [original / *translated*] words.

Finally Table 4 provides examples of cases where augmentation results in incorrect sentences. In the first example, the sentence is ungrammatical after substitution (*of / yearly*), which can be the result of choosing substitutions with low probabilities from the English LM topK suggestions.

Errors can also occur during translation selection, as in the second example where *betraut* is an acceptable translation of *entrusted* but would require a rephrasing of the German sentence to be grammatically correct. Problems of this kind can be attributed to the German LM, but also to the lack of a more suitable translation in the lexicon extracted from the bitext. Interestingly, this noise seems to affect NMT only to a limited extent.

5 Conclusion

We have proposed a simple but effective approach to augment the training data of Neural Machine Translation for low-resource language pairs. By leveraging language models trained on large amounts of monolingual data, we generate new sentence pairs containing rare words in new, synthetically created contexts. We show that this approach leads to generating more rare words during translation and, consequently, to higher translation quality. In particular we report substantial improvements in simulated low-resource English→German and German→English settings, outperforming another recently proposed data augmentation technique.

Acknowledgments

This research was funded in part by the Netherlands Organization for Scientific Research (NWO) under project numbers 639.022.213 and 639.021.646, and a Google Faculty Research Award. We also thank NVIDIA for their hardware support, Ke Tran for providing the neural machine translation baseline system, and the anonymous reviewers for their helpful comments.

References

Dzmitry Bahdanau, Kyunghyun Cho, and Yoshua Bengio. 2015. Neural machine translation by jointly learning to align and translate. In *Proceedings of the International Conference on Learning Representations (ICLR)*.

Ondřej Bojar, Rajen Chatterjee, Christian Federmann, Yvette Graham, Barry Haddow, Matthias Huck, Antonio Jimeno Yepes, Philipp Koehn, Varvara Logacheva, Christof Monz, Matteo Negri, Aurelie Neveol, Mariana Neves, Martin Popel, Matt Post, Raphael Rubino, Carolina Scarton, Lucia Specia, Marco Turchi, Karin Verspoor, and Marcos Zampieri. 2016. Findings of the 2016 conference on machine translation. In *Proceedings of the First Conference on Machine Translation*. Association for Computational Linguistics, Berlin, Germany, pages 131–198. http://www.aclweb.org/anthology/W/W16/W16-2301.

Ken Chatfield, Karen Simonyan, Andrea Vedaldi, and Andrew Zisserman. 2014. Return of the devil in the details: Delving deep into convolutional nets. In *Proceedings of the British Machine Vision Conference*. BMVA Press. https://doi.org/http://dx.doi.org/10.5244/C.28.6.

Kyunghyun Cho, B van Merrienboer, Dzmitry Bahdanau, and Yoshua Bengio. 2014. On the properties of neural machine translation: Encoder-decoder approaches. In *Eighth Workshop on Syntax, Semantics and Structure in Statistical Translation (SSST-8), 2014*.

Long Duong, Trevor Cohn, Steven Bird, and Paul Cook. 2015. A neural network model for low-resource universal dependency parsing. In *Proceedings of the 2015 Conference on Empirical Methods in Natural Language Processing*. Association for Computational Linguistics, Lisbon, Portugal, pages 339–348. http://aclweb.org/anthology/D15-1040.

Chris Dyer, Victor Chahuneau, and Noah A. Smith. 2013. A simple, fast, and effective reparameterization of ibm model 2. In *Proceedings of the 2013 Conference of the North American Chapter of the Association for Computational Linguistics: Human Language Technologies*. Association for Computational Linguistics, Atlanta, Georgia, pages 644–648. http://www.aclweb.org/anthology/N13-1073.

Sepp Hochreiter and Jürgen Schmidhuber. 1997. Long short-term memory. *Neural Computation* 9(8):1735–1780.

Rafal Jozefowicz, Wojciech Zaremba, and Ilya Sutskever. 2015. An empirical exploration of recurrent network architectures. In Francis Bach and David Blei, editors, *Proceedings of the 32nd International Conference on Machine Learning*. PMLR, Lille, France, volume 37 of *Proceedings of Machine Learning Research*, pages 2342–2350. http://proceedings.mlr.press/v37/jozefowicz15.pdf.

Alex Krizhevsky, Ilya Sutskever, and Geoffrey E Hinton. 2012. Imagenet classification with deep convolutional neural networks. In F. Pereira, C. J. C. Burges, L. Bottou, and K. Q. Weinberger, editors, *Advances in Neural Information Processing Systems 25*, Curran Associates, Inc., pages 1097–1105. http://papers.nips.cc/paper/4824-imagenet-classification-with-deep-convolutional-neural-networks.pdf.

Thang Luong, Hieu Pham, and Christopher D. Manning. 2015. Effective approaches to attention-based neural machine translation. In *Proceedings of the 2015 Conference on Empirical Methods in Natural Language Processing*. Association for Computational Linguistics, Lisbon, Portugal, pages 1412–1421. http://aclweb.org/anthology/D15-1166.

Yuval Marton, Chris Callison-Burch, and Philip Resnik. 2009. Improved statistical machine translation using monolingually-derived paraphrases. In *Proceedings of the 2009 Conference on Empirical Methods in Natural Language Processing*. Association for Computational Linguistics, Singapore, pages 381–390. http://www.aclweb.org/anthology/D/D09/D09-1040.

Kishore Papineni, Salim Roukos, Todd Ward, and Wei-Jing Zhu. 2002. Bleu: a method for automatic evaluation of machine translation. In *Proceedings of 40th Annual Meeting of the Association for Computational Linguistics*. Association for Computational Linguistics, Philadelphia, Pennsylvania, USA, pages 311–318. https://doi.org/10.3115/1073083.1073135.

Rico Sennrich, Barry Haddow, and Alexandra Birch. 2016a. Improving neural machine translation models with monolingual data. In *Proceedings of the 54th Annual Meeting of the Association for Computational Linguistics (Volume 1: Long Papers)*. Association for Computational Linguistics, Berlin, Germany, pages 86–96. http://www.aclweb.org/anthology/P16-1009.

Rico Sennrich, Barry Haddow, and Alexandra Birch. 2016b. Neural machine translation of rare words with subword units. In *Proceedings of the 54th Annual Meeting of the Association for Computational Linguistics (Volume 1: Long Papers)*. Association for Computational Linguistics, Berlin, Germany, pages 1715–1725. http://www.aclweb.org/anthology/P16-1162.

Ilya Sutskever, Oriol Vinyals, and Quoc V Le. 2014. Sequence to sequence learning with neural networks. In Z. Ghahramani, M. Welling, C. Cortes, N. D. Lawrence, and K. Q. Weinberger, editors, *Advances in Neural Information Processing Systems 27*, Curran Associates, Inc., pages 3104–3112. http://papers.nips.cc/paper/5346-sequence-to-sequence-learning-with-neural-networks.pdf.

Barret Zoph, Deniz Yuret, Jonathan May, and Kevin Knight. 2016. Transfer learning for low-resource neural machine translation. In *Proceedings of the 2016 Conference on Empirical Methods in Natural Language Processing*. Association for Computational Linguistics, Austin, Texas, pages 1568–1575. https://aclweb.org/anthology/D16-1163.

Speeding Up Neural Machine Translation Decoding by Shrinking Run-time Vocabulary

Xing Shi and Kevin Knight
Information Sciences Institute & Computer Science Department
University of Southern California
{xingshi,knight}@isi.edu

Abstract

We speed up Neural Machine Translation (NMT) decoding by shrinking run-time target vocabulary. We experiment with two shrinking approaches: Locality Sensitive Hashing (LSH) and word alignments. Using the latter method, we get a 2x overall speed-up over a highly-optimized GPU implementation, without hurting BLEU. On certain low-resource language pairs, the same methods improve BLEU by 0.5 points. We also report a negative result for LSH on GPUs, due to relatively large overhead, though it was successful on CPUs. Compared with Locality Sensitive Hashing (LSH), decoding with word alignments is GPU-friendly, orthogonal to existing speedup methods and more robust across language pairs.

1 Introduction

Neural Machine Translation (NMT) has been demonstrated as an effective model and been put into large-scale production (Wu et al., 2016; He, 2015). For online translation services, decoding speed is a crucial factor to achieve a better user experience. Several recently proposed training methods (Shen et al., 2015; Wiseman and Rush, 2016) aim to solve the *exposure bias* problem, but require decoding the whole training set multiple times, which is extremely time-consuming for millions of sentences.

Slow decoding speed is partly due to the large target vocabulary size V, which is usually in the tens of thousands. The first two columns of Table 1 show the breakdown of the runtimes required by sub-modules to decode 1812 Japanese sentences to English using a sequence-to-sequence model with local attention (Luong et al., 2015).

Sub-module	Full vocab	WA50	Speedup
Total	1002.78 s	481.52 s	2.08
– Beam expansion	174.28 s	76.52 s	2.28
– Source-side	83.67 s	83.44 s	1
– Target-side	743.25 s	354.52 s	2.1
– – Softmax	402.77 s	20.68 s	19.48
– – Attention	123.05 s	123.12 s	1
– – 2nd layer	64.72 s	64.76 s	1
– – 1st layer	88.02 s	87.96 s	1
Shrink vocab	-	0.39 s	-
BLEU	25.16	25.13	-

Table 1: Time breakdown and BLEU score of full vocabulary decoding and our "WA50" decoding, both with beam size 12. WA50 means decoding informed by word alignments, where each source word can select at most 50 relevant target words. The model is a 2-layer, 1000-hidden dimension, 50,000-target vocabulary LSTM seq2seq model with local attention trained on the ASPEC Japanese-to-English corpus (Nakazawa et al., 2016). The time is measured on a single Nvidia Tesla K20 GPU.

Softmax is the most computationally intensive part, where each hidden vector $h_t \in \mathbb{R}^d$ needs to dot-product with V target embeddings $e_i \in \mathbb{R}^d$. It occupies 40% of the total decoding time. Another sub-module whose computation time is proportional to V is *Beam Expansion*, where we need to find the top B words among all V vocabulary according to their probability. It takes around 17% of the decoding time.

Several approaches have proposed to improve decoding speed:

1. Using special hardware, such as GPU and Tensor Processing Unit (TPU), and low-precision calculation (Wu et al., 2016).

2. Compressing deep neural models through knowledge distillation and weight pruning (See et al., 2016; Kim and Rush, 2016).

Proceedings of the 55th Annual Meeting of the Association for Computational Linguistics (Short Papers), pages 574–579
Vancouver, Canada, July 30 - August 4, 2017. ©2017 Association for Computational Linguistics
https://doi.org/10.18653/v1/P17-2091

3. Several variants of *Softmax* have been proposed to solve its poor scaling properties on large vocabularies. Morin and Bengio (2005) propose *hierarchical softmax*, where at each step $\log_2 V$ binary classifications are performed instead of a single classification on a large number of classes. Gutmann and Hyvärinen (2010) propose *noise-contrastive estimation* which discriminate between positive labels and k ($k << V$) negative labels sampled from a distribution, and is applied successfully on natural language processing tasks (Mnih and Teh, 2012; Vaswani et al., 2013; Williams et al., 2015; Zoph et al., 2016). Although these two approaches provide good speedups for training, they still suffer at test time. Chen et al. (2016) introduces *differentiated softmax*, where frequent words have more parameters in the embedding and rare words have less, offering speedups on both training and testing.

In this work, we aim to speed up decoding by shrinking the run-time target vocabulary size, and this approach is **orthogonal** to the methods above. It is important to note that approaches 1 and 2 will maintain or even increase the ratio of target word embedding parameters to the total parameters, thus the *Beam Expansion* and *Softmax* will occupy the same or greater portion of the decoding time. A small run-time vocabulary will dramatically reduce the time spent on these two portions and gain a further speedup even after applying other speedup methods.

To shrink the run-time target vocabulary, our first method uses Locality Sensitive Hashing. Vijayanarasimhan et al. (2015) successfully applies it on CPUs and gains speedup on single step prediction tasks such as image classification and video identification. Our second method is to use word alignments to select a very small number of candidate target words given the source sentence. Recent works (Jean et al., 2015; Mi et al., 2016; L'Hostis et al., 2016) apply a similar strategy and report speedups for decoding on CPUs on rich-source language pairs.

Our major contributions are:

1. To our best of our knowledge, this work is the first attempt to apply LSH technique on sequence generation tasks on GPU other than single-step classification on CPU. We find current LSH algorithms have a poor performance/speed trade-off on GPU, due to the large overhead introduced by many hash table lookups and list-merging involved in LSH.

2. For our word alignment method, we find that only the candidate list derived from lexical translation table of IBM model 4 is adequate to achieve good BLEU/speedup trade-off for decoding on GPU. There is no need to combine the top frequent words or words from phrase table, as proposed in Mi et al. (2016).

3. We conduct our experiments on GPU and provide a detailed analysis of BLEU/speedup trade-off on both resource-rich/poor language pairs and both attention/non-attention NMT models. We achieve more than 2x speedup on 4 language pairs with only a tiny BLEU drop, demonstrating the robustness and efficiency of our methods.

2 Methods

At each step during decoding, the *softmax* function is calculated as:

$$P(y = j|h_i) = \frac{e^{h_i^T w_j + b_j}}{\sum_{k=1}^{V} e^{h_i^T w_k + b_k}} \qquad (1)$$

where $P(y = j|h_i)$ is the probability of word $j = 1...V$ given the hidden vector $h_i \in \mathbb{R}^d, i = 1...B$. B represents the beam size. $w_j \in \mathbb{R}^d$ is output word embedding and $b_j \in \mathbb{R}$ is the corresponding bias. The complexity is $\mathcal{O}(dBV)$. To speed up *softmax*, we use *word frequency*, *locality sensitive hashing*, and *word alignments* respectively to select C ($C << V$) potential words and evaluate their probability only, reducing the complexity to $\mathcal{O}(dBC + overhead)$.

2.1 Word Frequency

A simple baseline to reduce target vocabulary is to select the top C words based on their frequency in the training corpus. There is no run-time overhead and the overall complexity is $\mathcal{O}(dBC)$.

2.2 Locality Sensitive Hashing

The word $j = \arg\max_k P(y = k|h_i)$ will have the largest value of $h_i^T w_j + b_j$. Thus the $\arg\max$ problem can be converted to finding the nearest neighbor of vector $[h_i; 1]$ among the vectors $[w_j; b_j]$ under the distance measure of dot-product.

Locality Sensitive Hashing (LSH) is a powerful technique for the nearest neighbor problem. We employ the winner-take-all (WTA) hashing (Yagnik et al., 2011) defined as:

$$WTA(x \in \mathbb{R}^d) = [I_1; ...; I_p; ...; I_P] \quad (2)$$
$$I_p = \arg\max_{k=1}^{K} Permute_p(x)[k] \quad (3)$$
$$WTA_{band}(x) = [B_1; ...; B_w; ...; B_W] \quad (4)$$
$$B_w = [I_{(w-1)*u+1}; ...; I_{(w-1)*u+i}; ...; I_{w*u}] \quad (5)$$
$$u = P/W \quad (6)$$

where P distinct permutations are applied and the index of the maximum value of the first K elements of each permutations is recorded. To perform approximate nearest neighbor searching, we follow the scheme used in (Dean et al., 2013; Vijayanarasimhan et al., 2015):

1. Split the hash code $WTA(x)$ into W bands (as shown in equation 4), with each band $\frac{P}{W}\log_2(K)$ bits long.

2. Create W hash tables $[T_1, ..., T_w, ..., T_W]$, and hash every word index j into every table T_w using $WTA_{band}(w_j)[w]$ as the key.

3. Given the hidden vector h_i, extract a list of word indexes from each table T_w using the key $WTA_{band}(h_i)[w]$. Then we merge the W lists and count the number of the occurrences of each word index. Select the top C word indexes with the largest counts, and calculate their probability using equation 1.

The 4 hyper-parameters that define a WTA-LSH are $\{K, P, W, C\}$. The run-time overhead comprises hashing the hidden vector, W times hash table lookups and W lists merging. The overall complexity is $\mathcal{O}(B(dC+K*P+W+W*N_{avg})))$, where N_{avg} is the average number of the word indexes stored in a hash bin of T_w. Although the complexity is much smaller than $\mathcal{O}(dBV)$, the runtime in practice is not guaranteed to be shorter, especially on GPUs, as hash table lookups introduce too many small kernel launches and list merging is hard to parallelize.

2.3 Word Alignment

Intuitively, LSH shrinks the search space utilizing the spatial relationship between the query vector and database vectors in high dimension space. It is a task-independent technique. However, when focusing on our specific task (MT), we can employ translation-related heuristics to prune the run-time vocabulary precisely and efficiently.

One simple heuristic relies on the fact that each source word can only be translated to a small set of target words. The word alignment model, a foundation of phrase-base machine translation, also follows the same spirit in its generative story: each source word is translated to zero, one, or more target words and then reordered to form target sentences. Thus, we apply the following algorithm to reduce the run-time vocabulary size:

1. Apply IBM Model 4 and the *grow-diag-final* heuristic on the training data to get word alignments. Calculate the lexical translation table $P(e|f)$ based on word alignments.

2. For each word f in the source vocabulary of the neural machine translation model, store the top M target words according to $P(e|f)$ in a hash table $T_{f2e} = \{f : [e_1, ...e_M]\}$

3. Given a source sentence $s = [f_1, ..., f_N]$, extract the candidate target word list from T_{f2e} for each source word f_i. Merge the N lists to form the reduced target vocabulary V_{new};

4. Construct the new embedding matrix and bias vector according to V_{new}, then perform the normal beam search on target side.

The only hyper-parameter is $\{M\}$, the number of candidate target words for each source word. Given a source sentence of length L_s, the run-time overhead includes L_s times hash table lookups and L_s lists merging. The complexity for each decoding step is $\mathcal{O}(dB|V_{new}|+(L_s+L_sM)/L_t)$, where L_t is the maximum number of decoding steps. Unlike LSH, these table lookups and list mergings are performed once per sentence, and do not depend on the any hidden vectors. Thus, we can overlap the computation with source side forward propagation.

3 Experiments

To examine the robustness of these decoding methods, we vary experiment settings in different ways: 1) We train both attention (Luong et al., 2015) and non-attention (Sutskever et al., 2014) models; 2) We train models on

	J2E			E2J			F2E			U2E		
	TC	BLEU	X	TC	BLEU	X	TC	BLEU	X	TC	BLEU	X
Full	0.87	25.16	1	0.95	33.87	1	0.84	**28.12**	1	0.9	11.67	1
TF1K	0.14	13.42	2.11	0.15	18.91	2.42	0.1	12.1	2.32	0.29	8.78	1.65
TF5K	0.49	21.31	1.93	0.56	29.77	2.23	0.38	21.98	2.04	0.67	11.54	1.51
TF10K	0.67	23.62	1.76	0.75	32.28	2.04	0.56	24.88	1.78	0.81	11.67	1.33
TF20K	0.78	24.61	1.48	0.87	33.41	1.74	0.72	26.95	1.42	0.89	11.66	1.09
LSH1K	-	19.45	0.026	-	22.23	0.027	-	3.43	0.036	-	9.41	0.025
LSH5K	-	23.43	0.023	-	30.63	0.025	-	12.81	0.031	-	11.41	0.022
LSH10K	-	24.82	0.022	-	32.63	0.024	-	18.45	0.028	-	11.63	0.020
LSH20K	-	**25.20**	0.020	-	33.78	0.022	-	24.31	0.025	-	11.73	0.018
WA10	0.75	24.74	2.12	0.77	33.24	2.46	0.72	27.9	2.37	0.66	**12.17**	1.7
WA50	0.82	25.13	2.08	0.85	33.79	2.43	0.77	27.94	2.34	0.71	12.01	1.67
WA250	0.84	25.13	1.89	0.88	**34.05**	2.27	0.8	27.95	2.1	0.73	11.94	1.62
WA1000	0.85	25.17	1.57	0.9	33.97	1.93	0.82	28.08	1.67	0.75	11.89	1.58

Table 2: Word type coverage (TC), BLEU score, and speedups (X) for full-vocabulary decoding (Full), top frequency vocabulary decoding (TF*), LSH decoding (LSH*), and decoding with word alignments(WA*). TF10K represents decoding with top 10,000 frequent target vocabulary ($C = 10,000$). WA10 means decoding with word alignments, where each source word can select at most 10 candidate target words ($M = 10$). For LSH decoding, we choose (32, 5000, 1000) for (K,P,W), and vary C.

both resource-rich language pairs, French to English (F2E) and Japanese to English (J2E), and a resource-poor language pair, Uzbek to English (U2E); 3) We translate both to English (F2E, J2E, and U2E) and from English (E2J). We use 2-layer LSTM seq2seq models with different attention settings, hidden dimension sizes, dropout rates, and initial learning rates, as shown in Table 3. We use the ASPEC Japanese-English Corpus (Nakazawa et al., 2016), French-English Corpus from WMT2014 (Bojar et al., 2014), and Uzbek-English Corpus (Linguistic Data Consortium, 2016).

Table 2 shows the decoding results of the three methods. Decoding with word alignments achieves the best performance/speedup trade-off across all four translation directions. It can halve the overall decoding time with less than 0.17 BLEU drop. Table 1 compares the detailed time breakdown of full-vocabulary decoding and WA50 decoding. WA50 can gain a speedup of 19.48x and 2.28x on *softmax* and *beam expansion* respectively, leading to an overall 2.08x speedup with only 0.03 BLEU drop. In contrast, decoding with top frequent words will hurt the BLEU rapidly as the speedup goes higher. We calculate the word type coverage (TC) for the test reference data as

	J2E	E2J	F2E	U2E
Source Vocab	80K	88K	200K	50K
Target Vocab	50K	66K	40K	25K
#Tokens	70.4M	70.4M	652M	3.3M
#Sent pairs	1.4M	1.4M	12M	88.7K
Attention	Yes	Yes	No	Yes
Dimension	1000	1000	1000	500
Dropout	0.2	0.2	0.2	0.5
Learning rate	0.5	1	0.35	0.5

Table 3: Training configurations on different language pairs.

follows:

$$TC = \frac{|\{\text{run-time vocab}\} \cap \{\text{word types in test}\}|}{|\{\text{word types in test}\}|}$$

The top 1000 words only cover 14% word types of J2E test data, whereas WA10 covers 75%, whose run-time vocabulary is no more than 200 for a 20 words source sentence.

The speedup of English-to-Uzbek translation is relatively low (around 1.7x). This is because the original full vocabulary size is small (25k), leaving less room for shrinkage.

LSH achieves better BLEU than decoding with top frequent words of the same run-time vocabulary size C on attention models. However, it introduces too large an overhead (50 times slower), especially when *softmax* is highly optimized on GPU. When doing sequential beam search, search error accumulates rapidly. To reach reasonable performance, we have to apply an adequately large number of permutations ($P = 5000$).

We also find that decoding with word alignments can even improve BLEU on resource-poor languages (12.17 vs. 11.67). Our conjecture is that rare words are not trained enough, so neural models confuse them, and word alignments can provide a hard constraint to rule out the unreasonable word choices.

4 Conclusion

We apply word alignments to shrink run-time vocabulary to speed up neural machine translation decoding on GPUs, and achieve more than 2x speedup on 4 translation directions without hurting BLEU. We also compare with two other speedup methods: decoding with top frequent words and decoding with LSH. Experiments and analyses demonstrate that word alignments provides accurate candidate target words and introduces only a tiny overhead over a highly-optimized GPU implementation.

References

Ondrej Bojar, Christian Buck, Christian Federmann, Barry Haddow, Philipp Koehn, Matous Machacek, Christof Monz, Pavel Pecina, Matt Post, Herv Saint-Amand, Radu Soricut, and Lucia Specia, editors. 2014. *Proc. Ninth Workshop on Statistical Machine Translation*.

Welin Chen, David Grangier, and Michael Auli. 2016. Strategies for training large vocabulary neural language models. In *Proc. ACL*.

Thomas Dean, Mark A Ruzon, Mark Segal, Jonathon Shlens, Sudheendra Vijayanarasimhan, and Jay Yagnik. 2013. Fast, accurate detection of 100,000 object classes on a single machine. In *Proc. CVPR*.

Michael Gutmann and Aapo Hyvärinen. 2010. Noise-contrastive estimation: A new estimation principle for unnormalized statistical models. In *Proc. AISTATS*.

Zhongjun He. 2015. Baidu translate: research and products. In *Proc. ACL-IJCNLP*.

Sébastien Jean, Kyunghyun Cho, Roland Memisevic, and Yoshua Bengio. 2015. On using very large target vocabulary for neural machine translation. In *Proc. ACL*.

Yoon Kim and Alexander M Rush. 2016. Sequence-level knowledge distillation. In *Proc. EMNLP*.

Gurvan L'Hostis, David Grangier, and Michael Auli. 2016. Vocabulary Selection Strategies for Neural Machine Translation. *Arxiv preprint* arXiv:1610.00072.

Linguistic Data Consortium. 2016. (bolt lrl uzbek representative language pack v1.0. ldc2016e29.

Minh-Thang Luong, Hieu Pham, and Christopher D. Manning. 2015. Effective approaches to attention-based neural machine translation. In *Proc. EMNLP*.

Haitao Mi, Zhiguo Wang, and Abraham Ittycheriah. 2016. Vocabulary Manipulation for Neural Machine Translation. In *Proc. ACL*.

Andriy Mnih and Yee Whye Teh. 2012. A fast and simple algorithm for training neural probabilistic language models. *Proc. ICML* .

Frederic Morin and Yoshua Bengio. 2005. Hierarchical probabilistic neural network language model. In *Proc. AISTATS*.

Toshiaki Nakazawa, Manabu Yaguchi, Kiyotaka Uchimoto, Masao Utiyama, Eiichiro Sumita, Sadao Kurohashi, and Hitoshi Isahara. 2016. ASPEC: Asian Scientific Paper Excerpt Corpus. In *Proc. LREC*.

Abigail See, Minh-Thang Luong, and Christopher D Manning. 2016. Compression of neural machine translation models via pruning.

Shiqi Shen, Yong Cheng, Zhongjun He, Wei He, Hua Wu, Maosong Sun, and Yang Liu. 2015. Minimum risk training for neural machine translation. In *Proc. ACL*.

Ilya Sutskever, Oriol Vinyals, and Quoc V Le. 2014. Sequence to sequence learning with neural networks. In *Proc. NIPS*.

Ashish Vaswani, Yinggong Zhao, Victoria Fossum, and David Chiang. 2013. Decoding with large-scale neural language models improves translation. In *Proc. EMNLP*.

Sudheendra Vijayanarasimhan, Jonathon Shlens, Rajat Monga, and Jay Yagnik. 2015. Deep networks with large output spaces. In *Proc. ICLR*.

Will Williams, Niranjani Prasad, David Mrva, Tom Ash, and Tony Robinson. 2015. Scaling recurrent neural network language models. In *Proc. ICASSP*.

Sam Wiseman and Alexander M Rush. 2016. Sequence-to-sequence learning as beam-search optimization. In *Proc. EMNLP*.

Yonghui Wu, Mike Schuster, Zhifeng Chen, Quoc V Le, Mohammad Norouzi, Wolfgang Macherey, Maxim Krikun, Yuan Cao, Qin Gao, Klaus

Macherey, et al. 2016. Google's neural machine translation system: Bridging the gap between human and machine translation. *arXiv preprint arXiv:1609.08144* .

Jay Yagnik, Dennis Strelow, David A Ross, and Ruei-sung Lin. 2011. The power of comparative reasoning. In *Proc. ICCV*.

Barret Zoph, Ashish Vaswani, Jonathan May, and Kevin Knight. 2016. Simple, fast noise-contrastive estimation for large rnn vocabularies. In *Proc. NAACL-HLT*.

Chunk-Based Bi-Scale Decoder for Neural Machine Translation

Hao Zhou[*]
Nanjing University
zhouh@nlp.nju.edu.cn

Zhaopeng Tu[*]
Tencent AI Lab
tuzhaopeng@gmail.com

Shujian Huang
Nanjing University
huangsh@nlp.nju.edu.cn

Xiaohua Liu
Huawei Noah's Ark Lab
liuxiaohua3@huawei.com

Hang Li
Huawei Noah's Ark Lab
hangli.hl@huawei.com

Jiajun Chen
Nanjing University
chenjj@nlp.nju.edu.cn

Abstract

In typical neural machine translation (NMT), the decoder generates a sentence word by word, packing all linguistic granularities in the same time-scale of RNN. In this paper, we propose a new type of decoder for NMT, which splits the decode state into two parts and updates them in two different time-scales. Specifically, we first predict a chunk time-scale state for phrasal modeling, on top of which multiple word time-scale states are generated. In this way, the target sentence is translated hierarchically from chunks to words, with information in different granularities being leveraged. Experiments show that our proposed model significantly improves the translation performance over the state-of-the-art NMT model.

1 Introduction

Recent work of neural machine translation (NMT) models propose to adopt the *encoder-decoder* framework for machine translation (Kalchbrenner and Blunsom, 2013; Cho et al., 2014; Sutskever et al., 2014), which employs a recurrent neural network (RNN) *encoder* to model the source context information and a RNN *decoder* to generate translations, which is significantly different from previous statistical machine translation systems (Koehn et al., 2003; Chiang, 2005). This framework is then extended by an attention mechanism, which acquires source sentence context dynamically at different decoding steps (Bahdanau et al., 2014; Luong et al., 2015).

The decoder state stores translation information at different granularities, determining which segment should be expressed (phrasal), and which word should be generated (lexical), respectively. However, due to the extensive existence of multi-word phrases and expressions, the varying speed of the lexical component is much faster than the phrasal one. As in the generation of "*the French Republic*", the lexical component in the decoder will change thrice, each of which for a separate word. But the phrasal component may only change once. The inconsistent varying speed of the two components may cause translation errors.

Typical NMT model generates target sentences in the word level, packing the phrasal and lexical information in one hidden state, which is not necessarily the best for translation. Much previous work propose to improve the NMT model by adopting fine-grained translation levels such as the character or sub-word levels, which can learn the intermediate information inside words (Ling et al., 2015; Costa-jussà and Fonollosa, 2016; Chung et al., 2016; Luong et al., 2016; Lee et al., 2016; Sennrich and Haddow, 2016; Sennrich et al., 2016; García-Martínez et al., 2016). However, high level structures such as phrases has not been explicitly explored in NMT, which is very useful for machine translation (Koehn et al., 2007).

We propose a chunk-based bi-scale decoder for NMT, which explicitly splits the lexical and phrasal components into different time-scales.[1] The proposed model generates target words in a hierarchical way, which deploys a standard word time-scale RNN (lexical modeling) on top of an additional chunk time-scale RNN (phrasal modeling). At each step of decoding, our model first predict a chunk state with a *chunk attention*, based on which multiple word states are generated with-

---

[*]Work was done when Hao Zhou was interning and Zhaopeng Tu was working at Huawei Noah's Ark Lab.

[1]In this work, we focus on chunk-based well-formed phrases, which generally contain two to five words.

Proceedings of the 55th Annual Meeting of the Association for Computational Linguistics (Short Papers), pages 580–586
Vancouver, Canada, July 30 - August 4, 2017. ©2017 Association for Computational Linguistics
https://doi.org/10.18653/v1/P17-2092

out attention. The word state is updated at every step, while the chunk state is only updated when the chunk boundary is detected by a *boundary gate* automatically. In this way, we incorporate *soft phrases* into NMT, which makes the model flexible at capturing both *global reordering* of phrases and *local translation* inside phrases. Our model has following benefits:

1. The chunk-based NMT model explicitly splits the lexical and phrasal components of the decode state for different time-scales, which addresses the issue of inconsistent updating speeds of different components, making the model more flexible.

2. Our model recognizes phrase structures explicitly. Phrase information are then used for word predictions, the representations of which are then used to help predict corresponding words.

3. Instead of incorporating source side linguistic information (Eriguchi et al., 2016; Sennrich and Haddow, 2016), our model incorporates linguistic knowledges in the target side (for deciding chunks), which will guide the translation more in line with linguistic grammars.

4. Given the predicted phrase representation, our NMT model could extract attentive source context by *chunk attention*, which is more specific and thus more useful compared to the word-level counterpart.

Experiments show that our proposed model obtains considerable BLEU score improvements upon an attention-based NMT baseline on the Chinese to English and the German to English datasets simultaneously.

2 Standard Neural Machine Translation Model

Generally, neural machine translation system directly models the conditional probability of the translation y word by word (Bahdanau et al., 2014). Formally, given an input sequence $\mathbf{x} = [x_1, x_2, \ldots, x_J]$, and the previously generated sequence $\mathbf{y}_{<t} = [y_1, y_2, \ldots, y_{t-1}]$, the probability of next target word y_t is

$$P(y_t|\mathbf{x}) = softmax(f(e_{y_{t-1}}, s_t, c_t)) \quad (1)$$

where $f(\cdot)$ is a non-linear function, $e_{y_{t-1}}$ is the embedding of y_{t-1}; s_t is the *decode state* at the time step t, which is computed by

$$s_t = g(s_{t-1}, e_{y_{t-1}}, c_t) \quad (2)$$

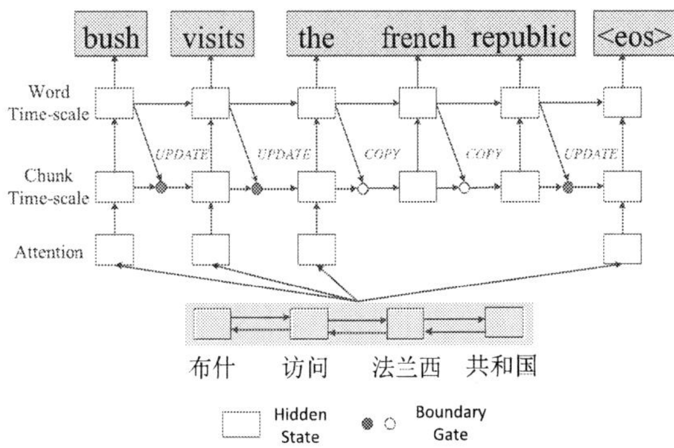

Figure 1: The architecture of the chunk-based bi-scale NMT.

Here $g(\cdot)$ is a transition function of decoder RNN. c_t is the context vector computed by

$$c_t = \sum_{j=1}^{J} \text{ATT}(s_{t-1}, h_j) \cdot h_j = \sum_{j=1}^{J} \alpha_{t,j} \cdot h_j \quad (3)$$

where ATT is an attention operation, which outputs alignment distribution α:

$$\alpha_{t,j} = \frac{exp(e_{t,j})}{\sum_{k=1}^{T_x} exp(e_{t,k})} \quad (4)$$

$$e_{t,j} = v_a^T \tanh(W_a s_{t-1} + U_a h_j) \quad (5)$$

and h is the annotation of $\mathbf{x}$ from a bi-directional RNNs. The training objective is to maximize the likelihood of the training data. Beam search is adopted for decoding.

3 Chunk-Based Bi-Scale Neural Machine Translation Model

Instead of the word-based decoder, we propose to use a chunk-based bi-scale decoder, which generates translation hierarchically with *chunk* and *word* time-scales, as shown in Figure 1. Intuitively, we firstly generate a chunk state with the attention model, which extracts the source context for the current phrasal scope. Then we generate multiple lexical words based on the same chunk state, which does not require attention operations. The boundary of a chunk is determined by a *boundary gate*, which decides whether to update the chunk state or not at each step.

Formally, the probability of next word y_t is

$$P(y_t|\mathbf{x}) = softmax(f(e_{y_{t-1}}, s_t, p_t)) \quad (6)$$
$$s_t = g(s_{t-1}, e_{y_{t-1}}, p_t) \quad (7)$$

here p_t is the chunk state at step t. Compared with Equations 1 and 2, the generation of target word is based on the chunk state instead of the context vector c_t produced by the attention model.

Since a chunk may correspond to multiple words, we employ a *boundary gate* b_t to decide the boundary of each chunk:

$$p(b_t) = softmax(s_{t-1}, e_{y_{t-1}}) \qquad (8)$$

b_t will be 0 or 1, where 1 denotes this is the boundary of a new chunk while 0 denotes not. Two different operations would be executed:

$$p_t = \begin{cases} p_{t-1}, & b_t = 0 \text{ (COPY)} \\ g(p_{t-1}, e_{p_{t-1}}, pc_t), & b_t = 1 \text{ (UPDATE)} \end{cases}$$

In the COPY operation, the chunk state is kept the same as the previous step. In the UPDATE operation, $e_{p_{t-1}}$ is the representation of last chunk, which is computed by the LSTM-minus approach (Wang and Chang, 2016):

$$e_{p_{t-1}} = m(s_{t-1}, e_{y_{t-1}}) - m(s_{t'}, e_{y_{t'}}) \qquad (9)$$

here t' is the boundary of last chunk and $m(\cdot)$ is a linear function. pc_t is the context vector for chunk p_t, which is calculated by a *chunk attention* model:

$$pc_t = \sum_{j=1}^{T_s} \text{ATT}(p_{t-1}, h_j) \cdot h_j \qquad (10)$$

The chunk attention model differs from the standard word attention model (i.e., Equation 3) at: 1) it reads chunk state p_{t-1} rather than word state s_{t-1}, and 2) it is only executed at boundary of each chunk rather than at each decoding step.

In this way, our model only extracts source context once for a chunk, and the words in one chunk will share the same context for word generation. The chunk attention mechanism adds a constrain that target words in the same chunk shares the same source context.

Training To encourage the proposed model to learn reasonable chunk state, we add two additional objectives in training:

Chunk Tag Prediction: For each chunk, we predict the probability of its tag $P(l_k|\mathbf{x}) = softmax(f(p_t, e_{p_t}, c_t))$, where l_k is the syntactic tag of the k-th chunk such as *NP* (noun phrase) and *VP* (verb phrase), and t is time step of its boundary.

Chunk Boundary Prediction: At each decoding step, we predict the probability of chunk boundary $P(b_t|\mathbf{x}) = softmax(s_{t-1}, e_{y_{t-1}})$.

Accordingly, given a set of training examples $\{[\mathbf{x}_n, \mathbf{y}_n]\}_{n=1}^{N}$, the new training objective is

$$J(\theta, \gamma) = \arg\max \sum_{n=1}^{N} \left\{ \log P(\mathbf{y_n}|\mathbf{x_n}) \right.$$
$$\left. + \log P(\mathbf{l_n}|\mathbf{x_n}) + \log P(\mathbf{b_n}|\mathbf{x_n}) \right\} \qquad (11)$$

where $\mathbf{l_n}$ and $\mathbf{b_n}$ are chunk tag sequence and boundary sequence on $\mathbf{y_n}$, respectively.

4   Experiments

We carry out experiments on a Chinese-English translation task. Our training data consists of $1.16M^2$ sentence pairs extracted from LDC corpora, with 25.1M Chinese words and 27.1M English words, respectively. We choose the NIST 2002 (MT02) dataset as our development set, and the NIST 2003 (MT03), 2004 (MT04) 2005 (MT05) datasets as our test sets. We also evaluate our model on the WMT translation task of German-English, newstest2014 (DE14) is adopted as development set and newstest2012, newstest2013 (DE1213) are adopted as testing set. The English sentences are labeled by a neural chunker, which is implemented according to Zhou et al. (2015). We use the case-insensitive 4-gram NIST BLEU score as our evaluation metric (Papineni et al., 2002).

In training, we limit the source and target vocabularies to the most frequent 30K words. We train each model with the sentences of length up to 50 words. Sizes of the chunk representation and chunk hidden state are set to 1000. All the other settings are the same as in Bahdanau et al. (2014).

4.1   Results on Chinese-English

We list the BLEU score of our proposed model in Table 1, comparing with Moses (Koehn et al., 2007) and dl4mt[3] (Bahdanau et al., 2014), which are state-of-the-art models of SMT and NMT, respective. For Moses, we use the default configuration with a 4-gram language model trained on the target portion of the training data. For dl4mt, we also report the results (dl4mt-2) by using two

---

[2] 3LDC2002E18, LDC2003E14, the Hansards portion of LDC2004T08, and LDC2005T06.

[3] `https://github.com/nyu-dl/dl4mt-tutorial`

System	MT02	MT03	MT04	MT05	Ave.
Moses	30.10	28.82	31.22	27.78	29.48
dl4mt	31.66	29.92	32.76	28.88	30.81
dl4mt-2	31.01	28.74	31.71	27.95	29.85
This Work	**33.43**	**32.06**	**34.21**	**30.01**	**32.42**

Table 1: BLEU scores for different systems.

Attention	MT02	MT03	MT04	MT05	Ave.
Word	32.69	31.36	33.55	29.77	31.56
Chunk	33.43	32.06	34.21	30.01	32.42

Table 2: Results with different attention models.

decoder layers (Wu et al., 2016) for better comparison.

As shown in Table 1, our proposed model outperforms different baselines on all sets, which verifies that the chunk-based bi-scale decoder is effective for NMT. Our model gives a 1.6 BLEU score improvement upon the standard NMT baseline (dl4mt). We conduct experiment with dl4mt-2 to see whether the neural NMT system can model the bi-scale components with different varying speeds automatically. Surprisingly, we find that dl4mt-2 obtains lower BLEU scores than dl4mt. We speculate that the more complex model dl4mt-2 may need more training data for obtaining reasonable results.

Effectiveness of Chunk Attention As described in Section 3, we propose to use the *chunk attention* to replace the word level attention in our model, in which the source context extracted by the chunk attention will be used for the corresponding word generations in the chunk. We also report the result of our model using conventional word attention for comparison. As shown in Table 2, our model with the chunk attention gives higher BLEU score than the word attention.

Intuitively, we think chunks are more specific in semantics, thus could extract more specific source context for translation. The chunk attention could be considered as a compromise approach between encoding the whole source sentence into decoder without attention (Sutskever et al., 2014) and utilizing word level attention at each step (Bahdanau et al., 2014). We also draw the figure of alignments by chunk attention (Figure 2), from which we can see that our chunk attention model can well explore the alignments from phrases to words.

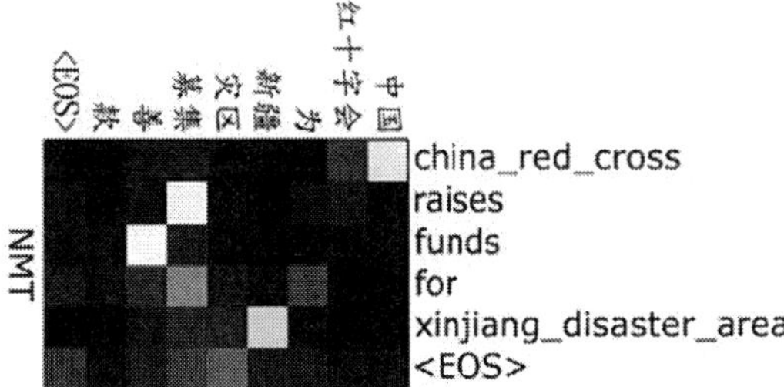

Figure 2: Alignments with chunk attention.

	MT02	MT03	MT04	MT05
Boundary	89.97	88.81	89.64	89.25
Label	47.00	44.75	45.54	44.41

Table 3: Accuracies of predicted chunk boundary and chunk label.

Predictions of the Chunk Boundary and Chunk Label We also compute predicted accuracies of chunk boundaries and chunk labels on the auto-chunked development and testing data (Table 3). We find that the chunk boundary could be predicted well, with an average accuracy of 89%, which shows that our model could capture the phrasal boundary information in the translation process. However, our model could not predict chunk labels as well as chunk boundaries. We speculate that more syntactic context features should be added to improve the performance of predicting chunk labels.

Subjective Evaluation Following Tu et al. (2016, 2017a,b), we also compare our model with the dl4mt baseline by subjective evaluation. Two human evaluators are asked to evaluate the translations of 100 source sentences randomly sampled from the test sets without knowing which system

Model	dl4mt	Our Work
Adequacy	3.26	3.35
Fluency	3.69	3.71
Under-Translation	50%	47%
Over-Translation	32%	26%

Table 4: Subjective evaluation results.

System	DE-14	DE-1213
dl4mt	16.53	16.78
This Work	17.40	17.45

Table 5: Results on German-English

the translation is translated by. The human evaluator is asked to give 4 scores: adequacy score and fluency score, which are between 0 and 5, the larger, the better; under-translation score and over-translation score, which are set to 1 when under or over translation errors occurs, otherwise set to 0.

We list the averaged scores in Table 5. We find that our proposed model improves the dl4mt baseline on both the translation adequacy and fluency aspects. Specifically, the over translation error rate drops by 6%, which confirms the assumption in the introduction that splitting the fast and slow varying components in different time-scales could help alleviate the over translation errors.

4.2 Results on German-English

We evaluate our model on the WMT15 translation task from German to English. We find that our proposed chunk-based NMT model also obtains considerable accuracy improvements on German-English. However, the BLEU score gains are not as significant as on Chinese-English. We speculate that the difference between Chinese and English is larger than German and English. The chunk-based NMT model may be more useful for bilingual data with bigger difference.

5 Related Work

NMT with Various Granularities. A line of previous work propose to utilize other granularities besides words for NMT. By further exploiting the character level (Ling et al., 2015; Costajussà and Fonollosa, 2016; Chung et al., 2016; Luong et al., 2016; Lee et al., 2016), or the sub-word level (Sennrich and Haddow, 2016; Sennrich et al., 2016; García-Martínez et al., 2016) information, the corresponding NMT models capture the infor-

mation inside the word and alleviate the problem of unknown words. While most of them focus on decomposing words into characters or sub-words, our work aims at composing words into phrases.

Incorporating Syntactic Information in NMT
Syntactic information has been widely used in SMT (Liu et al., 2006; Marton and Resnik, 2008; Shen et al., 2008), and a lot of previous work explore to incorporate the syntactic information in NMT, which shows the effectiveness of the syntactic information (Stahlberg et al., 2016). Shi et al. (2016) give some empirical results that the deep networks of NMT are able to capture some useful syntactic information implicitly. Luong et al. (2016) propose to use a multi-task framework for NMT and neural parsing, achieving promising results. Eriguchi et al. (2016) propose a string-to-tree NMT system by end-to-end training. Different to previous work, we try to incorporate the syntactic information in the target side of NMT. Ishiwatari et al. (2017) concurrently propose to use chunk-based decoder to cope with the problem of free word-order languages. Differently, they adopt word-level attention, and predict the end of chunk by generating end-of-chunk tokens instead of using boundary gate.

6 Conclusion

We propose a chunk-based bi-scale decoder for neural machine translation, in which way, the target sentence is translated hierarchically from chunks to words, with information in different granularities being leveraged. Experiments show that our proposed model outperforms the standard attention-based neural machine translation baseline. Future work includes abandoning labeled chunk data, adopting reinforcement learning to explore the boundaries of phrase automatically (Mou et al., 2016). Our code is released on `https://github.com/zhouh/chunk-nmt`.

Acknowledge

We would like to thank the anonymous reviewers for their insightful comments. We also thank Lili Mou for helpful discussion and Hongjie Ji, Zhenting Yu, Xiaoxue Hou and Wei Zou for their help in data preparation and subjective evaluation. This work was partially founded by the Natural Science Foundation of China (61672277, 71503124) and the China National 973 project 2014CB340301.

References

Dzmitry Bahdanau, Kyunghyun Cho, and Yoshua Bengio. 2014. Neural machine translation by jointly learning to align and translate. In *ICLR 2015*.

David Chiang. 2005. A hierarchical phrase-based model for statistical machine translation. In *Proceedings of the 43rd Annual Meeting on Association for Computational Linguistics*. Association for Computational Linguistics, pages 263–270.

Kyunghyun Cho, Bart van Merrienboer, Caglar Gulcehre, Dzmitry Bahdanau, Fethi Bougares, Holger Schwenk, and Yoshua Bengio. 2014. Learning phrase representations using rnn encoder–decoder for statistical machine translation. In *Proceedings of the 2014 Conference on Empirical Methods in Natural Language Processing (EMNLP)*. Association for Computational Linguistics, pages 1724–1734. https://doi.org/10.3115/v1/D14-1179.

Junyoung Chung, Kyunghyun Cho, and Yoshua Bengio. 2016. A character-level decoder without explicit segmentation for neural machine translation. In *Proceedings of the 54th Annual Meeting of the Association for Computational Linguistics (Volume 1: Long Papers)*. Association for Computational Linguistics, Berlin, Germany, pages 1693–1703. http://www.aclweb.org/anthology/P16-1160.

R. Marta Costa-jussà and R. José A. Fonollosa. 2016. Character-based neural machine translation. In *Proceedings of the 54th Annual Meeting of the Association for Computational Linguistics (Volume 2: Short Papers)*. Association for Computational Linguistics, pages 357–361. https://doi.org/10.18653/v1/P16-2058.

Akiko Eriguchi, Kazuma Hashimoto, and Yoshimasa Tsuruoka. 2016. Tree-to-sequence attentional neural machine translation. In *Proceedings of the 54th Annual Meeting of the Association for Computational Linguistics (Volume 1: Long Papers)*. Association for Computational Linguistics, pages 823–833. https://doi.org/10.18653/v1/P16-1078.

Mercedes García-Martínez, Loïc Barrault, and Fethi Bougares. 2016. Factored neural machine translation. *arXiv preprint arXiv:1609.04621* .

Shonosuke Ishiwatari, Jingtao Yao, Shujie Liu, Mu Li, Ming Zhou, Naoki Yoshinaga, Masaru Kitsuregawa, and Weijia Jia. 2017. Chunk-based decoder for neural machine translation. In *Proceedings of the 55th annual meeting of the Association for Computational Linguistics*. Association for Computational Linguistics.

Nal Kalchbrenner and Phil Blunsom. 2013. Recurrent continuous translation models. In *Proceedings of the 2013 Conference on Empirical Methods in Natural Language Processing*. Association for Computational Linguistics, pages 1700–1709. http://aclweb.org/anthology/D13-1176.

Philipp Koehn, Hieu Hoang, Alexandra Birch, Chris Callison-Burch, Marcello Federico, Nicola Bertoldi, Brooke Cowan, Wade Shen, Christine Moran, Richard Zens, et al. 2007. Moses: Open source toolkit for statistical machine translation. In *Proceedings of the 45th annual meeting of the ACL on interactive poster and demonstration sessions*. Association for Computational Linguistics, pages 177–180.

Philipp Koehn, Franz Josef Och, and Daniel Marcu. 2003. Statistical phrase-based translation. In *Proceedings of the 2003 Conference of the North American Chapter of the Association for Computational Linguistics on Human Language Technology-Volume 1*. Association for Computational Linguistics, pages 48–54.

Jason Lee, Kyunghyun Cho, and Thomas Hofmann. 2016. Fully character-level neural machine translation without explicit segmentation. *arXiv preprint arXiv:1610.03017* .

Wang Ling, Isabel Trancoso, Chris Dyer, and Alan W Black. 2015. Character-based neural machine translation. *arXiv preprint arXiv:1511.04586* .

Yang Liu, Qun Liu, and Shouxun Lin. 2006. Tree-to-string alignment template for statistical machine translation. In *Proceedings of the 21st International Conference on Computational Linguistics and the 44th annual meeting of the Association for Computational Linguistics*. Association for Computational Linguistics, pages 609–616.

Minh-Thang Luong, Quoc V. Le, Ilya Sutskever, Oriol Vinyals, and Lukasz Kaiser. 2016. Multi-task sequence to sequence learning. In *International Conference on Learning Representations (ICLR)*. San Juan, Puerto Rico.

Thang Luong, Hieu Pham, and D. Christopher Manning. 2015. Effective approaches to attention-based neural machine translation. In *Proceedings of the 2015 Conference on Empirical Methods in Natural Language Processing*. Association for Computational Linguistics, pages 1412–1421. https://doi.org/10.18653/v1/D15-1166.

Yuval Marton and Philip Resnik. 2008. Soft syntactic constraints for hierarchical phrased-based translation. In *ACL*. pages 1003–1011.

Lili Mou, Zhengdong Lu, Hang Li, and Zhi Jin. 2016. Coupling distributed and symbolic execution for natural language queries. *arXiv preprint arXiv:1612.02741* .

Kishore Papineni, Salim Roukos, Todd Ward, and Wei-Jing Zhu. 2002. Bleu: a method for automatic evaluation of machine translation. In *Proceedings of the 40th annual meeting on association for computational linguistics*.

Rico Sennrich and Barry Haddow. 2016. Linguistic input features improve neural machine translation. In *Proceedings of the First Conference on Machine Translation*. Association for Computational Linguistics, Berlin, Germany, pages 83–91. http://www.aclweb.org/anthology/W16-2209.

Rico Sennrich, Barry Haddow, and Alexandra Birch. 2016. Neural machine translation of rare words with subword units. In *Proceedings of the 54th Annual Meeting of the Association for Computational Linguistics (Volume 1: Long Papers)*. Association for Computational Linguistics, pages 1715–1725. https://doi.org/10.18653/v1/P16-1162.

Libin Shen, Jinxi Xu, and Ralph M Weischedel. 2008. A new string-to-dependency machine translation algorithm with a target dependency language model. In *ACL*. pages 577–585.

Xing Shi, Inkit Padhi, and Kevin Knight. 2016. Does string-based neural mt learn source syntax? In *Proceedings of the 2016 Conference on Empirical Methods in Natural Language Processing*. Association for Computational Linguistics, pages 1526–1534. http://aclweb.org/anthology/D16-1159.

Felix Stahlberg, Eva Hasler, Aurelien Waite, and Bill Byrne. 2016. Syntactically guided neural machine translation. In *Proceedings of the 54th Annual Meeting of the Association for Computational Linguistics (Volume 2: Short Papers)*. Association for Computational Linguistics, pages 299–305. https://doi.org/10.18653/v1/P16-2049.

Ilya Sutskever, Oriol Vinyals, and Quoc V Le. 2014. Sequence to sequence learning with neural networks. In *Advances in neural information processing systems*. pages 3104–3112.

Zhaopeng Tu, Yang Liu, Zhengdong Lu, Xiaohua Liu, and Hang Li. 2017a. Context gates for neural machine translation. *Transactions of the Association for Computational Linguistics* 5:87–99.

Zhaopeng Tu, Yang Liu, Lifeng Shang, Xiaohua Liu, and Hang Li. 2017b. Neural machine translation with reconstruction. In *Proceedings of AAAI 2017*. pages 3097–3103.

Zhaopeng Tu, Zhengdong Lu, Yang Liu, Xiaohua Liu, and Hang Li. 2016. Modeling coverage for neural machine translation. In *Proceedings of the 54th Annual Meeting of the Association for Computational Linguistics (Volume 1: Long Papers)*. Association for Computational Linguistics, pages 76–85. https://doi.org/10.18653/v1/P16-1008.

Wenhui Wang and Baobao Chang. 2016. Graph-based dependency parsing with bidirectional lstm. In *Proceedings of ACL*. volume 1, pages 2306–2315.

Yonghui Wu, Mike Schuster, Zhifeng Chen, Quoc V Le, Mohammad Norouzi, Wolfgang Macherey, Maxim Krikun, Yuan Cao, Qin Gao, Klaus Macherey, et al. 2016. Google's neural machine translation system: Bridging the gap between human and machine translation. *arXiv preprint arXiv:1609.08144* .

Hao Zhou, Yue Zhang, Shujian Huang, and Jiajun Chen. 2015. A neural probabilistic structured-prediction model for transition-based dependency parsing. In *Proceedings of the 53rd Annual Meeting of the Association for Computational Linguistics and the 7th International Joint Conference on Natural Language Processing (Volume 1: Long Papers)*. Association for Computational Linguistics, Beijing, China, pages 1213–1222. http://www.aclweb.org/anthology/P15-1117.

Model Transfer for Tagging Low-resource Languages using a Bilingual Dictionary

Meng Fang and **Trevor Cohn**
School of Computing and Information Systems
The University of Melbourne
`meng.fang@unimelb.edu.au`, `t.cohn@unimelb.edu.au`

Abstract

Cross-lingual model transfer is a compelling and popular method for predicting annotations in a low-resource language, whereby parallel corpora provide a bridge to a high-resource language and its associated annotated corpora. However, parallel data is not readily available for many languages, limiting the applicability of these approaches. We address these drawbacks in our framework which takes advantage of cross-lingual word embeddings trained solely on a high coverage bilingual dictionary. We propose a novel neural network model for joint training from both sources of data based on cross-lingual word embeddings, and show substantial empirical improvements over baseline techniques. We also propose several active learning heuristics, which result in improvements over competitive benchmark methods.

1 Introduction

Part-of-speech (POS) tagging is an important first step in most natural language processing (NLP) applications. Typically this is modelled using sequence labelling methods to predict the conditional probability of taggings given word sequences, using linear graphical models (Lafferty et al., 2001), or neural network models, such as recurrent neural networks (RNN) (Mikolov et al., 2010; Huang et al., 2015). These supervised learning algorithms rely on large labelled corpora; this is particularly true for state-of-the-art neural network models. Due to the expense of annotating sufficient data, such techniques are not well suited to applications in low-resource languages.

Prior work on low-resource NLP has primarily focused on exploiting parallel corpora to project information between a high- and low-resource language (Yarowsky and Ngai, 2001; Täckström et al., 2013; Guo et al., 2015; Agić et al., 2016; Buys and Botha, 2016). For example, POS tags can be projected via word alignments, and the projected POS is then used to train a model in the low-resource language (Das and Petrov, 2011; Zhang et al., 2016; Fang and Cohn, 2016). These methods overall have limited effectiveness due to errors in the alignment and fundamental differences between the languages. They also assume a large parallel corpus, which may not be available for many low-resource languages.

To address these limitations, we propose a new technique for low resource tagging, with more modest resource requirements: 1) a bilingual dictionary; 2) monolingual corpora in the high and low resource languages; and 3) a small annotated corpus of around $1,000$ tokens in the low-resource language. The first two resources are used as a form of distant supervision through learning cross-lingual word embeddings over the monolingual corpora and bilingual dictionary (Ammar et al., 2016). Additionally, our model jointly incorporates the language-dependent information from the small set of gold annotations. Our approach combines these two sources of supervision using multi-task learning, such that the kinds of errors that occur in cross-lingual transfer can be accounted for, and corrected automatically.

We empirically demonstrate the validity of our observation by using distant supervision to improve POS tagging performance with little supervision. Experimental results show the effectiveness of our approach across several low-resource languages, including both simulated and true low-resource settings. Furthermore, given the clear superiority of training with manual annotations, we compare several active learning heuristics. Active learning using uncertainty sampling with a word-

Proceedings of the 55th Annual Meeting of the Association for Computational Linguistics (Short Papers), pages 587–593
Vancouver, Canada, July 30 - August 4, 2017. ©2017 Association for Computational Linguistics
https://doi.org/10.18653/v1/P17-2093

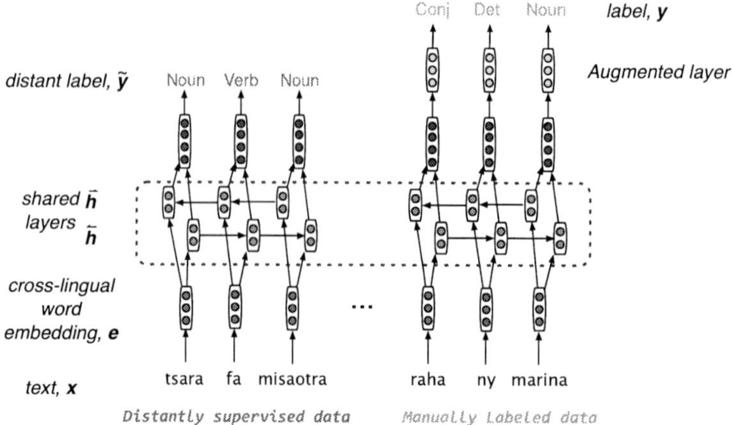

Figure 1: Illustration of the architecture of the joint model, which performs joint inference over both distant supervision (left) and manually labelled data (right).

type bias leads to substantial gains over benchmark methods such as token or sentence level uncertainty sampling.

2   Related work

POS tagging has been studied for many years. Traditionally, probabilistic models are a popular choice, such as Hidden Markov Models (HMM) and Conditional Random Fields (CRF) (Lafferty et al., 2001). Recently, neural network models have been developed for POS tagging and achieved good performance, such as RNN and bidirectional long short-term memory (BiLSTM) and CRF-BiLSTM models (Mikolov et al., 2010; Huang et al., 2015). For example, the CRF-BiLSTM POS tagger obtained the state-of-the-art performance on Penn Treebank WSJ corpus (Huang et al., 2015).

However, in low-resource languages, these models are seldom used because of limited labelled data. Parallel data therefore appears to be the most realistic additional source of information for developing NLP systems in low-resource languages (Yarowsky and Ngai, 2001; Das and Petrov, 2011; Täckström et al., 2013; Fang and Cohn, 2016; Zhang et al., 2016). Yarowsky and Ngai (2001) pioneered the use of parallel data for projecting POS tag information from one language to another language. Das and Petrov (2011) used parallel data and exploited graph-based label propagation to expand the coverage of labelled tokens.

Täckström et al. (2013) constructed tag dictionaries by projecting tag information from a high-resource language to a low-resource language via alignments in the parallel text. Fang and Cohn (2016) used parallel data to obtain projected tags as distant labels and proposed a joint BiLSTM model trained on both the distant data and $1,000$ tagged tokens. Zhang et al. (2016) used a few word translations pairs to find a linear transformation between two language embeddings. Then they used unsupervised learning to refine embedding transformations and model parameters. Instead we use minimal supervision to refine 'distant' labels through modelling the tag transformation, based on a small set of annotations.

3   Model

We now describe the modelling framework for POS tagging in a low-resource language, based on very limited linguistic resources. Our approach extends the work of Fang and Cohn (2016), who present a model based on distant supervision in the form of cross-lingual projection and use projected tags generated from parallel corpora as distant annotations. There are three main differences between their work and ours: 1) We do not use parallel corpora, but instead use a bilingual dictionary for knowledge transfer. 2) Our model uses a more expressive multi-layer perceptron when generating the gold standard tags. The multi-layer perceptron can capture both language-specific infor-

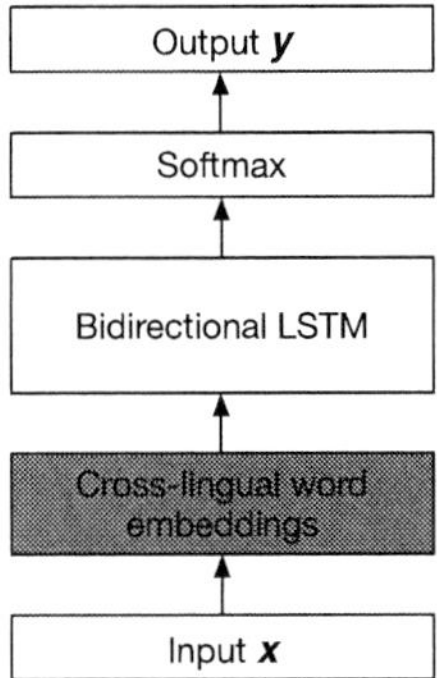

Figure 2: Architecture of the universal POS tagger. Cross-lingual word embeddings are pretrained using monolingual corpora and bilingual dictionaries.

mation and consistent tagging errors arising from this method of supervision. 3) We propose a number of active learning methods to further reduces the annotation requirements. Our method is illustrated in Figure 1, and we now elaborate on the model components.

Distant cross-lingual supervision In order to transfer tag information between the high- and low-resource languages, we start by learning cross-lingual word embeddings, which operate by learning vector valued embeddings such that words and their translations tend to be close together in the vector space. We use the embeddings from Ammar et al. (2016) which trains monolingual `word2vec` distributional representations, which are then projected into a common space, learned from bilingual dictionaries.

We then train a POS tagger on the high-resource language, using the cross-lingual word embeddings as the first, fixed, layer of a bidirectional LSTM tagger. The tagger is a language-universal model based on cross-lingual word embeddings, for processing an arbitrary language, given a monolingual corpus and a bilingual dictionary, as shown in Figure 2. Next we apply this tagger to unannotated text in the low-resource language; this application is made possible through the use of cross-lingual word embeddings. We refer to text tagged this way as *distantly supervised data*, and emphasize that although much better than chance, the outputs are often incorrect and are of limited utility on their own.

As illustrated in Figure 1, the distant components are generated directly as softmax outputs,

$y_t \sim \text{Categorial}(\mathbf{o}_t)$, with parameters $\mathbf{o}_t = \text{Softmax}(W\mathbf{h}_t + \mathbf{b})$ as a linear classifier over a sentence encoding, $\mathbf{h}_t$, which is the output of a bidirectional LSTM encoder over the words.

Ground truth supervision The second component of the model is manually labelled text in the low-resource language. To model this data we employ the same model structure as above but augmented with a second perceptron output layer, as illustrated in Figure 1 (right). Formally, $\tilde{y}_t \sim \text{Categorial}(\tilde{\mathbf{o}}_t)$ where $\tilde{\mathbf{o}}_t = \text{MLP}(\mathbf{o}_t)$ is a single hidden layer perceptron with tanh activation and softmax output transformation. This component allows for a more expressive label mapping than Fang and Cohn (2016)'s linear matrix translation.

Joint multi-task learning To combine the two sources of information, we use a joint objective,

$$\mathcal{J} = -\gamma \sum_{t \in \mathcal{N}} \langle \tilde{y}_t, \log \tilde{o}_t \rangle - \sum_{t \in \mathcal{M}} \langle y_t, \log o_t \rangle , \quad (1)$$

where $\mathcal{N}$ and $\mathcal{M}$ index the token positions in the distant and ground truth corpora, respectively, and γ is a constant balancing the two components which we set for uniform weighting, $\gamma = \frac{|\mathcal{M}|}{|\mathcal{N}|}$.

Consider the training effect of the true POS tags: when performing error backpropagation, the cross-entropy error signal must pass through the transformation linking $\tilde{o}$ with o, which can be seen as a language-specific step, after which the generalised error signal can be further backpropagated to the rest of the model.

Active learning Given the scarcity of ground truth labels and the high cost of annotation, a natural question is whether we can optimise which text to be annotated in order achieve the high accuracy for the lowest cost. We now outline a range of active learning approaches based on the following heuristics, which are used to select the instances for annotation from a pool of candidates:

TOKEN Select the token x_t with the highest uncertainty, $H(\mathbf{x}, t) = -\sum_y P(y|\mathbf{x}, t) \log P(y|\mathbf{x}, t)$;

SENT Select the sentence $\mathbf{x}$ with the highest aggregate uncertainty, $H(\mathbf{x}) = \sum_t H(\mathbf{x}, t)$;

FREQTYPE Select the most frequent unannotated word type (Garrette and Baldridge, 2013), in which case all token instances are annotated with the most frequent label for the type in the training corpus;[1]

SUMTYPE Select a word type, z, for annotation with the highest aggregate uncertainty over token occurrences, $H(z) = \sum_{i \in \mathcal{D}} \sum_{x_{i,t}=z} H(\mathbf{x}_i, t)$, which effectively combines uncertainty sampling with a bias towards high frequency types; and

RANDOM Select word types randomly.

4 Experiments

We evaluate the effectiveness of the proposed model for several different languages, including both simulated low-resource and true low-resource settings. The first evaluation set uses the CoNLL-X datasets of European languages (Buchholz and Marsi, 2006), comprising Danish (da), Dutch (nl), German (de), Greek (el), Italian (it), Portuguese (pt), Spanish (es) and Swedish (sv). We use the standard corpus splits. The first 20 sentences of training set are used for training as the tiny labelled (gold) data and the last 20 sentences are used for development (early stopping). We report accuracy on the held-out test set.

The second evaluation set includes two highly challenging languages, Turkish (tk) and Malagasy (mg), both having high morphological complexity and the latter has truly scant resources. Turkish data was drawn from CoNLL 2003[2] and Malagasy data was collected from Das and Petrov (2011), in both cases using the same training configuration as above.

In all cases English is used as the source 'high resource' language, on which we train a tagger using the Penn Treebank, and we evaluate on each of the remaining languages as an independent target. For cross-lingual word embeddings, we evaluate two techniques from Ammar et al. (2016): CCA-based word embeddings and cluster-based word embeddings. Both types of word embedding techniques are based on bilingual dictionaries. The dictionaries were formed by translating the $20k$ most common words in the En-

glish monolingual corpus with Google Translate.[3] The monolingual corpora were constructed from a combination of text from the Leipzig Corpora Collection and Europarl. We trained the language-universal POS tagger based on the cross-lingual word embeddings with the universal POS tagset (Petrov et al., 2011), and then applied to the target language using the embedding lookup table for the corresponding language embeddings. We implement our learning procedure with the DyNet toolkit (Neubig et al., 2017).[4] The BiLSTM layer uses 128 hidden units, and 32 hidden units for the transformation step. We used SGD with momentum to train models, with early stopping based on development performance.

For benchmarks, we compare the proposed model against various state-of-the-art supervised learning methods, namely: a BiLSTM tagger, BiLSTM-CRF tagger (Huang et al., 2015), and a state-of-the-art semi-supervised POS tagging algorithm, MINITAGGER (Stratos and Collins, 2015), which is also focusing on minimising the amount of labelled data. Note these methods do not use cross-lingual supervision. For a more direct comparison, we include BiLSTM-DEBIAS (Fang and Cohn, 2016), applied using our proposed cross-lingual supervision based on dictionaries, instead of parallel corpora; accordingly the key difference is their linear transformation for the distant data, versus our non-linear transformation to the gold data.

Results Table 1 reports the tagging accuracy, showing that our models consistently outperform the baseline techniques. The poor performance of the supervised methods suggests they are overfitting the small training set, however this is much less of a problem for our approach (labelled Joint). Note that distant supervision alone gives reasonable performance (labelled DISTANT) however the joint modelling of the ground truth and distant data yields significant improvements in almost all cases. BiLSTM-DEBIAS (Fang and Cohn, 2016) performs worse than our proposed method, indicating that a linear transformation is insufficient for modelling distant supervision. The accuracies are higher overall for the European cf. Turkic languages, presumably because these languages are

---

[1]We could support more than one class label, by marginalising over the set of valid labels for all tokens in the training objective.

[2]http://www.cnts.ua.ac.be/conll2003/ner/

[3]Although the use of a translation system conveys a dependence on parallel text, high quality word embeddings can be learned directly from bilingual dictionaries such as Panlex (Kamholz et al., 2014).

[4]Code available at https://github.com/mengf1/trpos

	da	nl	de	el	it	pt	es	sv	tk	mg
Random	23.2	30.5	27.1	23.2	25.9	24.3	26.9	21.6	36.9	34.5
BiLSTM	61.8	62.1	60.5	70.1	73.6	67.6	63.6	57.2	44.0	63.4
BiLSTM-Crf	46.3	47.7	53.2	35.1	41.2	44.1	25.5	54.9	43.1	41.4
MiniTagger	77.0	72.5	75.9	75.7	67.3	75.1	73.5	77.7	49.8	67.2
Distant +CCA	73.5	64.5	57.7	53.1	59.5	67.8	63.5	66.0	57.2	49.7
Distant +Cluster	70.4	61.7	65.9	65.5	64.8	66.9	68.4	64.1	51.7	50.2
BiLSTM-Debias +CCA	73.2	72.8	72.5	71.2	70.7	72.1	71.1	73.1	49.2	65.9
BiLSTM-Debias +Cluster	72.5	70.1	71.2	68.7	69.1	72.5	70.6	73.3	48.7	64.5
Joint +CCA	81.1	**82.3**	76.1	77.5	75.9	**82.1**	79.7	**78.1**	**72.6**	75.3
Joint +Cluster	**81.9**	81.5	**78.9**	**80.1**	**81.9**	76.7	**81.2**	78.0	70.4	**75.7**

Table 1: POS tagging accuracy on over the ten target languages, showing first approaches using only the gold data; next methods using only distant cross-lingual supervision, and lastly joint multi-task learning. English is used as the source language and columns correspond to a specific target language.

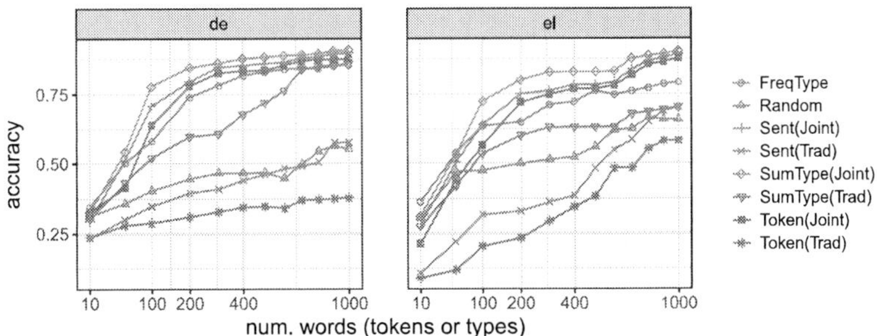

Figure 3: Active learning evaluation on German and Greek, using CCA trained cross-lingual word embeddings. Trad means traditional active learning; Joint means joint multi-task learning.

closer to English, have higher quality dictionaries and in most cases are morphologically simpler. Finally, note the difference between CCA and Cluster methods for learning word embeddings which arise from the differing quality of distant supervision between the languages.

Figure 3 compares various active learning heuristics (see §3) based on different taggers, either a supervised BiLSTM (labelled Trad) or our multi-task model which also includes cross-lingual supervision (JOINT).

Traditional uncertainty-based sampling strategies (TOKEN(Trad) and SENT(Trad)) do not work well because models based on limited supervision do not provide accurate uncertainty information,[5] and moreover, annotating at the type rather than token level provides a significantly stronger supervision signal. The difference is apparent from the decent performance of Random sampling over word types. Overall, SUMTYPE(Joint) outperforms the other heuristics consistently, underlining the importance of cross-lingual distant super-

vision, as well as combining the benefits of uncertainty sampling, type selection and a frequency bias. Comparing the amount of annotation required between the best traditional active learning method SUMTYPE(Trad) and our best method SUMTYPE(Joint), we achieve the same performance with an order of magnitude less annotated data (100 vs. 1,000 labelled words).

5   Conclusion

In this paper, we proposed a means of tagging a low-resource language without the need for bilingual parallel corpora. We introduced a new cross-lingual distant supervision method based on a bilingual dictionary. Furthermore, deep neural network models can be effective with limited supervision by incorporating distant supervision, in the form of model transfer with cross-lingual word embeddings. We show that traditional uncertainty sampling strategies do not work well on low-resource settings, and introduce new methods based around labelling word types. Overall our approach leads to consistent and substantial improvements over benchmark methods.

---

[5] Sentence level annotation is likely to be much faster than token or type level annotation, however even if it were an order of magnitude faster it is still not a competitive active learning strategy.

Acknowledgments

This work was sponsored by the Defense Advanced Research Projects Agency Information Innovation Office (I2O) under the Low Resource Languages for Emergent Incidents (LORELEI) program issued by DARPA/I2O under Contract No. HR0011-15-C-0114. The views expressed are those of the author and do not reflect the official policy or position of the Department of Defense or the U.S. Government. Trevor Cohn was supported by the Australian Research Council Future Fellowship (project number FT130101105).

References

Željko Agić, Anders Johannsen, Barbara Plank, Héctor Alonso Martínez, Natalie Schluter, and Anders Søgaard. 2016. Multilingual projection for parsing truly low-resource languages. *Transactions of the Association for Computational Linguistics* 4:301–312.

Waleed Ammar, George Mulcaire, Yulia Tsvetkov, Guillaume Lample, Chris Dyer, and Noah A Smith. 2016. Massively multilingual word embeddings. *Transactions of the Association for Computational Linguistics* 4:431–444.

Sabine Buchholz and Erwin Marsi. 2006. Conll-x shared task on multilingual dependency parsing. In *Proceedings of the Tenth Conference on Computational Natural Language Learning*. Association for Computational Linguistics, pages 149–164.

Jan Buys and Jan A. Botha. 2016. Cross-lingual morphological tagging for low-resource languages. In *Proceedings of the 54th Annual Meeting of the Association for Computational Linguistics (ACL)*. Association for Computational Linguistics, Berlin, Germany, pages 1954–1964.

Dipanjan Das and Slav Petrov. 2011. Unsupervised part-of-speech tagging with bilingual graph-based projections. In *Proceedings of the 49th Annual Meeting of the Association for Computational Linguistics: Human Language Technologies (ACL-HLT)*. pages 600–609.

Meng Fang and Trevor Cohn. 2016. Learning when to trust distant supervision: An application to low-resource pos tagging using cross-lingual projection. In *Proceedings of the 20th SIGNLL Conference on Computational Natural Language Learning (CoNLL)*. Berlin, Germany.

Dan Garrette and Jason Baldridge. 2013. Learning a part-of-speech tagger from two hours of annotation. In *Proceedings of the 2013 Conference of the North American Chapter of the Association for Computational Linguistics: Human Language Technologies (NAACL-HLT)*. Citeseer, pages 138–147.

Jiang Guo, Wanxiang Che, David Yarowsky, Haifeng Wang, and Ting Liu. 2015. Cross-lingual dependency parsing based on distributed representations. In *Proceedings of the 53rd Annual Meeting of the Association for Computational Linguistics (ACL)*. Association for Computational Linguistics, pages 1234–1244.

Zhiheng Huang, Wei Xu, and Kai Yu. 2015. Bidirectional lstm-crf models for sequence tagging. *arXiv preprint arXiv:1508.01991* .

David Kamholz, Jonathan Pool, and Susan M Colowick. 2014. Panlex: Building a resource for panlingual lexical translation. In *Proceedings of the Ninth International Conference on Language Resources and Evaluation (LREC)*. pages 3145–3150.

John Lafferty, Andrew McCallum, and Fernando Pereira. 2001. Conditional random fields: Probabilistic models for segmenting and labeling sequence data. In *Proceedings of the 8th International Conference on Machine Learning (ICML)*. volume 1, pages 282–289.

Tomas Mikolov, Martin Karafiát, Lukas Burget, Jan Cernockỳ, and Sanjeev Khudanpur. 2010. Recurrent neural network based language model. In *Interspeech*. volume 2, page 3.

Graham Neubig, Chris Dyer, Yoav Goldberg, Austin Matthews, Waleed Ammar, Antonios Anastasopoulos, Miguel Ballesteros, David Chiang, Daniel Clothiaux, Trevor Cohn, Kevin Duh, Manaal Faruqui, Cynthia Gan, Dan Garrette, Yangfeng Ji, Lingpeng Kong, Adhiguna Kuncoro, Gaurav Kumar, Chaitanya Malaviya, Paul Michel, Yusuke Oda, Matthew Richardson, Naomi Saphra, Swabha Swayamdipta, and Pengcheng Yin. 2017. Dynet: The dynamic neural network toolkit. *arXiv preprint arXiv:1701.03980* .

Slav Petrov, Dipanjan Das, and Ryan McDonald. 2011. A universal part-of-speech tagset. *arXiv preprint arXiv:1104.2086* .

Karl Stratos and Michael Collins. 2015. Simple semi-supervised pos tagging. In *Proceedings of the 2015 Conference of the North American Chapter of the Association for Computational Linguistics: Human Language Technologies (NAACL-HLT)*. pages 79–87.

Oscar Täckström, Dipanjan Das, Slav Petrov, Ryan McDonald, and Joakim Nivre. 2013. Token and type constraints for cross-lingual part-of-speech tagging. *Transactions of the Association for Computational Linguistics* 1:1–12.

David Yarowsky and Grace Ngai. 2001. Inducing multilingual POS taggers and NP brackets via robust projection across aligned corpora. In *Proceedings of the 2001 Conference of the North American Chapter of the Association for Computational Linguistics (NAACL)*.

Yuan Zhang, David Gaddy, Regina Barzilay, and
Tommi Jaakkola. 2016. Ten pairs to tag–
multilingual pos tagging via coarse mapping between embeddings. In *Proceedings of the 2016 Conference of the North American Chapter of the Association for Computational Linguistics: Human Language Technologies (NAACL-HLT).* pages 1307–
1317.

EuroSense: Automatic Harvesting of Multilingual Sense Annotations from Parallel Text

Claudio Delli Bovi, Jose Camacho-Collados, Alessandro Raganato and Roberto Navigli
Department of Computer Science
Sapienza University of Rome
{dellibovi,collados,raganato,navigli}@di.uniroma1.it

Abstract

Parallel corpora are widely used in a variety of Natural Language Processing tasks, from Machine Translation to cross-lingual Word Sense Disambiguation, where parallel sentences can be exploited to automatically generate high-quality sense annotations on a large scale. In this paper we present EuroSense, a multilingual sense-annotated resource based on the joint disambiguation of the Europarl parallel corpus, with almost 123 million sense annotations for over 155 thousand distinct concepts and entities from a language-independent unified sense inventory. We evaluate the quality of our sense annotations intrinsically and extrinsically, showing their effectiveness as training data for Word Sense Disambiguation.

1 Introduction

One of the long-standing challenges in Natural Language Processing (NLP) lies in automatically identifying the meaning of words in context. Various lines of research have been geared towards achieving this goal, most notably Word Sense Disambiguation (Navigli, 2009, WSD) and Entity Linking (Rao et al., 2013, EL). In both tasks, supervised approaches (Zhong and Ng, 2010; Melamud et al., 2016; Iacobacci et al., 2016; Kågebäck and Salomonsson, 2016) tend to obtain the best performances over standard benchmarks but, from a practical standpoint, they lose ground to knowledge-based approaches (Agirre et al., 2014; Moro et al., 2014b; Weissenborn et al., 2015), which scale better in terms of scope and number of languages. In fact, the development of supervised disambiguation systems depends crucially on the availability of re-liable sense-annotated corpora, which are indispensable in order to provide solid training and testing grounds (Pilehvar and Navigli, 2014). However, hand-labeled sense annotations are notoriously difficult to obtain on a large scale, and manually curated corpora (Miller et al., 1993; Passonneau et al., 2012) have a limited size. Given that scaling the manual annotation process becomes practically unfeasible when both lexicographic and encyclopedic knowledge is addressed (Schubert, 2006), recent years have witnessed efforts to produce larger sense-annotated corpora automatically (Moro et al., 2014a; Taghipour and Ng, 2015a; Scozzafava et al., 2015; Raganato et al., 2016). Even though these automatic approaches produce noisier corpora, it has been shown that training on them leads to better supervised and semi-supervised models (Taghipour and Ng, 2015b; Raganato et al., 2016; Yuan et al., 2016; Raganato et al., 2017), as well as to effective embedded representations for senses (Iacobacci et al., 2015; Flekova and Gurevych, 2016).

A convenient way of generating sense annotations is to exploit parallel corpora and word alignments (Taghipour and Ng, 2015a): indeed, parallel corpora exist in many flavours (Tiedemann, 2012) and are widely used across the NLP community for a variety of different tasks. In this paper we focus on Europarl (Koehn, 2005)[1], one of the most popular multilingual corpora, originally designed to provide aligned parallel text for Machine Translation (MT) systems. Extracted from the proceedings of the European Parliament, the latest release of the Europarl corpus comprises parallel text for 21 European languages, with more than 743 million tokens overall.

Apart from its prominent role in MT as a training set, the Europarl corpus has been used

---

[1] http://opus.lingfil.uu.se/Europarl.php

Proceedings of the 55th Annual Meeting of the Association for Computational Linguistics (Short Papers), pages 594–600
Vancouver, Canada, July 30 - August 4, 2017. ©2017 Association for Computational Linguistics
https://doi.org/10.18653/v1/P17-2094

for cross-lingual WSD (Lefever and Hoste, 2010, 2013), including, more recently, preposition sense disambiguation (Gonen and Goldberg, 2016), and widely exploited to develop cross-lingual word embeddings (Hermann and Blunsom, 2014; Gouws et al., 2015; Coulmance et al., 2015; Vyas and Carpuat, 2016; Vulić and Korhonen, 2016; Artetxe et al., 2016) as well as multi-sense embeddings (Ettinger et al., 2016; Šuster et al., 2016).

In this paper, our aim is to augment Europarl with sense-level information for multiple languages, thereby constructing a large-scale sense-annotated multilingual corpus which has the potential to boost both WSD and MT research.

We follow an approach that has already proved effective in a definitional setting (Camacho-Collados et al., 2016a): unlike previous cross-lingual approaches, we do not rely on word alignments against a pivot language, but instead leverage all languages at the same time in a joint disambiguation procedure that is subsequently refined using distributional similarity. We draw on the wide-coverage multilingual encyclopedic dictionary of BabelNet (Navigli and Ponzetto, 2012)[2], which enables us to seamlessly cover lexicographic and encyclopedic knowledge in multiple languages within a unified sense inventory.

As a result of our disambiguation pipeline we obtain and make available to the community EU-ROSENSE, a multilingual sense-annotated corpus with almost 123 million sense annotations of more than 155 thousand distinct concepts and named entities drawn from the multilingual sense inventory of BabelNet, and covering all the 21 languages of the Europarl corpus. As such EUROSENSE constitutes, to our knowledge, the largest corpus of its kind.

2   Related Work

Extending sense annotations to multiple languages is a demanding endeavor, especially when manual intervention is required. Despite the fact that sense-annotated corpora for a number of languages have been around for more than a decade (Petrolito and Bond, 2014), they either include few samples per word sense, or only cover a restricted set of ambiguous words (Passonneau et al., 2012); as a result, multilingual WSD was until recently almost exclusively tackled using knowledge-based approaches (Agirre et al., 2014;

Moro et al., 2014b). Nowadays, however, the rapid development of NLP pipelines for languages other than English has been opening up the possibilities for the automatic generation of multilingual sense-annotated data. Nevertheless, the few approaches that have been proposed so far are either focused on treating each individual language in isolation (Otegi et al., 2016), or limited to short and concise definitional text (Camacho-Collados et al., 2016a).

On the other hand, the use of parallel text to perform WSD (Ng et al., 2003; Lefever et al., 2011; Yao et al., 2012; Bonansinga and Bond, 2016) or even Word Sense Induction (Apidianaki, 2013) has been widely explored in the literature, and has demonstrated its effectiveness in producing high-quality sense-annotated data (Chan and Ng, 2005). This strategy, however, requires word alignments for each language pair to be taken into account, with alignment errors that might propagate and hamper subsequent stages unless human supervision is employed to correct erroneous annotations (Taghipour and Ng, 2015a). Moreover, cross-language disambiguation using parallel text requires a language-independent annotation framework that goes beyond monolingual WordNet-like sense inventories (Lefever et al., 2011) in order for the annotations obtained to be used effectively within end-to-end applications.

With EUROSENSE, instead, the key idea is to exploit at best parallel sentences to provide enriched context for a joint multilingual disambiguation. Using BabelNet, a unified multilingual sense inventory, we obtain language-independent sense annotations for a wide variety of concepts and named entities, which can be seamlessly mapped to individual semantic resources (e.g WordNet, Wikipedia, DBpedia) via Babel-Net's inter-resource mappings.

3   Building EUROSENSE

Following Camacho-Collados et al. (2016a), our fully automatic disambiguation pipeline for constructing EUROSENSE couples a graph-based multilingual joint WSD/EL system, Babelfy (Moro et al., 2014b)[3], and a language-independent vector representation of concepts and entities, NASARI (Camacho-Collados et al., 2016b).[4] It comprises two stages: multilingual disambiguation (Section 3.1) and refinement based on distributional similarity (Section 3.2).

3.1 Stage 1: Multilingual Disambiguation

As a preprocessing step, we part-of-speech tag and lemmatize the whole corpus using TreeTagger (Schmid, 1995)[5]. We perform disambiguation at the sentence level. However, instead of disambiguating each sentence in isolation, language by language, we first identify all available translations of a given sentence and then gather these together into a single multilingual text.

Then, we disambiguate this multilingual text using Babelfy. Given that Babelfy is capable of handling text with multiple languages at the same time, this multilingual extension effectively increases the amount of context for each sentence, and directly helps in dealing with highly ambiguous words in any particular language (as the translations of these words may be less ambiguous in some different language). Moreover, given the multilingual nature of our sense inventory, Babelfy's high-coherence approach favors naturally sense assignments that are consistent across languages at the sentence level (i.e. those having fewer distinct senses shared by more translations of the same sentence).

As a result, we obtain a full, high-coverage version of EUROSENSE where each disambiguated word or multi-word expression (*disambiguated instance*) is associated with a coherence score.[6]

3.2 Stage 2: Similarity-based Refinement

In this stage we aim at improving the sense annotations obtained in the previous step (Section 3.1), with a procedure specifically targeted at correcting and extending these sense annotations. In general, graph-based WSD systems, such as Babelfy, have been shown to be heavily biased towards the Most Common Sense (MCS) (Calvo and Gelbukh, 2015). In order to get a handle on this bias and improve our pipeline's disambiguation accuracy we adopt a refinement based on distributional similarity, which is not affected by the MCS.

To this end, we exploit the 300-dimensional embedded representations of concepts and entities of NASARI to discard or refine disambiguated instances that are less semantically coherent. These NASARI vector representations were constructed by combining structural and distributional knowledge from Wikipedia and WordNet with Word2Vec word embeddings (Mikolov et al., 2013) trained on textual corpora.

For each sentence, we first identify a subset D of high-confidence disambiguations[7] from among those given by Babelfy in the previous step. Then, we calculate the centroid of all the NASARI vectors corresponding to the elements of D, and we re-disambiguate the mentions associated with the remaining low-confidence disambiguated instances (i.e. those not in D), by picking, for each mention w, the concept or entity $\hat{s}$ whose NASARI vector[8] is closest to the centroid of the sentence:

$$\hat{s} = \underset{s \in S_w}{\operatorname{argmax}} \, cos\left(\frac{\sum_{d \in D} \vec{d}}{|D|}, \vec{s}\right) \quad (1)$$

where S_w is the set of all candidate senses for mention w according to BabelNet. Cosine similarity (cos) is used as similarity measure. Finally, in order to discard less confident annotations, we consider the cosine value associated with each refined disambiguation as confidence score, and use it to compare each disambiguated instance against an empirically validated threshold of 0.75.

As a result, we obtain the refined high-precision version of EUROSENSE, where each disambiguated instance is associated with both a coherence score and a distributional similarity score.

4 Corpus and Statistics

Table 1 reports general statistics on EUROSENSE regarding both its high-coverage (cf. Section 3.1) and high-precision (cf. Section 3.2) versions. Joint multilingual disambiguation with Babelfy generated more than 215M sense annotations of 247k distinct concepts and entities, while similarity-based refinement retained almost 123M high-confidence instances (56.96% of the total), covering almost 156k distinct concepts and entities. 42.40% of these retained annotations were corrected or validated using distributional similarity. As expected, the distribution over parts of speech is skewed towards nominal senses (64.79% before refinement and 81.79% after refinement)

---

[5]We rely on the internal preprocessing pipeline of Babelfy for those languages not supported by TreeTagger.

[6]As in Camacho-Collados et al. (2016a), coherence score is given by the normalized number of connections of a given concept within the sentence.

[7]We follow Camacho-Collados et al. (2016a) and consider disambiguated instances with a coherence score above 0.125.

[8]Given a concept or entity s we indicate with $\vec{s}$ its corresponding NASARI vector.

		Total	EN	FR	DE	ES
Full	# Annotations	215 877 109	26 455 574	22 214 996	16 888 108	21 486 532
	Distinct lemmas covered	567 378	60 853	30 474	66 762	43 892
	Distinct senses covered	247 706	138 115	65 301	75 008	74 214
	Average coherence score	0.19	0.19	0.18	0.18	0.18
Refined	# Annotations	122 963 111	15 441 667	12 955 469	9 165 112	12 193 260
	Distinct lemmas covered	453 063	42 947	23 603	50 681	31 980
	Distinct senses covered	155 904	86 881	49 189	52 425	52 859
	Average coherence score	0.29	0.28	0.25	0.28	0.27

Table 1: General statistics on EUROSENSE before *(full)* and after refinement *(refined)* for all the 21 languages. Language-specific figures are also reported for the 4 languages of the intrinsic evaluation.

followed by verbs (19.26% and 12.22%), adjectives (11.46% and 5.24%) and adverbs (4.48% and 0.73%). We note that the average coherence score increases from 0.19 to 0.29 after refinement, suggesting that distributional similarity tends to favor sense annotations that are also consistent across different languages. Table 1 also includes language-specific statistics on the 4 languages of the intrinsic evaluation, where the average lexical ambiguity ranges from 1.12 senses per lemma (German) to 2.26 (English) and, as expected, decreases consistently after refinement.

Interestingly enough, if we consider all the 21 languages, the total number of distinct lemmas covered is more than twice the total number of distinct senses: this is a direct consequence of having a unified, language-independent sense inventory (BabelNet), a feature that sets EUROSENSE apart from previous multilingual sense-annotated corpora (Otegi et al., 2016). Finally we note from the global figures on the number of covered senses that 109 591 senses (44.2% of the total) are not covered by the English sense annotations: this suggests that EUROSENSE relies heavily on multilinguality in integrating concepts or named entities that are tied to specific social or cultural aspects of a given language (and hence would be underrepresented in an English-specific sense inventory).

5 Experimental Evaluation

We assessed the quality of EUROSENSE's sense annotations both intrinsically, by means of a manual evaluation on four samples of randomly extracted sentences in different languages (Section 5.1), as well as extrinsically, by augmenting the training set of a state-of-the-art supervised WSD system (Zhong and Ng, 2010) and showing that it leads to consistent performance improvements over two standard WSD benchmarks (Section 5.2).

5.1 Intrinsic Evaluation: Annotation Quality

In order to assess annotation quality directly, we carried out a manual evaluation on 4 different languages (English, French, German and Spanish) with 2 human judges per language. We sampled 50 random sentences across the subset of sentences in EUROSENSE featuring a translation in all 4 languages, totaling 200 sentences overall.

For each sentence, we evaluated all sense annotations both before and after the refinement stage, along with the sense annotations obtained by a baseline that disambiguates each sentence in isolation with Babelfy. Overall, we manually verified a total of 5818 sense annotations across the three configurations (1518 in English, 1564 in French, 1093 in German and 1643 in Spanish). In every language the two judges agreed in more than 85% of the cases, with an inter-annotator agreement in terms of Cohen's kappa (Cohen, 1960) above 60% in all evaluations (67.7% on average).

Results, reported in Table 2, show that joint multilingual disambiguation improves consistently over the baseline. The similarity-based refinement boosts precision even further, at the expense of a reduced coverage (whereas both Babelfy and the baseline attempt an answer for every disambiguation target). Over the 4 languages, sense annotations appear to be most reliable for German, which is consistent with its lower lexical ambiguity on the corpus (cf. Section 4).

5.2 Extrinsic Evaluation: Word Sense Disambiguation

We additionally carried out an extrinsic evaluation of EUROSENSE by using its refined sense an-

	EN		FR		DE		ES	
	Prec.	**Cov.**	**Prec.**	**Cov.**	**Prec.**	**Cov.**	**Prec.**	**Cov.**
Babelfy	76.1	100	59.1	100	80.4	100	67.5	100
EuroSense (full)	80.3	100	67.9	100	84.6	100	76.7	100
EuroSense (refined)	**81.5**	75.0	**71.8**	63.5	**89.3**	53.8	**82.5**	62.9

Table 2: Precision *(Prec.)* and coverage *(Cov.)* of EuroSense, manually evaluated on a random sample in 4 languages. Precision is averaged between the two judges, and coverage is computed assuming each content word in the sense inventory to be a valid disambiguation target.

notations for English as a training set for a supervised all-words WSD system, It Makes Sense (Zhong and Ng, 2010, IMS). Following Taghipour and Ng (2015a), we started with SemCor (Miller et al., 1993) as initial training dataset, and then performed a subsampling of EuroSense up to 500 additional training examples per word sense. We then trained IMS on this augmented training set and tested on the two most recent standard benchmarks for all-words WSD: the SemEval-2013 task 12 (Navigli et al., 2013) and the SemEval-2015 task 13 (Moro and Navigli, 2015) test sets. As baselines we considered IMS trained on SemCor only and OMSTI, the sense-annotated dataset constructed by Taghipour and Ng (2015a) which also includes SemCor. Finally, we report the results of UKB, a knowledge-based system (Agirre et al., 2014).[9] As shown in Table 3, IMS trained on our augmented training set consistently outperforms all baseline models, showing the reliability of EuroSense as training corpus, even against sense annotations obtained semi-automatically (Taghipour and Ng, 2015a).

6 Release

EuroSense is available at `http://lcl. uniroma1.it/eurosense`. We release two different versions of the corpus:

- A *high-coverage version*, obtained after the first stage of the pipeline, i.e. multilingual joint disambiguation with Babelfy. Here, each sense annotation is associated with a coherence score (cf. Section 3.1);

- A *high-precision version*, obtained after the similarity-based refinement with Nasari. In this version, sense annotations are associated

	SemEval-2013	SemEval-2015
IMS$_{SemCor}$	65.3	69.3
IMS$_{OMSTI}$	65.0	69.1
IMS$_{EuroSense}$	**66.4**	**69.5**
UKB	59.0	61.2
UKB$_{w2w}$	62.9	63.3
MCS	63.0	67.8

Table 3: F-Score on all-words WSD.

with both a coherence score and a distributional similarity score (cf. Section 3.2).

7 Conclusion

In this paper we presented EuroSense, a large multilingual sense-annotated corpus based on Europarl, and constructed automatically via a disambiguation pipeline that exploits the interplay between a joint multilingual disambiguation algorithm and a language-independent vector-based representation of concepts and entities. Crucially, EuroSense relies on the wide-coverage unified sense inventory of BabelNet, which enabled the disambiguation process to exploit at best parallel text and enforces cross-language coherence among sense annotations. We evaluated EuroSense both intrinsically and extrinsically, showing that it provides reliable sense annotations that improve supervised models for WSD.

Acknowledgments

The authors gratefully acknowledge the support of the ERC Consolidator Grant MOUSSE Contract No. 726487.

Claudio Delli Bovi is supported by a Sapienza Research Grant 'Avvio alla Ricerca 2016'. Jose Camacho-Collados is supported by a Google PhD Fellowship in Natural Language Processing.

---

[9] We include its two implementations using the full WordNet graph and the disambiguated glosses of WordNet as connections: default and word by word (*w2w*).

References

Eneko Agirre, Oier Lopez de Lacalle, and Aitor Soroa. 2014. Random Walks for Knowledge-Based Word Sense Disambiguation. *Computational Linguistics* 40(1):57–84.

Marianna Apidianaki. 2013. LIMSI: Cross-lingual Word Sense Disambiguation using Translation Sense Clustering. In *Proc. of SemEval*. pages 178–182.

Mikel Artetxe, Gorka Labaka, and Eneko Agirre. 2016. Learning Principled Bilingual Mappings of Word Embeddings while Preserving Monolingual Invariance. In *Proc. of EMNLP*. pages 2289–2294.

Giulia Bonansinga and Francis Bond. 2016. Multilingual Sense Intersection in a Parallel Corpus with Diverse Language Families. In *Proc. of the 8th Global WordNet Conference*. pages 44–49.

Hiram Calvo and Alexander Gelbukh. 2015. Is the most frequent sense of a word better connected in a semantic network? In *International Conference on Intelligent Computing*. Springer, pages 491–499.

José Camacho-Collados, Claudio Delli Bovi, Alessandro Raganato, and Roberto Navigli. 2016a. A Large-Scale Multilingual Disambiguation of Glosses. In *Proc. of LREC*. pages 1701–1708.

José Camacho-Collados, Mohammad Taher Pilehvar, and Roberto Navigli. 2016b. Nasari: Integrating explicit knowledge and corpus statistics for a multilingual representation of concepts and entities. *Artificial Intelligence* 240:36–64.

Yee Seng Chan and Hwee Tou Ng. 2005. Scaling Up Word Sense Disambiguation via Parallel Texts. In *Proc. of AAAI*. volume 5, pages 1037–1042.

J. A. Cohen. 1960. A coefficient of agreement of nominal scales. *Educational and Psychological Measurement* 20(1):37–46.

Jocelyn Coulmance, Jean-Marc Marty, Guillaume Wenzek, and Amine Benhalloum. 2015. Transgram, Fast Cross-lingual Word-embeddings. In *Proc. of EMNLP*. pages 1109–1113.

Allyson Ettinger, Philip Resnik, and Marine Carpuat. 2016. Retrofitting Sense-Specific Word Vectors Using Parallel Text. In *Proc. of NAACL-HLT*. pages 1378–1383.

Lucie Flekova and Iryna Gurevych. 2016. Supersense Embeddings: A Unified Model for Supersense Interpretation, Prediction and Utilization. In *Proc. of ACL*. pages 2029–2041.

Hila Gonen and Yoav Goldberg. 2016. Semi Supervised Preposition-Sense Disambiguation using Multilingual Data. In *Proc. of COLING*. pages 2718–2729.

Stephan Gouws, Yoshua Bengio, and Greg Corrado. 2015. BilBOWA: Fast Bilingual Distributed Representations without Word Alignments. In *Proc. of ICML*. pages 748–756.

Karl Moritz Hermann and Phil Blunsom. 2014. Multilingual Distributed Representations without Word Alignment. In *Proc. of ICLR*. pages 1–9.

Ignacio Iacobacci, Mohammad Taher Pilehvar, and Roberto Navigli. 2015. SensEmbed: Learning Sense Embeddings for Word and Relational Similarity. In *Proc. of ACL*. pages 95–105.

Ignacio Iacobacci, Mohammad Taher Pilehvar, and Roberto Navigli. 2016. Embeddings for Word Sense Disambiguation: An Evaluation Study. In *Proc. of ACL*. pages 897–907.

Mikael Kågebäck and Hans Salomonsson. 2016. Word Sense Disambiguation using a Bidirectional LSTM. In *Proc. of CogALex*. pages 51–56.

Philipp Koehn. 2005. Europarl: A Parallel Corpus for Statistical Machine Translation. In *Proc. of MT summit*. volume 5, pages 79–86.

Els Lefever and Veronique Hoste. 2010. SemEval-2010 Task 3: Cross-lingual Word Sense Disambiguation. In *Proc. of SemEval*. pages 15–20.

Els Lefever and Véronique Hoste. 2013. SemEval-2013 task 10: Cross-lingual Word Sense Disambiguation. In *Proc. of SemEval*. pages 158–166.

Els Lefever, Véronique Hoste, and Martine De Cock. 2011. ParaSense or How to Use Parallel Corpora for Word Sense Disambiguation. In *Proc. of ACL-HLT*. pages 317–322.

Oren Melamud, Jacob Goldberger, and Ido Dagan. 2016. context2vec: Learning Generic Context Embedding with Bidirectional LSTM. In *Proc. of CONLL*. pages 51–61.

Tomas Mikolov, Kai Chen, Greg Corrado, and Jeffrey Dean. 2013. Efficient Estimation of Word Representations in Vector Space. *CoRR* abs/1301.3781.

George A. Miller, Claudia Leacock, Randee Tengi, and Ross T. Bunker. 1993. A semantic concordance. In *Proc. of HLT*. pages 303–308.

Andrea Moro and Roberto Navigli. 2015. SemEval-2015 Task 13: Multilingual All-Words Sense Disambiguation and Entity Linking. *Proc. of SemEval* pages 288–297.

Andrea Moro, Roberto Navigli, Francesco Maria Tucci, and Rebecca J. Passonneau. 2014a. Annotating the MASC Corpus with BabelNet. In *Proc. of LREC*. pages 4214–4219.

Andrea Moro, Alessandro Raganato, and Roberto Navigli. 2014b. Entity Linking meets Word Sense Disambiguation: a Unified Approach. *Transactions of the Association for Computational Linguistics* 2:231–244.

Roberto Navigli. 2009. Word Sense Disambiguation: A survey. *ACM Computing Surveys* 41(2):1–69.

Roberto Navigli, David Jurgens, and Daniele Vannella. 2013. SemEval-2013 Task 12: Multilingual Word Sense Disambiguation. In *Proc. of SemEval*. pages 222–231.

Roberto Navigli and Simone Paolo Ponzetto. 2012. BabelNet: The Automatic Construction, Evaluation and Application of a Wide-Coverage Multilingual Semantic Network. *Artificial Intelligence* 193:217–250.

Hwee Tou Ng, Bin Wang, and Yee Seng Chan. 2003. Exploiting Parallel Texts for Word Sense Disambiguation: An Empirical Study. In *Proc. of ACL*. pages 455–462.

Arantxa Otegi, Nora Aranberri, Antonio Branco, Jan Hajic, Steven Neale, Petya Osenova, Rita Pereira, Martin Popel, Joao Silva, Kiril Simov, and Eneko Agirre. 2016. QTLeap WSD/NED Corpora: Semantic Annotation of Parallel Corpora in Six Languages. In *Proc. of LREC*. pages 3023–3030.

Rebecca J. Passonneau, Collin Baker, Christiane Fellbaum, and Nancy Ide. 2012. The MASC Word Sense Sentence Corpus. In *Proc. of LREC*. pages 3025–3030.

Tommaso Petrolito and Francis Bond. 2014. A Survey of WordNet Annotated Corpora. In *Proc. of the 7th Global WordNet Conference*. pages 236–245.

Mohammad Taher Pilehvar and Roberto Navigli. 2014. A large-scale pseudoword-based evaluation framework for state-of-the-art Word Sense Disambiguation. *Computational Linguistics* 40(4):837–881.

Alessandro Raganato, Claudio Delli Bovi, and Roberto Navigli. 2016. Automatic Construction and Evaluation of a Large Semantically Enriched Wikipedia. In *Proc. of IJCAI*. pages 2894–2900.

Alessandro Raganato, Jose Camacho-Collados, and Roberto Navigli. 2017. Word Sense Disambiguation: A Unified Evaluation Framework and Empirical Comparison. In *Proc. of EACL*. pages 99–110.

Delip Rao, Paul McNamee, and Mark Dredze. 2013. Entity Linking: Finding extracted entities in a knowledge base. *Multi-Source, Multilingual Information Extraction and Summarization* 11:93–115.

Helmut Schmid. 1995. Improvements In Part-of-Speech Tagging With an Application To German. In *Proc. of the ACL SIGDAT-Workshop*. pages 47–50.

Lenhart Schubert. 2006. Turing's Dream and the Knowledge Challenge. In *Proc. of AAAI*. pages 1534–1538.

Federico Scozzafava, Alessandro Raganato, Andrea Moro, and Roberto Navigli. 2015. Automatic identification and disambiguation of concepts and named entities in the multilingual Wikipedia. In *AI*IA*, Springer, pages 357–366.

Simon Šuster, Ivan Titov, and Gertjan van Noord. 2016. Bilingual Learning of Multi-sense Embeddings with Discrete Autoencoders. In *Proc. of NAACL-HLT*. pages 1346–1356.

Kaveh Taghipour and Hwee Tou Ng. 2015a. One Million Sense-Tagged Instances for Word Sense Disambiguation and Induction. In *Proc. of CoNLL*. pages 338–344.

Kaveh Taghipour and Hwee Tou Ng. 2015b. Semi-Supervised Word Sense Disambiguation Using Word Embeddings in General and Specific Domains. *Proc. of NAACL-HLT* pages 314–323.

Jörg Tiedemann. 2012. Parallel Data, Tools and Interfaces in OPUS. In *Proc. of LREC*. pages 2214–2218.

Ivan Vulić and Anna Korhonen. 2016. On the Role of Seed Lexicons in Learning Bilingual Word Embeddings. In *Proc. of ACL*. pages 247–257.

Yogarshi Vyas and Marine Carpuat. 2016. Sparse Bilingual Word Representations for Cross-lingual Lexical Entailment. In *Proc. of NAACL-HLT*. pages 1187–1197.

Dirk Weissenborn, Leonhard Hennig, Feiyu Xu, and Hans Uszkoreit. 2015. Multi-Objective Optimization for the Joint Disambiguation of Nouns and Named Entities. In *Proc. of ACL*. pages 596–605.

Xuchen Yao, Benjamin Van Durme, and Chris Callison-Burch. 2012. Expectations of Word Sense in Parallel Corpora. In *Proc. of NAACL-HLT*. pages 621–625.

Dayu Yuan, Julian Richardson, Ryan Doherty, Colin Evans, and Eric Altendorf. 2016. Semi-supervised Word Sense Disambiguation with Neural Models. In *Proc. of COLING*. pages 1374–1385.

Zhi Zhong and Hwee Tou Ng. 2010. It Makes Sense: A Wide-Coverage Word Sense Disambiguation System for Free Text. In *Proc. of ACL System Demonstrations*. pages 78–83.

Challenging Language-Dependent Segmentation for Arabic:
An Application to Machine Translation and Part-of-Speech Tagging

Hassan Sajjad   Fahim Dalvi   Nadir Durrani   Ahmed Abdelali
Yonatan Belinkov*   Stephan Vogel

Qatar Computing Research Institute – HBKU, Doha, Qatar
{hsajjad, faimaduddin, ndurrani, aabdelali, svogel}@qf.org.qa

*MIT Computer Science and Artificial Intelligence Laboratory, Cambridge, MA 02139, USA
belinkov@mit.edu

Abstract

Word segmentation plays a pivotal role in improving any Arabic NLP application. Therefore, a lot of research has been spent in improving its accuracy. Off-the-shelf tools, however, are: i) complicated to use and ii) domain/dialect dependent. We explore three language-independent alternatives to morphological segmentation using: i) data-driven sub-word units, ii) characters as a unit of learning, and iii) word embeddings learned using a character CNN (Convolution Neural Network). On the tasks of Machine Translation and POS tagging, we found these methods to achieve close to, and occasionally surpass state-of-the-art performance. In our analysis, we show that a neural machine translation system is sensitive to the ratio of source and target tokens, and a ratio close to 1 or greater, gives optimal performance.

1 Introduction

Arabic word segmentation has shown to significantly improve output quality in NLP tasks such as machine translation (Habash and Sadat, 2006; Almahairi et al., 2016), part-of-speech tagging (Diab et al., 2004; Habash and Rambow, 2005), and information retrieval (M. Aljlayl and Grossman, 2002). A considerable amount of research has therefore been spent on Arabic morphological segmentation in the past two decades, ranging from rule-based analyzers (Beesley, 1996) to state-of-the-art statistical segmenters (Pasha et al., 2014; Abdelali et al., 2016; Khalifa et al., 2016). Morphological segmentation splits words into morphemes. For example, "*wktAbnA*" "وكتابنا" (gloss: and our book) is decomposed into its stem and affixes as: "*w+ ktAb +nA*" "و+ كتاب +نا".

Despite the gains obtained from using morphological segmentation, there are several caveats to using these tools. Firstly, they make the training pipeline cumbersome, as they come with complicated pre-processing (and additional post-processing in the case of English-to-Arabic translation (El Kholy and Habash, 2012)). More importantly, these tools are dialect- and domain-specific. A segmenter trained for modern standard Arabic (MSA) performs significantly worse on dialectal Arabic (Habash et al., 2013), or when it is applied to a new domain.

In this work, we explore whether we can avoid the *language-dependent* pre/post-processing components and learn segmentation directly from the training data being used for a given task. We investigate data-driven alternatives to morphological segmentation using i) unsupervised sub-word units obtained using byte-pair encoding (Sennrich et al., 2016), ii) purely character-based segmentation (Ling et al., 2015), and iii) a convolutional neural network over characters (Kim et al., 2016).

We evaluate these techniques on the tasks of machine translation (MT) and part-of-speech (POS) tagging and compare them against morphological segmenters MADAMIRA (Pasha et al., 2014) and Farasa (Abdelali et al., 2016). On the MT task, byte-pair encoding (BPE) performs the best among the three methods, achieving very similar performance to morphological segmentation in the Arabic-to-English direction and slightly worse in the other direction. Character-based methods, in comparison, perform better on the task of POS tagging, reaching an accuracy of 95.9%, only 1.3% worse than morphological segmentation. We also analyze the effect of segmentation granularity of Arabic on the quality of MT. We observed that a neural MT (NMT) system is sensitive to source/target token ratio and performs best when this ratio is close to or greater than 1.

Proceedings of the 55th Annual Meeting of the Association for Computational Linguistics (Short Papers), pages 601–607
Vancouver, Canada, July 30 - August 4, 2017. ©2017 Association for Computational Linguistics
https://doi.org/10.18653/v1/P17-2095

2 Segmentation Approaches

We experimented with three data-driven segmentation schemes: i) morphological segmentation, ii) sub-word segmentation based on BPE, and iii) two variants of character-based segmentation. We first map each source word to its corresponding segments (depending on the segmentation scheme), embed all segments of a word in vector space and feed them one-by-one to an encoder-decoder model. See Figure 1 for illustration.

2.1 Morphological Segmentation

There is a vast amount of work on statistical segmentation for Arabic. Here we use the state-of-the-art Arabic segmenter MADAMIRA and Farasa as our baselines. MADAMIRA involves a morphological analyzer that generates a list of possible word-level analyses (independent of context). The analyses are provided with the original text to a `Feature Modeling` component that applies an SVM and a language model to make predictions, which are scored by an `Analysis Ranking` component. Farasa on the other hand is a light weight segmenter, which ignores context and instead uses a variety of features and lexicons for segmentation.

2.2 Data Driven Sub-word Units

A number of data-driven approaches have been proposed that learn to segment words into smaller units from data (Demberg, 2007; Sami Virpioja and Kurimo, 2013) and shown to improve phrase-based MT (Fishel and Kirik, 2010; Stallard et al., 2012). Recently, with the advent of neural MT, a few sub-word-based techniques have been proposed that segment words into smaller units to tackle the limited vocabulary and unknown word problems (Sennrich et al., 2016; Wu et al., 2016).

In this work, we explore *Byte-Pair Encoding* (BPE), a data compression algorithm (Gage, 1994) as an alternative to morphological segmentation of Arabic. BPE splits words into symbols (a sequence of characters) and then iteratively replaces the most frequent symbols with their merged variants. In essence, frequent character n-gram sequences will be merged to form one symbol. The number of merge operations is controlled by a hyper-parameter OP which directly affects the granularity of segmentation: a high value of OP means coarse segmentation and a low value means fine-grained segmentation.

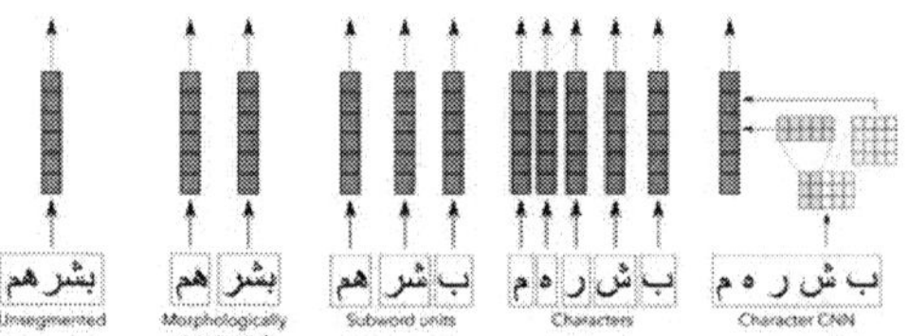

Figure 1: Segmentation approaches for the word "b$rhm" "بشرهم"; the blue vectors indicate the embedding(s) used before the encoding layer.

2.3 Character-level Encoding

Character-based models have been found to be effective in translating closely related language pairs (Durrani et al., 2010; Nakov and Tiedemann, 2012) and OOV words (Durrani et al., 2014). Ling et al. (2016) used character embeddings to address the OOV word problem. We explored them as an alternative to morphological segmentation. Their advantage is that character embeddings do not require any complicated pre- and post-processing step other than segmenting words into characters. The fully character-level encoder treats the source sentence as a sequence of letters, encoding each letter (including white-space) in the LSTM encoder (see Figure 1). The decoding may follow identical settings. We restricted the character-level representation to the Arabic side of the parallel corpus and use words for the English side.

Character-CNN   Kim et al. (2016) presented a neural language model that takes character-level input and learns word embeddings using a CNN over characters. The embedding are then provided to the encoder as input. The intuition is that the character-based word embedding should be able to learn the morphological phenomena a word inherits. Compared to fully character-level encoding, the encoder gets word-level embeddings as in the case of unsegmented words (see Figure 1). However, the word embedding is intuitively richer than the embedding learned over unsegmented words because of the convolution over characters. The method was previously shown to help neural MT (Belinkov and Glass, 2016; Costa-jussà and Fonollosa, 2016). Belinkov et al. (2017) also showed character-based representations learned using a CNN to be superior, at learning word morphology, than their word-based counter-parts. However, they did not compare these against BPE-based segmentation. We use character-CNN to aid Arabic word segmentation.

# SEG	Arabic-to-English					English-to-Arabic				
	tst11	tst12	tst13	tst14	AVG.	tst11	tst12	tst13	tst14	AVG.
UNSEG	25.7	28.2	27.3	23.9	26.3	15.8	17.1	18.1	15.5	16.6
MORPH	29.2	33.0	32.9	28.3	30.9	16.5	18.8	20.4	17.2	**18.2**
cCNN	29.0	32.0	32.5	28.0	30.3	14.3	12.8	13.6	12.6	13.3
CHAR	28.8	31.8	32.5	27.8	30.2	15.3	17.1	18.0	15.3	16.4
BPE	29.7	32.5	33.6	28.4	**31.1**	17.5	18.0	20.0	16.6	18.0

Table 1: Results of comparing several segmentation strategies.

3 Experiments

In the following, we describe the data and system settings and later present the results of machine translation and POS tagging.

3.1 Settings

Data The MT systems were trained on 1.2 Million sentences, a concatenation of TED corpus (Cettolo et al., 2012), LDC NEWS data, QED (Guzmán et al., 2013) and an MML-filtered (Axelrod et al., 2011) UN corpus.[1] We used dev+test10 for tuning and tst11-14 for testing. For English-Arabic, outputs were detokenized using MADA detokenizer. Before scoring the output, we normalized them and reference translations using the QCRI normalizer (Sajjad et al., 2013).

POS tagging We used parts 2-3 (v3.1-2) of the Arabic Treebank (Mohamed Maamouri, 2010). The data consists of 18268 sentences (483,909 words). We used 80% for training, 5% for development and the remaining for test.

Segmentation MADAMIRA and Farasa normalize the data before segmentation. In order to have consistent data, we normalize it for all segmentation approaches. For BPE, we tuned the value of merge operations OP and found 30k and 90k to be optimal for Ar-to-En and En-to-Ar respectively. In case of *no segmentation* (UNSEG) and *character-CNN* (cCNN), we tokenized the Arabic with the standard Moses tokenizer, which separates punctuation marks. For *character-level* encoding (CHAR), we preserved word boundaries by replacing space with a special symbol and then separated every character with a space. English-side is tokenized/truecased using Moses scripts.

Neural MT Settings We used the *seq2seq-attn* (Kim, 2016) implementation, with 2 layers of LSTM in the (bidirectional) encoder and the decoder, with a size of 500. We limit the sentence length to 100 for MORPH, UNSEG, BPE, cCNN, and 500 for CHAR experiments. The source and target vocabularies are limited to 50k each.

3.2 Machine Translation Results

Table 1 presents MT results using various segmentation strategies. Compared to the UNSEG system, the MORPH system[2] improved translation quality by 4.6 and 1.6 BLEU points in Ar-to-En and En-to-Ar systems, respectively. The results also improved by up to 3 BLEU points for cCNN and CHAR systems in the Ar-to-En direction. However, the performance is lower by at least 0.6 BLEU points compared to the MORPH system.

In the En-to-Ar direction, where cCNN and CHAR are applied on the target side, the performance dropped significantly. In the case of CHAR, mapping one source word to many target characters makes it harder for NMT to learn a good model. This is in line with our finding on using a lower value of OP for BPE segmentation (see paragraph **Analyzing the effect of OP**). Surprisingly, the cCNN system results were inferior to the UNSEG system for En-to-Ar. A possible explanation is that the decoder's predictions are still done at word level even when using the cCNN model (which encodes the target input during training but not the output). In practice, this can lead to generating unknown words. Indeed, in the Ar-to-En case cCNN significantly reduces the unknown words in the test sets, while in the En-to-Ar case the number of unknown words remains roughly the same between UNSEG and cCNN.

The BPE system outperformed all other systems in the Ar-to-En direction and is lower than MORPH by only 0.2 BLEU points in the opposite direction. This shows that machine translation involving the

---

[1]We used 3.75% as reported to be optimal filtering threshold in (Durrani et al., 2016).

[2]Farasa performed better in the Ar-to-En experiments and MADAMIRA performed better in the En-to-Ar direction. We used best results as our baselines for comparison and call them MORPH.

Arabic language can achieve competitive results with data-driven segmentation. This comes with an additional benefit of *language-independent* pre-processing and post-processing pipeline. In an attempt to find, whether the gains obtained from data-driven segmentation techniques and morphological segmentation are additive, we applied BPE to morphological segmented data. We saw further improvement of up to 1 BLEU point by using the two segmentations in tandem.

Analyzing the effect of OP: The unsegmented training data consists of 23M Arabic tokens and 28M English tokens. The parameter OP decides the granularity of segmentation: a higher value of OP means fewer segments. For example, at OP=50k, the number of Arabic tokens is greater by 7% compared to OP=90k. We tested four different values of OP (15k, 30k, 50k, and 90k). Figure 2 summarizes our findings on test-2011 dataset, where x-axis presents the ratio of source to target language tokens and y-axis shows the BLEU score. The boundary values for segmentation are character-level segmentation (OP=0) and unsegmented text (OP=N).[3] For both language directions, we observed that a source to target token ratio close to 1 and greater works best provided that the boundary conditions (unsegmented Arabic and character-level segmentation) are avoided. In the En-to-Ar direction, the system improves for coarse segmentation whereas in the Ar-to-En direction, a much finer-grained segmentation of Arabic performed better. This is in line with the ratio of tokens generated using the MORPH systems (Ar-to-En ratio = 1.02). Generalizing from the perspective of neural MT, the system learns better when total numbers of source and target tokens are close to each other. The system shows better tolerance towards modeling many source words to a few target words compared to the other way around.

Discussion: Though BPE performed well for machine translation, there are a few reservations that we would like to discuss here. Since the main goal of the algorithm is to compress data and segmentation comes as a by-product, it often produces different segmentations of a root word when occurred in different morphological forms. For example, the words *driven* and *driving* are segmented as *driv en* and *drivi ng* respectively. This adds ambiguity to the data and may result in un-

---

[3] N is the number of types in the unsegmented corpus.

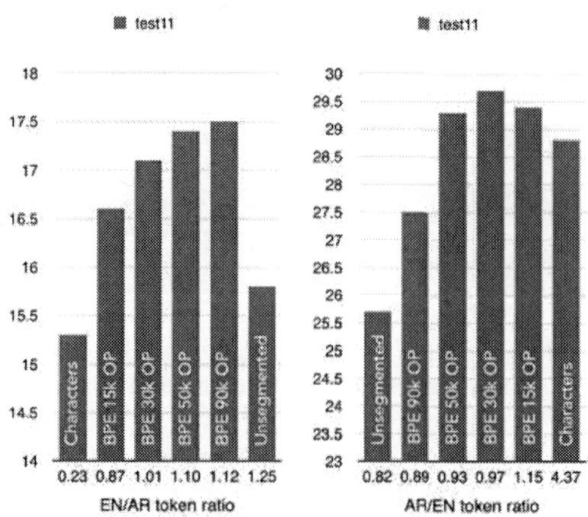

Figure 2: Source/Target token ratio with varying OP versus BLEU. Character and unsegmented systems can be seen as BPE with OP=0 and OP=N.

expected translation errors. Another limitation of BPE is that at test time, it may divide the unknown words to semantically different known sub-word units which can result in a semantically wrong translation. For example, the word "قطر" is unknown to our vocabulary. BPE segmented it into known units which ended up being translated to *courage*. One possible solution to this problem is; at test time, BPE is applied to those words only which were known to the full vocabulary of the training corpus. In this way, the sub-word units created by BPE for the word are already seen in a similar context during training and the model has learned to translate them correctly. The downside of this method is that it limits BPE's power to segment unknown words to their correct sub-word units and outputs them as *UNK* in translation.

3.3 Part of Speech Tagging

We also experimented with the aforementioned segmentation strategies for the task of Arabic POS tagging. Probabilistic taggers like HMM-based (Brants, 2000) and sequence learning models like CRF (Lafferty et al., 2001) consider previous words and/or tags to predict the tag of the current word. We mimic a similar setting but in a sequence-to-sequence learning framework. Figure 3 describes a step by step procedure to train a neural encoder-decoder tagger. Consider an Arabic phrase "klm >SdqA}k b$rhm" "كلم أصدقائك بشرهم" (gloss: call your friends give them the good news), we want to learn the tag

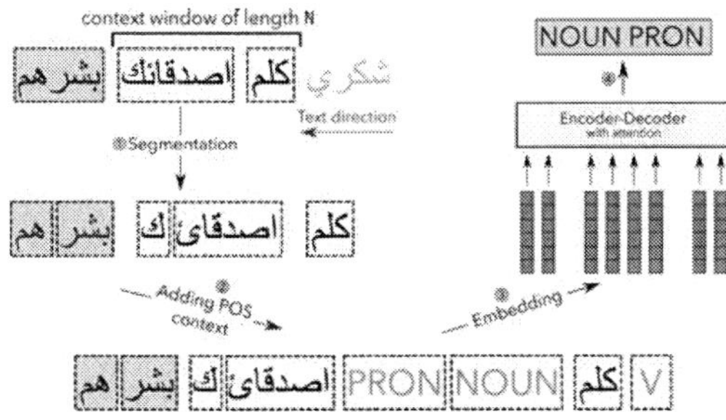

Figure 3: Seq-to-Seq POS Tagger: The number of segments and the embeddings depend on the segmentation scheme used (See Figure 1).

of the word "بشرهم" using the context of the previous two words and their tags. First, we segment the phrase using a segmentation approach (step 1) and then add POS tags to context words (step 2). The entire sequence with the words and tags is fed to the sequence-to-sequence framework. The embeddings (for both words and tags) are learned jointly with other parameters in an end-to-end fashion, and optimized on the target tag sequence; for example, "NOUN PRON" in this case.

For a given word w_i in a sentence $s = \{w_1, w_2, ..., w_M\}$ and its POS tag t_i, We formulate the neural TAGGER as follows:

$$\text{SEGMENTER}(\tau) : \forall w_i \mapsto S_i$$
$$\text{TAGGER} : S_{i-2} \ S_{i-1} \ S_i \mapsto t_i$$

where S_i is the segmentation of word w_i. In case of UNSEG and cCNN, S_i would be same as w_i. SEGMENTER here is identical to the one described in Figure 1. TAGGER is a NMT architecture that learns to predict a POS tag of a segmented/unsegmented word given previous two words.[4]

Table 2 summarizes the results. The MORPH system performed best with an improvement of 5.3% over UNSEG. Among the data-driven methods, CHAR model performed best and was behind MORPH by only 0.3%. Even though BPE was inferior compared to other methods, it was still better than UNSEG by 4%.[5]

Analysis of POS outputs We performed a comparative error analysis of predictions made

SEG	UNSEG	MORPH	CHAR	cCNN	BPE
ACC	90.9	96.2	95.9	95.8	94.9

Table 2: POS tagging with various segmentations

through MORPH, CHAR and BPE based segmentations. MORPH and CHAR observed very similar error patterns, with most confusion between *Foreign* and *Particle* tags. In addition to this confusion, BPE had relatively scattered errors. It had lower precision in predicting nouns and had confused them with adverbs, foreign words and adjectives. This is expected, since most nouns are out-of-vocabulary terms, and therefore get segmented by BPE into smaller, possibly known fragments, which then get confused with other tags. However, since the accuracies are quite close, the overall errors are very few and similar between the various systems. We also analyzed the number of tags that are output by the sequence-to-sequence model using various segmentation schemes. In 99.95% of the cases, the system learned to output the correct number of tags, regardless of the number of source segments.

4 Conclusion

We explored several alternatives to language-dependent segmentation of Arabic and evaluated them on the tasks of machine translation and POS tagging. On the machine translation task, BPE segmentation produced the best results and even outperformed the state-of-the-art morphological segmentation in the Arabic-to-English direction. On the POS tagging task, character-based models got closest to using the state-of-the-art segmentation. Our results showed that data-driven segmentation schemes can serve as an alternative to heavily engineered language-dependent tools and achieve very competitive results. In our analysis we showed that NMT performs better when the source to target token ratio is close to one or greater.

Acknowledgments

We would like to thank the three anonymous reviewers for their useful suggestions. This research was carried out in collaboration between the HBKU Qatar Computing Research Institute (QCRI) and the MIT Computer Science and Artificial Intelligence Laboratory (CSAIL).

---

[4]We also tried using previous words with their POS tags as context but did not see any significant difference in the end result.

[5]Optimizing the parameter OP did not yield any difference in accuracy. We used $10k$ operations.

References

Ahmed Abdelali, Kareem Darwish, Nadir Durrani, and Hamdy Mubarak. 2016. Farasa: A fast and furious segmenter for arabic. In *Proceedings of the 2016 Conference of the North American Chapter of the Association for Computational Linguistics: Demonstrations*. San Diego, California.

Amjad Almahairi, Cho Kyunghyun, Nizar Habash, and Aaron Courville. 2016. First result on Arabic neural machine translation. In *https://arxiv.org/abs/1606.02680*.

Amittai Axelrod, Xiaodong He, and Jianfeng Gao. 2011. Domain adaptation via pseudo in-domain data selection. In *Proceedings of the Conference on Empirical Methods in Natural Language Processing*. Edinburgh, United Kingdom, EMNLP '11.

Kenneth R Beesley. 1996. Arabic finite-state morphological analysis and generation. In *ACL*. pages 89–94.

Yonatan Belinkov, Nadir Durrani, Fahim Dalvi, Hassan Sajjad, and James Glass. 2017. What do Neural Machine Translation Models Learn about Morphology? In *Proceedings of the 55th Annual Meeting of the Association for Computational Linguistics*. Association for Computational Linguistics, Vancouver, Canada.

Yonatan Belinkov and James Glass. 2016. Arabic and hebrew: Available corpora and initial results. In *Proceedings of the Workshop on Semitic Machine Translation*.

Thorsten Brants. 2000. Tnt: A statistical part-of-speech tagger. In *Proceedings of the Sixth Conference on Applied Natural Language Processing*. ANLC '00, pages 224–231. https://doi.org/10.3115/974147.974178.

Mauro Cettolo, Christian Girardi, and Marcello Federico. 2012. WIT^3: Web Inventory of Transcribed and Translated Talks. In *Proceedings of the 16th Conference of the European Association for Machine Translation (EAMT)*. Trento, Italy, pages 261–268.

Marta R. Costa-jussà and José A. R. Fonollosa. 2016. Character-based neural machine translation. In *Proceedings of the 54th Annual Meeting of the Association for Computational Linguistics (Volume 2: Short Papers)*. Association for Computational Linguistics, Berlin, Germany, pages 357–361. http://anthology.aclweb.org/P16-2058.

Vera Demberg. 2007. A language independent unsupervised model for morphological segmentation. In *In Proceedings of the 45th Annual Meeting of the Association of Computational Linguistics*.

Mona Diab, Kadri Hacioglu, and Daniel Jurafsky. 2004. Automatic tagging of arabic text: From raw text to base phrase chunks. In *Proceedings of HLT-NAACL 2004: Short Papers*. Stroudsburg, PA, USA, HLT-NAACL-Short '04.

Nadir Durrani, Fahim Dalvi, Hassan Sajjad, and Stephan Vogel. 2016. QCRI machine translation systems for IWSLT 16. In *Proceedings of the 15th International Workshop on Spoken Language Translation*. Seattle, WA, USA, IWSLT '16.

Nadir Durrani, Hassan Sajjad, Alexander Fraser, and Helmut Schmid. 2010. Hindi-to-Urdu Machine Translation through Transliteration. In *Proceedings of the 48th Annual Meeting of the Association for Computational Linguistics*. Association for Computational Linguistics, Uppsala, Sweden, pages 465–474. http://www.aclweb.org/anthology/P10-1048.

Nadir Durrani, Hassan Sajjad, Hieu Hoang, and Philipp Koehn. 2014. Integrating an unsupervised transliteration model into statistical machine translation. In *Proceedings of the 15th Conference of the European Chapter of the ACL (EACL 2014)*. Gothenburg, Sweden.

Ahmed El Kholy and Nizar Habash. 2012. Orthographic and morphological processing for English–Arabic statistical machine translation. *Machine Translation* 26(1-2).

Mark Fishel and Harri Kirik. 2010. Linguistically motivated unsupervised segmentation for machine translation. In *In Proceedings of the seventh International Conference on Language Resources and Evaluation (LREC*.

Philip Gage. 1994. A new algorithm for data compression. *C Users J.* 12(2):23–38. http://dl.acm.org/citation.cfm?id=177910.177914.

Francisco Guzmán, Hassan Sajjad, Stephan Vogel, and Ahmed Abdelali. 2013. The AMARA corpus: Building resources for translating the web's educational content. In *Proceedings of the 10th International Workshop on Spoken Language Technology (IWSLT-13)*.

Nizar Habash and Owen Rambow. 2005. Arabic tokenization, part-of-speech tagging and morphological disambiguation in one fell swoop. In *Proceedings of the 43rd Annual Meeting on Association for Computational Linguistics*. Stroudsburg, PA, USA, ACL '05.

Nizar Habash, Ryan Roth, Owen Rambow, Ramy Esk, and Nadi Tomeh. 2013. Morphological analysis and disambiguation for dialectal arabic. In *In Proceedings of the 2013 Conference of the North American Chapter of the Association for Computational Linguistics: Human Language Technologies (NAACL-HLT)*.

Nizar Habash and Fatiha Sadat. 2006. Arabic preprocessing schemes for statistical machine translation. In *Proceedings of the Human Language Technology Conference of the North American Chapter of the Association for Computational Linguistics (HLT-NAACL'06)*. New York, NY, USA.

Salam Khalifa, Nasser Zalmout, and Nizar Habash. 2016. Yamama: Yet another multi-dialect arabic morphological analyzer. *Proceedings of COLING 2016, the 26th International Conference on Computational Linguistics: System Demonstrations* pages 223–227.

Yoon Kim. 2016. Seq2seq-attn. https://github.com/harvardnlp/seq2seq-attn.

Yoon Kim, Yacine Jernite, David Sontag, and Alexander Rush. 2016. Character-Aware Neural Language Models. In *AAAI Conference on Artificial Intelligence*.

John D. Lafferty, Andrew McCallum, and Fernando C. N. Pereira. 2001. Conditional random fields: Probabilistic models for segmenting and labeling sequence data. In *Proceedings of the Eighteenth International Conference on Machine Learning*. ICML '01, pages 282–289.

Wang Ling, Isabel Trancoso, Chris Dyer, and Alan W. Black. 2015. Character-based neural machine translation. *CoRR* abs/1511.04586. http://arxiv.org/abs/1511.04586.

Wang Ling, Isabel Trancoso, Chris Dyer, and Alan W. Black. 2016. Character-based neural machine translation. *arXiv preprint arXiv:1511.04586* .

O. Frieder M. Aljlayl and D. Grossman. 2002. On Arabic-English cross-language information retrieval: A machine translation approach. In *IEEE Third International Conference on Information Technology: Coding and Computing (ITCC)*.

Ann Bies Seth Kulick Sondos Krouna Fatma Gaddeche Wajdi Zaghouani Mohamed Maamouri. 2010. Arabic treebank: Part 3 v 3.2 ldc2010t08. web download. *Philadelphia: Linguistic Data Consortium* .

Preslav Nakov and Jörg Tiedemann. 2012. Combining word-level and character-level models for machine translation between closely-related languages. In *Proceedings of the 50th Annual Meeting of the Association for Computational Linguistics (Volume 2: Short Papers)*. Jeju, Korea, ACL '12, pages 301–305.

Arfath Pasha, Mohamed Al-Badrashiny, Mona Diab, Ahmed El Kholy, Ramy Eskander, Nizar Habash, Manoj Pooleery, Owen Rambow, and Ryan M Roth. 2014. MADAMIRA: A fast, comprehensive tool for morphological analysis and disambiguation of Arabic. In *Proceedings of the Language Resources and Evaluation Conference*. Reykjavik, Iceland, LREC '14, pages 1094–1101.

Hassan Sajjad, Francisco Guzmn, Preslav Nakov, Ahmed Abdelali, Kenton Murray, Fahad Al Obaidli, and Stephan Vogel. 2013. QCRI at IWSLT 2013: Experiments in Arabic-English and English-Arabic spoken language translation. In *Proceedings of the 10th International Workshop on Spoken Language Technology (IWSLT-13)*.

Peter Smit Stig-Arne Grnroos Sami Virpioja and Mikko Kurimo. 2013. Morfessor 2.0: Python implementation and extensions for morfessor baseline. In *Technical Report, Aalto University publication series SCIENCE + TECHNOLOGY*.

Rico Sennrich, Barry Haddow, and Alexandra Birch. 2016. Neural machine translation of rare words with subword units. In *Proceedings of the 54th Annual Meeting of the Association for Computational Linguistics (Volume 1: Long Papers)*. Berlin, Germany.

David Stallard, Jacob Devlin, Michael Kayser, Yoong Keok Lee, and Regina Barzilay. 2012. Unsupervised morphology rivals supervised morphology for arabic mt. In *Proceedings of the 50th Annual Meeting of the Association for Computational Linguistics: Short Papers - Volume 2*. ACL '12.

Yonghui Wu, Mike Schuster, Zhifeng Chen, Quoc V. Le, Mohammad Norouzi, Wolfgang Macherey, Maxim Krikun, Yuan Cao, Qin Gao, Klaus Macherey, Jeff Klingner, Apurva Shah, Melvin Johnson, Xiaobing Liu, ukasz Kaiser, Stephan Gouws, Yoshikiyo Kato, Taku Kudo, Hideto Kazawa, Keith Stevens, George Kurian, Nishant Patil, Wei Wang, Cliff Young, Jason Smith, Jason Riesa, Alex Rudnick, Oriol Vinyals, Greg Corrado, Macduff Hughes, and Jeffrey Dean. 2016. Google's neural machine translation system: Bridging the gap between human and machine translation. *CoRR* abs/1609.08144. http://arxiv.org/abs/1609.08144.

Fast and Accurate Neural Word Segmentation for Chinese

Deng Cai[1,2], Hai Zhao[1,2,*], Zhisong Zhang[1,2], Yuan Xin[3], Yongjian Wu[3], Feiyue Huang[3]

[1]Department of Computer Science and Engineering, Shanghai Jiao Tong University
[2]Key Lab of Shanghai Education Commission for Intelligent Interaction
and Cognitive Engineering, Shanghai Jiao Tong Univeristy, Shanghai, China
thisisjcykcd@gmail.com, {zhaohai@cs, zzs2011@}sjtu.edu.cn
[3]Tencent Youtu Lab, Shanghai, China
{macxin,littlekenwu,garyhuang}@tencent.com

Abstract

Neural models with minimal feature engineering have achieved competitive performance against traditional methods for the task of Chinese word segmentation. However, both training and working procedures of the current neural models are computationally inefficient. This paper presents a greedy neural word segmenter with balanced word and character embedding inputs to alleviate the existing drawbacks. Our segmenter is truly end-to-end, capable of performing segmentation much faster and even more accurate than state-of-the-art neural models on Chinese benchmark datasets.

1 Introduction

Word segmentation is a fundamental task for processing most east Asian languages, typically Chinese. Almost all practical Chinese processing applications essentially rely on Chinese word segmentation (CWS), e.g., (Zhao et al., 2017).

Since (Xue, 2003), most methods formalize this task as a sequence labeling problem. In a supervised learning fashion, sequence labeling may adopt various models such as Maximum Entropy (ME) (Low et al., 2005) and Conditional Random Fields (CRF) (Lafferty et al., 2001; Peng et al., 2004). However, these models rely heavily on hand-crafted features.

To minimize the efforts in feature engineering, neural word segmentation has been actively studied recently. Zheng et al. (2013) first adapted the sliding-window based sequence labeling (Collobert et al., 2011) with character embeddings as input. A number of other researchers have attempted to improve the segmenter of (Zheng et al., 2013) by augmenting it with additional complexity. Pei et al. (2014) introduced tag embeddings. Chen et al. (2015a) proposed to model n-gram features via a gated recursive neural network (GRNN). Chen et al. (2015b) used a Long short-term memory network (LSTM) (Hochreiter and Schmidhuber, 1997) to capture long-distance context. Xu and Sun (2016) integrated both GRNN and LSTM for deeper feature extraction.

Besides sequence labeling schemes, Zhang et al. (2016) proposed a transition-based framework. Liu et al. (2016) used a zero-order semi-CRF based model. However, these two models rely on either traditional discrete features or non-neural-network components for performance enhancement, their performance drops rapidly when solely depending on neural models. Most closely related to this work, Cai and Zhao (2016) proposed to score candidate segmented outputs directly, employing a gated combination neural network over characters for word representation generation and an LSTM scoring model for segmentation result evaluation.

Despite the active progress of most existing works in terms of accuracy, their computational needs have been significantly increased to the extent that training a neural segmenter usually takes days even using cutting-edge hardwares. Meanwhile, different applications often require diverse segmenters and offer large-scale incoming data. The efficiency of a word segmenter either for training and decoding is crucial in practice. In this paper, we propose a simple yet accurate neu-

---
[*]Corresponding author. This paper was partially supported by Cai Yuanpei Program (CSC No. 201304490199 and No. 201304490171), National Natural Science Foundation of China (No. 61170114, No. 61672343 and No. 61272248), National Basic Research Program of China (No. 2013CB329401), Major Basic Research Program of Shanghai Science and Technology Committee (No. 15JC1400103), Art and Science Interdisciplinary Funds of Shanghai Jiao Tong University (No. 14JCRZ04), Key Project of National Society Science Foundation of China (No. 15-ZDA041), and the joint research project with Youtu Lab of Tencent.

Proceedings of the 55th Annual Meeting of the Association for Computational Linguistics (Short Papers), pages 608–615
Vancouver, Canada, July 30 - August 4, 2017. ©2017 Association for Computational Linguistics
https://doi.org/10.18653/v1/P17-2096

ral word segmenter who searches greedily during both training and working to overcome the existing efficiency obstacle. Our evaluation will be performed on Chinese benchmark datasets.

2 Related Work

Statistical Chinese word segmentation has been studied for decades (Huang and Zhao, 2007). (Xue, 2003) was the first to cast it as a character-based tagging problem. Peng et al. (2004) showed CRF based model is particularly effective to solve CWS in the sequence labeling fashion. This method has been followed by most later segmenters (Tseng et al., 2005; Zhao et al., 2006; Zhao and Kit, 2008c; Zhao et al., 2010; Sun et al., 2012; Zhang et al., 2013). The same spirit has also be followed by most neural models (Zheng et al., 2013; Pei et al., 2014; Qi et al., 2014; Chen et al., 2015a,b; Ma and Hinrichs, 2015; Xu and Sun, 2016).

Word based CWS to conveniently incorporate complete word features has also be explored. Andrew (2006) proposed a semi-CRF model. Zhang and Clark (2007, 2011) used a perceptron algorithm with inexact search. Both of them have been followed by neural model versions (Liu et al., 2016) and (Zhang et al., 2016) respectively. There are also works integrating both character-based and word-based segmenters (Huang and Zhao, 2006; Sun, 2010; Wang et al., 2014) and semi-supervised learning (Zhao and Kit, 2008b, 2011; Zeng et al., 2013; Zhang et al., 2013).

Unlike most previous works, which extract features within a fixed sized sliding window, Cai and Zhao (2016) proposed a direct segmentation framework that extends the feature window to cover complete input and segmentation history and uses beam search for decoding. In this work, we will make a series of significant improvement over the basic framework and especially adopt greedy search instead.

Another notable exception of embedding based methods is (Ma and Hinrichs, 2015), which used character-specified tags matching for fast decoding and resulted in a character-based greedy segmenter.

3 Models

To segment a character sequence, we employ neural networks to score the likelihood of a candidate segmented sequence being a true sentence, and the

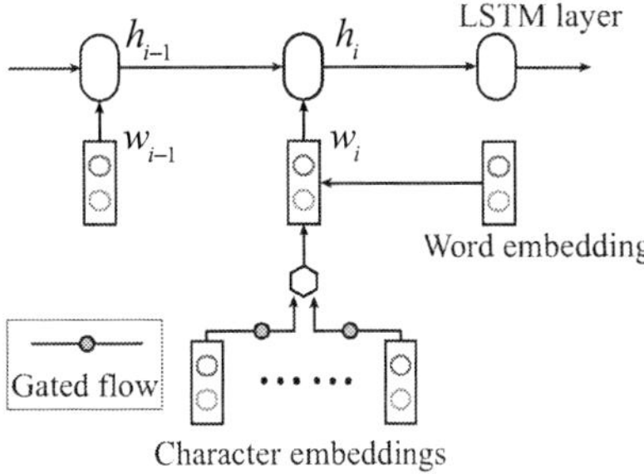

Figure 1: Neural network scoring for word candidate w_i in a possible word sequence $(..., w_i, ...)$.

one with the highest score will be picked as output.

3.1 Neural Scorer

Our neural architecture to score a segmented sequence (word sequence) can be described in the following three steps (illustrated in Figure 1).

Encoding To make use of neural networks, symbolic data needs to be transformed into distributed representations. The most straightforward solution is to use a lookup table for word vectors (Bengio et al., 2003). However, in the context of neural word segmentation, it will generalize poorly due to the severe word sparsity in Chinese. An alternative is employing neural networks to compose word representations from character embedding inputs. However, it is empirically hard to learn a satisfactory composition function. In fact, quite a lot of Chinese words, like "沙(sand)发(issue)" (sofa) , are not semantically character-level compositional at all.

For the dilemma that composing word representations from character may be insufficient while the direct use of word embedding may lose generalization ability, we propose a hybrid mechanism to alleviate the problem. Concretely, we keep a short list $\mathcal{H}$ of the most frequent words $w = c_1..c_l$ to balance character composition. If w in $\mathcal{H}$, the immediate word embedding $\mathbf{w} \in \mathbb{R}^{d_w}$ is attached via average pooling[1], otherwise, the character composition is used alone.

$$\text{WORD}(c_1..c_l) = \begin{cases} \frac{\text{COMP}(c_1..c_l)+\mathbf{w}[w]}{2} & \text{if } c_1..c_l \in \mathcal{H} \\ \text{COMP}(c_1..c_l) & \text{otherwise} \end{cases}$$

Our character composition function $\text{COMP}(\cdot)$ for

---

[1]We tried other two integration functions, concatenation and adaptive gating mechanism, but it finally shows that the simplest averaging works best.

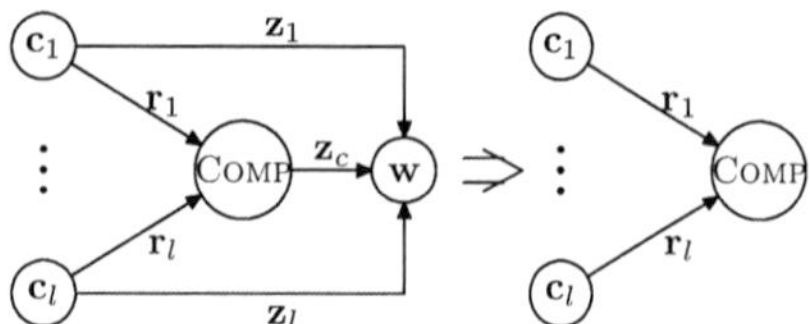

Figure 2: The difference between (Cai and Zhao, 2016) (left) and our model (right).

l-length word is

$$\text{COMP}(c_1..c_l) = \tanh(\mathbf{W}_l^c[\mathbf{r}_1 \odot \mathbf{c}_1; \dots; \mathbf{r}_l \odot \mathbf{c}_l] + \mathbf{b}_l^c)$$

where $\odot$ denotes the element-wise multiplication. $\mathbf{r}_i \in \mathbb{R}^{d_c}$ is the gate that controls the information flow from character embedding $\mathbf{c}_i \in \mathbb{R}^{d_c}$ to word. Intuitively, the gating mechanism is used to determine which part of the character vectors should be retrieved when composing a certain word. This is indeed important due to the ambiguity of individual Chinese characters.

$$[\mathbf{r}_1; \dots; \mathbf{r}_l] = \text{sigmoid}(\mathbf{W}_l^r[\mathbf{c}_1; \dots; \mathbf{c}_l] + \mathbf{b}_l^r)$$

In contrast, the model in (Cai and Zhao, 2016) further combined $\text{COMP}(\cdot)$ and character embeddings $\mathbf{c}_i$ via an update gate $\mathbf{z}$ (As in Figure 2), which has been shown helpless to the performance but requires huge computational cost according to our empirical study.

Linking To capture word interactions within a word sequence, the resulted word vectors are then linked sequentially via an LSTM (Sundermeyer et al., 2012). At each time step i, a prediction about next word is made according to the current hidden state $\mathbf{h}_i \in \mathbb{R}^H$ of LSTM. The procedure can be described as the following equation.

$$\mathbf{p}_{i+1} = \tanh(\mathbf{W}^p \mathbf{h}_i + \mathbf{b}^p)$$

The predictions $\mathbf{p} \in \mathbb{R}^{d_w}$ will then be used to evaluate how reasonable the transition is between next word and the preceding word sequence.

Scoring The segmented sequence is evaluated from two perspectives, (i) the legality of individual words, (ii) the smoothness or coherence of the word sequence. The former is judged by a trainable parameter vector $\mathbf{u} \in \mathbb{R}^{d_w}$, which is supposed to work like a hyperplane separating legal and illegal words. For the latter, the prediction $\mathbf{p}$ made for each position can be used to score the fitness of the

actual word. Both scoring operations are implemented via dot product in our settings. Summing up all scores, the segmented sequence (sentence) is scored as follow.

$$s([w_1, w_2, \dots, w_n]) = \sum_{i=1}^{n} (\mathbf{u} + \mathbf{p}_i)^{\mathrm{T}} \text{WORD}(w_i)$$

3.2 Search

The number of possible segmented sentences grows exponentially with the length of the input character sequence. Most existing methods made Markov assumptions to keep the exact search tractable.[2] However, such assumptions cannot be made in our model as the LSTM component takes advantage of the full segmentation history. We then adopt a beam search scheme, which works iteratively on every prefix of the input character sequence, approximating the k highest-scored word sequences of each prefix (i.e., k is the beam size). The time complexity of our beam search is $O(wkn)$, where w is the maximum word length and n is the input sequence length.

3.3 Training Criteria

Our segmenter is trained using max-margin methods (Taskar et al., 2005) where the structured margin loss is defined as μ times the number of incorrectly segmented characters (Cai and Zhao, 2016). However, according to (Huang et al., 2012), **standard** parameter update cannot guarantee convergence in the case of inexact search. We thus additionally examine two strategies as follows.

Early update This strategy proposed in (Collins and Roark, 2004) can be simplified into "update once the golden answer is unreachable". In our case, when the considering character prefix can be correctly segmented but the correct one falls off the beam, an update operation will be conducted and the rest part will be ignored.

LaSO update One drawback of early update is that the search may never reach the end of a training instance, which means the rest part of the instance is "wasted". Differently, LaSO method of (Daumé III and Marcu, 2005) continues on the same instance with correct hypothesis after each update. In our case, the beam will be emptied and the corresponding prefix of the correct word sequence will be inserted into the beam.

---

[2] By assuming that tag interactions or word interactions only exist in adjacent positions.

	PKU		MSR	
	Train	Test	Train	Test
#sentences	19K	2K	87K	4K
#words	1,110K	104K	2,368K	107K
#characters	1,788K	169K	3,981K	181K

Table 1: Data statistics.

Character embedding size	$d_c = 50$
Word embedding size	$d_w = 50$
Hidden unit number	$H = 50$
Margin loss discount	$\mu = 0.2$
Maximum word length	$w = 4$

Table 2: Model setting.

4 Experiments

4.1 Datasets and Settings

We conduct experiments on two popular benchmark datasets, namely PKU and MSR, from the second international Chinese word segmentation bakeoff (Emerson, 2005) (Bakeoff-2005). Data statistics are in Table 1.

Throughout this paper, we use the same model setting as shown in Table 2. These numbers are tuned on development sets.[3] We follow (Dyer et al., 2015) to train model parameters. The learning rate at epoch t is set as $\eta_t = 0.2/(1 + \gamma t)$, where $\gamma = 0.1$ for PKU dataset and $\gamma = 0.2$ for MSR dataset. The character embeddings are either randomly initialized or pre-trained by word2vec (Mikolov et al., 2013) toolkit on Chinese Wikipedia corpus (which will be indicated by *+pre-train* in tables.), while the word embeddings are always randomly initialized. The beam size is kept the same during training and working. By default, early update strategy is adopted and the word table H is top half of in-vocabulary (IV) words by frequency.

4.2 Model Analysis

Beam search collapses into greedy search Figure 3 demonstrates the effect of beam size. To our surprise, beam size change has little influence on the performance. Namely, simple stepwise greedy search nearly achieves the best performance, which suggests that word segmentation can be greedily solvable at word-level. It may be due to that right now the model is optimal

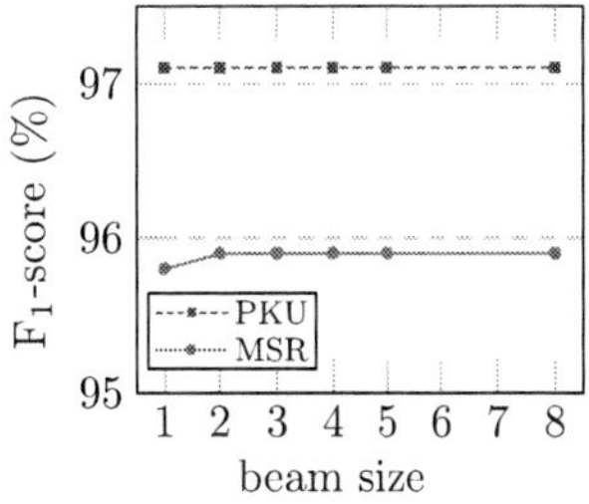

Figure 3: The effect of different beam sizes.

Methods	PKU		MSR	
	F_1	#epochs	F_1	#epochs
Standard	95.6	50	96.7	50
Early update	**95.8**	**30**	**97.1**	**30**
LaSO update	95.7	45	97.0	30

Table 3: The effect of different update methods. #epochs denotes the number of training epochs to convergence.

enough to make correct decisions at the first position. In fact, similar phenomenon was observed at character-level (Ma and Hinrichs, 2015). The rest experiments will thus only report the results of our greedy segmenter.

Comparing different update methods Table 3 compares the concerned three training strategies. We find that early update leads to faster convergence and a bit better performance compared to both standard and LaSO update.

Character composition versus word embedding Following Section 3.1, direct use of word embedding may bring efficiency and effectiveness for identifying IV words, but weaken the ability to recognize out-of-vocabulary (OOV) words. We accordingly conduct experiments on different sizes of word table $\mathcal{H}$. Concretely, sorting all IV words by frequency, the first $\{0, 25\%, 50\%, 75\%, 100\%\}$ fraction of them respectively forms the word table. The corresponding results on PKU in Figure 4 demonstrate that by the use of direct word embedding, F_1 score increases first but then drops rapidly. In contrast, OOV recall, which partially reflects the model generalization ability, decreases consistently. In addition, we also found the number of training epochs to convergence decreases continually. Overall, the results indicate that word-aware segmenter learns faster and fits better on training set, but generalizes relatively poorly.

---

[3]Following conventions, the last 10% sentences of training corpus are used as development set.

Models	PKU				MSR			
	F_1 + pre-train	F_1	Training (hours)	Test (sec.)	F_1 + pre-train	F_1	Training (hours)	Test (sec.)
(Zhao and Kit, 2008c)	-	95.4	-	-	-	**97.6**	-	-
(Chen et al., 2015a)	94.5*	94.4*	50	105	95.4*	95.1*	100	120
(Chen et al., 2015b)	94.8*	94.3*	58	105	95.6*	95.0*	117	120
(Ma and Hinrichs, 2015)	-	95.1	**1.5**	**24**	-	96.6	**3**	**28**
(Zhang et al., 2016)	95.1	-	6	110	97.0	-	13	125
(Liu et al., 2016)	93.91	-	-	-	95.21	-	-	-
(Cai and Zhao, 2016)	95.5	95.2	48	95	96.5	96.4	96	105
Our results	**95.8**	**95.4**	3	25	**97.1**	97.0	6	30

Table 4: Comparison with previous models. Results with * are from (Cai and Zhao, 2016).[4]

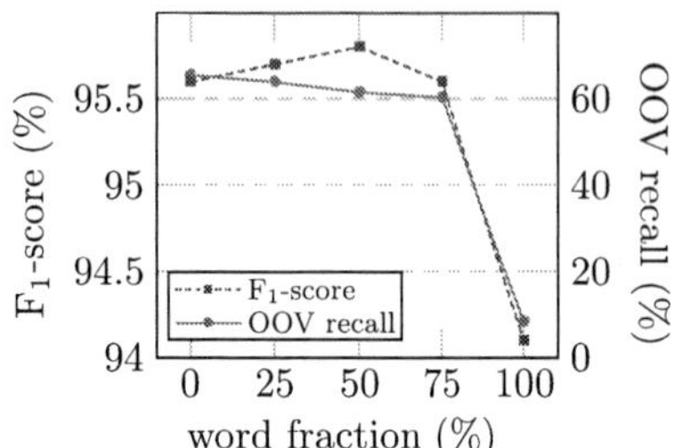

Figure 4: Performance with different sizes of word table on PKU test set.

4.3 Main Results

Table 4 compares our final results (greedy search is adopted by setting k=1) to prior neural models. Pre-training character embeddings on large-scale unlabeled corpus (not limited to the training corpus) has been shown helpful for extra performance improvement. The results with or without pre-trained character embeddings are listed separately for following the strict closed test setting of SIGHAN Bakeoff in which no linguistic resource other than training corpus is allowed. We also show the state-of-the-art results in (Zhao and Kit, 2008b) of traditional methods. The comparison shows our neural word segmenter outperforms all state-of-the-art neural systems with much less computational cost.

Finally, we present the results on all four Bakeoff-2005 datasets compared to (Zhao and Kit, 2008c) in Table 5. Note (Zhao and Kit, 2008c) used AV features, which are derived from global

Models	PKU	MSR	CityU	AS
(Zhao and Kit, 2008c)	95.4	97.6	96.1	95.7
–AV	95.2	**97.4**	94.8	**95.3**
ours	**95.4**	97.0	**95.4**	95.2
+pre-train	95.8	97.1	95.6	95.3

Table 5: Results on all four Bakeoff-2005 datasets.

statistics over entire training corpus in a similar way of unsupervised segmentation (Zhao and Kit, 2008a), for performance enhancement.[5] The comparison to their results without AV features show that our neural models for the first time present comparable performance against state-of-the-art traditional ones under strict closed test setting.[6]

5 Conclusion

In this paper, we presented a fast and accurate word segmenter using neural networks. Our experiments show a significant improvement over existing state-of-the-art neural models by adopting the following key model refinements.

(1) A novel character-word balanced mechanism for word representation generation. (2) A more efficient model for character composition by dropping unnecessary designs. (3) Early update strategy during max-margin training. (4) With the above modifications, we discover that beam size has little influence on the performance. Actually, greedy search achieves very high accuracy.

Through these improvement from both neural models and linguistic motivation, our model becomes simpler, faster and more accurate.[7]

---

[4]To distinguish the performance improvement from model optimization, we especially list the results of stand-alone neural models in (Zhang et al., 2016) and (Liu et al., 2016). All the running time results are from our runs of released implementations on a single CPU (Intel i7-5960X) with two threads only, except for those of (Zhang et al., 2016) which are from personal communication. The results of (Xu and Sun, 2016) are not listed due to their use of external Chinese idiom dictionary.

[5]In fact, this kind of features may also be incorporated to our model. We leave it as future work.

[6]To our knowledge, none of previous neural models has ever performed a complete evaluation over all four segmentation corpora of Bakeoff-2005, in which only two, PKU and MSR, are used since (Pei et al., 2014).

[7]Our code based on Dynet (Neubig et al., 2017) is released at https://github.com/jcyk/greedyCWS.

References

Galen Andrew. 2006. A hybrid markov/semi-markov conditional random field for sequence segmentation. In *Proceedings of the 2006 Conference on Empirical Methods in Natural Language Processing*. Sydney, Australia, pages 465–472.

Yoshua Bengio, Réjean Ducharme, Pascal Vincent, and Christian Janvin. 2003. A neural probabilistic language model. *The Journal of Machine Learning Research* 3:1137–1155.

Deng Cai and Hai Zhao. 2016. Neural word segmentation learning for Chinese. In *Proceedings of the 54th Annual Meeting of the Association for Computational Linguistics (Volume 1: Long Papers)*. Berlin, Germany, pages 409–420.

Xinchi Chen, Xipeng Qiu, Chenxi Zhu, and Xuanjing Huang. 2015a. Gated recursive neural network for Chinese word segmentation. In *Proceedings of the 53rd Annual Meeting of the Association for Computational Linguistics and the 7th International Joint Conference on Natural Language Processing (Volume 1: Long Papers)*. Beijing, China, pages 1744–1753.

Xinchi Chen, Xipeng Qiu, Chenxi Zhu, Pengfei Liu, and Xuanjing Huang. 2015b. Long short-term memory neural networks for Chinese word segmentation. In *Proceedings of the 2015 Conference on Empirical Methods in Natural Language Processing*. Lisbon, Portugal, pages 1197–1206.

Michael Collins and Brian Roark. 2004. Incremental parsing with the perceptron algorithm. In *Proceedings of the 42nd Meeting of the Association for Computational Linguistics, Main Volume*. Barcelona, Spain, pages 111–118.

Ronan Collobert, Jason Weston, Léon Bottou, Michael Karlen, Koray Kavukcuoglu, and Pavel Kuksa. 2011. Natural language processing (almost) from scratch. *The Journal of Machine Learning Research* 12:2493–2537.

Hal Daumé III and Daniel Marcu. 2005. Learning as search optimization: Approximate large margin methods for structured prediction. In *Proceedings of the 22nd international conference on Machine learning*. Bonn, Germany, pages 169–176.

Chris Dyer, Miguel Ballesteros, Wang Ling, Austin Matthews, and Noah A. Smith. 2015. Transition-based dependency parsing with stack long short-term memory. In *Proceedings of the 53rd Annual Meeting of the Association for Computational Linguistics and the 7th International Joint Conference on Natural Language Processing (Volume 1: Long Papers)*. Beijing, China, pages 334–343.

Thomas Emerson. 2005. The second international Chinese word segmentation bakeoff. In *Proceedings of the fourth SIGHAN workshop on Chinese language Processing*. Jeju Island, Korea, pages 123–133.

Sepp Hochreiter and Jürgen Schmidhuber. 1997. Long short-term memory. *Neural computation* 9(8):1735–1780.

Chang-Ning Huang and Hai Zhao. 2006. Which is essential for Chinese word segmentation: Character versus word. In *The 20th Pacific Asia Conference on Language, Information and Computation*. Wuhan, China, pages 1–12.

Changning Huang and Hai Zhao. 2007. Chinese word segmentation: A decade review. *Journal of Chinese Information Processing* 21(3):8–20.

Liang Huang, Suphan Fayong, and Yang Guo. 2012. Structured perceptron with inexact search. In *Proceedings of the 2012 Conference of the North American Chapter of the Association for Computational Linguistics: Human Language Technologies*. Montréal, Canada, pages 142–151.

John Lafferty, Andrew McCallum, and Fernando CN Pereira. 2001. Conditional random fields: Probabilistic models for segmenting and labeling sequence data. In *Proceedings of the Eighteenth Interntional Conference on Machine Learning*. San Francisco, USA, volume 1, pages 282–289.

Yijia Liu, Wanxiang Che, Jiang Guo, Bing Qin, and Ting Liu. 2016. Exploring segment representations for neural segmentation models. In *Proceedings of the Twenty-Fifth International Joint Conference on Artificial Intelligence*. New York, USA, pages 2880–2886.

Jin Kiat Low, Hwee Tou Ng, and Wenyuan Guo. 2005. A maximum entropy approach to Chinese word segmentation. In *Proceedings of the Fourth SIGHAN Workshop on Chinese Language Processing*. Jeju Island, Korea, pages 448–455.

Jianqiang Ma and Erhard Hinrichs. 2015. Accurate linear-time Chinese word segmentation via embedding matching. In *Proceedings of the 53rd Annual Meeting of the Association for Computational Linguistics and the 7th International Joint Conference on Natural Language Processing (Volume 1: Long Papers)*. Beijing, China, pages 1733–1743.

Tomas Mikolov, Kai Chen, Greg Corrado, and Jeffrey Dean. 2013. Efficient estimation of word representations in vector space. *arXiv preprint arXiv:1301.3781*.

Graham Neubig, Chris Dyer, Yoav Goldberg, Austin Matthews, Waleed Ammar, Antonios Anastasopoulos, Miguel Ballesteros, David Chiang, Daniel Clothiaux, Trevor Cohn, Kevin Duh, Manaal Faruqui, Cynthia Gan, Dan Garrette, Yangfeng Ji, Lingpeng Kong, Adhiguna Kuncoro, Gaurav Kumar, Chaitanya Malaviya, Paul Michel, Yusuke Oda, Matthew Richardson, Naomi Saphra, Swabha Swayamdipta, and Pengcheng Yin. 2017. Dynet: The dynamic neural network toolkit. *arXiv preprint arXiv:1701.03980*.

Wenzhe Pei, Tao Ge, and Baobao Chang. 2014. Max-margin tensor neural network for Chinese word segmentation. In *Proceedings of the 52nd Annual Meeting of the Association for Computational Linguistics (Volume 1: Long Papers)*. Baltimore, Maryland, pages 293–303.

Fuchun Peng, Fangfang Feng, and Andrew McCallum. 2004. Chinese segmentation and new word detection using conditional random fields. In *Proceedings of the 20th international conference on Computational Linguistics*. Geneva, Switzerland, pages 562–568.

Yanjun Qi, Sujatha G Das, Ronan Collobert, and Jason Weston. 2014. Deep learning for character-based information extraction. In *Advances in Information Retrieval*, pages 668–674.

Weiwei Sun. 2010. Word-based and character-based word segmentation models: Comparison and combination. In *Proceedings of the 23rd International Conference on Computational Linguistics*. Beijing, China, pages 1211–1219.

Xu Sun, Houfeng Wang, and Wenjie Li. 2012. Fast online training with frequency-adaptive learning rates for Chinese word segmentation and new word detection. In *Proceedings of the 50th Annual Meeting of the Association for Computational Linguistics*. Jeju Island, Korea, pages 253–262.

Martin Sundermeyer, Ralf Schlüter, and Hermann Ney. 2012. LSTM neural networks for language modeling. In *13th Annual Conference of the International Speech Communication Association*. Portland, Oregon, USA, pages 194–197.

Ben Taskar, Vassil Chatalbashev, Daphne Koller, and Carlos Guestrin. 2005. Learning structured prediction models: A large margin approach. In *Proceedings of the 22nd international conference on Machine learning*. Bonn, Germany, pages 896–903.

Huihsin Tseng, Pichuan Chang, Galen Andrew, Daniel Jurafsky, and Christopher Manning. 2005. A conditional random field word segmenter for SIGHAN bakeoff 2005. In *Proceedings of the fourth SIGHAN workshop on Chinese language Processing*. Jeju Island, Korea, pages 168–171.

Mengqiu Wang, Rob Voigt, and Christopher D. Manning. 2014. Two knives cut better than one: Chinese word segmentation with dual decomposition. In *Proceedings of the 52nd Annual Meeting of the Association for Computational Linguistics (Volume 2: Short Papers)*. Baltimore, Maryland, pages 193–198.

Jingjing Xu and Xu Sun. 2016. Dependency-based gated recursive neural network for Chinese word segmentation. In *Proceedings of the 54th Annual Meeting of the Association for Computational Linguistics (Volume 2: Short Papers)*. Berlin, Germany, pages 567–572.

Nianwen Xue. 2003. Chinese word segmentation as character tagging. *Computational Linguistics and Chinese Language Processing* 8(1):29–48.

Xiaodong Zeng, Derek F. Wong, Lidia S. Chao, and Isabel Trancoso. 2013. Graph-based semi-supervised model for joint Chinese word segmentation and part-of-speech tagging. In *Proceedings of the 51st Annual Meeting of the Association for Computational Linguistics (Volume 1: Long Papers)*. Sofia, Bulgaria, pages 770–779.

Longkai Zhang, Houfeng Wang, Xu Sun, and Mairgup Mansur. 2013. Exploring representations from unlabeled data with co-training for Chinese word segmentation. In *Proceedings of the 2013 Conference on Empirical Methods in Natural Language Processing*. Seattle, USA, pages 311–321.

Meishan Zhang, Yue Zhang, and Guohong Fu. 2016. Transition-based neural word segmentation. In *Proceedings of the 54nd Annual Meeting of the Association for Computational Linguistics*. Berlin, Germany, pages 421–431.

Yue Zhang and Stephen Clark. 2007. Chinese segmentation with a word-based perceptron algorithm. In *Proceedings of the 45th Annual Meeting of the Association of Computational Linguistics*. Prague, Czech Republic, pages 840–847.

Yue Zhang and Stephen Clark. 2011. Syntactic processing using the generalized perceptron and beam search. *Computational linguistics* 37(1):105–151.

Hai Zhao, Deng Cai, Yang Xin, Wang Yuzhu, and Zhongye Jia. 2017. A hybrid model for Chinese spelling check. *ACM Transactions on Asian and Low-Resource Language Information Processing* 16(3).

Hai Zhao, Chang-Ning Huang, Mu Li, and Bao-Liang Lu. 2006. Effective tag set selection in Chinese word segmentation via conditional random field modeling. In *The 20th Pacific Asia Conference on Language, Information and Computation*. Wuhan, China, pages 87–94.

Hai Zhao, Chang-Ning Huang, Mu Li, and Bao-Liang Lu. 2010. A unified character-based tagging framework for Chinese word segmentation. *ACM Transactions on Asian Language Information Processing* 16(21).

Hai Zhao and Chunyu Kit. 2008a. An empirical comparison of goodness measures for unsupervised Chinese word segmentation with a unified framework. In *Proceedings of the Third International Joint Conference on Natural Language Processing*. Hyderabad, India, pages 9–16.

Hai Zhao and Chunyu Kit. 2008b. Exploiting unlabeled text with different unsupervised segmentation criteria for Chinese word segmentation. *Research in Computing Science* 33:93–104.

Hai Zhao and Chunyu Kit. 2008c. Unsupervised segmentation helps supervised learning of character tagging for word segmentation and named entity recognition. In *The Sixth SIGHAN Workshop on Chinese Language Processing*. Hyderabad, India, pages 106–111.

Hai Zhao and Chunyu Kit. 2011. Integrating unsupervised and supervised word segmentation: The role of goodness measures. *Information Sciences* 181(1):163–183.

Xiaoqing Zheng, Hanyang Chen, and Tianyu Xu. 2013. Deep learning for Chinese word segmentation and POS tagging. In *Proceedings of the 2013 Conference on Empirical Methods in Natural Language Processing*. Seattle, Washington, USA, pages 647–657.

Pay Attention to the Ending:
Strong Neural Baselines for the ROC Story Cloze Task

Zheng Cai[1]   Lifu Tu[2]   Kevin Gimpel[2]

[1]University of Chicago, Chicago, IL, 60637, USA
[2]Toyota Technological Institute at Chicago, Chicago, IL, 60637, USA

jontsai@uchicago.edu, {lifu, kgimpel}@ttic.edu

Abstract

We consider the ROC story cloze task (Mostafazadeh et al., 2016) and present several findings. We develop a model that uses hierarchical recurrent networks with attention to encode the sentences in the story and score candidate endings. By discarding the large training set and only training on the validation set, we achieve an accuracy of 74.7%. Even when we discard the story plots (sentences before the ending) and only train to choose the better of two endings, we can still reach 72.5%. We then analyze this "ending-only" task setting. We estimate human accuracy to be 78% and find several types of clues that lead to this high accuracy, including those related to sentiment, negation, and general ending likelihood regardless of the story context.

1   Introduction

The ROC story cloze task (Mostafazadeh et al., 2016) tests a system's ability to choose the more plausible of two endings to a story. The incorrect ending is written to still fit the world of the story, e.g., the protagonist typically appears in both endings. The task is designed to test for "common-sense" knowledge, where the difference between the two endings lies in the plausibility of the characters' actions. The best system of Mostafazadeh et al. (2016) achieves 58.5% accuracy.

The ROC training and evaluation data differ in a key way. The training set contains 5-sentence stories. But the evaluation datasets (the validation and test sets) contain both a correct ending and an incorrect ending. This means that the task is one of outlier detection: systems must estimate the density of correct endings in the training data and then detect which of the two endings is an outlier. This becomes difficult when the evaluation contains distractors that are still somewhat plausible. For example, a model may place mass on stories that consistently mention the same characters, but this will not be useful for the task because even the incorrect ending uses the correct character names.

In this paper, we discard the 50k training stories and train only on the 1871-story validation set. We develop several neural models based on recurrent networks, comparing flat and hierarchical models for encoding the sentences in the story. We also use an attention mechanism based on the ending to identify useful parts of the plot. Our final model achieves 74.7% on the test set, outperforming all systems of Mostafazadeh et al. (2016) and approaching the state of the art results of concurrent work (Schwartz et al., 2017b).

We then discard the first four sentences of each story and use our model to score endings alone. We achieve 72.5% on the test set, outperforming most prior work without even looking at the story plots. We do a small-scale manual study of this ending-only task, finding that humans can identify the better ending in approximately 78% of cases. We report several reasons for the high accuracy of this ending-only setting, including some that are readily captured by automatic methods, such as sentiment analysis and the presence of negation words, as well as others that are more difficult, like those derived from world knowledge. Our results and analysis, combined with the similar concurrent observations of Schwartz et al. (2017a), suggest that any meaningful system for the ROC task must outperform the best ending-only baselines.

2   Task and Datasets

We refer to a 5-sentence sequence as a **story**, the incomplete 4-sentence sequence as a **plot**, and the

Proceedings of the 55th Annual Meeting of the Association for Computational Linguistics (Short Papers), pages 616–622
Vancouver, Canada, July 30 - August 4, 2017. ©2017 Association for Computational Linguistics
https://doi.org/10.18653/v1/P17-2097

fifth sentence as an **ending**. The ROC story corpus (Mostafazadeh et al., 2016) contains training, validation, and test sets. The training set contains 5-sentence stories. The validation and test sets contain 4-sentence plots followed by two candidate endings, with only one correct.

Mostafazadeh et al. (2016) evaluated several methods for solving the task. Since the training set does not contain incorrect endings, their methods are based on computing similarity between the plot and ending. Their best results were obtained with the Deep Structured Semantic Model (DSSM) (Huang et al., 2013) which represents texts using character trigram counts followed by neural network layers and a similarity function.

Concurrently with our work, the LSDSem 2017 shared task was held (Mostafazadeh et al., 2017), focusing on the ROC story cloze task. Several of the participants made similar observations to what we describe here, namely that supervised learning on the validation set is more effective than learning directly from the training set, as well as noting certain biases in the endings (Schwartz et al., 2017a,b; Bugert et al., 2017; Flor and Somasundaran, 2017; Schenk and Chiarcos, 2017; Roemmele et al., 2017; Goel and Singh, 2017; Mihaylov and Frank, 2017).

3 Models and Training

We now describe our model variations. The first (ENCPLOTEND) encodes the plot and ending separately, then scores them with a scoring function. The second (ENCSTORY) concatenates the plot and ending to form a story, then encodes that story and scores its representation with a scoring function. When encoding a sequence of multiple sentences, whether with ENCPLOTEND or ENCSTORY, we consider two choices: a hierarchical encoder (HIER) that first encodes each sentence and then encodes the sentence representations, and a non-hierarchical encoder (FLAT) that simply encodes the concatenation of all sentences. We also consider the possibility of including an ending-oriented attention mechanism (ATT). For training, we use a simple supervised hinge loss objective.

3.1 Encoders

Our encoders encode text sequences into representations. When using our HIER model, we use a hierarchical recurrent neural network (RNN) (Li et al., 2015) with two levels. The first RNN encodes the sequence of words in a sentence; the same RNN is used for sentences in the plot and for each candidate ending. The second RNN encodes the sequence of sentence representations in a plot or story. When using our FLAT model, we only use the first RNN described above; the only change is that the input becomes the concatenation of multiple sentences (separated by sentence boundary tokens).

Below we use i as a subscript to index sentences in the story or plot, and j as a superscript to index individual words in sentences. E.g., we use $\boldsymbol{w}_i$ to indicate the ith sentence of the story/plot and we use $\boldsymbol{w}_i^{(j)}$ to denote the word embedding vector of the jth word in the ith sentence.

3.1.1 Encoding Word Sequences

We use a bidirectional long short-term memory (BiLSTM) RNN (Hochreiter and Schmidhuber, 1997) to encode a sentence. For sentence $\boldsymbol{w}_i$:

$$\boldsymbol{f}_i = \text{forward-LSTM}_1(\boldsymbol{w}_i)$$
$$\boldsymbol{b}_i = \text{backward-LSTM}_1(\boldsymbol{w}_i)$$

where $\boldsymbol{f}_i$ and $\boldsymbol{b}_i$ are hidden vector sequences. We add the forward and backward vectors at each step to obtain vectors $\boldsymbol{h}_i$, then average to obtain sentence representation $\boldsymbol{S}_i$:

$$\boldsymbol{h}_i = \boldsymbol{f}_i + \boldsymbol{b}_i \qquad \boldsymbol{S}_i = \frac{1}{|\boldsymbol{w}_i|}\sum_{j=1}^{|\boldsymbol{w}_i|} \boldsymbol{h}_i^{(j)} \qquad (1)$$

We define this function from word sequence $\boldsymbol{w}_i$ to sentence representation $\boldsymbol{S}_i$ by ENCWORDS($\boldsymbol{w}_i$).

3.1.2 Adding Attention

Attention mechanisms (Bahdanau et al., 2015; Mnih et al., 2014) have yielded considerable performance gains for machine comprehension (Hermann et al., 2015; Sukhbaatar et al., 2015; Chen et al., 2016), parsing (Vinyals et al., 2015), and machine translation (Luong et al., 2015).

After generating the representation $\boldsymbol{e} = \boldsymbol{S}_5 = \text{ENCWORDS}(\boldsymbol{w}_5)$ for candidate ending $\boldsymbol{w}_5$, we use it to compute the attention over the individual hidden vectors of each sentence to compute modified sentence representations $\boldsymbol{S}_i^{\dagger}$. That is:

$$\alpha_i^{(j)} = \boldsymbol{e}^{\top} \boldsymbol{M} \boldsymbol{h}_i^{(j)} \qquad \beta_i^{(j)} \propto \exp\{\alpha_i^{(j)}\}$$
$$\boldsymbol{S}_i^{\dagger} = \sum_{j=1}^{|\boldsymbol{w}_i|} \beta_i^{(j)} \boldsymbol{h}_i^{(j)} \qquad (2)$$

where $h_i^{(j)}$ is the jth entry of h_i and M is a bilinear attention matrix.[1] Figure 1 shows this architecture. We define this attention-augmented encoder as $\textsc{AttEncWords}(w_i, e)$.

3.1.3 Encoding Sentence Sequences

We use another BiLSTM to encode the sequence S of sentence representations S_i:

$$F = \text{forward-LSTM}_2(S)$$
$$B = \text{backward-LSTM}_2(S)$$
$$\textsc{EncSents}(S) = F_{-1} + B_{-1}$$

where F_{-1} is the final hidden vector in F. We also use this encoder to encode the ending e by treating it as a sequence containing only one element.

3.2 Model Variations

Given our encoders, we now define the final representations D for our modeling variations, combining each of Hier and Flat with each of Enc-Story and EncPlotEnd:

$$w_1^k = \langle w_1, ..., w_{k-1}, w_k \rangle \quad S_1^k = \langle S_1, ..., S_k \rangle$$
$$D_{\textsc{FlatS}} = \textsc{EncWords}(w_1^5)$$
$$S_i = \textsc{EncWords}(w_i)$$
$$D_{\textsc{FlatPE}} = \langle \textsc{EncWords}(w_1^4), S_5 \rangle$$
$$D_{\textsc{HierS}} = \textsc{EncSents}(S_1^5)$$
$$D_{\textsc{HierPE}} = \langle \textsc{EncSents}(S_1^4), \textsc{EncSents}(S_5) \rangle$$

When using attention, we replace $\textsc{EncWords}$ above with $\textsc{AttEncWords}$.

After encoding the story as D, we use a feed-forward network to act as a score function that takes D as input and generates a one-dimensional (scalar) output. We use tanh as the activation function on each layer of the feed-forward network and tune the numbers of hidden layers and the layer widths.

3.3 Training

Since we are training on the validation set which contains both correct and incorrect endings, we minimize the following hinge loss:

$$L = \max(0, -\text{score}(D^+) + \text{score}(D^-) + \delta)$$

where D^+ is the representation of the correct story, D^- is the representation of the incorrect story, and $\delta = 1$ is the margin.

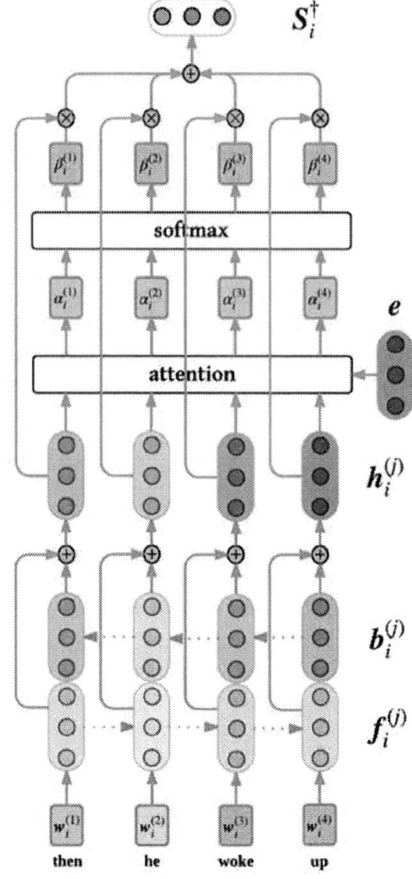

Figure 1: Attention-augmented BiLSTM for encoding a 4-word sentence w_i into a 3-dimensional representation $S_i^\dagger$. The attention function uses the ending representation e.

4 Experimental Setup

We shuffle and split the validation set into 5 folds and do 5-fold cross validation. For modeling decisions, we tune based on the average accuracy of the held-out folds. For final experiments, we choose the fold with the best held-out accuracy and report its test set accuracy. We use Adam (Kingma and Ba, 2015) for optimization with learning rate 0.001 and mini-batch size 50. We use pretrained 300-dimensional GloVe embeddings trained on Wikipedia and Gigaword (Pennington et al., 2014) and keep them fixed during training. We use L_2 regularization for the score feed-forward network, which has a single hidden layer of size 512. We use 300 for the LSTM hidden vector dimensionality for both encoders.

---

[1] In preliminary experiments we found bilinear attention to work better than attention based on cosine similarity.

	FLAT	HIER
ENCSTORY	79.08	80.22
ENCPLOTEND	71.75	79.84

Table 1: Accuracies (%) averaged over held-out folds of 5-fold cross validation. Comparing hierarchical (HIER) and non-hierarchical (FLAT) encoders, and encoding story (ENCSTORY) vs. separately encoding plot and ending (ENCPLOTEND). No attention is used.

	-ATT	+ATT
ENCSTORY	80.22	79.95
ENCPLOTEND	79.84	81.24

Table 2: For the ENCSTORY and ENCPLOTEND models, showing the contribution of adding attention (+ATT). All models use the HIER encoder.

5 Results

Modeling Decisions. We first evaluate our modeling decisions, using the averaged held-out fold accuracy as our model selection criterion. Table 1 shows results when comparing FLAT/HIER and ENCSTORY/ENCPLOTEND. Hierarchical modeling helps especially with ENCPLOTEND.

Table 2 shows the contribution of attention when using HIER. Attention helps when separately encoding the plot and ending, but not when encoding the entire story. We suspect this is because when we use ENCSTORY, the higher BiLSTM processes the sequence $\langle S_1^\dagger, S_2^\dagger, S_3^\dagger, S_4^\dagger, S_5 \rangle$. That is, the first four sentence representations are in a different space from the ending due to the use of attention.

Final Results. Table 3 shows final results. We report the best result from Mostafazadeh et al. (2016), the best result from the concurrently-held LSDSem shared task (Schwartz et al., 2017b), and our final system configuration (with decisions tuned via cross validation as shown in Tables 1-2, then using the model with the best held-out fold accuracy). Our model achieves 74.7%, which is close to the state of the art result of 75.2%.[2]

We also report the results of stripping away the plots and running our system on just the endings ("ending only"). We use the FLAT BiLSTM model on the ending followed by the feed-forward scoring function, using the same loss as above for training. We again use 5-fold cross validation

---

[2]We also tried to train the DSSM on the validation set, but were unable to approach the performance of our model. The DSSM appears to benefit greatly from the training set.

	val	test
DSSM[‡]	60.4	58.5
UW (Schwartz et al., 2017b)	-	75.2
UW (ending only)	-	72.4
trigram LM (estimated from stories)	52.4	53.6
trigram LM (estimated from endings)	53.8	54.6
Our model (HIER, ENCPLOTEND, ATT)	-	74.7
Our model (ending only)	-	72.5
Human[‡] (story + ending)	100	100
Human (ending only)	78*	-

Table 3: Final results. * = estimate from 100; see Section 6.1. ‡ = from Mostafazadeh et al. (2016).

on the validation set and choose the model with the highest held-out fold accuracy. We achieve 72.5%, matching the similar ending-only result of Schwartz et al. (2017b). We estimate human performance in the ending-only setting to be 78%. We provide more details in Section 6.1. These results suggest that the dataset contains systematic biases in the composition of its endings and that any meaningful system for the task must outperform the best ending-only baseline.

We also report the results of two n-gram language model baselines. We estimated trigram models using KenLM (Heafield, 2011) from two different datasets: (1) the entire training stories, and (2) only the endings from the training stories. Using only the endings works better, even though it uses one fifth of the data; this further shows the importance of focusing on endings for this task.

6 Analysis

We analyze the attention weights in our final model. Figure 2 shows the distribution of attention weights over position bins, aggregated over the plot sentences in the test set. We find that the attentions generated by the correct ending show higher weight for words early in the sentences, while the attentions for incorrect endings are higher at the ends of the sentences.

We also study the ending-only task to uncover the different kinds of bias that lead to high accuracies in this setting. We consider automatic features that can be computed on the endings and evaluate the accuracy of relying solely upon each feature as a classification rule. We then compute correlations between our ending-only model and each feature. In addition to the trigram model described above, we consider the following rules:

- **sentiment**: choose ending with higher predicted sentiment score from the Stanford sentiment an-

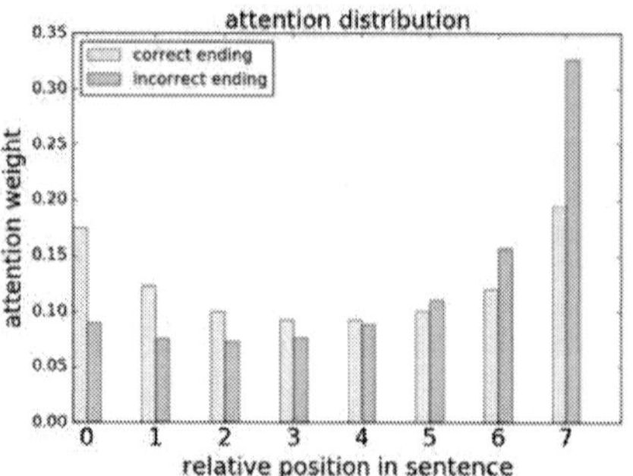

Figure 2: Attention weight distribution in test set plot sentences. Sentences were divided into eighths, then attention weights were averaged for each and normalized. For correct endings, there is more attention on early words in plot sentences.

rule	rule applicability	test accuracy	Spearman correlation
sentiment	65.9%	58.7%	0.214
negation words	20.7%	55.4%	-
length	100%	53.2%	0.047
language model	100%	54.6%	0.135

Table 4: Ending selection rules exhibiting biases in endings. Final column shows correlation between each feature and the score of our model.

alyzer (Socher et al., 2013).

- **negation**: choose ending with fewer words from {*not, neither, nor, never, n't, no, rarely*}.

- **length**: choose the longer ending.

Table 4 shows the results. Each rule yields accuracy at least 53%, with the sentiment rule nearing 59%. Even though the negation rule is only applicable in 20% of cases, its bias is strong enough to yield 5% improvement over the random baseline. These results show several reasons why an ending-only model can perform well, and suggests that our model may be identifying positive sentiment, due to its correlation of 0.214 with that feature.

We counted words in the correct and incorrect endings and in Table 5 we show some that differ between the top-50 lists for each category. E.g., "never" appears among the top 50 words in incorrect endings but not correct endings. The word count differences are accordant with the results from the sentiment and negation word rules, with non-overlapping words showing significant sentiment difference and that correct endings are more neutral or positive than incorrect ones.

correct endings:	out, !, great, new, found
incorrect endings:	n't, did, not, never, hated

Table 5: Non-overlapping words in the top 50 most frequent word list of each category.

6.1 Human Ending-Only Performance

In order to assess human performance, we randomly chose 100 ending pairs from the validation set and gave them to a human annotator, a native speaker of English who is familiar with the ROC task. The annotator was asked to select the more likely ending based only on the two endings provided. He was correct on 78, observing several kinds of cues in the endings alone in addition to those mentioned above.

In some cases, one ending sentence is simply much more likely than the other based on world knowledge. For example, the ending "the glasses fixed his headaches immediately" is much more likely than "the optometrist gave him comfortable sneakers". It is possible that the plot could change the preferred ending to the second, but this appears to be rare in the ROC dataset. In another example, "I practice all the time now" is more likely than "I hope I drop the batons" because it seems unlikely that anyone would ever hope to drop batons in the surmised world of the story. While these instances still test for a kind of "commonsense" or "world" knowledge, they do not require the plot to answer.

7 Conclusions and Future Work

Our models use none of the ROC training data but achieve strong performance, even when discarding the story plots. We uncovered several sources of bias in the endings that make the ending-only task solvable with greater than 70% accuracy. Our results suggest that any meaningful system for the ROC story cloze task should perform better than the best ending-only system. In future work, we will experiment with additional modeling choices, including adding attention to the higher BiLSTM and adding a decoder and a multi-task objective during training to improve stability.

Acknowledgments

We acknowledge Zhongtian Dai for his assistance and expertise and we thank Yejin Choi, Nasrin Mostafazadeh, Michael Roth, Roy Schwartz, and the anonymous reviewers for valuable discussions and insights.

References

Dzmitry Bahdanau, Kyunghyun Cho, and Yoshua Bengio. 2015. Neural machine translation by jointly learning to align and translate. In *Proceedings of International Conference on Learning Representations*.

Michael Bugert, Yevgeniy Puzikov, Andreas Rücklé, Judith Eckle-Kohler, Teresa Martin, Eugenio Martínez-Cámara, Daniil Sorokin, Maxime Peyrard, and Iryna Gurevych. 2017. LSDSem 2017: Exploring data generation methods for the story cloze test. In *Proceedings of the 2nd Workshop on Linking Models of Lexical, Sentential and Discourse-level Semantics*.

Danqi Chen, Jason Bolton, and Christopher D. Manning. 2016. A thorough examination of the CNN/Daily Mail reading comprehension task. In *Proceedings of the 54th Annual Meeting of the Association for Computational Linguistics (ACL)*.

Michael Flor and Swapna Somasundaran. 2017. Sentiment analysis and lexical cohesion for the story cloze task. In *Proceedings of the 2nd Workshop on Linking Models of Lexical, Sentential and Discourse-level Semantics*.

Pranav Goel and Anil Kumar Singh. 2017. IIT (BHU): System description for LSDSem'17 shared task. In *Proceedings of the 2nd Workshop on Linking Models of Lexical, Sentential and Discourse-level Semantics*.

Kenneth Heafield. 2011. KenLM: faster and smaller language model queries. In *Proceedings of the EMNLP 2011 Sixth Workshop on Statistical Machine Translation*.

Karl Moritz Hermann, Tomáš Kočiský, Edward Grefenstette, Lasse Espeholt, Will Kay, Mustafa Suleyman, and Phil Blunsom. 2015. Teaching machines to read and comprehend. In *Advances in Neural Information Processing Systems (NIPS)*.

Sepp Hochreiter and Jürgen Schmidhuber. 1997. Long short-term memory. *Neural Computation* 9(8).

Po-Sen Huang, Xiaodong He, Jianfeng Gao, Li Deng, Alex Acero, and Larry Heck. 2013. Learning deep structured semantic models for web search using clickthrough data. In *Proceedings of the 22nd ACM International Conference on Information & Knowledge Management (CIKM)*.

Diederik P. Kingma and Jimmy Ba. 2015. Adam: A method for stochastic optimization. In *Proceedings of International Conference on Learning Representations*.

Jiwei Li, Minh-Thang Luong, and Dan Jurafsky. 2015. A hierarchical neural autoencoder for paragraphs and documents. In *Proceedings of the 53rd Annual Meeting of the Association for Computational Linguistics (ACL) and the 7th International Joint Conference on Natural Language Processing (Volume 1: Long Papers)*.

Thang Luong, Hieu Pham, and Christopher D. Manning. 2015. Effective approaches to attention-based neural machine translation. In *Proceedings of the 2015 Conference on Empirical Methods in Natural Language Processing (EMNLP)*.

Todor Mihaylov and Anette Frank. 2017. Story cloze ending selection baselines and data examination. In *Proceedings of the 2nd Workshop on Linking Models of Lexical, Sentential and Discourse-level Semantics*.

Volodymyr Mnih, Nicolas Heess, Alex Graves, and Koray Kavukcuoglu. 2014. Recurrent models of visual attention. In *Advances in Neural Information Processing Systems (NIPS)*.

Nasrin Mostafazadeh, Nathanael Chambers, Xiaodong He, Devi Parikh, Dhruv Batra, Lucy Vanderwende, Pushmeet Kohli, and James Allen. 2016. A corpus and cloze evaluation for deeper understanding of commonsense stories. In *Proceedings of the 2016 Conference of the North American Chapter of the Association for Computational Linguistics: Human Language Technologies*.

Nasrin Mostafazadeh, Michael Roth, Annie Louis, Nathanael Chambers, and James Allen. 2017. LSDSem 2017 shared task: The story cloze test. In *Proceedings of the 2nd Workshop on Linking Models of Lexical, Sentential and Discourse-level Semantics*.

Jeffrey Pennington, Richard Socher, and Christopher D. Manning. 2014. GloVe: Global vectors for word representation. In *Proceedings of Empirical Methods in Natural Language Processing (EMNLP)*.

Melissa Roemmele, Sosuke Kobayashi, Naoya Inoue, and Andrew Gordon. 2017. An RNN-based binary classifier for the story cloze test. In *Proceedings of the 2nd Workshop on Linking Models of Lexical, Sentential and Discourse-level Semantics*.

Niko Schenk and Christian Chiarcos. 2017. Resource-lean modeling of coherence in commonsense stories. In *Proceedings of the 2nd Workshop on Linking Models of Lexical, Sentential and Discourse-level Semantics*.

Roy Schwartz, Maarten Sap, Ioannis Konstas, Leila Zilles, Yejin Choi, and Noah A. Smith. 2017a. The effect of different writing tasks on linguistic style: A case study of the ROC story cloze task. *CoRR* abs/1702.01841.

Roy Schwartz, Maarten Sap, Ioannis Konstas, Leila Zilles, Yejin Choi, and Noah A. Smith. 2017b. Story cloze task: UW NLP system. In *Proceedings of the 2nd Workshop on Linking Models of Lexical, Sentential and Discourse-level Semantics*.

Richard Socher, Alex Perelygin, Jean Y Wu, Jason
Chuang, Christopher D Manning, Andrew Y Ng,
Christopher Potts, et al. 2013. Recursive deep models for semantic compositionality over a sentiment
treebank. In *Proceedings of the Conference on Empirical Methods in Natural Language Processing
(EMNLP)*.

Sainbayar Sukhbaatar, arthur szlam, Jason Weston, and
Rob Fergus. 2015. End-to-end memory networks.
In *Advances in Neural Information Processing Sys-
tems (NIPS)*.

Oriol Vinyals, Ł ukasz Kaiser, Terry Koo, Slav Petrov,
Ilya Sutskever, and Geoffrey Hinton. 2015. Gram-
mar as a foreign language. In *Advances in Neural
Information Processing Systems (NIPS)*.

Neural Semantic Parsing over Multiple Knowledge-bases

Jonathan Herzig[1,2] and **Jonathan Berant**[1]

[1]Tel-Aviv University, Tel Aviv-Yafo, Israel
[2]IBM Research, Haifa 31905, Israel
`jherzig@gmail.com, joberant@cs.tau.ac.i`

Abstract

A fundamental challenge in developing semantic parsers is the paucity of strong supervision in the form of language utterances annotated with logical form. In this paper, we propose to exploit structural regularities in language in different domains, and train semantic parsers over multiple knowledge-bases (KBs), while sharing information across datasets. We find that we can substantially improve parsing accuracy by training a single sequence-to-sequence model over multiple KBs, when providing an encoding of the domain at decoding time. Our model achieves state-of-the-art performance on the OVERNIGHT dataset (containing eight domains), improves performance over a single KB baseline from 75.6% to 79.6%, while obtaining a 7x reduction in the number of model parameters.

1 Introduction

Semantic parsing is concerned with translating language utterances into executable logical forms and constitutes a key technology for developing conversational interfaces (Zelle and Mooney, 1996; Zettlemoyer and Collins, 2005; Kwiatkowski et al., 2011; Liang et al., 2011; Artzi and Zettlemoyer, 2013; Berant and Liang, 2015).

A fundamental obstacle to widespread use of semantic parsers is the high cost of annotating logical forms in new domains. To tackle this problem, prior work suggested strategies such as training from denotations (Clarke et al., 2010; Liang et al., 2011; Artzi and Zettlemoyer, 2013), from paraphrases (Berant and Liang, 2014; Wang et al., 2015) and from declarative sentences (Krishnamurthy and Mitchell, 2012; Reddy et al., 2014).

Example 1
Domain: HOUSING
*"Find a housing that is **no more than** 800 square feet.",*
`Type.HousingUnit` ⊓ `Size.`≤`.800`
Domain: PUBLICATIONS
*"Find an article with **no more than** two authors"*
`Type.Article` ⊓ $\mathbf{R}[\lambda x.\text{count}(\texttt{AuthorOf}.x)]$.≤`.2`

Example 2
Domain: RESTAURANTS
*"which restaurant has **the most ratings**?"*
$\text{argmax}(\texttt{Type.Restaurant}, \mathbf{R}[\lambda x.\text{count}(\mathbf{R}[\texttt{Rating}].x)])$
Domain: CALENDAR
*"which meeting is attended by **the most people**?"*
$\text{argmax}(\texttt{Type.Meeting}, \mathbf{R}[\lambda x.\text{count}(\mathbf{R}[\texttt{Attendee}].x)])$

Figure 1: Examples for natural language utterances with logical forms in lambda-DCS (Liang, 2013) in different domains that share structural regularity (a comparative structure in the first example and a superlative in the second).

In this paper, we suggest an orthogonal solution: to pool examples from multiple datasets in different domains, each corresponding to a separate knowledge-base (KB), and train a model over all examples. This is motivated by an observation that while KBs differ in their entities and properties, the structure of language composition repeats across domains (Figure 1). E.g., a superlative in language will correspond to an 'argmax', and a verb followed by a noun often denotes a join operation. A model that shares information across domains can improve generalization compared to a model that is trained on a single domain only.

Recently, Jia and Liang (2016) and Dong and Lapata (2016) proposed sequence-to-sequence models for semantic parsing. Such neural models substantially facilitate information sharing, as both language and logical form are represented with similar abstract vector representations in all domains. We build on their work and examine models that share representations across domains during encoding of language and decoding of logical form, inspired by work on domain adaptation

623

Proceedings of the 55th Annual Meeting of the Association for Computational Linguistics (Short Papers), pages 623–628
Vancouver, Canada, July 30 - August 4, 2017. ©2017 Association for Computational Linguistics
https://doi.org/10.18653/v1/P17-2098

(Daume III, 2007) and multi-task learning (Caruana, 1997; Collobert et al., 2011; Luong et al., 2016; Firat et al., 2016; Johnson et al., 2016). We find that by providing the decoder with a representation of the domain, we can train a single model over multiple domains and substantially improve accuracy compared to models trained on each domain separately. On the OVERNIGHT dataset, this improves accuracy from 75.6% to 79.6%, setting a new state-of-the-art, while reducing the number of parameters by a factor of 7. To our knowledge, this work is the first to train a semantic parser over multiple KBs.

2 Problem Setup

We briefly review the model presented by Jia and Liang (2016), which we base our model on.

Semantic parsing can be viewed as a sequence-to-sequence problem (Sutskever et al., 2014), where a sequence of input language tokens $x = x_1, \ldots, x_m$ is mapped to a sequence of output logical tokens $y_1, \ldots, y_n$.

The **encoder** converts $x_1, \ldots, x_m$ into a sequence of context sensitive embeddings $b_1, \ldots, b_m$ using a bidirectional RNN (Bahdanau et al., 2015): a forward RNN generates hidden states $h_1^F, \ldots, h_m^F$ by applying the LSTM recurrence (Hochreiter and Schmidhuber, 1997): $h_i^F = LSTM(\phi^{(in)}(x_i), h_{i-1}^F)$, where $\phi^{(in)}$ is an embedding function mapping a word x_i to a fixed-dimensional vector. A backward RNN similarly generates hidden states $h_m^B, \ldots, h_1^B$ by processing the input sequence in reverse. Finally, for each input position i, the representation b_i is the concatenation $[h_i^F, h_i^B]$. An attention-based **decoder** (Bahdanau et al., 2015; Luong et al., 2015) generates output tokens one at a time. At each time step j, it generates y_j based on the current hidden state s_j, then updates the hidden state s_{j+1} based on s_j and y_j. Formally, the decoder is defined by the following equations:

$$
\begin{aligned}
s_1 &= \tanh(W^{(s)}[h_m^F, h_1^B]), \\
e_{ji} &= s_j^\top W^{(a)} b_i, \\
\alpha_{ji} &= \frac{\exp(e_{ji})}{\sum_{i'=1}^m e_{ji'}}, \\
c_j &= \sum_{i=1}^m \alpha_{ji} b_i, \\
p(y_j = w \mid x, y_{1:j-1}) &\propto \exp(U[s_j, c_j]), \\
s_{j+1} &= LSTM([\phi^{(out)}(y_j), c_j], s_j),
\end{aligned}
\tag{1}
$$

where $i \in \{1, \ldots, m\}$ and $j \in \{1, \ldots, n\}$. The matrices $W^{(s)}$, $W^{(a)}$, U, and the embedding function $\phi^{(out)}$ are decoder parameters. We also employ attention-based copying as described by Jia and Liang (2016), but omit details for brevity.

The entire model is trained end-to-end by maximizing $p(y \mid x) = \prod_{j=1}^n p(y_j \mid x, y_{1:j-1})$.

3 Models over Multiple KBs

In this paper, we focus on a setting where we have access to K training sets from different domains, and each domain corresponds to a different KB. In all domains the input is a language utterance and the label is a logical form (we assume annotated logical forms can be converted to a single formal language such as lambda-DCS in Figure 1). While the mapping from words to KB constants is specific to each domain, we expect that the manner in which language expresses composition of meaning to be shared across domains. We now describe architectures that share information between the encoders and decoders of different domains.

3.1 One-to-one model

This model is similar to the baseline model described in Section 2. As illustrated in Figure 2, it consists of a single encoder and a single decoder, which are used to generate outputs for all domains. Thus, all model parameters are shared across domains, and the model is trained from all examples. Note that the number of parameters does not depend on the number of domains K.

Since there is no explicit representation of the domain that is being decoded, the model must learn to identify the domain given only the input. To alleviate that, we encode the k'th domain by a one-hot vector $d_k \in \mathbb{R}^K$. At each step, the decoder updates the hidden state conditioned on the domain's one-hot vector, as well as on the previous hidden state, the output token and the context. Formally, for domain k, Equation 1 is changed:[1]

$$
s_{j+1} = LSTM([\phi^{(out)}(y_j), c_j, d_k], s_j). \tag{2}
$$

Recently Johnson et al. (2016) used a similar intuition for neural machine translation, where they added an artificial token at the beginning of each source sentence to specify the target language. We implemented their approach and compare to it in Section 4.

---

[1] For simplicity, we omit the domain index k from our notation whenever it can be inferred from context.

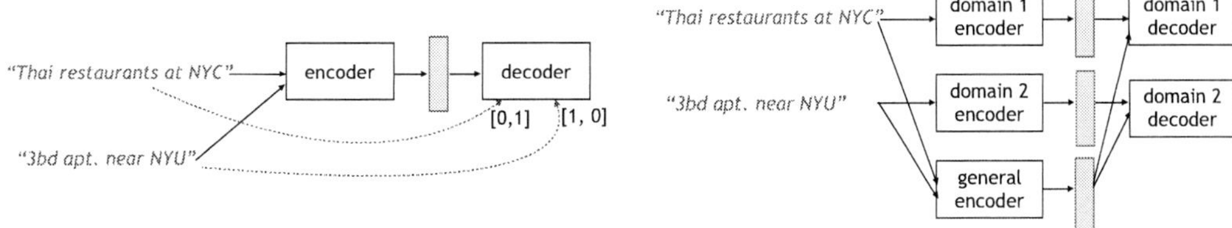

Figure 2: Illustration of models with one example from the RESTAURANTS domain and another from the HOUSING domain. Left: One-to-one model with optional domain encoding. Right: many-to-many model.

Since we have one decoder for multiple domains, tokens which are not in the domain vocabulary could possibly be generated. We prevent that at test time by excluding out-of-domain tokens before the softmax ($p(y_j \mid x, y_{1:j-1})$) takes place.

3.2 Many-to-many model

In this model, we keep a separate encoder and decoder for every domain, but augment the model with an additional encoder that consumes examples from all domains (see Figure 2). This is motivated by prior work on domain adaptation (Daume III, 2007; Blitzer et al., 2011), where each example has a representation that captures domain-specific aspects of the example and a representation that captures domain-general aspects. In our case, this is achieved by encoding examples with a domain-specific encoder as well as a domain-general encoder, and passing both representations to the decoder.

Formally, we now have $K + 1$ encoders and K decoders, and denote by $h_i^{F,k}, h_i^{B,k}, b_i^k$ the forward state, backward state and their concatenation at position i (the domain-general encoder has index $K + 1$). The hidden state of the decoder in domain k is initialized from the domain-specific and domain-general encoder:

$$s_1 = \tanh(W^{(s)}[h_m^{F,k}, h_1^{B,k}, h_m^{F,K+1}, h_1^{B,K+1}]).$$

Then, we compute unnormalized attention scores based on both encoders, and represent the language context with both domain-general and domain-specific representations. Equation 1 for domain k is changed as follows:

$$e_{ji} = s_j^\top W^{(a)}[b_i^k, b_i^{K+1}],$$

$$c_j = \sum_{i=1}^{m} \alpha_{ji}[b_i^k, b_i^{K+1}].$$

In this model, the number of encoding parameters grows by a factor of $\frac{1}{k}$, and the number of decoding parameters grows by less than a factor of 2.

3.3 One-to-many model

Here, a single encoder is shared, while we keep a separate decoder for each domain. The shared encoder captures the fact that the input in each domain is a sequence of English words. The domain-specific decoders learn to output tokens from the right domain vocabulary.

4 Experiments

4.1 Data

We evaluated our system on the OVERNIGHT semantic parsing dataset, which contains $13,682$ examples of language utterances paired with logical forms across eight domains. OVERNIGHT was constructed by generating logical forms from a grammar and annotating them with language through crowdsourcing. We evaluated on the same train/test split as Wang et al. (2015), using the same accuracy metric, that is, the proportion of questions for which the denotations of the predicted and gold logical forms are equal.

4.2 Implementation Details

We replicate the experimental setup of Jia and Liang (2016): We used the same hyper-parameters without tuning; we used 200 hidden units and 100-dimensional word vectors; we initialized parameters uniformly within the interval $[-0.1, 0.1]$, and maximized the log likelihood of the correct logical form with stochastic gradient descent. We trained the model for 30 epochs with an initial learning rate of 0.1, and halved the learning rate every 5 epochs, starting from epoch 15. We replaced word vectors for words that occur only once in the training set with a universal <unk> word vector. At test time, we used beam search with beam size 5. We then picked the highest-scoring logical form that does not yield an executor error when its denotation is computed. Our models were implemented in Theano (Bergstra et al., 2010).

Model	Basketball	Blocks	Calendar	Housing	Publications	Recipes	Restaurants	Social	Avg.	# Model Params
INDEP	85.2	61.2	77.4	67.7	74.5	79.2	79.5	80.2	75.6	14.1 M
MANY2MANY	83.9	63.2	79.8	75.1	75.2	81.5	79.8	**82.4**	77.6	22.8 M
ONE2MANY	84.4	59.1	79.8	74.6	80.1	81.5	80.7	81.1	77.7	8.6 M
INPUTTOKEN	85.9	63.2	79.2	77.8	75.8	80.6	**82.5**	81.0	78.2	2 M
ONE2ONE	84.9	**63.4**	75.6	76.7	78.9	**83.8**	81.3	81.4	78.3	2 M
DOMAINENCODING	**86.2**	62.7	**82.1**	**78.3**	80.7	82.9	82.2	81.7	**79.6**	2 M

Table 1: Test accuracy for all models on all domains, along with the number of parameters for each model.

4.3 Results

For our main result, we trained on all eight domains all models described in Section 3: ONE2ONE, DOMAINENCODING and INPUTTOKEN representing respectively the basic one-to-one model, with extensions of one-hot domain encoding or an extra input token, as described in Section 3.1. MANY2MANY and ONE2MANY are the models described in Sections 3.2 and 3.3, respectively. INDEP is the baseline sequence-to-sequence model described in Section 2, which trained independently on each domain.

Results show (Table 1) that training on multiple KBs improves average accuracy over all domains for all our proposed models, and that performance improves as more parameters are shared. Our strongest results come when parameter sharing is maximal (i.e., single encoder and single decoder), coupled with a one-hot domain representation at decoding time (DOMAINENCODING). In this case accuracy improves not only on average, but also for each domain separately. Moreover, the number of model parameters necessary for training the model is reduced by a factor of 7.

Our baseline, INDEP, is a reimplementation of the NORECOMBINATION model described in Jia and Liang (2016), which achieved average accuracy of 75.8% (corresponds to our 75.6% result). Jia and Liang (2016) also introduced a framework for generating new training examples in a single domain through *recombination*. Their model that uses the most training data achieved state-of-the-art average accuracy of 77.5% on OVERNIGHT. We show that by training over multiple KBs we can achieve higher average accuracy, and our best model, DOMAINENCODING, sets a new state-of-the-art average accuracy of 79.6%.

Figure 3 shows a learning curve for all models on the test set, when training on a fraction of the training data. We observe that the difference between models that share parameters (INPUTTOKEN, ONE2ONE and DOMAINEN-CODING) and models that keep most of the pa-

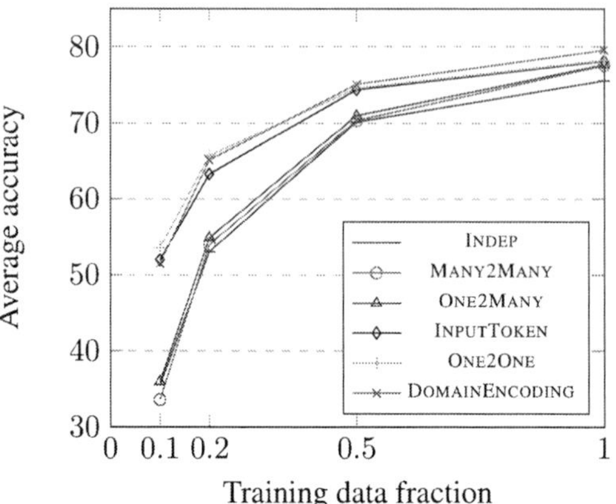

Figure 3: Learning curves for all models on the test set.

rameters separate (INDEP, MANY2MANY and ONE2MANY) is especially pronounced when the amount of data is small, reaching a difference of more than 15 accuracy point with 10% of the training data. This highlights the importance of using additional data from a similar distribution without increasing the number of parameters when there is little data. The learning curve also suggests that the MANY2MANY model improves considerably as the amount of data increases, and it would be interesting to examine its performance on larger datasets.

4.4 Analysis

Learning a semantic parser involves mapping language phrases to KB constants, as well as learning how language composition corresponds to logical form composition. We hypothesized that the main benefit of training on multiple KBs lies in learning about compositionality. To verify that, we append the domain index to the name of every constant in every KB, and therefore constant names are disjoint across datasets. We train DOMAINEN-CODING on this dataset and obtain an accuracy of 79.1% (comparing to 79.6%), which hints that most of the gain is attributed to compositionality rather than mapping of language to KB constants.

We also inspected cases where DOMAINEN-

CODING performed better than INDEP, by analyzing errors on a development set (20% of the training data). We found 45 cases where INDEP makes an error (and DOMAINENCODING does not) by predicting a wrong comparative or superlative structure (e.g., $>$ instead of $\geq$). However, the opposite case occurs only 29 times. This reiterates how we learn structural linguistic regularities when sharing parameters.

Lastly, we observed that the domain's training set size negatively correlates with its relative improvement in performance (DOMAINENCODING accuracy compared to INDEP), where Spearman's $\rho = -0.86$. This could be explained by the tendency of smaller domains to cover a smaller fraction of structural regularities in language, thus, they gain more by sharing information.

5 Conclusion

In this paper we address the challenge of obtaining training data for semantic parsing from a new perspective. We propose that one can improve parsing accuracy by training models over multiple KBs and demonstrate this on the eight domains of the OVERNIGHT dataset.

In future work, we would like to further reduce the burden of data gathering by training character-level models that learn to map language phrases to KB constants across datasets, and by pre-training language side models that improve the encoder from data that is independent of the KB. We also plan to apply this method on datasets where only denotations are provided rather than logical forms.

Reproducibility

All code, data, and experiments for this paper are available on the CodaLab platform at `https://worksheets.codalab.org/worksheets/0xdec998f58deb4829aba80fbf49f69236/`.

Acknowledgments

We thank Shimi Salant and the anonymous reviewers for their constructive feedback. This work was partially supported by the Israel Science Foundation, grant 942/16.

References

Y. Artzi and L. Zettlemoyer. 2013. Weakly supervised learning of semantic parsers for mapping instructions to actions. *Transactions of the Association for Computational Linguistics (TACL)* 1:49–62.

D. Bahdanau, K. Cho, and Y. Bengio. 2015. Neural machine translation by jointly learning to align and translate. In *International Conference on Learning Representations (ICLR)*.

J. Berant and P. Liang. 2014. Semantic parsing via paraphrasing. In *Association for Computational Linguistics (ACL)*.

J. Berant and P. Liang. 2015. Imitation learning of agenda-based semantic parsers. *Transactions of the Association for Computational Linguistics (TACL)* 3:545–558.

J. Bergstra, O. Breuleux, F. Bastien, P. Lamblin, R. Pascanu, G. Desjardins, J. Turian, D. Warde-Farley, and Y. Bengio. 2010. Theano: a CPU and GPU math expression compiler. In *Python for Scientific Computing Conference*.

J. Blitzer, S. Kakade, and D. P. Foster. 2011. Domain adaptation with coupled subspaces. In *Artificial Intelligence and Statistics (AISTATS)*. pages 173–181.

R. Caruana. 1997. Multitask learning. *Machine Learning* 28:41–75.

J. Clarke, D. Goldwasser, M. Chang, and D. Roth. 2010. Driving semantic parsing from the world's response. In *Computational Natural Language Learning (CoNLL)*. pages 18–27.

R. Collobert, J. Weston, L. Bottou, M. Karlen, K. Kavukcuoglu, and P. Kuksa. 2011. Natural language processing (almost) from scratch. *Journal of Machine Learning Research (JMLR)* 12:2493–2537.

H. Daume III. 2007. Frustratingly easy domain adaptation. In *Association for Computational Linguistics (ACL)*.

L. Dong and M. Lapata. 2016. Language to logical form with neural attention. In *Association for Computational Linguistics (ACL)*.

O. Firat, K. Cho, and Y. Bengio. 2016. Multi-way, multilingual neural machine translation with a shared attention mechanism. In *North American Association for Computational Linguistics (NAACL)*.

S. Hochreiter and J. Schmidhuber. 1997. Long short-term memory. *Neural Computation* 9(8):1735–1780.

R. Jia and P. Liang. 2016. Data recombination for neural semantic parsing. In *Association for Computational Linguistics (ACL)*.

M. Johnson, M. Schuster, Q. V. Le, M. Krikun, Y. Wu, Z. Chen, N. Thorat, F. Vigas, M. Wattenberg, G. Corrado, M. Hughes, and J. Dean. 2016. Google's multilingual neural machine translation system: Enabling zero-shot translation. *arXiv preprint arXiv:1611.04558* .

J. Krishnamurthy and T. Mitchell. 2012. Weakly supervised training of semantic parsers. In *Empirical Methods in Natural Language Processing and Computational Natural Language Learning (EMNLP/CoNLL)*. pages 754–765.

T. Kwiatkowski, L. Zettlemoyer, S. Goldwater, and M. Steedman. 2011. Lexical generalization in CCG grammar induction for semantic parsing. In *Empirical Methods in Natural Language Processing (EMNLP)*. pages 1512–1523.

P. Liang. 2013. Lambda dependency-based compositional semantics. *arXiv* .

P. Liang, M. I. Jordan, and D. Klein. 2011. Learning dependency-based compositional semantics. In *Association for Computational Linguistics (ACL)*. pages 590–599.

M. Luong, Q. V. Le, I. Sutskever, O. Vinyals, and L. Kaiser. 2016. Multi-task sequence to sequence learning. In *International Conference on Learning Representations (ICLR)*.

M. Luong, H. Pham, and C. D. Manning. 2015. Effective approaches to attention-based neural machine translation. In *Empirical Methods in Natural Language Processing (EMNLP)*. pages 1412–1421.

S. Reddy, M. Lapata, and M. Steedman. 2014. Large-scale semantic parsing without question-answer pairs. *Transactions of the Association for Computational Linguistics (TACL)* 2(10):377–392.

I. Sutskever, O. Vinyals, and Q. V. Le. 2014. Sequence to sequence learning with neural networks. In *Advances in Neural Information Processing Systems (NIPS)*. pages 3104–3112.

Y. Wang, J. Berant, and P. Liang. 2015. Building a semantic parser overnight. In *Association for Computational Linguistics (ACL)*.

M. Zelle and R. J. Mooney. 1996. Learning to parse database queries using inductive logic programming. In *Association for the Advancement of Artificial Intelligence (AAAI)*. pages 1050–1055.

L. S. Zettlemoyer and M. Collins. 2005. Learning to map sentences to logical form: Structured classification with probabilistic categorial grammars. In *Uncertainty in Artificial Intelligence (UAI)*. pages 658–666.

Representing Sentences as Low-Rank Subspaces

Jiaqi Mu, Suma Bhat, and **Pramod Viswanath**
University of Illinois at Urbana Champaign
{jiaqimu2, spbhat2, pramodv}@illinois.edu

Abstract

Sentences are important semantic units of natural language. A generic, distributional representation of sentences that can capture the latent semantics is beneficial to multiple downstream applications. We observe a simple geometry of sentences – the word representations of a given sentence (on average 10.23 words in all SemEval datasets with a standard deviation 4.84) roughly lie in a *low-rank* subspace (roughly, rank 4). Motivated by this observation, we represent a sentence by the low-rank *subspace* spanned by its word vectors. Such an unsupervised representation is empirically validated via semantic textual similarity tasks on 19 different datasets, where it outperforms the sophisticated neural network models, including skip-thought vectors, by 15% on average.

1 Introduction

Real-valued word representations have brought a fresh approach to classical problems in NLP, recognized for their ability to capture linguistic regularities: similar words tend to have similar representations; similar word pairs tend to have similar difference vectors (Bengio et al., 2003; Mnih and Hinton, 2007; Mikolov et al., 2010; Collobert et al., 2011; Huang et al., 2012; Dhillon et al., 2012; Mikolov et al., 2013; Pennington et al., 2014; Levy and Goldberg, 2014; Arora et al., 2015; Stratos et al., 2015). Going beyond words, sentences capture much of the semantic information. Given the success of lexical representations, a natural question of great topical interest is how to extend the power of distributional representations to sentences.

There are currently two approaches to represent sentences. A sentence contains rich syntactic information and can be modeled through sophisticated neural networks (e.g., convolutional neural networks (Kim, 2014; Kalchbrenner et al., 2014), recurrent neural networks (Sutskever et al., 2014; Le and Mikolov, 2014; Kiros et al., 2015; Hill et al., 2016) and recursive neural networks (Socher et al., 2013)). Another simple and common approach ignores the latent structure of sentences: a prototypical approach is to represent a sentence by summing or averaging over the vectors of the words in this sentence (Wieting et al., 2015; Adi et al., 2016; Kenter et al., 2016).

Recently, Wieting et al. (2015); Adi et al. (2016) reveal that even though the latter approach ignores all syntactic information, it is simple, straightforward, and remarkably robust at capturing the sentential semantics. Such an approach successfully outperforms the neural network based approaches on textual similarity tasks in both supervised and unsupervised settings.

We follow the latter approach but depart from representing sentences in a vector space as in these prior works; we present a novel Grassmannian property of sentences. The geometry is motivated by (Gong et al., 2017; Mu et al., 2016) where an interesting phenomenon is observed – the local context of a given word/phrase can be well represented by a low rank subspace. We propose to generalize this observation to sentences: not only do the word vectors in a snippet of a sentence (i.e., a context for a given word defined as several words surrounding it) lie in a low-rank subspace, but the entire sentence (on average 10.23 words in all SemEval datasets with standard deviation 4.84) follows this geometric property as well:

Geometry of Sentences: The word representations lie in a low-rank subspaces (rank 3-5) for all words in a target sen-

Proceedings of the 55th Annual Meeting of the Association for Computational Linguistics (Short Papers), pages 629–634
Vancouver, Canada, July 30 - August 4, 2017. ©2017 Association for Computational Linguistics
https://doi.org/10.18653/v1/P17-2099

tence.

The observation indicates that the subspace contains most of the information about this sentence, and therefore motivates a sentence representation method: the sentences should be represented in the space of subspaces (i.e., the Grassmannian manifold) instead of a vector space; formally:

> **Sentence Representation:** A sentence can be represented by a low-rank subspace spanned by its word representations.

Analogous to word representations of similar words being similar vectors, the principle of sentence representations is: similar sentences should have similar subspaces. Two questions arise: (a) how to define the similarity between sentences and (b) how to define the similarity between subspaces.

The first question has been already addressed by the popular semantic textual similarity (STS) tasks. Unlike textual entailment (which aims at inferring directional relation between two sentences) and paraphrasing (which is a binary classification problem), STS provides a unified framework of measuring the degree of semantic equivalence (Agirre et al., 2012, 2013, 2014, 2015) in a continuous fashion. Motivated by the cosine similarity between vectors being a good index for word similarity, we generalize this metric to subspaces: the similarity between subspaces defined in this paper is the ℓ_2-norm of the singular values between two subspaces; note that the singular values are in fact the cosine of the principal angles.

The key justification for our approach comes from empirical results that outperform state-of-the-art in some cases, and being comparable in others. In summary, representing sentences by subspaces outperforms representing sentences by averaged word vectors (by 14% on average) and sophisticated neural networks (by 15%) on 19 different STS datasets, ranging over different domains (News, WordNet definition, and Twitter).

2   Geometry of Sentences

Assembling successful distributional word representations (for example, GloVe (Pennington et al., 2014)) into sentence representations is an active research topic. Different from previous studies (for example, doc2vec (Mikolov et al., 2013), skip-thought vectors (Kiros et al., 2015), Siamese

CBOW (Kenter et al., 2016)), our main contribution is to represent sentences using *non-vector* space representations: a sentence can be well represented by the subspace spanned by the context word vectors – such a method naturally builds on any word representation method. Due to the widespread use of word2vec and GloVe, we use their publicly available word representations – word2vec(Mikolov et al., 2013) trained using Google News[1] and GloVe (Pennington et al., 2014) trained using Common Crawl[2] – to test our observations.

Observation Let $v(w) \in \mathbb{R}^d$ be the d-dimensional word representation for a given word $w \in V$, and $s = (w_1, \ldots, w_n)$ be a given sentence. Consider the following sentence where $n = 32$:

> They would not tell me if there was any pension left here, and would only tell me if there was (and how much there was) if they saw I was entitled to it.

After stacking the (non-functional) word vectors $v(w)$ to form a $d \times n$ matrix, we observe that most energy (80% for GloVe and 72% for word2vec) of such a matrix is contained in a rank-N subspace, where N is much smaller than n (for comparison, we choose N to be 4 and therefore $N/n \approx 13\%$). Figure 1 provides a visual representation of this geometric phenomenon, where we have projected the d-dimensional word representations into 3-dimensional vectors and use these 3-dimensional word vectors to get the subspace for this sentence (we set $N = 2$ here for visualization), and plot the subspaces as 2-dimensional planes.

Geometry of Sentences The example above generalizes to a vast majority of the sentences: the word representations of a given sentence roughly reside in a low-rank subspace, which can be extracted by principal component analysis (PCA).

Verification We empirically validate this geometric phenomenon by collecting 53,396 sentences from the SemEval STS share tasks (Agirre et al., 2012, 2013, 2014, 2015) and plotting the fraction of energy being captured by the top N components of PCA in Figure 2 for $N = 3, 4, 5,$

---

[1] https://code.google.com/archive/p/word2vec/

[2] http://nlp.stanford.edu/projects/glove/

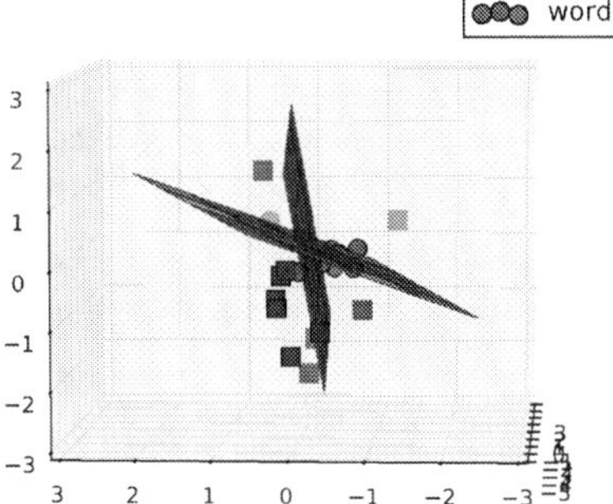

Figure 1: Geometry of sentences.

from where we can observe that on average 70% of the energy is captured by a rank-3 subspace, and 80% for a rank-4 subspace and 90% for rank-5 subspace. For comparison, the fraction of energy of random sentences (generated i.i.d. from the unigram distribution) are also plotted in Figure 2.

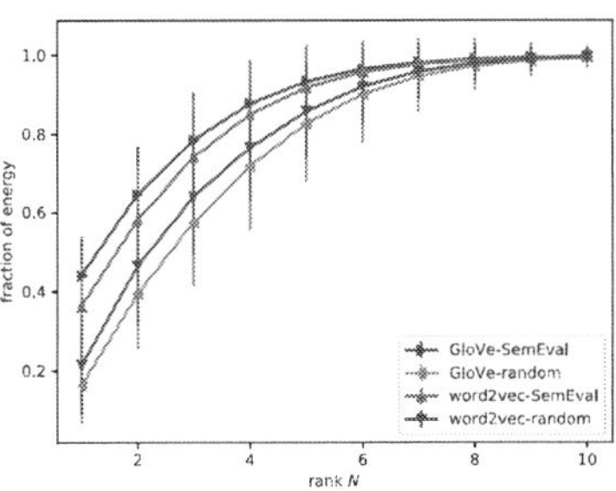

Figure 2: Fraction of energy captured by the top principal components.

Representation The observation above motivates our sentence representation algorithm: since the words in a sentence concentrate on a few directions, the subspace spanned by these directions could in principle be a proper representation for this sentence. The direction and subspace in turn can be extracted via PCA as in Algorithm 1.

Similarity Metric The principle of sentence representations is that similar sentences should have similar representations. In this case, we expect the similarity between subspaces to be a good index for the semantic similarity of sentences. In our paper, we define the similarity between subspaces as follows: let $u_1(s), ..., u_N(s)$ be the N orthonormal basis for a sentence s. After stacking the N vectors in a $d \times N$ matrix

---

Algorithm 1: The algorithm for sentence representations.

Input : a sentence s, word embeddings $v(\cdot)$, and a PCA rank N.

1 Compute the first N principle components of samples $v(w'), w' \in c$,

$$u_1, ..., u_N \leftarrow \mathrm{PCA}(v(w'), w' \in s),$$

$$S \leftarrow \left\{ \sum_{n=1}^{N} : \alpha_n u_n, \alpha_n \in R \right\}$$

Output: N orthonormal basis $u_1, ..., u_N$ and a subspace S.

$U(s) = (u_1(s), ..., u_N(s))$, we define the corresponding cosine similarity as, $\mathrm{CosSim}(s_1, s_2) = \sqrt{\sum_{t=1}^{N} \sigma_t^2}$, where σ_t is the t-th singular value of $U(s_1)^{\mathrm{T}} U(s_2)$.

Note that $\sigma_t = \cos(\theta_t)$ where θ_t is the t-th "principle angle" between two subspaces. Such a metric is naturally related to the cosine similarity between vectors, which has been empirically validated to be a good measure of word similarity.

3 Experiments

In this section we evaluate our sentence representations empirically on the STS tasks. The objective of this task is to test the degree to which the algorithm can capture the semantic equivalence between two sentences. For example, the similarity between "a kid jumping a ledge with a bike" and "a black and white cat playing with a blanket" is 0 and the similarity between "a cat standing on tree branches" and "a black and white cat is high up on tree branches" is 3.6. The algorithm is then evaluated in terms of Pearson's correlation between the predicted score and the human judgment.

Datasets We test the performances of our algorithm on 19 different datasets, which include SemEval STS share tasks (Agirre et al., 2012, 2013, 2014, 2015), sourced from multiple domains (for example, News, WordNet definitions and Twitter).

Baselines and Preliminaries Our main comparisons are with algorithms that perform unsupervised sentence representation: average of word representations (i.e., avg. (of GloVe and skipgram) where we use the average of word vectors), doc2vec (D2V) (Le and Mikolov, 2014) and sophisticated neural networks (i.e., skip-thought vectors (ST) (Kiros et al., 2015), Siamese CBOW (SC) (Kenter et al., 2016)). In order to enable a fair comparison, we use the Toronto Book Corpus (Zhu et al., 2015) to train word embeddings. In our experiment, we adapt the same setting as in (Kenter et al., 2016) where we use skip-gram (Mikolov et al., 2013) of and GloVe (Pennington et al., 2014) to train a 300-dimensional word vectors for the words that occur 5 times or more in the training corpus. The rank of subspaces is set to be 4 for both word2vec and GloVe.

Results The detailed results are reported in Table 1, from where we can observe two phenomena: (a) representing sentences by its averaged word vectors provides a strong baseline and the performances are remarkably stable across different datasets; (b) our subspace-based method outperforms the average-based method by 14% on average and the neural network based approaches by 15%. This suggests that representing sentences by subspaces maintains more information than simply taking the average, and is more robust than highly-tuned sophisticated models.

When we average over the words, the average vector is biased because of many irrelevant words (for example, function words) in a given sentence. Therefore, given a longer sentence, the effect of useful word vectors become smaller and thus the average vector is less reliable at capturing the semantics. On the other hand, the subspace representation is immune to this phenomenon: the word vectors capturing the semantics of the sentence tend to concentrate on a few directions which dominate the subspace representation.

4   Conclusion

This paper presents a novel unsupervised sentence representation leveraging the Grassmannian geometry of word representations. While the current approach relies on the pre-trained word representations, the *joint learning* of both word and sentence representations and in conjunction with supervised datasets such the Paraphrase Database (PPDB) (Ganitkevitch et al., 2013) is left to future research. Also interesting is the exploration of neural network architectures that operate on subspaces (as opposed to vectors), allowing for downstream evaluations of our novel representation.

References

Yossi Adi, Einat Kermany, Yonatan Belinkov, Ofer Lavi, and Yoav Goldberg. 2016. Fine-grained analysis of sentence embeddings using auxiliary prediction tasks. *arXiv preprint arXiv:1608.04207* .

Eneko Agirre, Carmen Banea, Claire Cardie, Daniel Cer, Mona Diab, Aitor Gonzalez-Agirre, Weiwei Guo, Inigo Lopez-Gazpio, Montse Maritxalar, Rada Mihalcea, et al. 2015. Semeval-2015 task 2: Semantic textual similarity, english, spanish and pilot on interpretability. In *Proceedings of the 9th international workshop on semantic evaluation (SemEval 2015)*. pages 252–263.

Eneko Agirre, Carmen Banea, Claire Cardie, Daniel Cer, Mona Diab, Aitor Gonzalez-Agirre, Weiwei Guo, Rada Mihalcea, German Rigau, and Janyce Wiebe. 2014. Semeval-2014 task 10: Multilingual semantic textual similarity. In *Proceedings of the 8th international workshop on semantic evaluation (SemEval 2014)*. pages 81–91.

Eneko Agirre, Daniel Cer, Mona Diab, Aitor Gonzalez-Agirre, and Weiwei Guo. 2013. sem 2013 shared task: Semantic textual similarity, including a pilot on typed-similarity. In *In* SEM 2013: The Second Joint Conference on Lexical and Computational Semantics. Association for Computational Linguistics*. Citeseer.

Eneko Agirre, Mona Diab, Daniel Cer, and Aitor Gonzalez-Agirre. 2012. Semeval-2012 task 6: A pilot on semantic textual similarity. In *Proceedings of the First Joint Conference on Lexical and Computational Semantics-Volume 1: Proceedings of the main conference and the shared task, and Volume 2: Proceedings of the Sixth International Workshop on Semantic Evaluation*. Association for Computational Linguistics, pages 385–393.

Sanjeev Arora, Yuanzhi Li, Yingyu Liang, Tengyu Ma, and Andrej Risteski. 2015. Rand-walk: A latent variable model approach to word embeddings. *arXiv preprint arXiv:1502.03520* .

Yoshua Bengio, Réjean Ducharme, Pascal Vincent, and Christian Jauvin. 2003. A neural probabilistic language model. *journal of machine learning research* 3(Feb):1137–1155.

Ronan Collobert, Jason Weston, Léon Bottou, Michael Karlen, Koray Kavukcuoglu, and Pavel Kuksa. 2011. Natural language processing (almost) from scratch. *Journal of Machine Learning Research* 12(Aug):2493–2537.

Paramveer Dhillon, Jordan Rodu, Dean Foster, and Lyle Ungar. 2012. Two step cca: A new spectral method for estimating vector models of words. *arXiv preprint arXiv:1206.6403* .

Juri Ganitkevitch, Benjamin Van Durme, and Chris Callison-Burch. 2013. PPDB: The paraphrase database. In *Proceedings of NAACL-*

HLT. Association for Computational Linguistics, Atlanta, Georgia, pages 758–764. http://cs.jhu.edu/ ccb/publications/ppdb.pdf.

Hongyu Gong, Suma Bhat, and Pramod Viswanath. 2017. Geometry of compositionality. *Association for Advancement of Artificial Intelligence (AAAI)* .

Felix Hill, Kyunghyun Cho, and Anna Korhonen. 2016. Learning distributed representations of sentences from unlabelled data. *arXiv preprint arXiv:1602.03483* .

Eric H Huang, Richard Socher, Christopher D Manning, and Andrew Y Ng. 2012. Improving word representations via global context and multiple word prototypes. In *Proceedings of the 50th Annual Meeting of the Association for Computational Linguistics: Long Papers-Volume 1*. Association for Computational Linguistics, pages 873–882.

Nal Kalchbrenner, Edward Grefenstette, and Phil Blunsom. 2014. A convolutional neural network for modelling sentences. *arXiv preprint arXiv:1404.2188* .

Tom Kenter, Alexey Borisov, and Maarten de Rijke. 2016. Siamese cbow: Optimizing word embeddings for sentence representations. *arXiv preprint arXiv:1606.04640* .

Yoon Kim. 2014. Convolutional neural networks for sentence classification. *arXiv preprint arXiv:1408.5882* .

Ryan Kiros, Yukun Zhu, Ruslan R Salakhutdinov, Richard Zemel, Raquel Urtasun, Antonio Torralba, and Sanja Fidler. 2015. Skip-thought vectors. In *Advances in neural information processing systems*. pages 3294–3302.

Quoc V Le and Tomas Mikolov. 2014. Distributed representations of sentences and documents. In *ICML*. volume 14, pages 1188–1196.

Omer Levy and Yoav Goldberg. 2014. Neural word embedding as implicit matrix factorization. In *Advances in neural information processing systems*. pages 2177–2185.

Tomas Mikolov, Kai Chen, Greg Corrado, and Jeffrey Dean. 2013. Efficient estimation of word representations in vector space. *arXiv preprint arXiv:1301.3781* .

Tomas Mikolov, Martin Karafiát, Lukas Burget, Jan Cernockỳ, and Sanjeev Khudanpur. 2010. Recurrent neural network based language model. In *Interspeech*. volume 2, page 3.

Andriy Mnih and Geoffrey Hinton. 2007. Three new graphical models for statistical language modelling. In *Proceedings of the 24th international conference on Machine learning*. ACM, pages 641–648.

Jiaqi Mu, Suma Bhat, and Pramod Viswanath. 2016. Geometry of polysemy. *arXiv preprint arXiv:1610.07569* .

Jeffrey Pennington, Richard Socher, and Christopher D Manning. 2014. Glove: Global vectors for word representation. In *EMNLP*. volume 14, pages 1532–43.

Richard Socher, Alex Perelygin, Jean Y Wu, Jason Chuang, Christopher D Manning, Andrew Y Ng, and Christopher Potts. 2013. Recursive deep models for semantic compositionality over a sentiment treebank. In *Proceedings of the conference on empirical methods in natural language processing (EMNLP)*. Citeseer, volume 1631, page 1642.

Karl Stratos, Michael Collins, and Daniel Hsu. 2015. Model-based word embeddings from decompositions of count matrices. In *Proceedings of ACL*. pages 1282–1291.

Ilya Sutskever, Oriol Vinyals, and Quoc V Le. 2014. Sequence to sequence learning with neural networks. In *Advances in neural information processing systems*. pages 3104–3112.

John Wieting, Mohit Bansal, Kevin Gimpel, and Karen Livescu. 2015. Towards universal paraphrastic sentence embeddings. *arXiv preprint arXiv:1511.08198* .

Yukun Zhu, Ryan Kiros, Richard Zemel, Ruslan Salakhutdinov, Raquel Urtasun, Antonio Torralba, and Sanja Fidler. 2015. Aligning books and movies: Towards story-like visual explanations by watching movies and reading books. In *arXiv preprint arXiv:1506.06724*.

dataset		l	ST	SC	D2V	GloVe		skip-gram	
						avg.	subspace	avg.	subspace
2012	MSRpar	17.70	5.60	43.79	14.85	**<u>46.18</u>**	40.74	16.82	35.71
	MSRvid	6.63	58.07	45.22	19.82	<u>63.75</u>	**73.90**	<u>58.28</u>	<u>63.19</u>
	OnWn	7.57	60.45	**64.44**	35.73	56.72	63.21	42.22	58.43
	SMTeuroparl	10.70	42.03	45.03	36.18	**<u>52.51</u>**	<u>45.83</u>	37.99	<u>45.35</u>
	SMTnews	11.72	39.11	39.02	52.78	38.99	**45.73**	23.44	37.73
2013	FNWN	19.90	31.24	23.22	**51.07**	39.29	41.03	19.35	26.43
	OnWn	7.17	24.18	49.85	49.26	<u>52.48</u>	**72.03**	<u>58.30</u>	<u>56.52</u>
	headlines	7.21	38.61	65.34	28.90	49.07	**66.13**	41.53	62.84
2014	OnWn	7.74	48.82	60.73	60.84	60.15	**76.28**	55.38	<u>67.13</u>
	deft-forum	8.38	37.36	40.82	22.63	22.75	<u>42.60</u>	32.87	**45.30**
	deft-news	15.78	46.17	59.13	18.93	<u>62.91</u>	**64.40**	38.72	53.62
	headlines	7.43	40.31	**63.64**	24.31	46.00	62.42	36.46	61.44
	images	9.12	42.57	64.97	39.92	55.19	**73.38**	45.17	**71.84**
	tweet-news	10.03	51.38	73.15	33.56	60.45	**74.29**	44.16	<u>73.87</u>
2015	answer-forum	15.03	27.84	21.81	28.59	<u>31.39</u>	**69.50**	<u>34.83</u>	<u>57.62</u>
	answer-studetns	10.44	26.61	36.71	11.14	<u>48.46</u>	**63.43**	<u>43.85</u>	<u>59.01</u>
	belief	13.00	45.84	47.69	30.58	44.73	**69.65**	<u>49.24</u>	<u>64.48</u>
	headlines	7.50	12.48	21.51	22.64	<u>44.80</u>	<u>65.67</u>	<u>44.23</u>	**68.02**
	images	9.12	21.00	25.60	34.14	<u>66.40</u>	**80.12**	56.47	<u>70.53</u>

Table 1: Pearson's correlation (x100) on SemEval textual similarity task using 19 different datasets, where l is the average sentence length of each dataset. Results that are better than the baselines are marked with underlines and the best results are in bold.

Improving Semantic Relevance for Sequence-to-Sequence Learning of Chinese Social Media Text Summarization

Shuming Ma[1,2], Xu Sun[1,2], Jingjing Xu[1,2], Houfeng Wang[1,2], Wenjie Li[3], Qi Su[4]

[1]MOE Key Laboratory of Computational Linguistics, Peking University
[2]School of Electronics Engineering and Computer Science, Peking University
[3]Department of Computing, The Hong Kong Polytechnic University
[4]School of Foreign Languages, Peking University
{shumingma, xusun, jingjingxu, wanghf, sukia}@pku.edu.cn
cswjli@comp.polyu.edu.hk

Abstract

Current Chinese social media text summarization models are based on an encoder-decoder framework. Although its generated summaries are similar to source texts literally, they have low semantic relevance. In this work, our goal is to improve semantic relevance between source texts and summaries for Chinese social media summarization. We introduce a Semantic Relevance Based neural model to encourage high semantic similarity between texts and summaries. In our model, the source text is represented by a gated attention encoder, while the summary representation is produced by a decoder. Besides, the similarity score between the representations is maximized during training. Our experiments show that the proposed model outperforms baseline systems on a social media corpus.

1 Introduction

Text summarization is to produce a brief summary of the main ideas of the text. For long and normal documents, extractive summarization achieves satisfying performance by selecting a few sentences from source texts (Radev et al., 2004; Woodsend and Lapata, 2010; Cheng and Lapata, 2016). However, it does not apply to Chinese social media text summarization, where texts are comparatively short and often full of noise. Therefore, abstractive text summarization, which is based on encoder-decoder framework, is a better choice (Rush et al., 2015; Hu et al., 2015).

For extractive summarization, the selected sentences often have high semantic relevance to the text. However, for abstractive text summarization, current models tend to produce grammatical

Text: 昨晚，中联航空成都飞北京一架航班被发现有多人吸烟。后因天气原因，飞机备降太原机场。有乘客要求重新安检，机长决定继续飞行，引起机组人员与未吸烟乘客冲突。
Last night, several people were caught to smoke on a flight of China United Airlines from Chendu to Beijing. Later the flight temporarily landed on Taiyuan Airport. Some passengers asked for a security check but were denied by the captain, which led to a collision between crew and passengers.

RNN: 中联航空机场发生爆炸致多人死亡。
China United Airlines exploded in the airport, leaving several people dead.

Gold: 航班多人吸烟机组人员与乘客冲突。
Several people smoked on a flight which led to a collision between crew and passengers.

Figure 1: An example of RNN generated summary. It has high similarity to the text literally, but low semantic relevance.

and coherent summaries regardless of its semantic relevance with source texts. Figure 1 shows that the summary generated by a current model (RNN encoder-decoder) is similar to the source text literally, but it has low semantic relevance.

In this work, our goal is to improve the semantic relevance between source texts and generated summaries for Chinese social media text summarization. To achieve this goal, we propose a Semantic Relevance Based neural model. In our model, a similarity evaluation component is introduced to measure the relevance of source texts and generated summaries. During training, it maximizes the similarity score to encourage high semantic relevance between source texts and sum-

Proceedings of the 55th Annual Meeting of the Association for Computational Linguistics (Short Papers), pages 635–640
Vancouver, Canada, July 30 - August 4, 2017. ©2017 Association for Computational Linguistics
https://doi.org/10.18653/v1/P17-2100

maries. The representation of source texts is produced by an encoder, while that of summaries is computed by a decoder. We introduce a gated attention encoder to better represent the source text. Besides, our decoder generates summaries and provide the summary representation. Experiments show that our proposed model has better performance than baseline systems on the social media corpus.

2 Background: Chinese Abstractive Text Summarization

Current Chinese social media text summarization model is based on encoder-decoder framework. Encoder-decoder model is able to compress source texts $x = \{x_1, x_2, ..., x_N\}$ into continuous vector representation with an encoder, and then generate the summary $y = \{y_1, y_2, ..., y_M\}$ with a decoder. In the previous work (Hu et al., 2015), the encoder is a bi-directional gated recurrent neural network, which maps source texts into sentence vector $\{h_1, h_2, ..., h_N\}$. The decoder is a unidirectional recurrent neural network, which produces the distribution of output words y_t with previous hidden state s_{t-1} and word y_{t-1}:

$$p(y_t|x) = softmax f(s_{t-1}, y_{t-1}) \quad (1)$$

where f is recurrent neural network output function, and s_0 is the last hidden state of encoder h_N.

Attention mechanism is introduced to better capture context information of source texts (Bahdanau et al., 2014). Attention vector c_t is represented by the weighted sum of encoder hidden states:

$$c_t = \sum_{i=1}^{N} \alpha_{ti} h_i \quad (2)$$

$$\alpha_{ti} = \frac{e^{g(s_t, h_i)}}{\sum_{j=1}^{N} e^{g(s_t, h_j)}} \quad (3)$$

where $g(s_t, h_i)$ is a relevant score between decoder hidden state s_t and encoder hidden state h_i. When predicting an output word, the decoder takes account of attention vector, which contains the alignment information between source texts and summaries.

3 Proposed Model

Our assumption is that source texts and summaries have high semantic relevance, so our proposed model encourages high similarity between

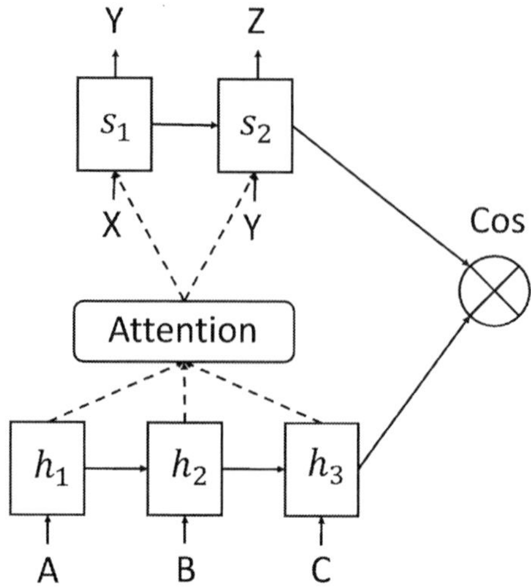

Figure 2: Our Semantic Relevance Based neural model. It consists of decoder (above), encoder (below) and cosine similarity function.

their representations. Figure 2 shows our proposed model. The model consists of three components: encoder, decoder and a similarity function. The encoder compresses source texts into semantic vectors, and the decoder generates summaries and produces semantic vectors of the generated summaries. Finally, the similarity function evaluates the relevance between the sematic vectors of source texts and generated summaries. Our training objective is to maximize the similarity score so that the generated summaries have high semantic relevance with source texts.

3.1 Text Representation

There are several methods to represent a text or a sentence, such as mean pooling of RNN output or reserving the last state of RNN. In our model, source text is represented by a gated attention encoder (Hahn and Keller, 2016). Every upcoming word is fed into a gated attention network, which measures its importance. The gated attention network outputs the important score with a feedforward network. At each time step, it inputs a word vector e_t and its previous context vector h_t, then outputs the score β_t. Then the word vector e_t is multiplied by the score β_t, and fed into RNN encoder. We select the last output h_N of RNN encoder as the semantic vector of the source text V_t.

A natural idea to get the semantic vector of a summary is to feed it into the encoder as well. However, this method wastes much time because we encode the same sentence twice. Actually, the last output s_M contains information of both source text and generated summaries. We simply compute the semantic vector of the summary by subtracting h_N from s_M:

$$V_s = s_M - h_N \qquad (4)$$

Previous work has proved that it is effective to represent a span of words without encoding them once more (Wang and Chang, 2016).

3.2 Semantic Relevance

Our goal is to compute the semantic relevance of source text and generated summary given semantic vector V_t and V_s. Here, we use cosine similarity to measure the semantic relevance, which is represented with a dot product and magnitude:

$$cos(V_s, V_t) = \frac{V_s \cdot V_t}{\|V_s\|\|V_t\|} \qquad (5)$$

Source text and summary share the same language, so it is reasonable to assume that their semantic vectors are distributed in the same space. Cosine similarity is a good way to measure the distance between two vectors in the same space.

3.3 Training

Given the model parameter θ and input text x, the model produces corresponding summary y and semantic vector V_s and V_t. The objective is to minimize the loss function:

$$L = -p(y|x;\theta) - \lambda cos(V_s, V_t) \qquad (6)$$

where $p(y|x;\theta)$ is the conditional probability of summaries given source texts, and is computed by the encoder-decoder model. $cos(V_s, V_t)$ is cosine similarity of semantic vectors V_s and V_t. This term tries to maximize the semantic relevance between source input and target output.

4 Experiments

In this section, we present the evaluation of our model and show its performance on a popular social media corpus. Besides, we use a case to explain the semantic relevance between generated summary and source text.

4.1 Dataset

Our dataset is Large Scale Chinese Short Text Summarization Dataset (LCSTS), which is constructed by Hu et al. (2015). The dataset consists of more than 2.4 million text-summary pairs, constructed from a famous Chinese social media website called Sina Weibo[1]. It is split into three parts, with 2,400,591 pairs in PART I, 10,666 pairs in PART II and 1,106 pairs in PART III. All the text-summary pairs in PART II and PART III are manually annotated with relevant scores ranged from 1 to 5, and we only reserve pairs with scores no less than 3. Following the previous work, we use PART I as training set, PART II as development set, and PART III as test set.

4.2 Experiment Setting

To alleviate the risk of word segmentation mistakes (Xu and Sun, 2016), we use Chinese character sequences as both source inputs and target outputs. We limit the model vocabulary size to 4000, which covers most of the common characters. Each character is represented by a random initialized word embedding. We tune our parameter on the development set. In our model, the embedding size is 400, the hidden state size of encoder-decoder is 500, and the size of gated attention network is 1000. We use Adam optimizer to learn the model parameters, and the batch size is set as 32. The parameter λ is 0.0001. Both the encoder and decoder are based on LSTM unit. Following the previous work (Hu et al., 2015), our evaluation metric is F-score of ROUGE: ROUGE-1, ROUGE-2 and ROUGE-L (Lin and Hovy, 2003).

4.3 Baseline Systems

RNN. We denote RNN as the basic sequence-to-sequence model with bi-directional GRU encoder and uni-directional GRU decoder. It is a widely used language generated framework, so it is an important baseline.

RNN context. RNN context is a sequence-to-sequence framework with neural attention. Attention mechanism helps capture the context information of source texts. This model is a stronger baseline system.

4.4 Results and Discussions

We compare our model with above baseline systems, including RNN and RNN context. We refer to our proposed Semantic Relevance Based neural model as **SRB**. Besides, SRB with a gated attention encoder is denoted as **+Attention**. Table 1

---

[1] weibo.sina.com

Model	ROUGE-1	ROUGE-2	ROUGE-L
RNN (W) (Hu et al., 2015)	17.7	8.5	15.8
RNN (C) (Hu et al., 2015)	21.5	8.9	18.6
RNN context (W) (Hu et al., 2015)	26.8	16.1	24.1
RNN context (C) (Hu et al., 2015)	29.9	17.4	27.2
RNN context + SRB (C)	32.1	18.9	29.2
+Attention (C)	**33.3**	**20.0**	**30.1**

Table 1: Results of our model and baseline systems. Our models achieve substantial improvement of all ROUGE scores over baseline systems. (W: Word level; C: Character level).

Text:仔细一算，上海的互联网公司不乏成功案例，但最终成为BAT一类巨头的几乎没有，这也能解释为何纳税百强的榜单中鲜少互联网公司的身影。有一类是被并购，比如：易趣、土豆网、PPS、PPTV、一号店等；有一类是数年偏安于细分市场。

With careful calculation, there are many successful Internet companies in Shanghai, but few of them becomes giant company like BAT. This is also the reason why few Internet companies are listed in top hundred companies of paying tax. Some of them are merged, such as Ebay, Tudou, PPS, PPTV, Yihaodian and so on. Others are satisfied with segment market for years.

Gold:为什么上海出不了互联网巨头？
Why Shanghai comes out no giant company?

RNN context:上海的互联网巨头。
Shanghai's giant company.

SRB:上海鲜少互联网巨头的身影。
Shanghai has few giant companies.

Figure 3: An Example of RNN generated summary on LCSTS corpus.

Model	level	R-1	R-2	R-L
RNN context	Word	26.8	16.1	24.1
(Hu et al., 2015)	Char	29.9	17.4	27.2
COPYNET	Word	35.0	22.3	32.0
(Gu et al., 2016)	Char	34.4	21.6	31.3
this work	Char	33.3	20.0	30.1

Table 2: Results of our model and state-of-the-art systems. COPYNET incorporates copying mechanism to solve out-of-vocabulary problem, so its has higher ROUGE scores. Our model does not incorporate this mechanism currently. In the future work, we will implement this technic to further improve the performance. (Word: Word level; Char: Character level; R-1: F-score of ROUGE-1; R-2: F-score of ROUGE-2; R-L: F-score of ROUGE-L)

shows the results of our models and baseline systems. We can see SRB outperforms both RNN and RNN context in the F-score of ROUGE-1, ROUGE-2 and ROUGE-L. It concludes that SRB generates more key words and phrases. With a gated attention encoder, SRB achieves a better performance with 33.3 F-score of ROUGE-1, 20.0 ROUGE-2 and 30.1 ROUGE-L. It shows that the gated attention reduces noisy and unimportant information, so that the remaining information represents a clear idea of source text. The better representation of encoder leads to a better semantic relevance evaluation by the similarity function. Therefore, SRB with gated attention encoder is able to generate summaries with high semantic relevance to source text.

Figure 3 is an example to show the semantic relevance between the source text and the summary. It shows that the main idea of the source text is about the reason why Shanghai has few giant company. RNN context produces "Shanghai's giant companies" which is literally similar to the source text, while SRB generates "Shanghai has few giant companies", which is closer to the main idea in semantics. It concludes that SRB produces summaries with higher semantic similarity to texts.

Table 2 summarizes the results of our model and state-of-the-art systems. COPYNET has the highest socres, because it incorporates copying mechanism to deals with out-of-vocabulary word problem. In this paper, we do not implement this mechanism in our model. In the future work, we will try to incorporates copying mechanism to our model to solve the out-of-vocabulary problem.

5 Related Work

Abstractive text summarization has achieved successful performance thanks to the sequence-to-sequence model (Sutskever et al., 2014) and attention mechanism (Bahdanau et al., 2014). Rush et al. (2015) first used an attention-based encoder to compress texts and a neural network language decoder to generate summaries. Following this work, recurrent encoder was introduced to text summarization, and gained better performance (Lopyrev, 2015; Chopra et al., 2016). Towards Chinese texts, Hu et al. (2015) built a large corpus of Chinese short text summarization. To deal with unknown word problem, Nallapati et al. (2016) proposed a generator-pointer model so that the decoder is able to generate words in source texts. Gu et al. (2016) also solved this issue by incorporating copying mechanism.

Our work is also related to neural attention model. Neural attention model is first proposed by Bahdanau et al. (2014). There are many other methods to improve neural attention model (Jean et al., 2015; Luong et al., 2015) and accelerate the training process (Sun, 2016).

6 Conclusion

Our work aims at improving semantic relevance of generated summaries and source texts for Chinese social media text summarization. Our model is able to transform the text and the summary into a dense vector, and encourage high similarity of their representation. Experiments show that our model outperforms baseline systems, and the generated summary has higher semantic relevance.

Acknowledgements

This work was supported in part by National High Technology Research and Development Program of China (863 Program, No. 2015AA015404), and National Natural Science Foundation of China (No. 61673028). Xu Sun is the corresponding author of this paper.

References

Dzmitry Bahdanau, Kyunghyun Cho, and Yoshua Bengio. 2014. Neural machine translation by jointly learning to align and translate. *CoRR* abs/1409.0473.

Jianpeng Cheng and Mirella Lapata. 2016. Neural summarization by extracting sentences and words. In *Proceedings of the 54th Annual Meeting of the Association for Computational Linguistics, ACL 2016, August 7-12, 2016, Berlin, Germany, Volume 1: Long Papers.*

Sumit Chopra, Michael Auli, and Alexander M. Rush. 2016. Abstractive sentence summarization with attentive recurrent neural networks. In *NAACL HLT 2016, The 2016 Conference of the North American Chapter of the Association for Computational Linguistics: Human Language Technologies, San Diego California, USA, June 12-17, 2016.* pages 93–98.

Jiatao Gu, Zhengdong Lu, Hang Li, and Victor O. K. Li. 2016. Incorporating copying mechanism in sequence-to-sequence learning. In *Proceedings of the 54th Annual Meeting of the Association for Computational Linguistics, ACL 2016, August 7-12, 2016, Berlin, Germany, Volume 1: Long Papers.*

Michael Hahn and Frank Keller. 2016. Modeling human reading with neural attention. In *Proceedings of the 2016 Conference on Empirical Methods in Natural Language Processing, EMNLP 2016, Austin, Texas, USA, November 1-4, 2016.* pages 85–95.

Baotian Hu, Qingcai Chen, and Fangze Zhu. 2015. LCSTS: A large scale chinese short text summarization dataset. In *Proceedings of the 2015 Conference on Empirical Methods in Natural Language Processing, EMNLP 2015, Lisbon, Portugal, September 17-21, 2015.* pages 1967–1972.

Sébastien Jean, KyungHyun Cho, Roland Memisevic, and Yoshua Bengio. 2015. On using very large target vocabulary for neural machine translation. In *Proceedings of the 53rd Annual Meeting of the Association for Computational Linguistics and the 7th International Joint Conference on Natural Language Processing of the Asian Federation of Natural Language Processing, ACL 2015, July 26-31, 2015, Beijing, China, Volume 1: Long Papers.* pages 1–10.

Chin-Yew Lin and Eduard H. Hovy. 2003. Automatic evaluation of summaries using n-gram co-occurrence statistics. In *Human Language Technology Conference of the North American Chapter of the Association for Computational Linguistics, HLT-NAACL 2003, Edmonton, Canada, May 27 - June 1, 2003.*

Konstantin Lopyrev. 2015. Generating news headlines with recurrent neural networks. *CoRR* abs/1512.01712.

Thang Luong, Hieu Pham, and Christopher D. Manning. 2015. Effective approaches to attention-based neural machine translation. In *Proceedings of the 2015 Conference on Empirical Methods in Natural Language Processing, EMNLP 2015, Lisbon, Portugal, September 17-21, 2015.* pages 1412–1421.

Ramesh Nallapati, Bowen Zhou, Cícero Nogueira dos Santos, Çaglar Gülçehre, and Bing Xiang. 2016.

Abstractive text summarization using sequence-to-sequence rnns and beyond. In *Proceedings of the 20th SIGNLL Conference on Computational Natural Language Learning, CoNLL 2016, Berlin, Germany, August 11-12, 2016*. pages 280–290.

Dragomir R. Radev, Timothy Allison, Sasha Blair-Goldensohn, John Blitzer, Arda Çelebi, Stanko Dimitrov, Elliott Drábek, Ali Hakim, Wai Lam, Danyu Liu, Jahna Otterbacher, Hong Qi, Horacio Saggion, Simone Teufel, Michael Topper, Adam Winkel, and Zhu Zhang. 2004. MEAD - A platform for multidocument multilingual text summarization. In *Proceedings of the Fourth International Conference on Language Resources and Evaluation, LREC 2004, May 26-28, 2004, Lisbon, Portugal*.

Alexander M. Rush, Sumit Chopra, and Jason Weston. 2015. A neural attention model for abstractive sentence summarization. In *Proceedings of the 2015 Conference on Empirical Methods in Natural Language Processing, EMNLP 2015, Lisbon, Portugal, September 17-21, 2015*. pages 379–389.

Xu Sun. 2016. Asynchronous parallel learning for neural networks and structured models with dense features. In *COLING 2016, 26th International Conference on Computational Linguistics, Proceedings of the Conference: Technical Papers, December 11-16, 2016, Osaka, Japan*. pages 192–202.

Ilya Sutskever, Oriol Vinyals, and Quoc V. Le. 2014. Sequence to sequence learning with neural networks. In *Advances in Neural Information Processing Systems 27: Annual Conference on Neural Information Processing Systems 2014, December 8-13 2014, Montreal, Quebec, Canada*. pages 3104–3112.

Wenhui Wang and Baobao Chang. 2016. Graph-based dependency parsing with bidirectional LSTM. In *Proceedings of the 54th Annual Meeting of the Association for Computational Linguistics, ACL 2016, August 7-12, 2016, Berlin, Germany, Volume 1: Long Papers*.

Kristian Woodsend and Mirella Lapata. 2010. Automatic generation of story highlights. In *ACL 2010, Proceedings of the 48th Annual Meeting of the Association for Computational Linguistics, July 11-16, 2010, Uppsala, Sweden*. pages 565–574.

Jingjing Xu and Xu Sun. 2016. Dependency-based gated recursive neural network for chinese word segmentation. In *Meeting of the Association for Computational Linguistics*. pages 567–572.

Determining Whether and When People Participate
in the Events They Tweet About

Krishna C. Sanagavarapu, **Alakananda Vempala** and **Eduardo Blanco**
Human Intelligence and Language Technologies Lab
University of North Texas
Denton, TX, 76203
{KrishnaSanagavarapu, AlakanandaVempala}@my.unt.edu, eduardo.blanco@unt.edu

Abstract

This paper describes an approach to determine whether people participate in the events they tweet about. Specifically, we determine whether people are participants in events with respect to the tweet timestamp. We target all events expressed by verbs in tweets, including past, present and events that may occur in the future. We present new annotations using 1,096 event mentions, and experimental results showing that the task is challenging.

1 Introduction

Twitter has quickly become one of the most popular social media sites: it has 313 million monthly active users, and 500 million tweets are published daily. People tweet about breaking news, world and local events (e.g., eclipses, road closures), and personal events ranging from important life events (e.g., graduating from college) to mundane events such as commuting and attending a party.

People tweet not only about events in which they participate, but also events in which they do not participate but are somehow relevant (e.g., John Doe may tweet about his nephew graduating from college). More specifically, people can participate in the events they tweet about (underlining indicates events of interest below) prior to tweeting (e.g., *When I come back to London, I realise how much I miss <u>living</u> here*), while tweeting (e.g., *Nope. Not yet. Still in my car, <u>enjoying</u> traffic*), or after tweeting (e.g., *Can't wait to <u>fly</u> home this summer*). In the third example, it is not guaranteed that *fly* will occur, so one can only say that the author will probably participate in *fly*.

In this paper, we determine whether people participate in the events they tweet about. More specifically, we determine whether they are par-

ticipants before tweeting, while tweeting and after tweeting, and define event participants as people directly involved in an event, regardless of whether they are the agent, recipient or play another role. The main contributions of this paper are: (a) annotations using 1,096 events from 826 tweets; (b) analysis showing that authors of tweets are often not participants in the events they tweet about before or after tweeting; and (c) experimental results showing that the task can be automated.

2 Previous Work

Most previous efforts on detecting events from Twitter focus on events of general importance (e.g., death of a celebrity, natural disasters) or major life events of individuals (e.g. John Doe getting married, having a baby, being promoted).

Extracting events of general importance often includes extracting the entities involved, date and location, and classifying events into classes such as *trial*, *product launch* or *death* (Ritter et al., 2012). Exploiting redundancy in tweets to extract events is common (Zhou et al., 2014), as well as spatio-temporal information (Cheng and Wicks, 2014), i.e., when and where tweets originate from.

Extracting major life events consists on pinpointing significant events from mundane events (e.g., having lunch, exercising) (Di Eugenio et al., 2013; Li et al., 2014; Dickinson et al., 2015), and determining whether significant events are relevant to Twitter users (e.g., *Why doesn't John <u>marry</u> Mary already?* [not relevant to the author]).

Unlike these previous efforts, the work proposed here determines whether people participate in the events they tweet about, and specifies when with respect to tweet timestamps. As a result, we target past events, ongoing events, and events likely to occur in the future. Additionally, we target all events regardless of importance.

Proceedings of the 55th Annual Meeting of the Association for Computational Linguistics (Short Papers), pages 641–646
Vancouver, Canada, July 30 - August 4, 2017. ©2017 Association for Computational Linguistics
https://doi.org/10.18653/v1/P17-2101

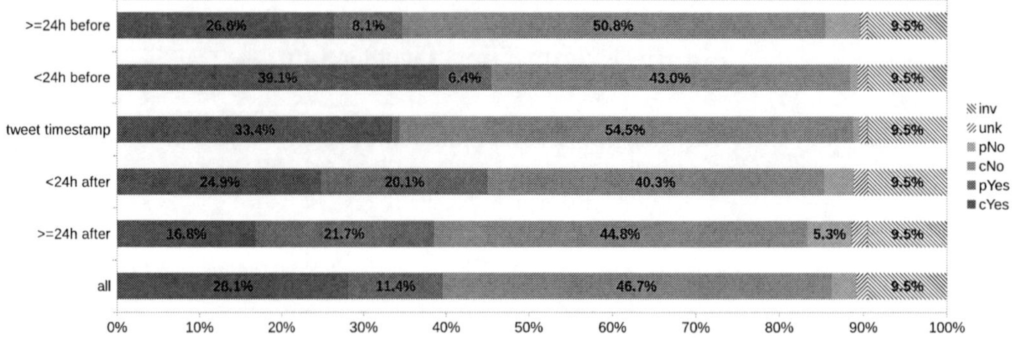

Figure 1: Label distribution per temporal span. Percentages are shown if they are greater or equal than 2%, e.g., percentages for unk label are not shown because they range between 0.91% and 1.91%.

3 Corpus Creation

We created a corpus of tweets, events and annotations indicating whether and when the authors of tweets participate in the events as follows.

Selecting Tweets and Events. First, we collected 5,017 tweets from corpora released by previous projects (Owoputi et al., 2013; Kong et al., 2014; Ritter et al., 2011). Second, we run an event detector to tag tokens that are events (Ritter et al., 2012). Third, we selected as events all tokens tagged as events that are verbs. Fourth, we filtered out tweets that did not contain pronouns *I*, *me* or *we* in order to target tweets that are likely to discuss events that involve the author. Finally, we run a dependency parser for tweets (Kong et al., 2014). We decided to work with an automated event detector and parser to experiment with a system that could be deployed in the real world, and discarded events that are nouns because manual inspection revealed that the event detector makes many more mistakes with nouns than with verbs.

The steps above resulted in 1,096 events from 826 tweets. The part-of-speech tags of events are as follows: VBP: 553 (verb, non-3rd person singular present), VBG: 345 (verb, gerund or present participle), VBN: 198 (verb, past participle).

Annotation Process and Quality. For each event in each tweet, we asked annotators "Is the author of the tweet a participant in the *event*?" During pilot annotations with two graduate students, it became clear that a major source of disagreements was due to annotators answering the question for different times with respect to the tweet timestamp. After discussing errors, we decided to ask for five answers: over 24 hours and within

24 hours before tweeting, when tweeting (tweet timestamp), and within 24 hours and over 24 hours after tweeting. Additionally, we allow for six answers partially inspired by previous work on factuality (Sauri and Pustejovsky, 2009):

- cYes, cNo: I am certain that the author is (or is not) a participant in the event.
- pYes, pNo: It is probably the case that the author is (or is not) a participant in the event.
- unk: the question is intelligible, but none of the four labels above would be correct.
- inv: the event at hand is not an event.

The temporal spans and labels were tuned until the two annotators obtained 0.70 Kappa agreement with 10% of selected events. Kappa agreement between 0.60 and 0.80 is considered *substantial* agreement (Landis and Koch, 1977). After tuning, the remaining events were annotated once.[1]

4 Corpus Analysis

In this section, we present a corpus analysis consisting of label distribution per temporal span, label distribution for the top 5 most frequent events, and label distribution per part-of-speech tag.

Figure 1 plots percentages of each label per temporal span. Overall (bottom bar), 28.1% of answers are cYes, and 46.7% are cNo, i.e., annotators are certain that the author of the tweet is or is not a participant in the event. Percentages for pYes and pNo are much lower: 11.4% and 2.9%. Regarding time spans, people do not usually tweet about events in which they participate while tweeting (cYes: 33.4% vs. cNo: 54.5%). People are more likely to tweet about

---

[1]Available at `http://www.cse.unt.edu/~blanco/`

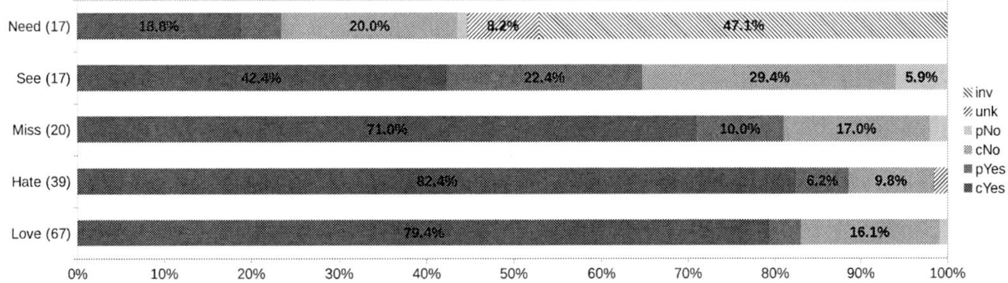

Figure 2: Label distribution for the top 5 most frequent events (frequency is shown between parentheses beside the event). Percentages are shown if they are greater or equal than 5%.

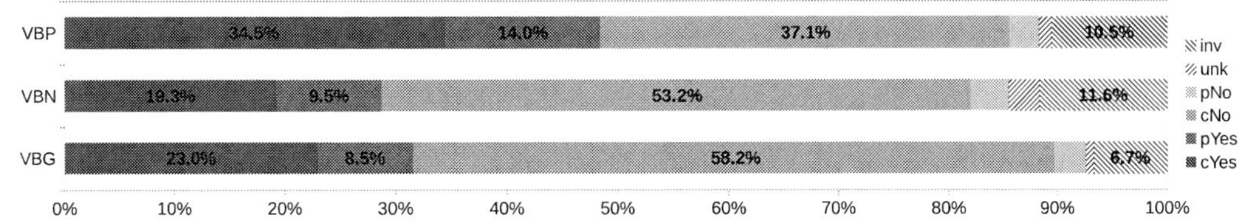

Figure 3: Label distribution per part-of-speech tags of the event. Percentages are shown if they are greater or equal than 5%.

events in which they participated within the last 24 hours (39.1%) than longer before (26.6%), and after tweeting (24.9% and 16.8%). Finally, the percentages of pYes and pNo are below 2% for *tweet timestamp*. Intuitively, it is easier to determine whether somebody participates in the event he tweets about when tweeting rather than before or after. Percentages for labels that do not indicate event participation (unk and inv) are low: unk ranges from 0.91% to 1.91%, and inv is 9.5% for all spans. inv is often used for automatically detected events that are actually states, e.g., *been*.

In Figure 2, we portray the label distribution for the top 5 frequent events and all temporal spans. The top 3 most frequent events (*love, hate* and *miss*) have the highest percentages of cYes and pYes labels ($>$ 80% combined), and the fourth most frequent verb (*see*) a lower percentage (cYes: 42.4%, pYes: 22.4%). *Need* has a high percentage of inv (47.1%). This is due to the fact the *need* is often a state (e.g., *Look, I need less friends more bread, less talk, more head*), and asking whether the author is a participant in the event before, during or after the tweet timestamp is nonsensical.

Figure 3 presents the label distribution per part-of-speech tag of the event. VBP (non-3rd person singular present) has the highest percentage of

cYes + pYes (48.5% vs. 28.8% and 31.5%), indicating that the author is likely to participate in such events. VBG (gerund or present participle) has highest percentage of cNo + pNo (61.1%), indicating that the author is not likely to participate in those events.

Annotation Examples. Table 1 presents real annotation examples. In Tweet (1), annotators understood that the author has certainly been *addicted to Twitter* for 24 hours before and after tweeting, and probably longer. The author of Tweet (2) was clearly *talking about YOU* before but not after tweeting; annotators indicated that talking most likely occurred within 24 hours before tweeting. The annotations in Tweet (3) indicate that the author was certainly a participant of *selling* when he tweeted and within 24 hours after tweeting, and probably also within 24 hours before and over 24 hours after. Event *seeing* in Tweet (4) may occur *next week*, and annotations capture this information (all cNo except 24h after, which is pYes). Finally, the author of Tweet (5) was never a participant in *scrapbooking* despite she witnessed it.

Note that the annotations also provide information regarding event durations, e.g., *addicted* in Tweet (1) is likely ongoing a day after, but *talking* in Tweet (2) has ended and was a short event.

	Tweet	before		tweet	after	
		≥24h	<24h	ts.	<24h	≥24h
1	I'm so addicted to Twitter now that I can tweet all the time. Not good.	pYes	cYes	cYes	cYes	pYes
2	I wonder if you realize we were talking about YOU.	pNo	cYes	cNo	cNo	cNo
3	I'm selling my snorkle, text me for details.	cNo	pYes	cYes	cYes	pYes
4	@Genuine Will I be seeing you at #typeamom next week?	cNo	cNo	cNo	cNo	pYes
5	Today the mall was full of moms who love scrapbooking. kill me.	cNo	cNo	cNo	cNo	cNo

Table 1: Annotation examples. We show annotations for the underlined events only. Recall that events are detected automatically (Section 3). *Tweet ts.* stands for *twitter timestamp*.

Type	No.	Description
Event	1–2	*Event* word form and POS tag
	3	Token number of *event* within the tweet
Situation Entities	7–8	*Event* tense and flag indicating whether *event* tense is perfect tense
	9	Modal type of *event*, if any
	10	Flag indicating whether *event* is a reporting verb
	11	WordNet lexical file name of *event*
Context	12	Position of any pronouns with respect to *event*: left, right, both or none
	13	Position of pronouns *I*, *me*, *we* with respect to *event*: left, right, both or none
	14	Number of outgoing dependencies from *event*
	15	Flag indicating whether there is a dependency between *event* and pronouns *I*, *me*, or *we*

Table 2: Features to determine whether the author of a tweet is a participant in the events he tweets about.

5 Experiments and Results

We follow a standard supervised machine learning approach. We divided the 826 tweets into training and test splits (80% / 20%), and created an instance for each event and temporal span (1,096 × 5 = 5,480 instances). We trained a Support Vector Machine with RBF kernel per temporal span using scikit-learn (Pedregosa et al., 2011) and tuned SVM parameters (C and γ) using 5-fold cross-validation with the training set. We report results when evaluating with the test set.

5.1 Feature Selection

The feature set is presented in Table 2. Most features are fairly simple and well-known, but we borrow some features from previous work on identifying situation entity types (Friedrich et al., 2016) and include features especially designed to capture context around the event we work with.

Event features include the actual event (word form and part-of-speech tag) and number of tokens to left of the event. *Situation Entities* features further characterize the event at hand. To extract them, we first retrieve the clause containing the event by collecting all tokens to the left of the event until we reach a token that is not a verb (including auxiliaries), a modal, or adverb. Friedrich et al. (2016) propose many more features for identifying situation entities, but we selected those that are useful for our task: fine event tense, flag indicating whether the event is in perfect tense (past perfect, present perfect, etc.), the type of modals present in the verb clause (if any), whether the event is in a list of 88 reporting verbs, and the WordNet lexical file containing the event (Miller, 1995). Finally, *Context* features mostly indicate the presence of pronouns in the tweet. Specifically, we include the position of any pronoun with respect to the event, and a specialization of this feature for pronouns *I*, *me*, and *we*. We also extract the number of outgoing dependencies from the event, and whether one of those dependencies is between the event and a pronoun *I*, *me* or *we*. Note that the dependency parser for tweets extracts untyped dependencies (Kong et al., 2014), thus we have available information about syntactic dependents but not about specific syntactic relationships (nsubj, dobj, auxpass, etc.).

5.2 Experimental Results

Results obtained in the test split with several combinations of features are depicted in Table 3. The baseline always predicts the majority label (cNo for all temporal spans), and is outperformed by all feature combinations.

Feature ablation experiments show (a) little improvement with respect to only training with *Event* features, i.e., the simplest features, and (b) that the optimal combination of features depends on the temporal span for which author participation is being predicted. More specifically, including *Situation Entities* features yields the same results for

	Label	$\geq$24h Before			<24h Before			tweet timestamp			<24h After			$\geq$24h After		
		P	R	F	P	R	F	P	R	F	P	R	F	P	R	F
Baseline	cNo	0.45	1.00	0.62	0.38	1.00	0.55	0.50	1.00	0.67	0.33	1.00	0.49	0.39	1.00	0.56
	others	0.00	0.00	0.00	0.00	0.00	0.00	0.00	0.00	0.00	0.00	0.00	0.00	0.00	0.00	0.00
	Avg.	0.20	0.45	0.28	0.15	0.38	0.21	0.25	0.50	0.34	0.11	0.33	0.16	0.15	0.39	0.22
Event	cYes	0.60	0.51	0.55	0.71	0.71	0.71	0.94	0.69	0.79	0.84	0.59	0.69	0.85	0.69	0.76
	pYes	0.00	0.00	0.00	0.33	0.06	0.10	0.00	0.00	0.00	0.51	0.33	0.40	0.37	0.25	0.30
	cNo	0.56	0.85	0.67	0.54	0.74	0.63	0.69	0.93	0.79	0.45	0.79	0.58	0.48	0.74	0.59
	pNo	0.00	0.00	0.00	0.00	0.00	0.00	0.00	0.00	0.00	0.00	0.00	0.00	0.14	0.11	0.12
	unk	0.00	0.00	0.00	0.00	0.00	0.00	0.00	0.00	0.00	0.00	0.00	0.00	0.00	0.00	0.00
	Avg.	0.48	0.56	0.50	0.57	0.61	**0.57**	0.74	0.75	0.73	0.55	0.53	**0.51**	0.50	0.52	0.49
Event + Situation Entities	cYes	0.61	0.52	0.56	0.71	0.69	0.70	0.91	0.73	0.81	0.75	0.60	0.67	0.85	0.71	0.78
	pYes	0.00	0.00	0.00	0.50	0.06	0.11	0.00	0.00	0.00	0.50	0.30	0.37	0.42	0.31	0.36
	cNo	0.57	0.81	0.67	0.56	0.73	0.64	0.72	0.87	0.79	0.46	0.74	0.57	0.49	0.69	0.58
	pNo	0.00	0.00	0.00	0.00	0.00	0.00	0.00	0.00	0.00	0.00	0.00	0.00	0.25	0.11	0.15
	unk	0.00	0.00	0.00	0.00	0.00	0.00	0.00	0.00	0.00	0.00	0.00	0.00	0.00	0.00	0.00
	Avg.	0.47	0.55	0.50	0.58	0.60	**0.57**	0.74	0.74	0.73	0.52	0.51	0.49	0.51	0.53	**0.51**
Event + Situation Entities + Context	cYes	0.71	0.55	0.62	0.69	0.69	0.69	0.91	0.73	0.81	0.73	0.56	0.63	0.85	0.69	0.76
	pYes	0.00	0.00	0.00	0.50	0.06	0.11	0.00	0.00	0.00	0.55	0.40	0.46	0.35	0.31	0.33
	cNo	0.57	0.84	0.68	0.55	0.69	0.61	0.73	0.89	0.80	0.42	0.61	0.49	0.50	0.65	0.56
	pNo	0.00	0.00	0.00	0.00	0.00	0.00	0.00	0.00	0.00	0.00	0.00	0.00	0.20	0.11	0.14
	unk	0.00	0.00	0.00	0.00	0.00	0.00	0.00	0.00	0.00	0.00	0.00	0.00	0.00	0.00	0.00
	Avg.	0.50	0.58	**0.52**	0.57	0.59	0.56	0.75	0.76	**0.74**	0.50	0.48	0.48	0.49	0.50	0.49

Table 3: Results obtained with several feature combinations in the test split. *Average* is the weighted average; we do not show results for *invalid* but they are included in the averages.

$\geq$*24h before*, <*24h before* and *tweet timestamp*, slightly worse results for < *24h after* (F-measures: 0.51 vs. 0.49) and slightly better for $\geq$*24h after* (F-measures: 0.49 vs. 0.51). Training with all features (Event + Situation Entities + Context), obtains the best results for $\geq$*24h before* (F-measure: 0.52) and *tweet timestamp* (F-measure: 0.74), but results are slightly lower for the other time spans.

Note that while the results with *Event* features are only outperformed for some temporal spans when training with all features, information beyond the event at hand is needed to solve this task. For example, the correct labels for *I love living in NYC* and *I miss living in NYC* are different (*living* is an ongoing and past event respectively).

6 Conclusions

We have presented a corpus and machine learning models to predict whether people participate in the events they tweet about. More specifically, we determine whether people participate in events when they tweet about them, and also before and after.

Unlike most previous work, we target any event in a tweet regardless of its importance. While major life events (e.g., graduating from college) are arguably more important, we believe that mundane events (e.g., studying for an exam) provide key information to retrieve major life events and predict future events, e.g., *studying for an exam* is (most probably) more likely to lead to *graduating from* *college* than *going to parties on a regular basis*.

Experimental results show that the task can be automated but is challenging. We believe that features derived from subsequent tweets by the same author and tweet replies would yield better results, and plan to incorporate them in future work.

References

Tao Cheng and Thomas Wicks. 2014. Event detection using twitter: A spatio-temporal approach. *PLOS ONE* 9(6):1–10.

Barbara Di Eugenio, Nick Green, and Rajen Subba. 2013. Detecting life events in feeds from twitter. In *Semantic Computing (ICSC), 2013 IEEE Seventh International Conference on*. Ieee, pages 274–277.

Thomas Dickinson, Miriam Fernandez, Lisa A. Thomas, Paul Mulholland, Pam Briggs, and Harith Alani. 2015. Identifying prominent life events on twitter. In *Proceedings of the 8th International Conference on Knowledge Capture*. ACM, New York, NY, USA, K-CAP 2015, pages 4:1–4:8.

Annemarie Friedrich, Alexis Palmer, and Manfred Pinkal. 2016. Situation entity types: automatic classification of clause-level aspect. In *Proceedings of the 54th Annual Meeting of the Association for Computational Linguistics (Volume 1: Long Papers)*. Association for Computational Linguistics, Berlin, Germany, pages 1757–1768. http://www.aclweb.org/anthology/P16-1166.

Lingpeng Kong, Nathan Schneider, Swabha Swayamdipta, Archna Bhatia, Chris Dyer, and

Noah A. Smith. 2014. A dependency parser for tweets. In *Proceedings of the 2014 Conference on Empirical Methods in Natural Language Processing (EMNLP)*. Association for Computational Linguistics, Doha, Qatar, pages 1001–1012. http://www.aclweb.org/anthology/D14-1108.

J. Richard Landis and Gary G. Koch. 1977. The measurement of observer agreement for categorical data. *Biometrics* 33(1).

Jiwei Li, Alan Ritter, Claire Cardie, and Eduard Hovy. 2014. Major life event extraction from twitter based on congratulations/condolences speech acts. In *Proceedings of the 2014 Conference on Empirical Methods in Natural Language Processing (EMNLP)*. Association for Computational Linguistics, Doha, Qatar, pages 1997–2007. http://www.aclweb.org/anthology/D14-1214.

George A. Miller. 1995. Wordnet: A lexical database for english. *Commun. ACM* 38(11):39–41. https://doi.org/10.1145/219717.219748.

Olutobi Owoputi, Brendan O'Connor, Chris Dyer, Kevin Gimpel, Nathan Schneider, and Noah A. Smith. 2013. Improved part-of-speech tagging for online conversational text with word clusters. In *Proceedings of the 2013 Conference of the North American Chapter of the Association for Computational Linguistics: Human Language Technologies*. Association for Computational Linguistics, Atlanta, Georgia, pages 380–390. http://www.aclweb.org/anthology/N13-1039.

F. Pedregosa, G. Varoquaux, A. Gramfort, V. Michel, B. Thirion, O. Grisel, M. Blondel, P. Prettenhofer, R. Weiss, V. Dubourg, J. Vanderplas, A. Passos, D. Cournapeau, M. Brucher, M. Perrot, and E. Duchesnay. 2011. Scikit-learn: Machine learning in Python. *Journal of Machine Learning Research* 12:2825–2830.

Alan Ritter, Sam Clark, Mausam, and Oren Etzioni. 2011. Named entity recognition in tweets: An experimental study. In *Proceedings of the 2011 Conference on Empirical Methods in Natural Language Processing*. Association for Computational Linguistics, Edinburgh, Scotland, UK., pages 1524–1534. http://www.aclweb.org/anthology/D11-1141.

Alan Ritter, Mausam, Oren Etzioni, and Sam Clark. 2012. Open domain event extraction from twitter. In *Proceedings of the 18th ACM SIGKDD International Conference on Knowledge Discovery and Data Mining*. ACM, New York, NY, USA, KDD '12, pages 1104–1112.

Roser Sauri and James Pustejovsky. 2009. Factbank: a corpus annotated with event factuality. *Language Resources and Evaluation* 43(3):227–268.

Deyu Zhou, Liangyu Chen, and Yulan He. 2014. A simple bayesian modelling approach to event extraction from twitter. In *Proceedings of the 52nd Annual Meeting of the Association for Computational Linguistics (Volume 2: Short Papers)*. Association for Computational Linguistics, Baltimore, Maryland, pages 700–705. http://www.aclweb.org/anthology/P14-2114.

Separating Facts from Fiction: Linguistic Models to Classify Suspicious and Trusted News Posts on Twitter

Svitlana Volkova, Kyle Shaffer, Jin Yea Jang and Nathan Hodas
Data Sciences and Analytics Group, National Security Directorate
Pacific Northwest National Laboratory
902 Battelle Blvd, Richland, WA 99354
`firstname.lastname@pnnl.gov`

Abstract

Pew research polls report 62 percent of U.S. adults get news on social media (Gottfried and Shearer, 2016). In a December poll, 64 percent of U.S. adults said that "made-up news" has caused a "great deal of confusion" about the facts of current events (Barthel et al., 2016). Fabricated stories in social media, ranging from deliberate propaganda to hoaxes and satire, contributes to this confusion in addition to having serious effects on global stability.

In this work we build predictive models to classify 130 thousand news posts as suspicious or verified, and predict four subtypes of suspicious news – satire, hoaxes, clickbait and propaganda. We show that neural network models trained on tweet content and social network interactions outperform lexical models. Unlike previous work on deception detection, we find that adding syntax and grammar features to our models does not improve performance. Incorporating linguistic features improves classification results, however, social interaction features are most informative for finer-grained separation between four types of suspicious news posts.

1 Introduction

Popular social media platforms such as Twitter and Facebook have proven to be effective channels for disseminating falsified information, unverified claims, and fabricated attention-grabbing stories due to their wide reach and the speed at which this information can be shared. Recently, there has been an increased number of disturbing incidents of fabricated stories proliferated through social media having a serious impact on real-world events (Perrott, 2016; Connolly et al., 2016)

False news stories distributed in social media vary depending on the intent behind falsification. Unlike verified news, suspicious news tends to build narratives rather than report facts. On one extreme is *disinformation* which communicates false facts to deliberately deceive readers or promote a biased agenda. These include posts generated and retweeted from propaganda and so-called clickbait ("eye-catching" headlines) accounts. The intent behind **propaganda** and **clickbait** varies from opinion manipulation and attention redirection to monetization and traffic attraction. **Hoaxes** are another type of *disinformation* that aims to deliberately deceive the reader (Tambuscio et al., 2015; Kumar et al., 2016). On the other extreme is **satire**, e.g., `@TheOnion`, where the writer's primary purpose is not to mislead the reader, but rather entertain or criticize (Conroy et al., 2015). However, satirical news and hoaxes may also be harmful, especially when they are shared out of context (Rubin et al., 2015).

Our novel contributions in this paper are twofold. We first investigate several features and neural network architectures for automatically classifying verified and suspicious news posts, and four sub-types of suspicious news. We find that incorporating linguistic and network features via a "late fusion" technique boosts performance. We then investigate differences between verified and suspicious news tweets by conducting a statistical analysis of linguistic features in both types of account. We show significant differences in use of biased, subjective language and moral foundations behind suspicious and trustworthy news posts.

Our analysis and experiments rely on a large Twitter corpus[1] collected during a two-week pe-

---

[1] Data available at: http://www.cs.jhu.edu/~svitlana/

Proceedings of the 55th Annual Meeting of the Association for Computational Linguistics (Short Papers), pages 647–653
Vancouver, Canada, July 30 - August 4, 2017. ©2017 Association for Computational Linguistics
https://doi.org/10.18653/v1/P17-2102

TYPE	NEWS	POSTS	RTPA	EXAMPLES
Propaganda	99	56,721	572	ActivistPost
Satire	9	3,156	351	ClickHole
Hoax	8	4,549	569	TheDcGazette
Clickbait	18	1,366	76	chroniclesu
Verified	166	65,792	396	USATODAY

Table 1: Twitter dataset statistics: news accounts, posts and retweets per account (RTPA).

riod around terrorist attacks in Brussels in 2016. Our method of collection ensures that our models learn from verified and suspicious news within a predefined timeframe, and further ensures homogeneity of deceptive texts in length and writing manner (Rubin et al., 2015).

Several tools have been recently developed to verify and reestablish trusted sources of information online e.g., Google fact checking (Gindras, 2016) and Facebook repost verification (Mosseri, 2016). These projects, among others, teach news literacy[2] and contribute to fact-checking online.[3] We believe our models and novel findings on linguistic differences between suspicious and verified news will contribute to these fact-checking systems, as well as help readers to judge the accuracy of information they consume in social media.

2 Data

Suspicious News We relied on several public resources that annotate suspicious Twitter accounts or their corresponding websites as propaganda, hoax, clickbait and satire. They include propaganda accounts identified by PropOrNot,[4] satire, clickbait and hoax accounts.[5] In total we collected 174 suspicious news accounts.[6] In addition, we manually confirmed that accounts and their corresponding webpages labeled by PropOrNot have one or more signs of propaganda listed below: (a) tries to persuade; (b) influences the specific emotions, attitudes, opinions, and actions; (c) target audiences for political, ideological, and religious purposes; and (d) contains selectively-omitting and one-sided messages.

Figure 1 presents a communication network between verified and suspicious news accounts. We observe that verified accounts are connected to

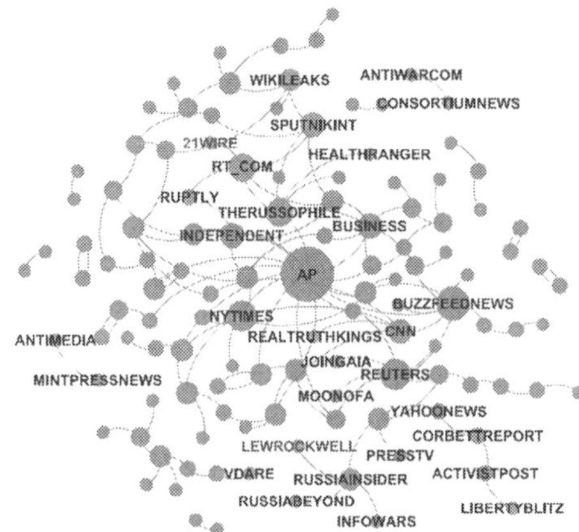

Figure 1: Communication network (@mention) among verified (blue), propaganda (pink), and clickbait (orange) accounts (no shared edges with Hoax and Satire accounts).

(via RTs and mentions) some suspicious news accounts – clickbaits and propaganda.

Verified News We manually constructed a list of 252 "trusted" news accounts that tweet in English and checked whether they are verified on Twitter. We release the final verified list of trusted and suspicious news accounts used in our analysis.[7]

Tweet Corpus We query the Twitter firehose from Mar 15 to Mar 29 2016 – one week before and after Brussels bombing on Mar 22 2016 for 174 suspicious and 252 verified news accounts. We collected retweets generated by any user that mentions one of these accounts and assign the corresponding label propagated from suspicious or trusted news.[8] We de-duplicated, lowercased, and tokenized these posts and applied standard NLP preprocessing. We extracted part-of-speech tags and dependency parses for 130 thousand tweets using SyntaxNet (Petrov, 2016).

3 Models

We propose linguistically-infused neural network models to classify social media posts retweeted from news accounts into verified and suspicious categories – propaganda, hoax, satire and clickbait. Our models incorporate tweet text, social graph, linguistic markers of bias and subjectivity, and moral foundation features. We experiment with several baseline models, and develop neural network architectures presented in Figure 2 in the

---

[2]News Literacy: http://www.thenewsliteracyproject.org/

[3]Fact checking: http://reporterslab.org/fact-checking/ Hoaxy: http://hoaxy.iuni.iu.edu/

[4]Propaganda: http://www.propornot.com/p/the-list.html

[5]http://www.fakenewswatch.com/

[6]To ensure the quality of suspicious account labels we manually verified them.

[7]The lists of verified and suspicious news: http://www.cs.jhu.edu/~svitlana/TwitterList

[8]Suspicious news annotations should be done on a tweet rather than an account level. However, these annotations are extremely costly and time consuming.

Keras framework.[9] We rely on state-of-the-art layers effectively used in text classification – Long Short-Term Memory (LSTM) and Convolutional Neural Networks (CNN) (Johnson and Zhang, 2014; Zhang and Wallace, 2015). The content sub-network consists of an embedding layer and either (a) one LSTM layer or (b) two 1-dimensional convolution layers followed by a max-pooling layer.

We initialize our embedding layer with pre-trained GloVe embeddings (Pennington et al., 2014). The social graph sub-network is a simple feed-forward network that takes one-hot vectors of user interactions, e.g. @mentions, as input. We are careful to exclude source @mentions from these vectors, as these were used to derive labels for our networks and would likely lead to overfitting. In addition to content and network signals, we incorporate other linguistic cues into our networks. For this we rely on the "late fusion" approach that has been shown to be effective in vision tasks (Karpathy et al., 2014; Park et al., 2016). "Fusion" allows for a network to learn a combined representation of multiple input streams. This fusion can be done early (in the feature extraction layers) or later (in the later extraction layers, or in classification layers). In our case, we use fusion as a technique for training networks to learn how to combine data representations from different modalities (network and text features) to boost performance. We train our models for 10 epochs using the ADAM optimization algorithm, and evaluate them using 10 fold cross-validation (Kingma and Ba, 2014).

Baselines We compare our neural network architectures to several baselines. Word- and document-level embeddings have been shown to be effective as input to simpler classifiers. We experiment with several feature inputs for testing baseline classifiers: (a) TFIDF features, (b) Doc2Vec vectors and (c) Doc2Vec or TFIDF features concatenated with linguistic or network features. In the case of Doc2Vec features, we induce 200-dimensional vectors for each tweet using the gensim library,[10] training for 15 epochs.

Bias cues Inspired by earlier work on identifying *biased language* on Wikipedia (Recasens et al., 2013) we extract *hedges* (expressions of tentativeness and possibility) (Hyland, 2005), *assertive verbs* (the level of certainty in the complement

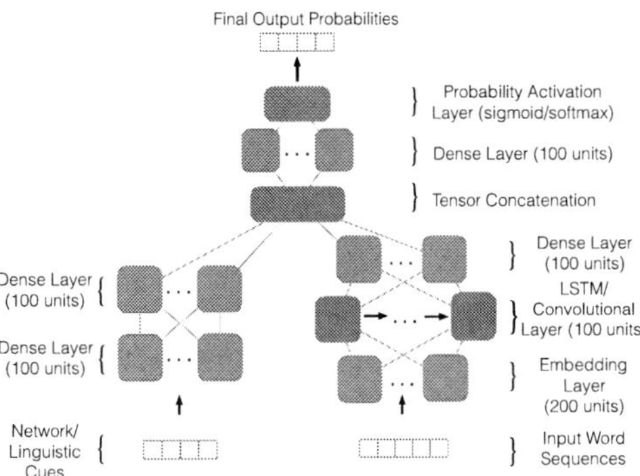

Figure 2: Neural network architecture for news classification fused with social network and linguistic cues.

clause) (Hooper, 1975), *factive verbs* (presuppose the truth of their complement clause) (Kiparsky and Kiparsky, 1968), implicative verbs (imply the truth or untruth of their complement) (Karttunen, 1971) and report verbs (Recasens et al., 2013) from preprocessed tweets.

Subjectivity cues We rely on external publicly available subjectivity, and positive and negative opinion lexicons to extract strongly and weakly subjective words (Riloff and Wiebe, 2003), positive and negative opinion words (Liu et al., 2005).

Psycholinguistic cues In addition to biased and subjective language cues, we extract Linguistic Inquiry Word Count (LIWC) features (Pennebaker et al., 2001) to capture additional signals of persuasive and biased language in tweets. LIWC features have been successfully used for deception detection before (Hancock et al., 2007; Vrij et al., 2007; Mihalcea and Strapparava, 2009). For example, persuasive language cues in LIWC include statistics and factual data, rhetorical questions, imperative commands, personal pronouns, and emotional language. Additional biased language cues captured by LIWC are quotations, markers of certainty, inclusions and conjunctions. Extra subjective language cues in LIWC cover positive and negative emotion and anxiety words.

Moral foundation cues According to Haidt and Graham (2007); Graham et al. (2009), there is a small number of basic widely supported moral values, and people differ in the way they endorse these values. Moral foundations include care and harm, fairness and cheating, loyalty and betrayal, authority and subversion, and purity and degradation. We hypothesize that suspicious news could appeal to specific moral foundations of their read-

---

[9]Keras: https://keras.io/

[10]https://radimrehurek.com/gensim/models/doc2vec.html

ers in a way that is distinct from verified news accounts. Thus, they could help in predicting verified vs. suspicious news, as well as different suspicious news types.

4 Results

4.1 Classification

Table 2 presents classification results for Task 1 (binary) – suspicious vs. verified news posts and Task 2 (multi-class) – four types of suspicious tweets e.g., propaganda, hoaxes, satire and clickbait. We report performance for different model and feature combinations.

We find that our neural network models (both CNNs and RNNs) significantly outperform logistic regression baselines learned from all feature combinations.[11] The accuracy improvement for the binary task is 0.2 and F1-macro boost for the multi-class task is 0.07. We also observe that all models learned from network and tweet text signals outperform models trained exclusively on tweets. We report 0.05 accuracy improvement for Task 1, and 0.02 F1 boost for Task 2. Adding linguistic cues to basic tweet representations significantly improves results across all models. Finally, by combining basic content with network and linguistic features via late fusion, our neural network models achieve best results in binary experiments. Interestingly, models perform best in the multi-class case when trained on tweet embeddings and fused network features alone. We report 0.95 accuracy when inferring suspicious vs. verified news posts, and 0.7 F1-macro when classifying types of suspicious news.

Syntax and grammar features have been predictive of deception in the product review domain (Feng et al., 2012; Pérez-Rosas and Mihalcea, 2015). However, unlike earlier work we find that fusing these features into our models significantly decreases performance – by 0.02 accuracy for the binary task and 0.02 F1 for multi-class. This may be explained by the domain differences between reviews and tweets which are shorter, more noisy and difficult to parse.

4.2 Linguistic Analysis

We measure statistically significant differences in linguistic markers of bias, subjectivity and moral

Features	BINARY			MULTI-CLASS	
	A	ROC	AP	F1	F1 macro
BASELINE 1: LOGISTIC REGRESSION (DOC2VEC)					
Tweets	0.65	0.70	0.68	0.82	0.40
+ network	0.72	0.80	0.82	0.88	0.57
+ cues	0.69	0.74	0.73	0.83	0.46
ALL	**0.75**	**0.84**	**0.84**	**0.88**	**0.59**
BASELINE 2: LOGISTIC REGRESSION (TFIDF)					
Tweets	0.72	0.81	0.81	0.84	0.48
+ network	0.78	0.87	0.88	0.88	0.59
+ cues	0.75	0.85	0.85	0.86	0.49
ALL	**0.79**	**0.88**	**0.89**	**0.89**	**0.59**
RECURRENT NEURAL NETWORK					
Tweets	0.78	0.87	0.88	0.90	0.63
+ network	0.83	0.91	0.92	**0.92**	**0.71**
+ cues	0.93	0.98	0.99	0.90	0.63
+ syntax	0.93	0.96	0.96	0.90	0.64
ALL	**0.95**	**0.99**	**0.99**	0.91	0.66
CONVOLUTIONAL NEURAL NETWORK					
Tweets	0.76	0.85	0.87	0.91	0.63
+ network	0.81	0.9	0.91	**0.92**	**0.70**
+ cues	0.93	0.98	0.98	0.90	0.61
ALL	**0.95**	**0.98**	**0.99**	0.91	0.64

Table 2: Classification results: predicting suspicion and verified posts reported as A – accuracy, AP – average precision, ROC – the area under the receiver operator characteristics curve, and inferring types of suspicious news reported using F1 micro and F1 macro scores.

foundations across different types of suspicious news, and contrast them with verified news using resources described in Section 3. These novel findings presented in Table 3 provide deeper understanding of model performance in Table 2.

Verified news tweets contain significantly less bias markers, hedges and subjective terms and less harm/care, loyalty/betrayal and authority moral cues compared to suspicious news tweets. Satirical news are the most different from propaganda and hoaxes; and propaganda, hoax and clickbait news are the most similar based on moral, bias and subjectivity cues.

Propaganda news target morals more than satire and hoaxes, but less than clickbait. Satirical news contains more loyalty and less betrayal morals compared to propaganda, hoaxes and clickbait news. Propaganda news target authority more than satire and hoaxes, and fairness more than satire.

Hoaxes and propaganda news contain significantly less bias markers (e.g, hedging, implicative and factive verbs) compared to satire. However, propaganda and clickbait news contain significantly more factive verbs and bias language markers compared to hoaxes. Satirical news use significantly more subjective terms compared to other news, while clickbait news use more subjective cues than propaganda and hoaxes.

---

[11]We experimented with other baseline models, such as Random Forest, but found negligible difference between these results and those obtained via logistic regression.

CUES	V ↔ F	P ↔ S	P ↔ H	P ↔ C	S ↔ H	S ↔ C	H ↔ C
MORAL FOUNDATION CUES							
Harm	2.1↓↓↓ 2.8	2.8↑ 2.1	–	–	2.0↓↓ 2.6	–	–
Care	5.8↓↓↓ 9.0	9.4↑↑↑ 6.3	9.4↑↑↑ 5.1	9.4↓ 11.3	–	6.3↓↓↓ 11.3	5.1↓↓↓ 11.3
Fairness	–	0.8↑ 0.4	–	–	–	0.4↓ 1.0	–
Cheating	0.3↑ 0.2	–	–	–	–	–	–
Loyalty	2.1↓↓↓ 2.5	2.2↓↓↓ 7.6	–	–	7.6↑↑↑ 2.0	7.6↑↑↑ 2.3	–
Betrayal	1.7↓↓↓ 3.1	3.4↑↑↑ 0.2	3.4↑↑↑ 2.2	–	0.2↓↓↓ 2.2	0.2↓↓↓ 3.0	–
Authority	2.4↓↓↓ 2.9	3.0↑ 2.1	3.0↑ 2.3	–	–	–	–
BIASED LANGUAGE CUES							
Assertive	12.6↓↓↓ 13.8						
Bias	142.6↓↓↓ 164.4	–	165.5↑↑↑ 148.8	–	165↑↑↑ 148.8	–	148.8↓↓167.1
Factive	4.9↓↓↓ 5.5	5.5↓ 6.3	5.5↑ 4.7	5.5↓ 6.8	6.3↑ 4.7	–	4.7↓↓ 6.8
Hedges	14.2↓↓↓ 15.7	15.6↓↓↓ 20.0	–	–	20↑↑↑ 15.8	20↑↑↑ 13.4	–
Implicative	7.6↓↓↓ 8.9	8.6↓↓↓ 15.2	–	–	15.2↑↑↑ 8.8	15.2↑↑↑ 8.3	–
Report	30↓↓↓ 34.5	34.3↓ 36.0	–	–	–	–	–
SUBJECTIVE LANGUAGE CUES							
Subjective	28.8↓↓↓ 32.8	32.6↓↓↓ 39.5	–	–	39.5↑↑↑ 30.9	39.5↑↑↑ 32.5	–
Strong Subj	23.5↓↓↓ 25.3	24.8↓↓↓ 31.5	24.8↓↓↓ 26.3	24.8↓↓↓ 27.5	31.5↑↑↑ 26.3	–	–
Weak Subj	24.8↓↓↓ 30.8	31.2↓↓↓ 32.8	31.2↑↑↑ 24.1	–	32.8↑↑↑ 24.1	32.8↑↑ 30.7	24.1↓↓↓ 30.7

Table 3: Linguistic analysis of moral foundations, bias and subjective language shown as the **percentage of tweets with one or more cues** across verified (V) and suspicious (F) news – propaganda (P), hoaxes (H), satire (S) and clickbait (C). We report only statistically significant differences: p-value ≤ 0.05↑, ≤ 0.01↑↑, ≤ 0.001↑↑↑ estimated using the Mann-Whitney U test. Subjective lexicon is from (Liu et al., 2005), weekly and strongly subjective terms are from (Riloff and Wiebe, 2003).

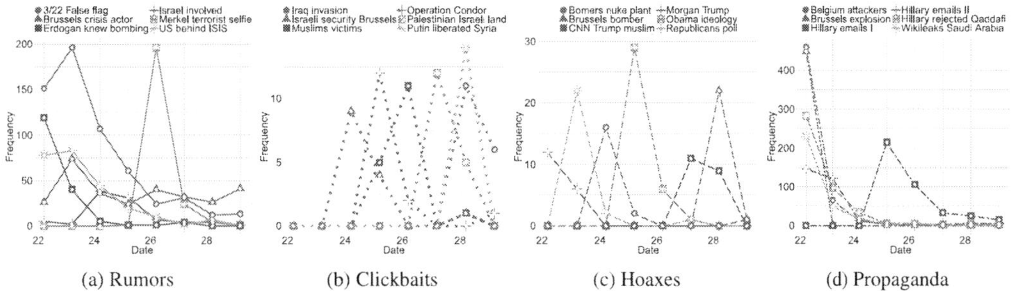

(a) Rumors   (b) Clickbaits   (c) Hoaxes   (d) Propaganda

Figure 3: The most popular retweets over time across suspicious news types in contrast to rumors.

4.3 Suspicious News Retweet Patterns

In addition to contrasting linguistic realizations behind different types of suspicious news on Twitter, we are interested in qualitatively evaluating differences in retweet patterns across suspicious news types (Lumezanu and Klein, 2012; Mendoza et al., 2010; Kumar et al., 2016). Figure 3 presents top retweeted tweets over time across three types of suspicious news – hoaxes, propaganda, and clickbaits and contrasts them to well-studied retweeting behaviors of rumors. We observe that users retweeting propaganda, clickbaits and hoaxes send high volumes of tweets over short periods of time. Rumors[12] are less spiky but active over significantly longer periods of time compared to other suspicious news. We also notice that rumors and propaganda contain the majority of topics related to Brussels bombing, but clickbaits and hoaxes promote very divergent set of topics.

5 Summary

We built linguistically-infused neural network models that jointly learn from tweet content and social network interactions to classify suspicious and verified news tweets and infer specific types of suspicious news. Future work may focus on utilizing more sophisticated discourse and pragmatics features, and inferring degrees of credibility. We hope our findings on bias and subjectivity in suspicious news will help readers to better judge about credibility of news in social media.

6 Acknowledgments

The research described in this paper was conducted under the High-Performance Analytics Program and the Laboratory Directed Research and Development Program at Pacific Northwest National Laboratory, a multiprogram national laboratory operated by Battelle for the U.S. Department of Energy.

---

[12]We identified rumors relevant to Brussels bombing: http://www.cs.jhu.edu/~svitlana/BrusselsRumorList

References

Michael Barthel, Amy Mitchell, and Jesse Holcomb. 2016. Many americans believe fake news is sowing confusion. http://www.journalism.org/2016/12/15/many-americans-believe-fake-news-is-sowing-confusion/. Accessed: 2017-01-31.

Kate Connolly, Angelique Chrisafis, Poppy McPherson, Stephanie Kirchgaessner, Benjamin Haas, Dominic Phillips, Elle Hunt, and Michael Safi. 2016. Fake news: an insidious trend that's fast becoming a global problem. https://www.theguardian.com/media/2016/dec/02/fake-news-facebook-us-election-around-the-world. Accessed: 2017-01-30.

Niall J Conroy, Victoria L Rubin, and Yimin Chen. 2015. Automatic deception detection: methods for finding fake news. *Proceedings of the Association for Information Science and Technology* 52(1):1–4.

Song Feng, Ritwik Banerjee, and Yejin Choi. 2012. Syntactic stylometry for deception detection. In *Proceedings of ACL*. pages 171–175.

Richard Gindras. 2016. Labeling fact-check articles in google news. https://blog.google/topics/journalism-news/labeling-fact-check-articles-google-news/. Accessed: 2016-12-12.

Jeffrey Gottfried and Elisa Shearer. 2016. News use across social media platforms 2016. http://www.journalism.org/2016/05/26/news-use-across-social-media-platforms-2016. Accessed: 2017-01-30.

Jesse Graham, Jonathan Haidt, and Brian A Nosek. 2009. Liberals and conservatives rely on different sets of moral foundations. *Journal of personality and social psychology* 96(5):1029.

Jonathan Haidt and Jesse Graham. 2007. When morality opposes justice: Conservatives have moral intuitions that liberals may not recognize. *Social Justice Research* 20(1):98–116.

Jeffrey T Hancock, Lauren E Curry, Saurabh Goorha, and Michael Woodworth. 2007. On lying and being lied to: A linguistic analysis of deception in computer-mediated communication. *Discourse Processes* 45(1):1–23.

Joan B. Hooper. 1975. On assertive predicates. In J. Kimball, editor, *Syntax and Semantics*. volume 4, pages 91–124.

Ken Hyland. 2005. *Metadiscourse*. Wiley Online Library.

Rie Johnson and Tong Zhang. 2014. Effective use of word order for text categorization with convolutional neural networks. *arXiv preprint arXiv:1412.1058* .

Andrej Karpathy, George Toderici, Sanketh Shetty, Thomas Leung, Rahul Sukthankar, and Li Fei-Fei. 2014. Large-scale video classification with convolutional neural networks. In *Proceedings of CVPR*. pages 1725–1732.

Lauri Karttunen. 1971. Implicative verbs. *Language* pages 340–358.

Diederik P. Kingma and Jimmy Ba. 2014. Adam: A method for stochastic optimization. *CoRR* abs/1412.6980. http://arxiv.org/abs/1412.6980.

Paul Kiparsky and Carol Kiparsky. 1968. *Fact*. Indiana University.

Srijan Kumar, Robert West, and Jure Leskovec. 2016. Disinformation on the web: Impact, characteristics, and detection of wikipedia hoaxes. In *Proceedings of WWW*. pages 591–602.

Bing Liu, Minqing Hu, and Junsheng Cheng. 2005. Opinion observer: analyzing and comparing opinions on the web. In *Proceedings of WWW*. pages 342–351.

Feamster Lumezanu and H Klein. 2012. Measuring the tweeting behavior of propagandists. In *Proceedings of ICWSM*.

Marcelo Mendoza, Barbara Poblete, and Carlos Castillo. 2010. Twitter under crisis: can we trust what we rt? In *Proceedings of the first workshop on social media analytics*. ACM, pages 71–79.

Rada Mihalcea and Carlo Strapparava. 2009. The lie detector: Explorations in the automatic recognition of deceptive language. In *Proceedings of the ACL-IJCNLP*. pages 309–312.

Adam Mosseri. 2016. News feed fyi: Addressing hoaxes and fake news. http://newsroom.fb.com/news/2016/12/news-feed-fyi-addressing-hoaxes-and-fake-news/. Accessed: 2017-01-30.

Eunbyung Park, Xufeng Han, Tamara L Berg, and Alexander C Berg. 2016. Combining multiple sources of knowledge in deep cnns for action recognition. In *Proceedings of AWACV*. IEEE, pages 1–8.

James W Pennebaker, Martha E Francis, and Roger J Booth. 2001. Linguistic inquiry and word count: Liwc 2001. *Mahway: Lawrence Erlbaum Associates* 71:2001.

Jeffrey Pennington, Richard Socher, and Christopher D. Manning. 2014. Glove: Global vectors for word representation. In *EMNLP*. pages 1532–1543.

Verónica Pérez-Rosas and Rada Mihalcea. 2015. Experiments in open domain deception detection. *Proceedings of EMNLP* pages 1120–1125.

Kathryn Perrott. 2016. 'fake news' on social media influenced us election voters, experts say. http://www.abc.net.au/news/2016-11-14/fake-news-would-have-influenced-us-election-experts-say/8024660. Accessed: 2017-01-30.

Slav Petrov. 2016. Announcing syntaxnet: The world's most accurate parser goes open source. *Google Research Blog, May* 12:2016.

Marta Recasens, Cristian Danescu-Niculescu-Mizil, and Dan Jurafsky. 2013. Linguistic models for analyzing and detecting biased language. In *Proceedings of ACL*. pages 1650–1659.

Ellen Riloff and Janyce Wiebe. 2003. Learning extraction patterns for subjective expressions. In *Proceedings of EMNLP*. pages 105–112.

Victoria L Rubin, Yimin Chen, and Niall J Conroy. 2015. Deception detection for news: three types of fakes. *Proceedings of the Association for Information Science and Technology* 52(1):1–4.

Marcella Tambuscio, Giancarlo Ruffo, Alessandro Flammini, and Filippo Menczer. 2015. Fact-checking effect on viral hoaxes: A model of misinformation spread in social networks. In *Proceedings of WWW*. pages 977–982.

Aldert Vrij, Samantha Mann, Susanne Kristen, and Ronald P Fisher. 2007. Cues to deception and ability to detect lies as a function of police interview styles. *Law and human behavior* 31(5):499–518.

Ye Zhang and Byron Wallace. 2015. A sensitivity analysis of (and practitioners' guide to) convolutional neural networks for sentence classification. *arXiv preprint arXiv:1510.03820* .

Recognizing Counterfactual Thinking in Social Media Texts

**Youngseo Son[†], Anneke Buffone[§], Anthony Janocko[§], Allegra Larche[§],
Joseph Raso[§], Kevin Zembroski[§], H Andrew Schwartz[†], Lyle Ungar[§]**
[†]Stony Brook University, [§]University of Pennsylvania
yson@cs.stonybrook.edu, ungar@cis.upenn.edu

Abstract

Counterfactual statements, describing events that did *not* occur and their consequents, have been studied in areas including problem-solving, affect management, and behavior regulation. People with more counterfactual thinking tend to perceive life events as more personally meaningful. Nevertheless, counterfactuals have not been studied in computational linguistics. We create a counterfactual tweet dataset and explore approaches for detecting counterfactuals using rule-based and supervised statistical approaches. A combined rule-based and statistical approach yielded the best results (F1 = 0.77) outperforming either approach used alone.

1 Introduction

Counterfactuals describe events that did not occur, and what would have happened (or not happened), had the event occurred (e.g., "If I hadn't broken my arm, I never would have met her."). More precisely, counterfactual conditionals have the form "If it had been the case that A (or not A), it would have been the case that B (or not B)."

Counterfactuals have been studied in many different domains. Logicians and philosophers focus on literally logical relations between the antecedent and consequent of counterfactual forms and the outcomes (Goodman, 1947). In contrast, political scientists usually conduct counterfactual thought experiments for hypothetical tests on historical events, policies, or other aspects of a society and assess them (Tetlock, 1996).

Counterfactual thoughts are defined, especially in psychology, as mental representations of alternatives to past events, actions, or states. Their use has been explored for correlations with many different demographics (age, gender) and psychological variables (depression, religiosity) (Kray et al., 2010; Markman and Miller, 2006). Counterfactual thinking has been linked to perceiving life events as more meaningful, fated, and even as influenced by the divine (Kray et al., 2010; Buffone et al., 2016), as well as with problem-solving, because imagining alternate outcomes can easily bring to mind the steps needed for improvement (Epstude and Roese, 2008; Roese, 1994). It has also been shown to be associated with affect management, particularly when imagining realities that are worse than what actually happened (Epstude and Roese, 2008; Roese, 1994)

Despite the extensive research on counterfactual *thinking*, counterfactual *language forms* have not been studied in computational linguistics. Language-based models to recognize counterfactual thinking in social media would potentially allow for psychological analysis on users based on their everyday language, avoiding the high expense of capturing counterfactual thinking at a large scale using traditional psychological assessments.

Therefore, in this paper, we build a language-based model to recognize counterfactual forms in social media texts of Twitter and Facebook. There are many challenges for this task. First, counterfactual statements have a low base rate; we found only 2% of status updates on Facebook and 1% of tweets contain counterfactual statements. Secondly, counterfactual statements can take on many forms in natural language.[1] For example, they may or may not use explicit if- or then- clauses (e.g, consider "If I had not met him then I would be better off" versus "I wish I had not met him").

---

[1] Simply looking for words like 'if' fails to produce useful results; only 2 percent of sentences of tweets containing 'if' are counterfactuals.

Proceedings of the 55th Annual Meeting of the Association for Computational Linguistics (Short Papers), pages 654–658
Vancouver, Canada, July 30 - August 4, 2017. ©2017 Association for Computational Linguistics
https://doi.org/10.18653/v1/P17-2103

The low base rate and high variability of natural language counterfactuals in social media texts make them difficult recognize using simple linguistic or statistical features. We address theses challenges by using a combined rule-based and statistical approach. Key to our success is defining seven sub-types of counterfactuals, allowing better coverage of rarer sub-types.

2 Related Work

Identifying counterfactuals is in many ways similar to identifying discourse relations. In terms of relation classification, the counterfactual conditionals can be viewed as a subset of Condition type of Contingency class in the Penn Discourse Treebank (PDTB) (Prasad et al., 2008) or the Condition relation of Rhetorical Structure Theory (RST) (Mann and Thompson, 1987). Also, like all discourse relations in the PDTB, counterfactuals have implicit and explicit forms, and so cannot by uniquely identified by the presence of specific words.

There have been many researchers who have tried end-to-end discourse relation parsing with the PDTB and RST(Biran and McKeown, 2015; Lin et al., 2009; Ji and Eisenstein, 2014). Many of them used dependency parsing or constituency parsing for argument detection or elementary discourse unit (EDU) segmentation to infer the relation between them. However, the short lengths and poor quality of parses of social media texts make dependency constituents unreliable.[2] For example, posters frequently drop the subject of a sentence.

Other work mostly focuses on relation classification with an assumption that arguments of the given relations are already identified (Park and Cardie, 2012; Pitler et al., 2009). They explore various learning algorithms and types of features in the given arguments of discourse relations. Then, they report which combinations give the best performance of each discourse relation.

Our work, while possible to view as a task in discourse relation classification, focuses on critical features of counterfactuals rather than on accurate demarcation of each argument of the relation. Most downstream applications, such as psychological studies, require knowing the presence/absence of counterfactuals rather than their exact extent.

3 Method

We use a combination of a rule-based approach and a supervised classifier to capture counterfactual statements from Twitter.

3.1 Data Set

No existing corpus of counterfactual statements was available, so we collected our own data set, starting from a random set of tweets from May 2014 and July 2014. As noted previously, couterfactual statements are rare, so we first limited the random tweet set to 1,637 containing keywords[3] that can signal counterfactuals (Train and Test row from Table 1). Keywords were in part based on prior literature on spontaneous counterfactual generation, such as should have, could have, at least, if only, or next time (Sanna and Turley, 1996). We identified further counterfactual forms (e.g. wish) based on visual inspection of the data. Next we used the overall list of keywords to draw samples of 500 Tweets for further visual inspection. Words or phrases which had an unreasonably high false positive rate for containing counterfactuals were eliminated. Well-trained annotators then manually labeled each of the 1,637 tweets for counterfactuals with a 10% postive rate, results in 166 counterfactuals and 1,471 negative samples. A random set of 500 of these instances were used in training and the rest were reserved for testing. To build out our training set to capture examples of all forms of counterfactuals, we added a *train supplement* from random tweets from 2012 – at least thirty tweets from each of seven counterfactual forms we defined for our statistical model using the regular expressions[4] with brown-clusters and the tweet PTB tagging model (described next). With this process, we enabled the model to be less biased towards only the samples with the counterfactual cue phrases used for data collection. Additionally, the model learned syntactically different forms of counterfactuals identified in prior work. To evaluate counterfactual form annotation, inter-annotator agreement was established on 1,637 tweets with a

---

[2] In our preliminary experiments on our causality tweet dataset ($\kappa = 0.61$), Lin's parser (Lin et al., 2009) obtained 0.45 F1 while a linear support vector machine (SVM) with n-gram obtained 0.58 F1 for causality detection.

[3] e.g., 'should', 'shulda'; full list available in our supplementary data.

[4] The regular expression table is included in our supplementary data.

Dataset	CF	Non-CF	Total
Train	49	451	500
+ Supplement	768	498	1,266
Test	84	1,053	1,137

Table 1: Data Collection. 'CF' is counterfactual and 'Non-CF' is non-counterfactual

second rater with achieving $\kappa = 0.774$ and human annotation F1 0.791.

3.2 Classification

We first use a rule-based model to capture counterfactual patterns from social media texts. We then use a statistical model (Linear SVM) to increase precision by identifying tricky false positives with forms similar to counterfactuals (e.g., "wish you the best").

Rule-based Classification. Our rule-based approach is based on seven forms of counterfactuals (Table 2). Central to our method is our theorizing, based on reading the literature, especially (Kray et al., 2010) and examining many counterfactual examples, that counterfactuals come in seven different forms, shown with examples in (Table 2). First, we remove sentences ending in question marks predicted as 'end of sentence' by the tweet part-of-speech (POS) tagger (Gimpel et al., 2011). We then use pattern matching with regular expression using a combination of cue phrases (bold), POS tags, and word clusters. The word clusters, based on a set of Twitter Brown clusters[5] are used to capture the numerous variations of words in social media texts (e.g., 'shuldve' for 'should have'). This approach requires matching both the token and its part-of-speech, since the POS tag of each token is important for counterfactual form.

The rule-based approach is also useful in that it allows us to detect the arguments for counterfactual relations; conditional statement and consequent statement from *Conjunctive Normal/ Converse* form and *Verb Inversion* form, one counterfactual statement from *Wish Verb* and *Could / Would / Should have*. We customized Biran's demarcation methods using the first verb phrase or the connective as a boundary to capture the more informative argument of the statement: For one argument detection, we demarcate from the cue phrase (e.g., would have) to the end of sentence. For two arguments, we demarcate from conditional word (e.g., if, unless) to the end of statement or before the start of the second verb phrase.

Part of Speech Tagging We use the Penn Treebank (PTB)-style Tweet POS tags[6] instead of Tweet POS tags (Gimpel et al., 2011) as it contains more fine-grained categories and yields higher accuracy of pattern matching. For instance, Tweet POS tags do not differentiate modal verbs, past tense verbs, and other types of verbs, but categorize all of them as 'V'. However, in many forms of counterfactuals, the distinction between modal verbs and past particles from other types of verbs are critical (e.g., in *Should / Could / Would Have* forms). Finally, we conduct a postprocessing on the Tweet POS parsing results for the more accurate prediction. First, we delete RT tags along with the token since it is not informative for our task. Then, we convert 'USR' to nouns because the word token tagged as 'user' usually plays the role of a common noun from the discourse relation perspective. Additionally, in order to enhance the POS tagging, we use the brown clusters to tag empirical variations of modal verbs as 'MD' and we define 'CCJ', a new tag to distinguish conditional conjunctions (i.e. Brown clusters for 'if') from other types of conjunctions.

Statistical Modeling. Each counterfactual form has a different number of arguments for the relation, and different types of features that cause the most errors. Therefore, we analyze the errors of each form separately and use different approaches expected to ensure the best performance.

If a tweet matches rules for counterfactual forms 1, 2, 3, 4, or 5, it is further classified using a statistical model trained with features of sequential words (n-gram) and POS tags of demarcated arguments and the whole sentence.

A statistical model is expected to capture some implicit relations between arguments as well as lexical and part-of-speech patterns, but may also hurt performance in situations where the rule-based approach achieves high precision. Therefore, we applied statistical approaches to counterfactual forms which cannot be easily differentiated by their superficial patterns. These forms were selected by both theoretical and empirical analysis; we discuss these forms further in our evaluation section.

---

[5]http://www.cs.cmu.edu/~ark/TweetNLP/clusters/50mpaths2

[6]http://www.cs.cmu.edu/~ark/TweetNLP/model.ritter_ptb_alldata_fixed.20130723

Counterfactual Form	Example
1.Wish Verb	**I wish I had** been richer
2. Conjunctive Normal	**If** everyone **put** differences aside and get along, everything would be so much enjoyable
3. Conjunctive Converse	**I would** be stronger, if **I had lifted** weights
4. Modal Normal	They **should of shown** this guy gettin shot, that **woulda been** TV gold.
5. Verb Inversion	**Had I left** the event early, **I would not have met** John
6. Should Have	**I should have** joined the event early
7. (Would / Could) Have	**I would have been happier** without John

Table 2: Counterfactual Forms

Performance	CF Parser	Rules only	SVM
Precision	0.7131	0.5864	**0.7143**
Recall	0.8365	**0.9134**	0.2791
F1	**0.7699**	0.7143	0.4013

Table 3: Performance of Classifiers

Process	F1	Precision	Recall
Whole Pipeline	0.7699	0.7131	0.8365
- Args	0.7595	0.6767	0.8653
- PTB	0.7456	0.6854	0.8173
- Form 1	0.7447	0.6592	0.8557
- Form 2,3,4,5	0.7352	0.6241	0.8942

Table 4: Ablation Test for Each Process

4 Evaluation

As discussed, counterfactuals are not easily identified by rules or specific words. Given their low base rate and multiplicity of forms, traditional machine learning approaches trained on a random tweet sample tend to label all tweets as the most frequent class (non-counterfactual). Use of a counterfactual-enriched training set increases precision, but still gives a low F1 on the imbalanced test set.

Thus, in order to make the classifier robust to the imbalanced dataset, we designed a rule-based model with counterfactual forms, which resulted in significantly lower false negative rate of the statistical model. Moreover, the rule-based model captured more positive samples of all possible forms, despite its lack of presence in the training set. This results in a substantial increase in overall performance F1. However, the precision is extremely low because of its incapability to detect negative sample with subtle differences inside the pattern.

A combined approach therefor gives the best result. As Table 3 shows, the statistical model obtained the highest precision, while the rule-based model obtained, by a large margin, the highest recall. However, our whole pipeline ('CF Parser' in Table 3) obtained the best overall performance with the combination of both approaches.

For *Wish Verb* form prediction gets a big performance boost from the statistical model because of highly frequent false positives which have counterfactual-like forms such as birthday wishes or new year's day wishes. Among samples classified as *Wish Verb* form the counterfactual prediction F1 increased from 0.82 to 0.90 after the final prediction by the statistical model.

Finally, we conducted an ablation test to analyze how each process of the pipeline affects the overall performance of the classifier (Table 4). The argument detection was less effective (F1 0.01 drop) than we expected due to the relatively simple and concise structure of tweets in general (Args in Table 4).

Using only n-grams as features for the statistical model without PTB-style Tweet POS tags gives a relatively large drop (0.02) from F1. From the grammatical perspective, n-grams are less informative than POS tags for counterfactuals especially considering that there are so many variations of each word token in social media (e.g., 'clda', 'coulda', and 'couldve' for 'could have').

We examined how the statistical model affected the final performance of each counterfactual form. The model we used for filtering out frequent false positives (e.g., birth day wishes) of *Wish Verb* form caused 0.03 F1 drop when it is removed. Also, the models trained with two-argument-relation forms (*Conjunctive Normal / Converse*, *Modal Normal*, and *Verb Inversion*) caused 0.04 F1 drop when they are removed from the pipeline, since the classifier cannot use subtle relations between arguments for its counterfactual prediction.

5 Conclusion

This is the first work to identify counterfactuals in social media, a task we hope more people will address. Our best results came from combining rule-based methods that exploit a theory of the different forms of counterfactual with focused statistical methods for reclassification of challenging forms. Our counterfactual predictor can now be applied to large collections of tweets and Facebook posts from people of known education, religiosity, political orientation, well-being, and other attributes of interest to psychologists and political scientists, allowing further study of their theories of counterfactual use.

References

Or Biran and Kathleen McKeown. 2015. Pdtb discourse parsing as a tagging task: The two taggers approach. In *Proceedings of the 16th Annual Meeting of the Special Interest Group on Discourse and Dialogue*. pages 96–104.

Anneke Buffone, Shira Gabriel, and Michael Poulin. 2016. There but for the grace of god counterfactuals influence religious belief and images of the divine. *Social Psychological and Personality Science* 7(3):256–263.

Kai Epstude and Neal J Roese. 2008. The functional theory of counterfactual thinking. *Personality and Social Psychology Review* 12(2):168–192.

Kevin Gimpel, Nathan Schneider, Brendan O'Connor, Dipanjan Das, Daniel Mills, Jacob Eisenstein, Michael Heilman, Dani Yogatama, Jeffrey Flanigan, and Noah A Smith. 2011. Part-of-speech tagging for twitter: Annotation, features, and experiments. In *Proceedings of the 49th Annual Meeting of the Association for Computational Linguistics: Human Language Technologies: short papers-Volume 2*. Association for Computational Linguistics, pages 42–47.

Nelson Goodman. 1947. The problem of counterfactual conditionals. *The Journal of Philosophy* 44(5):113–128.

Yangfeng Ji and Jacob Eisenstein. 2014. Representation learning for text-level discourse parsing. In *ACL (1)*. pages 13–24.

Laura J Kray, Linda G George, Katie A Liljenquist, Adam D Galinsky, Philip E Tetlock, and Neal J Roese. 2010. From what might have been to what must have been: counterfactual thinking creates meaning. *Journal of personality and social psychology* 98(1):106.

Ziheng Lin, Min-Yen Kan, and Hwee Tou Ng. 2009. Recognizing implicit discourse relations in the penn discourse treebank. In *Proceedings of the 2009 Conference on Empirical Methods in Natural Language Processing: Volume 1-Volume 1*. Association for Computational Linguistics, pages 343–351.

William C Mann and Sandra A Thompson. 1987. *Rhetorical structure theory: A theory of text organization*. University of Southern California, Information Sciences Institute.

Keith D Markman and Audrey K Miller. 2006. Depression, control, and counterfactual thinking: Functional for whom? *Journal of Social and Clinical Psychology* 25(2):210–227.

Joonsuk Park and Claire Cardie. 2012. Improving implicit discourse relation recognition through feature set optimization. In *Proceedings of the 13th Annual Meeting of the Special Interest Group on Discourse and Dialogue*. Association for Computational Linguistics, pages 108–112.

Emily Pitler, Annie Louis, and Ani Nenkova. 2009. Automatic sense prediction for implicit discourse relations in text. In *Proceedings of the Joint Conference of the 47th Annual Meeting of the ACL and the 4th International Joint Conference on Natural Language Processing of the AFNLP: Volume 2-Volume 2*. Association for Computational Linguistics, pages 683–691.

Rashmi Prasad, Nikhil Dinesh, Alan Lee, Eleni Miltsakaki, Livio Robaldo, Aravind Joshi, and Bonnie Webber. 2008. The penn discourse treebank 2.0. In *In Proceedings of LREC*.

Neal J Roese. 1994. The functional basis of counterfactual thinking. *Journal of personality and Social Psychology* 66(5):805.

Lawrence J Sanna and Kandi Jo Turley. 1996. Antecedents to spontaneous counterfactual thinking: Effects of expectancy violation and outcome valence. *Personality and Social Psychology Bulletin* 22(9):906–919.

Philip E Tetlock. 1996. *Counterfactual thought experiments in world politics: Logical, methodological, and psychological perspectives*. Princeton University Press.

Temporal Orientation of Tweets for Predicting Income of Users

Mohammed Hasanuzzaman[1], Sabyasachi Kamila[2], Mandeep Kaur[2],
Sriparna Saha[2] and Asif Ekbal[2]

[1]ADAPT Centre, School of Computing, Dublin City University, Dublin, Ireland
[2]Department of Computer Science and Engineering,
Indian Institute of Technology Patna, India
`hasanuzzaman.im@gmail.com`

Abstract

Automatically estimating a user's socio-economic profile from their language use in social media can significantly help social science research and various downstream applications ranging from business to politics. The current paper presents the first study where user cognitive structure is used to build a predictive model of income. In particular, we first develop a classifier using a weakly supervised learning framework to automatically time-tag tweets as past, present, or future. We quantify a user's overall temporal orientation based on their distribution of tweets, and use it to build a predictive model of income. Our analysis uncovers a correlation between future temporal orientation and income. Finally, we measure the predictive power of future temporal orientation on income by performing regression.

1 Introduction

User-generated content in social media such as Twitter has enabled the study of author profiling on an unprecedented scale. Author profiling in social media aims at inferring various attributes of the user from the text that they have written. Most of the prior studies in this field have focused on age, gender prediction (Marquardt et al., 2014; Sap et al., 2014), psychological well-being (Dodds et al., 2011; Choudhury et al., 2013), and a host of other behavioural, psychological and medical phenomena (Kosinski et al., 2013). However, there has been a lack of work looking at the socio-economic characteristics of Twitter users. In this paper, we focus on automatic estimation of Twitter users' income from their Twitter language. An income predictor of social media users can be useful for both social science research and a range of downstream applications in banking, marketing, and politics.

Previous social science studies on income demonstrate that income of people is correlated with various factors such as demographic feature (the congressional district in which the respondent lived), educational categories, sex, age, age squared, gender, race categories, marital status categories, and height (Kahneman and Deaton, 2010). Other studies reveal that psychological traits related to extroversion (e.g. larger social networks) and conscientiousness (e.g. orderliness) have a positive correlation with income, while neurotic traits (e.g. anger, anxiety) are anti-correlated (Roberts et al., 2007). Human temporal orientation refers to individual differences in the relative emphasis one places on the past, present, or future (Zimbardo and Boyd, 2015). Past studies have established consistent links between temporal orientation and most of the above-mentioned income predictor factors such as age, sex, gender, education, and psychological traits (Webley and Nyhus, 2006; Adams and Nettle, 2009; Schwartz et al., 2013; Zimbardo and Boyd, 2015). Accordingly, this begs the question as to whether there is any link between an individual's temporal orientation and their income level. Traditionally, temporal orientation has been assessed by self-report questionnaires. In this paper, we assess temporal orientation based on language use in Twitter. Our method uses a tweet-level classifier of past, present, and future, grouped over users to create user-level assessments.

Our learning framework uses convolutional neural networks (CNNs) (Goodfellow et al., 2016) to infer tweet vector representations, and considers them as the feature to develop a classification model that can automatically detect the time orientation (oriented towards *past, present*, and *future*) of tweets. The framework leverages weak supervision signals provided by a list of manu-

659

Proceedings of the 55th Annual Meeting of the Association for Computational Linguistics (Short Papers), pages 659–665
Vancouver, Canada, July 30 - August 4, 2017. ©2017 Association for Computational Linguistics
https://doi.org/10.18653/v1/P17-2104

ally selected eighty (80) high-precision seed terms (and automatically extracted similar terms) representing past, present, and future to train the CNN. For example, tweets exclusively containing *past* (resp. *present* and *future*) seed terms were marked with weak labels *past* (resp. *present* and *future*). We used the tweet-level temporal classifier to automatically classify a large dataset consisting of ≈ 10 million tweets from 5,191 users mapped to their income, using fine-grained user occupation as a proxy. Finally, we tested whether individual differences in past, present, and future orientation are related to income. In particular, we frame the income prediction task as regression using linear as well as non-linear learning algorithms where temporal orientation served as predictive features. To the best of our knowledge, this represents the first work to study a temporal orientation-based income prediction using Twitter language.

In summary the proposed approach is different from the previous works (Schwartz et al., 2015; Preoţiuc-Pietro et al., 2015; Park et al., 2017) in several ways. Unlike Schwartz et al. (2015), we used a weakly supervised approach. The generation of training data is semi-automatic in our case. Rather than manually identifying features, tweet vectors are fed to a CNN classifier. Furthermore while Schwartz et al. (2015) studied temporal orientation of facebook data in order to predict different human correlates like conscientiousness, age, and gender, our current work focuses on predicting the income of a user using temporal orientation of their tweets. In Preoţiuc-Pietro et al. (2015), the authors predict user income based on different demographic and psychological features of users. However, the process of extracting these features is computationally complex. The current study is therefore, the first of its kind to explore the use of temporal orientation of user-tweets to predict income.

2 Related Work

Existing message-/sentence-level temporal classification methods generally fall into two categories: (1) rule-based methods, and (2) supervised machine-learning methods. Rule-based methods mainly rely on manually designed classification rules for each temporal class (Nie et al., 2015). Despite their effectiveness, this kind of method requires substantial efforts in rule design. Most research on machine learning-based sentence tem-

poral classification has revolved around feature engineering for better classification performance. Different kinds of features have been explored such as bag-of-words, time expressions, part-of-speech tags, and temporal class-specific lexicons (Schwartz et al., 2015). Temporal class specific lexicon creation and feature engineering also cost a lot of human efforts. In addition, creation of a large-scale training data set for supervised machine-learning approaches is also very laborious.

3 Methodology

In this section, we describe our proposed methodology to identify the underlying temporal orientation of tweets and a set of contrastive systems that we used as baselines for comparative study.

3.1 Tweet Temporal Orientation Classifier

The task can be defined as given a tweet t and its posting date d, predict its temporal class $c \in \{$ *past, present*, or *future*$\}$ with reference to its issuing date.

Proposed Architecture: The proposed framework has two main steps as: (i) training the model parameters, and (ii) using the model to tag unseen tweets. During training, we use the weakly labeled tweets to learn the parameters of the CNN and temporal orientation classifier. For classification, a linear Support Vector Machine (lSVM)[1] is used. In particular, we trained three binary classifiers (one per class)[2] using one-vs.-rest, and label a tweet with the class that assigned the highest score. In the second step, we pass tweets through these two optimized components to detect their temporal orientation.

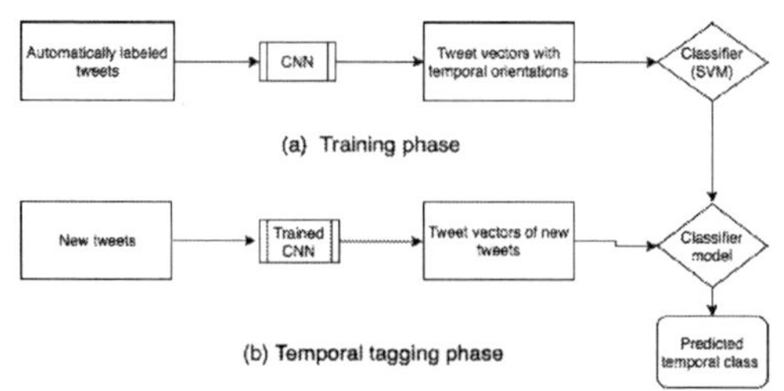

Figure 1: Proposed learning architecture.

---

[1]Trained using the Weka implementation of LIBSVM with linear kernels (polynomial kernels yielded worse performance).

[2]Multi-class classification yielded worse performance.

The choice of CNN for feature extraction is motivated by:

- CNNs have been successfully used as feature extractors in various computer vision tasks and achieved better results compared to hand-crafted features. Research has shown that CNN feature maps can be used with SVM to yield classification results that outperform the original CNN (Athiwaratkun et al., 2015)

- Superior accuracies have also been achieved by following a similar line of research in the context of NLP tasks (Kim, 2014; Poria et al., 2015).

Convolutional Neural Networks (CNNs): The task is challenging as tweets are short and noisy. Moreover, English, like many languages, uses a wide variety of ways to refer to the past, present, and future. Unlike previous approaches which mainly rely on hand-crafted rules and feature engineering, we automatically extract features for tweets to build our tweet-level Temporal Orientation Classifier. In particular, we use CNNs to automatically extract tweet vectors as the features for classification. Recently, CNNs have been shown to be useful in many natural language processing and information retrieval tasks by effectively modeling natural language semantics (Collobert et al., 2011). For our experiments, we trained a simple CNN with one convolution layer followed by one max pooling layer (Collobert et al., 2011; Kim, 2014). In the CNN model, we use 3 filters with window sizes of 5, 6 and 7 with 100 feature maps each. These window sizes will capture 5-gram, 6-gram, and 7-gram information in the tweets. We employ dropout for regularization with a dropout rate of 0.5 which is a reasonable default. We also use rectified linear units and mini-batches with size of 50. The parameters of the CNN were fixed based on the performance of 3-fold cross-validation. The tweet representations are trained on top of pre-trained word vectors which are updated during CNN training. We use the publicly available word2vec[3] vectors that are trained on Google News corpus as well our own Word2vec vectors[4] trained during the labeled-data creation phase. During the training phase, the parameters

of the CNN model are learned by passing multiple filters over word vectors and then applying the max-over-time pooling operation to generate features which are used in a fully connected softmax layer. Finally, we use the cross-entropy loss function for learning the parameters of the model. Similar to Kim (2014), we use dropout (Hinton et al., 2012) to regularize the change of parameters by randomly setting some weights to zero that prevents overfitting.

3.2 Income Predictor Model

Similar to Preoţiuc-Pietro et al. (2015), we formulate the income prediction task as regression using user-level temporal orientation as features. First, the tweet temporal orientation classifier is used to label whether a tweet focuses on past, present, or future. Afterwards, at user-level, we produce three categories of temporal orientation (three separate variables summing to one), defined simply as the proportion of a user's total tweets ($tweets(user)_{all}$) classified in the given temporal category ($c \in \{$ *past, present,* or *future*$\}$), as in (1):

$$orientation_c(user) = \frac{|tweets_c(user)|}{|tweets_{all}(user)|} \quad (1)$$

We use linear and non-linear methods. The linear method is logistic regression (LR) (Freedman, 2009) with Elastic Net regularisation. In order to capture the non-linear relationship between a user's temporal orientation and their income, we use Gaussian Processes (GP) (Rasmussen and Nickisch, 2010) for regression. Given that our dataset is very large and the number of features is high, for GP inference we use the fully independent training conditional approximation (Snelson and Ghahramani, 2005) with 500 random inducing points.

4 Data Sets

4.1 Training Data

Tweets are collected using the Twitter streaming API.[5] We downloaded English tweets during the period 01.01.2015–31.01.2015, which generated about 40 million tweets. After collecting the tweets, we filter past-, present-, and future-oriented tweets using a manually selected high precision list of 50 seed terms. These are terms

---

[3]https://code.google.com/p/word2vec/
[4]trained using gensim library available at https://radimrehurek.com/gensim/intro.html

[5]https://dev.twitter.com/streaming/overview.

that capture temporal dimensions of tweets with very few false positives, though the recall of these terms is low. In order to increase the recall, and to capture new terms that are good paradigms of past, present, and future, we expand our initial seed terms using a query expansion technique. We employ a continuous distributed vector representation of words using the continuous Skip-gram model (also known as Word2Vec) proposed by Mikolov et al. (2013). The model is trained on the whole collection of 40 million tweets with dimension and window size set to 300 and 7, respectively.

Given the vector representations for the terms, we calculate the similarity scores between pairs of terms in our vocabulary using cosine similarity. The top 10 similar terms for each seed term are selected for the expansion of the initial seed list. We again filter the whole collection of tweets using the newly added seed terms. We finally select 120,000 tweets equally distributed in past (=40,000 tweets), present (=40,000), and future (=40,000) temporal categories.[6] Examples of filtered tweets are as follows:

- *Thank you so much for coming in for our show yesterday.* (**seed=yesterday**)

- *@**** is currently out of the office working his other job.* (**seed=currently**)

- *I promise you don't have to be afraid.* (**seed=promise**)

Table 1 shows some examples of expanded terms for some of the initial seed terms. There are some unrelated keywords in the expanded seed list due to the automatic process of keyword selection.

4.2 Test Set

In order to evaluate the tweet temporal orientation classification model, 2035 tweets were manually annotated by three human annotators in four different categories: past, present, future and doubtful. Majority voting is applied to assign the final output class to a given tweet. Tweets whose temporal orientation was not resolved by majority voting were deleted from the test set.[7] The final distribution of annotated tweets was: past=423, present=1252, future=325, doubtful=35.

---

[6] Similar to Schwartz et al. (2015), we only considered past, present and future categories.

[7] Note that we approached the authors of Schwartz et al. (2015) to obtain their dataset but they did not share the data because of copyright issues. This is the reason for generating our own gold-standard test set.

4.3 Income data of Users

We used a dataset developed by Preoţiuc-Pietro et al. (2015), which contains 5,191 Twitter users along with their platform statistics and ≈ 10 million historical tweets. The dataset is based on mapping a Twitter user to a job title and using this as a proxy for the mean income for that specific occupation.

5 Experimental Results

Temporal Orientation Classification Results: The performance of our tweet temporal orientation classifier is evaluated using the manually annotated test set. We compare our approach with two baselines that are the most relevant for our research: (i) Baseline1: a rule-based method (Nie et al., 2015) and (ii) Baseline2: a supervised learning strategy with bag-of-words, time expressions, part-of-speech tags, and temporal class-specific lexicon features (Schwartz et al., 2015). Comparative evaluation results are presented in Table 2. The results show that our weakly supervised framework outperforms rule-based and supervised learning technique in terms of accuracy.

We examine the impact of the size of labeled training data on each method's performance. Baseline1 (rule-based approach) is not involved since this does not depend on labeled training data. We randomly select $d\%$ of the training data to train the classifiers and test them on the test set, with d ranging from 10 to 90. For each d, we generate the training set 20 times and the averaged performance is recorded. Accuracies of both approaches over the test data are presented in Table 3. Results show that our proposed framework performs consistently better than its counterpart. In particular, results show that with 30K training examples, better results can be obtained by our approach than relying on 120K training items for the state-of-the-art supervised machine learning approach (Baseline2).

Income Prediction Results: Similar to Preoţiuc-Pietro et al. (2015), we measure the predictive power of temporal orientation by performing regression on the user income. Performance is measured using 10-fold cross-validation: in each round, 80% of the data is used to train the model, 10% is used to tune model parameters using grid search and a different 10% is held out for testing. The final results are computed over the aggregate set of results of all 10 folds. Results us-

Initial Seed Terms (Temporal Orientation)	Extended Seed Terms
Yesterday (Past)	yesterday!, started, yday, finished, already, yest, earlier, held, arrived
Currently (Present)	now, still, presently, available, whilst, actively, contemplating, considering
Promise (Future)	guarantee, expect, doubt, commitment, think, hope, opportunity, tomorrow

Table 1: Examples of initial seed terms and expanded seed terms.

Method	Baseline1	Baseline2	Proposed Method[1]	Proposed Method[2]
Accuracy	48.8	67.4	**74.4**	72.7
Past (p, r, f1)	(52.0, 56.3, 54.0)	(67.4, 81.9, 73.9)	(84.5, 79.8, 82.0)	(71.1, 79.5, 75.0)
Present (p, r, f1)	(58.2, 54.2, 56.1)	(69.3, 82.6, 75.3)	(81.3, 86.6, 83.8)	(73.0, 71.5, 72.2)
Future (p, r, f1)	(51.0, 53.3, 52.1)	(64.4, 77.9, 70.5)	(78.5, 79.8, 79.1)	(79.4, 69.5, 74.0)

Table 2: Accuracy for *past, present, future* classifications using different methods measured over test data. Results are broken down by precision (p), recall (r), and f1-measure (f1) scores. Proposed Method[1] and Proposed Method[2] represent our classification framework with Word2vec vectors derived from our collected tweet and pre-trained Google News corpus, respectively.

Training data size	Baseline2	Proposed Method[1]
10k	57.5	61.3
20k	60.2	66.4
30k	63.5	71.7
50k	65.4	73.6
70k	66.1	74.2
90k	67.4	74.1
120K (all)	67.4	**74.4**

Table 3: Tweets temporal orientation classification accuracies with different sizes of training data.

ing linear and non-linear regression methods and past, present, future temporal orientation features are presented in Table4. Performance is measured using two standard metrics: Pearson's correlation coefficient r and Mean Absolute Error (MAE) between inferred and target values. Results show that

Method	Temporal Orientation	Correlation coefficient	MAE
LR	Past	0.1449	£12365
	Present	0.0998	£14365
	Future	**0.4505**	£ 10850
GP	Past	0.1849	£11200
	Present	0.1099	£12125
	Future	**0.5104**	£ 10235

Table 4: Prediction of income using temporal orientation features

correlation between a user's future temporal orientation and their income is the highest, i.e. people with higher future temporal orientation tend to have higher income levels. Results also demonstrate that predictive models with future temporal orientation as a feature can predict income with high accuracy compared to past and present temporal orientation. Our findings are consistent with previous research that suggests that future-oriented thinking is linked to academic achievement, increased social involvement, lower distress, extroversion, and conscientiousness. These factors are also positively correlated with income (Kahana et al., 2005; Roberts et al., 2007). Note also that, the non-linear methods outperform the linear methods by a wide margin, showing the importance of modeling non-linear relationships in our data.

6 Conclusions

We presented the first large-scale study aiming to predict the income of Twitter users from their temporal orientation. Temporal orientation of users is assessed from their tweets. Our weakly supervised learning framework automatically time-tags tweets according to its underlying temporal orientation: past, present, or future. The associations we found between user-level future temporal orientation and income are novel in the context of well-established temporal orientation correlates. As future work, we are in the process of improving the temporal orientation classification accuracy by incorporating linguistic and sentiment related features into the deep learning phase.

Acknowledgments

The ADAPT Centre for Digital Content Technology is funded under the SFI Research Centres Programme (Grant 13/RC/2106) and is co-funded under the European Regional Development Fund.

References

Jean Adams and Daniel Nettle. 2009. Time perspective, personality and smoking, body mass, and physical activity: An empirical study. *British journal of health psychology* 14(1):83–105.

Munmun De Choudhury, Scott Counts, and Eric Horvitz. 2013. Predicting postpartum changes in emotion and behavior via social media. In *2013 ACM SIGCHI Conference on Human Factors in Computing Systems, CHI '13, Paris, France, April 27 - May 2, 2013*. pages 3267–3276.

Ronan Collobert, Jason Weston, Léon Bottou, Michael Karlen, Koray Kavukcuoglu, and Pavel Kuksa. 2011. Natural language processing (almost) from scratch. *Journal of Machine Learning Research* 12(Aug):2493–2537.

Peter Sheridan Dodds, Kameron Decker Harris, Isabel M Kloumann, Catherine A Bliss, and Christopher M Danforth. 2011. Temporal patterns of happiness and information in a global social network: Hedonometrics and twitter. *PloS one* 6(12):e26752.

David A Freedman. 2009. *Statistical models: theory and practice*. Cambridge University Press, Cambridge, UK.

Ian Goodfellow, Yoshua Bengio, and Aaron Courville. 2016. *Deep Learning*. MIT Press, Massachusetts, US. http://www.deeplearningbook.org.

Geoffrey E Hinton, Nitish Srivastava, Alex Krizhevsky, Ilya Sutskever, and Ruslan R Salakhutdinov. 2012. Improving neural networks by preventing co-adaptation of feature detectors. *arXiv preprint arXiv:1207.0580* .

Eva Kahana, Boaz Kahana, and Jianping Zhang. 2005. Motivational antecedents of preventive proactivity in late life: Linking future orientation and exercise. *Motivation and emotion* 29(4):438–459.

Daniel Kahneman and Angus Deaton. 2010. High income improves evaluation of life but not emotional well-being. *Proceedings of the national academy of sciences* 107(38):16489–16493.

Yoon Kim. 2014. Convolutional neural networks for sentence classification. *arXiv preprint arXiv:1408.5882* .

Michal Kosinski, David Stillwell, and Thore Graepel. 2013. Private traits and attributes are predictable from digital records of human behavior. *Proceedings of the National Academy of Sciences* 110(15):5802–5805.

James Marquardt, Golnoosh Farnadi, Gayathri Vasudevan, Marie-Francine Moens, Sergio Davalos, Ankur Teredesai, and Martine De Cock. 2014. Age and gender identification in social media. In *Working Notes for CLEF 2014 Conference, Sheffield, UK, September 15-18, 2014.*. pages 1129–1136.

Tomas Mikolov, Ilya Sutskever, Kai Chen, Gregory S. Corrado, and Jeffrey Dean. 2013. Distributed representations of words and phrases and their compositionality. In *Advances in neural information processing systems, Lake Tahoe, Nevada, United States, December 5-8, 2013*. pages 3111–3119.

Aiming Nie, Jason Shepard, Jinho Choi, Bridget Copley, and Phillip Wolff. 2015. Computational exploration of the linguistic structures of future-oriented expression: Classification and categorization. In *NAACL-HLT 2015 Student Research Workshop (SRW), Denver, Colorado, USA*. volume 867, page 168.

Gregory Park, H. Andrew Schwartz, Maarten Sap, Margaret L. Kern, Evan Weingarten, Johannes C. Eichstaedt, Jonah Berger, David J. Stillwell, Michal Kosinski, Lyle H. Ungar, and Martin E. P. Seligman. 2017. Living in the past, present, and future: Measuring temporal orientation with language. *Journal of Personality* 85(2):270–280.

Soujanya Poria, Erik Cambria, and Alexander F. Gelbukh. 2015. Deep convolutional neural network textual features and multiple kernel learning for utterance-level multimodal sentiment analysis. In *Proceedings of the 2015 Conference on Empirical Methods in Natural Language Processing, EMNLP 2015, Lisbon, Portugal, September 17-21, 2015*. pages 2539–2544.

Daniel Preoţiuc-Pietro, Svitlana Volkova, Vasileios Lampos, Yoram Bachrach, and Nikolaos Aletras. 2015. Studying user income through language, behaviour and affect in social media. *PloS one* 10(9):e0138717.

Carl Edward Rasmussen and Hannes Nickisch. 2010. Gaussian processes for machine learning (GPML) toolbox. *Journal of Machine Learning Research* 11:3011–3015.

Brent W Roberts, Nathan R Kuncel, Rebecca Shiner, Avshalom Caspi, and Lewis R Goldberg. 2007. The power of personality: The comparative validity of personality traits, socioeconomic status, and cognitive ability for predicting important life outcomes. *Perspectives on Psychological Science* 2(4):313–345.

Maarten Sap, Gregory J. Park, Johannes C. Eichstaedt, Margaret L. Kern, David Stillwell, Michal Kosinski, Lyle H. Ungar, and Hansen Andrew Schwartz. 2014. Developing age and gender predictive lexica over social media. In *Proceedings of the 2014 Conference on Empirical Methods in Natural Language Processing, EMNLP 2014, October 25-29, 2014, Doha, Qatar, A meeting of SIGDAT, a Special Interest Group of the ACL*. pages 1146–1151.

H Andrew Schwartz, Johannes C Eichstaedt, Margaret L Kern, Lukasz Dziurzynski, Stephanie M Ramones, Megha Agrawal, Achal Shah, Michal Kosinski, David Stillwell, Martin EP Seligman, et al.

2013. Personality, gender, and age in the language of social media: The open-vocabulary approach. *PloS one* 8(9):e73791.

H. Andrew Schwartz, Greg Park, Maarten Sap, Evan Weingarten, Johannes Eichstaedt, Margaret Kern, Jonah Berger, Martin Seligman, and Lyle Ungar. 2015. Extracting human temporal orientation in facebook language. In *Proceedings of The 2015 Conference of the North American Chapter of the Association for Computational Linguistics-Human Language Technologies (NAACL), Denver, Colorado, USA*. pages 409–419.

Edward Snelson and Zoubin Ghahramani. 2005. Sparse gaussian processes using pseudo-inputs. In *Advances in Neural Information Processing Systems 18 [Neural Information Processing Systems, NIPS 2005, December 5-8, 2005, Vancouver, British Columbia, Canada]*. pages 1257–1264.

Paul Webley and Ellen K Nyhus. 2006. Parents influence on childrens future orientation and saving. *Journal of Economic Psychology* 27(1):140–164.

Philip G Zimbardo and John N Boyd. 2015. Putting time in perspective: A valid, reliable individual-differences metric. In *Time Perspective Theory; Review, Research and Application*, Springer, Berlin, Germany, pages 17–55.

Character-Aware Neural Morphological Disambiguation

Alymzhan Toleu   **Gulmira Tolegen**   **Aibek Makazhanov**

National Laboratory Astana, Nazarbayev University
53 Kabanbay batyr ave., Astana, Kazakhstan
`alymzhan.toleu@gmail.com, gulmira.tolegen.cs@gmail.com,`
`aibek.makazhanov@nu.edu.kz`

Abstract

We develop a language-independent, deep learning-based approach to the task of morphological disambiguation. Guided by the intuition that the correct analysis should be "most similar" to the context, we propose dense representations for morphological analyses and surface context and a simple yet effective way of combining the two to perform disambiguation. Our approach improves on the language-dependent state of the art for two agglutinative languages (Turkish and Kazakh) and can be potentially applied to other morphologically complex languages.

1 Introduction

Morphological disambiguation (MD) is a long standing problem in processing morphologically complex languages (MCL). POS tagging is a somewhat related problem, however in MD, in addition to POS tags, one typically has to predict lemmata (roots hereinafter) that surface forms stem from and morphemes[1] they bear. For example, depending on the context, a Turkish word *adam* can be analyzed as: (i) *a man* – $[adam]_1+[Noun]_2+[A3sg+Pnon+Nom]_3$ or (ii) *my island* – $[ada]_1+[Noun]_2+[A3sg+P1sg +Nom]_3$ (Hakkani-Tür et al., 2002). Thus, if one counts analyses as tags, MD can be cast as a tagging problem with an extremely large tagset. This fact discourages direct application of the state of the art approaches designed for small fixed tagsets.

To develop a language independent dense representation of the analyses, we segment[2] an analysis

---

[1] We use the term *morpheme* for its universal recognition within the community. A more appropriate term might be *grammeme*, i.e. a value of grammatical category.

[2] Such a segmentation is denoted by the squared brackets numbered in the respective order (cf. Turkish example).

into (i) the root, (ii) its POS and (iii) the morpheme chain (MC). We then proceed to jointly learn the embeddigns for the root and the POS segments and to combine them and the MC segment representation into a single dense representation. MC segments are represented as binary vectors that, for a given analysis, encode presence or absence of *each* morpheme found in the train set. This ensures language independence and contrasts previous work (at least on Turkish and Kazakh), where only certain morphemes are chosen as features depending on their position (Assylbekov et al., 2016; Hakkani-Tür et al., 2002) or presence (Makhambetov et al., 2015) in an analysis, or the authors' intuition (Yildiz et al., 2016; Tolegen et al., 2016; Sak et al., 2007).

Apart from the sparseness of analyses distribution MCL notoriously raise free word order and long dependency issues. Thus, decoding analysis sequences using only the leftmost context may not be enough. To address this we leverage the rightmost context as well. We model the left- and rightmost surface context in two ways: using (i) BiL-STM (Greff et al., 2015) with a character-based sub-layer (Ling et al., 2015) and (ii) with a feed forward network on word embeddings. We then entertain the idea that given a word with multiple analyses and its surface context, the correct analysis might be "closer" to the context. Following our intuition, we have tried computing the distance between the analysis and the context representations, and a simple dot product (as in unnormalized cosine similarity) has yielded the best performance.

We evaluate our approach on Turkish and Kazakh data sets, using several baselines (including the state of the art methods for both languages) and a variety of settings and metrics. In terms of general accuracy our approach has achieved a nearly 1% improvement over the state of the art for Turkish and a marginal improvement for Kazakh.

Proceedings of the 55th Annual Meeting of the Association for Computational Linguistics (Short Papers), pages 666–671
Vancouver, Canada, July 30 - August 4, 2017. ©2017 Association for Computational Linguistics
https://doi.org/10.18653/v1/P17-2105

Our contribution amounts to the following: (i) a general MD framework for MCL that can be analyzed in <root, POS, MC> triplets; (ii) improvement on language-dependent state of the art for Turkish and Kazakh.

2 Models

In this section we describe our approach to encoding morphological analyses and the context into the embeddings and combining them to perform morphological disambiguation.

2.1 Morphological Representation

We treat a morphological analysis as a combination of three main constituents: the root, its POS and the morpheme chain. These constituents are represented as d_r, d_p, and d_m-dimensional vectors respectively. The former two vectors correspond to dense word embeddings (Collobert et al., 2011), and the latter is a binary vector which encodes the presence of a certain morpheme in the chain. The size of the binary vector, d_m, is equal to the size of the morpheme dictionary obtained from the data.

Given a sentence and the j-th surface word form with N analyses, we represent the k-th analysis as:

$$\mathbf{A}_j^k = tanh(\mathbf{W}^r r_k + \mathbf{W}^p p_k + \mathbf{W}^m m_k) \qquad (1)$$

where $A_j \in \mathbf{R}^{d_h \times |N|}$, d_h is the dimension of each analysis embedding, $r_k \in \mathbf{R}^{d_r \times 1}, p_k \in \mathbf{R}^{d_p \times 1}, m_k \in \{0,1\}^{d_p \times 1}$ are constituent vectors of the k-th analysis, and $\mathbf{W}^r \in \mathbf{R}^{d_h \times d_r}$, $\mathbf{W}^p \in \mathbf{R}^{d_h \times d_p}, \mathbf{W}^m \in \mathbf{R}^{d_h \times d_m}$ are the model parameters. The bias term was left out for clarity. This representation is shown on Figure 1 (bottom).

2.2 Recurrent Neural Disambiguation

The model architecture is shown on Figure 1. It consists of two main blocks that learn the surface context (top) and the morphological analyses representations (bottom).

When it comes to modeling context via word embeddings for morphologically complex languages, it is impractical to actually store vectors for all words, since majority of words in such languages has a large number of surface realizations. Our solution to this problem is to construct a surface word representation from characters that not only reduces data sparseness, but also help in dealing with the out-of-vocabulary (OOV) words (Ling et al., 2015). We represent each character of each word as a vector $x_i \in \mathbf{R}^{d_c}$ and the

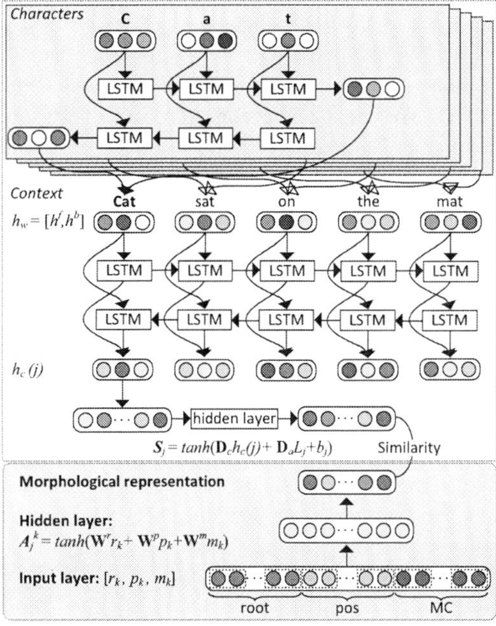

Figure 1: Model architecture

entire embedding matrix as $\mathbf{E}^c \in \mathbf{R}^{d_c \times |C|}$, where C is the character vocabulary extracted from the training set including alphanumeric characters and other possible symbols. Given an input surface word w_i with its character embeddings $x_1, ..., x_n$, the hidden state h_t at the time step t can be computed via the following Vanilla LSTM calculations:

$$i_t = \sigma(\mathbf{W}^i x_t + \mathbf{U}^i h_{t-1} + b^i) \qquad (2)$$
$$f_t = \sigma(\mathbf{W}^f x_t + \mathbf{U}^f h_{t-1} + b^f) \qquad (3)$$
$$o_t = \sigma(\mathbf{W}^o x_t + \mathbf{U}^o h_{t-1} + b^o) \qquad (4)$$
$$z_t = tanh(\mathbf{W}^z x_t + \mathbf{U}^z h_{t-1} + b^z) \qquad (5)$$
$$c_t = f_t \odot c_{t-1} + i_t \odot z_t \qquad (6)$$
$$h_t = o_t \odot tanh(c_t) \qquad (7)$$

where $\sigma(\cdot)$ and $tanh(\cdot)$ are the non-linear functions. i_t, f_t, o_t are referred to three gates: *input, forget, output* that control the information flow of inputs. Parameters of the LSTM are W^*, U^*, b^*, where $*$ can be any of $\{i, f, o, g\}$. The peephole connections were left out for clarity.

We use both forward and backward LSTM to learn word representations obtained by concatenation of the last states in both direction h^f and h^b, e.g. $h_w = [h^f, h^b]$. Character-based word embeddings obtained in this manner do not yet contain the context information on a sentence level. Thus, we adopt another LSTM to learn context-sensitive information for each word in both directions. We denote the concatenation of the embeddings learned from the forward and backward LSTM states as $h_c(j) \in \mathbf{R}^{2hs \times 1}$ (where hs is the output size for the j-th word), and represent surface context as:

$$S_j = tanh(\mathbf{D}_c h_c(j) + b_j) \qquad (8)$$

where $S_j \in \mathbf{R}^{d_h \times 1}$ is a hidden layer output, $h_c(j) \in \mathbf{R}^{2hs \times 1}$ is a context vector of the j-th word, and $b_j \in \mathbf{R}^{d_h \times 1}$ is a bias term.

For the final prediction, we score each analysis by computing the inner product between its representation and the context's representations:

$$P_j^k = S_j \cdot \mathbf{A}_j^k \qquad (9)$$

where S_j and A_j^k are computed as equations (8) and (1) respectively. We normalize the obtained scores using softmax and choose the analysis with the maximum score as the correct one. In what follows we refer to this model as **BiLSTM**.

Finally, in a separate setting, in addition to the surface context in the hidden layer we also incorporate the immediate (left and right) morphological context in the form of the average of the analyses representations:

$$S_j^* = tanh(\mathbf{D}_c h_c(j) + \mathbf{D}_a L_j + b_j) \qquad (10)$$

where $L_j \in \mathbf{R}^{2d_h \times 1}$ is concatenation of averaged representations of the leftmost and rightmost analyses, and $\mathbf{D}_c \in \mathbf{R}^{d_h \times 2hs}$ and $\mathbf{D}_a \in \mathbf{R}^{d_h \times 2d_h}$ are the model parameters. This advanced variation is referred to as **BiLSTM***.

2.3 Alternative Context Representation

We also experiment with an alternative context model that uses a feed-forward NN architecture (Collobert et al., 2011; Zheng et al., 2013). In this model word embeddings of fixed window size are fed to the hidden layer, and the output represents the context. The remaining parts of the architecture stay the same: we use the same morphological representation and choose the correct analysis exactly as we did for BiLSTM model. As in the case with BiLSTM, we leverage morphological context, by performing a Viterbi decoding conditioned on the leftmost analysis. We refer to this

Lang.	Train	Test	OOV	ΔAT
Kazakh	16,624	2,324	43.9%	2.85
Turkish	752,332	20,536	10.24%	1.76

Table 1: Corpora statistics: ΔAT denotes the average number of analysis per token.

model as **DNN** (Deep NN), an advanced variation of which uses the averaged rightmost morphological context as well, and is referred to as **DNN***.

2.4 Training

In all models, the top layer of the networks has a softmax that computes the normalized scores over morphological candidates given the input word. The networks are trained to minimize the cross entropy of the predicted and true morphological analyses. Back-propagation is employed to compute the gradient of the corresponding object function with respect to the model parameters.

3 Experiments and Evaluation

3.1 Data Sets

We conduct our experiments on Kazakh (Assylbekov et al., 2016) and Turkish (Yuret and Türe, 2006) data sets[3]. Table 1 shows the corpora statistics. Kazakh data set is almost 50 times smaller than that of Turkish, with four times the OOV rate and almost twice as many analyses per word on average. Given such a drastic difference in the resources it would be interesting to see how our models perform on otherwise similar languages (both Turkic). Lastly, while the corpora provide train and test splits, there are no tuning sets, so we withdraw small portions from the training sets for tuning hyper-parameters[4].

3.2 Baselines

We compare our models to three other approaches. For Kazakh we use an HMM based tagger and its version extended with the rule-based constraint grammar (Assylbekov et al., 2016), which is considered the state of the art for the language. We

---

[3]For Turkish, we used a test set that was manually re-annotated by Yildiz et al. (2016).

[4]The following hyper-parameters are used in all the experiments: character embedding size $d_c = 35$, character and context LSTM states are 50, root and POS embedding sizes are all set to 50, hidden layer size $d_h = 200$, learning rate is set to 0.01. The window size of DNN is set to 5. For regularization we use dropout (Srivastava et al., 2014) with probability 0.5 on the hidden layers. We further constrain the norm of gradient to be below 2 by using gradient clipping.

Models	Kazakh					Turkish				
	tok. acc.	tok. amb.acc.	OOV acc.	OOV amb.acc.	sen. acc.	tok. acc.	tok. amb.acc.	OOV acc.	OOV amb.acc.	sen. acc.
HMM	83.82	74.98	80.90	73.89	32.41	-	-	-	-	-
MANN	85.56	77.66	81.68	74.96	32.80	91.35	82.32	86.72	74.09	40.38
Voted Perceptron	88.41	82.07	86.19	81.12	40.31	91.89	83.47	87.98	76.87	41.52
DNN	86.33	78.86	84.13	78.31	40.71	92.24	84.14	87.05	74.74	41.16
DNN*	87.25	80.28	85.99	80.85	40.31	92.22	84.12	87.24	75.11	40.38
DNN*‡	88.26	81.85	86.77	81.92	39.52	**92.32**	**84.32**	87.95	76.50	**41.55**
BiLSTM	87.49	80.65	85.21	79.78	39.52	91.37	82.39	86.91	74.46	38.13
BiLSTM*	90.92	85.95	88.73	84.60	50.19	92.03	83.73	88.01	76.60	40.54
BiLSTM*‡	**91.06**	**86.40**	**88.93**	**85.27**	**50.98**	92.16	84.01	**88.24**	**77.06**	41.01
HMMCG	90.39	85.88	88.83	86.07	53.75	-	-	-	-	-
BiLSTM*‡+CG	91.74	87.45	90.00	86.74	54.54	-	-	-	-	-

Table 2: Results: here, *tok. acc.* and *tok. amb. acc.* denote the accuracy over all and ambiguous tokens respectively. Same goes for *OOV acc.* and *OOV amb. acc.*. Sentence accuracy is denoted as *sen. acc.*.

refer to these baselines as HMM and HMMCG. Another baseline is a voted perceptron (Collins, 2002) based tagger. We use our implementation of this baseline for Kazakh and the model developed by Sak et al. (2007) for Turkish. Lastly, we use a neural network model proposed by Yildiz et al. (2016), which is considered state of the art for Turkish. For this baseline too we use our own implementation (for both languages) and refer to it as MANN[5].

3.3 Experimental Setup

As described in the previous section, each of our models has two settings: the one that does not incorporate *surrounding* morphological context and the one that does (the starred one). In addition to that we use pre-trained embeddings, by training *word2vec* (Mikolov et al., 2013) skip-gram model on Wikipedia texts. This setting is denoted by a double dagger (‡).

We perform a single run evaluation in terms of token- and sentence- based accuracy. We consider four types of tokens: (i) all tokens; (ii) ambiguous tokens (the ones with at least two analyses); (iii) OOV tokens; (iv) ambiguous OOV tokens. Thus, we use a total of five metrics. In terms of strictness we deem correct only the predictions that match the golden truth completely, i.e. in root, POS and MC (up to a single morpheme tag).

---

[5]Note that all of the baselines are language dependent to a certain degree, with MANN being the least dependent and HMMCG the most. The latter baseline employs hand-engineered constraint grammar rules to perform initial disambiguation, followed by application of the HMM tagger, which cherry-picks the most informative grammatical features.

3.4 Results and Discussion

The results are given in Table 2. Unless stated otherwise we refer to the general (all tokens) accuracy when comparing model performances.

For Kazakh, DNN conditioned on the leftmost analysis yields 86.33% accuracy. DNN* that in addition uses the rightmost analysis embeddings, improves almost 1% over that result (87.25%). On the other hand BiLSTM, whose context representation uses surface forms only, performs even better (87.49%). When this model incorporates immediate morphological context, it (BiLSTM*) performs at 90.92% and beats the HMMCG baseline. However, the latter being a very strong language dependent baseline still outperforms our model in ambiguous OOV and sentence accuracy. When we evaluate our model under equal conditions (BiLSTM*‡+CG) it beats HMMCG on all of the metrics. We separate this comparison from the rest because of a language-dependent set up.

In contrast, for Turkish DNN models outperform BiLSTM on seen tokens and yield an almost equal 92.2% accuracy regardless of using the rightmost morphological context. This performance is also higher than that of all baselines, including the state of the art MANN. However BiLSTM* is still better than DNN* in OOV token accuracy, both overall and ambiguous.

As it can be seen, pre-training boosts the performance of DNN* and BiLSTM* across all metrics. For Kazakh pre-training results in .14% improvement in general token accuracy for BiLSTM*, which amounts to .67% improvement over the state of the art. For Turkish this results in an almost 1% net improvement in overall token accuracy over MANN, the state of the art[6].

A cross-linguistic comparison reveals that although Kazakh data set is much smaller than that of Turkish and has more analyses per word on average and higher OOV rate, on certain metrics the models perform on par or even better for Kazakh[7]. To investigate this further we have made data sets comparable in size by randomly choosing 20.6K+ and 3.4K from Turkish training and test sets. On this data BiLSTM*‡ yields 91.18, 82.0% general and ambiguous token accuracy and respective scores for OOV are 87.0, 74.6%. This result follows the pattern, where for Turkish only the general accuracy is higher than that of Kazakh. It turns out that Turkish data contains many unambiguous tokens: 49% and 48% for full and small data sets (train + test average), against 36% for Kazakh. This suggests that the higher general accuracy on Turkish data can be explained by the higher rate of the unambiguous tokens. Also Turkish has a more complex derivational morphology, which "lengthens" the analyses, e.g. an average number of morphemes per analysis is higher for Turkish (5.25) than for Kazakh (4.6). This adds sparseness to the morpheme chains and certainly further complicates disambiguation, especially in an OOV scenario.

We also observe that BiLSTM*‡ works best on all metrics for Kazakh, but for Turkish it beats DNN*‡ only on the OOV part. Due to BiLSTM*‡ being computationally prohibitive we ran it with significantly less number of epochs than DNN, and it also being a character-based model, we speculate that it was able to learn character aware context embeddings hence better at OOV.

4 Related Work

A morphology-aware NN (MANN) for MD was proposed by Yildiz et al. (2016), and has been reported to achieve ambiguous token accuracies of 84.12, 88.35 and 93.78% for Turkish, Finish and Hungarian respectively. This approach differs from ours in a number of ways. (i) Our analysis representation treats morpheme tags in a language-independent manner considering every tag found in the training set, whereas in MANN certain tags are chosen with a specific language in mind. (ii) MANN is a feed-forward NN that, unlike our approach, does not account for the surface context. (iii) As we understood, at the decoding step MANN makes use of the golden truth, whereas our models have no need for that.

Although several statistical models have been proposed for Kazakh MD, such as HMM- (Makazhanov et al., 2014; Makhambetov et al., 2015; Assylbekov et al., 2016), voted perceptron- (Tolegen et al., 2016) and transformation-based (Kessikbayeva and Cicekli, 2016) taggers, to our knowledge ours is the first deep learning-based approach to the problem that is also purely language independent.

It is becoming increasingly popular to use richer architectures to learn better embeddings from characters/words (Yessenbayev and Makazhanov, 2016; Ling et al., 2015; Wieting et al., 2016). Ling et al. (2015) used a BiLSTM to learn word vectors, showing strong performance on language modeling and POS tagging. Melamud et al. (2016) proposed *context2vec*, a BiLSTM based model to learn context embedding of target words and achieved state-of-the-art results on sentence completion and word sense disambiguation.

5 Conclusion

We have proposed a general MD framework for MCL that can be analyzed in <root, POS, MC> triplets. We have showed that the surface context can be useful to MD, especially if combined with morphological context. Our next step would be to assess our claims on a larger number of typologically distant languages.

Acknowledgments

This work has been conducted under the targeted program O.0743 (0115PK02473) of the Committee of Science of the Ministry of Education and Science of the Republic of Kazakhstan, and the research grant 129-2017/022-2017 of the Nazarbayev University.

The authors would like to thank Xiaoqing Zheng for tremendously helpful discussions, as well as Eray Yildiz and Zhenisbek Assylbekov for the data sets used in this study and prompt replies to all questions regarding those.

---

[6]For the un-pretrained model original work reports 84.12% accuracy on ambiguous tokens (Yildiz et al., 2016), which is lower than 84.14% that un-pretrained DNN achieves on this metric.

[7] For instance, BiLSTM*‡ applied to Kazakh performs better than any other model for Turkish in terms of sentence, ambiguous and OOV token accuracy. Moreover all of the models (including the baselines) perform better on Kazakh in terms of ambiguous OOV accuracy.

References

Zhenisbek Assylbekov, Jonathan Washington, Francis Tyers, Assulan Nurkas, Aida Sundetova, Aidana Karibayeva, Balzhan Abduali, and Dina Amirova. 2016. A free/open-source hybrid morphological disambiguation tool for Kazakh. In *TurCLing 2016*. pages 18–26.

Michael Collins. 2002. Discriminative Training Methods for Hidden Markov Models: Theory and Experiments with Perceptron Algorithms. In *Proceedings of the ACL-02 Conference on Empirical Methods in Natural Language Processing - Volume 10*. Association for Computational Linguistics, Stroudsburg, PA, USA, EMNLP '02, pages 1–8.

Ronan Collobert, Jason Weston, Léon Bottou, Michael Karlen, Koray Kavukcuoglu, and Pavel Kuksa. 2011. Natural Language Processing (Almost) from Scratch. *J. Mach. Learn. Res.* 12:2493–2537.

Klaus Greff, Rupesh Kumar Srivastava, Jan Koutník, Bas R. Steunebrink, and Jürgen Schmidhuber. 2015. LSTM: A Search Space Odyssey. *CoRR* abs/1503.04069.

Dilek Z. Hakkani-Tür, Kemal Oflazer, and Gökhan Tür. 2002. Statistical Morphological Disambiguation for Agglutinative Languages. *Computers and the Humanities* 36(4):381–410.

Gulshat Kessikbayeva and Ilyas Cicekli. 2016. A Rule Based Morphological Analyzer and a Morphological Disambiguator for Kazakh Language. *Linguistics and Literature Studies* 4(4):96–104.

Wang Ling, Chris Dyer, Alan W. Black, Isabel Trancoso, Ramon Fermandez, Silvio Amir, Lus Marujo, and Tiago Lus. 2015. Finding Function in Form: Compositional Character Models for Open Vocabulary Word Representation. In *EMNLP*. The Association for Computational Linguistics, pages 1520–1530.

Aibek Makazhanov, Zhandos Yessenbayev, Islam Sabyrgaliyev, Anuar Sharafudinov, and Olzhas Makhambetov. 2014. On certain aspects of Kazakh part-of-speech tagging. In *Application of Information and Communication Technologies (AICT), 2014 IEEE 8th International Conference on*. pages 1–4.

Olzhas Makhambetov, Aibek Makazhanov, Islam Sabyrgaliyev, and Zhandos Yessenbayev. 2015. Data-Driven Morphological Analysis and Disambiguation for Kazakh. In *Computational Linguistics and Intelligent Text Processing - 16th International Conference, CICLing 2015, Cairo, Egypt, April 14-20, 2015, Proceedings Part I*. pages 151–163.

Oren Melamud, Jacob Goldberger, and Ido Dagan. 2016. context2vec: Learning Generic Context Embedding with Bidirectional LSTM. In *CoNLL*.

Tomas Mikolov, Ilya Sutskever, Kai Chen, Greg S Corrado, and Jeff Dean. 2013. Distributed Representations of Words and Phrases and their Compositionality. In C. J. C. Burges, L. Bottou, M. Welling, Z. Ghahramani, and K. Q. Weinberger, editors, *Advances in Neural Information Processing Systems 26*, Curran Associates, Inc., pages 3111–3119.

Haşim Sak, Tunga Güngör, and Murat Saraçlar. 2007. Morphological Disambiguation of Turkish Text with Perceptron Algorithm. In *Proceedings of CICLing 2007*. volume LNCS 4394, pages 107–118.

Nitish Srivastava, Geoffrey Hinton, Alex Krizhevsky, Ilya Sutskever, and Ruslan Salakhutdinov. 2014. Dropout: A Simple Way to Prevent Neural Networks from Overfitting. *Journal of Machine Learning Research* 15:1929–1958.

Gulmira Tolegen, Alymzhan Toleu, and Zheng Xiaoqing. 2016. Named Entity Recognition for Kazakh Using Conditional Random Fields. In *Proceedings of the 4-th International Conference on Computer Processing of Turkic Languages TurkLang 2016*. Izvestija KGTU im.I.Razzakova. TurkLang 2016, pages 122–129.

John Wieting, Mohit Bansal, Kevin Gimpel, and Karen Livescu. 2016. Charagram: Embedding Words and Sentences via Character n-grams. In *Proceedings of the 2016 Conference on Empirical Methods in Natural Language Processing*. Association for Computational Linguistics, Austin, Texas, pages 1504–1515.

Zhandos Yessenbayev and Aibek Makazhanov. 2016. Character-based Feature Extraction with LSTM Networks for POS-tagging Task. In *Application of Information and Communication Technologies (AICT), 2016 IEEE 10th International Conference on*. pages 62–66.

Eray Yildiz, Caglar Tirkaz, H. Bahadir Sahin, Mustafa Tolga Eren, and Omer Ozan Sonmez. 2016. A Morphology-Aware Network for Morphological Disambiguation. In *Proceedings of AAAI*. AAAI Press, pages 2863–2869.

Deniz Yuret and Ferhan Türe. 2006. Learning Morphological Disambiguation Rules for Turkish. In *Proceedings of the Main Conference on Human Language Technology Conference of the North American Chapter of the Association of Computational Linguistics*. Association for Computational Linguistics, Stroudsburg, PA, USA, HLT-NAACL '06, pages 328–334.

Xiaoqing Zheng, Hanyang Chen, and Tianyu Xu. 2013. Deep learning for Chinese word segmentation and POS tagging. In *Proceedings of the 2013 Conference on Empirical Methods in Natural Language Processing*. Association for Computational Linguistics, Seattle, Washington, USA, pages 647–657.

Character Composition Model with Convolutional Neural Networks for Dependency Parsing on Morphologically Rich Languages

Xiang Yu and **Ngoc Thang Vu**
Institut für Maschinelle Sprachverarbeitung
Universität Stuttgart
`{xiangyu,thangvu}@ims.uni-stuttgart.de`

Abstract

We present a transition-based dependency parser that uses a convolutional neural network to compose word representations from characters. The character composition model shows great improvement over the word-lookup model, especially for parsing agglutinative languages. These improvements are even better than using pre-trained word embeddings from extra data. On the SPMRL data sets, our system outperforms the previous best greedy parser (Ballesteros et al., 2015) by a margin of 3% on average.[1]

1 Introduction

As with many other NLP tasks, dependency parsing also suffers from the out-of-vocabulary (OOV) problem, and probably more than others since training data with syntactical annotation is usually scarce. This problem is particularly severe when the target is a morphologically rich language. For example, in the SPMRL shared task data sets (Seddah et al., 2013, 2014), 4 out of 9 treebanks contain more than 40% word types in the development set that are never seen in the training set.

One way to tackle the OOV problem is to pre-train the word embeddings, *e.g.*, with word2vec (Mikolov et al., 2013), from a large set of unlabeled data. This comes with two main advantages: (1) more word types, which means that the vocabulary is extended by the unlabeled data, so that some of the OOV words now have a learned representation; (2) more word tokens per type, which means that the syntactic and semantic similarities of the words are better modeled than only using the parser training data.

Pre-trained word embeddings can alleviate the OOV problem by expanding the vocabulary, but it does not model the morphological information. Instead of looking up word embeddings, many researchers propose to compose the word representation from characters for various tasks, *e.g.*, part-of-speech tagging (dos Santos and Zadrozny, 2014; Plank et al., 2016), named entity recognition (dos Santos and Guimarães, 2015), language modeling (Ling et al., 2015), machine translation (Costa-jussà and Fonollosa, 2016). In particular, Ballesteros et al. (2015) use a bidirectional long short-term memory (LSTM) character model for dependency parsing. Kim et al. (2016) present a convolutional neural network (CNN) character model for language modeling, but make no comparison among the character models, and state that "it remains open as to which character composition model (*i.e.*, LSTM or CNN) performs better".

We propose to apply the CNN model by Kim et al. (2016) in a greedy transition-based dependency parser with feed-forward neural networks (Chen and Manning, 2014; Weiss et al., 2015). This model requires no extra unlabeled data but performs better than using pre-trained word embeddings. Furthermore, it can be combined with word embeddings from the lookup table since they capture different aspects of word similarities.

Experimental results show that the CNN model works especially well on agglutinative languages, where the OOV rates are high. On other morphologically rich languages, the CNN model also performs at least as good as the word-lookup model.

Furthermore, our CNN model outperforms both the original and our re-implementation of the bidirectional LSTM model by Ballesteros et al. (2015) by a large margin. It provides empirical evidence to the aforementioned open question, suggesting that the CNN is the better character composition model for dependency parsing.

---

[1]The parser is available at `http://www.ims.uni-stuttgart.de/institut/mitarbeiter/xiangyu/index.en.html`

Proceedings of the 55th Annual Meeting of the Association for Computational Linguistics (Short Papers), pages 672–678
Vancouver, Canada, July 30 - August 4, 2017. ©2017 Association for Computational Linguistics
https://doi.org/10.18653/v1/P17-2106

2   Parsing Models

2.1   Baseline Parsing Model

As the baseline parsing model, we re-implement the greedy parser in Weiss et al. (2015) with some modifications, which brings about 0.5% improvement, outlined below.[2]

Since most treebanks contain non-projective trees, we use an approximate non-projective transition system similar to Attardi (2006). It has two additional transitions (LEFT-2 and RIGHT-2) to the Arc-Standard system (Nivre, 2004) that attach the top of the stack to the third token on the stack, or *vice versa*. We also extend the feature templates in Weiss et al. (2015) by extracting the children of the third token in the stack. The complete transitions and feature templates are listed in Appendix A.

The feature templates consist of 24 tokens in the configuration, we look up the embeddings of the word forms, POS tags and dependency labels of each token.[3] We then concatenate the embeddings $\mathbf{E}_{word}(t_i)$, $\mathbf{E}_{tag}(t_i)$, $\mathbf{E}_{label}(t_i)$ for each token t_i, and use a dense layer with ReLU non-linearity to obtain a compact representation $\mathbf{f}(t_i)$ of the token:

$$\mathbf{x}(t_i) = [\mathbf{E}_{word}(t_i); \mathbf{E}_{tag}(t_i); \mathbf{E}_{label}(t_i)] \quad (1)$$
$$\mathbf{f}(t_i) = \max\{\mathbf{0}, \mathbf{W}_f \mathbf{x}(t_i) + \mathbf{b}_f\}$$

We concatenate the representations of the tokens and feed them through two hidden layers with ReLU non-linearity, and finally into the softmax layer to compute the probability of each transition:

$$\mathbf{h}_0 = [\mathbf{f}(t_1); \mathbf{f}(t_2); ...; \mathbf{f}(t_{24})]$$
$$\mathbf{h}_1 = \max\{\mathbf{0}, \mathbf{W}_1 \mathbf{h}_0 + \mathbf{b}_1\}$$
$$\mathbf{h}_2 = \max\{\mathbf{0}, \mathbf{W}_2 \mathbf{h}_1 + \mathbf{b}_2\}$$
$$p(\cdot|t_1, ..., t_{24}) = \mathrm{softmax}(\mathbf{W}_3 \mathbf{h}_2 + \mathbf{b}_3)$$

$\mathbf{E}_{word}$, $\mathbf{E}_{tag}$, $\mathbf{E}_{label}$, $\mathbf{W}_f$, $\mathbf{W}_1$, $\mathbf{W}_2$, $\mathbf{W}_3$, $\mathbf{b}_f$, $\mathbf{b}_1$, $\mathbf{b}_2$, $\mathbf{b}_3$ are all the parameters that will be learned through back propagation with averaged stochastic gradient descent in mini-batches.

Note that Weiss et al. (2015) directly concatenate the embeddings of the words, tags, and labels of all the tokens together as input to the hidden layer. Instead, we first group the embeddings of the word, tag, and label of each token and compute

an intermediate representation with shared parameters, then concatenate all the representations as input to the hidden layer.

2.2   LSTM Character Composition Model

To tackle the OOV problem, we want to replace the word-lookup table with a function that composes the word representation from characters.

As a baseline character model, we re-implement the bidirectional LSTM character composition model following Ballesteros et al. (2015). We replace the lookup table $\mathbf{E}_{word}$ in the baseline parser with the final outputs of the forward and backward LSTMs $\overleftarrow{\mathbf{lstm}}$ and $\overrightarrow{\mathbf{lstm}}$. Equation (1) is then replaced with

$$\mathbf{x}(t_i) = [\overleftarrow{\mathbf{lstm}}(t_i); \overrightarrow{\mathbf{lstm}}(t_i); \mathbf{E}_{tag}(t_i); \mathbf{E}_{label}(t_i)].$$

We refer the readers to Ling et al. (2015) for the details of the bidirectional LSTM.

2.3   CNN Character Composition Model

In contrast to the LSTM model, we propose to use a "flat" CNN as the character composition model, similar to Kim et al. (2016).[4]

Equation (1) is thus replaced with

$$\mathbf{x}(t_i) = [\mathbf{cnn}^{l_1}(t_i); \mathbf{cnn}^{l_2}(t_i); ...; \mathbf{cnn}^{l_k}(t_i);$$
$$\mathbf{E}_{tag}(t_i); \mathbf{E}_{label}(t_i)]. \quad (2)$$

Concretely, the input of the model is a concatenated matrix of character embeddings $\mathbf{C} \in \mathbb{R}^{d_i \times w}$, where d_i is the dimensionality of character embeddings (number of input channels) and w is the length of the padded word.[5] We apply k convolutional kernels $\mathcal{K} \in \mathbb{R}^{d_o \times d_i \times l_k}$ with ReLU non-linearity on the input, where d_o is the number of output channels and l_k is the length of the kernel. The output of the convolution operation is $\mathbf{O}_{conv} \in \mathbb{R}^{d_o \times (l-k+1)}$, and we apply a max-over-time pooling that takes the maximum activations of the kernel along each channel, obtaining the final output $\mathbf{O}_{final} \in \mathbb{R}^{d_o}$, which corresponds to the most salient n-gram representation of the word, denoted $\mathbf{cnn}^{l_k}$ in Equation (2). We then concatenate the outputs of several such CNNs with different lengths, so that the information from different n-grams are extracted and can interact with each other.

---

[2] We only experiment with the greedy parser, since this paper focuses on the character-level input features and is independent of the global training and inference as in Weiss et al. (2015); Andor et al. (2016).

[3] The tokens in the stack and buffer do not have labels yet, we use a special label <NOLABEL> instead.

[4] We do not use the highway networks since it did not improve the performance in preliminary experiments.

[5] The details of the padding is in Appendix B.

	Model	Ara	Baq	Fre	Ger	Heb	Hun	Kor	Pol	Swe	Avg
Int	WORD	84.50	77.87	82.20	85.35	**74.68**	76.17	84.62	80.71	79.14	80.58
	W2V	**85.11**	79.07	**82.73**	**86.60**	74.55	78.21	85.30	82.37	79.67	81.51
	LSTM	83.42	82.97	81.35	85.34	74.03	83.06	86.56	80.13	77.44	81.48
	CNN	84.65	**83.91**	82.41	85.61	74.23	**83.68**	**86.99**	**83.28**	**80.00**	**82.75**
	LSTM+WORD	**84.75**	83.43	**82.25**	85.56	74.62	83.43	86.85	82.30	79.85	82.56
	CNN+WORD	84.58	**84.22**	81.79	**85.85**	**74.79**	**83.51**	**87.21**	**83.66**	**80.52**	**82.90**
	LSTM+W2V	85.35	83.94	83.04	86.38	**75.15**	83.30	87.35	83.00	79.38	82.99
	CNN+W2V	**85.67**	**84.37**	**83.09**	**86.81**	74.95	**84.08**	**87.72**	**84.44**	**80.35**	**83.50**
Ext	B15-WORD	**83.46**	73.56	**82.03**	**84.62**	**72.70**	69.31	83.37	**79.83**	**76.40**	78.36
	B15-LSTM	83.40	**78.61**	81.08	84.49	72.26	**76.34**	**86.21**	78.24	74.47	**79.46**
	BestPub	86.21	85.70	85.66	89.65	81.65	86.13	87.27	87.07	82.75	85.79

Table 1: LAS on the test sets, the best LAS in each group is marked in bold face.

3 Experiments

3.1 Experimental Setup

We conduct our experiments on the treebanks from the SPMRL 2014 shared task (Seddah et al., 2013, 2014), which includes 9 morphologically rich languages: Arabic, Basque, French, German, Hebrew, Hungarian, Korean, Polish, and Swedish. All the treebanks are split into training, development, and test sets by the shared task organizers. We use the fine-grained predicted POS tags provided by the organizers, and evaluate the labeled attachment scores (LAS) including punctuation.

We experiment with the CNN-based character composition model (CNN) along with several baselines. The first baseline (WORD) uses the word-lookup model described in Section 2.1 with randomly initialized word embeddings. The second baseline (W2V) uses pre-trained word embeddings by word2vec (Mikolov et al., 2013) with the CBOW model and default parameters on the unlabeled texts from the shared task organizers. The third baseline (LSTM) uses a bidirectional LSTM as the character composition model following Ballesteros et al. (2015). Appendix C lists the hyper-parameters of all the models.

Further analysis suggests that combining the character composition models with word-lookup models could be beneficial since they capture different aspects of word similarities (orthographic vs. syntactic/semantic). We therefore experiment with four combined models in two groups: (1) randomly initialized word embeddings (LSTM+WORD vs. CNN+WORD), and (2) pre-trained word embeddings (LSTM+W2V vs. CNN+W2V).

The experimental results are shown in Table 1, with Int denoting internal comparisons (with three groups) and Ext denoting external comparisons, the highest LAS in each group is marked in bold face.

3.2 Internal Comparisons

In the first group, we compare the LAS of the four single models WORD, W2V, LSTM, and CNN. In macro average of all languages, the CNN model performs 2.17% higher than the WORD model, and 1.24% higher than the W2V model. The LSTM model, however, performs only 0.9% higher than the WORD model and 1.27% lower than the CNN model.

The CNN model shows large improvement in four languages: three agglutinative languages (Basque, Hungarian, Korean), and one highly inflected fusional language (Polish). They all have high OOV rate, thus difficult for the baseline parser that does not model morphological information. Also, morphemes in agglutinative languages tend to have unique, unambiguous meanings, thus easier for the convolutional kernels to capture.

In the second group, we observe that the additional word-lookup model does not significantly improve the CNN moodel (from 82.75% in CNN to 82.90% in CNN+WORD on average) while the LSTM model is improved by a much larger margin (from 81.48% in LSTM to 82.56% in LSTM+WORD on average). This suggests that the CNN model has already learned the most important information from the the word forms, while the LSTM model has not. Also, the combined CNN+WORD model is still better than the LSTM+WORD model, despite the large improvement in the latter.

In the third group where pre-trained word embeddings are used, combining CNN with W2V brings an extra 0.75% LAS over the CNN model. Combining LSTM with W2V shows similar trend but with much larger improvement, yet again, CNN+W2V outperforms LSTM+W2V both on average and individually in 8 out of 9 languages.

Model	Case	Ara	Baq	Fre	Ger	Heb	Hun	Kor	Pol	Swe	Avg
CNN	ΔIV	0.12	2.72	-0.44	0.13	-0.35	1.48	1.30	0.98	1.39	0.81
CNN	ΔOOV	0.03	5.78	0.33	0.10	-1.04	5.04	2.17	2.34	0.95	1.74
LSTM	ΔIV	-0.58	1.98	-0.55	-0.08	-1.23	1.62	1.12	-0.49	0.21	0.22
LSTM	ΔOOV	-0.32	5.09	0.12	-0.21	-1.99	4.74	1.51	0.10	0.38	1.05

Table 2: LAS improvements by CNN and LSTM in the IV and OOV cases on the development sets.

Mod	Ara	Baq	Fre	Ger	Heb	Hun	Kor	Pol	Swe	Avg
♣bc	-1.23	-1.94	-1.35	-1.57	-0.79	-3.23	-1.22	-2.53	-1.54	-1.71
a♣c	-3.47	-3.96	-2.39	-2.54	-1.24	-4.52	-3.21	-4.47	-4.19	-3.33
ab♣	-1.52	-15.31	-0.72	-1.23	-0.26	-13.97	-10.22	-3.52	-2.61	-5.48
a♣♣	-3.73	-19.29	-3.30	-3.49	-1.21	-17.89	-12.95	-6.22	-6.01	-8.23
♣b♣	-3.02	-18.06	-2.60	-3.54	-1.42	-18.43	-11.69	-6.22	-3.85	-7.65
♣♣c	-5.11	-7.90	-4.05	-4.86	-2.50	-9.75	-4.56	-6.71	-6.74	-5.80

Table 3: Degradation of LAS of the CNN model on the masked development sets.

3.3 External Comparisons

We also report the results of the two models from Ballesteros et al. (2015): B15-WORD with randomly initialized word embeddings and B15-LSTM as their proposed model. Finally, we report the best published results (BestPub) on this data set (Björkelund et al., 2013, 2014).

On average, the B15-LSTM model improves their own baseline by 1.1%, similar to the 0.9% improvement of our LSTM model, which is much smaller than the 2.17% improvement of the CNN model. Furthermore, the CNN model is improved from a strong baseline: our WORD model performs already 2.22% higher than the B15-WORD model.

Comparing the individual performances on each language, we observe that the CNN model almost always outperforms the WORD model except for Hebrew. However, both LSTM and B15-LSTM perform higher than baseline only on the three agglutinative languages (Basque, Hungarian, and Korean), and lower than baseline on the other six.

Ballesteros et al. (2015) do not compare the effect of adding a word-lookup model to the LSTM model as in our second group of internal comparisons. However, Plank et al. (2016) show that combining the same LSTM character composition model with word-lookup model improves the performance of POS tagging by a very large margin. This partially confirms our hypothesis that the LSTM model does not learn sufficient information from the word forms.

Considering both internal and external comparisons in both average and individual performances, we argue that CNN is more suitable than LSTM as character composition model for parsing.

While comparing to the best published results

(Björkelund et al., 2013, 2014), we have to note that their approach uses explicit morphological features, ensemble, ranking, etc., which all can boost parsing performance. We only use a greedy parser with much fewer features, but bridge the 6 points gap between the previous best greedy parser and the best published result by more than one half.

3.4 Discussion on CNN and LSTM

We conjecture that the main reason for the better performance of CNN over LSTM is its flexibility in processing sub-word information. The CNN model uses different kernels to capture n-grams of different lengths. In our setting, a kernel with a minimum length of 3 can capture short morphemes; and with a maximum length of 9, it can practically capture a normal word. With the flexibility of capturing patterns from morphemes up to words, the CNN model almost always outperforms the word-lookup model.

In theory, LSTM has the ability to model much longer sequences, however, it is composed step by step with recurrence. For such deep network architectures, more data would be required to learn the same sequence, in comparison to CNN which can directly use a large kernel to match the pattern. For dependency parsing, training data is usually scarce, this could be the reason that the LSTM has not utilized its full potential.

3.5 Analyses on OOV and Morphology

The motivation for using character composition models is based on the hypothesis that it can address the OOV problem. To verify the hypothesis, we analyze the LAS improvements of the CNN and LSTM model on the development sets in two cases: (1) both the head and the dependent are in vocabulary or (2) at least one of them is out of vocabulary. Table 2 shows the results, where the two cases are denoted as ΔIV and ΔOOV. The general trend in the results is that the improvements of both models in the OOV case are larger than in the IV case, which means that the character composition models indeed alleviates the OOV problem. Also, CNN improves on seven languages in the IV case and eight languages in the OOV case, and it performs consistently better than LSTM in both cases.

To analyze the informativeness of the morphemes at different positions, we conduct an ablation experiment. We split each word equally into three thirds, approximating the prefix, stem, and suffix. Based on that, we construct six modified versions of the development sets, in which we mask one or two third(s) of the characters in each word. Then we parse them with the CNN models trained on normal data. Table 3 shows the degradations of LAS on the six modified data sets compared to parsing the original data, where the position of ♣ signifies the location of the masks. The three agglutinative languages Basque, Hungarian, and Korean suffer the most with masked words. In particular, the suffixes are the most informative for parsing in these three languages, since they cause the most loss while masked, and the least loss while unmasked. The pattern is quite different on the other languages, in which the distinction of informativeness among the three parts is much smaller.

4 Conclusion

In this paper, we propose to use a CNN to compose word representations from characters for dependency parsing. Experiments show that the CNN model consistently improves the parsing accuracy, especially for agglutinative languages. In an external comparison on the SPMRL data sets, our system outperforms the previous best greedy parser.

We also provide empirical evidence and analysis, showing that the CNN model indeed alleviates the OOV problem and that it is better suited than the LSTM in dependency parsing.

Acknowledgements

This work was supported by the German Research Foundation (DFG) in project D8 of SFB 732. We also thank our collegues in the IMS, especially Anders Björkelund, for valuable discussions, and the anonymous reviewers for the suggestions.

References

Daniel Andor, Chris Alberti, David Weiss, Aliaksei Severyn, Alessandro Presta, Kuzman Ganchev, Slav Petrov, and Michael Collins. 2016. Globally normalized transition-based neural networks. In *Proceedings of the 54th Annual Meeting of the Association for Computational Linguistics (Volume 1: Long Papers)*. Association for Computational Linguistics, pages 2442–2452. https://doi.org/10.18653/v1/P16-1231.

Giuseppe Attardi. 2006. Experiments with a multilanguage non-projective dependency parser. In *Proceedings of the Tenth Conference on Computational Natural Language Learning (CoNLL-X)*. Association for Computational Linguistics, pages 166–170. http://aclweb.org/anthology/W06-2922.

Miguel Ballesteros, Chris Dyer, and A. Noah Smith. 2015. Improved transition-based parsing by modeling characters instead of words with lstms. In *Proceedings of the 2015 Conference on Empirical Methods in Natural Language Processing*. Association for Computational Linguistics, pages 349–359. https://doi.org/10.18653/v1/D15-1041.

Anders Björkelund, Özlem Çetinoğlu, Agnieszka Faleńska, Richárd Farkas, Thomas Müller, Wolfgang Seeker, and Zsolt Szántó. 2014. The ims-wrocław-szeged-cis entry at the spmrl 2014 shared task: Reranking and morphosyntax meet unlabeled data. *Notes of the SPMRL* .

Anders Björkelund, Özlem Çetinoğlu, Richárd Farkas, Thomas Mueller, and Wolfgang Seeker. 2013. (re)ranking meets morphosyntax: State-of-the-art results from the spmrl 2013 shared task. In *Proceedings of the Fourth Workshop on Statistical Parsing of Morphologically-Rich Languages*. Association for Computational Linguistics, pages 135–145. http://aclweb.org/anthology/W13-4916.

Danqi Chen and Christopher Manning. 2014. A fast and accurate dependency parser using neural networks. In *Proceedings of the 2014 Conference on Empirical Methods in Natural Language Processing (EMNLP)*. Association for Computational Linguistics, pages 740–750. https://doi.org/10.3115/v1/D14-1082.

R. Marta Costa-jussà and R. José A. Fonollosa. 2016. Character-based neural machine translation. In *Proceedings of the 54th Annual Meeting of the Association for Computational Linguistics (Volume 2: Short Papers)*. Association for Computational Linguistics, pages 357–361. https://doi.org/10.18653/v1/P16-2058.

Cicero dos Santos and Victor Guimarães. 2015. Boosting named entity recognition with neural character embeddings. In *Proceedings of the Fifth Named Entity Workshop*. Association for Computational Linguistics, pages 25–33. https://doi.org/10.18653/v1/W15-3904.

Cicero dos Santos and Bianca Zadrozny. 2014. Learning character-level representations for part-of-speech tagging. In *Proceedings of the 31st International Conference on Machine Learning (ICML-14)*. pages 1818–1826.

Kaiming He, Xiangyu Zhang, Shaoqing Ren, and Jian Sun. 2015. Delving deep into rectifiers: Surpassing human-level performance on imagenet classification. In *Proceedings of the IEEE international conference on computer vision*. pages 1026–1034.

Yoon Kim, Yacine Jernite, David Sontag, and Alexander M. Rush. 2016. Character-aware neural language models. In *Proceedings of the Thirtieth AAAI Conference on Artificial Intelligence, February 12-17, 2016, Phoenix, Arizona, USA.*. AAAI Press, pages 2741–2749.

Wang Ling, Chris Dyer, W. Alan Black, Isabel Trancoso, Ramon Fermandez, Silvio Amir, Luis Marujo, and Tiago Luis. 2015. Finding function in form: Compositional character models for open vocabulary word representation. In *Proceedings of the 2015 Conference on Empirical Methods in Natural Language Processing*. Association for Computational Linguistics, pages 1520–1530. https://doi.org/10.18653/v1/D15-1176.

Tomas Mikolov, Ilya Sutskever, Kai Chen, Greg S Corrado, and Jeff Dean. 2013. Distributed representations of words and phrases and their compositionality. In C. J. C. Burges, L. Bottou, M. Welling, Z. Ghahramani, and K. Q. Weinberger, editors, *Advances in Neural Information Processing Systems 26*, Curran Associates, Inc., pages 3111–3119.

Joakim Nivre. 2004. Incrementality in deterministic dependency parsing. In *Proceedings of the Workshop on Incremental Parsing: Bringing Engineering and Cognition Together*. http://aclweb.org/anthology/W04-0308.

Barbara Plank, Anders Søgaard, and Yoav Goldberg. 2016. Multilingual part-of-speech tagging with bidirectional long short-term memory models and auxiliary loss. In *Proceedings of the 54th Annual Meeting of the Association for Computational Linguistics (Volume 2: Short Papers)*. Association for Computational Linguistics, pages 412–418. https://doi.org/10.18653/v1/P16-2067.

Djamé Seddah, Sandra Kübler, and Reut Tsarfaty. 2014. Introducing the spmrl 2014 shared task on parsing morphologically-rich languages. In *Proceedings of the First Joint Workshop on Statistical Parsing of Morphologically Rich Languages and Syntactic Analysis of Non-Canonical Languages*. Dublin City University, pages 103–109. http://aclweb.org/anthology/W14-6111.

Djamé Seddah, Reut Tsarfaty, Sandra Kübler, Marie Candito, D. Jinho Choi, Richárd Farkas, Jennifer Foster, Iakes Goenaga, Koldo Gojenola Galletebeitia, Yoav Goldberg, Spence Green, Nizar Habash, Marco Kuhlmann, Wolfgang Maier, Joakim Nivre, Adam Przepiórkowski, Ryan Roth, Wolfgang Seeker, Yannick Versley, Veronika Vincze, Marcin Woliński, Alina Wróblewska, and Villemonte Eric de la Clergerie. 2013. Overview of the spmrl 2013 shared task: A cross-framework evaluation of parsing morphologically rich languages. In *Proceedings of the Fourth Workshop on Statistical Parsing of Morphologically-Rich Languages*. Association for Computational Linguistics, pages 146–182. http://aclweb.org/anthology/W13-4917.

David Weiss, Chris Alberti, Michael Collins, and Slav Petrov. 2015. Structured training for neural network transition-based parsing. In *Proceedings of the 53rd Annual Meeting of the Association for Computational Linguistics and the 7th International Joint Conference on Natural Language Processing (Volume 1: Long Papers)*. Association for Computational Linguistics, pages 323–333. https://doi.org/10.3115/v1/P15-1032.

A Transitions and Feature Templates

Transition	Configurations (Before $\Rightarrow$ After)
SHIFT	$(\sigma, [w_i|\beta], A) \Rightarrow ([\sigma|w_i], \beta, A)$
LEFT	$([\sigma|w_i, w_j], \beta, A)$
	$\Rightarrow ([\sigma|w_j], \beta, A \cup (w_j \to w_i))$
RIGHT	$([\sigma|w_i, w_j], \beta, A)$
	$\Rightarrow ([\sigma|w_i], \beta, A \cup (w_i \to w_j))$
LEFT-2	$([\sigma|w_i, w_j, w_k], \beta, A)$
	$\Rightarrow ([\sigma|w_j, w_k], \beta, A \cup (w_k \to w_i))$
RIGHT-2	$([\sigma|w_i, w_j, w_k], \beta, A)$
	$\Rightarrow ([\sigma|w_i, w_j], \beta, A \cup (w_i \to w_k))$

Table 4: The transition system in our experiments, where the configuration is a tuple of (stack, buffer, arcs).

$s_1, s_2, s_3, s_4, b_1, b_2, b_3, b_4,$
$s_1.lc_1, s_1.lc_2, s_1.rc_1, s_1.rc_2,$
$s_2.lc_1, s_2.lc_2, s_2.rc_1, s_2.rc_2,$
$s_3.lc_1, s_3.lc_2, s_3.rc_1, s_3.rc_2,$
$s_1.lc_1.lc_1, s_1.lc_1.rc_1, s_1.rc_1.lc_1, s_1.rc_1.rc_1$

Table 5: The list of tokens to extract feature templates, where s_i denotes the i-th token in the stack, b_i the i-th token in the buffer, lc_i denotes the i-th leftmost child, rc_i the i-th rightmost child.

B Character Input Preprocessing

For the CNN input, we use a list of characters with fixed length to for batch processing. We add some special symbols apart from the normal alphabets, digits, and punctuations: <SOW> as the start of the word, <EOW> as the end of the word, <MUL> as multiple characters in the middle of the word squeezed into one symbol, <PAD> as padding equally on both sides, and <UNK> as characters unseen in the training data.

For example, if we limit the input length to 9, a short word *ein* will be converted into <PAD>-<PAD>-<SOW>-e-i-n-<EOW>-<PAD>-<PAD>; a long word *prächtiger* will be <SOW>-p-r-ä-<MUL>-g-e-r-<EOW>. In practice, we set the length as 32, which is long enough for almost all the words.

C Hyper-Parameters

The common hyper-parameters of all the models are tuned on the development set in favor of the WORD model:

- 100,000 training steps with random sampling of mini-batches of size 100;
- test on the development set every 2,000 steps;
- early stop if the LAS on the development does not improve for 3 times in a row;
- learning rate of 0.1, with exponential decay rate of 0.95 for every 2,000 steps;
- L2-regularization rate of 10^{-4};
- averaged SGD with momentum of 0.9;
- parameters are initialized following He et al. (2015);
- dimensionality of the embeddings of each word, tag, and label are 256, 32, 32, respectively;
- dimensionality of the hidden layers are 512, 256;
- dropout on both hidden layers with rate of 0.1;
- total norm constraint of the gradients is 10.

The hyper-parameters for the CNN model are:

- dimensionality of the character embedding is 32;
- 4 convolutional kernels of lengths 3, 5, 7, 9;
- number of output channels of each kernel is 64;
- fixed length for the character input is 32.

The hyper-parameters for the LSTM model are:

- 128 hidden units for both LSTMs;
- all the gates use orthogonal initialization;
- gradient clipping of 10;
- no L2-regularization on the parameters.

How (not) to train a dependency parser:
The curious case of jackknifing part-of-speech taggers

Željko Agić and **Natalie Schluter**

Department of Computer Science
IT University of Copenhagen
Rued Langgaards Vej 7, 2300 Copenhagen S, Denmark
`zeag@itu.dk nael@itu.dk`

Abstract

In dependency parsing, jackknifing taggers is indiscriminately used as a simple
adaptation strategy. Here, we empirically
evaluate when and how (not) to use jackknifing in parsing. On 26 languages, we
reveal a preference that conflicts with, and
surpasses the ubiquitous ten-folding. We
show no clear benefits of tagging the training data in cross-lingual parsing.

1 Introduction

Dependency parsers are trained over manually annotated treebank data. By contrast, when applied
in the real world, they parse over sequences of predicted parts of speech. As POS tagging accuracy
drops due to domain change, the parsing quality
declines proportionally. Bringing these two POS
tag sources closer together thus makes for a reasonable adaptation strategy.

Arguably the simplest of such adaptations is n-
fold **jackknifing**. In it, a treebank is divided into n
equal parts, and the n-th part is POS-tagged with
a tagger trained on the remainder. The procedure
is repeated until all n parts are assigned with predicted POS tags. A parser is then trained over the
thus altered treebank, under the assumption that
its POS features will now more closely resemble
those of the input data.

Jackknifing is simplistic as it i) has a very lim-
ited adaptation range for $n \in \mathbb{N}^+$, and it ii) does not
in any way take the input data into account, other
than through a vague assumption of an undefined
amount of tagging noise in the input. As such, it
exhibits very mixed results. Still, the method is
now ubiquitous in the parsing literature.

In Figure 1, we survey the ACL Anthology[1] for
POS jackknifing. We uncover that ~80% of the 70

[1] `http://aclweb.org/anthology/`

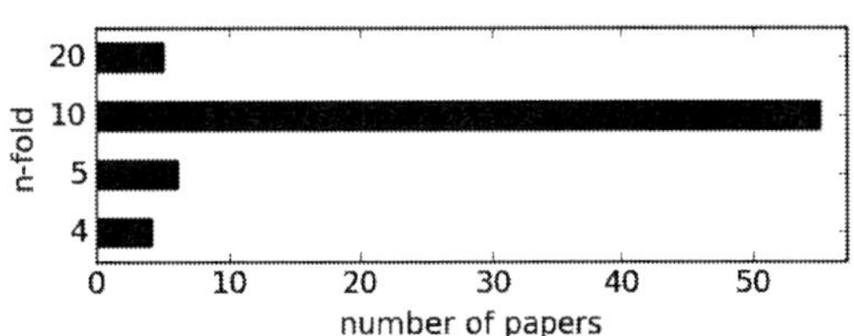

Figure 1: Jackknifing in the ACL Anthology. Distribution of n over 70 parsing papers that use tagger n-folding.

parsing papers we retrieved make use of **ten-fold**
jackknifing. This choice spans across the various
languages and domains parsed in these papers, and
is even motivated by simply "following the tradi-
tions in literature".[2]

Our contributions. We evaluate jackknifing to
establish whether its use is warranted in dependency parsing. Controlling for tagging quality in
training and testing, we experiment with monolingual and delexicalized cross-lingual parsers over
26 languages, showing that:

i) Indiscriminate use of ten-fold jackknifing results in sub-optimal parsing.
ii) Tagging the training data does not yield clear
benefits in realistic cross-lingual parsing.
iii) Our jackknifing extension improves parsing
through finer-grained adaptation.

2 Method

Jackknifing generally refers to a leave-one-out
procedure for reducing bias in parameter estimation from an unbiased sample (Quenouille, 1956;
Tukey, 1958). More recently, in machine learning the term is used synonymously with "cross-

[2] Incidentally, using ten-folds with the WSJ data yields
roughly the same train- and test-set tagging accuracy, and
seems to be where the choice originated.

Proceedings of the 55th Annual Meeting of the Association for Computational Linguistics (Short Papers), pages 679–684
Vancouver, Canada, July 30 - August 4, 2017. ©2017 Association for Computational Linguistics
https://doi.org/10.18653/v1/P17-2107

validation" for estimation of predictive model performance measures. In NLP, jackknifing has commonly been used to describe a procedure by which the training input is adjusted to correspond more closely to the expected test input, and it is in this latter sense that we use the term here.

In particular, in parsing research, the n-**fold jackknifing** proceeds as follows. The treebank is first partitioned into n non-overlapping subsets of equal size. Then, iteratively, each part acts as a *test subset* and is tagged using a model induced by the remaining $n-1$ parts, the *training subset*, until the entire treebank is tagged.

We want to control for POS tagging accuracy through the jackknifing method. To do this, we train a tagger on increasing sized subsets of the training set. In fold terminology, this corresponds to dividing the training set into equal parts of size $\frac{1}{n}$, training on $\frac{n-1}{n}$ths of the training set and testing on the remaining $\frac{1}{n}$th. However, this constrains the size of the training subset to be larger than half the original data, and thus concentrates our study on models that use almost all the data, since the non-linear curve $f(n) = \frac{n-1}{n}$ becomes very flat very fast. Thus, varying fold numbers reveals very little variation in terms of POS tagging accuracy in the lower accuracy range.

Linear extension. We now propose a simple extension of the jackknifing paradigm to study parser accuracy given a percentage p of the training set: **linear jackknifing**.

Let $p \in (0, 1)$ be the percentage of the randomly shuffled training set D used to induce a model to tag some remaining number of instances. A training subset of this size allows a test subset of size at most $\lceil |D| \cdot (1-p) \rceil$. Given a test subset to tag, we can induce a model from a random subset of the remaining examples of size approximately $p \cdot |D|$ to become our training subset. We randomize the choice of examples in the training subset to avoid introducing bias. In order to tag all of D, the minimum number of models we need to generate is $\lceil 1/(1-p) \rceil$. We thus separate D into test subsets $f_1, \ldots, f_{\lceil 1/(1-p) \rceil}$ each of size approximately $\lceil |D| \cdot (1-p) \rceil$. For each f_i, we randomly sample a training subset of size approximately $\lceil p \cdot |D| \rceil$ from the remainder of D, induce a model and then tag f_i. This results in the original full training set tagged with an accuracy corresponding to the performance of a randomly selected tagger trained on approximately $p \cdot |D|$ of the examples.

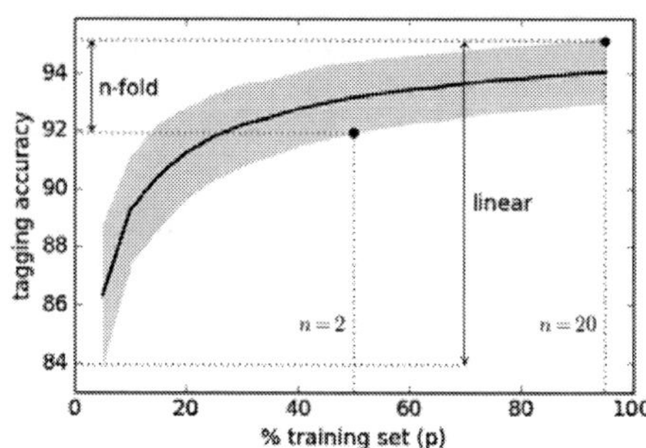

Figure 2: Tagger learning curve for 26 languages: mean tagging accuracy with 95% confidence intervals. Accuracy ranges for n-fold and linear jackknifing are indicated.

Intrinsic evaluation. For increasing values of p, at 5% increments, we carried out linear jackknifing on 26 languages. For each p, we averaged the performance of the induced taggers on the respective gold standards. Figure 2 illustrates the difference in informativeness of the two approaches, where each tagging accuracy score is averaged across the 26 languages. We see that with n-fold jackknifing, tagging accuracy is constrained to between approximately 92% and 95%, whereas linear jackknifing explores accuracies as low as approximately 86%. Moreover, the confidence intervals are consistent across the p, demonstrating unbiased tagging models generated on less data (lower p). We now show that these smaller levels of p are essential for good parser performance in some cases of jackknifing.

3 Experiments

Our experiment aims at judging the adequacy of jackknifing in dependency parsing. First, we outline the experiment setup, where we conduct two sets of experiments:

i) **monolingual**, where lexicalized parsers are trained on treebanks for their respective languages, and

ii) **cross-lingual**, that features **SINGLE**-best and **MULTI**-source delexicalized parsers.

Tagging sources. By jackknifing we explore how the mismatch between training and test POS affects parsing. Our setup thus critically relies on the sources of tags. We tag our test sets using:

i) **PRED**, the monolingual taggers, and

ii) **PROJ**, the low-resource taggers by Agić et al. (2016), based on annotation projection.

| | Monolingual parsing | | | | | | | | | | |
| **Train:** | GOLD | | linear jackknifing | | | | n-fold jackknifing | | | | PROJ | |
Test:	PRED	PROJ	PRED	p_{max}	PROJ	p_{max}	PRED	n_{max}	PROJ	n_{max}	PRED	PROJ
Arabic (ar)	79.4	51.4	**79.5**	90	64.0	5	**79.5**	12	55.3	2	73.5	**74.4**
Bulgarian (bg)	86.8	56.4	**87.2**	80	66.7	5	**87.2**	12	60.2	2	82.2	**78.0**
Czech (cs)	81.0	58.2	**81.6**	85	62.5	5	**81.6**	8	60.1	2	77.3	**70.7**
Danish (da)	74.4	65.7	78.2	95	71.8	5	**78.3**	11	68.5	2	75.1	**76.0**
German (de)	79.0	51.8	**80.2**	20	56.6	5	80.1	2	54.4	7	75.6	**69.2**
Greek (el)	81.1	59.4	**81.4**	70	64.7	5	**81.4**	20	61.2	2	74.7	**75.6**
English (en)	80.9	71.6	**82.3**	80	77.6	5	**82.3**	17	76.0	2	80.2	**80.9**
Spanish (es)	80.7	75.4	**82.1**	20	78.3	5	81.8	9	77.3	4	80.2	**80.2**
Estonian (et)	74.3	61.6	76.0	55	67.1	5	**76.1**	13	65.0	2	73.3	**70.5**
Persian (fa)	82.3	25.8	**83.2**	35	46.3	5	83.1	4	35.1	2	66.3	**71.9**
Finnish (fi)	72.0	53.9	72.9	75	60.4	5	**73.0**	18	56.6	2	69.2	**64.7**
French (fr)	80.9	65.4	81.7	90	72.7	5	**81.8**	19	68.7	2	79.2	**77.1**
Hebrew (he)	80.6	54.2	**81.5**	75	68.1	5	**81.5**	7	61.7	2	77.9	**75.7**
Hindi (hi)	89.1	51.0	**91.0**	70	70.1	5	**91.0**	11	63.1	2	84.8	**85.5**
Croatian (hr)	78.1	54.6	78.2	45	62.9	5	**78.4**	19	56.3	20	73.6	**72.5**
Hungarian (hu)	74.3	55.4	74.9	95	63.2	5	**75.2**	17	58.3	2	71.0	**66.8**
Indonesian (id)	79.4	70.6	**79.6**	90	74.9	5	**79.6**	9	72.3	2	77.8	**77.7**
Italian (it)	86.2	76.2	**87.6**	55	82.9	5	**87.6**	2	80.6	2	86.2	**85.5**
Dutch (nl)	72.1	60.2	**73.8**	50	67.9	5	**73.8**	12	65.6	8	67.6	**72.6**
Norwegian (no)	83.7	74.8	**85.3**	95	79.9	5	**85.3**	8	78.0	2	83.7	**82.6**
Polish (pl)	83.7	69.8	84.7	30	75.8	5	**84.9**	20	73.0	2	81.4	**78.6**
Portuguese (pt)	82.2	75.7	**83.2**	30	78.8	5	83.1	2	77.7	19	80.2	**82.0**
Romanian (ro)	81.8	66.8	**82.5**	85	72.9	5	**82.5**	5	69.0	2	79.7	**79.1**
Slovene (sl)	82.0	62.5	**84.2**	55	71.4	5	**84.2**	16	68.9	7	79.3	**77.4**
Swedish (sv)	80.9	74.4	81.9	90	77.3	10	**82.0**	19	76.8	7	80.0	**79.1**
Tamil (ta)	65.1	33.4	**65.8**	95	49.5	5	65.6	5	42.5	2	51.5	**56.3**
Mean	79.7	60.6	80.8	67.5	68.6	5.2	80.8	11.4	64.7	4.2	76.2	75.4
Best for #/26	0	0	18	–	0	–	21	–	0	–	0	26

Table 1: Parsing accuracy (UAS) in relation to the underlying sources of POS tags in training and at runtime. **Bold:** best result for language, separately for PRED and PROJ test sets.

We do not experiment with gold POS tags in the test sets. Instead, we only focus on realistic parsing over predicted tags. The tags in our training sets can be **GOLD**, PROJ, or they can be predicted through n-fold or linear jackknifing.

In n-fold jackknifing, we experiment with $n \in \{2, 3, .., 20\}$, while for the linear extension we set $p \in \{5, 10, ..., 95\}$. We report the average parsing scores over 5 runs for each n and p so as to mitigate the effects of random shuffling in the two jackknifing procedures. In finding the optimal values of the parameters n_{max} and p_{max}, we report the highest values in case of ties. For example, if $n = 5$ and $n = 10$ both yield the same maximum UAS, we set $n_{max} = 10$.

We emphasize the importance of realistic set-

tings especially in cross-lingual parsing. Thus, we commit to using PROJ taggers with an outlook on true low-resource languages.

Data. We use the Universal Dependencies (UD) treebanks version 1.2 (Nivre et al., 2016).[3] As the projection-based taggers are trained on the WTC dataset by Agić et al. (2016), we intersect the list of WTC languages with the UD list for a total of 26 languages.

Tagging and parsing. For POS tagging, we use the TNT tagger by Brants (2000). The PRED taggers score 94.1±1.1%, while the low-resource PROJ taggers are on average 71.7±5.7% accurate. We experiment with two parsers. Bohnet's (2010)

---

[3] http://universaldependencies.org/

	Delexicalized transfer				
Train:	GOLD↝PROJ			PROJ↝PROJ	
Test:	MULTI	SINGLE		MULTI	SINGLE
Arabic (ar)	**34.2**	he **38.3**		28.3	id 37.0
Bulgarian (bg)	49.5	cs 50.1		**50.2**	cs **51.1**
Czech (cs)	**50.4**	sl 50.7		48.4	sl **50.8**
Danish (da)	58.0	no 58.5		**58.1**	no **61.4**
German (de)	43.9	no 45.0		**45.8**	sv **45.4**
Greek (el)	56.3	it **55.4**		**57.3**	no 55.3
English (en)	55.8	no 56.7		**57.2**	sv **58.2**
Spanish (es)	**67.9**	it **68.5**		64.9	it 67.6
Estonian (et)	**45.8**	fi **53.1**		43.9	fi 50.8
Persian (fa)	**21.5**	ar **25.7**		18.9	pl 24.2
Finnish (fi)	38.8	et 45.1		**40.0**	et **45.5**
French (fr)	52.8	it 54.4		**54.9**	it **58.9**
Hebrew (he)	**44.6**	ro **45.1**		41.7	ro 44.0
Hindi (hi)	16.9	ta **38.1**		**18.0**	ta 31.0
Croatian (hr)	**50.9**	sl **50.8**		46.8	cs 49.3
Hungarian (hu)	39.9	sv 46.4		**40.1**	et **49.3**
Indonesian (id)	**54.5**	ro **56.6**		48.7	ro 54.4
Italian (it)	67.0	es 67.8		**67.4**	es **69.2**
Dutch (nl)	**55.1**	es **53.9**		52.2	sv 52.5
Norwegian (no)	**63.5**	sv 64.3		62.4	sv **64.4**
Polish (pl)	**62.9**	cs **64.2**		57.3	cs 59.2
Portuguese (pt)	**65.7**	es **67.7**		64.7	it 66.9
Romanian (ro)	**53.6**	it 53.7		50.5	es **53.9**
Slovene (sl)	50.5	cs 53.4		**52.6**	cs **56.3**
Swedish (sv)	**62.7**	no 66.8		61.9	no **67.1**
Tamil (ta)	21.2	hu 28.9		**24.6**	hi **33.8**
Mean	49.4	– 52.3		48.3	– 52.2
Best for #/26	14	– 12		12	– 14

Table 2: UAS scores for the delexicalized transfer parsers. TRAIN↝TEST indicates the training and testing POS. **Bold:** best result for language, separate for MULTI and SINGLE transfer. For SINGLE, best source names are also reported.

second-order graph-based system MATE[4] is the primary. Further, we verify all parsing results by using a transition-based parser YARA[5] with dynamic oracles (Rasooli and Tetreault, 2015).

The following CoNLL 2009 features are used for training the parsers:[6] ID, FORM (in monolingual parsing only), POS, and HEAD. Since ours is not a benchmarking effort, we apply all systems with their default settings.

3.1 Results

In **monolingual parsing** over PRED tags (Table 1), we achieve an identical average UAS with lin-

[4] https://code.google.com/archive/p/mate-tools/
[5] https://github.com/yahoo/YaraParser
[6] https://ufal.mff.cuni.cz/conll2009-st/

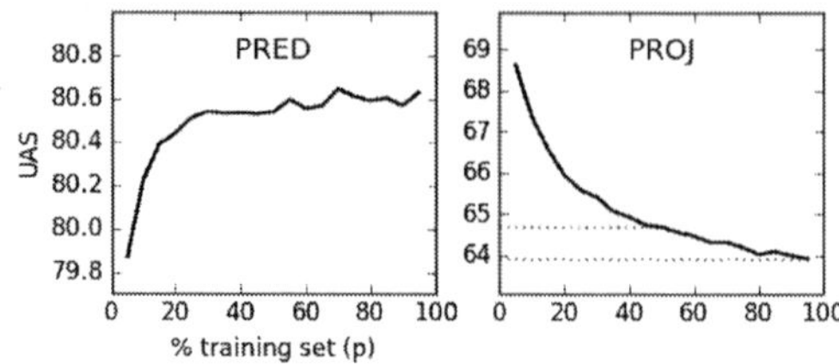

Figure 3: Parsing accuracy (UAS) in relation to linear jackknifing over 26 languages, with two sources of test set POS tags.

ear and n-fold jackknifing. Our adaptations surpass training with GOLD data by +1.1 UAS. Linear jackknifing improves over GOLD training by +8.1 UAS when parsing over low-resource PROJ tags. There, we top GOLD training by n-fold jackknifing as well, but it trails the linear variant by -3.9 UAS. In the low-resource PROJ setup, PROJ-trained parsers are dominant. They score +6.8 UAS over linear, +10.7 UAS over n-folding, and +14.8 UAS over GOLD training.

Figure 3 plots the relation between the sample size p in linear jackknifing and the resulting UAS in parsing, split for PRED and PROJ test-set taggings. Parsing over PRED tags, the UAS generally increases with p, but we note that this increase is rather small: over 26 languages, moving p from 5% to 95% yields only +0.7 UAS on average. By contrast, adapting to the lower-quality PROJ tags sees a larger +5 UAS benefit from decreasing p all the way to 5%, which is well outside the n-fold range, as indicated for $n \in \{2, ..., 20\}$ by the dotted lines in the figure.

Our **cross-lingual parsing** experiment (Table 2) contrasts two options: we either tag (PROJ↝) or do not tag (GOLD↝) the parser training data. To reflect realistic low-resource parsing, the test data is tagged with PROJ taggers only. On average, the unadapted parsers are slightly better (UAS: +1.1 MULTI, +0.1 SINGLE). However, they are almost evenly split with the adapted ones in terms of offering the best performance for 12-14 out of the 26 test languages each. These results suggest, at least for simplicity, a preference for not tagging the treebanks.

4 Discussion

Linear or n-fold? In resource-rich PRED parsing, the two jackknifing methods are evenly split, with identical average UAS score and an overlap on 13 languages. In low-resource PROJ parsing, n-folding falls far behind as the constraint for $n \geq 2$ prevents it from adapting accordingly. The median p_{max} in PRED and PROJ are 75% and 5%. The first one roughly corresponds to 4-fold jackknifing, while the second one is far below the two-fold range. The median n_{max} are 11 and 2, and we note that n_{max} is rarely ~10 in Table 1.

If we simply use ten-fold jackknifing for PRED tags, we manage to match the p_{max} scores for only 9 of 26 languages, and we score -0.2 UAS on average. If using $n = 10$ with PROJ tags, the disconnect is much more substantial, and we are unable to reach p_{max} (-4.6 UAS).

The GOLD training data is *never* the best choice in our monolingual parsing experiment, regardless of whether the test tags are PRED or PROJ. This result in itself justifies the usage of jackknifing as adaptation for the monolingual setting, provided that it is not indiscriminate.

Finding $\hat{p}_{\mathrm{max}}$. For choosing the optimal linear jackknifing in real-world parsing, we note that p_{max} closely correlates with test set tagging accuracy (Spearman's $\rho = 0.76$), and negatively with treebank size ($\rho = -0.42$, for $|D| \leq$ 10k sentences). Thus, to adapt via linear jackknifing, we must i) approximate the expected input data tagging accuracy, while at the same time ii) accounting for the fact that the accuracy associated with any p depends on treebank size as well. In other words, given two treebanks $|D_1| < |D_2|$, we would typically need $p_1 > p_2$ with the goal of matching the same test-set accuracy.

The other parser. Replacing the MATE parser with the transition-based YARA does not change the outcome of our monolingual parsing experiment, save for the average 0.58–1.65 drop in UAS. On the other hand, in cross-lingual parsing, YARA highlights the benefits of *not* tagging the training data, as the GOLD↝PROJ parsers are there the best choice for parsing 17/26 languages. On average, we see +2.1 UAS for MULTI, and +0.7 for SINGLE over PROJ↝PROJ. This is especially worth noting since large-scale parsing generally favors transition-based systems.

GOLD test tags. Thus far, we have shown the need for more careful jackknifing in parser training with respect to the expected tagging quality at parse time. Fixing $n = 10$ was suboptimal in parsing over the fully supervised PRED tags, while $n = 2, 10$ were way below the threshold in low-resource parsing over our cross-lingual PROJ tags. We have purposely excluded GOLD test tags from the discussion so far.

Still, while parsing over GOLD POS input does not hold much significance for real-world applications, it is worth noting how jackknifing performs in the upper limit: trying to reach the accuracy of parsers trained and tested on GOLD tags. In that particular setup, we observe the maximum UAS of 83.8 for median $n_{\mathrm{max}} = 12$ and $p_{\mathrm{max}} = 80\%$. The respective modal values are $n = 20$ and $p = 95\%$, meaning that for most languages, we come closest to GOLD↝GOLD by maximizing the tagging accuracy. The overall score amounts to -0.7 UAS below the upper bound.

5 Related work

Jackknifing itself is for the most part incidental to the work that employs it. Here, we mention a few notable exceptions.

Che et al. (2012) compare jackknifing to using gold tags in parsing Chinese for constituents and dependencies, where they observe mixed results: improvement with one parser, and decrease with the other. Seeker and Kuhn (2013) briefly touch upon the importance of jackknifing in bridging the gap between training and test data, and experiment with 5- and 10-folds. Honnibal and Johnson (2015) passingly contrast jackknifing to joint learning, giving precedence to the latter for simplicity. Finally, Kong et al. (2015) follow Zhu et al. (2013) in ten-folding for Chinese and English, citing 2.0% and 0.4% improvements. Incidentally, jackknifing parsers then hurts their performance in tree conversions.

6 Conclusions

The parsing literature is riddled with indiscriminate use of n-fold part-of-speech tagger jackknifing as makeshift domain adaptation.

In this paper we have proposed a careful empirical treatment of jackknifing in dependency parsing, far surpassing ten-folding via fine-grained control over the data adjustment.

Acknowledgements. We thank Barbara Plank and Djamé Seddah for their valuable comments on an earlier version of this paper. We appreciate the incisive feedback by the anonymous reviewers. Finally, we acknowledge the NVIDIA Corporation for supporting our research.

References

Željko Agić, Anders Johannsen, Barbara Plank, Héctor Martínez Alonso, Natalie Schluter, and Anders Søgaard. 2016. Multilingual projection for parsing truly low-resource languages. *Transactions of the Association of Computational Linguistics* 4:301–312. http://aclweb.org/anthology/Q16-1022.

Bernd Bohnet. 2010. Top accuracy and fast dependency parsing is not a contradiction. In *Proceedings of the 23rd International Conference on Computational Linguistics (Coling 2010)*. Coling 2010 Organizing Committee, pages 89–97. http://aclweb.org/anthology/C10-1011.

Thorsten Brants. 2000. Tnt - a statistical part-of-speech tagger. In *Proceedings of the Sixth Applied Natural Language Processing Conference*. http://aclweb.org/anthology/A00-1031.

Wanxiang Che, Valentin Spitkovsky, and Ting Liu. 2012. A comparison of chinese parsers for stanford dependencies. In *Proceedings of the 50th Annual Meeting of the Association for Computational Linguistics (Volume 2: Short Papers)*. Association for Computational Linguistics, pages 11–16. http://aclweb.org/anthology/P12-2003.

Matthew Honnibal and Mark Johnson. 2015. An improved non-monotonic transition system for dependency parsing. In *Proceedings of the 2015 Conference on Empirical Methods in Natural Language Processing*. Association for Computational Linguistics, pages 1373–1378. https://doi.org/10.18653/v1/D15-1162.

Lingpeng Kong, M. Alexander Rush, and A. Noah Smith. 2015. Transforming dependencies into phrase structures. In *Proceedings of the 2015 Conference of the North American Chapter of the Association for Computational Linguistics: Human Language Technologies*. Association for Computational Linguistics, pages 788–798. https://doi.org/10.3115/v1/N15-1080.

Joakim Nivre, Marie-Catherine de Marneffe, Filip Ginter, Yoav Goldberg, Jan Hajic, Christopher D. Manning, Ryan McDonald, Slav Petrov, Sampo Pyysalo, Natalia Silveira, Reut Tsarfaty, and Daniel Zeman. 2016. Universal dependencies v1: A multilingual treebank collection. In *Proceedings of the Tenth International Conference on Language Resources and Evaluation (LREC 2016)*. European Language Resources Association (ELRA), Paris, France, pages 1659–1666.

Maurice H. Quenouille. 1956. Notes on Bias in Estimation. *Biometrika* 61:1–17. https://doi.org/10.2307/2332914.

Mohammad Sadegh Rasooli and Joel Tetreault. 2015. Yara Parser: A Fast and Accurate Dependency Parser. *arXiv preprint arXiv:1503.06733* .

Wolfgang Seeker and Jonas Kuhn. 2013. The effects of syntactic features in automatic prediction of morphology. In *Proceedings of the 2013 Conference on Empirical Methods in Natural Language Processing*. Association for Computational Linguistics, pages 333–344. http://aclweb.org/anthology/D13-1033.

John W. Tukey. 1958. Bias and Confidence in Not Quite Large Samples. *Annals of Mathematical Statistics* 29:614. https://doi.org/10.1214/aoms/1177706647.

Muhua Zhu, Yue Zhang, Wenliang Chen, Min Zhang, and Jingbo Zhu. 2013. Fast and accurate shift-reduce constituent parsing. In *Proceedings of the 51st Annual Meeting of the Association for Computational Linguistics (Volume 1: Long Papers)*. Association for Computational Linguistics, pages 434–443. http://aclweb.org/anthology/P13-1043.

Author Index